Lecture Notes in Computer Science 2421

Edited by G. Goos, J. Hartmanis, and J. van Leeuwen

Lecture Notes in Computer Science 2121
Edited by G. Goos, J. Hartmanis, and J. van Leeuwen

Springer
Berlin
Heidelberg
New York
Barcelona
Hong Kong
London
Milan
Paris
Tokyo

Luboš Brim   Petr Jančar
Mojmír Křetínský   Antonín Kučera (Eds.)

CONCUR 2002 –
Concurrency Theory

13th International Conference
Brno, Czech Republic, August 20-23, 2002
Proceedings

Springer

Series Editors

Gerhard Goos, Karlsruhe University, Germany
Juris Hartmanis, Cornell University, NY, USA
Jan van Leeuwen, Utrecht University, The Netherlands

Volume Editors

Luboš Brim
Mojmír Křetínský
Antonín Kučera
Masaryk University Brno, Faculty of Informatics
Botanicka 68a, 60200 Brno, Czech Republic
E-mail: {brim, mojmir, kucera}@fi.muni.cz

Petr Jančar
Technical University of Ostrava (VSB)
Faculty of Electrical Engineering and Informatics, Department of Computer Science
17. listopadu 15, 70833 Ostrava-Poruba, Czech Republic
E-mail: petr.jancar@vsb.cz

Cataloging-in-Publication Data applied for

Die Deutsche Bibliothek - CIP-Einheitsaufnahme

Concurrency theory : 13th international conference ; proceedings / CONCUR
2002, Brno, Czech Republic, August 20 - 23, 2002. Lubos Brim ... (ed.). -
Berlin ; Heidelberg ; New York ; Barcelona ; Hong Kong ; London ; Milan ;
Paris ; Tokyo : Springer, 2002
  (Lecture notes in computer science ; Vol. 2421)
  ISBN 3-540-44043-7

CR Subject Classification (1998): F.3, F.1, D.3, D.1, C.2

ISSN 0302-9743
ISBN 3-540-44043-7 Springer-Verlag Berlin Heidelberg New York

Springer-Verlag Berlin Heidelberg New York,
a member of BertelsmannSpringer Science+Business Media GmbH

http://www.springer.de

© Springer-Verlag Berlin Heidelberg 2002
Printed in Germany

Typesetting: Camera-ready by author, data conversion by DA-TeX Gerd Blumenstein
Printed on acid-free paper   SPIN: 10873811   06/3142   5 4 3 2 1 0

Preface

This volume contains the proceedings of the 13th International Conference on Concurrency Theory (CONCUR 2002) held in Brno, Czech Republic, August 20–23, 2002.

The purpose of the CONCUR conferences is to bring together researchers, developers and students in order to advance the theory of concurrency, and promote its applications. Interest in this topic is continuously growing, as a consequence of the importance and ubiquity of concurrent systems and their applications, and of the scientific relevance of their foundations. The scope covers all areas of semantics, logics and verification techniques for concurrent systems. Topics include concurrency-related aspects of models of computation and semantic domains, process algebras, Petri nets, event structures, real-time systems, hybrid systems, probabilistic systems, model-checking, verification techniques, refinement techniques, term and graph rewriting, distributed programming, logic constraint programming, object-oriented programming, typing systems and algorithms, security, case studies, tools and environments for programming and verification.

The first two CONCUR conferences were held in Amsterdam (The Netherlands) in 1990 and 1991, the following ones in Stony Brook (USA), Hildesheim (Germany), Uppsala (Sweden), Philadelphia (USA), Pisa (Italy), Warsaw (Poland), Nice (France), Eindhoven (The Netherlands), University Park (Pennsylvania, USA), and Aalborg (Denmark). The proceedings have appeared in Springer LNCS, as Vols. 458, 527, 630, 715, 836, 962, 1119, 1243, 1466, 1664, 1877, and 2154.

Out of 101 regular papers submitted this year, 32 were accepted for presentation at the conference and are included in this volume. The conference also included five talks by invited speakers: Amir Pnueli (Weizmann Institute of Science, Rehovot, Israel) and Vaughan Pratt (Stanford University, USA) reappeared as CONCUR invited speakers after 10 years, and further invited talks were given by Wan Fokkink (CWI Amsterdam, The Netherlands), Alexander Rabinovich (Tel Aviv University, Israel) and Davide Sangiorgi (INRIA Sophia Antipolis, France). Additionally, there were two invited tutorials, given by Julian Bradfield (University of Edinburgh, UK) and Andrew D. Gordon (Microsoft Research, Cambridge, UK).

CONCUR 2002 was accompanied by a special event called Tools Day, organized by Ivana Černá, and by the following satellite workshops:

- CMCIM'02 (Categorical Methods for Concurrency, Interaction, and Mobility), organized by Alexander Kurz, held on 24 August 2002.
- EXPRESS'02 (9th International Workshop on Expressiveness in Concurrency), organized by Uwe Nestmann and Prakash Panangaden, held on 19 August 2002.

- FATES'02 (Formal Approaches to Testing of Software), organized by Robert M. Hierons and Thierry Jéron, held on 24 August 2002.
- FOCLASA'02 (1st International Workshop on Foundations of Coordination), organized by Antonio Brogi and Jean-Marie Jacquet, held on 24 August 2002.
- INFINITY'02 (4th International Workshop on Verification of Infinite State Systems), organized by Antonín Kučera and Richard Mayr, held on 24 August 2002.
- MTCS'02 (3rd International Workshop on Models for Time-Critical Systems), organized by Kim Larsen and Walter Vogler, held on 24 August 2002.
- PDMC'02 (1st International Workshop on Parallel and Distributed Model Checking), organized by Luboš Brim and Orna Grumberg, held on 19 August 2002.

We would like to thank all the Program Committee members, and their sub-referees, for their meritorious work and for establishing the selective program of the conference. We also thank the invited speakers for their talks, and tutorials, all the authors of submitted papers, and all the participants of the conference. Our thanks also go to the organizers of the affiliated events whose efforts contributed to the attractiveness of CONCUR 2002.

Special thanks are due to the organizing committee chaired by Jan Staudek. Jiří Barnat, Jan Strejček and David Šafránek took care of the CONCUR 2002 web pages, including the submission server and the software systems for electronic PC and OC management. They effectively managed many other aspects of the organization; their assistance has been indispensable. Tomáš Staudek designed the logo and the poster of the conference.

The conference was run under the auspices of Jiří Zlatuška, the Rector of Masaryk University. A lot of advice on how to prepare the conference was kindly provided by Jozef Gruska. We also gratefully acknowledge financial support from the European Research Consortium in Informatics and Mathematics (ERCIM), as well as support from the Faculty of Informatics, Masaryk University in Brno.

June 2002   Luboš Brim
                                                             Petr Jančar
                                                        Mojmír Křetínský
                                                         Antonín Kučera

CONCUR Steering Committee

Jos C.M. Baeten (Chair, Eindhoven University of Technology, The Netherlands)
Eike Best (University of Oldenburg, Germany)
Kim G. Larsen (Aalborg University, Denmark)
Ugo Montanari (University of Pisa, Italy)
Scott A. Smolka (State University of New York, USA)
Pierre Wolper (Université de Liège, Belgium)

CONCUR 2002 Program Committee

Roberto M. Amadio (Université de Provence, F)
Ralph-Johan Back (Abo Akademi University, SF)
Jos C.M. Baeten (Eindhoven University of Technology, NL)
Eike Best (University of Oldenburg, D)
Ahmed Bouajjani (Université Paris 7, F)
Javier Esparza (University of Edinburgh, UK)
Rob van Glabbeek (Stanford University, USA)
Matthew Hennessy (University of Sussex, UK)
Thomas A. Henzinger (University of California at Berkeley, USA)
Petr Jančar (Technical University of Ostrava, CZ, co-chair)
Mojmír Křetínský (Masaryk University Brno, CZ, co-chair)
Orna Kupferman (Hebrew University, IL)
Faron Moller (University of Wales, Swansea, UK)
Ugo Montanari (University of Pisa, I)
Rocco De Nicola (University of Florence, I)
Mogens Nielsen (Aarhus University, DK)
Catuscia Palamidessi (Pennsylvania State University, USA)
Prakash Panangaden (McGill University, CAN)
Joachim Parrow (Uppsala University, S)
Philippe Schnoebelen (Ecole Normale Supérieure de Cachan, F)
Scott A. Smolka (State University of New York, USA)
Walter Vogler (University of Augsburg, D)
Igor Walukiewicz (Warsaw University, PL)

CONCUR 2002 Organizing Committee

J. Barnat	M. Jaroš	R. Pelánek
T. Brázdil	D. Komárková	J. Staudek, Chair
J. Crhová	M. Komárková	T. Staudek
I. Černá	P. Krčál	J. Strejček
R. Havelková	P. Lidman	D. Šafránek
J. Holeček	J. Měkota	P. Šimeček
D. Janoušková	J. Obdržálek	

Referees

P. A. Abdulla
L. Aceto
T. Amtoft
G. Auerbach
P. Baldan
J. Barnat
T. Basten
G. Beaulieu
E. Best
L. Bettini
E. Bihler
R. Bloo
M. Bojanczyk
R. Bol
M. Boreale
J. Borgström
V. Bos
D. Bosnacki
G. Boudol
P. Bouyer
J. Bradfield
F. van Breugel
L. Brim
R. Bruni
G. Bruns
M. Bugliesi
M. Buscemi
N. Busi
D. R. Cacciagrano
B. Caillaud
M. Carbone
L. Cardelli
F. Cassez
D. Caucal
H. Chockler
R. Cleaveland
S. Conchon
M. Coppo
A. Corradini
F. Corradini
F. Crazzolara

I. Černá
M. Dam
P. Degano
J. Desharnais
K. Etessami
G. Ferrari
H. Fleischhack
W. Fokkink
L. Fribourg
P. Gastin
B. Genest
S. Gnesi
J. C. Godskesen
R. Gorrieri
J. Goubault-Larrecq
R. Grosu
D. Gruska
P. Habermehl
K. Heljanko
T. Hildebrandt
D. Hirschkoff
B. Horowitz
R. Jagadeesan
A. Jeffrey
R. Jhala
B. Jonsson
G. Juhas
M. Jurdzinski
Y. Jurski
V. Khomenko
E. Kindler
H. Klaudel
B. Klin
M. Koutny
A. Kučera
M. Kwiatkowska
A. Labella
F. Laroussinie
S. Lasota
M. Loreti
D. Lugiez

M. Maidl
T. Mailund
R. Majumdar
S. Mauw
C. Meadows
M. Merro
C. Middelburg
D. Miller
E. Moggi
U. Montanari
R. Morin
A. Muscholl
F. Z. Nardelli
P. Niebert
D. Niwinski
G. Norman
J. Obdržálek
D. Pavlovicć
J. Pearson
D. Peled
W. Penczek
N. Piterman
A. Polrola
F. Pommereau
V. Prabhu
S. Prasad
R. Pugliese
A. Rabinovich
S. K. Rajamani
C. Ramakrishnan
J. Raskin
J. Rathke
M. Reniers
A. Rensink
A. Sabelfeld
D. Sands
D. Sangiorgi
Z. Sawa
A. Schmitt
S. Schneider
C. Schröter

R. Segala
P. Sewell
N. Sidorova
S. Sims
P. Sobocinski
A. Sokolova
J. Srba
E. W. Stark
I. Stark
A. Stefanescu
C. Stehno
C. Stirling
S. Stoller
J. Strejček
S. Tiga
S. Tini
E. Tuosto
M. Turuani
F. Valencia
A. Valmari
V. Vanackere
D. Varacca
B. Victor
E. de Vink
H. Völzer
T. Vojnar
M. Voorhoeve
S. Vorobyov
E. Wilkeit
H. Wimmel
L. Wishick
J. Worrell
J. von Wright
P. Yang
K. Yemane
M. Ying
M. Zenger
W. Zielonka
S. D. Zilio
P. Zimmer

Table of Contents

Models of Computation, Process Algebra

Security

Petri Nets

Bisimulation

Refinement and Verification Applied to an In-Flight Data Acquisition Unit*

Wan Fokkink[1], Natalia Ioustinova[1], Ernst Kesseler[2], Jaco van de Pol[1], Yaroslav S. Usenko[1], and Yuri A. Yushtein[2]

[1] Centre for Mathematics and Computer Science (CWI)
Department of Software Engineering
PO Box 94079, 1090 GB Amsterdam, The Netherlands
{wan,ustin,vdpol,ysu}@cwi.nl
[2] National Aerospace Laboratory (NLR), Department of Embedded Systems
PO Box 90502, 1006 MB Amsterdam, The Netherlands
{kesseler,yushtein}@nlr.nl

Abstract. In order to optimise maintenance and increase safety, the Royal Netherlands Navy initiated the development of a multi-channel on-board data acquisition system for its Lynx helicopters. This AIDA (Automatic In-flight Data Acquisition) system records usage and loads data on main rotor, engines and airframe. We used refinement in combination with model checking to arrive at a formally verified prototype implementation of the AIDA system, starting from the functional requirements.

Keywords: refinement, verification, B-method, model checking, μCRL.

1 Introduction

A good method for developing (safety-critical) software is by means of a stepwise refinement, starting from the original user requirements. Furthermore, formal methods can be applied to guarantee correctness at the different stages of refinement.

B method [1] provides a notation and a toolset for requirements modelling, software interface specification, software design, implementation and maintenance. It targets software development from specification through refinement, down to implementation and automatic code generation, with verification at each stage. Refinement via incremental construction of layered software is the guiding principle of B.

Refinement verification is a methodology for verifying that the functionality of an abstract system model is correctly implemented by a low-level implementation. By breaking a large verification problem into small, manageable parts, the refinement methodology makes it possible to verify designs that are much too large to be handled directly. This decomposition of the verification problem is enabled by specifying refinement maps that translate the behaviour of

---

* This research was carried out in the framework of the KTV-FM project funded by the Dutch Ministry of Defense under the order #726/1/00301.

L. Brim et al. (Eds.): CONCUR 2002, LNCS 2421, pp. 1–23, 2002.

the abstract model into the behaviour of given interfaces and structures in the low-level design.

Refinement verification targets safety properties, which guarantee that a bad thing will never happen. However, in general one also wants to verify progress properties, which guarantee that a good thing will eventually happen. Special purpose theorem provers and model checkers have been developed which can check progress properties. Since these tools use their own languages, they cannot be applied to B specifications directly.

μCRL [3,9] provides a notation and a toolset for the specification and verification of distributed systems in an algebraic fashion. It targets the specification of system behaviour in a process-algebraic style and of data elements in the form of abstract data types. The μCRL toolset, together with the CADP toolset [6], which acts as a back-end for the μCRL toolset, features visualisation, simulation, state space generation, model checking, theorem proving and state bit hashing capabilities. It has been successfully applied in the analysis of a wide range of protocols and distributed systems.

In this paper we combine the B refinement paradigm based on imperative programming with the μCRL verification support based on algebraic specification. The idea is that the models that are produced during the subsequent refinement stages in B can be quite easily transformed into μCRL specifications, where excellent tool support is available for the verification of these models.

In order to reduce maintenance costs and increase safety, the Royal Netherlands Navy initiated the development of a multi-channel on-board data acquisition system for its Lynx helicopters [19]. This AIDA (Automatic In-flight Data Acquisition) system records usage and loads data on main rotor, engines and airframe, thus making it possible to optimise the maintenance of Lynx helicopters. In a project funded by the Royal Netherlands Navy, the National Aerospace Laboratory (NLR) in collaboration with the Centre for Mathematics and Computer Science (CWI), made an effort to arrive at a formally verified implementation of the AIDA system, starting from the functional requirements, using refinement.

We built B models of the AIDA system, including a number of its monitoring tasks. These models are based on the functional requirements document for the AIDA system [5]. We started with a high level abstract description in the form of abstract machines; on this level we performed animation, and a number of internal consistency proof obligations were generated and discharged. Next, some of the machines were refined, and once more internal consistency proof obligations were generated and discharged. As a final refinement step, all abstract machines were implemented, and the resulting executable specification was tested. We also built a μCRL model of the AIDA system, including the same monitoring tasks, based on the B model. Moreover, correctness criteria for the AIDA system were formalised in modal logic. Using the μCRL toolset, we verified the system does not contain deadlocks. Furthermore, using a model checker within the CADP verification toolbox we verified that all usage and loads data are recorded, and that no recordings are made without reason. For the validity of these properties it turned out to be essential that some of the requirements in the original requirements document were strengthened.

Concluding, we found that the refinement paradigm together with formal verification methods can be successfully applied in the development of naval equipment.

This paper is set up as follows. Section 2 contains a description of the AIDA system and of the formal model that we designed. Section 3 sets forth the methodology behind our approach. Section 4 explains the basics of refinement in general and B in particular, and describes how refinement was applied to the formal model of the AIDA system. Section 5 deals with the μCRL model of the system and with the model checking analysis. Section 6 gives references to related work. Finally, Section 7 sums up our conclusions.

2   System Overview

2.1   AIDA

The Lynx helicopter is in service with the Royal Netherlands Navy since the late 70's. In September 1994, a fatal accident with a UK Lynx helicopter occurred in Germany as a result of failure of a tie-bar, which connects the rotor hub with the blade. In response, at the end of 1996, the Royal Netherlands Navy initiated the development of an Automatic In-flight Data Acquisition Unit (AIDA) for its Lynx helicopters, in order to optimise maintenance and increase safety.

As inputs, the AIDA system gathers data from 15 analog and 2 discrete signals produced by several measurement and control devices. 39 different tasks of the AIDA system are responsible for data storage, conditioning and processing. The AIDA system performs several logging tasks simultaneously. Each of the tasks checks values of one or more input signals and depending on them performs some logging activities, such as writing to a data acquisition file, or producing a signal via an audio or video channel. Some of the tasks use timers to check whether a particular situation persists for some period of time, and only after that period the logging is performed.

In Figure 1, an overview of a part of the system is presented. The environment represents the measurement and control devices of a helicopter. *TASK2* receives *NR* (main rotor rotational speed) and *WOW* (weight-on-wheels) signals from the environment and uses timer *TIMER2*. The task can write data to the data administration file (*DAF*) and can set video warnings for the crew. *TASK27* performs activities similar to the activities of *TASK2*, but according to *NR* and *LHMY* (strain in left-hand side of rear spar sponson) signals. *TASK3* produces an audio warning depending on the values of *NR* and *WOW* signals. *TASK4* also sets an audio warning according to the value of *NR* signal.

With respect to the functional requirements of the AIDA system [5], there are the following groups of tasks:

– *Data reduction tasks* monitor and process signals using standard algorithms, with subsequent storage of data into memory. (For example, the so-called

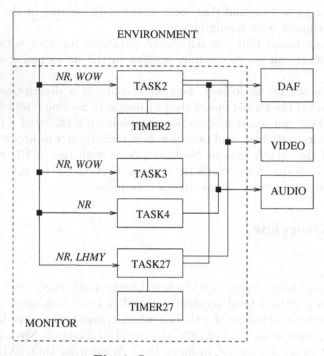

Fig. 1. System overview

SPTTS algorithm searches the load trace for successive peaks and troughs and stores them with time stamps and momentary values of any slaved signals.)
- *Level crossing detection tasks* monitor signals to check whether a predefined level is crossed upwards or downwards. If so, audio or video warnings are given and relevant information is stored into AIDA memory. (A typical example is main rotor overspeed or underspeed.) Such tasks are usually a safety issue for the helicopter and its crew.
- *Event count and event duration tasks* provide signal monitoring, count the number of times that a signal reaches a certain predefined level, and determine the time span that the signal is at this pre-defined level. (A typical example is the weight-on-wheels task, which determines whether or not a helicopter is at the ground.) Such tasks provide direct compact event information without a further need for processing.
- *System integrity tasks* verify the status of the AIDA recorder and monitor various signals during the AIDA recorder operation to check whether a predefined malfunctioning condition is met. If so, integrity of the signals and/or the total system is considered questionable.

Since the AIDA system handles critical flight data, it should not change the data content or influence timing in any way. On the other hand, the monitoring system should not miss or discard the data on any of the monitored channels, as this could lead to incorrect calculations of the estimated helicopter operational status and required maintenance cycle.

2.2 Formal Specification

Our goal was to build a formal specification of the AIDA system and to verify the specification with respect to functional requirements for an on-board loads and usage monitoring system for the Lynx helicopter. Considering the functional requirements we identified the following key entities of the system: monitor, tasks, data administration file, input and output channels. The monitor schedules the tasks, and also plays the role of system clock. The data administration file is used to store the data and the results of data processing.

Since AIDA is a real-time system, some primitives are needed to represent time aspects of the system. We employed a concept of timers, where a timer can be either active or deactivated, and time progression is discretised. An active timer is represented by a variable that is set to the delay left until expiration of the timer. System time elapses by counting down all the active timers present in the system. We refer to a segment of time separated by the transitions decrementing active timers as a time slice. A timer with zero delay expires, and in the next time slice is deactivated.

Since the specification of the system should abstract from details that depend on the hardware implementation of the system, we assume that operations performed by tasks are atomic and can be handled within a time slice.

All tasks are triggered by some kind of condition (either a safety-critical condition, a level crossing condition, or a condition checking whether a predefined level is reached). Considering the functional requirements, we divided tasks into three groups with respect to the activities that the tasks should perform:

- Tasks that use a timer, can write data to the data acquisition file and can produce a warning signal for the crew.
- Tasks that only produce a warning signal for the crew.
- Tasks that only write to the data acquisition file.

Tasks of the first type are usually triggered by a safety-critical condition. Being triggered, the task sets a timer and waits until the timer expires. After the timer is expired, the task checks whether the safety critical condition is still satisfied. If the condition is still true, then the data and time when the condition was recognised are stored into the data acquisition file and a warning signal is provided for the crew.

Tasks of the second type are triggered when a predefined level is crossed. Being triggered, the task provides a warning signal for the crew. The third kind of tasks mostly detect when a signal reaches a predefined level, process data with respect to some standard algorithm, and store the data. Since tasks of the same group show similar observable behaviour, we have decided to concentrate our attention on the refinement and verification of a part of the system.

3   Combining Refinement and Model Checking

3.1   Refinement

A good method for developing safety-critical software is by means of a stepwise refinement, starting from the original user requirements. Formal methods can be applied to guarantee correctness at the different stages of refinement.

Refinement verification is a methodology for verifying that the functionality of an abstract system model is correctly implemented by a low-level implementation. By breaking a large verification problem into small, manageable parts, the refinement methodology makes it possible to verify designs that are too large to be handled directly. This decomposition of the verification problem is enabled by specifying refinement maps that translate the behaviour of the abstract model into the behaviour of given interfaces and structures in the low-level design. This makes it possible to verify small parts of the low-level design in the context of the abstract model. Thus, proof obligations can be reduced to a small enough scale.

B [1] provides a notation and a toolset for requirements modelling, software interface specification, software design, implementation and maintenance. It targets software development from specification through refinement, down to implementation and automatic code generation, with verification at each stage. Refinement via incremental construction of layered software is the guiding principle of B. Development with B is based on the concept of an abstract machine, a refinement and an implementation of the machine. The B Abstract Machine Notation [1] is used with many alternative development processes and with a number of existing development methods [18].

3.2   Model Checking

Model checking is a completely different approach. Here we have one system model, described in some high-level programming language. Separately, we formulate a number of user requirements in some temporal logic. The model checker generates all reachable program states exhaustively (in principle) in order to check that the user requirements hold in all possible runs.

Several efficient algorithms exist, in order to verify that all states in a state space satisfy a certain formula from temporal logic. The main bottleneck of model checking is the state explosion problem: the size of the state space of a system tends to grow exponentially with respect to the number of concurrent components of the system. However, owing to recent advances such as model checking of symbolic representations of state spaces and state bit hashing, model checking is by now a mature technique for the analysis of real-life hardware and software systems.

μCRL [9] is a language for specifying and verifying distributed systems in an algebraic fashion. It targets the specification of system behaviour in a process-algebraic style and of data elements in the form of abstract data types. The

μCRL toolset [3,20] supports efficient state space generation of μCRL specifications. The CADP toolset [6] acts as a back-end for the μCRL toolset, so that model checking can be applied with respect to the state spaces generated from μCRL specifications.

3.3 The Combination

We note that in a refinement step from an abstract to a concrete model, new details are added. In refinement tools it is only checked that the concrete model is internally consistent (by invariants and preconditions) and consistent with the abstract model. Except consistency, nothing is checked about the initial most abstract model, nor about the added details. So refinement verification is limited to safety properties, which guarantee that a bad thing will never happen.

However, in general one wants to verify that the initial model and the refined model satisfy certain user requirements. In particular, one also wants to verify progress properties, which guarantee that a good thing will eventually happen. Model checking can be applied for the verification of progress properties [13].

Another reason to apply model checking could be that the automated proof search capabilities of B turn out to be relatively limited; model checking can be used as a debugging device for proof obligations [16].

For these reasons we combined the refinement paradigm and verification of safety properties using B with the verification of progress properties using the model checking capabilities of μCRL and CADP. We applied this combination with respect to the functional requirements of the AIDA system. In the next two sections, refinement using B and model checking using μCRL are explained, respectively.

4 Refinement Using B

4.1 The B Method

A typical development process using B [14] might cover requirement analysis, specification development, design, and coding, integration and test phases of software development. For all these phases, some tool support exists. The B-Toolkit of the company B-Core in the UK supports the incremental construction of software, where validation is supported by static analysis such as type checking, by dynamic analysis using simulation, and by proof of correctness using an integrated theorem prover. An alternative commercial toolset that supports the B method is offered by Atelier B in France.

Informal structured models of the problem domain are created during requirement analysis. Specification development results in formalisation of analysis models in terms of abstract machines. The specification can be validated by animation in B-Toolkit. Internal consistency obligations can be generated and proved to check whether all operations of the machines respect their invariants. During the design phase, the decomposition of the system is identified and selected components of the system are refined. The proof obligations generated by B-Toolkit during this phase are used to prove whether refinements are correct with respect to the specification. At the end, a code generator can be applied to the model. Generated code can be tested using test cases based on the requirements.

4.2 Specification Design

To get a more concrete picture, we focus on one of the tasks within AIDA, viz. *TASK2*. Some tasks of the system, including *TASK2*, use timers. For this reason we specified timer machines; the timer for *TASK2* is called `Timer2`. The timer can be either active (`on`) or deactivated (`off`). The state of the timer is represented by two variables `tstat2` and `tval2`. The first one shows whether the timer is active or deactivated, the second one represents the delay left until expiration of the active timer.

Each timer machine contains the following operations: `reset` deactivates the timer, `set` activates and sets up the timer, `expire` returns `true` if and only if the timer is active and expired, and `tick` decreases the value of the timer if it is active and carries a value greater than zero (see Figure 2). The invariant of the machine imposes a restriction on the possible value of the delay as well as typing constraints for variables `tval2` and `tstat2`. The precondition of operation `set` states that the delay should not exceed the maximum prescribed by the system requirements.

Figure 3 shows a high-level machine specification of *TASK2*. It has two operations: initialisation `tinit` and "do some work" `work`. Doing some work depends on the state, which is one of `idle`, `wait` or `check`:

```
MACHINE   Timer2
SEES      Bool_TYPE, CommDefs
VARIABLES tval2, tstat2
INVARIANT tval2:0..max & tstat2:TISTATE
INITIALISATION tval2:=0 || tstat2:=off
OPERATIONS
reset2    = BEGIN tstat2 := off END ;
set2(del) = PRE del:NAT & del <= max
            THEN tval2 := del || tstat2:=on END;
ok <-- expire2 = IF tval2 = 0 & tstat2=on
                THEN ok := TRUE ELSE ok := FALSE END;
tick2 = IF tstat2=on & tval2>0
        THEN tval2 := tval2-1 ELSE tval2:=tval2 END
END
```

Fig. 2. High-level machine description for `Timer2`

- in the state `idle`, the condition is watched. If it holds, the timer is set and we go to state `wait`.
- in the state `wait`, the timer has been set. If it expires we go to state `check`.
- in the state `check`, the condition is checked again, and we go to state `idle`.

On this abstract level, it is only defined which transitions are possible, but not when they are taken. Machines `Bool_TYPE` and `CommDefs` are seen by `Task2`. `Bool_TYPE` contains a specification of the Boolean operators. `CommDefs` defines sets, constants and their properties reused by several components of the specification. The invariant defined for `Task2` provides a typing constraint for the variable of the machine. Operation `ttick2` calls operation `tick2` of the timer. This operation is invoked itself by the monitor to decrease values of all active timers at the same time.

To make the definition of task behaviour independent on particular values of signals triggering the task, we defined a condition machine for each task. We can easily change the condition without modifying the specification of the task. Initially, the condition machine (see Figure 4) has only one operation `issatisfied2`, which returns either `TRUE` or `FALSE`.

To mimic the input channels, we developed sensor machines. We consider the operations of a sensor machine using the weight-on-wheels (*WOW*) sensor as an illustrative example. Since the *WOW* signal can be either `high` or `low`, the operation `refreshWOW` of `SensorWOW` is defined as a non-deterministic choice of the machine state between `high` or `low` (see Figure 5). Operation `getstateWOW` returns the current state of the sensor. This approach to specification of the input channels allows us to cover the possible inputs of the system.

```
MACHINE    Task2
SEES       Bool_TYPE, CommDefs
INCLUDES   Timer2
VARIABLES  tstate2
INVARIANT  tstate2:TSTATE
INITIALISATION tstate2:=idle
OPERATIONS
tinit2 = BEGIN reset2 || tstate2:=idle END;
work2 = CASE tstate2 OF
          EITHER idle THEN CHOICE tstate2:=wait || set2(5)
                           OR tstate2:=idle END
            OR wait THEN CHOICE tstate2:=check OR tstate2:=wait END
            OR check THEN tstate2:=idle END
          END;
ss <-- getstate2 = ss:=tstate2;
ttick2 = tick2
END
```

Fig. 3. High-level machine description for `Task2`

```
MACHINE         Condition2
SEES            Bool_TYPE, CommDefs
OPERATIONS
xx <-- issatisfied2 = CHOICE xx := FALSE OR xx := TRUE END
END
```

Fig. 4. High-level machine description for *WOW* sensor

```
MACHINE         SensorWOW
SEES            Bool_TYPE, CommDefs
VARIABLES       sstateWOW
INVARIANT       sstateWOW:LHLEVELS
INITIALISATION  sstateWOW:=low
OPERATIONS
refreshWOW = CHOICE sstateWOW := high OR sstateWOW := low END;
xx <-- getstateWOW = xx := sstateWOW
END
```

Fig. 5. High-level machine description for *WOW* sensor

Audio and video output channels and the data administration file are shared by several tasks. Therefore we specified a controller for each output channel and for the data administration file.

4.3   Refinement and Implementation

A B development consists of a set of components defined by abstract specification machines and a path of refinement steps down to an executable description, called an implementation. An implementation of the component is decomposed via IMPORTS and SEES clauses. A specification of the component may itself be constructed from a set of machines using INCLUDES, USES, SEES and EXTENDS mechanisms.

Usage of IMPORTS and SEES constructs implies a layered approach to system development whereby the internal details of implementation of one layer are hidden from the next layer. Such a structure improves the maintainability of the system because higher layers are independent of the internal details of lower layers and rely only on the specification of these layers.

The implementation of Monitor relies only on the specifications of tasks, sensors and controllers of output channels and data administration file. Since we have no information about scheduling the tasks, we have chosen one of the possible scenarios. To simulate fresh inputs, the monitor refreshes values of the sensors at the beginning. Then it allows each task to do some work and finally

```
IMPLEMENTATION   MonitorI
REFINES          Monitor
SEES             CommDefs, Bool_TYPE, basic_io, String_TYPE
IMPORTS          Monitor_Vvar(MSTATE),
                 Task4, Task2, Task27, Task3,
                 SensorLHMY, SensorWOW, SensorNR,
                 OutChController, DAFController, AudioChController
INVARIANT        (mstate=Monitor_Vvar)
INITIALISATION   Monitor_STO_VAR(start)
OPERATIONS
minit = BEGIN
      Monitor_STO_VAR(monitor);
      tinit1; tinit2; tinit3; tinit27;
      resetanalog;resetaudio
      END;
monitortask = VAR curmstate IN
                    curmstate<--Monitor_VAL_VAR;
                    IF curmstate=monitor THEN
                        refreshWOW; refreshNR; refreshLHMY;
                        work2; work3; work4; work27;
                        ttick2; ttick27
                        ELSE PUT_STR("Initialisation error"); END
              END
END
```

Fig. 6. Implementation of Monitor machine

it decreases the values of all active timers, by which the system time elapses
(Figure 6).

The implementation of Condition2 refines operation issatisfied2 as is
shown on the Figure 8. Now issatisfied2 returns TRUE only if the condition
triggering Task2 is satisfied, i.e. the value of the *NR* sensor is below 50%RPM
and the *WOW* signal is low.

The refinement of Task2 (Figure 7) defines INCLUDES and SEES relations
for Task2 and the other components of the system. A task sees the condition Condition2 that acts as its trigger, the data acquisition file controller
DAFController, the video channel controller OutChController and includes the
Timer2 machine. The controllers of the data administration file and the video
channel regulate access to these entities by the tasks of the system.

Figure 7 contains a refinement of Task2. The refinement not only specifies
possible transitions but also defines enabling conditions for those transitions.
For example, after refinement, the operation work2 changes the state of the task
from wait to check only if the timer is expired. The timer is deactivated by
reset, after the task state is changed to check. If the condition triggering the
task is still satisfied after timer expiration, the task writes data to the data

```
REFINEMENT       Task2R
REFINES          Task2
SEES             Bool_TYPE, CommDefs, Condition2, OutChController,
                 DAFController
INCLUDES         Timer2
VARIABLES        tstate2
INVARIANT        tstate2:TSTATE
INITIALISATION   tstate2:=idle
OPERATIONS
tinit2 = BEGIN reset2 END;
work2 = VAR exp IN
        CASE tstate2 OF
        EITHER idle THEN exp<--issatisfied2;
                      IF exp=TRUE THEN tstate2:=wait; set2(5)
                      ELSE tstate2:=idle END
        OR wait THEN exp <--expire2;
                      IF exp=TRUE THEN tstate2:=check ; reset2
                      ELSE tstate2:=wait END
        OR check THEN exp <--issatisfied2;
                      IF exp=TRUE THEN tstate2:=idle;
                                       setanalogon; writetodaf
                      ELSE tstate2:=idle END
                END
            END
        END;
ss <-- getstate2 = ss:=tstate2;
ttick2 = tick2
END
```

Fig. 7. Refinement of Task2

acquisition file (by means of the `writetodaf` operation of the data acquisition file controller), sets up an output signal (by means of the `setanalogon` operation of the output channel controller) and becomes `idle`. Otherwise, the task just goes back to state `idle`.

4.4 Proof and Validation

B-Toolkit generates and assists to prove a number of proof obligations. In our development we have proved that all operations of the machines respect their invariants and that the invariants are established by the initialisation. We proved that preconditions for any invoked machine operations are satisfied. For example, it was shown that the specification, the refinement and the implementation of `Task2` do not violate the precondition imposed on the input parameter of the operation `set2` of the machine `Timer2`.

```
xx <-- issatisfied2 = VAR currNR, currWOW IN
                      currNR <-- getstateNR;
                      currWOW <-- getstateWOW;
                      IF (currNR=110 or currNR=meq10150) & currWOW=low
                      THEN xx:=TRUE ELSE xx:=FALSE END
                      END
```

Fig. 8. Refinement of `issatisfied2` operation of `Condition2` machine

At the specification development phase, we also used animation supported by B-Toolkit. The animation can be really helpful for debugging the specification. It allows to test the specification against various scenarios. At the design phase we used B-Toolkit's theorem prover to check whether the refinement and implementation machines satisfy the refinement constraints and whether the implementations are correct refinements of machines.

Since the development of test cases for this kind of the systems is not a trivial task, we used the code, generated by B-Toolkit, to test the system against a "chaotic" environment. In this case "chaotic" means that we abstracted from real values of analog signals NR and $LHMY$ and implemented the **refresh** operation of the sensors as a random choice (provided by B-Toolkit) on the set of abstract values. So we have specified an environment that covers all combinations of input signals.

5   Model Checking Using μCRL

5.1   The μCRL Toolset

μCRL [9] is a language for specifying and verifying distributed systems in an algebraic fashion. It targets the specification of system behaviour in a process-algebraic style and of data elements in the form of abstract data types. System specification takes place in the form of recursive equations that include recursion variables, the basic process algebraic constructors (atomic actions, alternative and sequential composition), parallelism, synchronous communication, encapsulation of actions, and hiding of internal activity. Furthermore, atomic actions and recursion variables can carry data parameters, data elements can influence the course of a process via an if-then-else construct , and a summation operator allows to take the alternative composition with respect to all possible values of some data parameter.

The μCRL toolset [3,20] supports the analysis and manipulation of μCRL specifications, based on term rewriting and linearisation techniques. It supports efficient state space generation, deadlock detection, interactive simulation, and theorem proving. The CADP toolset [6] acts as a back-end for the μCRL toolset, so that state spaces can be visualised, analysed and minimised, and model checking and state bit hashing are available.

The toolset is constructed around a restricted linear form of μCRL specifications, which does not include parallelism, encapsulation and hiding. The tool mcrl checks whether a certain specification is well-formed and brings it into linear form, which is stored as a binary file. All other tools use this linear form as their starting point. These tools come in four kinds:

1. (msim) steps through a process described in μCRL;
2. (instantiator) generates a state space that can serve as input to the CADP toolset;
3. several tools optimise linearised specifications:
   (a) rewr applies the equations of the data types as rewrite rules;
   (b) constelm removes data parameters that are constant throughout any run of the process;
   (c) parelm removes data and process parameters that do not influence the behaviour of the system;
   (d) structelm, expands variables of compound data types;
4. a tool (pp) to print the linearised specification.

An overview of the relations between the tools in the μCRL toolset is sketched in Figure 9. Some other tools rely on a recently developed automated theorem prover. These tools implement reachability and confluence analysis, and some sophisticated control flow analysis methods.

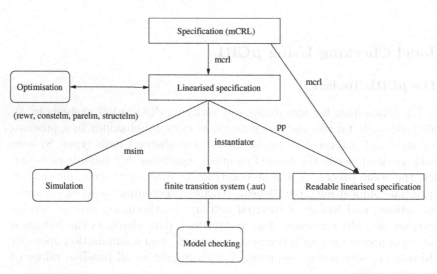

Fig. 9. The main relations between the tools in the μCRL toolset

μCRL was successfully applied in the analysis of a wide range of protocols and distributed systems. Recently it was used to support the optimised redesign of the Transactions Capabilities Procedures in the SS No. 7 protocol stack for telephone exchanges [2], to detect a number of mistakes in an industrial protocol over the CAN bus for lifting trucks [8], and to analyse the coordination languages SPLICE [4,11] and JavaSpaces [17].

5.2   AIDA Model in μCRL

We specified the different components of the AIDA system (tasks, sensors, buttons, monitor, data acquisition file, output channels, environment) as independent μCRL processes. These components communicate synchronously by performing communication actions. During these communications data can be transferred between the components.

The μCRL specification of the AIDA system consists of several parts. The first part specifies the data types used by means of equations. Some of them are general data structures, like booleans, natural numbers and lists. Others are specific to AIDA, like states of tasks, sensors, buttons, data acquisition file, output channels, etc. Next, the atomic actions are specified, and it is declared which actions can communicate. The different processes are defined by means of recursive equations. Finally, the initial state of the whole system is given, being a parallel composition of components where some actions are encapsulated or hidden. Figure 10 shows the various processes in the μCRL specification

Figure 11 shows the definition of Task 2 as a μCRL process. According to this definition *TASK2* has one state variable. It can synchronise on init, run and tick actions (+ is alternative choice). After an init action the timer is reset ($\cdot$ denotes sequential composition), and the state is set to idle. If a run action occurs the process *TASK2RUN* is executed, *provided* the state is either idle or wait ($x \triangleleft b \triangleright y$ means do x if b, else do y). A tick action results in ticking the accompanying timer, provided the task is in waiting state. *TASK2RUN* first checks the state. If the state is wait, the timer value is obtained (sum denotes alternative choice over a data sort). If no timeout occurs, *TASK2RUN* finishes. Otherwise, the timer is reset, the sensors are inspected, and depending on the safety condition a logging action is performed. If the state is not wait, the sensors are inspected, and depending on the safety condition, either the timer is set and the state is changed to wait, or we stay in idle. Eventually, in all cases, control is returned to the *TASK2* process.

The mcrl tool was used to check the syntax and static semantics of the specification, and also to transpose it to linear form. The specification was thoroughly simulated using the msim tool in a way that all parts of the code were reached. Several specification errors were discovered and corrected. The linear form of the ultimate (after corrections of section 5.3) μCRL specification contained 47 data parameters and 132 summands. Using the tool constelm, the number of parameters was reduced to 32, and the number of summands to 85.

State space generation took approximately 1 minute and 10 seconds on an AMD Athlon 1.4GHz machine, and resulted in a state space with approximately 250,000 states and 900,000 transitions. The state space did not contain deadlocks (checked with the μCRL toolset) and livelocks (checked with the CADP toolset).

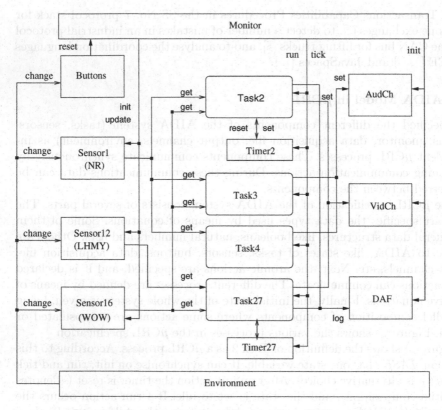

Fig. 10. System decomposition in the μCRL model

Reduction of the state space (modulo branching bisimulation equivalence [7]) took approximately 47 seconds on the same machine and produced 1,072 states and 5,855 transitions.

5.3 Validation of User Requirements

The informal description of the AIDA system contains a rather technical specification. It provides several kinds of operational details, for instance when timers must be set and reset. This made it difficult to validate the specification. We took the following approach: we invented "reasonable" user requirements for the system, formalised them in temporal logic, and checked automatically whether the μCRL model of the AIDA system satisfies these requirements.

We formulated the following user requirements, that seemed plausible to us. For each task, it should hold that:

Property 1. if the condition checked by some task is satisfied during a certain period of time, then this task will perform its logging activity.

```
TASK2(st:TaskSt)=
  init_task(2)._reset_timer(2).TASK2(TST_IDLE)
+
  run_task(2).
    ( TASK2RUN(st)
    <|or(eq(st,TST_IDLE),eq(st,TST_WAIT))|>
       TASK2(st)
    )
+
  tick_task(2).
    ( _tick_timer(2).TASK2(st)
    <|eq(st,TST_WAIT)|>
       TASK2(st)
    )

TASK2RUN(st:TaskSt)=
       sum(t:Nat,_get_timer(2,t).
         (TASK2(st)
          <|gt(TIMEOUT2,t)|>
          _reset_timer(2).
          sum(sst:SensorSt,_get_state_sensor(1,sst).
            sum(sst1:SensorSt,_get_state_sensor(16,sst1).
               ( TASK2LOG.TASK2(TST_IDLE)
               <|and(eq(sst,sst1(1)),eq(sst1,sst16(F)))|>
                  TASK2(TST_IDLE)
          )) )))
          <|eq(st,TST_WAIT)|>
          sum(sst:SensorSt,_get_state_sensor(1,sst).
            sum(sst1:SensorSt,_get_state_sensor(16,sst1).
               ( _set_timer(2).TASK2(TST_WAIT)
               <|and(eq(sst,sst1(1)),eq(sst1,sst16(F)))|>
                  TASK2(TST_IDLE)
          )))

TASK2LOG=_log(LogEntryTask(2))._set_vidch(VidchSt1)
```

Fig. 11. Specification of Task2

Property 2. the task only performs a logging activity if the condition checked
   by it was satisfied during a certain period of time.

The first requirement indicates that all strains and loads are logged, and the
second one indicates that no false alarms are logged.

The properties were formulated in the regular alternation-free μ-calculus [15].
We show this for Task2, which watches the sensors NR and WOW (see Figure 1).
The following abbreviations are used (in CADP these are defined as macros):

```
[true*.( (NR.OTHER.WOW) | (WOW.OTHER.NR) )
  .OTHER.( (NR.OTHER.WOW) | (WOW.OTHER.NR) )

... dropped 19 similar lines

  .OTHER.( (NR.OTHER.WOW) | (WOW.OTHER.NR) )
  .OTHER.( (NR.OTHER.WOW) | (WOW.OTHER.NR) )
] false
```

Fig. 12. Modal formula expressing Property 1

NR – indicates the event that the NR-sensor is below 50%RPM. WOW – indicates the event that the weight is not on the wheels (so the combination NR and WOW indicates that the helicopter is probably falling down). OTHER – any sequence of actions that does not contain logging actions, reset buttons, or changes to NR-sensor and WOW-sensor.

From now on we assume that the timeout value TIMEOUT2 is equal to 20 time units. The first property can be expressed as follows: There is no execution trace of the AIDA system with a subsequence consisting of 23 (NR,WOW) or (WOW,NR) pairs, interspersed only with OTHER sequences (see Figure 12).

The second property can be expressed as follows: there is no execution trace of the AIDA system ending in a logging activity, preceded by at most 20 time slices where $WOW = $ low (see Figure 13). A similar formula is needed for the NR-sensor. The full source code of the properties will be available in a technical report.

```
[              (not(WOW)*.
        (true|nil).(not WOW)*.

... dropped 17 similar lines ...

        (true|nil).(not WOW)*.
        (true|nil).(not WOW)*
    ).
  "__log(LogEntryTask(x2p2(0)))"
]false
```

Fig. 13. Modal formula expressing Property 2

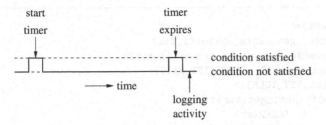

Fig. 14. Spurious logging activity

The next step is to verify that these properties hold for the AIDA system. To this end we applied the CADP model checker to the reduced transition system generated by the μCRL toolset. The first formula holds straight away, but surprisingly, the second formula failed. In this case, the model checker provided a counter-example in the form of a wrong execution trace. This trace was carefully inspected, and appeared to correspond to the following situation (see Figure 14): The condition on *WOW* and *NR* holds in the first time slice, and the timer is correctly set. After some time slices, the timer expires, and the condition on *WOW* and *NR* holds again. However, *it was not checked by the system whether the condition holds between setting and expiration of the timer.*

We could now proceed in two ways: either adapt the model, or the user requirements. As our properties seem quite natural we adapted the μCRL model. In the modified version, a task goes from idle to wait if the condition checked by it is satisfied. In the wait phase, it continuously checks the condition, and if it fails it returns to idle and resets the timer. If the condition remains true until the timer expires a logging action is performed. This is implemented in the μCRL specification by modifying the *TASK2RUN* process according to Figure 15 (cf. Figure 11).

In this new model, both properties appear to hold. It is interesting to remark that the mentioned time slices (20 and 23) are strict boundaries. This means that if the condition holds during exactly 21 or 22 time slices, then the system may or may not log this event, depending on the exact order in which the *NR*- and *WOW*-sensors are changed by the environment and read by the *TASK2* process.

We conclude that the informal specification was too operational, in the sense that the user requirements were missing, only the solution in terms of timers was mentioned. At the same time, they were ambiguous, because it was not indicated what the system should do between starting the timer and expiration of the timer. In the formal specification this ambiguity must be resolved in some way. We showed two ways to resolve this ambiguity, and proved that one of the solutions is preferable, because it meets certain plausible user requirements.

```
TASK2RUN(st:TaskSt)=
  sum(sst:SensorSt,_get_state_sensor(1,sst).
    sum(sst1:SensorSt,_get_state_sensor(16,sst1).
      (  (  _set_timer(2).TASK2(TST_WAIT)
         <|eq(st,TST_IDLE)|>
            sum(t:Nat,_get_timer(2,t).
              (  TASK2(st)
                 <|gt(TIMEOUT2,t)|>
                 _reset_timer(2).TASK2LOG.TASK2(TST_IDLE)
            )  )  )
      <|and(eq(sst,sst1(1)),eq(sst1,sst16(F)))|>
         (  _reset_timer(2).TASK2(TST_IDLE)
         <|eq(st,TST_WAIT)|>
            TASK2(TST_IDLE)
      )  )  )  )
```

Fig. 15. Modified specification of `Task2`

6 Related Work

Combination of different formal techniques to support the development of verifiable correct systems is an active line of research. Our work is closely related in spirit and techniques to [13] and [16].

Julliand, Legeard, Machicoane, Parreaux and Tatibouët [13] used B Atelier in combination with the model checker Spin [10] to analyse a protocol within the Integrated Circuit Card (European Standard EN 27816). First a B model of the protocol was constructed, which was manually translated to a PROMELA specification (the input language for Spin). Similar to our approach, safety properties were verified within B, while progress properties were verified using temporal logic.

Mikhailov and Butler [16] used the B Method in combination with the state-based model checker Alloy Constraint Analyser [12] to derive the proof obligations generated by B. Their approach is motivated by the fact that a formal proof using a theorem prover of all proof obligations generated by B is often practically unfeasible. Sometimes, proof obligations are actually false, due to underspecification or to a specification error. Detecting such flaws by means of theorem proving is very difficult indeed. Therefore, in [16] model checking was used as a debugging device. The B specification of a student grades data base was manually translated to an Alloy specification. In cases where proof obligations were left unproved, these were transposed to the Alloy language, and the Alloy constraint analyser was applied. The counter-examples that the Aloy constraint analyser can generate are usually suggestive, so that the developer may realise how and why a certain property is invalidated. This leads to a debugging process with a shorter life-cycle than when only an interactive theorem prover is used.

7   Conclusion

We have shown that one can perform a whole cycle of software development from an informal task description to a specification close to an executable prototype implementation within the B-Method. By identifying the key entities in the informal description, a designer can easily develop the needed data structures. We captured the functional requirements of the system in a stepwise manner. The layered design method advocated with B allowed us to obtain an elegant and succinct implementation.

The relationship between the initial formal requirements and the final implementation is given by formal refinement maps, whose correctness is expressed by proof obligations. For the developed system, 127 nontrivial proof obligations of internal consistency of the system were generated and proved. Also invariants led to proof obligations and were proved. Generation of these proof obligations was sometimes time consuming. The automated proof search capabilities of the B-Toolkit are rather limited. It is time consuming for the user to decide whether a failed proof indicates an error in the specification. In some cases, we adapted the specification in order to assist the theorem prover.

In a refinement step many details are added. Even formally correct refinement steps can introduce new errors, so there is a need to validate the models at various levels. To this end we used a model checker. This also makes it possible to check a wider set of properties. In B only safety properties can be checked (a bad thing will never happen). Using model checking, we can also check progress properties (something good will eventually happen). Therefore, the core part of AIDA system was formally specified in μCRL, and absence of deadlocks and some temporal properties were established using the model checker CADP. For the validity of these temporal properties, the original model had to be modified.

Although the μCRL toolset is not directly applicable to the B model, the translation from B to μCRL turned out to be relatively straightforward. The specification language of μCRL is sufficiently expressive for this kind of applications. Also the specification of the user requirements was rather straightforward owing to the use of regular expressions. The combination of the μCRL and CADP toolsets turned out to be very effective for a completely automated verification of properties with respect to the AIDA model.

Compared to the informal requirements we started with, the formal description is much better structured. Also, we concluded that the informal specification was not abstract enough, in the sense that operational details were given instead of user requirements. On the other hand, many ambiguities were detected, and had to be resolved in the formal specification. The analysis carried out on the formal models (e.g. exact conditions on when safety conditions lead to logging activity) cannot be performed on the informal models. Also, formal analysis was used to choose how to resolve certain types of ambiguity.

The industrial partners could use the B specification, extend it to contain descriptions of the other tasks, refine it to the special purposes of the implementation, and use the μCRL toolset to verify additional properties. For these activities, however, some expert knowledge is still needed in order to understand the specification languages and make effective use of the tools.

Acknowledgement

This research was funded by the Dutch Ministry of Defense. We would like to thank Wim Pelt and Jan Friso Groote for their support and valuable input, and Radu Mateescu for his advice on using the regular alternation-free μ-calculus.

References

1. J. R. Abrial. *The B-Book.* Cambridge University Press, 1996. 1, 6
2. Th. Arts and I. A. van Langevelde. Correct performance of transaction capabilities. In *Proceedings 2nd Conference on Applications of Concurrency to System Design (ICACSD'2001)*, Newcastle upon Tyne, UK, pp. 35–42. IEEE Computer Society Press, 2001. 15
3. S. C. C. Blom, W. J. Fokkink, J. F. Groote, I. A. van Langevelde, B. Lisser, and J. C. van de Pol. μCRL: a toolset for analysing algebraic specifications. In G. Berry, H. Comon, and A. Finkel, eds, *Proceedings 13th Conference on Computer Aided Verification (CAV'01)*, Paris, France, LNCS 2102, pp. 250–254. Springer-Verlag, July 2001. 2, 7, 13
4. P. F. G. Dechering and I. A. van Langevelde. The verification of coordination. In A. Porto and G.-C. Roman, *Proceedings 4th Conference on Coordination Languages and Models (COORDINATION'2000)*, Limmasol, Cyprus, LNCS 1906, pp. 335–340. Springer-Verlag, 2000. 15
5. J. A. J. A. Dominicus, A. A. ten Have, M. C. Buitelaar, P. R. Hoek, and F. J. Carati. Functional requirements for an on-board loads and usage monitoring system for the WHL Lynx SH-14D helicopter. Report CR 97568, National Aerospace Laboratory, November 1997. 2, 3
6. J.-C. Fernandez, H. Garavel, A. Kerbrat, L. Mounier, R. Mateescu, and M. Sighireanu. CADP – a protocol validation and verification toolbox. In R. Alur and T. A. Henzinger, eds, *Proceedings 8th Conference on Computer-Aided Verification (CAV'96)*, New Brunswick, New Jersey, LNCS 1102, pp. 437–440. Springer-Verlag, 1996. 2, 7, 13
7. R. J. van Glabbeek and W. P. Weijland. Branching time and abstraction in bisimulation semantics. *Journal of the ACM*, 43(3):555–600, 1996. 16
8. J. F. Groote, J. Pang, and A. G. Wouters. A balancing act: Analyzing a distributed lift system. In S. Gnesi and U. Ultes-Nitsche, eds, *Proceedings 6th Workshop on Formal Methods for Industrial Critical Systems (FMICS'2001)*, Paris, France, pp. 1–12, 2001. 15
9. J. F. Groote and A. Ponse. The syntax and semantics of μCRL. In A. Ponse, C. Verhoef, and S. F. M. van Vlijmen, editors, *Algebra of Communicating Processes 1994*, pages 26–62. Workshop in Computing Series, Springer-Verlag, 1995. 2, 6, 13
10. G. J. Holzmann. The model checker Spin. *IEEE Transactions on Software Engineering*, 23(5):279–295, 1997. 20

11. J. Hooman and J. C. van de Pol. Formal verification of replication on a distributed data space architecture. In *Proceedings 17th Symposium on Applied Computing (SAC'2002) – Coordination Models, Languages and Applications*, Madrid, Spain, pp. 351–358. ACM Press, 2002. 15

12. D. Jackson, I. Schechter, and I. Shlyakhter. Alcoa: the alloy constraint analyzer. In *Proceedings 22nd Conference on Software Engineering (ICSE'2000)*, Limerick, Ireland, pp. 730–733. ACM Press, 2000. 20

13. J. Julliand, B. Legeard, T. Machicoane, B. Parreaux, and B. Tatibouët. Specification of an integrated circuit card protocol application using the B method and linear temporal logic. In D. Bert, ed., *Proceedings 2nd B Conference (B'98) – Recent Advances in the Development and Use of the B Method*, Montpellier, France, pp. 273–292, LNCS 1393. Springer-Verlag, 1998. 7, 20

14. K. Lano and H. Haughton. *Specification in B: An Introduction Using the B Toolkit*. World Scientific, 1996. 7

15. R. Mateescu and M. Sighireanu. Efficient on-the-fly model-checking for regular alternation-free mu-calculus. Technical Report 3899, INRIA, March 2000. To appear in *Science of Computer Programming*. 17

16. L. Mikhailov and M. Butler. An approach to combining B and Alloy. In D. Bert, J. P. Bowen, M. C. Henson, and K. Robinson, eds, *Proceedings 2nd Conference of B and Z Users (ZB'2002) – Formal Specification and Development in Z and B*, Grenoble, France, pp. 140–161, LNCS 2272. Springer-Verlag, 2002. 7, 20

17. J. C. van de Pol and M. Valero Espada. Formal specification of JavaSpaces architecture using μCRL. In F. Arbab and C. L. Talcott, eds, *Proceedings 5th Conference on Coordination Languages and Models (COORDINATION'2002)*, York, UK, LNCS 2315, pp. 274–290. Springer-Verlag, 2002. 15

18. E. Sekerinski and K. Sere (eds). *Program Development by Refinement*. Springer-Verlag, 1999. 6

19. A. L. Vergroesen, P. R. Hoek, F. J. Carati, J. A. J. A. Dominicus, A. A. ten Have, and D. Schütz. An automatic in-flight data acquisition system for the RNLN Lynx helicopter. In *Proceedings 19th International Symposium on Aircraft Integrated Monitoring Systems (AIMS'98)*, Garmisch Partenkirchen, Germany, May 1998. 2

20. A. G. Wouters. Manual for the μCRL tool set (version 2.8.2). Report SEN-R0130, CWI, December 2001. 7, 13

A Deductive Proof System for CTL*

Amir Pnueli[1] and Yonit Kesten[2]

[1] Weizmann Institute of Science
amir@wisdom.weizmann.ac.il
[2] Ben Gurion University
ykesten@bgumail.bgu.ac.il

Abstract. The paper presents a sound and (relatively) complete deductive proof system for the verification of CTL* properties over possibly infinite-state reactive systems. The proof system is based on a set of proof rules for the verification of *basic* CTL* formulas, namely CTL* formulas with no embedded path quantifiers. We first show how to decompose the proof of a general (non-basic) CTL* formula into proofs of basic CTL* formulas. We then present proof rules for some of the most useful basic CTL* formulas, then present a methodology for transforming an arbitrary basic formula into one of these special cases.

1 Introduction

The paper presents a sound and (relatively) complete deductive proof system for the verification of CTL* properties over possibly infinite-state reactive systems. The logic CTL* is a temporal logic which can express linear-time as well as branching-time temporal properties, and combinations thereof, and contains both LTL and CTL as sub-logics. A complete deductive proof system for linear-time temporal logic (LTL) has been presented in [16] and further elaborated in [17] and [18]. This proof system has been successfully implemented in the Stanford Temporal Verifier STEP [15]. The presented work can be viewed as an extension of the approach of [16] to the logic CTL*.

A deductive proof system for CTL* is valuable for several reasons. In spite of the impressive progress in the various versions of model-checking and other algorithmic verification techniques, they are still restricted to finite-state systems. The only verification method known to be complete for all programs is still the method of deductive verification. There are special benefits to the extension of the deductive methodology from the linear-time framework to the more expressive branching semantics of CTL*:

1. Some important system properties are expressible in CTL* but not in LTL. Typically, these are "possibility" properties, such as the *viability* of a system, stating that any reachable state can spawn a fair computation. This is strongly related to the non-zeno'ness of real-time and hybrid systems.

---

* This research was supported in part by the John von Newman Minerva Center for the Verification of Reactive Systems.

L. Brim et al. (Eds.): CONCUR 2002, LNCS 2421, pp. 24–40, 2002.
© Springer-Verlag Berlin Heidelberg 2002

2. As shown in [21], the problem of synthesis of a reactive module can be solved by checking for validity of a certain CTL* formula, even if the original specification is a pure LTL formula.

Deductive verification of CTL* formulas is valuable even in the context of finite-state systems which can be model-checked:

3. A counter-example of even simple CTL formulas such as $E\Box\, p$ is no longer a simple finite printable trace. A convincing evidence of a counter-example could be an automatically produced *proof* of its existence.
4. In general, model-checking is useful if it produces a counter-example. However, when it terminates declaring the property to be valid, the user is not always convinced. A *deductive proof* can provide a convincing argument of such a validity [19,20].

The proof system presented here is based on a set of proof rules for *basic* CTL* formulas, which are CTL* formulas with no embedded path quantifiers. Thus, a basic CTL* formula has the form $\mathcal{Q}\varphi$, where $\mathcal{Q}$ is a path quantifier and φ is a *path formula* (according to the CTL* terminology) or, equivalently, can be described as an LTL formula. As a first step, we reduce the problem of verifying an arbitrary CTL* formula into a set of verification tasks of the form $p_i \Rightarrow \beta_i$ where p_i is an assertion and β_i is a basic CTL* formula. This reduction is based on the following observation: Let $f(\beta)$ be a CTL* formula which contains one or more occurrences of the basic CTL* formula β. Then, a sufficient condition for $f(\beta)$ to be valid over the computation tree of system $\mathcal{D}$ ($\mathcal{D}$-valid) is the $\mathcal{D}$-validity of the formulas $p \Rightarrow \beta$ and $f(p)$, for some assertion p, where $f(p)$ is obtained from $f(\beta)$ by replacing all occurrences of β by the assertion p. By repeated application of such replacements (for appropriately designed assertions p), we reduce the verification problem of an arbitrary CTL* formula to a set of verification problems, each requiring a proof of a formula of the form $p_i \Rightarrow \beta_i$.

In the context of finite-state model checking, this decomposition of the verification task based on the path quantifiers has been first proposed by Emerson and Lei in [5]. It has been used again in [12] for the construction of a symbolic model checker (SMC) for CTL* properties over finite state systems.

Concentrating on rules for verifying properties of the form $p \Rightarrow \beta$, we present first a set of rules for the special cases of basic formulas of the forms $A\Box\, q$, $E\bigcirc q$, $q\,E\mathcal{U}\,r$, $E_f\Box\, q$, and $A_f\Diamond\, q$. For the universal path quantifiers, these rules are adapted versions of corresponding LTL rules taken from [16].

To deal with *arbitrary* basic CTL* formulas, we introduce another reduction principle which replaces each *basic path formula* by a newly introduced boolean variable which is added to the system $\mathcal{D}$. This reduction can be viewed as a simplified version of the tableau construction proposed in [14] and later referred to as the construction of a *tester* [11]. A basic path formula is a path formula whose principal operator is temporal and it contains no other nested temporal operators.

Thus, our proof method is based on two *statification* transformations which successively replace temporal formulas by assertions which contain no path quantifiers or temporal operators. The first transformation replaces a basic CTL* formula β by an assertion p, provided that we can independently establish the $\mathcal{D}$-validity of the entailment $p \Rightarrow \beta$. The second transformation replaces the basic path formula φ by the single boolean variable x_φ (which is also a trivial assertion) at the price of augmenting the system $\mathcal{D}$ by a temporal tester T_φ.

It is interesting to compare the general structure of this proof system with the LTL deductive proof system presented in [16] and elaborated in [17,18,15]. Similar to the approach presented here, the system lists first useful rules for special form formulas, the most important of which are formulas of the form $p \Rightarrow \Box q$, $p \Rightarrow \Diamond q$, and $\Box \Diamond p \Rightarrow \Box \Diamond q$, where p and q are arbitrary *past formulas*. To deal with the general case, [16] invokes a general canonic-form theorem, according to which every (quantifier-free) LTL formula is equivalent to a conjunction of formulas of the form $\Box \Diamond p_i \Rightarrow \Box \Diamond q_i$, for some past formulas p_i and q_i.

While this approach is theoretically adequate, it is not a practically acceptable solution to the verification of arbitrary LTL formulas. This is because the best known algorithms for converting an arbitrary LTL formula into canonic form are at least exponential (e.g., [6] which is actually non-elementary). A better approach to the verification of arbitrary LTL formulas is based on the notion of *deductive model checking* [23], which can also be described as a tableau-based construction.

The approach presented here, based on successive elimination of temporal operators, can be viewed as an incremental tableau construction and offers a viable new approach to the verification of arbitrary LTL formulas, even though it is presented as a part of a deductive proof system for CTL*, which is a more complex logic than LTL.

There have been two earlier complete axiomatizations of propositional CTL*. The work reported in [22] provides (the first) complete axiomatization of pure propositional CTL*, thus solving a long standing open problem in branching-time temporal logic. Comparing this impressive result with our work, we should remind the reader of our motivation which is to provide a deductive system to verify first-order CTL* expressible properties of reactive systems, where the computational model includes a full fledged set of weak and strong fairness assumptions. Our goal is to derive a deductive system for CTL* which extends the LTL deductive methodology expounded in [18] and provides realistic tools for verifying non-trivial reactive systems, such as those implemented in the STeP system [15]. Theoretically, this goal can be implemented even within the pure-logic axiomatization of [22], because CTL* (being more expressive than LTL) can certainly capture the computation tree of a reactive system including all fairness assumptions. This allows us to reduce the verification problem $\mathcal{D} \models \varphi$ into the pure validity problem $\models S_\mathcal{D} \rightarrow \varphi$, where $S_\mathcal{D}$ is the CTL* formula characterizing the computation tree of system $\mathcal{D}$. While this is possible in theory, it is highly impractical and leads to very obscure and unreadable proofs. A similar dichotomy exists in finite-state LTL verification. On one hand, one can use the special LTL model checking technique proposed in [14] for verifying $\mathcal{D} \models \varphi$ whose complexity is exponential in φ but only linear in $\mathcal{D}$. On the other hand, one can reduce this to the problem of checking the validity of the implication $S_{\mathcal{D}} \rightarrow \varphi$ which is exponential in both φ and $\mathcal{D}$. It is obvious that the specialized technique which does not transform the system into a formula is (exponentially) better than the reductionist approach. While the analogy between finite-state model checking and deductive verification is not perfect, this argument serves to indicate the inherent rise in complexity when using pure temporal logic techniques for practical verification.

Another related work is that of Sprenger [25]. This approach is much closer to our own, because it preserves the distinction between the system and the formula, and contains a special treatment of the different kinds of fairness. The advantage of our approach is that it proceeds at a coarser level of granularity, and therefore yields a much simpler proof system. Sprenger's method of local model checking proceeds at steps analogous to the basic steps of a tableau construction, including step by step handling of the boolean connectives. Our approach attempts to get rid of one temporal operator at each step, applying the appropriate rule for this operator, with no need to trace cycles and close leaves in the tableau. We believe that our proof system and its application to be significantly more succinct and effective and, therefore, more amenable to the construction of support systems for serious reactive verification.

The paper is organized as follows. In section 2 we present the FDS computation model. In Section 3, we present the logic CTL*. In Section 4, we show how to decompose the task of verifying a general CTL* formula into tasks, each verifying a basic CTL* formula. In Section 5, we present the methodology by which we propose to prove a basic CTL* formula. This methodology starts by presenting a set of proof rules for some of the most useful basic CTL* properties, and claim soundness and completeness of these rules. We then show how to reduce an arbitrary basic CTL* formula to one of these special cases. Finally, in Section 6, we present an example of the application of these rules.

2   The Computational Model

As a computational model for reactive systems, we take the model of *fair discrete system* (FDS). An FDS $\mathcal{D} : \langle V, \Theta, \rho, \mathcal{J}, \mathcal{C} \rangle$ consists of the following components.

- $V = \{u_1, ..., u_n\}$: A finite set of typed *state variables* over possibly infinite domains. We define a *state* s to be a type-consistent interpretation of V, assigning to each variable $u \in V$ a value $s[u]$ in its domain. We denote by Σ the set of all states.
- Θ : The *initial condition*. This is an assertion characterizing all the initial states of the FDS. A state is called *initial* if it satisfies Θ.
- ρ : A *transition relation*. This is an assertion $\rho(V, V')$, relating a state $s \in \Sigma$ to its $\mathcal{D}$-successor $s' \in \Sigma$ by referring to both unprimed and primed versions of the state variables. The transition relation $\rho(V, V')$ identifies state s' as a $\mathcal{D}$-*successor* of state s if $\langle s, s' \rangle \models \rho(V, V')$, where $\langle s, s' \rangle$ is the joint interpretation which interprets $x \in V$ as $s[x]$, and x' as $s'[x]$.

- $\mathcal{J} = \{J_1, \ldots, J_k\}$: A set of assertions expressing the *justice (weak fairness)* requirements. Intentionally, the justice requirement $J \in \mathcal{J}$ stipulates that every computation contains infinitely many J-states (states satisfying J).
- $\mathcal{C} = \{\langle p_1, q_1 \rangle, \ldots \langle p_n, q_n \rangle\}$: A set of assertions expressing the *compassion (strong fairness)* requirements . Intentionally, the compassion requirement $\langle p, q \rangle \in \mathcal{C}$ stipulates that every computation containing infinitely many p-states also contains infinitely many q-states.

Let $\sigma : s_0, s_1, \ldots$, be a sequence of states, φ be an assertion, and $j \geq 0$ be a natural number. We say that j is a φ-position of σ if s_j is a φ-state. Let $\mathcal{D}$ be an FDS for which the above components have been identified. We define a *run* of $\mathcal{D}$ to be a finite or infinite sequence of states $\sigma : s_0, s_1, \ldots$, satisfying the requirement of

- *Consecution:* For each $j = 0, 1, \ldots$, the state s_{j+1} is a $\mathcal{D}$-successor of the state s_j.

and such that it is either infinite, or terminates at a state s_k which has no $\mathcal{D}$-successors.

We denote by $runs(\mathcal{D})$ the set of runs of $\mathcal{D}$. An infinite run of $\mathcal{D}$ is called *fair* if it satisfies the following:

- *Justice:*   For each $J \in \mathcal{J}$, σ contains infinitely many J-positions
- *Compassion:* For each $\langle p, q \rangle \in \mathcal{C}$, if σ contains infinitely many p-positions, it must also contain infinitely many q-positions.

We say that a fair run $\sigma : s_0, s_1, \ldots$ is a *computation* of $\mathcal{D}$ if it satisfies

- *Initiality:* s_0 is initial, i.e., $s_0 \models \Theta$.

We denote by $\mathcal{C}omp(\mathcal{D})$ the set of all computations of $\mathcal{D}$.

A state s is said to be *reachable* if there exists a run $s_0, s_1, s_2, \ldots, s_k = s, \ldots$ such that $s_0 \models \Theta$. We say that a state s is *feasible* if it participates in some computation of $\mathcal{D}$. An FDS $\mathcal{D}$ is *feasible* if it has at least one computation, i.e., if $\mathcal{C}omp(\mathcal{D}) \neq \emptyset$. We say that an FDS $\mathcal{D}$ is *viable* if every reachable state is feasible. Note that the FDS model does not guarantee viability.

Parallel Composition of FDS's

Fair discrete systems can be composed in parallel. Let $\mathcal{D}_i = \langle V_i, \Theta_i, \rho_i, \mathcal{J}_i, \mathcal{C}_i \rangle$, $i \in \{1, 2\}$, be two fair discrete systems. Two versions of parallel composition are used. Asynchronous composition is used to assemble an asynchronous system from its components (see [KP00]). Synchronous composition is used in some cases, to assemble a system from its components (in particular when considering hardware designs which are naturally synchronous). However, our primary use of synchronous composition is for combining a system with a *tester* T_φ for a basic LTL formula φ, as described in section 5. We define the *synchronous* parallel composition of two FDS's to be

$$\mathcal{D} = \langle V, \Theta, \rho, \mathcal{J}, \mathcal{C} \rangle \quad = \quad \langle V_1, \Theta_1, \rho_1, \mathcal{J}_1, \mathcal{C}_1 \rangle \parallel\!\parallel \langle V_2, \Theta_2, \rho_2, \mathcal{J}_2, \mathcal{C}_2 \rangle, \quad \text{where}$$
$$V = V_1 \cup V_2 \quad \Theta = \Theta_1 \wedge \Theta_2, \quad \rho = \rho_1 \wedge \rho_2, \quad \mathcal{J} = \mathcal{J}_1 \cup \mathcal{J}_2, \quad \mathcal{C} = \mathcal{C}_1 \cup \mathcal{C}_2.$$

We can view the execution of $\mathcal{D}$ as the *joint execution* of $\mathcal{D}_1$ and $\mathcal{D}_2$.

3   Branching Temporal Logic

In the following we define the branching temporal logic CTL* (see [4]). We assume a finite set of variables V over possibly infinite domains, and an underlying assertion language $\mathcal{L}$ which contains the predicate calculus augmented with fix-point operators.[1] We assume that $\mathcal{L}$ contains interpreted symbols for expressing the standard operations and relations over some concrete domains, such as the integers. A CTL* formula is constructed out of *assertions* (formulas over $\mathcal{L}$) to which we apply the boolean operators, temporal operators and path quantifiers. The basic temporal operators are

$\bigcirc$ – Next $\mathcal{U}$ – Until $\mathcal{W}$ – waiting-for

Additional temporal operators may be defined as follows:

$$\Diamond p = \text{T}\mathcal{U}p, \quad \Box p = \neg\Diamond\neg p,$$

The path quantifiers are E, A, E_f and A_f. We refer to E_f and A_f as the *fair* path quantifiers and to E and A as the *unrestricted* path quantifiers. In the following, we present the syntax and semantics of the logic which is interpreted over the computation tree generated by an FDS. We use the terms *path* and *fair path* as synonymous to a *run* and a *fair run* respectively, over an FDS. Let $\pi : s_0, s_1, \ldots$ be a run of $\mathcal{D}$. Then, we write $\pi[0]$ to denote s_0, the first state in π and, for $j \geq 0$, we write $\pi[j..] = s_j, s_{j+1}, \ldots$ to denote the suffix of π obtained by omitting the first j states. If the path π is finite, we use $|\pi|$ to denote its length.

The Logic CTL*

There are two types of sub-formulas in CTL*: *state formulas* that are interpreted over states, and *path formulas* that are interpreted over paths. The syntax of a CTL* formula is defined inductively as follows.

State formulas:
- Every assertion in $\mathcal{L}$ is a state formula.
- If p is a *path formula*, then Ep, Ap, E_fp and A_fp are state formulas.
- If p and q are state formulas then so are $p \vee q$ and $p \wedge q$.

Path formulas:
- Every state formula is a path formula.
- If p and q are path formulas then so are $p \vee q, p \wedge q, \bigcirc p, p\mathcal{U}q$ and $p\mathcal{W}q$.

The formulas of CTL* are all the state formulas generated by the above rules.

We say that p is a *basic* CTL* *formula* if p is a CTL* formula with no embedded path quantifiers. A basic CTL* formula of the form $A\psi$ or $A_f\psi$ ($E\psi$ or $E_f\psi$) is called a basic *universal* (*existential*) formula. We define a basic *path formula* to be a path formula φ whose principal operator is temporal, and such that φ

---

[1] As is well known ([13],) a first-order language is not adequate for (relative) completeness of a temporal proof system for infinite state reactive programs. The use of minimal and maximal fix-points for relative completeness of the liveness rules is discussed in [16], based on [26].

contains no other temporal operators. Note that the set of basic universal CTL*
formulas corresponds to the set of linear temporal logic formulas (LTL). We refer
to the set of variables that occur in a formula p as the *vocabulary of p*. The
semantics of a CTL* formula p is defined with respect to an FDS $\mathcal{D}$ over the
vocabulary of p. The semantics is defined inductively as follows.

State formulas are interpreted over states in $\mathcal{D}$. We define the notion of a
CTL* formula p holding at a state s in $\mathcal{D}$, denoted $(\mathcal{D}, s) \models p$, as follows:

- For an assertion p,
  $$(\mathcal{D}, s) \models p \qquad \Leftrightarrow \qquad s \models p$$
- For state formulas p and q,
  $$(\mathcal{D}, s) \models p \vee q \quad \Leftrightarrow \quad (\mathcal{D}, s) \models p \text{ or } (\mathcal{D}, s) \models q$$
  $$(\mathcal{D}, s) \models p \wedge q \quad \Leftrightarrow \quad (\mathcal{D}, s) \models p \text{ and } (\mathcal{D}, s) \models q$$
- For a path formula p,
  $$(\mathcal{D}, s) \models Ep \quad \Leftrightarrow \quad (\mathcal{D}, \pi) \models p \text{ for some path } \pi \in runs(\mathcal{D}) \text{ satisfying}$$
  $$\pi[0] = s.$$
  $$(\mathcal{D}, s) \models Ap \quad \Leftrightarrow \quad (\mathcal{D}, \pi) \models p \text{ for all paths } \pi \in runs(\mathcal{D}) \text{ satisfying}$$
  $$\pi[0] = s.$$

The semantics of $E_f p$ and $A_f p$ are defined similar to Ep and Ap respectively,
replacing *path* (run) by *fair path* (fair runs).

Path formulas are interpreted over runs of $\mathcal{D}$. We define the notion of a CTL*
formula p holding at a run $\pi \in runs(\mathcal{D})$, denoted $(\mathcal{D}, \pi) \models p$, as follows:

- For a state formula p,
  $$(\mathcal{D}, \pi) \models p \qquad \Leftrightarrow \qquad (\mathcal{D}, \pi[0]) \models p.$$
- For path formulas p and q,
  $$(\mathcal{D}, \pi) \models p \vee q \quad \Leftrightarrow \quad (\mathcal{D}, \pi) \models p \text{ or } (\mathcal{D}, \pi) \models q$$
  $$(\mathcal{D}, \pi) \models p \wedge q \quad \Leftrightarrow \quad (\mathcal{D}, \pi) \models p \text{ and } (\mathcal{D}, \pi) \models q$$
  $$(\mathcal{D}, \pi) \models \bigcirc p \quad \Leftrightarrow \quad |\pi| > 1 \text{ and } (\mathcal{D}, \pi[1..]) \models p$$
  $$(\mathcal{D}, \pi, j) \models p \mathcal{U} q \quad \Leftrightarrow \quad (\mathcal{D}, \pi[k..]) \models q \text{ for some } k \geq 0, \text{ and}$$
  $$(\mathcal{D}, \pi[i..]) \models p \text{ for every } i, 0 \leq i < k$$
  $$(\mathcal{D}, \pi, j) \models p \mathcal{W} q \quad \Leftrightarrow \quad (\mathcal{D}, \pi) \models p \mathcal{U} q, \text{ or } (\mathcal{D}, \pi[i..]) \models p \text{ for all } i < |\pi|.$$

Let p be a CTL* formula. We say that p *holds* on $\mathcal{D}$ (p is $\mathcal{D}$-valid), denoted $\mathcal{D} \models p$,
if $(\mathcal{D}, s) \models p$, for every initial state s in $\mathcal{D}$. A CTL* formula p is called *satisfiable*
if it holds on some model. A CTL* formula is called *valid* if it holds on all models.

We refer to a state which satisfies p as a *p-state*. Let p and q be CTL* formulas.
We introduce the abbreviation

$$p \Rightarrow q \quad \text{for} \quad A \square (p \rightarrow q).$$

where $p \rightarrow q$ is the logical implication equivalent to $\neg p \vee q$. Thus, the formula
$p \Rightarrow q$ holds at $\mathcal{D}$ if the implication $p \rightarrow q$ holds at all reachable states.

Let V be a set of variables and ψ be a CTL* formula over V. We denote
by ψ' the formula ψ in which every variable $v \in V$ is replaced by the primed
variable v'.

Without loss of generality, we assume that a formula is given in *positive
normal form*, which means that negation is only applied to assertions, namely, to
formulas with no temporal or path operators. Any CTL* formula can be brought

> For a formula $f(\varphi)$,
> a basic CTL* formula φ,
> and an assertion p,
>
> $$\text{R1. } p \Rightarrow \varphi$$
> $$\frac{\text{R2. } \ f(p)}{f(\varphi)}$$

Fig. 1. BASIC-STATE

to a congruent positive form by a repeated application of the following rewriting rules.

$$
\begin{aligned}
\neg\neg p &\rightarrow p \\
\neg(p \wedge q) &\rightarrow (\neg p \vee \neg q) \\
\neg(p \vee q) &\rightarrow (\neg p \wedge \neg q) \\
\neg \bigcirc p &\rightarrow \bigcirc \neg p \\
\neg(p \, \mathcal{U} \, q) &\rightarrow (\neg q) \, \mathcal{W} \, (\neg p \wedge \neg q) \\
\neg(p \, \mathcal{W} \, q) &\rightarrow (\neg q) \, \mathcal{U} \, (\neg p \wedge \neg q) \\
\neg A_f p &\rightarrow E_f \neg p \\
\neg E_f p &\rightarrow A_f \neg p
\end{aligned}
$$

4   Decomposing a Formula into Basic CTL* Formulas

Consider a CTL* formula φ which we wish to verify over an FDS $\mathcal{D}$. As a first step, we show how to reduce the task of verifying the formula φ into simpler subtasks, each required to verify a basic CTL* formula over $\mathcal{D}$. This reduction repeatedly applies rule BASIC-STATE which is presented in Fig. 1.

The rule considers an arbitrary formula f which contains one or more occurrences of the basic CTL* formula φ. The rule calls for an identification of an assertion p which characterizes all states which satisfy the formula φ. It then reduces the task of verifying $f(\varphi)$ into the two simpler tasks of verifying the entailment $p \Rightarrow \varphi$, where φ is a basic CTL* formula, and the formula $f(p)$ obtained from f by substituting the assertion p for all occurrences of φ.

Example

Consider the system $\mathcal{D}$ presented in Fig. 2.

This system has a single state variable x and no fairness conditions. For this system we wish to prove the property $f : E\Box \, E\Diamond(x = 1)$, claiming the existence of a run from each of whose states it is possible to reach a state at which $x = 1$.

Using BASIC-STATE, it is possible to reduce the task of verifying the non-basic formula $E\Box \, E\Diamond(x = 1)$ into the two tasks of verifying

R1. $(x = 0) \Rightarrow E\Diamond(x = 1)$
R2. $E\Box(x = 0)$

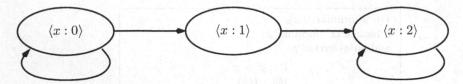

Fig. 2. An example system $\mathcal{D}$

Note that, as the assertion p, we have chosen $x = 0$. The design of an appropriate assertion p which characterizes states satisfying φ is the part which requires creativity and ingenuity in the application of BASIC-STATE.

In the following section, we will present methods which can be used to prove entailments of the form $p \Rightarrow \varphi$ for an assertion p and basic CTL* formula φ.

5   Proof Rules for Basic CTL* Properties

In this section we present a set of proof rules for proving entailments of the form $p \Rightarrow \varphi$ for an assertion p and a basic CTL* formula φ. To simplify the presentation, we consider only systems with no compassion requirements, and deal only with the *justice* requirements ($\mathcal{J}$).

5.1   Preliminary Inference Rules

We introduce two basic inference rules as part of the deductive system. Let $\mathcal{D}$ be an FDS and p, q be assertions. The first rule is *generalization*, presented in Figure 3. The rule transforms a state validity (denoted by $\Vdash$) into a temporal validity (denoted by $\models$). The premise $\Vdash p$ states that assertion p holds at every possible state. Then obviously, p holds at every reachable state of every model, and therefore the basic universal CTL* formula $A \square p$ holds at the initial state of every model (equivalently, $\mathcal{D} \models A \square p$ for every FDS $\mathcal{D}$).

The second rule is *entailment modus ponens*, presented in Figure 4. The rule states that if every reachable state satisfies both p and the implication $p \rightarrow q$ (i.e., $\mathcal{D}$ satisfies $A \square p$ and $A \square (p \rightarrow q)$), then q holds at every reachable state ($\mathcal{D}$ satisfies $A \square q$).

In the following we present a set of proof rules all having a common structure. Premises are stated above the line and the conclusion is presented below the line.

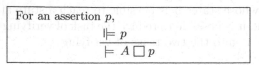

Fig. 3. GEN (generalization)

For assertions p and q,

$$\frac{\models A \,\square\, p, \quad \models p \Rightarrow q}{\models A \,\square\, q}$$

Fig. 4. EMP (entailment modus ponens)

Each rule claims that if the premises hold over $\mathcal{D}$, then so does the conclusion. When the validities of the premises and the conclusion are over different FDS's, the relevant FDS are stated explicitly, otherwise the common FDS is omitted.

5.2   Safety Rules

First we consider safety formulas of the form $\mathcal{Q} \,\square\, q$, where q is an assertion and $\mathcal{Q} \in \{A, A_f, E, E_f\}$ is a path quantifier. We refer to such formulas as *invariance* formulas. We use the terms *universal* and *existential* invariance for the CTL* formulas $\{A \,\square\, q, A_f \,\square\, q\}$ and $\{E \,\square\, q, E_f \,\square\, q\}$ respectively.

Universal Invariance In Figure 5, we present the rule for universal invariance, which is similar to the rule for LTL invariance. Rule A-INV states that if the set of premises $I1 - I3$ are $\mathcal{D}$-valid, then the conclusion is $\mathcal{D}$-valid. Premise I1 and I2 are shorthand notations for $\mathcal{D} \models A \,\square\, (p \rightarrow \varphi)$ and $\mathcal{D} \models A \,\square\, (\varphi \rightarrow q)$ respectively. Premise I1 states that every reachable p-state is also a φ-state. Similarly, premise I2 states that every reachable φ-state is a q-state. Assertion φ is introduced to strengthen assertion q in case q is not *inductive*, namely, in case q does not satisfy I3 (see [18] for a discussion on inductive assertions). Premise I3 is a shorthand notation for $\mathcal{D} \models A \,\square\, (\varphi(V) \;\wedge\; \rho(V,V') \rightarrow \varphi(V'))$. The premise states that every ρ-successor of a reachable φ-state is a φ-state (equivalently, all transitions of $\mathcal{D}$ preserve φ). Rule A-INV establishes the invariance formula $A \,\square\, q$ over all reachable p-states, for some assertion p.

Claim (universal invariance). Let $\mathcal{D}$ be an FDS. Rule A-INV is sound and relatively complete, for proving unrestricted universal (state) invariance over $\mathcal{D}$.

Proof Sketch The proof of completeness is based on the identification of an assertion φ, expressible in our assertional language, which satisfies the premises

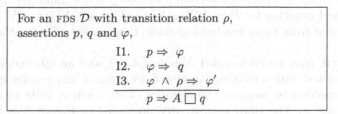

Fig. 5. A-INV (universal invariance)

For an FDS $\mathcal{D}$ with transition relation ρ,
assertions p, q, φ

> N1. $p \Rightarrow \varphi$
> N2. $\varphi \Rightarrow \exists V' : \rho \wedge q'$
> ——————————————
> $p \Rightarrow E \bigcirc q$

Fig. 6. E-NEXT

For an FDS $\mathcal{D}$ with transition relation ρ,
assertions p, q, r and φ,
a well-founded domain $(\mathcal{A}, \succ)$, and a ranking function $\delta : \Sigma \mapsto \mathcal{A}$

> U1. $p \Rightarrow \varphi$
> U2. $\varphi \Rightarrow r \vee (q \wedge \exists V' : (\rho \wedge \varphi' \wedge \delta' < \delta))$
> ——————————————
> $p \Rightarrow qE\mathcal{U}r$

Fig. 7. E-UNTIL

of rule A-INV. We follow the construction of [16] (further elaborated in [17]) to show the existence of an assertion characterizing all the states that can appear in a finite run of a system $\mathcal{D}$. □

Existential Invariance We define a *well-founded domain* $(\mathcal{A}, \succ)$ to consist of a set $\mathcal{A}$ and a *well-founded order* relation $\succ$ on $\mathcal{A}$. The order relation $\succ$ is called *well-founded* if there does not exist an infinitely descending sequence $a_0, a_1, \ldots$ of elements of $\mathcal{A}$ such that $a_0 \succ a_1 \succ \ldots$

Next, we present three proof rules which together constitute a sound and (relatively) complete set for proving existential (state) invariance. The first rules, E-NEXT and E-UNTIL presented in Figures 6 and 7, prove the validity of the CTL* properties $E \bigcirc q$ and $qE\mathcal{U}r$ respectively, over all reachable p-states, where p, q and r are assertions.

Both rules are defined for the unrestricted existential path quantifier E which quantifies over any path, not necessarily a fair path (recall that E is weaker than E_f). While not being invariance rules by themselves, the E-NEXT and E-UNTIL rules are included in this subsection because they are essential for the invariance rule E_f-INV presented in Figure 8. Rule E-NEXT uses an intermediate assertion φ which strengthen assertion p in case p is not inductive. Premise N2 is a shorthand notation for $\mathcal{D} \models A \square (\varphi(V) \rightarrow \exists V' : \rho(V, V') \wedge q(V'))$. The premise states that from every reachable φ-state, there exists a $\mathcal{D}$-transition into a q-state.

The rule E-UNTIL uses a well-founded domain $(\mathcal{A}, \succ)$, and an intermediate assertion φ, associated with a ranking function δ. Function δ maps states into the set $\mathcal{A}$ and is intended to measure the distance of the current state to a state satisfying the goal r. The third rule, E_f-INV presented in Figure 8, is the existential invariance rule. We use the notation $(i \oplus_m 1)$ for $(i + 1) mod\ m$. Rule

For assertions $p, \varphi_0, \ldots, \varphi_m$,
an FDS $\mathcal{D}$ with justice requirements $J_0 = \text{T}, J_1, \ldots, J_m \in \mathcal{J}$,

$$\text{I1.} \qquad p \Rightarrow \bigvee_{i=0}^{m} \varphi_i$$

For $i = 0, \ldots, m$,

$$\text{I2.} \qquad \varphi_i \Rightarrow J_i$$

$$\text{I3.} \qquad \varphi_i \Rightarrow q \wedge E \bigcirc (q E \mathcal{U} \varphi_{i \oplus_m 1})$$
$$\overline{p \Rightarrow E_f \,\Box\, q}$$

Fig. 8. E_f-INV

E_f-INV proves a temporal property using three premises. Premises I1 and I2 use state reasoning, and premise I3 requires temporal reasoning. Premise I3 is resolved by the rules E-NEXT and E-UNTIL which transform the temporal reasoning into state reasoning. For the special case that $p = \Theta$ and $q = \text{T}$, rule E_f-INV proves *feasibility* of $\mathcal{D}$. For the case that $p = q = \text{T}$, the rule proves *viability* of $\mathcal{D}$.

Claim (existential invariance). Let $\mathcal{D}$ be an FDS. Rules E-NEXT, E-UNTIL, and E_f-INV are sound and relatively complete, for proving their respective conclusions.

Proof Sketch: For rule E-NEXT, it is straightforward to write a first-order assertion φ which characterizes all the reachable p-states, i.e. all p-states participating in a run of $\mathcal{D}$. For rule E-UNTIL, we can use again an assertion φ which characterizes all the reachable p-states. We can use a ranking function δ which measures the number of steps from a reachable p-state s to its closest r-state reachable by a continuous q-path. It only remains to show that these two constructs are expressible within our assertional language. For rule E_f-INV, we can use a maximal fix-point expression to construct an assertion φ characterizing all accessible states initiating a continuous-q fair path. For the sub-assertions φ_i, we can take $\varphi \wedge J_i$. $\qquad \Box$

5.3   Liveness Properties

Universal Liveness Under Justice In Figure 9, we present the rule for *universal eventuality* properties of the form $p \Rightarrow A_f \Diamond r$. The rule uses a well-founded domain $(\mathcal{A}, \succ)$, and a set of intermediate assertions $\varphi_1, \ldots, \varphi_m$, each associated with its own ranking function δ_i. Each function δ_i is intended to measure the distance of the current state to a state satisfying the goal q. Premise W1 states that every p-state satisfies q or one of $\varphi_1, \ldots, \varphi_m$. Premise W2 states that for every i, $1 \leq i \leq m$, a φ_i-state with rank $\delta_i = u$ is followed by either a q-state or a φ_i-state that does not satisfy J_i and has the same rank u, or by a φ_j-state ($1 \leq j \leq m$) with a smaller rank (i.e., $u \succ \delta_j$). The rule claims that if

For an FDS $\mathcal{D}$ with transition relation ρ and justice set $\mathcal{J} = \{J_1, \ldots, J_m\}$,
assertions $p, q, \varphi_1, \ldots, \varphi_m$,
well-founded domain $(\mathcal{A}, \succ)$ and ranking functions $\delta_1, \ldots, \delta_m : \Sigma \mapsto \mathcal{A}$

W1. $p \qquad\qquad \Rightarrow \quad q \vee \bigvee_{j=1}^{m} \varphi_j$

W2. For $i = 1, \ldots, m$

$$\varphi_i \wedge \rho \quad \Rightarrow \quad q' \vee (\neg J_i' \wedge \varphi_i' \wedge \delta_i = \delta_i') \vee \left(\bigvee_{j=1}^{m} \varphi_j' \wedge (\delta_i \succ \delta_j') \right)$$

$p \Rightarrow A_f \Diamond q$

Fig. 9. Rule A_f-EVENT (universal well-founded eventuality under justice)

For assertions p and q,

$$p \wedge \neg q \Rightarrow A_f \Diamond \text{F}$$

$p \Rightarrow A_f q$

Fig. 10. A_f-ASRT

premise W1, and the set of m premises W2 are $\mathcal{D}$-valid, then the (fair) universal
eventuality property $A_f \Diamond q$ is satisfied by all reachable p-states.

Claim (Completeness of universal eventuality). Rule A_f-EVENT is sound and
relatively complete, for proving the $\mathcal{D}$-validity of universal eventuality formulas.

Proof Sketch: This rule is semantically equivalent to the LTL rule for the
property $p \Rightarrow \Diamond q$. We refer the reader to [16] for the non-trivial proof of relative
completeness of this rule.   □

5.4 Assertional Basic CTL* Formulas

As the last rules for special cases, we present two rules dealing with the entailments $p \Rightarrow Qq$, where p and q are assertions and $Q \in \{A_f, E_f\}$ is a fair path
quantifier.

Rule A_f-ASRT, presented in Fig. 10, can be used in order to establish the
validity of the entailment $p \Rightarrow A_f q$, for the case that p and q are assertions.

The rule claims that, in order to prove the validity of $p \Rightarrow A_f q$, it is sufficient
to show that no fair runs can depart from a reachable state satisfying $p \wedge \neg q$.
This is shown by proving (using rule A_f-EVENT) that every fair run departing
from a reachable $(p \wedge \neg q)$-state satisfies $A_f \Diamond \text{F}$ ("eventually false"), which is
obviously impossible. Thus there can be no fair runs departing from such a state
and, therefore, no such states are reachable as part of a computation.

The dual rule E_f-ASRT is presented in Fig. 11.

$$\text{For assertions } p \text{ and } q,$$
$$\frac{p \Rightarrow q \wedge E_f \,\square\, \text{T}}{p \Rightarrow E_f q}$$

Fig. 11. E_f-ASRT

This rule claims that, in order to prove $p \Rightarrow E_f q$, it is sufficient to show that every reachable p-state satisfies q and initiates at least one fair run.

5.5   Basic CTL* Properties: The General Case

Finally, we present our general approach to the verification of an entailment of the form $p \Rightarrow \varphi$ for an assertion p and a general basic CTL* formula φ.

The approach is based on a successive elimination of temporal operators from the formula φ until it becomes an assertional basic CTL* formula, to which we can apply rules A_f-ASRT or E_f-ASRT. Elimination of the temporal operators is based on the construction of *temporal testers*, as follows.

We define a temporal tester for each of the three temporal operators $\bigcirc$, $\mathcal{U}$ and $\mathcal{W}$. These testers are a simplified version of the tableau construction presented in [14] and its later symbolic version which was referred to as *tester* [11]. For an assertion p, we denote by V_p the set of variables occuring in p. For the basic path formula $\bigcirc p$, we construct the tester $T_{\bigcirc p}$ as follows:

$$
\begin{aligned}
V &\quad : V_p \cup \{x_\bigcirc\} \\
\Theta &\quad : \text{T} \\
\rho &\quad : x_\bigcirc = p' \\
\mathcal{J} = \mathcal{C} &: \emptyset
\end{aligned}
$$

For the basic path formula $p\,\mathcal{U}\,q$, we construct the tester $T_{p\mathcal{U}q}$ as follows:

$$
\begin{aligned}
V &: V_p \cup V_q \cup \{x_\mathcal{U}\} \\
\Theta &: \text{T} \\
\rho &: x_\mathcal{U} = (q \vee p \wedge x'_\mathcal{U} \\
\mathcal{J} &: \{\neg x_\mathcal{U} \vee q\} \\
\mathcal{C} &: \emptyset
\end{aligned}
$$

For the basic path formula $p\,\mathcal{W}\,q$, we construct the tester $T_{p\mathcal{W}q}$ as follows:

$$
\begin{aligned}
V &: V_p \cup V_q \cup \{x_\mathcal{W}\} \\
\Theta &: \text{T} \\
\rho &: x_\mathcal{W} = (q \vee p \wedge x'_\mathcal{W} \\
\mathcal{J} &: \{x_\mathcal{W} \vee (\neg p \wedge \neg q)\} \\
\mathcal{C} &: \emptyset
\end{aligned}
$$

Let $f(\varphi)$ be an arbitrary CTL* formula containing one or more occurrences of the basic path formula φ. In Fig. 12, we present the rule BASIC-PATH which reduces the proof of $f(\varphi)$ to the proof of $f(x_\varphi)$, where x_φ is a boolean variable, and $f(x_\varphi)$ is obtained from $f(\varphi)$ by replacing every occurrence of φ by x_φ.

For a CTL* formula $f(\varphi)$,
a basic path formula φ,
and an FDS $\mathcal{D}$,

$$\frac{\mathcal{D} \,\|\|\, T_\varphi \models \quad f(x_\varphi)}{\mathcal{D} \quad \models \quad f(\varphi)}$$

Fig. 12. BASIC-PATH

6 An Example

In this section, we present an example system and a deductive proof of a property it has. In Fig. 13, we present the system $\mathcal{D}$. This system has a single state variable x and no fairness conditions. For this system we wish to prove the property $\mathrm{T} \Rightarrow A_f \Diamond \Box \, even(x)$, stating that every computation eventually stabilizes with an even value of the state variable x.

Following are the first steps of the deductive proof for this property. The proof is presented in a goal-oriented style, where we identify for each goal the subgoals which are necessary in order to establish the goal and the rule which justifies the deductive step.

$$
\begin{array}{lll}
\mathcal{D} & \models \quad \mathrm{T} \Rightarrow A_f \Diamond \Box \, even(x) & \text{A tester for } x_\Box = \Box \, even(x) \\
\mathcal{D} \,\|\|\, T_\Box & \models \quad \mathrm{T} \Rightarrow A_f \Diamond \, x_\Box & \text{A tester for } x_\Diamond = \Diamond \, x_\Box \\
\mathcal{D} \,\|\|\, T_\Box \,\|\|\, T_\Diamond & \models \quad \mathrm{T} \Rightarrow A_f x_\Diamond &
\end{array}
$$

Thus, these proof steps reduced the task of verifying the formula $\mathrm{T} \Rightarrow A_f \Diamond \Box \, even(x)$ over system $\mathcal{D}$ to the verification of the simpler formula $\mathrm{T} \Rightarrow A_f x_\Diamond$ over the system $\mathcal{D}^* = \mathcal{D} \,\|\|\, T_\Box \,\|\|\, T_\Diamond$. The transition relation of system $\mathcal{D}^*$ is presented in Fig. 14.

The justice requirements associated with $\mathcal{D}^*$ are

$$J_1 : x_\Box \, \vee \, \neg even(x), \qquad J_2 : \neg x_\Diamond \, \vee \, x_\Box$$

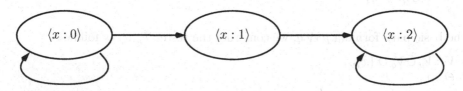

Fig. 13. An example system $\mathcal{D}$

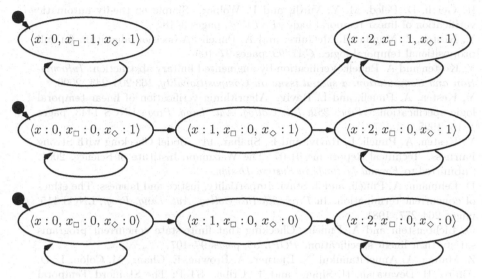

Fig. 14. The augmented system $\mathcal{D}^*$

We now use rule A_f-ASRT in order to reduce the goal $\mathcal{D}^* \models \text{T} \Rightarrow A_f x_\diamond$ into the goal $\mathcal{D}^* \models \neg x_\diamond \Rightarrow A_f \diamondsuit \text{F}$. This goal is proven using rule A_f-EVENT with the following choices:

$$p: \quad \neg x_\diamond$$
$$q: \quad \text{F}$$

$$\varphi_1: \neg x_\square \wedge \neg x_\diamond \wedge \quad even(x) \qquad\qquad \delta_1: 2 - x$$
$$\varphi_2: \neg x_\square \wedge \neg x_\diamond \wedge \neg even(x) \qquad\qquad \delta_2: 2 - x$$

References

1. E. Clarke, E. Emerson, and A. Sistla. Automatic verification of finite state concurrent systems using temporal logic specifications. *ACM Trans. Prog. Lang. Sys.*, 8:244–263, 1986.
2. E. Clarke, O. Grumberg, and K. Hamaguchi. Another look at LTL model checking. *CAV'94*, LNCS 818, pages 415–427.
3. M. Daniele, F. Giunchiglia, and M. Y. Vardi. Improved automata generation for linear time temporal logic. *CAV'99*, LNCS 1633, pages 255–265.
4. E. Emerson. Temporal and modal logics. In J. van Leeuwen, editor, *Handbook of theoretical computer science*, volume B, pages 995–1072. Elsevier, 1990. 29
5. E. Emerson and C. Lei. Modalities for model checking: Branching time strikes back. *POPL'85*, pages 84–96. 25
6. D. Gabbay. The declarative past and imperative future. In B. Banieqbal, H. Barringer, and A. Pnueli, editors, *Temporal Logic in Specification*, volume 398 of *Lect. Notes in Comp. Sci.*, pages 407–448. Springer-Verlag, 1987. 26
7. P. Gastin and D. Oddoux. Fast LTL to Büchi automata translation. *CAV'01*, LNCS 2102.

8. R. Gerth, D. Peled, M. Y. Vardi, and P. Wolper. Simple on-the-fly automatic verification of linear temporal logic. *PSTV'95*, pages 3–18.
9. Y. Kesten, Z. Manna, H. McGuire, and A. Pnueli. A decision algorithm for full propositional temporal logic. *CAV'93*, pages 97–109.
10. Y. Kesten and A. Pnueli. Verification by augmented finitary abstraction. *Information and Computation, a special issue on Compositionality*, 163:203–243, 2000.
11. Y. Kesten, A. Pnueli, and L. Raviv. Algorithmic verification of linear temporal logic specifications. *Proc. 25th Int. Colloq. Aut. Lang. Prog.*, LNCS 1443, pages 1–16, 1998. 25, 37
12. Y. Kesten, A. Pnueli, L. Raviv, and E. Shahar. LTL Model Checking with Strong Fairness. Technical Report mcs01-07, The Weizmann Institute of Science, 2001. Submitted to *Formal Methods in System Design*. 25
13. D. Lehmann, A. Pnueli, and J. Stavi. Impartiality, justice and fairness: The ethics of concurrent termination. In *Proc. 8th Int. Colloq. Aut. Lang. Prog.*, LNCS 115, pages 264–277, 1981. 29
14. O. Lichtenstein and A. Pnueli. Checking that finite-state concurrent programs satisfy their linear specification. *POPL'85*, pages 97–107. 25, 26, 37
15. Z. Manna, A. Anuchitanukul, N. Bjørner, A. Browne, E. Chang, M. Colón, L. D. Alfaro, H. Devarajan, H. Sipma, and T. Uribe. STeP: The Stanford Temporal Prover. Stanford University, 1994. 24, 26
16. Z. Manna and A. Pnueli. Completing the temporal picture. *Theor. Comp. Sci.*, 83(1):97–130, 1991. 24, 25, 26, 29, 34, 36
17. Z. Manna and A. Pnueli. *The Temporal Logic of Reactive and Concurrent Systems: Specification.* Springer Verlag, New York, 1991. 24, 26, 34
18. Z. Manna and A. Pnueli. *Temporal Verification of Reactive Systems: Safety.* Springer-Verlag, New York, 1995. 24, 26, 33
19. K. Namjoshi. Certifying model checkers. *CAV'01*, LNCS 2102. 25
20. D. Peled, A. Pnueli, and L. Zuck. From falsification to verification. *FTTCS'01*, LNCS 2245, pages 292–304. 25
21. A. Pnueli and R. Rosner. A framework for the synthesis of reactive modules. *Concurrency 88*, LNCS 335, pages 4–17. 25
22. M. Reynolds. An axiomatization of full computation tree logic. *Journal of Symbolic Logic*, 66(3):1011–1057, 2001. 26
23. H. Sipma, T. Uribe, and Z. Manna. Deductive model checking. *Formal Methods in System Design*, 15(1):49–74, 1999. 26
24. F. Somenzi and R. Bloem. Efficient Büchi automata from LTL formulae. *CAV'00*, LNCS 1855, pages 248–263.
25. C. Sprenger. *On the Verification of CTL* Properties of Infinite-State Reactive Systems.* PhD thesis, Swiss Federal Institute of Technology, Lausanne, 2000. 27
26. F. Stomp, W.-P. de Roever, and R. Gerth. The μ-calculus as an assertion language for fairness arguments. *Inf. and Comp.*, 82:278–322, 1989. 29
27. M. Y. Vardi and P. Wolper. Reasoning about infinite computations. *Inf. and Comp.*, 115(1):1–37, 1994.

Event-State Duality: The Enriched Case

Vaughan R. Pratt

Stanford University
Stanford CA 94305, USA
pratt@cs.stanford.edu
http://boole.stanford.edu/pratt.html

Abstract. Enriched categories have been applied in the past to both event-oriented true concurrency models and state-oriented information systems, with no evident relationship between the two. Ordinary Chu spaces expose a natural duality between partially ordered temporal spaces (pomsets, event structures), and partially ordered information systems. Barr and Chu's original definition of Chu spaces however was for the general V-enriched case, with ordinary Chu spaces arising for $V = \mathbf{Set}$ (equivalently $V = \mathbf{Pos}$ at least for biextensional Chu spaces). We extend time-information duality to the general enriched case, and apply it to put on a common footing event structures, higher-dimensional automata (HDAs), a cancellation-based approach to branching time, and other models treatable by enriching either event (temporal) space or state (information) space.

1 Introduction

Although the present paper is about enrichment in concurrency, the framework facilitating this treatment is the duality of time and information, the title of the author's CONCUR'92 talk [1] at Stonybrook NY exactly a decade ago. The abstract began with

> The states of a computing system bear information and change time, while its events bear time and change information.

The introduction expanded on this by beginning

> The behavior of an automaton is to alternately wait in a *state* and perform a transition or *event*. We may think of the state as bearing information representing the "knowledge" of the automaton when in that state, and the event as modifying that information. At the same time we may think of the event as taking place at a moment in time, and the state as modifying or whiling away time.

This view organizes states and events into two complementary spaces, state spaces or automata and event spaces or schedules, whose distances are respectively information deltas and time deltas. The two spaces are interderivable, and

L. Brim et al. (Eds.): CONCUR 2002, LNCS 2421, pp. 41–56, 2002.

are shaped similarly (linearly) by sequential behavior but strikingly differently by concurrency.

This was then and remains today the underlying principle of our event-state symmetric view of behavior, independently of whether sequential or concurrent. The basic framework for this view then was complete semilattices, modified to cater for conflict by replacing bottom by top. Within a month of writing [1], V. Gupta and I [2] had simplified and generalized this framework via Chu spaces [3], which has remained our current view for the past decade [http://chu.stanford.edu/].

Yet earlier [4] we had applied categorical enrichment to a unified treatment of ordered time, real time, etc., but at that stage of thinking did not have the notion of information as dual to time. What we did have was a puzzle as to why Girard's Linear Logic (LL) should look so like our Process Specification Language (PSL) except for the self-duality of LL, which PSL lacked. We raised this issue at the end of [4] in the following paragraph.

A recent noncartesian logic is Girard's linear logic [5]. Like PSL, linear logic distinguishes ordinary and tensor product. Like Boolean logic but unlike PSL, Girard's linear logic is self-dual, giving rise by de Morgan's law to two binary operations dual to the two products. This prompts the following question. Why should self-duality survive the diverging of the two products?

But while [1] answered that puzzle with time-information duality it did so only for ordered time and not for the generalized metrics of [4], leaving this as a loose end.

In between [4] and [1] we introduced the notion of higher dimensional automaton (HDA) [6] as an algebraic topological form of automata theory supporting Papadimitriou's geometric view of concurrency control [7] in terms of higher-dimensional state spaces, in which mutual exclusion takes the form of a hole. At that time we were unable to answer Boris Trakhtenbrot's question after our POPL talk as to how HDAs were related to event spaces, leaving another loose end which we only recently tied up using triadic Chu spaces [8].

We found ourselves subsequently drawn more strongly to the duality puzzle than to HDAs, intuiting that the latter should rest on the former which therefore needed to be understood first. We have since written extensively on this topic [http://chu.stanford.edu/], and with V. de Paiva also organized a LICS workshop on Chu spaces. This is not to say that HDAs have gone neglected: thanks to the efforts of a number of researchers, in particular Eric Goubault, HDA theory has since ripened into a relatively popular research area with some dozens of papers, two workshops, and a special issue of MSCS [9]. The upshot has been that both Chu spaces and HDAs have received their fair share of attention during the past several years.

The purpose of this paper is to tie up the remaining loose end involving enrichment, accomplished by passing from ordinary to enriched Chu spaces. This passage provides a common framework with the metric space approaches to both information systems [10] and temporal systems [4], not by unifying them however but by placing them on opposite sides of the duality of states and events. The key idea is to apply the way a metric on V lifts to a metric on a V-category to the rows and columns of a matrix to yield separate metrics of time and information.

Enriched Chu spaces greatly simplify this reconciliation to the point of automating it. Ordinary Chu spaces are a sort of halfway-house between universal algebra and category theory. Enriched Chu spaces make the corresponding connection for enriched categories, in the process enriching universal algebra analogously.

Ironically the original definition of Chu spaces [3] was for the enriched case, with ordinary Chu spaces receiving only a passing mention.[1] The first detailed treatment of ordinary Chu spaces was by Lafont and Streicher, and they were subsequently adopted by Gupta and Pratt [2, 11] for the purpose of modeling behavior at a more fundamental level than possible with higher dimensional automata.

2 Event-State Duality

Computation is traditionally taught with a focus on states, a point of view that has permeated computer science so thoroughly that event-oriented models are in a distinct minority even at CONCUR. One could imagine a parallel universe in which computer science had focused instead on events, with advocates of a state-oriented perspective in the minority. The situation is rather like the old philosophical problem of the primacy of mind or matter, with science having chosen Hume over Berkeley, matter over mind. Or for that matter the general preference in mathematics of sets over categories.

Just as Russell along with Eccles and Popper advocated a return to the more symmetric view of matter and mind contemplated both by millennia-old yin-yang philosophy and by Descartes in 1647, so does event-state duality take a more symmetric view of events and states, defining them in such a way that each can be understood in terms of the other. The duality of events and states goes hand in hand with that of time and information as the respective metrics on event spaces and state spaces. Event-state duality permits a process to be viewed equally well as a state-based automaton or an event-based schedule. These views are structurally different: automata (or transition systems) are state-based, and branching is disjunctive: the process goes down only one branch. Schedules are event-based, and branching is conjunctive: parallel events all occur. These structural differences notwithstanding, each view fully determines the other, and moreover simply by matrix transposition!

---

[1] This exclusive attention to the enriched case in the original literature has created the impression in some quarters that Chu spaces are an inaccessibly abstract notion. This does not do justice to the simplicity of ordinary Chu spaces as mere matrices, and moreover matrices over a mere set, unlike the matrices of linear algebra which are over a field.

Event-state duality can be understood in terms of element-predicate duality. The essence of duality is reversal, as with negation of reals which reverses their order while interchanging max and min as well as floor and ceiling. Complementing the elements of a Boolean algebra, De Morgan duality, similarly reverses its order while interchanging the roles of true and false and of conjunction and disjunction. And taking the opposite $\mathcal{C}^{\mathrm{op}}$ of a category $\mathcal{C}$ reverses its morphisms while interchanging limits and colimits, categorical duality. This third example generalizes the first two when made categories by interpreting $a \leq b$ as a morphism from a to b.

Element-predicate duality arises as an instance of categorical duality for a category $\mathcal{C}$ as follows. Two objects g and k (not necessarily distinct) are chosen to play the roles of respectively a singleton object and a truth values object. (An obvious and natural choice for the category of sets is $g = 1 = \{0\}$ and $k = 2 = \{0, 1\}$. Less obvious but equally natural choices exist for many popular categories, e.g. for (locally compact) Abelian groups the integers under addition as the free group on one generator and the unit circle of the complex plane under multiplication as its dual.) This choice determines for every object a both the elements of a and the predicates on a, as respectively the morphisms from g to a, and from a to k. When necessary for disambiguation we refer to these as g-elements and k-predicates. Note that the set $\mathcal{C}(g, k)$ of morphisms from g to k are simultaneously the g-elements of k and the k-predicates on g, constituting the set of truth values which we denote henceforth by K. Application of a predicate to an element is accomplished by composition to yield a truth value.

Categorical duality reverses the orientation of the morphisms of $\mathcal{C}$ while interchanging elements and predicates by interchanging the roles of g and k: g now serves as the truth values object while k acts as the singleton. In this process *the set of truth values remains unchanged*, since what used to be both g-elements of k and k-predicates on g have become both g-predicates on k and k-elements of g. That is, the set K is invariant under dualization! Furthermore application of predicate y to element x prior to dualization yields the same truth value as application of x (now a predicate) to y (now an element) after dualization.

A given choice of g and k establishes for every object a of $\mathcal{C}$ a triple (A, r, X) where A is the set $\mathcal{C}(g, a)$ of elements of a, X is the set $\mathcal{C}(a, k)$ of predicates on a, and $r : A \times X \to K$ is the application function defined by $r(a, x) = x(a)$. Such a triple expresses those aspects of a that can be understood in terms of the interaction of its elements and predicates via application (realized as composition).

A ***Chu space over*** K is any triple $\mathcal{A} = (A, r, X)$ where A and X are sets and $r : A \times X \to K$ is an arbitrary function called the *matrix* of the Chu space. Dualization exchanges A and X and transposes the matrix.

Besides viewing elements and predicates more symmetrically, this element-predicate approach to Chu spaces also views set theory and category theory more symmetrically. From the categorical perspective a Chu space is an object of a category $\mathcal{C}$ together with some[2] incident arrows. From the set perspective a Chu space is a generalized topological space whose set X of "open sets" need not be closed under union or finite intersection, and which allows $|K| > 2$; its morphisms can be understood as simply those functions for which the inverse image of open sets is open, exactly as for topological continuity.

Event-state duality arises as the case of element-predicate duality in which a process $\mathcal{A}$ as an object of a category $\mathcal{C}$ of processes is understood as having events for elements and states for predicates. We call such a process a *schedule*. Dualizing $\mathcal{C}$ as $\mathcal{C}^{\mathrm{op}}$ turns states into elements and events into predicates; we call the objects of $\mathcal{C}^{\mathrm{op}}$ *automata*. Dualizing an object leaves it as the same process with the same events and the same states, changing only which are the elements and which the predicates.

A morphism of Chu spaces $(A, r, X) \rightarrow (B, s, Y)$ is a pair of functions $(f : A \rightarrow B, g : Y \rightarrow X)$ satisfying the **adjointness** condition $s(f(a), y) = r(a, g(y))$ for all $a \in A$ and $y \in Y$. Dualizing interchanges f and g, thereby reversing the morphism since f and g are oppositely orientated. The category of Chu spaces over K and their morphisms is denoted **Chu(Set**, $K)$.

Define $\hat{r} : A \rightarrow K^X$ as $\hat{r}(a)(x) = r(a, x)$ and $\check{r} : X \rightarrow K^A$ as $\check{r}(x)(a) = r(a, x)$. We refer to $\hat{r}(a)$ as row a of the matrix r, and $\check{r}(x)$ as column x.

A Chu space is **extensional** when $\check{r} : X \rightarrow K^A$ is an injection (no repeated columns in the matrix), **separable** when $\hat{r} : A \rightarrow K^X$ is an injection (no repeated rows), and **biextensional** when both extensional and separable. Biextensional Chu spaces are to Chu spaces as posets are to preordered sets: the former collapses "isomorphic" elements (those lying on a cycle in the case of preordered sets, those indexing equal rows or columns in the case of Chu spaces) to a single element. The subcategory of **Chu(Set**, $K)$ consisting of its biextensional Chu spaces has been denoted **chu(Set**, $K)$, or "little Chu" by Barr. Every morphism (f, g) of little Chu from $\mathcal{A} = (A, r, X)$ to $\mathcal{B} = (B, s, Y)$ is representable as the Chu space (A, t, Y) where $t(a, y) = s(f(a), y) = r(a, g(y))$: the columns of t come from $\mathcal{A}$ and its rows from $\mathcal{B}$, and t uniquely determines f and g. (f, g) is reconstructed from (A, t, Y) by taking $f(a)$ to be the location in $\mathcal{B}$ of row a of t, and dually $g(y)$ for the location in $\mathcal{A}$ of column y of t.

For extensional Chu spaces we can identify each state x with the column $\lambda a.r(a, x)$, a function $A \rightarrow K$. This identification permits r to be dropped because we can recover it via $r(a, x) = x(a)$. In this case a Chu space is a pair (A, X) where $X \subseteq K^A$.

3   Examples

The table in Figure 1 below is taken from [12]. Each of the four columns (a)-(d) corresponds to a choice of K, respectively $\{0, 1\}$, $\{0, \lrcorner, 1\}$, $\{0, \times, 1\}$, and

---

[2] Replacing "some" by "all" when $\mathcal{C}$ is small embeds $\mathcal{C}$ fully in **chu(Set**, ob$(\mathcal{C}))$ [13]. That is, taking K to be sufficiently large permits the objects of any small category to be represented as Chu spaces in such a way that the morphisms of $\mathcal{C}$ become exactly the Chu morphisms between the representing Chu spaces.

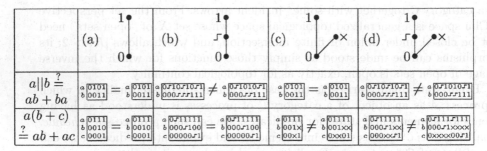

Fig. 1. Examples of event-state duality

$\{0, \digamma, 1, \times\}$. The elements of K are the possible values of an event in a given state, with $0, \digamma, 1, \times$ corresponding to the respective adverbs *before*, *during*, *after*, and *instead*. In a given state an event has value 0 when it has not yet started, $\digamma$ when it is happening, 1 when it is finished, and $\times$ if it has been canceled. The four corresponding automata, with edges oriented to point upwards, indicate the transitions an event may make. These transitions enrich the structure of K and we shall ignore them for the moment, treating K as merely a set, i.e. focusing only on its points.

The 16 matrices denote the Chu spaces corresponding to the four processes $a\|b$, $ab+ba$, $a(b+c)$, and $ab+ac$ for each of the four choices of K. Rows represent events and columns states. The first matrix, expressing $a\|b$ with $K = \{0,1\}$, has all possible states for two events, respectively neither a nor b done, a done, b done, and both done. The matrix under it also has four states: nothing done, a done, a and b done, and a and c done. All 16 spaces are biextensional.

The table shows how adding a third value to K serves to distinguish either $a\|b$ from $ab+ba$ or $a(b+c)$ from $ab+ac$, but not both, depending on whether the value is $\digamma$ or $\times$. To make both distinctions requires both additional values. This is developed in considerably more detail in [12]. The point here is to illustrate and motivate the kinds of primitive structures that might play a role in enrichment-based semantics, in particular as the V we now describe.

4   Enrichment

Posets abstract the notion of a set of sets ordered by inclusion: the elements of the inner sets disappear. The ordinary category **Pos** of posets is even more abstract: the elements of the outer sets also disappear, but we still have one straw left to grasp at: the monotone functions between two posets form a mere set. The notion of a poset as a category whose "homsets" are not sets but objects of a certain symmetric monoidal closed category V, the chain 2 in the case of posets, is abstract nonsense taken to the max. The defining characteristic of a V-category or enriched category is that its morphisms from object a to object b band together not as a set but as an object of V, with the characteristic features of a category being reformulated in terms of V.

Lawvere [14] has provided an attractive way of conceptually taming V-categories, by viewing the objects of V as distances, and V-categories as generalized metric spaces satisfying a suitable triangle inequality over such distances. Besides being good pedagogy, this view nicely connects enrichment with the Gauss-Kleene-Floyd-Warshall connection that was emerging in computer science simultaneously with and completely independently of the development of enriched categories [15]. That connection applied semirings to create a common algebraic framework for the Roy-Warshall transitive closure algorithm [16, 17], Floyd's shortest path algorithm [18], Kleene's algorithm for translating nondeterministic finite state automata into regular expressions [19], and even Gauss's algorithm for inverting a matrix. These $O(n^3)$ algorithms can be made instances of the same algorithm parametrized only by choice of semiring, which plays the role for this common algorithm that V plays for enrichment. The uniform expression of this common algorithm in terms of semirings was first described by Robert and Ferland [20].

The ordinary triangle inequality takes the form

$$d(a, b) + d(b, c) \geq d(a, c)$$

where $d(a, b)$ is a nonnegative real constituting the distance from point a to point b of a space. The Fréchet axioms for ordinary metric spaces are the ordinary triangle inequality together with

$$
\begin{aligned}
d(x, y) &= d(y, x) \quad \text{(symmetry)} \\
d(x, x) &= 0 \\
d(x, y) = 0 &\supset x = y
\end{aligned}
$$

The first step in generalizing the Fréchet axioms is to restate $d(x, x) = 0$ as $d(x, x) \leq 0$, or better yet as $0 \geq d(x, x)$ to give it the same orientation as the triangle inequality. Absent negative distances this rewording changes nothing.

The next step is to drop the second and fourth axioms. Not only do they get in the way of the connection to enrichment, they are not even well motivated in many practical situations. Counterexamples to symmetry abound: the distance between the base and the summit of a mountain measured in climbing days, the distance along an asymmetric toll road measured in dollars, and so on.

If we view points zero distance apart as somehow isomorphic, the fourth axiom identifies isomorphic points. This is analogous to the role of antisymmetry in partially ordering a preordered set (one whose order relation $\leq$ is reflexive and transitive) by identifying points x, y that are isomorphic by virtue of lying on a cycle $x \leq y \leq x$. The practice in surveying of measuring only the horizontal component of distance refutes the fourth axiom in that it makes vertically aligned points isomorphic; the axiom is restored however in the plan view projecting vertical lines to points.

The third step is to view the ordering $\geq$ on ordinary real-valued distances as an instance of $\sqsubseteq$, the generic ordering relation for generalized distances (the reversal is intentional), and real addition as an instance of a commutative monoid operation $x \cdot y$. Here distances are viewed as forming a preordered monoid $(V, \sqsubseteq, \cdot, 1)$, with $\sqsubseteq$ being a reflexive transitive binary relation on V and $\cdot$ and 1 furnishing V with the structure of a commutative monoid. That is, $\cdot$ is associative and commutative, and 1 is the identity for $\cdot$. (Caveat: the generic $\cdot$ and 1 typically revert to $+$ and 0 when the objects of V are numeric.) We also require that $\cdot$ be monotone in each argument with respect to $\sqsubseteq$; the property of being closed actually makes it additive $(s \cdot (t \vee t') = s \cdot t \vee s \cdot t')$.

We can now define the notion of **generalized metric space** over a generalized metric $(V, \sqsubseteq, \cdot, 1)$, namely as a set X of points with a metric $d : X^2 \to V$ satisfying the following generalizations of the remaining two Fréchet axioms.

$$d(x, y) \cdot d(y, z) \sqsubseteq d(x, z)$$
$$1 \sqsubseteq d(x, x)$$

The preorder $\sqsubseteq$ and the monoid $\cdot$ are to be understood as essentially independent structures on V, associated with respectively strength and length of distances. Whereas strengths are compared via the preorder, lengths are added via the monoid. Borrowing a convention from 2-categories, we picture length as horizontal (like a road) and strength as vertical (as in a Hasse diagram).

Strength and length are sometimes incorporated into a single number. The canonical example is distance as an upper bound, where $d(a, b) = 3$ means that any trip from a to b traverses *at most* 3 units of length. For example a process presented with different inputs of the same length may follow state trajectories of different lengths. If some path from state x to state z passes through state y, and all paths from x to y take at most 5 seconds, and from y to z at most 7 seconds, then any path from x to z via y can take at most 12 seconds. But paths through some other state w may have $d(x, w) = 4$ and $d(w, z) = 9$, preventing us from ruling out the possibility of taking 13 seconds to get from x to z. This reasoning shows why the relevant form of the triangle inequality for upper bounds is $d(a, b) + d(b, c) \leq d(a, c)$.

Geodesics constitute *lower* bounds: the length of a geodesic from a to b is a lower bound on the length of an arbitrary path from a to b. Ordinary metric spaces are based on geodesic distance and therefore instantiate the generic comparison relation $\sqsubseteq$ with the reverse order $\geq$ on the reals, the appropriate order for lower bounds, with the geodesic triangle inequality being the ordinary $d(a, b) + d(b, c) \geq d(a, c)$.

Distances need not be simple numbers. A natural notion of distance is an interval $[s, t]$ giving a range of possible distances. In this case $[s, t] \sqsubseteq [s', t']$ defined as $s \geq s'$ for the lower bounds and $t \leq t'$ for the upper as per the preceding two paragraphs. But this makes $\sqsubseteq$ reverse inclusion for intervals, the natural information ordering for such applications of intervals as interval arithmetic where strength is measured by the narrowness of the interval. Upper and lower bound distances t can be seen to be the respective special cases $[-\infty, t]$ and $[t, \infty]$ of interval distances. Intervals are added via $[s, t] + [s', t'] = [s + s', t + t']$, with the identity interval being $[0, 0]$.

One last generalization remains, namely of the preorder $\sqsubseteq$ on V to the morphisms of a category structure on V. Viewing a preorder as a category with at most one morphism between any two objects, this generalization amounts to dropping the cardinality bound $|V(a, b)| \leq 1$ on homsets of V.

The elements of the preorder are now understood as objects. The $\cdot$ operation becomes a functor $V^2 \rightarrow V$, and is renamed $\otimes$; likewise 1 becomes an object of V and is renamed I (except in linear logic where it remains 1 and the terminal object is denoted $\top$). The result is a **symmetric monoidal category** V, a category equipped with a monoid in the form of a tensor product $\otimes$ and tensor unit I, whose monoid laws now take the form of suitable natural transformations which join $\otimes$ and I as part of the signature: α_{stu} expressing associativity and λ_s and ρ_s expressing the identity laws. These natural transformations themselves obey certain nonobvious *coherence laws*, most notably a pentagonal diagram for α and a triangular diagram for λ and ρ [21, §VII-1] [22, §1.1]. When these three natural transformations are identities V is called **strict monoidal**.

We further require that V be **closed**, meaning that tensor have a right adjoint in each argument. That is, to each object s of V is associated an isomorphism

$$V(s \otimes t, u) \cong V(t, s\multimap u)$$

natural in t and u, that is, an adjunction, with the functor $s\multimap-$ right adjoint to the functor $s \otimes -$. The functor $s\multimap-$ is called the *internal hom*, and serves as a generalized metric on V.

We are now ready for the general notion of enriched category or V-category.

Definition. A **V-category** $A = (O, d, m, j)$, or **category enriched in V**, consists of a set O of objects, a function $d : O^2 \rightarrow \mathrm{ob}(V)$ constituting the metric, and families of morphisms of V, namely compositions $m_{uvw} : d(u, v) \otimes d(v, w) \rightarrow d(u, w)$ and identities $j_u : I \rightarrow d(u, u)$, such that certain reasonably obvious diagrams commute expressing associativity of composition and the left and right identity laws [22, §1.2].

The class of V-categories is itself a category V-**Cat** whose morphisms are V-functors. The basic constituents of a V-functor $F : A \rightarrow B$ are a function $F_O : \mathrm{ob}(A) \rightarrow \mathrm{ob}(B)$ and an $\mathrm{ob}(A)^2$-indexed family $F_{uv} : d(u, v) \rightarrow d(F_O(u), F_O(v))$ of morphisms of V such that certain diagrams commute expressing functoriality [22, §1.2], or [4] for definitions coordinated with this process perspective.

V itself is a V-category whose homobjects are given by its internal hom $a\multimap b$. We use this fact later in Plotkin's theorem about $\mathbf{chu}(Q\text{-}\mathbf{Cat}, Q)$.

5   Quantales

A large and useful class of monoidal closed categories is given by quantales [23]. A **quantale with unit** $(Q, \bigvee, \otimes, 1)$ is a complete-semilattice-ordered monoid, equivalently a one-object[3] V-category where V is the category **CSLat** of complete semilattices, equivalently a monoid object in **CSLat**. As such it is a (pose-

---

[3] Dropping the one-object restriction yields the more general notion of *quantaloid* [24].

tal) monoidal closed cocomplete category, the symmetric case of which is obtained as commutative quantales ($s \otimes t = t \otimes s$). This case provides a suitable V for constructing V-categories. A number of quantales (not under that name) applicable to various metrics of computational interest are described in [4].

The finite linearly ordered commutative quantales with bottom 0 and unit 1 form an interesting and useful special case. As shown in [4] there are 2^{n-2} such having $n \geq 2$ elements, necessarily satisfying $0 \neq 1$ (if $0 = 1$ then $s = s \otimes 1 = s \otimes 0 = 0$ violating $n \geq 2$).

These have the following picturesque characterization. Pick any chain $(Q, \bigvee)$ with n elements. Holding it vertically with smaller elements lower, grasp the j-th element from the top, $1 \leq j \leq n-1$ (so the bottom element is not eligible). Let the portion of the chain above the grasped element fall over (i.e. rotate 180 degrees about the grasped element) so as to dangle down beside the other half of the chain. Arbitrarily interleave the two halves, preserving their respective orders, to give a second linear order on Q, while keeping the original bottom at the bottom and the grasped element at the top. The first and second orders on Q have the same bottom element.

We now define $(Q, \bigvee, \otimes, 1)$ as follows. Take $\bigvee$ to be supremum (least upper bound) in the first linear order, so 0 (sup of the empty set) is its bottom (the original bottom). Define $\otimes$ to be infimum (greatest lower bound) in the second linear order, with 1 as its top (the grasped element).

This interleaving can be done in $\binom{n-2}{j-1}$ ways. Summing this over $1 \leq j \leq n-1$ yields the promised result 2^{n-2}. Exactly one of these ways is a Heyting algebra or cartesian closed poset, namely when $j = 1$, the one case in which the two orders are the same, making $\otimes$ infimum (greatest lower bound) in the first linear order.

The unique such quantale for $n = 2$ is not only a Heyting algebra but a Boolean algebra, unlike the rest. As such it is the quantale to use for V in the analysis of partial orders (more generally preorders) as a V-category. For $n = 3$ we have one Heyting algebra and one non-Heyting algebra, denoted 3 and 3' in [4]. 3' is the quantale structure implicit in the "prossets" of [25], which are 3'-categories, and is also the appropriate quantale structure to impose on $K = \{0, r, 1\}$ for modeling HDAs as triadic Chu spaces [8]. 3 is the quantale structure implicit in Gaifman's treatment of the distinction between incidental and causal order [26], where the schedules he defines amount to V-categories for $V = 3$.

Ordinary metric spaces restricted to nonnegative integer distances but supplemented with distance ∞ can be understood as the quantale $(\mathbb{N} \cup \{\infty\}, \bigwedge, +, 0)$ (taking the quantale's $\bigvee$ operation to be $\mathbb{N}$'s $\bigwedge$ amounts to reversing the standard order on $\mathbb{N}$).[4] It does not fit the preceding pattern because it is infinite, and because $\otimes$ as integer addition is not idempotent.

The ordinary metric is appropriate for delay between events in sequential computation. When n unit-time events must happen sequentially the time to

---

[4] Some useful variations: $(\mathbb{Z} \cup \{\infty, -\infty\}, \bigwedge, +, 0)$, $(\mathbb{R}^{\geq 0} \cup \{\infty\}, \bigwedge, +, 0)$, $(\mathbb{R} \cup \{\infty, -\infty\}, \bigwedge, +, 0)$.

pass through the resulting $n+1$ states is n, which the ordinary metric arrives at by adding the distance vector between the initial and final state, which consists of n 1's. This remains the case whether the sequentiality is a consequence either of the order being specified, or of the events being performable in any order (but pairwise mutually exclusively, e.g. $ab + ba$), or anything in between (e.g. $abc + cba + cab$, omitting the other three permutations).

While this metric is exactly right for sequential computation, it fails to recognize the performance benefits of concurrency. If instead of addition we take $\otimes$ to be $\bigvee$ in $\mathbb{N}$ ($\bigwedge$ in the quantale's order), we obtain an *ultrametric* space which in this case is also a (complete) Heyting algebra. This metric is appropriate when all events are performed in parallel, giving the expected result that n unit-time events performed in parallel need take only unit time; more generally when the events take different times, their max.

Practical computation is of course somewhere in between these extremes of sequential and concurrent, entailing an appropriate blend of the two metrics to get a satisfactory estimate of running time. We return to this later.

6 Enriched Chu Spaces

An ordinary Chu space is a triple (A, r, X) where A, X are sets, i.e. objects of the category **Set**, and $r : A \times X \to K$ is a function, a morphism of **Set**. The passage to the enriched case generalizes **Set** to an arbitrary monoidal closed category V with pullbacks. A and X are objects of V, r is a morphism of V, and Chu morphisms are pairs $(f : A \to B, g : Y \to B)$ of morphisms of V. The adjointness condition is rephrased in the evident way as the diagram

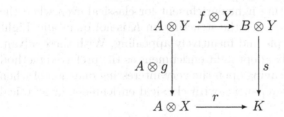

The enriched case of little $\mathbf{chu}(V, k)$ is defined so that $\hat{r} : A \to K^X$ and $\check{r} : X \to K^A$ are not merely monos but extremal monos. A mono f is **extremal** when for all factorizations of f as the composition $g \circ e$ of a morphism g with an epi e, e is an isomorphism. In **Set** every mono is extremal, which is why we did not need this distinction for ordinary Chu spaces. In **Pos** extremal monos satisfy not only monotonicity as usual but also its converse $f(x) \le f(y) \to x \le y$.

The idea is that the monotonicity of $\hat{r}$ and $\check{r}$ put upper bounds on the structure of A and X respectively, while extremality forces those upper bounds to be attained. This is intended to pin down the structure on each of A and X to exactly that determined by the induced structure on respectively the rows and columns of the matrix.

For example if K is furnished with a binary operation $+$, this operation lifts pointwise to both the rows and columns of r, thereby furnishing both A and X

with that operation. Any equational properties enjoyed by the operation in K, such as associativity or commutativity, lift to these induced operations on A and X.

For at least one large and useful class of symmetric monoidal categories this works sufficiently well as to make this induced structure on A and X redundant: A and X can be left discrete and their structure inferred entirely from the matrix, made precise by the following unpublished theorem of G. Plotkin.

Theorem 1. *(Plotkin) For any quantale Q, $\mathbf{chu}(Q\text{-}\mathbf{Cat}, Q)$ is equivalent (in fact isomorphic) to $\mathbf{chu}(\mathbf{Set}, |Q|)$.*

This theorem is remarkable in that alterations to the structure of a given quantale Q leaves the ordinary category $\mathbf{chu}(Q\text{-}\mathbf{Cat}, Q)$ unchanged. What does change is the induced structure on A and X, but such changes have no impact on the morphisms! The changes are felt only for $\mathbf{chu}(Q\text{-}\mathbf{Cat}, Q)$ understood as a Q-category, where the induced structures on A, X, $A\!-\!\circ B$ and so on track changes to the structure on Q.

Plotkin's isomorphism in the ordinary case covers many choices of V of practical interest, though certainly not all. In these cases enrichment can be made attractively simple: start with ordinary Chu spaces over K, enrich K in the usual manner of furnishing a set with algebraic or relational structure, enrich A from the matrix by reflecting the structure of K^X into A via $\hat{r} : A \to K^X$, and dually for X via $\check{r}$. Call this simplistic approach to enriched Chu spaces *light enrichment*.

Plotkin's theorem gives enough situations in which light and classical enrichment agree up to category isomorphism that it is natural to ask what the downside might be of substituting light enrichment for classical even when the results are not identical, that is, when the structure on K is not quantalic. Light enrichment is conceptually simple and intuitively appealing. With these advantages in mind we experimentally adopt light enrichment as the preferred method of enrichment for Chu spaces, leaving open the very interesting question of when this can cause problematic discrepancies with classical enrichment in practical situations.

7   Time and Information as Induced Metrics

We define time and information as generalized metrics on the spaces of events and states respectively. Classical enrichment provides these directly in the objects A and X when these are drawn from a suitable category of generalized metric spaces. Light enrichment allows the metrics on A and X to be inferred via the matrix r from the structure assigned to $K = \mathrm{ob}(V)$, as follows.

The distance between two vectors (either rows or columns) over K is itself a vector over K determined pointwise from the given vectors via the distance metric on V as the enrichment of K, namely its internal hom $s\!-\!\circ t$. This vector distance is then converted to a scalar distance by combining the components of the vector with the tensor product of V. This calculation of metrics on rows and columns is a core part of the proof of Plotkin's theorem.

For ordered time, the case $V = 2$ where 2 is the 2-element chain understood as a commutative quantale (hence as a symmetric monoidal closed category) makes V-Cat the category **Ord** of preordered sets. Here distances $d(u, v)$ are 0 and 1 giving the truth value of $u \leq v$, respectively false and true. Bit vectors $\mathbf{u}, \mathbf{v}$ are compared coordinatewise, with 0 in those positions where $\mathbf{u}$ is 1 and $\mathbf{v}$ is 0, and 1 in all other positions. The tensor product here is conjunction and so the corresponding scalar is 1 just when every bit in the comparison vector is 1: a single counterexample makes it false. For example the comparison of 010011101 with 010010101 first yields the vector distance 111110111, which is then converted to a scalar distance by forming the conjunction of those 9 bits to yield 0, the truth value of $010011101 \leq 010010101$. In this way the order on 2 lifts to a preordering of A and of X (a partial ordering, i.e. satisfying antisymmetry, in the biextensional case).

For real time, the ordinary metric space $(\mathbb{N} \cup \{\infty\}, \wedge, +, 0)$ encountered earlier provides a notion of sequential time. If n events happen sequentially their respective durations should be combined with $+$. This is true regardless of what order is specified for them. In particular ab, ba, $ab + ba$, and $a\|b$ all take the same time.

Parallel time recognizes the performance gain possible with $a\|b$ over ab, ba, and $ab + ba$. For $a\|b$ the appropriate metric is $(\mathbb{N} \cup \{\infty\}, \wedge, \vee, 0)$. If n events happen independently then the time required is that of the slowest, whence their times should be combined with $\vee$. For the other three combinations we retain the sequential metric.

The situation becomes more interesting with arbitrary processes (A, X) whose set X of states is an arbitrary subset of K^A. The first question to ask here is whether any reasonable notion of running time is possible for such general processes, independently of whether enrichment is of any use here.

As shown in [12], the presence of Γ in K permits a very simple yet natural notion of distance between any two states x, y of (A, X). Form the power graph K^A derived from any of the four graphs of Figure 1, each understood as being reflexive but not transitive (unless vacuously so as in 1(a) and 1(d)), as proposed in [12]. For any given process (A, X) take its transition system to be the full subgraph of K^A having as vertices the states of X, denoted $K^A \cap X$. Define the distance between states to be one less than the usual shortest-path metric in a directed graph, or ∞ when there is no path or only infinite paths.

In the absence of value Γ the primitive transition systems for single events are those of Figure 1 (a) and (c). These are automatically transitive by virtue of having only paths of length one, whence the power graph K^A is transitive and hence in fact a power poset. This means that if there is a path from x to y in K^A, there is a path of length 0 directly from x to y that survives the removal of any states other than x or y; if not then the distance is ∞. This is effectively the all-or-nothing poset metric; substituting 1 for 0 and 0 for ∞ yields the conventional values for this metric.

Now we could instead take the distance from x to y to be the Hamming metric, which counts the number of events that change in that passage. This metric, which satisfies the ordinary triangle inequality, has two drawbacks. First it does not take the efficiencies of concurrency into account, corresponding instead to the time required to perform the events sequentially. Second, like the all-or-nothing poset metric it is invariant under removal of intermediate states.

Both these drawbacks are overcome with the metric obtained via K^A as above with the graphs K of either Figure 1 (b) or (d), in which an event requires 2 steps, or time 1 after subtracting the 1, to get from 0 to 1, namely via Γ. There is a path of length 1 from the initial (all-zero) state to a given final state (all events done or cancelled) if and only if the state in which the events that are done in the final state are all in state Γ (assuming at least one of these) and the rest are 0 or ×. Removal of that state constitutes an obstacle, calling for a longer path around that obstacle, provided one exists (otherwise that final state is deemed unreachable).

Taking $K = \{0, \Gamma, 1\}$, we may illustrate this with the example of three children ($A = 3$) taking turns riding n ponies. For $n = 3$ the relevant process (A, X) is the 3-cube with $|X| = 27$ states, whose cells consist of the 3^3 triples over K, broken down as 8 0-cells or vertices, 12 1-cells or edges, 6 2-cells or faces, and 1 3-cell or interior, the usual organization of the 3-cube. In this case we can pass from 000 via $\Gamma\Gamma\Gamma$ to 111 in two steps, which the subtraction of 1 makes time 1. For $n = 2$, $\Gamma\Gamma\Gamma$ is no longer available and a shortest path (by no means unique) is 000 to $\Gamma\Gamma 0$ to 11Γ to 111, taking time 2, the time required for two children to ride both ponies and then let the third child have its turn. For $n = 1$ we cannot do better than 000 to $\Gamma 00$ to $1\Gamma 0$ to 11Γ to 111, or time 3, the completely sequential case.

8   Process Algebra

The method of shortest paths in $K^A \cap X$ is a globally defined measure. For programs built up by composition, a more appropriate way to compute running time is by induction on program structure. We repeat here the Chu space definitions of four basic process algebra operations given in [12]. These are based on the following notions of conjunction, disjunction, and termination $\sqrt{[A]}$ for Chu spaces. Note that these definitions do not assume disjointness of A and B, although some applications will force them to be disjoint. For more details see [13].

$$\mathcal{A} \wedge \mathcal{B} \stackrel{\text{def}}{=} (A \cup B, \{z \in 2^{A \cup B} \mid z \upharpoonright A \in X \ \wedge \ z \upharpoonright B \in Y\})$$

$$\mathcal{A} \vee \mathcal{B} \stackrel{\text{def}}{=} (A \cup B, \{z \in 2^{A \cup B} \mid z \upharpoonright A \in X \ \vee \ z \upharpoonright B \in Y\})$$

$$\sqrt{[A]} \stackrel{\text{def}}{=} (A, \{1, \times\}^A)$$

We then use these operations to define the following four basic process algebra operations, respectively *concurrence*, *sequence*, *choice*, and *orthocurrence*.

$$\mathcal{A} \| \mathcal{B} \stackrel{\text{def}}{=} \mathcal{A} \wedge \mathcal{B}$$

$$\mathcal{AB} \overset{\text{def}}{=} \mathcal{A} \wedge \mathcal{B} \wedge (B - A = 0 \vee \sqrt{[A]}) \wedge (B = 0 \vee \sqrt{[A-B]})$$

$$\mathcal{A} + \mathcal{B} \overset{\text{def}}{=} (A \cup B = 0) \vee (A \not\leq \times \wedge B - A = \times) \vee (B \not\leq \times \wedge A - B = \times)$$

$$\mathcal{A} \otimes \mathcal{B} \overset{\text{def}}{=} (A \times B, \{z \in K^{A \times B} \mid z(\lambda, \forall) \in X \wedge z(\forall, \lambda) \in Y\})$$

Concurrence $\mathcal{A}\|\mathcal{B}$ simply collects the events of $\mathcal{A}$ and $\mathcal{B}$ subject to the separate constraints of each (conjunction). Sequence $\mathcal{AB}$ is the same with the additional constraint that in every state either $\mathcal{B}$ has not yet started or $\mathcal{A}$ has terminated (the nondisjoint case treats A and B even-handedly). Choice $\mathcal{A} + \mathcal{B}$ starts out in the all-zero (initial) state and embarks on one of $\mathcal{A}$ or $\mathcal{B}$ ($A \not\leq \times$ consists of those states of $\mathcal{A}$ in which at least one event has progressed to r or 1) while simultaneously cancelling the unchosen events. Orthocurrence $\mathcal{A} \otimes \mathcal{B}$ forms all states on $A \times B$ that are "bilinear" in both $\mathcal{A}$ and $\mathcal{B}$. (Here $z(\lambda, \forall)$ denotes $\lambda a.z(a, b)$ with b universally quantified in the containing proposition, and dually for $z(\forall, \lambda)$. This makes $z(\lambda, \forall)$ and $z(\forall, \lambda)$ respectively the columns and rows of the $A \times B$ matrix z.)

We now specify the distance between states of each of these combinations. For the first three (all but orthocurrence) we are comparing two vectors x, y indexed by the event set $A \cup B$, with no assumption that the event sets A and B are disjoint. We are given the distances from $x \upharpoonright A$ to $y \upharpoonright A$ and $x \upharpoonright B$ to $y \upharpoonright B$, call these s and t respectively. For all three operations we combine s and t as $s \otimes t$.

What varies between the operations is the choice of $\otimes$. For $\mathcal{A}\|\mathcal{B}$ and $\mathcal{A} + \mathcal{B}$ we take $\otimes$ to be $\wedge$. Thus for $V = 2$, mere reachability, we require that $y \upharpoonright A$ be reachable from $x \upharpoonright A$ and $y \upharpoonright B$ from $x \upharpoonright B$. For numeric metrics $\wedge$ becomes max. For $\mathcal{AB}$, in the reachability case we continue to take $\otimes$ to be $\wedge$ (to complete $\mathcal{AB}$ we must complete both $\mathcal{A}$ and $\mathcal{B}$). In the numeric case however we take $\otimes$ to be $+$.

Having abruptly exhausted the space-time side of this instance of writer-reader duality, we content ourselves with foreshadowing a future expansion of this paper addressing the following concern. Metrics based on enrichment via the simple V's considered here are calculated only from path endpoint information, making them intrinsically oblivious to intermediate obstacles of the kind so adroitly handled by the intransitive $K^A \cap X$ metric. Moreover the metrics computed inductively on process algebra terms employ mixed metrics, which only gets worse with expansions of process algebra to additional operations such as mutual exclusion, asymmetric conflict, etc. Thus the elegant and accurate $K^A \cap X$ metric would appear hard to arrive at either via enrichment or inductively, a serious concern for both techniques!

References

1. Pratt, V.: The duality of time and information. In: Proc. of CONCUR'92. Volume 630 of Lecture Notes in Computer Science., Stonybrook, New York, Springer-Verlag (1992) 237–253
2. Gupta, V., Pratt, V.: Gates accept concurrent behavior. In: Proc. 34th Ann. IEEE Symp. on Foundations of Comp. Sci. (1993) 62–71

3. Barr, M.: *-Autonomous categories. Volume 752 of Lecture Notes in Mathematics. Springer-Verlag (1979)
4. Casley, R., Crew, R., Meseguer, J., Pratt, V.: Temporal structures. Math. Structures in Comp. Sci. **1** (1991) 179–213
5. Girard, J. Y.: Linear logic. Theoretical Computer Science **50** (1987) 1–102
6. Pratt, V.: Modeling concurrency with geometry. In: Proc. 18th Ann. ACM Symposium on Principles of Programming Languages. (1991) 311–322
7. Papadimitriou, C.: The Theory of Database Concurrency Control. Computer Science Press (1986)
8. Pratt, V.: Higher dimensional automata revisited. Math. Structures in Comp. Sci. **10** (2000) 525–548
9. Goubault, E.: (ed.) geometry and concurrency. Mathematical Structures in Computer Science, special issue **10** (2000) 409–573 (7 papers)
10. America, P., Rutten, J.: Solving reflexive domain equations in a category of complete metric spaces. Journal of Computer and System Sciences **39** (1989) 343–375
11. Gupta, V.: Chu Spaces: A Model of Concurrency. PhD thesis, Stanford University (1994) Tech. Report, available as http://boole.stanford.edu/pub/gupthes.ps.gz.
12. Pratt, V.: Transition and cancellation in concurrency and branching time. Math. Structures in Comp. Sci., special issue on the difference between sequentiality and concurrency, to appear (2002)
13. Pratt, V.: Chu spaces as a semantic bridge between linear logic and mathematics. Theoretical Computer Science (2002) to appear, preprint at http://boole.stanford.edu/pub/bridge.ps.gz.
14. Lawvere, W.: Metric spaces, generalized logic, and closed categories. In: Rendiconti del Seminario Matematico e Fisico di Milano, XLIII. Tipografia Fusi, Pavia (1973)
15. Pratt, V.: Enriched categories and the Floyd-Warshall connection. In: Proc. First International Conference on Algebraic Methodology and Software Technology, Iowa City (1989) 177–180
16. Roy, B.: Transitivité et connexité. Comptes Rendues Acad. Sci. **249** (1959) 216–218
17. Warshall, S.: A theorem on Boolean matrices. Journal of the ACM **9** (1962) 11–12
18. Floyd, R.: Algorithm 97: shortest path. Communications of the ACM **5** (1962) 345
19. Kleene, S.: Representation of events in nerve nets and finite automata. In: Automata Studies. Princeton University Press, Princeton, NJ (1956) 3–42
20. Robert, P., Ferland, J.: Généralisation de l'algorithme de Warshall. Revue Française d'Informatique et de Recherche Operationnelle **2** (1968) 13–25
21. Mac Lane, S.: Categories for the Working Mathematician. Springer-Verlag (1971)
22. Kelly, G.: Basic Concepts of Enriched Category Theory: London Math. Soc. Lecture Notes. 64. Cambridge University Press (1982)
23. Rosenthal, K.: Quantales and their applications. Longman Scientific and Technical (1990)
24. Rosenthal, K.: The theory of quantaloids. Longman Scientific and Technical (1996)
25. Gaifman, H., Pratt, V.: Partial order models of concurrency and the computation of functions. In: Proc. 2nd Annual IEEE Symp. on Logic in Computer Science, Ithaca, NY (1987) 72–85
26. Gaifman, H.: Modeling concurrency by partial orders and nonlinear transition systems. In: Proc. REX School/Workshop on Linear Time, Branching Time and Partial Order in Logics and Models for Concurrency, Noordwijkerhout, The Netherlands, Springer-Verlag (1989) 467–488

Expressive Power of Temporal Logics

Alexander Rabinovich

School of Computer Science, Tel Aviv University
Israel 69978
rabino@cs.tau.ac.il
http://www.cs.tau.ac.il/~rabino

Abstract. The objectives of this paper is to survey classical and recent expressive completeness results and to provide some external yardsticks by which the expressive power of temporal logics can be measured.

1 Introduction

Various temporal logics have been proposed for reasoning about so-called "reactive" systems, computer hardware or software systems which exhibit (potentially) a non-terminating and a non-deterministic behavior. Such a system is typically represented by (potentially) infinite sequences of computation states through which it may evolve, where we associate with each state the set of atomic propositions which are true in that state, along with the possible next state transitions to which it may evolve. Thus, its behavior is denoted by a (potentially) infinite rooted tree, with the initial state of the system represented by the root of the tree.

Temporal Logic (*TL*) introduced to Computer Science by Pnueli in [28] is a convenient framework for the specification properties of "reactive" systems. This made temporal logics a popular subject in the Computer Science community and it enjoyed an extensive research during the last 20 years. In temporal logic the relevant properties of the system are described by *atomic propositions* that hold at some points in time, but not at others. More complex properties are described by formulas built from the atoms using Boolean connectives and *Modalities* (temporal connectives): a k-place modality C transforms statements $\varphi_1, \ldots, \varphi_k$ on points possibly other than the given point t_0 to a statement $C(\varphi_1, \ldots, \varphi_k)$ on the point t_0. The rule that specifies when the statement $C(\varphi_1, \ldots, \varphi_k)$ is true for the given point is called *Truth Table*. The choice of the particular modalities with their truth tables determines the different temporal logics. A Temporal Logic with modalities $M_1, \ldots M_k$ is denoted by $TL(M_1, \ldots, M_k)$.

The most basic modality is the one place modality **F**X saying "X holds some time in the future". Its truth table is usually formalized by $\varphi_{\mathbf{F}}(t_0, X) \equiv (\exists t > t_0) t \in X$. This is a formula of the Monadic Logic of Order (*MLO*). The Monadic Logic of Order is a fundamental formalism in Mathematical Logic. Its formulas are built using atomic propositions $t \in X$, atomic relations between elements $t_1 = t_2$, $t_1 < t_2$, Boolean connectives, first-order quantifiers $\exists t$ and $\forall t$,

L. Brim et al. (Eds.): CONCUR 2002, LNCS 2421, pp. 57–76, 2002.
© Springer-Verlag Berlin Heidelberg 2002

and second-order (set) quantifiers $\exists X$ and $\forall X$. Practically, all the modalities used in the literature have their truth tables defined in MLO, and as a result every formula of a temporal logic translates directly into an equivalent formula of MLO. Therefore, the different temporal logics may be considered a convenient way to use fragments of MLO. MLO can also serve as a yardstick by which to check the strength of the temporal logic chosen: a temporal logic is *expressively complete* for a fragment L of MLO if every formula of L with a single free variable t_0 is equivalent to a temporal formula.

Actually, the notion of expressive completeness refers to a temporal logic and to a model (or a class of models) since the question if two formulas are equivalent depends on the domain over which they are evaluated. Any (partially) ordered set with monadic predicates is a model for TL and MLO, but the main, *canonical*, linear time intended models are the non-negative integers $\langle N, < \rangle$ for discrete time and the non-negative reals $\langle R^+, < \rangle$ for continuous time.

A major result concerning TL is Kamp's theorem [19,12] which states that the pair of modalities X *until* Y and X *since* Y is expressively complete for the first-order fragment of MLO over the above two linear time canonical models.

The objectives of this paper is to survey classical and recent expressive completeness results and to provide some external yardsticks by which the expressive power of the temporal logics can be measured. We consider natural fragments of MLO, and for each of these fragment L we address the question whether there is a temporal logic with a finite set of modalities which has the same expressive power of L. It turns out that for most of these fragments the answer is negative.

The paper is organized as follows. In the next section we review basic definitions about monadic logic of order and its fragments. In Section 3 we review basic definitions about temporal logics and modalities. Section 4 provides the definition of expressive completeness. Section 5 surveys classical and recent results for expressive completeness over linear time models. The temporal logic with one modality **U** *"until"* is usually referred to as the standard linear time temporal logic (see e.g. survey [8]). The "linear time" appears in the name of this logic probably because when it was introduced by Pnueli its intended models were linear orders. The adjective "standard" is probably used due to the Kamp theorem which states that it is expressively equivalent to the first-order fragment of MLO - a very robust formalism.

Sections 6 and 7 deal with temporal logic interpreted over trees - branching time models. In contrast to the linear case many temporal logics over branching time models were suggested and investigated starting from [20,3,31,9,10]. In section 6 the expressive power of temporal logics over branching time models is compared with the fragments of MLO and some objective yardsticks by which to measure the expressive power are suggested. In Section 7 we offer an explanation for the multiplicity of temporal logics over branching time and discuss the complexity of the model checking problem for finite base temporal logics.

2   Monadic Logic of Order

Monadic logic of order is a fundamental formalism in mathematical logic and the theory of computation. In this section we recall basic definitions about monadic logic of order; we also define its important fragments.

2.1   Notations

We use standard notations and abbreviations. A (relational) signature is given by a set of relational symbols and their arity. Let A be a structure for a signature τ. We use $|\ A\ |$ for the universe of A and R^A for the interpretation of the relational symbol R in A. However, whenever there is no confusion we will also use A for the universe of A; sometimes, we use "$a \in A$" instead of "$a \in|\ A\ |$" and "$\langle a_1, \ldots, a_n \rangle \in R$" instead of "$\langle a_1, \ldots, a_n \rangle \in R^A$". For a structure A over a signature $\tau = \{\ldots, R_i, \ldots\}$ we use notations $\langle |\ A\ |, \ldots, R_i^A, \ldots \rangle$ which we also abbreviated to $\langle |\ A\ |, \ldots, R_i, \ldots \rangle$.

2.2   Syntax

The syntax of the **second-order Monadic Logic of Order (MLO)** has in its vocabulary individual first-order variables $x_0, x_1, x_2, \ldots$, set variables $X_0, X_1, X_2, \ldots$ and set constants (monadic predicates names).

The atomic formulas are of the form $x_1 = x_2, x_1 < x_2$, $x \in X$ and $x \in P$, where x_i (respectively, X and P) ranges over individual variables (respectively, set variables and monadic predicate names). Formulas are built up from the atomic formulas using the propositional connectives $\wedge$ and $\neg$, and the quantifiers $\exists x$ and $\exists X$.

We shall write $\varphi(x_1, x_2, \ldots, x_k, X_1, X_2, \ldots, X_m)$ to indicate that the free variables of φ are among $x_1, x_2, \ldots, x_k, X_1, X_2, \ldots, X_m$.

The **quantifier-depth** of a formula φ, denoted by $\mathrm{qd}(\varphi)$, is defined as usual: $\mathrm{qd}(\varphi) = 0$ for atomic formulas; $\mathrm{qd}(\varphi \wedge \varphi') = \max(\mathrm{qd}(\varphi), \mathrm{qd}(\varphi'))$; $\mathrm{qd}(\neg\varphi) = \mathrm{qd}(\varphi)$; and $\mathrm{qd}(\exists x\varphi) = \mathrm{qd}(\exists X\varphi) = 1 + \mathrm{qd}(\varphi)$.

2.3   Semantics

The semantics of *MLO* follows classical lines. A structure for *MLO* is a tuple $M = \langle |\ M\ |, <, \mathcal{P}_1, \ldots, \mathcal{P}_n, \ldots \rangle$ where $<$ is a partial order over a set $|\ M\ |$ and $\mathcal{P}_1, \ldots, \mathcal{P}_n, \ldots \subseteq |\ M\ |$ are monadic predicates. If M is such a structure, $s_1, \ldots, s_m \in |\ M\ |$ are elements of M and $S_1, \ldots, S_n \subseteq |\ M\ |$ are sets of elements, we write

$$(M, s_1, s_2, \ldots, s_m, S_1, S_2, \ldots, S_n) \models \varphi(x_1, x_2, \ldots, x_m, X_1, X_2, \ldots, X_n)$$

if the formula φ is satisfied in the structure M with x_i interpreted as s_i ($i = 1, \ldots, m$) and X_j interpreted as S_j ($j = 1, \ldots, n$). The definition is a standard one, so we omit it.

We will be mainly interested in partial orders which are either linear orders or tree orders.

Chains. A structure $M = \langle \mid M \mid, <, \mathcal{P}_1, \ldots, \mathcal{P}_n, \ldots \rangle$ where $<$ is a linear order over $\mid M \mid$ and $\mathcal{P}_1, \ldots, \mathcal{P}_n, \ldots$ are monadic predicates is called a *colored (or labelled) chain*, or for brevity simply a *chain*.

The important examples of chains are $\langle R^+, < \rangle$ and $\langle N, < \rangle$ - the non-negative real line and the non-negative integers. A labelled chain over the non-negative integers is often called ω-model or ω-structure.

Trees. A structure $T = \langle \mid T \mid, <^T \rangle$ is a *tree* if $<^T$ is a binary relation such that

1. The set $\mid T \mid$ is partially ordered by $<^T$.
2. There is a unique $<^T$ minimal element.
3. For every element $a \in \mid T \mid$ the set $\{ b \in \mid T \mid \; : \; b <^T a \}$ is finite and $<^T$ is a linear order on this set.

The elements of $\mid T \mid$ are called *nodes* of the tree (sometimes we call them *time points*). The minimal element is denoted by ε_T or by $root_T$, and referred to as the *root of the tree*. A node s is an *ancestor* of a node s' in T if $s \leq^T s'$. A node s is a *successor* (in T) of a node s' if $s' <^T s$ and there is no element between s and s'.

A structure $(\mid T \mid, <^T, \ldots, P_i^T, \ldots)$ is a *labelled or computation tree* if $\langle \mid T \mid, <^T \rangle$ is a tree and P_i^T are unary predicates (subsets of $\mid T \mid$). We say that a node $s \in \mid T \mid$ is *labelled by* P_i if $s \in P_i^T$.

When s is a node in a computation tree T, we write $T_{\geq s}$ to denote the *subtree of T rooted at s*. Formally, the nodes of $T_{\geq s}$ are $\mid T_{\geq s} \mid \stackrel{\triangle}{=} \{ t : t \in \mid T \mid \text{ and } t \geq s \}$, P_i is interpreted as $P_i^T \cap \mid T_{\geq s} \mid$ and $<$ is interpreted as $<^T \cap \mid T_{\geq s} \mid \times \mid T_{\geq s} \mid$.

A *path through T starting at* $s_1 \in \mid T \mid$ is a maximal linearly ordered sequence of successive nodes $\pi = \langle s_1, s_2, s_3, \ldots \rangle$ through the tree. A path π through T induces a substructure, denoted by T_π; the set of nodes of T_π is $\{ s_1, s_2, \ldots \}$, s is labelled by P_i in T_π iff s is labelled by P_i in T, and s is an ancestor of s' in T_π iff $s \leq^T s'$.

2.4 Fragments of Monadic Logic of Order

We denote by *FOMLO* the subset of *first-order formulas of MLO*, i.e., formulas where the second-order quantifier $\exists X$ does not occur. Note that formulas of this fragment may contain free set variables.

We also consider *MPL*, the *monadic path logic* [16,14]: its syntax is the same as that of monadic second-order logic. However, unlike *MLO*, the bound set variables range over all the paths (not over arbitrary sets of nodes); the monadic predicate names (set constants) and the free set variables are interpreted by arbitrary sets of nodes.

Therefore, the corresponding clause for the second-order quantification is

$$(T, s_1, s_2, \ldots, s_m, S_1, , \ldots, S_n) \models \exists X_n \varphi(x_1, x_2, \ldots, x_m, X_1, \ldots, X_n) \text{ iff}$$
$$(T, s_1, s_2, \ldots, s_m, S_1, , \ldots, S_{n-1}, S) \models \varphi(x_1, x_2, \ldots, x_m, X_1, \ldots, X_n)$$
$$\text{for the set of nodes } S \text{ of a path in } T.$$

Since "X is a path" can be expressed in $FOMLO$, there is a meaning preserving translation from MPL into a fragment of MLO.

Though the syntax of MPL is the same as the syntax of MLO, the expressive power of MPL is very closely related to the expressive power of first-order logic [14]. In particular, for every MPL sentence φ there is a $FOMLO$ sentence ψ such that for every finite tree T

$$T \models \varphi \text{ if and only if } T \models \psi.$$

Definition 2.1 (Future formula [13]). *A formula $\varphi(x_0, X_1, \ldots, X_k)$ of MLO with one free first-order variable x_0 is a future formula if for every tree T and node $s \in |T|$, and for every subsets $S_1, \ldots, S_k$ of $|T|$, the following holds:*

$$T, s, S_1, \ldots, S_k \models \varphi \quad iff \quad T_{\geq s}, s, S_1', \ldots, S_k' \models \varphi$$

where, for $i = 1, \ldots, k$, S_i' is the restriction of S_i to $|T_{\geq s}|$.

In other words, a future formula is a formula with one free individual variable x_0 whose value depends only on nodes higher than x_0 in the tree. Observe that this is a semantic notion, not a syntactic one.

Remark 2.2 (Syntactical conditions for the property to be a future formula). Let $\varphi(x_0, X_1, \ldots X_k)$ be a formula. Let $\tilde{\varphi}$ be obtained from φ by relativizing all first-order quantifiers to the elements greater than or equal to x_0, i.e., when "$\exists x. \ldots$" and "$\forall x. \ldots$" are replaced by "$\exists x(x \geq x_0 \wedge \ldots)$" and by "$\forall x(x \geq x_0 \rightarrow \ldots)$", respectively. Note that the formula $\tilde{\varphi}$ obtained in such a way is always a future formula. Moreover, $\psi(x_0)$ is a future formula if and only if it is equivalent to a formula $\tilde{\varphi}(x_0)$ with all quantifies relativized to the elements greater than or equal to x_0.

3 Temporal Logics

In this section, we recall the syntax and semantics of temporal logics and how temporal modalities are defined using MLO truth tables.

3.1 Temporal Logics and Modalities

The syntax of **Temporal Logic (TL)** has in its vocabulary a set of variables (sometimes called propositional names) and a set B of **modality names** (sometimes called "temporal connectives" or "temporal operators") with prescribed arity $B = \{\#_1^{l_1}, \#_2^{l_2}, \ldots\}$ (we usually omit the arity notation). The set of modality names B might be infinite. A temporal logic based on a set of modalities B is denoted $TL(B)$; B is called the **basis** of $TL(B)$. Atomic temporal formulas are just variables and other formulas are obtained from the atoms using Boolean connectives and applying the modalities. Formally, the syntax of $TL(B)$ is given by the following grammar:

$$\varphi ::= P \mid \varphi_1 \wedge \varphi_2 \mid \neg\varphi_1 \mid \#_i^{l_i}(\varphi_1, \varphi_2, \ldots, \varphi_{l_i}), \text{ where}$$

P ranges over the variable names.

The **nesting-depth** of a temporal formula φ, denoted by $\mathrm{nd}(\varphi)$, is defined as usual: $\mathrm{nd}(\varphi) = 0$ for atomic formulas; $\mathrm{nd}(\varphi \wedge \varphi') = \max(\mathrm{nd}(\varphi), \mathrm{nd}(\varphi'))$; $\mathrm{nd}(\neg\varphi) = \mathrm{nd}(\varphi)$; and $\mathrm{nd}(\#_i^{l_i}(\varphi_1, \varphi_2, \ldots, \varphi_{l_i})) = 1 + \max\limits_{1 \le j \le l_i} (\mathrm{nd}(\varphi_j))$.

Temporal formulas are interpreted over partially ordered sets with monadic predicates, in particular over computation trees and over labelled chains. Every modality $\#^l$ is interpreted in every structure T as an operator

$$\#_T^l : [\mathcal{P}(\mid T \mid)]^l \to \mathcal{P}(\mid T \mid)$$

which assigns "the set of points where $\#^l(Q_1, \ldots, Q_l)$ holds" to the l–tuple $\langle Q_1, \ldots, Q_l \rangle$. (Here $\mathcal{P}$ is the power set notation, and $\mathcal{P}(\mid T \mid)$ denotes the set of all subsets of the universe of T.)

Formally, we define when a temporal formula φ holds in a node s of a structure $T = \langle \mid T \mid, <^T, P_1^T, \ldots P_n^T, \ldots \rangle$, written $T, s \models \varphi$, by the following inductive clauses:

1. For atomic formulas $T, s \models P_i$ iff $s \in P_i^T$.
2. The semantics of Boolean combinations is defined as usual, and
3. The semantics of modalities is defined by:

$$T, s \models \#^l(\varphi_1, \varphi_2, \ldots, \varphi_l) \text{ iff } s \in \#_T^l(R_{\varphi_1}, R_{\varphi_2}, \ldots, R_{\varphi_l})$$

where $R_{\varphi_i} = \{a : T, a \models \varphi_i\}$ for all $i, 1 \le i \le l$.

Notes.

1. In temporal and modal logics, formulas are constructed from atoms by applying Boolean connectives and modalities. Formalisms like *MLO* and μ-calculus can specify properties of trees. However, they use binding, quantifiers, fixed-points; hence, they are not temporal logics according to our definition.
2. Strictly speaking what we call temporal logic is called *one-dimensional temporal logic*. The syntax of k-dimensional temporal logic is the same as that of one-dimensional temporal logic. However, atomic formulas (variables) are interpreted as k-ary relations; accordingly, every l-place modality $\#^l$ is interpreted in every structure T as an operator which assigns a k-ary relation (over $\mid T \mid$) to every l-tuple of k-ary relations [12].

3.2   Truth Tables

There is not much interest in a modality $\#$ whose interpretation is arbitrary and is defined ad-hoc in each and every structure where the temporal logic is to be interpreted. To be of interest a modality needs to have a uniform description in some metalanguage that connects the set of points where $\#(\varphi_1, \ldots, \varphi_k)$ holds to the sets of points where each of the φ_i holds. It is an empirical fact that all the temporal modalitities considered in the literature are defined in MLO in the following way: for every l-place modality $\#$ there is a formula $\bar{\#}(x_0, X_1, X_2, \ldots, X_l)$ of MLO with one free first-order variable x_0 and l set variables, such that for every structure T and subsets $R_i \subseteq |T|$:

$$\#_T(R_1, R_2, \ldots, R_l) = \{s : (T, s, R_1, R_2, \ldots, R_l) \models \bar{\#}(x_0, X_1, X_2, \ldots, X_l)\}.$$

The formula will be called the *truth table* of this modality. Let M be a temporal modality defined by a formula $\varphi_M \in MLO$ serving as a truth table. We say that M has the quantifier-depth k if $\mathrm{qd}(\varphi_M) = k$.

Example 3.1 (Some common modalities and their truth tables).

- The one-place modality **F** (*"eventually"*); its truth table is

$$\varphi_{\mathbf{F}}(x_0, X_1) \triangleq \exists y(y > x_0 \wedge y \in X_1).$$

- The one-place modality **G** (*"globally"*); its truth table is

$$\varphi_{\mathbf{G}}(x_0, X_1) \triangleq \forall y(y > x_0 \rightarrow y \in X_1).$$

- The one-place modality **X** (*"next"*); its truth table is

$$\varphi_{\mathbf{X}}(x_0, X_1) \triangleq \exists y(y > x_0 \wedge y \in X_1 \wedge \forall z(z < y \rightarrow z \leq x_0)).$$

- The two-place modality **U** (*"until"*); its truth table is

$$\varphi_{\mathbf{U}}(x_0, X_1, X_2) \triangleq \exists y(y > x_0 \wedge y \in X_2 \wedge \forall z(x_0 < z < y \rightarrow z \in X_1)).$$

In the literature sometimes a "nonstrict" definition of Until is given: the "nonstrict until" $\mathbf{U}_{ns}$ modality has the truth table

$$\varphi_{\mathbf{U}_{ns}}(x_0, X_1, X_2) \triangleq \exists y(y \geq x_0 \wedge y \in X_2 \wedge \forall z(x_0 \leq z < y \rightarrow z \in X_1)).$$

Clearly, $\mathbf{U}_{ns}$ can be defined using $\mathbf{U}$:

$$X_1 \mathbf{U}_{ns} X_2 \leftrightarrow X_2 \vee (X_1 \wedge (X_1 \mathbf{U} X_2)).$$

- The one-place modality $\mathbf{F}^\infty$ (*"infinitely often"*); its truth table is

$$\varphi_{\mathbf{F}^\infty}(x_0, X_1) \triangleq \forall y(y > x_0 \rightarrow \exists z(z > y \wedge z \in X_1)).$$

- The two-place modality **S** (*"since"*); its truth table is

$$\varphi_{\mathbf{S}}(x_0, X_1, X_2) \triangleq \exists y(y < x_0 \wedge y \in X_2 \wedge \forall z(x_0 > z > y \rightarrow z \in X_1)).$$

The choice of the particular modalities with their truth tables determines the different temporal logics.

Most of the temporal logics studied in Computer Science use only modalities having truth tables definable by future MLO formulas (see Definition 2.1).

Definition 3.2 (First-Order Future Modality). *A temporal modality M is a first-order future modality if its truth table is a future formula of FOMLO.*

Second-order future modalities are defined similarly. The modalities defined in the above example $\mathbf{F}$, $\mathbf{G}, \mathbf{X}, \mathbf{U}$ and $\mathbf{F}^\infty$ are first-order future modalities; the modality $\mathbf{S}$ is not a future modality.

For reasoning about the branching structure of computation trees, so-called *branching-time* temporal logics have been introduced, with CTL and CTL^* as main representatives. These temporal logics use special modalities whose truth table starts with a path quantifier, as we now explain.

Definition 3.3 (Path Modalities). *For every first-order future formula $\varphi(x_0, X_1, \ldots, X_l)$, we define an l-place path modality $\mathbf{E}\varphi$ as follows:*

$$T, a \models \mathbf{E}\varphi \text{ if and only if}$$
there is a path π from a in T, such that[1] $T_\pi, a \models \varphi(x_0, X_1, \ldots, X_l)$.

The modality $\mathbf{E}\varphi$ is said to be the path modality which corresponds to $\varphi(x_0, X_1, \ldots, X_l)$.

If $\varphi(x_0, X_1, \ldots, X_l)$ is a future $FOMLO$ formula, the truth table of the path modality $\mathbf{E}\varphi$ is the MPL formula $\exists Y\big(x_0 \in Y \ \wedge \ \varphi'(x_0, X_1, \ldots, X_l, Y)\big)$ where $\varphi'(x_0, X_1, \ldots, X_l, Y)$ is obtained from $\varphi(x_0, X_1, \ldots, X_l)$ by relativising all its quantifiers to Y. Thus, the following proposition holds:

Proposition 3.4. *For every first-order future formula $\varphi(x_0, X_1, \ldots, X_l)$, the path modality $\mathbf{E}\varphi$ has an MPL truth table.*

4   Expressive Completeness - Basic Definitions

Different temporal logics may be considered a convenient way to use fragments of MLO. The following are standard definitions and notations to discuss the expressive power of temporal logics. A temporal logic formula φ is *equivalent* to an MLO formula $\psi(x_0, X_1, \ldots, X_l)$ with a single free first-order variable (or to a temporal logic formula ψ) over a structure T iff for every $a \in |\,T\,|$:

$$T, a \models \varphi \text{ if and only if } T, a \models \psi.$$

φ is equivalent to ψ (over a set C of structures) iff for every T (respectively, for every $T \in C$), φ is equivalent to ψ over T.

---

[1] Recall that T_π is the substructure of T over the set of nodes π (see Subsection 2.3)

Definition 4.1. *Let C be a set of structures. TL_1 is **less or equally expressive** than TL_2 over C (notation $TL_1 \preceq_{exp}^C TL_2$), if for every formula $\varphi_1 \in TL_1$ there is a formula $\varphi_2 \in TL_2$ which is equivalent to φ_1 over C. The relations **equally expressive** (notation $\equiv_{exp}^C$) and **strictly less expressive** (notation $\prec_{exp}^C$) are defined from the relation $\preceq_{exp}^C$ as expected. When C is the class of all trees, we write $\preceq_{exp}$ for $\preceq_{exp}^C$. The relations $\equiv_{exp}$ and $\prec_{exp}$ are defined similarly.*

Definition 4.2 (Expressive Completeness). *Let L be a fragment of MLO and let C be a set of structures. A temporal logic TL_1 is **expressively complete** for L over C if for every formula $\psi(x_0) \in L$ with a single free first-order variable x_0 there is a formula $\varphi \in TL_1$ which is equivalent to ψ over C, and for every formula $\varphi \in TL_1$ there is a formula $\psi(x_0) \in L$ with a single free first-order variable x_0 which is equivalent to φ over C.*

By a straightforward induction on the structure of TL formulas one can show

Proposition 4.3. 1. *If every modality of a temporal logic TL is defined by a FOMLO truth table then every formula φ of TL is equivalent to a FOMLO formula.*
2. *If every modality of a temporal logic TL is defined by a future FOMLO truth table then every formula φ of TL is equivalent to a future FOMLO formula.*
3. *Similar to (1) and (2) with "MPL" or "MLO" replacing "FOMLO".*

We say that a fragment L of MLO (or a temporal logic L) has (or admits) a **finite basis** over a class C of structures if there is a finite set of modalities $M_1, \ldots, M_k$ such that L is expressively equivalent over C to $TL(M_1, \ldots, M_k)$.

5   Linear Time

In the next subsection we recall classical theorems which show that over linear time models $FOMLO$ is expressively equivalent to a finite base temporal logic (i.e., temporal logic with a finite set of modalities). In the second subsection we show that there is no finite base temporal logic which is expressively equivalent to MLO. The third subsection shows that there is no finite base temporal logic which is expressively equivalent over the reals to the future fragment of $FOMLO$.

5.1   Kamp's and Stavi's Theorems

A major result concerning TL and $FOMLO$ is Kamp's theorem which implies that $TL(\mathbf{U}, \mathbf{S})$, the temporal logic having "*Until*" and "*Since*" as the only modalities, is expressively complete for $FOMLO$ over the two canonical models - real numbers and natural numbers. There is a technical property which unifies in the general case the treatment of real and discrete time: recall that a chain is Dedekind complete iff every non empty bounded subset has a lowest upper bound. The natural numbers are trivially Dedekind complete since every bounded set is finite and has a maximal element. The real line is also Dedekind complete. Kamp's result applies to both these models:

Theorem 5.1 (Kamp [19,12]**).** *The temporal logic with two modalities* **U** *("until") and* **S** *("since") is expressively complete for FOMLO over the class of Dedekind complete chains.*

Observe that the rationals are not Dedekind complete. It turns out that the temporal logic with **U** and **S** modalities is less expressive than *FOMLO* over the rationals [34,12]. Stavi introduced two more modalities $\mathbf{U}^{Stavi}$ and $\mathbf{S}^{Stavi}$ and proved

Theorem 5.2 (Stavi [34,12]**).** *The temporal logic with four modalities* **U, S,** $\mathbf{U}^{Stavi}$ *and* $\mathbf{S}^{Stavi}$ *is expressively complete for FOMLO over the class of all linear orders.*

5.2 No Finite Base for *MLO*

Some natural properties are not expressible in the first-order logic [23]. For example, in the first-order fragment of *MLO* it is impossible to specify any of the following properties $Mult_p(x_0, X)$ $(1 < p \in \mathbb{N})$:

$Mult_p(x_0, X)$**:** $Mult_p(x_0, X)$ holds at point x_0 iff there is exactly one $x > x_0$ such that X holds at x, and the number of elements between x_0 and this x is a multiple of p plus one.

However, for every p, the property $Mult_p(x_0, X)$ is easily expressible in the future fragment of *MLO*.

In [1] we addressed the question of existence of a finite base temporal logic which is expressively equivalent (over the naturals) to *MLO*.

The main technical lemma implies

Lemma 5.3 ([1]**).** *For every finite set of modalities* $\{M_1, \ldots M_k\}$ *with truth tables in MLO there is* $p \in \mathbb{N}$ *such that the property* $Mult_p(x_0, X)$ *is not expressible (over the naturals) in* $TL(M_1, \ldots M_k)$.

As a consequence of this lemma we obtain

Theorem 5.4 ([1]**).** *There is no finite base temporal logic which is expressively equivalent (over the naturals) to monadic logic of order.*

The above theorem can be strengthened as follows:

Theorem 5.5. *Let C be a set of linear orders which is either infinite or contains an infinite linear order. There is no finite set of modalities such that the temporal logic over this set of modalities is expressively equivalent over C to monadic logic of order.*

5.3   No Finite Base for the Future Fragment of *FOMLO*

Most of the temporal formalisms studied in Computer Science concern only future-time modalities (see [21] for the discussion of past-time modalities in specification formalisms). Is there also a natural temporal logic that is expressively complete for the fragment of future *FOMLO* formulas with respect to the canonical models? Is it simply $TL(\mathsf{U})$, and if not, can we add some naturally defined modalities to obtain an expressively complete future logic?

Theorem 5.6 ([13]). *The temporal logic with the single modality* U *("until") is expressively equivalent (over the naturals) to the future fragment of FOMLO.*

Thus, in the discrete case $TL(\mathsf{U})$ is as strong as the future fragment of *FOMLO*. The following theorem from [17] shows that for continuous time the situation is radically different.

Theorem 5.7 ([17]). *There is no finite base temporal logic which is expressively equivalent (over the reals) to the future fragment of FOMLO.*

Let $\langle A, \ < \rangle$ be a linear order and let $P \subseteq A$. A point x is a left limit point of P if for every $y < x$, the interval $(y, \ x)$ contains a point from P. Let $P^{(1)}$ be the set of left limit points of P and let $P^{(m+1)}$ be the set of left limit points of $P^{(m)}$. It is easy to express in *FOMLO* the following property of an unary predicate P.

$Prop_m(P)$: "there is in the future a point in $P^{(m)}$.

The main technical lemma in [17] shows that if a temporal logic L has modalities definable by future *FOMLO* formulas of quantifier depth at most m, then $Prop_m(P)$ is not expressible in L. Theorem 5.7 is an easy consequence of this lemma.

6   Branching Time

Milner and Park [24,27] pointed out that for the specification of concurrent systems we need a model finer than just the set of possible (linear) runs; this led to the computation tree model. The logic $TL(\mathsf{U})$ is usually referred to as the standard linear time temporal logic (see e.g., survey [8]). Of course, $TL(\mathsf{U})$ is interpreted not only over linear orders, but also over arbitrary partial orders; in particular, over trees. The "linear time" appears in the name of this logic probably because when it was introduced by Pnueli its intended models were linear orders; more precisely, ω-models. The adjective "standard" is probably used due to the Kamp theorem which states that it is expressively equivalent (over the ω-models) to (the future fragment of) *FOMLO* - a very robust formalism.

Recall that $TL(\mathsf{U})$ as any logic with modalities defined in *MLO* is interpreted not only over linear orders, but over arbitrary partial orders (according to the truth table of U); in particular, over the trees. However, the expressive power of $TL(\mathsf{U})$ over the trees is very limited. For instance, a very basic property "along all futures, eventually p" (that is, "p is inevitable") is not expressible in $TL(\mathsf{U})$.

In order to reflect branching properties of computations many temporal logics were suggested starting from [20,3,31,9,10]. The basic modalities of these logics (which are often called branching time logics) are either of the form **E** ("there exists a linear run") followed by a formula in $TL(\mathbf{U})$ or of the form **A** ("for every linear run") followed by a formula in $TL(\mathbf{U})$. $\mathbf{E}\varphi$ (respectively $\mathbf{A}\varphi$) holds at a moment t_0 if for a path π (respectively, for every path π) starting at t_0 the $TL(\mathbf{U})$ formula φ holds along π. For example, one commonly used branching time logic is CTL [3]. It is based on two binary modalities **EU** and **AU** ; $\mathbf{AU}(X,Y)$ (respectively $\mathbf{EU}(X,Y)$) holds at a current moment t_0 if "for all (respectively, for some) runs from the current moment, X until Y holds". In contrast to the expressive completeness of $TL(\mathbf{U})$ over the canonical linear models, there is no natural predicate logic which corresponds to $TL(\mathbf{EU},\mathbf{AU})$ (i.e., to CTL) over the trees. Moreover, it turns out that CTL cannot express many natural fairness properties [10].

The logic CTL^* suggested in [10] has the same expressive power as the temporal logic with infinite set of modalities $\{\mathbf{E}\varphi : \varphi$ is a formula of $TL(\mathbf{U})\} \cup \{\mathbf{A}\varphi : \varphi$ is a formula of $TL(\mathbf{U})\}$. Many temporal logics were suggested as branching time specification formalisms (see [10,11,7,35]) by imposing some syntactical restrictions on CTL^* formulas. The lack of a yardstick was emphasized by Emerson in words very similar to the above [7,8]:

> "... While less is known about comparisons of Branching time logics against external "yardsticks", a great deal is known about comparisons of $BTLs$ against each other. This contrasts with the reversed situation for Linear-Time Logics." (page 44 in [8]).

In Section 7 we offer an explanation for the multiplicity of temporal logics over branching time. In Section 6 we suggest some yardsticks by which to measure the expressive power of these logics.

One popular equivalence between computation trees is that of bisimulation equivalence. This equivalence catches subtle differences between trees based on their branching structures. It is generally regarded as the finest behavioral equivalence of interest for concurrency (it is often argued that concurrent systems giving rise to bisimulation equivalent computation trees are indistinguishable for all reasonable notions of observation). In [25], CTL^* was shown to be expressively equivalent to the bisimulation invariant fragment of monadic path logic [14,16]. Thus, at least CTL^* represents an objectively quantified expressive power.

In Subsection 6.3 we describe a sequence TLQ_k ($k \in N$) of temporal logics. All these logics are (expressively equivalent to) fragments of CTL^* and their union has the same expressive power as CTL^*. Roughly speaking, the modalities of TLQ_k correspond to formulas with quantifier-depth at most k. However, for every m and k there is a TLQ_k formula which is equivalent to no MLO formula with quantifier-depth $\leq m$. It turns out that the sequence TLQ_k ($k \in N$) of temporal logics forms a hierarchy according to the expressive power [32], i.e., TLQ_{k+1} is strictly more expressive than TLQ_k. Consequently, we obtain that there is no finite base temporal logic which is expressively equivalent to CTL^*, and hence there is no finite base temporal logic which is expressively equivalent to the bisimulation invariant fragment of monadic path logic.

In Subsection 6.4 and in Subsection 6.5 we present two additional hierarchies of temporal logics. The first hierarchy is based on the alternation depth of the truth tables for the logical modalities and the second one is based on the arity of the logical modalities.

6.1 CTL^*

Computation Tree Logic (CTL) was introduced in [3]. It is based on two binary modalities **EU** and **AU**; $\mathbf{AU}(X,Y)$ (respectively $\mathbf{EU}(X,Y)$) holds at a current moment t_0 if "for all (respectively, for some) paths from the current moment, X until Y holds". The modality **EU** is equivalent to **U**. The truth table for $\mathbf{AU}(X,Y)$ is $\neg\mathbf{E}\neg\varphi_{\mathbf{U}}$, where $\varphi_{\mathbf{U}}$ is the truth table of **U**.

In contrast to the expressive completeness of $TL(\mathbf{U})$ over ω-models (the canonical discrete-time linear models), there is no natural predicate logic which corresponds to CTL ($= TL(\mathbf{EU},\mathbf{AU}) \equiv_{exp} TL(\mathbf{U},\mathbf{E}\neg\varphi_{\mathbf{U}})$) over the class of trees. Moreover, it turns out that CTL cannot express many natural properties over trees [10].

The logic CTL^* suggested in [10] is much more expressive. The definition of CTL^* [10] uses an interplay between state formulas (which correspond to genuine modalities) and path formulas (which play an auxiliary role) to generate infinitely many modalities by a finite syntax. CTL^* is expressively equivalent to the temporal logic based on the infinite set of modalities $\{E\varphi : \varphi$ is a formula of $TL(\mathbf{U})\} \cup \{A\varphi : \varphi$ is a formula of $TL(\mathbf{U})\}$ [7,32]. $\mathbf{A}\varphi$ (respectively $\mathbf{E}\varphi$) holds at a current moment t_0 if "for all (respectively, for some) paths from the current moment, φ holds". Formally, $T,t_0 \models \mathbf{E}\varphi$ iff $T_\pi,t_0 \models \varphi$ for some path π starting at t_0.

The modalities of the form $\mathbf{A}\varphi$ are expressible from $\mathbf{E}\varphi$ since for every φ in $TL(\mathbf{U})$, $\mathbf{A}\varphi$ means the same as $\neg\mathbf{E}\neg\varphi$. Thus, the set of modalities $\{\mathbf{E}\varphi : \varphi \in TL(\mathbf{U})\}$ is a base for CTL^*.

Observe that if $\varphi(X_1,\ldots,X_l)$ is a $TL(\mathbf{U})$ formula, then by Proposition 4.3(1) there is a future $FOMLO$ formula $\psi(x_0,X_1,\ldots,X_l)$ which is equivalent to φ. Moreover, the path modality $\mathbf{E}\psi$ (see Definition 3.3) defines the same temporal operators as $\mathbf{E}\varphi$. Let M be the set of modalities

$$M \triangleq \{\mathbf{E}\varphi : \varphi \in TL(\mathbf{U})\}.$$

Let H be the set of modalities

$$H \triangleq \{\mathbf{E}\psi : \psi \text{ is } FOMLO \text{ future formula}\}.$$

From the above observation it follows that $TL(M) \preceq_{exp} TL(H)$. Theorem 5.6 implies that for every formula $\psi(x_0,X,\ldots,X_l)$ in the future fragment of $FOMLO$ there is φ in $TL(\mathbf{U})$ such that the temporal operators $\mathbf{E}\varphi$ and $\mathbf{E}\psi$ are the same. Therefore, the temporal logics $TL(M)$ and $TL(H)$ are expressively equivalent.

To summarize, we have that the following temporal logics are expressively equivalent:

Lemma 6.1. *CTL^* is expressively equivalent to $TL(\{\mathbf{E}\varphi : \varphi \in TL(\mathbf{U})\}) \equiv_{exp}$ $TL(\{\mathbf{E}\psi : \psi$ is FOMLO future formula$\}$.*

6.2   CTL* versus Monadic Path Logic

Bisimulation equivalence [24,27] plays a very important role in concurrency. This equivalence catches subtle differences between trees based on their branching structures. It is generally regarded as the finest behavioral equivalence of interest for concurrency. A (future MLO) formula $\varphi(x_0, X_1, \ldots, X_l)$ is *bisimulation invariant* if $T, root \models \varphi(x_0, X_1, \ldots, X_l)$ implies $T', root' \models \varphi(x_0, X_1, \ldots, X_l)$ whenever T and T' are bisimulation equivalent.

Theorem 6.2 ([25]). *CTL^* is expressively equivalent (over trees) to the bisimulation invariant future fragment of MPL.*

Thus, CTL^* represents an objectively quantified expressive power.

The counting operator $\mathbf{D}^n X$ with $n>0$ expresses *"for at least $n>0$ different successors have property X"*. The truth table for $\mathbf{D}^n$ is

$$\exists y_1 \ldots \exists y_n (\bigwedge_{i \neq j} y_i \neq y_j) \wedge (\bigwedge_{i=1}^{n} (y_i \in X \wedge Succ(x_0, y_i))), \text{ where}$$

$Succ(x,y)$ (y is a successor of x) is $x < y \wedge \neg\exists z(x < z < y)$. One can easily describe bisimilar trees T and T' such that $T, root \models \mathbf{D}^2 X$, but $T', root' \not\models \mathbf{D}^2 X$. Hence, modalities $\mathbf{D}^n$ are not bisimulation invariant.

Theorem 6.3 ([26]). *The extension of CTL^* by the counting operators $\{\mathbf{D}^n\}_{n=1}^{\infty}$ is expressively equivalent (over trees) to the future fragment of MPL.*

Theorem 6.4. *The extension of CTL^* by the counting operators $\{\mathbf{D}^n\}_{n=1}^{\infty}$ and by $\mathbf{S}$ ("since") is expressively equivalent (over trees) to MPL.*

6.3   Quantifier Hierarchy

The quantifier depth of a modality (i.e. of its truth table) is a natural measure of its complexity.

Definition 6.5 (Logic TLQ_k). *For every $k \geq 1$, let TLQ_k be the temporal logic with the set of basic modalities defined by the following set Q_k of truth tables:*

$$Q_k = \{\mathbf{E}\varphi : qd(\varphi(x_0, X_1, \ldots, X_l)) \leq k \text{ and } \varphi \text{ is a first-order future formula}\}.$$

Notes.

1. The basic modalities of TLQ_k are path modalities. Their truth tables can be defined by MPL formulas with only one path quantifier. However, formulas of TLQ_k (as formulas of every temporal logic) permit arbitrarily deep nesting of modalities and can express "branching" properties which require many path quantifiers.

2. The basic modalities of TLQ_k have a bounded quantifier depth, but formulas of TLQ_k permit arbitrarily deep nesting of modalities. Properties of "an arbitrary quantifier depth" can be expressed even in TLQ_1. More precisely, for every n, there is a TLQ_1 formula φ_n which is equivalent to no MLO formula of quantifier-depth $\leq n$ [32].

3. Observe that Lemma 6.1 implies that $\bigcup_{k=1}^{\infty} TLQ_k \equiv_{exp} CTL^*$.

Theorem 6.6 (Quantifier Depth Hierarchy [32]). TLQ_{k+1} *is strictly more expressive than* TLQ_k.

On the Expressive Power of TLQ_2. Many temporal logics were suggested as branching time specification formalisms (see [11,7]) by imposing some syntactic restrictions on CTL^* formulas. In [32] we examined the expressive power of commonly used branching time temporal logics. It turns out that almost all of these logics are inside TLQ_2 - the second level of our hierarchy. The modalities for these logics were suggested by the desire to formalize some pragmatic properties which often occur in specifications of hardware and software systems. It is instructive to observe that most of these properties can be formalized by TLQ_2 formulas constructed from basic modalities of quantifier-depth two.

In [33] it was shown that $B(\mathbf{U}, \mathbf{F}, \mathbf{F}^{\infty}, \mathbf{G}^{\infty}, \wedge, \neg)$, the classical extension of CTL with fairness properties [10], is expressively equivalent to TLQ_2. This result, linking $B(\mathbf{U}, \mathbf{F}, \mathbf{F}^{\infty}, \mathbf{G}^{\infty}, \wedge, \neg)$ to a natural fragment of the monadic logic of order, provides a characterization that other branching time logics, e.g., CTL, lack.

It was also shown in [33] that TLQ_2 does not admit a finite base (i.e., it is expressively equivalent to no temporal logic with a finite set of modalities).

6.4   Alternation Depth Hierarchy

An alternation type of a first-order formula is a finite sequence of positive natural numbers. We define below when a formula φ has an alternation type $\langle n_1, \ldots n_k \rangle$. However, unlike the quantifier depth, a formula has many alternation types.

1. If $\bar{n}$ is an alternation type and φ is atomic then $\bar{n}$ is an alternation type of φ.
2. If $\bar{n}$ is an alternation type of φ_1 and of φ_2 then $\bar{n}$ is an alternation type of $\neg\varphi_1$, of $\varphi_1 \wedge \varphi_2$ and of $\varphi_1 \vee \varphi_2$.
3. If $\langle n_1, \ldots n_k \rangle$ is an alternation type of φ then $\langle n_0, n_1, \ldots n_k \rangle$ is an alternation type of $\forall u_1 \ldots \forall u_m \varphi$ and of $\exists u_1 \ldots \exists u_m \varphi$ for $n_0 \geq m$.

For example, if φ is in prenex normal form with the quantifier prefix $\forall^2 \exists^3$ then $\langle 2, 3 \rangle$, $\langle 1, 1, 1, 1, 1 \rangle$ and $\langle 2, 2, 1 \rangle$ are alternation types of φ, but $\langle 1, 3, 1 \rangle$ is not one of its alternation types. Finally, we say that φ has an alternation depth (or rank) k if φ has an alternation type of the length k.

Definition 6.7 (Logic $TLAL_k$). *For every $k \geq 1$, let $TLAL_k$ be the temporal logic with the set of basic modalities defined by the following set AL_k of truth tables:*

$$AL_K = \{ \mathbf{E}\varphi : \text{alternation depth of } \varphi(x_0, X_1, \ldots, X_l) \leq k$$
$$\text{and } \varphi \text{ is a first-order future formula} \}.$$

Theorem 6.8 (Alternation Hierarchy). $TLAL_{k+1}$ *is strictly more expressive than* $TLAL_k$.

6.5   Arity Hierarchies

Let $Fair_k(X_1, \ldots, X_k)$ be the modality such that $T, s \models Fair_k(X_1, \ldots, X_k)$ iff there is a path from s along which every X_i is satisfied infinitely often and where only nodes satisfying some of the X_is are encountered.

It is clear that $Fair_k$ has a truth table in Monadic path logic; moreover, $Fair_k$ is TLQ_2 modality. It was shown in [33]

Lemma 6.9 ([33]). *The modality* $Fair_{k+1}$ *is not expressible in* $TL(\mathbf{U}, \{Fair_n\}_{n=1}^k)$ *for every* k.

Definition 6.10 (Logic $TLAR_k$). *For every* $k \geq 1$, *let* $TLAR_k$ *be the temporal logic based on all modalities of arity at most* k *defined by MLO future formulas.*

Lemma 6.9 can be strengthened as follows:

Lemma 6.11. *The modality* $Fair_{k+1}$ *is not expressible in* $TLAR_k$ *for every* k.

As a consequence one obtains

Theorem 6.12 (Arity Hierarchy). $TLAR_{k+1}$ *is strictly more expressive than* $TLAR_k$.

Corollary 6.13. *Let* M_k *be the set of all modalities of arity at most* k, *which are definable by* CTL^* *formulas.* $TL(M_k)$ *is strictly less expressive than* $TL(M_{k+1})$ *for every* k.

7   Why so Many Temporal Logics Climb Up the Trees

Two of the most important characteristics of a TL are (1) its expressive power and (2) the complexity of its model checking problem [8]. Theorem 7.1 shows that for natural fragments of MLO there is no expressive equivalent finite base temporal logics. On the other hand, Theorem 7.2 below shows that for every finite set of modalities $M_1, M_2, \ldots, M_r$, the complexity of model checking for $TL(M_1, M_2, \ldots, M_r)$ is linear both in the size of structure and the size of formula. We believe, therefore, that these are the reasons for so many suggestions for temporal logics over branching time models.

7.1   There Is No Natural Finite Base TL over Trees

Theorem 7.1. *There are no finite base temporal logics which are expressive equivalent over trees to the the the following fragments of MLO.*

1. *FOMLO and the future fragment of FOMLO.*
2. *Like in (1) with "MPL" or "MLO" replacing "FOMLO".*
3. *The future bisimulation invariant fragment[2] of MPL.*
4. *Like in (3) with "FOMLO" or "MLO" replacing "MPL".*

About proofs: (1) Recall that $\mathbf{D}^n$ is the counting operator and $\mathbf{D}^n X$ says "*at least n different successors* have property X". The truth table for $\mathbf{D}^n$ (see Sect. 6.2) uses n different bound variables. Moreover, any *FOMLO* formula which is equivalent (over trees) to $\mathbf{D}^n X$ should use at least $n+1$ different variables. From this observation it is derived in [12] (see Section 1.8) that there is no finite base temporal logic which is expressive equivalent over trees to *FOMLO* [12]. The arguments for the future fragment of *FOMLO* and for (2) are similar to (1).

   (3)-(4) can be derived from the Hierarchy Theorems (Theorems 6.6, 6.8, 6.12) or their proofs. For example, to prove (3) recall that CTL^* is equivalent to $\bigcup TLQ_k$ and by Theorem 6.6 $\{TLQ_k\}_{k=1}^{\infty}$ contains a strict hierarchy. Hence, CTL^* cannot have a finite base. This together with 6.2 establish (3).

7.2   Complexity of Model Checking

The model checking problem for a logic L is as follows [3,31,7,5]. Given a finite Kripke structure K and a formula $\varphi \in L$, determine whether $T_K, root \models \varphi$, where T_K is the tree that corresponds to the unwinding of K from its initial state.

   CTL is based on four modalities. The model checking problem for CTL has the linear time complexity $O(|\,K\,| \times |\,\varphi\,|)$. CTL^* is based on an infinite set of modalities. Unlike CTL, the model checking problem for CTL^* is PSPACE complete [4]. The next Theorem shows that for a temporal logic based on a finite set of modalities, the model checking problem has a low complexity. Its proof is based on techniques from [11].

Theorem 7.2 (Complexity of Model Checking [32]). *Let $TL(M_1, M_2, \ldots, M_k)$ be a TL based on a finite set of modalities.*

1. *Assume that M_i $(i = 1, 2, \ldots, k)$ are definable by CTL^* formulas. Then the model checking problem for $TL(M_1, M_2, \ldots, M_k)$ has time complexity $O(|\,K\,| \times |\,\varphi\,|)$.*
2. *Assume that M_i $(i = 1, 2, \ldots, k)$ are of the form $E\varphi$, where φ is a future monadic second-order formula. Then the model checking problem for $TL(M_1, M_2, \ldots, M_k)$ has time complexity $O(|\,K\,| \times |\,\varphi\,|)$.*

---

[2] This fragment is equivalent to CTL^*

Acknowledgments

I am grateful to Danièle Beauquier, Yoram Hirshfeld, Shahar Maoz, Faron Moller, Philippe Schnoebelen and Boris Trakhtenbrot. Many results reported in this paper were obtained in our joint work.

References

1. D. Beauquier and A. Rabinovich (2002). Monadic Logic of Order over Naturals Has no Finite Base. Journal on Logic and Computations **12**:(2) pp 243-253. 66
2. M. Ben-Ari, Z. Manna and A. Pnueli (1981). The temporal logic of branching time. In *Proceedings of the 8th Annual ACM Symposium on Principles of Programming Languages*, ACM, New York, pp. 164-176.
3. E.M. Clarke and E.A. Emerson (1981). Design and verification of synchronous skeletons using branching time temporal logic. *Lecture Notes in Computer Science* **131**:52–71. 58, 68, 69, 73
4. E.M. Clarke, E.A. Emerson and A.P. Sistla (1983). Automatic verification of finite state concurrent system using temporal logic. In *Proceedings of the 10th Annual ACM Symposium on Principles of Programming Languages*. 73
5. E. Clarke and B.H. Schlingloff (1999). Model checking. In A. Robinson and A. Voronkov, editors, *Handbook on Automated Reasoning*, pages 3–157. Elsevier Science Publishers B.V. 73
6. E. A. Emerson and E. M. Clarke (1980). Characterizing correctness properties of parallel programs using fixpoints. In *Proc. 7th Coll. Automata, Languages and Programming (ICALP'80), Noordwijkerhout, NL,* , volume 85 of *Lecture Notes in Computer Science*, pages 169–181. Springer, 1980.
7. E.A. Emerson (1990). Temporal and modal logic. In J. van Leeuwen, editor, *Handbook of Theoretical Computer Science*, volume B. Elsevier, Amsterdam, 1990. 68, 69, 71, 73
8. E.A. Emerson (1996). Automated temporal reasoning about reactive systems. *Logics for Concurrency: Structure versus Automata*, F. Moller and G. Birtwistle (eds.), Springer LNCS no. 1043, pp. 41–101, 1996. 58, 67, 68, 72
9. E.A. Emerson and J.Y. Halpern (1982). Decision procedures and expressiveness in the temporal logic of branching time. In *Proceedings of the 14th Annual ACM Symposium of Theory of Computing*, ACM, New York, 1982. pp. 169-180. 58, 68
10. E.A. Emerson and J.Y. Halpern (1986). 'Sometimes' and 'not never' revisited: on branching versus linear time temporal logics. *Journal of the ACM* **33**(1):151–178. 58, 68, 69, 71
11. E.A. Emerson and C.L. Lei. Modalities for model checking: branching time strikes back. *12th ACM Symp. on Principles of Prog. Lang.*, pp. 84-96, 1985. 68, 71, 73
12. D. Gabbay, I. Hodkinson and M. Reynolds (1994). *Temporal Logic*. Oxford University Press. 58, 62, 66, 73
13. D. Gabbay, A. Pnueli, S. Shelah and J. Stavi (1980). On the temporal analysis of fairness. *7th ACM Symp. on Principles of Prog. Lang.*, pp. 163-173, 1980. 61, 67
14. Y. Gurevich and S. Shelah, "To the decision problem for branching time logic", In "Foundations of Logic and Linguistics: Problems and their Solutions" (ed. P. Weingartner and G. Dold), Plenum, 1985, 181–198. 60, 61, 68
15. Y. Gurevich and S. Shelah (1985). The decision problem for branching time logic. *Journal of Symbolic Logic* **50**(3):668–681.

16. T. Hafer and W. Thomas (1987). Computation tree logic CTL* and path quantifiers in the monadic theory of the binary tree. In *Proceedings of ICALP'87: International Colloquium on Automata, Languages and Programming, Lecture Notes in Computer Science* **267**:269–279, Springer-Verlag.

17. Y. Hirshfeld and A. Rabinovich (2000). Future temporal logic needs infinitely many modalities. *Technical Report*, Tel-Aviv University.

18. D. Janin and I. Walukiewicz (1996). On the expressive completeness of the propositional mu-calculus with respect to monadic second order logic. In *Proceedings of CONCUR'96: International Conference on Concurrency Theory, Lecture Notes in Computer Science* **1119**:263–277, Springer-Verlag.

19. H. W. Kamp (1968). *Tense logic and the theory of linear order*. PhD Thesis, University of California, Los Angeles.

20. L. Lamport (1980). "Sometimes" is sometimes "not never" - On the temporal logic of programs. In *Proceedings of the 7th Annual ACM Symposium on Principles of Programming Languages*, ACM, New York, 1980. pp. 174-185.

21. F. Laroussinie and Ph. Schnoebelen(2000). Specification in CTL+Past for verification in CTL. Information and Computation, 156(1/2):236-263.

22. S. Maoz (2000). Infinite Hierarchy of Temporal Logics over Branching Time Models. M.Sc. Thesis, Tel-Aviv University.

23. R. McNaughton and S. Papert (1971). Counter-Free Automata. *MIT Press*, 1971.

24. R. Milner (1989). *Communication and Concurrency*. Prentice-Hall.

25. F. Moller and A. Rabinovich (1999). On the expressive power of CTL*. *Proceedings of fourteenth IEEE Symposium on Logic in Computer Science*, 360-369.

26. F. Moller and A. Rabinovich (2001). Counting on CTL*: On the Expressive power of Monadic Path Logic. Submitted.

27. D.M.R. Park (1981). Concurrency and automata on infinite sequences. *Lecture Notes in Computer Science* **104**:168–183.

28. A. Pnueli (1977). The temporal logic of programs. In *Proc. IEEE 18th Annu. Symp. on Found. Comput. Sci.*, pages 46–57, New York, 1977. IEEE.

29. A. Prior (1967). Past, Present and Future. Claredon Press, Oxford.

30. M. O. Rabin (1969). Decidability of second order theories and automata on infinite trees. In *Trans. Amer. Math. Soc.*,**141**,pp 1-35.

31. J.-P. Queille and J. Sifakis (1983). Fairness and related properties in transition systems. A temporal logic to deal with fairness. *Acta Informatica*, 19(3):195–220.

32. A. Rabinovich and S. Maoz (2001). An Infinite Hierarchy of Temporal Logics over Branching Time. Information and Computation, 171:306-332, 2001.

33. A. Rabinovich and Ph. Schnoebelen (2000). BTL_2 and expressive completeness for $ECTL^+$. Research Report LSV-00-8, Lab. Specification and Verification, ENS de Cachan, Cachan, France, October 2000.

34. J. Stavi (1979). Functional Completeness over the rationals. Unpublished, Bar Ilan University, Israel, 1979.

35. C. Stirling (1992). Modal and temporal logics. In *Handbook of Logic in Computer Science*, Oxford University press, 476-567.

36. W. Thomas 1990). Automata on Infinite Objects. In J. van Leeuwen editor *Handbook of Theoretical Computer Science*, The MIT Press.

37. W. Thomas (1997). Languages, Automata, and Logic. In Handbook of Formal Language Theory (G. Rozenberg, A. Salomaa, Eds.),Vol. III, Springer-Verlag , New York, pp. 389-455.

38. M. Vardi and P. Wolper (1984). Yet another process logic. *In Logics of Programs, Lecture Notes in Computer Science* **164**, 501-512, Springer-Verlag.

Types, or:
Where's the Difference Between CCS and π?

Davide Sangiorgi*

INRIA
Davide.Sangiorgi@inria.fr

Abstract. The π-calculus is the paradigmatic calculus of mobile processes. With respect to previous formalisms for concurrency, most notably CCS, the most novel aspect of π-calculus is probably its rich theory of *types*. We explain the importance of types in the π-calculus on a concrete example: the *termination* property.

A process M terminates if it cannot produce an infinite sequence of reductions $M \xrightarrow{\tau} M_1 \xrightarrow{\tau} M_2 \ldots$. Termination is a useful property in concurrency. For instance, a terminating applet, when loaded on a machine, will not run for ever, possibly absorbing all computing resources (a 'denial of service' attack). Similarly, termination guarantees that queries to a given service originate only finite computations.

We consider the problem of proving termination of non-trivial subsets of CCS and π-calculus. In CCS the proof is purely combinatorial, and is very simple. In the π-calculus, by contrast, combinatorial proofs appear to be very hard. We show how to solve the problem by taking into account type information.

1 Introduction

The π-calculus is the paradigmatic calculus of mobile processes. With respect to previous formalisms for concurrency, most notably CCS, the most novel aspect of π-calculus is probably its rich theory of *types*. We explain the importance of types in the π-calculus on a concrete example: the *termination* property.

'Terminating' is different from 'convergent'. A convergent term has *at least one* finite (complete) internal run; in a terminating term, by contrast, *all* internal runs are finite (there may even be an infinity of internal runs, and of unbounded length). For instance, the process

$$(a.\overline{c} + !a.\overline{a}) \mid \overline{a}$$

is convergent but non-terminating. (When the values communicated are not important, we abbreviate inputs $a(x).M$ and outputs $\overline{a}v.M$ as $a.M$ and $\overline{a}.M$. The replication operator $!\pi.M$ can be thought of as an infinite number of copies of $\pi.M$ in parallel; in a language with recursion, it can be taken as an abbreviation

---

* Work supported by the EC project "PROFUNDIS" (IST-2001-33100)

for $\mu X.\,(\pi.\,(M \mid X))$.) Also, 'terminating' is different from 'finite'. In a terminating process, only the internal runs are required to be finite. In a finite process, by contrast, all runs are finite, including runs consisting of external actions such as inputs and outputs. For instance, $!a.\,\overline{b}$ is terminating but is not finite.

Termination is a useful property, especially for mobile processes. For instance, if we interrogate a process, we may want to know that an answer is eventually produced. Similarly, when we load an applet we may like to know that the applet will not run for ever on our machine, possibly absorbing all the computing resources (a 'denial of service' attack). In general, if the lifetime of a process can be infinite, we may want to know that the process does not remain alive simply because of non-terminating internal activity, and that, therefore, the process will always accept interactions with the environment. For similar reasons of protection, all programs of languages for active networks such as Plan [HKM^{+}99] must terminate.

We consider the problem of proving termination of a non-trivial subset of the π-calculus. The corresponding problem in CCS has a simple solution, and the proof is purely combinatorial. In the π-calculus, by contrast, a combinatorial proof appears to be very hard. We shall solve the problem by taking into account type information.

We explain why the termination problem is much harder in the π-calculus than in CCS. Consider the process language given by the grammar production

$$M ::= (\boldsymbol{\nu} a_1, \dots, a_n)(!a_1(x).\,M_1 \mid \dots \mid !a_n(x).\,M_n \mid \overline{b_1}v_1 \mid \dots \mid \overline{b_r}v_r) \qquad (1)$$

where $n, r \geq 0$. This language includes non-terminating processes, such as

$$\boldsymbol{\nu} a\,(\overline{a} \mid !a.\,\overline{a})\,,$$

and

$$(\boldsymbol{\nu} a, b)(\overline{a} \mid !a.\,\overline{b} \mid !b.\,\overline{a}),$$

in which the inputs at a and b are mutually recursive. Further, regardless of what the values v_j are, the size of a process may grow with reduction, because replications are persistent and reductions may liberate new processes (which can themselves be replicated). We can avoid mutual recursions by imposing an order on the inputs: require that in any term $(\boldsymbol{\nu} a_1, \dots, a_n)(!a_1(x).\,M_1 \mid \dots \mid !a_n(x).\,M_n \mid \overline{b_1}v_1 \mid \dots \mid \overline{b_r}v_r)$ process M_i only uses names a_j with $j < i$. This condition does indeed guarantee termination if, as in CCS, values are first order and therefore cannot be links.[1] For the proof, it suffices to define a measure that decreases after each reduction. This is easy to do because a process liberated by a replication satisfies the same condition on the usage of names as the replication itself.

The same argument does not work if values can be links, as in the π-calculus. For instance, the process liberated by a replication $!a_i(x).\,M_i$ can be $M_i\{v_j/x\}$

---

[1] We prefer the word 'link' to 'channel' because the latter has a more restrictive connotation.

with $v_j = a_j$ and $j > i$. Indeed if values can be links, then the language (1) does include non-terminating processes even if inputs are ordered; an example is

$$R \stackrel{\text{def}}{=} \nu a \, (!a(x). \, \overline{x}x \mid \overline{a}a).$$

Modulo structural congruence ($\equiv$), a relation that allows us some simple rearrangements of the structure of a process, R reduces to itself.

Intuitively, R does not terminate because it has self-applications, that is, outputs in which the value emitted is related to the link along which the output occurs. A discussion on the (very subtle) problems given by self-application is worthwhile. These problems are well-known in the λ-calculus. The process R, as well as the other examples of self-applications below, are not translations of λ-expressions, but are inspired by the λ-calculus.

In R, the self-applications are syntactic: in $\overline{x}x$ and $\overline{a}a$ the link of the output and the value emitted are identical. If all self-applications were syntactic, then termination could be ensured, operationally, by checking that after each reduction no output of the form $\overline{a}a$ exists. Unfortunately, non-termination may also arise because of 'implicit' self-applications: these are outputs $\overline{a}b$ in which the link b emitted is different from the link a of the output, but b may be used by a recipient to access a. An example of implicit self-application is the process $\overline{a}b. \, !b(x). \, \overline{a}x$. Indeed, under certain hypothesis the process is behaviourally equivalent to $\overline{a}a$ [Mer01]. This form of implicit self-application is the reason for the divergence of

$$Q \stackrel{\text{def}}{=} \nu b \, (\overline{a}b \mid !b(z). \, \overline{a}z) \mid !a(x). \, (\nu y \, (\overline{x}y \mid !y(z). \, \overline{x}z)),$$

which in two steps can reduce to a process weakly bisimilar to Q itself.

Here is however an example of a process that does not terminate because of self-application but that cannot possibly be considered behaviourally equivalent to a process with syntactic self-applications:

$$M \stackrel{\text{def}}{=} \begin{aligned}&!a(x). \, \nu b \, (\overline{x}b \mid b(y). \, \overline{y}x) \\ &\mid !v(z). \, \overline{z}a \\ &\mid \overline{a}v.\end{aligned}$$

M has the following divergent computation:

$$
\begin{aligned}
M \; = \; & !a(x). \, \nu b \, (\overline{x}b \mid b(y). \, \overline{y}x) \mid !v(z). \, \overline{z}a \mid \overline{a}v \\
\stackrel{\tau}{\longrightarrow} \; & \overline{v}b \mid b(y). \, \overline{y}v \mid !a(x). \, \nu b \, (\overline{x}b \mid b(y). \, \overline{y}x) \mid !v(z). \, \overline{z}a && [av] \\
\stackrel{\tau}{\longrightarrow} \; & b(y). \, \overline{y}v \mid !a(x). \, \nu b \, (\overline{x}b \mid b(y). \, \overline{y}x) \mid \overline{b}a \mid !v(z). \, \overline{z}a && [vb] \\
\stackrel{\tau}{\longrightarrow} \; & \overline{a}v \mid !a(x). \, \nu b \, (\overline{x}b \mid b(y). \, \overline{y}x) \mid !v(z). \, \overline{z}a && [ba] \\
\equiv \; & M \\
\stackrel{\tau}{\longrightarrow} \; & \dots
\end{aligned}
$$

where the column on the right indicates the action performed in the reduction, that is, the link along which the reduction occurs and the value exchanged. The culprit of the non-termination of M is the subterm $\overline{x}b \mid b(y). \, \overline{y}x$. This process, although behaviourally quite different from a syntactic self-application, does represent a self-application because the name b transmitted at x is used in an input inside which x appears in an output.

But self-applications can be even more nasty. They can arise in processes that, at the beginning, contain no patterns of dependencies between inputs and outputs – not even a 'weak' pattern as the one of M above. An example is the process N below. It is hard to see where an implicit self-application is located in the syntax of N. For instance, there is an output $\overline{a_2}a_1$ but the input at a_1 does not use a_2. However, recursive dependencies among names can arise dynamically in N, at run time.

$$N \stackrel{\text{def}}{=} !a(x).\,(\boldsymbol{\nu}a_1, a_2\,)(\overline{a_2}a_1 \mid !a_1(y).\,\overline{x}y \mid !a_2(y).\,\overline{x}y)$$
$$\mid !a_0(z).\,\overline{a}z$$
$$\mid \overline{a}a_0$$

Moreover, whereas the divergent run of M has at least one action – $[av]$ – that repeats itself an infinite number of times, N has a divergent computation in which all actions performed are different. The infinite computation of N consists of cycles of increasing length; a cycle begins with a reduction at a and ends with a reduction at a_0. These are the actions for the first three cycles:

$$[a\,a_0],\,[a_2\,a_1],\,[a_0\,a_1],$$
$$[a\,a_1],\,[a_4\,a_3],\,[a_1\,a_3],\,[a_0\,a_3]\,,$$
$$[a\,a_3],\,[a_6\,a_5],\,[a_3\,a_5],\,[a_1\,a_5],\,[a_0\,a_5]\,.$$

We shall avoid the problems given by self-applications by means of types, moving to the *simply-typed π-calculus* (Section 3).

Besides mutual recursion and self-application, the other major issue for the termination of π-calculus processes is *state*. In all examples of processes seen so far, all links are *functional*, in the sense that each link appears only once in input, and the input is replicated. In other words, the service offered by the link is always available and does not change over time. Here are examples of stateful terms:

$$N_1 \stackrel{\text{def}}{=} a(x).\,M \qquad\qquad N_3 \stackrel{\text{def}}{=} a(x).\,(N \mid a(y).\,M)$$
$$N_2 \stackrel{\text{def}}{=} !a(x).\,M + N \qquad\qquad N_4 \stackrel{\text{def}}{=} !b(x).\,(N \mid !a(y).\,M)$$
$$N_5 \stackrel{\text{def}}{=} \mu X(y).\,a(x).\,\overline{y}v.\,X\lfloor x \rfloor$$

(where $\mu X(y).\,M$ is a recursive definition with formal parameter y and body M, and $X\lfloor v \rfloor$ is a recursive call with actual parameter v). In N_1, the input at a is ephemeral and can therefore vanish. In N_2 the input at a vanishes if the summand N is used first. In N_3 and N_5, different outputs at a may activate different processes (in N_5 this happens because the continuation of the input uses the parameter y of the recursive definition). Finally, in N_4 the input at a is not immediately available.

It is known that in imperative sequential languages higher-order references can break termination [HMST95]. Since higher-order references can be modeled in π-calculus, using recursion, some constraints on state are expected. It is not sufficient, however, to transport the conditions for imperative sequential languages onto the π-calculus, which has more diverse forms of state. We will impose two constraints on state: the parameters of recursive definitions should be first order; certain forms of nesting between inputs are disallowed.

Thus, our language $\mathcal{P}$ of terminating π-calculus processes has the constraints on recursive inputs, self-applications, and state mentioned above. The proof of termination is in two parts. The first part uses the technique of logical relations. Logical relations are well-known in functional languages and are used, in particular, to prove termination of typed λ-calculi. We have not been able to apply the technique to the whole language $\mathcal{P}$. We have only been able to apply it to a small sublanguage, $\mathcal{P}^-$. This is a non-deterministic language, with only asynchronous outputs, and in which all names are functional. One of the reasons for restricting the logical-relation technique to $\mathcal{P}^-$ is that we need several times the Replication Theorems (laws for the distributivity of replicated processes). These theorems hold only if the names are functional.

The language $\mathcal{P}^-$ is not very expressive. It is however a powerful language for the termination property. The second part of our proof shows that the termination of $\mathcal{P}^-$ implies that of $\mathcal{P}$. For this, we use process calculus techniques, most notably techniques for behavioural preorders.

In this paper, some proofs are only sketched. For more details, we refer to [San01], where, moreover, the language of processes is richer. For instance, here the only first-order value is unit, whereas in [San01] arbitrary first-order values are allowed.

Structure of the paper Sections 2 and 3 contain background material on the π-calculus. In Section 4 we define termination and the language $\mathcal{P}$. The proof of termination of $\mathcal{P}$ is developed in the Section 5 to 8. First, we prove the termination of the language $\mathcal{P}^-$ (Section 5-7). Then, in Section 8, we sketch how the termination of $\mathcal{P}$ is derived from that of $\mathcal{P}^-$.

Related work Termination has been widely studied in sequential languages (see [GLT88, Mit96]), but very little has been done in concurrency. Kobayashi's type system [Kob00] ensures that in every fair reduction sequence a process trying to perform a communication will eventually succeed. Types can express causality, obligation, and time limit on the usage of a link. The main differences with our work are: the types of [Kob00] are rather sophisticated; the properties guaranteed are different (a well-typed process in [Kob00] may still have a divergent computation); the system of [Kob00] cannot handle various forms of replications, for instance it cannot handle the processes encoding the simply-typed λ-calculus.

The closest to our work is Berger, Honda, and Yoshida's [YBK01], which is the first study of termination in the π-calculus. The main differences with our work are the following. First, the conditions that [YBK01] impose for termination are almost entirely expressed by means of *graph types* [Yos96]. By contrast, we separate typing and syntactic conditions. This allows us, for instance, to use more standard notions of types. Second, the language $\mathcal{P}^{\mathrm{BHY}}$ of [YBK01] is a language of functional processes. For instance, every name has only one input occurrence, and reduction is confluent. It is indeed close to the subset of $\mathcal{P}^-$ (Section 5) without sums. Thus, the λ-calculus with resources (Section 9, [BL00]), or deterministic subsets of it such as the λ-calculus with multiplicities, cannot not be encoded in $\mathcal{P}^{\mathrm{BHY}}$. Also, in $\mathcal{P}^{\mathrm{BHY}}$ all outputs are bound; that is, only private names can be transmitted. Third, the encoding of the simply-typed (call-by-name) λ-calculus into the π-calculus is fully abstract if the π-calculus language is taken to be $\mathcal{P}^{\mathrm{BHY}}$. By contrast, the encoding is not fully abstract with respect to $\mathcal{P}$: standard counterexamples to full abstraction of λ-calculus encodings [SW01] live in $\mathcal{P}$. Fourth, the technique of logical relations is used by both us and [YBK01], but the details are quite different. For instance, the proof in [YBK01] exploits the property that the processes are confluent, by allowing also certain outputs underneath prefixes to be consumed. Finally, the types of [YBK01] also guarantee that certain visible actions will eventually be performed. This property does not hold in our case.

2   The Localised π-Calculus

The syntax of the calculus, in Table 1, has the process constructs of the standard (monadic) π-calculus [Mil99, SW01]. The calculus is *localised* [Mer01], that is, the recipient of a link cannot use it in input. Formally, in an input $a(x). M$, name x cannot appear free in M as subject of an input. (The subject of an input is the name at which the input is performed; for instance, the subject of $a(x). M$ is a.) Locality has been found useful in practice – it is adopted by a number of experimental languages derived from the π-calculus, most notably Join [FG96] – and has also useful consequences on the theory [Mer01]. In our work, locality is essential: most of our results rely on it.

Bound names, free names, and names of a process M, respectively written $\mathsf{bn}(M)$, $\mathsf{fn}(M)$, and $\mathsf{n}(M)$, are defined in the usual way. We do not distinguish α-convertible terms. Unless otherwise stated, we also assume that, in any term, each bound name is different from the free names of the term and from the other bound names. In a statement, we sometimes say that a name is *fresh* to mean that it does not occur in the objects of the statement, like processes and actions. A name a is *fresh for M* if a does not occur in M. If R' is a subterm of R we say that R' is *guarded in R* if R' is underneath a prefix of R; otherwise R' is *unguarded in R*. We use a tilde to indicate a tuple. All notations are extended to tuples in the usual way.

In a recursive definition $\mu X(\widetilde{x}). M$, the recursion variable is X and the formal parameters are $\widetilde{x}$. The actual parameters of a recursion are supplied in a recursion call $H\lfloor\widetilde{v}\rfloor$. We require that, in a recursive definition $\mu X(\widetilde{x}). M$, the only free recursion variable of M is X. This constraint simplifies some of our proofs, but can be lifted. Moreover, the recursion variable X should be guarded in the body M of the recursion.

Table 1. Syntax of processes

$$a, b, c, d, \ldots, x, y, z \ldots \quad Names$$

$$Values$$

$$v, w ::= a \qquad \qquad \text{name}$$

$$\Big| \quad \star \qquad \qquad \text{unit value}$$

$$Processes$$

$$M, N ::= \mathbf{0} \qquad \qquad \text{nil process}$$

$$\Big| \quad H\lfloor \tilde{v} \rfloor \qquad \text{recursion call}$$

$$\Big| \quad a(x).M \qquad \text{input}$$

$$\Big| \quad \overline{v}w.M \qquad \text{output}$$

$$\Big| \quad M \mid M \qquad \text{parallel}$$

$$\Big| \quad M + M \qquad \text{sum}$$

$$\Big| \quad \nu \tilde{a}\, M \qquad \text{restriction}$$

$$H ::= X \qquad \qquad \text{recursion variable}$$

$$\Big| \quad \mu X(\tilde{x}).M \quad \text{recursive definition}$$

When a recursion has no parameters we abbreviate $\mu X().R$ as $\mu X.R$, and calls $(\mu X.R)\lfloor\,\rfloor$ and $X\lfloor\,\rfloor$ as $\mu X.R$ and X, respectively. For technical reasons, we find it convenient a restriction operator that introduces several names at once.

A *first-order value* is a value that does not contain links. Examples are: an integer, a boolean value, a pair of booleans, a list of integers. To facilitate the reading of the proofs, in this paper the only first-order value is the *unit* value, $\star$. (Arbitrary first-order values are studied in [San01].)

The SOS rules for the transition relation of the processes of the calculus are presented in Table 2, where α ranges over actions. (The symmetric of PAR-1, COM-1, CLOSE-1, and SUM-1 have been omitted.) They are the usual transition rules for the π-calculus, in the early style.

Table 2. Transition rules

INP: $a(x).\, M \xrightarrow{av} M\{v/x\}$

OUT: $\overline{a}v.\, M \xrightarrow{\overline{a}v} M$

$$\text{REC: } \frac{M\{\mu X(\widetilde{x}).\, M/X\}\{\widetilde{v}/\widetilde{x}\} \xrightarrow{\alpha} M'}{(\mu X(\widetilde{x}).\, M)\lfloor \widetilde{v}\rfloor \xrightarrow{\alpha} M'}$$

$$\text{RES: } \frac{\nu \widetilde{b}\, M \xrightarrow{\alpha} M'}{(\nu a, \widetilde{b}\,)M \xrightarrow{\alpha} \nu a\, M'} \quad a \notin \mathsf{n}(\alpha)$$

$$\text{OPEN: } \frac{\nu \widetilde{b}\, M \xrightarrow{\overline{x}a} M'}{(\nu a, \widetilde{b}\,)M \xrightarrow{(\nu a\,)\overline{x}a} M'} \quad x \neq a$$

$$\text{SUM-1: } \frac{M \xrightarrow{\alpha} M'}{M + N \xrightarrow{\alpha} M'} \qquad \text{PAR-1: } \frac{M \xrightarrow{\alpha} M'}{M \mid N \xrightarrow{\alpha} M' \mid N} \text{ if } \mathsf{bn}(\alpha) \cap \mathsf{fn}(N) = \emptyset$$

$$\text{COM-1: } \frac{M \xrightarrow{av} M' \qquad N \xrightarrow{\overline{a}v} N'}{M \mid N \xrightarrow{\tau} M' \mid N'}$$

$$\text{CLOSE-1: } \frac{M \xrightarrow{ab} M' \qquad N \xrightarrow{\nu b\, \overline{a}b} N'}{M \mid N \xrightarrow{\tau} \nu b\, (M' \mid N')} \text{ if } b \notin \mathsf{fn}(M)$$

2.1 Other Process Operators

For the proofs in the paper, we consider various π-calculus languages. They are defined from the operators introduced above, with transition rules as by Table 2, plus: *asynchronous output*, $\overline{v}w$, that is, output without continuation; and *replication*, $!M$, which represents an infinite parallel composition of copies of M. Their transition rules are:

$$\overline{a}v \xrightarrow{\overline{a}v} 0 \qquad\qquad \frac{M \mid !M \xrightarrow{\alpha} M'}{!M \xrightarrow{\alpha} M'}$$

3 The Simply-Typed Calculus

The grammar of types for the simply-typed π-calculus is:

$$T ::= \sharp T \mid \texttt{unit}$$

where the *connection type* $\sharp T$ is the type of a link that carries tuples of values of type T, and $\texttt{unit}$ is the only *first-order type* (that is, the type of a first-order value).

A *link* is a name of a connection type. A link is *first order* if it carries first-order values. It is *higher order* if it carries higher-order values (i.e., links). Note that 'first-order name' is different from 'first-order link': a first-order name has a type $\texttt{unit}$, whereas a first-order link has a type $\sharp\, \texttt{unit}$.

Table 3. Typing rules

T-Par : $\dfrac{\vdash M \qquad \vdash N}{\vdash M \mid N}$ 　　　　　 T-Sum : $\dfrac{\vdash M \qquad \vdash N}{\vdash M + N}$

T-Rec : $\dfrac{X \in \langle \widetilde{T} \rangle \qquad \widetilde{x} \in \widetilde{T} \qquad \vdash \widetilde{v} : \widetilde{T} \qquad \vdash M}{\vdash (\mu X(\widetilde{x}).\, M)\lfloor \widetilde{v} \rfloor}$

T-Rvar : $\dfrac{X \in \langle \widetilde{T} \rangle \qquad \vdash \widetilde{v} : \widetilde{T}}{\vdash X\lfloor \widetilde{v} \rfloor}$

T-Out : $\dfrac{\vdash v : \sharp T \qquad \vdash w : T \qquad \vdash M}{\vdash \overline{v}w.\, M}$ T-Inp : $\dfrac{\vdash v : \sharp T \qquad x \in T \qquad \vdash M}{\vdash v(x).\, M}$

T-Res : $\dfrac{x_i \in \sharp T_i \text{ for some } T_i \ (1 \le i \le n) \qquad \vdash M}{\vdash (\boldsymbol{\nu} x_1 \ldots x_n)M}$

T-Nil : $\vdash \mathbf{0}$ 　　　　 T-Unit : $\vdash \star : \mathtt{unit}$ 　　　　 T-Var : $\dfrac{x \in T}{\vdash x : T}$

Our type system is à la Church, thus each name has a predefined type. We assume that for each type there is an infinite number of names with that type. We write $x \in T$ to mean that the name x has type T. Similarly, each recursion variable X has a predefined tuple of types, written $X \in \langle \widetilde{T} \rangle$, indicating the types of the arguments of the recursion. A judgment $\vdash M$ says that M is a well-typed process; a judgment $\vdash v : T$ says that v is a well-typed value of type T. For values v, w we write $v : w$ to mean that v and w have the same type.

The typing rules are in Table 3. The typing rules for the operators of Section 2.1 (asynchronous output, replication) are similar to those of (standard) output and parallel composition.

A process is *closed* if all its free names have a connection type (i.e., they are links). The closed processes are the 'real' processes, those that, for instance, are supposed to be run, or to be tested. If a process is not closed, it has some names yet to be instantiated. A *closing substitution* for a process R is a substitution σ such that $R\sigma$ is closed (R may already be closed, and σ may just rename some of its links).

4 　Terminating Processes

Our goal in this paper is to isolate a subset of processes as large as possible that terminate.

Definition 1. *A process M diverges (or is divergent) if there is an infinite sequence of processes $M_1, \ldots, M_n, \ldots$ with $M_1 = M$, such that, for all i,*

$$M_i \xrightarrow{\tau} M_{i+1}.$$

M terminates (or is terminating), written $M \in \mathrm{TER}$, if M is not divergent. □

We have explained in Section 1 what makes termination hard: self-applications, recursive inputs, state. Our language of terminating processes is defined by four constraints. Three of them, mostly syntactic, are reported in Condition 1. The first condition is for recursive inputs; the second and third conditions control state. The last constraint – condition 1 of Definition 2 – controls self-applications.

We explain the new terminology used in the conditions. A name a appears free in *output position in N* if N has a free occurrence of a in an output prefix. An input is *replicated* if the input is inside the body of a recursive definition. Thus, a process M has free replicated first-order inputs if M contains a free first-order input inside the body of a recursive definition. For instance, if a is a first-order link then

$$\mu X. a(y). (\mathbf{0} \mid X)$$

has free replicated first-order inputs, whereas

$$\nu a \, (\mu X. a(y). (\mathbf{0} \mid X)) \mid b(z). \mathbf{0}$$

has not.

Condition 1 (Termination constraints on the grammar)

1. *Let $\widetilde{a} = a_1, \ldots, a_n$. In a process $\nu\widetilde{a}\, M$, if $a_i(x). N$ is a free input of M, then the following holds:*
   (a) $a_i \in \widetilde{a}$,
   (b) *names a_j with $j \geq i$ do not appear free in output position in N.*
2. *In an higher-order input $a(x). M$, the continuation M does not contain free higher-order inputs, and does not contain free replicated first-order inputs.*
3. *In a recursive definition $\mu X(\widetilde{x}). M$:*
   (a) *$\widetilde{x}$ are first order,*
   (b) *M has no unguarded output and no unguarded if-then-else.* □

Condition (1b) poses no constraints on occurrences of names not in $\widetilde{a}$. The condition can be made simpler, but weaker, by requiring that names $\widetilde{a}$ do not appear free in output position in M.

To illustrate the meaning of condition (3a), consider a 1-place buffer, that receives values at a link a and retransmits them at a link b:

$$\mu X. a(x). \overline{b} x. X$$

This process respects the condition regardless of whether the values transmitted are first order or higher order. By contrast, a delayed 1-place buffer

$$\mu X(x).\, a(y).\, \overline{b}x.\, X\lfloor y\rfloor\,,$$

which emits at b the second last value received by a, respects the condition only if the values transmitted are first order.

We say that a process M respects the constraints of Condition 1 to mean that M itself and all its process subterms respect the constraints.

Definition 2 (Language $\mathcal{P}$). $\mathcal{P}$ *is the set of processes such that $M \in \mathcal{P}$ implies:*

1. *M is typable in the simply-typed π-calculus;*
2. *$\nu\widetilde{a}\, M$ respects the constraints of Condition 1, where $\widetilde{a} = \mathsf{fn}(M)$.* □

Theorem 1. *All processes in $\mathcal{P}$ terminate.*

The proof of this theorem is in two parts; one in Sections 5-7, the other is sketched in Section 8. In the remainder of the paper, all processes and values are well typed, and substitutions map names onto values of the same type. Moreover, processes have no free recursion variables.

5 $\mathcal{P}^-$: Monadic Functional Non-deterministic Processes

We define a very constrained calculus $\mathcal{P}^-$ whose processes will be proved to terminate using the technique of logical relations. We will then use $\mathcal{P}^-$ to derive the termination of the processes of the language $\mathcal{P}$ of Theorem 1.

The processes of $\mathcal{P}^-$ are functional, that is, the input end of each link occurs only once, is replicated, and is immediately available (cf., the uniform-receptiveness discipline, [San99]). To emphasize the 'functional' nature of these processes, we use the (input-guarded) replication operator $!a(x).\, M$ instead of recursion. Processes can however exhibit non-determinism, due to the presence of the sum operator. Outputs are asynchronous, that is, they have no continuations.

For the definition of $\mathcal{P}^-$, and elsewhere in the paper, it is useful to work up to structural congruence, a relation that allows us to abstract from certain details of the syntax of processes.

Definition 3 (Structural congruence). *Let R be a process of a language $\mathcal{L}$ whose operators include parallel composition, restriction, replication, and $\mathbf{0}$. We write $R \equiv_1 R'$ if R' is obtained from R by rewriting, in one step, a subterm of R using one of the rules below (from left to right, or from right to left)*

$$!R = R \mid !R$$
$$\nu\widetilde{a}\,\nu\widetilde{b}\, R = (\nu\widetilde{a}, \widetilde{b}\,)R$$
$$(\nu\widetilde{a}, a, b, \widetilde{b}\,)R = (\nu\widetilde{a}, b, a, \widetilde{b}\,)R$$
$$R_1 \mid R_2 = R_2 \mid R_1$$
$$R_1 \mid (R_2 \mid R_3) = (R_1 \mid R_2) \mid R_3$$
$$R \mid \mathbf{0} = R$$

Table 4. The normal forms

Pre-processes

$$P^{\mathrm{NF}} ::= \boldsymbol{\nu} a\,(I_a^{\mathrm{NF}} \mid P^{\mathrm{NF}})\ \text{with}\ \mathsf{fn}(I_a^{\mathrm{NF}}) \cap \mathsf{in}(P^{\mathrm{NF}}) = \emptyset$$
$$\mid\ M^{\mathrm{NF}}$$
$$\mid\ I_a^{\mathrm{NF}}$$

Resources

$$I_a^{\mathrm{NF}} ::=\ !a(x).\,M^{\mathrm{NF}} \qquad \text{with}\ a \notin \mathsf{fn}(M^{\mathrm{NF}})$$

Processes

$$M^{\mathrm{NF}} ::= \boldsymbol{\nu} a\,(I_a^{\mathrm{NF}} \mid M^{\mathrm{NF}})$$
$$\mid\ M^{\mathrm{NF}} + M^{\mathrm{NF}}$$
$$\mid\ M^{\mathrm{NF}} \mid M^{\mathrm{NF}}$$
$$\mid\ \overline{v}w$$
$$\mid\ \mathbf{0}$$

Values

$$v ::= a \qquad\qquad\ \text{name}$$
$$\mid\ \star \qquad\qquad\ \text{unit value}$$

(Note that if $R \equiv_1 R'$ then R' need not be in $\mathcal{L}$.) Structural congruence, $\equiv$, is the reflexive and transitive closure of $\equiv_1$. □

The definition of $\mathcal{P}^-$ uses the syntactic categories of *processes*, *pre-processes*, and *resources*. The *normal forms* for processes, pre-processes and resources of $\mathcal{P}^-$ are given in Table 4, where $\mathsf{in}(P)$ are the names that appear free in P in input position. Each new name is introduced with a construct of the form $\boldsymbol{\nu}a\,(!a(x).\,N \mid P)$ where the resource $!a(x).\,N$ is the only process that can ever input at a. In the definition of resources, the constraint $a \notin \mathsf{fn}(M^{\mathrm{NF}})$ prevents mutual recursion (calls of the replication from within its body).

Normal forms are not closed under reduction. For instance, if $M^{\mathrm{NF}} \xrightarrow{\tau} N$ then N may not be a process of the grammar in the table. However, N is structurally congruent to a normal form. We therefore define processes, resources, pre-processes by closing the normal forms with structural congruence. We need the reduction-closure property (Lemma 8) in later proofs.

Definition 4 (Language $\mathcal{P}^-$). *The sets $\mathcal{PR}$ of processes, $\mathcal{RES}$ of resources, and $\mathcal{P}^-$ of pre-processes are obtained by closing under $\equiv$ the corresponding (well-typed) normal forms in Table 4.*   □

Thus $M \in \mathcal{PR}$ if there is M^{NF} with $M \equiv M^{\mathrm{NF}}$. Pre-processes include resources and processes (which explains why pre-processes are indicated with the symbol $\mathcal{P}^-$). Pre-processes are ranged over by P, Q; resources by I_a, processes by M, N. If $\tilde{a}$ is $a_1, \ldots, a_n$ then $\nu\tilde{a}\,(I_{\tilde{a}} \mid P)$ abbreviates $\nu a_1\,(I_{a_1} \mid \ldots \nu a_n\,(I_{a_n} \mid P)\ldots)$, and similarly for $\nu\tilde{a}\,(I_{\tilde{a}}^{\mathrm{NF}} \mid P)$.

6 Logical Relations on Processes

We recall the main steps of the technique of logical relations in the λ-calculus:

1. assignment of types to terms;
2. definition of a typed logical predicate on terms, by induction on the structure of types; the base case uses the termination property of interest;
3. proof that the logical terms (i.e., those in the logical predicate) terminate;
4. proof, by structural induction, that all well-typed terms are logical.

For applying logical relations to the π-calculus we follow a similar structure. Some of the details however are rather different. For instance, in the π-calculus an important role is played by a closure property of the logical predicate with respect to bisimilarity, and by the (Sharpened) Replication Theorems. Further, in the λ-calculus typing rules assign types to terms; in the π-calculus, by contrast, types are assigned to names. To start off the technique (step 1), we therefore force an assignment of types to the pre-processes. We use A to range over the types for pre-processes:

$$A ::= \diamond \mid b_\sharp T$$

where T is an ordinary type, as by the grammar in Section 3. If $R, R' \in \mathcal{P}^-$ then R' *is a normal form of R* if R' is a normal form and $R \equiv R'$.

Definition 5 (Assignment of types to pre-processes). *A normal form of a (well-typed) pre-process P is either of the form*

- $\nu\tilde{a}\,(I_{\tilde{a}} \mid M)$, *or*
- $\nu\tilde{a}\,(I_{\tilde{a}} \mid I_b)$, *with $b \notin \tilde{a}$.*

In the first case we write $P : \diamond$, in the latter case we write $P : b\_T$, where T is the type of b.   □

Lemma 1. *A pre-process has a unique type.*   □

We define the logical predicate $\mathcal{L}^A$ by induction on A.

Definition 6 (Logical relations).

- $P \in \mathcal{L}^\diamond$ *if $P : \diamond$ and $P \in \mathrm{TER}$.*

– $P \in \mathcal{L}^{a\text{-}\sharp\, \text{unit}}$ if $P : a_{\text{-}\sharp}\, \text{unit}$, and for all $v : \text{unit}$,

$$\nu a \,(P \mid \overline{a}v) \in \mathcal{L}^\diamond \,.$$

– $P \in \mathcal{L}^{a\text{-}\sharp\, T}$, where T is a connection type, if $P : a_{\text{-}\sharp}\, T$, and, for all b fresh for P and for all $I_b \in \mathcal{L}^{b\text{-}T}$,

$$\nu b \,(I_b \mid \nu a \,(P \mid \overline{a}b)) \in \mathcal{L}^\diamond \,. \tag{2}$$

We write $P \in \mathcal{L}$ if $P \in \mathcal{L}^A$, for some A. □

In Definition 6, the most important clause is the last one. The process in (2) is similar to those used for translating function application into π-calculus [SW01]. Therefore a possible reading of (2) is that P is a function and I_b its argument. In (2), P does not know b (because fresh), and I_b does not know a (because restricted). However, P and I_b may have common free names, in output position.

7 Termination of $\mathcal{P}^-$

We first present (Sections 7.1 and 7.2) some general results on the π-calculus. We present them on $A\pi_+$: this is the π-calculus of Section 2, well-typed, without recursion, with only asynchronous outputs, and with the addition of replication. Here is the grammar of $A\pi_+$:

$$M ::= a(x).\, M \ \Big| \ \overline{v}w \ \Big| \ M + M \ \Big| \ M \mid M \ \Big| \ !M \ \Big| \ \nu\widetilde{a}\, M$$

where values $v, w, \ldots$ are as in Table 4.

In the second part (Sections 7.3-7.5), we derive the termination of $\mathcal{P}^-$.

7.1 The Replication Theorems

In the proofs with the logical relations we make extensive use of the Sharpened Replication Theorems [SW01]. These express distributivity properties of private replications, and are valid for (strong) barbed congruence. We write $M \downarrow_a$ if $M \xrightarrow{\alpha} M'$ where α is an input or an output along link a.

Definition 7 (Barbed congruence).

A relation $\mathcal{R}$ on closed processes is a barbed bisimulation if whenever $(M, N) \in \mathcal{R}$,

1. $M \downarrow_a$ implies $N \downarrow_a$, for all links a;
2. $M \xrightarrow{\tau} M'$ implies $N \xrightarrow{\tau} N'$ for some N' with $(M', N') \in \mathcal{R}$;
3. the variants of (1) and (2) with the roles of M and N swapped.

Two closed processes M and N are barbed bisimilar if $(M, N) \in \mathcal{R}$ for some barbed bisimulation $\mathcal{R}$.

Two processes M and N are barbed congruent, $M \sim N$, if $C[M]$ and $C[N]$ are barbed bisimilar, for every context C such that $C[M]$ and $C[N]$ are closed. □

Lemma 2. *Relation $\sim$ is a congruence on $A\pi_+$.*   □

Lemma 3 (Sharpened Replication Theorems, for $A\pi_+$). *Suppose a does not appear free in input position in $M, N, N_1, N_2, \pi. N$. We have:*

1. $\nu a\, (!a(x).\, M \mid !N) \sim !\nu a\, (!a(x).\, M \mid N);$
2. $\nu a\, (!a(x).\, M \mid N_1 \mid N_2) \sim \nu a\, (!a(x).\, M \mid N_1) \mid \nu a\, (!a(x).\, M \mid N_2);$
3. $\nu a\, (!a(x).\, M \mid \pi. N) \sim \pi. \nu a\, (!a(x).\, M \mid N)$, *where π is any input or output prefix;*
4. $\nu a\, (!a(x).\, M \mid (N_1 + N_2)) \sim \nu a\, (!a(x).\, M \mid N_1) + \nu a\, (!a(x).\, M \mid N_2).$ □

7.2   Wires

A *wire* is a process of the form $!a(x).\, \bar{b}x$. The main result in this section says that, under certain conditions, wires do not affect termination. We write $R \longrightarrow_E R'$ if a transition $R \overset{\tau}{\longrightarrow} R'$ can be inferred using the transition rules of $A\pi_+$ plus the rule

$$\text{SUM-INT-1:}\quad M_1 + M_2 \overset{\tau}{\longrightarrow} M_1$$

and its symmetric. We say that R *E-diverges* if R has a divergent computation $R \longrightarrow_E R_1 \longrightarrow_E R_2 \ldots$.

Lemma 4 (in $A\pi_+$). *If R E-diverges, then R diverges.*   □

Lemma 5 (in $A\pi_+$). *Suppose c' is a name that does not occur free in R in input position, and that R only uses input-guarded replications. If $R \mid !c'(x).\, \bar{c}x$ diverges, then $R\{c/c'\}$ E-diverges.*

Proof. The proof is in two parts. First, one shows that a reductions for $R \mid !c'(x).\, \bar{c}x \overset{\tau}{\longrightarrow} R' \mid !c'(x).\, \bar{c}x$ can be mimicked by sequence of reductions $R\{c/c'\}(\longrightarrow_E)^* \equiv R'\{c/c'\}$. This sequence can however be empty if the reduction from $R \mid !c'(x).\, \bar{c}x$ is a communication at c' (and the output consumed is not part of a sum); the sequence is non-empty otherwise.

In the second part of the proof one shows that in a divergent computation from $R \mid !c'(x).\, \bar{c}x$ there are an infinite number of steps that are not communications at c'. This implies, by the arguments above, that also $R\{c/c'\}$ E-diverges.

□

Lemma 6 (in $A\pi_+$). *Suppose c' is a name that does not occur free in R in input position, and R only uses input-guarded replication. Then $\nu c'\, (R \mid !c'(x).\, \bar{c}x)$ diverges iff $R\{c/c'\}$ diverges.*

Proof. The hard implication is the one from left to right, and follows from Lemmas 5 and 4, and the fact that a top restriction preserves divergences.   □

7.3   Closure Properties

Lemma 7. *Suppose $R \in \mathcal{P}^-$. If $R \equiv \xrightarrow{\alpha} R'$ then $R \xrightarrow{\alpha} \equiv R'$.* $\square$

Lemma 8 (Closure under reduction for $\mathcal{P}^-$). *$R \in \mathcal{P}^-$ and $R \xrightarrow{\tau} R'$ imply $R' \in \mathcal{P}^-$.*

Proof. Because of Lemma 7, it is sufficient to prove the result when R is a normal form. Moreover, it suffices to prove it for processes: resources have no reductions; only pre-processes of type $\diamond$ can reduce, and these are also processes. The proof is by structural induction. $\square$

Lemma 9 (Closure under $\sim$ for the logical relations). *Suppose $P, Q \in \mathcal{P}^-$, and $P \sim Q$. If $P \in \mathcal{L}^A$, then also $Q \in \mathcal{L}^A$.*

Proof. First, note that if P and Q are barbed congruent, then they must have the same type. Then the thesis, for $A = \diamond$, follows from the fact that $\sim$ preserves termination.

Suppose $A = a\_\sharp T$, and T is a connection type (the case of unit type is simpler): we have to show that if b is a fresh name, for any $I_b \in \mathcal{L}^{b\text{-}T}$,

$$\nu b \, (I_b \mid \nu a \, (Q \mid \overline{a}b)) \in \mathcal{L}^\diamond \, .$$

We can assume that b is fresh also for P, and therefore, since $P \in \mathcal{L}^{a\text{-}\sharp T}$,

$$\nu b \, (I_b \mid \nu a \, (P \mid \overline{a}b)) \in \mathcal{L}^\diamond \, .$$

But since $\sim$ is a congruence, we are done, using the result of the lemma for $A = \diamond$. $\square$

Lemma 10. *If $P \in \mathcal{L}$ then $P \in \text{TER}$.*

Proof. If $P \in \mathcal{L}^\diamond$ then the result follows by definition of $\mathcal{L}^\diamond$. Otherwise $P \in \mathcal{L}^{a\text{-}T}$, for some a, T, and P cannot reduce. $\square$

We write $R \xrightarrow{\tau}_d R'$ if $R \xrightarrow{\tau} R'$ and this is the only possible transition for R (i.e., for all α, R'' such that $R \xrightarrow{\alpha} R''$, we have $\alpha = \tau$ and $R' \equiv R''$).

Lemma 11. *If $R \xrightarrow{\tau}_d R'$ and $R' \in \text{TER}$ then also $R \in \text{TER}$.* $\square$

Lemma 12. *If $a, b : T$ then $!a(x).\overline{b}x \in \mathcal{L}^{a\text{-}T}$.*

Proof. Suppose $T = \sharp\,\text{unit}$. Then

$$\nu a \, (!a(x).\overline{b}x \mid \overline{a}v) \xrightarrow{\tau}_d \sim \overline{b}v$$

(it terminates after one step), therefore by Lemma 11 and 9 $\nu a \, (!a(x).\overline{b}x \mid \overline{a}v) \in \text{TER}$.

Otherwise, take a fresh c and any I_c, and consider the process

$$P \overset{\text{def}}{=} \nu c \, (I_c \mid \nu a \, (!a(x).\overline{b}x \mid \overline{a}c))$$

We have $P \xrightarrow{\tau}_d \sim \nu c \, (I_c \mid \overline{b}c)$, and the latter process cannot reduce further, therefore $P \in \text{TER}$, reasoning as above. $\square$

Lemma 13. *Let c be a higher-order name. We have $\nu b\,(I_b \mid \bar{b}c) \in$ TER iff $(\nu b\,,c')(I_b \mid \bar{b}c' \mid !c'(x).\bar{c}x) \in$ TER, where c' is fresh.*

Proof. Follows from Lemma 6.   □

Lemma 14. $M_1 \mid M_2 \in$ TER *iff, for each i, $M_i \in$ TER.*

Proof. M_1 and M_2 have no free input. This means that M_1 and M_2 cannot interact.   □

7.4   Relatively Independent Resources

Definition 8. *Resources $I_{a_1},\ldots,I_{a_n}$ are relatively independent if none of the names $a_1,\ldots,a_n$ appears free in output position in any of the resources $I_{a_1},\ldots,I_{a_n}$.*

A term $P \in \mathcal{P}^-$ has relatively independent resources if, for all subterms P' of P, the resources that are unguarded in P' are relatively independent.   □

Lemma 15. *For each $I_a \in \mathcal{RES}$ there is $J_a \in \mathcal{RES}$ with $I_a \sim J_a$ and J_a has relatively independent resources.*

Proof. Induction on the structure of a normal form of I_a, using the Replication Theorems.   □

Lemma 16. *For each $P \in \mathcal{P}^-$ there is $Q \in \mathcal{P}^-$ with $P \sim Q$ and Q has relatively independent resources.*

Proof. Similar to the previous lemma.   □

Lemma 17. *For each $P \in \mathcal{P}^-$ there is a normal form $Q \in \mathcal{P}^-$ with $P \sim Q$ and Q has relatively independent resources.*

Proof. If in the previous lemmas the initial process is in normal form, then also the transformed process is. The result then follows from the fact that $\equiv \subseteq \sim$.   □

7.5   Main Theorem

Theorem 2. *Let $\tilde{a} = a_1,\ldots,a_n$. Suppose that resources $I_{a_1},\ldots,I_{a_n}$ are relatively independent, and $I_{a_i} \in \mathcal{L}$ for each i. Then $P : A$ and $\mathrm{in}(P) \cap \mathrm{fn}(I_{\tilde{a}}) = \emptyset$ imply $\nu\tilde{a}\,(I_{\tilde{a}} \mid P) \in \mathcal{L}^A$.*

Proof. By Lemmas 17 and 9 we can assume that P is a normal form and has relatively independent resources. We proceed by induction on the structure of P. We call Q the process $\nu\tilde{a}\,(I_{\tilde{a}} \mid P)$. We consider the most interesting cases.

– $P = \bar{b}c$.
  In this case, $A = \Diamond$. We have to show that $Q \in$ TER. We have:

$$Q = \nu\tilde{a}\,(I_{\tilde{a}} \mid P) \sim \nu\tilde{a}'\,(I_{\tilde{a}'} \mid P) \stackrel{\mathrm{def}}{=} Q'$$

  where $\tilde{a}' = \tilde{a} \cap \{b,c\}$ (here we exploit the fact that the resources are relatively independent).
  There are 4 subcases:

- $\widetilde{a'} = \emptyset$. Then $Q' \sim \bar{b}c$, which is in TER.
- $\widetilde{a'} = \{b\}$. Then $Q' \sim \nu b\,(I_b \mid \bar{b}c)$ and the latter process is in TER iff the process $(\nu b\,, c')(I_b \mid !c'(x).\,\bar{c}x \mid \bar{b}c')$ is in TER (Lemma 13), where c' is fresh. And now we are done, exploiting the definition of $\mathcal{L}$ on the type of b, for $!c'(x).\,\bar{c}x \in \mathcal{L}$ (Lemma 12) and we know that $I_b \in \mathcal{L}$.
- $\widetilde{a'} = \{c\}$. Then $Q' \sim \nu c(I_c \mid \bar{b}c)$ and the latter process is in TER because cannot reduce.
- $\widetilde{a'} = \{b, c\}$. Then

$$Q' \sim (\nu b, c)(I_b \mid I_c \mid \bar{b}c)$$
$$\sim \nu c\,(I_c \mid \nu b\,(I_b \mid \bar{b}c)) \stackrel{\text{def}}{=} Q''$$

since c is fresh for I_b (the relatively-independence hypothesis). Now, Q'' is in TER by definition of $\mathcal{L}$ on higher types (precisely, the type of b).

- $P = M_1 \mid M_2$. (Thus $P : \diamond$)
We have to show that $Q = \nu\widetilde{a}\,(I_{\widetilde{a}} \mid M_1 \mid M_2) \in$ TER. Using the Replication Theorems we have

$$Q \sim Q_1 \mid Q_2$$

where

$$Q_i \stackrel{\text{def}}{=} \nu\widetilde{a}\,(I_{\widetilde{a}} \mid M_i)\,.$$

By Lemma 14, $Q \in$ TER iff each Q_i is so. The latter is true by the induction on the structure.

- $P = !b(x).\,M$. Then $Q : b\_\sharp\,T$. We assume that T is a connection type. Then $Q \in \mathcal{L}$ if for a fresh c, for any $I_c \in \mathcal{L}^{c\text{-}T}$,

$$R \stackrel{\text{def}}{=} \nu c\,(I_c \mid \nu b\,(Q \mid \bar{b}c)) \in \text{TER}\,.$$

Since c is fresh, we can assume $c = x$. We thus have

$$R = \nu x\,(I_x \mid \nu b\,(\nu\widetilde{a}\,(I_{\widetilde{a}} \mid !b(x).\,M) \mid \bar{b}x))$$
$$\equiv (\nu x, b, \widetilde{a}\,)(I_x \mid I_{\widetilde{a}} \mid !b(x).\,M \mid \bar{b}x)$$

and

$$R \stackrel{\tau}{\longrightarrow}_{\text{d}}\sim (\nu x, \widetilde{a}\,)(I_x \mid I_{\widetilde{a}} \mid M) \stackrel{\text{def}}{=} R'$$

(here we exploit the fact that replications are not recursive, and that $b \notin \text{fn}(I_{\widetilde{a}})$).

Using the induction on the structure we derive $R' \in$ TER (note that $I_x, I_{\widetilde{a}}$ are relatively independent).

- $P = \nu x\,(I_x \mid P')$, where $I_x = !x(y).\,M$.
We have, using the Replication Theorems:

$$Q = \nu\widetilde{a}\,(I_{\widetilde{a}} \mid \nu x\,(I_x \mid P'))$$
$$\sim \nu x\,(\nu\widetilde{a}\,(I_{\widetilde{a}} \mid I_x) \mid \nu\widetilde{a}\,(I_{\widetilde{a}} \mid P')) \stackrel{\text{def}}{=} Q'$$

Call $R \stackrel{\text{def}}{=} \boldsymbol{\nu}\tilde{a}(I_{\tilde{a}} \mid I_x)$. Then $R \in \mathcal{L}$ using the inductive hypothesis. Moreover, using the Replication Theorems,

$$R \sim !x(y). \boldsymbol{\nu}\tilde{a} \, (I_{\tilde{a}} \mid M) \stackrel{\text{def}}{=} J_x$$

and $J_x \in \mathcal{L}$, using Lemma 9. Thus we have

$$Q' \sim (\boldsymbol{\nu}x, \tilde{a})(J_x \mid I_{\tilde{a}} \mid P') \stackrel{\text{def}}{=} Q''$$

where $J_x, I_{\tilde{a}}$ are relatively independent. Finally we can apply the induction hypothesis to P' and infer $Q'' \in \text{TER}$.   □

Corollary 1. *If $P \in \mathcal{P}^-$ then $P \in \mathcal{L}$.*   □

8 Proofs Based on Simulation

The language $\mathcal{P}^-$ is non-trivial, but not very expressive. It is however a powerful language for the termination property, in the sense that the termination of the processes in $\mathcal{P}^-$ implies that of a much broader language, namely the language $\mathcal{P}$ of Theorem 1.

We move to $\mathcal{P}$ by progressively extending the language $\mathcal{P}^-$. The technique for proving termination of the extensions is as follows. The extensions define a sequence of languages $\mathcal{P}_0, \ldots, \mathcal{P}_{11}$, with $\mathcal{P}_0 = \mathcal{P}^-$, $\mathcal{P}_{11} = \mathcal{P}$, and $\mathcal{P}_i \subset \mathcal{P}_{i+1}$ for all $0 \leq i < 11$. For each i, we exhibit a transformation $[\![\cdot]\!]_i$, defined on the normal forms of $\mathcal{P}_{i+1}$, with the property that a transformed process $[\![M]\!]_i$ belongs to $\mathcal{P}_i$ and $[\![M]\!] \in \text{TER}$ implies $M \in \text{TER}$. We then infer the termination of the processes in $\mathcal{P}_{i+1}$ from that of the processes in $\mathcal{P}_i$.

For this kind of proofs we use process calculus techniques, especially techniques for *simulation*. If R' simulates R, then R' can do everything R can, but the other way round may not be true. For instance, $a. (b. c+d)$ simulates $a. b$, but the other way round is false. Simulation is not much interesting as a behavioural equivalence. Simulation is however interesting for reasoning about termination, and is handy to use because of its co-inductive definition.

Definition 9. *A relation $\mathcal{R}$ on closed processes is a strong simulation if $(M, N) \in \mathcal{R}$ implies:*

- *whenever $M \stackrel{\alpha}{\longrightarrow} M'$ there is N' such that $N \stackrel{\alpha}{\longrightarrow} N'$ and $(M', N') \in \mathcal{R}$.*

A process N simulates M, written $M \preceq N$, if for all closing substitutions σ there is a strong simulation $\mathcal{R}$ such that $(M\sigma, N\sigma) \in \mathcal{R}$.   □

Relation $\preceq$ is reflexive and transitive, and is preserved by all operators of the π-calculus. Hence $\preceq$ is a precongruence in all languages $\mathcal{P}_i$. An important property of $\preceq$ for us is:

Lemma 18. *If $M \preceq M'$ then $M' \in \text{TER}$ implies $M \in \text{TER}$.*   □

Each language $\mathcal{P}_i$ $(i > 0)$ is defined by exhibiting the additional productions for the normal forms of the processes and the resources of the language. We only show a few examples of extensions and their correctness proofs. We refer to [San01] for the details.

$$M^{\mathrm{NF}} ::= \ldots \mid \bar{a}v.\, M^{\mathrm{NF}}$$

Proof. Consider a transformation $[\![\cdot]\!]$ that acts on outputs thus:

$$[\![\bar{b}v.\, M]\!] \stackrel{\mathrm{def}}{=} \bar{b}v \mid [\![M]\!].$$

and is an homomorphism elsewhere. Its correctness is given by the law

$$\bar{b}v.\, M \preceq \bar{b}v \mid M$$

and Lemma 18. □

$$I_a^{\mathrm{NF}} ::= \ldots \mid I_a^{\mathrm{NF}} \mid I_a^{\mathrm{NF}}$$

Proof. With the addition of this production, there can be several input-replicated processes at the same link. The correctness of this extension is inferred using the law

$$!a(x).\, R \mid !a(x).\, R' \preceq !a(x).\, (R \mid R').$$

□

$$I_{\tilde{a}}^{\mathrm{NF}} ::= \ldots \mid I_{\tilde{a}}^{\mathrm{NF}} + I_{\tilde{a}}^{\mathrm{NF}}$$

Proof. We use the law $R_1 + R_2 \preceq R_1 \mid R_2$. □

The addition of nested inputs and of recursion with first-order state are more difficult, though the basis of the proof is the same. Again, we refer to [San01]. Also, we refer to [San01] for more discussions on the importance of the clauses (2) and (3) of Condition 1 (on nesting of inputs and on state) for the termination of the processes of $\mathcal{P}$.

9 Conclusions and Future Work

We have proved termination of $\mathcal{P}$, the simply-typed (localised) π-calculus subject to three syntactic conditions that constrain recursive inputs and state. In the proof, we have first applied the logical-relation technique to a subset of processes with only functional names, and then we have extended the termination property to the whole language by means of techniques of behavioural preorders.

The termination of $\mathcal{P}$ implies that of various forms of simply-typed λ-calculus: usual call-by-name, call-by-value, and call-by-need, but also enriched λ-calculi such as concurrent λ-calculi [DCdLP94], λ-calculus with resources and λ-calculus with multiplicities [BL00]. Indeed all encodings of λ-calculi into π-calculus we are aware of, restricted to simply-typed terms, are also encodings into $\mathcal{P}$. The λ-calculus with resources, λ^{res}, is a form of non-deterministic λ-calculus with explicit substitutions and with a parallel composition. Substitutions have a multiplicity, telling us how many copies of a given resource can be made. Due to non-determinism, parallelism, and the multiplicity in substitutions (which implies that a substitution cannot be distributed over a composite term), a direct proof of termination of λ^{res}, with the technique of logical relations, although probably possible, is non-trivial.

The main focus of this paper have been the proof techniques of termination for processes. For future work, an important issue to look at is the expressiveness of the language $\mathcal{P}$ obtained. At present we know little about it, other than $\mathcal{P}$ can encode various λ-calculus dialects. We are particularly interested in applications to parallel and distributed object-oriented languages. This will probably require extending $\mathcal{P}$ with other features, such as primitives for distribution and migration.

We have only considered the simply-typed π-calculus – the process analogous of the simply-typed λ-calculus. It should be possible to adapt our work to more complex types, such as those of the polymorphic π-calculus [Tur96, SW01] – the process analogous of the polymorphic λ-calculus.

We have been able to apply the logical-relation technique only to a small set of 'functional' processes. Then we have had to use ad hoc techniques to prove the termination of a larger language. To obtain stronger results, and to extend the results more easily to other languages (for instance, process languages with communication of terms such as the Higher-Order π-calculus) a deeper understanding of the logical-relation technique in concurrency would seem necessary.

References

[BL00]   G. Boudol and C. Laneve. λ-calculus, multiplicities and the π-calculus. In G. Plotkin, C. Stirling, and M. Tofte, editors, *Proof, Language and Interaction: Essays in Honour of Robin Milner.* MIT Press, 2000. 81, 96

[DCdLP94] M. Dezani-Ciancaglini, U. de Liguoro, and U. Piperno. Fully abstract semantics for concurrent λ-calculus. In M. Hagiya and J. C. Mitchell, editors, *Theoretical Aspects of Computer Software*, volume 789 of *Lecture Notes in Computer Science*, pages 16–35. Springer Verlag, 1994. 96

[FG96]   C. Fournet and G. Gonthier. The Reflexive Chemical Abstract Machine and the Join calculus. In *Proc. 23th POPL*. ACM Press, 1996. 81

[GLT88]   J.-Y. Girard, Y. Lafont, and P. Taylor. *Proofs and Types.* Cambridge Tracts in Theoretical Computer Science 7. Cambridge University Press, 1988. 80

[HKM+99] M. Hicks, P. Kakkar, J. T. Moore, C. A. Gunter, and S. Nettles. PLAN: A packet language for active networks. In *Conf. on Functional Programming (ICFP'98)*, volume 34(1) of *ACM SIGPLAN Notices*, pages 86–93. ACM, June 1999. 77

[HMST95] F. Honsell, I. A. Mason, S. F. Smith, and C. L. Talcott. A Variable Typed Logic of Effects. *Information and Computation*, 119(1):55–90, 1995. 79

[Kob00] N. Kobayashi. Type systems for concurrent processes: From deadlock-freedom to livelock-freedom, time-boundedness. In J. van Leeuwen, O. Watanabe, M. Hagiya, P. D. Mosses, and T. Ito, editors, *IFIP Conf. TCS 2000*, volume 1872 of *Lecture Notes in Computer Science*, pages 365–389. IFIP, Springer Verlag, August 2000. 80

[Mer01] M. Merro. Locality in the π-calculus and applications to object-oriented languages. PhD thesis, Ecoles des Mines de Paris, 2001. 78, 81

[Mil99] R. Milner. *Communicating and Mobile Systems: the π-Calculus*. Cambridge University Press, 1999. 81

[Mit96] J. C. Mitchell. *Foundations for Programming Languages*. MIT Press, Cambridge, MA, 1996. 80

[San99] D. Sangiorgi. The name discipline of uniform receptiveness. *Theoretical Computer Science*, 221:457–493, 1999. 86

[San01] D. Sangiorgi. Termination of processes. ftp://ftp-sop.inria.fr/mimosa/personnel/davides/ter.ps, December 2001. 80, 82, 95

[SW01] D. Sangiorgi and D. Walker. *The π-calculus: a Theory of Mobile Processes*. Cambridge University Press, 2001. 81, 89, 96

[Tur96] N. D. Turner. *The polymorphic pi-calculus: Theory and Implementation*. PhD thesis, Department of Computer Science, University of Edinburgh, 1996. 96

[YBK01] N. Yoshida, M. Berger, and Honda. K. Strong normalisation in the π-Calculus. In *16th Annual IEEE Symposium on Logic in Computer Science (LICS-01)*, pages 311–322. IEEE Computer Society, 2001. 80, 81

[Yos96] N. Yoshida. Graph types for monadic mobile processes. In *Proc. FST & TCS*, volume 1180 of *Lecture Notes in Computer Science*, pages 371–386. Springer Verlag, 1996. Full paper appeared as Technical Report, ECS-LFCS-96-350, 1996, Edinburgh. 80

Introduction to Modal and Temporal Mu-Calculi
(Abstract)

Julian C. Bradfield

Laboratory for Foundations of Computer Science
Division of Informatics, University of Edinburgh
Edinburgh, EH9 3JZ United Kingdom
jcb@dcs.ed.ac.uk

Modal mu-calculus is a logic obtained by adding *fixpoint operators* to ordinary modal logic, or Hennessy–Milner logic. The result is a very expressive logic, sufficient to subsume many other temporal logics such as CTL and CTL*. The modal mu-calculus is easy to model-check, and so makes a good 'back-end' logic for tools; it has an interesting theory, with some major problems still open; but it also has a certain reputation for being hard to read and write.

This tutorial provides an introduction to the modal mu-calculus and related logics, suitable for those with some exposure to modal or temporal logic, but without prior knowledge of fixpoint logics.

I start by reviewing the basic semantic setting of processes modelled as transition systems, and briefly review basic modal logic and temporal logics such as CTL.

I then introduce the modal mu-calculus itself. I cover the formal syntax and semantics, and then give more informally the game-based intuition that is most useful in understanding formulae of the logic.

I next describe global and local model-checking techniques.

Finally, I discuss the relationship between modal mu-calculus, automata and games, and some of the theoretical questions that have been and are now of interest.

The tutorial is based around the handbook chapter [1], written with Colin Stirling, which forms the text for the tutorial.

References

1. J. C. Bradfield and C. P. Stirling, 'Modal logics and mu-calculi: an introduction', in: *Handbook of Process Algebra* (ed. Bergstra, Ponse and Smolka), pp. 293–330, Elsevier, 2001. Preprint at
   http://www.dcs.ed.ac.uk/home/jcb/Research/papers.html#HPA-preprint 98

L. Brim et al. (Eds.): CONCUR 2002, LNCS 2421, p. 98, 2002.
© Springer-Verlag Berlin Heidelberg 2002

Types for Cryptographic Protocols

Andrew D. Gordon

Microsoft Research

One of the many different approaches to proving properties of a cryptographic security protocol is to encode it within a process calculus [6,7,11,12,14,20], and then to apply standard techniques from concurrency theory such as model-checking [19] or equational reasoning [4,5,8,9,13,15]. A promising recent development is to verify properties such as secrecy and authenticity via behavioural type systems [1,2,3,10,16,17,18]. This tutorial reviews the known type systems and results in this area, and suggests areas for further research.

References

1. M. Abadi. Secrecy by typing in security protocols. *Journal of the ACM*, 46(5):749–786, September 1999. 99
2. M. Abadi and B. Blanchet. Secrecy types for asymmetric communication. In *Foundations of Software Science and Computation Structures (FoSSaCS 2001)*, volume 2030 of *Lecture Notes in Computer Science*, pages 25–41. Springer, 2001. 99
3. M. Abadi and B. Blanchet. Analyzing security protocols with secrecy types and logic programs. In *29th ACM Symposium on Principles of Programming Languages (POPL'02)*, pages 33–44, 2002. 99
4. M. Abadi, C. Fournet, and G. Gonthier. Secure communications implementation of channel abstractions. In *13th IEEE Symposium on Logic in Computer Science (LICS'98)*, pages 105–116, 1998. 99
5. M. Abadi and A. D. Gordon. A bisimulation method for cryptographic protocols. *Nordic Journal of Computing*, 5:267–303, 1998. 99
6. M. Abadi and A. D. Gordon. A calculus for cryptographic protocols: The spi calculus. *Information and Computation*, 148:1–70, 1999. 99
7. R. Amadio and S. Prasad. The game of the name in cryptographic tables. In *Advances in Computing Science (ASIAN'99)*, volume 1742 of *Lecture Notes in Computer Science*, pages 5–26. Springer, 1999. 99
8. M. Boreale, R. De Nicola, and R. Pugliese. Proof techniques for cryptographic processes. In *14th IEEE Symposium on Logic in Computer Science*, pages 157–166, 1999. 99
9. B. Borgström and U. Nestmann. On bisimulations for the spi calculus. In *International Conference on Algebraic Methodology And Software Technology (AMAST2002)*, Lecture Notes in Computer Science. Springer, 2002. To appear. 99
10. I. Cervesato. Typed MSR: Syntax and examples. In *First International Workshop on Mathematical Methods, Models and Architectures for Computer Network Security (MMM'01)*, volume 2052 of *Lecture Notes in Computer Science*, pages 159–177. Springer, 2001. 99

L. Brim et al. (Eds.): CONCUR 2002, LNCS 2421, pp. 99–100, 2002.
© Springer-Verlag Berlin Heidelberg 2002

11. M. Dam. Proving trust in systems of second-order processes. In *31st Hawaii International Conference on System Sciences*, volume VII, pages 255–264, 1998. 99

12. N. Durgin, J. C. Mitchell, and D. Pavlovic. A compositional logic for protocol correctness. In *14th IEEE Computer Security Foundations Workshop*, pages 241–255. IEEE Computer Society Press, 2001. 99

13. A. S. Elkjær, M. Höhle, H. Hüttel, and K. Overgård. Towards automatic bisimilarity checking in the spi calculus. *Australian Computer Science Communications*, 21(3):175–189, 1999. 99

14. R. Focardi and R. Gorrieri. A classification of security properties for process algebra. *Journal of Computer Security*, 3(1):5–33, 1994. 99

15. R. Focardi, R. Gorrieri, and F. Martinelli. Message authentication through non-interference. In *International Conference on Algebraic Methodology And Software Technology (AMAST2000)*, volume 1816 of *Lecture Notes in Computer Science*, pages 258–272. Springer, 2000. 99

16. A. D. Gordon and A. Jeffrey. Authenticity by typing for security protocols. In *14th IEEE Computer Security Foundations Workshop*, pages 145–159. IEEE Computer Society Press, 2001. 99

17. A. D. Gordon and A. Jeffrey. Typing correspondence assertions for communication protocols. In *Mathematical Foundations of Programming Semantics 17*, volume 45 of *Electronic Notes in Theoretical Computer Science*. Elsevier, 2001. Pages 99–120 of the Preliminary Proceedings, BRICS Notes Series NS-01-2, BRICS, University of Aarhus, May 2001. Extended version to appear in *Theoretical Computer Science*. 99

18. A. D. Gordon and A. Jeffrey. Types and effects for asymmetric cryptographic protocols. In *15th IEEE Computer Security Foundations Workshop*. IEEE Computer Society Press, 2002. To appear. 99

19. G. Lowe. Breaking and fixing the Needham-Schroeder public-key protocol using CSP and FDR. In T. Margaria and B. Steffen, editors, *Tools and Algorithms for the Construction and Analysis of Systems (TACAS'96)*, volume 1055 of *Lecture Notes in Computer Science*, pages 147–166. Springer, 1996. 99

20. P. Ryan and S. Schneider. *Modelling and Analysis of Security Protocols*. Addison-Wesley, 2001. 99

Network Invariants in Action[*]

Yonit Kesten[1], Amir Pnueli[2], Elad Shahar[2], and Lenore Zuck[3]

[1] Ben Gurion University
ykesten@bgumail.bgu.ac.il
[2] Weizmann Institute of Science
{amir,elad}@wisdom.weizmann.ac.il
[3] New York University, New York
zuck@cs.nyu.edu

Abstract. The paper presents the method of *network invariants* for verifying a wide spectrum of LTL properties, including liveness, of parameterized systems. This method can be applied to establish the validity of the property over a system $S(n)$ for every value of the parameter n. The application of the method requires checking abstraction relations between two finite-state systems. We present a proof rule, based on the method of Abstraction Mapping by Abadi and Lamport, which has been implemented on the TLV model checker and incorporates both history and prophecy variables. The effectiveness of the network invariant method is illustrated on several examples, including a deterministic and probabilistic versions of the dining-philosophers problem.

1 Introduction

The emerging interest in embedded systems brought forth a surge of research in *automatic uniform verification* of *parameterized systems*: Given a parameterized system $S(n) : P_1 \| \cdots \| P_n$ and a property p, uniform verification attempts to verify $S(n) \models p$ for every $n > 1$. Verification of such systems is known to be undecidable [2]; much of the recent research has been devoted to identifying conditions that enable their automatic verification and abstraction tools to facilitate the task (e.g., [7,6,19,21,22].)

One of the promising approaches to the uniform verification of parameterized systems is the method of *network invariants*, first mentioned in [3,23], further developed in [25] (who also coined the name "network invariant"), and elaborated in [13] into a working method. The formulation here follows [10], which is somewhat akin in spirit to both [25] and [13]. A significant improvement of our approach over [25] and [13] and most other works that use abstraction for verification is that our notion of abstraction takes into account the fairness properties of the compared systems. Consequently, our abstraction can support and

---

[*] This research was supported in part by the John von Neumann Minerva Center for Verification of Reactive Systems, The European Community IST project "Advance", and ONR grant N00014-99-1-0131.

simplify proofs of liveness properties as well as any other property expressible by LTL.

The main idea of the method is to abstract $n-1$ of the processes, say the composition $P_2 \parallel \cdots \parallel P_n$, into a single finite-state process $\mathcal{I}$, independent of n. We refer to $\mathcal{I}$ as the *network invariant*. If possible, this reduces the parameterized verification problem $(P_1 \parallel \cdots \parallel P_n) \models p$ into the fixed-size verification problem $(P_1 \parallel \mathcal{I}) \models p$. In order to show that $\mathcal{I}$ is a correct abstraction of any number of processes (assuming that $P_2, \ldots, P_n$ are all identical except for renaming), it is sufficient to apply an inductive argument, using $P \sqsubseteq \mathcal{I}$ as the induction base, and $(P \parallel \mathcal{I}) \sqsubseteq \mathcal{I}$ as the induction step. These two abstraction proof obligations compare two finite-state systems and can, in principle, be performed algorithmically by a model checker.

Unfortunately this approach is intractable. The obvious way to establish algorithmically that a concrete system S_c is abstracted by the abstract system S_a is by showing that $S_c \cap \bar{S}_a$ admits no computations, where $\bar{S}_a$ is the complement of S_a. Since fair systems are equivalent to Streett automata, the set of states obtained by complementing S_a is usually prohibitively large. Consequently, abstraction is accomplished by establishing a step-by-step simulation relation between a concrete computation and an abstract one, following the *abstraction mapping* method of Abadi and Lamport [1]. This approach has been implemented on the Weizmann Institute Temporal Logic Verifier TLV.

In this paper we present our theory of abstraction which can be used for the verification of arbitrary LTL formulas (including liveness). We introduce the method of network invariants and the abstraction proof rule used for discharging the abstraction proof obligations. The method is then illustrated over several examples of parameterized systems for which we uniformly verify their essential safety and liveness properties.

The two examples we study deal with a solution to the dining philosophers problem. In the first example, we consider the case in which each of the philosophers follows a deterministic protocol. The property we establish is individual accessibility, that is, every hungry philosopher eventually eats. We present two network invariants for this problem. The first invariant is a carefully designed abstraction of the two end processes in a string of philosophers. While the design of this invariant took a long time to develop, its proof obligations were very straightforward to establish. At the other end of the spectrum, we present a very natural invariant, which is just a string of 3 philosophers. The main proof obligation here was to show that a string of 4 philosophers is abstracted by a string of 3. This required an abstraction mapping which uses prophecy variables. We then turn to a solution of the dining philosophers which is a variant of the probabilistic "Courteous Philosophers" protocol of [14]. For this protocol, we also succeeded in automatically verifying individual accessibility using a two-halves abstraction. As a third example, we considered the distributed termination algorithm of [5]. This algorithm also considers a ring of processes. However, unlike the two preceding cases, in addition to the communication with its two close neighbors, a process also maintains a communication of a different kind with (potentially) every other process. In order to make this problem amenable to treatment by the network-invariants method, we had first to abstract this "unconstrained" model of communication into a simpler representation. Details about the successful and effective application of the method to this case study are provided in [12]. [1]

The variety of examples of application of the network invariant method to automatic verification of liveness properties of parameterized system, demonstrates the power of the methodology and the wide range of its applicability.

Many methods have been proposed for the uniform verification of parameterized systems. These include methods based on explicit induction ([24,22]) network invariants that can be viewed as implicit induction ([13], [25], [8], [15]), methods that can be viewed as abstraction and approximation of network invariants ([3], [23], [4]), and other methods that can be viewed as based on abstraction ([9], [7]).

Our approach to verification by network invariants has been presented first in [10]. The work in [10] was based on a significantly weaker proof rule than the one we present here. For example, the proof rule presented there could not handle prophecy variables and was therefore inherently incomplete. Also, some of the solutions presented in [10] used the construct of *chaos* in cases where it was not necessary, leading to overly cumbersome abstractions. Relative to [10], this paper presents a more powerful rule and additional interesting examples, such as the verification of a probabilistic protocol.

2   Fair Discrete Systems

As a computational model for reactive systems we take the model of *fair discrete systems* (FDS) [10], which is a slight variation on the model of *fair transition system* [18]. Under this model, a system $\mathcal{D} : \langle V, \mathcal{O}, W, \Theta, \rho, \mathcal{J}, \mathcal{C} \rangle$ consists of the following components:

- V: A finite set of typed *system variables*, containing data and control variables. A state s is an assignment of type-compatible values to the system variables V. For a set of variables $U \subseteq V$, we denote by $s[U]$ the values assigned by state s to the variables U. The set of states over V is denoted by Σ. In this paper, we assume that Σ is finite.
- $\mathcal{O} \subseteq V$: A subset of *observable variables*. These are the variables which can be externally observed.
- $W \subseteq V$: A subset of *owned* variables. These are variables which only the system itself can modify. All other variables can also be modified by steps of the environment.
- Θ: The *initial condition* – an *assertion* (first-order state formula) characterizing the initial states.
- ρ: A *transition relation* – an assertion $\rho(V, V')$, relating the values V of the variables in state $s \in \Sigma$ to the values V' in a ρ-successor state $s' \in \Sigma$.

---

[1] The TLV code of all examples presented in this paper can be found in www.wisdom.weizmann.ac.il/ verify/publications/2002/KPZ02.html#explanation.

- $\mathcal{J}$: A set of *justice (weak fairness) requirements*. Each justice requirement $J \in \mathcal{J}$ is an assertion, intended to guarantee that every computation contains infinitely many J-states (states satisfying J.)
- $\mathcal{C}$: A set of *compassion (strong fairness) requirements*. Each compassion requirement is a pair $\langle p, q \rangle \in \mathcal{C}$ of assertions, intended to guarantee that every computation containing infinitely many p-states also contains infinitely many q-states.

We require that every state $s \in \Sigma$ has at least one ρ-successor. This is often ensured by including in ρ the *idling* disjunct $V = V'$ (also called the *stuttering* step). In such cases, every state s is its own ρ-successor. A system is said to be *closed* if $W = V$, i.e., all variables are owned by the system. Otherwise, the system is said to be *open*. Let $\sigma: s_0, s_1, s_2, ...$, be an infinite sequence of states, φ be an assertion and $j \geq 0$ be a natural number. We say that s_j is a φ-state if it satisfies φ, and we say that j is a φ-position of σ if s_j is a φ-state.

Let $\mathcal{D}$ be an FDS as above. We define an (*open*) *run* of $\mathcal{D}$ to be an infinite sequence of states $\sigma: s_0, s_1, s_2, ...$, satisfying the following requirements:

- *Initiality:* s_0 is initial, i.e., $s_0 \models \Theta$.
- *Consecution:*   For each $j = 0, 1, ...$,
  - $s_{2j+1}[W] = s_{2j}[W]$. That is, s_{2j+1} and s_{2j} agree on the interpretation of the owned variables W.
  - s_{2j+2} is a ρ-successor of s_{2j+1}.

Thus, an open run of a system consists of a strict interleaving of system with environment actions, where the system action has to satisfy the transition relation ρ, while the environment step is only required to preserve the values of the owned variables. We say that a run of $\mathcal{D}$ is a *computation* if it satisfies the following requirements:

- *Justice:*   For each $J \in \mathcal{J}$, σ contains infinitely many J-positions
- *Compassion:*   For each $\langle p, q \rangle \in \mathcal{C}$, if σ contains infinitely many p-positions, it must also contain infinitely many q-positions.

We denote by $Comp(\mathcal{D})$ the set of all computations of $\mathcal{D}$.

Systems $\mathcal{D}_1$ and $\mathcal{D}_2$ are *compatible* if their sets of owned variables are disjoint, and the intersection of their variables is observable in both systems. For compatible systems $\mathcal{D}_1$ and $\mathcal{D}_2$, we define their *asynchronous parallel composition*, denoted by $\mathcal{D}_1 \| \mathcal{D}_2$, as the FDS whose sets of variables, observable variables, owned variables, justice, and compassion sets are the unions of the corresponding sets in the two systems, whose initial condition is the conjunction of the initial conditions, and whose transition relation is the disjunction of the two transition relations. Thus, a step in an execution of the composed system is a step of system $\mathcal{D}_1$, or a step of system $\mathcal{D}_2$, or an environment step. We also provide a *restriction* operation, which moves a specified variable to the category of owned variables and makes it non-observable. We denote by [**restrict** x **in** $\mathcal{D}$] the system obtained by restricting variable x in system $\mathcal{D}$.

An *observation* of $\mathcal{D}$ is a projection of a $\mathcal{D}$-computation onto $\mathcal{O}$. We denote by $Obs(\mathcal{D})$ the set of all observations of $\mathcal{D}$. Systems $\mathcal{D}_C$ and $\mathcal{D}_A$ are said to be *comparable* if they have the same sets of observable variables, i.e., $\mathcal{O}_C = \mathcal{O}_A$ or, alternatively, if there is a 1-1 correspondence between $\mathcal{O}_C$ and $\mathcal{O}_A$. System $\mathcal{D}_A$ is said to be an *abstraction* of the comparable system $\mathcal{D}_C$, denoted $\mathcal{D}_C \sqsubseteq \mathcal{D}_A$, if $Obs(\mathcal{D}_C) \subseteq Obs(\mathcal{D}_A)$. The abstraction relation is reflexive, transitive, and compositional, that is, whenever $\mathcal{D}_C \sqsubseteq \mathcal{D}_A$ then $(\mathcal{D}_C \| Q) \sqsubseteq (\mathcal{D}_A \| Q)$. It is also *property restricting*. That is, if $\mathcal{D}_C \sqsubseteq \mathcal{D}_A$ then $\mathcal{D}_A \models p$ implies that $\mathcal{D}_C \models p$ (see [10] for more details).

All our concrete examples are given in SPL (Simple Programming Language), which is used to represent concurrent programs (e.g., [18,16]). Every SPL program can be compiled into an FDS in a straightforward manner. In particular, every statement in an SPL program contributes a disjunct to the transition relation. For example, the assignment statement "$\ell_0 : y := x + 1; \ \ell_1 :$" contributes to ρ the disjunct

$$\rho_{\ell_0} : \quad at\_\ell_0 \ \wedge \ at\_\ell_1' \ \wedge \ y' = x + 1 \ \wedge \ x' = x.$$

The predicates at_ℓ_0 and at_ℓ_1' stand, respectively, for the assertions $\pi_i = 0$ and $\pi_i' = 1$, where π_i is the control variable denoting the current location within the process to which the statement belongs. Every variable declared in an SPL program is specified as having one of the modes *in*, *out*, *in-out*, or *local*. All but the local variables are observable. The non-input (out and local) variables are owned, while the input variables (in and in-out) are not owned.

Properties are specified in propositional linear time temporal logic (LTL) over the states of $\mathcal{D}$ (see [17], [18] for LTL). A property φ is *valid* over $\mathcal{D}$ if $\sigma \models \varphi$ for every $\sigma \in Comp(\mathcal{D})$.

3   Verification by Abstract Network Invariants

We define a *binary process* $Q(\boldsymbol{x}; \boldsymbol{y})$ to be a process with two ordered sequences of observable variables $\boldsymbol{x}$ and $\boldsymbol{y}$. When $\boldsymbol{x}$ and $\boldsymbol{y}$ consist of a single variable we use the notation $Q(x; y)$. Two binary processes Q and R can be composed to yield another binary process, using the *modular composition* operator $\circ$ defined by

$$(Q \circ R)(\boldsymbol{x}; \boldsymbol{z}) \quad = \quad [\textbf{restrict } \boldsymbol{y} \textbf{ in } Q(\boldsymbol{x}; \boldsymbol{y}) \ \| \ R(\boldsymbol{y}; \boldsymbol{z})]$$

Binary processes $P_1, \dots, P_m$ can be composed into a closed ring structure (having no observables) defined by

$$(P_1 \circ \cdots \circ P_m \circ) = [\textbf{restrict } \boldsymbol{x}_1, \dots, \boldsymbol{x}_m \textbf{ in } \ P_1(\boldsymbol{x}_1; \boldsymbol{x}_2) \ \| \ \cdots \ \| \ P_m(\boldsymbol{x}_m; \boldsymbol{x}_1)]$$

The dangling $\circ$ denotes that process P_m is composed with P_1. In this work we deal with parameterized systems of the form $P(n) = (P_1 \circ \cdots \circ P_n \circ)$, where each P_i is a finite state binary process. Such a system represents an infinite *family* of systems (one for each value of n). Our objective is to verify uniformly (i.e., for every value of $n > 1$) that property p is valid. For simplicity of presentation, assume that the property p only refers to the observable variables of P_1 and that processes $P_1, \ldots, P_{n-1}$ are identical (up to renaming) and can be represented by the generic binary process Q. That is, $P_1(x; y) = \cdots = P_{n-1}(x; y) = Q(x; y)$. The *network invariants method* can be summarized as follows:

1. Devise a *network invariant* $\mathcal{I} = \mathcal{I}(x, y)$ which is an FDS intended to provide an abstraction for the (open) modular composition $Q^k = \underbrace{Q \circ \cdots \circ Q}_{k}$ for any $k \geq 2$.
2. Confirm that $\mathcal{I}$ is indeed a network invariant, by establishing that $Q \sqsubseteq \mathcal{I}$ and $(Q \circ \mathcal{I}) \sqsubseteq \mathcal{I}$.
3. Model check $(P_1 \circ \mathcal{I} \circ P_n \circ) \models p$.

As presented here, the rule is adequate for proving properties of P_1. Another typical situation is when we wish to prove properties of a generic P_j for $j < n$. In this case, we model check in step 3 that $(\mathcal{I} \circ P \circ \mathcal{I} \circ P_n \circ) \models p$.

Verification by the network invariants method entails *model checking* (step 3) and *verifying abstraction* (step 2). Most of the available computer aided verification (CAV) tools for LTL are designed to support verification tasks: They accept a system and an LTL formula as input, and check whether the formula is valid over the system.

Based on the *abstraction mapping* of [1], we present in Fig. 1 a proof rule that reduces the abstraction problem into a verification problem. There, we assume two comparable FDS's, a *concrete* $\mathcal{D}_C : \langle V_C, \mathcal{O}_C, W_C, \Theta_C, \rho_C, \mathcal{J}_C, \mathcal{C}_C \rangle$ and an *abstract* $\mathcal{D}_A : \langle V_A, \mathcal{O}_A, W_A, \Theta_A, \rho_A, \mathcal{J}_A, \mathcal{C}_A \rangle$, and we wish to establish that $\mathcal{D}_C \sqsubseteq \mathcal{D}_A$. Without loss of generality, we assume that $V_C \cap V_A = \emptyset$, and that there exists a 1-1 correspondence between the concrete observables $\mathcal{O}_C$ and the abstract observables $\mathcal{O}_A$.

The method assumes the identification of an *abstraction mapping* $\alpha : (U = \mathcal{E}_\alpha(V_C))$ which assigns expressions over the concrete variables to *some* of the abstract variables $U \subseteq V_A$. For an abstract assertion φ, we denote by $\varphi[\alpha]$ the assertion obtained by replacing the variables in U by their concrete expressions. We say that the abstract state S is an α-image of the concrete state s if the values of $\mathcal{E}_\alpha$ in s equal the values of the variables U in S.

$$
\begin{array}{ll}
\textbf{A1. } \Theta_C \to \exists V_A : \Theta_A[\alpha] & \\
\textbf{A2. } \mathcal{D}_C \models \square(\rho_C \quad \to \quad \exists V'_A : \rho_A[\alpha][\alpha']) & \\
\textbf{A3. } \mathcal{D}_C \models \square(\alpha \to \mathcal{O}_C = \mathcal{O}_A) & \\
\textbf{A4. } \mathcal{D}_C \models \square \Diamond J[\alpha], & \text{for every } J \in \mathcal{J}_A \\
\textbf{A5. } \mathcal{D}_C \models \square \Diamond p[\alpha] \to \square \Diamond q[\alpha], & \text{for every } (p, q) \in \mathcal{C}_A \\
\hline
\multicolumn{2}{c}{\mathcal{D}_C \sqsubseteq \mathcal{D}_A}
\end{array}
$$

Fig. 1. Rule AL-ABS

Premise A1 of the rule states that for every initial concrete state s, it is possible to find an initial abstract state $S \models \Theta_A$, such that $\langle s, S \rangle \models \alpha$. The existential quantification allows to choose arbitrary values for the abstract variables not mapped by α, i.e. the variables in $V_A - U$.

Premise A2 states that for every pair of concrete states, s_1 and s_2, such that s_2 is a ρ_C-successor of s_1, and an abstract state S_1 which is a α-image of s_1, it is possible to find an abstract state S_2 such that S_2 is an α-image of s_2 and is also a ρ_A-successor of S_1. Together, A1 and A2 guarantee that, for every run $s_0, s_1, \ldots$ of $\mathcal{D}_C$ there exists a run $S_0, S_1, \ldots$ of $\mathcal{D}_A$, such that S_j is an α-image of s_j for every $j \geq 0$. Premise A3 states that whenever an abstract state S is an α-image of a concrete state s, then the values of the corresponding observables in the two states match. Premises A4 and A5 ensure that the abstract fairness requirements (justice and compassion, respectively) hold in any abstract state sequence which is a (point-wise) α-image of a concrete computation. It follows that every α-image of a concrete computation σ obtained by applications of premises A1 and A2 is an abstract computation whose observables match the observables of σ. This leads to the following claim:

Claim. If the premises of rule AL-ABS are valid for some choice of α, then $\mathcal{D}_A$ is an abstraction of $\mathcal{D}_C$.

Rule AL-ABS has been implemented in the current TLV-BASIC implementation of the abstraction checker within TLV [20].

As explained in [1], a rule such as AL-ABS cannot be complete unless we allow the mapping at position j to refer to concrete states at positions other than j. This is handled in [1] by augmenting the concrete system by *history* and *prophecy* variables. Following this recommendation, we allow the concrete system to be augmented with a set V_H of *history variables* and a set V_P of *prophecy variables*. We assume that the three sets, V_C, V_H, and V_P, are pairwise disjoint. The result is an augmented concrete system $\mathcal{D}_C^* : \langle V_C^*, \mathcal{O}, W_C^*, \Theta_C^*, \rho_C^*, \mathcal{J}_C, \mathcal{C}_C \rangle$, where

$$V_C^* = V_C \cup V_H \cup V_P \qquad\qquad W_C^* = W \cup V_H$$
$$\Theta_C^* = \Theta_C \wedge \bigwedge_{x \in V_H} (x = f_x(V_C, V_P))$$
$$\rho_C^* = \rho_C \wedge \bigwedge_{x \in V_H} x' = g_x(V_C^*, V_C', V_P') \wedge \bigwedge_{y \in V_P} y = \varphi_y(V_C)$$

In these definitions, each f_x and g_x are state functions, while each $\varphi_y(V_C)$ is a future temporal formula referring only to the variables in V_C. Thus, unlike [1], we use *transition relations* to define the values of history variables, and *future* LTL *formulas* to define the values of prophecy variables. The clause $y = \varphi_y(V_C)$ added to the transition relation implies that at any position $j \geq 0$, the value of the boolean variable y is 1 iff the formula $\varphi_y(V_C)$ holds at this position.

It is not difficult to see that the augmentation scheme proposed above is *non-constraining*. Namely, for every computation σ of the original concrete system $\mathcal{D}_C$ there exists a computation σ^* of $\mathcal{D}_C^*$ such that σ and σ^* agree on the values of the variables in V_C. It follows that rule AL-ABS can be applied to $\mathcal{D}_C^*$

an arbitrary non-constraining augmentation of $\mathcal{D}_C$ and if the premises are valid, then so is the conclusion. This extended version of the rule has been implemented within the TLV model checker. Handling of the prophecy variables definitions is performed by constructing an appropriate *temporal tester* [11] for each of the future temporal formulas appearing in the prophecy schemes, and composing it with the concrete system.

The presented version of the rule is formulated for the case that the abstraction mapping is a *function*. We do have extensions of the rule for the more general case that α is a *relation* rather than a function.

4 Deterministic Dining Philosophers

As a first example, we apply the network invariant method to a deterministic solution to the dining philosophers problem (DDP). As originally described by Dijkstra, n philosophers are seated at a round table, with a fork placed in between each two neighbors. Each philosopher alternates between a thinking phase and a phase in which he becomes hungry and wishes to eat. In order to eat, a philosopher needs to acquire the forks on both its sides. A solution to the problem consists of protocols to the philosophers (and, possibly, forks) that guarantees that no two adjacent philosophers eat at the same time (mutual exclusion) and that every hungry philosopher eventually gets to eat (individual accessibility). It is well known that there are no symmetric deterministic solutions to the problem. In this section we explore a deterministic asymmetric solution. In the next section we explore a non-deterministic symmetric solution.

A deterministic solution to the problem that uses semaphores for forks, is given by a modular composition $(Q^{n-1} \circ C \circ)$, where the binary processes $Q(left; right)$ and $C(left; right)$ are presented in Fig. 2. In this program, $n - 1$ philosophers reach first for the fork on their left, and then for their right fork. One philosopher, C, is a *contrary philosopher*, reaching first for its right fork and only later for its left fork.

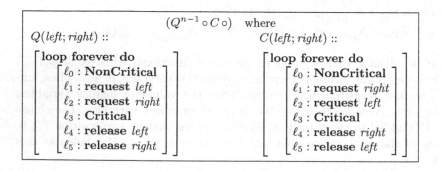

Fig. 2. Program DINE-CONTR: solution with one contrary philosopher

Our goal is to prove the liveness property of individual accessibility (starvation freedom), specified by the formula φ : $at\_\ell_1[j] \implies \Diamond at\_\ell_3[j]$, for every philosopher $j = 1, \ldots, n$. Our strategy is to construct a network invariant $\mathcal{I}(left; right)$ that abstracts a philosophers chain Q^k for any $k \geq 2$. In the following we present two such network invariants.

The *"Two-Halves"* Abstraction

The first network invariant $\mathcal{I}(left; right)$ is presented in Fig. 3 and can be viewed as the parallel composition of two "one-sided" philosophers. The compassion requirement reflects the fact that $\mathcal{I}$ can deadlock at location ℓ_1 only if, from some point on, the fork on the right (*right*) remains continuously unavailable. To establish that $\mathcal{I}$ is a network invariant, we use rule AL-ABS to verify $(Q \circ Q) \sqsubseteq \mathcal{I}$ and $(Q \circ \mathcal{I}) \sqsubseteq \mathcal{I}$, using an obvious abstraction mapping with no augmentation of the concrete system. To show that an arbitrary regular philosopher never starves, we model check

$$(\mathcal{I} \circ Q \circ \mathcal{I} \circ C \circ) \models at\_\ell_1[Q] \implies \Diamond at\_\ell_3[Q]$$

where C is a contrary philosopher.

In [10] we presented a similar two-halves abstraction, that contained a special *chaos* state, used as an escape state for both components of the abstraction, whenever an environment fault is detected. As can be seen by the current abstraction, the use of *chaos* is unnecessary.

The *"Four-by-Three"* Abstraction with Prophecy

An alternative network invariant is obtained by taking $\mathcal{I} = Q^3$, i.e. a chain of 3 philosophers. To prove that this is an invariant, it is sufficient to establish the abstraction $Q^4 \sqsubseteq Q^3$, that is, to prove that 3 philosophers can faithfully emulate 4 philosophers.

Let $Q_1 \circ Q_2 \circ Q_3 \circ Q_4$ and $Q_5 \circ Q_6 \circ Q_7$ be the modular composition of four and three regular philosophers. The abstraction mapping is defined such that Q_5 mimics Q_1 and Q_7 mimics Q_4. As to Q_6, it remains idle until $Q_1 \circ Q_2 \circ Q_3 \circ Q_4$ reaches a *deadlock* ($Q_1, \ldots, Q_4$ all remain at location ℓ_2 with their right forks

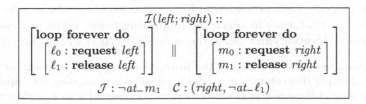

Fig. 3. The Two-Halves Network Invariant

being used), at which point Q_6 joins Q_5 and Q_7 to form a similar deadlock at the abstract level. To sense a guaranteed deadlock, we augment the concrete system with a *prophecy variable* $v \in V_P$ and associate v with the temporal formula $\psi : \Box$ *deadlock*. Namely, v is true in all states of the concrete system which satisfy ψ. The new variable v is then used in the definition of the abstraction mapping.

5   Probabilistic Courteous Philosophers

As a second example, we consider Lehman and Rabin's *courteous philosophers* protocol [14]. The protocol gives a symmetric, distributed solution to the dining philosophers problem, by introducing probabilistic transitions. An SPL code of the protocol is presented in Fig. 4.[2] In this protocol, the forks (represented by the array $y[1..n]$) are shared variables that are reset when held and set when on the table. In addition to the forks, adjacent philosophers $P[i]$ and $P[i \oplus 1]$[3] share a $last[i \oplus 1]$ variable which indicates whether $P[i]$ is the last to have eaten between the two. Each philosopher $P[i]$ has two additional variables $signL[i]$ and $signR[i]$ that signal its wish to eat to its left and right neighbors. In order to choose the first fork to be picked, a philosopher flips a coin, represented by the probabilistic statement **goto** $\{0.5 : \ell_2; 0.5 : \ell_5\}$ at location ℓ_1. A philosopher can pick its first fork (ℓ_2 and ℓ_5) only when the neighbor with whom it shares the fork is either not hungry or is the last to have eaten between the two. Once it gains the first fork, the philosopher checks whether its second fork is available. If it is, it proceeds to eat (ℓ_8). Else, it returns the *first* fork (ℓ_4 and ℓ_7) and returns to flipping the coin (ℓ_1). The justice requirements of the system are the obvious ones, and there are no compassion requirements.

In [14], the protocol is claimed to satisfy individual accessibility to ℓ_8 with probability 1, under the obvious justice requirements and appropriate assumptions about the probabilistic choices. To provide an automatic proof, we perform the following transformations. First, as we prove in [26], in order to prove the accessibility property of the protocol, it suffices to consider a non-probabilistic version of it, where the coin flips in location ℓ_1 are replaced by non-deterministic choices, and compassion requirements are added to capture the fairness required of the coin flips. Next, we reduce the state space by eliminating the variables $y[i]$, $signL[i]$ and $signR[i]$, whose values can be uniquely determined by the locations of the relevant processes.

The result is program DINE presented in Fig. 5. Process Q has the interface list ($lloc, last, loc; loc, rlast, rloc$) in which loc (appearing twice) is the process own program counter (location) and $last$ is the variable declared within the process.

---

[2] In the protocol, as presented in [14], the instructions appearing at location 8 are not atomic. Making them atomic, as we did in our presentation, does not impair the proof since none of these non-atomic assignments are observable to a single process. It does, however, reduce state space for model-checking.

[3] We define $i \oplus 1 = (i \bmod n) + 1$ and $i \ominus 1 = (i - 2 \bmod n) + 1$, so that $n \oplus 1 = 1$ and $1 \ominus 1 = n$.

$$\|_{i=1}^{n} \ P[i] ::$$

```
in     n :              integer where n ≥ 2
local y :               array [1..n] of boolean init 1
local signL, signR :    array [1..n] of boolean init 0
local last :            array [1..n] of {−1, 0, 1} init −1
⌈ loop forever do
  ⌈ ℓ₀ : non-critical
    ℓ₁ : signL[i] := 1; signR[i] := 1; goto {0.5 : ℓ₂; 0.5 : ℓ₅}
    ℓ₂ : await y[i] ∧ (¬signR[i ⊖ 1] ∨ last[i] = 1)
         and then y[i] := 0
    ℓ₃ : If y[i ⊕ 1] = 1
         then y[i ⊕ 1] := 0; goto ℓ₈
    ℓ₄ : y[i] := 1; goto ℓ₁
    ℓ₅ : await y[i ⊕ 1] ∧ (¬signL[i ⊕ 1] ∨ last[i ⊕ 1] = 0)
         and then y[i ⊕ 1] := 0
    ℓ₆ : If y[i] = 1
         then y[i] := 0; goto ℓ₈
    ℓ₇ : y[i ⊕ 1] := 1; goto ℓ₁
    ℓ₈ : ⟨ Critical;   signL[i] := 0; signR[i] := 0
           last[i] := 0; last[i ⊕ 1] := 1;   y[i] := 1; y[i ⊕ 1] := 1 ⟩
```

Fig. 4. The Courteous Philosophers

Variables *lloc* and *rloc* are the locations of the left and right neighbors of Q, respectively, while *rlast* is the *last* variable declared in the right neighbor of Q. Every process in the program is associated with a set of *justice* requirements and a set of *compassion* requirements. The justice requirements are

$$\{loc \neq 1, \quad loc \neq 3, \quad loc \neq 4, \quad loc \neq 6, \quad loc \neq 7, \quad loc \neq 8,$$
$$\neg(loc = 2 \ \wedge \ (lloc = 0 \ \vee \ lloc \in \{0..5\} \wedge last \neq 0)),$$
$$\neg(loc = 5 \ \wedge \ (rloc = 0 \ \vee \ rloc \in \{1, 2, 5..7\} \wedge rlast \neq 1))\}$$

The justice requirements guarantee that no process can get stuck forever at any of the locations $\ell_1, \ell_3, \ell_4, \ell_6, \ell_7, \ell_8$ or at locations ℓ_2, ℓ_5 when their exit conditions are continuously true.

The role of the compassion requirements is to emulate the probabilistic choice at location ℓ_1. The compassion requirements are:

$$\{(entered\_\ell_{2,5} \ \wedge \ cond, \quad entered\_\ell_2 \ \wedge \ cond),$$
$$(entered\_\ell_{2,5} \ \wedge \ cond, \quad entered\_\ell_5 \ \wedge \ cond)\}$$

for each choice of *cond* taken from the following set:

$$\{rloc \in \{0, 8\}, \ rloc \in \{2, 3\}, \ rloc = 4, \ rloc \in \{5, 6\}, \ rloc = 7,$$
$$lloc \in \{0, 8\}, \ lloc \in \{2, 3\}, \ lloc = 4, \ lloc \in \{5, 6\}, \ lloc = 7\}$$

For a location ℓ_i, the predicate *entered*$\_\ell_i$ characterizes all states in which control has just entered ℓ_i. The above requirements guarantee, for each of the conditions

$$Q^n \quad \text{where}$$
$$Q(lloc, last, loc; \ loc, rlast, rloc) ::$$

> ⌈ **local** $last : [-1..1]$ **init** -1
>
> **loop forever do**
>> ⌈ ℓ_0: **Think**
>> ℓ_1: **go to** $\{\ell_2, \ \ell_5\}$
>> ℓ_2: **await** $lloc = 0 \ \lor \ lloc \in \{0..5\} \land last \neq 0$
>> ℓ_3: **if** $rloc \in \{0..2, 5..7\}$ **then go to** ℓ_8
>> ℓ_4: **go to** ℓ_1
>> ℓ_5: **await** $rloc = 0 \ \lor \ rloc \in \{1, 2, 5..7\} \land rlast \neq 1$
>> ℓ_6: **if** $lloc \in \{0..5\}$ **then go to** ℓ_8
>> ℓ_7: **go to** ℓ_1
>> ⌊ ℓ_8: **Eat**; $\quad last := 0$; $\quad rlast := 1$

Fig. 5. Program DINE: Location-based Courteous Philosophers

cond, that if the choice at location ℓ_1 is taken infinitely many times while cond holds, then the computation proceeds infinitely many times from ℓ_1 to ℓ_2 while cond holds and infinitely many times from ℓ_1 to ℓ_5 while cond holds.

Our goal is to establish the accessibility property for the protocol, specified by: $at\_\ell_1[i] \implies \Diamond \ at\_\ell_8[i]$ for every $n \geq 2$ and every $i = 1, \ldots, n$ The proof proceeds in several steps, described below.

No Process Can Get Stuck at Either ℓ_2 or ℓ_5

Consider the closed ring $(Q^n \circ) = (Q_1 \circ \cdots \circ Q_n \circ)$. First, we establish

$$\Box(loc = 5) \quad \implies \quad \Diamond \Box(rloc = 5 \land rlast = 1) \tag{1}$$

for every Q_i within the ring. To establish this property, we consider the open composition $Q^2 = Q_1 \circ Q_2$ consisting of two composed processes in an unrestricted environment and model check property (1) for Q_1 within Q^2. From property (1) we conclude by induction the property

$$\Box \ at\_\ell_5[i] \quad \implies \quad \forall j : [1..n] : \Diamond \Box (at\_\ell_5[j] \land last[j] = 1), \tag{2}$$

claiming that if process Q_i get stuck at ℓ_5 then, eventually all processes get stuck at ℓ_5 with $last[1] = \cdots = last[n] = 1$. We proceed to show that such a situation is impossible. This is due to the invariance of the assertion

$$last[i] \neq -1 \quad \rightarrow \quad \exists j \neq k : last[j] = 0 \land last[k] = 1 \tag{3}$$

The invariance of this assertion follows from the observation that the only transition which can modify the values of $last[i]$ is the exit from ℓ_8 and any execution of this transition sets $last[i] = Q_i.last$ to 0 and $last[i \oplus 1] = Q_i.rlast$ to 1. We conclude that no process can ever get stuck at ℓ_5. In a completely symmetric way we show that no process can ever get stuck at ℓ_2. This allows us to replace binary process Q by a process R which is identical to Q, except that the justice requirements associated with locations ℓ_2 and ℓ_5 are, respectively, $loc \neq 2$ and $loc \neq 5$.

Proving Accessibility for ($R^n \circ$)

We can now prove accessibility for the parametric system $(R_1 \circ \cdots \circ R_n \circ)$, using the network invariants method.

For the network invariant we use a *Two-Halves* abstraction $\mathcal{I} = Left \circ Right$, where process $Left = Left(lloc, last, loc;\ loc, rloc)$ is presented in Fig. 6. Process $Right = Right(lloc, loc;\ loc, rlast, rloc)$ is a mirror image of $Left$ (see [12]), communicating with its right neighbor wherever $Left$ communicates with its left neighbor. Process $Left$ behaves like a regular philosopher with respect to its left fork, but its behavior with respect to the right fork is abstracted by non-deterministic steps (ℓ_3 and ℓ_5). To compensate for the non-determinism and ensure accessibility, the following compassion requirement is added to the process:

$$(loc \in \{2..4\} \ \wedge \ rloc \in \{5..7\}, \quad loc = 8 \ \vee \ rloc = 8)$$

Process $Right$ is defined symmetrically.

For the first step of establishing that $\mathcal{I}$ is a network invariant, we show that $(R_1 \circ R_2 \circ R_1) \sqsubseteq Left \circ Right$. We use the abstraction mapping α given by

$$Left.lloc = R_1.lloc, \quad Left.last = R_1.last, \quad Left.loc = R_1.loc,$$
$$Right.last = R_3.last,$$
$$Right.loc = R_3.loc, \quad Right.rlast = R_3.rlast, \quad Right.rloc = R_3.rloc$$

With this abstraction mapping, it is not difficult to check that premises A1, A2 and A3 hold. In particular, the concrete processes have tests for the statements at locations $\ell_2, \ell_3, \ell_5, \ell_6$ which some of the abstract versions transform into non-deterministic choices. Most of the instances of premises A4 and A5 need not be checked because they are equivalent to their concrete counterparts. The only exception is the abstract compassion requirement

$$(Left.loc \in \{2..4\} \ \wedge \ Right.loc \in \{5..7\}, \quad Left.loc = 8 \ \vee \ Left.loc = 8)$$

which has no concrete counterpart. Consequently, we model check that the system $(R_1 \circ R_2 \circ R_3)$ satisfies

$$\square \diamondsuit (R_1.loc \in \{2..4\} \ \wedge \ R_3.loc \in \{5..7\}) \ \rightarrow \ \square \diamondsuit (R_1.loc = 8 \ \vee \ R_3.loc = 8)$$

Next, we have to show that $(R \circ \mathcal{I}) \sqsubseteq \mathcal{I}$. This task calls for establishing that $(R \circ Left \circ Right) \sqsubseteq (Left \circ Right)$. The proof of this abstraction is similar to the previous one, using a similar abstraction mapping.

Finally, we conclude the verification by model checking the accessibility property

$$(R \circ Left \circ Right \circ) \ \models \ (R.loc = 1) \ \implies \ \diamondsuit (R.loc = 8).$$

114   Yonit Kesten et al.

$Left(lloc, last, loc;\ loc, rloc) ::$

$$
\begin{aligned}
&\textbf{local } last : [-1..1] \textbf{ init } -1 \\
&\textbf{loop forever do} \\
&\quad \ell_0: \quad \textbf{Think} \\
&\quad \ell_1: \quad \textbf{go to } \{\ell_2,\ \ell_5\} \\
&\quad \ell_2: \quad \textbf{await } lloc = 0\ \lor\ lloc \in \{0..5\} \land last \neq 0 \\
&\quad \ell_3: \quad \textbf{go to } \{\ell_4,\ \ell_8\} \\
&\quad \ell_4: \quad \textbf{go to } \ell_1 \\
&\quad \ell_5: \quad \textbf{go to } \{\ell_5,\ \ell_6\} \\
&\quad \ell_6: \quad \textbf{if } lloc \in \{0..5\} \textbf{ then go to } \ell_8 \\
&\quad \ell_7: \quad \textbf{go to } \ell_1 \\
&\quad \ell_8: \quad \textbf{Eat;} \quad last := 0;
\end{aligned}
$$

JUSTICE

$loc \neq 1,\ loc \neq 2,\ loc \neq 3,\ loc \neq 4,$
$loc \neq 5,\ loc \neq 6,\ loc \neq 7,\ loc \neq 8$

COMPASSION

$(loc \in \{2..4\}\ \land\ rloc \in \{5..7\},\quad loc = 8\ \lor\ rloc = 8),$
$(entered\_\ell_{2,5}\ \land\ cond,\quad entered\_\ell_2\ \land\ cond)$
$(entered\_\ell_{2,5}\ \land\ cond,\quad entered\_\ell_5\ \land\ cond)$
for $cond \in \{lloc \in \{0,8\},\ lloc \in \{2,3\},\ lloc = 4,\ lloc \in \{5,6\},\ lloc = 7\}$

Fig. 6. Process *Left*

References

1. M. Abadi and L. Lamport. The existence of refinement mappings. *Theoretical Computer Science*, 82(2):253–284, May 1991. 102, 106, 107
2. K. R. Apt and D. Kozen. Limits for automatic program verification of finite-state concurrent systems. *Information Processing Letters*, 22(6), 1986. 101
3. M. Browne, E. Clarke, and O. Grumberg. Reasoning about networks with many finite state processes. *PODC'86*, pages 240–248. 101, 103
4. E. Clarke, O. Grumberg, and S. Jha. Verifying parametrized networks using abstraction and regular languages. *CONCUR'95*, pages 395–407. 103
5. E. Dijkstra, W. Feijen, and A. van Gasteren. Derivation of a termination detection algorithm for disrtibued computations. *Info. Proc. Lett.*, 16:217–219, 1983. 102
6. E. Emerson and V. Kahlon. Reducing model checking of the many to the few. In *CADE-17*, pages 236–255, 2000. 101
7. E. Emerson and K. Namjoshi. Automatic verification of parameterized synchronous systems. *CAV'96*, LNCS 1102. 101, 103
8. N. Halbwachs, F. Lagnier, and C. Ratel. An experience in proving regular networks of processes by modular model checking. *Acta Informatica*, 29(6/7):523–543, 1992. 103
9. C. Ip and D. Dill. Verifying systems with replicated components in Murφ. *CAV'96*, LNCS 1102. 103
10. Y. Kesten and A. Pnueli. Control and data abstractions: The cornerstones of formal verification. *Software Tools for Technology Transfer*, 2(4):328–342, 2000. 101, 103, 105, 109

11. Y. Kesten and A. Pnueli. Verification by augmented finitary abstraction. *Information and Computation, a special issue on Compositionality*, 163:203–243, 2000. 108

12. Y. Kesten, A. Pnueli, E. Shahar, and L. D. Zuck. Network invariant in action. Technical report, The weizmann Institute of Science, 2002. 103, 113

13. R. P. Kurshan and K. L. McMillan. A structural induction theorem for processes. *Information and Computation*, 117:1–11, 1995. 101, 103

14. D. Lehmann and M. O. Rabin. On the advantages of free choice: A symmetric and fully distributed solution to the dining philosophers problem. *POPL'81*, pages 133–138. 102, 110

15. D. Lesens, N. Halbwachs, and P. Raymond. Automatic verification of parameterized linear networks of processes. *POPL'97*. 103

16. Z. Manna, A. Anuchitanukul, N. Bjørner, A. Browne, E. Chang, M. Colón, L. D. Alfaro, H. Devarajan, H. Sipma, and T. Uribe. STeP: The Stanford Temporal Prover. Stanford, California, 1994. 105

17. Z. Manna and A. Pnueli. *The Temporal Logic of Reactive and Concurrent Systems: Specification*. Springer Verlag, New York, 1991. 105

18. Z. Manna and A. Pnueli. *Temporal Verification of Reactive Systems: Safety*. Springer-Verlag, New York, 1995. 103, 105

19. A. Pnueli, S. Ruah, and L. Zuck. Automatic deductive verification with invisible invariants. *TACAS'01*, LNCS 2031, pages 82–97. 101

20. A. Pnueli and E. Shahar. A platform for combining deductive with algorithmic verification. *CAV'96*, LNCS 1102, pages 184–195. 107

21. A. Pnueli, J. Xu, and L. Zuck. Liveness with $(0, 1, \infty)$-counter abstraction. To appear in *CAV'02*. 101

22. A. Roychoudhury and I. Ramakrishnan. Automated inductive verification of parameterized protocols. *CAV'01*, LNCS 2102. 101, 103

23. Z. Shtadler and O. Grumberg. Network grammars, communication behaviors and automatic verification. *CAV'89*, LNCS 407, pages 151–165. 101, 103

24. A. Sistla and S. German. Reasoning about systems with many processes. *J. ACM*, 39:675–735, 1992. 103

25. P. Wolper and V. Lovinfosse. Verifying properties of large sets of processes with network invariants. *CAV'89*, LNCS 407, pages 68–80. 101, 103

26. L. Zuck, A. Pnueli, and Y. Kesten. Automatic verification of free choice. In *Proc. of the 3rd workshop on Verification, Model Checking, and Abstract Interpretation*, LNCS 2294, 2002. 110

Regular Model Checking Made Simple and Efficient*

Parosh Aziz Abdulla, Bengt Jonsson, Marcus Nilsson**, and Julien d'Orso***

Department of Computer Systems
P.O. Box 337, S-751 05 Uppsala, Sweden
{parosh,bengt,marcusn,juldor}@docs.uu.se

Abstract. We present a new technique for computing the transitive closure of a regular relation characterized by a finite-state transducer. The construction starts from the original transducer, and repeatedly adds new transitions which are compositions of currently existing transitions. Furthermore, we define an equivalence relation which we use to merge states of the transducer during the construction. The equivalence relation can be determined by a simple local check, since it is syntactically characterized in terms of "columns" that label constructed states. This makes our algorithm both simpler to present and more efficient to implement, compared to existing approaches. We have implemented a prototype and carried out verification of a number of parameterized protocols.

1 Introduction

Regular model checking has been proposed as a uniform paradigm for algorithmic verification of several classes of infinite-state systems; in particular *parameterized systems* [KMM+97, ABJN99, BJNT00, PS00]. Such systems arise naturally in many applications. For instance, the specification of a protocol may be parameterized by the number of components which may participate in a given session of the protocol. In such a case, it is interesting to verify the correctness of the protocol, regardless of the number of participants in a particular session. The idea of regular model checking is to perform symbolic reachability analysis, using words over a finite alphabet to represent states, and using finite-state transducers to describe transitions between states. Such an approach has been advocated by, e.g., Kesten et al. [KMM+97], Boigelot and Wolper [WB98], and implemented, e.g., in the Mona [HJJ+96], MoSel [KMMG97], or LASH [BFL] packages.

A generic task in most symbolic model checking paradigms is to compute a representation for the transitive closure of the transition relation. Such a characterization can then be used to compute the set of reachable states (e.g. for

* This work was supported in part by the European Commission (FET project ADVANCE, contract No IST-1999-29082).
** This author is supported in part by Vetenskapsrådet, the Swedish Research Council (http://www.vr.se/).
*** This author is supported in part by ARTES, the Swedish network for real-time research (http://www.artes.uu.se/).

verifying safety properties), or to find loops when verifying liveness properties [BJNT00, PS00].

A central problem in regular model checking is that the standard iteration-based methods for computing transitive closures, which are used for finite-state systems (e.g., [BCMD92]), are guaranteed to terminate only if there is a bound on the distance (in number of transitions) from the initial configurations to any reachable configuration. In general, a parameterized or infinite-state system does not have such a bound. For instance, consider a transition of a parameterized system in which a process passes a token to its neighbour. The transitive closure of such a transition relation will be to pass the token to any other process through an arbitrary sequence of neighbours, for which the number of transitions is unbounded. Therefore, an important challenge in the design of algorithms for computing transitive closures, is to invent techniques in order to enhance the performances of iteration-based methods. One such a technique is that of *accelerations*: try to calculate the effect of arbitrarily long sequences of transitions. Although such an effect is in general not computable, accelerations have successfully been applied for several classes of parameterized and infinite-state systems, e.g., systems with unbounded FIFO channels [BG96, BGWW97, BH97, ABJ98], systems with stacks [BEM97, Cau92, FWW97, ES01] systems with counters [BW94, CJ98], and several classes of parameterized systems [ABJN99, PS00].

In our work [JN00], we gave an explicit representation of a finite-state transducer accepting the transitive closure, for the case that the transition relation satisfies a condition of *bounded local depth*. A related automata-based construction was presented in [BJNT00]. Both these works employ a direct construction of some form of "column transducer", whose states are sequences (columns) of states of the original transducer.

In this paper, we present a technique for computing transitive closures, which is more light-weight than our previous automata-based solutions. The technique uses post-image computation augmented with identification of "equivalent" states. Roughly, the construction of transitive closure proceeds by starting from the original transducer, then repeatedly adding new transitions by simple matching of already constructed transitions. During the construction, equivalent states are merged, using an equivalence relation which preserves the set of traces of the transducer. More precisely, our equivalence relation is the combination of a forward simulation and a backward simulation relation. This makes sure that no prefix/suffix combinations are added to the set of traces. The technique represents a substantial simplification over the previous approaches [JN00, BJNT00], where several layers of automata-theoretic constructions were used. An important property of the equivalence relation is that it can be syntactically characterized in terms of "columns" that label constructed states, and therefore it can be determined by a simple local check. This allows for a much more efficient implementation of the algorithm. In fact, a first implementation of the new, simplified, technique improves the running times of examples by up to a factor of ten. At the same time, the technique does not substantially sacrifice completeness. Completeness results, similar to those in [JN00, BJNT00] can be proven.

Related Work Previous work on the general aspects of regular model checking, and on analyzing classes of systems, e.g., pushdown systems, parameterized systems, systems with FIFO channels, or with counters, has already been mentioned earlier in this introduction.

In [BJNT00], we present a technique for computing the transitive closure of a regular transducer. The technique relies on several potentially expensive operations on automata such as checking language equivalence, computing post-images of regular sets, and saturating regular sets with respect to members of the alphabet. These operations are not needed in the present algorithm, leading to a much more efficient implementation (see Section 5).

Dams et al. [DLS01] present a related approach, which differs from ours in the way states are merged. Dams et al. use an extensional equivalence, which is computed by a global analysis of the current approximation of the transitive closure. It appears that this calculation is very expensive, and the paper does not report successful application of the techniques to examples of similar complexity as the more complex examples in Section 5. In contrast, we base the equivalence on a relation defined in terms of the "columns" that label constructed states, which can be determined by a simple local check. The technique in our proof of Theorem 2 is inspired by the proof technique of their paper.

Caucal [Cau00] presents a class of rewriting systems, called *right-overlapping systems* (and symmetrically also *left-overlapping systems*) for which the transitive closure can be computed as a transducer. A simple instance is the token-passing example mentioned at the beginning of this introduction. Our algorithm is guaranteed to terminate on all overlapping rewriting systems.

Touili [Tou01] presents a technique for computing transitive closures of regular transducers based on *widening*, and shows that the method is sufficiently powerful to simulate earlier constructions described in [ABJN99] and [BMT01]. However, these are substantially weaker than the automata-based techniques. Another approach, based on second order monadic logic [PS00], covers some commonly occurring patterns of successive transduction.

Outline In the next section, we present a simple example which we will use to illustrate our algorithm. In Section 3 we describe the algorithm for computing transitive closures. In Section 4, we show soundness and completeness of the algorithm and present sufficient conditions for termination. Section 5 contains a description of an implementation of the algorithm and the result of applying it to a number of mutual exclusion protocols. Concluding remarks and directions for future research are given in Section 6.

2   An Example

In this section, we present informally, through a simple example, an algorithm which computes R^+, for a regular relation R. It computes successively larger under-approximations of R^+, starting from R. The algorithm consists of repeatedly performing a small basic step which combines two matching transitions of the current approximation. It also uses an equivalence relation on states, for on-the-fly identification of newly produced states.

Preliminaries Let Σ be a finite alphabet of symbols. Let R be a regular relation on Σ, represented by a deterministic finite-state *transducer* $T = \langle Q, q_0, \longrightarrow, F \rangle$ where Q is the set of states, q_0 is the initial state, $\longrightarrow : (Q \times (\Sigma \times \Sigma)) \mapsto Q$ is the transition function, and $F \subseteq Q$ is the set of accepting states. We use $q_1 \xrightarrow{(a,b)} q_2$ to denote that $\longrightarrow (q_1, (a, b)) = q_2$. We use a similar notation also for other types of transition relations introduced later in the paper.

Our goal is to construct a transducer that recognizes the relation R^+, where $R^+ = \cup_{i>0} R^i$.

Starting from T, we can in a straight-forward way construct a transducer for R^+ whose states, called *columns*, are sequences of states in Q, where runs of transitions between columns of length i accept pairs of words in R^i. More precisely, define the *column transducer* for T as the tuple $T^+ = \langle Q^+, q_0^+, \Longrightarrow, F^+ \rangle$ where

- Q^+ is the set of non-empty sequences of states of T,
- q_0^+ is the set of non-empty sequences of the initial state of T,
- $\Longrightarrow : (Q^+ \times (\Sigma \times \Sigma)) \mapsto 2^{Q^+}$ is defined as follows: for any columns $q_1 q_2 \cdots q_m$ and $r_1 r_2 \cdots r_m$, and pair (a, a'), we have $q_1 q_2 \cdots q_m \xRightarrow{(a,a')} r_1 r_2 \cdots r_m$ iff there are $a_0, a_1, \ldots, a_m$ with $a = a_0$ and $a' = a_m$ such that $q_i \xrightarrow{(a_{i-1}, a_i)} r_i$ for $1 \leq i \leq m$,
- F^+ is the set of non-empty sequences of accepting states of T.

Note that although T is deterministic, T^+ needs not be. It is easy to see that T^+ accepts exactly the relation R^+: runs of transitions from q_0^i to columns in F^i accept transductions in R^i. The problem is that T^+ has infinitely many states.

We will use x, y, etc. to denote columns in Q^+ and regular expressions notation for representing sets. In this paper, we present a procedure for incrementally generating a transducer which accepts the same relation as T^+. The procedure starts from T; by successively adding transitions of T^+ we compute a sequence of successively larger (in terms of sets of accepted pairs of words) transducers, all of which under-approximate R^+. Each new approximation is generated through performing a basic step. The step constructs transitions by combining already constructed transitions. Furthermore, all the time during this procedure, "equivalent" columns will be merged, in order to hopefully arrive at a finite-state result.

Example As a running example, consider the transducer below over the alphabet $\{\bot, a, b\}$. It relates a word of the form $\bot^i ab \bot^j$ with $\bot^{i+1} ab \bot^{j-1}$, moving the sequence ab one step to the right. This could be a computation step in a token-passing algorithm.

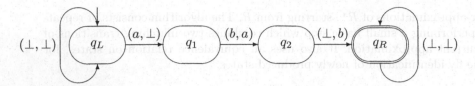

Our algorithm identifies pairs of transitions (of the automaton) and combines them in the following way. When we have a transition from x to x' on (a, b), and a transition from y to y' on (b, c) we add the transition xy to $x'y'$ on (a, c). Furthermore, we define an equivalence relation which enables us to merge columns in the following way. A state in Q is *left-copying* if all words in its prefix consist of pairs of identical symbols. A state in Q is *right-copying* if all words in its suffixes consist of pairs of identical symbols. In the above example, the states q_L and q_R are left- and right-copying, respectively. Now, two columns are *equivalent* if they can be made equal by ignoring repetitions of identical neighbours which are either left- or right-copying. For instance the columns $q_L q_L x q_R$ and $q_L x q_R q_R$ are equivalent. Applying this to our example, we get the following transitions.

- $q_L \overset{(a,\perp)}{\Longrightarrow} q_1$ and $q_L \overset{(\perp,\perp)}{\Longrightarrow} q_L$ give us $q_L q_L \overset{(a,\perp)}{\Longrightarrow} q_1 q_L$. We merge $q_L q_L$ and q_L (both their prefix is $(\perp, \perp)^*$).
- $q_1 \overset{(b,a)}{\Longrightarrow} q_2$ and $q_L \overset{(a,\perp)}{\Longrightarrow} q_1$ give us $q_1 q_L \overset{(b,\perp)}{\Longrightarrow} q_2 q_1$.
- $q_2 \overset{(\perp,b)}{\Longrightarrow} q_R$ and $q_1 \overset{(b,a)}{\Longrightarrow} q_2$ give us $q_2 q_1 \overset{(\perp,a)}{\Longrightarrow} q_R q_2$.
- $q_R \overset{(\perp,\perp)}{\Longrightarrow} q_R$ and $q_2 \overset{(\perp,b)}{\Longrightarrow} q_R$ give us $q_R q_2 \overset{(\perp,b)}{\Longrightarrow} q_R q_R$. We merge $q_R q_R$ and q_R (both their suffix is $(\perp, \perp)^*$).

The new transducer (equivalent to running one step of our algorithm) thus becomes:

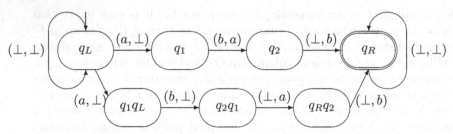

3   Algorithm

In this section, we will formally present our algorithm. The main idea behind the algorithm is to define an equivalence relation on the set Q^+ of columns of T^+, which is used to merge columns during the computation of R^+. Correctness of the algorithm will crucially depend on the property that merging equivalent columns does not change the relation accepted by T^+; this will be proven in Section 4.

Consider first the set Q of states of the transducer T. The set of *left-copying* states in Q is the largest subset of Q such that whenever $q \overset{(a,a')}{\Longrightarrow} q'$ and $q' \in Q$, then $a = a'$ and $q \in Q$. Analogously, the set of *right-copying* states in Q is the largest subset of Q such that whenever $q \overset{(a,a')}{\Longrightarrow} q'$ and $q \in Q$, then $a = a'$ and $q' \in Q$. In other words, prefixes of left-copying states only copy input symbols to output symbols, and similarly for suffixes of right-copying states.

Let us now define $\simeq$. The equivalence classes of $\simeq$ will be sets denoted by regular expressions of form $e_1 e_2 \cdots e_n$ where each e_i is one of the following:

1. q_L^+, for some left-copying state q_L,
2. q_R^+, for some right-copying state q_R,
3. q, for some state q which is neither left-copying nor right-copying,

and where two consecutive e_i can be identical only if they are neither left-copying nor right-copying. For a column x, let $[x]_\simeq$ denote the equivalence class for x. We will use X, Y, etc. to denote equivalence classes of columns.

Define the operator $\star$ as the natural concatenation operator on equivalence classes:

$$[x]_\simeq \star [y]_\simeq = [x \cdot y]_\simeq$$

where $\cdot$ denotes concatenation of columns. It is easy to check that this operation is well-defined. If equivalence classes are represented by their defining regular expressions, this means that $e_1 \cdots e_n \star f_1 \cdots f_m$ is $e_1 \cdots e_n f_1 \cdots f_m$, except when e_n and f_1 are both q^+ for some left- or right-copying state q, in which case it is $e_1 \cdots e_n f_2 \cdots f_m$.

Having defined an equivalence relation $\simeq$ on Q^+, we define the *quotient transducer* $T_\simeq$ as $T_\simeq = \langle Q^+/\simeq, \{q_0\}^+, \Longrightarrow_\simeq, F^+/\simeq \rangle$ where

- $Q^+/\simeq$ is the set of equivalence classes of columns,
- q_0^+ is the initial equivalence class (this will indeed be one equivalence class of $\simeq$),
- $\Longrightarrow_\simeq: ((Q^+/\simeq) \times (\Sigma \times \Sigma)) \mapsto 2^{(Q^+/\simeq)}$ is defined in the natural way as follows. For any columns x, x' and symbols a, a':

$$x \overset{(a,a')}{\Longrightarrow} x' \quad \Rightarrow \quad [x]_\simeq \overset{(a,a')}{\Longrightarrow}_\simeq [x']_\simeq$$

- $F^+/\simeq$ is the partitioning of F^+ with respect to $\simeq$ (this will be well-defined since, as we shall see later, F^+ is a union of equivalence classes).

Our proposed algorithm now builds a sequence $\widetilde{T}_0, \widetilde{T}_1, \widetilde{T}_2, \cdots$ of transducers. The states of each $\widetilde{T}_i$ is $Q^+/\simeq$, and its transition relation will be a subset of $\Longrightarrow_\simeq$. The procedure incrementally adds transitions in $\Longrightarrow_\simeq$ between equivalence classes, and therefore the relations accepted by $\widetilde{T}_0, \widetilde{T}_1, \cdots$ will be successively larger subsets of the relation accepted by $T_\simeq$.

Based on these ideas, here is the **algorithm** for computing a transducer for the transitive closure.

- The initial transducer $\widetilde{T}_0$ is obtained from T by taking all transitions in $\longrightarrow$ and replacing all left- or right-copying states q by q^+.
- In each step of the procedure, $\Longrightarrow_{i+1}$ is obtained from $\Longrightarrow_i$ by adding transitions of form $X \star X' \overset{(a,c)}{\Longrightarrow}_{i+1} Y \star Y'$ such that $X \overset{(a,b)}{\Longrightarrow}_i Y$ and $X' \overset{(b,c)}{\Longrightarrow}_0 Y'$.
- The algorithm terminates when the relation R^+ is accepted by $\widetilde{T}_i$. This can be tested by checking if the language of $\widetilde{T}_i \circ R$ is included in $\widetilde{T}_i$.

Example (ctd.) Continuing our example from Section 2, we arrive at the below transducer after adding some more transitions. At this point, the termination test succeeds, implying that the below transducer indeed accepts the transitive closure of the original relation.

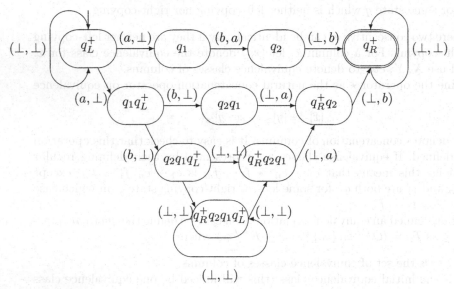

4   Correctness

In this section we show correctness (soundness and completeness) of our construction. We do this in two steps. First, we prove (Corollary 1) that $T_{\simeq}$ is equivalent to T^+ in the sense that both transducers accept the same relation on words. Then, we relate the transducer generated by the algorithm in Section 3 to $T_{\simeq}$ proving its soundness (Theorem 3) and completeness (Theorem 4).

We also present sufficient conditions for termination of the algorithm, which implies that our approach is sufficiently general to cover several classes of systems considered in earlier works.

Before doing this, we need a technical result saying that, since T is deterministic, we can ignore columns containing distinct consecutive left-copying states.

Lemma 1. *Any column x which contains two distinct consecutive left-copying states, i.e., is of form $x = x_1 \cdot q_1 \cdot q_2 \cdot x_2$ where q_1 and q_2 are distinct left-copying states, is unreachable in T^+.*

Proof. Follows directly from the fact that T is deterministic, and that the set of initial states of T^+ is q_0^+. □

Lemma 2. *The relation accepted by T^+ remains the same if we remove all columns that contain two distinct consecutive left-copying states. Analogously, the relation accepted by $T_\simeq$ remains the same if we remove all equivalence classes that contain two distinct consecutive left-copying states.*

Proof. Follows directly from Lemma 1, and the observation that if some column in an equivalence class contains two distinct consecutive left-copying states, then all columns in this equivalence class will also do so. □

In the rest of this paper, we will thus assume that all columns with two distinct consecutive left-copying states are removed from T^+ and $T_\simeq$.

Equivalence of $T_\simeq$ and T^+   The crucial part in proving the equivalence of $T_\simeq$ and T^+ (Corollary 1) is to show (Theorem 1) that the equivalence relation $\simeq$ contains a forward simulation and a backward simulation relation with certain properties.

A relation $\leq_F$ on the set Q^+ of columns is a *forward simulation* if whenever $x \leq_F y$ and $x \overset{(a,b)}{\Longrightarrow} x'$ for columns x, y, x', and symbols a, b, there is a column y' such that $y \overset{(a,b)}{\Longrightarrow} y'$ and $x' \leq_F y'$. Analogously, a relation $\leq_B$ on the set of columns is a *backward simulation* if whenever $x \leq_B y$ and $x' \overset{(a,b)}{\Longrightarrow} x$ for columns x, y, x', and symbols a, b, there is a column y' such that $y' \overset{(a,b)}{\Longrightarrow} y$ and $x' \leq_B y'$.

Theorem 1. *There is a forward simulation $\leq_F$ and a backward simulation $\leq_B$ with $\leq_F \subseteq \simeq$ and $\leq_B \subseteq \simeq$ such that for all columns x and y with $x \simeq y$, there is some column z such that $x \leq_F z$ and $y \leq_B z$.*

Proof. We must define the forward simulation $\leq_F$ and the backward simulation $\leq_B$ on columns. Let x and y be two equivalent columns. Then they must be of form $x = e_1 e_2 \cdots e_n$ and $y = f_1 f_2 \cdots f_n$, where for each k, we have either $e_k = f_k = q$ for some state q, or that $e_k = q^i$ and $f_k = q^j$ for some left- or right-copying state q. Furthermore, no consecutive e_k (or f_k) contain the same left- or right-copying state. Define

 - $e_1 e_2 \cdots e_n \leq_F f_1 f_2 \cdots f_n$ iff in addition $e_k = f_k$ whenever $e_k = q^i$ for some left-copying state q,
 - $e_1 e_2 \cdots e_n \leq_B f_1 f_2 \cdots f_n$ iff in addition $e_k = f_k$ whenever $e_k = q^i$ for some right-copying state q.

Intuitively, $\leq_F$ ignores the number of repetitions of consecutive right-copying states, and $\leq_B$ ignores the number of repetitions of consecutive left-copying states. We must prove that $\leq_F$ is a forward simulation, and that $\leq_B$ is a backward simulation. Let $x = e_1 e_2 \cdots e_n$ and $y = f_1 f_2 \cdots f_n$ be as above.

$\leq_F$: Assume $x \leq_F y$. If $x \overset{(a,b)}{\Longrightarrow} x'$, then x' is of form $x' = e_1'e_2' \cdots e_n'$. We can choose y' as $f_1'f_2' \cdots f_n'$, where $f_k' = e_k'$, except when e_k is of the form q^i for a right-copying state q. However, in this case, since T is deterministic, e_k' will be of form q'^i for a right-copying state q', whence we can choose f_k' as q'^j.

$\leq_B$: Assume $x \leq_B y$. If $x' \overset{(a,b)}{\Longrightarrow} x$, then x' is of form $x' = e_1'e_2' \cdots e_n'$. We can choose y' as $f_1'f_2' \cdots f_n'$, where $f_k' = c_k'$, except when e_k is of the form q^i for a left-copying state q. However, in this case, by Lemma 2, e_k' will be of form q'^i for a left-copying state q', whence we can choose f_k' as q'^j.

For each pair $x = e_1e_2 \cdots e_n$ and $y = f_1f_2 \cdots f_n$ of equivalent columns, we can now find a z with $x \leq_F z$ and $y \leq_B z$ by taking z as $g_1g_2 \cdots g_n$, where g_k is

- e_k if $e_k = f_k$,
- $g_k = e_k$ whenever $e_k = q^i$ for some left-copying state q,
- $g_k = f_k$ whenever $e_k = q^i$ for some right-copying state q.   □

We are now ready to prove the main theorem of this section, namely that the set of traces of $T_{\sim}$ is included in the set of traces of T^+.

Theorem 2. $T_{\sim}$ and T^+ have the same set of traces.

Proof. Notice that since $T_{\sim}$ is a collapsed version of T^+, it will obviously have more traces. We just need to show the inclusion in the other direction.

We will show that for each sequence of transitions of $T_{\sim}$

$$X_0 \overset{(a_1,b_1)}{\Longrightarrow_{\sim}} X_1 \overset{(a_2,b_2)}{\Longrightarrow_{\sim}} \cdots \overset{(a_{n-1},b_{n-1})}{\Longrightarrow_{\sim}} X_{n-1} \overset{(a_n,b_n)}{\Longrightarrow_{\sim}} X_n$$

there is a corresponding sequence of transitions of T^+.

$$x_0 \overset{(a_1,b_1)}{\Longrightarrow} x_1 \overset{(a_2,b_2)}{\Longrightarrow} \cdots \overset{(a_{n-1},b_{n-1})}{\Longrightarrow} x_{n-1} \overset{(a_n,b_n)}{\Longrightarrow} x_n$$

where $x_i \in X_i$ for $i = 0, \ldots, n$. We show this by induction on the length n of the sequence.

- **Base case:** The empty trace is trivially in both $T_{\sim}$ and T^+.
- **Inductive case:** Assume that the property is true for n. Let $w = w_1 \cdot (a_{n+1}, b_{n+1})$ be a trace of length $n + 1$. Then w_1 is a trace of length n, and by the induction hypothesis, there exists a trace of T^+ for w_1 as in the display above. Let w be accepted by the sequence of transitions

$$X_0 \overset{(a_1,b_1)}{\Longrightarrow_{\sim}} \cdots \overset{(a_n,b_n)}{\Longrightarrow_{\sim}} X_n \overset{(a_{n+1},b_{n+1})}{\Longrightarrow_{\sim}} X_{n+1}$$

meaning that there are $y_n \in X_n$ and $y_{n+1} \in X_{n+1}$ such that $y_n \overset{(a_{n+1},b_{n+1})}{\Longrightarrow} y_{n+1}$. Since $x_n \in X_n$ we have $x_n \simeq y_n$, and hence there is a z_n such that $x_n \leq_B z_n$ and $y_n \leq_F z_n$. From $y_n \leq_F z_n$ we infer that there is a $z_{n+1} \in X_{n+1}$ such that

$$z_n \overset{(a_{n+1},b_{n+1})}{\Longrightarrow} z_{n+1}$$

From $x_n \leq_B z_n$ we infer that there is a sequence

$$z_0 \overset{(a_1,b_1)}{\Longrightarrow} \quad \dots \quad \overset{(a_n,b_n)}{\Longrightarrow} z_n$$

such that $x_i \leq_B z_i$ for $i = 0, \dots, n$, implying that $z_i \in X_i$ for $i = 0, \dots, n$. We can thus conclude that the sequence

$$z_0 \overset{(a_1,b_1)}{\Longrightarrow} \quad \dots \quad \overset{(a_n,b_n)}{\Longrightarrow} z_n \overset{(a_{n+1},b_{n+1})}{\Longrightarrow} z_{n+1}$$

satisfies the conditions for the inductive step.

$\square$

From this theorem, we can deduce that $T_\simeq$ and T^+ accept the same relation.

Corollary 1. *$T_\simeq$ and T^+ accept the same relation.*

Proof. We notice that the union of the sets attached to each final state of $T_\simeq$ is the set of final columns of T^+ (they form a partition of it w.r.t $\simeq$). Thus we can conclude that any trace that is an accepting run in one automaton is also an accepting run in the other automaton. $\square$

Soundness and Completeness We are now ready to prove the soundness and completeness of the algorithm. For soundness, we show that the transition relation obtained in each step of the algorithm is contained in $\Longrightarrow_\simeq$.

Theorem 3. *For every k, $\Longrightarrow_k \subseteq \Longrightarrow_\simeq$.*

Proof. For $k = 0$, let X, Y be two equivalence classes such that $X \overset{(a,a')}{\Longrightarrow}_0 Y$ for some pair (a, a'). Since $\Longrightarrow_0$ is obtained from T by substituting each state with its equivalence-class, we must have that $X = [q]_\simeq$ and $Y = [q']_\simeq$ for some states q, q' such that $q \overset{(a,a')}{\longrightarrow} q'$. Thus $X \overset{(a,a')}{\Longrightarrow}_\simeq Y$.

Now take $k > 0$ and assume that for all $k' < k$ we have $\Longrightarrow_{k'} \subseteq \Longrightarrow_\simeq$. Let X, X', Y, Y' be equivalence classes such that $X \overset{(a,b)}{\Longrightarrow}_{k-1} Y$ and $X' \overset{(b,c)}{\Longrightarrow}_0 Y'$. Then we have to show that $X \star X' \overset{(a,c)}{\Longrightarrow}_\simeq Y \star Y'$. By induction, we have that $X \overset{(a,b)}{\Longrightarrow}_\simeq Y$ and $X' \overset{(b,c)}{\Longrightarrow}_\simeq Y'$. Then we must have $x \overset{(a,b)}{\Longrightarrow} y$ and $x' \overset{(b,c)}{\Longrightarrow} y'$ for some x, x', y, y' where $[x]_\simeq = X$, $[x']_\simeq = X'$, $[y]_\simeq = Y$ and $[y']_\simeq = Y'$. We get $x \cdot x' \overset{(a,c)}{\Longrightarrow} y \cdot y'$, and thus by definition of concatenation of equivalence classes, $X \star X' \overset{(a,c)}{\Longrightarrow}_\simeq Y \star Y'$.

$\square$

The following completeness theorem states that any pair in the transitive closure will eventually be generated by the algorithm.

Theorem 4. *Let (w, w') be a word in R^+. Then there is some k such that $\widetilde{T}_k$ accepts (w, w').*

Proof. Let $x_1, x_2, \cdots, x_n$ be a run of T^+ accepting (w, w'). This run can be organized as columns of the following matrix:

$$q_1^1 \xrightarrow{(a_1^0, a_1^1)} q_2^1 \xrightarrow{(a_2^0, a_2^1)} \cdots q_{n-1}^1 \xrightarrow{(a_{n-1}^0, a_{n-1}^1)} q_n^1$$

$$q_1^2 \xrightarrow{(a_1^1, a_1^2)} q_2^2 \xrightarrow{(a_2^1, a_2^2)} \cdots q_{n-1}^2 \xrightarrow{(a_{n-1}^1, a_{n-1}^2)} q_n^2$$

$$\vdots$$

$$q_1^m \xrightarrow{(a_1^{m-1}, a_1^m)} q_2^m \xrightarrow{(a_2^{m-1}, a_2^m)} \cdots q_{n-1}^m \xrightarrow{(a_{n-1}^{m-1}, a_{n-1}^m)} q_n^m$$

where for all i with $1 \leq i < n$ and all j with $1 \leq j \leq m$ we have that $q_i^j \xrightarrow{(a_i^{j-1}, a_i^j)} q_{i+1}^j$. Note that we have $w = a_1^0 \ldots a_{n-1}^0$, $w' = a_1^m \ldots a_{n-1}^m$, and for each i, $x_i = q_i^1 \ldots q_i^m$.

We now prove by induction on the number of rows of this matrix that the pair (w, w') is eventually accepted by the transducer built by the algorithm.

By the definition of $\Longrightarrow_0$ we get that $[q_i^j]_\simeq \xrightarrow{(a_i^{j-1}, a_i^j)}_0 [q_{i+1}^j]_\simeq$, for all i with $1 \leq i < n$ and all j with $1 \leq j \leq m$. Taking $j = 1$, we get that $[q_1^1]_\simeq, [q_2^1]_\simeq, \ldots, [q_n^1]_\simeq$ is a run of $\widetilde{T}_0$ accepting $(a_1^0, a_1^1) \cdot (a_2^0, a_2^1) \ldots (a_{n-1}^0, a_{n-1}^1)$.

Now suppose that in some step i in the algorithm, for some k we have built the transition relation $\Longrightarrow_i$ such that $X_1, X_2, \ldots, X_n$ is a run of $\widetilde{T}_i$ accepting $(a_1^0, a_1^k) \cdot (a_2^0, a_2^k) \cdots (a_{n-1}^0, a_{n-1}^k)$. Then since $[q_1^{k+1}]_\simeq, [q_2^{k+1}]_\simeq, \ldots, [q_n^{k+1}]_\simeq$ is a run of $\widetilde{T}_0$ accepting $(a_1^k, a_1^{k+1}) \cdot (a_2^k, a_2^{k+1}) \cdots (a_{n-1}^k, a_{n-1}^{k+1})$, transitions will be in $\Longrightarrow_{i+1}$ such that $X_1 \star [q_1^{k+1}]_\simeq, X_2 \star [q_2^{k+1}]_\simeq \ldots X_n \star [q_n^{k+1}]_\simeq$ is a run of $\widetilde{T}_{i+1}$ accepting $(a_1^0, a_1^{k+1}) \cdot (a_2^0, a_2^{k+1}) \cdots (a_{n-1}^0, a_{n-1}^{k+1})$. □

Termination The termination of our method is dependent on the number of different equivalence classes of the form $e_1 e_2 \cdots e_n$ which might be generated during construction of the transitive closure. This number in turn depends on two parameters:

1. the number of non-copying states in columns, and
2. the number of alternations of copying states in columns.

Therefore a bound on these two parameters is a sufficient condition for termination.

In [JN00], we introduced a class of systems which satisfied the *bounded local depth* property. Roughly speaking, this property means that there is a bound on the number of times each position in a word is rewritten when applying the transducer to the word an arbitrary number of times. For example, a system passing a token to the right has local depth 2, since each position can be rewritten at most twice; once when passing the token, and once when receiving it. In [JN00], we also assumed that there could only be at most one left-copying state and one right-copying state. For this class of systems, it can be shown that for each pair of words in the transitive closure, there is a run of the column transducer having at most two alternations of the left-copying state and the right-copying state. Thus, our construction will also terminate under the condition of bounded local depth.

Caucal [Cau00] presents a construction of a transducer for the transitive closure of rewriting relations which are called *right-overlapping* (or symmetrically *left-overlapping*). Roughly, this means that each rewritings must occur at the same position or further to the right than the previous. We can adapt these definitions to our framework. Space does not permit a thorough development, but the transducer in Section 2 defines a right-overlapping relation. We can show that our algorithm is able to compute the transitive closure of such relations.

5   Implementation

We have implemented the technique presented in this paper and run it on a number of mutual exclusion and termination detection protocols. We have compared the performance of the algorithm with our earlier work [BJNT00].

The technique in [BJNT00] is based on applying subset construction to the column transducer and on-the-fly identification of equivalent (w.r.t. suffixes) states. The subset construction technique represents sets of states (columns) by finite-state automata and involves several operations on regular sets, such as

- computing post-images of sets of columns represented by finite-state automata,
- *saturating* generated sets of columns, a technique for detecting equivalent sets by adding columns to them, and
- testing saturated sets for equality against all previous sets.

All the above operations can potentially be expensive. In contrast, our new algorithm represents the equivalence classes as vectors of states. The concatenation operator is a variant of concatenation of vectors, and equivalence checking of vectors is fast and can be hashed effectively.

We have implemented an obvious optimization to our new method to avoid generating useless states, namely, in each step, we only merge transitions where $X \stackrel{(a,b)}{\Longrightarrow} X'$ and $Y \stackrel{(b,c)}{\Longrightarrow} Y'$ only if all X, X', Y, Y' are both reachable and productive in the transducer obtained in the previous step. Using this technique, we substantially reduce the number of generated useless states. It should be mentioned that it is not clear whether all operations in the subset construction method are implemented in the most efficient way, since there are many ways to represent automata. Nevertheless, the initial experiments indicate that the new method runs several times faster.

We have measured the BDD node usage and execution times for computing transitive closures of relations used in the mutual exclusion algorithm of Szymanski and the mutual exclusion algorithm of Dijkstra. The results follow the same pattern for all relations. In Fig. 1, the execution time for relations from the algorithms are shown. In Fig. 2, the number of BDD nodes used over time for the computation of the transitive closure for one relation is shown, the

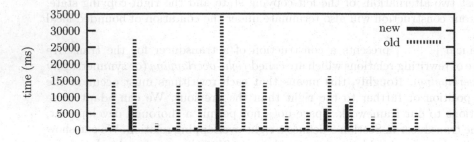

Fig. 1. Execution times for transitive closures of relations. Each relation is a statement in the algorithm of Szymanski or Dijkstra

other relations follow a similar pattern. Note that the instrumentation for this measurement adds to the execution time by a factor up to two.

For all relations, the new algorithm performs better than the old one. However, the difference in BDD node usage is the most dramatic. For the old algorithm, each peak corresponds to finding post-images and then adding them to the current automaton. Each BDD peak for the new method corresponds to a semantic check to see if we have computed the transitive closure. The dramatic usage of BDD nodes for the old method can be explained by the many complicated automata operations described earlier. The new method is simpler, it just combines and adds transitions, giving a low BDD node usage.

We expect to be able to improve the new method further by considering different ways of scheduling the matching operations. Also, it may be possible to find ways to remember already tried combinations to avoid repeated work.

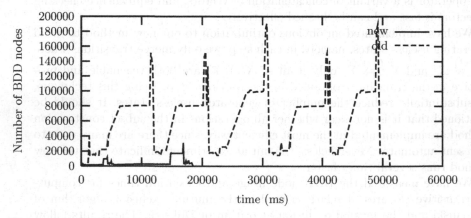

Fig. 2. Typical BDD node usage for transitive closures of relations, in this case a statement in Dijkstra's Algorithm

6 Conclusions and Future Research

We have presented a new technique for performing regular model checking. More precisely, given a finite-state transducer, our algorithm generates a new transducer corresponding to the transitive closure of the original one. The algorithm involves two ingredients, namely a matching operation which combines existing transitions to add new ones, and an equivalence relation which enables us to merge states. An important property of the equivalence relation is that it is syntactically characterized and hence possible to decide locally.

A crucial aspect in the application of the algorithm is the order in which the matching operation is performed on transitions. By defining appropriate matching strategies, we believe that our algorithm can be made both to uniformly simulate existing algorithms for parameterized protocols [JN00, BJNT00], rewriting systems [Cau00], push-down systems [BEM97, Cau92, FWW97], etc, and to produce more efficient versions of these algorithms. Furthermore, we think that the generality of construction will enable us to extend the algorithm to other classes of relations than those on words, e.g., relations on trees and graphs. This would allow us to verify systems with dynamic behaviours such as data security protocols, mobile protocols, etc.

References

[ABJ98]   Parosh Aziz Abdulla, Ahmed Bouajjani, and Bengt Jonsson. On-the-fly analysis of systems with unbounded, lossy fifo channels. In *Proc. CAV '98*, volume 1427 of *LNCS*, pages 305–318, 1998.

[ABJN99]   Parosh Aziz Abdulla, Ahmed Bouajjani, Bengt Jonsson, and Marcus Nilsson. Handling global conditions in parameterized system verification. In *Proc. CAV '99*, volume 1633 of *LNCS*, pages 134–145, 1999.

[BCMD92]   J. R. Burch, E. M. Clarke, K. L. McMillan, and D. L. Dill. Symbolic model checking: 10^{20} states and beyond. *Information and Computation*, 98:142–170, 1992.

[BEM97]   A. Bouajjani, J. Esparza, and O. Maler. Reachability Analysis of Pushdown Automata: Application to Model Checking. In *Proc. CONCUR'97*. LNCS 1243, 1997.

[BFL]   B. Boigelot, J.-M. François, and L. Latour. The Liége automata-based symbolic handler (lash). Available at
           http://www.montefiore.ulg.ac.be/~boigelot/ research/lash/.

[BG96]   B. Boigelot and P. Godefroid. Symbolic verification of communication protocols with infinite state spaces using QDDs. In Alur and Henzinger, editors, *Proc. CAV '96*, volume 1102 of *LNCS*, pages 1–12. Springer Verlag, 1996.

[BGWW97]   B. Boigelot, P. Godefroid, B. Willems, and P. Wolper. The power of QDDs. In *Proc. of the Fourth International Static Analysis Symposium*, LNCS. Springer Verlag, 1997.

[BH97]   A. Bouajjani and P. Habermehl. Symbolic reachability analysis of fifo-channel systems with nonregular sets of configurations. In *Proc. ICALP '97*, 24th *International Colloquium on Automata, Lnaguages, and Programming*, volume 1256 of *LNCS*, 1997.

[BJNT00]   A. Bouajjani, B. Jonsson, M. Nilsson, and T. Touili. Regular model checking. In Emerson and Sistla, editors, *Proc. CAV '00*, volume 1855 of *LNCS*, pages 403–418, 2000.

[BMT01]   A. Bouajjani, A. Muscholl, and T. Touili. Permutation rewriting and algorithmic verification. In *Proc. LICS' 01* 17th *IEEE Int. Symp. on Logic in Computer Science.* IEEE, 2001.

[BW94]   B. Boigelot and P. Wolper. Symbolic verification with periodic sets. In *Proc. CAV '94*, volume 818 of *LNCS*, pages 55–67. Springer Verlag, 1994.

[Cau92]   Didier Caucal. On the regular structure of prefix rewriting. *Theoretical Computer Science*, 106(1):61–86, Nov. 1992.

[Cau00]   Didier Caucal. On word rewriting systems having a rational derivation. In *FOSSACS 2000*, volume 1784 of *LNCS*, pages 48–62, April 2000.

[CJ98]   H. Comon and Y. Jurski. Multiple counters automata, safety analysis and presburger arithmetic. In *CAV'98*. LNCS 1427, 1998.

[DLS01]   D. Dams, Y. Lakhnech, and M. Steffen. Iterating transducers. In G. Berry, H. Comon, and A. Finkel, editors, *Proc. CAV '01*, volume 2102 of *LNCS*, 2001.

[ES01]   J. Esparza and S. Schwoon. A bdd-based model checker for recursive programs. In *Proc. CAV '01*, volume 2102 of *LNCS*, pages 324–336, 2001.

[FWW97]   A. Finkel, B. Willems, and P. Wolper. A direct symbolic approach to model checking pushdown systems (extended abstract). In *Proc. Infinity'97, Electronic Notes in Theoretical Computer Science*, Bologna, 1997.

[HJJ+96]   J. G. Henriksen, J. Jensen, M. Jørgensen, N. Klarlund, B. Paige, T. Rauhe, and A. Sandholm. Mona: Monadic second-order logic in practice. In *Proc. TACAS '95*, volume 1019 of *LNCS*, 1996.

[JN00]   Bengt Jonsson and Marcus Nilsson. Transitive closures of regular relations for verifying infinite-state systems. In S. Graf and M. Schwartzbach, editors, *Proc. TACAS '00*, volume 1785 of *LNCS*, 2000.

[KMM+97]   Y. Kesten, O. Maler, M. Marcus, A. Pnueli, and E. Shahar. Symbolic model checking with rich assertional languages. In O. Grumberg, editor, *Proc. CAV '97*, volume 1254, pages 424–435, Haifa, Israel, 1997. Springer Verlag.

[KMMG97]   P. Kelb, T. Margaria, M. Mendler, and C. Gsottberger. Mosel: A flexible toolset for monadic second–order logic. In *Proc. TACAS '97*, volume 1217 of *LNCS*, pages 183–202, Heidelberg, Germany, March 1997. Springer Verlag.

[PS00]   A. Pnueli and E. Shahar. Liveness and acceleration in parameterized verification. In *Proc. CAV '00*, volume 1855 of *LNCS*, pages 328–343, 2000.

[Tou01]   T. Touili. Regular Model Checking using Widening Techniques. *Electronic Notes in Theoretical Computer Science*, 50(4), 2001. Proc. Workshop on Verification of Parametrized Systems (VEPAS'01), Crete, July, 2001.

[WB98]   Pierre Wolper and Bernard Boigelot. Verifying systems with infinite but regular state spaces. In *Proc. CAV '98*, volume 1427 of *LNCS*, pages 88–97, Vancouver, July 1998. Springer Verlag.

A Hierarchy of Polynomial-Time Computable Simulations for Automata

Kousha Etessami

Bell Labs, Murray Hill, NJ
kousha@research.bell-labs.com

Abstract. We define and provide algorithms for computing a natural hierarchy of simulation relations on the state-spaces of ordinary transition systems, finite automata, and Büchi automata. These simulations enrich ordinary simulation and can be used to obtain greater reduction in the size of automata by computing the automaton quotient with respect to their underlying equivalence. State reduction for Büchi automata is useful for making explicit-state model checking run faster ([EH00, SB00, EWS01]).

We define k-simulations, where 1-simulation corresponds to ordinary simulation and its variants for Büchi automata ([HKR97, EWS01]), and k-simulations, for $k > 1$, generalize the game definition of 1-simulation by allowing the Duplicator to use k pebbles instead of 1 (to "hedge its bets") in response to the Spoiler's move of a single pebble. As k increases, k-simulations are monotonically non-decreasing relations. Indeed, when k reaches n, the number of states of the automaton, the n-simulations defined for finite-automata and for labeled transition systems correspond precisely to language containment and trace containment, respectively. But for each fixed k, the maximal k-simulation relation is computable in polynomial time: $n^{O(k)}$.

This provides a mechanism with which to trade off increased computing time for larger simulation relation size, and more potential reduction in automaton size. We provide algorithms for computing k-simulations using a natural generalization of a prior efficient algorithm based on parity games ([EWS01]) for computing various simulations. Lastly, we observe the relationship between k-simulations and a k-variable interpretation of modal logic.

1 Introduction

Computing simulation relationships between the states of transition systems (Kripke structures), NFAs, and Büchi automata is useful for several purposes. One purpose is to efficiently establish language containment between automata and/or to establish the preservation of properties from fragments of various modal logics. Another important use of simulation is to reduce the state space of an automaton while preserving the underlying language it accepts. This is done by computing the quotient of the automaton with respect to the equivalence underlying a simulation preorder. Smaller Büchi automata obtained in such a

L. Brim et al. (Eds.): CONCUR 2002, LNCS 2421, pp. 131–144, 2002.

manner can be used in the standard algorithms for explicit-state model checking based on Büchi automata ([VW86]), like those used in the tool SPIN ([Hol97]), to make the model checking computation more efficient (see, e.g., [EH00, SB00]).

Thus, in order to obtain the greatest possible state reduction, it is desirable to have as large a "simulation relation" as possible, which still has a quotient that preserves the language of the automaton, and which still remains efficiently computable. Finding the optimal nondeterministic automaton, or computing language containment in general, are well-known PSPACE-hard problems, so one can only hope for efficient solutions that achieve substantial size reduction in practice.

In prior work by this author together with Wilke and Schuller [EWS01], we provided efficient algorithms for computing a variety of simulations (and bisimulations) on the state-space of Büchi automata. These simulations included among them *fair* simulation, introduced by Henzinger, et. al. ([HKR97]), but we also introduced a new notion of simulation called *delayed* simulation, and showed that while *fair* simulation quotients do not preserve the language of an automaton, delayed simulation quotients do and yet they can be arbitrarily coarser (i.e., larger) than standard direct simulation, used in the past for quotienting automata. Our algorithms for computing these simulations used a parity game framework, employing an algorithm by Jurdzinski ([Jur00]) for computing the winner in a parity game. These algorithms have been implemented, and an executable for an optimized translation from temporal logic to Büchi automata using them is available[1].

In this paper we vastly generalize the game-theoretic simulation framework, providing a natural hierarchy of ever-coarser polynomial time computable simulations for labeled transition systems (LTSs), NFAs, and Büchi automata. In the setting of finite automata, these k-simulations allow the Duplicator in the simulation game to perform a kind of partial subset construction, restricted to subsets of size at most k, as it tries to "match" the moves of the Spoiler on nondeterministic automata. Indeed, in the finite automaton case, if n is the number of states of an automaton, then n-simulation corresponds precisely to finite language containment. This is so because subsets of size n suffice to perform the full-fledged subset construction. The situation in the Büchi automaton case is more subtle, but there as well k-simulations can be appropriately defined to generalize the notions of fair and delayed simulation. k-simulations thus provide a parameterized way to trade off the use of more computing resources to obtain larger simulations and hence improved reduction in automaton size via quotients.

The k-simulation games we define are related to, but markedly different from, well-known Ehrenfeucht-Fraisse games for, e.g., k-variable first-order logic (see, e.g., [IK89]). The most important difference is that k-simulation games are peculiarly asymmetric: the Duplicator controls a different number of pebbles than the Spoiler.

---

[1] http://cm.bell-labs.com/who/kousha.

We also observe how k-simulations are naturally related to k-variable interpretations of modal logic and the μ-calculus. This characterization is analogous to the well-known fact that states in a transition system are bisimilar iff they agree on all modal logic properties ([HM85]).

In recent research, simulation quotients have been used for a variety of purposes, including, e.g., indexing and describing the structure of XML data ([ABS99, KSBG02]). We envision that k-simulations, for small k, can be used as richer notions of simulation in any setting where some extra computing time is affordable in order to obtain a larger simulation relation on the state space. This will however be more practical and plausible if the space bounds of our algorithms can be improved upon.

In the next section we present background and definitions, and in the two subsequent sections we prove the desirable properties of k-simulations and we describe the algorithmic framework for computing them using parity games. In the last section we describe the connection to modal logic interpreted over k variables.

2   Background and Definitions

We will not review the standard definition of simulation and its variants incorporating acceptance notions (see [EWS01, HKR97]). Instead we go directly to the general definition of k-simulations and point out how specializing to $k = 1$ naturally yields the standard simulations. We then motivate the general definition with examples. All definitions are presented from a game-theoretic viewpoint.

Our definitions focus on Büchi automata, but many results are relevant for finite automata as well as state machines without acceptance criteria, i.e., labeled transition systems (LTSs). Recall that a Büchi automaton $A = \langle \Sigma, Q, q_I, \Delta, F \rangle$ has an alphabet Σ, a state set Q, an initial state $q_I \in Q$, a transition relation $\Delta \subseteq Q \times \Sigma \times Q$, and a set of final states $F \subseteq Q$. We will henceforth assume that a Büchi automaton has no *dead ends*: from each state there is a path of length ≥ 1 to *some* state in F. It is easy to assure this property without changing the accepting runs from any state, using a simple search to eliminate unnecessary states and transitions.

Recall that a *run* of A is a sequence $\pi = q_0 a_0 q_1 a_1 q_2 \ldots$ of states alternating with letters such that for all i, $(q_i, a_i, q_{i+1}) \in \Delta$. The ω-word associated with π is $w_\pi = a_0 a_1 a_2 \ldots$ The run π is *initial* if it starts with q_I; it is *accepting* if there exist infinitely many i with $q_i \in F$. The ω-language defined by A is $L_\omega(A) = \{ w_\pi \mid \pi \text{ is an initial, accepting run of } A \}$. When we ignore the accepting states F, A can be viewed a basic LTS where every infinite run is considered an accepting run. The set of traces of A, denoted $Tr(A) = \{ w_\pi \mid \pi \text{ is an initial run of } A \}$, constitutes all words over which a run exists. Finally, when A is viewed as an ordinary NFA, the language of finite strings it accepts is denoted $L(A)$. We may want to change the start state of A to a different state q; the revised automaton will be denoted by $A[q]$. We are ready to define the k-simulation game.

Given a Büchi automaton A, $q_0 \in Q$, and a k-tuple[2] (a.k.a., k-vector) $\mathbf{q}'_0 = (q'_{0,1}, \ldots, q'_{0,k}) \in Q^k$ we define the k-*simulation* game $G_A(q_0, \mathbf{q}'_0)$. The game is played by two players, *Spoiler* and *Duplicator*, in rounds. Initially, round 0, a pebble, *Red*, is placed on q_0, and k pebbles ($Blue_1, Blue_2, \ldots, Blue_k$) are placed, respectively, on $q'_{0,1}, \ldots, q'_{0,k}$. We will refer to this vector of blue pebbles as *Blue*. We define a transition relation $\Gamma_{A,k}$ on k-vectors as follows (we write Γ_A when k is apparent from the context). Given $\mathbf{q}_0 = (q_{0,1}, \ldots, q_{0,k})$ and $\mathbf{q}'_0 = (q'_{0,1}, \ldots, q'_{0,k})$, $(\mathbf{q}_0, a, \mathbf{q}'_0) \in \Gamma_A$ iff for each $i \in [k]$ there is some $j \in [k]$ such that $(q_{0,j}, a, q'_{0,i}) \in \Delta$. Note that i and j need not be the same! Assume that at the beginning of round i *Red* is on state q_i and *Blue* is on $\mathbf{q}'_i$. Then:

1. Spoiler chooses a transition $(q_i, a, q_{i+1}) \in \Delta$ and moves *Red* to q_{i+1}.
2. Duplicator, responding, chooses a transition $(\mathbf{q}'_i, a, \mathbf{q}'_{i+1}) \in \Gamma_A$ and moves the vector of *Blue* pebbles to $\mathbf{q}'_{i+1}$. If no such transition exists (i.e., Duplicator can't move) then the game halts and Spoiler wins.

Either the game halts, in which case Spoiler wins, or the game produces two infinite sequences: a run $\pi = q_0 a_0 q_1 a_1 q_2 \ldots$ and a sequence $\pi' = \mathbf{q}'_0 a_0 \mathbf{q}'_1 a_1 \mathbf{q}'_2 \ldots$, built from the transitions taken by the *Red* pebble and the vector of *Blue* pebbles. Given these infinite sequences, there are several ways one can define the winner of the game. Each determines a different notion of k-simulation. Two of the basic notions related to ordinary transition systems and to finite automata, respectively, are as follows:

1. *Ordinary k-simulation game:* denoted $\mathbf{G}^o_A(q_0, \mathbf{q}'_0)$. Duplicator wins, regardless. (In other words, acceptance conditions are ignored; Duplicator wins as long as the game does not halt).
2. *Direct k-simulation game:* denoted $\mathbf{G}^{di}_A(q_0, \mathbf{q}'_0)$. Duplicator wins iff, for all i, if $q_i \in F$, then also $q'_{i,j} \in F$ for <u>some</u> $j \in \{1, \ldots, k\}$.

We will need some definitions in order to present the other notions of k-simulation, designed for Büchi automata. We want to define what it means for a vector of states $\mathbf{q}'_i$ to be *good* since some prior round, which roughly speaking is analogous to a single state q being an accept state.

The vector $\mathbf{q}'_i$ defines the location of all blue pebbles at round i. We will first define what it means for a pebble $Blue_j$ at some round m to have *"seen"* a state q since some prior round i. As a base case, we say $Blue_j$ at round $m = i$ has seen state q since round i if indeed $q'_{i,j} = q$. Inductively, $Blue_j$, at round $m > i$ has seen state q since round i if either $q'_{m,j} = q$ or if there is some r such that $(q'_{m-1,r}, a_{m-1}, q'_{m,j}) \in \Delta$, and such that $Blue_r$ at round $m-1$ has seen state q since round i.

---

[2] We have chosen to describe the states covered by Blue pebbles as a tuple rather than a set. This is done only to make some parts of the presentation more convenient, and in fact the only information from a tuple $\mathbf{q}'$ that matters for all our simulations is the set of states in it; even the mapping of pebbles to states can be taken to be a canonical mapping. This will be described further in the proof of theorem 3 which appears in the appendix.

Now to define goodness of a vector at round m: $\mathbf{q}'_m$ is *good* since round $m' \leq m$ if at round m every pebble $Blue_j$ has seen some accept state since round m' and m is the least round for which this holds. Now we can define the notions of simulation designed for Büchi automata:

3. *Delayed k-simulation game:* denoted $\mathbf{G}_A^{de}(q_0, \mathbf{q}'_0)$. Duplicator wins iff, for all i, if $q_i \in F$, then there exists $j \geq i$ such that $\mathbf{q}'_j$ is good since round i.

4. *Fair k-simulation game:* denoted $\mathbf{G}_A^{f}(q_0, \mathbf{q}'_0)$. Duplicator wins iff $\forall i \exists j \geq i$ such that $\mathbf{q}'_j$ is good since round i, or else there are only finitely many i such that $q_i \in F$ (in other words, if there are infinitely many i such that $q_i \in F$, then for each such i, there exists $j \geq i$ such that $\mathbf{q}'_j$ is good since round i).

Given these notions for simulation games, we now define what it means for a state vector $\mathbf{q}'$ to k-simulate a state q, and using this we also define what it means for a single state q' to k-simulate another state q. We will speak of strategy and winning strategy without formally defining them here. These are standard game theoretic notions (see [EWS01]).

Definition 1. *For an automaton A,*

1. *For each simulation type $\tau \in \{$ordinary, direct, delayed, fair$\}$, we say k-vector $\mathbf{q}'$ τ-k-simulates state q, denoted $q \sqsubseteq_k^\tau \mathbf{q}'$, if Duplicator has a winning strategy in $G_A^\tau(q, \mathbf{q}')$.*
2. *For a single state q', we say q' τ-k-simulates q if $\mathbf{q}' = (q', q', \ldots, q')$ τ-k-simulates q. We overload $\sqsubseteq_k^\tau$ to denote the binary τ-k-simulation relation on states of A. We denote by $\preceq_k^\tau$ the* *transitive closure* *of the binary relation $\sqsubseteq_k^\tau$.*
3. *We define $q \approx_k^\tau q'$ to hold if and only if $q \preceq_k^\tau q'$ and $q' \preceq_k^\tau q$.*

It is not hard to show that for $k > 1$, $\sqsubseteq_k^\tau$ itself is not in general a transitive relation. That is why we define $\preceq_k^\tau$ as the transitive closure. Consequently, $\approx_k^\tau$ is an equivalence. If we restrict attention to 1-simulations, the definition of "goodness" for a 1-vector amounts to nothing more than the state being an accept state, and hence all variants of 1-simulation amount to the same variants of standard simulation given in [EWS01].

To begin to understand the motivation for k-simulations with $k > 1$, consider the automata depicted in Figure 1.

The state q'_0 obviously does not simulate the state q_0. This is because there must be a way for Duplicator to counter a move by Spoiler's *Red* pebble from q_0 to q_1. However, Duplicator, with its single *Blue* pebble, has to choose either to move from q'_0 to q'_1 or to q'_2, and with either choice the Spoiler defeats her in the next move. On the other hand, if Duplicator had two Blue pebbles with which to "hedge its bets" it could move one pebble to q'_1 and the other to q'_2, and in so doing be prepared for any subsequent move by Spoiler. It is trivial to generalize these automata so that exactly k pebbles are necessary and sufficient, rather than 2, for duplicator to be able to win the game. From the definitions, using the example in figure 1, and the examples given in [EWS01], we can establish the following:

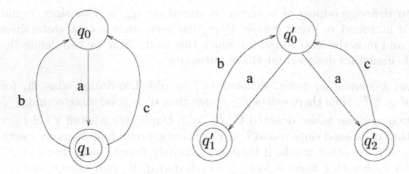

Fig. 1. q_0' 2-simulates q_0 but does not 1-simulate it

Theorem 1. *For $k \geq 1$, $\tau \in \{o, di, de, f\}$, for any A, the following containments hold:*

1. $\preceq_k^\tau \subseteq \preceq_{k+1}^\tau$. *Furthermore, $\forall k$, there are A over which the containment is strict.*
2. $\preceq_k^{di} \subseteq \preceq_k^o$, *and* $\preceq_k^{de} \subseteq \preceq_k^f \subseteq \preceq_k^o$. *Furthermore, for each k there are automata over which all these containments are strict ([EWS01]).*

The example of Figure 1 is a textbook case of why standard simulation is too weak to capture language containment. However, whereas it is PSPACE-complete to compute language containment, as we will see it will only require polynomial time to compute 2-simulations, or k-simulations for any fixed k. Quotients of automata are defined as follows:

Definition 2. For a Büchi automaton A, and an equivalence relation $\approx$ on the states of A, let $[q]$ denote the equivalence class of $q \in Q$ with respect to $\approx$. The *quotient* of A with respect to $\approx$ is the automaton $A/\approx = \langle \Sigma, Q/\approx, \Delta_\approx, [q_I], F_\approx \rangle$ where $\Delta_\approx = \{([q], a, [q']) \mid \exists\, q_0 \in [q],\ q_0' \in [q'],\ \text{such that } (q_0, a, q_0') \in \Delta\}$, and where $F_\approx = \{[q] \mid \exists\, q_0 \in [q] \text{ such that } q_0 \in F\}$.

3   Useful Properties of k-Simulations

In this section we show some basic properties of k-simulations that make them useful for checking language containment and for state space reduction.

Theorem 2. *For $k \geq 1$, for $q, q' \in Q$, where $|Q| = n$:*

1. *If $q \preceq_k^o q'$ then $Tr(A[q]) \subseteq Tr(A[q'])$. Moreover, $q \preceq_n^o q'$ iff $Tr(A[q]) \subseteq Tr(A[q'])$.*
2. *If $q \preceq_k^{di} q'$ then $L(A[q]) \subseteq L(A[q'])$. Furthermore $q \preceq_n^{di} q'$ if and only if $L(A[q]) \subseteq L(A[q'])$.*
3. *For $\tau \in \{de, f\}$: if $q \preceq_k^\tau q'$ then $L_\omega(A[q]) \subseteq L_\omega(A[q'])$.*

Proof. For part 1 and 2, the claim that if $q \preceq_k^{di(o)} q'$ then $L(A[q]) \subseteq L(A[q'])$ ($Tr(A[q]) \subseteq Tr(A[q'])$) follows readily from definitions. The converse for $k = n$, namely that if $L(A[q]) \subseteq L(A[q'])$ then $q \preceq_n^{di} q'$, holds because the Duplicator's strategy will be the standard subset construction: at each round the Duplicator will maintain a pebble on each of the at most n possible states that one could reach from q' using the prefix of the string traversed so far. It is easily seen that the subset construction can also be used to determinize LTSs, and hence $Tr(A[q]) \subseteq Tr(A[q'])$ implies that $q \preceq_n^o q'$.

For part 3, it suffices to prove the statement for $\tau = f$ because by the second part of Proposition 1, $\preceq_k^f$ is larger than $\preceq_k^{de}$. Since set containment is transitive, all we need to show is that if $q \sqsubseteq_k^f q'$ then $L_\omega(A[q]) \subseteq L_\omega(A[q'])$. Suppose $q \sqsubseteq_k^f q'$, and let $\pi = q a_0 q_1 a_1 \ldots$ be an accepting run of Büchi automaton $A[q]$. We want to find an accepting run of $A[q']$ over the same word $w_\pi = a_0 a_1 \ldots$. We know from Duplicator's winning strategy in $G_A^f(q, \mathbf{q}')$ that there exists a sequence $\pi' = \mathbf{q}' a_0 \mathbf{q}'_1 a_1 \ldots$ that witnesses Duplicator's win if the Spoiler's strategy is to play the run π. We will construct an accepting run of $A[q']$ over w using π'. We know that for infinitely many rounds, $i_1 < i_2 < i_3 < \ldots$, $\mathbf{q}'_{i_j}$ is good in π' since prior round $i_{j-1} < i_j$ (setting $i_0 = 0$). By induction on j, we can construct a run such that the run's prefix of length i_j traverses an accept state at least j times. $\qquad\square$

Next, we show that quotienting with respect to delayed k-simulation preserves the ω-language of automaton A, while quotienting with respect to direct k-simulation preserves the finite language. As noted in [EWS01], fair (1-)simulation quotients do not preserve the ω-language of A. Also, as we will see in Proposition 2, unlike direct 1-simulation, direct k-simulation does not preserve the ω-language either.

Proposition 1. *Given a finite automaton A, $L(A/\approx_k^{di}) = L(A)$.*

Proof. We simply observe that the largest direct simulation equivalence, $\approx_n^{di}$, where $n = |A|$, is the language equivalence relation, i.e., $q \approx_n^{di} q'$ iff $L(A[q]) = L(A[q'])$. It is known and easy to show that quotienting a finite automaton with respect to finite language equivalence does not alter the (finite) language of the automaton. Since $\approx_k^{di}$ is a refinement of language equivalence, the claim follows. $\qquad\square$

We now come to a theorem which justifies our definitions for the purpose of state space reduction on Büchi automata.

Theorem 3. *For a Büchi automaton A, $L_\omega(A/\approx_k^{de}) = L_\omega(A)$.*

The proof is involved and is given in the appendix. We now observe that finite language equivalence quotients, and direct k-simulation equivalence quotients, do not preserve ω-languages. This is in contrast to the case of direct 1-simulation ([EH00, SB00]). (We could have defined direct k-simulation is such a way that duplicator must respond to a move to an accept state with a move to a vector

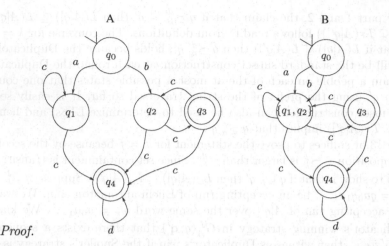

Fig. 2. $A/\approx_2^{di} = B$

all of whose states are accept states, making direct k-simulation strictly weaker than delayed k-simulation. But that definition would have the disadvantage that direct k-simulations would not reach finite language containment as k increases to n.)

Proposition 2. *There are Büchi automata A such that $L_\omega(A/\approx_2^{di}) \neq L_\omega(A)$.* (Hence quotienting with respect to finite language equivalence, i.e., $\approx_{|A|}^{di}$, also does not preserve the ω-language of A.)

Consider the automaton A depicted on the left of Figure 2. The finite language accepted starting at states q_1 and q_2 is identical: c^+d^*. In other words, $q_1 \approx_5^{di} q_2$, and in fact $q_1 \approx_2^{di} q_2$. Hence, the quotient $A/\approx_2^{di}$ is given by the automaton B on the right of Figure 2. However, q_1 and q_2 do not share the same ω-language: $ac^\omega \in L_\omega(B) \setminus L_\omega(A)$. ☐

4   Computing k-Simulations

Our algorithms for computing τ-k-simulations are based on the same framework as the algorithms for computing τ-1-simulations described in [EWS01]. We reduce each simulation computation to a parity game computation, by building an appropriate parity game graph $\mathbf{G}_A^{\tau,k}$, such that q' τ-k-simulates q if an only if Player Zero has a winning strategy from a corresponding node $v_{q,q'}$ in the game graph $\mathbf{G}_A^{\tau,k}$. These parity game graphs have nodes labeled by at most 3 distinct priorities. We then apply an algorithm by Jurdzinski ([Jur00]), along with some enhancements described in [EWS01] which allow us to achieve the desired time and space bounds, to compute the winning nodes in the parity games and thus to compute the simulation relation.

We will not review in full the definition of parity games. See [Jur00, EWS01] for notation that matches ours. A parity game graph $\mathbf{G} = \langle V_0, V_1, E, p \rangle$ has two disjoint sets of vertices, V_0 and V_1 (nodes where it is player *Zero* and player *One*'s turn to play, respectively), whose union is denoted V. There is an edge set $E \subseteq V \times V$, and $p: V \rightarrow \{0, \ldots, d-1\}$ is a mapping that assigns a *priority* to each vertex.

Because these constructions are quite similar to those given in [EWS01], we only describe the most complicated parity game graph here, corresponding to delayed k-simulation, $\mathbf{G}_A^{de,k} = \langle V_0^{de,k}, V_1^{de,k}, E^{de,k}, p^{de,k} \rangle$. Please see [EWS01] for several examples of how parity game graphs are constructed from simulation games. For each state $q \in Q$ and each k-vector $\mathbf{q}' \in Q^k$, each binary bit b, and each binary k-vector $\overline{b}'$ there will be a vertex $v_{(q,\mathbf{q}',b,\overline{b}')} \in V_1^{de,k}$. The bit b will be used to record whether, thus far in the simulation game, the *Red* pebble has seen an accept state without the vector of *Blue* pebbles having been on a good vector since then. The vector $\overline{b}'$ will be used to record, for each pebble $Blue_i$ whether it has seen an accept state since the last time *Red* was on an accept state. The vertices $V_0^{de,k}$ will be similar, but each node $v_{(q,\mathbf{q}',b,\overline{b}',a)}$ will also record the label a of the last transition taken by the *Red* pebble in spoiler's move. The vertices of $\mathbf{G}_A^{de,k}$ are thus as follows:

$$V_1^{de,k} = \{v_{(q,\mathbf{q}',b,\overline{b}')} \mid q \in Q,\ \mathbf{q}' \in Q^k,\ b \in \{0,1\},\ \overline{b}' \in \{0,1\}^k\}\ ,$$

$$V_0^{de,k} = \{v_{(q,\mathbf{q}',b,\overline{b}',a)} \mid \exists q''((q'',a,q) \in \Delta)\}\ .$$

The edges of the game graph reflect the possible moves of spoiler and duplicator in the k-simulation game. Thus edge $(v_{(q,\mathbf{q}',b,\overline{b}')}, v_{(q'',\mathbf{q}',b'',\overline{b}'',a)}) \in E^{de,k}$ corresponds to a move by spoiler of the *Red* pebble from q to q'' using a transition $(q, a, q'') \in \Delta$, while *Blue* is on $\mathbf{q}'$. The bit b is adjusted in b'', so that if q'' is an accept state then b'' is set to 1. Likewise, the bits $\overline{b}'$ are adjusted in $\overline{b}'''$, so that if q'' is an accept state then $\overline{b}'''$ is reset to the all 0 vector. Here, a bit of $\overline{b}'''$ will be set to 1 if the corresponding blue pebble has seen an accept state since the last time *Red* saw an accept state. When all these bits have been set to 1, the bit b will be reset to 0. The edges from vertices in $V_0^{de,k}$ to those in $V_1^{de,k}$ are described similarly, using the appropriate rules that dictate how the bits b and $\overline{b}$ should be modified. The priorities $p^{de,k}(v)$ will be assigned as follows: nodes $v_{(q,\mathbf{q}',b,\overline{b}')}$ in V_1 will get priority b, while nodes in V_0 will get priority 2.

The game graph is such that Zero has a winning strategy from $v_{(q,\mathbf{q}',b,\overline{0})}$ if and only if $\mathbf{q}'$ delayed-k-simulates q, where $b = 1$ if $q \in F$ and $\mathbf{q}'$ is not a vector of final states, and $b = 0$ otherwise. $\mathbf{G}_A^{de,k}$ has $O(2^k n^k m)$ vertices, where m is the number of transitions of A, and it has at most $O(n^{2k-1}2^{2k}m)$ edges. Using the parity game algorithms described in [Jur00, EWS01], and parity game constructions for the other k-simulations, we get:

Theorem 4. *Given a Büchi automaton A with n states and m transitions:*

- *The relations $\sqsubseteq_k^{de}$ and $\sqsubseteq_k^f$ can each be computed in time $O(n^{3k}2^{2k}m)$ and space $O(n^{2k-1}2^{2k}m)$.*

– *The relations $\sqsubseteq_k^{di}$ and $\sqsubseteq_k^o$ can both be computed in time and space $O(n^{2k-1}m)$.*

To compute $\preceq_k^\tau$, we compute the transitive closure of $\sqsubseteq_k^\tau$. Note $\sqsubseteq_1^\tau$ is already transitive ([EWS01]).

5 k-Simulations and Modal Logic

It is well known that finite transition systems are bisimilar iff they satisfy the same propositional modal logic formulas ([HM85]). More generally, the same is true for modal μ-calculus formulas. Related observations regarding fair simulation and bisimulation and fragments of alternation-free μ-calculus have been made in [HKR97, HR00], who introduced an interpretation of alternation-free μ-calculus over fair transition systems. We observe here the analogous relationship between k-simulations and a k-variable interpretation of modal logic and μ-calculus. Consider the basic propositional modal μ-calculus, a logic whose formulas $\mathcal{L}_\mu$ are generated by the following (redundant) grammar:

$$\Phi ::= true \mid \neg\Phi \mid \Phi \vee \Phi \mid \Phi \wedge \Phi \mid \langle a\rangle\Phi \mid X \mid \mu X.\Phi \mid \nu X.\Phi$$

Here a can be any symbol of the alphabet Σ, and X can be any variable from a set $\mathcal{X}$ of propositional variables. The grammar is given redundantly so we can consider several fragments of $\mathcal{L}_\mu$. First, if we restrict the grammar to disallow the three last forms: X, $\mu X.\Phi$, and $\nu X.\Phi$, we obtain ordinary propositional modal logic, $\mathcal{L}_M$. We consider the restriction of $\mathcal{L}_M$ to its existential fragment, $\exists\mathcal{L}_M$, where negation is eliminated, except only when applied to $true$. Also, we consider a similar restriction of $\mathcal{L}_\mu$ to its existential fragment, $\exists\mathcal{L}_\mu$, where again, negation is eliminated except when applied to $true$. Recall the interpretation of a $\mathcal{L}_M$ formula on a transition system $A = (\Sigma, Q, \Delta)$ and distinguished state $q \in Q$ is as follows. $(A, q) \models true$ always holds, boolean combinations are interpreted in the obvious way, and: $(A, q) \models \langle a\rangle\varphi$ iff $\exists q'$ s.t. $(q, a, q') \in \Delta$ and $(A, q') \models \varphi$. The interpretation of $\mathcal{L}_\mu$ follows the usual fixed point semantic which we will not repeat here. We introduce the following k-variable interpretation of formulas in $\mathcal{L}_M$, derived from the definition of k-simulation. Given $(A, q_1, \ldots, q_k)$, where $\mathbf{q} = (q_1, \ldots, q_k) \in Q^k$: again $(A, q_1, \ldots, q_k) \models^k true$, boolean combinations are obvious, and: $(A, q_1, \ldots, q_k) \models^k \langle a\rangle\varphi$ iff $\exists\mathbf{q}' = (q_1' \ldots q_k')$ such that, $(\mathbf{q}, a, \mathbf{q}') \in \Gamma_A$ and $(A, q_1', \ldots, q_k') \models^k \varphi$. The simple relationship to k-simulations, analogous to the Henessey-Milner characterization of bisimulations ([HM85]), is as follows:

Proposition 3. *For any finite transition system A, $q \in Q$, $\mathbf{q}' = (q_1', \ldots, q_k') \in Q^k$, TFAE:*

1. *$q \sqsubseteq_k^o \mathbf{q}'$*
2. *For every $\exists\mathcal{L}_M$ formula φ, if $(A, q) \models \varphi$ then $(A, \mathbf{q}') \models^k \varphi$.*
3. *For every $\exists\mathcal{L}_\mu$ formula ψ, if $(A, q) \models \psi$ then $(A, \mathbf{q}') \models^k \psi$.*

To generalize this to fair structures would first require a suitable k-variable interpretation of alternation-free modal μ-calculus over automata with fairness constraints, analogous to the single variable interpretation defined in [HKR97]. We do not attempt to provide such a definition here.

6 Conclusions

We have shown how simulation can be understood as the first step in a natural progression towards trace containment and language containment for labeled transition systems and finite automata. We have similarly generalized definitions of fair and delayed simulation for Büchi automata to a progression of ever richer k-simulations; these k-simulations, by contrast, do not "reach" ω-language containment as k grows. This is unavoidable if we wish to be able to use quotients for state space reduction, because quotienting with respect to ω-language equivalence itself does not preserve the ω-language of a Büchi automaton. For the purpose of state reduction we have defined the k-simulation variant of delayed simulation, and shown that it does preserve the ω-language upon quotienting. It will be interesting to find an alternative to our definition of fair k-simulation which does "reach" ω-language containment. Such a simulation likely must more closely mimic Safra's construction [Saf88], and since that construction requires Rabin acceptance conditions, it is not likely that the game graph for it will be encodable with 3-priority parity games like our definition.

Our algorithms for computing k-simulations, based on parity games, can be implemented atop the same parity game framework for computing simulations ([EWS01]) that has already been implemented in our Temporal Massage Parlor platform for generating optimized Büchi automata from temporal logic formulas[3]. However, without substantial heuristic optimization the algorithms are inefficient as k grows, because of k's role in the exponents of both the running time and space. Particularly problematic is the space inefficiency of the algorithms, but there is some reason to believe that the worst case space efficiency of the algorithms can be improved. One obvious optimization which mildly mitigates the space inefficiency is to use, rather than k-vectors, k-sets as described in the appendix, to define the position of the *Blue* pebbles at any given round.

Acknowledgement

Thanks to Thomas Wilke for helpful discussions.

References

[ABS99]   S. Abiteboul, P. Buneman, and D. Suciu. *Data on the Web*. Morgan Kaufmann, 1999. 133

[EH00]   K. Etessami and G. Holzmann. Optimizing Büchi automata. In *Proc. of 11th Int. Conf on Concurrency Theory (CONCUR)*, pages 153–167, 2000. 131, 132, 137

[EWS01]   K. Etessami, T. Wilke, and R. Schuller. Fair simulation relations, parity games, and state space reduction for Büchi automata. In *Proc. of ICALP'2001*, pages 694–707, 2001. 131, 132, 133, 135, 136, 137, 138, 139, 140, 141

---

[3] http://cm.bell-labs.com/kousha

[HKR97]   T. Henzinger, O. Kupferman, and S. Rajamani. Fair simulation. In *Proc. of 9th Int. Conf. on Concurrency Theory (CONCUR'97)*, number 1243 in LNCS, pages 273–287, 1997. 131, 132, 133, 140

[HM85]   M. Hennessey and R. Milner. Algebraic laws for nondeterminism and concurrency. *J. of the ACM*, 32(1):137–161, 1985. 133, 140

[Hol97]   G. J. Holzmann. The model checker SPIN. *IEEE Transactions on Software Engineering*, 23(5):279–295, 1997. 132

[HR00]   T. Henzinger and S. Rajamani. Fair bisimulation. In *6th Int. Conf. on Tools and Algorithms for Construction and Analysis of Systems (TACAS'2000)*, LNCS 1785, pages 299–314, 2000. 140

[IK89]   N. Immerman and K. Kozen. Definability with bounded number of bound variables. *Inform. and Comput.*, 83:121–139, 1989. 132

[Jur00]   M. Jurdziński. Small progress measures for solving parity games. In *Proc. 17th Symp. Theoretical Aspects of Comp. Sci. (STACS)*, pages 290–301, 2000. 132, 138, 139

[KSBG02]   R. Kaushik, P. Shenoy, P. Bohannon, and E. Gudes. Exploiting local similarity for indexing of paths in graph structured data. In *Proc. of 18th Int. Conf. on Data Engineering (ICDE)*, 2002. 133

[Saf88]   S. Safra. On the complexity of ω-automata. In *Proc. of 29th Ann. Symp. on Foundations of Comp. Sci.*, pages 319–327, 1988. 141

[SB00]   F. Somenzi and R. Bloem. Efficient Büchi automata from LTL formulae. In *Proceedings of 12th Int. Conf. on Computer Aided Verification*, 2000. 131, 132, 137

[VW86]   M. Y. Vardi and P. Wolper. An automata-theoretic approach to automatic program verification. In *Proc. 1st Symp. on Logic in Comp. Sci. (LICS)*, pages 322–331, 1986. 132

A   Proof of Theorem 3

One direction of the proof is easy: $L_\omega(A) \subseteq L_\omega(A/\approx_k^{de})$. Suppose $q_0 a_0 q_1 a_1 \ldots$ is an accepting run of A, then $[q_0]a_0[q_1]a_1 \ldots$ constitutes an accepting run of $A/\approx_k^{de}$.

The other direction, $L_\omega(A/\approx_k^{de}) \subseteq L_\omega(A)$, will require some lemmas. Before going into the lemmas, we note that for any type of k-simulation, including delayed k-simulation, we need not consider k-tuples $\mathbf{q}_i$, but rather we can view $\mathbf{q}_i$ as sets of at most k states (call them "k-sets") together with a canonical mapping, to be described, from pebbles to those states. Assume the states $Q = \{q_1, \ldots, q_n\}$ are ordered 1 through n. Instead of viewing $\mathbf{q}_i$ as a k-tuple, the only thing that matters is the set of states $\{q_{i_1}, \ldots, q_{i_d}\}$ that are in the k-tuple $\mathbf{q}_i$. Assume $i_1 < i_2 < \ldots < i_d$. We can assume that pebbles are always mapped to states in the following canonical way: for pebbles $j \in \{1, \ldots, d\}$, $Blue_j$ gets mapped to q_{i_j}, and for $j \in \{d+1, \ldots, k\}$, $Blue_j$ gets mapped to q_{i_d}. Note that the transition relation $\Gamma_{A,k}$ remains identical on k-sets as on k-tuples, i.e., whether or not a transition $(\mathbf{q}_i, a, \mathbf{q}_j)$ is in $\Gamma_{A,k}$ is unaffected by whether we view $\mathbf{q}_i, \mathbf{q}_j$ as k-vectors or k-sets. Moreover, a k-vector $\mathbf{q}_j$ in a sequence $\pi = \mathbf{q}_0 a_0 \mathbf{q}_1 \ldots$ will be good since some prior round i if and only if the corresponding k-set $\mathbf{q}_j$ is also good since round i, meaning that each pebble has seen an accept state since round i and j is the least such round $\geq i$.[4] Thus there is no loss of power on the part of Duplicator in viewing $\mathbf{q}_i$ as k-sets, and in fact we could have defined k-simulations in terms of k-sets, but didn't do so only for convenience in some other proofs. Henceforth, we assume $\mathbf{q}_i$ are k-sets.

Lemma 1. *On an automaton A with n states, the binary relation $\sqsubseteq_n^{de}$ is transitive. Hence $q \preceq_n^{de} q' \iff q \sqsubseteq_n^{de} q'$.*

Proof. Suppose, using the n-set notation, that $q \sqsubseteq_n^{de} \{q'\}$ and that $q' \sqsubseteq_n^{de} \{q''\}$. We will show that $q \sqsubseteq_n^{de} \{q''\}$.

Suppose Spoiler plays a run $\pi = q_0 a_0 q_1 a_1 \ldots$ in the game $\mathbf{G}_A^{de}(q, \mathbf{q}_0')$, where $q_0 = q$ and $\mathbf{q}_0' = \{q'\}$. Duplicator's winning strategy in that game supplies a sequence $\pi' = \mathbf{q}_0' a_0 \mathbf{q}_1' a_1 \ldots$, where each $\mathbf{q}_i'$ is an n-set.

We want to supply a sequence $\pi'' = \mathbf{q}_0'' a_0 \mathbf{q}_1'' a_1 \mathbf{q}_2'' \ldots$ such that $\mathbf{q}_0'' = \{q''\}$ and such that Duplicator wins the game $\mathbf{G}_A^{de}(q_0, \mathbf{q}_0'')$ when Spoiler and Duplicator play π and π'', respectively. In constructing π'', we can use Duplicator's winning strategy in the game $\mathbf{G}_A^{de}(q', \mathbf{q}_0'')$. Consider any run $\rho = q_0^\rho a_0 q_1^\rho a_1 \ldots$, such that $q_i^\rho \in \mathbf{q}_i'$. Duplicator, according to its winning strategy, can respond to this run with a winning sequence $\pi_\rho'' = \mathbf{q}_0^\rho a_0 \mathbf{q}_1^\rho a_1 \ldots$. We use these sequences to construct Duplicator's response in the game $\mathbf{G}_A^{de}(q_0, \mathbf{q}_0'')$.

Duplicator's strategy is as follows: suppose that thus far Duplicator has constructed a response $\mathbf{q}_0'' a_0 \mathbf{q}_1'' \ldots \mathbf{q}_i''$ to $q_0 a_0 \ldots a_{i-1} q_i$. In response to the move to q_{i+1} via a_i, duplicator will respond with $\mathbf{q}_{i+1}'' = \cup_\rho \mathbf{q}_{i+1}^\rho$, where the union is over all runs ρ with each $q_i^\rho \in \mathbf{q}_i'$. In other words, Duplicator's response will be to move to the <u>union</u> of all sets that are responses of Duplicator in its winning strategy against any run in the sequence π', which is itself the sequence that provides a win for Duplicator in the game $\mathbf{G}_A^{de}(q, \mathbf{q}')$.

Note that since there are at most n states, we need not worry that the size of the union is too large to be accommodated by n pebbles. We need only show that indeed π'' provides a win for Duplicator in response to π. For this we have to establish that if $q_i \in F$ then there is some $\mathbf{q}_i''$ which is good since round i. We use the fact that if $q_i \in F$ then for each π_ρ', there exists a $j \geq i$ such that $\mathbf{q}_j^\rho$ is good since round i. The crucial observation is that since every pebble in $\mathbf{q}_j^\rho$ has seen an accept state since round i, then for every $j' \geq j$ also, every pebble in $\mathbf{q}_{j'}^\rho$ has seen an accept state since round i. Thus, we let $j^\star$ be the maximum, over all ρ, of the minimum $j \geq i$ such that $\mathbf{q}_j^\rho$ is good since round i, then by construction of π'', there is a j'', $i \leq j'' \leq j^\star$, such that $\mathbf{q}_{j''}''$ is good since round i. That establishes the Lemma. □

Lemma 2. *For a state $q_0 \in Q$ and an n-set $\mathbf{q}_0'$:*

1. *If $q_0 \sqsubseteq_n^{de} \mathbf{q}_0'$ and $(q_0, a, q_1) \in \Delta$, then there is an n-set $\mathbf{q}_1'$ such that $(\mathbf{q}_0', a, \mathbf{q}_1') \in \Gamma_A$, and such that $q_1 \sqsubseteq_n^{de} \mathbf{q}_1'$. Moreover, $\mathbf{q}_1'$ can be taken to be Duplica-*

---

[4] The order in which pebbles see accept states might change, because of the canonical mapping of pebbles to states, but this is irrelevant. Note that if two pebbles in a tuple $\mathbf{q}_j$ are on the same state, then they either both have seen an accept state since some prior round i or they both have not.

tor's response, according to its winning strategy in $\mathbf{G}_A^{de}(q_0, \mathbf{q}_0')$, *to a move by spoiler using* (q_0, a, q_1).

2. *If* $q_0 \sqsubseteq_n^{de} \mathbf{q}_0'$ *and* $[q_0]a_0[q_1]a_1 \ldots$ *is a run of* $A/\approx_n^{de}$ *then there exists a sequence* $\pi' = \mathbf{q}_0' a_0 \mathbf{q}_1' a_1 \ldots$ *such that* $q_i \sqsubseteq_n^{de} \mathbf{q}_i'$ *and* $(\mathbf{q}_i', a_i, \mathbf{q}_{i+1}') \in \Gamma_A$. *Moreover, if* $q_i \in F$ *then for some* $r \geq i$, $\mathbf{q}_r'$ *is good since round* i.

Proof. For the first part, we know Duplicator has a winning strategy in $\mathbf{G}_A^{de}(q_0, \mathbf{q}_0')$. Let $\mathbf{q}_1'$ be Duplicator's response, according to its winning strategy, to a move by Spoiler using edge (q_0, a, q_1). Then $(\mathbf{q}_0', a, \mathbf{q}_1') \in \Gamma_A$. Now, it isn't hard to see that a winning strategy for Duplicator in $\mathbf{G}_A^{de}(q_1, \mathbf{q}_1')$ is given by playing according to Duplicator's winning strategy in $\mathbf{G}_A^{de}(q_0, \mathbf{q}_0')$ after the initial moves of *Red* to q_1 and *Blue* to $\mathbf{q}_1'$.

The second part can be established from the first by induction, using the transitivity of $\sqsubseteq_n^{de}$ established in Lemma 1. The proof is similar to the proof of Lemma 1, and we will not provide all the details here. In constructing the sequence π', we repeatedly combine duplicator strategies by taking the union of the n-sets in those strategies. Note that for all i, there are states $q_i^\star$ and $q_{i+1}^\star$ in $[q_i]$ and $[q_{i+1}]$, respectively, such that $(q_i^\star, a_i, q_{i+1}^\star) \in \Delta$. Thus, since $q_i^\star \sqsubseteq_n^{de} q_i$, and using the transitivity established in Lemma 1, there is a set $\mathbf{q}_{i+1}''$ such that $(\{q_i\}, a_i, \mathbf{q}_{i+1}'') \in \Gamma_A$, and such that $q_{i+1} \sqsubseteq_n^{de} \mathbf{q}_{i+1}''$. Having, by induction, already constructed $\mathbf{q}_i'$, we now construct $\mathbf{q}_{i+1}'$ as the union $\cup_\lambda \mathbf{q}^\lambda$ of the sets $\mathbf{q}^\lambda$ which would constitute a response by duplicator from $\mathbf{q}_i'$ to a move by spoiler from q_i to each $q_\lambda \in \mathbf{q}_{i+1}''$. $\square$

To complete the proof of Theorem 3, we need to establish that if $\pi = [q_0]a_0[q_1]a_1 \ldots$ is an accepting run of $A/\approx_k^{de}$, then there is an accepting run π' of A over the same word w_π. Note that by part 1 of Theorem 1, delayed n-simulation is at least as large a relation as delayed k-simulation, and thus $\pi = [q_0]a_0[q_1]a_1 \ldots$ can also be viewed as an accepting run of $A/\approx_n^{de}$. Hence, using the sequence π' obtained in part 2 of Lemma 2, we can build an accepting run of A on w_π using the same construction as that used to prove part 3 of Theorem 2. This completes the proof.

A Decidable Class
of Asynchronous Distributed Controllers

P. Madhusudan[1*] and P. S. Thiagarajan[2]

[1] Department of Computer and Information Science, University of Pennsylvania
madhusudan@saul.cis.upenn.edu
[2] Department of Computer Science, National University of Singapore
thiagu@comp.nus.edu.sg

Abstract. We study the problem of synthesizing controllers in a natural distributed asynchronous setting: a finite set of plants interact with their local environments and communicate with each other by synchronizing on common actions. The controller-synthesis problem is to come up with a *local* strategy for each plant such that the controlled behaviour of the network meets a specification. We consider linear time specifications and provide, in some sense, a minimal set of restrictions under which this problem is effectively solvable: we show that the controller-synthesis problem under these restrictions is decidable while the problem becomes undecidable if any one or more of these three restrictions are dropped.

1 Introduction

An *open* reactive system interacts with its environment in a sustained fashion and its behaviour crucially depends on this interaction. The key feature of such a system is that one is required to distinguish between the capabilities of the system and its environment. In particular, while the actions performed by the system can be controlled, actions performed by the environment— typically modelling inputs— are uncontrollable. The *controller synthesis* problem arises naturally in such a setting: One starts with an open system— often called a *plant* in this context— and a specification of the desired behaviour of the plant. In this paper, we will be concerned only with *linear time* specifications which typically describe a language of action sequences. The goal now is come up with a strategy to control the actions of the plant so that the overall behaviour meets the specification. Thus the strategy will serve as a *controller* which restricts the behaviour of the plant— and not that of the environment— so that the controlled sequences satisfy the specification.

There is a wealth of literature on this problem and the related problem of *realizability* (which we shall not be concerned with here) for both linear time specifications and branching time specifications [Chu63, BL69, ALW89, PR89a, KV99, KV00]. However, all these studies are carried out in a *sequential* setting.

---

* Supported in part by NSF awards CCR99-70925 and ITR/SY 0121431

L. Brim et al. (Eds.): CONCUR 2002, LNCS 2421, pp. 145–160, 2002.

Controller synthesis problems, however, arise naturally in a distributed framework and here the main results in the literature are the ones due to Pnueli and Rosner [PR90] and some recent extensions [KV01, MT01]. Phrased in the context of the present paper— and in line with the results reported in [MT01]— Pnueli and Rosner exploit the notion of an *architecture* which basically consists of a set of sites and some communication channels between them. In the control-synthesis problem, each site has a plant associated with it which can interact with its local environment. The plants evolve together in lock-step synchronous fashion. One is also given a specification of the action sequences that this network of sites is permitted to generate. The problem is to come with a local strategy at each site so that the distributed controlled behaviour meets the specification. By a local strategy we mean one which knows only about the action sequence that the site has participated in (and any information that it may have thus gained via the communications). The surprising fact is that the controller synthesis problem is undecidable for almost all architectures [PR90, MT01, Mad01]. In [KV01], the authors extend the small class of acyclic decidable architectures to related cyclic architectures.

In this paper, we study the distributed controller synthesis problem in a more general setting, where the processes at the sites can evolve asynchronously with respect to each other. (The framework of [PR89b] is different; there, the interaction between a *global* plant and its environment is asynchronous.) The sites interact with their environments locally and communicate with each other by synchronizing on common actions. We are also given a linear time specification in terms of a regular set of action sequences that this network of sites is allowed to generate. The problem is to come up with local strategies for the sites so that the controlled distributed behaviour meets the specification.

Our main result in this setting is that we can provide a minimal set of restrictions under which the controller synthesis problem becomes decidable. We impose three restrictions R1, R2 and R3 ; while R1 is a restriction on the specification, R2 and R3 have to do with the nature of the local strategies that are permitted.

In the distributed setting we consider, an execution of the network can be naturally viewed as a labelled partial order, rather than as a linear order (i.e. a word). Roughly speaking if there is an execution of the network after which two actions a and b occur, and the processes that are involved with a and b are disjoint, then the actions are not causally dependent on each other and can be viewed as occuring in no particular order. The labelled partial order reflects the events and their causal relation.

R1 demands that the specification must be *robust* in that if one linearization of an execution is in the specification then all its linearizations must also be. Such robust specifications are well studied and there are a number of temporal logics developed in the literature that are, by design, robust (the survey article [HT98] provides a detailed summary). Here, for convenience, we shall be using ω-automata instead of temporal logics to capture specifications, with or without the restriction R1.

Turning now to the other two restrictions, R2 demands that each local strategy can only keep track of the local time and not the local history. More precisely, the strategy can only remember the *length* of the local history but not the history itself. Such a strategy will then be a function of the length of the local history *and* of course the current local state of the plant.

Finally R3 requires that the local strategies follow a *rigid* communication pattern. In other words, at a given stage in the computation, a local strategy cannot recommend two synchronizations that involve two different sets of sites; the synchronization actions recommended must all involve the same set of sites.

Our main positive result is that, if the specification satisfies R1, then determining if there exists a controller that satisfies R2 and R3 is decidable for *all* architectures. Further, whenever a controller exists, we show that we can synthesize a finite-state one. Our main negative result is that if *any* one (or more) of these restrictions is dropped then the corresponding controller synthesis problem is undecidable. For instance, suppose one does not impose any condition on the specifications except that it is regular (i.e. we drop restriction R1). Then determining if there exists a distributed controller is undecidable, whether or not we impose conditions R2 and/or R3. Similarly, we show that we cannot drop the conditions R2 or R3 and retain decidability. It is in this sense R1, R2 and R3 form a minimal set of restrictions in whose presence the controller synthesis problem can be effectively solved in a natural distributed asynchronous framework.

The most severe restriction of the above is R2 which requires that strategies are "clocked" — i.e. that they can only remember the length of the history and not the history itself. We can drop the restriction R2 and instead parameterize the control problem with a number b and require that strategies, in addition to the lengths of the local histories, use no more than b bits to remember information about the local past histories. We believe that this "graded" relaxation of R2 will frequently and quickly yield through an iterative process, a valid controller that meets the specification. However, since the introduction of this bounded memory complicates the technical presentation, we shall not deal with it here except for some additional remarks in the concluding section.

We believe our positive results are relevant for synthesizing distributed controllers for discrete event systems (DES). The objective here is to synthesize a controller for each agent (interacting with its environment) in the plant such that the controlled plant meets the specification. The requirement that the controllers are local and communicate with each other but evolve at different speeds is often essential when modelling spatially separate agents (for example, robots with embedded local control software).

Our results are also relevant to the setting of [PR90], where the model is a synchronous one and all the sites operate in a lock-step fashion. Since the communication pattern can be fixed in such a setting, condition R3 has no effect. Also, one can add a process that acts as a global observer by synchronizing with all the other processes. The specification can then be stated as a local specification (which is always robust) of this observer, and hence we can drop restriction

R1 as well. As a result, in the [PR90] framework, the controller synthesis problem is undecidable for almost all architectures if one imposes no restrictions and it becomes decidable for *all* architectures if we demand R2.

Turning briefly to the proof of decidability, the key insight is that in the presence of R2 and R3, our strategies can be encoded as restricted labelled partial orders called *Mazurkiewicz traces* which have a rich theory [DR95]. We handle these partial orders here via their linearizations. We show then that we can design an automaton to check whether a strategy (encoded as linearizations of a trace) is winning or not. The major technical hurdle is that we need to ensure that the choice of the linearization used to represent strategies does not interfere with the correctness of the decision procedure, and this crucially requires the fact that the specification satisfies R1.

The key technique for all the undecidability results is a reduction borrowed from [PR90] (see also [PR79]) with some insights provided by the undecidability arguments developed in

2   The Problem Setting

We fix a finite set of processes $\mathcal{P}$ for the rest of the paper and let p, q range over $\mathcal{P}$. A distributed alphabet over $\mathcal{P}$ is a pair (Σ, θ) where Σ is a finite alphabet of actions and $\theta : \Sigma \to 2^{\mathcal{P}} \setminus \{\emptyset\}$ identifies for each action, a nonempty set of processes that take part in each execution of the action. Let $\Sigma_p = \{a \in \Sigma \mid p \in \theta(a)\}$ denote the set of actions the process p partakes in. Fix such a distributed alphabet (Σ, θ) for the rest of this section.

Definition 1. *A product system $\mathcal{S}$ over (Σ, θ) is a family of transition systems, $\{(S_p^E, S_p^C, \Sigma_p^E, \Sigma_p^C, \to_p, s_{in}^p)\}_{p \in \mathcal{P}}$, where for each process $p \in \mathcal{P}$:*

- $S_p = S_p^E \uplus S_p^C$ *is the finite set of local states of p, with S_p^E denoting environment states and S_p^C denoting controller states. S_p^E and S_p^C are disjoint;*
- Σ_p^E *and Σ_p^C form a partition of Σ_p and denote the* environment actions *and* controllable actions, *respectively. We also require that environment actions are local— i.e. for every $e \in \Sigma_p^E$, $\theta(e) = \{p\}$;*
- $\to_p \subseteq (S_p^E \times \Sigma_p^E \times S_p^C) \cup (S_p^C \times \Sigma_p^C \times S_p^E)$ *is the deterministic localized transition relation (i.e. if $(s, a, s'), (s, a, s'') \in \to_p$, then $s' = s''$). Note that the system alternates between system states and environment states;*
- $s_{in}^p \in S_p^C$ *is the local initial state and is a controller state.* □

A product system is hence a set of local systems, one for each process, where each local system alternately performs controllable actions and environment actions. The coordination among the processes is achieved by synchronizing on common actions as dictated by the distribution function θ. We write $s \xrightarrow{a}_p s'$ to denote $(s, a, s') \in \to_p$. A state in S_p is called a p-state. A state $s \in \bigcup_{p \in \mathcal{P}} S_p$ is called a *local state*. For a p-state $s \in S_p$, let $en(s)$ denote the set of actions locally enabled at s— i.e. $en(s) = \{a \in \Sigma_p \mid \exists s' \in S_p, s \xrightarrow{a}_p s'\}$.

A global state of a product system $\mathcal{S}$ is a function $\mathbf{s} : \mathcal{P} \to \bigcup_{p \in \mathcal{P}} S_p$ such that $\mathbf{s}(p) \in S_p$, for each $p \in \mathcal{P}$. Let $S_\mathcal{P}$ be the set of all global states. The *global system* associated with a product system $\mathcal{S}$ is the transition system $\mathcal{G}_\mathcal{S} = (S_\mathcal{P}, \Sigma, \Rightarrow, \mathbf{s}_{in})$ where $\mathbf{s}_{in} \in S_\mathcal{P}$ is the global initial state with $\mathbf{s}_{in}(p) = s_{in}^p$, for each $p \in \mathcal{P}$. As usual, the transition relation $\Rightarrow \subseteq S_\mathcal{P} \times \Sigma \times S_\mathcal{P}$ is given by: $(\mathbf{s}, a, \mathbf{s}') \in \Rightarrow$ iff $\mathbf{s}(p) \xrightarrow{a}_p \mathbf{s}'(p)$, for every $p \in \theta(a)$ and $\mathbf{s}(p') = \mathbf{s}'(p')$, for every $p' \notin \theta(a)$.

Example 1. Consider the *dining-philosophers problem*. There are n philosophers (processes) P_i, $0 \le i < n$ in a ring and there are n forks f_i, $0 \le i < n$ — one fork between each neighbouring pair of processes. The philosophers can be thinking and when they get hungry, they need both forks (look upon these as resources) to eat. When they finish eating, they go back to the thinking state.

This problem can be modelled by having $2n$ processes, one for each philosopher and one for each fork — say $\{P_i, f_i \mid 0 \le i < n\}$. The philosopher P_i, when thinking, can go into a state of hunger at any time, and send requests for the neighbouring forks f_{i-1} and f_i, in any order (addition and subtraction are modulo n). When (s)he gets both, (s)he goes into a state where (s)he eats and after finishing, goes back to the thinking state. We model this by having:
$$\Sigma_{P_i} = \{hungry_i, reqf_{(i,i)}, reqf_{(i,i-1)}, grf_{(i,i)}, grf_{(i,i-1)}, eat_i, finish_i, \tau_i, \beta_i\} \text{ and}$$
$$\Sigma_{f_i} = \{reqf_{(i,i)}, reqf_{(i+1,i)}, grf_{(i,i)}, grf_{(i+1,i)}, \tau_i'\}$$
The action $reqf_{(i,j)}$ is interpreted as the i'th philosopher requesting the j'th fork and $grf_{(i,j)}$ means the i'th philosopher is granted the j'th fork.

We can now have a transition system, for each philosopher, that models the philosopher getting hungry, requesting for his left and right forks (he can request in any order), getting them, eating and going back to the thinking state. Forks are also modelled as processes that get requests and grant them to philosophers requesting them. The environment actions are the local actions of the kind $hungry_i$, $finish_i$, τ_i and τ_i'. The τ_i and τ_i' actions are "dummy" actions used to interleave system actions with environment actions. Similarly, β_i actions are dummy system actions. We shall return to this example after introducing strategies.

Let Σ^* denote the set of finite words over Σ, Σ^ω denote the set of infinite words over Σ and $\Sigma^\infty = \Sigma^* \cup \Sigma^\omega$. For a word $\alpha \in \Sigma^\omega$ and $i, j \in \mathbb{N}$, let $\alpha[i]$ denote the ith letter of α and $\alpha[i, j]$ denote the subsequence $\alpha[i]\alpha[i+1] \ldots \alpha[j]$. This notation is extended to finite words as well, for appropriate values of i and j. Also, for a language of finite words $L \subseteq \Sigma^*$, let L^* and L^ω denote the languages obtained by finite and infinite iterations of words in L. These notations are transported to other alphabets as well in the obvious way.

The distributed alphabet (Σ, θ) induces a natural equivalence relation over words over Σ. For a word $\alpha \in \Sigma^\infty$ and $\Sigma' \subseteq \Sigma$, let $\alpha \restriction \Sigma'$ denote the projection of α to the letters in Σ'. By abuse of notation, let $\alpha \restriction p$ denote $\alpha \restriction \Sigma_p$. The *Mazurkiewicz trace relation* (or just *trace relation*) associated with (Σ, θ) is the relation $\approx \subseteq \Sigma^\infty \times \Sigma^\infty$ given by $\alpha \approx \beta$ iff for every $p \in \mathcal{P}$, $\alpha \restriction p = \beta \restriction p$. We say a language $L \subseteq \Sigma^\infty$ is *trace-closed* if for every $\alpha \in L$ and $\beta \in \Sigma^\infty$ such that $\alpha \approx \beta$, we have $\beta \in L$. This is just a way of specifying a Mazurkiewicz trace language where a trace is a $\approx$-equivalence class or equivalently a suitably axiomatized Σ-labelled poset (see [DR95]).

A transition system over Σ is a tuple $TS = (S, \Sigma, \delta, s_{in})$ where S is a finite set of states, $s_{in} \in S$ is the initial state and $\delta \subseteq S \times \Sigma \times S$ is the transition relation. TS is said to be total if for every $s \in S$, $a \in \Sigma$, there is at least one transition of the form $(s, a, s') \in \delta$. For a word $\alpha \in \Sigma^\omega$, a run of a transition system $TS = (S, \Sigma, \delta, s_{in})$ on α is a sequence of states $\rho = s_1, s_2, \ldots$ such that $s_1 = s_{in}$ and $\forall i \in \mathbb{N}$, $s_i \xrightarrow{\alpha[i]} s_{i+1}$. Runs of TS on finite words are defined similarly. The set of infinite words over which TS has a run is called the language of TS (denoted $\mathcal{L}(TS)$).

For a product system $\mathcal{S}$ over (Σ, θ), the language of infinite words of $\mathcal{S}$ is the language of the global system associated with $\mathcal{S}$. In other words, $\mathcal{L}(\mathcal{S}) = \mathcal{L}(\mathcal{G}_\mathcal{S})$. It is easy to see that $\mathcal{L}(\mathcal{S})$ is trace-closed with respect to the equivalence relation induced by (Σ, θ).

A *plant* $\mathcal{S}$ is a product system over (Σ, θ), $\mathcal{S} = \{(S_p^E, S_p^C, \Sigma_p^E, \Sigma_p^C, \rightarrow_p , s_{in}^p)\}_{p \in \mathcal{P}}$. Let us fix such a plant. For $p \in \mathcal{P}$, an *advice function* for p is a map $\xi_p : S_p \rightarrow 2^{\Sigma_p}$ such that $\xi_p(s) \subseteq en(s)$, for each $s \in S_p$, and further, if $s \in S_p^E$, then $\xi_p(s) = en(s)$. The advice function thus recommends a subset of the enabled actions at each state s in S_p, while recommending all the enabled actions at s, if s is an environment state. Let Δ_p denote the set of advice functions for p.

For $p \in \mathcal{P}$, a *local strategy for p* is a function $f_p : \Sigma_p^* \rightarrow \Delta_p$. If p executes a sequence of actions $w \in \Sigma_p^*$ and reaches a state $s \in S_p$, the strategy recommends that the actions in $(f_p(w))(s)$ be offered as possible moves by the plant. A *controller* (or *strategy*) is a set of local strategies, $Str = \{f_p\}_{p \in \mathcal{P}}$, where each f_p is a local strategy for p.

Let us fix a strategy $Str = \{f_p\}_{p \in \mathcal{P}}$ for $\mathcal{S}$. A word $\alpha \in \Sigma^\infty$ is said to be a *play according to* the strategy Str if there is a run $\rho = \mathbf{s}_1, \mathbf{s}_2, \ldots$ of $\mathcal{G}_\mathcal{S}$ on α such that for every $0 \leq i < |\alpha|$:

$$\alpha[i+1] \in f_p(\alpha[1, i] \upharpoonright p)(\mathbf{s}_{i+1}(p)), \text{ for every } p \in \theta(\alpha[i+1])$$

Thus a play under a strategy is just a word that can be executed by the plant when it respects the moves suggested by the strategy. At any stage the strategies of the components that take part in an action are consulted and the move can be made provided all of them are willing to make the move. Note that the strategy for a process p "knows" only the history of local events ($\alpha[1, i] \upharpoonright p$) that have taken place. We denote the set of finite plays and infinite plays according to Str as $plays_\mathcal{S}^f(Str)$ and $plays_\mathcal{S}(Str)$, respectively. It is easy to see that these sets are in fact trace-closed, with respect to (Σ, θ).

A strategy Str for $\mathcal{S}$ is said to be *non-blocking* if every finite play can be extended— i.e. $\forall x \in plays_\mathcal{S}^f(Str), \exists a \in \Sigma : xa \in plays_\mathcal{S}^f(Str)$.

A local strategy $f_p : \Sigma_p^* \rightarrow \Delta_p$ is said to be *finite-state* if there is a deterministic total transition system $TS_{f_p} = (R, \Sigma_p, \delta, r_{in})$ and a function $h : R \rightarrow \Delta_p$ such that for any $w \in \Sigma_p^*$, if the state reached by TS_{f_p} on w is r, then $h(r) = f_p(w)$. A strategy Str is said to be finite-state if each of its local strategies is finite-state.

Specifications that the controlled plant has to satisfy are given as ω-regular languages over Σ. A Büchi automaton over Σ is a structure $\mathcal{A} = (Q, \Sigma, \delta, q_{in}, F)$ where $(Q, \Sigma, \delta, q_{in})$ is a total transition system and $F \subseteq Q$ is the set of *good* states (see [Tho90]). A run of $\mathcal{A}$ over a word $\alpha \in \Sigma^\omega$ is a run over the underlying transition system. For a run $\rho \in Q^\omega$, let $inf(\rho)$ denote the set of states that occur infinitely often in ρ. A run ρ is said to accepting if $inf(\rho) \cap F \neq \emptyset$. A word α is accepted by $\mathcal{A}$ if there is an accepting run of $\mathcal{A}$ on α. The set of words accepted by $\mathcal{A}$ is called the language of $\mathcal{A}$ and denoted by $\mathcal{L}(\mathcal{A})$. A language $\mathcal{L} \subseteq \Sigma^\omega$ is said to be an ω-regular language if there is a Büchi automaton $\mathcal{A}$ over Σ such that $\mathcal{L}(\mathcal{A}) = \mathcal{L}$.

The general control-synthesis problem in our setting is: Given a finite plant S over (Σ, θ) and an ω-regular language $\mathcal{L}_{spec} \subseteq \Sigma^\omega$, is there a nonblocking controller Str for S such that $plays_S(Str) \subseteq \mathcal{L}_{spec}$?

Consider the dining-philosophers' problem described earlier. The specification can now include all sequences α where a philosopher, when (s)he gets hungry, always gets to eat (along with some fairness assumptions that one can enforce on α). A valid controller now will be a local program at each site (typically modelling in which way each philosopher requests for forks — left first or right first *and* in which way the fork-processes grant these requests) and will ensure that no philosopher starves.

As we show later, the general control-synthesis problem is undecidable. We impose three restrictions on the problem, which we now describe formally.

A local strategy f_p for p is said to be *clocked* if the advice the strategy offers depends only on the *length* of the history and not on the history itself. Formally, $f_p : \Sigma_p^* \to \Delta_p$ is clocked if for every $x, y \in \Sigma_p^*$ such that $|x| = |y|$, $f_p(x) = f_p(y)$. A strategy Str for S is said to be clocked if all the local strategies of Str are clocked. Note that since clocked strategies map into advice functions, the recommendation of the strategy also depends on the current local plant state.

A strategy $Str = \{f_p\}_{p \in \mathcal{P}}$ for S is called a *com-rigid* ("communication-rigid") strategy if, for every $p \in \mathcal{P}$, $w \in \Sigma_p^*$, there exists a set $X \subseteq \mathcal{P}$ such that for every $s \in S_p^C$ and $a \in f_p(w)(s)$, $\theta(a) = X$. In other words, if at any stage a local strategy offers a set of actions, the processes involved in these actions must be identical.

Through the rest of the paper we will refer to clocked, com-rigid controllers as *strict* controllers. The restricted control problem is then:

Definition 2 (Restricted control-synthesis problem). *Given a finite plant S over (Σ, θ) and a trace-closed ω-regular language $\mathcal{L}_{spec} \subseteq \Sigma^\omega$, is there a nonblocking strict controller Str for S such that $plays_S(Str) \subseteq \mathcal{L}_{spec}$?* ☐

The control-synthesis problem is hence restricted in three ways: (R1) the specification $\mathcal{L}_{spec}$ is trace-closed, (R2) the controller is a clocked strategy and (R3) the controller is a com-rigid strategy. (The nonblocking property is essential for otherwise the problem will become trivial). The main result of the paper is:

Theorem 1. *The restricted control-synthesis problem is decidable. Also, if there is a nonblocking strict controller, one can effectively synthesize a finite-state one. Moreover, if one or more of the restrictions R1, R2 or R3 are removed, the corresponding control-synthesis problem is undecidable.* □

For the dining philosophers problem as formulated above, there appears to be no natural local strategies that satisfy R2 and R3 for the robust specification demanding that no philosopher starves. However, as we point out in the concluding section, we can model this problem in our framework with an additional bounded memory. It then turns out that some standard solutions to the problem do fall into the restricted class of winning strategies we consider.

3   Decidability of Restricted Control Synthesis

Since the complement of a trace-closed language is also trace-closed and since Büchi automata can be effectively complemented, we assume, without loss of generality, that we are presented a Büchi automaton $\bar{\mathcal{A}}_{spec}$ whose language is trace-closed and is the complement of $\mathcal{L}_{spec}$. Our goal is to show that given a plant $\mathcal{S}$ and such a specification automaton $\bar{\mathcal{A}}_{spec}$, whether there is a nonblocking strict controller for the plant such that $plays_{\mathcal{S}}(Str) \cap \mathcal{L}(\bar{\mathcal{A}}_{spec}) = \emptyset$, is decidable.

Let us fix an instance of the problem by fixing a distributed alphabet $\tilde{\Sigma} = (\Sigma, \theta)$, a plant $\mathcal{S} = \{(S_p^E, S_p^C, \Sigma_p^E, \Sigma_p^C, \rightarrow_p, s_{in}^p)\}_{p \in \mathcal{P}}$ over (Σ, θ) and also a specification automaton $\bar{\mathcal{A}}_{spec}$ whose language is trace-closed with respect to (Σ, θ).

The key technical idea is that strict strategies can be represented as traces (i.e. equivalence classes of strings) over an appropriate distributed alphabet. A number of preliminaries are required before we can arrive at this representation. First, consider a strict strategy $Str = \{f_p\}_{p \in \mathcal{P}}$ for $\mathcal{S}$, where $f_p : \Sigma_p^* \rightarrow \Delta_p$. Since the strategy is clocked, we can view this instead as $\{g_p\}_{p \in \mathcal{P}}$, where $g_p : \mathbb{N}_0 \rightarrow \Delta_p$, for each $p \in \mathcal{P}$, by setting for each $i \in \mathbb{N}_0$, $g_p(i) = f_p(w)$ for some $w \in \Sigma_p^*$ such that $|w| = i$ ($\mathbb{N}_0$ denotes the set of nonnegative integers).

Next consider a strict strategy $Str = \{g_p\}_{p \in \mathcal{P}}$ for $\mathcal{S}$, where $g_p : \mathbb{N}_0 \rightarrow \Delta_p$. We say Str is proper if for every $p \in \mathcal{P}$, $n \in \mathbb{N}_0$ and $s \in S_p^C$, if $a \in g_p(n)(s)$, then there is a finite play $xa \in plays_{\mathcal{S}}^f(Str)$ such that $xa \upharpoonright p = w'a$, $|w'| = n$ and the p-state after executing x is s. That is, if a local strategy recommends a letter a at a controller state s after a history length n, then there must be some play according to the strategy that uses this recommendation. Note that this demand is only w.r.t. the controller states. It is not difficult to see that we can restrict our attention to proper clocked strategies without loss of generality.

Let $\xi_p^{\perp}$ represent the advice function that maps each $s \in S_p^C$ to the empty-set and maps each $s \in S_p^E$ to $en(s)$. If Str is a proper strict strategy, then it is clear that for every $p \in \mathcal{P}$, $n \in \mathbb{N}_0$, if n is odd, then $g_p(n) = \xi_p^{\perp}$ (since the local plant is at an environment state). Moreover, if there is some $n \in \mathbb{N}_0$, n even and $g_p(n) = \xi_p^{\perp}$, then the local plant is at a controller state where the strategy recommends no action. Hence, every play that reaches this stage has no more actions that involve p, and hence for every $n' \in \mathbb{N}_0$ such that $n' \geq n$, $g_p(n') = \xi_p^\perp$ (since Str is proper).

An advice function $\xi_p : S_p \to 2^{\Sigma_p}$ is said to be a *fixed-communication advice function* if there is a set $X \subseteq \mathcal{P}$ such that for every $s \in S_p^C$ and $a \in \xi_p(s)$, we have $\theta(a) = X$. If $\xi_p \neq \xi_p^\perp$, then this set X is unique and we denote it as $loc(\xi_p)$. Also, by convention, let $loc(\xi_p^\perp) = \{p\}$. Let $\widehat{\Delta}_p$ denote the set of all fixed-communication advice functions for p and let $\widehat{\Delta} = \bigcup_{p \in \mathcal{P}} \widehat{\Delta}_p$. Clearly for a proper strict strategy, for every $p \in \mathcal{P}$, $n \in \mathbb{N}$, $g_p(n) \in \widehat{\Delta}_p$.

We now introduce the distributed alphabet $\widetilde{\Pi} = (\Pi, \theta_\Pi)$ over $\mathcal{P}$; strategies will be represented as a single trace equivalence class over this distributed alphabet and our decision procedure will work over the words in this class. Let $Loc = \{\theta(a) \mid a \in \Sigma\}$ and $\Pi = \widehat{\Delta} \cup Loc$. Let $\theta_\Pi : \Pi \to 2^{\mathcal{P}} \setminus \emptyset$ be given by: $\theta_\Pi(\xi_p) = \{p\}$, if $\xi_p \in \widehat{\Delta}_p$ and $\theta_\Pi(X) = X$, $\forall X \in Loc$. Let $\approx_\Pi$ denote the equivalence relation induced by (Π, θ_Π).

Let Loc_p denote the collection of sets $X \in Loc$ such that $p \in X$. A word $\sigma \in \Pi^\omega$ is said to be an *str-linearization* if (i) $\sigma \upharpoonright \widehat{\Delta}_p \in ((\widehat{\Delta}_p \setminus \{\xi_p^\perp\}) \cdot \{\xi_p^\perp\})^\infty$, for each $p \in \mathcal{P}$, and (ii) for each $p \in \mathcal{P}$, $\sigma \upharpoonright p \in (\widehat{\Delta}_p \cdot Loc_p)^\infty$ such that for every prefix $\tau \cdot \xi_p \cdot X$ of $\sigma \upharpoonright p$ (where $\tau \in \Pi^*$, $\xi_p \in \widehat{\Delta}_p$ and $X \in Loc_p$), we have $X = loc(\xi_p)$. An str-linearization σ is said to *represent* the strict strategy $Str = \{g_p\}_{p \in \mathcal{P}}$ if for every $n \in \mathbb{N}$, $g_p(n-1) = (\sigma \upharpoonright p)[n]$, if $n \leq |\sigma \upharpoonright p|$ and $g_p(n) = \xi_p^\perp$ for other values of n.

An str-linearization σ is, in some sense, intended to be one member of the equivalence class of strings (i.e. a trace) whose p-projections are captured by the strategy Str that σ is representing. More crucially, σ describes, in an interleaved fashion, how a play according to Str may evolve. For example, if $\sigma = \xi_p^1 \xi_q^1 \{p, q\} \xi_p^2 \{p\} \ldots$, then, by definition, $loc(\xi_p^1) = loc(\xi_q^1) = \{p, q\}$ and $loc(\xi_p^2) = \{p\}$, and σ intuitively represents a high-level description of a set of plays where the processes p and q first synchronize, followed by a local p-action, etc.

Some easy facts to establish are: Not every member of Π^ω is an str-linearization. An str-linearization represents exactly one strict strategy. Every non-blocking strict strategy has an str-linearization that represents it. Let $Lin(Str)$ be the set of str-linearizations that represent Str. Then $Lin(Str)$ is exactly one $\approx_\Pi$-equivalence class of strings in case Str is a non-blocking strict strategy.

For a finite or infinite play $\alpha \in \Sigma^\infty$, let $com(\alpha)$ denote the string $\pi \in Loc^\infty$ where $|\pi| = |\alpha|$ and for every $1 \leq i \leq |\alpha|$, $\pi[i] = \theta(\alpha[i])$. A play $\alpha \in plays_S(Str)$ *corresponds* to an str-linearization σ of Str if for every $p \in \mathcal{P}$, $com(\alpha \upharpoonright p) = \sigma \upharpoonright Loc_p$. That is, α corresponds to σ if both of them follow the same pattern of communication, when σ is regarded without its $\widehat{\Delta}$-letters. For an str-linearization σ, let $plays_{Lin}(\sigma)$ denote the plays of Str that σ corresponds to. One can show that every play according to Str corresponds to some str-linearization of Str (i.e. $\bigcup_{\sigma \in Lin(Str)} plays_{Lin}(\sigma) = plays_S(Str)$).

Our decision procedure is designed to work over inputs that are str-linearizations of strategies. The "false" inputs will be treated in a "don't-care" fashion and will be filtered out by a separate automaton. We will run an automaton T over the distributed alphabet $\tilde{\Pi}$ which, when supplied with an str-linearization $\sigma \in \Pi^*$ representing some strict strategy Str, will use the plant structure to non-deterministically emit (one of the) the plays according to Str, in the form of a string over the distributed alphabet (Σ, θ). We will then run in tandem, a Büchi automaton B which will check if the output produced by T is accepted by $\bar{A}_{spec}$. A strict controller will exist iff the complement of B accepts some str-linearization.

Let us now introduce asynchronous transducers. Let $\tilde{\Sigma}_I = (\Sigma_I, \theta_I)$ and $\tilde{\Sigma}_O = (\Sigma_O, \theta_O)$ be two distributed alphabets over P and let $\approx_I$ and $\approx_O$ be the equivalence relations induced by them.

Definition 3. *An* asynchronous transducer *over* $(\tilde{\Sigma}_I, \tilde{\Sigma}_O)$ *is a transition system* $T = (\{U_p, u_{in}^p\}_{p\in P}, \{\delta_a\}_{a\in \Sigma_I})$ *where each* U_p *is a finite set of states and* $u_{in}^p \in U_p$ *is the local initial state of p. For $a \in \Sigma_I$, let U_a denote the set of functions* $\mathbf{v}_a : \theta_I(a) \to \bigcup_{p\in\theta_I(a)} U_p$ *such that* $\mathbf{v}_a(p) \in U_p$, *for each $p \in \theta_I(a)$. Then, for each $a \in \Sigma_I$, $\delta_a \subseteq (U_a \times (\{b \in \Sigma_O \mid \theta_O(b) = \theta_I(a)\} \cup \{\varepsilon\}) \times U_a)$.* □

An asynchronous transducer hence has a state-space which resembles that of a product system over P. The main difference is that transitions are not entirely local: a transition on an action a depends on the states of the processes that are involved in the action. An element $\mathbf{v}_a \in U_a$ represents some set of states which the processes involved in a are in, and are called a-states. A transition for a is a tuple $(\mathbf{v}_a, b, \mathbf{v}_a')$, where $\mathbf{v}_a$ and $\mathbf{v}_a'$ are a-states, and b is the letter output when this transition is taken (there is no output if $b = \varepsilon$). Note that if $b \in \Sigma_O$, we require that the processes that are involved in b are precisely those that are involved in a. The global system associated with an asynchronous transducer T is defined in the natural way: $\mathcal{G}(T) = (\hat{U}, \mathbf{u}_{in}, \delta)$ where $\hat{U}$ is the set of functions $\mathbf{u} : P \to \bigcup_{p\in P} U_p$ such that $\mathbf{u}(p) \in U_p$ (for each $p \in P$), $\mathbf{u}_{in} \in \hat{U}$ such that $\mathbf{u}_{in}(p) = u_{in}^p$ (for each $p \in P$). $\delta \subseteq \hat{U} \times \Sigma_I \times (\Sigma_O \cup \{\varepsilon\}) \times \hat{U}$ is given by: $(\mathbf{u}, a, b, \mathbf{u}') \in \delta$ iff for each $p \notin \theta(a)$, $\mathbf{u}(p) = \mathbf{u}(p')$ and there exists a transition $(\mathbf{v}_a, b, \mathbf{v}_a') \in \delta_a$ such that for each $p \in \theta(a)$, $\mathbf{u}(p) = \mathbf{v}_a(p)$ and $\mathbf{u}'(p) = \mathbf{v}_a'(p)$.

For a word $\alpha \in (\Sigma_I)^\omega$, a run of $\mathcal{G}(T)$ on α is sequence of transitions over δ, $(\mathbf{u}_1, a_1, b_1, \mathbf{u}_1')(\mathbf{u}_2, a_2, b_2, \mathbf{u}_2') \ldots$ such that $\alpha = a_1 a_2 \ldots$, $\mathbf{u}_1 = \mathbf{u}_{in}$ and, for each $i \in \mathbb{N}$, $\mathbf{u}_i' = \mathbf{u}_{i+1}$. The *output* of such a run is the word $\beta = b_1 b_2 \ldots \in (\Sigma_O)^\infty$ (where ε is treated as the empty word). Again, one can show that the set of words over which $\mathcal{G}(T)$ has a run is trace-closed with respect to (Σ_I, θ_I). Further, one can easily show using trace theory:

Lemma 1. *Let T be an asynchronous transducer over $(\tilde{\Sigma}_I, \tilde{\Sigma}_O)$. If there is a run of $\mathcal{G}(T)$ on $\alpha \in (\Sigma_I)^\omega$ that outputs $\beta \in (\Sigma_O)^\infty$, then for every $\alpha' \in \Sigma_I^\omega$ such that $\alpha \approx_I \alpha'$, there exists β' such that $\beta' \approx_O \beta$ and $\mathcal{G}(T)$ has a run on α' that outputs β'.* □

Let us now return to deciding the restricted control-synthesis problem. We show now that we can design an asynchronous transducer which, when supplied an str-linearization of a strict strategy Str, will non-deterministically produce the set of plays corresponding to the str-linearization as output.

Lemma 2. *There is an asynchronous transducer $\mathcal{T}$ over $(\widetilde{\Sigma}, \widetilde{\Pi})$ that, on any input σ which is an str-linearization of a strategy Str, produces non-deterministically as output the set plays$_{Lin}(Str)$.*

Proof: The automaton reads an str-linearization of a strategy and keeps track of the local p-states of the plant in its local p-state. When it encounters a local advice function ξ_p, it consults it to see which moves are recommended from the current state, and records this set of enabled actions. When it encounters a letter $X \in Loc$, it nondeterministically guesses an action $a \in \Sigma$, such that $\theta(a) = X$, which all the participating agents are willing to perform— it then updates its a-state according to the plant's transitions and outputs the letter a. If there is no such action a, then the local plant states move to a special state— from this point on, these processes never allow any other action a that involves them to occur in a play. In this way, the automaton working on an input str-linearization σ, has many runs on σ, and produces the plays in $plays_{Lin}(\sigma)$. $\qquad\square$

We can now show that the set of str-linearizations σ such that there is a play corresponding to σ which is not in $\mathcal{L}_{spec}$, is regular.

Lemma 3. *There is a Büchi automaton $\mathcal{B}$ over Π that accepts an str-linearization σ iff there is a play $\alpha \in plays_{Lin}(\sigma)$ such that $\alpha \in \mathcal{L}(\bar{\mathcal{A}}_{spec})$, or the strategy that σ represents is blocking. Further, the set of str-linearizations accepted by $\mathcal{B}$ is trace-closed.*

Proof: Consider the asynchronous transducer $\mathcal{T}$ constructed in Lemma 2 that, on every str-linearization σ, produces the plays according to the strategy represented by σ. The state-space of $\mathcal{B}$ will be the product of the spaces of $\mathcal{G}(\mathcal{T})$ and $\bar{\mathcal{A}}_{spec}$. $\mathcal{B}$ will read an input σ and run $\mathcal{T}$ on it. Simultaneously, whenever $\mathcal{T}$ produces an output $a \in \Sigma$, it will simulate $\bar{\mathcal{A}}_{spec}$ on this output. The acceptance condition for $\mathcal{B}$ will be inherited from $\bar{\mathcal{A}}_{spec}$.

It is easy to construct the automaton $\mathcal{B}$ and show that it has the required properties. The one catch is we will have to also check if the strategy (represented by one of its str-linearizations that the automaton is running over) is blocking. But this can be detected by looking for a finite play which gets stuck and then, by moving to a good state, accept this blocking strategy.

Finally, $\mathcal{L}(\mathcal{B})$ being trace-closed can be shown using Lemma 1 and the fact that $\mathcal{L}(\bar{\mathcal{A}}_{spec})$ is trace-closed. $\qquad\square$

Theorem 2. *The restricted control-synthesis problem is decidable. Moreover, if there is a restricted controller, we can effectively synthesize a finite-state strategy.*

Proof: By Lemma 3, we construct the automaton $\mathcal{B}$, and complement it to get $\mathcal{B}'$. Now $\mathcal{B}'$ will accept an str-linearization σ iff $plays_{Lin}(\sigma) \subseteq \mathcal{L}_{spec}$ *and the* strategy represented by σ is nonblocking. (Note that the strategy represented by σ is strict). Now, if $\alpha \in plays_S(Str)$ where Str is the strategy represented by σ, then there is an str-linearization σ' that corresponds to α. But since all such str-linearizations are trace-equivalent, $\sigma' \approx_\Pi \sigma$ and hence σ' is accepted by $\mathcal{B}'$; thus $\alpha \in \mathcal{L}_{spec}$. Hence Str is a winning nonblocking strict strategy.

$\mathcal{B}'$ may however accept strings that are not str-linearizations of strategies at all. However, one can easily construct an automaton $\mathcal{B}_r$ that accepts the set of all str-linearizations over Π. The existence of a controller can now be determined by testing the intersection of the automata $\mathcal{B}'$ and $\mathcal{B}_r$, for emptiness: the intersection is nonempty iff there is a controller for the plant. If the intersection is nonempty then the emptiness test will exhibit an ultimately periodic word $\sigma = \tau \cdot (\tau')^\omega$ in the intersection. The p-projection of this word can be realized as a finite state controller for each p.   □

4   Undecidability of Partially Restricted Control-Synthesis Problems

Now, we claim that the restrictions R1, R2 and R3 are, in a sense, necessary in that if one imposes just one or two restrictions of the three, then the problem is still undecidable. Note that removing restriction R2 (or R3) does not a priori mean that the problem is simpler to handle — hence we have to prove undecidability for all the possible combinations of dropping R1, R2 and R3.

The main argument is based on an undecidability proof presented in [PR90], where the the reduction is from the halting problem for Turing machines on a blank tape. Let us fix a Turing machine $M = (\Gamma, \#, Q, q_{in}, \delta, q_h)$ where Γ denotes the tape alphabet, $\# \in \Gamma$ is a special 'blank' symbol, Q is the finite set of states of M, $q_{in} \in Q$ is the initial state and $\delta : Q \times \Gamma \to Q \times \Gamma \times \{l, r\}$ is the transition relation. A move $(q', b, d) \in \delta(q, a)$ means that M, when in state q and reading letter a, replaces a by b, changes to state q', and moves the tape-head one position in direction d (where l denotes 'left' and r denotes 'right').

A configuration of M is a string $C \in \Gamma^* \cdot (Q \times \Gamma) \cdot \Gamma^*$— a configuration $x.(q, a).y$ means that M is in state q, the tape content is $x.a.y$ and the tape-head is at cell $(|x|+1)$. The initial configuration C_{in} is $(q_{in}, \#)$. We write $C \vdash C'$ to denote that C' is the successor configuration of C. A run of M is a sequence of configurations $C_1, C_2, \ldots C_k$, $k \in \mathbb{N}$, where $C_1 = C_{in}$ and where $\forall 1 \leq i < k$, $C_i \vdash C_{i+1}$. Configurations of the form $(q_h, \#).(\#)^*$ are called halting configurations. A run of M is halting if the last configuration is halting; M is said to halt if there is a run of M that is halting.

Consider two sequences of configurations, where configurations are separated by a special symbol '\$': $\tau = C_1 \cdot \$ \cdot C_2 \cdot \$ \cdot \ldots$ and $\tau' = C_1' \cdot \$ \cdot C_2' \cdot \$ \cdot \ldots$. Consider now a system that reads these sequences in an interleaved manner. In particular, we are interested in two such interleavings, called *useful* interleavings— the interleavings where one sequence starts ahead of another by exactly one configuration and from then on the sequences strictly alternate. That is, one useful interleaving is where C_1 occurs first, then C_2 and C_1' occur interleaved letter-by-letter, followed by C_3 and C'_2 interleaved letter-by-letter, etc. The other interleaving is the analogous one where C'_1 occurs first.

The crucial point is that a finite-state device can, from these two interleavings, determine whether both of them represent the correct run of M or not. First, it can determine whether both C_1 and C'_1 are the initial configuration of M. When reading the interleaving where C_1 is read first, whenever it gets two configurations C_{i+1} and C'_i interleaved, it checks whether $C'_i \vdash C_{i+1}$. On the other interleaving, while reading C_i and C'_{i+1} interleaved, it checks whether $C_i \vdash C'_{i+1}$. Since a successor configuration is different in at most three places, a finite-state device can check these properties. We say a useful interleaving is *correct* if it satisfies these conditions and also both sequences include a halting configuration. It is easy to show then that the configuration sequences τ and τ' both represent configuration runs of M that halt iff their two useful interleavings are correct.

For grouping together our undecidability arguments succinctly, let $\mathcal{R}$ range over the *proper* subsets of $\{R1, R2, R3\}$. Then the $\mathcal{R}$-controller synthesis problem is the general control-synthesis problem along with the restrictions in $\mathcal{R}$.

Theorem 3. *Given a finite-state plant S and an ω-regular language specification $\mathcal{L}_{spec}$, the problem of checking if there is a $\mathcal{R}$-controller is undecidable for every $\mathcal{R}$.*   □

Proof: First assume that $\mathcal{R} = \{R2, R3\}$. Let $\mathcal{P} = \{p, q\}$ and $\Sigma = (\Gamma \cup \{e, \$\}) \times \{p, q\}$ where $\theta((a, p)) = p$ and $\theta((a, q)) = q$ for every $a \in \Gamma \cup \{e, \$\}$. Thus p and q do not synchronize for any action, and evolve independent of each other. Also, p and q have exactly one environment action— (e, p) and (e, q), respectively, which are enabled at every alternate state. The plant at p is a two-state system that can generate, at the controller state, any letter in $(\Gamma \cup \{\$\}) \times \{p\}$; the plant at q is similar. The specification demands the following: (i) The plants locally produce sequences of configurations and the first configuration output is C_{in} and (ii) If the plants happen to evolve in such a way so as to produce a useful interleaving, then the interleaving is correct.

Note that the specification is not trace-closed. We can show that there is a controller that meets the specification iff M halts, and hence the control-synthesis problem for $\mathcal{R} = \{R2, R3\}$ is undecidable. Now note that any controller that meets the specification needs to recommend only one move for p and q at each stage. Also, since there is only one environment action, *any* such controller is a clocked strategy. Further, all actions are local and thus any controller is com-rigid as well. It is hence clear that the problem remains undecidable for $\mathcal{R} = \{R2\}$, $\mathcal{R} = \{R3\}$ and $\mathcal{R} = \emptyset$.

Next assume that $\mathcal{R} = \{R1, R3\}$. We have two processes p and q, as in the above proof, that generate configurations. However, there are two environment actions at p— $Start_p$, $Next_p$. The plant at p is constructed so that it starts outputting a configuration only if the last environment action is $Start_p$— otherwise, it can only do the action $\$$. The plant at q is constructed in a similar fashion. The environment hence stutters the actions of p and q that encode configurations.

We also have a new process r, which synchronizes alternately with p and q, observes their controllable actions, and determines whether, when the actions occur according to a useful interleaving, they are correct. The specification is a local specification on the actions of r, and is hence trace-closed. This shows that the control-synthesis problem in this setting with $\mathcal{R} = \{R1, R3\}$ is undecidable. Also, since r alternately synchronizes with p and q, any strategy is a com-rigid strategy. Hence it follows that the problem remains undecidable for $\mathcal{R} = \{R1\}$.

Finally assume that $\mathcal{R} = \{R1, R2\}$. We have three processes as in the previous proof, with process r observing the actions of p and q. However, there is only one environment action at p and at q, while we have two environment actions e_p and e_q at r. The process r decides which process to communicate with first (p or q), depending on the first environment action that occurs. The process r proceeds then, as usual, to check whether the two useful interleavings are correct. Note that a nonblocking strategy for r cannot be com-rigid. One can now show that there is a controller in this setting iff M halts.

In all the above proofs, it is easy to see that if there is a controller then there is a finite-state controller as well; hence in all the above problems, even searching for a finite-state controller is undecidable.   □

5   Conclusions

We have considered a class of effectively synthesizable controllers in a natural asynchronous distributed setting. We have shown that when the specification is restricted to be robust (R1) and the controllers are restricted to follow a clocked (R2) rigid-communication-pattern (R3) strategy, the controller synthesis problem is effectively decidable. And when controllers exist, a finite state controller also exists and can be effectively synthesized. Further, the controller synthesis problem becomes undecidable if one or more of these restrictions are dropped.

Regarding the complexity of our decision procedure, it is easy to see that our algorithm works in time doubly exponential in the size of the input. This is a sharp drop in complexity from the non-elementary results reported in the [PR90] framework for even restricted synchronous architectures.

A number of extensions to our work are worth studying. Firstly, we could generalize our results to handle locally nondeterministic systems — where each local plant is nondeterministic on action labels. A local controller then has to recommend not only an action (which will decide what is to be communicated with the other processes) but also a transition on this action. Our decidability results can be easily modified to handle this (the encoding of strategies now have to encode the recommended transitions).

With this extension, we can relax the restriction R2, as mentioned in the introduction, and endow each local controller with a bounded amount of memory, say b bits, to remember information of its local past. We do this by blowing up the state-space of each local plant by all possible valuations of these b bits and make the transitions nondeterministic on this update of the b bits of information. A clocked controller then, looking at the length of the history *and* the current state of the plant and the b-bits of information, recommends a move as well as an update of its b bits. For example, in the dining philosophers' problem, it turns out that the solutions in the literature (see [Lyn96]) require very few bits of memory for each process (2 bits for the Right-Left dining philosophers' algorithm). Indeed, a variety of resource allocation problems (for example, round-robin based and turn-based solutions to mutual exclusion problems) can be modeled in our framework and this will be explored in future work.

Secondly, in the current setting the plant's transition relations are purely local. A good deal of additional modeling power can be obtained by making the local moves depend also on the states of the other agents involved in a synchronization action. Our results still go through with some additional notational complications.

A different line of research to pursue would be to impose some architectural restrictions and then look for suitable conditions (other than R1, R2 and R3) to achieve decidability. Since R1 and R3 are fairly natural, we suspect that the main challenge will be to replace R2 with suitable conditions that exploit the architectural constraints.

References

[ALW89]   M. Abadi, L. Lamport, and P. Wolper. Realizable and unrealizable concurrent program specifications. In *Proc. 16th Int. Coll. on Automata, Languages and Programming*, volume 372 of *LNCS*, pages 1–17. Springer-Verlag, 1989. 145

[BL69]   J. R. Büchi and L. H. Landweber. Solving sequential conditions by finite-state strategies. *Trans. AMS*, 138:295–311, 1969. 145

[Chu63]   A. Church. Logic, arithmetics, and automata. In *Proc. International Congress of Mathematicians, 1962*, pages 23–35. institut Mittag-Leffler, 1963. 145

[DR95]   V. Diekert and G. Rozenberg, editors. *The Book of Traces*. World Scientific, Singapore, 1995. 148, 150

[HT98]   J. G. Henriksen and P. S. Thiagarajan. Distributed versions of Linear time temporal logic. In *Lectures on Petri Nets: Basic Models*, volume 1491 of *Lecture Notes in Computer Science*, pages 643–682. Springer-Verlag, (1998). 146

[KV99]   O. Kupferman and M. Y. Vardi. Church's problem revisited. *The Bulletin of Symbolic Logic*, 5(2):245 – 263, June 1999. 145

[KV00]   O. Kupferman and M. Vardi. μ-calculus synthesis. In *MFCS: Symposium on Mathematical Foundations of Computer Science*, vol. 1893 of *LNCS*, 2000. 145

[KV01]   O. Kupferman and M. Vardi. Synthesizing distributed systems. In *16th Annual IEEE Symp on Logic in Computer Science*, pages 16–19, USA, 2001. IEEE Comp. Society. 146

[Lyn96]   N. A. Lynch. *Distributed Algorithms* Morgan Kaufmann Publ. Inc., 1996. 159

[Mad01]   P. Madhusudan. *Control and synthesis of open reactive systems*. PhD thesis, Institute of Mathematical Sciences, 2001. 146

[MT01]   P. Madhusudan and P. S. Thiagarajan. Distributed control and synthesis for local specifications. In *Proc., ICALP '01*, volume 2076 of *LNCS*, July 2001. 146

[PR79]   G. L. Peterson and J. H. Reif. Multiple-person alternation. In *Proc. 20th IEEE Symposium on Foundation of Computer Science*, pages 348–363, 1979. 148

[PR89a]   A. Pnueli and R. Rosner. On the synthesis of a reactive module. In *Proc. 16th ACM Symposium on Principles of Programming Languages*, 1989. 145

[PR89b]   A. Pnueli and R. Rosner. On the synthesis of an asynchronous reactive module. In *Proc. 16th ICALP*, volume 372, pages 652–671. LNCS, 1989.

[PR90]   A. Pnueli and R. Rosner. Distributed reactive systems are hard to synthesize. In *Proc. 31st IEEE Symp. on Foundation of Comp. Sc.*, pages 746–757, 1990. 146, 147, 148, 156, 158

[Tho90]   W. Thomas. Automata on Infinite Objects. In *Handbook of Theoretical Comp. Sc.*, volume B, pages 135–191, Elsevier, 1995. 151

Alphabet-Based Synchronisation
is Exponentially Cheaper

Antti Valmari and Antti Kervinen

Tampere University of Technology, Institute of Software Systems
PO Box 553, FIN-33101 Tampere, FINLAND
{ava,ask}@cs.tut.fi

Abstract. We study the complexity of verification problems in which a preorder relation between an implementation and a specification is checked, when the specification is given as a parallel composition of processes. This problem turns out to be **PSPACE**- or **EXPSPACE**-complete, depending on the type of the parallel composition operator that is used in the construction of the specification. This implies that confusion with different parallel composition operators may lead to erroneous complexity claims. We fix one such erroneous result presented in an earlier publication. We also show that the application of hiding, renaming or just one interleaving parallel composition operation to a specification for which the problem is in **PSPACE**, may raise the complexity of the problem to **EXPSPACE**-hard.

1   Introduction

In this paper we study the complexity of the verification of $Impl \leq Spec$ in the case where at least the specification and possibly also the implementation are given as a parallel composition of processes, and where "$\leq$" is a linear time preorder. The preorders we investigate are trace inclusion $Tr(Impl) \subseteq Tr(Spec)$, and the main preorders in the CSP [3,12] and CFFD [16] theories. The preorders express that the implementation may exhibit only the behaviour that is accepted by the specification. The literature presents also numerous other similar preorders, but these three suffice to illustrate the phenomenon we are interested in and the proof techniques.

Checking whether a system satisfies a linear time temporal logic formula is **PSPACE**-complete [14] in the length of the formula. Verification is **PSPACE**-complete also when *Impl* and *Spec* are single processes and the preorder is trace inclusion. This result is rather easily obtained from the classic **PSPACE**-complete problem: do two finite automata accept the same language [8]. The result is valid also for CSP- or CFFD-preorders [6,2].

When the specification is a parallel composition of processes, verification tasks easily require exponential space. Let "||" denote the parallel composition operator that synchronises processes according to their alphabets. **EXPSPACE**-completeness for deciding trace equivalence between systems where actions may be hidden after the "||" parallel composition is shown in [11].

L. Brim et al. (Eds.): CONCUR 2002, LNCS 2421, pp. 161–176, 2002.
© Springer-Verlag Berlin Heidelberg 2002

If the hiding is not allowed, the problem is in **PSPACE** as shown in [13]. It is claimed in [7] that trace equivalence and trace inclusion are **EXPSPACE**-hard for every "non-flat" system. The claim contradicts the result of [13] and our Theorem 1. This issue will be discussed in Section 3.

In this paper we journey to the borderline between **PSPACE** and **EX-PSPACE** to study what elements in the construction of a specification make the complexity of checking linear-time preorders to grow **EXPSPACE**-hard. We show that the verification problem is in **PSPACE** when the specification is constructed with "||", despite the kind of synchronisation used in the implementation. The problem is shown to become **EXPSPACE**-hard when actions of the specification may be hidden or renamed after the parallel composition. **EXPSPACE**-hardness results also if the CCS [10] parallel composition operator "|" or Lotos [1] operator "|[···]|" is used instead of "||", or if one of the "||" operators is replaced by the interleaving parallel composition "|||". We consider this difference in the complexities of the three parallel composition operators "||", "|" and "|[···]|" as the main observation of this paper.

In Section 2 we introduce the notations, operators and semantics needed in the results. The upper bound results of this paper are proven in Section 3. In Section 4 we show our main result: when "|[···]|" is used, the problems become **EXPSPACE**-hard. Then, in Section 5, various corollaries are presented to clarify the complexity jump from **PSPACE** to **EXPSPACE**-hard. The paper ends in conclusions in Section 6.

2   Framework

In this section we will define labelled transition systems (LTSs), some operations on them, and the trace, CFFD and CSP semantics on LTSs.

Definition 1 (LTS). *A labelled transition system, abbreviated LTS, is a qua-druple* $(S, \Sigma, \Delta, \hat{s})$ *where* S *is a set of states,* Σ *is a set of visible actions (alphabet),* $\Delta \subseteq S \times (\Sigma \cup \{\tau\}) \times S$ *is a set of transitions where* $\tau \notin \Sigma$ *is an invisible action, and* $\hat{s} \in S$ *is an initial state.*   □

$\Sigma(L)$ is used to denote the alphabet of LTS L.

The size of an LTS is the sum of the numbers of its states, visible actions and transitions.

Definition 2 (Size). *Let* L *be an LTS* $(S, \Sigma, \Delta, \hat{s})$. *The size of* L *is* $|L| = |S| + |\Sigma| + |\Delta|$.   □

We will use the following arrow notation.

Definition 3 (Arrow Notation). *Let* $L = (S, \Sigma, \Delta, \hat{s})$ *be an LTS;* $s, s' \in S$; *and* $a \in \Sigma \cup \{\tau\}$. *We denote*

- $s -a\rightarrow s'$ *iff* $(s, a, s') \in \Delta$.
- $s -a\rightarrow$ *iff there exists* s' *so that* $s -a\rightarrow s'$.

- $s -a^\omega \to$ iff there exist $s_1, s_2, \ldots$ so that $s -a\to s_1 -a\to s_2 -a\to \ldots$
- $s =\varepsilon\Rightarrow s'$ iff there exist $n \geq 0$ and $s_0, s_1, \ldots, s_n$, where $s_0 = s$ and $s_n = s'$, so that $s_0 -\tau\to s_1 -\tau\to \ldots -\tau\to s_n$.
- $s =a\Rightarrow s'$ iff $a \neq \tau$ and there exist s_1 and s_2 so that $s =\varepsilon\Rightarrow s_1 -a\to s_2 =\varepsilon\Rightarrow s'$.
- $s =a_1 a_2 \cdots a_n\Rightarrow s'$, where $n \geq 1$, if and only if there exist $s_0, s_1, \ldots, s_n$ so that $s = s_0$, $s' = s_n$, and $s_0 =a_1\Rightarrow s_1 =a_2\Rightarrow \ldots =a_n\Rightarrow s_n$. $\qquad\square$

Definition 4 (Trace). *LTS* $L = (S, \Sigma, \Delta, \hat{s})$ *has a trace* σ, *if and only if* $\exists s \in S : \hat{s} =\sigma\Rightarrow s$. *The set of traces is denoted* $Tr(L)$. $\qquad\square$

We will use a projection operator for traces and sets of traces. The projection of a trace σ against an alphabet Σ is what remains when all symbols in σ that do not belong to Σ are removed. The projection of a set of traces T is the set that consists of the projection of every trace in T.

Definition 5 (Projection "$\downarrow$"). *Let* Σ *and* Σ_{proj} *be alphabets,* $a_1 a_2 \cdots a_n \in \Sigma^*$ *a trace, and* $T \subseteq \Sigma^*$ *a set of traces.*

- $a_i\downarrow\Sigma_{\mathrm{proj}} = a_i$ *if* $a_i \in \Sigma_{\mathrm{proj}}$, *otherwise* ε *(that is, the empty trace).*
- $a_1 a_2 \cdots a_n\downarrow\Sigma_{\mathrm{proj}} = (a_1\downarrow\Sigma_{\mathrm{proj}})(a_2\downarrow\Sigma_{\mathrm{proj}}) \cdots (a_n\downarrow\Sigma_{\mathrm{proj}})$.
- $T\downarrow\Sigma_{\mathrm{proj}} = \{ \sigma \mid \exists\sigma' \in T : \sigma'\downarrow\Sigma_{\mathrm{proj}} = \sigma \}$. $\qquad\square$

Next we define operators for hiding and renaming actions in LTSs. Hiding removes a set of visible actions from the alphabet of an LTS and relabels corresponding transitions with the invisible action τ.

Definition 6 (Hide). *Let* L *be an LTS* $(S, \Sigma, \Delta, \hat{s})$ *and* A *a set of actions.* **hide** A **in** L *is the LTS* $(S, \Sigma', \Delta', \hat{s})$ *where* $\Sigma' = \Sigma - A$ *and* $(s, a, s')\acute{a} \in \Delta'$ *if and only if* $\exists(s, b, s') \in \Delta$ *such that either* $b \notin A$ *and* $a = b$ *or* $b \in A$ *and* $a = \tau$. $\qquad\square$

Renaming changes the names of some visible actions and relabels the corresponding transitions. Actions can not be renamed to τ.

Definition 7 (Rename). *Let* $L = (S, \Sigma, \Delta, \hat{s})$ *be an LTS and* R *be a set of pairs* (a, a') *(written as* $a'_1/a_1, \ldots, a'_n/a_n$) *where* τ *does not appear in any pair.* **rename** R **in** L *is the LTS* $(S, \Sigma', \Delta', \hat{s})$ *where* $\Sigma' = (\Sigma - \{ a \mid (a, a') \in R \}) \cup \{ a' \mid \exists a \in \Sigma : (a, a') \in R \}$ *and* $(s, a, s') \in \Delta'$ *if and only if* $\exists(s, b, s') \in \Delta$ *such that either* $b \notin \{ a \mid (a, a') \in R \}$ *and* $a = b$ *or* $(b, a) \in R$. $\qquad\square$

The definition allows multiple renaming, that is, the mapping of one action name to several action names. This is not important for the results of this paper, however.

The main theorems of this paper compare the effects of three different parallel composition operators on the complexity of a verification task. All operators take LTSs as input and produce an LTS as output.

In the parallel composition with the "$\|$" operator a visible action a is executed if and only if every LTS that has a in its alphabet executes it. Invisible actions are not synchronised, that is, when an LTS executes the invisible action τ, other LTSs do nothing.

Definition 8 (Parallel Composition "$\|$"). *Let $P_i = (S_i, \Sigma_i, \Delta_i, \hat{s}_i)$ be LTSs for $1 \leq i \leq n$. Then $P_1 \| \cdots \| P_n$ is the LTS $(S, \Sigma, \Delta, \hat{s})$ where*

- $S = S_1 \times \cdots \times S_n$
- $\Sigma = \Sigma_1 \cup \cdots \cup \Sigma_n$
- $(s, a, s') \in \Delta$, *where* $s = (s_1, \ldots, s_n)$ *and* $s' = (s'_1, \ldots, s'_n)$ *iff either*
  - $a = \tau$ *and for some* $i, 1 \leq i \leq n : (s_i, \tau, s'_i) \in \Delta_i$ *and for the other* $j \neq i, 1 \leq j \leq n : s_j = s'_j$ *or*
  - $a \in \Sigma$ *and for every* $i, 1 \leq i \leq n :$ *if* $a \in \Sigma_i$, *then* $(s_i, a, s'_i) \in \Delta_i$ *and if* $a \notin \Sigma_i$, *then* $s_i = s'_i$.
- $\hat{s} = (\hat{s}_1, \ldots, \hat{s}_n)$. □

In the second parallel composition operator, "$\|[\cdots]\|$" [1], a set of actions according to which the LTSs synchronise is explicitly given. The remaining (visible and invisible) actions of LTSs behave like the invisible action τ in the parallel composition operator "$\|$".

Definition 9 (Parallel Composition "$\|[\cdots]\|$"). *Let $P_i = (S_i, \Sigma_i, \Delta_i, \hat{s}_i)$ be LTSs for $1 \leq i \leq 2$. Then $P_1 \|[a_1, \ldots, a_n]\| P_2$ is the LTS $(S, \Sigma, \Delta, \hat{s})$ where*

- $S = S_1 \times S_2$
- $\Sigma = \Sigma_1 \cup \Sigma_2$
- $(s, a, s') \in \Delta$, *where* $s = (s_1, s_2)$ *and* $s' = (s'_1, s'_2)$ *if and only if either*
  - $a \notin \{a_1, \ldots, a_n\}$ *and* $(s_1, a, s'_1) \in \Delta_1$ *and* $s_2 = s'_2$,
  - $a \notin \{a_1, \ldots, a_n\}$ *and* $s_1 = s'_1$ *and* $(s_2, a, s'_2) \in \Delta_2$, *or*
  - $a \in \{a_1, \ldots, a_n\}$, $(s_1, a, s'_1) \in \Delta_1$ *and* $(s_2, a, s'_2) \in \Delta_2$.
- $\hat{s} = (\hat{s}_1, \hat{s}_2)$. □

When the set of synchronised actions is empty, instead of "$\|[\,]\|$" the operator is written as "$\|\|\|$". This is (essentially) the same as the interleaving operator of CSP and Lotos.

The binary version of the parallel composition operator "$\|$" is a special case of "$\|[\cdots]\|$". Let $P_1 = (S_1, \Sigma_1, \Delta_1, \hat{s}_1)$ and $P_2 = (S_2, \Sigma_2, \Delta_2, \hat{s}_2)$, now $P_1 \| P_2 = P_1 \|[\Sigma_1 \cap \Sigma_2]\| P_2$.

The third parallel composition operator "$|$" is from CCS [10]. In CCS, every visible action a has its co-action $\bar{a}$. Actions and co-actions reflect sending and receiving. Processes are synchronised by executing an action and its co-action simultaneously. The synchronous execution produces an invisible action. Actions can also be executed independently of their co-actions. When this is not desired, it can be prevented with a CCS operator that is not discussed in this paper.

Definition 10 (Parallel Composition "$|$"). *Let $P_i = (S_i, \Sigma_i, \Delta_i, \hat{s}_i)$ be LTSs for $1 \leq i \leq 2$. Then $P_1 \mid P_2$ is the LTS $(S, \Sigma, \Delta, \hat{s})$ where*

- $S = S_1 \times S_2$
- $\Sigma = \Sigma_1 \cup \Sigma_2$
- $(s, a, s') \in \Delta$, *where* $s = (s_1, s_2)$ *and* $s' = (s'_1, s'_2)$ *if and only if either*
  - $a = \tau$ *and*

* there is a visible action b so that $(s_1, b, s_1') \in \Delta_1$ and $(s_2, \overline{b}, s_2') \in \Delta_2$
* there is a visible action b so that $(s_1, \overline{b}, s_1') \in \Delta_1$ and $(s_2, b, s_2') \in \Delta_2$
* either $(s_1, \tau, s_1') \in \Delta_1$ and $s_2 = s_2'$, or $s_1 = s_1'$ and $(s_2, \tau, s_2') \in \Delta_2$

or
- a is a visible action and either $(s_1, a, s_1') \in \Delta_1$ and $s_2 = s_2'$, or $s_1 = s_1'$ and $(s_2, a, s_2') \in \Delta_2$.
- $\hat{s} = (\hat{s}_1, \hat{s}_2)$. ☐

We will show our complexity results to hold for checking trace preorder (essentially language inclusion), but also for CSP and CFFD preorders. They will be defined after first defining some auxiliary concepts.

Definition 11. Let $L = (S, \Sigma, \Delta, \hat{s})$ be an LTS.

- A state s is stable iff $\neg(s -\tau\rightarrow)$.
- L is stable, denoted stable(L), iff $\hat{s}$ is stable.
- Let $\sigma \in Tr(L)$ and $A \subseteq \Sigma$. (σ, A) is a stable failure of L, if and only if there is $s \in S$ such that $\hat{s} =\sigma\Rightarrow s$ and $\forall a \in A \cup \{\tau\} : \neg(s -a\rightarrow)$. The set of stable failures is denoted SFail(L).
- $\sigma \in Tr(L)$ is a divergence trace of L, if and only if there is $s \in S$ such that $\hat{s} =\sigma\Rightarrow s$ and $s -\tau^\omega\rightarrow $. The set of divergence traces is denoted DivTr(L).
- Let $a_1, a_2, a_3, \ldots \in \Sigma$. $a_1 a_2 a_3 \cdots$ is an infinite trace of L, if and only if there exist $s_1, s_2, s_3, \ldots \in S$ so that $\hat{s} =a_1\Rightarrow s_1 =a_2\Rightarrow s_2 =a_3\Rightarrow \cdots$. The set of infinite traces is denoted InfTr(L). ☐

That is, a state of an LTS is stable if the invisible action τ can not be executed in it. An LTS is stable if and only if its initial state is stable. Stable failures are pairs consisting of a trace and an action set where the trace may lead to a stable state where continuing the execution with any action in the set fails. Divergence traces are traces that may lead to states from which the invisible action τ can be executed infinitely many times. Infinite traces are infinite sequences of visible actions that can be executed starting from the initial state of an LTS.

We have $Tr(P) = DivTr(P) \cup \{ \sigma \mid (\sigma, \emptyset) \in SFail(P) \}$ [16].

Definition 12 (CFFD-preorder "$\leq_{CFFD}$"). Let P and Q be LTSs. $P \acute{a} \leq_{CFFD} Q$ if and only if $\Sigma(P) = \Sigma(Q)$, stable(Q)$\acute{a} \Rightarrow$ stable(P), SFail(P)$\acute{a} \subseteq$ SFail(Q), DivTr(P)$\acute{a} \subseteq$ DivTr(Q) and InfTr(P)$\acute{a} \subseteq$ InfTr(Q). ☐

If P and Q are finite LTSs, then InfTr(P)$\acute{a} \subseteq$ InfTr(Q) is implied by SFail(P) $\acute{a} \subseteq$ SFail(Q) and DivTr(P)$\acute{a} \subseteq$ DivTr(Q) [16]. As a consequence, the infinite traces are insignificant for this paper, and will not be mentioned any more.

The CSP-divergence traces are those visible action sequences whose prefix is a divergence trace. Stable failures are CSP-failures, and so are also CSP-divergence traces with any subset of the alphabet as the refusal set.

Definition 13 (CSP-divergences and CSP-failures). Let $L = (S, \Sigma, \Delta, \hat{s})$ be an LTS. $CSPdiv(L) = \{ a_1 a_2 \cdots a_n \in \Sigma^* \mid \exists i, 0 \leq i \leq n : a_1 a_2 \cdots a_i \in DivTr(L) \}$. $CSPfail(L) = SFail(L)\acute{a} \cup (CSPdiv(L)\acute{a} \times 2^\Sigma)$. ☐

Definition 14 (CSP-preorder "$\leq_{CSP}$"). Let P and Q be LTSs. $P\acute{a} \leq_{CSP} Q$ iff $\Sigma(P) = \Sigma(Q)$, CSPfail(P)$\acute{a} \subseteq$ CSPfail(Q) and CSPdiv(P) $\subseteq$ CSPdiv(Q). ☐

3   Upper Bounds

Upper bounds on complexity of linear-time verification hold for a large class of operators. Because of this, we introduce the notion of *small-space operators*. Let P be a process expression, and let $L = (S, \Sigma, \Delta, \hat{s})$ be the LTS obtained by evaluating P. We say that P can be *simulated* in memory M, if, given any $s, s' \in S$ and $a \in \Sigma \cup \{\tau\}$, M suffices for representing s and for nondeterministically checking that $(s, a, s') \in \Delta$. For instance, an individual LTS L can be simulated in memory $O(\log |L|)$. If P_1 to P_n can be simulated in memory M_1 to M_n, respectively, then $P_1 \parallel \cdots \parallel P_n$ can be simulated in $M_1 + \cdots + M_n + O(1)$.

We define that an n-ary process operator f is a small-space operator, if $f(P_1, \ldots, P_n)$ can be simulated in memory $M_1 + \cdots + M_n + M_f$, where M_1 to M_n are the amounts of memory needed to simulate P_1 to P_n, respectively, and M_f is a constant that may depend on f, but not on the P_i. The hiding, renaming and three parallel composition operators defined in Section 2 are small-space, and so are all operators of the Basic Lotos language [1]. (We assume that the lowest-level constituents of process expressions are explicit LTSs. Therefore, we do not consider recursive process invocation such as $P := a; P$ as a process operator.) Indeed, most process composition operators presented in the literature are small-space. As an artificial example of an operator that is *not* small-space we define "squaring" $sq(P)$ as an abbreviation of $P \parallel\parallel P$.

It is well known that the problem of deciding $Tr(P) \subseteq Tr(Q)$ is **PSPACE**-complete, if P and Q are given as LTSs. We will now show that the problem remains in **PSPACE** even if P and Q are replaced by significantly more complicated process expressions. This result slightly extends Theorem 3.12 of [13] by allowing a large variety of operators on the left hand side of the preorder. The proofs are based on the same ideas.

Theorem 1. *Let P_1 to P_n and Q_1 to Q_m be LTSs, and let $f(P_1, \ldots, P_n)$ be a process expression composed of small-space operators. The problem* "does $Tr(f(P_1, \ldots, P_n)) \subseteq Tr(Q_1 \parallel \cdots \parallel Q_m)$ hold?" *is in* **PSPACE**.

Proof. We will present a nondeterministic algorithm that answers the question in polynomial space, if the answer is "no". Because **NPSPACE = PSPACE**, this implies the claim.

Let Σ_P be the alphabet of $f(P_1, \ldots, P_n)$, and let $Q_i = (S_i, \Sigma_i, \Delta_i, \hat{s}_i)$ for $1 \leq i \leq m$. Let $\Sigma_Q = \Sigma_1 \cup \cdots \cup \Sigma_m$. Without loss of generality we may assume that $\Sigma_P \subseteq \Sigma_Q$, because otherwise we may add to the right hand side an extra LTS Q_{m+1} that has one state and no transitions, and whose alphabet is $\Sigma_P - \Sigma_Q$.

For any $\sigma \in \Sigma_Q^*$, let S_i^σ be the set of states that Q_i can be in after executing its part of σ. That is, $S_i^\sigma = \{ s \in S_i \mid \hat{s}_i =\sigma\downarrow\Sigma_i\Rightarrow s \}$. The crucial point of the proof is that the set of states that $Q_1 \parallel \cdots \parallel Q_m$ can be in after executing σ is $S_1^\sigma \times \cdots \times S_m^\sigma$. This can be verified from Definition 8 with a simple induction proof on the length of σ.

Because f is composed of small-space operators, a nondeterministic algorithm can simulate $f(P_1, \ldots, P_n)$ in polynomial (actually $O(\log |P_1| + \cdots + \log |P_n|)$)

space. During the simulation, the set of the states of $Q_1 \| \cdots \| Q_m$ is maintained as follows. Initially the sets S_1^ε to S_m^ε are computed. Whenever the label of a simulated transition of $f(P_1, \ldots, P_m)$ is a visible action a, each set S_i^σ is updated to become $S_i^{\sigma a}$. If any S_i^σ becomes empty, then the algorithm stops and replies "no". Each S_i^σ can be maintained in $O(|Q_i|)$ space, so altogether only a polynomial amount of space is needed.   □

Theorem 1 is in contradiction with Theorem 5.1 in [7]. That theorem claims that the checking of trace inclusion (and some other preorders) is **EXPSPACE**-hard for "non-flat" systems. The non-flat systems of that paper are systems of the form $P_1 \| \cdots \| P_n$, where the P_i are LTSs without τ-transitions. The proof (called "sketch of proof" in the paper) of the theorem refers to a construction in [5] without describing it, and adds a small change to it. The latter paper, in turn, refers to [9]. However, [9] uses the interleaving parallel composition operator "$\|\|$" which can be immediately simulated by the formalism in [5], but not by "$\|$". We conclude that there has been a confusion with different types of parallel composition operators.

The result of Theorem 1 extends to the checking of the CFFD- and CSP-preorders.

Theorem 2. *Let P_1 to P_n and Q_1 to Q_m be LTSs, and let $f(P_1, \ldots, P_n)$ be a process expression composed of small-space operators. The following problems are in* **PSPACE***:*

- *Does $f(P_1, \ldots, P_n) \leq_{\mathsf{CFFD}} Q_1 \| \cdots \| Q_m$ hold?*
- *Does $f(P_1, \ldots, P_n) \leq_{\mathsf{CSP}} Q_1 \| \cdots \| Q_m$ hold?*

Proof. Let $Impl = f(P_1, \ldots, P_n)$ and $Spec = Q_1 \| \cdots \| Q_m$. We consider first the checking of $Impl \leq_{\mathsf{CFFD}} Spec$. The equality of alphabets is easy to check, and so is also the claim $stable(Spec) \Rightarrow stable(Impl)$. If neither of these checks yields a "no"-answer, then $Impl \not\leq_{\mathsf{CFFD}} Spec$ if and only if there is some $\sigma \in Tr(Impl) \cap Tr(Spec)$ such that at least one of the following three holds [2]:

1. There is such an a that $\sigma a \in Tr(Impl)$ but $\sigma a \notin Tr(Spec)$.
2. There is such an A that $(\sigma, A) \in SFail(Impl)$ but $(\sigma, A) \notin SFail(Spec)$.
3. $\sigma \in DivTr(Impl)$ but $\sigma \notin DivTr(Spec)$.

The first of these three conditions is checked by the algorithm in the proof of Theorem 1. To cover the remaining two, we add two "test modes" to the algorithm. The algorithm may nondeterministically decide to enter either of these modes at any time.

As the first thing after entering the "$DivTr$-checking mode" the algorithm stores the state of $Impl$. Then it simulates τ-transitions of $Impl$ until $Impl$ gets back to the stored state. (Of course, it is possible that this never happens, but this is not a problem in a nondeterministic algorithm.) At that point it has proven that the trace σ executed so far is in $DivTr(Impl)$. Then it verifies that none of the Q_i contains a cycle that consists only of τ-transitions and states of S_i^σ.

This can be done by a depth-first search, for instance. If that succeeds, the algorithm stops and replies "no", as it has proven that $DivTr(Impl) \not\subseteq DivTr(Spec)$. This kind of proof is available for every member of $DivTr(Impl) \cap Tr(Spec) - DivTr(Spec)$.

In the "$SFail$-checking mode" the algorithm first investigates each alternative next transition of $Impl$ and collects their labels into a set B. Storing B does not require much memory, because $B \subseteq \Sigma(Impl) \cup \{\tau\}$. The algorithm then verifies that $\tau \notin B$. Then it goes through each $s \in S_1^\sigma \times \cdots \times S_m^\sigma$. For each such s, it computes a set B' on the basis of the next possible transitions of s similarly to the computation of B, and checks whether $B' \subseteq B$ holds. If $B' \subseteq B$ holds for no s, the algorithm has proven that $(\sigma, \Sigma(Impl) - B)$ is a counter-example, so the algorithm replies "no" and terminates. Again, this test can detect any instance of number 2 in the above list.

The checking of $Impl \leq_{\mathsf{CSP}} Spec$ is otherwise similar to $Impl \leq_{\mathsf{CFFD}} Spec$, except that the claim about "$stable$" is not checked, and the algorithm is immediately stopped with no reply when the trace executed so far is a divergence trace of $Spec$. This is correct, because if $\sigma \in DivTr(Spec)$, then $\sigma\rho \in CSPdiv(Spec)$ and $(\sigma\rho, A) \in CSPfail(Spec)$ for any $\rho \in \Sigma(Spec)^*$ and $A \subseteq \Sigma(Spec)$. If $\sigma \notin CSPdiv(Spec)$, then the $DivTr$-checking mode reports "no" on some prefix of σ if and only if $\sigma \in CSPdiv(Impl)$. If $\sigma \notin CSPdiv(Spec) \cup CSPdiv(Impl)$, then (σ, A) is a counter-example if and only if $(\sigma, A) \in SFail(Impl)$ and $(\sigma, A) \notin SFail(Spec)$, so the $SFail$-checking mode reveals the remaining "no"-cases. That $Spec$ has diverged is detected by checking each S_i^σ against τ-cycles, as was explained above in the description of the $DivTr$-checking mode.   □

If $Spec$ is made more complicated than in the previous theorems, then we only can prove a weaker result.

Theorem 3. *Let P_1 to P_n and Q_1 to Q_m be LTSs, and let $f(P_1, \ldots, P_n)$ and $g(Q_1, \ldots, Q_m)$ be process expressions composed of small-space operators. The following problems are in* **EXPSPACE***:*

- *Does $Tr(f(P_1, \ldots, P_n)) \subseteq Tr(g(Q_1, \ldots, Q_m))$ hold?*
- *Does $f(P_1, \ldots, P_n) \leq_{\mathsf{CFFD}} g(Q_1, \ldots, Q_m)$ hold?*
- *Does $f(P_1, \ldots, P_n) \leq_{\mathsf{CSP}} g(Q_1, \ldots, Q_m)$ hold?*

Proof. Exponential memory suffices for constructing the LTS of $g(Q_1, \ldots, Q_m)$. Application of Theorems 1 and 2 with that LTS on the right hand side and $f(P_1, \ldots, P_m)$ on the left hand side then yields the result. The amount of memory used is polynomial in the size of the expression $f(P_1, \ldots, P_n)$ and polynomial in the size of the explicit LTS, thus being exponential in the size of the expression $g(Q_1, \ldots, Q_m)$.   □

As a matter of fact, $f(P_1, \ldots, P_n)$ could have been allowed to use exponential memory in the theorem.

From the first two theorems it follows that *implementation complexity*, that is the complexity of checking linear time preorders against a fixed specification, does not grow out of **PSPACE** in ordinary cases. The problem is actually

PSPACE-complete because deciding "Can *Impl* ever execute action a after trace σ?" is **PSPACE**-hard. This well known result can be found, for example, in [15].

4   Exponential Space Lower Bounds for "$||[\cdots]||$"

This section is devoted to a proof that the decision problem in Theorem 1 becomes **EXPSPACE**-hard, if the operator "$||[\cdots]||$" is used instead of "$||$" on the right hand side. As a matter of fact, it suffices that just one of the "$||$" operators is replaced with a "$||[\cdots]||$", and the set within the "$||[\cdots]||$" may be empty. Furthermore, the expression on the left hand side does not need to be more than just one LTS.

Theorem 4. $Tr(P)$á $\subseteq Tr(Q_1 ||[\cdots]|| \cdots ||[\cdots]|| Q_m)$ *is* **EXPSPACE**-*complete.*

Proof. Theorem 3 says that it is in **EXPSPACE**. The problem whether a language over the alphabet $\{0,1\}$ expressed as a regular expression r with squaring is equal to $\{0,1\}^*$ is **EXPSPACE**-complete, as was shown by Meyer and Stockmeyer in [8]. We shall describe a polynomial time reduction from this problem to the problem

$$Tr(P)\text{á} \subseteq Tr(Spec),$$

where *Spec* is a short hand notation for the expression

$$(R\,||[mid_1, end_1, \ldots, mid_q, end_q]||\,(Q_1 ||| \cdots ||| Q_q))\,|||\,O.$$

The architecture of *Spec* is as shown in Figure 1.

In the above, q is the number of occurrences of the squaring operator in r. Most of r will be represented by R. The Q_i will keep track of the status of each squaring operation. The negotiations between R and the Q_i add some undesired visible actions to the behaviour of *Spec*, but their effect to the trace comparison is compensated by O. O generates "noise" that covers up any information on the negotiations.

The $2q$ actions $mid_1, end_1, \ldots, mid_q, end_q$ are all different from "0" and "1" and from each other. As it was mentioned earlier, "$|||$" stands for "$||[]||$", that is, parallel composition without synchronisation. The processes O, P, Q_1 to Q_q, and R have the following alphabets: $\Sigma(O) = \{mid_1, end_1, \ldots, mid_q, end_q\}$, $\Sigma(Q_i) = \{mid_i, end_i\}$ for $1 \leq i \leq q$, and $\Sigma(P) = \Sigma(R) = \Sigma(O) \cup \{0,1,\delta\}$ where δ is yet another new action. It will be used to express the acceptance of a word. The details of the processes will be described below.

A comparison of the alphabets shows that *Spec* can be written equivalently as

$$(R\,||\,Q_1\,||\,\cdots\,||\,Q_q)\,|||\,O.$$

Each Q_i, illustrated in Figure 2, is a two-state LTS with the alphabet $\Sigma(Q_i) = \{mid_i, end_i\}$. There are two transitions: one from the initial state to the other state, labelled mid_i, and one from the other state back to the initial state, labelled end_i. When synchronised with R, this process will ensure that the ith squaring operation works correctly.

The process O, also presented in Figure 2, is the one-state LTS with a transition from the initial state to itself for each action in the alphabet. Thus, O can execute any number of actions in $\Sigma(O)$ in any order and nothing else. O is composed in parallel with other processes without synchronisation. Therefore, *Spec* is allowed to execute any number of actions in $\Sigma(O)$ in any order at any time.

The process P is sketched in Figure 3. Its alphabet is $\{0, 1, \delta\} \cup \Sigma(O)$, and it contains $4q^2 + 1$ states. The initial state of P has a transition to the second state for each action in $\{0, 1, \delta\}$. The remaining transitions and states form a chain that leads back to the initial state. The chain is composed of $2q$ identical subchains, each of whose transitions are labelled mid_1, end_1, mid_2, ..., end_q in this order. (As a matter of fact, the ordering of the actions within a subchain does not matter.) Thus **hide** $mid_1, \ldots, end_q$ **in** P can execute any string in $\{0, 1, \delta\}^*$, but between any two actions from $\{0, 1, \delta\}$, P is guaranteed to execute $(mid_1 \cdots end_q)^{2q}$. We will later see that this makes it possible for R to negotiate with $Q_1, \ldots, Q_n$ via the *mid*- and *end*-actions without affecting the validity of the property $Tr(P)á \subseteq Tr(Spec)$. Thanks to O, *Spec* can also execute those *mid*- and *end*-actions of P that are not used in the negotiation.

We shall next construct R by a translation from the squaring-regular expression r. The translation is a variant of the well-known construction presented in many textbooks like [4, pages 102–104]. Of course, the presence of squaring operators makes a difference from the standard construction. Another important difference is that the empty string "ε" is treated as a special case. Namely, the possibility of accepting ε is not represented in the translations of subexpressions. Instead, it is kept track of in a separate attribute "$p\varepsilon(r)$" attached to each subexpression r. The purpose of this is to ensure that there is a reasonable upper limit to the number of mid_i- and end_i-actions that R must do between any two actions from $\{0, 1\}$. The construction of P relied on that limit.

The construction is shown in Figure 4. In the figure, states with a small inner circle are end states of the translations of sub-subexpressions and with a large inner circle end states of the translation of the subexpression. It is an invariant property of the construction that the translations of subexpressions cannot reach their end states without executing at least once "0" or "1". To guarantee that the construction can be executed in polynomial time, the translation of each sub-subexpression appears only once in the translation of a subexpression.

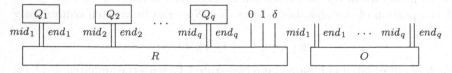

Fig. 1. The structure of the parallel composition

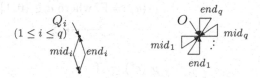

Fig. 2. Processes Q_i and O

The translation of the squaring operator relies on its corresponding Q_i-process to ensure that the executions of mid_i and end_i alternate. This forces the translation of the sub-subexpression to be executed the correct number of times. This correct number is precisely two, if the sub-subexpression does not produce ε. In the opposite case, also a single execution is allowed, to take into account the possibility that one of the applications of the r in r^2 produces ε. The possibility of both applications yielding ε is catered for by "$p\varepsilon$". Furthermore, the translation guarantees that before the first and between any two executions of mid_i, the action 0 or 1 is executed at least once; and similarly for end_i.

If $p\varepsilon(r) = \mathsf{F}$ when r is the whole expression, the problem whether $\mathcal{L}(r) = \{0,1\}^*$ has been solved: the answer is no, $\varepsilon \notin \mathcal{L}(r)$. In the opposite case, the construction of R is completed by adding one more state and five transitions as is shown in Figure 5.

Now we are ready to show that $\mathcal{L}(r) = \{0,1\}^*$ holds if and only if $\mathit{Tr}(P) \subseteq \mathit{Tr}(\mathit{Spec})$. First, assume that $\mathcal{L}(r) = \{0,1\}^*$. Let $a_1a_2 \cdots a_n\acute{a} \in \mathit{Tr}(P)$. It is of the form $b_1\pi b_2\pi \cdots \pi b_m\pi'$, where $\pi = (mid_1end_1 \cdots mid_qend_q)^{2q}$, π' is a prefix of π, and each b_i belongs to $\{0,1,\delta\}$. Let then $b_1b_2 \cdots b_k$ be the longest prefix of $b_1b_2 \cdots b_m$ that does not contain δ.

Since $\mathcal{L}(r) = \{0,1\}^*$, the string $b_1b_2 \cdots b_k$ is generated by r, and therefore R has an execution with the following properties. It leads to a starting state of a transition labelled δ. Furthermore, the trace it produces is of the form $b_1\sigma_1b_2\sigma_2 \cdots b_k\sigma_k$, where $\sigma_1\sigma_2 \cdots \sigma_k \in \Sigma_O^*$, each $a\acute{a} \in \Sigma(O)$ appears at most once in each σ_i, and $(\sigma_1\sigma_2 \cdots \sigma_k){\downarrow}\{mid_i, end_i\}$ is of the form $(mid_iend_i)^*$ for every $1 \leq i \leq q$. As a consequence, also $R \,\|\, Q_1 \,\|\, \cdots \,\|\, Q_q$ has an execution that produces the same trace, and leaves R in a start state of a δ-transition.

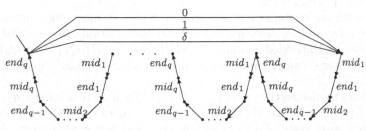

Fig. 3. Process P

$p\varepsilon(\varepsilon) := \mathsf{T}$

$p\varepsilon(a) := \mathsf{F}$, where $a \in \{0, 1\}$

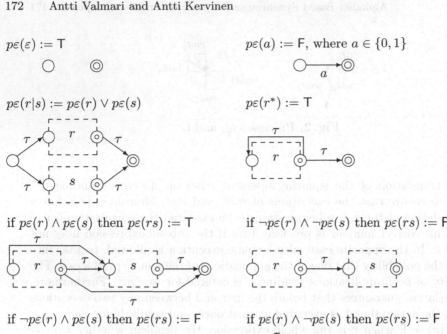

$p\varepsilon(r|s) := p\varepsilon(r) \vee p\varepsilon(s)$

$p\varepsilon(r^*) := \mathsf{T}$

if $p\varepsilon(r) \wedge p\varepsilon(s)$ then $p\varepsilon(rs) := \mathsf{T}$

if $\neg p\varepsilon(r) \wedge \neg p\varepsilon(s)$ then $p\varepsilon(rs) := \mathsf{F}$

if $\neg p\varepsilon(r) \wedge p\varepsilon(s)$ then $p\varepsilon(rs) := \mathsf{F}$

if $p\varepsilon(r) \wedge \neg p\varepsilon(s)$ then $p\varepsilon(rs) := \mathsf{F}$

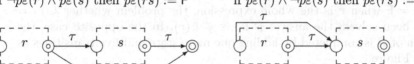

if $\neg p\varepsilon(r)$ then $p\varepsilon(r^2) := \mathsf{F}$

if $p\varepsilon(r)$ then $p\varepsilon(r^2) := \mathsf{T}$

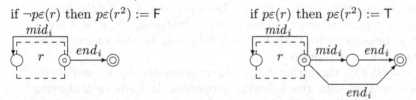

Fig. 4. Translation of subexpressions of r

Thanks to the state and transitions added in the last stage of the construction of R, $R \,||\, Q_1 \,||\, \cdots \,||\, Q_q$ can continue the execution and produce the trace $b_1\sigma_1 b_2\sigma_2 \cdots \sigma_{m-1} b_m \sigma_m$, where $\sigma_{k+1} = \sigma_{k+2} = \ldots = \sigma_m = \varepsilon$.

Because each σ_i contains any element of $\Sigma(O)$ at most once, it can be extended to π by adding elements from $\Sigma(O)$ into suitable places. The process O can execute the added actions. Therefore, $Spec = (R \,||\, Q_1 \,||\, \cdots \,||\, Q_q) \,|||\, O$ can execute $b_1\pi b_2\pi \cdots \pi b_m\pi$, and also its prefix $b_1\pi b_2\pi \cdots \pi b_m\pi'$. So $Tr(P)$á $\subseteq$ $Tr(Spec)$.

We still have to discuss the case $\mathcal{L}(r) \neq \{0, 1\}^*$. Then there is some $a_1 a_2 \cdots a_n \in \{0, 1\}^* - \mathcal{L}(r)$. If π is like above, then $a_1\pi a_2\pi \cdots a_n\pi\delta \in Tr(P)$. However, R cannot be in a start state of a δ-transition after $Spec$ has read $a_1\pi a_2\pi \cdots a_n\pi$, so $a_1\pi a_2\pi \cdots a_n\pi\delta \notin Tr(Spec)$. □

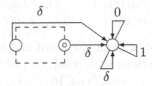

Fig. 5. Completion of process R

Next we show that **EXPSPACE**-hardness holds also for checking CSP- and CFFD-preorders when $Spec$ is composed using the "$\|[\cdots]\|$" operator.

Theorem 5. *The following problems are* **EXPSPACE**-*complete.*

- *Does* $P\acute{a} \leq_{\mathsf{CSP}} Q_1 \|[\cdots]\| \cdots \|[\cdots]\| Q_m$ *hold?*
- *Does* $P\acute{a} \leq_{\mathsf{CFFD}} Q_1 \|[\cdots]\| \cdots \|[\cdots]\| Q_m$ *hold?*

Proof. Theorem 3 says that they are in **EXPSPACE**. We modify slightly the LTSs O and R in the proof of Theorem 4. Namely, we add to both of them one extra state, and a τ-transition from each original state to the added state. This modification does not change the traces or divergence traces of O and R, but makes it possible for both of them to deadlock at any time. Thus also $Spec$ can deadlock at any time, and $SFail(Spec) = Tr(Spec) \times 2^{\Sigma(Spec)}$. The modification also guarantees that $stable(O) = stable(Spec) = \mathsf{F}$.

The construction of R guarantees that each cycle of R contains at least one transition whose label is in $\{0, 1, \delta\}$, so $DivTr(Spec) = CSPdiv(Spec) = \emptyset$. Clearly also $DivTr(P) = CSPdiv(P) = \emptyset$.

So $stable(Spec) \Rightarrow stable(P)$, $DivTr(P) \subseteq DivTr(Spec)$, and $CSPdiv(P) \subseteq CSPdiv(Spec)$. Furthermore, if $Tr(P) \subseteq Tr(Spec)$ then also $SFail(P) \subseteq Tr(Spec)$ $\times 2^{\Sigma(Spec)} = SFail(Spec)$ and $CSPfail(P) = SFail(P) \cup (\emptyset \times 2^{\Sigma(P)}) \subseteq SFail(Spec) \cup$ $(\emptyset \times 2^{\Sigma(Spec)}) = CSPfail(Spec)$. On the other hand, if $Tr(P) \not\subseteq Tr(Spec)$, then $SFail(P) \not\subseteq SFail(Spec)$ and $CSPfail(P) \not\subseteq CSPfail(Spec) = SFail(Spec) \cup (\emptyset \times 2^{\Sigma(Spec)})$. Thus $P\acute{a} \leq_{\mathsf{CFFD}} Spec$ if and only if $Tr(P) \subseteq Tr(Spec)$, and similarly with "$\leq_{\mathsf{CSP}}$". □

5 Corollaries

The construction that was used in the **EXPSPACE**-hardness proofs in Section 4 can be modified to obtain some additional **EXPSPACE**-hardness results. A crucial element in the proofs was that the presence of the interleaving operator "$|||$" made it impossible to uniquely reason which subprocesses of $Spec$ participate a visible action. The same effect can also be obtained with the renaming operator.

Corollary 1 (Renaming on top of "$\|$").
The following problems are **EXPSPACE**-*complete:*

- *Does* $Tr(P)\acute{a} \subseteq Tr(\mathbf{rename} \cdots \mathbf{in}\ (Q_1 \| \cdots \| Q_m))$ *hold?*

– *Does* $P\acute{a} \leq_{\mathsf{CFFD}}$ **rename** $\cdots$ **in** $(Q_1 \,\|\, \cdots \,\|\, Q_m)$ *hold?*
– *Does* $P\acute{a} \leq_{\mathsf{CSP}}$ **rename** $\cdots$ **in** $(Q_1 \,\|\, \cdots \,\|\, Q_m)$ *hold?*

Proof. Let P, Q_1 to Q_q and R be as in the proof of Theorem 5, and let O be changed such that it uses new actions mid_1', end_1', ..., mid_q', end_q' instead of mid_1 etc. Then **rename** mid_1/mid_1', ..., end_q/end_q' **in** $(R \,\|\, Q_1 \,\|\, \cdots \,\|\, Q_q \,\|\, O)$ behaves just like the original *Spec*.   □

Alternatively, one can hide the negotiation between R and the Q_i.

Corollary 2 (Hiding on top of "$\|$").
The following problems are **EXPSPACE**-*complete:*

– *Does* $Tr(P)\acute{a} \subseteq Tr(\mathbf{hide} \cdots \mathbf{in}\,(Q_1 \,\|\, \cdots \,\|\, Q_m))$ *hold?*
– *Does* $P\acute{a} \leq_{\mathsf{CFFD}}$ **hide** $\cdots$ **in** $(Q_1 \,\|\, \cdots \,\|\, Q_m)$ *hold?*
– *Does* $P\acute{a} \leq_{\mathsf{CSP}}$ **hide** $\cdots$ **in** $(Q_1 \,\|\, \cdots \,\|\, Q_m)$ *hold?*

Proof. The P in the proof of Theorem 5 is replaced with a single-state LTS that has a transition for each $a\acute{a} \in \{0, 1, \delta\}$, and O is omitted altogether. Instead of *Spec*, $Spec_2 = \mathbf{hide}\,mid_1, end_1, ..., mid_q, end_q\,\mathbf{in}\,(R \,\|\, Q_1 \,\|\, \cdots \,\|\, Q_q)$ is used.   □

Because the CCS parallel composition operator "$|$" automatically hides all synchronising actions, the previous result implies the following:

Corollary 3 (CCS-parallel composition).
The following problems are **EXPSPACE**-*complete:*

– *Does* $Tr(P)\acute{a} \subseteq Tr(Q_1 \,|\, \cdots \,|\, Q_m)$ *hold?*
– *Does* $P\acute{a} \leq_{\mathsf{CFFD}} Q_1 \,|\, \cdots \,|\, Q_m$ *hold?*
– *Does* $P\acute{a} \leq_{\mathsf{CSP}} Q_1 \,|\, \cdots \,|\, Q_m$ *hold?*

Proof. The Q_i of the previous corollary are changed to use co-actions $\overline{mid_i}$ and $\overline{end_i}$, the "$\|$" operators are replaced by "$|$" operators, and the hiding operator is discarded. Furthermore, an extra deadlock state is added to each Q_i, and a τ-transition to it is added from each original state of Q_i. The resulting $Spec_3 = R \,|\, Q_1 \,|\, \cdots \,|\, Q_q$ can execute all the traces that $Spec_2$ can. Because "$|$" does not *enforce* synchronisation, $Spec_3$ can also execute additional traces, but they all contain *mid* or *end*-actions or their co-actions, so they do not confuse the comparison of traces, stability, or divergence traces. They do affect stable failures, but the effect is cancelled by the addition of the deadlock states.   □

6   Conclusions

We saw that the complexity jumps from polynomial to exponential space when one of the "$\|$" operators in *Spec* is replaced with "$\|\|$". Intuitively, the reason for the complexity jump is that with "$\|$", the subprocesses of *Spec* that participate a visible action can always be reasoned from the name of the action, whereas in the presence of one "$\|\|$" this is no more possible. The reasoning can also be confused and the complexity jump caused by hiding some synchronisation actions in the specification, or renaming actions to the same.

If the total number of parallel composition operators is restricted from above by a constant k, then $O((max|S_i|)^k)$ memory suffices for constructing the state space. Therefore, an unbounded number of parallel composition operators is needed to obtain **EXPSPACE**-hardness. It is interesting that only one of them needs to be "|||".

Acknowledgements

Thanks to Antti Puhakka for good comments. The work was in part funded by the Academy of Finland, project Covera.

References

1. Bolognesi, T. & Brinksma, E.: "Introduction to the ISO Specification Language LOTOS". *Computer Networks and ISDN Systems* 14, 1987, pp. 25–59. 162, 164, 166
2. Helovuo, J. & Valmari, A.: "Checking for CFFD-Preorder with Tester Processes". *Proc. TACAS'2000, 6th International Conference on Tools and Algorithms for the Construction and Analysis of Systems*, Lecture Notes in Computer Science 1785, Springer-Verlag 2000, pp. 283–298. 161, 167
3. Hoare, C. A. R.: *Communicating Sequential Processes*. Prentice-Hall 1985, 256 p. 161
4. Hopcroft, J. E., Motwani, R. & Ullman, J. D.: *Introduction to Automata Theory, Languages, and Computation*. Addison-Wesley 2001, 521 p. 170
5. Jategaonkar, L. & Meyer, A. R.: "Deciding True Concurrency Equivalences on Finite Safe Nets". *Theoretical Computer Science* 154 (1), 1996, pp. 107–143. 167
6. Kanellakis, P. & Smolka, S.: "CCS Expressions, Finite State Processes, and Three Problems of Equivalence". *Information and Computation* 86 (1), Academic Press 1990, pp. 43–68. 161
7. Laroussinie, F. & Schnoebelen, P.: "The State Explosion Problem from Trace to Bisimulation Equivalence". *Proc. FoSSaCS'2000, 3rd International Conference on Foundations of Software Science and Computation Structures*, Lecture Notes in Computer Science 1784, Springer-Verlag 2000, pp. 192–207. 162, 167
8. Meyer, A. L. & Stockmeyer, L. J.: "The Equivalence Problem for Regular Expressions with Squaring Requires Exponential Time". *Proc. 13th Annual Symposium on Switching and Automata Theory*, IEEE 1972, pp. 125–129. 161, 169
9. Meyer, A. L. & Stockmeyer, L. J.: "Word Problems—This Time with Interleaving". *Information and Computation* 115 (2), 1994, pp. 293–311. 167
10. Milner, R.: *Communication and Concurrency*. Prentice Hall 1989. 162, 164
11. Rabinovich, A.: "Complexity of Equivalence Problems for Concurrent Systems of Finite Agents". *Information and Computation* 139 (2), Academic Press 1997, pp. 111–129. 161
12. Roscoe, A. W.: *The Theory and Practice of Concurrency*. Prentice-Hall 1998, 565 p. 161

13. Shukla, S. K., Hunt III, H. B., Rosenkrantz, D. J. & Stearns, R. E.: "On the Complexity of Relational Problems for Finite State Processes". *Proc. ICALP'96, 23rd International Colloquium on Automata, Languages and Programming*, Lecture Notes in Computer Science 1099, Springer-Verlag, 1996, pp. 466–477. 162, 166

14. Sistla, A. P. & Clarke, E. M.: "The Complexity of Propositional Linear Temporal Logics". *Journal of the ACP* 32 (3), 1985, pp. 733–749. 161

15. Valmari, A.: "Failure-based Equivalences Are Faster Than Many Believe". *Proc. STRICT'95, Structures in Concurrency Theory*, Workshops in Computing, Springer-Verlag 1995, pp. 326–340. 169

16. Valmari, A. & Tienari, M.: "Compositional Failure-Based Semantic Models for Basic LOTOS". *Formal Aspects of Computing* 7, 1995, pp. 440–468. 161, 165

Safe Realizability of High-Level Message Sequence Charts*

Markus Lohrey

Institut für Informatik, Universität Stuttgart
Breitwiesenstr. 20-22, 70565 Stuttgart, Germany
lohrey@informatik.uni-stuttgart.de

Abstract. We study the notion of safe realizability for high-level message sequence charts (HMSCs), which was introduced in [2]. We prove that safe realizability is EXPSPACE-complete for bounded HMSCs but undecidable for the class of all HMSCs. This solves two open problems from [2]. Moreover we prove that safe realizability is also EXPSPACE-complete for the larger class of transition-connected HMSCs.

1 Introduction

Message sequence charts (MSCs) are a popular visual formalism for specifying the communication of asynchronous processes, where most of the details (variables, timing constraints, etc) are abstracted away. They are part of the ITU standard [14]. *High-level message sequence charts* (HMSCs) extend MSCs by allowing iteration and non-deterministic choices. In this way infinite sets of MSCs can be described.

Due to the abstract nature of HMSCs, the question of realizability (or implementability) arises: Given an HMSC (the specification), is it possible to implement it as a communicating protocol (the implementation), which shows the same behaviour as the original HMSC? This is a highly nontrivial problem, properties like for instance non-local choices in HMSCs [4] may constitute nontrivial obstacles for obtaining realizations, see e.g. [10].

Concerning the formal definition of realizability, we follow Alur et al [1,2], which define two notions of realizability: *weak realizability* and *safe realizability*. Both are based on the model of *communicating finite state machines* (CFMs) with FIFO-queues for describing the implementation. CFMs appeared as one of the earliest abstract models for concurrent systems [5,18], and are used for instance in the specification language SDL [13]. An accepting run of a CFM generates in a canonical way an MSC. Thus, in [2] an HMSC H is called weakly realizable, if there exists a CFM $\mathcal{A}$ such that the set of all MSCs generated by the accepting runs of $\mathcal{A}$ is precisely the set of MSCs defined by H. In practice, such an implementation may be considered as being too weak. A very desirable further property of the implementation $\mathcal{A}$ is *deadlock-freeness*: every partial run

---

* This work was done while the author was on leave at IRISA, Campus de Beaulieu, 35042 Rennes, France and supported by the INRIA cooperative research action FISC.

L. Brim et al. (Eds.): CONCUR 2002, LNCS 2421, pp. 177–192, 2002.

of $\mathcal{A}$ can be completed to a run that terminates in a final state of $\mathcal{A}$. Thus, in [2] an HMSC H is called safely realizable, if there exists a *deadlock-free* CFM $\mathcal{A}$ such that the set of all MSCs generated by the accepting runs of $\mathcal{A}$ is precisely the set of MSCs defined by H.

In [2] it is shown that weak realizability is already undecidable for *bounded HMSCs*, a class of HMSCs, which was introduced in [3,16] because of its nice model-checking properties. As shown in [15], FIFO communication is crucial for this result: for non-FIFO communication weak realizability is decidable for bounded HMSCs. Concerning safe realizability, Alur et al prove in [2] that for bounded HSMCs safe realizability is in EXPSPACE but PSPACE-hard, but the exact complexity remained open. In Section 3.1, we will prove that safe realizability is in fact EXPSPACE-complete for bounded HMSCs. Moreover, using the same technique, we will also prove that safe realizability is undecidable for the class of all HMSCs, which solves the second open problem from [2]. Finally, in Section 3.2, we will establish EXPSPACE-completeness of safe realizability also for the class of *transition-connected HMSCs* [8,15]. This class strictly contains the class of bounded HSMC but shares many of the nice properties of the latter.

Let us also remark that the notion of realizability used in this paper is a quite strict one in the sense that it allows on the implementation-side neither the introduction of new messages nor the addition of further content to already existing messages. More liberal realizations that allow the latter were studied in [8]. Another approach to realization based on Petri nets is studied in [6].

Proofs that are omitted in this extended abstract will appear in the full version of this paper.

2   Preliminaries

For complexity results we will use standard classes like PSPACE (polynomial space) and EXPSPACE (exponential space), see [17] for definitions.

Let Σ be an alphabet of symbols and $\Gamma \subseteq \Sigma$. We denote with $\pi_\Gamma : \Sigma^* \to \Gamma^*$ the projection morphism onto the subalphabet Γ. The empty word is denoted by ϵ. The length of the word $w \in \Sigma^*$ is $|w|$. For $k \in \mathbb{N}$ let $w[1,k]$ be the prefix of w of length $\min\{k, |w|\}$. For $u, v \in \Sigma^*$ we write $u \sqsubseteq v$, if u is a prefix of v.

A *pomset* is a labeled partial order $\mathcal{P} = (A, \lambda, \prec)$, i.e., $(A, \prec)$ is a partial order and $\lambda : A \to \Sigma$ is a labeling function. For $B \subseteq A$ we define the restricted pomset $\mathcal{P}\restriction_B = (B, \lambda\restriction_B, \prec\restriction_B)$. A word $\lambda(a_1)\lambda(a_2)\cdots\lambda(a_n) \in \Sigma^*$ is a *linearization* of $\mathcal{P}$ if $A = \{a_1, a_2, \ldots, a_n\}$, $a_i \neq a_j$ for $i \neq j$, and $a_i \prec a_j$ implies $i < j$ for all i, j. With $\mathrm{lin}(\mathcal{P}) \subseteq \Sigma^*$ we denote the set of all linearizations of $\mathcal{P}$.

For this paper, we use some basic notions from trace theory, see [7] for more details. An *independence relation* on the alphabet Σ is a symmetric and irreflexive relation $I \subseteq \Sigma \times \Sigma$. The complementary relation $(\Sigma \times \Sigma) \setminus I$ is also called a *dependence relation*. On Σ^* we define the equivalence relation $\equiv_I$ as the transitive reflexive closure of the symmetric relation $\{(uabv, ubav) \mid u, v \in \Sigma^*, (a, b) \in I\}$. The *I-closure* of $L \subseteq \Sigma^*$ is $[L]_I = \{v \in \Sigma^* \mid \exists u \in L : u \equiv_I v\} \subseteq \Sigma^*$. Let $\mathcal{A}$ be a finite automaton over the alphabet Σ, and assume that $\to \subseteq Q \times \Sigma \times Q$ is the transition relation of $\mathcal{A}$. Then $\mathcal{A}$ is called *loop-connected with respect to* I, if for every loop $q_1 \xrightarrow{a_1} q_2 \xrightarrow{a_2} \cdots \xrightarrow{a_{n-1}} q_n \xrightarrow{a_n} q_1$ of $\mathcal{A}$, the set $\{a_1, \ldots, a_n\} \subseteq \Sigma$ induces a connected subgraph of $(\Sigma, (\Sigma \times \Sigma) \backslash I)$. For a loop connected automaton $\mathcal{A}$, one can construct an automaton $\mathcal{A}'$ of size bounded exponentially in the size of $\mathcal{A}$ such that $L(\mathcal{A}') = [L(\mathcal{A})]_I$ [16]. In general, this exponential blow-up cannot be avoided, see [16] for an example.

2.1 Message Sequence Charts

For the rest of this paper let P be a finite set of *processes* ($|P| \geq 2$) and $\mathfrak{C}$ be a finite set of *message contents*. With $\mathrm{Ch} = \{(p,q) \in P \times P \mid p \neq q\}$ we denote the set of all *channels*. With $\Sigma_p = \{p!q(c), p?q(c) \mid q \in P \backslash \{p\}, c \in \mathfrak{C}\}$ we denote the set of all *types of process* $p \in P$. The set of all *types* is $\Sigma = \bigcup_{p \in P} \Sigma_p$. With $p!q(c)$ we denote the type of an event that sends from process p a message with content c to process q, whereas $p?q(c)$ denotes the type of an event that receives on process p a message with content c from process q. A *partial message sequence chart (pMSC)* over P and $\mathfrak{C}$ is a tuple $M = (E, t, m, \prec)$, where:

- E is a finite set of *events*.
- $t : E \to \Sigma$ labels each event with its type. The set of events *located on process* $p \in P$ is $E_p = t^{-1}(\Sigma_p)$. Let $E_! = \{e \in E \mid \exists p, q \in P, c \in \mathfrak{C} : t(e) = p!q(c)\}$ be the set of *send events* and $E_? = E \backslash E_!$ be the set of *receive events*.
- $m : D \to E_?$ is a bijection between a subset $D \subseteq E_!$ of the send events and the receive events such that $m(s) = r$ and $t(s) = p!q(c)$ implies $t(r) = q?p(c)$. In this case we also say that (s, r) is a *message* from process p to q with content c. If $s \in E_! \backslash D$, then s is called an *unmatched send event* in M from p to q.
- $\prec$ is a partial order on E, called the *visual order of* M, such that for every $p \in P$, the restriction of $\prec$ to E_p is a total order, and $\prec$ is equal to the transitive closure of

$$\{(e_1, e_2) \mid e_1 \prec e_2, \exists p \in P : e_1, e_2 \in E_p\} \cup \{(s, m(s)) \mid s \in D\}.$$

Often pMSCs are further restricted to satisfy the *FIFO-condition*, which means that for all $s_1, s_2 \in E_!$, if $s_1 \prec s_2$, $t(s_1) = p!q(c)$, $t(s_2) = p!q(d)$, and $s_2 \in D$, then also $s_1 \in D$ and $m(s_1) \prec m(s_2)$, i.e., message overtaking on any channel is disallowed. *For the main part of this paper we always assume the FIFO-restriction without mention it explicitly*, only in Section 4 we briefly discuss the non-FIFO case. The pMSC definition may also include local actions, however this is not important in the present setting. We use the usual graphical representation of pMSCs, where time flows top-down and processes are drawn as vertical lines.

Let $M = (E, t, m, \prec)$ be a pMSC, where $m : D \to E_?$ for $D \subseteq E_!$. We also write $E(M) = E$. We identify M with the pomset $(E, t, \prec)$, and we identify pMSCs if they are isomorphic as pomsets. If $D = E_!$, i.e., if there are no unmatched send events, then M is called a *message sequence chart* (MSC) over P and $\mathfrak{C}$. With $\mathrm{pMSC}_{P,\mathfrak{C}}$ (resp. $\mathrm{MSC}_{P,\mathfrak{C}}$) we denote the set of all pMSCs (resp. MSCs) over P and $\mathfrak{C}$. In the sequel, we will omit the subscripts P and $\mathfrak{C}$, if they are clear from the context. Let $|M| = |E|$ denote the *size of M*. Let $P(M) = \{p \in P \mid E_p \neq \emptyset\}$, more generally, let $P(M{\upharpoonright}_F) = \{p \in P \mid E_p \cap F \neq \emptyset\}$ for $F \subseteq E$. The *communication graph* $G(M)$ of M is defined as the directed graph $G(M) = (P(M), \mapsto)$, where $p \mapsto q$ if and only if there exists in M a message from p to q (with arbitrary content). For $p \in P$ let $\pi_p(M) = \pi_{\Sigma_p}(w)$, where $w \in \mathrm{lin}(M)$ is chosen arbitrarily (the actual choice of $w \in \mathrm{lin}(M)$ is irrelevant).

Let $M_i = (E_i, t_i, m_i, \prec_i)$, $i = 1, 2$, be two pMSCs over P and $\mathfrak{C}$ such that $E_1 \cap E_2 = \emptyset$ and for all $(p, q) \in \mathrm{Ch}$, if there is an unmatched send event from p to q in M_1, then there is no message from p to q in M_2 (there may be unmatched sends from p to q in M_2). Then the *concatenation* of M_1 and M_2 is the pMSC $M_1 {\cdot} M_2 = (E_1 \cup E_2, t_1 \cup t_2, m_1 \cup m_2, \prec)$, where $\prec$ is the transitive closure of

$$\prec_1 \cup \prec_2 \cup \{(e_1, e_2) \in E_1 \times E_2 \mid \exists p \in P : e_1 \text{ and } e_2 \text{ are located on process } p\}.$$

For the case that $M_1, M_2 \in \mathbb{MSC}$ this corresponds to the usual definition of MSC-concatenation. Note that concatenation is only partially defined on pMSC.

Let $F \subseteq E(M)$ be an arbitrary set of events of the pMSC M. Note that the pomset $N = M{\upharpoonright}_F$ is in general not a pMSC. On the other hand, if F is *downward-closed*, i.e., $e \prec f \in F$ implies $e \in F$, then $N = M{\upharpoonright}_F$ it is again a pMSC over P and $\mathfrak{C}$. We write $N \leq M$ in this case, this defines a partial order $(\mathbb{pMSC}, \leq)$ on the set of pMSCs. The pomset $M{\upharpoonright}_{E \setminus F}$ will be denoted by $M \backslash N$. In general, $M \backslash N$ is not a pMSC. On the other hand, if a send event $s \in F$ is unmatched in M whenever it is unmatched in N (i.e., no message arrows are crossing from F to its complement $E \backslash F$, this happens in particular if N is an MSC), then $M \backslash N \in \mathbb{pMSC}$ and moreover $M = N \cdot (M \backslash N)$.

We say that an MSC $M \in \mathbb{MSC}$ is *atomic* if M cannot be written as $M = M_1 \cdot M_2$ for MSCs $M_1, M_2 \in \mathbb{MSC} \backslash \{\emptyset\}$, where $\emptyset$ stands for the MSC with an empty set of events. With $\mathbb{A}_{P,\mathfrak{C}}$ (briefly $\mathbb{A}$) we denote the set of atomic MSCs over P and $\mathfrak{C}$. Already for $|P| = 2$, the set $\mathbb{A}$ is easily seen to be infinite, see e.g. [9, Sec. 3] for an example. On $\mathbb{A}$ we define an independence relation $\mathcal{I}$ by $(A, B) \in \mathcal{I}$ if $P(A) \cap P(B) = \emptyset$. Obviously, every $M \in \mathbb{MSC}$ can be written as $M = A_1 \cdot A_2 \cdots A_m$, where $A_i \in \mathbb{A}$. Furthermore, this factorization is unique up to $\mathcal{I}$-commutations, a fact which will be crucial in Section 3.2, see [11,15]:

Lemma 1. *If $A_1, \ldots, A_m, B_1, \ldots, B_n \in \mathbb{A}$ are such that the MSCs $A_1 {\cdot} A_2 \cdots A_m$ and $B_1 \cdot B_2 \cdots B_n$ are equal then the words $A_1 A_2 \cdots A_n$, $B_1 B_2 \cdots B_m \in \mathbb{A}^*$ satisfy $A_1 A_2 \cdots A_n \equiv_{\mathcal{I}} B_1 B_2 \cdots B_m$.*

The *supremum* (resp. *infimum*) of two pMSCs $M_1, M_2 \in \mathbb{pMSC}$ in the partial order $(\mathbb{pMSC}, \leq)$ is denoted by $\sup(M_1, M_2)$ (resp. $\inf(M_1, M_2)$). In general, $\sup(M_1, M_2)$ does not exist:

Lemma 2. *Let $M_1, M_2 \in \mathbb{pMSC}$. Then $\sup(M_1, M_2)$ exists if and only if for all $p \in P$, either $\pi_p(M_1) \sqsubseteq \pi_p(M_2)$ or $\pi_p(M_2) \sqsubseteq \pi_p(M_1)$. Moreover, if $\sup(M_1, M_2)$ exists, then $\inf(M_1, M_2) = \emptyset$ if and only if $P(M_1) \cap P(M_2) = \emptyset$.*

The following picture visualizes the general situation. Arrows that are leafing some region correspond to unmatched sends, and the whole region corresponds to the supremum.

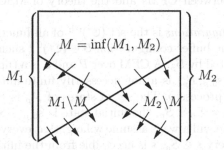

The ITU standard Z.120 defines *high-level message sequence charts (HMSCs)* as finite transition systems with nodes labeled by MSCs. Here we prefer to label edges by MSCs, which does not change the expressive power of HMSCs. Thus, an HMSC H over P and $\mathfrak{C}$ is a tuple $H = (V, \rightarrow, v_0, F)$, where V is a finite set of nodes, $\rightarrow \subseteq V \times \mathbb{MSC}_{P,\mathfrak{C}} \times V$ is a finite set of labeled edges, $v_0 \in V$ is the initial state, and $F \subseteq V$ is the set of final nodes. Instead of $(u, M, v) \in \rightarrow$, we write $u \xrightarrow{M}_H v$. The MSC-language $\mathrm{msc}(H)$ defined by H is the set of all MSCs $M_1 \cdot M_2 \cdots M_n$, where $v_0 \xrightarrow{M_1}_H v_1 \xrightarrow{M_2}_H \cdots \xrightarrow{M_n}_H v_n \in F$ for some $v_1, \ldots, v_n \in V$. We impose the restriction that for every node $v \in V$, v is accessible from the initial node v_0, and some node from F is accessible from v. Furthermore, we assume that $\rightarrow \subseteq V \times \mathbb{A}_{P,\mathfrak{C}} \times V$. Both of these assumptions do not change the expressiveness of HMSCs and can be easily established by polynomial time constructions. Let $\mathbb{A}_H = \{A \in \mathbb{A} \mid \exists u, v \in V : u \xrightarrow{A}_H v\}$. We may view H also as a finite automaton over the alphabet $\mathbb{A}_H$ of atoms, which accepts a set $L(H) \subseteq \mathbb{A}_H^*$ of words over $\mathbb{A}_H$. We will denote this automaton by H as well. An HMSC H is called *bounded* [3,16] if for every cycle

$$v_1 \xrightarrow{A_1}_H v_2 \xrightarrow{A_2}_H \cdots \xrightarrow{A_{n-1}}_H v_n \xrightarrow{A_n}_H v_1,$$

the communication graph $G(A_1 \cdot A_2 \cdots A_n)$ is strongly connected (recall that the set of nodes of $G(M)$ is $P(M)$). In [3] it is shown that for a bounded HMSC H the language $\mathrm{lin}(\mathrm{msc}(H)) \subseteq \Sigma^*$ of all linearizations of MSCs generated by H is regular. We say that H is *transition-connected* [8] if H, viewed as a finite automaton over the alphabet $\mathbb{A}_H$, is loop-connected with respect to the independence relation $\mathcal{I} \subseteq \mathbb{A} \times \mathbb{A}$. It is easy to see that every bounded HMSC is transition-connected. Finally, H is called $\mathcal{I}$-*closed* if H, viewed as a finite automaton over $\mathbb{A}_H$, satisfies $L(H) = [L(H)]_\mathcal{I}$. Thus, by [16], for a transition-connected HMSC H there exists an $\mathcal{I}$-closed HMSC H' of size bounded exponentially in the size of H such that $L(H') = [L(H)]_\mathcal{I}$ and thus, $\mathrm{msc}(H) = \mathrm{msc}(H')$.

2.2   Communicating Finite State Machines

In this section we briefly introduce *communicating finite state machines* (CFMs) The tight relationship between CFMs and the theory of MSCs is well-known, see e.g. [12].

The set of *buffer configurations* is the set $(\mathfrak{C}^*)^{\text{Ch}}$ of all functions from the set of channels Ch to $\mathfrak{C}^*$. The buffer configuration $\mathcal{B} \in (\mathfrak{C}^*)^{\text{Ch}}$ such that $\mathcal{B}(p,q) = \epsilon$ for all $(p,q) \in$ Ch is denoted by $\mathcal{B}_\emptyset$. A CFM over P and $\mathfrak{C}$ is a tuple $\mathcal{A} = (\mathcal{A}_p)_{p \in P}$, where $\mathcal{A}_p = (S_p, \Sigma_p, \delta_p, s_{0,p}, F_p)$ is a not necessarily finite automaton over the alphabet Σ_p of types of process p. The set of states of $\mathcal{A}_p$ is S_p, the transition relation of $\mathcal{A}_p$ is $\delta_p \subseteq S_p \times \Sigma_p \times S_p$, the initial state is $s_{0,p} \in S_p$, and the set of final states is $F_p \subseteq S_p$. We will always assume w.l.o.g. that every local automaton $\mathcal{A}_p$ is *reduced*, i.e., for every $s \in S_p$, s is accessible from the initial state $s_{0,p}$ and some state from F_p is accessible from s. The infinite set $\mathbf{S}$ of *global states of $\mathcal{A}$* and the set $\mathbf{F}$ of *final states of $\mathcal{A}$* are defined by

$$\mathbf{S} = \prod_{p \in P} S_p \times (\mathfrak{C}^*)^{\text{Ch}} \quad \text{and} \quad \mathbf{F} = \prod_{p \in P} F_p \times \{\mathcal{B}_\emptyset\}.$$

The *initial state of $\mathcal{A}$* is $(\mathbf{s}_0, \mathcal{B}_\emptyset)$, where $\mathbf{s}_0 = (s_{0,p})_{p \in P}$. The *global transition relation δ of $\mathcal{A}$* is defined as follows: Let $(\mathbf{s}, \mathcal{B}) \in \mathbf{S}$, where $\mathbf{s} = (s_p)_{p \in P}$. If $(s_i, i!j(c), t) \in \delta_i$ then $((\mathbf{s}, \mathcal{B}), i!j(c), (\mathbf{t}, \mathcal{C})) \in \delta$, where $\mathbf{t} = (t_p)_{p \in P}$, $t_p = s_p$ for $p \neq i$, $t_i = t$, $\mathcal{C}(p,q) = \mathcal{B}(p,q)$ for $(p,q) \neq (i,j)$, and $\mathcal{C}(i,j) = c\mathcal{B}(i,j)$. On the other hand, if $(s_i, i?j(c), t) \in \delta_i$ and $\mathcal{B}(j,i) = wc$ for some $w \in \mathfrak{C}^*$, then $((\mathbf{s}, \mathcal{B}), i?j(c), (\mathbf{t}, \mathcal{C})) \in \delta$, where $\mathbf{t} = (t_p)_{p \in P}$, $t_p = s_p$ for $p \neq i$, $t_i = t$, $\mathcal{C}(q,p) = \mathcal{B}(q,p)$ for $(q,p) \neq (j,i)$, and $\mathcal{C}(j,i) = w$. We extend the relation $\delta \subseteq \mathbf{S} \times \Sigma \times \mathbf{S}$ in the usual way to a relation $\delta \subseteq \mathbf{S} \times \Sigma^* \times \mathbf{S}$. Instead of $((\mathbf{s}, \mathcal{B}), w, (\mathbf{t}, \mathcal{C})) \in \delta$, $w \in \Sigma^*$, we write $(\mathbf{s}, \mathcal{B}) \xrightarrow{w}_{\mathcal{A}} (\mathbf{t}, \mathcal{C})$. We write $(\mathbf{s}, \mathcal{B}) \xrightarrow{*}_{\mathcal{A}} (\mathbf{t}, \mathcal{C})$ if $(\mathbf{s}, \mathcal{B}) \xrightarrow{w}_{\mathcal{A}} (\mathbf{t}, \mathcal{C})$ for some $w \in \Sigma^*$. We write $(\mathbf{s}, \mathcal{B}) \xrightarrow{w}_{\mathcal{A}}$ if $(\mathbf{s}, \mathcal{B}) \xrightarrow{w}_{\mathcal{A}} (\mathbf{t}, \mathcal{C})$ for some $(\mathbf{t}, \mathcal{C})$. Let $L(\mathcal{A}) = \{w \in \Sigma^* \mid \exists(\mathbf{t}, \mathcal{B}_\emptyset) \in \mathbf{F} : (\mathbf{s}_0, \mathcal{B}_\emptyset) \xrightarrow{w}_{\mathcal{A}} (\mathbf{t}, \mathcal{B}_\emptyset)\}$.

It is easy to see that for every word $w \in \Sigma^*$ such that $(\mathbf{s}, \mathcal{B}_\emptyset) \xrightarrow{w}_{\mathcal{A}}$ for some $\mathbf{s}$, there exists a unique pMSC pmsc(w) with $w \in \text{lin}(\text{pmsc}(w))$. Furthermore, if $(\mathbf{s}_\emptyset, \mathcal{B}_\emptyset) \xrightarrow{w}_{\mathcal{A}} (\mathbf{t}, \mathcal{B}_\emptyset)$ for some $\mathbf{s}, \mathbf{t}$, then pmsc$(w) \in$ MSC, and we write msc(w) instead of pmsc(w). Thus, we can define msc$(\mathcal{A}) = \{\text{msc}(w) \mid w \in L(\mathcal{A})\}$. It is also easy to see that if $w_1, w_2 \in \text{lin}(M)$ for $M \in$ pMSC, then $(\mathbf{s}, \mathcal{B}_\emptyset) \xrightarrow{w_1}_{\mathcal{A}} (\mathbf{t}, \mathcal{B})$ if and only if $(\mathbf{s}, \mathcal{B}_\emptyset) \xrightarrow{w_2}_{\mathcal{A}} (\mathbf{t}, \mathcal{B})$. Thus, we may write $(\mathbf{s}, \mathcal{B}_\emptyset) \xrightarrow{M}_{\mathcal{A}} (\mathbf{t}, \mathcal{B})$ in this case. Finally, we say that $\mathcal{A}$ is *deadlock-free* if for all states $(\mathbf{s}, \mathcal{B}) \in \mathbf{S}$ such that $(\mathbf{s}_0, \mathcal{B}_\emptyset) \xrightarrow{*}_{\mathcal{A}} (\mathbf{s}, \mathcal{B})$ we have $(\mathbf{s}, \mathcal{B}) \xrightarrow{*}_{\mathcal{A}} (\mathbf{t}, \mathcal{B}_\emptyset)$ for some $(\mathbf{t}, \mathcal{B}_\emptyset) \in \mathbf{F}$.

3   Weak and Safe Realizability

Let $L \subseteq \text{MSC}_{P,\mathfrak{C}}$. Following [1], we say that L is *weakly realizable* if there exists a CFM $\mathcal{A}$ over P and $\mathfrak{C}$ such that msc$(\mathcal{A}) = L$. We say that L is *safely realizable* if there exists a deadlock-free CFM $\mathcal{A}$ over P and $\mathfrak{C}$ such that msc$(\mathcal{A}) = L$. These definitions allow local automata with infinite state sets, but this case will never occur in this paper, since we only consider sets of MSCs that are generated by HMSCs. An HMSC H is called *weakly realizable* (*safely realizable*) if msc(H) is weakly realizable (safely realizable). Given H, we can construct in polynomial time *finite* automata $\mathcal{A}_p$, $p \in P$, with $L(\mathcal{A}_p) = \pi_p(\text{msc}(H))$. We call the CFM $\mathcal{A} = (\mathcal{A}_p)_{p \in P}$ the *canonical implementation* of H. Then H is weakly realizable if and only if msc($\mathcal{A}$) = msc(H) [1]. Note that the inclusion msc(H) $\subseteq$ msc($\mathcal{A}$) always holds. Furthermore, H is safely realizable if and only if $\mathcal{A}$ is deadlock-free and msc($\mathcal{A}$) = msc(H) [1]. In [1] it is also shown that $L \subseteq \text{MSC}$ is weakly realizable if and only if the following closure condition CC_w (called CC2 in [1]) holds:

Closure condition CC_w. If $M \in \text{MSC}$ is such that for all $p \in P$ there exists $N \in L$ with $\pi_p(M) = \pi_p(N)$ then $M \in L$.

Furthermore, it is claimed that $L \subseteq \text{MSC}$ is safely realizable if and only if the following closure condition CC_s (called CC3 in [1]) holds:

Closure condition CC_s. If $M \in \text{pMSC}$ is such that for all $p \in P$ there exists $N \in L$ with $\pi_p(M) \sqsubseteq \pi_p(N)$ then $M \leq N$ for some $N \in L$.

But this is in fact false, the set L consisting of the following 6 MSCs satisfies CC_s but it does not satisfy CC_w, and hence, it is not even weakly realizable.

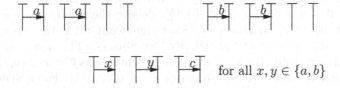

for all $x, y \in \{a, b\}$

On the other hand, using arguments from [1], one can easily prove

Lemma 3. $L \subseteq \text{MSC}$ *is safely realizable if and only if L satisfies CC_w and CC_s.*

As already mentioned, the notions of weak and safe realizability were introduced in [1], where it was shown that for finite sets of MSCs, safe realizability can be tested in polynomial time, whereas weak realizability is coNP-complete. In [2], realizability was studied for HMSCs. It was shown that weak realizability is already undecidable for bounded HMSCs, [1] whereas safe realizability for bounded HMSCs is in EXPSPACE but PSPACE-hard. In Section 3.1, we will close this latter gap by proving that safe realizability for bounded HMSCs is EXPSPACE-complete. The proof technique used for this result will be also applied in order to show that safe realizability is undecidable for the class of all HMSCs.

---

[1] For this result, FIFO-communication is important: Under non-FIFO communication, weak realizability is decidable for bounded HMSCs [15].

3.1   Bounded HMSCs

Theorem 1. *The following problem is EXPSPACE-complete:*
INPUT: Set P of processes, set $\mathfrak{C}$ of message contents, and a bounded HMSC H
over P and $\mathfrak{C}$
QUESTION: Is H safely realizable?
Furthermore, this problem is also EXPSPACE-complete if P and $\mathfrak{C}$ are fixed,
i.e., do not belong to the input.

Proof. Membership in EXPSPACE is shown in [2] (for variable P and $\mathfrak{C}$),
or follows from Theorem 5. For the lower bound we combine ideas from [2]
and [16,19]. Let $\mathcal{M}$ be a fixed Turing-machine with an EXPSPACE-complete
acceptance problem (such a machine exists, take any machine, which accepts an
EXPSPACE-complete language). W.l.o.g. $\mathcal{M}$ works on an input of length n in
space $2^n - 1$. Let Q be the set of states of $\mathcal{M}$ and let Δ be the tape alphabet.
Furthermore, let q_0 be the initial state of $\mathcal{M}$ and q_f be the final state of $\mathcal{M}$.
Let $\square \in \Delta$ be the blank symbol. The machine $\mathcal{M}$ accepts if it reaches the final
state q_f. Let us fix an input $w \in \Delta^*$ for $\mathcal{M}$ with $|w| = n$ for the further discus-
sion. Configurations of $\mathcal{M}$ are represented as a word from $\Delta^* Q \Delta^*$ of length 2^n.
A sequence $(u_1, \dots, u_m)$ of words $u_i \in \Delta^* Q \Delta^*$ is called an *accepting compu-*
tation of $\mathcal{M}$ if $u_1 = q_0 w \square^{2^n - n - 1}$, $|u_i| = 2^n$ $(1 \leq i \leq m)$, u_{i+1} is a successor
configuration of u_i with respect to $\mathcal{M}$ $(1 \leq i < m)$, and $u_m \in \Delta^* q_f \Delta^*$.

For a number $0 \leq i < 2^n$ let $\langle i \rangle \in \{0,1\}^n$ denote the binary representation of i of length n, where moreover the least significant bit is the left-most
bit. For $w = a_0 \cdots a_{2^n - 1}$, $a_i \in Q \cup \Delta$, let $\beta(w) = \langle 0 \rangle a_0 \cdots \langle 2^n - 1 \rangle a_{2^n - 1}$. Let
$\Gamma = Q \cup \Delta \cup \{0, 1\}$ and define the set $\mathfrak{C}$ of message contents as $\mathfrak{C} = \Gamma \cup \{\$, \ell, r\}$.
[2] We will deal with the fixed set of processes $P = \{0, \dots, 5\}$. For a symbol
$a \in \Gamma$ we define the MSC $a^{(2,1)}$ (resp. $a^{(4,5)}$) over P and $\mathfrak{C}$ as the unique
MSC with the only linearization $2!1\langle a \rangle 1?2\langle a \rangle 1!2\ 2?1$ (resp. $4!5\langle a \rangle 5?4\langle a \rangle 5!4\ 4?5$),
thus, the symbol a is send from 2 to 1 (resp. 4 to 5) and immediately con-
firmed. For $C = b_1 \cdots b_m \in \Gamma^*$ define $C^{(2,1)} = b_1^{(2,1)} \cdots b_m^{(2,1)}$ and $C^{(4,5)} =$
$b_1^{(4,5)} \cdots b_m^{(4,5)}$. For words $C_1, D_1, \dots, C_m, D_m \in \Gamma^*$ $(m \geq 1)$ we define the MSC
$M(C_1, D_1, \dots, C_m, D_m)$ over P and $\mathfrak{C}$ as shown in Figure 1, where the case
$m = 3$ is shown (process 0 is not involved into this MSC, and hence not drawn).
Finally define the following two sets of MSCs:

$$L_\ell = \{M(C_1, D_1, \dots, C_m, D_m) \mid m \geq 1,\ C_1, D_1, \dots, C_m, D_m \in \Gamma^*\}$$

$$L_r = L_\ell \backslash \{M(\beta(u_1), \beta(u_1), \dots, \beta(u_m), \beta(u_m)) \mid (u_1, \dots, u_m) \text{ is an}$$

$$\text{accepting computation of } \mathcal{M}\}$$

Claim 1. There exist bounded HMSCs H_ℓ and H_r that can be constructed in
time polynomial in n such that $\mathrm{msc}(H_\ell) = L_\ell$ and $\mathrm{msc}(H_r) = L_r$.

---

[2] In the following, we will also use messages without any content, the corresponding types are written as $p!q$ and $p?q$, respectively. Formally, one can introduce an
additional message content nil for these messages.

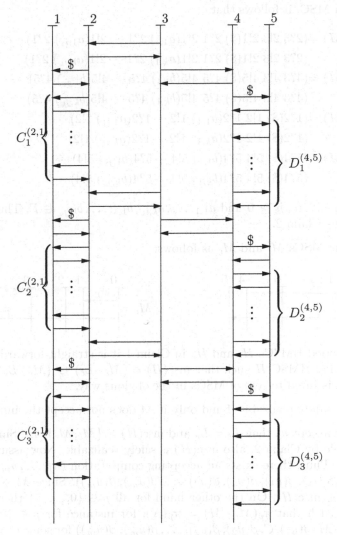

Fig. 1. $M(C_1, D_1, C_2, D_2, C_3, D_3)$

For L_ℓ this is clear, since all messages are immediately confirmed by messages back to the sending process. For L_r the construction follows [16, Prop. 7].

Claim 2. L_ℓ is safely realizable.

We will only check condition CC_w, condition CC_s can be verified analogously. Thus, assume that M is an MSC such that for each $p \in \{0, \ldots, 5\}$ there exists $N \in L_\ell$ with $\pi_p(M) = \pi_p(N)$. Thus, $\pi_3(M) = (3!2\ 3?2\ 3!4\ 3?4)^k$ for some $k \geq 1$.

Since M is an MSC, it follows that

$$\pi_2(M) =(2?3\ 2!3\ 2!1(\$)\ 2?1\ 2!1(a_{1,1})\ 2?1\cdots 2!1(a_{1,i_1})\ 2?1)\cdots$$
$$(2?3\ 2!3\ 2!1(\$)\ 2?1\ 2!1(a_{k,1})\ 2?1\cdots 2!1(a_{k,i_k})\ 2?1)$$
$$\pi_4(M) =(4?3\ 4!3\ 4!5(\$)\ 4?5\ 4!5(b_{1,1})\ 4?5\cdots 4!5(b_{1,j_1})\ 4?5)\cdots$$
$$(4?3\ 4!3\ 4!5(\$)\ 4?5\ 4!5(b_{k,1})\ 4?5\cdots 4!5(b_{k,j_k})\ 4?5)$$
$$\pi_1(M) =(1?2(\$)\ 1!2\ 1?2(a_{1,1})\ 1!2\cdots 1?2(a_{1,i_1})\ 1!2)\cdots$$
$$(1?2(\$)\ 1!2\ 1?2(a_{k,1})\ 1!2\cdots 1?2(a_{k,i_k})\ 1!2)$$
$$\pi_5(M) =(5?4(\$)\ 5!4\ 5?4(b_{1,1})\ 5!4\cdots 5?4(b_{1,j_1})\ 5!4)\cdots$$
$$(5?4(\$)\ 5!4\ 5?4(b_{k,1})\ 5!4\cdots 5?4(b_{k,j_k})\ 5!4)$$

for some $i_1, j_1, \ldots, i_k, j_k \geq 0$ and $a_{1,1}, \ldots, a_{k,i_k}, b_{1,1}, \ldots, b_{k,j_k} \in \Gamma$. Thus, $M \in L_\ell$. This proves Claim 2.

Now define the MSCs M_ℓ and M_r as follows:

From the bounded HMSCs H_ℓ and H_r in Claim 1 it is straight-forward to construct a bounded HMSC H such that $\mathrm{msc}(H) = (M_\ell \cdot L_\ell) \cup (M_r \cdot L_r)$, where concatenation is lifted to sets of MSCs in the obvious way.

Claim 3. H is safely realizable if and only if $\mathcal{M}$ does not accept the input w.

If $\mathcal{M}$ does not accept w, then $L_\ell = L_r$ and $\mathrm{msc}(H) = \{M_\ell, M_r\} \cdot L_\ell$. Since L_ℓ is safely realizable by Claim 2, also $\mathrm{msc}(H)$ is safely realizable. Now assume that $\mathcal{M}$ accepts w. Thus, there exists an accepting computation $(u_1, \ldots, u_m)$ of $\mathcal{M}$. Let $M = M(\beta(u_1), \beta(u_1), \beta(u_2), \beta(u_2), \ldots, \beta(u_m), \beta(u_m))$. Since $M \notin L_r$, we have $M_r \cdot M \notin \mathrm{msc}(H)$. On the other hand for all $p \in \{0, \ldots, 5\}$ there exists $N \in \mathrm{msc}(H)$ such that $\pi_p(M_r \cdot M) = \pi_p(N)$, for instance for $p \in \{0, 1, 2, 3\}$ take $N = M_r \cdot M(\beta(u_1), C, \beta(u_2), \beta(u_2), \ldots, \beta(u_m), \beta(u_m))$ for some $C \neq \beta(u_1)$. Thus, $\mathrm{msc}(H)$ is not weakly realizable and hence not safely realizable. This proves Claim 3 and hence the theorem. □

By applying the reduction from the previous proof (without the use of binary counters) to a Turing-machine with an undecidable acceptance problem, we obtain the following result.

Theorem 2. *There exist fixed sets P and $\mathfrak{C}$ of processes and message contents, respectively, such that the following problem is undecidable:*
    INPUT: An HMSC H over P and $\mathfrak{C}$
    QUESTION: Is H safely realizable?

3.2   Transition-Connected HMSCs

In [15] it is shown that weak realizability can be decided for transition-connected HMSCs if non-FIFO communication is supposed. Moreover, it is argued that the methods used in the proof of this result can be also applied in order to show that safe realizability is decidable for transition-connected HMSCs, both for FIFO and non-FIFO communication. In this section, we will prove that safe realizability is in fact EXPSPACE-complete for transition-connected HMSCs.

For the further discussion we have to introduce a few new notations. Let us fix an arbitrary HMSC $H = (V, \rightarrow, v_0, F)$ over P and $\mathfrak{C}$, which is not necessarily transition-connected. Recall that $\mathbb{A}_H = \{A \in \mathbb{A} \mid \exists u, v \in V : u \xrightarrow{A}_H v\}$. With $\langle \mathbb{A}_H \rangle$ we denote the set of all MSCs of the form $A_1 \cdot A_2 \cdots A_n$ with $A_i \in \mathbb{A}_H$ (possibly $n = 0$, i.e., $\emptyset \in \langle \mathbb{A}_H \rangle$). Let $\mathcal{A} = (\mathcal{A}_p)_{p \in P}$ be the canonical implementation of H, thus $L(\mathcal{A}_p) = \pi_p(\mathrm{msc}(H))$. Let $\mathcal{A}_p = (S_p, \Sigma_p, \delta_p, s_{0,p}, F_p)$. Recall that $\mathcal{A}$ can be constructed in polynomial time from H, in particular the size of every S_p is bounded polynomially in the size of H. Finally, following [15], let us define a finite automaton $\mathcal{A}_\emptyset = (\mathbf{S}_\emptyset, \mathbb{A}_H, \delta_\emptyset, \mathbf{s}_0, \mathbf{F}_\emptyset)$ over the alphabet of atoms $\mathbb{A}_H$, where $\mathbf{s}_0 = (s_{0,p})_{p \in P}$ is the initial state, $\mathbf{S}_\emptyset \subseteq \prod_{p \in P} S_p$ is the set of all tuples $\mathbf{s}$ such that there exists $K \in \langle \mathbb{A}_H \rangle$ with $(\mathbf{s}_0, \mathcal{B}_\emptyset) \xrightarrow{K}_{\mathcal{A}} (\mathbf{s}, \mathcal{B}_\emptyset)$, $\mathbf{F}_\emptyset = \mathbf{S}_\emptyset \cap \prod_{p \in P} F_p$, and the transition relation $\delta_\emptyset$ is defined as follows: If $\mathbf{s}, \mathbf{t} \in \mathbf{S}_\emptyset$ and $A \in \mathbb{A}_H$ then $(\mathbf{s}, A, \mathbf{t}) \in \delta_\emptyset$ if and only if $(\mathbf{s}, \mathcal{B}_\emptyset) \xrightarrow{A}_{\mathcal{A}} (\mathbf{t}, \mathcal{B}_\emptyset)$. Notations like $\mathbf{s} \xrightarrow{A}_{\mathcal{A}_\emptyset} \mathbf{t}$ are defined as for CFMs in Section 2.2. Note that $u \equiv_{\mathcal{I}} v$ for words $u, v \in \mathbb{A}_H^*$ implies that for all $\mathbf{s}, \mathbf{t} \in \mathbf{S}_\emptyset$, $\mathbf{s} \xrightarrow{u}_{\mathcal{A}_\emptyset} \mathbf{t}$ if and only if $\mathbf{s} \xrightarrow{v}_{\mathcal{A}_\emptyset} \mathbf{t}$, in fact, $\mathcal{A}_\emptyset$ is an asynchronous automaton in the sense of [20]. Thus, by Lemma 1, for $K \in \langle \mathbb{A}_H \rangle$ and $\mathbf{s}, \mathbf{t} \in \mathbf{S}_\emptyset$ we can write $\mathbf{s} \xrightarrow{K}_{\mathcal{A}_\emptyset} \mathbf{t}$, with the obvious meaning.

The main technical result of this section is stated in the following theorem. Note that it does not restrict to transition-connected HMSCs.

Theorem 3. *The following problem is in PSPACE:*
   INPUT: Set P of processes, set $\mathfrak{C}$ of message contents, and an arbitrary HMSC H over P and $\mathfrak{C}$
   QUESTION: Does the canonical implementation $\mathcal{A}$ of H satisfy the following two properties: (i) $\mathcal{A}$ is deadlock-free and (ii) $\mathrm{msc}(\mathcal{A}) \subseteq \langle \mathbb{A}_H \rangle$?

Using Theorem 3, we can prove the next two results.

Theorem 4. *The following problem is PSPACE-complete:*
   INPUT: Set P of processes, set $\mathfrak{C}$ of message contents, and an $\mathcal{I}$-closed HMSC H over P and $\mathfrak{C}$
   QUESTION: Is H safely realizable?
Furthermore, this problem is also PSPACE-complete if P and $\mathfrak{C}$ are fixed.

Proof. For PSPACE-hardness we can use the construction from the proof of [2, Thm. 3]. In fact, the HMSC H constructed there satisfies the property that $u \xrightarrow{A}_H v \xrightarrow{B}_H w$ implies $P(A) \cap P(B) \neq \emptyset$, thus, H is $\mathcal{I}$-closed. Moreover, P and $\mathfrak{C}$ are fixed in the construction. Thus, it remains to show membership in

PSPACE. Using Theorem 3, we first verify in PSPACE whether the canonical implementation $\mathcal{A}$ of H is both deadlock-free and satisfies $\mathrm{msc}(\mathcal{A}) \subseteq \langle \mathbb{A}_H \rangle$. If this is not the case then we can reject. Thus, let us assume that $\mathcal{A}$ is deadlock-free and $\mathrm{msc}(\mathcal{A}) \subseteq \langle \mathbb{A}_H \rangle$. It remains to show that $\mathrm{msc}(\mathcal{A}) = \mathrm{msc}(H)$, where the inclusion $\mathrm{msc}(H) \subseteq \mathrm{msc}(\mathcal{A})$ is trivial. Thus, we have to check whether $\mathrm{msc}(\mathcal{A}) \subseteq \mathrm{msc}(H)$. Since $\mathrm{msc}(\mathcal{A}) \subseteq \langle \mathbb{A}_H \rangle$, this is equivalent to $\mathrm{msc}(\mathcal{A}) \cap \langle \mathbb{A}_H \rangle \subseteq \mathrm{msc}(H)$. The following argument follows [15]. First note that for all $A_1, \ldots, A_m \in \mathbb{A}_H$, we have $A_1 \cdot A_2 \cdots A_m \in \mathrm{msc}(\mathcal{A})$ if and only if the *word* $A_1 A_2 \cdots A_m \in \mathbb{A}_H^*$ belongs to $L(\mathcal{A}_\emptyset)$. Thus, we have $\mathrm{msc}(\mathcal{A}) \cap \langle \mathbb{A}_H \rangle \subseteq \mathrm{msc}(H)$ if and only if $L(\mathcal{A}_\emptyset) \subseteq [L(H)]_{\mathcal{I}}$ (where H is viewed as a finite automaton over the alphabet $\mathbb{A}_H$) if and only if $L(\mathcal{A}_\emptyset) \subseteq L(H)$ (H is $\mathcal{I}$-closed) if and only if $L(\mathcal{A}_\emptyset) \cap (\mathbb{A}_H^* \backslash L(H)) = \emptyset$. This can be checked in polynomial space by guessing a word in the intersection and storing only the current state of $\mathcal{A}_\emptyset$ and the current state of the automaton for $\mathbb{A}_H^* \backslash L(H)$ resulting from the subset construction for H, which is a subset of the set of states of H.   □

Theorem 5. *The following problem is EXPSPACE-complete:*

INPUT: Set P of processes, set $\mathfrak{C}$ of message contents, and a transition-connected HMSC H over P and $\mathfrak{C}$

QUESTION: Is H safely realizable?

Furthermore, this problem is also EXPSPACE-complete if P and $\mathfrak{C}$ are fixed.

Proof. The lower bound follows from Theorem 1. For the upper bound we can argue as follows: By the proof of Theorem 4, we have to check whether $L(\mathcal{A}_\emptyset) \subseteq [L(H)]_{\mathcal{I}}$. But since H is assumed to be transition-connected, we can construct an HMSC H' of at most exponential size such that $L(H') = [L(H)]_{\mathcal{I}}$, and then verify $L(\mathcal{A}_\emptyset) \subseteq L(H')$ in space bounded polynomially in the size of H' (and thus, in space bounded exponentially in the size of H).   □

The proof of Theorem 3 is based on the following lemma.

Lemma 4. *The following two statements are equivalent:*

(A) $\mathcal{A}$ *is deadlock-free and* $\mathrm{msc}(\mathcal{A}) \subseteq \langle \mathbb{A}_H \rangle$.

(B) $\mathcal{A}_\emptyset$ *is deadlock-free, and for all* $\mathbf{s} \in \mathbf{S}_\emptyset$ *and all* $M \in \mathrm{pMSC} \backslash \{\emptyset\}$ *such that* $(\mathbf{s}, \mathcal{B}_\emptyset) \xrightarrow{M}_{\mathcal{A}}$ *it holds*

$$\exists K \in \langle \mathbb{A}_H \rangle \; \exists A \in \mathbb{A}_H \left\{ \begin{array}{l} \mathbf{s} \xrightarrow{K \cdot A}_{\mathcal{A}_\emptyset}, \; P(K) \cap P(M) = \emptyset, \\ \sup(A, M) \text{ exists and, } \inf(A, M) \neq \emptyset \end{array} \right\}. \quad (1)$$

For the further consideration, assume that $\mathbf{s} \in \mathbf{S}_\emptyset$ and $M \in \mathrm{pMSC} \backslash \{\emptyset\}$ are such that $(\mathbf{s}, \mathcal{B}_\emptyset) \xrightarrow{M}_{\mathcal{A}}$ but (1) from Lemma 4 *is not satisfied* for $\mathbf{s}$ and M. Furthermore, let us assume that M is chosen such that $|M|$ is minimal. We will show that we can bound the size of M. For this we need the following lemma, which can be shown by induction on $|N|$.

Lemma 5. *Let* $\mathbf{t} \in \mathbf{S}_\emptyset$ *and* $N \in \mathrm{pMSC}$ *such that* $(\mathbf{t}, \mathcal{B}_\emptyset) \xrightarrow{N}_\mathcal{A}$ *and* $|N| < |M|$. *Then there exist atoms* $A_1, \ldots, A_m \in \mathbb{A}_H$ *and non-empty prefixes* $B_i \leq A_i$, $1 \leq i \leq m$, *such that the following holds:*

- *For all send types* $p!q(c) \in \Sigma$, *if there is an unmatched send event of type* $p!q(c)$ *in* B_i *then* $q \notin P(B_{i+1} \cdots B_m)$.
- $N = B_1 \cdot B_2 \cdots B_m$ *(by the first point, concatenation of the* B_i *is defined)*

Now choose an arbitrary maximal event e of $M \neq \emptyset$, and let $N = M{\upharpoonright}_{E(M) \setminus \{e\}} \in$ pMSC, i.e., remove e from M. Since $|N| < |M|$ and $(\mathbf{s}, \mathcal{B}_\emptyset) \xrightarrow{N}_\mathcal{A}$, Lemma 5 applies to N. Thus, we get the following two properties (C1) and (C2) for M:

(C1) There is a maximal event e of M such that $N = M{\upharpoonright}_{E(M) \setminus \{e\}}$ satisfies $N = B_1 \cdot B_2 \cdots B_m$ for non-empty prefixes $B_i \leq A_i$ of atoms $A_i \in \mathbb{A}_H$.
(C2) For all send types $p!q(c) \in \Sigma$, if there is an unmatched send event of type $p!q(c)$ in B_i then $q \notin P(B_{i+1} \cdots B_m)$.

Now let $(\mathbf{s}, \mathcal{B}_\emptyset) = (\mathbf{s}_1, \mathcal{B}_1) \xrightarrow{B_1}_\mathcal{A} (\mathbf{s}_2, \mathcal{B}_2) \xrightarrow{B_2}_\mathcal{A} \cdots \xrightarrow{B_m}_\mathcal{A} (\mathbf{s}_{m+1}, \mathcal{B}_{m+1})$ be a run of $\mathcal{A}$ and assume that $\mathbf{s}_k = \mathbf{s}_\ell$ (but possibly $\mathcal{B}_k \neq \mathcal{B}_\ell$) for some $k < \ell$. Due to (C2), the CFM $\mathcal{A}$ can process, starting from $(\mathbf{s}_k, \mathcal{B}_k)$, also the suffix $B_\ell \cdots B_m$, i.e., $(\mathbf{s}, \mathcal{B}_\emptyset) \xrightarrow{B_1 \cdots B_{k-1} \cdot B_\ell \cdots B_m}_\mathcal{A} (\mathbf{s}_{m+1}, \mathcal{C})$ for some buffer configuration $\mathcal{C}$ (in general $\mathcal{C} \neq \mathcal{B}_{m+1}$). We can use this observation for a kind of pumping argument, in order to prove that additionally to (C1) and (C2), the following property (C3) holds, where $\alpha = \max\{|A| \mid A \in \mathbb{A}_H\}$.

(C3) The number m in (C1) satisfies $m < (|P| + \alpha \cdot |P| + 2) \cdot (1 + \prod_{p \in P} |S_p|)$.

Proof of Theorem 3 (sketch). It suffices to check property (B) from Lemma 4 in PSPACE. Whether $\mathcal{A}_\emptyset$ is deadlock-free can be easily checked in PSPACE without explicitly constructing $\mathcal{A}_\emptyset$ (states of $\mathcal{A}_\emptyset$ can be encoded in polynomial space). It remains to check, whether a situation of the form $(\mathbf{s}, \mathcal{B}_\emptyset) \xrightarrow{M}_\mathcal{A}$ exists such that (1) from Lemma 4 becomes false. A first approach would be to guess such a situation, but note that the size bound for M that results from (C3) is exponential in the size of H. On the other hand, all one has to remember from M in order to check, whether $\mathbf{s}$ and M do not satisfy (1) from Lemma 4, is the set of processes $P(M)$ and the tuple of prefixes $(\pi_p(M)[1, \alpha_p])_{p \in P}$ of the projections onto the processes, where $\alpha_p = \max\{|\pi_p(A)| \mid A \in \mathbb{A}_H\}$ for $p \in P$ (whether $\sup(A, M)$ exists for some $A \in \mathbb{A}_H$ depends by Lemma 2 only on the prefixes $\pi_p(M)[1, \alpha_p]$), which can be stored in polynomial space. Hence, one can guess M "slice by slice", according to (C1), (C2), and (C3), and thereby accumulate only the data $P(M)$ and $(\pi_p(M)[1, \alpha_p])_{p \in P}$ (and forget everything else).   □

4   Non-FIFO Communication

For all results in Section 3 we have restricted to FIFO communication. In this section we briefly discuss the non-FIFO case. Note that the obvious fact that under FIFO communication, every MSC M can be recovered from its projections $\pi_p(M)$, $p \in P$, is false for non-FIFO communication (take two messages with identical contents, which are received in M_1 in the order in which they were sent, whereas in M_2 they are received in reverse order). On the other hand if we forbid at least overtaking of messages with identical message contents, this fact still holds, see also [15]. Let us assume this for the further discussion. Note also that for the non-FIFO case, our CFM-model has to be slightly altered. The set $\mathfrak{C}^{Ch}$ of buffer configurations has to be replaced by $\mathbb{N}^{Ch \times \mathfrak{C}}$. For a given buffer configuration $\mathcal{B} \in \mathbb{N}^{Ch \times \mathfrak{C}}$, the value $\mathcal{B}((p,q),c)$, where $(p,q) \in Ch$ and $c \in \mathfrak{C}$, represents the number of messages with content c in the channel from p to q, see also [15]. Transitions in this CFM model are defined analogously to the FIFO-case in Section 2.2.

With the modifications described above, all results from Section 3 can be also shown for non-FIFO communication. First, thanks to our assumption that overtaking of identical messages is disallowed, Lemma 3 remains true. Concerning the EXPSPACE-hardness proof for Theorem 1, note that in the construction there, every message is immediately confirmed, which implies that the absence of the FIFO-restriction has no effect. Of course, the same holds for the undecidability proof of Theorem 2. Note also that the HMSC H in the proof of Theorem 2 (resp. Theorem 1) is either safely realizable (if $\mathcal{M}$ does not accept w) or not even weakly realizable (if $\mathcal{M}$ accepts w). It follows that also under non-FIFO communication, weak realizability is undecidable for the class of all HMSCs and EXPSPACE-hard for bounded HMSCs. For the latter problem, no primitive recursive upper bound is presently known, since the decidability proof in [15] uses a reduction to the reachability problem for Petri nets, for which no primitive recursive upper bound is known. Finally, also the proof of Theorem 3 (and hence of Theorem 4 and Theorem 5) works after some slight adaptations for non-FIFO communication.

Acknowledgments

I am grateful to Anca Muscholl for many fruitful discussions on the topic of this paper.

References

1. R. Alur, K. Etessami, and M. Yannakakis. Inference of message sequence charts. In *Proceedings of the 22nd International Conference on on Software Engineering (ICSE 2000), Limerick (Ireland)*, pages 304–313. ACM Press, 2000. 177, 182, 183
2. R. Alur, K. Etessami, and M. Yannakakis. Realizability and verification of MSC graphs. In *Proceedings of the 28th International Colloquium on Automata, Languages and Programming (ICALP 2001), Crete (Greece)*, number 2076 in Lecture Notes in Computer Science, pages 797–808. Springer, 2001. 177, 178, 183, 184, 187

3. R. Alur and M. Yannakakis. Model checking of message sequence charts. In *Proceedings of the 9th International Conference on Concurrency Theory (CONCUR 99), Eindhoven (The Netherlands)*, number 1664 in Lecture Notes in Computer Science, pages 114–129. Springer, 1999. 178, 181

4. H. Ben-Abdallah and S. Leue. Syntactic detection of process divergence and non-local choice in message sequence charts. In *Proceedings of the Third International Workshop on Tools and Algorithms for Construction and Analysis of Systems (TACAS '97), Enschede (The Netherlands)*, number 1217 in Lecture Notes in Computer Science, pages 259–274, 1997. 177

5. D. Brand and P. Zafiropulo. On communicating finite-state machines. *Journal of the Association for Computing Machinery*, 30(2):323–342, 1983. 177

6. B. Caillaud, P. Darondeau, L. Hélouët, and G. Lesventes. HMSCs as partial specifications . . . with Petri nets as completion. In *Modelling and Verification of Parallel Processes (MOVEP), Nantes (France)*, number 2067 in Lecture Notes in Computer Science, pages 125–152, 2000. 178

7. V. Diekert and G. Rozenberg, editors. *The Book of Traces*. World Scientific, Singapore, 1995. 178

8. B. Genest, A. Muscholl, H. Seidl, and M. Zeitoun. Infinite-state high-level MSCs: Model-checking and realizability. to appear in Proceedings of the 29th International Colloquium on Automata, Languages and Programming (ICALP 2002), Malaga (Spain), 2002. 178, 181

9. E. Gunter, A. Muscholl, and D. Peled. Compositional message sequence charts. In T. Margaria and W. Yi, editors, *Tools and Algorithms for the Construction and Analysis of Systems, 7th International Conference (TACAS), Genova (Italy)*, volume 2031 of *Lecture Notes in Computer Science*, pages 496–511. Springer, 2001. 180

10. L. Hélouët and C. Jard. Conditions for synthesis of communicating automata from HMSCs. In *5th International Workshop on Formal Methods for Industrial Critical Systems (FMICS), Berlin (Germany)*, 2000. 177

11. L. Hélouët and P. Le Maigat. Decomposition of message sequence charts. In *2nd Workshop on SDL and MSC (SAM 2000), Grenoble (France)*, pages 46–60, 2000. 180

12. J. G. Henriksen, M. Mukund, K. N. Kumar, and P. Thiagarajan. Regular collections of message sequence charts. In U. Montanari, J. D. P. Rolim, and E. Welzl, editors, *Proceedings of the 25th International Symposium onMathematical Foundations of Computer Science (MFCS'2000), Bratislava, (Slovakia)*, number 1893 in Lecture Notes in Computer Science, pages 675–686. Springer, 2000. 182

13. ITU. Recommendation Z.100. Specification and Description Language (SDL). 1994. 177

14. ITU. Recommendation Z.120. Message Sequence Charts. 1996. 177

15. R. Morin. Recognizable sets of message sequence charts. In H. Alt and A. Ferreira, editors, *Proceedings of the19th Annual Symposium on Theoretical Aspects of Computer Science (STACS 2002), Juan les Pins (France)*, number 2285 in Lecture Notes in Computer Science, pages 523–534. Springer, 2002. 178, 180, 183, 187, 188, 190

16. A. Muscholl and D. Peled. Message sequence graphs and decision problems on Mazurkiewicz trace. In M. Kutylowski, L. Pacholski, and T. Wierzbicki, editors, *Proceedings of the 24th Mathematical Foundations of Computer Science (MFCS'99), Szklarska Poreba (Poland)*, number 1672 in Lecture Notes in Computer Science, pages 81–91. Springer, 1999. 178, 179, 181, 184, 185

17. C. H. Papadimitriou. *Computational Complexity*. Addison Wesley, 1994. 178
18. G. von Bochmann. Finite state description of communication protocols. *Computer Networks*, 2:361–372, 1978. 177
19. I. Walukiewicz. Difficult configurations – on the complexity of LTrL. In *Proceedings of the25th International Colloquium on Automata, Languages and Programming (ICALP 98), Aalborg (Denmark)*, number 1443 in Lecture Notes in Computer Science, pages 140–151. Springer, 1998. 184
20. W. Zielonka. Notes on finite asynchronous automata. *R. A. I. R. O. — Informatique Théorique et Applications*, 27:99–135, 1985. 187

Widening the Boundary between Decidable and Undecidable Hybrid Systems[*]

Eugene Asarin and Gerardo Schneider

VERIMAG, Centre Equation
2 ave de Vignate, 38610, Gières, France
Eugene.Asarin@imag.fr
Gerardo.Schneider@imag.fr

Abstract. We revisited decidability of the reachability problem for low dimensional hybrid systems. Even though many attempts have been done to draw the boundary between decidable and undecidable hybrid systems there are still many open problems in between. In this paper we show that the reachability question for some two dimensional hybrid systems are undecidable and that for other 2-dim systems this question remains unanswered, showing that it is as hard as the reachability problem for Piecewise Affine Maps, that is a well known open problem.

1 Introduction

Although many intense research activity in the last years have been done in the domain of hybrid systems (systems combining discrete and continuous behaviors), there is no clear boundary between what is decidable or not on such systems. In this paper we address only the reachability problem, we refer the reader interested in decidability of other problems, such as stability, to [10].

It is well known that for particular cases the reachability question is decidable. For continuous-time hybrid systems, the reachability is decidable for timed automata (TA) [3], their generalizations such as multirate automata [2,30], some kinds of updatable timed automata [12,13] and initialized rectangular automata [20,32]. For all these models the decidability depends on existence of a finite bisimulation and holds for systems of any dimensions. Another class of decidability results concerns planar systems. The method was suggested in [27], where decidability was stated for 2-dim PCD (systems with the dynamics given by Piecewise Constant Derivatives). The results were extended to planar multipolynomial systems in [16] and to non-deterministic planar polygonal systems (SPDI) in [8]. All these results are based on topological properties of the plane and the method does not work neither in higher dimension nor for systems with "jumping" discontinuous trajectories. On the negative side there are many undecidability results, and we cannot give an exhaustive list. For dimension 3 or more the reachability is undecidable for Linear Hybrid Automata [20], and even

---

[*] Partially supported by CNRS Project MathSTIC "Squash - Analyse Qualitative de Systèmes Hybrides".

L. Brim et al. (Eds.): CONCUR 2002, LNCS 2421, pp. 193–208, 2002.
© Springer-Verlag Berlin Heidelberg 2002

for PCDs [7]. Undecidability proofs are based on simulation of Turing or Minsky (counter) machines. A more economic simulation allows to prove undecidability for systems with stringent restrictions on the continuous dynamics, guards and resets: for example reachability is undecidable for rectangular automata with at least 5 clocks and one two-slope variable [20], or for TA with two skewed clocks [2].

Another group of results is related to the reachability problem for discrete-time dynamical systems, in particular iterations of piecewise affine or more complex functions. Roughly speaking, as it is well known since Poincaré's work, continuous-time systems of dimension $n + 1$ are "as complex as" discrete iterations in dimension n. On the negative side, as stated in [25], TM can be simulated by iterations of 2-dim piecewise affine maps(PAM), and hence reachability is undecidable in dimension 2. In dimension one the known undecidable discrete-time systems involve rather complex dynamics, e.g. in [26] an elementary function (a combination of sines an cosines) that simulates Turing machines (TM) with an exponential slowdown is constructed. Another class of systems with undecidable reachability in dimension one are countable PAMs (PAMs with an infinite number of intervals). As for the most natural class of one dimensional systems: finite PAMs, the decidability of reachability is an old standing open question (see [24,11] for a thorough discussion), related to other open questions in number theory and linear algebra. This problem (we call it REACH$_{PAM}$) plays the key rôle in this paper.

In this paper we analyze continuous-time hybrid systems which are close to the boundary between decidable and undecidable. As it was mentioned, planar systems with continuous trajectories are decidable, 3-dim are not. That is why we explore planar systems with jumps, and also systems with continuous trajectories on 2-dim manifolds. For such systems instead of proving decidability or undecidability, we establish an equivalence to the problem REACH$_{PAM}$. A finer analysis allows to show that the reachability for some constrained systems (e.g. with 2 clocks and affine resets) is also as hard as for REACH$_{PAM}$. For a little bit more complex 2-dim systems with a simple infinitary pattern we prove undecidability.

The paper is organized as follows. In section 2 we define several classes of hybrid automata, two dimensional manifolds, and our reference model: Piecewise affine maps (PAM). In section 3 we introduce Hierarchical PCDs (HPCD) and we show that the reachability problem for HPCD, PCD on manifolds, and some other classes of 2-dim systems is as hard as the reachability for PAM. In section 4 we show that enriching HPCD with one counter, or an infinite partition leads to the undecidability of the reachability question. We conclude in the last section with a summary. Due to space limitations we give only sketches of proofs for most results. The reader can find more details in the thesis [33].

2 Preliminaries

2.1 Hybrid Automata

There are many (more or less) equivalent definitions of hybrid systems/automata (see for example [1,21,35]). We will adopt in this paper the following definition.

A hybrid system is a dynamical system that combines discrete and continuous components. A natural model for hybrid systems is *hybrid automata* [21] that are automata such that at each discrete location the dynamics is governed by a differential equation (over continuous variables) and whose transitions (between locations) are enabled by conditions on the values of the variables.

Formally, an *n-dimensional hybrid automaton* is a tuple $\mathcal{H} = (\mathcal{X}, Q, f, \mathsf{I}_0, \mathsf{Inv}, \delta)$ where

- $\mathcal{X} \subseteq \mathbb{R}^n$ is the *continuous state space*. Elements of $\mathcal{X}$ are written as $\mathbf{x} = (x_1, x_2, \ldots, x_n)$, for $\{x_1, x_2, \ldots, x_n\} \in \mathsf{V}$, where V is a finite set of variables;
- Q is a finite set of *discrete locations*;
- $f : Q \to (\mathcal{X} \to \mathbb{R}^n)$ assigns a continuous vector field on $\mathcal{X}$ to each discrete location. While in discrete location $\ell \in Q$, the evolution of the continuous variables is governed by the differential equation $\dot{\mathbf{x}} = f_\ell(\mathbf{x})$. We say that the differential equation defines the *dynamics* of location ℓ;
- The *initial condition* $\mathsf{I}_0 : Q \to 2^{\mathcal{X}}$ is a function that for each state defines the initial values of the variables of $\mathcal{X}$;
- The *invariant* or *staying* conditions $\mathsf{Inv} : Q \to 2^{\mathcal{X}}$, $\mathsf{Inv}(\ell)$ is the condition that must be satisfied by the continuous variables in order to stay in location $\ell \in Q$;
- δ is a set of transitions of the form $tr = (\ell, g, \gamma, \ell')$ with $\ell, \ell' \in Q$. Such a quadruple means that a transition from ℓ to ℓ' can be taken whenever the guard $g \subset \mathcal{X}$ is satisfied and then the reset $\gamma : \mathcal{X} \to \mathcal{X}$ is applied.

In what follows we will consider deterministic systems unless the contrary be specified.

A *state* is a pair $(\ell, \mathbf{x})$ consisting of a location $\ell \in Q$ and $\mathbf{x} \in \mathcal{X}$. A state can change in two ways: (1) by *discrete* and *instantaneous* transition that changes both the location and the values of the variables according to the transition relation, and (2) by a *time delay* that changes only the values of the variables according to the dynamics of the current location. The system may stay at a location only if the invariant is true, and a transition must be taken before the invariant becomes false.

A *trajectory* of a hybrid automaton $\mathcal{H}$ is a function $\Theta : [0, T] \to Q \times \mathcal{X}$, $\Theta(t) = (\ell(t), \xi(t))$ such that there exists a sequence of times values $t_0 = 0 < t_1 < \ldots < t_n = T$ for which the following holds for each $1 \leq i \leq n$: (1) ℓ is constant on (t_i, t_{i+1}) (we describe its value there by ℓ_i) and ξ is derivable on (t_i, t_{i+1}), it is left continuous and with right limits everywhere; (2) There is a transition $(\ell(t_i), g, \gamma, \ell(t_{i+1})) \in \delta$ such that $\xi^-(t_{i+1}) \in g(\ell_i, \ell_{i+1})$ and $\xi(t_{i+1}) = \gamma(\xi^-(t_{i+1}))$[1]; (3) For any $0 \leq i \leq n$, for any $t \in (t_i, t_{i+1})$, $\dot{\xi}(t) = f_{l(t)}(\xi(t))$.

---

[1] $\xi^-(t)$ is the left limit of $\xi(t)$.

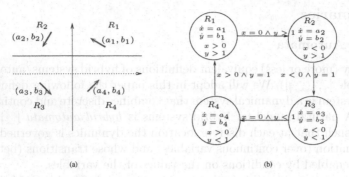

Fig. 1. (a) A simple PCD; (b) Its corresponding hybrid automaton

2.2 Rectangular and Linear Hybrid Automata

A hybrid automaton $\mathcal{H}$ is *linear* [21,1] if the following restrictions are met: (1) The initial and invariant conditions as well as the guard are boolean combinations of linear inequalities; (2) The dynamics are defined by differential equations of the form $\dot{x} = k_x$, one for each variable $x \in V$, where $k_x \in \mathbb{Z}$ is an integer constant. We say that k_x is the *slope* (or *rate*) of the variable x at a given location.

We say that a variable x is a *memory cell* if it has slope 0 in every location of $\mathcal{H}$. A variable x is a *clock* if it has slope 1 in every location. A variable x is a *skewed clock* if there is a rational $k \in \mathbb{Q}\backslash\{0,1\}$ such that x has slope k in each location. The variable x is a *two-slope clock* if there is a rational k such that for each location $\dot{x} = k$ or $\dot{x} = 1$. A *stopwatch* is a two-slope clock with $k = 0$.

A *rectangle of dimension n* $R = \prod_{1 \leq i \leq n} I_i$ is the product of n intervals $I_i \subseteq \mathbb{R}$ of the real line with rational or infinite extremities.

A hybrid automaton is a *rectangular automaton* [21,20,32] if (1) all the initial conditions, invariants and graphs of resets are rectangles; (2) for each location ℓ, the dynamics has the form $\dot{\mathbf{x}} \in R_\ell$, where R_ℓ is a rectangle.

Another special case of linear hybrid automata are PCDs, that are described in next section.

2.3 PCD

A *piecewise constant derivative system* (PCD) [7,27] is a pair $\mathcal{H} = (\mathbb{P}, \mathbb{F})$ with $\mathbb{P} = \{P_s\}_{s \in S}$ a finite family of non-overlapping convex polygonal sets in $\mathbb{R}^2$ with non-empty interiors, and $\mathbb{F} = \{\mathbf{c}_s\}_{s \in S}$ a family of vectors in $\mathbb{R}^2$. The dynamics of the PCD is determined by the equation $\dot{\mathbf{x}} = \mathbf{c}_s$ for $\mathbf{x} \in P_s$. Hence trajectories are broken lines.

A well known technique for planar differential equations and in particular for PCD is to replace the analysis of those systems by analysis of edge-to-edge discrete successors [7,8,27] (also known as Poincaré map [22]). Given an edge e, each point on e can be represented by a local one dimensional coordinate. A one-step

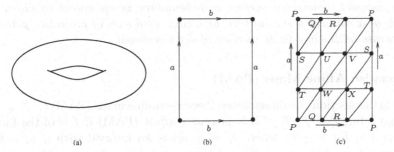

Fig. 2. Representations of a Torus: (a) a surface in $\mathbb{R}^3$; (b) a square with identified edges; (c) a triangulated surface

edge-to-edge successor in such coordinates can be written as $\mathsf{Succ}_{ee'}(x) = ax + b$. In general, a n-step successor for a given sequence of edges $\sigma = e_1, e_2, \ldots, e_n$ is again a function of the above form (see for example [7] for a better understanding).

Notice that PCDs can be viewed as linear hybrid automata without reset. In Figure 1 a simple PCD and its corresponding hybrid automata are shown.

2.4 Two Dimensional Manifolds

All the (topological) definitions, examples and results of this section are done following the *combinatorial method* and follow [19].

A topological space is *triangulable* if it can be obtained from a set of triangles by the identification of edges and vertices subject to the restriction that any two triangles are identified either along a single edge or at a single vertex, or are completely disjoint. The identification should be done via an affine bijection.

A *surface* (or *2-dim manifold*) is a triangulable space for which in addition: (1) each edge is identified with exactly one other edge; and (2) the triangles identified at each vertex can always be arranged in a cycle $T_1, \ldots, T_k, T_1$ so that adjacent triangles are identified along an edge. Typical examples are the sphere, the torus (see Figure 2) or the Klein's bottle.

A *surface with boundary* is a topological space obtained by identifying edges and vertices of a set of triangles as for surfaces except that certain edges may not be identified with another edge. These edges, which violate the definition of a surface, are called *boundary edges*, and their vertices, which also violate the definition of surface, are called *boundary vertices*. Typical examples of surfaces with boundary are the cylinder and the Möbius strip. Indeed, the cylinder is equivalent to a sphere with two disks cut out.

We state now an important theorem in the topological theory of surfaces:

Theorem 1 (Classification theorem(see [19], p.122)).

– *Every compact, connected surface is topologically equivalent to a sphere, or a connected sum of tori, or a connected sum of projective planes.*

— *Every compact, connected surface with boundary is equivalent to either a sphere, or a connected sum of tori, or a connected sum of projective planes, in any case with some finite number of disks removed.*

2.5   Piecewise Affine Maps (PAM)

We define in this section one dimensional Piecewise affine maps (PAM) [11,24,25]. We say that a function $f : \mathbb{R} \to \mathbb{R}$ is *piecewise affine* (PAM) if f is of the form $f(x) = a_i x + b_i$ for $x \in I_i$, where $I_i = [l_i, u_i]$ is an interval with $l_i, u_i \in \mathbb{Q}$. Coefficients a_i, b_i and the extremities of I_i are supposed to be rational.

Let REACH$_{PAM}$, the reachability problem for PAMs, be the following problem.

Problem 1. Given a PAM $\mathcal{A}$ and two points x and y, is y reachable from x?

Even for a function f with just two linear pieces, there is no known decision algorithm for the above problem. The same problem is known to be undecidable in dimension 2 and if piecewise affine maps are replaced by polynomials, the problem is open for any dimension [11,24,25].

3   Between Decidability and Undecidability

We show in this section that for several natural classes of 2-dim hybrid systems the reachability problem is s as hard as for 1-dim PAMs, for which such problem is known to be open. Recall that the reachability problem is decidable [27] for planar PCDs and undecidable for dimensions greater than two [6].

3.1   HPCD

Hierarchical piecewise constant derivative systems (HPCDs) can be seen as hybrid automata such that at each location the dynamics is given by a PCD. More formally, an HPCD is a hybrid automaton $H_{PCD} = (\mathcal{X}, Q, f, l_0, \mathsf{Inv}, \delta)$ such that Q and l_0 are as before while the dynamics at each ℓ is a PCD and each transition $tr = (\ell, g, \gamma, \ell')$ is such that (1) its guard g is a predicate of the form $P(x, y) \equiv (ax + by + c = 0 \land x \in I \land y \in J)$ where I and J are intervals and a, b, c and the extremities of I and J are rational-valued and (2) the reset functions γ are affine functions: $\gamma(\mathbf{x}) = A\mathbf{x} + \mathbf{b}$. Last, Inv is defined as the negation of the union of the guards, i.e. we can stay in location ℓ as long as no guard is satisfied. If all the PCDs are bounded, then the HPCD is said to be *bounded*.

We need to introduce a 1-dim coordinate system on each edge e. We will denote a point with local coordinates x on edge e by (e, x) or whenever no confusion may arise, just as x.

It can be argued that the term *hierarchical* in the above definition is superfluous and that in fact HPCDs are just 2 dimensional linear hybrid automata. Even though this is true, the definition is intentional since we want to emphasize

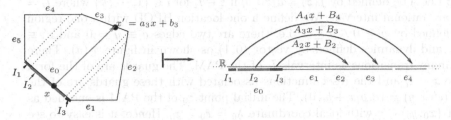

Fig. 3. Sketch of the simulation of a HPCD by a PAM

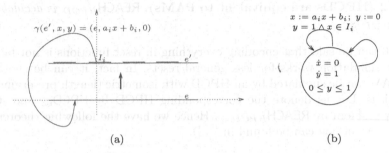

(a)   (b)

Fig. 4. (a) The HPCD that simulates a PAM. (b) An equivalent RA_{1cl1mc}

the fact that there are just "few" real discontinuities due to jumps and reset and that in general the trajectory behaves like a PCD.

Let $REACH_{HPCD}$ be the following problem:

Problem 2. Given a HPCD $\mathcal{H}$ and two points $\mathbf{x}_0$ and $\mathbf{x}_f$, is $\mathbf{x}_f$ reachable from $\mathbf{x}_0$?

We will prove that HPCDs can simulate PAMs and vice versa. For that we show first that each HPCD $\mathcal{H}$ is simulated by a PAM $\mathcal{A}$ and that for each PAM $\mathcal{A}$ there is a HPCD $\mathcal{H}$ such that $\mathcal{H}$ simulates $\mathcal{A}$. For proving the first, we should: (1) Encode an initial and final point of $\mathcal{H}$ by points on some intervals of $\mathcal{A}$; (2) Represent a configuration of $\mathcal{H}$ by a configuration of $\mathcal{A}$; (3) Simulate an edge-to-edge transition of $\mathcal{H}$ by some function application on $\mathcal{A}$.

Lemma 1 (PAMs simulate HPCDs). *Every bounded 2-dimensional HPCD $\mathcal{H}$ can be simulated by a PAM.*

Sketch of the proof: We arrange all the edges of $\mathcal{H}$ in the Real line (in an arbitrary order) and we represent each edge-to-edge successor function and each reset function by an affine map (restricted to an interval). Assembling all those affine maps together yields the PAM $\mathcal{A}$ simulating $\mathcal{H}$ (see Figure 3). $\square$

Lemma 2 (HPCDs simulate PAMs). *Every PAM $\mathcal{A}$ can be simulated by a 2-dim HPCD.*

Proof: Let $\mathcal{A}$ be defined by $f(z) = a_i z + b_i$ if $z \in I_i$ for $i \in \{1, \cdots, k\}$ where $I_i = [l_i, u_i]$ are rational intervals. We define a one-location HPCD with a one-region PCD defined by $y \geq 0 \wedge y \leq 1$, i.e. there are two edges $e \equiv y = 0$ and $e' \equiv y = 1$, and dynamics defined by vector $(0, 1)$ as shown in figure 4-(a). There are as many transitions as intervals I_i of the PAM. The guards are of the form $y \in e \wedge x \in I_i$ and the reset functions associated with these guards are of the form $\gamma(e', x, y) = (e, a_i x + b_i, 0)$. The initial point z_0 of the PAM is encoded as a point $(x_0, y_0) \in e$ with local coordinate $\lambda_0 = x_0 = z_0$. Hence, it is easy to see that $z_f = f(z_0)$ iff $\lambda_f = \gamma(e', \lambda')$ where $\lambda' = \mathsf{Succ}_{ee'}(\lambda_0)$. $\square$
From the above two lemmas, we have then the following theorem.

Theorem 2 (HPCDs are equivalent to PAMs). REACH$_{HPCD}$ *is decidable iff* REACH$_{PAM}$ *is.* $\square$

Remark. It can be said that encoding everything in reset functions is not fair. Indeed, the simulation works for less general resets. In fact, it can be shown that any PAM can be simulated by an HPCD with isometric (length preserving) reset functions. Let us denote the corresponding HPCD by HPCD$_{\mathsf{iso}}$ and its reachability problem by REACH$_{HPCD_{iso}}$. Hence we have the following theorem (the exact construction can be found in [33]).

Theorem 3 (HPCD$_{\mathsf{iso}}$ are equivalent to PAMs). REACH$_{HPCD_{iso}}$ *is decidable iff* REACH$_{PAM}$ *is.* $\square$

3.2 About Rectangular and Linear 2-Dimensional Hybrid Automata

In this section we prove some corollaries of Theorem 2 and Theorem 3.

The class of rectangular hybrid automata with one clock y, one memory cell x, invariants of the form $C \leq y \leq D$, guards of the form $y = D$ and resets of the form $\gamma(x, y) = (ax + b, 0)$ will be denoted as RA$_{\mathsf{1cl1mc}}$. It is easy to observe that the HPCD defined for simulating a PAM (see Figure 4-(a)) is in fact a RA$_{\mathsf{1cl1mc}}$ (see Figure 4-(b)) and to deduce the following result.

Corollary 1 (RA$_{\mathsf{1cl1mc}}$ are equivalent to PAMs). *Reachability for* RA$_{\mathsf{1cl1mc}}$ *is decidable iff reachability for PAMs is. The same is true for one-state* RA$_{\mathsf{1cl1mc}}$.

The class of rectangular hybrid automata with two clocks x and y, invariants of the form $C \leq y \leq D$, guards of the form $y = D$ and resets of the form $\gamma(x, y) = (ax + b, 0)$ will be denoted as RA$_{\mathsf{2cl}}$.

Corollary 2 (RA$_{\mathsf{2cl}}$ are equivalent to PAMs). *Reachability for* RA$_{\mathsf{2cl}}$ *is decidable iff reachability for PAMs is.*

Sketch of the proof: In Lemma 2 an HPCD $\mathcal{H}$ (see Figure 4) that simulates a PAM was built. We obtain another HPCD $\mathcal{H}'$ applying an affine transformation to $\mathcal{H}$, where the edge e remains unchanged whereas e' is translated by one unit to the right. $\mathcal{H}'$ is represented in Figure 5-(a), where given $I = [l, u]$ $I + 1$ is a

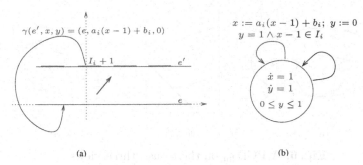

$$\gamma(e', x, y) = (e, a_i(x-1) + b_i, 0)$$

$$x := a_i(x-1) + b_i; \; y := 0$$
$$y = 1 \wedge x - 1 \in I_i$$

$$I_i + 1 \qquad e'$$

$$e$$

$$\dot{x} = 1$$
$$\dot{y} = 1$$
$$0 \le y \le 1$$

(a)   (b)

Fig. 5. (a) Another HPCD that simulates a PAM; (b) The corresponding RA_{2cl}

short for $[l+1, u+1]$. It is not difficult to see that the automaton of Figure 5-(b) is a RA_{2cl} equivalent to $\mathcal{H}'$.   □

Notice that RA_{2cl} automata can be considered as *updatable* timed automata [12,13] with more general resets (of the form $y := ax + b$).

The next two corollaries are consequences of Theorem 3.

We denote by RA_{1sk1sl}, the class of rectangular hybrid automata with one two-slope clock x (taking values on $\{-1, 1\}$) and one positive n-skewed clock y with the following restrictions: (1) on each transition, x is reset to function of y of the form $x := y + d$ and y is reinitialized with a constant value c, where c is the inferior bound of y in ℓ'; (2) the values of the two variables are never compared, and (3) the guard of a transition from location ℓ to ℓ' is of the form $x = A$, where A is one of the bounds of x in the invariant of location ℓ.

It can be seen that the construction of Theorem 3 gives in fact a RA_{1sk1sl}.

Corollary 3 (RA_{1sk1sl} are equivalent to PAMs). *Reachability for RA_{1sk1sl} is decidable iff reachability for PAMs is.*

Let $\mathcal{H}$ be a linear hybrid automaton with just two (mutually exclusive) stop-watches x and y with the following restriction: (1') whenever a transition is taken, x and y remain unchanged or the new value of x is a function of y of the form $x := y + d$ and y is reinitialized with a constant value c, where c is the inferior bound of y in ℓ'; (2') the guard of a transition from ℓ to ℓ' is of the form $x = A$ or $ax + by + c = 0$, where A is one of the bounds of x in the invariant of location ℓ and a, b and c are rational constants. We denote this class by LA_{St}.

It can be shown that LA_{St} can simulate any RA_{1sk1sl} which implies the last result of this subsection.

Corollary 4 (LA_{St} are equivalent to PAMs). *Reachability for LA_{St} is decidable iff reachability for PAMs is.*

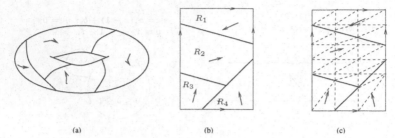

Fig. 6. A PCD_{2m} on the torus : three views

3.3 PCD_{2m}: PCDs on 2-Dimensional Manifolds

Surfaces (or 2-dimensional manifolds) were introduced in section 2.4. To define a PCD on a triangulated surface S, a PCD should be defined on each of its triangles. We call this class of systems *PCD on 2-dimensional manifolds* (PCD_{2m}).

In figure Figure 6 we define a PCD on a torus and show how to represent it as a family of PCDs on triangles.

A point x_f is *reachable* from another point x_0 if there exists a trajectory from x_0 to x_f. We consider the following problem:

Problem 3. Given a PCD_{2m} $\mathcal{H}$ and two points x_0 and x_f, is x_f reachable from x_0?

Lemma 3 (PAM_{inj} **simulate** PCD_{2m}). *Every PCD_{2m} can be simulated by an injective PAM.*

Sketch of the proof: Let $\mathcal{H}$ be a PCD_{2m}. The reduction is analog to the simulation of HPCDs by PAMs. Notice that $\mathcal{H}$ is in fact an HPCD where a jump is produced each time we reach an identified edge and the resets are the identifying bijections between the identified edges. We will not reproduce the proof here, see Lemma 1. The requirement that each edge is identified with exactly one other edge ensures injectivity.   □

Lemma 4 (PCD_{2m} **simulate** PAM_{inj}). *Every injective (bounded) PAM can be simulated by a PCD_{2m}.*

Sketch of the proof: Let $\mathcal{A}$ be an injective PAM defined as $f(z) = f_i(z) = a_i z + b_i$ if $z \in I_i$ for $1 \le i \le n$. We obtain a PCD_{2m} in the following way similar to the construction of lemma 2. In the rectangle $R = [-M; M] \times [0; 1]$ (with M large enough) the dynamics is defined by vector $(0, 1)$. In order to realize the function f by identification of edges, we introduce several new edges (see Figure 7: on the bottom side of the rectangle R we define $I_i^k = (f_i(I_i) \cap I_k) \times \{0\}$, on the top side we define $J_i^k = (I_i \cap f_i^{-1}(I_k)) \times \{1\}$). Injectivity of the PAM $\mathcal{A}$ guarantees that these intervals do not overlap.

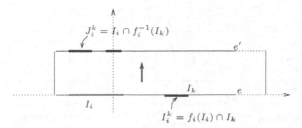

Fig. 7. Simulation of a PCD$_{2m}$ by a PAM$_{inj}$: edge J_i^k identified with I_i^k via f_i

Next we identify each non-empty J_i^k with I_i^k via the function f_i (which is an affine bijection between these two edges). It is easy to find a triangulation such that I_i^k and J_i^k are its edge, hence we have represented our system as a PCD on a compact surface with boundary.

By the Classification Theorem for Surfaces with Boundary (see Theorem 1) we have that this surface is equivalent to a sphere with some disks removed and we obtain then a PCD$_{2m}$ just "sewing" the disks. We associate with these disks a zero slope vector. □

From the above two lemmas we have that $z_f = f^*(z_0)$ iff Reach($\mathcal{H}, \mathbf{x}_0, \mathbf{x}_f$), where $\mathbf{x}_0$ has local coordinate $\lambda_0 = z_0$ on a given edge e and $\mathbf{x}_f$ has local coordinate $\lambda_f = z_f$ on an edge e'. Then the following theorem holds.

Theorem 4 (PCD$_{2m}$ are equivalent to PAM$_{inj}$). *Reachability for* PCD$_{2m}$ *is decidable iff reachability for injective PAMs is.*

4 Undecidability Results

We show in this section that modifying HPCD slightly by adding "something infinite" (a counter, an infinite partition, etc.) yields undecidable systems.

4.1 HPCD with One Counter (HPCD$_{1c}$)

Consider the class of HPCD$_{1c}$ which are HPCD augmented with a counter c. In each location ℓ the state vector (x, y) evolves according to a PCD, while c remains constant. Guards have the form $P(x, y) \wedge Q(c)$ where $P(x, y)$ is as for HPCDs and $Q(c) \equiv c = 0 \mid c > 0 \mid$ **true**. Resets are as for HPCDs, but they can also increment or decrement c.

We prove that the reachability problem for HPCD$_{1c}$ is undecidable showing that a HPCD$_{1c}$ $\mathcal{H}$ can simulate Minsky (two counter) machines [28] for which reachability is known to be undecidable.

Proposition 1 (HPCD$_{1c}$ simulates MM). *Every Minsky Machine* $\mathcal{M}$ *can be simulated by a 2-dim HPCD with one counter. Hence reachability is undecidable for* HPCD$_{1c}$.

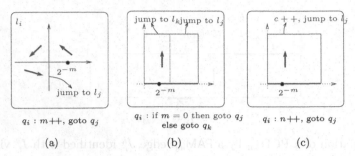

Fig. 8. Sketch of the simulation of a MM by a HPCD$_{1c}$: location l_i

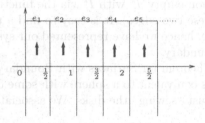

Fig. 9. Sketch of the simulation of a TM by a HPCD$_\infty$

Sketch of the proof: We associate with each q_i of $\mathcal{M}$ a location ℓ_i of HPCD$_{1c}$. In order to encode a configuration of $\mathcal{M}$ which is a triple (q_i, m, n) (with m and n standing for contents of the two counters), we represent it in $\mathcal{H}$ by (ℓ_i, x, y, c) with the point $(x, y) = (2^{-m}, 0)$ representing the first counter of $\mathcal{M}$, and $c = n$ storing the second one. In any case, the PCD associated to the location ℓ_i simulates the instruction for the state q_i. Informally speaking, in order to increment or decrement m we just divide or multiply x by 2 (it can be easily done by a PCD). In order to test whether $m = 0$ we check whether $x > 0.75$. All the operations on n are done directly on the counter c. Figure 8 represents PCD simulating instructions $m++$, $m = 0$? and $n++$. PCD for the three other instructions of Minsky machine ($m--$, $n--$ and $n = 0$?) are similar.

Putting all those PCDs together we obtain a HPCD$_{1c}$ which simulates $\mathcal{M}$.   □

4.2   HPCDs with Infinite Partition (HPCD$_\infty$)

We will consider in this section HPCDs for which we relax the condition of having a finite number of regions. We call this class of systems, *HPCDs with infinite partition* (HPCD$_\infty$). We are not going to define this class formally, since we are just interested in showing that this additional feature (having an infinite partition) leads immediately to the undecidability of the reachability problem for HPCD$_\infty$.

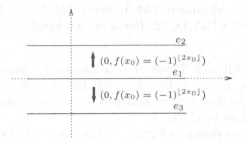

Fig. 10. Simulation of a TM by a HPCD_x

Proposition 2 (HPCD_∞ simulate TMs). *Every TM $\mathcal{M}$ with alphabet $\{0; 1\}$ can be simulated by a 2-dimensional (unbounded) HPCD with infinite partition. Hence reachability is undecidable for HPCD_∞.*

Sketch of the proof: The system $\mathcal{H}$ will have a location l_k for each state q_k of the TM. We represent the TM tape contents by a point on the x-axis with the abscissa $x = \sum_{i=-\infty}^{\infty} a_i 2^i$ (here a_0 is the symbol under the head of the TM) in a HPCD with infinite partition as in Figure 9. With such a partition it is easy to test whether the current symbol is 0 or 1: whenever an "even" edge is reached (e_i with $i = 2k$ for $k \in \mathbb{N}$), that corresponds to $\text{frac}_x > \frac{1}{2}$, and hence the current symbol is 1, otherwise it is 0.

Hence, to simulate an instruction of the form $q_k 0 \to \dots$ we make a jump from all the odd e_i edges of the location l_k. For an instruction $q_k 1 \to \dots$ we make a jump from all the even edges. It is easy to see that this jump is always affine: shifting the head corresponds to division or multiplication of x by 2, and replacing the current symbol corresponds to addition or substraction of $\frac{1}{2}$.   □

4.3   Origin-Dependent Rate HPCDs (HPCD_x)

Another way of introducing "infinite patterns" is allowing continuous dynamics with some periodic behavior that depends on the initial points after a reset is done. An *origin-dependent rate PCD* is a PCD $\mathcal{H} = (\mathbb{P}, \mathbb{F})$ such that each region P_s has dynamics $\dot{\mathbf{x}} = \phi_s(\mathbf{x_0})$ (as before, given a generic region P we will also use the notation $\phi(P, \mathbf{x_0})$).

Notice, that after reaching an edge, the system evolves according to a fixed rate that depends on the initial value $\mathbf{x_0}$ of the variables when entering the region. The idea of having flows (dynamics) that depend on initial sates has been taken from [5].

In the construction of Proposition 3 we will use rather particular ϕ_s functions.

We extend the above definition to HPCDs: an *origin-dependent rate HPCD* (HPCD_x) is a HPCD with an origin-dependent rate PCD at each location.

Proposition 3 (HPCD$_x$ simulate TMs). *Every TM $\mathcal{M}$ can be simulated by a 2-dimensional unbounded* HPCD$_x$ $\mathcal{H}$. *Hence the reachability is undecidable for such systems.*

Proof: We associate with each TM-state q_i a location ℓ_i, where the PCD_i is defined by four regions: R_1, $(y > 0) \wedge (y < 1)$; R_2, $(y < 0) \wedge (y > -1)$; R_3, $y < -1$; R_4, $y > 1$. The first two regions have dynamics given by the vector $(0, f(x_0))$ and the last two by $(0,1)$.

Let e_1, e_2 and e_3 be as shown in Figure 10. Let $f(x_0) = (-1)^{\lfloor 2x_0 \rfloor}$, where x_0 is the first coordinate on edge e_0 of the initial point $\mathbf{x}_0$. Notice that $f(x) = 1$ if frac$_x < \frac{1}{2}$ and $f(x) = -1$ otherwise.

There are two transitions from ℓ_i: (1) $tr_1 = (\ell_i, g_1, \gamma_1, \ell_j)$ where $g_1 \equiv e_2$ and $\gamma_1(e_2, x) = (e_1', f'(x))$; (2) $tr_2 = (\ell_i, g_2, \gamma_2, \ell_h)$ where $g_2 \equiv e_3$ and $\gamma_2(e_3, x) = (e_1, f''(x))$. Transitions tr_1 and tr_2 allow the trajectory to continue in locations ℓ_j and ℓ_h with a reset function that implement the instructions of the Turing machine as before. $\square$

Notice that the above definition allows the dynamics to be defined by any function of the initial point, but in order to simulate a TM we need very particular kind of functions, those that have a periodic pattern. We could have chosen any periodic function like sine or cosine. In any case, the key idea is to obtain an "infinite pattern" as before.

5   Conclusion

The contribution of this paper is twofold. First, we have shown that between 2 dimensional PCDs (for which the reachability problem is decidable [27]) and 3 dimensional PCDs (reachability is undecidable [7]) there exist an interesting class, *2-dim HPCD*, for which the reachability question is still open. We have also shown that the same is true for other similar systems, namely 2-dim rectangular automata and 2-dim linear hybrid automata with some restrictions as well as for PCD on 2-dim manifolds. Second, we have proved that 2-dim HPCD are really in the boundary between decidability and undecidability, since adding a simple counter or allowing some kind of "infinite pattern" to these systems, makes the reachability problem undecidable.

References

1. R. Alur, C. Courcoubetis, N. Halbwachs, T. A. Henzinger, P.-H. Ho, X. Nicollin, A. Olivero, J. Sifakis, and S. Yovine. The algorithmic analysis of hybrid systems. *TCS*, 138:3–34, 1995. 195, 196
2. R. Alur, C. Courcoubetis, T. A. Henzinger, and P.-H. Ho. Hybrid automata: An algorithmic approach to the specification and verification of hybrid systems. LNCS 736, p. 209–229. Springer-Verlag, 1993. 193, 194
3. R. Alur and D. L. Dill. A theory of timed automata. *TCS*, 126:183–235, 1994. 193

4. R. Alur, T. A. Henzinger, and M. Y. Vardi. Parametric real-time reasoning. In *25th ACM STOC*, p. 592–601, 1993.
5. R. Alur, S. Kannan, and S. La Torre. Polyhedral flows in hybrid automata. In *HSCC'99*, LNCS 1569, p. 5–18. Springer-Verlag, 1999. 205
6. E. Asarin and O. Maler. On some relations between dynamical systems and transition systems. In *ICALP'94*, LNCS 820. Springer, 1994. 198
7. E. Asarin, O. Maler, and A. Pnueli. Reachability analysis of dynamical systems having piecewise-constant derivatives. *TCS*, 138:35–65, 1995. 194, 196, 197, 206
8. E. Asarin, G. Schneider, and S. Yovine. On the decidability of the reachability problem for planar differential inclusions. In *HSCC'2001*, LNCS 2034, p. 89–104. 193, 196
9. L. S. Bobrow and M. A. Arbib. *Discrete Mathematics*. W. B. Saunders, 1974.
10. V. Blondel and J. Tsitsilkis. Complexity of stability and controllability of elementary hybrid systems. *Automatica*, 35:479–489, 1999. 193
11. O. Bournez. *Complexité algorithmique des systèmes dynamiques continus et hybrides*. PhD thesis, ENS de Lyon, 1999. 194, 198
12. P. Bouyer, C. Dufourd, E. Fleury, and A. Petit. Are timed automata updatable? In *CAV'2000*, LNCS 1855, p. 464–479. 193, 201
13. P. Bouyer, C. Dufourd, E. Fleury, and A. Petit. Expressiveness of updatable timed automata. In *MFCS'2000*, LNCS 1893, p. 232–242. 193, 201
14. M. S. Branicky. Universal computation and other capabilities of hybrid and continuous dynamical systems. *TCS*, 138(1), 1995.
15. K. Čerāns. *Algorithmic problems in analysis of real-time systems specifications*. PhD thesis, Univ. of Latvia, 1992.
16. K. Čerāns and J. Vīksna. Deciding reachability for planar multi-polynomial systems. In *Hybrid Systems III*, LNCS 1066. Springer, 1996. 193
17. R. L. Devaney. *An Introduction to Chaotic Dynamical Systems*. Addison-Wesley, Redwood City, 2nd edition, 1989.
18. J. Guckenheimer and P. Holmes. *Nonlinear Oscillations, Dynamical Systems and Linear Algebra*. Springer-Verlag, New York, 1990.
19. M. Henle. *A combinatorial introduction to topology*. Dover publications, Inc., 1979. 197
20. T. A. Henzinger, P. W. Kopke, A. Puri, and P. Varaiya. What's decidable about hybrid automata? In *STOC'1995*, p. 373–382. ACM Press. 193, 194, 196
21. T. A. Henzinger. The theory of hybrid automata. In *LICS'96*, p. 278–292, 1996. 195, 196
22. M. W. Hirsch and S. Smale. *Differential Equations, Dynamical Systems and Linear Algebra*. Academic Press Inc., 1974. 196
23. Y. Kesten, A. Pnueli, J. Sifakis, and S. Yovine. Integration graphs: a class of decidable hybrid systems. In *Hybrid Systems*, LNCS 736, p. 179–208, 1993.
24. P. Koiran. My favourite problems. www.ens-lyon.fr/~koiran/problems.html. 194, 198
25. P. Koiran, M. Cosnard, and M. Garzon. Computability with low-dimensional dynamical systems. *TCS*, 132(1):113–128, 1994. 194, 198
26. P. Koiran and C. Moore. Closed-form analytic maps in one and two dimensions can simulate universal Turing machines. *TCS*, 210:217–223, 1999. 194
27. O. Maler and A. Pnueli. Reachability analysis of planar multi-linear systems. In *CAV'93*, LNCS 697, p. 194–209. Springer-Verlag, 1993. 193, 196, 198, 206
28. M. L. Minsky. *Computation: Finite and Infinite Machines*. Prentice-Hall, 1967. 203

29. C. Moore. Unpredictability and undecidability in dynamical systems. *Physical Review Letters*, 64(20), 1990.

30. X. Nicollin, A. Olivero, J. Sifakis, and S. Yovine. An approach to the description and analysis of hybrid systems. In *Hybrid Systems*, LNCS 736, p. 149–178, 1993. 193

31. C. H. Papadimitriou. *Computational complexity*. Addison-Wesley, 1994.

32. A. Puri and P. Varaiya. Decidability of hybrid systems with rectangular differential inclusions. In *CAV'94*, LNCS 818, p. 95–104. Springer, 1994. 193, 196

33. G. Schneider. *Algorithmic Analysis of Polygonal Hybrid Systems*. PhD thesis, VERIMAG – UJF, Grenoble, 2002. 194, 200

34. K. S. Sibirsky. *Introduction to Topological Dynamics*. Noordhoff International Publishing, Leyden, 1975.

35. S. Simić, K. Johansson, S. Sastry, and J. Lygeros. Towards a geometric theory of hybrid systems. In *HSCC'00*, LNCS 1790. Springer, 2000. 195

A Spatial Logic for Concurrency (Part II)

Luís Caires[1] and Luca Cardelli[2]

[1] Departamento de Informática FCT/UNL
Lisboa, Portugal
[2] Microsoft Research
Cambridge, UK

Abstract. We present a modal logic for describing the spatial organization and the behavior of distributed systems. In addition to standard logical and temporal operators, our logic includes spatial operations corresponding to process composition and name hiding, and a fresh quantifier.

1   Introduction

We develop a logic to describe properties of distributed concurrent systems, for specification and model-checking purposes; we believe that the peculiar characteristics of such systems justify the introduction of new logical constructs. Our first emphasis is on *distributed* systems, meaning that we should be able to talk about properties of distinct subsystems, such as subsystems that reside at different locations, and subsystems that privately share hidden resources. For this purpose, we introduce *spatial* (as opposed to temporal) logical operators; for example, we may talk about a property holding somewhere (as opposed to sometimes). Our second emphasis is on *concurrent* systems: we want a logic that unambiguously talks about concurrency and (nowadays) privacy. For this purpose, the intended model of our logic is built explicitly from a standard process calculus (an asynchronous π-calculus). Our formulas denote collections of processes subject to certain closure conditions, with some logical operators mapping directly to process composition and name hiding. In Part I of this paper [2,4] we study this intended model, which is used here to establish the soundness of the logical rules. The central focus of this Part II, however, is proof theory. We regularize and generalize the logics introduced in [1,7,8], and we prove a cut-elimination result for the first-order fragment, including cut-elimination for a fresh name quantifier (*cf.* Nominal Logic [13]).

A formula in our logic describes a property of a particular part of a concurrent system (a *world*) at a particular time; therefore it is modal in space as well as in time. In our sequents, formulas are indexed by the worlds they predicate over [17], so a sequent can talk about many distinct worlds at once. Each sequent incorporates also a finite set of constraints over the worlds, including process reduction and congruence constraints. In general, the constraint structure can be fashioned as an algebra [18]; which in our case is a relatively complex process algebra.

L. Brim et al. (Eds.): CONCUR 2002, LNCS 2421, pp. 209–225, 2002.

The fragment of our logic that deals with process composition is relatively straightforward: composition shows up in the logic as a tensor, which is strongly related to linear connectives. The sequent-style presentation of this fragment should look relatively familiar, except for the constraints part. The relevant constraints are essentially constraints over a (concurrency) monoid, with some specific interactions with reduction. Along these lines, we could also easily add an explicit structure of locations to the process calculus, and related logical operators, as done in [7].

Far less obvious is what to do about hiding of private resources, which is represented in π-calculus by the name hiding operator. The hiding of a name in a process should correspond, logically, to a "hiding quantifier" that binds a private name in a formula; such a formula could then describe the use of that private name in the process. The study of such a quantifier, from a logical point of view, was started in [5,1], and later independently in [8]. Our current understanding is that it is best to decompose such a hiding quantifier into two operators: a modal version of the fresh quantifier of Gabbay and Pitts [10], and a logical operator, called *revelation* [8], that relates to name hiding in strong analogy to the way tensor relates to process composition. A simple combination of fresh quantification and revelation then yields hiding, in the intuitive sense that if something is hidden, we can choose to name it (reveal it) by any name that is fresh.

Many natural examples of use of our logic involve recursive formulas. Two typical examples of recursion that attract us in our context are: (1) a process having an arbitrary number of hidden resources, and (2) a process generating an infinite supply of fresh names. Particularly, the interaction of recursion and freshness is semantically quite challenging, and was investigated in Part I. In this paper we go one step further and introduce second-order quantification in the logic, from which we can define least and greatest fixpoints of formulas, almost along standard lines [14].

Structurally, our logic consists of a collection of left-right rules for logical operators, including essentially the standard rules of classical sequent calculus, plus the ones for temporal and spatial operators. In addition, there are special rules about the worlds: they add meaning to the logical operators, allowing us to capture deep properties of process calculi without interfering very much with the core left-right rules.

We highlight here the left and right rules for composition, $A|B$, which include many of the interesting features of our sequents. Sequents have the form $\langle S \rangle\, \Gamma \vdash \Delta$, where $\langle S \rangle$ is a finite set of constraints, and Γ , Δ are multisets of indexed formulas.

$$\frac{[\mathcal{X} \text{ and } \mathcal{Y} \text{ not free in the conclusion}]}{\langle S, u \doteq \mathcal{X}|\mathcal{Y} \rangle\, \Gamma, \mathcal{X} : A, \mathcal{Y} : B \vdash \Delta}{\langle S \rangle\, \Gamma, u : A|B \vdash \Delta} \quad (|\text{L})$$

$$\frac{\langle S \rangle\, \Gamma \vdash v : A, \Delta \quad \langle S \rangle\, \Gamma \vdash t : B, \Delta \quad u \doteq_S v|t}{\langle S \rangle\, \Gamma \vdash u : A|B, \Delta} \quad (|\text{R})$$

The $(|\text{R})$ rule says: if we can show that index v satisfies formula A (i.e, that A holds at world v, written $v : A$), and that t satisfies B, and if we can show from the constraints in S that $u \doteq v|t$, then we can conclude that u satisfies $A|B$. Hence, the reading of this logical rules incorporates much of the intended satisfaction semantics [17]. The $(|L)$ rule features the assumption "X and Y not free in the conclusion (of the rule)". This assumption means, in particular, that X and Y are completely generic and unconstrained variables. A reading is: to show that $u : A|B$ entails Δ, we must show that for an arbitrary decomposition of u as $X|Y$, we have that $X : A$ and $Y : B$ entail Δ.

Composition also has a number of "rules about the world", as mentioned above. Here is a simple one:

$$\frac{\langle S, u \doteq \mathbf{0} \rangle\, \Gamma \vdash \Delta \quad u|v \doteq_S \mathbf{0}}{\langle S \rangle\, \Gamma \vdash \Delta} \ (\mathrm{S}|\mathbf{0})$$

Note that these world rules do not involve the logical connectives (we have $\Gamma \vdash \Delta$ above and below), and instead affect the $\langle S \rangle$ part. In most process calculi we have that if $u|v \equiv 0$ then both $u \equiv 0$ and $v \equiv 0$. This property does not derive from $(|L)$ and $(|R)$, but is embedded in $(\mathrm{S}|\mathbf{0})$. The rule reads as follows: if we can already infer from the S part of the constraints that $u|v \doteq_S \mathbf{0}$, and we have an additional constraint that $u \doteq \mathbf{0}$, that constraint is redundant and we can remove it. In this style, we can incorporate many peculiar properties of process calculi as world rules; many such rules analyze the consequences of an equation between two spatial operators (above, | vs. $\mathbf{0}$), and are listed in Figure 8. All such rules have a similar reading in terms of eliminating "redundant" constraints.

Because of the regular left-right structure of our core rules, cut elimination falls largely along predictable lines; the indexes do not hinder, and rules such as $(\mathrm{S}|\mathbf{0})$ can be dealt with separately. The main difficulty is in the cut elimination case for the freshness quantifier. As in Nominal Logic, the result depends on an "equivariance" property of the logic [13], which is used to perform an α-conversion of fresh names over a whole derivation. Equivariance is embedded, in our case, in the (τ) rule in Figure 7, whose soundness depends on the main theorem of Part I. Expressing this rule in the general case of open formulas, requires introducing explicit transpositions over formulas, which entail some technical complications.

Related Work A logic for a process calculus including a tensor operator and a hiding quantifier was developed by Luís Caires in [5,1], but a satisfactory semantic treatment for the latter connective not was achieved before the contributions of [8,2]. Andy Gordon was a coauthor with Luca Cardelli of initial versions of spatial logics for the Ambient Calculus [7,8], which also investigated connections with linear logic. The present paper contains the first presentation of such a logic as a proper sequent calculus. Moreover, we now target the logic towards a more standard π-calculus.

The first main difference between our logic and standard logics of concurrency (e.g. [11]) is the presence in our case of a tensor operator that corresponds to process composition. Usually, those other logics require formulas to denote processes up to bisimulation, which is difficult to reconcile with a tensor operator that can make distinctions between bisimilar processes (however, such an operator was anticipated by Dam [9]). In our case, we only require formulas to denote processes up to structural equivalence, so that a tensor operator makes easy sense. Sangiorgi has shown, for a closely related logic, that the equivalence induced by the logic is then essentially structural equivalence [16].

The work of Gabbay and Pitts on the freshness quantifier [10] has become central to our logic. The work of O'Hearn and Pym on Bunched Logics [12] and of Reynolds on Separation Logic [15] is closely related to ours, at least in intent. The style in which the logic is formalized is an extension of work by Alex Simpson [17], and is also related, at least superficially, to labeled deductive systems [18]. A decidable and complete propositional fragments of a related logic has been recently investigated [6].

In Section 2 we introduce the algebra of constraints. In Section 3 we introduce our sequent calculus, which can be shown sound by an interpretation in the model of Part I. In Section 4 we investigate proof theory, and in particular cut elimination for the first-order fragment of our logic. In Section 5 we go through a set of basic examples, to illustrate the expressive power of the logic.

2　Preliminaries

In this Section we introduce π-algebras, and constraint theories over the term π-algebra. A π-algebra is a two sorted algebra, with a sort for names and a sort for processes, and equipped with the basic process operations of composition, name hiding and name transposition. Hence, many process calculi are π-algebras, in particular the asynchronous π-calculus Aπ which is the intended model of our logic. We summarize the main concepts needed for our current purposes, a more detailed presentation can be found in [3].

Definition 2.1 (π-Algebra). *A π-algebra is a structure $\langle \mathcal{L}, \mathcal{P}, \mathbf{0}, |, \nu, (\leftrightarrow)_{\mathcal{L}},$ $(\leftrightarrow)_{\mathcal{P}} \rangle$ such that $\mathcal{L}$ is a countable set of labels (ℓ), $\mathcal{P}$ is a set of processes (P, Q, R), $\mathbf{0}$ (void) is a distinguished process in $\mathcal{P}$, $-|-$ (composition) is an operation $\mathcal{P} \times \mathcal{P} \to \mathcal{P}$, $(\nu-)-$ (name hiding, a.k.a. restriction) is an operation $\mathcal{L} \times \mathcal{P} \to \mathcal{P}$, $(-\leftrightarrow-)_{\mathcal{L}}-$ (transposition on labels) is an operation $\mathcal{L} \times \mathcal{L} \times \mathcal{L} \to \mathcal{P}$ and $(-\leftrightarrow-)_{\mathcal{P}}-$ (transposition on processes) is an operation $\mathcal{L} \times \mathcal{L} \times \mathcal{P} \to \mathcal{L}$. We refer to the $\mathcal{L}$ part of a π-algebra Π by $\Pi_{\mathcal{L}}$, and likewise for the remaining components (e.g., $\Pi_{\mathcal{P}}$).*

Of special interest is the term π-algebra **P**, whose terms of sort process (called *indexes*) will be used to label formulas in sequents and denote the worlds of our modal logic, while terms of sort name (called *name terms*) denote the pure names used in processes. Given a set $\mathcal{V}$ of names variables and a set χ of process variables, the term π-algebra **P** is the free π-algebra over a set of variables $x \in \mathcal{V}$ for the sort of *name terms* $\mathcal{N}$, and over a set of variables $X \in \chi$ for the sort of *indexes* $\mathcal{I}$. We use the meta-variables $m, n, p \in \mathcal{N}$; $u, v, t \in \mathcal{I}$; $X, \mathcal{Y}, \mathcal{Z} \in \chi$; $x, y, z \in \mathcal{V}$; $\gamma \in \mathcal{G} = \mathcal{I} \cup \mathcal{N}$. Given an index or name term γ, we denote by $afv(\gamma)$ its set of algebraic free (name and process) variables, defined simply as the collection of all the variables in $\mathcal{V}$ and χ occurring in such terms.

Processes relate to each other both by spatial and temporal constraints: in the term π-algebra such constraints are represented by *spatial constraints*, expressing that the processes denoted by the equated indexes have the same spatial structure (*cf.* π-calculus structural congruence), and *temporal constraints*, expressing that the processes denoted by the given indexes are related by a reduction (*cf.* π-calculus reduction).

Definition 2.2 (Constraint). *A constraint c is either an index equation, a reduction, a name apartness, or a set apartness, defined by*

$$
\begin{array}{ll}
c ::= & \text{Constraints} \\
& u \doteq v \;\text{Index equation }\; (u,v \in \mathcal{I}) \quad u \to v \;\text{Reduction}\quad (u,v \in \mathcal{I}) \\
& m \,\#\, n \;\text{Name apartness }\; (m,n \in \mathcal{N}) \quad m \,\#\, X \;\text{Set apartness }\; (m \in \mathcal{N}, X \in \mathcal{X})
\end{array}
$$

In order to handle freshness explicitly, we also introduce *apartness constraints*: $m \,\#\, n$ meaning that the name terms m and n denote distinct names, and $m \,\#\, X$ meaning that the name term m denotes a name distinct from any name in the (finite) support [2] of the property denoted by the propositional variable X (see Section 3.1).

A *constraint theory* is a finite set of constraints, presenting a particular world structure. Such a structure enjoys a number of structural properties, axiomatized by the set of closure rules in Fig. 1. For instance, (Spatial) characterizes properties of structural congruence (*e.g.*, monoidal laws for composition and name extrusion). We write $S \vdash c$ to say that the constraint c holds in the closure of S, writing $\gamma \doteq_S \gamma'$ for $S \vdash \gamma \doteq \gamma'$, and likewise for the relations $\#_S$ and $\to_S$.

3 Sequent Calculus

3.1 Formulas and Sequents

Formulas, defined in Fig. 2, include classical propositional connectives, $\mathbf{F}$, $\wedge$, $\Rightarrow$, and the basic spatial operators: $A|B$ (the tensor, representing the parallel composition of processes), $\mathbf{0}$ (the unit of the tensor, representing the collection of void processes), and $A \triangleright B$ (the linear implication associated with the tensor). This last operator corresponds to context-system specification of processes, which are the concurrency-theory equivalent of pre/post conditions. Name hiding induces a pair of adjunct logical operators. The formula $n \circledR A$ means that a hidden name, which we choose to call n, exists in a restricted scope that satisfies property A. It is matched by a π-calculus term $(\nu n)u$ provided that u satisfies A (see rule ($\circledR$R) in Fig. 4, and the example in Section 5; see [8,2] for further details.) The formula $A \oslash n$ is the logical adjunct of $n \circledR A$. The notion of *fresh name* is introduced by a quantifier $\mathsf{V}x.A$; this means that x denotes a name that is fresh with respect to the names used either in A or in processes satisfying A. $\mathsf{V}x.A$ is defined along the lines of the freshness quantifier of Gabbay-Pitts [10,13], and its semantics is designed to be compatible with recursive formulas. A logical operator $n\langle m \rangle$ allows us to assert that a message m is present over channel n,

(Basic)

$u \doteq v \in S \Rightarrow u \doteq_S v$

$m \# n \in S \Rightarrow m \#_S n$

$u \to v \in S \Rightarrow u \to_S v$

(Spatial)

$u|0 \doteq_S u$

$u|v \doteq_S v|u$

$(u|v)|t \doteq_S u|(v|t)$

$(\nu n)0 \doteq_S 0$

$(\nu n)(\nu n)u \doteq_S (\nu n)u$

$(\nu m)(\nu n)u \doteq_S (\nu n)(\nu m)u$

$(\nu n)(u|(\nu n)v) \doteq_S ((\nu n)u)|(\nu n)v$

(Congruence)

$\gamma \doteq_S \gamma$

$\gamma \doteq_S \gamma' \Rightarrow \gamma' \doteq_S \gamma$

$\gamma \doteq_S \gamma', \gamma' \doteq_S \gamma'' \Rightarrow \gamma \doteq_S \gamma''$

$u \doteq_S v \Rightarrow u|t \doteq_S v|t$

$u \doteq_S v, m \doteq_S n \Rightarrow (\nu m)u \doteq_S (\nu n)v$

$m \doteq_S n, \gamma \doteq_S \gamma' \Rightarrow (m \leftrightarrow r)\gamma \doteq_S (r \leftrightarrow n)\gamma'$

(Apartness)

$m \#_S p, n \#_S p \Rightarrow (m \leftrightarrow n)p \doteq_S p$

$m \#_S n \Rightarrow n \#_S m$

$p \#_S q, p \doteq_S p', q \doteq_S q' \Rightarrow p' \#_S q'$

$p \#_S X, p \doteq_S q \Rightarrow q \#_S X$

(Transposition)

$\tau 0 \doteq_S 0$

$\tau(u|v) \doteq_S \tau u | \tau v$

$\tau(\nu p)u \doteq_S (\nu \tau p)\tau u$

$\tau(p \leftrightarrow q)\gamma \doteq_S (\tau p \leftrightarrow \tau q)\tau \gamma$

$\tau \tau \gamma \doteq_S \gamma$

$(n \leftrightarrow n)\gamma \doteq_S \gamma$

$(m \leftrightarrow n)m \doteq_S n$

$u \doteq_S (\nu n)t, u \doteq_S (\nu m)v \Rightarrow$
$\qquad (n \leftrightarrow m)u \doteq_S u$

(Reduction)

$u \to_S t, v \doteq_S u, t \doteq_S w \Rightarrow v \to_S w$

$u \to_S t \Rightarrow u|v \to_S t|v$

$u \to_S t \Rightarrow (\nu n)u \to_S (\nu n)t$

$u \to_S t \Rightarrow \tau u \to_S \tau t$

Fig. 1. Closure of constraint theories

giving us some minimal power to observe the behavior of processes. A next-step temporal operator, $\Diamond A$, allows us to talk about the behavior of a process after a single (unspecified) reduction step. Finally, we have a second-order quantifier and related propositional variables.

Formulas are the same as in Part I [4], except that we now allow formulas to contain general name terms (including explicit transpositions), and not only variables and pure names. Therefore, we will refer to the formulas as defined in [2] by *simple* formulas.

In $\forall x.A$, $\mathsf{N} x.A$ (and $\forall X.A$), the variables x (and X) are bound with scope the formula A. We assume defined on formulas the standard relation $\equiv_\alpha$ of α-conversion (safe renaming of bound variables), but will never implicitly take formulas "up to α-conversion": our manipulation of variables via α-conversion steps will always be quite explicit. We also assume defined as usual the set $fv(A)$ of *free name variables* in A, and the set $fpv(A)$ of *free propositional variables* in A. Then, we define the set of *logically free variables* of a formula A by $lfv(A) \triangleq fv(A) \cup fpv(A)$. If m is a name term and A is a formula then $A\{x \leftarrow m\}$ denotes the formula obtained by replacing all free occurrences of x in A by the name term m, (nondeterministically) renaming bound variables as needed to avoid capture of names in m.

$m, n, p ::=$	Name Terms	$(m, n, p \in \mathcal{N})$
x	Name variable	$(x \in \mathcal{V})$
$(m \leftrightarrow n)p$	Transposition term	

A, B	::=	Formulas			
	$\mathbf{F}$	False	$m \oslash A$	Hiding
	$A \wedge B$	Conjunction	$m \langle n \rangle$	Message
	$A \Rightarrow B$	Implication	$\Diamond A$	Next
	$\mathbf{0}$	Void	$\forall x.A$	Name quantification
	$A \vert B$	Composition	$\mathsf{N}x.A$	Freshness quantification
	$A \triangleright B$	Guarantee	X	Propositional variable
	$m \circledR A$	Revelation	$\forall X.A$	Property quantification

Formulas are subject to: no occurrence of a variable x in a transposition term is under the scope of a $\forall x.$ or a $\mathsf{N}x.$

Fig. 2. Formulas

Any substitution $I_{\mathcal{L}} : \mathcal{V} \to \Lambda$ of pure names for name variables acts on a formula A (respectively, on a name term p) yielding a simple formula $I_{\mathcal{L}}(A)$ (respectively a pure name), defined as expected. The following definition lifts the equational theory of name terms to the level of formulas: $A \equiv_S B$ asserts that, under any substitution that satisfies all constraints in S, A and B denote the same simple formula.

Definition 3.1 (Equational Equivalence of Formulas). *Given a constraint theory S, $\equiv_S$ is the least equivalence relation on formulas such that $A\{x \leftarrow m\} \equiv_S A\{x \leftarrow n\}$ for all name terms m, n such that $m \doteq_S n$.*

The semantics of the freshness quantifier requires names to be chosen fresh with respect to the free names of both processes and formulas. By the formation condition at the bottom of Fig. 2, transposition terms in formulas *never contain bound occurrences of name variables*. Hence, a maximal term in a formula is either a bound name variable, or a term completely built out of free name variables: explicit transpositions in formulas just swap *free names*. Thus, it is sensible to define the set $ft(A)$ of *free terms* of a formula A to be the set of maximal name terms occurring in A which are not a bound occurrence of a variable. Given a constraint theory S and a formula A, we write $n \#_S A$ as an abbreviation of $n \#_S ft(A)$: $n \#_S A$ asserts that, under the constraints in S, n denotes a name *distinct* from all names denoted by the (free) terms in formula A. We can verify that the relations $\equiv_S$ (between formulas) and $\#_S$ (between name terms and formulas) defined are sound with respect to their intended interpretation.

A context (Γ, Δ) is a finite multiset of indexed formulas of the form $u : A$ where u is an index and A is a formula.

Definition 3.2 (Sequent). *A sequent is a judgment $\langle S \rangle \Gamma \vdash \Delta$ where S is a constraint theory, and Δ and Γ are logical contexts.*

The *right context* Δ is interpreted as the disjunction of its formulas, the *left context* Γ is interpreted as the conjunction of the formulas in it. Defining contexts as multisets allows for the implicit use of exchange in proofs.

Definition 3.3 (Variables in Sequents). *The set of free (name, process, and propositional) variables of a context Δ is given by $lfv(\Delta) = \bigcup\{afv(u) \cup lfv(A) \mid u : A \in \Delta\}$. The set of free (name, process, and propositional) variables in a sequent $\langle S \rangle \, \Gamma \vdash \Delta$ is given by $afv(S) \cup fv(\Gamma) \cup fv(\Delta)$.*

N.B.: name variables x occur both in indexes u and in formulas A; process variables X occur only in indexes; propositional variables X occur only in formulas.

We now define the semantics of sequents, namely validity. To that end we need to interpret both constraints and formulas: this will be achieved by logical interpretations.

Definition 3.4 (Logical Interpretation). *A logical interpretation $\mathcal{J}$ is pair (v, I) where $I_{\mathcal{P}}$ is a map of process variables into $A\pi$ processes, $I_{\mathcal{L}}$ is a map name of variables into $A\pi$ names , and v is a map of propositional variables into property sets.*

Hence, I is an homomorphism I of $\mathbf{P}$ into $A\pi$, and v is a valuation as defined in Part I.

Definition 3.5 (Satisfaction and Validity). *The relation of satisfaction between logical interpretations $\mathcal{J} = (v, I)$ into $A\pi$ and constraints is defined thus:*

$\mathcal{J}$ *satisfies* $u \doteq v \Leftrightarrow I_{\mathcal{P}}(u) \equiv I_{\mathcal{P}}(v)$ $\mathcal{J}$ *satisfies* $u \to v \Leftrightarrow I_{\mathcal{L}}(u) \to I_{\mathcal{L}}(v)$
$\mathcal{J}$ *satisfies* $n \, \# \, m \Leftrightarrow I_{\mathcal{L}}(n) \neq I_{\mathcal{L}}(m)$ $\mathcal{J}$ *satisfies* $n \, \# \, X \Leftrightarrow I_{\mathcal{L}}(n) \notin supp(v(X))$

$\mathcal{J}$ satisfies *the constraint theory S if $\mathcal{J}$ satisfies all constraints in S. A constraint $S \vdash c$ is valid if every interpretation that satisfies S also satisfies c.*

Semantics of formulas is defined in Part I by a mapping $[\![-]\!]_v$ that assigns a property set $[\![A]\!]_v$ to any simple formula A, given a valuation v.

Definition 3.6 (Valid Sequent in $A\pi$). *A sequent $\langle S \rangle \, \Gamma \vdash \Delta$ is valid in $A\pi$ if for all logical interpretations $\mathcal{J} = (v, I)$ such that $\mathcal{J}$ satisfies all constraints in S and $I(u) \in [\![I_{\mathcal{L}}(A)]\!]_v$ for all $u : A \in \Gamma$, then $I(v) \in [\![I_{\mathcal{L}}(A)]\!]_v$ for some $v : A \in \Delta$.*

3.2   Inference Rules

Inference rules may have for premises both sequents $\langle S \rangle \, \Gamma \vdash \Delta$ and assertions over the closure of the theory S of the form $u \doteq_S v$ (mostly in the rules for spatial connectives), $A \equiv_S B$ (in the identity axiom), $u \to_S v$ (in the temporal rules) or $n \, \#_S \, A$ (in the freshness rules).

The rules in the identity, structural and propositional groups (see Fig. 3) follow the standard. Note that in (Id) indexes are identified up to $\doteq_S$, while formulas are identified up to $\equiv_S$: (Id) absorbs the simple theory of equality

$$\frac{u \doteq_S u' \quad A \equiv_S A'}{\langle S \rangle\, \Gamma, u : A \vdash u' : A', \Delta}\;\text{(Id)} \qquad \frac{\langle S \rangle\, \Gamma \vdash u : A, \Delta \quad \langle S \rangle\, \Gamma, u : A \vdash \Delta}{\langle S \rangle\, \Gamma \vdash \Delta}\;\text{(Cut)}$$

$$\frac{\langle S \rangle\, \Gamma, u : A, u : A \vdash \Delta}{\langle S \rangle\, \Gamma, u : A \vdash \Delta}\;\text{(CL)} \qquad \frac{\langle S \rangle\, \Gamma \vdash u : A, u : A, \Delta}{\langle S \rangle\, \Gamma \vdash u : A, \Delta}\;\text{(CR)}$$

$$\frac{}{\langle S \rangle\, \Gamma, u : \mathbf{F} \vdash \Delta}\;\text{(FL)} \qquad \frac{\langle S \rangle\, \Gamma \vdash \Delta}{\langle S \rangle\, \Gamma \vdash u : \mathbf{F}, \Delta}\;\text{(FR)}$$

$$\frac{\langle S \rangle\, \Gamma, u : A, u : B \vdash \Delta}{\langle S \rangle\, \Gamma, u : A \wedge B \vdash \Delta}\;\text{(}\wedge\text{L)} \qquad \frac{\langle S \rangle\, \Gamma \vdash u : A, \Delta \quad \langle S \rangle\, \Gamma \vdash u : B, \Delta}{\langle S \rangle\, \Gamma \vdash u : A \wedge B, \Delta}\;\text{(}\wedge\text{R)}$$

$$\frac{\langle S \rangle\, \Gamma \vdash u : A, \Delta \quad \langle S \rangle\, \Gamma, u : B \vdash \Delta}{\langle S \rangle\, \Gamma, u : A \Rightarrow B \vdash \Delta}\;\text{(}\Rightarrow\text{L)} \qquad \frac{\langle S \rangle\, \Gamma, u : A \vdash u : B, \Delta}{\langle S \rangle\, \Gamma \vdash u : A \Rightarrow B, \Delta}\;\text{(}\Rightarrow\text{R)}$$

Fig. 3. Propositional rules

$$\frac{\langle S, t \doteq \mathbf{0} \rangle\, \Gamma \vdash \Delta}{\langle S \rangle\, \Gamma, t : \mathbf{0} \vdash \Delta}\;\text{(0L)} \qquad \frac{u \doteq_S \mathbf{0}}{\langle S \rangle\, \Gamma \vdash u : \mathbf{0}, \Delta}\;\text{(0R)}$$

$$\frac{[X \text{ and } Y \text{ not free in the conclusion}]}{\dfrac{\langle S, u \doteq X | Y \rangle\, \Gamma, X : A, Y : B \vdash \Delta}{\langle S \rangle\, \Gamma, u : A | B \vdash \Delta}}\;\text{(|L)} \qquad \frac{\langle S \rangle\, \Gamma \vdash v : A, \Delta \quad \langle S \rangle\, \Gamma \vdash t : B, \Delta \quad u \doteq_S v | t}{\langle S \rangle\, \Gamma \vdash u : A | B, \Delta}\;\text{(|R)}$$

$$\frac{\langle S \rangle\, \Gamma \vdash t : A, \Delta \quad \langle S \rangle\, \Gamma, t | u : B \vdash \Delta}{\langle S \rangle\, \Gamma, u : A \triangleright B \vdash \Delta}\;\text{(}\triangleright\text{L)} \qquad \frac{[X \text{ not free in the conclusion}]}{\dfrac{\langle S \rangle\, \Gamma, X : A \vdash v : B, \Delta \quad v \doteq_S X | u}{\langle S \rangle\, \Gamma \vdash u : A \triangleright B, \Delta}}\;\text{(}\triangleright\text{R)}$$

$$\frac{[X \text{ not free in the conclusion}]}{\dfrac{\langle S, u \doteq (\nu n) X \rangle\, \Gamma, X : A \vdash \Delta}{\langle S \rangle\, \Gamma, u : n\textcircled{R}A \vdash \Delta}}\;\text{(}\textcircled{R}\text{L)} \qquad \frac{\langle S \rangle\, \Gamma \vdash u : A, \Delta \quad t \doteq_S (\nu n) u}{\langle S \rangle\, \Gamma \vdash t : n\textcircled{R}A, \Delta}\;\text{(}\textcircled{R}\text{R)}$$

$$\frac{\langle S \rangle\, \Gamma, t : A \vdash \Delta \quad t \doteq_S (\nu n) u}{\langle S \rangle\, \Gamma, u : A \oslash n \vdash \Delta}\;\text{(}\oslash\text{L)} \qquad \frac{\langle S \rangle\, \Gamma \vdash u : A, \Delta \quad u \doteq_S (\nu n) t}{\langle S \rangle\, \Gamma \vdash t : A \oslash n, \Delta}\;\text{(}\oslash\text{R)}$$

Fig. 4. Spatial rules

$$\frac{[X \text{ not free in the conclusion}]}{\dfrac{\langle S, u \to X \rangle\, \Gamma, X : A \vdash \Delta}{\langle S \rangle\, \Gamma, u : \Diamond A \vdash \Delta}}\;\text{(}\Diamond\text{L)} \qquad \frac{\langle S \rangle\, \Gamma \vdash v : A, \Delta \quad u \to_S v}{\langle S \rangle\, \Gamma \vdash u : \Diamond A, \Delta}\;\text{(}\Diamond\text{R)}$$

Fig. 5. Temporal rules

captured by $\equiv_S$, thus axiomatizing the principle of substitution of equals for equals of name terms in formulas. We include explicit contraction rules (CL) and (CR); weakening is admissible, and exchange may be dealt with implicitly, since sequent contexts are multisets. In the rules for propositional connectives, indexes keep track of the processes for which the formulas are asserted to hold, but do not interfere in any way with the constraint part of sequents.

The rules for the spatial connectives (Fig. 4) make essential use of the constraint theories in sequents. Note that the left rules, when read bottom-up, introduce spatial constraints into the constraint theories, and the respective right rules, when read top-down, check corresponding constraints. While spatial rules rely on spatial constraints, temporal rules (Fig. 5) rely on reduction constraints.

The rules for first and second order quantifiers have the expected form (Fig. 6). We then introduce the rules for freshness (Fig. 7). Rule ($И$) asserts, when read bottom-up, that there is always a name (denoted by) x that is fresh with respect to the free names of (the process denoted by) the index u, and that is also fresh with respect to a set of names (denoted by the name and propositional variables in) N. Hence, rule ($И$) corresponds to the (Fresh) axiom of Pitts' Nominal Logic [13]. The transposition rule (τ) captures the property of invariance of the semantics under transposition of names (see the main theorem of Part I). Moreover, as we shall discuss below, explicit transpositions and the transposition rule play an crucial role in obtaining cut-elimination for the freshness quantifier. By $\{m \leftrightarrow n\} \cdot A$ we denote the formula obtained by swapping occurrences of m and n in A, possibly by introducing explicit transpositions: if $A[n_1, \ldots, n_k]$ is a formula with free terms $n_1, \ldots, n_k$, then $\tau \cdot A[n_1, \ldots, n_k]$ is the formula $A[\tau \cdot n_1, \ldots, \tau \cdot n_k]$.

The rules ($ИL/R$) for the fresh quantifier do not show the symmetry one might expect of a left / right rule pair. This fact relates to the existential / universal ambivalence of freshness quantification (the Gabbay-Pitts property): note that ($ИL$) follows the pattern of ($\forall L$), while ($ИR$) follows the pattern of ($\exists R$). Then, ($И$) embodies the introduction of fresh witnesses usually present in *both* ($\forall R$) and ($\exists L$). Besides the freshness condition $n \#_S Иx.A$ of the name denoted by n with respect to the free names in the formula $Иx.A$, the assumption $u \doteq_S (\nu n)v$ ensures that n denotes a name that does not occur free in the process denoted by u, cf. the semantics of $Иx.A$.

As discussed in Section 1, world rules (Fig. 8) axiomatize certain deep (extralogical) properties of the worlds (inversion principles for structural congruence and process reduction). We assert $\vdash \langle S \rangle \Gamma \vdash \Delta$ to state that the sequent $\langle S \rangle \Gamma \vdash \Delta$ has a derivation. We can show that all rules are sound with respect to the $A\pi$ model of Part I:

Theorem 3.7 (Soundness). *All derivable sequents are valid in* $A\pi$.

4 Basic Proof Theory

In this Section we develop some proof-theory for our logic, stating several admissible proof principles and a cut elimination result for the first-order fragment.

$$\frac{\langle S \rangle\, \Gamma, u : A\{x\leftarrow n\} \vdash \Delta}{\langle S \rangle\, \Gamma, u : \forall x.A \vdash \Delta}\ (\forall\mathrm{L}) \qquad \frac{[\ y\ not\ free\ in\ the\ conclusion]}{\dfrac{\langle S \rangle\, \Gamma \vdash u : A\{x\leftarrow y\}, \Delta}{\langle S \rangle\, \Gamma \vdash u : \forall x.A, \Delta}}\ (\forall\mathrm{R})$$

$$\frac{\langle S \rangle\, \Gamma, u : A\{X\leftarrow B\} \vdash \Delta}{\langle S \rangle\, \Gamma, u : \forall X.A \vdash \Delta}\ (\forall^2\mathrm{L}) \qquad \frac{[\ Y\ not\ free\ in\ the\ conclusion]}{\dfrac{\langle S \rangle\, \Gamma \vdash u : A\{X\leftarrow Y\}, \Delta}{\langle S \rangle\, \Gamma \vdash u : \forall X.A, \Delta}}\ (\forall^2\mathrm{R})$$

(In (∀L) and (∀R), the formula $\forall x.A$ must verify the condition in Fig. 2)

Fig. 6. Quantifier rules

$$\frac{[X, x\ not\ free\ in\ the\ conclusion,\ u\ or\ N]}{\dfrac{\langle S, x \,\#\, N, u \doteq (\boldsymbol{\nu}x)X \rangle\, \Gamma \vdash \Delta}{\langle S \rangle\, \Gamma \vdash \Delta}}\ (\textit{И}) \qquad \frac{m, n \,\#_S\, fpv(A)}{\dfrac{\langle S \rangle\, \Gamma, (m\leftrightarrow n)u : \{m\leftrightarrow n\}\cdot A \vdash \Delta}{\langle S \rangle\, \Gamma, u : A \vdash \Delta}}\ (\tau)$$

$$\frac{\begin{array}{c} u \doteq_S (\boldsymbol{\nu}n)v \\ n \,\#_S\, \textit{И}x.A \\ \langle S \rangle\, \Gamma, u : A\{x\leftarrow n\} \vdash \Delta \end{array}}{\langle S \rangle\, \Gamma, u : \textit{И}x.A \vdash \Delta}\ (\textit{И}\mathrm{L}) \qquad \frac{\begin{array}{c} u \doteq_S (\boldsymbol{\nu}n)v \\ n \,\#_S\, \textit{И}x.A \\ \langle S \rangle\, \Gamma \vdash u : A\{x\leftarrow n\}, \Delta \end{array}}{\langle S \rangle\, \Gamma \vdash u : \textit{И}x.A, \Delta}\ (\textit{И}\mathrm{R})$$

(In (ИL) and (ИR), the formula $\textit{И}x.A$ must verify the condition in Fig. 2)

Fig. 7. Freshness rules

$$\frac{\langle S, u \doteq \mathbf{0} \rangle\, \Gamma \vdash \Delta \quad u|v \doteq_S \mathbf{0}}{\langle S \rangle\, \Gamma \vdash \Delta}\ (\mathrm{S}|\mathbf{0}) \qquad \frac{\langle S, u \doteq \mathbf{0} \rangle\, \Gamma \vdash \Delta \quad (\boldsymbol{\nu}n)u \doteq_S \mathbf{0}}{\langle S \rangle\, \Gamma \vdash \Delta}\ (\mathrm{S}\boldsymbol{\nu}\mathbf{0})$$

$$\frac{[X\ and\ Y\ not\ free\ in\ the\ conclusion]}{\dfrac{\langle S, u \doteq X|Y, (\boldsymbol{\nu}n)X \doteq t, (\boldsymbol{\nu}n)Y \doteq v \rangle\, \Gamma \vdash \Delta \quad (\boldsymbol{\nu}n)u \doteq_S t|v}{\langle S \rangle\, \Gamma \vdash \Delta}}\ (\mathrm{S}\boldsymbol{\nu}|)$$

$$\frac{[X, X', Y\ and\ Y'\ not\ free\ in\ the\ conclusion]}{\dfrac{\langle S, u \doteq X|X', w \doteq Y|Y', t \doteq X|Y, v \doteq X'|Y' \rangle\, \Gamma \vdash \Delta \quad u|w \doteq_S t|v}{\langle S \rangle\, \Gamma \vdash \Delta}}\ (\mathrm{S}||)$$

$$\frac{[X\ not\ free\ in\ the\ conclusion]}{\dfrac{\langle S, u \doteq (m\leftrightarrow n)v \rangle\, \Gamma \vdash \Delta}{\langle S \rangle\, \Gamma \vdash \Delta}}\ ?$$

$$\frac{[X\ not\ free\ in\ the\ conclusion]}{\dfrac{\langle S, u \doteq (\boldsymbol{\nu}m)X, v \doteq (\boldsymbol{\nu}n)X \rangle\, \Gamma \vdash \Delta \quad (\boldsymbol{\nu}n)u \doteq_S (\boldsymbol{\nu}m)v}{\langle S \rangle\, \Gamma \vdash \Delta}}\ (\mathrm{S}\boldsymbol{\nu}\boldsymbol{\nu})$$

$$\frac{\mathbf{0} \to_S u}{\langle S \rangle\, \Gamma \vdash \Delta}\ (\mathrm{S0}\to) \qquad \frac{[X\ not\ free\ in\ the\ conclusion]}{\dfrac{\langle S, u \to X, v \doteq (\boldsymbol{\nu}n)X \rangle\, \Gamma \vdash \Delta \quad (\boldsymbol{\nu}n)u \to_S v}{\langle S \rangle\, \Gamma \vdash \Delta}}\ (\mathrm{S}\boldsymbol{\nu}\to)$$

Fig. 8. World rules

Most of the presented proof principles are size-preserving, and instrumental to the proof of cut elimination. We introduce a measure for the *size* of a derivation, in which certain occurrences of the (τ) rule are not weighted. An occurrence of the inference rule (τ) in a derivation is *simple* if it applies either to an instance of (Id) or to another simple occurrence of (τ). We define the *size of a derivation* as the number of rule occurrences it contains, other than simple occurrences of rule (τ). We then assert $\vdash_n \langle S \rangle \Gamma \vdash \Delta$ to state that the given sequent has a derivation of size not exceeding n. We have the following useful admissible rules

Lemma 4.1 (Basic). *The following proof principles are admissible:*

$$
[\; \Gamma \equiv_\alpha \Gamma' \text{ and } \Delta \equiv_\alpha \Delta' \;] \qquad [\varphi, \varphi' \in \chi \text{ or } \varphi, \varphi' \in \mathcal{V}, \; \varphi' \text{ not free in the premise}]
$$

$$
\frac{\vdash_n \langle S \rangle \Gamma \vdash \Delta}{\vdash_n \langle S \rangle \Gamma' \vdash \Delta'} \; (\alpha) \qquad \frac{\vdash_n \langle S \rangle \Gamma \vdash \Delta}{\vdash_n \langle S\{\varphi \leftarrow \varphi'\} \rangle \Gamma\{\varphi \leftarrow \varphi'\} \vdash \Delta\{\varphi \leftarrow \varphi'\}} \; (\text{Ren})
$$

$$
\frac{\vdash_n \langle S \rangle \Gamma \vdash \Delta}{\vdash_n \langle S, S' \rangle \Gamma, \Gamma' \vdash \Delta, \Delta'} \; (\text{W}) \qquad \frac{\vdash_n \langle S \rangle \Gamma \vdash \Delta}{\vdash_n \langle S\{X \leftarrow u\} \rangle \Gamma\{X \leftarrow u\} \vdash \Delta\{X \leftarrow u\}} \; (\text{Inst}\mathcal{I})
$$

$$
\frac{\vdash_n \langle S, c \rangle \Gamma \vdash \Delta \quad S \vdash c}{\vdash_n \langle S \rangle \Gamma \vdash \Delta} \; (\text{CS}) \qquad \frac{\vdash_n \langle S \rangle \Gamma \vdash \Delta}{\vdash_n \langle S\{x \leftarrow m\} \rangle \Gamma\{x \leftarrow m\} \vdash \Delta\{x \leftarrow m\}} \; (\text{Inst}\mathcal{N})
$$

N.B. We write $\Delta \equiv_\alpha \Delta'$ if Δ' is obtained from Δ by α-converting some formulas in it.

Lemma 4.2 (Replacement and Instantiation). *The following rules are admissible*

$$
\frac{[\; X \text{ not free in } S \;]}{\langle S \rangle X : A \vdash X : B \quad \langle S \rangle X : B \vdash X : A} \qquad \frac{[\; X \text{ not free in the conclusion} \;]}{\langle S \rangle \Gamma \vdash \Delta}
$$

$$
\frac{}{\langle S \rangle \mathcal{Y} : C[A] \vdash \mathcal{Y} : C[B]} \qquad \frac{}{\langle S \rangle \Gamma\{X \leftarrow A\} \vdash \Delta\{X \leftarrow A\}}
$$

The first-order fragment of the spatial logic enjoys the cut elimination property, and therefore the subformula property. This result is a reasonable evidence that our addition of structural and freshness constraints to sequents and inference rules is rather canonical. For instance, cuts on spatial formulas are eliminated in a rather uniform way, by matching process eigenvariables (on one side) against the given witnesses (on the other), and then eliminating the remaining (redundant) structural constraints. The cut case for freshness quantifications is more interesting, since it relies on a proof transformation that can be interpreted as α-conversion in elements of the intended model (processes) *inside our logic* (to be distinguished from (α) in Lemma 4.1, which is about the syntax of the derivations). For this transformation to go through, explicit transpositions needed to be included both in the π-algebra and in the syntax of terms in formulas.

Theorem 4.3 (Cut Elimination). *If a sequent has a first-order derivation then it has a derivation without instances of the* (Cut) *rule.*

Full proofs of Theorem 4.3 and related results can be found in [3], where a set of derived connectives and respective proof rules is also presented.

5   Examples

We now go through a sequence of short examples to show how our logic is applicable to reasoning about distributed concurrent systems. We are necessarily brief here, and show only very elementary examples, but most interesting logical operators are covered.

A Simple Property We show a simple derivation of the fact that $(A|B) \land \mathbf{0}$ entails A, meaning that if a process satisfies $(A|B) \land \mathbf{0}$ then it satisfies A. The intuition is that if a process P satisfies both $(A|B)$ and $\mathbf{0}$, then P is (structurally equivalent to) the $\mathbf{0}$ process, which is the same as $\mathbf{0}|\mathbf{0}$; so $\mathbf{0}$ satisfies A (and B). We conclude that P satisfies A. This derivation illustrates: a property combining spatial and propositional operators; the use of constraint manipulation; and the use of one of the world rules, namely, $(S|\mathbf{0})$ corresponding to the "zero law" of Aπ processes: if $P|Q \equiv \mathbf{0}$ then $P \equiv \mathbf{0}$.

5. $\langle S, u \doteq x | \mathcal{Y}, u \doteq \mathbf{0}, X \doteq \mathbf{0} \rangle \, \Gamma, X : A, \mathcal{Y} : B \vdash u : A, \Delta$ (by (Id) since $u \doteq_S X$)

4. $\langle S, u \doteq x | \mathcal{Y}, u \doteq \mathbf{0} \rangle \, \Gamma, X : A, \mathcal{Y} : B \vdash u : A, \Delta$ (by 5, $(S|\mathbf{0})$ since $x | \mathcal{Y} \doteq_S \mathbf{0}$)

3. $\langle S, u \doteq x | \mathcal{Y} \rangle \, \Gamma, X : A, \mathcal{Y} : B, u : \mathbf{0} \vdash u : A, \Delta$ (by 4, (OL))

2. $\langle S \rangle \, \Gamma, u : (A|B), u : \mathbf{0} \vdash u : A, \Delta$ (by 3, (|L))

1. $\langle S \rangle \, \Gamma, u : (A|B) \land \mathbf{0} \vdash u : A, \Delta$ (by 2, ($\land$L))

Note that the proof is fairly simple, particularly if conducted bottom up. Most constraints are generated from the goal by using all the applicable left rules, and the final constraint $X \doteq \mathbf{0}$ is generated by closing up the constraint set under deduction, via $(S|\mathbf{0})$. Finally, (Id) involves a simple equivalence check in S. It is common for our derivations, when read bottom-up, to have this mechanical flavor.

Freshness We show a derivation of the fact that $\neg \mathsf{U}x.A$ entails $\mathsf{U}x.\neg A$. This (and its converse) is a well-known property of $\mathsf{U}x.A$ [10]; the purpose here is to show the use of the rules for freshness in a simple case. We abbreviate by $y \# \mathsf{U}x.A$ the set of constraints $y \# \mathit{lfv}(\mathsf{U}x.A)$.

6. $\langle S, y \# \mathsf{U}x.A, u \doteq (\nu y)X \rangle \, \Gamma, \text{á}u : A\{x \leftarrow y\} \vdash u : A\{x \leftarrow y\}, \text{á}\Delta$
   (by (Id) choose y, X fresh)

5. $\langle S, y \# \mathsf{U}x.A, u \doteq (\nu y)X \rangle \, \Gamma \vdash u : A\{x \leftarrow y\}, u : \neg A\{x \leftarrow y\}, \text{á}\Delta$ (by 6, ($\neg$ R))

4. $\langle S, y \# \mathsf{U}x.A, u \doteq (\nu y)X \rangle \, \Gamma \vdash u : \mathsf{U}x.A, u : \neg A\{x \leftarrow y\}, \text{á}\Delta$ (by 5, (UR))

3. $\langle S, y \# \mathsf{U}x.A, u \doteq (\nu y)X \rangle \, \Gamma \vdash u : \mathsf{U}x.A, u : \mathsf{U}x.\neg A, \text{á}\Delta$ (by 4, (UR))

2. $\langle S, y \# \mathsf{U}x.A, u \doteq (\nu y)X \rangle \, \Gamma, \text{á}u : \neg \mathsf{U}x.A \vdash u : \mathsf{U}x.\neg A, \text{á}\Delta$ (by 3, ($\neg$ L))

1. $\langle S \rangle \, \Gamma, \text{á}u : \neg \mathsf{U}x.A \vdash u : \mathsf{U}x.\neg A, \text{á}\Delta$ (by 2, (U) y, X not in conclusion)

We start with $A\{x \leftarrow y\}$ for a fresh y, instead of simply with A, so that we can apply (U) in the last step even when x occurs free in Γ, Δ. It is usually the case that an application of rules (U L) or (U R) is followed by an application of rule (U), to clean up the constraints. Note, however, that having (U) decoupled from (UL) and (UR) allow us to apply, in this case, (UR) twice before applying (U).

Along similar lines, we can derive interesting properties combining $\mathsf{N}x.A$ with spatial operators, for example the following one, which is important for deriving properties of the hiding quantifier (it takes about eight steps in each direction, but with a rather more involved set of constraints):

$$\langle S \rangle \; \Gamma, u : (\mathsf{N}x.A)|(\mathsf{N}x.B) \;\dashv\vdash\; u : \mathsf{N}x.(A|B), \acute{a}\Delta$$

This derivation uses the world rule $(S\nu|)$, which embeds a rather deep lemma about π-calculus structural congruence; namely, that if $(\nu n)P \equiv Q|R$ then there exist P', Q' such that $P \equiv P|P''$ and $(\nu n)P' \equiv Q$ and $(\nu n)P'' \equiv R$.

Equivariance In general, we have that a process P satisfies the formula $n\textcircled{R}A$ if $P \equiv (\nu n)Q$, where Q is a process that satisfies A. Then n is a name which is hidden, and hence not free, in P. So, the revelation operator has a useful meaning also in the special case $n\textcircled{R}\mathbf{T}$: the process P satisfies $n\textcircled{R}\mathbf{T}$ if and only if the name n is fresh in P ($\textcircled{c}n$ abbreviates $\neg n\textcircled{R}A$). We can show than $A \wedge m\textcircled{R}\mathbf{T} \wedge n\textcircled{R}\mathbf{T}$ entails $\{m \leftrightarrow n\}\cdot A$:

3. $\langle Z \doteq (\nu n)X, u \doteq (\nu m)\mathcal{Y} \rangle \, \acute{a}(m \leftrightarrow n)Z : \{m \leftrightarrow n\}\cdot A, X : \mathbf{T}, \mathcal{Y} : \mathbf{T} \vdash Z : \{m \leftrightarrow n\}\cdot A$ (Id)

2. $\langle Z \doteq (\nu n)X, u \doteq (\nu m)\mathcal{Y} \rangle \, \acute{a}Z : A, X : \mathbf{T}, \mathcal{Y} : \mathbf{T} \vdash Z : \{m \leftrightarrow n\}\cdot A$ (by 3, (τ))

1. $\langle \rangle \, \acute{a}Z : A \wedge m\textcircled{R}\mathbf{T} \wedge n\textcircled{R}\mathbf{T} \vdash u : \{m \leftrightarrow n\}\cdot A$ (by 2, ($\wedge$L and $\textcircled{R}$L))

(Note the use of (Swap Erase) in step 3) This property can be interpreted as saying that, for any process P, if it satisfies A, it also satisfies $\{m \leftrightarrow n\}\cdot A$ for any fresh names m and n. This fact is a consequence of the equivariance property of the semantics: intuitively, if the name denoted by (say) m occurs in the formula A but not in the process P, then we would expect the name m to be irrelevant to the fact that P satisfies A. This means that if we swap in formula A the name m by any other fresh name n, we would expect that P would still satisfy it (since a fresh name is as good as any other fresh name). For example, the following provable sequent

$$\langle n \# p, m \# p \rangle \; n\textcircled{R}(p\langle n \rangle | \mathbf{T}) \wedge m\textcircled{R}\mathbf{T} \wedge n\textcircled{R}\mathbf{T} \vdash m\textcircled{R}(p\langle m \rangle | \mathbf{T})$$

says that if a process is about to send a fresh name on a public channel p, it can send any other fresh name as well.

Input In our logic we have a primitive formula to observe messages, $n\langle m \rangle$, corresponding to the output operator of the asynchronous π-calculus. We do not have a corresponding input formula, but it can be expressed from output along the lines of [16]. The guarantee operator is crucial to this; recall that a process P satisfies $A \triangleright B$ if for any Q that satisfies A, we have that $P|Q$ satisfies B (this can be read out from $(\triangleright R)$). We say that P satisfies B "in presence" of any Q that satisfies A. We can take the following definition of input: $x(y).A \stackrel{\Delta}{=} \forall y.x\langle y \rangle \triangleright \Diamond A$.

The intention is that a process satisfies the input specification $x(y).A$ if it performs an input over a given channel x of any name y (with y bound in A), and then satisfies the property A. The above definition says literally, that an input process is one that, in presence of any output message y over the given channel x, at the next step (after input) it behaves according to A.

It is then easy to verify that because of the adjunction between $|$ and $\triangleright$, input and output interact as expected in $A\pi$ communication, that is, $x\langle z\rangle|x(y).A$ entails $\Diamond A\{y\leftarrow z\}$:

4.2. $\langle S, u = X|\mathcal{Y}\rangle\ \Gamma, X : x\langle z\rangle$á $\vdash X : x\langle z\rangle, u : \Diamond A\{y\leftarrow z\}, \Delta$ (by (Id) choose $X, \mathcal{Y}$ fresh)

4.1. $\langle S, u = X|\mathcal{Y}\rangle\ \Gamma, X : x\langle z\rangle, X|\mathcal{Y} : \Diamond A\{y\leftarrow z\}$á $\vdash u : \Diamond A\{y\leftarrow z\}, \Delta$
    (by (Id), for $X|\mathcal{Y} \doteq_S u$)

3. $\langle S, u = X|\mathcal{Y}\rangle\ \Gamma, X : x\langle z\rangle, \mathcal{Y} : x\langle z\rangle \triangleright \Diamond A\{y\leftarrow z\}$á $\vdash u : \Diamond A\{y\leftarrow z\}, \Delta$á
    (by 4.1, 4.2, ($\triangleright$L))

2. $\langle S, u = X|\mathcal{Y}\rangle\ \Gamma, X : x\langle z\rangle, \mathcal{Y} : \forall y.x\langle y\rangle \triangleright \Diamond A$á $\vdash u : \Diamond A\{y\leftarrow z\}, \Delta$ (by 3, ($\forall$L))

1. $\langle S\rangle\ \Gamma, u : x\langle z\rangle|(\forall y.x\langle y\rangle \triangleright \Diamond A)$á $\vdash u : \Diamond A\{y\leftarrow z\}, \Delta$á
    (by 2, ($|$L) $X, \mathcal{Y}$ not in conclusion)

Hiding In Part I we defined a hiding quantifier: $\mathsf{H}x.A \triangleq \mathsf{V}x.x\circledR A$ which is related to π-calculus name restriction in an appropriate way; namely, that if process P satisfies formula $A\{x\leftarrow n\}$, then $(\nu n)P$ satisfies $\mathsf{H}x.A$. An interesting use of $\mathsf{H}x.A$ is in specifying "nonce generators", that is processes that output freshly generated names on a given channel. In π-calculus, a nonce generator can be written simply as $(\nu n)nc\langle n\rangle$, for a given channel nc. A nonce generator over nc can then be specified by the following formula: $\mathcal{N}_c \triangleq \mathsf{H}x.nc\langle x\rangle$. We can show that, when a nonce generator interacts with an input, the result is the acquisition of a private name:

$$\langle S\rangle\ \Gamma, \text{á}u : \mathcal{N}_c|nc(y).A \vdash u : \Diamond\mathsf{H}z.A\{y\leftarrow z\}, \text{á}\Delta$$

Before input we have a nonce generator $\mathcal{N}_c$ separate from the input process. After one step, we have that the A part has acquired a name z; but noticeably this z is "hidden" within $A\{y\leftarrow z\}$ by the scope of the hiding quantifier. Hence the A part of the system has acquired, from the nonce generator, a private name not shared with other parts of the system (at least, not yet).

Inductive Definitions We just sketch here our treatment of recursive formulas. First, we can combine the spatial operator $\triangleright$ with classical negation to obtain an operator $!A \triangleq (A \Rightarrow \mathbf{F}) \triangleright \mathbf{F}$ that has the meaning that A is valid (is satisfied by any process). Through second-order quantification, we can then define least and greatest fixpoint operators in a style similar to F-algebraic encodings.

$$\mu X.A \triangleq \forall Y.(!(A\{X\leftarrow Y\} \Rightarrow Y)) \Rightarrow Y \ \text{(where } Y \text{ is not free in } A)$$
$$\nu X.A \triangleq \neg\mu X.\neg A\{X\leftarrow\neg X\}$$

These definitions turn out to enjoy the expected properties of recursive formulas, in the form of derivable left and right rules; for example the derivable rule (νR) corresponds to a coinduction principle. The folding and unfolding of $\mu X.A$ and

$\nu X.A$ can be derived under an assumption of monotonicity of $A\{X\}$; this can be expressed via the ! operator. As an example of the use of recursion, we can specify a recursive nonce generator (a process producing an unbounded number of fresh names) as follows: $\mathcal{UN}_c \triangleq \nu X.\mathcal{N}_c|X$. By a standard coinductive argument, we can then show that $\mathcal{UN}_c|\mathcal{UN}_c$ entails $\mathcal{UN}_c$. This is simple but significant: it means that (without any knowledge of the π-calculus implementation) two recursive nonce generators running in parallel behave like a single recursive nonce generator; in particular, the two generators do not risk generating independently the same name twice.

6   Conclusion

We have presented a sequent calculus that has a direct interpretation in terms of distributed concurrent behaviors, including notions of resource hiding.

We believe we have obtained a unique combination of, on one hand, good proof-theoretical structures and properties, and, on the other hand, direct applicability to concurrency. These twin aims have driven us towards a "many worlds" formulation of modal sequents that has been able to accommodate a wide range of unusual but strongly motivated logical constructions.

Acknowledgements

Andy Gordon contributed to early stages of Part I of this paper. Thanks also to Peter O'Hearn for early discussions on substructural logics. Caires acknowledges Microsoft Research and Profundis IST200133100.

References

1. L. Caires. *A Model for Declarative Programming and Specification with Concurrency and Mobility*. PhD thesis, Dept. de Informática, FCT, Universidade Nova de Lisboa, 1999. 209, 210, 211
2. L. Caires and L. Cardelli. A Spatial Logic for Concurrency (Part I). In N. Kobayashi and B. C. Pierce, editors, *Proceedings of the 10th Symposium on Theoretical Aspects of Computer Science (TACS 2001)*, volume 2215 of *Lecture Notes in Computer Science*, pages 1–30. Springer-Verlag, 2001. 209, 211, 213, 214
3. L. Caires and L. Cardelli. A Spatial Logic for Concurrency (Part II). Technical Report 3/2002/DI/PLM/FCTUNL, DI/PLM FCT Universidade Nova de Lisboa, 2002. 212, 220
4. L. Caires and L. Cardelli. A Spatial Logic for Concurrency (Part I). *Information and Computation*, to appear. 209, 214
5. L. Caires and L. Monteiro. Verifiable and Executable Specifications of Concurrent Objects in $\mathcal{L}_\pi$. In C. Hankin, editor, *Programming Languages and Systems: Proceedings of the 7th European Symp. on Programming (ESOP 1998)*, number 1381 in Lecture Notes in Computer Science, pages 42–56. Springer-Verlag, 1998. 210, 211

6. C. Calcagno, Luca Cardelli, and Andrew Gordon. Deciding Validity in a Spatial Logic of Trees. to appear, 2002. 212

7. L. Cardelli and A. D. Gordon. Anytime, Anywhere. Modal Logics for Mobile Ambients. In *27th ACM Symp. on Principles of Programming Languages*, pages 365–377. ACM, 2000. 209, 210, 211

8. L. Cardelli and A. D. Gordon. Logical Properties of Name Restriction. In S. Abramsky, editor, *Typed Lambda Calculi and Applications*, number 2044 in Lecture Notes in Computer Science. Springer-Verlag, 2001. 209, 210, 211, 213

9. M. Dam. Relevance Logic and Concurrent Composition. In *Proceedings, Third Annual Symposium on Logic in Computer Science*, pages 178–185, Edinburgh, Scotland, 5–8 July 1988. IEEE Computer Society. 212

10. M. Gabbay and A. Pitts. A New Approach to Abstract Syntax Involving Binders. In *14th Annual Symposium on Logic in Computer Science*, pages 214–224. IEEE Computer Society Press, Washington, 1999. 210, 212, 213, 221

11. M. Hennessy and R. Milner. Algebraic laws for Nondeterminism and Concurrency. *JACM*, 32(1):137–161, 1985. 211

12. P. O'Hearn and D. Pym. The Logic of Bunched Implications. *The Bulletin of Symbolic Logic*, 5(2):215–243, 1999. 212

13. A. Pitts. Nominal Logic: A First Order Theory of Names and Binding. In B. C. Pierce N. Kobayashi, editor, *Proceedings of the 10th Symposium on Theoretical Aspects of Computer Science (TACS 2001)*, volume 2215 of *Lecture Notes in Computer Science*, pages 219–235. Springer-Verlag, 2001. 209, 211, 213, 218

14. G. Plotkin and M. Abadi. A logic for parametric polymorphism. In M. Bezem and J. F. Groote, editors, *International Conference on Typed Lambda Calculi and Applications*, number 664 in Lecture Notes in Computer Science, pages 361–375, Utrecht, The Netherlands, March 1993. Springer-Verlag. TLCA'93. 210

15. J. C. Reynolds. Separation Logic: A Logic for Shared Mutable Data Structures. In *Proceedings of the Third Annual Symposium on Logic in Computer Science*, Copenhagen, Denmark, 2002. IEEE Computer Society. 212

16. D. Sangiorgi. Extensionality and Intensionality of the Ambient Logics. In *28th Annual Symposium on Principles of Programming Languages*, pages 4–13. ACM, 2001. 212, 222

17. A. Simpson. *The Proof Theory and Semantics of Intuitionistic Modal Logic*. Ph.D. thesis, Dept. of Computer Science, Edingburgh University, 1994. 209, 211, 212

18. Luca Viganò. *Labelled Non-Classical Logics*. Kluwer Academic Publishers, Dordrecht, 2000. 209, 212

Reducing Model Checking
from Multi-valued CTL* to CTL*

Beata Konikowska[1] and Wojciech Penczek[1,2]*

[1] Institute of Computer Science, PAS
01-237 Warsaw, ul. Ordona 21, Poland
{beatak,penczek}@ipipan.waw.pl
[2] Podlasie Academy, Institute of Informatics
Siedlce, Poland

Abstract. A multi-valued version of CTL* (mv-CTL*), where both the propositions and the accessibility relation are multi-valued taking values in a finite quasi-boolean algebra, is considered. A general translation from mv-CTL* to CTL* model checking is defined. An application of the translation is shown for the most commonly used quasi-boolean algebras.

1 Introduction

Model checking is one of the most popular methods used in automated verification of concurrent systems like hardware circuits, communication protocols, and distributed programs [12]. It consists in verifying that a finite state program P satisfies a property φ (denoted $P \models \varphi$). When P is represented by its model M_P and the property φ is given by a temporal logic formula, one checks whether $M_P \models \varphi$. The process of generating M_P for P and checking that $M_P \models \varphi$ is automated. The complexity of model checking methods strongly depends on the translation from P to M_P and on the type of the temporal logic that the formula φ belongs to.

In this paper we consider model checking algorithms for Computation Tree Logic* (CTL*) [16]. We are not concerned with the problem of getting a model M_P from a program P and just assume that such a model is provided. Two-valued models and logics, like CTL*, are sufficient for proving properties of standard concurrent systems. However, there is a number of problems for which we need to reason under uncertainty or to use models containing inconsistency. Uncertainty can occur either when complete information is not known or cannot be obtained, or when this information has been abstracted away [6,13]. On the other hand, models can be inconsistent because they combine conflicting points of view or contain components developed by different designers [15].

Multi-valued modal logics provide a solution to both reasoning under uncertainty and reasoning under inconsistency. Several model checkers based on

* Partly supported by the State Committee for Scientific Research under the grant No. 7T11C 00620, and by the EU Framework V research project ALFEBIITE.

multi-valued logics have been already defined [2,3,6,21,10]. We discuss the existing model checking algorithms in detail in Section 2 of our paper.

There are two different approaches to extending modal logics to multi-valued versions. Either solely the interpretation of propositional variables is extended to a multi-valued one, or in addition the accessibility relation becomes a multi-valued one [18,19]. Moreover, there can also be various approaches to selecting the domain of logical values to be used. Here some kind of a (partially) ordered set is usually considered, with the most common choices being either a finite totally ordered set or, more generally, a finite quasi-boolean lattice. In order to define a model checking algorithm for a selected multi-valued modal logic mv-L (which extends a two-valued modal logic L), one can either design a new model checking algorithm for mv-L by extending an existing algorithm for L or define a translation from model checking for mv-L to model checking for L.

The latter approach is usually more efficient. Indeed: with a simple translation, it allows us to use the benefits of well-developed and verified, standard model checking algorithms for L without having to rediscover things from the start. Clearly, the latter is usually connected with a greater work outlay, plus some practically inevitable faults and/or inefficiencies of the resulting new algorithm. Moreover, such an approach provides greater flexibility, since it is not restricted to any specific model checking method for the logic L. Therefore, it allows us to use any existing (present or future) model checking algorithm for L to provide model checking for mv-L.

This is the approach we follow in this paper, which generalizes our results presented in [22]. We define a general translation method to be applied for all the finite and distributive quasi-boolean lattices considered in the literature. Our method consists in finding a proper injection f on a lattice $\mathcal{L}$ which preserves arbitrary bounds. Then, the model checking problem of mv-CTL* over $\mathcal{L}$ is translated to the model checking problem of mv-CTL* over $f(\mathcal{L})$. If $f(\mathcal{L})$ is two-valued, then we deal with the standard model checking for CTL*, for which numerous solutions are available. Using our method we explain the existing translations as well as design new ones, e.g. for product lattices.

The rest of the paper is organized as follows. The next section discusses the related work, whereas Section 3 introduces quasi-boolean lattices. In Section 4, we start with defining mv-CTL*, where both the propositions and the accessibility relation are multi-valued and take values in a finite quasi-boolean algebra. In Section 5, we define a general translation from mv-CTL* model checking to mv-CTL* model checking. Next, we show how to design a translation algorithm for the most commonly applied quasi-boolean algebras. Final remarks are given in Section 6.

2   Related Work

A translation from a 3-valued model checking problem for CTL* and the modal μ-calculus to a standard model checking problem has been defined in [2,3]. The authors have considered a restricted version of the logics with the 2-valued interpretation of the accessibility-relation. Our translation can be viewed as a generalization of these results for CTL*.

Another approach has been taken by Chechik et al. A new model checking algorithm for a multi-valued CTL has been defined exploiting mv-BDD's [7] for unrestricted interpretations and MTBDD's [8] for distributive quasi-boolean algebras. Moreover, a model checker for mv-LTL under restricted interpretations (a 2-valued accessibility relation and totally ordered sets for the propositions) has been implemented, based on a translation to (mv)-Büchi automata [9].

In our former paper [22], we showed a translation from mv-CTL* to CTL* model checking for models over selected finite lattices including: total orders and two quasi-boolean algebras with four and six elements.

3　Quasi-Boolean Lattices

This section deals with quasi-boolean lattices and finite totally ordered sets, which are used as logical domains of interpretations for the formulas of our multi-valued logics.

Definition 1. *A lattice is a partial order $\mathcal{L} = (L, \leq)$ satisfying the following conditions:*

- *for any two elements $x, y \in L$, there exists their greatest lower bound $(x \cap y)$ and their least upper bound $(x \cup y)$.*[1]

Definition 2. *A lattice $\mathcal{L} = (L, \leq)$ is quasi-boolean if there exists a unary operator $\sim$ having the following properties for any $x, y \in L$:*

- $\sim (x \cap y) = \sim x \cup \sim y,$
- $\sim (x \cup y) = \sim x \cap \sim y,$
- $x \leq y$ *iff* $\sim y \leq \sim x,$
- $\sim\sim x = x.$

$\mathcal{L}$ is distributive if the following conditions hold for any $x, y, z \in L$:

- $z \cup (x \cap y) = (z \cup x) \cap (z \cup y),$
- $z \cap (x \cup y) = (z \cap x) \cup (z \cap y).$

Definition 3. *A lattice $\mathcal{L} = (L, \leq)$ is a finite total order (FTO) if the following conditions hold:*

- *L is a finite set,*
- *for each two elements $x, y \in L$, either $x \leq y$ or $y \leq x$.*

Example 1. In Figure 1 we show an FTO denoted **K** representing uncertainty, and two well-known finite lattices, the use of which is motivated by clear practical intuitions: the lattice **K** × **L** representing disagreement, and the lattice **2** × **2** + **2** representing both uncertainty and disagreement. (Note that **K** and **K** × **L** represent in fact two sets of lattices.)

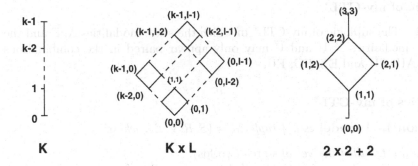

Fig. 1. Standard multi-valued lattices

When discussing the translations, we will identify each linear order **K** and the lattices **2 × 2** and **2 × 2 + 2** with their isomorphic images in the considered quasi-boolean lattices.

4   MV-Temporal Logics: mv-CTL*, mv-CTL

Syntax of mv-CTL*

Let PV be a finite set of propositions, $\overline{PV} = \{\neg p \mid p \in PV\}$, and let $true$ and $false$ be two constants. First, we give the syntax of mv-CTL*, and then restrict it to its standard sublanguages. To simplify subsequent technical issues connected with proving the correctness of translations, we define the positive version of the language, which does not influence the expressiveness of the language. The set of state formulas and the set of path formulas of mv-CTL* are defined inductively:

S1. every element of $PV \cup \overline{PV} \cup \{true, false\}$ is a state formula,
S2. if φ and ψ are state formulas, then so are $\varphi \vee \psi$ and $\varphi \wedge \psi$,
S3. if φ is a path formula, then Aφ and Eφ are state formulas,
P1. any state formula φ is also a path formula,
P2. if φ, ψ are path formulas, then so are $\varphi \wedge \psi$ and $\varphi \vee \psi$,
P3. if φ, ψ are path formulas, then so are $X\varphi$, U(φ, ψ), and $\overline{U}(\varphi, \psi)$.

The modal operator A has the intuitive meaning "for all paths", E - "there is a path", U denotes the standard Until, whereas $\overline{U}$ denotes Release (dual to Until). The language of mv-CTL* consists of the set of all state formulas.
    The following abbreviations will be used:

- G$\varphi \stackrel{def}{=} \overline{U}(\varphi, false)$,
- F$\varphi \stackrel{def}{=}$ U$(true, \varphi)$.

---

[1] Obviously, from antisymmetry of a partial order it follows that both the greatest lower bound and least upper bound of x, y are uniquely determined elements of L.

Sublogic of mv-CTL*

mv-CTL: The sublogic of mv-CTL* in which the state modalities A, E and the path modalities X, U and $\overline{U}$ may only appear paired in the combinations AX, AU, A$\overline{U}$ and EX, EU, E$\overline{U}$.

Semantics of mv-CTL*

Definition 4. *A model is a 4-tuple* $M = (S, R, V, \mathcal{L})$, *where*

- S *is a set, called the set of* states (worlds),
- $R : S \times S \longrightarrow L$ *is a function, called the* accessibility function,
- $V : S \times (PV \cup \overline{PV}) \longrightarrow L$ *is a function, called the* valuation function,
- $\mathcal{L} = (L, \leq)$ *is a finite quasi-boolean lattice, with the least element* **F** *and the greatest element* **T**.[2]

We assume that R satisfies the condition $(\forall s \in S)(\exists s' \in S)\, R(s, s') > \mathbf{F}$.

The latter requirement for R is aimed at keeping the semantics of mv-CTL* as close as possible to that of CTL*. Define

$$\Pi(s) = \{s_0 s_1 \ldots \mid s_0 = s \wedge (\forall i \geq 0)\, R(s_i, s_{i+1}) > \mathbf{F}\}, \quad \Pi = \bigcup_{s \in S} \Pi(s)$$

to be the set of all the paths starting at s in M, and the set of all the paths in M, respectively.

For $\pi = s_0 s_1 \ldots \in \Pi(s)$, let $\pi_i = s_i s_{i+1} \ldots$ denote the i-th suffix of π, and let $\pi(i) = s_i$ be the i-th state of π.

Then, $[\varphi]_s^M$ and $[\varphi]_\pi^M$ is defined inductively as follows (as before we omit M when it is understood):

S1. $[true]_s = \mathbf{T}$, $[false]_s = \mathbf{F}$, $[p]_s = V(s, p)$ for $p \in PV \cup \overline{PV}$,

S2. $[\varphi \wedge \psi]_s = [\varphi]_s \cap [\psi]_s$, $[\varphi \vee \psi]_s = [\varphi]_s \cup [\psi]_s$,

S3. $[A\varphi]_s = \bigcap_{\pi \in \Pi(s)} [\varphi]_\pi$, $[E\varphi]_s = \bigcup_{\pi \in \Pi(s)} [\varphi]_\pi$,

P1. $[\varphi]_\pi = [\varphi]_{\pi(0)}$ for any state formula φ,

P2. $[\varphi \wedge \psi]_\pi = [\varphi]_\pi \cap [\psi]_\pi$, $[\varphi \vee \psi]_\pi = [\varphi]_\pi \cup [\psi]_\pi$,

P3. $[X\varphi]_\pi = R(\pi(0), \pi(1)) \cap [\varphi]_{\pi_1}$,
$[U(\varphi, \psi)]_\pi =$
$\bigcup_{i>0}([\psi]_{\pi_i} \cap \bigcap_{0<j<i}(R(\pi(j-1), \pi(j)) \cap [\varphi]_{\pi_j}) \cap [\varphi]_{\pi_0}) \cup [\psi]_{\pi(0)}$,
$[\overline{U}(\varphi, \psi)]_\pi =$
$\bigcap_{i\geq0}((R(\pi(i), \pi(i+1)) \cap [\psi]_{\pi_i}) \cup (\bigcup_{0<j<i}(R(\pi(j-1), \pi(j)) \cap [\varphi]_{\pi_j}) \cup [\varphi]_{\pi_0}))$.

---

[2] In the examples, **F** and **T** are denoted by sequences of natural numbers in order to simplify the definition of the order in lattices.

Note that under the above semantics we need not have $V(s, \neg p) = \sim V(s, \neg p)$ for all $p \in PV$. If the above condition holds in a multi-valued model, then the model is called *standard*.

Given a finite-state model M, a state s of S, and a mv-CTL* formula φ, the model checking problem is defined as that of finding the value of $[\varphi]_s^M$.

Example 2. In Figure 2 we show an example of a standard multi-valued model representing our requirements for a simple coffee machine (a modified example from [7]). The model uses multiple truth values to distinguish between transitions and propositions that **must**, **should**, **should not**, or **must not** be true. Two types of unknown values are used: **do not know** for values controlled by the system, but not yet decided, and **do not care** for values controlled by the environment. Labelling a state s with $p = x$ means that $V(s, p) = x$, where p is a proposition and x is a truth value. Labelling a transition with x means that its truth value is x. In the figure we omit all the transitions labelled **F**, i.e., "prohibited". The coffee machine starts in the state **OFF**, where it is irrelevant whether a cup is provided or not, which is modeled by $cup = $ **DC**. Since it has not been decided yet whether the machine should be able to go directly to IDLE, the corresponding transition is labelled **DK**. On the other hand, all the transitions labelled **T** represent the required changes of states. Note that the transitions from the states **Delivers ...** to **OFF** are labelled **N**. As they are dependent on the environment they cannot be prohibited, i.e., labelled **F**. The value **DK** of the proposition *power* in the state **IDLE** represents the fact that it has not yet been decided whether the power should be ON or OFF on idle. Notice that the model abstracts away from the payments required from clients for simplicity sake.

There are several properties that can be specified and then checked in the model:

1. The machine must eventually be able to deliver coffee,
2. Coffee is always delivered in a cup,
3. After coffee has been delivered, coffee cannot be immediately delivered again.

The properties of the coffee machine model can be specified by the following formulas:

1. EF *coffee*,
2. AG($\neg coffee \vee cup$),
3. AG($\neg coffee \vee$ AX($\neg coffee$)).

5   Model Checking for mv-CTL*

In this section we show that the model checking problem for mv-CTL* can be translated to the model checking problem for CTL*. We start with a basic result which will underlie all of the above-mentioned translations.

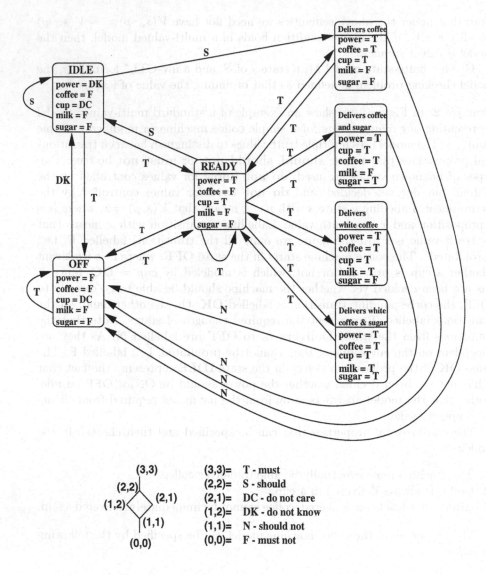

$$(3,3)= \text{T - must}$$
$$(2,2)= \text{S - should}$$
$$(2,1)= \text{DC - do not care}$$
$$(1,2)= \text{DK - do not know}$$
$$(1,1)= \text{N - should not}$$
$$(0,0)= \text{F - must not}$$

Fig. 2. A coffee machine model over the lattice $2 \times 2 + 2$

Theorem 1. *Let $\mathcal{L} = (L, \leq)$ be an arbitrary finite quasi-boolean lattice, and let $f : L \to L$ be a proper injection with $f(L) \neq L$, which preserves arbitrary bounds in $\mathcal{L}$, i.e.,*

$$f(\bigcap_{i \in I} x_i) = \bigcap_{i \in I} f(x_i), \qquad f(\bigcup_{i \in I} x_i) = \bigcup_{i \in I} f(x_i) \qquad (1)$$

where I is an arbitrary set of indices. Further, let $M = (S, R, V, \mathcal{L})$ be an L-valued model of mv-CTL*, and let $M_1 = (S, R_1, V_1, f(\mathcal{L}))$ be a model with values in $f(L)$

obtained out of M by replacing each value $x \in L$ returned by V and R in M with $f(x)$, i.e., $R_1(s, s') = f(R(s, s'))$ and $V_1(s, q) = f(V(s, q))$, for $s, s' \in S$ and $q \in PV \cup \overline{PV}$.

Then, for any state (path) formula φ of mv-CTL over $\mathcal{L}$ and any state (path, resp.) ι, we have*

$$[\varphi]_\iota^{M_1} = x \text{ iff } [\varphi]_\iota^M \in f^{-1}(x) \tag{2}$$

First and foremost, the bounds preservation condition (1) implies clearly that $(f(L), \leq \cap (f(L) \times f(L)))$ is a sublattice of $\mathcal{L}$ - hence we can indeed consider a model M_1 valued over $f(L)$. Note that this model need not be standard even if M was, since $V(s, \neg q) = \sim V(s, q)$ in general does not imply $f(V(s, \neg q)) = \sim f(V(s, q))$. However, non-standard models do not pose any problem from the viewpoint of model checking, since they are just equivalent to standard models of a negation-free sublanguage.

The proof of the theorem is based on the following key result:

Lemma 1. *Assume a formula φ is such that $[\varphi]_\iota^{M'} = \bigcap_{i \in I}[\varphi_i]_\iota^{M'}$ or $[\varphi]_\iota^{M'} = \bigcup_{i \in I}[\varphi_i]_\iota^{M'}$ for any model M' and any state (path) ι of M', where φ_i are some state (path, resp.) formulas of mv-CTL*, I is an arbitrary set, and the thesis (2) holds for each φ_i. Then (2) holds for φ.*

Proof. To prove the lemma, consider the case when $[\varphi]_\iota^{M'} = \bigcap_{i \in I}[\varphi_i]_\iota^{M'}$; the other case follows by symmetry.

(=>)
Assume $[\varphi]_\iota^{M_1} = x$. Then by the assumption on φ we have $[\varphi]_\iota^{M_1} = \bigcap_{i \in I}[\varphi_i]_\iota^{M_1}$, and, denoting $[\varphi_i]_\iota^{M_1} = x_i, i \in I$, we get $x = \bigcap_{i \in I} x_i$. Further, since each φ_i satisfies (2), then $[\varphi_i]_\iota^M \in f^{-1}(x_i)$ for $i \in I$. As f preserves the bounds, by the assumption on φ we have $f([\varphi]_\iota^M) = f(\bigcap_{i \in I}[\varphi_i]_\iota^M) = \bigcap_{i \in I} f([\varphi_i]_\iota^M) = \bigcap_{i \in I} x_i = x$ whence $[\varphi]_\iota^M \in f^{-1}(x)$.

(<=)
Assume now $[\varphi]_\iota^M \in f^{-1}(x)$. Then $f([\varphi]_\iota^M) = f(\bigcap_{i \in I}[\varphi_i]_\iota^M) = \bigcap_{i \in I} f([\varphi_i]_\iota^M) = x$. Denoting $f([\varphi_i]_\iota^M) = x_i$, we get $\bigcap_{i \in I} x_i = x$ and $[\varphi_i]_\iota^M \in f^{-1}(x_i)$ for $i \in I$. Thus by assumption on φ_i we get $[\varphi_i]_\iota^{M_1} = x_i$ for $i \in I$, whence $[\varphi]_\iota^{M_1} = \bigcap_{i \in I}[\varphi_i]_\iota^{M_1} = \bigcap_{i \in I} x_i = x$.

Now we can prove the theorem itself.

Proof. (Sketch) We use induction on the length of formula. The hypothesis clearly holds for propositional variables and their negations. Assume it holds for formulas of length at most k. Then we have the following cases:

(a) $\varphi = \varphi_1 \wedge \varphi_2$ or $\varphi = \varphi_1 \vee \varphi_2$, where each φ_i is state (or path) formula of length at most k. Then φ satisfies (2) by Lemma 1 for $I = \{1, 2\}$.

(b) $\varphi = A\psi$ or $\varphi = E\psi$, where ψ is of length at most k. Then φ satisfies (2) by Lemma 1 for $I = \mathbf{N}$, where $\mathbf{N}$ is the set of natural numbers.

(c) $\varphi = X\psi$. The reasoning is similar to (a).

(f) $\varphi = U\psi$ or $\varphi = \overline{U}\psi$. Since on the semantic side both the operators correspond to a combination of finite and infinite lower and upper bounds, the proof is a combination of those used in (a) and (b).

This theorem provides the basis for reducing the model-checking problem over a lattice $\mathcal{L}$ to the model-checking problems over its proper sublattices $f(\mathcal{L}) = (f(L), \leq \cap (f(L) \times f(L)))$, where f is a bounds-preserving mapping like in Theorem 1. The general method defines k mappings (translations) $f_1, \ldots, f_k$ such that:

- $f_1(\mathcal{L}), \ldots, f_k(\mathcal{L})$ are lattices for which we already have model-checking algorithms,
- for any $x \in L$ there exist some $x_i \in f_i(L), i = 1, \ldots, k$, such that $\bigcap_{i=1}^{k} f_i^{-1}(x_i) = \{x\}$.

Indeed: in such a case, Theorem 1 implies that, for any mv-CTL* formula φ, any model M over $\mathcal{L}$ and any state or path ι of M, $[\varphi]_\iota^M = x$ iff $[\varphi]_\iota^{M_i} = x_i$ for all $i = 1, \ldots, k$, where each M_i is the model over $f_i(L)$ obtained out of M using the mapping (translation) f_i. Hence the model-checking problem for $\mathcal{L}$ reduces to the model-checking problems over $f_1(\mathcal{L}), \ldots, f_k(\mathcal{L})$.

The application of our translation will be shown first for mv-CTL* interpreted over FTO's $\mathcal{L}$. Here the functions f_i are such that $f_i(\mathcal{L})$ is two-valued, i.e., each $f_i(\mathcal{L})$ is a two-valued linear order, for which we already have the usual model-checking algorithms. Then, we show functions f_i defining translations for other typical finite quasi-boolean lattices $\mathcal{L}$. In case of the lattice $\mathbf{K} \times \mathbf{L}$ for all our functions f_i, the sublattice $f_i(\mathcal{L})$ is an FTO, whereas in case of the lattice $\mathbf{2} \times \mathbf{2} + \mathbf{2}$ for all our functions f_i, the sublattice $f_i(\mathcal{L})$ is an FTO or the lattice $\mathbf{2} \times \mathbf{2}$. Therefore, eventually we have a translation to the two valued case.

5.1   Translation for FTO's

We assume that $\mathcal{L} = (L, \leq)$ is an FTO, denoted by $\mathbf{K+1}$, such that $L = \{0, 1, \ldots, k-1, k\}$. Let $M = (S, R, V, \mathcal{L})$ be an L-valued model, and let φ be an mv-CTL* formula. For each $1 \leq i \leq k$, define the function $f_i : L \longrightarrow L$ as follows:

- $f_i(x) = 0$ iff $x < i$,
- $f_i(x) = 1$ iff $x \geq i$.

Lemma 2. *The functions f_i (for $i \in \{1, \ldots, k\}$) satisfy the condition (1) in the assumption of Theorem 1.*

Proof. For any $i, 0 \leq i \leq k$, we have: $f_i(\bigcap_{l \in L} x_l) = f_i(\min_{l \in L} x_l)$, whence $f_i(\bigcap_{l \in L} x_l) = 0$ iff $x_l < i$ for some $l \in L$ iff $f_i(x_l) = 0$ for some $l \in L$ iff $\bigcap_{l \in L} f_i(x_l) = \min_{l \in L} f_i(x_l) = 0$. Further, $f_i(\bigcap_{l \in L} x_l) = 1$ iff $x_l \geq i$ for each $l \in L$ iff $f_i(x_l) = 1$ for each $l \in L$ iff $\bigcap_{l \in L} f_i(x_l) = \min_{l \in L} f_i(x_l) = 1$. Thus we indeed have $f_i(\bigcap_{l \in L} x_l) = \bigcap_{l \in L} f_i(x_l)$. The proof for $\bigcup$ is just dual, so each f_i indeed satisfies the condition (1).

In what follows, $[\varphi]_s$ denotes $[\varphi]_s^M$, and $[\varphi]_s^i$ denotes $[\varphi]_s^{M_i}$ for $i = 1, \ldots, k$, where M_i is the model over **2** obtained from M using the translation f_i.

Theorem 2. *The following condition holds for each $s \in S$:*

- $[\varphi]_s = i$ *iff* $[\varphi]_s^i = 1$ *and* $(\forall i < j \leq k) [\varphi]_s^j = 0$.

Proof. Follows directly from Theorem 1 and the fact that
$$f_i^{-1}(1) \cap \bigcap_{i<j\leq k} f_j^{-1}(0) = \{x \mid x \geq i\} \cap \bigcap_{i<j\leq k}\{x \mid x < j\} = \{i\}.$$

5.2   Translation for the Lattice **K** × **L**

Consider the standard product lattice $\mathcal{L} = \mathbf{K} \times \mathbf{L}$, where $\mathbf{K} = (\{0, 1, \ldots, k-1\},$ $\leq)$ and $\mathbf{L} = (\{0, 1, \ldots, l-1\}, \leq)$ are linear orders with $0 \leq 1 \leq \cdots \leq k-1$, $0 \leq 1 \leq \cdots \leq l-1$. The order $\leq$ is defined componentwise, i.e.,

$$(x, y) \leq (x', y') \text{ iff } x \leq x' \text{ and } y \leq y'$$

(for simplicity sake, we use the same symbol $\leq$ for the ordering in $\mathcal{L}$ and the component linear orders, but its interpretation is clear from the context). In consequence, the bounds are also taken componentwise, whence

$$(x, y) \cap (x', y') = (\min(x, x'), \min(y, y')),$$
$$(x, y) \cup (x', y') = (\max(x, x'), \max(y, y'))$$

and, in general,

$$\bigcap_{i\in I}(x_i, y_i) = (\inf_{i\in I} x_i, \inf_{i\in I} y_i),$$
$$\bigcup_{i\in I}(x_i, y_i) = (\sup_{i\in I} x_i, \sup_{i\in I} y_i)$$

We define two mappings

$$f_k : \mathrm{L} \to \mathrm{L}, \qquad f_l : \mathrm{L} \to \mathrm{L}$$

as projections on **K** and **L**, respectively, i.e.,

$$f_k((x, y)) = (x, l-1), \qquad f_l((x, y)) = (k-1, y)$$

Lemma 3. *The functions f_k and f_l satisfy the condition (1) in the assumption of Theorem 1.*

Proof. We must prove that f_k and f_l preserve the bounds in $\mathcal{L}$. Indeed: we have $f_k(\bigcap_{i\in I}(x_i, y_i)) = f_k((\inf_{i\in I} x_i, \inf_{i\in I} y_i)) = (\inf_{i\in I} x_i, l-1) = \bigcap_{i\in I}(x_i, l-1) = \bigcap_{i\in I} f_k((x_i, y_i))$. As the proof for $\bigcup$ and f_l is dual, then the functions f_i indeed satisfy the condition (1), and hence the assumption of Theorem 1.

Next, we formulate the main theorem of this section. In what follows, $[\varphi]_s$ denotes $[\varphi]_s^M$, and $[\varphi]_s^r$ denotes $[\varphi]_s^{M_r}$ for $r = k, l$, where M_k is the model over **K** obtained from M using the translation f_k, while M_l is the model over **L** obtained from M using the translation f_l.

Theorem 3. *The following condition holds for every $s \in S$:*

- $[\varphi]_s = (i,j)$ *iff* $[\varphi]_s^k = (i, l-1)$ *and* $[\varphi]_s^l = (k-1, j)$.

Proof. Follows from Theorem 1 and the fact that $f_k^{-1}((i, l-1)) \cap f_l^{-1}((k-1, j)) = \{(i,r) \mid 0 \le r \le l-1\} \cap \{(s,j) \mid 0 \le s \le k-1\} = \{(i,j)\}$.

Thus model checking over $\mathbf{K} \times \mathbf{L}$ can be reduced to model checking over the linear orders $\mathbf{K}$ and $\mathbf{L}$, for which we already have the algorithm shown in the previous section.

5.3   Translation for the Lattice $2 \times 2 + 2$

Consider the lattice $\mathcal{L} = 2 \times 2 + 2$. Let $M = (S, R, V, \mathcal{L})$ be a 6-valued model, where $L = \{(0,0), (1,1), (1,2), (2,1), (2,2), (3,3)\}$, and let φ be an mv-CTL* formula. The order in $\mathcal{L}$ is defined componentwise according to the standard order $\le$ on integers.

Define the functions $f_1, f_2 : L \longrightarrow L$ as follows:

- $f_1((0,0)) = (0,0)$,
- $f_1((i,j)) = (2,2)$ for $1 \le i, j \le 2$,
- $f_1((3,3)) = (3,3)$,

- $f_2((i,j)) = (1,1)$ for $i, j \le 1$,
- $f_2((i,j)) = (i,j)$ for $i + j = 3$,
- $f_2((i,j)) = (2,2)$ for $i, j \ge 2$.

Lemma 4. *The functions f_i $(i = 1, 2)$ satisfy the condition (1) in the assumption of Theorem 1.*

Proof. Similar to the proofs of Lemma 2 and 3.

In what follows, $[\varphi]_s$ denotes $[\varphi]_s^M$, and $[\varphi]_s^r$ denotes $[\varphi]_s^{M_r}$ for $r = 1, 2$, where M_1 is the model over $\mathbf{3}$ obtained from M using the translation f_1, while M_2 is the model over $\mathbf{2} \times \mathbf{2}$ obtained from M using the translation f_2.

Theorem 4. *The following conditions hold for every $s \in S$:*

- $[\varphi]_s = [\varphi]_s^1$ *for* $[\varphi]_s^1 \in \{(0,0), (3,3)\}$,
- $[\varphi]_s = [\varphi]_s^2$ *for* $[\varphi]_s^1 = (2,2)$.

Proof. Follows directly from Theorem 1 and the following facts:

$$f_1^{-1}((x,y)) = \{(x,y)\} \text{ for } (x,y) \in \{(0,0), (3,3)\},$$
$$f_2^{-1}((x,y)) \cap f_1^{-1}((2,2)) = \{(x,y)\},$$
$$L = \{(0,0), (3,3)\} \cup f_1^{-1}((2,2)), \text{ and}$$
$$f_1(L) = \{(0,0), (2,2), (3,3)\}.$$

Complexity of mv-CTL* Model Checking depends on the structure of a lattice $\mathcal{L}$ and the complexity of the model checking problem for CTL*. It is easy to see that if deciding whether $[\varphi]_s^M = \mathbf{T}$ for a two valued model M requires time $O(Y)$, then the value of $[\varphi]_s^M$ for a many-valued model M can be found in time:

- $O((k-1) \times Y)$ for M over the lattice $\mathbf{K}$,
- $O((k+l-2) \times Y)$ for M over the lattice $\mathbf{K} \times \mathbf{L}$,
- $O(4 \times Y)$ for M over the lattice $\mathbf{2} \times \mathbf{2} + \mathbf{2}$.

Notice that for all the above lattices the running time of our model checking method for mv-CTL* is only linearly worse than for CTL*. The complexity of our algorithm can be compared with the model checking algorithm for mv-CTL of [8], where the running time depends on $|\mathbf{L}|^{3 \times |PV|-2}$. So, for each lattice $\mathbf{K} \times \mathbf{K}$, the running time of our algorithm is at least k times better.

6 Final Remarks

We have shown that a model checking algorithm for all multi-valued versions of CTL* over finite quasi-boolean distributive lattices considered in the literature can be obtained by making several queries to a standard model checking algorithm for CTL*. Such an approach does not restrict us to using any of the specific model checking methods for CTL*. The issue of existence of suitable translation mappings for other lattices will be the subject of further research.

The possibility of selecting any of the available model checking methods is not the only advantage of our approach. Another superiority is demonstrated by a possibility of applying different model reduction techniques directly. This is very important since practical applicability of model checking is strongly restricted by the state explosion problem. Thus, each of the two-valued models obtained via the translation can be reduced using the following methods: partial order reductions [24,28,20,25], symmetry reductions [17], abstraction techniques [14,11], and BDD-based symbolic storage methods, [4,5,23]. Moreover, our translation can be combined with SAT-related methods of model checking [1,26,27]. It is easy to notice that there is no need to make any changes to the above methods in order to use them in our approach.

References

1. A. Biere, A. Cimatti, E. Clarke, and Y. Zhu. Symbolic model checking without BDDs. In *Proc. of TACAS'99*, volume 1579 of *LNCS*, pages 193–207. Springer-Verlag, 1999. 237
2. G. Bruns and P. Godefroid. Model checking partial state spaces. In *Proc. of CAV'99*, volume 1633 of *LNCS*, pages 274–287. Springer-Verlag, 1999. 227
3. G. Bruns and P. Godefroid. Generalized model checking: reasoning about partial state spaces. In *Proc. of CONCUR'00*, volume 1877 of *LNCS*, pages 168–182. Springer-Verlag, 2000. 227

4. R. Bryant. Graph-based algorithms for boolean function manipulation. *IEEE Transaction on Computers*, 35(8):677–691, 1986. 237
5. R. Bryant. Binary Decision Diagrams and beyond: Enabling technologies for formal verification. In *Proc. of Int. Conf. on Computer-Aided Design (ICCAD'95)*, pages 236–243, 1995. 237
6. M. Chechik. On interpreting results of model-checking with abstraction. Technical Report 417, University of Toronto, 2000. 226, 227
7. M. Chechik, B. Devereux, and S. Easterbrook. Implementing a multi-valued symbolic model-checker. In *Proc. of TACAS'01*, volume 2031 of *LNCS*, pages 404–419. Springer-Verlag, 2001. 228, 231
8. M. Chechik, B. Devereux, S. Easterbrook, A. Y. C. Lai, and V. Petrovykh. Efficient multiple-valued model-checking using lattice representations. In *Proc. of CONCUR'01*, volume 2154 of *LNCS*, pages 441–455. Springer-Verlag, 2001. 228, 237
9. M. Chechik, B. Devereux, and A. Gurfinkel. Model checking infinite state-spaces systems with fine-grained abstractions using spin. In *Proc. of SPIN'01*, volume 2057 of *LNCS*, pages 16–36. Springer-Verlag, 2001. 228
10. M. Chechik, S. Easterbrook, and V. Petrovykh. Model checking over multi-valued temporal logics. In *Proc. of FME'01*, volume 2001 of *LNCS*, pages 72–98. Springer-Verlag, 2001. 227
11. E. M. Clarke, T. Filkorn, and S. Jha. Exploiting symmetry in temporal logic model checking. In *Proc. of CAV'93*, volume 697 of *LNCS*, pages 450–462. Springer-Verlag, 1993. 237
12. E. M. Clarke, O. Grümberg, and D. Peled. *Model Checking*. MIT Press, 1999. 226
13. D. Dams, R. Gerth, G. Dohmen, R. Herrmann, P. Kelb, and H. Pargmann. Model checking using adaptive state and data abstraction. In *Proc. of CAV'94*, volume 818 of *LNCS*, pages 455–467. Springer-Verlag, 1994. 226
14. D. Dams, O. Grümberg, and R. Gerth. Abstract interpretation of reactive systems: Abstractions preserving ACTL*, ECTL* and CTL*. In *Proceedings of the IFIP Working Conference on Programming Concepts, Methods and Calculi (PRO-COMET'94)*. Elsevier Science Publishers, 1994. 237
15. S. Easterbrook and M. Chechik. A framework for multi-valued reasoning over inconsistent viewpoints. In *Proc. of ICSE'01*, pages 411–420, 2001. 226
16. E. A. Emerson. *Handbook of Theoretical Computer Science*, volume B: Formal Methods and Semantics, chapter Temporal and Modal Logic, pages 995–1067. Elsevier, 1990. 226
17. E. A. Emerson and A. P. Sistla. Symmetry and model checking. *Formal Methods in System Design*, 9:105–131, 1995. 237
18. M. Fitting. Many-valued modal logics. *Fundamenta Informaticae*, 15(3-4):335–350, 1991. 227
19. M. Fitting. Many-valued modal logics II. *Fundamenta Informaticae*, 17:55–73, 1992. 227
20. R. Gerth, R. Kuiper, D. Peled, and W. Penczek. A partial order approach to branching time logic model checking. *Information and Computation*, 150:132–152, 1999. 237
21. S. Hazelhurst. *Compositional model checking of partially ordered state spaces*. PhD thesis, University of British Columbia, 1996. 227
22. B. Konikowska and W. Penczek. Model checking for multi-valued computation tree logics. In M. Fitting and E. Orlowska, editors, *Beyond Two: Theory and Applivations of Multiple Valued Logic*. to appear, 2002. 227, 228

23. K. L. McMillan. A technique of a state space search based on unfolding. *Formal Methods in System Design*, 6(1):45–65, 1995. 237
24. D. Peled. Partial order reduction: Linear and branching temporal logics and process algebras. In *Proc. of Partial Order Methods in Verification (POMIV'96)*, volume 29 of *ACM/AMS DIMACS Series*, pages 79–88. Amer. Math. Soc., 1996. 237
25. W. Penczek, M. Szreter, R. Gerth, and R. Kuiper. Improving partial order reductions for universal branching time properties. *Fundamenta Informaticae*, 43:245–267, 2000. 237
26. W. Penczek, B. Woźna, and A. Zbrzezny. Bounded model checking for the universal fragment of CTL. *Fundamenta Informaticae*, 50, 2002. to appear. 237
27. W. Penczek, B. Woźna, and A. Zbrzezny. Branching time bounded model checking for elementary net systems. *Report ICS PAS*, 940, January 2002. 237
28. A. Valmari. Stubborn sets for reduced state space generation. In *Proc. of the Int. Conf. on Applications and Theory of Petri Nets (ICATPN'89)*, volume 483 of *LNCS*, pages 491–515. Springer-Verlag, 1989. 237

Local Model Checking Games
for Fixed Point Logic with Chop

Martin Lange

Institut für Informatik
Ludwigs-Maximilian-Universität München
martin@dcs.ed.ac.uk

Abstract. The logic considered in this paper is FLC, fixed point logic with chop. It is an extension of modal μ-calculus $\mathcal{L}_\mu$ that is capable of defining non-regular properties which makes it interesting for verification purposes. Its model checking problem over finite transition systems is PSPACE-hard. We define games that characterise FLC's model checking problem over arbitrary transition systems. Over finite transition systems they can be used as a basis of a local model checker for FLC. I.e. the games allow the transition system to be constructed on-the-fly. On formulas with fixed alternation depth and so-called sequential depth deciding the winner of the games is PSPACE-complete. The best upper bound for the general case is EXPSPACE which can be improved to EXPTIME at the cost of losing the locality property. On $\mathcal{L}_\mu$ formulas the games behave equally well as the model checking games for $\mathcal{L}_\mu$, i.e. deciding the winner is in NP∩co-NP.

1   Introduction

Modal and temporal logics are well established research areas in computer science, artificial intelligence, philosophy, etc. [2, 5, 11]. An important temporal logic is Kozen's modal μ-calculus $\mathcal{L}_\mu$ [8] because it contains almost all other propositional temporal logics. In fact, it is equi-expressive to the bisimulation invariant fragment of monadic second-order logic over transition graphs [7]. Therefore, properties expressed by $\mathcal{L}_\mu$ formulas are essentially "regular".

In [10], Müller-Olm introduced FLC, fixed point logic with chop, that extends $\mathcal{L}_\mu$ with sequential composition. He showed that the expressive power of FLC is strictly greater than $\mathcal{L}_\mu$ because FLC can define non-regular properties. Whereas the semantics of a modal μ-calculus formula is a subset of states of a transition system, the semantics of an FLC formula is a predicate transformer, a function from sets of states to sets of states.

In [9] it is shown that FLC can express certain non-regular properties that are very interesting for verification of protocols for example. The reason for this is FLC's restricted ability to count similar to that of context-free languages. As Müller-Olm showed, FLC is even able to express certain non-context-free properties due to the presence of boolean operators.

L. Brim et al. (Eds.): CONCUR 2002, LNCS 2421, pp. 240–254, 2002.

He also proved that, because of FLC's expressive power, its satisfiability problem as well as the model checking problem for BPA processes is undecidable. However, he notes that model checking finite transition systems is decidable. It can be done using the Tarski-Knaster Theorem [13] in a function lattice using fixed point approximants. In [9] it has been proved to be PSPACE-hard and a model checker for FLC that avoids explicit calculation of functions has been given. It builds tableaux for formulas of FLC and sets of states of a transition system. These tableaux admit global model checking, i.e. they require the entire underlying transition system to be present in the memory. In general, they result in a model checking procedure that needs time exponential in the size of the transition system and the size of the formula. The space needed is quadratic in the size of the transition system and the size of the formula.

Here we show that FLC model checking can be done locally. We define games similar to the model checking games for $\mathcal{L}_\mu$ from [12]. They work on single states instead of sets and allow the transition system to be built up on demand. The sets of states in the tableaux of [9] are not used explicitly, but are implicitly present as stacks of FLC formulas in the games of this paper. This results in a better complexity for fixed formulas, PSPACE for the games as opposed to EXPTIME for the tableaux. Moreover, if the alternation depth and the sequential depth, which is to be defined, of the input formula are fixed, then the games like the tableaux from [9] yield a PSPACE algorithm as well. Therefore, the games behave better than the tableaux, i.e. they are more suitable for verification purposes.

Furthermore, games are naturally equipped with the ability to show the user of a verification tool why a formula is not fulfilled. This is simply done by playing a game according to a winning strategy. It is not obviously clear how to show the non-existence of a successful tableaux.

It is well known that a game graph for a finite transition system and a modal μ-calculus formula is nothing else but an alternating tree automaton. No automata-based model checker for FLC is known so far. The games of this paper suggest that alternating push-down tree automata might be the right machinery for this.

For a more thorough discussion of examples of FLC formulas and properties of the logic see [10] and [9]. The rest of the paper is structured as follows. In section 2 we recall the syntax and semantics of FLC. The model checking games are defined and shown to be sound and complete in section 3. Finally, section 4 analyses the complexity of game-based FLC model checking.

2   Preliminaries

Let $\mathcal{P} = \{\mathtt{tt}, \mathtt{ff}, q, \overline{q}, \ldots\}$ be a set of propositional constants that is closed under complementation, $\mathcal{V} = \{Z, Y, \ldots\}$ a set of propositional variables, and $\mathcal{A} = \{a, b, \ldots\}$ a set of action names. A labelled *transition system* is a graph $\mathcal{T} = (\mathcal{S}, \{\xrightarrow{a} \mid a \in \mathcal{A}\}, L)$ where $\mathcal{S}$ is a set of states, $\xrightarrow{a}$ for each $a \in \mathcal{A}$ is a binary relation on states and $L : \mathcal{S} \to 2^{\mathcal{P}}$ labels the states such that, for all $s \in \mathcal{S} : q \in L(s)$

iff $\bar{q} \notin L(s)$, $\mathbf{tt} \in L(s)$, and $\mathbf{ff} \notin L(s)$. We will use infix notation $s \xrightarrow{a} t$ for transition relations.

Formulas of FLC are given by

$$\varphi \quad ::= \quad q \mid Z \mid \tau \mid \langle a \rangle \mid [a] \mid \varphi \vee \varphi \mid \varphi \wedge \varphi \mid \mu Z.\varphi \mid \nu Z.\varphi \mid \varphi;\varphi$$

where $q \in \mathcal{P}$, $Z \in \mathcal{V}$, and $a \in \mathcal{A}$.[1] We will write σ for μ or ν. To save brackets we introduce the convention that ; binds stronger than $\wedge$ which binds stronger than $\vee$. Formulas are assumed to be well named in the sense that each binder variable is distinct. Our main interest is with closed formulas, that do not have free variables, in which case there is a function $fp : \mathcal{V} \to$ FLC that maps each variable to its defining fixed point formula (that may contain free variables).

The set $Sub(\varphi)$ of subformulas of φ is defined as usual, with $Sub(\sigma Z.\psi) = \{\sigma Z.\psi\} \cup Sub(\psi)$. We say that Z depends on Y in φ, written $Z \prec_\varphi Y$, if Y occurs free in $fp(Z)$. We write $Z <_\varphi Y$ iff (Z, Y) is in the transitive closure of $\prec_\varphi$. The *alternation depth* of φ, $ad(\varphi)$, is the maximal k in a chain $Z_0 <_\varphi Z_1 <_\varphi \ldots <_\varphi Z_k$ of variables in φ s.t. Z_{i-1} and Z_i are of different fixed point types for $0 < i \leq k$.

The *tail* of a variable Z in a formula φ, tl_Z is a set consisting of those formulas that occur "behind" Z in $fp(Z)$ in φ. We assume that φ is derivable from the context and avoid to put it into the subscript of tl. In order to define it technically we use sequential composition for sets of formulas in a straightforward way: $\{\varphi_0, \ldots, \varphi_n\}; \psi := \{\varphi_0; \psi, \ldots, \varphi_n; \psi\}$. We also use the eponymous function $tl_Z : Sub(\varphi) \to 2^{Sub(\varphi)}$ where

$$tl_Z(q) \quad := \{q\} \qquad\qquad tl_Z(\varphi \vee \psi) := tl_Z(\varphi) \cup tl_Z(\psi)$$

$$tl_Z(\langle a \rangle) \quad := \{\langle a \rangle\} \qquad\quad tl_Z(\varphi \wedge \psi) := tl_Z(\varphi) \cup tl_Z(\psi)$$

$$tl_Z([a]) \quad := \{[a]\} \qquad\quad tl_Z(\sigma Y.\psi) := tl_Z(\psi)$$

$$tl_Z(\varphi; \psi) := T_1 \cup T_2 \qquad tl_Z(Y) \quad := \begin{cases} \{Y\} & \text{if } Y \neq Z \\ \{\tau\} & \text{o.w.} \end{cases}$$

with

$$T_1 \quad := \begin{cases} tl_Z(\varphi); \psi & \text{if } Z \in Sub(\varphi) \\ \{\tau\} & \text{o.w.} \end{cases} \qquad T_2 \quad := \begin{cases} tl_Z(\psi) & \text{if } Z \in Sub(\psi) \\ \{\tau\} & \text{o.w.} \end{cases}$$

The tail of Z in φ is simply calculated as $tl_Z := tl_Z(fp(Z))$.

Like the alternation depth of a formula φ, its *sequential depth* $sd(\varphi)$ is an important factor in the complexity of the model checking problem. Informally the sequential depth of a formula is the maximal number of times a variable is sequentially composed with itself. It is defined as $sd(\varphi) := max\{sd_Z(fp(Z)) \mid Z \in Sub(\varphi)\} - 1$ where

---

[1] In [10], τ is called $\mathbf{term}$.

$$sd_Z(\varphi \vee \psi) := max\{sd_Z(\varphi), sd_Z(\psi)\} \qquad sd_Z(\varphi \wedge \psi) := max\{sd_Z(\varphi), sd_Z(\psi)\}$$

$$sd_Z(\varphi; \psi) := sd_Z(\varphi) + sd_Z(\psi) \qquad\qquad sd_Z(\sigma Y.\varphi) := sd_Z(\varphi)$$

$$sd_Z(\psi) := 0 \text{ if } \psi \in \{q, \tau, \langle a \rangle, [a]\} \qquad sd_Z(Y) := \begin{cases} 1 & \text{if } Y = Z \\ 0 & \text{o.w.} \end{cases}$$

Important syntactical fragments of FLC are those with fixed alternation and sequential depth.

$$\text{FLC}^{k,n} := \{\varphi \in \text{FLC} \mid ad(\varphi) \leq k, sd(\varphi) \leq n\}$$

$$\text{FLC}^{k,\omega} := \bigcup_{n \in \mathbb{N}} \text{FLC}^{k,n} \qquad \text{FLC}^{\omega,n} := \bigcup_{k \in \mathbb{N}} \text{FLC}^{k,n}$$

An *environment* $\rho : \mathcal{V} \to (2^S \to 2^S)$ maps variables to monotone functions of sets to sets. $\rho[Z \mapsto f]$ is the function that maps Z to f and agrees with ρ on all other arguments. The semantics $[\![\cdot]\!]_\rho^{\mathcal{T}} : 2^S \to 2^S$ of an FLC formula, relative to $\mathcal{T}$ and ρ, is a monotone function on subsets of states with respect to the inclusion ordering on 2^S. These functions together with the partial order given by

$$f \sqsubseteq g \text{ iff } \forall X \subseteq S : f(X) \subseteq g(X)$$

form a complete lattice with joins $\sqcup$ and meets $\sqcap$. By the Tarski-Knaster Theorem [13] the least and greatest fixed points of functionals $F : (2^S \to 2^S) \to (2^S \to 2^S)$ exist. They are used to interpret fixed point formulas of FLC.

To simplify the notation we assume a transition system $\mathcal{T}$ to be fixed for the remainder of the paper, and drop it from the semantic brackets.

$$[\![q]\!]_\rho = \lambda X.\{s \in S \mid q \in L(s)\}$$
$$[\![Z]\!]_\rho = \rho(Z)$$
$$[\![\tau]\!]_\rho = \lambda X.X$$
$$[\![\varphi \vee \psi]\!]_\rho = \lambda X.[\![\varphi]\!]_\rho(X) \cup [\![\psi]\!]_\rho(X)$$
$$[\![\varphi \wedge \psi]\!]_\rho = \lambda X.[\![\varphi]\!]_\rho(X) \cap [\![\psi]\!]_\rho(X)$$
$$[\![\langle a \rangle]\!]_\rho = \lambda X.\{s \in S \mid \exists t \in X, \text{ s.t. } s \xrightarrow{a} t\}$$
$$[\![[a]]\!]_\rho = \lambda X.\{s \in S \mid \forall t \in S, s \xrightarrow{a} t \Rightarrow t \in X\}$$
$$[\![\mu Z.\varphi]\!]_\rho = \bigsqcap\{f : 2^S \to 2^S \mid f \text{ monotone}, [\![\varphi]\!]_{\rho[Z \mapsto f]} \sqsubseteq f\}$$
$$[\![\nu Z.\varphi]\!]_\rho = \bigsqcup\{f : 2^S \to 2^S \mid f \text{ monotone}, f \sqsubseteq [\![\varphi]\!]_{\rho[Z \mapsto f]}\}$$
$$[\![\varphi; \psi]\!]_\rho = [\![\varphi]\!]_\rho \circ [\![\psi]\!]_\rho$$

A state s satisfies a formula φ under ρ, written $s \models_\rho \varphi$, iff $s \in [\![\varphi]\!]_\rho(S)$. If φ is a closed formula then ρ can be omitted and we write $[\![\varphi]\!](S)$ as well as $s \models \varphi$.

Two formulas φ and ψ are *equivalent*, written $\varphi \equiv \psi$, iff their semantics are the same, i.e. for every $\mathcal{T}$ and every ρ: $[\![\varphi]\!]_\rho^{\mathcal{T}} = [\![\psi]\!]_\rho^{\mathcal{T}}$.

In [10] it is shown how to embed $\mathcal{L}_\mu$ into FLC by using sequential composition: for instance, $\langle a \rangle \varphi$ becomes $\langle a \rangle; \varphi$. Therefore, we will sometimes omit the semicolon to maintain a strong resemblance to the syntax of $\mathcal{L}_\mu$. For example, $\langle a \rangle Z \langle a \rangle$ abbreviates $\langle a \rangle; Z; \langle a \rangle$. Note that $tl_Z = \emptyset$ for every Z in a formula that arises from this translation. We set $\text{FLC}^- := \{\varphi \in \text{FLC} \mid tl_Z = \emptyset \text{ for all}$

$$(\lor) : \frac{s,\delta \vdash \varphi_0 \lor \varphi_1}{s,\delta \vdash \varphi_i} \; \exists i \qquad\qquad (\land) : \frac{s,\delta \vdash \varphi_0 \land \varphi_1}{s,\delta \vdash \varphi_i} \; \forall i$$

$$\text{FP} : \frac{s,\delta \vdash \sigma Z.\varphi}{s,\delta \vdash Z} \qquad\qquad \text{VAR} : \frac{s,\delta \vdash Z}{s,\delta \vdash \varphi} \; \text{if } fp(Z) = \sigma Z.\varphi$$

$$(;) : \frac{s,\delta \vdash \varphi_0;\varphi_1}{s,\varphi_1 \delta \vdash \varphi_0} \qquad\qquad \text{TERM} : \frac{s,\psi\delta \vdash \tau}{s,\delta \vdash \psi}$$

$$\text{DIAM} : \frac{s,\psi\delta \vdash \langle a \rangle}{t,\delta \vdash \psi} \; \exists s \xrightarrow{a} t \qquad\qquad \text{BOX} : \frac{s,\psi\delta \vdash [a]}{t,\delta \vdash \psi} \; \forall s \xrightarrow{a} t$$

Fig. 1. The model checking game rules

$Z \in Sub(\varphi)\}$. The fragment of FLC that is the image of $\mathcal{L}_\mu$ under the described translation is a genuine subset of FLC$^-$.

We introduce *approximants* of fixed point formulas. Let $fp(Z) = \mu Z.\varphi$ for some φ and let $\alpha, \lambda \in \mathbb{O}\text{rd}$, the ordinals, where λ is a limit ordinal. Then $Z^0 := $ ff, $Z^{\alpha+1} = \varphi[Z^\alpha/Z]$, $Z^\lambda = \bigvee_{\alpha<\lambda} Z^\alpha$. If $fp(Z) = \nu Z.\varphi$ then $Z^0 := $ tt, $Z^{\alpha+1} = \varphi[Z^\alpha/Z]$, $Z^\lambda = \bigwedge_{\alpha<\lambda} Z^\alpha$. Note that $\mu Z.\varphi \equiv \bigvee_{\alpha \in \mathbb{O}\text{rd}} Z^\alpha$ and $\nu Z.\varphi \equiv \bigwedge_{\alpha \in \mathbb{O}\text{rd}} Z^\alpha$. If only finite transition systems are considered $\mathbb{O}\text{rd}$ can be replaced by $\mathbb{N}$. If the size $|\mathcal{S}|$ of the underlying transition system is fixed then it serves as an upper bound for the number of approximants needed. This is expressed in the following Lemma which was proved in [9].

Lemma 1. *(Approximants)* Let $\mathcal{T} = (\mathcal{S}, \{\xrightarrow{a} \mid a \in \mathcal{A}\}, L)$ be finite with $s \in \mathcal{S}, S \subseteq \mathcal{S}$.
a) $s \in [\![\mu Z.\varphi]\!]_\rho^{\mathcal{T}}(S)$ iff $\exists k \leq |\mathcal{S}|$, s.t. $s \in [\![Z^k]\!]_\rho^{\mathcal{T}}(S)$.
b) $s \in [\![\nu Z.\varphi]\!]_\rho^{\mathcal{T}}(S)$ iff $\forall k \leq |\mathcal{S}|: s \in [\![Z^k]\!]_\rho^{\mathcal{T}}(S)$.

3   Model Checking Games

Model checking games are played by two players, called $\exists$ and $\forall$, on a transition system and an FLC formula φ. Note that here we do not restrict ourselves to finite transition systems only. Player $\exists$ tries to establish that a given state s of a transition system $\mathcal{T}$ satisfies φ, whereas $\forall$ tries to show that $s \not\models \varphi$.

A play is a (possibly infinite) sequence $C_0, C_1, \ldots$ of configurations, and a configuration is an element of $Conf = \mathcal{S} \times Sub(\varphi)^* \times Sub(\varphi)$. It is written $s, \delta \vdash \psi$ where δ is interpreted as a stack of subformulas with its top on the left. The empty stack is denoted by ϵ. With a stack $\delta = \varphi_0 \ldots \varphi_k$ we associate the formula $\delta := \varphi_0; \ldots; \varphi_k$ while ϵ is associated with the formula τ.

Each play for s_0 of $\mathcal{T}$ and φ begins with $C_0 = s_0, \epsilon \vdash \varphi$. A play proceeds according to rules given in figure 1. Some of them require one of the players to choose a subformula or a state. This is indicated at the right side of a rule. Rules ($\vee$) and ($\wedge$) are straightforward. Rules VAR and FP are justified by the unfolding characterisations of fixed points: $\sigma Z.\varphi \equiv \varphi[\sigma Z.\varphi/Z]$. If a formula $\varphi; \psi$ is encountered ψ is stored on the stack with rule (;) to be dealt with later on while the players try to prove or refute φ. Modalities cause either of the players to choose a successor state. After that rules DIAM and BOX pop the top formula from the stack into the right side of the actual configuration. Rule TERM does the same without a choice of one of the players. In both cases the last formula on the right-hand side has been proved and those formulas that have been collected on the stack need to be proved or refuted.

Before we can define the winning conditions we need another definition. A variable Z is called *stack-increasing* in a play $C_0, C_1, \ldots$ if there are infinitely many configurations $C_{i_0}, C_{i_1}, \ldots$, s.t.

- $i_j < i_{j+1}$ for all $j \in \mathbb{N}$
- $C_{i_j} = s_j, \delta_j \vdash Z$ for some s_j and δ_j,
- for all $j \in \mathbb{N}$ exists $\gamma \in tl_Z \cup \{\epsilon\}$ s.t. $\delta_{j+1} = \gamma \delta_j$, and $\gamma = \epsilon$ iff $tl_Z = \emptyset$.

Player $\exists$ wins a play $C_0, \ldots, C_n, \ldots$ iff

1. $C_n = s, \delta \vdash q$ and $q \in L(s)$, or
2. $C_n = s, \epsilon \vdash \tau$, or
3. $C_n = s, \epsilon \vdash \langle a \rangle$ and there is a $t \in \mathcal{S}$, s.t. $s \xrightarrow{a} t$, or
4. $C_n = s, \delta \vdash [a]$, and $\delta = \epsilon$ or $\nexists t \in \mathcal{S}$, s.t. $s \xrightarrow{a} t$, or
5. the play is infinite, and there is a $Z \in \mathcal{V}$ s.t. Z is the greatest, w.r.t. $<_\varphi$, stack-increasing variable and $fp(Z) = \nu Z.\psi$ for some ψ.

Player $\forall$ wins such a play iff

6. $C_n = s, \delta \vdash q$ and $q \notin L(s)$, or
7. $C_n = s, \delta \vdash \langle a \rangle$, and $\nexists t \in \mathcal{S}$, s.t. $s \xrightarrow{a} t$, or
8. the play is infinite, and there is a $Z \in \mathcal{V}$ s.t. Z is the greatest, w.r.t. $<_\varphi$, stack-increasing variable and $fp(Z) = \mu Z.\psi$ for some ψ.

Winning conditions 1 and 6 suggest that game rule (;) can be refined. Whenever the formula to be put on the stack is a $q \in Prop$ then the existing stack can be discarded. This does not effect the worst-case complexities, therefore we merely mention this optimisation.

A player has a winning strategy, or simply wins the game, for $s, \delta \vdash \varphi$ if she can enforce a winning play for herself, starting with this configuration.

The *full game tree* T for $C = s, \delta \vdash \varphi$ is the tree of configurations whose paths are plays starting with C. If player p has a winning strategy for C then the *game tree for player* p arises from T in the following way. If the next move is deterministic or taken by player $\bar{p}$ preserve and continue with all successor nodes. If the next configuration is chosen by p then preserve one successor C' s.t. p wins the game starting with C'. Obviously, the game tree for p is a representation of a winning strategy for p on C.

$$s, \epsilon \vdash \mu Y.\langle b \rangle \vee \langle a \rangle \nu Z.Y; Z; Y$$
$$\overline{s, \epsilon \vdash Y}$$
$$\overline{s, \epsilon \vdash \langle b \rangle \vee \langle a \rangle \nu Z.Y; Z; Y}$$
$$\overline{s, \epsilon \vdash \langle a \rangle \nu Z.Y; Z; Y} \quad \exists \langle a \rangle \nu Z.Y; Z; Y$$
$$\overline{s, \nu Z.Y; Z; Y \vdash \langle a \rangle}$$
$$\overline{t, \epsilon \vdash \nu Z.Y; Z; Y} \quad \exists s \xrightarrow{a} t$$
$$\overline{t, \epsilon \vdash Z}$$
$$\overline{t, \epsilon \vdash Y; Z; Y}$$
$$\overline{t, Z; Y \vdash Y}$$
$$\overline{t, Z; Y \vdash \langle b \rangle \vee \langle a \rangle \nu Z.Y; Z; Y}$$
$$\overline{t, Z; Y \vdash \langle b \rangle} \quad \exists \langle b \rangle$$
$$\overline{t, Y \vdash Z} \quad \exists t \xrightarrow{b} t$$
$$\overline{t, Y \vdash Y; Z; Y}$$
$$\overline{t, Z; Y; Y \vdash Y}$$
$$\vdots$$

Fig. 2. $\exists$'s winning play from example 1

The following example illustrates the importance of being stack-increasing. Note that in a $\mathcal{L}_\mu$ model checking game the winner is determined by the outermost variable that occurs infinitely often. There, if two variables Y and Z occur infinitely often then, say, $Y <_\varphi Z$, and $fp(Y)$ occurs infinitely often, too. Thus two occurrences of Y cannot be related to each other in terms of approximants. FLC only has this property for stack-increasing variables.

Example 1. Let $\varphi = \mu Y.\langle b \rangle \vee \langle a \rangle \nu Z.Y; Z; Y$. $ad(\varphi) = 1$ and $sd(\varphi) = 2$. Let $\mathcal{T}$ be the transition system consisting of states $\{s, t\}$ and transitions $s \xrightarrow{a} t$ and $t \xrightarrow{b} t$. $s \models \varphi$. The game tree for player $\exists$ is shown in figure 2. Since φ does not contain any $\wedge$, $[a]$, or $[b]$ player $\forall$ does not make any choices and the tree is in fact a single play.

Y and Z occur infinitely often in the play. However, neither $fp(Y)$ nor $fp(Z)$ does. Note that $Z <_\varphi Y$. Y gets "fulfilled" each time it is replaced by its defining fixed point formula, but reproduced by Z. On the other hand, Y does not start a new computation of $fp(Z)$ each time it is reproduced. But Y is not stack-increasing whereas Z is. And Z denotes a greatest fixed point, therefore player $\exists$ wins this play.

Before we can prove soundness and completeness of the games we need a few technical lemmas. Let $\mathcal{T} = (\mathcal{S}, \{\xrightarrow{a} \mid a \in \mathcal{A}\}, L)$, $s \in \mathcal{S}$, $\varphi \in$ FLC, and $C = s, \delta \vdash \psi$ be a configuration in a game for s and φ. C is called *true* if $s \in \llbracket \varphi \rrbracket (\llbracket \delta \rrbracket (\mathcal{S}))$, and *false* otherwise.

Lemma 2. *Player* $\exists$ *preserves falsity and can preserve truth with her choices. Player* $\forall$ *preserves truth and can preserve falsity with his choices.*

Proof. First consider those choices involving disjuncts and conjuncts. Take a configuration $C = s, \delta \vdash \varphi_0 \vee \varphi_1$. Suppose C is false, i.e. $s \notin [\![\varphi_0]\!]([\![\delta]\!](\mathcal{S}))$ and $s \notin [\![\varphi_1]\!]([\![\delta]\!](\mathcal{S}))$. Regardless of which i player $\exists$ chooses, the configuration $s, \delta \vdash \varphi_i$ will be false. On the other hand, suppose C is true. Then $s \in [\![\varphi_0]\!]([\![\delta]\!](\mathcal{S}))$ or $s \in [\![\varphi_1]\!]([\![\delta]\!](\mathcal{S}))$, and player $\exists$ can preserve truth by choosing i accordingly.

Now consider a configuration $C = s, \psi\delta \vdash \langle a \rangle$. If C is true then there is a t s.t. $s \xrightarrow{a} t$ and $t \in [\![\psi; \delta]\!](\mathcal{S})$. By choosing this t, player $\exists$ can make the next configuration $t, \delta \vdash \psi$ true. If C is false then there is no such t and regardless of which transition $\exists$ chooses the following configuration will be false, too.

The proofs of the other cases are dual. $\qquad\square$

Note that the rules that do not require a player to make a choice preserve both truth and falsity if variables are interpreted via their approximants.

Lemma 3. *Let* $\mathcal{T} = (\mathcal{S}, \{\xrightarrow{a} \mid a \in \mathcal{A}\}, L)$, $s \in \mathcal{S}$, $\varphi \in FLC$. *In a play* $C_0, C_1, \ldots$ *for* s *and* φ *there is a unique greatest, with respect to* $<_\varphi$, *stack-increasing variable* Z, *if such one exists.*

Proof. Obviously, a finite play cannot have a stack-increasing variable. Let the infinite play at hand be $C_0, C_1, \ldots$. Suppose first there are two stack-increasing variables Z and Y. Then there must be two configurations $C_i = s, \delta \vdash Z$ and $C_j = t, \delta' \vdash Y$ with $i < j$. Either Y has been generated from the unfolding of Z in which case one of them is greater than the other. The reason is that the stack only contains elements of tl_V for some variable V. But $Y \in tl_Z$ implies either Y is free in $fp(Z)$ or $fp(Y) \in Sub(fp(Z))$. Therefore they must be comparable.

Suppose $\delta = \delta_0 Y \delta_1$. But then Z has either been generated from the unfolding of Y and they are comparable or $\delta' = \delta_0' Z \delta_1'$. At every configuration the stack can only hold a finite number of variables. Therefore, in such an infinite play it is not possible that neither of the variables generates the other one infinitely often, and they must be comparable.

It remains to show that at least one variable is stack-increasing. Obviously, there must be a variable Z that occurs infinitely often. Moreover, this Z must generate itself infinitely often. Let $fp(Z) = \sigma Z.\varphi$. This means that for every occurrence of Z in a $C_i = s, \delta \vdash Z$, when Z is replaced by φ, the play must follow the syntactical structure of φ to one occurrence of Z in φ. In order to pop an element from δ an atomic formula in φ must have been reached, and Z in C_i did no regenerate itself. Suppose it did and the stack has been increased. Since rule VAR replaces a variable Z with its defining fixed point formula φ the additional part of the stack must consist of subformulas of φ only. Moreover, every subformula that occurs "before" Z in φ must have been removed from the stack before Z can be reached again. Therefore, the extension of the stack must be an element of tl_Z. $\qquad\square$

One important property of a stack-increasing variable is: If its occurrence in a configuration $s, \delta \vdash Z$ is interpreted as the approximant Z^{α} then in its next occurrence Z will denote $Z^{\alpha-1}$. This is because Z is outermost in the play at hand and thus the computation of $fp(Z)$ does not get restarted.

Theorem 1. (Soundness) *Let* $\mathfrak{T} = (\mathcal{S}, \{\xrightarrow{a} \mid a \in \mathcal{A}\}, L)$ *with* $s \in \mathcal{S}$ *and* $\varphi, \delta_0 \in$ *FLC. If* $s \notin [\![\varphi; \delta_0]\!](\mathcal{S})$ *then* $\forall$ *wins* $s, \delta_0 \vdash \varphi$.

Proof. Suppose $s \notin [\![\varphi]\!]([\![\delta_0]\!](\mathcal{S}))$. We construct a (possibly infinite) game tree for $\forall$ starting with $s, \delta_0 \vdash \varphi$. If $\varphi = \varphi_0 \wedge \varphi_1$, $\forall$ chooses the φ_i that makes $s, \delta \vdash \varphi_i$ false. If $\varphi = \varphi_0 \vee \varphi_1$ then the game tree is extended with both false configurations $s, \delta \vdash \varphi_i$. Similar arguments hold for the applications of rules DIAM, BOX, and TERM. Since falsity is preserved no finite path can be won by player $\exists$ since a false leaf implies that $\forall$ is the winner of that particular play.

We show that the game tree can be constructed such that player $\exists$ cannot win an infinite play either. Suppose the construction of the game tree reaches a configuration $t, \delta \vdash \nu Z.\psi$, s.t. Z is the unique stack-increasing variable according to Lemma 3. In the following configuration $t, \delta \vdash Z$, Z is interpreted as the least approximant Z^{α} s.t. $t \notin [\![Z^{\alpha}]\!]([\![\delta]\!](\mathcal{S}))$ but $t \in [\![Z^{\alpha-1}]\!]([\![\delta]\!](\mathcal{S}))$. Note that α cannot be a limit ordinal λ since $t \notin [\![\bigwedge_{\beta<\lambda} Z^{\beta}]\!](S)$ for any $S \subseteq \mathcal{S}$ implies $t \notin [\![Z^{\beta}]\!](S)$ for some $\beta < \lambda$. The next time a configuration $t', \delta' \vdash Z$ is reached Z is consequently interpreted as $Z^{\alpha-1}$. Again, if $\alpha - 1$ is a limit ordinal λ, then there must be a $\beta < \alpha$ such that $t' \notin [\![Z^{\beta}]\!]([\![\delta']\!](\mathcal{S}))$.

But ordinals are well-founded, i.e. the play must eventually reach a false configuration $t'', \delta'' \vdash Z$ in which Z is interpreted as Z^0. But $Z^0 \equiv \mathsf{tt}$ and $t'' \notin [\![\mathsf{tt}]\!](S)$ is not possible for any $S \subseteq \mathcal{S}$. We conclude that there is no least α that makes $t, \delta \vdash Z^{\alpha}$ false and that therefore $t, \delta \vdash \nu Z.\psi$ could not have been false either.

Since player $\exists$ cannot win any play in the game tree that is constructed in the described way player $\forall$ must win the game on $s, \delta_0 \vdash \varphi$. □

Theorem 2. (Completeness) *Let* $\mathfrak{T} = (\mathcal{S}, \{\xrightarrow{a} \mid a \in \mathcal{A}\}, L)$ *with* $s \in \mathcal{S}$ *and* $\varphi, \delta_0 \in$ *FLC. If* $s \in [\![\varphi; \delta_0]\!](\mathcal{S})$ *then* $\exists$ *wins* $s, \delta_0 \vdash \varphi$.

Proof. The proof is dual to the proof of the soundness theorem. Here, assuming $s \in [\![\varphi]\!]([\![\delta_0]\!](\mathcal{S}))$ we build a game tree for player $\exists$ starting with the true configuration $s, \delta_0 \vdash \varphi$ and preserving truth. If the construction of the game tree reaches a leaf the corresponding play must be won by $\exists$ since only she wins a finite play that ends with a true configuration.

Again, we show that player $\forall$ cannot win an infinite play either. Suppose there is a configuration $t, \delta \vdash \mu Y.\psi$ with Y being stack-increasing according to Lemma 3. In the next step, Y is interpreted as the least approximant Y^{α} s.t. $t \in [\![Y^{\alpha}]\!]([\![\delta]\!](\mathcal{S}))$ but $t \notin [\![Y^{\alpha-1}]\!]([\![\delta]\!](\mathcal{S}))$. Again, α cannot be a limit ordinal. The next time a configuration $t', \delta' \vdash Y$ is reached it becomes true if Y is interpreted as $Y^{\alpha-1}$. If $\alpha - 1$ is a limit ordinal then there is a smaller one that makes the configuration true.

Because of well-foundedness of the ordinals every infinite play must reach a configuration $t'', \delta'' \vdash Y$ in which Y is interpreted as Y^0. But $Y^0 \equiv \text{ff}$ and therefore $t'', \delta'' \vdash Y$ cannot be true. Thus, $t, \delta \vdash \mu Y.\psi$ could not have been true either.

Since player $\forall$ cannot win any play of the game tree that is constructed in the described way player $\exists$ must win the game starting with $s, \delta_0 \vdash \varphi$.   □

From Theorem 1 and 2 follows that the model checking problem for FLC can be rephrased as: $s \models \varphi$ iff player $\exists$ wins $s, \epsilon \vdash \varphi$.

4   Decidability and Complexity

In [10] Müller-Olm has shown that FLC model checking is undecidable for BPA already. We show that this result can easily be improved a bit.

Theorem 3. *FLC model checking is undecidable for normed deterministic BPA.*

Proof. Based on an early result from language theory in [4] it is shown in [6] that the simulation problem for deterministic normed BPA is undecidable. Given a BPA process Q one can construct an FLC formula ϕ_Q, s.t. $P \models \phi_Q$ iff P simulates Q. The construction for arbitrary BPA processes is shown in [10] and works in particular for normed deterministic BPA.   □

However, over finite transition systems the model checking problem for FLC is decidable [10, 9]. We describe how the games of the previous section can be used to obtain a local model checker.

Theorem 4. *Let* $\mathcal{T} = (\mathcal{S}, \{\xrightarrow{a} \mid a \in \mathcal{A}\}, L)$ *be finite with* $s \in \mathcal{S}$ *and* $\varphi, \delta \in FLC^{k,n}$. *Deciding the winner of* $s, \delta \vdash \varphi$ *is in PSPACE for all* $k, n \in \mathbb{N}$.

Proof. If the underlying transition system is finite then the least approximants used in the proofs of Theorem 1 and 2 are bounded by $|\mathcal{S}|$ according to Lemma 1. An algorithm deciding the winner of $s, \delta \vdash \varphi$ can index variables occurring in a play as the corresponding approximant. This means, rules FP and VAR are used as

$$\frac{s, \delta \vdash \sigma Z.\varphi}{s, \delta \vdash Z^{|\mathcal{S}|}} \qquad \frac{s, \delta \vdash Z^k}{s, \delta \vdash \varphi[Z^{k-1}/Z]} \quad \text{if } fp(Z) = \sigma Z.\varphi$$

Then, configurations of the form $t, \delta \vdash Z^0$ with $fp(Z) = \sigma Z.\psi$ for some ψ, δ and t are winning for player $\exists$ if $\sigma = \nu$ and winning for player $\forall$ if $\sigma = \mu$.

Next we analyse the maximum length of a play of $s, \delta \vdash \varphi$. Suppose $ad(\varphi) = 0$. At most $O(|\mathcal{S}| \cdot |\varphi|)$ steps are possible before a terminal configuration with a Z^0 must be reached, if the sequential depth of φ is 0. However, if it is greater than 0 then at the beginning a $Z^{|\mathcal{S}|}$ can be pushed onto the stack where it remains while another Z^k gets unfolded at most $|\mathcal{S}|$ times before it might disappear. Then the $Z^{|\mathcal{S}|}$ from the stack can be popped and create the same situation by unfolding to more than one $Z^{|S|-1}$ of which one remains on the stack again. Generally, the maximum length of a play in this situation is $O((|S| \cdot |\varphi|)^{sd(\varphi)})$.

Let now $ad(\varphi) = k > 0$. Take the outermost variable Z that occurs in the play at hand. With each unfolding it can start a subplay on a formula with alternation depth $k - 1$. Therefore the overall maximum length of the play is $O(((|S| \cdot |\varphi|)^{sd(\varphi)})^{ad(\varphi)}) = O((|S| \cdot |\varphi|)^{sd(\varphi) \cdot ad(\varphi)})$.

An alternating algorithm can decide the winner of $s, \delta \vdash \varphi$ by simply playing the game for it. For input formulas $\delta, \varphi \in \mathrm{FLC}^{k,n}$ the alternation depth and sequential depth are bounded. Thus, the time needed is polynomial in the size of the formula and the size of the transition system. According to [1] there is a deterministic procedure that needs space which is polynomial in the size of the formula and in the size of the transition system.   □

This argument, applied to formulas of arbitrary alternation or sequential depth, yields an EXPSPACE procedure. This follows from the fact that the alternating algorithm needs time exponential in the alternation and sequential depth of the input formula, and AEXPTIME = EXPSPACE. To show that game-based model checking for FLC can be done in EXPTIME an alternating algorithm must not use more than polynomial space. Equally, a single play must be playable using at most polynomial space.

We show why this is not likely to be possible. First we consider a slightly different way of proving soundness and completeness of the games which only applies if the underlying transition system is finite. Remember that in the proofs of Theorem 1 and 2 variables are interpreted as approximants, and contradictions arise at configurations $t, \delta' \vdash Z^0$. Suppose $fp(Z) = \mu Z.\psi$ and the game tree is constructed preserving truth. Then at its first occurrence Z is interpreted as the least Z^k which makes the configuration, say, $t, \delta' \vdash Z^k$ true. However, if later another true configuration $t, \delta'' \vdash Z^j$ is seen and $[\![\delta'']\!](S) \subseteq [\![\delta']\!](S)$ then this contradicts the fact that k was chosen least.

This occurs trivially after $O(|S| \cdot 2^{|S|})$ steps since there are only $|S|$ many different states and $2^{|S|}$ many different sets of them. In most cases this situation will occur in a stack of polynomial size already. However, there are cases in which the stack can grow super-polynomially. That means there are m configurations $s_i, \delta_i \vdash Z$ s.t. $[\![\delta_i]\!](S) \not\subseteq [\![\delta_j]\!](S)$ for $j < i \leq m$ and m is not polynomially bounded by the input size.

Example 2. Let $a, b \in \mathcal{A}$. Take n pairwise different prime numbers $p_1, \ldots, p_n$. Let $P_0 = 0$ and $P_i = \Sigma_{j=1}^{i} p_j$ be the sum of the first i prime numbers for $i = 1, \ldots, n - 1$. We construct a transition system $\mathcal{T} = (S, \{\xrightarrow{a} \mid a \in \mathcal{A}\}, L)$ with $S = \{0, \ldots, P_n - 1\}$. Transitions in $\mathcal{T}$ are given by $j \xrightarrow{a} j + 1$ for all $j < P_n$, $j \neq P_i - 1$ for all $i \in \{1, \ldots, n\}$, and $P_i - 1 \xrightarrow{a} P_{i-1}$ for all $i \in \{1, \ldots, n\}$. Finally, $i \xrightarrow{b} j$ iff $j \xrightarrow{a} i$. $\mathcal{T}$ consists of n cycles of length $p_1, \ldots, p_n$ which can be traversed along a-transitions, say, clockwise and through b-transitions counterclockwise. Feel free to add as many c-transitions if $c \neq a$ and $c \neq b$ to make $\mathcal{T}$ connected. Finally, we use one proposition q which holds on one state of each cycle only. $q \in L(j)$ iff $j = P_i$ for some $i \in \{0, \ldots, n - 1\}$.

The formula under examination is $\varphi := (\nu Z.\tau \wedge \langle a \rangle Z \langle b \rangle); q$. It says that there is an a-path s.t. after each n a's another n b's can be done to satisfy q. $0 \not\models \varphi$ which can easily be seen using the games of the previous section. Player $\forall$ can never choose τ since $0 \models q$ and every sequence of m a-transitions away from 0 leads to a state that can do m b-transitions back to 0. But then player $\exists$ wins because the play repeats on a ν-variable. Her game tree is shown in figure 3.

If approximants are used explicitly as suggested in the proof of Theorem 4 the stack cannot grow larger than P_n. This is not surprising since $\varphi \in \text{FLC}^{0,0}$. However, let $S_q := \{P_i \mid i \in \{0, \dots, n-1\}\}$ be the set of all states satisfying q. We write $\langle b \rangle^i$ to abbreviate $\langle b \rangle; \dots; \langle b \rangle$, where it occurs exactly i times. We claim that $[\![\langle b \rangle^i]\!](S_q) \neq [\![\langle b \rangle^j]\!](S_q)$ for $i, j < \Pi_{i=1}^n p_i$, $i \neq j$. And, since $|[\![\langle b \rangle^i]\!](S_q)| = n$ for all $i < \Pi_{i=1}^n p_i$, even $[\![\langle b \rangle^i]\!](S_q) \not\subseteq [\![\langle b \rangle^j]\!](S_q)$ for $i, j < \Pi_{i=1}^n$, $i \neq j$. Take a state in the k-th cycle. It belongs to $[\![\langle b \rangle^i]\!](S_q)$ iff it is the $(i \bmod p_k)$-th b-predecessor of P_{k-1}. In other words, the sets $[\![\langle b \rangle^i]\!](S_q)$ can be defined by moving markers along a-transitions in each cycle starting with S_q. Since the lengths of the cycles are pairwise different prime numbers the same set is only marked after $\Pi_{i=1}^n p_i$ steps.

This means that the first $(\Pi_{i=1}^n p_i) - 1$ sequences $\langle b \rangle^i; q$ define pairwise uncomparable sets of states. Clearly, $\Pi_{i=1}^n p_i \notin O(n^k)$ for all $k \in \mathbb{N}$.

Corollary 1. *Let $\mathcal{T} = (\mathcal{S}, \{\xrightarrow{a} \mid a \in \mathcal{A}\}, L)$ be finite with $s \in \mathcal{S}$ and $\varphi, \delta \in FLC$. Deciding the winner of $s, \delta \vdash \varphi$ is in EXPSPACE.*

It should be mentioned that, if the requirement of locality is dropped, then model checking can be done in EXPTIME in the general case. For this, a configuration like $s, \delta \vdash \varphi; \psi$ can be model checked in the following way. Player $\exists$ chooses a set T s.t. $T = [\![\psi; \delta]\!](\mathcal{S})$. Then, player $\forall$ either selects to continue with $s, \epsilon \vdash \varphi$ and the additional winning requirement that player $\exists$ can only win if the last state reached in a subplay is a $t \in T$. Or he chooses a $t \in T$ and continues with $t, \delta \vdash \psi$. It is easy to see that the stack becomes obsolete and that therefore configurations are of polynomial size only. However, player $\exists$'s choice of T prevents the model checker from being local.

The next theorem analyses the complexity of the games if applied to $\mathcal{L}_\mu$ formulas. In this case it is helpful to start the game with an empty stack.

Theorem 5. *Let $\mathcal{T} = (\mathcal{S}, \{\xrightarrow{a} \mid a \in \mathcal{A}\}, L)$ be finite with $s \in \mathcal{S}$ and $\varphi \in FLC^-$. Deciding the winner of $s, \epsilon \vdash \varphi$ is in NP$\cap$co-NP.*

Proof. The stack can never grow larger than φ and will be empty each time a variable is reached. The resulting games are essentially the same as the model checking games for $\mathcal{L}_\mu$ from [12]. It is known from [3] for example that the winner of those games can be decided in NP$\cap$co-NP. The same technique applies here.

Clearly, the game graph for $s, \epsilon \vdash \varphi$ is finite and of size polynomial in the input. To decide whether player $\exists$ wins $s, \epsilon \vdash \varphi$ a nondeterministic algorithm can guess annotations $(k_1, \dots, k_n)$ for each μ-variable Y. The meaning of such an annotation is: Y has to be unfolded k_n times at this moment and there are

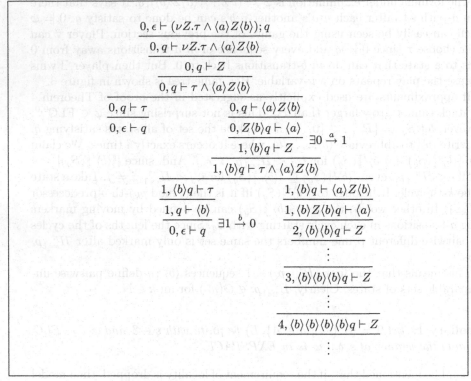

Fig. 3. ∃'s game tree from example 2

outer variables $Z_1, \ldots, Z_{n-1}$ which have been unfolded $k_1, \ldots, k_{n-1}$ times. The maximal size of such an annotation is $O(ad(\varphi) \cdot log|\mathcal{S}|)$.

Finally, the algorithm has to verify that the order of the annotations is well-founded, i.e. for every μ-variable Y: if there is a path from $s, \delta \vdash Y$ with annotation $K = k_1, \ldots, k_n$ to $t, \delta' \vdash Y$ with annotation $K' = k_1', \ldots, k_n'$ then K' is lexicographically smaller than K.

This proves that deciding the winner of $s, \epsilon \vdash \varphi$ is in NP. Inclusion in co-NP follows from the fact that the same argument applies to player ∀ and ν-variables to decide whether he wins $s, \epsilon \vdash \varphi$.   □

This is not a contradiction to the PSPACE-hardness proved in [9]. There, reductions from the validity problem for QBF and from the universal acceptance problem for NFAs are presented. In both cases the constructed formulas are not in FLC⁻.

Even if the starting stack in the game of Theorem 5 is non-empty the semantics of approximants will always be evaluated on the same set of states. However, if the stack is $\delta = \psi\delta'$ and deciding the winner of $t, \delta' \vdash \psi$ is in the complexity class $\mathcal{C}$ for any $t \in \mathcal{S}$, then deciding the winner of $s, \delta \vdash \varphi$ is in (NP∩co-NP)∪$\mathcal{C}$.

Theorem 5 becomes interesting if applied to formulas in FLC^- that are not a translation of a $\mathcal{L}_\mu$ formula but are equivalent to a formula in $\mathcal{L}_\mu$. One example is $\nu Z.(\langle a_0 \rangle \wedge \langle b_0 \rangle); \ldots; (\langle a_0 \rangle \wedge \langle b_0 \rangle); Z$ which is exponentially more succinct than its equivalent in $\mathcal{L}_\mu$, see [9]. Theorem 5 suggests that the model checking games for FLC behave better than those for $\mathcal{L}_\mu$ in this case, although equation-based model checkers for $\mathcal{L}_\mu$ can do equally well.

5   Conclusion

We have given a game-based account of the model checking problem for FLC. The main feature of the games is their ability to allow local model checking. This makes them suitable for verification purposes. We have also shown that the games are optimal for fixed alternation and sequential depth in terms of complexity bounds. These parameters can be assumed to be small for formulas that express properties desired in the verification of finite transition systems.

It is not known whether FLC's model checking problem for unbounded alternation depth is EXPTIME-hard. Compare this to the $\mathcal{L}_\mu$ situation: NP∩co-NP for the general case and P-complete for bounded alternation.

One candidate for establishing EXPTIME-hardness is the model checking problem for $\mathcal{L}_\mu$ and BPA or PDA. However, this cannot work since these problems are EXPTIME-complete for alternation free $\mathcal{L}_\mu$ formulas already. It remains to see whether EXPTIME-hardness can be established, and whether local FLC model checking for unbounded alternation depth is possible to do in EXPTIME.

References

[1] A. K. Chandra, D. C. Kozen, and L. J. Stockmeyer. Alternation. *Journal of the ACM*, 28(1):114–133, January 1981. 250

[2] E. A. Emerson. Temporal and modal logic. In J. van Leeuwen, editor, *Handbook of Theoretical Computer Science*, volume B: Formal Models and Semantics, chapter 14, pages 996–1072. Elsevier Science Publishers B. V.: Amsterdam, The Netherlands, New York, N. Y., 1990. 240

[3] E. A. Emerson, C. S. Jutla, and A. P. Sistla. On model checking for the μ-calculus and its fragments. *Theoretical Computer Science*, 258(1–3):491–522, 2001. 251

[4] E. P. Friedman. The inclusion problem for simple languages. *TCS*, 1(4):297–316, April 1976. 249

[5] R. Goré. Tableau methods for modal and temporal logics. In M. D'Agostino, D. Gabbay, R. Hähnle, and J. Posegga, editors, *Handbook of Tableau Methods*. Kluwer, Dordrecht, 1999. 240

[6] J. F. Groote and H. Hüttel. Undecidable equivalences for basic process algebra. *Information and Computation*, 115(2):354–371, December 1994. 249

[7] D. Janin and I. Walukiewicz. On the expressive completeness of the propositional μ-calculus with respect to monadic second order logic. In U. Montanari and V. Sassone, editors, *CONCUR '96: Concurrency Theory, 7th Int. Conf.*, volume 1119 of *LNCS*, pages 263–277, Pisa, Italy, 26–29 August 1996. Springer. 240

[8] D. Kozen. Results on the propositional mu-calculus. *TCS*, 27:333–354, December 1983. 240

[9] M. Lange and C. Stirling. Model checking fixed point logic with chop. In M. Nielsen and U. H. Engberg, editors, *Proc. Foundations of Software Science and Computation Structures, FOSSACS'02*, volume 2303 of *LNCS*, pages 250–263, Grenoble, France, 2002. Springer. 240, 241, 244, 249, 252, 253

[10] M. Müller-Olm. A modal fixpoint logic with chop. In C. Meinel and S. Tison, editors, *Proc. 16th Annual Symp. on Theoretical Aspects of Computer Science, STACS'99*, volume 1563 of *LNCS*, pages 510–520, Trier, Germany, 1999. Springer. 240, 241, 242, 243, 249

[11] C. Stirling. Modal and temporal logics. In *Handbook of Logic in Computer Science*, volume 2 (Background: Computational Structures), pages 477–563. Clarendon Press, Oxford, 1992. 240

[12] C. Stirling. Local model checking games. In I. Lee and S. A. Smolka, editors, *Proc. 6th Int. Conf. on Concurrency Theory, CONCUR'95*, volume 962 of *LNCS*, pages 1–11, Berlin, Germany, August 1995. Springer. 241, 251

[13] A. Tarski. A lattice-theoretical fixpoint theorem and its application. *Pacific J.Math.*, 5:285–309, 1955. 241, 243

A Decidable Fixpoint Logic for Time-Outs⋆

Maria Sorea⋆⋆

SRI International, Computer Science Laboratory
333 Ravenswood Avenue, Menlo Park, CA 94025, USA
sorea@csl.sri.com

Abstract. We show decidability of the satisfiability problem for an extension of the modal μ-calculus with event-recording clocks. Based on techniques for deciding the untimed μ-calculus, we present a complete set of reduction rules for constructing tableaux for formulas of this event-recording logic. To keep track of the actual value of the clocks, the premises and conclusions of our tableau rules are augmented with timing contexts, which are sets of timing constraints satisfied by the actual value of the clocks. The decidability problem is shown to be EXPTIME complete. In addition, we address the problem of model synthesis, that is, given a formula φ, we construct an event-recording automaton that satisfies φ.

1 Introduction

Real-time extensions of temporal logics use either a discrete or a continuous time model. Whereas the satisfiability problem for discrete time logics is usually decidable [12,6,7], many logics with a continuous time model are undecidable [15,2,4,14]. Decidable dense-time logics have been obtained by various restrictions on timing constraints as extensions of linear temporal logics [5,21]. Here, we present the first decidable dense real-time logic for specifying branching-time properties of timed systems.

Whereas most timed logics are based on the model of timed automata, we define satisfiability of our logic in terms of event-recording automata [3], which are a determinizable subclass of timed automata. In contrast to the timed automata model, where the clocks are maintained by the system, event-recording automata have a fixed, predefined association between clocks and symbols of the input alphabet. The event-recording clock $S(a)$ of the input symbol a gives the time of the last occurrence of the event a relative to the current time. As observed by Alur, Fix, and Henzinger [3], the key for the determinization of event-recording automata is the property that at each computation step, all clock values are determined only by the input word. We show that in the context of dense real-time logics, such a property yields decidability for the satisfiability problem.

⋆ This research was supported by the National Science Foundation under grants CCR-00-82560 and CCR-00-86096.
⋆⋆ Also affiliated with University of Ulm, Germany.

Our event-recording logic ERL is a real-time extension of the μ-calculus [16] with clocks for specifying timing constraints. As for the event-recording automata, the use of clocks is restricted to refer to the time of previous events only. ERL includes, for each possible event a, a *since* operator $S(a)$ that has the same meaning as an event-recording clock in the event-recording automata formalism. In addition, there are real-time modalities such as $\langle S(b) \leq 3, a \rangle$, which expresses the fact that event a must occur at most 3 time units after the last occurrence of event b. At each computation step, all clock values are determined only by the formula under consideration. Consider, for example, the formula $\langle \mathtt{tt}, a \rangle \langle S(a) = 1, b \rangle \varphi$, with two clocks, $S(a)$ and $S(b)$. This formula expresses the fact that after an a event (the occurrence time for a is not restricted) exactly 1 time unit later a b has to follow. At the beginning the values of the clocks are undefined, since no a and b events occurred previously. After the first computation step (first modality), the value of $S(a)$ equals 0, and after the second step (second modality) the value of $S(a)$ equals 1, and the value of $S(b)$ equals 0. ERL allows for specifying many properties of interest for real-time systems, such as time-out, bounded response, liveness, and safety. A fragment of ERL that contains only greatest fixpoints can be used to encode every event-recording automaton into a single characteristic formula [13,24] that uniquely characterizes the event-recording automaton up to timed bisimulation. Furthermore, the model checking problem for event-recording automata and ERL is PSPACE-hard. Thus, timed bisimulation for event-recording automata is also decidable, since it can be reduced to the model checking problem whether one automaton satisfies the characteristic formula of the other. See [23,22] for details on these results.

Here, we address the satisfiability problem for ERL, and show its decidability by constructing tableaux. Our contribution is based on techniques by Emerson and Streett [26], and by Niwiński and Walukiewicz [19] for deciding the (untimed) μ-calculus. We present a set of reduction rules for constructing tableaux for ERL formulas, and propose two systems of tableaux based on these rules. The first system is used to prove the satisfiability of a formula. In this case the tableau is also referred to as a *pre-model*. The second system, called a *refutation*, decides the unsatisfiability of a formula. Both systems are sound and complete in the sense that a formula is satisfiable iff there exists a pre-model for it, respectively unsatisfiable iff there exists a refutation. To keep track of the actual value of the clocks, the premises and conclusions of our tableau rules are augmented with *timing contexts*, which are sets of timing constraints satisfied by the actual value of the clocks. For example, the timing context $\{S(a) = 0, S(b) \geq 3\}$ states that the value of the event-recording clock $S(a)$ equals 0, and that the value of $S(b)$ is equal to or greater than 3. The main difference between the approaches advocated in [26,19] and the techniques presented in this paper is that the rules, used to construct a tableau for a given ERL formula, contain information about the value of the clocks of the formula. Thus, applying a rule not only reduces the formula but also changes the value of the clocks, by performing operations such as *time elapse* and *clock reset*. Time elapse adds a positive value to the values of all the clocks in the timing context, while resetting clock $S(a)$ in a timing context C assigns 0 to $S(a)$ without changing the value of the other clocks in C. In [26,19] it has been shown that every μ–calculus formula has a finite tableau, using a measure on formulas that decreases with every rule application. For ERL tableaux this criterion is not sufficient to ensure finiteness, since it may be the case that an unbounded number of timing contexts is produced during the tableau construction. We solve this problem by using *rounded timing contexts* [27,8,20,23] in which the clocks are compared only with constants less than or equal to the largest constant k appearing in the guards of the formula under consideration. In this way finitely many rounded timing contexts are obtained. We show that the satisfiability problem for ERL is EXPTIME complete, and address the problem of model construction, that is, given a formula φ, we construct an event-recording automaton that satisfies φ.

Related Work

Alur and Henzinger [7] introduce TPTL as an extension of the temporal logic PTL that uses a freeze quantifier whose bound variable binds the current value of time. Such clock variables are also used to extend the branching-time logic CTL to the timed computation tree logic TCTL [1], and the propositional μ-calculus to the timed μ-calculi T_μ [14] and $\mathcal{L}_\nu$ [17]. All these logics are undecidable when interpreted over dense-time domains. A characteristic of the logics with clock variables is that the set of clocks belonging to a formula is different from the set of clocks in the corresponding timed automata model. Laroussinie, Larsen, and Weise show [17] that the number of clocks in the automata cannot be deduced from the number of clocks in the formula, but that the bounded satisfiability problem for $\mathcal{L}_\nu$ is decidable, that is, given a $\mathcal{L}_\nu$ formula and bounds k and M a timed automaton with no more than k clocks and no clock being compared with constants greater than M can be found. In contrast to the logics mentioned above, ERL does not make a distinction between formula and automata clocks, since clocks are related in both formalisms to the same set of events. Another dense-time logic based on the event-recording model, the Event-Clock Logic (EventClockTL) is proposed by Raskin and Schobbens [21] as an extension of the linear time temporal logic LTL with event-recording and event-predicting operators. The satisfiability problem for the EventClockTL is PSPACE-complete [21]. D'Souza [9] gives a logical characterization of event-recording automata with a monadic second-order logic, MSO_{er}, interpreted over timed words that is expressively equivalent to the event-recording part of EventClockTL. ERL is more expressive than the event-recording part of EventClockTL since it includes arbitrary nested fixpoints.

Organization of the Paper

Event-recording automata are presented in Section 2. Section 3 introduces the event-recording fixpoint logic. Section 4 describes a system of rules for generating tableaux of ERL formulas. The notions of (real-time) refutation and (real-time) pre-model are introduced as a timing analogous of the corresponding concepts in [19], and we show that every ERL formula has either a refutation or a pre-model. Section 5 describes the model construction. In Section 6 the complexity of the tableau construction is analyzed. Finally, in Section 7 we draw conclusions.

2   Event-Recording Automata

This introduction to event-recording automata closely follows [3]. Given a finite alphabet Σ, every symbol $a \in \Sigma$ is associated with an event-recording clock $S(a)$. The set of event-recording clocks is denoted by $C_\Sigma = \{S(a)|a \in \Sigma\}$. An infinite *timed word* w over the alphabet Σ is an infinite sequence $(a_0, t_0)(a_1, t_1) \cdots$ of symbols $a_i \in \Sigma$, paired with nonnegative real numbers $t_i \in I\!\!R^{\geq 0}$ such that the sequence $t = t_0 t_1 \cdots$ of time-stamps is nondecreasing (that is, $t_i \leq t_{i+1}$, for all $i \geq 0$). We assume that $t_0 = 0$. Given an infinite timed word $w = (a_0, t_0)(a_1, t_1) \cdots$, the value of the clock variable $S(a)$ at position j of w equals $t_j - t_i$, where i is the last position preceding j with $a_i = a$. If there is no such position i then the value of $S(a)$ is undefined and is denoted by $\bot$. We write $I\!\!R^{\geq 0}_\bot$ ($\mathbb{Q}^{\geq 0}_\bot$) for the set of nonnegative real (rational) numbers together with the value $\bot$. A clock-valuation function $v : C_\Sigma \to I\!\!R^{\geq 0}_\bot$ assigns a (positive) real or the undefined value to each clock. Clock constraints compare clock values with rational constants or the undefined value $\bot$. Given a set C_Σ of clock variables (or simply *clocks*), $S(a) \in C_\Sigma$ an arbitrary clock, $\gamma \in \mathbb{Q}^{\geq 0}_\bot$, and $\sim \in \{\leq, \geq, <, >, =\}$, the set $\Phi(C_\Sigma)$ of *clock (or timing) constraints* over C_Σ is defined by the grammar

$$g := \mathtt{tt} \mid \mathtt{ff} \mid S(a) \sim \gamma \mid S(a) - S(b) \sim \gamma \mid g_1 \wedge g_2.$$

Clock constraints over C_Σ are interpreted with respect to clock-valuation functions: atomic constraints of the form $\bot \sim \bot$ and $\bot - \bot \sim \bot$ evaluate to true ($\mathtt{tt}$), and all other comparisons that involve $\bot$ (e.g., $\bot \leq 2$) evaluate to false ($\mathtt{ff}$). For a clock-valuation function v and a clock constraint g over C_Σ, we write $v \models g$ (to be read as "v satisfies g") to denote that according to the values given by v the constraint g evaluates to true. Formally, $v \models g$ is defined inductively over the syntactic structure of g, where $S(a), S(b) \in C_\Sigma$ are arbitrary clocks, $\gamma \in \mathbb{Q}^{\geq 0}_\bot$, and $\sim \in \{\leq, \geq, <, >, =\}$:

$$v \not\models \mathtt{ff} \qquad v \models \mathtt{tt} \qquad\qquad v \models S(a) - S(b) \sim \gamma \text{ iff } v(S(a)) - v(S(b)) \sim \gamma$$
$$v \models S(a) \sim \gamma \text{ iff } v(S(a)) \sim \gamma \qquad v \models g_1 \wedge g_2 \text{ iff } v \models g_1 \text{ and } v \models g_2$$

For $\delta \in I\!\!R^{\geq 0}$, $v + \delta$ denotes the clock valuation that maps each defined clock $S(a) \in C_\Sigma$ to the value $v(S(a)) + \delta$ and equals $\bot$ for all undefined clocks. For a clock $S(a) \in C_\Sigma$, $v[S(a) := 0]$ denotes the clock valuation for C_Σ that maps $S(a)$ to the value 0 and agrees with v over the rest of the clocks. Formally, an *event-recording automaton* A is a tuple $\langle L, L^0, \Sigma, E \rangle$ where Σ is a nonempty finite input alphabet, L is a nonempty finite set of locations, $L^0 \subseteq L$ is the set of initial locations, and $E \subseteq L \times L \times \Sigma \times \Phi(C_\Sigma)$ is a finite set of edges. An edge $e = \langle l, l', a, g \rangle$ represents a transition from location l to location l' with the symbol a.

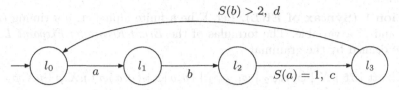

Fig. 1. An event-recording automaton

The clock constraint g specifies when the transition is enabled. Transitions are instantaneous, and time can elapse only in locations. On a transition the clock corresponding to the taken event is implicitly reset to zero. At any point the value of a clock $S(a)$ equals the time elapsed since the last occurrence of the event a.

The event-recording automaton of Figure 1, for example, has four locations and four clocks $S(a), S(b), S(c), S(d)$. Only $S(a)$ and $S(b)$ are explicitly referred within a clock constraint. The initial location is l_0. The first occurrence of event a is at time $t_0 = 0$. Whenever the system moves from location l_0 to location l_1 on input symbol a, the clock $S(a)$ is implicitly reset to 0. In l_2, the values of $S(a)$ and $S(b)$, yield the time since the last occurrence of event a and event b, respectively. The clock constraint $S(a) = 1$, associated with the edge from l_2 to l_3, ensures that each c occurs exactly 1 time unit after the preceding a (time-out requirement). The transition from l_3 to l_0 is enabled only if the value of $S(b)$ is greater than 2.

A *state* of an event-recording automaton A is a pair (l, v) where l is a location of A, and v a clock valuation for C_Σ. An *initial state* of A is of the form (l_0, v_0) where $l_0 \in L_0$ and v_0 maps all clocks in C_Σ to $\bot$. The semantics of an event-recording automaton A is defined by associating a labeled transition system $\mathcal{M} = \langle Q_A, Q_A^0, \Sigma \cup I\!\!R^{\geq 0}, \rightarrow \rangle$ with it, where Q_A is the set of states of A, and Q_A^0 is the set of initial states. Two types of transition are defined in $\mathcal{M}$. First, a state can change due to elapse of time: given a state (l, v) and $\delta \geq 0$, then $(l, v) \xrightarrow{\delta} (l', v')$ if and only if $l = l'$, and $v' = v + \delta$. Second, a state can change by taking a transition between two locations: $(l, v) \xrightarrow{a} (l', v')$ if and only if there is an edge $\langle l, l', a, g \rangle$ such that v satisfies g, and $v' = v[S(a) := 0]$. Both types of transition can be combined into a single transition of the form $(l, v) \xrightarrow{(\delta, a)} (l', v')$, where $(l, v) \xrightarrow{(\delta, a)} (l', v')$ iff there exists a state $(l'', v'') \in Q_A$ such that $(l, v) \xrightarrow{\delta} (l'', v'')$ and $(l'', v'') \xrightarrow{a} (l', v')$.

3   Event-Recording Fixpoint Logic

We consider the dense-time fixpoint logic ERL with event-recording clocks. ERL may be seen as a restriction of T_μ [14] in that clocks may refer only to the time of previous events, instead of specifying the time difference between arbitrary events.

Definition 1 (Syntax of ERL). Let Σ be a finite alphabet, g a timing constraint, and X a variable. The formulas of the *Event-Recording Fixpoint Logic* ERL are defined by the grammar

$$\varphi ::= \text{tt} \mid \text{ff} \mid X \mid \varphi_1 \wedge \varphi_2 \mid \varphi_1 \vee \varphi_2 \mid [g,a]\varphi \mid \langle g,a\rangle\varphi \mid \mu X.\varphi \mid \nu X.\varphi$$

Definition 2 (Semantics of ERL). Given an event-recording automaton $A = \langle L, L^0, \Sigma, E\rangle$ together with the corresponding labeled transition system $\mathcal{M} = \langle Q_A, Q_A^0, \Sigma \cup I\!\!R^{\geq 0}, \rightarrow\rangle$, the semantics of an ERL formula is given by the set of states $(l, v) \in Q_A$, for which the formula holds. Subformulas containing free variables are dealt with using *valuation functions* $\vartheta : V \rightarrow \mathcal{P}(Q_A)$, where V denotes the set of free variables. The updating notation $\vartheta[X := Q]$ denotes the valuation ϑ' that agrees with ϑ on all variables except X, where $\vartheta'(X) = Q \subseteq Q_A$. The semantics for $\langle g,a\rangle\varphi$ and $[g,a]\varphi$, for example, is given as follows

$$[\![\langle g,a\rangle\varphi]\!]_\vartheta^\mathcal{M} := \{(l,v) \in Q_A \mid \exists l', g', \delta \geq 0. \ \langle l,l',a,g'\rangle \in E \text{ and } v + \delta \approx g \wedge g'$$
$$\text{and } (l',v') \in [\![\varphi]\!]_\vartheta^\mathcal{M}, \text{ where } v' = (v + \delta)[S(a) := 0]\}$$
$$[\![[g,a]\varphi]\!]_\vartheta^\mathcal{M} := \{(l,v) \in Q_A \mid \forall l', g', \delta \geq 0. \ \langle l,l',a,g'\rangle \in E \text{ and } v + \delta \approx g \wedge g'$$
$$\text{implies } (l',v') \in [\![\varphi]\!]_\vartheta^\mathcal{M}, \text{ where } v' = (v + \delta)[S(a) := 0]\}$$

The functional $F(X) := [\![\varphi(X)]\!]_\vartheta^\mathcal{M}$ is monotonic in the sense that if $X \subseteq Y$ then $F(X) \subseteq F(Y)$. Then it follows from the Knaster-Tarski fixpoint theorem that the least (greatest) fixpoint $[\![\mu X.\varphi(X)]\!]_\vartheta^\mathcal{M}$ ($[\![\nu X.\varphi(X)]\!]_\vartheta^\mathcal{M}$) of this functional exists and can be computed by a successive iteration. We also write $\mathcal{M}, (l, v), \vartheta \models \varphi$, to denote that $(l, v) \in [\![\varphi]\!]_\vartheta^\mathcal{M}$. The subscript ϑ is omitted if the formula does not contain free variables (φ is a *sentence*). A variable X is *guarded* in a formula $\mu X.\varphi(X)$ ($\nu X.\varphi(X)$) iff every occurrence of X in $\varphi(X)$ is in the scope of some modality $\langle \cdot \rangle$ or $[\cdot]$. A formula is guarded iff every bounded variable in the formula is guarded. Every ERL formula is equivalent to some guarded formula. This can be shown as in [16]. We consider only guarded formulas.

Some examples illustrate the expressiveness of ERL. Consider the model $\mathcal{M}$ in Figure 2, where $\mathcal{M}, (l_2, v_2) \models \varphi_2$, and $\mathcal{M}, (l_3, v_3) \models \varphi_3$ with $\varphi_2 \wedge \varphi_3 = \text{ff}$, for some ERL formulas φ_2, φ_3. Suppose, we want to express the property that there is a time point at least 1 time unit later and not later than 3 time units than the precedent a, such that a b event occurs, which leads to a state in which the formula φ_2 is true. This property is expressed by the ERL formula

$$F_1 = \langle S(a) \geq 1 \wedge S(a) \leq 3, b\rangle\varphi_2.$$

$\mathcal{M}$ satisfies F_1 in state $(l_1, S(a) = 0 \wedge S(b) = \bot)$. The formula

$$F_2 = [S(a) \geq 1 \wedge S(a) \leq 3, b]\varphi_2$$

states, that for all time points between 1 and 3 time units after the precedent a, for all b that are then possible, a state in which φ_2 holds will be reached. This formula does not hold in $\mathcal{M}$ at state $(l_1, S(a) = 0 \wedge S(b) = \bot)$, since there is a b-transition from l_1 exactly 3 time units after the a, which leads to the state (l_3, v_3)

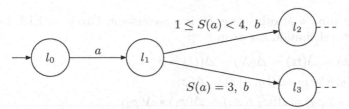

Fig. 2. Event-recording automaton for illustrating ERL

where φ_2 does not hold. The property of $\mathcal{M}$ in state $(l_1, S(a) = 0 \wedge S(b) = \bot)$, that 4 time units after an a no more b events are allowed to occur, is given as

$$F_3 = [\, S(a) \geq 4, b\,]\text{ff}.$$

Time-out properties as well as bounded response properties can be specified in ERL. For example the time-out requirement "if the last a event is exactly distant of 2 time units then a b event has to occur next" can be specified as

$$\langle\, S(a) = 2, b\,\rangle\text{tt} \wedge [\, S(a) < 2 \vee S(a) > 2, b\,]\text{ff}.$$

The requirement that "every request a is followed by a response b within 3 time units, and two requests are separated by at least 5 time units" [3] is expressed as follows ($[\, \text{tt}, \Sigma\,]$ denotes "next" over all events in Σ).

$$\nu X.(\langle\, S(a) = \bot \vee S(a) > 5, a\,\rangle\langle\, S(a) < 3, b\,\rangle\text{tt} \wedge [\, \text{tt}, \Sigma\,]X.$$

Note that the formula $\langle\, g_1 \vee g_2, a\,\rangle\varphi$ is equivalent to $\langle\, g_1, a\,\rangle\varphi \vee \langle\, g_2, a\,\rangle\varphi$ [22].

4   Tableaux

We present a tableau-based procedure that allows a decision of whether or not a given formula is satisfiable. The procedure is based on techniques by Emerson and Streett [26], and by Niwiński and Walukiewicz [19] for deciding the (untimed) μ-calculus. The main difference is that the reduction rules, used to construct a tableau for a given ERL formula, contain information about the value of the clocks of the formula. Thus, applying a rule not only reduces the formula but also changes the value of the clocks, by performing operations such as *time elapse* and *clock reset*.

The alphabet of the ERL logic is extended with a family of propositional constant symbols, also referred to as *definition constants* [25,19]. These constants are used to denote the fixpoint subformulas of a given formula in order of their nesting. A *definition list* is a sequence Δ of declarations $U_1 = \sigma X.\varphi_1(X), \ldots, U_n = \sigma X.\varphi_n(X)$, where $U_1, \ldots, U_n$ are definition constants such that $U_i \neq U_j$ whenever $i \neq j$ and each constant occurring in φ_i is one of $U_1, \ldots, U_{i-1}$. For a definition list Δ we define $dom(\Delta) = \{U_1, \ldots, U_n\}$ and $\Delta(U_i) = \sigma X.\varphi_i(X)$. U_i

is a μ-constant if $\sigma_i = \mu$; otherwise, U_i is a ν-constant. Given an ERL formula φ we construct a definition list as in [19]:

$$\Delta(\mathbf{tt}) = \Delta(\mathbf{ff}) = \Delta(X) = \Delta(U) = \emptyset$$
$$\Delta(\langle g, a \rangle \varphi) = \Delta([g, a] \varphi) = \Delta(\varphi)$$
$$\Delta(\varphi_1 \vee \varphi_2) = \Delta(\varphi_1 \wedge \varphi_2) = \Delta(\varphi_1) \bullet \Delta(\varphi_2)$$
$$\Delta(\mu X.\varphi(X)) = (U = \mu X.\varphi(X)) \circ \Delta(\varphi(U)), \text{ where } U \text{ is new}$$
$$\Delta(\nu X.\varphi(X)) = (U = \nu X.\varphi(X)) \circ \Delta(\varphi(U)), \text{ where } U \text{ is new}$$

where $\circ$ denotes the operation of appending a new definition to an existing definition list, while $\bullet$ appends two definition lists, and renames identical fixpoint subformulas by the same constant.

To keep track of the actual value of the clocks, the premises and conclusions of our tableau rules are augmented with *timing contexts*, which are sets of timing constraints satisfied by the actual value of the clocks in the formula.

Definition 3 (Timing Context). Let Σ be a finite alphabet. A *timing context* (for short "context") is generated by

$$C ::= \mathbf{ff} \mid \mathbf{tt} \mid S(a) \sim \gamma \mid S(a) - S(b) \sim \gamma \mid C_1 \wedge C_2$$

where $S(a), S(b)$ are arbitrary clocks, $\sim \in \{<, \leq, =, >, \geq\}$, and $\gamma \in \mathbb{Q}^{\geq 0}$.

Each context denotes a set of clock valuations in the obvious way: $\llbracket \mathbf{ff} \rrbracket = \emptyset$, $\llbracket \mathbf{tt} \rrbracket = \{v\}$, $\llbracket S(a) \sim \gamma \rrbracket = \{v \mid v(S(a)) \sim \gamma\}$, $\llbracket S(a) - S(b) \sim \gamma \rrbracket = \{v \mid v(S(a)) - v(S(b)) \sim \gamma\}$, $\llbracket C_1 \wedge C_2 \rrbracket = \{v \mid v \in \llbracket C_1 \rrbracket \text{ and } v \in \llbracket C_2 \rrbracket\}$.

For a clock valuation v and a timing context C we write $v \approx C$ if $v \in \llbracket C \rrbracket$. An *empty context*, denoted by $C = \mathbf{tt}$ corresponds to the initial clock valuation, that is $S(a_i) = \bot$, for all $a_i \in \Sigma$. A false context, $C = \mathbf{ff}$ is a context that cannot be satisfied by any clock valuation. For example, the contexts $C = S(a) > 1 \wedge S(a) < 1$ and $C = \mathbf{ff}$ are identical. Sometimes we write a context $C_1 \wedge \ldots \wedge C_n$ as a set $\{C_1, \ldots, C_n\}$.

Definition 4. An ERL-formula φ is satisfiable in a context C iff there exists a model $\mathcal{M}$ and a state $s = (l, v)$ with $v \approx C$ and $\mathcal{M}, s \models \varphi$.

On timing contexts two operations are defined: *time elapse* ($C\uparrow$), and *clock reset* ($C \odot \{S(a) := 0\}$). $C\uparrow$ is the largest set of clock valuations that will eventually be reached from C after some delay, and $C \odot \{S(a) := 0\}$ denotes the set of clock valuations obtained from C by setting the value of the clock $S(a)$ to 0.

Definition 5 (Operations on Timing Contexts). Let C be a timing context, $S(a)$ an arbitrary clock, and v a clock valuation function. Then $C\uparrow$ (time elapse) and $C \odot \{S(a) := 0\}$ (reset) are timing contexts satisfying the following equations.

$$\llbracket C\uparrow \rrbracket = \{v + \delta \mid v \in \llbracket C \rrbracket \text{ and } \delta \in \mathbb{R}^{\geq 0}\}$$
$$\llbracket C \odot \{S(a) := 0\} \rrbracket = \begin{cases} \llbracket C \wedge S(a) = 0 \rrbracket, & \text{if } S(a) \sim \gamma \notin C \\ \{v[S(a) := 0] \mid v \in \llbracket C \rrbracket\}, & \text{otherwise} \end{cases}$$

For the timing context $C = \{S(a) = 0, S(b) > 2\}$, for example, $C\!\uparrow\, = \{S(a) \geq 0,$ $S(b) > 2, S(b) - S(a) > 2\}$ denotes the new context obtained by letting time elapse in C.

Definition 6 (Time-Overlapping a-Boxes). Let $\varphi = \langle\, g, a \,\rangle\varphi'$ be an ERL formula, and Γ be a set of formulas, such that each formula in Γ is a variable X, or a formula of the form $\langle\, g', a' \,\rangle\psi$ or $[\, g', a' \,]\psi$ for some guards g', and events a'. Then the set of *time-overlapping a-boxes* of φ and Γ is defined as

$$\mathtt{tob}(g, a, \Gamma) \stackrel{\text{def}}{=} \{\, [\, g', a \,]\psi \in \Gamma \mid g' \wedge g \neq \mathtt{ff} \,\}.$$

A *tableau sequent* $C; \Gamma \vdash_\Delta$ is a triple $(C; \Delta; \Gamma)$, where C is a timing context, Γ is a finite set of formulas (i.e. conjunction of formulas), and Δ is a definition list that includes all definition constants occurring in Γ. A *tableau system* is a finite collection of tableau rules. The rules are written with the premises below the line and the conclusion above the line, since we regard a tableau as a tree that expands downwards.

Definition 7 (Tableau Rules). Let $\mathcal{R}$ be the following set of tableau rules:

$$\frac{C; \mathtt{tt}, \Gamma \vdash_\Delta}{C; \Gamma \vdash_\Delta} \ (\mathtt{tt}) \qquad \frac{C; \mathtt{ff}, \Gamma' \vdash_\Delta}{\mathtt{ff} \vdash_\Delta} \ (\mathtt{ff}_\Gamma) \qquad \frac{\mathtt{tt}; \Gamma \vdash_\Delta}{\mathtt{ff} \vdash_\Delta} \ (\mathtt{ff}_C)$$

$$\frac{C; \varphi \wedge \psi, \Gamma \vdash_\Delta}{C; \varphi, \psi, \Gamma \vdash_\Delta} \ (\wedge) \qquad \frac{C; \varphi \vee \psi, \Gamma \vdash_\Delta}{C; \varphi, \Gamma \vdash_\Delta \quad C; \psi, \Gamma \vdash_\Delta} \ (\vee)$$

$$\frac{C; \Gamma \vdash_\Delta}{\{\{C'_z; \Gamma'_z \vdash_\Delta \mid z \in Z_g\} \mid \langle\, g, a \,\rangle\varphi \in \Gamma\}} \ \eta \ \ (\forall\langle\rangle)$$

$$\frac{C; \nu X.\varphi(X), \Gamma \vdash_\Delta}{C; U, \Gamma \vdash_\Delta} \ \Delta(U) = \nu X.\varphi(X) \ \ (\nu)$$

$$\frac{C; \mu X.\varphi(X), \Gamma \vdash_\Delta}{C; U, \Gamma \vdash_\Delta} \ \Delta(U) = \mu X.\varphi(X) \ \ (\mu)$$

$$\frac{C; U, \Gamma \vdash_\Delta}{C; \varphi[X := U], \Gamma \vdash_\Delta} \ \zeta \text{ and } \Delta(U) = \sigma X.\varphi(X) \ \ (subst)$$

The rules for the boolean operators are straightforward. The rules (ν) and (μ) for fixpoint formulas introduce new definition constants for $\nu X.\varphi(X)$ and $\mu X.\varphi(X)$, while the rule *(subst)* unwinds the corresponding fixpoint when the condition ζ holds. This condition specifies that no node above the current node $C; U, \Gamma \vdash_\Delta$ in the proof tree, is labeled $C; U, \Gamma \vdash_\Delta$, where Γ consists only of definition constants. Now, consider rule $(\forall\langle\rangle)$. The condition η specifies that each formula in Γ is a variable or a formula of the form $\langle\, g', a' \,\rangle\psi$ or $[\, g', a' \,]\psi$ for some guards g', and events a' (that is, no other rule is applicable to Γ). Z_g denotes the set of all subguards of g that are defined as follows. Let $\mathtt{tob}(g, a, \Gamma)$ be the set of the time-overlapping a-boxes of φ and Γ. For every nonempty subset S of $\mathtt{tob}(g, a, \Gamma)$ a subguard z of g is the conjunction of g and of all guards of the boxes in S and all negated guards of the boxes in $\mathtt{tob}(g, a, \Gamma) \setminus S$. This construction corresponds to the determinization procedure for event-clock automata [3]. For every $z \in Z_g$,

$$C'_z;\ \Gamma'_z \overset{\text{def}}{=} \begin{cases} (C{\uparrow} \wedge g) \odot \{S(a) := 0\};\ \varphi, & \text{if } \Gamma = \emptyset \text{ or } \mathtt{tob}(g, a, \Gamma) = \emptyset \\ (C{\uparrow} \wedge z) \odot \{S(a) := 0\};\ \{\varphi, \Psi_z\}, & \text{otherwise} \end{cases}$$

where $\Psi_z = \{\psi \mid [\,g', a\,]\psi \in \mathtt{tob}(g, a, \Gamma) \text{ and } z \subseteq g'\}$.

We introduce a new system as a fragment of the system $\mathcal{R}$. The system $\mathcal{R}_{ref}$ is obtained from $\mathcal{R}$ by substituting the rule $(\forall\langle\rangle)$ with the rule

$$\frac{C;\ \langle g, a\rangle\varphi, \Gamma \vdash_\Delta}{\{C'_z;\ \Gamma'_z \vdash_\Delta \mid z \in Z_g\}}\ \eta\ \ (\langle\rangle)$$

with similar restriction on Γ as for $(\forall\langle\rangle)$. An example illustrates the applicability of the rule $(\langle\rangle)$. Given the sequent

$$\{S(b) \geq 0\};\ \langle\,S(b) \geq 1, a\,\rangle\varphi_1,\ \{[\,S(b) \leq 2, a\,]\varphi_2,\ [\,S(b) \geq 2, a\,]\varphi_3\} \vdash_\Delta$$

where the context $C = \{S(b) \geq 0\}$, $g = S(b) \geq 1$, and Γ is a conjunction of two formulas, $\Gamma = \{[\,S(b) \leq 2, a\,]\varphi_2,\ [\,S(b) \geq 2, a\,]\varphi_3\}$. First, the set of time-overlapping a-boxes is computed,

$$\mathtt{tob}(g, a, \Gamma) = \{[\,S(b) \leq 2, a\,]\varphi_2, [\,S(b) \geq 2, a\,]\varphi_3\}.$$

Then, all nonempty subsets of $\mathtt{tob}(g, a, \Gamma)$ are computed as, $S_1 = \{[\,S(b) \leq 2, a\,]\varphi_2\}$, $S_2 = \{[\,S(b) \geq 2, a\,]\varphi_3\}$, and $S_3 = \{[\,S(b) \leq 2, a\,]\varphi_2, [\,S(b) \geq 2, a\,]\varphi_3\}$. Let g_i denotes the conjunction of the guards in S_i, and g_{ti} denotes the conjunction of the negated guards in $\mathtt{tob}(g, a, \Gamma) \setminus S_i$. The subguards z_i of $g = S(b) \geq 1$, for $i = 1, 2, 3$ are given by $z_i = g \wedge g_i \wedge g_{ti}$.

$$\begin{aligned} z_1 &= S(b) \geq 1 \ \wedge\ S(b) \leq 2 \ \wedge\ S(b) < 2 &=& \ 1 \leq S(b) < 2 \\ z_2 &= S(b) \geq 1 \ \wedge\ S(b) \geq 2 \ \wedge\ S(b) > 2 &=& \ S(b) > 2 \\ z_3 &= S(b) \geq 1 \ \wedge\ S(b) = 2 \ \wedge\ \mathtt{tt} &=& \ S(b) = 2. \end{aligned}$$

For $i = 1, 2, 3$ the new context C'_{z_i} corresponding to the subguards z_i is computed as

$$C'_{z_i} \ =\ ((S(b) \geq 0){\uparrow} \ \wedge\ z_i) \odot \{S(a) := 0\}$$

while Γ'_{z_i} is given by $\{\varphi_1, \{\psi \mid [\,g', a\,]\psi \in \mathtt{tob}(g, a, \Gamma) \text{ and } z_i \subseteq g'\}\}$. We obtain

$$\begin{aligned} C'_{z_1} &= \{1 \leq S(b) < 2 \ \wedge\ S(a) = 0 \ \wedge\ 1 \leq S(b) - S(a) < 2\} & \Gamma'_{z_1} &= \{\varphi_1, \varphi_2\} \\ C'_{z_2} &= \{S(b) > 2 \ \wedge\ S(a) = 0 \ \wedge\ S(b) - S(a) > 2\} & \Gamma'_{z_2} &= \{\varphi_1, \varphi_3\} \\ C'_{z_3} &= \{S(b) = 2 \ \wedge\ S(a) = 0 \ \wedge\ S(b) - S(a) = 2\} & \Gamma'_{z_3} &= \{\varphi_1, \varphi_2, \varphi_3\} \end{aligned}$$

Note that by construction all zones $z \in Z_g$ are disjoint and $\bigvee_{z \in Z_g} z = g$.

Definition 8 (Tableau). Consider a guarded formula φ, together with an initial timing context C, and a system of rules $\mathcal{R}$. A *tableau* for φ is a labeled tree. The root of the tree is labeled by $C; \varphi \vdash_\Delta$, where Δ is the definition list corresponding to φ. A leaf is labeled by the formula $\mathbf{ff}$ or by an irreducible sequent. If a node n is not labeled by $\mathbf{ff}$ or by an irreducible sequent, then the sons of n are created and labeled according to the rules in the system $\mathcal{R}$.

For a node $n = C_n; \Gamma_n \vdash_\Delta$ we denote by $L(n)$ the label of n, that is $C_n; \Gamma_n$, by $C(n)$ the corresponding context C_n, and by $\Gamma(n)$ the set of formulas Γ_n.

The notions of quasi-model, quasi-refutation, regeneration, pre-model and refutation are taken from [19]. If the system $\mathcal{R}$ is used, and no leaf is labeled by $\mathbf{ff}$ then the tableau for φ is also referred to as a *quasi-model* of φ. A *quasi-refutation* of φ is a tableau for φ, where the system $\mathcal{R}_{ref}$ is used, and where every leaf is labeled by $\mathbf{ff}$. Given a tableau $\mathcal{T}$ for a guarded formula, and a path $\pi = (n_1, n_2, \ldots)$ in $\mathcal{T}$, a *trace* τ on π is a sequence $(\tau_1, \tau_2, \ldots)$ of formulas such that $\tau_i \in \Gamma(n_i)$ and τ_{i+1} is one of the formulas derived from $\tau_i \in \Gamma(n_i)$ by the rule applied in n_i. A constant $U = \sigma X.\varphi(X)$ *regenerates* on a trace $\tau = (\tau_1, \tau_2, \ldots)$ if there exists an i such that $U \in \tau_i$ and $\varphi(U) \in \tau_{i+1}$. A ν-*trace* is either finite and does not end with the formula $\mathbf{ff}$, or is an infinite trace on which the oldest constant in Δ that is regenerated infinitely often on τ is a ν-constant. A μ-*trace* is either finite and ends with $\mathbf{ff}$, or it is an infinite trace on which the oldest constant in Δ that is regenerated infinitely often on τ is a μ-constant. A quasi-model for a given ERL formula φ, where every trace on every path is a ν-trace, is a *pre-model* for φ. A quasi-refutation for φ, where on every path there exists a μ-trace, is a *refutation* of φ. It can be shown as in [19] that every ERL formula φ has either a pre-model or a refutation.

4.1   Contradiction in a Tableau

A leaf in a tableau is labeled by $\mathbf{ff}$ if there is a contradiction. In untimed settings this is the case if a formula and its negation occur in a sequent. If the tableau also contains information about values of clocks, a contradiction may occur if these values are inconsistent. Therefore we identify two types of contradictions in a given tableau, *atomic contradictions* and *timing contradictions*. An atomic contradiction may occur in Γ if some formula and its negation are contained in Γ. In this case $\Gamma = \mathbf{ff}$ and there is no model $\mathcal{M}$ such that $\mathcal{M}, s \models \mathbf{ff}$. Thus, according to Definition 4, Γ is unsatisfiable in context C. A timing contradiction is triggered by an inconsistent timing context. For example, the context $C = \{S(a) \geq 1 \wedge S(a) < 1\}$ is inconsistent since there is no clock valuation v that satisfies C. The rules $(\mathbf{ff}_\Gamma)$ and $(\mathbf{ff}_C)$ from Definition 7 are used to check for inconsistencies.

The formula $F_1 = \langle \mathbf{tt}, b \rangle (\langle S(b) = 1, a \rangle \mathbf{tt} \wedge [S(b) = 1, a] \mathbf{ff})$, for example, is unsatisfiable. This can be shown using the tableau $\mathcal{R}_{ref}$. A refutation, given by the atomic contradiction between the formulas $\mathbf{tt}$ and $\mathbf{ff}$, is illustrated below.

$$\frac{\dfrac{\{\text{tt}\};\ \langle\,\text{tt}, b\,\rangle(\langle\,S(b)=1,a\,\rangle\text{tt}\wedge[\,S(b)=1,a\,]\text{ff})\vdash_\Delta}{\{S(b)=0\};\ \langle\,S(b)=1,a\,\rangle\text{tt}\wedge[\,S(b)=1,a\,]\text{ff}\vdash_\Delta}\ (\langle\langle\rangle\rangle)}{\dfrac{\{S(b)=1,S(a)=0,S(b)-S(a)=1\};\ \boxed{\text{tt},\text{ff}}\ \vdash_\Delta}{\text{ff}}\ (\text{ff}_r)}\ (\langle\langle\rangle\rangle)$$

The formula $F_2 = \langle\,\text{tt}, a\,\rangle\langle\,S(a)=1,b\,\rangle\langle\,S(a)<1,c\,\rangle\text{tt}$ is also unsatisfiable, since the timing contradiction $S(a) \geq 1 \wedge S(a) < 1$ yields a refutation in $\mathcal{R}_{ref}$.

$$\frac{\dfrac{\dfrac{\{\text{tt}\};\ \langle\,\text{tt}, a\,\rangle\langle\,S(a)=1,b\,\rangle\langle\,S(a)<1,c\,\rangle\text{tt}\vdash_\Delta}{\{S(a)=0\};\ \langle\,S(a)=1,b\,\rangle\langle\,S(a)<1,c\,\rangle\text{tt}\vdash_\Delta}\ (\langle\langle\rangle\rangle)}{\{S(a)=1,S(b)=0,S(a)-S(b)=1\};\ \langle\,S(a)<1,c\,\rangle\text{tt}\vdash_\Delta}\ (\langle\langle\rangle\rangle)}{\dfrac{\{\{\,\boxed{S(a)\geq 1}\,,S(b)\geq 0,S(a)-S(b)=1,\boxed{S(a)<1}\,\}\odot\{S(c):=0\}\};\ \text{tt}\vdash_\Delta}{\text{ff}}\ (\text{ff}_C)}\ (\langle\langle\rangle\rangle)$$

4.2   Termination, Soundness and Completeness

The tableau system presented in this paper is sound and complete in the sense that a formula is satisfiable iff there exists a pre-model for it, respectively unsatisfiable iff there exists a refutation. First, we show that for a given formula every tableau is finite. As in [26,19] we introduce the notion of *signature* and show that in a pre-model (refutation) every regeneration of a μ-constant (ν-constant) always decreases the signature.

First recall the definition of least and greatest fixpoints of monotonic functionals φ over subsets of states of a set S: $\mu_0(\varphi) = \emptyset$, $\mu_\tau(\varphi) = \varphi(\mu_{\tau-1}(\varphi))$, for any ordinal τ, and $\mu_\lambda(\varphi) = \bigcup_{\tau<\lambda}\mu_\tau(\varphi)$ for the limit ordinal λ. Similarly, for the greatest fixpoint: $\nu_0(\varphi) = S$, $\nu_\tau(\varphi) = \varphi(\nu_{\tau-1}(\varphi))$, and $\nu_\lambda(\varphi) = \bigcap_{\tau<\lambda}\nu_\tau(\varphi)$.

A *signature* sig is a sequence of ordinals $(\tau_1,\ldots,\tau_n)$. A signature sig_1 is smaller than sig_2, $sig_1 < sig_2$, if sig_1 lexicographically precedes sig_2. The following definition and lemma are the timed counterpart of [26] and [19] in that timed modalities $\langle\,g,a\,\rangle$, and $[\,g,a\,]$ are used instead of the μ−calculus modalities $\langle\,a\,\rangle$, respectively $[\,a\,]$.

Definition 9. Consider a sentence φ together with the corresponding definition list Δ. Let $\mathcal{M}$ be a model, and $s = (l,v)$ a state in $\mathcal{M}$ such that $\mathcal{M}, (l,v) \models \varphi$. We say that φ has *signature* $sig = \tau_1,\ldots,\tau_n$ at s if sig is the lexicographically least signature such that $\mathcal{M}$ at s satisfies the sentence obtained by replacing the i-th μ-constant definition $\mu X.\varphi(X)$ by $\mu_{\tau_i}\varphi(X)$.

Lemma 1. Consider a model $\mathcal{M}$, a state $s = (l,v)$, and a formula φ, such that $\mathcal{M}, (l,v) \models \varphi$. Let sig be the signature of φ at (l,v). The following properties hold for signatures:

1. If $\varphi = \varphi_1 \vee \varphi_2$ then either φ_1 or φ_2 has signature $sig' \leq sig$ at (l,v).
2. If $\varphi = \varphi_1 \wedge \varphi_2$ then both φ_1 and φ_2 have signature $sig' \leq sig$ at s.

3. If $\varphi = \langle g, a \rangle \varphi_1$ then φ_1 has signature $sig' \leq sig$ at some (l', v'), with $\langle l, l', a, \tilde{g} \rangle \in E$, $v + \delta \approx g \wedge \tilde{g}$ for some $\delta \geq 0$, and $v' = (v + \delta)[S(a) := 0]$.
4. If $\varphi = [\,g, a\,] \varphi_1$ then φ_1 has signature $sig' \leq sig$ at all (l', v'), with $\langle l, l', a, \tilde{g} \rangle \in E$, $v + \delta \approx g \wedge \tilde{g}$ for all $\delta \geq 0$, and $v' = (v + \delta)[S(a) := 0]$.
5. If $\nu X.\varphi(X)$, where $\Delta(U) = \nu X.\varphi(X)$, has signature sig at s then U has signature sig at s.
6. If $\mu X.\varphi(X)$ has signature sig at s, and $\Delta(U_i) = \mu X.\varphi(X)$, where U_i is the i-th μ-constant in Δ then the prefix of length $i - 1$ of sig and the signature of U_i at s are equal.
7. If U has signature sig at s, and $\Delta(U) = \nu X.\varphi(X)$ then $\varphi(U)$ has signature sig at s.
8. If U has signature sig at s, and $\Delta(U) = \mu X.\varphi(X)$ then $\varphi(U)$ has signature $sig' < sig$ at s.

As the above lemma shows, regeneration always decreases signature. Unfortunately, it may be the case that regeneration produces new contexts every time. Let $\varphi = \nu X.\langle S(b) = 1, b \rangle X$ and $C = \{S(a) = 0, S(b) = 0\}$. Obviously, φ is satisfiable. A tableau for $C; \varphi$ is given by

$$\frac{\dfrac{\dfrac{\dfrac{\dfrac{\dfrac{\{S(a) = 0, S(b) = 0\}; \nu X.\langle S(b) = 1, b \rangle X \vdash_\Delta}{\{S(a) = 0, S(b) = 0\}; U \vdash_\Delta}\,(\nu)}{\{S(a) = 0, S(b) = 0\}; \langle S(b) = 1, b \rangle U \vdash_\Delta}\,(subst)}{\{S(a) = 1, S(b) = 0, S(a) - S(b) = 1\}; U \vdash_\Delta}\,(\forall\langle\rangle)}{\{S(a) = 1, S(b) = 0, S(a) - S(b) = 1\}; \langle S(b) = 1, b \rangle U \vdash_\Delta}\,(subst)}{\{S(a) = 2, S(b) = 0, S(a) - S(b) = 2\}; U \vdash_\Delta}\,(\forall\langle\rangle)}{}\,(subst)$$

$$\vdots$$

Every trace of the above tableau is a ν-trace. However, the tableau is infinite, since after every regeneration of U a new context is generated, $\{S(a) = i, S(b) = 0, S(a) - S(b) = i\}$ for $i \geq 1$.

Thus, in contrast to the untimed case, Lemma 1 is not sufficient to ensure finiteness of tableaux. The solution to this problem is to use *rounded contexts*, that is, to consider only contexts in which the clocks are compared only with constants less than or equal to the largest integer constant k appearing in the guards of the formula under consideration.[1] A rounded context is obtained from a context C by a $widening_k(C)$ operator. Intuitively, this operator removes for all clock constraints in C all upper bounds greater than k and replaces all lower bounds greater than k by k. Similar operators are considered also in [27,8,20,23]. There are only finitely many rounded contexts [8].

By using the widening operator after every application of the rule $(\forall\langle\rangle)$ on the resulting context, the following finite tableau is obtained for the above example.

---

[1] We assume here that all clock constraints of the formula contain only integer constants (otherwise, all constants need to be multiplied by the least common multiple of the denominators of all rational numbers that appear in clock constraints).

(∗)

$$
\begin{array}{c}
\dfrac{n_0:\quad \{S(a)=0,S(b)=0\};\nu X.\langle\,S(b)=1,b\,\rangle X\vdash_\Delta}{n_1:\quad \{S(a)=0,S(b)=0\};U\vdash_\Delta}\;(\nu)\\[2pt]
\dfrac{}{n_2:\quad \{S(a)=0,S(b)=0\};\langle\,S(b)=1,b\,\rangle U\vdash_\Delta}\;(subst)\\[2pt]
\dfrac{}{n_3:\quad \{S(a)=1,S(b)=0,S(a)-S(b)=1\};U\vdash_\Delta}\;(\forall\langle\rangle)\\[2pt]
\dfrac{}{n_4:\quad \{S(a)=1,S(b)=0,S(a)-S(b)=1\};\langle\,S(b)=1,b\,\rangle U\vdash_\Delta}\;(subst)\\[2pt]
\dfrac{}{n_5:\quad \{S(a)>1,S(b)=0,S(a)-S(b)>1\};U\vdash_\Delta}\;(\forall\langle\rangle)\\[2pt]
\dfrac{}{n_6:\quad \{S(a)>1,S(b)=0,S(a)-S(b)>1\};\langle\,S(b)=1,b\,\rangle U\vdash_\Delta}\;(subst)\\[2pt]
\dfrac{}{n_7:\quad \{S(a)>1,S(b)=0,S(a)-S(b)>1\};U\vdash_\Delta}\;(\forall\langle\rangle)
\end{array}
$$

In node n_7 no further rule is applicable, since the condition ζ of the rule *subst* is not satisfied. Thus, the tableau contains a cycle between nodes n_7 and n_5.

Proposition 1. Consider a formula φ with k the largest constant appearing in the guards of φ, and a context C. Then φ is satisfiable in the context C iff φ is satisfiable in the rounded context $widening_k(C)$.

Given an ERL formula φ with k the largest integer constant appearing in the guards of the formula, C an initial context, and Δ the definition list corresponding to φ. Consider a tableau for $C;\varphi\vdash_\Delta$. After every application of the rule $(\forall\langle\rangle)$ respectively $(\langle\rangle)$ the obtained contexts have to be rounded by using the widening operator $widening_k(\cdot)$. Since the number of rounded contexts is finite, after a finite number of applications of the $(\forall\langle\rangle)$ respectively $(\langle\rangle)$ rule, the context does not change any more. We obtain the following lemma.

Lemma 2. Consider an ERL formula φ, Δ the corresponding definition list, and C the initial context. Then every tableau for $C;\varphi\vdash_\Delta$ contains only finitely many rounded contexts.

Theorem 1 follows from Lemma 1 and Lemma 2.

Theorem 1 (Termination). Consider an ERL formula φ, Δ the corresponding definition list, and C the initial context. Every tableau for $C;\varphi\vdash_\Delta$ is finite.

Theorem 2. A guarded ERL formula φ is satisfiable iff there exists a pre-model for φ.

For proving the $(\Rightarrow)$ direction assume that φ is satisfiable. Let $\mathcal{T}$ be a tableau for φ. We show that $\mathcal{T}$ is a pre-model for φ. First, we prove that no leaf of $\mathcal{T}$ is labeled by ff, by showing that for each of the rule of the system $\mathcal{R}$ if the conclusion is satisfiable then the premises are also satisfiable. Second, as in [19] every infinite trace τ on every path in $\mathcal{T}$ is a ν-trace.

For the other direction $(\Leftarrow)$ consider a formula φ and $\mathcal{T}$ a pre-model for it with C an initial context. We show that φ is satisfiable in C. First, we show, that if a leaf is labeled by a satisfiable formula, then also the root, by proving that for each of the rule of the system $\mathcal{R}$ if the premises are satisfiable then also the conclusion. Second, we show, as in [19] that if every infinite trace τ on every path in $\mathcal{T}$ is a ν-trace, then φ is also satisfiable. Thus, φ is satisfiable in the initial context C.

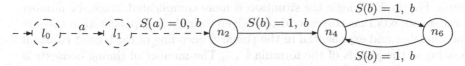

Fig. 3. An event-recording automaton satisfying $\varphi = \nu X.\langle S(b) = 1, b \rangle X$ in state $(n_2, S(a) = 0 \wedge S(b) = 0)$

5   Model Synthesis

We address the problem of model construction. Given a pre-model for a formula φ, we construct an event-recording automaton that satisfies φ. First, we introduce the notion of a *prefix-automaton* for initializing event-recording clocks with the value zero. Given a finite alphabet $\Sigma = \{a_1, a_2, \ldots, a_n\}$, a *prefix-automaton* $A = \langle L, l_0, \Sigma, E \rangle$ is an event-recording automaton of the following form

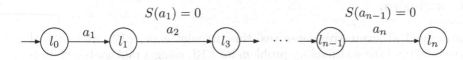

In the last state l_n all event-recording clocks $S(a_i)$ for all $a_i \in \Sigma$ are defined, and $S(a_i) = 0$.

Definition 10. Given a formula φ over the alphabet Σ, an initial context C, and a pre-model $\mathcal{T}$ for φ. An event-recording automaton $A = \langle L, l_0, \Sigma, E \rangle$ such that $A, (l, v) \models \varphi$ for a state (l, v) with $v \approx C$, can be constructed as follows.

- $L = L' \cup L''$, where L'' consists of all nodes of $\mathcal{T}$ that are either leaves, or to which the rule $(\forall\langle\rangle)$ was applied. L' are the nodes of the prefix automaton over the set of all events $a_i \in \Sigma$ with $S(a_i) \in C$. Note that if the initial context C is empty, then there is no prefix-automaton, and $L' = \emptyset$. For a node n of $\mathcal{T}$, d_n denotes the closest descendant of n that is contained in L''.
- $E = E' \cup E''$, where $\langle l, l', a, g \rangle \in E''$ iff there exists in $\mathcal{T}$ a son n of l with $d_n = l'$, such that the label of n was obtained from the label of l by reducing a formula of the form $\langle g, a \rangle\varphi$. E' denotes the edges of the prefix-automaton.

Consider the finite tableau $(*)$. $L'' = \{n_2, n_4, n_6\}$, since the rule $(\forall\langle\rangle)$ was applied to the nodes n_2, n_4, and n_6. Figure 3 shows the event-recording automaton that satisfies φ in state $s = (n_2, S(a) = 0 \wedge S(b) = 0)$. The dashed part illustrates the prefix automaton.

6   Complexity

In [11,19] it has been shown that for a μ-calculus sentence either a model or a refutation, both of size exponential in the size of the formula, can be constructed. The running time of the algorithm is also exponential in the size of the formula. For the ERL logic the situation is more complicated, since the number of timing contexts that correspond to a given formula is exponential in the size of the alphabet and exponential in the (binary) encoding of the largest constant appearing in the guards of the formula [4,3]. The number of timing contexts is bounded by $m! \cdot 2^m \cdot (2k + 2)^m$, where m is the size of the input alphabet, and k the largest constant.

Theorem 3. *The satisfiability problem for ERL is EXPTIME complete in the size of the formula, in the size of the alphabet, and in the size of the (binary) encoding of the largest constant appearing in the guards of the formula.*

The EXPTIME-hardness follows from the fact that the μ-calculus, which is EXPTIME hard [10] is contained in ERL. The EXPTIME-membership is given by the observation that a model or a refutation for φ can be constructed in time $O(m! \cdot 2^m \cdot (2k + 2)^m \cdot 2^{|\varphi|})$.

7 Conclusion

We introduced an expressive dense real-time fixpoint logic, ERL, and showed the decidability of the satisfiability problem for ERL using a tableau-based decision procedure. This decision procedure combines, in a modular way, techniques for constructing tableaux for the untimed μ-calculus, with methods used for verifying timed systems such as region constructions [4] and clock constraint systems [18]. In order to keep the technical overhead manageable, we restricted ourselves to event-recording logic, but similar techniques should be applicable to fixpoint logics with event-predicting clocks.

Acknowledgment

We would like to thank the anonymous referees for their helpful comments.

References

1. R. Alur. *Techniques for Automatic Verification of Real-Time Systems*. PhD thesis, Stanford University, 1991. 257
2. R. Alur, C. Courcoubetis, and D. Dill. Model checking in dense real-time. *Information and Computation*, 104(1):2–34, 1993. 255
3. R. Alur, L. Fix, and T. A. Henzinger. Event-clock automata: A determinizable class of timed automata. *Theoretical Computer Science*, 211(1–2):253–273, 1999. 255, 258, 261, 264, 270
4. Rajeev Alur and David L. Dill. A theory of timed automata. *Theoretical Computer Science*, 126(2):183–235, 25 April 1994. 255, 270
5. Rajeev Alur, Tomás Feder, and Thomas A. Henzinger. The benefits of relaxing punctuality. *Journal of the ACM*, 43(1):116–146, January 1996. 255

6. Rajeev Alur and Thomas Henzinger. Real-time logics: Complexity and expressiveness. *Information and Computation*, 104(1):35–77, May 1993. 255
7. Rajeev Alur and Thomas A. Henzinger. A really temporal logic. *Journal of the ACM*, 41(1):181–204, 1994. 255, 257
8. Conrado Daws and Stavros Tripakis. Model checking of real-time reachability properties using abstractions. *Lecture Notes in Computer Science*, 1384:313–329, 1998. 257, 267
9. Deepak D'Souza. A logical characterization of event recording automata. In *Proceedings of FTRTFT*, volume 1926 of *LNCS*, 2000. 257
10. E. Allen Emerson and Charanjit S. Jutla. The complexity of tree automata and logics of programs. In *29th Annual Symposium on Foundations of Computer Science*, pages 328–337. IEEE, 1988. 270
11. E. Allen Emerson and Charanjit S. Jutla. On simultaneously determinizing and complementing ω-automata (extended abstract). In *Proceedings, Fourth Annual Symposium on Logic in Computer Science*, pages 333–342, 1989. 269
12. E. Allen Emerson, A. K. Mok, A. Prasad Sistla, and Jai Srinivasan. Quantitative temporal reasoning. *LNCS*, 531:136–145, 1991. 255
13. S. Graf and J. Sifakis. A modal characterization of observational congruence on finite terms of CCS. *Information and Control*, 68(1–3):125–145, 1986. 256
14. T. A. Henzinger, X. Nicollin, J. Sifakis, and S. Yovine. Symbolic model checking for real-time systems. *Information and Computation*, 111(2):193–244, June 1994. 255, 257, 259
15. R. Koymans. Specifying real-time properties with metric temporal logic. *Real-Time Systems*, 2(4):255–299, November 1990. 255
16. D. Kozen. Results on the propositional mu-calculus. *Theoretical Computer Science*, 27(3):333–354, December 1983. 256, 260
17. F. Laroussinie, K. G. Larsen, and C. Weise. From timed automata to logic — and back. *Lecture Notes in Computer Science*, 969:529–539, 1995. 257
18. K. G. Larsen, P. Pettersson, and W. Yi. Model-checking for real-time systems. *Lecture Notes in Computer Science*, 965:62–88, 1995. 270
19. Damian Niwiński and Igor Walukiewicz. Games for the μ-calculus. *Theoretical Computer Science*, 163(1–2):99–116, 1996. 256, 257, 258, 261, 262, 265, 266, 268, 269
20. P. Pettersson. *Modelling and Verification of Real-Time Systems Using Timed Automata: Theory and Practice*. PhD thesis, Uppsala University, 1999. 257, 267
21. Jean-François Raskin and Pierre-Yves Schobbens. The logic of event clocks: Decidability, complexity and expressiveness. *Journal of Automata, Languages and Combinatorics*, 4(3):247–282, 1999. 255, 257
22. Maria Sorea. Results on event-recording logic. Technical Report SRI-CSL-01-06, Computer Science Laboratory, SRI International, 2001. http://www.csl.sri.com/papers/csl-01-06/. 256, 261
23. Maria Sorea. Tempo: A model-checker for event-recording automata. Technical Report SRI-CSL-01-04, Computer Science Laboratory, SRI International, 2001. A short version appeared at the Workshop on Real-Time Tools 2001, Aalborg, Denmark. http://www.csl.sri.com/papers/csl-01-04/. 256, 257, 267
24. B. Steffen and A. Ingólfsdóttir. Characteristic formulae for processes with divergence. *Information and Computation*, 110(1):149–163, April 1994. 256
25. C. Stirling and D. Walker. Local model checking in the modal mu-calculus. *Theoretical Computer Science*, 89(1):161–177, 1991. 261

26. R. S. Streett and E. A. Emerson. An automata theoretic decision procedure for the propositional mu-calculus. *Information and Computation*, 81(3):249–264, 1989. 256, 257, 261, 266

27. Howard Wong-Toi. *Symbolic Approximations for Verifying Real-Time Systems*. PhD thesis, Stanford University, November 1994. 257, 267

A Calculus of Mobile Resources*

Jens Chr. Godskesen[1], Thomas Hildebrandt[1], and Vladimiro Sassone[2]

[1] IT University of Copenhagen
{jcg,hilde}@itu.dk
[2] University of Sussex
vs@susx.ac.uk

Abstract. We introduce a calculus of *Mobile Resources* (MR) tailored for the design and analysis of systems containing mobile, possibly nested, computing devices that may have resource and access constraints, and which are not copyable nor modifiable per se. We provide a reduction as well as a labelled transition semantics and prove a correspondence between barbed bisimulation congruence and a higher-order bisimulation. We provide examples of the expressiveness of the calculus, and apply the theory to prove one of its characteristic properties.

Introduction

Mobile computing resources moving in and out of other computing resources abound in our daily life. Prime examples are smart cards [12] used e.g. in Subscriber Identity Module (SIM) cards or next generation credit cards, moving from card issuers to card holders and in and out of mobile phones or automatic teller machines (ATMs). Accordingly, the ability to reason about correctness of the behavior of concurrent systems containing such resources, as well as the need of design and implementation tools, will raise to an increasingly prominent role. We propose a calculus of *mobile resources* (MR) aimed at designing and analysing systems containing nested, mobile computing resources residing in named locations that have *capacity* constraints. Our goals include to devise a formal framework to express and prove properties that may depend on the assumption that such resources are neither *copyable* nor arbitrarily *modifiable* per se. These assumptions are crucial for the security of systems based on smart cards as trusted computing bases, such as e-cash and SIMs.

The calculus MR is inspired by the Mobile Ambient calculus [5, 16], bears relationships to Boxed Ambients [3] and the Seal calculus [23], and to distributed process algebras [13, 22, 10], but differs from all these in important ways, motivated by our specific goals. Building upon a CCS-like calculus [18] with prefix, restriction, parallel composition, replication, no summation nor recursion, we introduce *named slots*, i.e., if p is a process, then $n\lfloor p \rfloor$ represents a resource p in a slot named by n. In general, we allow slot aliasing, that is slots to be named

---

* The third author is supported by 'MyThS: Models and Types for Security in Mobile Distributed Systems', EU FET-GC IST-2001-32617.

L. Brim et al. (Eds.): CONCUR 2002, LNCS 2421, pp. 272–287, 2002.

by more than one name, writing $\tilde{n}\lfloor p \rfloor$ for a resource p in a slot named by a set of names $\tilde{n}$. We omit brackets around singleton sets.

We postulate that a resource can move from a location to another only if an empty slot can be found at the target location. This makes $n\lfloor \bullet \rfloor$ very different from a slot containing a terminated process, and allows us to model locations that can only contain a bounded number of resources, thus capturing a very relevant aspect of real-world devices carrying embedded processors. To abstract away from this, replication in the style of the π calculus can be used to recover the usual semantics of locations by generating unboundedly many slots at a location, as, e.g., in $!n\lfloor \bullet \rfloor$. Since resources are processes, they might themselves contain slots, giving rise to a nested spatial structure. By allowing restriction of location names, we can represent restricted access to a location.

To help focusing our ideas, let us consider the processes

$$\mathsf{Alice} \triangleq (m)(a\lfloor \mathsf{C} \rfloor \parallel \mathsf{A})$$
$$\mathsf{Bob} \triangleq (b)(n)(b\lfloor \bullet \rfloor \parallel \mathsf{B} \parallel \{d,n\}\lfloor \bullet \rfloor)$$
$$\mathsf{C} \triangleq c\lfloor c' \rfloor \parallel m$$
$$P \triangleq \mathsf{Alice} \parallel \mathsf{Bob}$$

consisting of a process Alice with a resource C in a public slot named a and a process Bob having an empty, private slot named b and an empty slot with a public name d and a private name n. For the sake of this discussion, the spatial structure of P can be depicted as in the labelled tree below, where edges represent slots, labels slot names, and nodes processes other than slots.

Mobility of resources in MR is 'objective,' as opposed to 'subjective,' i.e. the migration of a resource is initiated and controlled not by the resource itself, but by an external process. More precisely, a resource is controlled by a process *outside* the slot where the resource is placed, that is a process residing at a super location. We introduce this notion by means of *move actions* of the form $n \triangleright \overline{m}$, a capability that should be read 'move a resource from a slot at the location n to a slot at the location m.' We use a notation reminiscent of action/co-action pairs to stress the dual roles of n and m that, respectively, give and take a resource, and we will adopt consistent conventions throughout the paper. If for instance $\mathsf{A} \triangleq a \triangleright \overline{d} . \mathsf{A}'$, we would have

$$P \searrow (m)(b)(n)(a\lfloor \bullet \rfloor \parallel \mathsf{A}' \parallel b\lfloor \bullet \rfloor \parallel \mathsf{B} \parallel \{d,n\}\lfloor \mathsf{C} \rfloor)$$

whose spatial structure can be drawn as follows.

$$A' \parallel B$$

$$a \diagup \quad b\vert \quad \diagdown \{d,n\}$$

$$\lfloor \bullet \rfloor \quad \lfloor \bullet \rfloor \quad \lfloor m \rfloor$$

$$\vert c$$

$$\lfloor c' \rfloor$$

Observe that the movement of C from a to d causes a *scope extension* for m.

Carrying on with our example, supposing $B \triangleq d \triangleright \bar{b}.B'$ we have the reduction

$$(m)(b)(n)(a\lfloor \bullet \rfloor \parallel A' \parallel b\lfloor \bullet \rfloor \parallel d \triangleright \bar{b}.B' \parallel \{d,n\}\lfloor C \rfloor) \searrow$$

$$(m)(b)(n)(a\lfloor \bullet \rfloor \parallel A' \parallel b\lfloor C \rfloor \parallel B' \parallel \{d,n\}\lfloor \bullet \rfloor).$$

Observe that the last two reductions illustrate the passage of resource C from Alice to the private slot of Bob, without Alice's knowing the name of Bob's private slot.

In order to allow the number of slots to *decrease*, slots may be removed. We denote slot remotion with actions of the form $\natural \tilde{n}$. Thus, if $B' \triangleq \natural\{d,n\}.D$, the following reduction is possible.

$$(m)(b)(n)(a\lfloor \bullet \rfloor \parallel A' \parallel b\lfloor C \rfloor \parallel \natural\{d,n\}.D \parallel \{d,n\}\lfloor \bullet \rfloor) \searrow$$

$$(m)(b)(n)(a\lfloor \bullet \rfloor \parallel A' \parallel b\lfloor C \rfloor \parallel D).$$

The remarkable features here are that a slot can only be removed by processes knowing all its names. In particular, holding a private name to a slot will prevent the slot's deletion. In our example, the slot named $\{d,n\}$ cannot be deleted by Alice or by another process in the environment, even though it is globally accessible by name d.

While explicit mobility captures asynchronous communication via resource passing, *synchronous communication* is the second central concept of MR, covering several different aspects of process interaction in our application domain. As in CCS, co-located parallel processes can communicate synchronously by performing respectively an a-action and a $\bar{a}$-action. In addition, we allow a process to communicate with any of its descendants, by performing a *directed action* of the form δa, where δ is a sequence of slot names. For example, if $D = bc\bar{c}'.D'$ in our running example, we have the reduction

$$(m)(b)(n)(a\lfloor \bullet \rfloor \parallel A' \parallel b\lfloor c\lfloor c' \rfloor \parallel m \rfloor \parallel bc\bar{c}'.D') \searrow$$

$$(a')(b)(b')(a\lfloor \bullet \rfloor \parallel A' \parallel b\lfloor c\lfloor 0 \rfloor \parallel m \rfloor \parallel D'),$$

where the co-action from D synchronises with the corresponding action from slot c inside slot b. In this way, the actions of the resource C (and its sub-resources) are *dynamically bound* to the directed actions of Bob. Unlike e.g. the Seal calculus, we do not distinguish between undirected actions and actions that may synchronise with ascendants.

Using sequences of names in move actions as for the synchronisation, we can move a resource (subtree) from a slot at an arbitrarily deep sub-location to an empty slot (a black leaf) at another arbitrarily deep sub-location. For instance, if $D' = bc \triangleright \bar{a} \, . \, D''$ we have the reduction

$$(m)(b)(n)(a\lfloor \bullet \rfloor \parallel A' \parallel b\lfloor c\lfloor 0 \rfloor \rfloor \parallel m \rfloor \parallel bc \triangleright \bar{a} \, . \, D'' \,) \searrow$$

$$(m)(b)(n)(\, a\lfloor 0 \rfloor \parallel A' \parallel b\lfloor c'\lfloor \bullet \rfloor \rfloor \parallel m \rfloor \parallel D'' \,).$$

The reductions presented above constitute the primary mechanisms of MR.

Structure of the paper & Results. After introducing the syntax of MR in §1, in §2 we lay the foundations of its semantic theory by giving a reduction semantics formalising the different ways of interaction discussed above; §3 discusses several small examples aimed at illustrating some particularities of MR. We then proceed in §4 to give a labelled transition semantics to MR equivalent to the reduction one. This is well known to be a non-trivial task for calculi allowing (higher-order) process mobility and scope extension, as in MR when resources containing restricted names are moved. In §5 we provide a characterisation of the barbed congruence in terms of a higher-order labelled transition bisimulation. Predictably, the main difficulty in proving the transition bisimulation to be a congruence is the insertion of processes into slots. One of the examples in §3 will point out one of the reasons for that. The detailed proofs of our results can be found in [11]. As usual with higher-order bisimulations, the characterisation here uses a selected set of contexts that play the role of destructors for the higher-order values, namely *receiving contexts* dealing with the reception of resources into slots. We will return on this later on. In §6 we give an application of the characterisation, proving a linearity property of the calculus by giving a bisimulation of two processes.

Design issues & Related work. As already mentioned, MR shares ideas with the Mobile Ambients (MA) [5]. In both calculi, in fact, processes are equipped with nested, named locations – the ambients – containing processes, and the spatial structure can be dynamically extended or change due to movement. However, likewise the Seal calculus [23], it is the *anonymous contents* of locations to be moved in MR, and it is moved by a process *external* to the location. On the contrary, in MA it is the *named location* to be moved by a process *within* it. Another departure point with MA, where ambients communicate only asynchronously, processes in MR may communicate both *synchronously*, as in CCS and the π-calculus, and *asynchronously*, by exchanging resources. Resource movement is a three-party interaction in both MR and the Seal calculus. However, slots in Seal are pure references that disappear after interaction, while in MR they remain as empty slots until explicitly removed. Moreover, the reception of a resource is via a pair action/co-action in Seal.

To the best of our knowledge, the boundedness of resources is unique, among process algebras, to the calculus proposed in this paper. Similar ideas may of course be found in related area, most notably bounded places in Petri nets, but, besides the obvious analogies, there seem to be no formal relationships with our notion here.

Our calculus shares with Safe Ambients (SA) [16] – and with several other proposals that space does not allow us to survey upon – the wish to put a stricter control on mobility and access to locations, taking the objective mobility viewpoint. While this is realised by an action/co-action synchronisation between mover and movee in the SA approach, MR relies on move actions performed by the mover. Also, the idea of direct actions across location boundaries is reminiscent of the forms of communications found in the Seal calculus, Boxed Ambients, in Dπ [13] and in the distributed Join calculus[10], though in the latter communication is asynchronous and locations distributed.

Observe that, differently from all these, MR does not allow explicit communication of names. This design choice seems consistent with our application, in that it confines information inside resources and allows network topology evolution only by means of extensions and replacement of substructures, maintaining a strictly hierarchical network structure. We leave to future work the investigation of a capability-passing version of MR, as well as the impact of asynchronous communication between remote, non directly nested sites, and the expressiveness of movements that refer to sibling slots.

Concerning the choice of moves and communication that span multiple slot boundaries our hypothesis is that, slots do not necessarily represent physical location boundaries that enforce a notion of communication distance. Distance may be enforced by use of restricted slot names akin to private fields in Java. For this reason we prefer to develop the theory in full generality. After all, that a location may not be accessed from "grand parent nodes" is an issue that can easily be demanded to the control of a type system. Of course, this choice makes the calculus more complex; its price is a more complex semantic theory, yet – we believe – still manageable. For future reference, let us call MR_2 the calculus restricted to paths of length at most two, that is with only directed communication across at most one boundary and short moves of the form $a\triangleright\bar{c}$ (flat), $ab\triangleright\bar{c}$ (up), and $a\triangleright\overline{cb}$ (down). All the results in the paper carry naturally over for this sub-calculus.

1   The Calculus

We assume an infinite set of *names* $\mathcal{N}$ ranged over by n and m. Let $\tilde{n}$ range over sets of names. Let $\overline{\mathcal{N}} = \{\overline{n} \mid n \in \mathcal{N}\}$ be the set of *co-names*. We let α range over $\mathcal{A} = \mathcal{N} \cup \overline{\mathcal{N}}$ and γ over the set $\mathcal{N}^*$ of sequences of names, referred to as *direction paths*, with ϵ denoting the empty sequence. We use δ to denote elements of $\mathcal{N}^+$, the set of non-empty direction paths. The set $\mathcal{L}$ of *prefix labels* is then defined by:

$$\lambda ::= \gamma\alpha \mid \delta\triangleright\overline{\delta'} \mid \natural\tilde{n}.$$

The actions α play the same role as in CCS. However, as explained in the introduction, we allow actions to be extended with a sequence of slot names, so that $n\alpha$ is an action directed to a resource in a slot identified by n. An action $n\alpha$ synchronises with the corresponding co-action $\bar{\alpha}$ performed by a resource in a slot at n.

The sets $\mathcal{P}$ of *process expressions* is defined by:

$$p, q ::= \mathbf{0} \mid \lambda \cdot p \mid p \parallel q \mid !p \mid (n)p \mid \tilde{n}\lfloor r \rfloor \qquad (\mathcal{P})$$
$$r \quad ::= \bullet \mid p$$

Processes $\mathbf{0}$, $\lambda \cdot p$, and $p \parallel q$ are the ordinary CCS-like constructs, representing respectively the inactive process, the prefixed process, and the parallel composition of processes. The replicated process $!p$ provides as many parallel instances of p as required and adds to the calculus the power of recursive definitions. The restriction $(n)p$ makes name n local to p. The novelty of the calculus resides in the slot processes already described in the introduction: $\tilde{n}\lfloor \bullet \rfloor$, an empty *slot*, identified by the names in $\tilde{n}$, and $\tilde{n}\lfloor p \rfloor$ a slot identified by the names $\tilde{n}$ containing a process p. We will write $n\lfloor r \rfloor$ for a slot $\{n\}\lfloor r \rfloor$ possessing only one name. We refer to processes within slots as *resources*.

The restriction operator (n) is the only binding construct; the set $fn(p)$ of free names of p is defined accordingly as usual. By convenience, we omit trailing $\mathbf{0}$s and hence write λ instead of $\lambda \cdot \mathbf{0}$. As usual, we let prefixing, replication, and restriction be right associative and bind stronger than parallel composition hence writing e.g. $!(n)n \cdot p \parallel q$ instead of $(!((n)(n \cdot p))) \parallel q$. For at set of names $\tilde{n} = \{n_1, \ldots, n_k\}$ we let $(\tilde{n})p$ denote $(n_1) \cdots (n_k)p$.

2   Reduction Semantics

Contexts C are, as usual, terms with a hole $(-)$. We write $\mathrm{C}(p)$ for the insertion of p in the hole of context C. An equivalence relation S on $\mathcal{P}$ is a *congruence* if it is preserved by all contexts. As our calculus allows actions involving terms at depths arbitrarily far apart, in order to express its notions with formal precision, yet in succinct terms, we need to make an essential use of a particular kind of contexts throughout the paper. We define an $\mathcal{N}^*$-indexed family of *path contexts*, C_γ, inductively as:

$$\mathrm{C}_\epsilon ::= (-) \qquad \mathrm{C}_{n\gamma} ::= \tilde{n}\lfloor \mathrm{C}_\gamma \parallel p \rfloor , \qquad n \in \tilde{n}.$$

Observe that the direction path γ for a context C_γ indicates a path under which the context's 'hole' is found. We extend $fn()$ to path contexts by $fn(\mathrm{C}_\gamma) = fn(\mathrm{C}_\gamma(\mathbf{0}))$. We also define a family of resource contexts

$$\mathrm{D}_{\gamma n} ::= \mathrm{C}_\gamma\big(\tilde{n}\lfloor (-) \rfloor\big) , \qquad n \in \tilde{n},$$

for the special case where the hole is the only content of a slot.

The structural congruence relation $\equiv$ is the least congruence on $\mathcal{P}$ satisfying alpha-conversion and the rules in Table 1. The equations express that $(P, \parallel, \mathbf{0})$ is a commutative monoid (E_1–E_3) and enforce the usual rules for scope (E_4–E_6) and replication (E_7). We write $p \equiv_\alpha q$ if p and q are alpha-convertible.

Table 1. Structural equivalence

$E_1.\ p \parallel 0 \equiv p$	$E_4.\ (n)0 \equiv 0$	$E_7.\ !p \equiv p \parallel\ !p$
$E_2.\ p \parallel q \equiv q \parallel p$	$E_5.\ (n)p \parallel p' \equiv (n)(p \parallel p')$, if $n \notin fn(p')$	
$E_3.\ (p \parallel p') \parallel p'' \equiv p \parallel (p' \parallel p'')$	$E_6.\ (n)\tilde{n}\lfloor p \rfloor \equiv \tilde{n}\lfloor (n)p \rfloor$, if $n \notin \tilde{n}$	

Table 2. Reduction rules

$$\gamma\alpha \cdot p \parallel C_\gamma(\overline{\alpha} \cdot q) \searrow p \parallel C_\gamma(q)$$

$$\gamma\delta_1 \triangleright \overline{\gamma\delta_2} \cdot p \parallel C_\gamma(D_{\delta_1}(q) \parallel D_{\delta_2}(\bullet)) \searrow p \parallel C_\gamma(D_{\delta_1}(\bullet) \parallel D_{\delta_2}(q))$$

$$\natural\tilde{n} \cdot p \parallel \tilde{n}\lfloor r \rfloor \searrow p$$

Evaluation contexts E are contexts whose hole does not appear under prefix or replication, i.e.

$$E ::= (-) \mid \tilde{n}\lfloor E \rfloor \mid E \parallel p \mid (n)E$$

Define $\searrow$ as the least binary relation on $\mathcal{P}$ satisfying the rules in Table 2 and closed under $\equiv$ and under all evaluation contexts E.

The first rule captures both the standard CCS synchronous communication and a synchronisation reminiscent of the one found in the Seal calculus and in Boxed ambients, in that communication in $n\alpha$ is directed downward and may synchronize with a local communication on α inside n. The purpose of context C_γ there is to express that $\gamma\alpha$ synchronises with an $\overline{\alpha}$ found under path γ. The second rule defines movement of resources. This movement is '*objective*,' meaning that resources are moved from the outside and not by the resource itself, as in the Ambient calculus. The third rule defines deletion of slots. The process that performs it must hold all the names of the slot.

As already remarked, moves across multiple boundaries make the calculus formally more complex. The price we pay is a pervasive use of contexts, starting here in the reduction rules and with effects reaching – as we will see – our bisimulation congruence. We remark that in MR_2, where paths have length at most two, the movement rules above specialise to

$$a \triangleright \overline{cb} \cdot p \parallel a\lfloor s \rfloor \parallel c\lfloor q \parallel b\lfloor \bullet \rfloor \rfloor \searrow p \parallel a\lfloor \bullet \rfloor \parallel c\lfloor q \parallel b\lfloor s \rfloor \rfloor,$$

$$ab \triangleright \overline{c} \cdot p \parallel a\lfloor b\lfloor s \rfloor \parallel q \rfloor \parallel c\lfloor \bullet \rfloor \searrow p \parallel a\lfloor b\lfloor \bullet \rfloor \parallel q \rfloor \parallel c\lfloor s \rfloor,$$

$$a \triangleright \overline{b} \cdot p \parallel a\lfloor s \rfloor \parallel b\lfloor \bullet \rfloor \searrow p \parallel a\lfloor \bullet \rfloor \parallel b\lfloor s \rfloor,$$

and similarly for the communication rules.

We move now to study the semantic theory of MR. We start by discussing the notion of observation. It seems fair to observe the communication actions processes offer to the environment. We then define barbs as:

$$p \downarrow n \quad \text{if} \quad p \equiv (\tilde{n})(\alpha \cdot p' \parallel q), \quad \alpha \in \{n, \overline{n}\},$$

where $n \notin \tilde{n}$. This excludes observing restricted actions, as well as directed actions and move actions. Several alternative choices of observation appear natural, as e.g. observing at top level – i.e., not inside any slots – free slot names, empty slots, path actions, or movements. Our choice is robust, as none of these alternatives would actually give rise to a different semantic theory from the one we develop below.

Definition 1. A *barbed bisimulation* is a symmetric relation S on $\mathcal{P}$ such that whenever p S q

$$p \downarrow n \text{ implies } q \downarrow n$$
$$p \searrow p', \text{ then } \exists q \searrow q' \text{ with } p' \text{ S } q'$$

Barbed bisimulation congruence $\sim_b$ is the largest congruence that is a barbed bisimulation.

The definition above is in principle stricter than the classical notion of barbed congruence, defined as the largest congruence *contained* in the barbed bisimulation. It is however gaining credit in process algebra theory for its good properties (cf. e.g [9, 1]).

3   Examples

Slots with multiple names. As already remarked in the introduction, slots may be given multiple names and some of the names may be hidden. As a further example, consider

$$(a)(a')(\{a,b\}\lfloor \bullet \rfloor \parallel \{a',b\}\lfloor \bullet \rfloor \parallel a \triangleright \bar{a} . \natural \{a,b\} \parallel a \lfloor \bullet \rfloor).$$

Here the environment can insert resources non-deterministically into one of two slots using the name b. If a resource is inserted into the buffer slot named $\{a,b\}$ then it is moved to an internal slot and the buffer is removed.

Linearity. It is a fundamental property of MR that resources cannot be copied. This interacts with the usual scoping rules enforced by restriction to yield an interesting '*linearity*' property. Consider the term $P \triangleq (b)(a\lfloor b \rfloor \parallel !a\bar{b} . c)$. Because of the restriction (b) only the resource inside slot a will ever be able to use b to interact with the replicated term on its side. However, it may in principle be possible that exporting it to some external context, such a resource may be able to 'copy' itself, replicating the reference to b. This would be possible in several (higher-order) calculi. Yet, it is not possible in MR. In particular, if a resource containing a reference to a local name is given out, only (a residual of) *that* resource may in future refer that name. This is stated by the following equation, that we prove in §6.

$$(b)(a\lfloor b \rfloor \parallel !a\bar{b} . c) \sim_b (b)(a\lfloor b \rfloor \parallel a\bar{b} . c)$$

Suggestively, the process $(b)(a\lfloor b \rfloor \parallel !a\bar{b} . c)$ can be regarded as a model of a pre-paid cash card (the resource b) in the slot a of a vending machine $a\lfloor \bullet \rfloor \parallel !a\bar{b} . c$

that delivers a cup of coffee (action c) for each cash card of the right kind, b, inserted in a. The $\sim_b$-equation above then states that if there exists only *one* card of the 'right' type, then there will ever be only *one* cup of coffee; in other words, the cash card cannot be copied. This is the kind of properties relevant to our intended application area.

Scope extension and mobility The interplay of upward and downward moves and scope extension gives rise to interactions unexpected at first, and is a major challenge for the theory of the observational congruence presented in the next section. Here, we exemplify it as follows. Consider the contexts

$$C_1 \triangleq c\lfloor (-) \rfloor \parallel a, \qquad C_2 \triangleq d\lfloor (-) \rfloor \parallel d\bar{a} . b,$$

and the process $p \triangleq (a)C_1(C_2(\bullet)) = (a)\big(c\lfloor d\lfloor \bullet \rfloor \parallel d\bar{a} . b \rfloor \parallel a \big)$. Since name a is private, it would appear that no resource inserted into the empty slot d can synchronise with the $d\bar{a}$-action and, similarly, that no process can ever synchronise with the a action at top-level. It would then follow that the b action can never be revealed and, in particular, that p behaves like $q \triangleq (a)(c\lfloor d\lfloor \bullet \rfloor \rfloor)$, no matter the context. Yet, this is not the case. Under a suitable context, it is possible for the process a to change its role from being the parent of $d\bar{a} . b$ to being its child in the slot named d. Suppose in fact that p and q are inserted into the context

$$C = x\lfloor (-) \rfloor \parallel y\lfloor \bullet \rfloor \parallel xc\triangleright\bar{y} . x\triangleright\bar{y}d.$$

Then $C(p)$ reduces (in two steps) to

$$(a)\big(x\lfloor \bullet \rfloor \parallel y\lfloor C_2(C_1(\bullet)) \rfloor \big) = (a)(x\lfloor \bullet \rfloor \parallel y\lfloor d\lfloor c\lfloor \bullet \rfloor \parallel a \rfloor \parallel d\bar{a} . b \rfloor),$$

where C_1 and C_2 have swapped place. Now the b-action may be unleashed upon synchronisation on a. Since $b \notin fn(C(q))$, clearly $C(q)$ cannot reduce to a process with a b-action, so $p \not\sim_b q$.

Digital Signature Card. The following example models a digital signature card. For readability we use the names *reg*, *in* and *out* for slots representing respectively a *register*, an *in-buffer* and a *out-buffer*. We then give a model of a process Enc_k parametrized by a name k (the key) that (repeatedly) encrypts resources received in its *in*-buffer with key k, and returns the encrypted resource via its *out*-buffer.

$$Enc_k \triangleq !(reg)(in\triangleright\overline{reg\ k} . reg\triangleright\overline{out} \parallel reg\lfloor k\lfloor \bullet \rfloor \rfloor) \parallel in\lfloor \bullet \rfloor \parallel out\lfloor \bullet \rfloor$$

Dually, we can define a process Dec_k that (repeatedly) decrypts resources received in its *in*-buffer with key k and returns the decrypted resource via its *out*-buffer.

$$Dec_k \triangleq !(reg)(in\triangleright\overline{reg} . reg\ k\triangleright\overline{out} . \parallel reg\lfloor \bullet \rfloor) \parallel in\lfloor \bullet \rfloor \parallel out\lfloor \bullet \rfloor$$

If the name k is globally known, anyone can perform encryption and decryption. On the other hand, if k is a shared secret between two processes, e.g. Alice and Bob, and Alice (resp. Bob) possesses an encryption (resp. decryption) process as a private resource, then Alice can send messages secretly to Bob.

$$Alice_{k,M} \triangleq (m)(a)\left(\, a\lfloor Enc_k \rfloor \;\|\; m\lfloor M \rfloor \;\|\; m{\triangleright}\overline{a\ in}\,.\, a\ out{\triangleright}\overline{network}\,\right)$$

$$Bob_k \triangleq (m)(b)(b\lfloor Dec_k \rfloor \;\|\; m\lfloor\, \bullet\, \rfloor \;\|\; network{\triangleright}\overline{b\ in}\,.\, b\ out{\triangleright}\overline{m})$$

$$SecretCom_M \triangleq (k)\left(\, Alice_{k,M} \;\|\; Bob_k\,\right) \;\|\; network\lfloor\, \bullet\, \rfloor$$

We may prove the encryption property by showing that for any processes (messages) of the form $M = a_1\,.\,a_2\ldots.a_i$ and $M' = a'_1\,.\,a'_2\ldots.a'_j$, we have

$$SecretCom_M \sim_b SecretCom_{M'}.$$

We then may model a digital signature card which generates the key and exports the decryption resource (as many times as needed) but keeps the encryption resource private.

$$SignatureCard \triangleq (k)(\,!export\lfloor Dec_k \rfloor \;\|\; Enc_k\,)$$

4 Transition Semantics

In this section we set out to provide MR with a labelled transition semantics. The interplay of mobility and local names as illustrated by the two examples in the previous section has interesting consequences in this respect. The first example, in fact, shows that a certain amount of information must be retained about resources given out to the context. This is not similar to the transition semantics for the π calculus (cf. [18, 20]). In the π calculus the relevant information concerns the extruded names; in MR things may in principle be more complex, since interaction involves passing around resources, i.e. higher-order, evolving entities. The second example also points out that we must consider that exported resources may be received in arbitrarily complex contexts.

We focus on explaining the transition rules for the characteristic features of our calculus, i.e. slots, directed communication and objective mobility, which are shown in Table 4. Also, we explain the interplay between labels.

To capture directed communication, we introduce labels of the form $\overline{\delta}\alpha$ that may synchronise with the directed actions of the form $\delta\alpha$ that appear as prefixes in the calculus. We do this by defining $\overline{\overline{n}a} = n\overline{a}$. For example, we have

$$n\lfloor a.p \rfloor \xrightarrow{\overline{n}a} n\lfloor p \rfloor \qquad (nesting)$$

and the usual synchronisation rule yields

$$n\overline{a}\,.\,p \;\|\; n\lfloor a\,.\,q \rfloor \xrightarrow{\tau} p \;\|\; n\lfloor q \rfloor\ ,$$

The three-party interaction required for the movement of resources is modelled by means of higher-order labels. We introduce

$$\overline{\delta} \triangleright \langle p \rangle \quad (p \text{ exits from } \delta) \qquad \text{and} \qquad (p) \triangleright \delta \quad (p \text{ enters in } \delta).$$

The corresponding co-labels will be indicated by $\delta \triangleright (p)$ and $\langle p \rangle \triangleright \overline{\delta}$, respectively.

The move action $\delta_1 \triangleright \overline{\delta_2}$ – whose co-action we denote by $\overline{\delta_1} \triangleright \delta_2$ – and the two higher-order labels will partially match each other in pairs, so as to give rise to co-*label* corresponding to the third party, the one missing to perfection the three-way synchronisation. That is,

$$\begin{array}{lll}
\delta_1 \triangleright \overline{\delta_2} & \text{coalesces with} \quad \overline{\delta_1} \triangleright \langle p \rangle \quad \text{yielding} & \langle p \rangle \triangleright \overline{\delta_2}, \\
\delta_1 \triangleright \overline{\delta_2} & \text{coalesces with} \quad (p) \triangleright \delta_2 \quad \text{yielding} & \delta_1 \triangleright (p), \\
\overline{\delta_1} \triangleright \langle p \rangle & \text{coalesces with} \quad (p) \triangleright \delta_2 \quad \text{yielding} & \overline{\delta_1} \triangleright \delta_2.
\end{array}$$

Hence, the three labels match in any order and annihilate their matching action/co-action particles to yield, at last, a τ. For instance, a resource that exits a slot produces a transition

$$n \lfloor p \rfloor \xrightarrow{\overline{n} \triangleright \langle p \rangle} n \lfloor \bullet \rfloor \quad (\textit{exit}),$$

and similarly, an empty slot that receives a resource, gives rise to a higher-order transition

$$m \lfloor \bullet \rfloor \xrightarrow{(p) \triangleright m} m \lfloor p \rfloor \quad (\textit{enter}).$$

These 'exit' and 'enter' transitions may synchronise, yielding a *co-move* transition

$$n \lfloor p \rfloor \parallel m \lfloor \bullet \rfloor \xrightarrow{\overline{n} \triangleright m} n \lfloor \bullet \rfloor \parallel m \lfloor p \rfloor \quad (\textit{co-move})$$

which, in turn, can synchronise with the corresponding move action to yield a τ-action that represent the completed interaction:

$$n \lfloor p \rfloor \parallel m \lfloor \bullet \rfloor \parallel n \triangleright \overline{m} . q \xrightarrow{\tau} n \lfloor \bullet \rfloor \parallel m \lfloor p \rfloor \parallel q.$$

Symmetrically, 'exit' and 'move' transitions may synchronise, resulting in a 'give' transition

$$n \lfloor p \rfloor \parallel n \triangleright \overline{m} . q \xrightarrow{\langle p \rangle \triangleright \overline{m}} n \lfloor \bullet \rfloor \parallel q \quad (\textit{give})$$

which may synchronise with the dual 'enter' transition. Dually, 'enter' and 'move' transitions may synchronise, resulting in a 'take' transition

$$m \lfloor \bullet \rfloor \parallel n \triangleright \overline{m} . q \xrightarrow{n \triangleright (p)} m \lfloor p \rfloor \parallel q \quad (\textit{take}),$$

which is ready to synchronise with the dual 'exit' transition.

Rules (*exit*) and, in particular, (*enter*) may at first appear to be 'spontaneous' rules. A closer analysis though reveals that they are akin to 'output' and 'input' transitions in the 'early' labelled transitions semantics of the (higher-order) π calculus, rather than transition that may fire autonomously an unbounded number of times.

Table 3. Transition rules, standard

$$
(\text{prefix}) \; \frac{}{\lambda \cdot p \xrightarrow{\lambda} p} \qquad\qquad (\text{rest}) \; \frac{p \xrightarrow{\pi} p'}{(n)p \xrightarrow{\pi} (n)p'}, \; n \notin fn(\pi) \cup bn(\pi)
$$

$$
(\text{rep}) \; \frac{p \parallel !p \xrightarrow{\pi} p'}{!p \xrightarrow{\pi} p'} \qquad (\text{sync}) \; \frac{p_1 \xrightarrow{(\tilde{n})\overline{\pi}} p_1' \quad p_2 \xrightarrow{\pi} p_2'}{p_1 \parallel p_2 \xrightarrow{\tau} (\tilde{n})(p_1' \parallel p_2')}, \; fn(p_2) \cap \tilde{n} = \emptyset
$$

$$
(\text{par}) \; \frac{p \xrightarrow{\pi} p'}{p \parallel q \xrightarrow{\pi} p' \parallel q}, \; fn(q) \cap bn(\pi) = \emptyset \qquad (\text{sym}) \; \frac{p \parallel q \xrightarrow{\pi} p' \parallel q}{q \parallel p \xrightarrow{\pi} q \parallel p'}
$$

The last issue involved in the movement of resources is the treatment of scope extension when resources are moved. The phenomenon is totally analogous to that in the (higher-order) pi-calculus, and we handle it as usual (cf. [20]) by restrictions on the labels of (*exit*) and (*give*) transitions, e.g.,

$$
(m)n\lfloor m \rfloor \xrightarrow{(m)\overline{n}\triangleright\langle m\rangle} n\lfloor \bullet \rfloor \qquad (O1)
$$

and by explicit scope extension in the synchronisation rule.

The directed communication and movement actions are generalised to actions spanning several levels by the (*nesting*) rule. This uses an operation $n \cdot (\_)$ to prepend n to labels coming from processes enclosed into slot n defined as follows:

$$
n \cdot (\tau) = \tau, \qquad\qquad n \cdot (\overline{\gamma}\alpha) = \overline{n\gamma}\alpha, \qquad\qquad n \cdot (\overline{\delta_1}\triangleright\delta_2) = \overline{n\delta_1}\triangleright n\delta_2,
$$
$$
n \cdot ((p)\triangleright\delta) = (p)\triangleright n\delta, \quad n \cdot \big((\tilde{n})\overline{\delta}\triangleright\langle p\rangle\big) = (\tilde{n})\overline{n\delta}\triangleright\langle p\rangle,
$$

where $n \notin \tilde{n}$. By using $n \cdot (\pi)$, we implicitly assume that π is a label of one of the kinds above. Finally, the rule (*delete*) allows a slot to be deleted if all its names are free.

We let π range over the complete set Π of labels used in our transition semantics, defined formally as follows.

$$
\pi ::= \beta \mid (\tilde{n})\overline{\delta}\triangleright\langle p\rangle \mid (\tilde{n})\langle p\rangle\triangleright\overline{\delta} \quad \text{where} \quad \beta ::= \tau \mid \lambda \mid \overline{\delta}\alpha \mid \overline{\delta}\triangleright\delta \mid (p)\triangleright\delta \mid \delta\triangleright(p).
$$

The set of *bound names* in a label π, $bn(\pi)$, is $\tilde{n}$ if π is $(\tilde{n})\overline{\delta}\triangleright\langle p\rangle$ or $(\tilde{n})\langle p\rangle\triangleright\overline{\delta}$, and $\emptyset$ if π is a β-label.

The rules in Table 3 and 4 then define a labelled transition system

$$
(\mathcal{P}, \longrightarrow \subseteq \mathcal{P} \times \Pi \times \mathcal{P}).
$$

The following two propositions state the correspondence between the reduction semantics and the transition semantics.

Proposition 1. $p \xrightarrow{\tau} p'$ *if and only if* $p \searrow p'$.

Proposition 2. $p \xrightarrow{n}$ *or* $p \xrightarrow{\overline{n}}$ *if and only if* $p \downarrow n$.

Table 4. Transition rules for resources and mobility

$$(exit) \; \frac{}{\tilde{n}\lfloor p \rfloor \xrightarrow{\overline{n} \triangleright \langle p \rangle} \tilde{n}\lfloor \bullet \rfloor}, \; n \in \tilde{n} \qquad (enter) \; \frac{}{\tilde{n}\lfloor \bullet \rfloor \xrightarrow{\langle p \rangle \triangleright n} \tilde{n}\lfloor p \rfloor}, \; n \in \tilde{n}$$

$$(give) \; \frac{p_1 \xrightarrow{(\tilde{n})\overline{\delta_1} \triangleright \langle q \rangle} p_1' \quad p_2 \xrightarrow{\delta_1 \triangleright \overline{\delta_2}} p_2'}{p_1 \parallel p_2 \xrightarrow{(\tilde{n})\langle q \rangle \triangleright \overline{\delta_2}} p_1' \parallel p_2'}, \; fn(p_2) \cap \tilde{n} = \emptyset \qquad (take) \; \frac{p_2 \xrightarrow{\delta_1 \triangleright \overline{\delta_2}} p_2' \quad p_1 \xrightarrow{\langle q \rangle \triangleright \delta_2} p_1'}{p_1 \parallel p_2 \xrightarrow{\delta_1 \triangleright \langle q \rangle} p_1' \parallel p_2'}$$

$$(co\text{-}move) \; \frac{p_1 \xrightarrow{(\tilde{n})\overline{\delta_1} \triangleright \langle q \rangle} p_1' \quad p_2 \xrightarrow{\langle q \rangle \triangleright \delta_2} p_2'}{p_1 \parallel p_2 \xrightarrow{\delta_1 \triangleright \delta_2} (\tilde{n})(p_1' \parallel p_2')}, \; fn(p_2) \cap \tilde{n} = \emptyset$$

$$(nesting) \; \frac{p \xrightarrow{\pi} p'}{\tilde{n}\lfloor p \rfloor \xrightarrow{n \cdot (\pi)} \tilde{n}\lfloor p' \rfloor}, \; n \in \tilde{n} \qquad (delete) \; \frac{}{\tilde{n}\lfloor r \rfloor \xrightarrow{\overline{\natural}\tilde{n}} 0} \qquad (alpha) \; \frac{p \equiv_\alpha p' \quad p' \xrightarrow{\pi} q}{p \xrightarrow{\pi} q}$$

$$(O1) \; \frac{p \xrightarrow{(\tilde{n})\overline{\delta} \triangleright \langle q \rangle} p'}{(n)p \xrightarrow{(n\tilde{n})\overline{\delta} \triangleright \langle q \rangle} p'}, \; n \in fn(q) \backslash (fn(\delta) \cup \tilde{n}) \qquad (O2) \; \frac{p \xrightarrow{(\tilde{n})\langle q \rangle \triangleright \overline{\delta}} p'}{(n)p \xrightarrow{(n\tilde{n})\langle q \rangle \triangleright \overline{\delta}} p'}, \; n \in fn(q) \backslash (fn(\delta) \cup \tilde{n})$$

5   Bisimulation Congruence

In this section we provide a labelled transition bisimulation, and prove that it coincides with the barbed bisimulation congruence.

As remarked in §4, we need to take into account that resources may be moved at arbitrary depth. As often happens in higher-order bisimulations (cf. e.g. [19, 8, 17]), we need to use an appropriate selection of destructors in order to test and assess the higher-order values exchanged by interaction. Analogously to what is done in [17] for the ambient calculus, we embody such contexts – resource receptors in our case – in the label. That is, we replace the higher-order actions $(\tilde{n})\langle p \rangle \triangleright \overline{\delta}$ and $(\tilde{n})\overline{\delta} \triangleright \langle p \rangle$ with the family of actions $\triangleright \overline{\delta}(D_\delta)$ and $(C_\gamma)\overline{\delta'} \triangleright (D_\delta)$, respectively. The path contexts D_δ and C_γ represent the surrounding slots that the resource crosses during its movement.

Definition 2. *For D_δ and C_γ path contexts, we define:*

- $p \xrightarrow{\triangleright \overline{\delta}(D_\delta)} (\tilde{n})(p' \parallel D_\delta(q))$ *if* $p \xrightarrow{(\tilde{n})\langle q \rangle \triangleright \overline{\delta}} p'$, *and* $fn(D_\delta) \cap \tilde{n} = \emptyset$.
- $p \xrightarrow{(C_\gamma)\overline{\delta'} \triangleright (D_\delta)} (\tilde{n})(C_\gamma(p') \parallel D_\delta(q))$ *if* $p \xrightarrow{(\tilde{n})\overline{\delta'} \triangleright \langle q \rangle} p'$, *and* $(fn(C_\gamma) \cup fn(D_\delta)) \cap \tilde{n} = \emptyset$.

The set of actions considered in the bisimulation game below is thus:

$$\psi ::= \beta \mid \triangleright \overline{\delta}(D_\delta) \mid (C_\gamma)\overline{\delta'} \triangleright (D_\delta).$$

Definition 3. A *simulation* is a binary relation $\mathcal{S}$ over $\mathcal{P}$ such that whenever $p \, \mathcal{S} \, q$

$$\text{if } p \xrightarrow{\psi} p' \text{ then } \exists q \xrightarrow{\psi} q' \text{ such that } p' \, \mathcal{S} \, q'$$

$\mathcal{S}$ is a *bisimulation* if $\mathcal{S}$ and $\mathcal{S}^{-1}$ are simulations. We write $p \sim q$ if there exists a bisimulation $\mathcal{S}$ such that $p \, \mathcal{S} \, q$.

It follows immediately from the definition of bisimulation that it is an *equivalence relation*. Also, $\sim$ can be proved to be a congruence.

Theorem 1. $\sim$ *is a congruence.*

From the correspondence between τ transitions and reductions (Prop. 1 and 2), and from the fact that $\sim$ is a congruence (Thm. 1), it follows easily that $\sim$ is sound with respect to the barbed bisimulation congruence. On the other hand, the proof that $\sim_b$ is a bisimulation can be found in [11].

Theorem 2. $\sim_b = \sim$

It can be argued that the use of 'receptor embodying' labels and their employment in the bisimulation make the latter a form of contextual equivalence, so that proving processes bisimilarity becomes overly hard. We claim that establishing $\sim$ is still much easier than proving barbed congruence, since the needed contexts have a very simple structure. The next section aims at supporting this claim by analysing an example.

In [11] we show path contexts with paths at length most two are enough for MR *altogether*.

6   An Application

In this section we prove the $\sim_b$-equivalence illustrated in §3 about the vending machine and the 'linear' behaviour of resources, taking up the opportunity to put $\sim$ at work. Exploiting Thm. 2, we prove that

$$(b)\big(a\lfloor b\rfloor \;\|\; !a\overline{b}.c\big) \sim_b (b)\big(a\lfloor b\rfloor \;\|\; a\overline{b}.c\big)$$

by showing that the two processes are $\sim$-bisimilar that, by co-induction, can be proved by proving that $\mathcal{S} = \mathcal{S}_1 \cup \mathcal{S}_2 \cup \{(p,p)\}$ is a bisimulation where

$$\mathcal{S}_1 = \Big\{ \big\langle \, (b)\big(C_\gamma(C_{\gamma'}(!a\overline{b}.c) \;\|\; D_\delta(b)) \;\|\; p\big), (b)\big(C_\gamma(C_{\gamma'}(a\overline{b}.c) \;\|\; D_\delta(b)) \;\|\; p\big) \,\big\rangle$$
$$|b \notin fn(C_\gamma) \cup fn(C_{\gamma'}) \cup fn(D_\delta) \cup fn(p) \Big\}$$
$$\mathcal{S}_2 = \Big\{ \big\langle \, (b)\big(C_\gamma(!a\overline{b}.c) \;\|\; p\big), (b)\big(C_\gamma(q) \;\|\; p\big) \,\big\rangle |b \notin fn(C_\gamma) \cup fn(p) \wedge q \in \{0, a\overline{b}.c\}\Big\}$$

It is then relatively easy to verify that $\mathcal{S}$ is a bisimulation that contains the pair of processes under analysis. Note that it would have been considerably more difficult to prove barbed congruence directly, since that would have required considering *all* contexts, in particular arbitrary replication.

Conclusions and Further Work

We have presented MR, a calculus of nested mobile resources designed to provide fine control on the migration and duplication of resources, as relevant for application in the analysis of mobile embedded devices. Its key properties are: the enforcement of bounded capacity for locations; the synchronous communication between co-located processes and toward children location; and the objective mobility provided by move actions. We have studied a semantic theory for MR based on a reduction semantics and a labelled transition systems, culminating in a bisimulation congruence that coincides with the barbed bisimulation. We provided examples of the expressiveness of MR and put the theory at work by exploiting the correspondence between semantics to prove a characteristic 'linearity' property of the calculus.

Among the open issues we plan to address in future work, we mention the study of spatial logics in the style of [7], the provision of suitable type theories, as e.g. [6, 4], to enforce communication and migration safety as well as access control. We plan to extend MR with name-passing, while maintaining the orthogonality of communication by mobility and by exchange of messages. We also plan to explore expressiveness issues by considering alternative design choice and reduced versions of MR, including the absence of communication primitives, move actions that only span single slot boundaries, disallowing scope extension through slot-boundaries, asynchronous messaging, and the cohabitation of slots with 'soft' slots that allow copying resources. Also, we are working on an encoding of (a form of linear) capability-passing in MR, and studying the formal relationships with MR_2. We think the theory we have developed carries on smoothly to weak bisimulation; the details are under investigation.

We have applied Sewell's [21] to derive a transition semantics for a finitary fragment of MR_2 and proved that the bisimulation that so arises is included in ours. We conjecture that they coincide. It would then be interesting to carry on and recast (a larger fragment of) MR in a framework where to understand the relationship with Leifer-Milner's RPOs based bisimulation [15].

References

[1] Martin Abadi and Cédric Fournet. Mobile values, new names, and secure communication. In *Proceedings of POPL '01*. ACM, January 2001. 279
[2] ACM. *27th Annual Symposium an Principles of Programming Languages (POPL) (Boston, MA)*, January 2000.
[3] Michele Bugliesi, Giuseppe Castagna, and Silvia Crafa. Boxed ambients. In Benjamin Pierce, editor, *TACS'01*, volume 2215 of *Lecture Notes in Computer Science*, pages 38–63. Springer-Verlag, 2001. 272
[4] Luca Cardelli, Giorgio Ghelli, and Andrew D. Gordon. Ambient groups and mobility types. In J. van Leeuwen, O. Watanabe, M. Hagiya, P. D. Mosses, and T. Ito, editors, *Theoretical Computer Science: Exploring New Frontiers of Theoretical Informatics, Proceedings of the International IFIP Conference TCS 2000 (Sendai, Japan)*, volume 1872 of *LNCS*, pages 333–347. IFIP, Springer, August 2000. 286

[5] Luca Cardelli and Andrew D. Gordon. Mobile ambients. In Maurice Nivat, editor, *Proceedings of FoSSaCS'98*, volume 1378 of *LNCS*, pages 140-155. Springer, 1998. 272, 275

[6] Luca Cardelli and Andrew D. Gordon. Types for mobile ambients. In *Proceedings of POPL'99*, pages 79-92. ACM, 1999. 286

[7] Luca Cardelli and Andrew D. Gordon. Anytime, anywhere: Modal logics for mobile ambients. In *Proceedings of POPL'00 [2]*, pages 365-377. 286

[8] William Ferreira, Matthew Hennessy, and Alan Jeffrey. A theory of weak bisimulation for core CML. *Journal of Functional Programming*, 8(5):447–491, 1998. 284

[9] Cédric Fournet and Georges Gonthier. A hierarchy of equivalences for asynchronous calculi. In Larsen et al. [14], pages 844-855. 279

[10] Cédric Fournet, Georges Gonthier, Jean-Jacques Lévy, Luc Maranget, and Didier Rémy. A calculus of mobile agents. In Ugo Montanari and Vladimiro Sassone, editors, *Proceedings of CONCUR'96*, volume 1119 of *LNCS*, pages 406-421. Springer, 1996. 272, 276

[11] Jens Chr. Godskesen, Thomas Hildebrandt, and Vladimiro Sassone. A calculus of mobile resources. Technical Report TR-2002-16, The IT University of Copenhagen, 2002. 275, 285

[12] Uwe Hansmann, Martin S. Nicklous, Thomas Schäck, and Frank Seliger. *Smart Card Application Development Using Java*. Springer, 200. 272

[13] Matthew Hennessy and James Riely. Resource access control in systems of mobile agents. In Uwe Nestmann and Benjamin C. Pierce, editors, *Proceedings of HLCL'98*, volume 16.3 of *ENTCS*, pages 3-17. Elsevier Science Publishers, 1998. 272, 276

[14] Kim G. Larsen, Sven Skyum, and Glynn Winskel, editors. *25th Colloquium an Automutu, Lunguages und Progrnmming (ICALP) (Aalborg, Denmark)*, volume 1443 of *LNCS*. Springer, July 1998.

[15] James J. Leifer and Robin Milner. Deriving bisimulation congruences for reactive systems. In *Proceedings of CONCUR 2000*, volume 1877 of *LNCS*, pages 243–258, 2000. 286

[16] Francesca Levi and Davide Sangiorgi. Controlling interference in ambients. In *Proceedings of POPL'00 [2]*, pages 352-364. 272, 276

[17] Massimo Merro and Matthew Hennessy. Bisimulation congruences in safe ambients. *ACM SIGPLAN Notices*, 31(1):71–80, January 2002. 284

[18] Robin Milner. *Communicating und Mobile Systems: the π-Culculus*. Cambridge University Press, May 1999. 272, 281

[19] Davide Sangiorgi. Bisimulation for Higher-Order Process Calculi. *Information and Computation*, 131(2):141–178, 1996. 284

[20] Davide Sangiorgi and David Walker. *The pi-calculus: a Theory of Mobile Processes*. Cambridge Universtity Press, 2001. 281, 283

[21] Peter Sewell. From rewrite rules to bisimulation congruences. In D. Sangiorgi and R. de Simone, editors, *Proceedings CONCUR'98*, volume 1466, pages 269–284, 1998. 286

[22] Peter Sewell. Global/local subtyping and capability inference for a distributed pi-calculus. In Larsen et al. [14], pages 695-706. 272

[23] Jan Vitek and Giuseppe Castagna. Seal: A framework for secure mobile computations. In *Internet Progrnmming Lunguuaes*, 1999. 272, 275

Using Ambients to Control Resources[*]

David Teller[1], Pascal Zimmer[2], and Daniel Hirschkoff[1]

[1] LIP - ENS Lyon, France
{David.Teller,Daniel.Hirschkoff}@ens-lyon.fr
[2] INRIA Sophia Antipolis, France
Pascal.Zimmer@sophia.inria.fr

Abstract. Current software and hardware systems, being parallel and reconfigurable, raise new safety and reliability problems, and the resolution of these problems requires new methods. Numerous proposals attempt at reducing the threat of bugs and preventing several kinds of attacks. In this paper, we develop an extension of the calculus of Mobile Ambients, named *Controlled Ambients*, that is suited for expressing such issues, specifically Denial of Service attacks. We present a type system for Controlled Ambients, which makes resource control possible in our setting.

Introduction

The latest generation of computer software and hardware makes use of numerous new technologies in order to enhance flexibility or performances. Most current systems may be dynamically reconfigured or extended, allow parallelism or use it, and can communicate with other systems. This flexibility, however, induces the multiplication of subsystems and protocols. In turn, this multiplication greatly increases the possibility of bugs, the feasibility of attacks and the sensitivity to possible breakdown of individual subsystems.

This paper presents a formalism for *resource control* in parallel, distributed, mobile systems, called *Controlled Ambients* (CA for short). The calculus of CA is based on Mobile Ambients [2], and extends Safe Ambients [15], and is equipped with a type system to express and verify resource control policies.

In the first section, we present our point of view on the problem of resource control. We provide motivations for using ambient calculi to represent the notion of resource, and claim that a specific calculus should be designed for the purpose of guaranteeing some control on the use of resources. In Sec. 2, we introduce our calculus of Controlled Ambients and explain why it fits to our purposes. We then develop in Sec. 3 a type system which uses the specifics of this language to make resource control possible; we prove its correctness (i.e. that it does control the acquisition and release of resources), and use it to treat several examples. After this, we discuss some refinements of our type system, and, in the last section, we present possible extensions of this study as well as related works.

---

[*] Work supported by european project FET - Global Computing

1   Resource Control

We define a resource as an entity which may *at will* be acquired, used, then released. Thus, this notion encompasses ports, CPUs, computers or RAM, but not time, or (presumably) money. A *resource-controlled system* is a system in which no subsystem will ever require more resources than may be available.

In order to prevent problems such as Denial of Service attacks, we need a formalism making resource control possible. This formalism should in particular provide means to describe systems in terms of resource availability and resource requirement, and should also support the description of concurrent and mobile computations. Lastly, the model should provide some kind of entity that can be regarded as a resource. Ambient calculi can be used for these purposes.

Ambient Calculi. Ambient Calculi are based on locality: each *ambient* is a site. An ambient's evolution is controlled by the means of *capabilities*: in m and out m let an ambient move (resp. entering ambient m or leaving ambient m), while open m opens ambient m and releases its contents in the current ambient. To draw some analogies with real systems, in and out can represent the movement of data in a computer or in a network, while open could be used for cleaning memory, for reading data or for loading programs into memory. As for ambients, they could stand for computers, programs, data, components...

These correspondences open the way for a natural model of resource control, where each site may have a finite (or infinite) quantity of resources of a given category. Resources will be used for data, programs, ... In other words, each ambient has a given *capacity* and each subambient *uses* a part of this capacity. Basically, *controlling resources means checking the number of* **direct** *subambients (according to the amount of resources these are using) which may be present in one ambient at any time.*

Do note that we could have chosen different points of view and decided to count all subambients at all depths, or possibly only "leaf" ambients. Although these approaches seems equally valid, we have decided not to undertake them, since they did not seem more powerful, only slightly more complicated.

An example. Let us consider a cab protocol, as shown in Fig. 1, which we will use as our main running example. The system consists of one city, n sites, and several cabs and clients. Cabs may be either "anywhere in the city" or in a precise site. Each client may be either in a given site or in a cab. Any client may call a cab. If a cab is available, one (and only one) cab must come fetch the client and bring her to her destination. If we consider the unique passenger seat of a cab as a resource, the system will be resource-controlled if each cab contains at most one client at any time.

Fig. 1 presents the cab protocol as written in the original calculus of Mobile Ambients[1]. All entities involved in the protocol are represented by ambients. Ambient movements are used to simulate the movements in the protocol

---

[1] As a matter of fact, we are not exactly using the original MA calculus, since we have introduced the rec operator, for more readability.

Message emitted by client $client$ at site $from$ to call a cab

$call\ from\ client \triangleq call[\text{out}\ client.\text{out}\ from.\text{in}\ cab.\text{in}\ from.loading[\text{out}\ cab.\text{in}\ client]]$

Instructions given by client $client$ going from site $from$ to site to

$trip\ from\ to\ c\ \triangleq trip[\text{out}\ client.\text{out}\ from.\text{in}\ to.unloading[\text{in}\ c]]$

The client itself, willing to go from $from$ to to

$client\ from\ to\ \triangleq (\nu c)c[call\ from\ c\ |\ \text{open}\ loading.\text{in}\ cab.trip\ from\ to\ c$
$\qquad\qquad\qquad\qquad |\ \text{open}\ unloading.\text{out}\ cab.bye[\text{out}\ c.\text{in}\ cab.\text{out}\ to]]$

The cab and the city

$cab\ \triangleq cab[\text{rec}\ X.\text{open}\ call.\text{open}\ trip.\text{open}\ bye.X]$

$city\ \triangleq city[cab\ |\ cab\ |\cdots|\ site_1[client\ site_1 site_i\ |\ client\ site_1\ site_j\ |\cdots]\ |\cdots|\ site_i[\cdots]]$

Fig. 1. Cab protocol - first attempt

(client entering a cab, cab moving from site to site,...). Some additional ambients are used to synchronise parties: *call* carries the client's call, *loading* (resp. *unloading*) tells *client* to enter (resp. exit) *cab*, *trip* carries the trip directions, and *bye* is used at the end of the trip.

Limitations. By examining the code of Fig. 1, one may see that several aspects of this implementation may lead to unwanted behaviors. The most visible flaw is the sending of ambient *bye*: if, for any reason, there are several *cabs* in the site, nothing guarantees that *bye* will reach the right *cab*. And if it does not, it may completely break the system by making one *cab* wait forever for its client to exit, although it already has left, while making the other *cab* leave its destination site with its unwilling *client*. In turn, the *client* may then get out of the cab about anywhere.

   Although this problem is partly due to the way this implementation has been designed, its roots are deeply nested within the calculus of Mobile Ambients itself. One may notice that any malicious ambient may, at any time, enter the cab: in the calculus of Mobile Ambients, there is no such thing as a filtering of entries/exits. This lack of filtering and accounting is a security threat as well as an obstacle for resource control: for security, since it prevents modeling a system which could check and refuse entry to unwanted mobile code, and for control, since one cannot maintain any information about who is using which resources in a given ambient.

Towards a better control. Difficulties with security and control are due, for the greatest part, to the nature of capabilities in, out and open. Actually, the way these capabilities are used seems too simple: in any real system, arrival or departure of data cannot happen without the consent of the acting subsystem, much less go unnoticed, not to mention the opening of a program. In practice, if a program wishes to receive network information, it must first "listen" on some communication port. If a binary file is to be loaded and executed, it must have some executable structure and some given entry point.

A calculus derived from Mobile Ambients is presented in [15]; in this calculus of *Safe Ambients*, three *cocapabilities* are introduced, which we will note $\overline{\mathsf{SAin}}$, $\overline{\mathsf{SAout}}$ and $\overline{\mathsf{SAopen}}$. When executed in m, capability $\overline{\mathsf{SAin}}$ m allows an ambient to enter m (by execution of capability in m). Similarly, $\overline{\mathsf{SAout}}$ m allows an ambient to leave m using out m, while $\overline{\mathsf{SAopen}}$ m allows m's parent to open m using open m. These cocapabilities make synchronizations more explicit and considerably decrease the risk of security breaches. Thinking of the example above, a rewritten cab may thus easily refuse entry right to parasites as long as it is not in any site, or while it contains a client. Moreover, a form of resource control is indeed possible, since a full ambient may refuse entrance of new subambients.

However, in this model, ambients are not always warned when they receive or lose subambients by some kind of side effect: in $h[m[n[\text{out } m] \mid \overline{\mathsf{SAout}}\ m]]$, h receives n from m but is not made aware of this. Moreover, while $\overline{\mathsf{SAin}}$ m serves as a warning for m that it will receive a new subambient, m does not know which one. Since a subambient representing static data and another one modeling some internal message will not occupy the same amount of resources, this model is probably not sufficient for our purposes.

[11] offers an alternative to these cocapabilities, in order to further enhance systems' robustness: in this formalism, $\overline{\text{in}}$ m does not allow *entering m* but rather *m to enter*. This approach solves one of our problems: identifying incoming data. Controlled Ambients may be considered as a development of [11] towards even more robustness as well as resource control. Let us also mention [16], where a different mechanism for the $\overline{\mathsf{SAout}}$ cocapability w.r.t. [15] is introduced. Our proposal subsumes the solutions of [16] and [15].

Embedding resource control. In Sec. 3, we equip our langage with a type system for resource control. Basically, the type of an ambient carries two informations:
 - its *capacity* - how many resources the ambient offers to its subambients;
 - its *weight* - how many resources it requires from its parent ambients.
The type system allows one to statically divide the available resources between parallel processes, and check that resources will be controlled along movements and openings of ambients.

2   The Language of Controlled Ambients

2.1   Syntax and Semantics

In CA, each movement is subject to a 3-way synchronization between the moving ambient, the ambient welcoming a new subambient and the ambient letting a subambient go. As for the opening of an ambient, it is subject to some synchronization between the opener and the ambient being opened. These forms of synchronization are somewhat reminiscent of early versions of Seal [21]. Interaction is handled using *cocapabilities*: $\overline{\text{in}}_\uparrow$, $\overline{\text{out}}_\uparrow$, $\overline{\text{in}}_\downarrow$, $\overline{\text{out}}_\downarrow$ and $\overline{\text{open}}$.

$\overline{\mathsf{in}}_\uparrow$ m the *up coentry*, welcomes m coming from a subambient;
$\overline{\mathsf{in}}_\downarrow$ m the *down coentry*, welcomes m coming from the parent ambient;
$\overline{\mathsf{out}}_\uparrow$ m the *up coexit*, allows m to leave the current ambient by exiting it;
$\overline{\mathsf{out}}_\downarrow$ m the *down coexit*, allows m to leave by entering a subambient;
$\overline{\mathsf{open}}$ $\{m,h\}$ the *coopening*, allows the parent ambient h to open the current
    ambient m.

Do note that $\uparrow$ and $\downarrow$ are not necessary for resource control. We added them
since we found they ease the task of specification in mobile ambients. We will
return on the use of these annotations in Sec. 2.3.

The syntax of Controlled Ambients is presented in Fig. 2. We suppose we have
two infinite sets of term variables, ranged over with capital letters (X, Y), and
of names, ranged over with small letters $(m, n, h, x, \ldots)$. Name binders (input
and restriction) are decorated with some type information, that shall be made
explicit in the next section. While several proposals for Mobile Ambient calculi
use replication, infinite behaviour is represented using recursion in CA. This is
mostly due to the fact that recursion allows for an easier specification of loops,
especially in the context of resource consumption. Note also that, compared to
the original calculus of Mobile Ambients, we restrict ourselves to communication
of ambient names only, and we do not handle communicated capabilities.

The null process $\mathbf{0}$ does nothing. Process $M.P$ is ready to execute M, then to
proceed with P. $P|Q$ is the parallel composition of P and Q. $m[P]$ is the defini-
tion of an ambient with name m and contents P. The process $(\nu n : A)P$ creates
a new, private name n, then behaves as P. The recursive construct $\mathsf{rec}\ X.P$ behaves like P in which occurences of X have been replaced by $\mathsf{rec}\ X.P$. Process
$(n : A)Q$ is ready to accept a message, then to proceed with Q with the actual
message replacing the formal parameter n. $\langle m \rangle$ is the asynchronous emission of a
message m. In most cases, we omit the terminal $\mathbf{0}$ process. We say that a process
is *prefixed* if it is of the form $M.P$, $\mathsf{rec}\ X.P$ or $(x : A)P$.

The operational semantics is defined in two steps. Structural congruence ($\equiv$)
is the least congruence relation satisfying monoidal laws for $(|, \mathbf{0})$ and the usual
laws for restriction (permutation of consecutive restrictions, garbage collection
of useless restrictions, name extrusion, and restrictions crossing ambient constructs). Reduction ($\longrightarrow$) is defined by the rules of Fig. 3, plus the property that
$\longrightarrow$ is defined modulo $\equiv$ and is preserved by parallel composition, restriction
and ambient construct. $\longrightarrow^*$ stands for the reflexive transitive closure of $\longrightarrow$.

2.2   Examples

We omit in the examples given below type annotations in restrictions; these will
be made explicit in the next section.

Renaming. Since movements in Controlled Ambients require full knowledge
about the name of moving ambients (also in cocapabilites, which is not the
case in Safe Ambients), renaming may be useful in order to comply with some
protocols. One may write the renaming of ambient a to b as follows:

$P ::= \mathbf{0}$	null process	$M ::= \text{in } m$	enter m
$\mid M.P$	capability	$\mid \text{out } m$	leave m
$\mid m[P]$	ambient	$\mid \text{open } m$	open m
$\mid P_1 \mid P_2$	parallel composition	$\mid \overline{\text{in}}_\uparrow m$	m may climb in upwards
$\mid (\nu n : A)P$	restriction	$\mid \overline{\text{in}}_\downarrow m$	m may climb in downwards
$\mid \text{rec } X.P$	recursion	$\mid \overline{\text{out}}_\uparrow m$	m may climb out upwards
$\mid X$	process variable	$\mid \overline{\text{out}}_\downarrow m$	m may climb out downwards
$\mid (n : A)P$	abstraction	$\mid \overline{\text{open}} \{m,h\}$	h may open m
$\mid \langle m \rangle$	message emission		

Fig. 2. Controlled Ambients – Syntax

$$m[\text{in } n.P \mid Q] \mid n[\overline{\text{in}}_\downarrow m.R \mid S] \mid \overline{\text{out}}_\downarrow m.T \longrightarrow n[m[P \mid Q] \mid R \mid S] \mid T \quad (R-in)$$
$$n[m[\text{out } n.P \mid Q] \mid \overline{\text{out}}_\uparrow m.R \mid S] \mid \overline{\text{in}}_\uparrow m.T \longrightarrow m[P \mid Q] \mid n[R \mid S] \mid T \quad (R-out)$$
$$h[\text{open } m.P \mid Q \mid m[\overline{\text{open}} \{m,h\}.R \mid S]] \longrightarrow h[P \mid Q \mid R \mid S] \quad (R-open)$$
$$\langle n \rangle \mid (x : A)P \longrightarrow P\{x \leftarrow n\} \quad (R-msg)$$
$$\text{rec } X.P \longrightarrow P\{X \leftarrow \text{rec } X.P\} \quad (R-rec)$$

Fig. 3. Controlled Ambients – Reduction

$$a \text{ be } b.P \triangleq b[\text{out } a.\overline{\text{in}}_\downarrow a.\text{open } a] \mid \overline{\text{out}}_\uparrow b.\text{in } b.\overline{\text{open}} \{a,b\}.P.$$

We then have $\overline{\text{in}}_\uparrow b.\overline{\text{out}}_\downarrow a \mid a[a \text{ be } b.P] \longrightarrow^* b[P]$. This important example is also characteristic of Controlled Ambients, since $\overline{\text{in}}_\uparrow b.\overline{\text{out}}_\downarrow a$ illustrates a particular programming discipline: a's parent ambient must accept the replacement of a by b. This means that, at any time, the father ambient knows its own contents, that is both the number of subambients and their names.

Safe Ambients Cocapabilities. As mentioned above, Safe Ambients [15] introduce another kind of cocapabilities, similar to ours, though weaker. We concentrate here on the $\overline{\text{SAin}}$ cocapability (the case of $\overline{\text{SAout}}$ being symmetrical). Its semantics is defined by

$$a[\text{in } b.P \mid Q] \mid b[\overline{\text{SAin}} b.R \mid S] \longrightarrow b[R \mid S \mid a[P \mid Q]].$$

By carrying on the idea behind renaming, we can approximate the working of this cocapability in CA. In other words, $a[\text{in } b.P \mid Q] \mid b[\overline{\text{SAin}} b.R \mid S]$ may be written

$$(\nu m, n) \, (a[\overline{\text{out}}_\uparrow m.\text{in } b.(P \mid n[\text{out } a.\overline{\text{open}} \{n,b\}] \mid \overline{\text{out}}_\uparrow n) \mid Q$$
$$\mid m[\text{out } a.\text{in } b.\overline{\text{open}} \{m,b\}.\overline{\text{in}}_\downarrow a]]$$
$$\mid b[\overline{\text{in}}_\downarrow m.\text{open } m.\overline{\text{in}}_\uparrow n.\text{open } n.R \mid S] \mid \overline{\text{in}}_\uparrow m.\overline{\text{out}}_\downarrow m.\overline{\text{out}}_\downarrow a).$$

As specified, this expression reduces to $b[R \mid S \mid a[P \mid Q]]$. As was the case for renaming, the father must accept the transaction with $\overline{\text{in}}_\uparrow m.\overline{\text{out}}_\downarrow m.\overline{\text{out}}_\downarrow a$. This entails in particular that the father must know the existence of a.

call from	$\triangleq$ *call*[out *client*.out *from*. in *cab*.$\overline{\text{open}}$ {*call, cab*}.in *from*.$\overline{\text{in}}_\downarrow$ *client*]
trip from to	$\triangleq$ *trip*[out *client*.$\overline{\text{open}}$ {*trip, cab*}.out *from*. in *to*.*arrived*[$\overline{\text{open}}$ {*arrived, cab*}.*end*[$\overline{\text{open}}$ {*end, cab*}.out *to*]]]
client from to	$\triangleq$ *client*[*call from* | $\overline{\text{out}}_\uparrow$ *call*.in *cab*.*trip from to* | $\overline{\text{out}}_\uparrow$ *trip*.out *cab*]
cab	$\triangleq$ *cab*[rec X.$\overline{\text{in}}_\downarrow$ *call*.open *call*.$\overline{\text{in}}_\uparrow$ *trip*.open *trip*.open *arrived*. $\overline{\text{out}}_\uparrow$ *client*.open *end*.X]

Fig. 4. Cab protocol – CA-style (see Fig. 1)

Firewall. We revisit the firewall example of [2], and consider a system f, protected by a firewall. Only agents aware of the password g are allowed in f. This may be modeled as:

$$Agent\ P\ Q \triangleq agent[\text{in } g.\overline{\text{in}}_\downarrow \text{ entered.open entered}.P \mid Q]$$

$$System \triangleq (\nu f)f[\text{rec } X.(g[\text{out } f.\overline{\text{in}}_\downarrow \text{ agent.in } f.\overline{\text{open}} \{g,f\}]$$
$$\mid \overline{\text{out}}_\uparrow g.\overline{\text{in}}_\downarrow g.\text{open } g.(entered[\text{in } agent.\overline{\text{open}} \{entered, agent\}]$$
$$\mid \overline{\text{out}}_\uparrow entered.X))]$$
$$\mid \text{rec } Y.\overline{\text{in}}_\uparrow g.\overline{\text{out}}_\downarrow agent.\overline{\text{out}}_\downarrow g.Y$$

This system implements two authentifications: in the first place, the Agent must be named *agent* - it will not enter f by accident. In the second place, it must know the password. Note that this is not the Firewall described in the original paper on Mobile Ambients [2], which relied on the secrecy of three keys. This version only uses one key and takes advantage of the synchronization mechanism to execute correctly. The basic ideas are the following: *System* receives *agent* and then recovers its original structure thanks to rec . The structure of g guarantees that, at any time, g may only contain one *agent*. On the other hand, *System* may contain any number of *agents*.

Cab. Fig. 4 presents a CA version of the cab protocol. We do not give definitions for the city or for the sites, which only need to contain all movement authorizations, in addition to *clients* and *cabs*. Using cocapabilities, synchronizations in CA are both easier than in Mobile Ambients and atomic. Additionally, the system is not subject to the interferences we have presented: only *clients* may enter the cab, not just any "parasite" ambient which happens to contain capability in *cab*. Similarly, sites only welcome *clients*, *cabs* and *calls*.

Note that in this version, all clients must be named *client* in order to enter a *cab*. In order to relax this constraint, one could use *renaming* or the approximation of $\overline{\text{SAin}}$ (see above).

Additionally, as was planned, Controlled Ambients permit the control of resources such as available space in cabs. As opposed to the Mobile Ambients version, we may easily check that the cab may contain at most *only one pas-*

senger and possibly an auxiliary ambient *call*, *trip*, *arrived* or *end*. This will be
expressed formally using our type system in Sec. 3.

2.3   Benefits

We believe that the formalism of Controlled Ambients is more reasonable than
Mobile Ambients or Safe Ambients. More reasonable insofar as the implementation of movements in ambient calculi suggests this kind of three-way synchronization. Let us consider the following transition in Mobile Ambients:

$$h[m[\text{in } n] \mid n[\mathbf{0}]] \longrightarrow h[n[m[\mathbf{0}]]]\,.$$

As shown in [8,19], a practical implementation of this rule requires that h must
be aware of the presence of n, no matter how n may have entered h. More generally, the execution of this rule will need a synchronization between n (who is
present), m (who looks for n) and h (who knows about m and n). Similarly,
the opening of ambient m by ambient h requires some complex synchronization between m and h in order to recover all processes and subambients of m
in h and update presence registers of h. A prototype implementation has been
developped [9] in order to validate these assertions.

Controlled Ambients are also more realistic as modeling tools. When a system receives informations, it must be by some action of his: the operating system
"listens" on a device, the configuration server waits for a request by "listening"
on some given TCP/IP port... Unfortunately, this listening aspect is not ren-
dered at all by Mobile Ambients and only in half of the cases by Safe Ambients.
Similarly, a system must be able to wait for several kinds of informations and to
sort them according to their origin: the OS is able to differentiate data read on
a disk from data read on the network or on the keyboard, while software may
listen on several communication ports, for example. We can easily model such
phenomena in CA, and if necessary take into account situations where some part
of the system (like the network connexion itself) accepts data without listening
for it, using renaming and infinite loops of cocapacities.

3   Typing Controlled Ambients

This section is devoted to the presentation of a basic type system for resource
control in Controlled Ambients. We first describe the system and its properties,
and then show the kind of information it is liable to capture on some examples.

3.1   The Type System

Type Judgments. The grammar for types is given in Fig. 5, and includes entries
for the types of ambients, processes and messages ($\overline{\mathbb{N}}$ stands for $\mathbb{N} \cup \{\infty\}$).

Typing environments, ranged over with Γ, which are lists of associations
of the form $x : A$ (for ambient names) or $X : U$ (for process variables). We
write $\Gamma(x) = A$ (resp. $\Gamma(X) = U$) to represent the fact that environment Γ
associates A (resp. U) to x (resp. X). $\Gamma, x : A$ stands for the extension of Γ with

---

| $A ::= \mathrm{CAAM}(s,e)[T]$ | $s \in \overline{\mathbb{N}}, e \in \mathbb{N}$ ambients | $T ::= Ssh$ | messages |
| $U ::= \mathrm{CAPR}(t)[T]$ | $t \in \overline{\mathbb{N}}$ processes | $\mid t, A$ | $t \in \overline{\mathbb{N}}$ |

Fig. 5. Types

the association $x : A$, possibly hiding some previous binding for x (and similarly for $\Gamma, X : U$).

The typing judgment for ambient names is of the form
$$\Gamma \vdash n : \mathrm{CAAM}(s,e)[T],$$
and expresses the fact that under assumptions Γ, n is the name of an ambient of *capacity* s, *weight* e, and within which messages carrying information of type T may be exchanged. The capacity s represents the number of resource units that are available within n (i.e. the space available for subambients - or *resources* for short), while e is the number of resources this ambient is occupying in its surrounding ambient. Note that while an ambient may have an infinite capacity ($s = \infty$), it cannot manipulate infinitely many resources ($e < \infty$). The type T for messages captures the kind of names being exchanged within n, similarly to Cardelli and Gordon's *topics of conversation* [3], augmented with an information t which represents a higher bound on the effect of exchanging messages within n (we shall come back to this below).

The typing judgment for processes is written
$$\Gamma \vdash P : \mathrm{CAPR}(t)[T],$$
meaning that according to Γ, P is a process that may use up to t resources, and take part in conversations (that is, emit and receive messages) having type T.

Typing Rules. The rules defining the typing judgments are given on Fig. 6. We now comment on them. While typing (subjective) movements has no effect from the point of view of resources (rules $T - in$ and $T - out$), the rules $T - coin$ and $T - coout$, for the co-capabilities (in which δ ranges over a direction tag, which can be $\uparrow$ or $\downarrow$), express the meaning of types, according to the weight e of the moving ambient. Note that the number t of resources allocated to the process must remain positive after decreasing (rule $T - coout$). This is made possible by the subtyping property of the system (Lemma 1), together with rules $T - nil$ and $T - amb$, which allow one to allocate any number of resources to an inert process (inert from the point of view of the current ambient). This mechanism can be used for example to derive a typing for a process of the form $\overline{out_\uparrow}\, n.\mathbf{0}$. Note also that the side condition $a \leq s$ in rule $T - amb$ expresses conformity with the capacity of the ambient.

When opening an ambient, we release the resources it had acquired (e), but at the same time we have to provide at least as many resources as its original capacity (s). The $\overline{open}$ capability plays no role from the point of view of resource control, as illustrated by rule $T - coopen$ (note, still, that message types in the opening ambient and in the type of R are unified using this rule). We shall

$$\frac{\Gamma(n) = A}{\Gamma \vdash n : A} \; T - name \qquad \frac{\Gamma(X) = \mathrm{CAPR}(t)[T]}{\Gamma \vdash X : \mathrm{CAPR}(t')[T]} \; \begin{array}{l} T - var \\ t' \geq t \end{array}$$

$$\frac{\Gamma, X : \mathrm{CAPR}(t)[T] \vdash P : \mathrm{CAPR}(t)[T]}{\Gamma \vdash \mathsf{rec}\ X.P : \mathrm{CAPR}(t')[T]} \; \begin{array}{l} T - rec \\ t' \geq t \end{array}$$

$$\frac{\Gamma \vdash P : \mathrm{CAPR}(t)[T]}{\Gamma \vdash \mathsf{in}\ m.P : \mathrm{CAPR}(t)[T]} \; T - in \qquad \frac{\Gamma \vdash P : \mathrm{CAPR}(t)[T]}{\Gamma \vdash \mathsf{out}\ m.P : \mathrm{CAPR}(t)[T]} \; T - out$$

$$\frac{\Gamma \vdash P : \mathrm{CAPR}(t)[T] \quad \Gamma \vdash m : \mathrm{CAAM}(s, e)[T']}{\Gamma \vdash \overline{\mathsf{in}}_\delta\ m.P : \mathrm{CAPR}(t + e)[T]} \; T - coin$$

$$\frac{\Gamma \vdash P : \mathrm{CAPR}(t)[T] \quad \Gamma \vdash m : \mathrm{CAAM}(s, e)[T']}{\Gamma \vdash \overline{\mathsf{out}}_\delta\ m.P : \mathrm{CAPR}(t - e)[T]} \; \begin{array}{l} T - coout \\ t \geq e \end{array}$$

$$\frac{\Gamma \vdash m : \mathrm{CAAM}(s, e)[T] \quad \Gamma \vdash P : \mathrm{CAPR}(t)[T]}{\Gamma \vdash \mathsf{open}\ m.P : \mathrm{CAPR}(t - e + s)[T]} \; \begin{array}{l} T - open \\ t - e + s \geq 0 \end{array}$$

$$\frac{\Gamma \vdash m : \mathrm{CAAM}(s, e)[T] \quad \Gamma \vdash R : \mathrm{CAPR}(t)[T]}{\Gamma \vdash \overline{\mathsf{open}}\ \{m, h\}.R : \mathrm{CAPR}(t)[T]} \; T - coopen$$

$$\frac{}{\Gamma \vdash \mathbf{0} : U} \; T - nil \qquad \frac{\Gamma \vdash m : \mathrm{CAAM}(s, e)[T] \quad \Gamma \vdash P : \mathrm{CAPR}(a)[T]}{\Gamma \vdash m[P] : \mathrm{CAPR}(t)[T']} \; \begin{array}{l} T - amb \\ a \leq s, e \leq t \end{array}$$

$$\frac{\Gamma, n : A \vdash P : U}{\Gamma \vdash (\nu n : A)P : U} \; T - res \qquad \frac{\Gamma \vdash P : \mathrm{CAPR}(t)[T] \quad \Gamma \vdash Q : \mathrm{CAPR}(t')[T]}{\Gamma \vdash P|Q : \mathrm{CAPR}(t + t')[T]} \; T - par$$

$$\frac{\Gamma \vdash m : A}{\Gamma \vdash \langle m \rangle : \mathrm{CAPR}(t')[t, A]} \; \begin{array}{l} T - snd \\ t' \geq t \end{array} \qquad \frac{\Gamma, x : A \vdash P : \mathrm{CAPR}(t)[t, A]}{\Gamma \vdash (x : A)P : \mathrm{CAPR}(t')[t, A]} \; T - rcv$$

Fig. 6. Typing rules

present in Sec. 4 a richer system where a more precise typing of opening (and co-opening) permits a better control.

We now explain the typing rules for communication. Since reception of a message can trigger a process which will necessitate a certain amount of resources, we attach to the type of an ambient the maximum amount of resources needed by a receiving process running within it: this is information t in an ambient's topic of conversation. Put differently, messages are decorated with an integer representing at least as many resources as needed by the processes they are liable to trigger: we are thus somehow measuring an effect in this case. Note that our approach is based on the idea that one emission typically corresponds to several receptions. The dual approach could have been used, by putting in correspondence one reception and several concurrent emissions. Our experience in writing examples suggests that the first choice is more tractable.

Finally, rule $T - rec$ expresses the fact that a recursively defined process should run "in constant space".

3.2   Static Resource Control

We now present the main properties of the type system. Proofs are not given, but can be found in [20]. We start by some technical properties of typing derivations.

Lemma 1 (Subtyping). *Let P be a process and Γ an environment. Then:*
$$\text{if } \Gamma \vdash P : \text{CAPR}(t)[T] \text{ then } \forall t' \geq t, \Gamma \vdash P : \text{CAPR}(t')[T].$$

Corollary 1 (Minimal typing). *If a process P is typeable in Γ with a topic type T, then there is a minimal $t \in \bar{\mathbb{N}}$ such that $\Gamma \vdash P : \text{CAPR}(t)[T]$.*

Note that the minimal parameter t can be different for each possible value T (see for example rule $T - snd$).

Let us now examine resource control. In order to be able to state the properties we are interested in, we extend the notion of weight, which has been used for ambients, to processes, by introducing the notion of resource usage, together with a natural terminology:

Definition 1 (Resource policy and resource usage). *We call* resource policy *a typing context. Given a resource policy Γ, we define the* resource usage *of a process P according to Γ, written $Res_\Gamma(P)$, as follows:*

  – *if $\Gamma(a) = \text{CAAM}(s, e)[T]$, then $Res_\Gamma(a[P]) = e$;*
  – *$Res_\Gamma(P_1 | P_2) = Res_\Gamma(P_1) + Res_\Gamma(P_2)$;*
  – *$Res_\Gamma((\nu n : A)\, P) = Res_{\Gamma, n:A}(P)$.*
  – *in all other cases, $Res_\Gamma(P) = 0$;*

Note in particular that according to this definition, prefixed terms (capabilities, reception, recursion) do not contribute to a process' *current* resource usage (accordingly, their resource usage is equal to 0). We now define formally what it means for a process to respect a given resource policy.

Definition 2 (Resource policy compliance). *Given a resource policy Γ, we define the judgment $\Gamma \models P$ (pronounced "P complies with Γ"), as follows:*

  – *$\Gamma \models n[P]$ iff $\Gamma \models P$ and $Res_\Gamma(P) \leq s$, where capacity s is given by $\Gamma(n) = \text{CAAM}(s, e)[T]$;*
  – *$\Gamma \models P_1 | P_2$ iff $\Gamma \models P_1$ and $\Gamma \models P_2$;*
  – *$\Gamma \models (\nu n : A)\, P$ iff $\Gamma, n : A \models P$;*
  – *in all other cases, $\Gamma \models P$.*

The typing rules ensure that a typeable term complies with a resource policy:

Lemma 2 (Typeable terms comply with resource policies). *For any process P, resource policy Γ and process type U, if $\Gamma \vdash P : U$, then $\Gamma \models P$.*

The following theorem states that typability is preserved by the operational semantics of Controlled Ambients:

Theorem 1 (Subject reduction). *For any processes P, Q, resource policy Γ and type U, if $\Gamma \vdash P : U$ and $P \longrightarrow Q$, then $\Gamma \vdash Q : U$.*

As a direct consequence, we obtain our main result:

Theorem 2 (Resource control). *Consider a resource policy Γ and a process P such that $\Gamma \vdash P : U$ for some U. Then for any Q such that $P \longrightarrow^* Q$, it holds that $\Gamma \models Q$.*

3.3   Examples

We now revisit some examples of Sec. 2.2, and explain how they can be typed. **Notation:** We shall write $a \rightsquigarrow_\Gamma^T (s, e)$ as a shorthand for $\Gamma(a) = \text{CAam}(s, e)[T]$.

Renaming. The expression of renaming given in Sec. 2.2 is typeable as soon as there exists a typing environment Γ and a conversation type T such that
$$a \rightsquigarrow_\Gamma^T (s, e), , \quad b \rightsquigarrow_\Gamma^T (s, e) \text{ with } s \geq e, \quad \text{and} \quad \Gamma \vdash P : \text{CApr}(s)[T].$$
We can actually slightly relax the conditions on types. One can show that the least set of conditions to type the renaming is
$$t_P \leq s_a, \quad e_b \leq s_a, \quad s_a \leq s_b, \quad \text{and} \quad e_a \leq s_b,$$
where $a \rightsquigarrow_\Gamma^T (s_a, e_a)$, $b \rightsquigarrow_\Gamma^T (s_b, e_b)$ and $\Gamma \vdash P : \text{CApr}(t_P)[T]$.

Firewall. Similarly, the firewall in Controlled Ambients, as defined in subsection 2.2 can be typed in a context Γ such that:
$$agent \rightsquigarrow_\Gamma^T (a_P + a_Q, 1), \quad entered \rightsquigarrow_\Gamma^T (0, 0),$$
$$f \rightsquigarrow_\Gamma^T (\infty, 0), \quad \text{and} \quad g \rightsquigarrow_\Gamma^T (1, 0).$$
In particular, the typing of the recursive process rec X.... in *System* entails a constraint of the form $\text{CApr}(t)[T] = \text{CApr}(t+1)[T]$. This is possible if and only if $t = \infty$, and as a consequence the capacity of f should also be ∞, so that the firewall is supposed to have infinite size. This is no surprise, since it may actually receive any number of external ambients. However, these ambients are contained in the firewall. Hence, one may still integrate this firewall as a component in a system with limited resources and resource control.

Cab. Let us consider an environment Γ such that:
$$client \rightsquigarrow_\Gamma^T (0, 1), \quad call \rightsquigarrow_\Gamma^T (1, 0), \quad trip \rightsquigarrow_\Gamma^T (0, 0), \quad arrived \rightsquigarrow_\Gamma^T (0, 0),$$
$$end \rightsquigarrow_\Gamma^T (0, 0), \quad cab \rightsquigarrow_\Gamma^T (1, 0), \quad site_i \rightsquigarrow_\Gamma^T (\infty, 0), \quad \text{and} \quad city \rightsquigarrow_\Gamma^T (0, 0).$$
Note in particular that this resource policy specifies that among the ambients that may enter the cab, only those named *client* are actually "controlled": this corresponds to the property we focus on when analyzing the cab. With these assumptions, the complete cab system is typeable. This means that resources are statically controlled in cabs: *at any step of its execution, the cab may contain at most one client.* Moreover, by changing our resource policy in such a way that ambients *call*, *trip*, *arrived* and *end* have weight 1 while *client* has weight 0, we can type the cab as having size 1. This typing lets us control the number of "auxiliary" ambients: at any time, at most one of those may be present in *cab*.

4   Refining the Resource Policy

While the basic system we have presented so far allows one to type many interesting examples, some relatively simple examples show its limitations. We illustrate these on two examples; consider the terms:

$$T_1 \triangleq a[\overline{\mathsf{open}}\ \{a,b\}.\mathsf{rec}\ X.(X \mid b[\mathbf{0}])] \mid \mathsf{open}\ a$$

$$T_2 \triangleq h[\mathsf{rec}\ X.(m[\overline{\mathsf{in}_\downarrow}\ n.\overline{\mathsf{out}_\uparrow}\ n.\overline{\mathsf{open}}\ \{m,h\}] \mid \overline{\mathsf{out}_\downarrow}\ n.\overline{\mathsf{in}_\uparrow}\ n.\mathsf{open}\ m.X)$$
$$\mid n[\mathsf{rec}\ Y.\mathsf{in}\ m.\mathsf{out}\ m.Y]]$$

Suppose for T_1 that the weight of b is not 0. The construction $\mathsf{rec}\ X.(X \mid b[\mathbf{0}])$ then requires infinite resources. Although the execution would not use any resource inside a, the typing will require a to have an infinite capacity. Similarly, if in T_2 the weight of n is not 0, by following the evolution of this term, one may notice that a finite capacity for h *should be sufficient*. However, the typing rules we have presented compell the capacity of h to be infinite. In both cases, the typing system is not refined enough to express a resource control property, essentially because the rules for open and $\overline{\mathsf{open}}$ control resources too strictly. In order to be able to type such programs as "resource conscious", we have defined an extended version of our type system, in which ambient types are of the form $\mathrm{CAAM}(s,e,r,z)[T]$, $r \in \overline{\mathbb{N}}, z \in \mathbb{N}$ and $z \leq s$. The rules are almost the same as above, except for the following ones:

$$\frac{\Gamma \vdash m : \mathrm{CAAM}(s,e,r,z)[T] \quad \Gamma \vdash P : \mathrm{CAPR}(t)[T]}{\Gamma \vdash \mathsf{open}\ m.P : \mathrm{CAPR}(t-e+z+r)[T]} \quad \begin{array}{c} T - open \\ t-e+z+r \geq 0 \end{array}$$

$$\frac{\Gamma \vdash m : \mathrm{CAAM}(s,e,r,z)[T] \quad \Gamma \vdash R : \mathrm{CAPR}(t)[T]}{\Gamma \vdash \overline{\mathsf{open}}\ \{m,h\}.R : \mathrm{CAPR}(t')[T]} \quad \begin{array}{c} T - coopen \\ t \leq r, t' \geq s - z \end{array}$$

For lack of space, we do not discuss further this enriched type system. Let us just stress that the results of Sec. 3.2 also hold for it, and that "intermediate" type systems adopting only one of the two additional parameters could also be defined (for more details, see [20]).

5   Conclusion

The language of Controlled Ambients has been introduced to analyze resource control in a distributed and mobile setting through an accurate programming of movements and synchronisations. We have enhanced our formalism with a type system for the static control of resources, and extensions of the basic type system have also been presented. Further, examples show that indications on the maximal amount of resources needed by a process match rather closely the actual amount of resources which may be reached in the worst case, which suggests that the solution we propose could serve as the basis for a study of resource control properties on a larger scale.

Among extensions of the present work, we are currently enriching the language and type system to include communication of capabilities, as in the original Mobile Ambients calculus [2]. We are also studying type inference for our system.

It seems that by requiring the recursion variables to be explicitly typed, type inference is decidable, and a rather natural algorithm can compute a minimal type for a given process, if it exists. In particular, the "message" component of terms leads to a classical unification problem. The question becomes more problematic if no information is given for recursion variables: one can compute a set of inequalities (resembling those given for the example of renaming in Sec. 3), but solving it in the general case would require more work.

We plan to study whether our approach can be adapted to other formalisms for mobile and distributed computation such as the distributed π-calculus [18] or the distributed join-calculus [7]. Along the same ideas, in some process calculi without any primitive notion of site, we could choose to regard name creation as a form of resource allocation, and find out whether (some of) our ideas can be adapted to this setting.

We could also consider combining our type system for resource control with other typing disciplines, adapted from the Single Threadness types of [15], or the Mandatory Access Control of [1]. It seems that Controlled Ambients could also be used to approximate some of the analyses done in [6,?], where, in a context where *security levels* are associated with processes, types are used to check that no agent can access an information having a security level higher than its own. In the simple case where we have two security levels, we could attach weight 0 to agents of high level, and 1 to low-level agents, and store high-level information in ambients of size 0: in such a framework, our type system can guarantee that only high-level processes can enter high-level data. Of course this is a very rough approximation, and a more refined account of access control in Controlled Ambients needs further investigation.

We have not addressed the issue of behavioural equivalences for CA. A possible outcome of such a study could be to validate a more elaborate treatment of resources involving operations like garbage collection, which would allow one to make available uselessly occupied resources. An example is the perfect firewall equation of [10]: when $c \notin \mathrm{fn}(P)$, process $(\nu c)\, c[P]$ may manipulate some resources while being actually equivalent to **0**.

Other Related Works. Other projects aim at controlling resources in possibly mobile systems without resorting to mobile process algebras. [14] presents a modified ML language with sized types in which bounds may be given to stack consumption. Like in our framework, resources are releasable entities; however, this approach seems more specialized than ours, and moreover concentrates on a sequential model. Similarly, [5] introduces a variant of the Typed Assembly Language *"augmenting TAL's very low-level safety certification with running-time guarantees"*, while Quantum, [17] may be used to describe distributed systems from the point of view of their resource consumption. In contrast to our approach, both systems consider non-releasable resources. Another programming language, PLAN [13], has been designed specifically for active networks, and also handles some form of resource bounds. Although PLAN accounts for both releasable (space, bandwidth) and non-releasable (time) resources, it handles neither recursion nor concurrency on one node.

These works all focus on resource control; however, none of these approaches can be directly compared to ours. It might be interesting to study if and how our methods could be integrated to these works, in order to combine several forms of resource control.

Another form of accounting on mobile ambients is introduced in [4]. In a calculus with a slightly different form of recursion than in CA (and without cocapabilities), the authors introduce a type system to count the number of active outputs and ambients (at any depth) in a process. This analysis, however, is not aimed at resources: it tries and isolate a finite-control fragment of mobile ambients on which model checking w.r.t. the Ambient Logic is decidable through state-space exploration.

Acknowledgements

We would like to thank Davide Sangiorgi for suggesting the original idea behind CA and providing insightful suggestions along this work.

References

1. Michele Bugliesi, Giuseppe Castagna, and Silvia Crafa. Boxed ambients. In *Proc. TACS 2001*, LNCS 2215, pages 38–63. Springer Verlag, 2001. 301
2. Luca Cardelli and Andrew D. Gordon. Mobile ambients. In *Proc. of FOSSACS'98*, volume 1378, pages 140–155. Springer Verlag, 1998. 288, 294, 300
3. Luca Cardelli and Andrew D. Gordon. Types for mobile ambients. In *Symposium on Principles of Programming Languages (POPL'99)*, pages 79–92. ACM Press, 1999. 296
4. Witold Charatonik, Andrew D. Gordon, and Jean-Marc Talbot. Finite-control mobile ambients. In *Proc. of ESOP'02*, volume 2305 of *LNCS*, pages 295–313, 2002. 302
5. Karl Crary and Stephanie Weirich. Resource bound certification. In *Symposium on Principles of Programming Languages (POPL'00)*, pages 184–198. ACM Press, 2000. 301
6. Mariangiola Dezani-Ciancaglini and Ivano Salvo. Security types for mobile safe ambients. In *Proc. of ASIAN'00*, LNCS 1961, pages 215–236. Springer Verlag, 2000. 301
7. Cédric Fournet, Georges Gonthier, Jean-Jacques Lévy, Luc Maranget, and Didier Rémy. A calculus of mobile agents. In *Proc. of CONCUR'96*, pages 406–421. Springer Verlag, 1996. 301
8. Cédric Fournet, Jean-Jacques Lévy, and Alan Schmitt. A distributed implementation of mobile ambients. In *Proc. of IFIP TCS'00*, pages 348–364. Springer Verlag, 1872. 295
9. T. Gazagnaire and D. Pous. Implémentation des Controlled Ambients en JoCaml. Students project – Magistère d'Informatique ENS Lyon, 2002. 295
10. Andrew D. Gordon and Luca Cardelli. Equational properties of mobile ambients. In *Proc. of FOSSACS'99*, volume 1578 of *LNCS*, pages 212–226. Springer Verlag, 1999. 301

11. Xudong Guan, Yiling Yang, and Jinyuan You. Making ambients more robust. In *Proc. of the International Conference on Software: Theory and Practice*, pages 377–384, 2000. 291

12. Matthew Hennessy and James Riely. Resource access control in systems of mobile agents. In *Proceedings of HLCL '98*, number 16.3 in ENTCS, pages 3–17. Elsevier, 1998.

13. Michael Hicks, Pankaj Kakkar, Jonathan T. Moore, Carl A. Gunter, and Scott Nettles. PLAN: A Packet Language for Active Networks. In *Proc. ICFP'99*, pages 86–93. ACM Press, 1999. 301

14. John Hughes and Lars Pareto. Recursion and dynamic data-structures in bounded space: Towards embedded ML programming. In *Proc. of ICFP'99*, pages 70–81. ACM Press, 1999. 301

15. Francesca Levi and Davide Sangiorgi. Controlling interference in ambients. In *Symposium on Principles of Programming Languages*, pages 352–364. ACM Press, 2000. 288, 291, 293, 301

16. M. Merro and M. Hennessy. Bisimulation congruences in safe ambients. In *Proc. of POPL'02*, pages 71–80. ACM Press, 2002. 291

17. Luc Moreau. A distributed garbage collector with diffusion tree reorganisation and mobile objects. In *Proc. of ICFP'98*, pages 204–215. ACM Press, 1998. 301

18. James Riely and Matthew Hennessy. A typed language for distributed mobile processes. In *Proc. of POPL'98*, pages 378–390. ACM Press, 1998. 301

19. D. Sangiorgi and A. Valente. A distributed abstract machine for Safe Ambients. In *Proc. of ICALP'01*, 2001. 295

20. D. Teller, P. Zimmer, and D. Hirschkoff. Using Ambients to Control Resources. Technical Report 2002-16, LIP - ENS Lyon, 2002. 298, 300

21. Jan Vitek and Giuseppe Castagna. Seal: A Framework for Secure Mobile Computations. In *Internet Programming Languages*, volume 1686 of *LNCS*. Springer Verlag, 1999. 291

Typing and Subtyping Mobility
in Boxed Ambients*

Massimo Merro and Vladimiro Sassone

University of Sussex

Abstract. We provide a novel type system for Bugliesi *et al.*'s Boxed
Ambients that combines value subtyping with mobility types. The former
is based on read/write exchange types, the latter builds on the notion
of ambient group. Mobility types allow to specify where an ambient is
allowed to stay, closing existing expressiveness gaps in the literature at
no additional complexity costs. Subtyping is aimed at achieving maximal
generality on both communication and mobility types. We then introduce
co-capabilities to express explicit permissions to access ambients. In this
setting, ambient types are refined to specify who is allowed to enter an
ambient, making a promising framework to model open systems.

Introduction

The calculus of *Mobile Ambients*, [8], abbreviated MA, is a novel process calculus
to describe *mobile agents* which focuses on three fundamental notions: *location
awareness* [9], *mobile computation* [4], and *local communication*. Papers such
as [8,5,7,3] demonstrate that MA can describe the run-time behaviour of mobile
agents very effectively. In MA, the term $n[P]$ represents an agent, or *ambient*,
named n, executing the code P. Intuitively an ambient represents a *mobile*,
bounded, and *protected* space in which a computation takes place.

Ambient names, such as n, are used to control access to the ambient computation space and may be dynamically created, as in the π-calculus [16], by the
construct $(\nu n)P$ The ability to move and open ambients is regulated by *capabilities* that processes possess by prior knowledge or acquire by communication.
As an example, the system

$$k[\,\text{in}\,n.R_1 \mid R_2] \mid n[\,\text{open}\,k.P \mid m[\text{out}\,n.Q_1 \mid Q_2]\,]$$

contains two ambients, k and n, running concurrently. The first, k, can migrate
to n by virtue of its capability $\text{in}\,n$. The second, n, contains a sub-ambient
$m[\ldots]$, in addition to the capability $\text{open}\,k$ which allows the opening of any
ambient named k if any such ambient exists in the computation space of n.

---

* Research supported by 'MyThS: Models and Types for Security in Mobile Distributed Systems', EU FET-GC IST-2001-32617. The first author was funded by
  EPSRC grant GR/M71169.

L. Brim et al. (Eds.): CONCUR 2002, LNCS 2421, pp. 304–320, 2002.

Unlike other process calculi, MA focuses primarily on *process mobility* rather than *process communication*. As a consequence, the need emerged soon of studying static techniques for constraining the mobility behaviour of ambients. In [6], the authors exhibited a type system to control whether or not an ambient is mobile or may be opened. Subsequently, [5] refined that type system enriching the type of ambient name n with a description of the ambients n may cross. In order to circumvent the need for *dependent types*, ambients in programmer-defined *groups*. The type of an ambient is then annotated with the capability of crossing – either from outside, via **in**, or from inside, via **out** – the border of ambients of certain groups.

In our opinion, the current mobility types of [5] have some limitations:

▷ Types are rather complex, due to the presence of the **open** capability, which allows ambients to acquire new behaviours by opening contained ambients.
▷ No *subtyping* on mobility has been achieved.
▷ The interaction of subjective moves (triggered by a process running inside an ambient) with the **open** construct tends to produce typings where all ambients are typed mobile. This obliges the authors of [5] to extend MA with *objective moves*, which move ambients from the outside.
▷ An anomaly arises in border-crossing control. Consider the system:

Odysseus[in *Horse*.out *Horse*.DESTROY_TROY] | *Horse*[in *Troy*] | *Troy*[*TROJANS*]

where *Odysseus* plans to enter *Troy* for the well-known deed, with the well-known method. This system is typeable in [5] under type assumptions of the form: [1]

$$Odysseus : \mathsf{amb}[\mathtt{Achaean}, \mathtt{cross}[\mathtt{Toy}]]$$

$$Horse : \mathsf{amb}[\mathtt{Toy}, \mathtt{cross}[\mathtt{City}]]$$

$$Troy : \mathsf{amb}[\mathtt{City}, \_]$$

They express that *Odysseus* is an ambient of group **Achaean** which is allowed to cross the boundary of ambients of group **Toy**; *Horse* is an ambient of group **Toy**, which may cross ambients of group **City**; finally, *Troy* is an ambient of group **City**. Suppose now *Odysseus* moves into the *Horse*, which subsequently moves into *Troy*, so that the system evolves to:

Troy[*TROJANS* | *Horse*[*Odysseus*[out *Horse*.DESTROY_TROY]]].

Odysseus may then move out of the *Horse* and take the *TROJANS* by surprise whom believed he did not have permission to traverse *Troy*'s walls.
▷ Ambients cannot determine which agents are allowed to traverse their boundaries.

This paper aims at finding an appropriate formalism that addresses the questions above within the ambient framework. It is well-known that many of the difficulties of MA are caused by the **open** capability [2]; it thus seems a commendable endeavour to investigate variants of the ambient calculus that drop **open**.

---

[1] We use simplified types here; in [5] types are more complex.

Boxed Ambients [2], abbreviated BA, is a variant of MA, from which it inherits the primitives **in** and **out** with exactly the same semantics. As for communication, BA relies on a completely different model which results from dropping the **open** capability, and adopting communication across ambient boundaries, between parent and children, similar to those found in the Seal calculus [18]. As pointed out in [2], BA retains much of the expressive power of MA while enhancing the flexibility of typed communication with finer-grained, more effective mechanisms. This makes BA particularly suitable for modelling classical security policies for resource protection and access control. For instance, in [1] BA is used to model *mandatory access control* policies within a multilevel security system, including both *military security* (no read-up, no write-down) and *commercial security* (no read-up, no write-up).

We introduce a type system to control mobility in BA which profits of the absence of the **open** capability. As in [5], we use *ambient groups* to express and enforce properties of names indirectly, as properties of groups of names, but avoiding dependent types. The absence of **open** simplifies types considerably, as both communication and mobility behaviour of children do not influence the types of their parents. Our types for ambient names consist of four components: the group to which the ambient belongs; a component that describes the mobility constraints of the ambient, viz. where the ambient is allowed to go/reside; one that characterises the communications in which the ambient is involved; and, finally, a set of markers that specify what the ambient name can be used for. Processes and capabilities have similar types, though not identical. In particular, their mobility types express where processes and capabilities may drive to, rather than where they are allowed to stay.

We then equip our type system with a non-trivial form of *subtyping* which deals with both mobility and communication aspects. Subtyping on mobility is based on the idea that a process can be used wherever processes with a more liberal behaviour (in terms of potential moves) is expected. For communication, generality is again our motor. We employ read/write types which specify separately the type of legal inputs and outputs for processes, and allow a general subsumption rule, so as to push both kinds of subtyping as far as possible. For such a system of inference we prove a set of properties expressing formally the intuitions behind our types. These, together with a subject reduction theorem, make explicit the safety guarantees upheld by the present framework.

Our types for BA meet the first four requirements discussed previously. To go further and attack the last requirement, in §4 we extend the syntax of BA with co-capabilities, which express explicit permission to traverse boundaries. The idea of introducing co-actions is borrowed from process calculi such as CCS [15] or the π-calculus [16]. Our co-capabilities, are inspired by [19] and [13], where explicit information about the crossing ambient may be required. Thus, for example, in

$$m[\,\textbf{in}\,n.Q_1 \mid l[\,\textbf{out}\,m.Q_2]\,]\mid n[P]\mid R$$

m may move into n if P has the form $\overline{\mathsf{in}}\, m.P_1 \mid P_2$, in which case the system evolves to

$$n[\, m[\, Q_1 \mid l[\mathsf{out}\, m.Q_2]\,] \mid P_1 \mid P_2\,] \mid R$$

Alternatively, l may emigrate from m if R has the form $\overline{\mathsf{out}}\, l.R_1 \mid R_2$, and then the system evolves to

$$m[\,\mathsf{in}\, n.Q_1\,] \mid l[Q_2] \mid n[P] \mid R_1 \mid R_2.$$

We call the calculus with co-capabilities BSA, for *Boxed Safe Ambients*. Co-capabilities in BSA are exercised by the target computation by (possibly) naming the ambient allowed to traverse a boundary. In this manner, they allow to enhance ambient types by augmenting the type of n with the set of groups of the ambients allowed to cross n's boundary. The results for BA are smoothly lifted to BSA. We believe that BSA is a promising framework for the analysis of *open systems*, because no ambients can be entered – and thus attacked – by an intruder unless the intruder's group name appears in the type of the ambient.

The paper proceeds as follows. In §1 we review the untyped Boxed Ambients and their standard semantics; §2 introduces the typed variant of Boxed Ambients and presents the relative subject reduction theorem; §3 show how our types tackle the *Troy's war* example above. In §4, we introduce Boxed Safe Ambients and their typing rules, illustrating their expressiveness again on the example of §3. The paper ends with a discussion of related works. In this extended abstract all proof are omitted, as is much of the discussion; complete proofs can be found in [14].

1   The Boxed Ambients

In this section we review the Boxed Ambient calculus as introduced in [2]. The syntax of processes is given in Table 1, where $\mathbf{N}$ denotes an infinite set of names. Inactivity, composition, restriction and replication are inherited from mainstream concurrent calculi, most notably the π-calculus [16]. Specific of the ambient calculus are the *ambient* construct, $V[P]$, and the *prefix* via capabilities, $V.P$. Capabilities are obtained from names; given a name n, the capability $\mathsf{in}\, n$ allows entry into n, the capability $\mathsf{out}\, n$ allows exit out of n. Meaningless terms such as $\mathsf{in}\, n[P]$ or $n.P$ are ruled out by the type system in the next section.

Communication is (i) *synchronous* (though an asynchronous version has been considered [2]); (ii) *polyadic*, we use boldface when appropriate to represent tuples concisely, as in $(\boldsymbol{x})^\eta.P$ and $\langle \boldsymbol{V} \rangle^\eta.P$; and, most importantly, (iii) *located* and *across* boundaries. Syntactically, located communication is obtained by means of tags specifying the location where the communication has to take place. More precisely, outputs (and similarly inputs) can take one of three forms: (i) $\langle \boldsymbol{V} \rangle^n.P$, a message for sub-ambient n from its parent; (ii) $\langle \boldsymbol{V} \rangle^\uparrow.P$, a message for the parent from a sub-ambient; (iii) $\langle \boldsymbol{V} \rangle^\star.P$, a local communication within the current ambient boundaries. We will omit $\star$ in both $\langle \boldsymbol{V} \rangle^\star.P$ and $(\boldsymbol{x})^\star.P$, so recovering the usual MA notation.

Table 1 The Boxed Ambients

Names: $n, m, \ldots, x, y, \ldots \in \mathbf{N}$

Locations:

$\eta ::= $	n	names
	$\uparrow$	enclosing ambient
	$\star$	local

Processes: *Values:*

$P ::= $	$\mathbf{0}$	nil process	$V, U ::= $	n	name
	$P_1 \mid P_2$	composition		$\text{in } V$	may enter into V
	$(\nu n)P$	restriction		$\text{out } V$	may exit out of V
	$!P$	replication		$V_1.V_2$	path
	$V[P]$	ambient			
	$V.P$	prefixing			
	$(\boldsymbol{x})^{\eta}.P$	input			
	$\langle \boldsymbol{V} \rangle^{\eta}.P$	output			

We use a number of notational conventions. Parallel composition has the lowest precedence among the operators. The process $V.V'.P$ is read as $V.(V'.P)$. As usual, we omit trailing dead processes, writing V for $V.\mathbf{0}$, $\langle \boldsymbol{V} \rangle$ for $\langle \boldsymbol{V} \rangle.\mathbf{0}$, and $n[\ ]$ for $n[\mathbf{0}]$. Restriction $(\nu n)P$ and input prefix $(\boldsymbol{x})^{\eta}.P$ acts as binders for names n and $\boldsymbol{x}$, respectively. The set of *free names* of P, fn(P), is defined accordingly.

The dynamics of the calculus is given in the form of a reduction relation as in Table 2. As customary in process calculi, the *reduction semantics* is based on an auxiliary relation called *structural congruence*, $\equiv$, which brings the participants of a potential interaction to contiguous positions. The reader is referred to [2] for its formal definition. The reduction rules are divided in two groups: the mobility rules and the communication rules. The former are exactly as in MA; the latter add to the usual local communication of MA the location-based communication across boundaries. In the communication rules we assume that tuples have the same arity, a condition that later will be enforced by the type system.

2 Typing Mobility in Boxed Ambients

The original types for BA of [2] control that communication is well-typed, wherever it happens. As processes in BA can communicate both locally and upwards, each ambient needs to state explicitly both the local topic of conversation and the topic of the conversation in its parent ambient. There is no need to keep explicit track of communications in the children, as this information is available as the topic of conversation locally in each children.

In this section we extend the types of [2] to control both *communication* and *mobility*. The Typed Boxed Ambients are obtained by adding type annotations to the syntax of Table 1 and inheriting the construct $(\nu G)P$ of [5] for *group creation*.

Table 2 Reduction Rules

$\rightarrow$ is the least relation on processes closed under $\_ \mid Q$, $(\nu n)\_$, $n[\_]$ such that:

mobility

$$n[\text{in } m.P \mid Q] \mid m[R] \;\rightarrow\; m[n[P \mid Q] \mid R] \qquad\qquad (\text{RED In})$$

$$m[n[\text{out } m.P \mid Q] \mid R] \;\rightarrow\; n[P \mid Q] \mid m[R] \qquad\qquad (\text{RED Out})$$

communication

$$(\boldsymbol{x}).P \mid \langle V \rangle.Q \;\rightarrow\; P\{V/\!\!\boldsymbol{x}\} \mid Q \qquad\qquad (\text{RED Comm Local})$$

$$(\boldsymbol{x})^n.P \mid n[\langle V \rangle.Q \mid R] \;\rightarrow\; P\{V/\!\!\boldsymbol{x}\} \mid n[Q \mid R] \qquad (\text{RED Comm Input } n)$$

$$(\boldsymbol{x}).P \mid n[\langle V \rangle^{\uparrow}.Q \mid R] \;\rightarrow\; P\{V/\!\!\boldsymbol{x}\} \mid n[Q \mid R] \qquad (\text{RED Comm Output } \uparrow)$$

$$\langle V \rangle^n.P \mid n[(\boldsymbol{x}).Q \mid R] \;\rightarrow\; P \mid n[Q\{V/\!\!\boldsymbol{x}\} \mid R] \qquad (\text{RED Comm Output } n)$$

$$\langle V \rangle.P \mid n[(\boldsymbol{x})^{\uparrow}.Q \mid R] \;\rightarrow\; P \mid n[Q\{V/\!\!\boldsymbol{x}\} \mid R] \qquad (\text{RED Comm Input } \uparrow)$$

congruence

$$P \equiv Q \quad Q \rightarrow R \quad R \equiv S \text{ implies } P \rightarrow S \qquad (\text{RED Struct})$$

The operator $(\nu \text{G})P$ binds G in P; the set of *free groups* of P, $fg(P)$, is defined accordingly. As in [5], groups may appear in the type annotations of both input and name restriction, and the definition of structural congruence must be extended to keep into account the new group operator.

2.1 The Types

The type system revolves around three main types: *ambient types*, *process types* and *capability types*; these are all interrelated to each other (actually mutually recursive) and annotated with information on both communication and mobility. A grammar for the types is given in Table 3.

The first component of ambient types is the group G which the ambient belongs to. Process (resp. capability) types have a similar component that establishes the group of the ambients where the process (resp. capability) can be executed.

The second component of ambient types describes the *mobility* constraints within the ambient, expressed in terms of groups rather than actual names. More precisely, in the mobility type mob[S], S represents the (set of groups of) ambients where the ambient in question may reside. As ambients are finally moved by processes, information about mobility must be attached to processes too. Specifically, a process must declare the set of groups of ambients it may *drive* the enclosing ambient to. For the same reason, since capabilities can be used to form processes, we need to add the same component to capability types as well.

The third component of ambient types disciplines communication along the lines of [2]. In a *communication type* com[E, F], the *exchange type* E represents the local topic of conversation, and F the one in the parent. As processes communicate with each other both inside and across ambients, type safety requires

Table 3 Types for Boxed Ambients

Groups:	$G, H, \ldots$	
Finite sets of groups:	$\mathsf{G, D, S}, \ldots$ $\mathfrak{U}$	*The universal set of groups*
Ambients types:		
A ::=	$\mathtt{amb}_\chi[\mathsf{G}, M, C]$	ambient of group G, for χ-actions, $\chi \subseteq \{\mathtt{i, o, c, r, w}\}$, with mobility type M, and communication type C
Process types:		
Π ::=	$\mathtt{proc}[\mathsf{G}, M, C]$	process that can be enclosed in an ambient of group G, may drive it to ambients whose groups are in M, and communicates as described by type C
Capability types:		
K ::=	$\mathtt{cap}[\mathsf{G}, M, F]$	capability that can appear in an ambient of group G, may drive it to ambients whose groups are in M, with exchange type F for local communication
Mobility types:		
M ::=	$\mathtt{mob}[\mathsf{G}]$	mobility specifications
Communication types:		
C ::=	$\mathtt{com}[E, F]$	E is the exchange type for local communications, F is the exchange type for upward communications
Exchange types:		
E, F ::=	$\mathtt{rw}[I, O]$	read/write values of type I and O (valid if $O \lessdot I$)
Message types:		
I, O ::=	$\bot$	bottom message type
	$W_1 \times \ldots \times W_k$	tuple (**1** is the null product)
	$\top$	top message type
Value types:		
W, Y ::=	A	ambient name
	K	capability

that the exchange of messages must be compatible with the communication type associated to the ambient. It thus follows that processes have a communication type exactly as the above. Things are slightly different for capabilities. Capabilities determine where a process carries its enclosing ambient. Although ambients cannot be opened, the processes they contain can still interact with the receiving ambients by means of upward communication. As a consequence, in order to guarantee safety in mobility, capability types must contain the information about the type of the conversation at destination.

The final component of ambient types – that we denote as an index attached to the keyword $\mathtt{amb}$ – is a set $\chi \subseteq \{\mathtt{i, o, c, r, w}\}$ which determines the ambient name can be used for, viz. $\mathtt{in}$ and $\mathtt{out}$ actions, creation of an ambient, reading from and writing to a subambient. This allows to give out names together with restricted capabilities, and refines the capability-passing mechanism of the ambient calculus in that it transmits full knowledge of ambient names, yet selectively releasing rights to act on it. As a matter of notation, we write $\mathtt{amb}_{\mathtt{iow}}$ for $\mathtt{amb}_{\{\mathtt{i,o,w}\}}$ and similarly for all χ.

Values in BA consist of tuples of names and capabilities. Since our intention is to have subtyping on values, we must separate the read and write capabilities of exchange types, as initiated in [17]. We do this in a simple, standard way

Table 4 Subtype Relation

$$(\text{sAmb}) \quad \frac{\chi_1 \subseteq \chi_0 \subseteq \{\mathtt{i}, \mathtt{o}, \mathtt{c}, \mathtt{r}, \mathtt{w}\}}{\mathtt{amb}_{\chi_0}[\mathsf{G}, M, C] \prec \mathtt{amb}_{\chi_1}[\mathsf{G}, M, C]} \qquad (\text{sProc}) \quad \frac{M_0 \prec M_1; \quad C_0 \prec C_1}{\mathtt{proc}[\mathsf{G}, M_0, C_0] \prec \mathtt{proc}[\mathsf{G}, M_1, C_1]}$$

$$(\text{sCap}) \quad \frac{M_0 \prec M_1; \quad F_0 \prec F_1}{\mathtt{cap}[\mathsf{G}, M_0, F_0] \prec \mathtt{cap}[\mathsf{G}, M_1, F_1]} \qquad (\text{sMob}) \quad \frac{\mathsf{G}_0 \subseteq \mathsf{G}_1}{\mathtt{mob}[\mathsf{G}_0] \prec \mathtt{mob}[\mathsf{G}_1]}$$

$$(\text{sCom}) \quad \frac{E_0 \prec E_1; \quad F_0 \prec F_1}{\mathtt{com}[E_0, F_0] \prec \mathtt{com}[E_1, F_1]} \qquad (\text{sExc}) \quad \frac{I_1 \prec I_0; \quad O_0 \prec O_1}{\mathtt{rw}[I_0, O_0] \prec \mathtt{rw}[I_1, O_1]}$$

$$(\text{sMsg}) \quad \frac{-}{\bot \prec W_1 \times \ldots \times W_k \prec \top} \qquad (\text{sTuple}) \quad \frac{W_i \prec Y_i; \quad i \in 1..k}{W_1 \times \ldots \times W_k \prec Y_1 \times \ldots \times Y_k}$$

similar to [22,20]. Our *exchange types* have the form $\mathtt{rw}[I, O]$ and represent the capability of reading and writing values of, respectively, the message types I and O. Message types contain tuple types $W_1 \times \ldots \times W_k$ to exchange tuples of values. For $k = 0$, the empty tuple type allows the exchange of empty messages, that is, it allows pure synchronisation. Besides tuple types, message types include standard bottom ($\bot$) and top ($\top$) types that allow to express interesting types. One of these is $\mathtt{zero} \triangleq \mathtt{rw}[\top, \bot]$, the least exchange type, which describes processes that engage in no communication. As customary with input/output types, we require in $\mathtt{rw}[I, O]$ that O is a subtype of I, so that a process output is compatible with (and more specific than) its input. Because of such restriction, that will be assumed throughout the paper, the set of valid types is defined simultaneously with the subtype relation $\prec$, whose formal definition is given in Table 4. We will discuss the details in §2.3 below. For the purposes of this section it suffices to say what follows.

Subtyping on communication allows processes with a communication type C inside ambients with a communication type C' if $C \prec C'$. For instance, a process that exchanges no messages can reside in a ambient regardless of its topic of conversation.

Subtyping on mobility is essentially based on subsets of set of groups, as formalised by rule (sMob). A process driving to ambients with groups in D is allowed to reside in ambients which can move into ambients whose groups belongs to D', with D $\subseteq$ D'.

In §2.3 we will give a better account about subtyping.

2.2 Type Assignment

A type environment Γ is a list of assumptions about groups, names and their types of one of two forms: G, declaring the existence of group G, or $n : A$, declaring a name n of type A. Since types contain references to groups, the order of assumptions in Γ is relevant; to describe valid environments we use judgements of the form $\Gamma \vdash \diamond$ that make sure that names and groups are not repeated

Table 5 Good Values

$$(\text{VAL } n) \ \frac{\Gamma, n : W, \Gamma' \vdash \diamond}{\Gamma, n : W, \Gamma' \vdash n : W}$$

$$(\text{VAL PFX}) \ \frac{\Gamma \vdash V_0 : K; \ \Gamma \vdash V_1 : K}{\Gamma \vdash V_0.V_1 : K} \qquad (\text{VAL IN}) \ \frac{\Gamma \vdash V : \text{amb}_i[G, M, \text{com}[E, F]]}{\Gamma \vdash \text{in } V : \text{cap}[H, \text{mob}[\{G\}], E]} H \in \text{dom}(\Gamma)$$

$$(\text{VAL SUB}) \ \frac{\Gamma \vdash V : W; \quad W \ll W'}{\Gamma \vdash V : W'} \qquad (\text{VAL OUT}) \ \frac{\Gamma \vdash V : \text{amb}_o[G, M, \text{com}[E, F]]}{\Gamma \vdash \text{out } V : \text{cap}[H, M, F]} H \in \text{dom}(\Gamma)$$

and that groups are defined before being referred to. The formal definition of type environments and domain of an environment, and the inference rules for *well-formed environments* are standard [5].

Table 5 presents the typing rules for *well-formed values*. Rules (VAL n) and (VAL SUB) are straightforward. Rule (VAL PFX) decrees that the type of a path of capabilities is the common type of its components. Notice that, in the light of (VAL SUB) and of the subtyping rule (sCAP) of Table 4, this actually means that paths are assigned a common super type of their component capabilities. In rule (VAL IN), exploiting the subtyping rule (sAMB), we require the in-capability on ambient name n to form in n. The conclusion states that the capability in V can reside inside any ambient of group H, for any H $\in$ dom(Γ), and can drive its enclosing ambient into an ambient of group G (viz. V's group) with local exchange type E (viz. V's local exchange type). Rule (VAL OUT) is similar. Its conclusion states that out V can drive the enclosing ambient into ambients with groups mentioned in M (viz. V's mobility type) and local exchange type F (viz. V's upward exchange type).

The inference rules in Tables 6 and 7 are for *well-typed processes* as expressed by judgements of the form $\Gamma \vdash P : \Pi$. We divide the rules in two groups, dealing separately with mobility and communication. Table 6 focuses on mobility. Rule (PRO PFX) builds on the subtyping rules (sCAP) and (sPROC) to state that the characteristics of the capabilities present in a process must be subsumed in its type.

Rule (PRO AMB) is crucial. It says that a process $V[P]$ can be formed only if we have the capability to create an ambient called V. Furthermore, P can run inside V only if P and V agree on the group, the mobility type, and the communication type. The resulting ambient $V[P]$ is a process that (i) can be executed in any ambient of group G, provided G is a place where V is allowed to reside; (ii) will not drive an enclosing ambients anywhere; and (iii) inherits P's upward exchange type as its local exchange type and, finally, has a minimal upward exchange type. As a consequence of the requirement G $\in$ S, the set S is never empty; indeed an ambient, even if immobile, always resides somewhere. Notice the role played here by the subtyping rule (sPROC). The remaining rules in Table 6 are straightforward.

Table 7 adapts the rules for communication of [2] taking subtyping into account.

Table 6 Good Processes - Mobility

$$(\text{Pro Pfx}) \quad \frac{\Gamma \vdash V : \text{cap}[\text{G}, M, F]; \quad \Gamma \vdash P : \text{proc}[\text{G}, M, \text{com}[E, F]]}{\Gamma \vdash V.P : \text{proc}[\text{G}, M, \text{com}[E, F]]}$$

$$(\text{Pro Amb}) \quad \frac{\Gamma \vdash V : \text{amb}_c[\text{H}, \text{mob}[\text{S}], \text{com}[E, F]]; \quad \Gamma \vdash P : \text{proc}[\text{H}, \text{mob}[\text{S}], \text{com}[E, F]]}{\Gamma \vdash V[P] : \text{proc}[\text{G}, \text{mob}[\varnothing], \text{com}[F, \text{zero}]]} \text{G} \in \text{S}$$

$$(\text{Pro Res}) \quad \frac{\Gamma, n : A \vdash P : \Pi}{\Gamma \vdash (\nu n : A)P : \Pi} \qquad\qquad (\text{Pro Gres}) \quad \frac{\Gamma, \text{G} \vdash P : \Pi}{\Gamma \vdash (\nu \text{G})P : \Pi} \text{G} \notin \text{fg}(\Pi)$$

$$(\text{Pro 0}) \quad \frac{\text{G} \in \text{dom}(\Gamma)}{\Gamma \vdash \mathbf{0} : \text{proc}[\text{G}, \text{mob}[\varnothing], \text{com}[\text{zero}, \text{zero}]]} \qquad (\text{Pro Par}) \quad \frac{\Gamma \vdash P : \Pi; \quad \Gamma \vdash Q : \Pi}{\Gamma \vdash P \mid Q : \Pi}$$

$$(\text{Pro Rep}) \quad \frac{\Gamma \vdash P : \Pi}{\Gamma \vdash !P : \Pi} \qquad\qquad (\text{Pro Sub}) \quad \frac{\Gamma \vdash P : \Pi \quad \Pi \lessdot \Pi'}{\Gamma \vdash P : \Pi'}$$

Table 7 Good Processes - Communication

$$(\text{Pro Inp} \star) \quad \frac{\Gamma, x_1{:}W_1, \ldots, x_k{:}W_k \vdash P : \text{proc}[\text{G}, M, \text{com}[\text{rw}[I, O], F]]}{\Gamma \vdash (x_1{:}W_1, \ldots, x_k{:}W_k).P : \text{proc}[\text{G}, M, \text{com}[\text{rw}[I, O], F]]} I \lessdot W_1 \times \ldots \times W_k$$

$$(\text{Pro Out} \star) \quad \frac{\Gamma \vdash V_1{:}W_1, \ldots, V_k{:}W_k; \quad \Gamma \vdash P : \text{proc}[\text{G}, M, \text{com}[\text{rw}[I, W_1 \times \ldots \times W_k], F]]}{\Gamma \vdash \langle V_1, \ldots, V_k \rangle.P : \text{proc}[\text{G}, M, \text{com}[\text{rw}[I, W_1 \times \ldots \times W_k], F]]}$$

$$(\text{Pro Inp} \uparrow) \quad \frac{\Gamma, x_1{:}W_1, \ldots, x_k{:}W_k \vdash P : \text{proc}[\text{G}, M, \text{com}[E, \text{rw}[I, O]]]}{\Gamma \vdash (x_1{:}W_1, \ldots, x_k{:}W_k)^\uparrow.P : \text{proc}[\text{G}, M, \text{com}[E, \text{rw}[I, O]]]} I \lessdot W_1 \times \ldots \times W_k$$

$$(\text{Pro Out} \uparrow) \quad \frac{\Gamma \vdash V_1{:}W_1, \ldots, V_k{:}W_k; \quad \Gamma \vdash P : \text{proc}[\text{G}, M, \text{com}[E, \text{rw}[I, W_1 \times \ldots \times W_k]]]}{\Gamma \vdash \langle V_1, \ldots, V_k \rangle^\uparrow.P : \text{proc}[\text{G}, M, \text{com}[E, \text{rw}[I, W_1 \times \ldots \times W_k]]]}$$

$$(\text{Pro Inp} V) \quad \frac{\Gamma \vdash V{:}\text{amb}_r[\text{G}, M, \text{com}[\text{rw}[I, O], F]]; \quad \Gamma, x_1{:}W_1, \ldots, x_k{:}W_k \vdash P : \Pi}{\Gamma \vdash (x_1{:}W_1, \ldots, x_k{:}W_k)^V.P : \Pi} I \lessdot W_1 \times \ldots \times W_k$$

$$(\text{Pro Out} V) \quad \frac{\Gamma \vdash V{:}\text{amb}_w[\text{G}, M, \text{com}[\text{rw}[I, W_k \times \ldots \times W_k], F]]; \Gamma \vdash U_1{:}W_1, \ldots, U_k{:}W_k; \Gamma \vdash P : \Pi}{\Gamma \vdash \langle U_1, \ldots, U_k \rangle^V.P : \Pi}$$

2.3 Subtyping

Subtyping has a truly relevant impact on type systems for Ambients. Subtyping on communication allows to have processes that exchange no messages in ambients regardless of the local topic of conversation. This idea has been proposed in [22]. In the current paper we put forward the use of subtyping for mobility types, unveiling its beneficial impact and general usefulness for the purpose. The prime idea here is to allow a process that may drive ambients to D wherever a processes that travels to D', with D ⊆ D', is expected.

Our aim of fully integrating subtyping in both mobility and communication types is achieved in rules (sPROC) and (sCAP), that state the covariance of process and capability types with their mobility and communication components. Notice that ambient types must be kept invariant, apart from the capabilities χ that – as typical of these 'may-use-for' situations – follow a contravariant typing.

Indeed no kind of variance is admissible for mobility or communication, as they both give rise to phony capabilities that trick processes into runtime errors. For instance, if ambient types were to be covariant, their mobility assumptions could be easily defied. Processes might falsely believe that, say, any ambient n at type $\text{amb}_\chi[\_, \text{mob}[S], \_]$, with $G \nsubseteq S$, is allowed to stay in any (ambient of group) G. In this manner, n might end up sitting where it should not. The same net effect is obtained by assuming contravariance, due to the interplay with covariance of process types in their mobility components. Similar arguments can be used to show that (sAMB) must be invariant also in the communication component (details can be found in [14]).

Finally, although in [2] there is no explicit subtyping on names or capabilities, the rules corresponding to our (VAL IN) and (VAL OUT) allow in n and out n an exchange type that is a subtype of the one declared for n. This is effectively a form of contravariant subtyping on names. We believe that our approach has advantages over that, as it allows deep, general subtyping on exchange types which, as discussed in [14], constitutes a major difference with the approach of [2].

2.4   Properties of Typing

As stated below, our subtype relation satisfies a certain number of properties.

Theorem 1 (Properties of $<$). The subtype relation is a partial order with all bounded joins and meets.

Existing joins ($\sqcup$) and meets ($\sqcap$) can be expressed quite easily starting from componentwise set union and intersection for mobility types, e.g., $\text{mob}[S_0] \sqcup \text{mob}[S_1] \triangleq \text{mob}[S_0 \cup S_1]$, from the obvious roles of $\bot$ and $\top$ among message types, and from their covariant/contravariant extension to exchange types, that is

$$\text{rw}[I_0, O_0] \sqcup \text{rw}[I_1, O_1] \triangleq \text{rw}[I_0 \sqcap I_1, O_0 \sqcup O_1] \quad , \quad \text{rw}[I_0, O_0] \sqcap \text{rw}[I_1, O_1] \triangleq \text{rw}[I_0 \sqcup I_1, O_0 \sqcap O_1].$$

As a whole, our type systems admits a quite simple algorithmic version – i.e., an equivalent type system with no subsumption rules nor reflexivity and transitivity rules for $<$ – that helps to prove the following results, intended to formalise the safety guarantees provided by our type system. In the following, we use '$\_$' to avoid naming irrelevant parts of types.

Theorem 2 (Communication Properties). Whenever for some types $W_1 \times \ldots \times W_k$ and Π one of the following holds,

$$\Gamma \vdash (x_1{:}W_1, \ldots, x_k{:}W_k).P \mid \langle V \rangle.Q : \Pi;$$

$$\Gamma \vdash (x_1{:}W_1, \ldots, x_k{:}W_k).P \mid m[\langle V \rangle^\uparrow.Q] : \Pi; \quad \Gamma \vdash \langle V \rangle.Q \mid m[(x_1{:}W_1, \ldots, x_k{:}W_k)^\uparrow.P] : \Pi,$$

$$\Gamma \vdash (x_1{:}W_1, \ldots, x_k{:}W_k)^m.P \mid m[\langle V \rangle.Q] : \Pi; \quad \Gamma \vdash \langle V \rangle^m.Q \mid m[(x_1{:}W_1, \ldots, x_k{:}W_k).P] : \Pi$$

then $V = V_1, \ldots, V_k$ and $\Gamma \vdash V_1 : Y_1, \ldots, V_k : Y_k$ with $Y_1 \times \ldots \times Y_k < W_1 \times \ldots \times W_k$.

Theorem 3 (Mobility Properties). Whenever $\Gamma \vdash n[\text{in}\, m.P \mid Q] \mid m[R]$: Π, then

$$\Gamma \vdash m : \text{amb}_{\chi_0}[M, \_, \_] \quad \text{and} \quad \Gamma \vdash n : \text{amb}_{\chi_1}[\_, \text{mob}[S], \_]$$

with $M \in S$, $i, c \in \chi_0$ and $c \in \chi_1$.
Moreover, if for some type Π we have $\Gamma \vdash m[n[\text{out}\, m.P \mid Q] \mid R] : \Pi$, then

$$\Gamma \vdash m : \text{amb}_{\chi_0}[M, \text{mob}[S_m], \_] \quad \text{and} \quad \Gamma \vdash n : \text{amb}_{\chi_1}[N, \text{mob}[S_n], \_]$$

with $o, c \in \chi_0$, $c \in \chi_1$, $M \in S_n$ and $S_m \subseteq S_n$.

Theorem 4 (Subject Congruence and Reduction). If $\Gamma \vdash P : \Pi$ and $P \equiv Q$ or $P \to Q$, then there exist groups $G_0, \ldots G_k$ such that $G_0, \ldots, G_k, \Gamma \vdash Q : \Pi$.

3   Some MyThS

As pointed out in the introduction, the system

Odysseus[in *Horse*.out *Horse.DESTROY_TROY*] | *Horse*[in *Troy*] | *Troy*[*TROJANS*]

can be typed with the types of [5] under hypotheses that say very little about the intentions of *Odysseus* to traverse *Troy*'s walls or indeed about the permission he might hold for doing so. On the contrary, in our system the term above can be only typed under assumptions of the kind

Odysseus : $\text{amb}_c[\text{Achaean}, \text{mob}[\{\text{Ground}, \text{Toy}, \text{City}\}], \_]$
Horse : $\text{amb}_{ioc}[\text{Toy}, \text{mob}[\{\text{Ground}, \text{City}\}], \_]$
Troy : $\text{amb}_{ioc}[\text{City}, \_, \_]$

that make explicit the hypotheses that *Odysseus* is an Achaean intentioned to move into a City. Such information should be enough to alert the *TROJANS* about an attack on *Troy* by *Odysseus*. On the other hand, under assumptions of the form

Odysseus : $\text{amb}_c[\text{Achaean}, \text{mob}[\{\text{Ground}, \text{Toy}\}], \_]$

the *TROJANS* should not fear any attack from *Odysseus*.

So far so good. Provided the *TROJANS* are in a position of believing *Odysseus*'s declared intentions of just 'moving into some Toy' everything is in place. But what if they suspect that the wily *Odysseus* might be lying about his real intentions, that is about his real type? The situation would then be perfectly analogous to what happens in the real-world of *open-ended systems*, where we cannot ask – nor afford – to type-check all systems which we interact with and, at the same time, we cannot trust their declarations of goodwill. What precautions can be taken to avoid being attacked by a malicious agent? What precautions can the *TROJANS* take to avoid *Odysseus*'s ravage?

A first solution is to have a type inference algorithm to infer a proper type for the external code. Then, analysing the mobility type of *Odysseus*, *Troy* can check whether its enemy is intentioned to move in. A more robust alternative is to provide *Troy* with a tool to explicitly declare the ambients allowed to move in. For instance, one may extend the mobility types with a second component that records the groups of those agents which are allowed to move into the ambient (in this case *Troy*). This would permit checking in movements by simply testing whether the moving ambients is accepted at destination. Unfortunately, we could not do the same test for out actions because target ambients in out movements may vary at run-time.

We avoid the obstacle by introducing the Boxed Safe Ambients a variant of BA enriched with co-capabilities to express permissions to move into ambients.

4   Safe Boxed Ambients

The Boxed Safe Ambients, abbreviated BSA, are obtained by extending the definition of Values of Table 1 as follows:

$$
\begin{array}{llll}
V & ::= & \ldots & \text{as in Typed Boxed Ambients} \\
& \mid & \overline{\text{in}}\,\alpha & \alpha \in \{\, n, \star \} \quad \text{allow enter of } n \text{ or of all} \\
& \mid & \overline{\text{out}}\,\alpha & \alpha \in \{ n, \star \} \quad \text{allow exit of } n \text{ or of all}
\end{array}
$$

Using co-capabilities, a BSA ambient can discriminate which ambient groups are allowed to enter its computation space, and when. The co-capabilities of BSA, inspired by [12,13,19], are a novel combination of existing proposals. In particular, both $\overline{in}$ and $\overline{out}$ co-capabilities are placed in the target computation, as in [13]. However, unlike [13], we allow both explicit and anonymous co-capabilities as in [19] and [12], respectively. The former indicates explicitly the name of the ambient allowed to cross the ambient boundary; the latter represents a general permission to cross the boundary usable by all.

The reduction relation is obtained by replacing the rules (Red In) and (Red Out) of Table 2 with the following rules.

$$
n[\text{in}\,m.P \mid Q] \mid m[\overline{\text{in}}\,\alpha.R \mid S] \longrightarrow m[n[P \mid Q] \mid R \mid S] \quad \text{for } \alpha \in \{\star, n\} \quad \text{(RED IN)}
$$

$$
m[n[\text{out}\,m.P \mid Q] \mid R] \mid \overline{\text{out}}\,\alpha.S \longrightarrow n[P \mid Q] \mid m[R] \mid S \quad \text{for } \alpha \in \{\star, n\} \quad \text{(RED OUT)}
$$

The types for BSA are obtained by enriching the mobility types of Table 3 with an extra information about the groups of ambients allowed to stay in the given ambient:

$$
M \quad ::= \quad \text{mob}[S, C].
$$

The subtyping rules of Table 4 are adapted by replacing the rule (sMob) with:

$$
(\text{sMob}) \quad \frac{G_0 \subseteq G_1, \quad C_0 \subseteq C_1}{\text{mob}[G_0, C_0] \prec \text{mob}[G_1, C_1]}.
$$

The inference rules for well-typed values of Table 5 must be adapted to take into account the new component of the capability types, as in Table 8. Rules (Val in V) and (Val out V) are like the corresponding ones in Table 5.

Table 8 Good Values in BSA (overlay on Table 5)

(VAL in V)
$$\frac{\Gamma \vdash V : \mathrm{amb_i}[\mathrm{G}, M, \mathrm{com}[E, F]]}{\Gamma \vdash \mathrm{in}\, V : \mathrm{cap}[\mathrm{H}, \mathrm{mob}[\{\mathrm{G}\}, \varnothing], E]}$$

(VAL out V)
$$\frac{\Gamma \vdash V : \mathrm{amb_o}[\mathrm{G}, \mathrm{mob}[\mathrm{S}, \mathrm{C}], \mathrm{com}[E, F]]}{\Gamma \vdash \mathrm{out}\, V : \mathrm{cap}[\mathrm{H}, \mathrm{mob}[\mathrm{S}, \varnothing], F]}$$

(VAL $\overline{\mathrm{in}}\, V$)
$$\frac{\Gamma \vdash V : \mathrm{amb_i}[\mathrm{G}, M, \mathrm{com}[E, F]]}{\Gamma \vdash \overline{\mathrm{in}}\, V : \mathrm{cap}[\mathrm{H}, \mathrm{mob}[\varnothing, \{\mathrm{G}\}], F]}$$

(VAL $\overline{\mathrm{out}}\, V$)
$$\frac{\Gamma \vdash V : \mathrm{amb_o}[\mathrm{G}, M, \mathrm{com}[E, F]]}{\Gamma \vdash \overline{\mathrm{out}}\, V : \mathrm{cap}[\mathrm{H}, \mathrm{mob}[\varnothing, \{\mathrm{G}\}], F]}$$

(VAL $\overline{\mathrm{in}}\,\star$)
$$\frac{\mathrm{G} \in \mathrm{dom}(\Gamma)}{\Gamma \vdash \overline{\mathrm{in}}\,\star : \mathrm{cap}[\mathrm{G}, \mathrm{mob}[\varnothing, \mathfrak{U}], \mathrm{zero}]}$$

(VAL $\overline{\mathrm{out}}\,\star$)
$$\frac{\mathrm{G} \in \mathrm{dom}(\Gamma)}{\Gamma \vdash \overline{\mathrm{out}}\,\star : \mathrm{cap}[\mathrm{G}, \mathrm{mob}[\varnothing, \mathfrak{U}], \mathrm{zero}]}$$

In rules (VAL in V), (VAL out V), (VAL $\overline{\mathrm{in}}\, V$), and (VAL $\overline{\mathrm{out}}\, V$) we require $\mathrm{H} \in \mathrm{dom}(\Gamma)$.

Table 9 Good Processes - Mobility (overlay on Table 6)

(PRO PFX)
$$\frac{\Gamma \vdash V : \mathrm{cap}[\mathrm{G}, M, F]; \quad \Gamma \vdash P : \mathrm{proc}[\mathrm{G}, M, \mathrm{com}[E, F]]}{\Gamma \vdash V.P : \mathrm{proc}[\mathrm{G}, M, \mathrm{com}[E, F]]}$$

(PRO **0**)
$$\frac{\mathrm{G} \in \mathrm{dom}(\Gamma)}{\Gamma \vdash \mathbf{0} : \mathrm{proc}[\mathrm{G}, \mathrm{mob}[\varnothing, \varnothing], \mathrm{com}[\mathrm{zero}, \mathrm{zero}]]}$$

(PRO AMB)
$$\frac{\Gamma \vdash V : \mathrm{amb_c}[\mathrm{H}, \mathrm{mob}[\mathrm{S}, \mathrm{C}], \mathrm{com}[E, F]]; \quad \Gamma \vdash P : \mathrm{proc}[\mathrm{H}, \mathrm{mob}[\mathrm{S}, \mathrm{C}], \mathrm{com}[E, F]]}{\Gamma \vdash V[P] : \mathrm{proc}[\mathrm{G}, \mathrm{mob}[\varnothing, \{\mathrm{H}\}], \mathrm{com}[F, \mathrm{zero}]]} \quad \mathrm{G} \in \mathrm{S}$$

We simply add a second empty component to the mobility type, denoting that these capabilities allow no incoming code. Dually, rules (VAL $\overline{\mathrm{in}}\, V$) and (VAL $\overline{\mathrm{out}}\, V$) do not trigger movements, but allow inbound code. Thus, the resulting mobility types in both conclusions have the first component empty, while the second one record the groups of possible visitors (i.e. the group of V). The third component of both capability types is the upward exchange type of V. As for rules (VAL $\overline{\mathrm{in}}\,\star$) and (VAL $\overline{\mathrm{out}}\,\star$), they differ from the previous ones in the second component of the mobility types where the universal set of groups $\mathfrak{U}$ is used to reflect the anonymous nature of the construct. Moreover, in both cases the exchange type is **zero**, the least exchange type, because nothing is known about the communication types of the incoming ambients.

The inference rules for well-typed processes are changed as in Table 9; the remaining rules are changed in the obvious manner.

Our results extends smoothly to BSA. In particular, the Subject Reduction Theorem 4 can be restated in formally identical terms for BSA as for BA. The new results concern the added control power granted to BSA by co-capabilities.

Theorem 5 (Control Properties). In addition to the properties of Theorems 2 and 3, whenever

$$\Gamma \vdash m[\overline{\mathrm{in}}\,\alpha.P \mid Q] : \Pi \quad \text{or} \quad \Gamma \vdash m[\overline{\mathrm{out}}\,\alpha.P \mid Q] : \Pi \quad \text{with } \alpha \in \{\star, n\},$$

then $\Gamma \vdash m : \mathtt{amb}_{\chi_0}[\_, \mathtt{mob}[\_, C], \_]$ and

- either $\alpha = \star$ and $C = \mathfrak{U}$,
- or $\alpha = n$ with $\Gamma \vdash n : \mathtt{amb}_{\chi_1}[N, \_, \_]$ and $N \in C$.

4.1   Using Co-capabilities to Defend *Troy*

The system discussed in §3 can be rewritten in BSA as follows.

$$THE\_TROJAN\_WAR \triangleq Odysseus[\mathtt{in}\, Horse.\mathtt{out}\, Horse.DESTROY\_TROY\,]$$
$$|\ Horse[\overline{\mathtt{in}}\, \star .\mathtt{in}\, Troy\,]$$
$$|\ Troy[\overline{\mathtt{in}}\, Horse. TROJANS \ |\ \overline{\mathtt{out}}\, Odysseus.SINON\,]$$

Here, although the *TROJANS* let the *Horse* inside the city walls, *Odysseus* still needs a co-capability, such as $\overline{\mathtt{out}}\ Odysseus$ executed by *SINON* from *Troy*, to be able to get out of the *Horse*. However, a behaviour like *SINON*'s from a process running in *Troy* can only be well-typed if *Troy* has a type allowing ambients of group Achaean to enter *Troy*, as for instance the following one.

$$Troy : \mathtt{amb}_{ioc}[\mathtt{City}, \mathtt{mob}[\_, \{\mathtt{Toy}, \mathtt{Achaean}\}], \_]$$

Of course, such a choice would be suicidal for *Troy*!

On the other hand, consider the system below, where we remove the security breach represented by *SINON*.

$$THE\_TROJAN\_TRAP \triangleq Odysseus[\mathtt{in}\, Horse.\mathtt{out}\, Horse.DESTROY\_TROY\,]$$
$$|\ Horse[\overline{\mathtt{in}}\, \star .\mathtt{in}\, Troy\,] \ |\ Troy[\overline{\mathtt{in}}\, Horse. TROJANS\,]$$

This situation would be perfectly safe for *Troy* (but dangerous for *Odysseus*!) provided we can type it under the assumptions of the form

$$Odysseus : \mathtt{amb}_c[\mathtt{Achaean}, \_, \_]$$
$$Horse : \mathtt{amb}_{ioc}[\mathtt{Toy}, \_, \mathtt{com}[E, \mathtt{zero}]]$$
$$Troy : \mathtt{amb}_{ioc}[\mathtt{City}, \mathtt{mob}[\varnothing, C], \_]$$

with $\mathtt{Achaean} \notin C$. In fact, even though the *Horse* gets inside the walls no *TROJANS* will ever give *Odysseus* permission to get out of it (and he will be stuck to starvation inside it), as assured by the condition for $\mathtt{Achaean} \notin C$. Furthermore, the upward exchange type of the *Horse* prevents leakage of information from *Troy*.

5   Conclusion and Related Work

We have presented a powerful type system to control communication and mobility within Bugliesi *et al.*'s Boxed Ambients. A major feature of our approach is the extensive use of a subtyping relation well integrated and crucially relied upon within the system. Our type system as a whole enjoys the expected property of subject reduction and provides strong safety guarantees for well-typed terms. These results are formally stated in §2 and §4 and exemplified in §3. We are currently investigating *type inference* algorithms.

Our types and subtyping compare well with related proposals in the literature. In particular, while the treatment of exchange types is similar to Zimmer's [22] and Yoshida and Hennessy's [20] – in turn elaborations over Pierce and Sangiorgi's input/output types [17] – we know of no similar approaches to mobility types. Work of Yoshida and Hennessy's [21] and Castagna *et al.*'s [11] use subtyping on interface types for processes of, respectively, a higher-order π calculus and the Seal calculus. These approaches, however, are not directly concerned with control of subjective mobility. On the contrary, De Nicola *et al.*'s [10] focuses on mobility control using subtyping over process capabilities, but for a Linda-like language rather far from ours.

In the second part of the paper we extended the Boxed Ambients with a version of co-capabilities where the entering/exiting ambient can, though need not, be explicitly mentioned. The information gathered in ambient types, together with the power granted to the calculus by co-capabilities, allow to express properties not expressible in previous frameworks. In particular, they permit to deal with situations typical of open-ended systems, as we exemplified by means of the *Troy's War* example. We believe that our approach here is totally compatible with the *moded types* of [2] and plan in future work to investigate the matter further.

Finally, note that within our type theory it is possible to analyse immobility properties of ambients. Namely, $n[P]$ is immobile when P can be assigned a type of the form $\mathtt{proc}[\_,\mathtt{mob}[\varnothing],\_]$. However, prescribing that an ambient cannot be moved is a different matter. Recall that the mobility component of an ambient type describes where ambients are allowed to *stay*, and not to *travel to*, as for process types. Assigning $\mathtt{mob}[\varnothing]$ as mobility type will therefore not help. (As a matter of fact, and as revealed by inspection of rule (PRO AMB), S can never be empty.) This is, we believe, a minor point that can be handled on top of the existing framework with minimal changes. For instance, it would be enough to think of the set of group names as partitioned in two infinite subsets: the mobile and the immobile groups. Then, we only need to add to (VAL IN) and (VAL OUT) the side condition that H is mobile. Ambients could then be declared immobile by assigning them – either in $\varGamma$ or in a name declarations – to an immobile group.

References

1. M. Bugliesi, G. Castagna and S. Crafa. Reasoning about security in mobile ambients. In *Proc. CONCUR* 2001, volume 2154 Lecture Notes in Computer Science, Springer, 2001. 306
2. M. Bugliesi, G. Castagna, and S. Crafa. Boxed ambients. In *Proc. TACS* 2001, volume 2215 of Lecture Notes in Computer Science, Springer, 2001. 305, 306, 307, 308, 309, 312, 314, 319

3. L. Cardelli and G. Ghelli. A query language based an the ambient logic. In *Proc. ESOP* 2001, volume 2028of Lecture Notes in Computer Science, Springer, 2001. 304

4. L. Cardelli. Wide area computation, In *Proc. ICALP 1999,* volume 1644 of Lecture Notes in Computer Science, Springer, 1999. 304

5. L. Cardelli, G. Ghelli, and A. Gordon. Ambient groups and mobility types. In *Proc. IFIP* TCS 2000, volume 1872 of Lecture Notes in Computer Science, Springer, 2000. 304, 305, 306, 308, 309, 312, 315

6. L. Cardelli and A. Gordon. Types for mobile ambients. In *Proc. of POPL'99,* ACM Press, 1999. 305

7. L. Cardelli and A. Gordon. Anytime, anywhere: Modal logics for mobile ambients. In *Proc. of POPL* 2000, ACM Press, 2000. 304

8. L. Cardelli and A. Gordon. *Mobile nmbients.* Theoretical Computer Science, *240(1):177213, 2000.* An extended abstract appeared in *Proc. of FoSSaCS 1998,* volume 1378 of *Lecture Notes in Computer Science,* Springer, 1998. 304

9. I. Castellani. Process algebras with localities. In J. Bergstra, A. Ponse, and S. Smolka, (Eds), *Handbook of Process Algebra, 945-1045,* North-Holland, 2001. 304

10. R. De Nicola, G. Ferrari, and R. Pugliese. *Klaim: A kernel language for agents interaction und mobility.* IEEE Trans. an Software Engineering, 24(5), IEEE Press, 1998. 319

11. G. Ghelli G. Castagna and F. Zappa Nardelli. Typing mobility in the seal calculus. In *Proc. CONCUR* 2001, volume 2154 Lecture Notes in Computer Science, Springer, 2001. 319

12. E Levi and D. Sangiorgi. Controlling interference in ambients. In *Proc. POPL* 2000, ACM Press. 316

13. M. Merro and M. Hennessy. Bisimulation congruences in safe ambients. *Proc. POPL'02,* ACM Press, 2002 306, 316

14. M. Merro and V Sassone. Typing and subtyping mobility in boxed ambients. To appear as Technical Report available at http://www.cogs.susx.ac.uk/reports. University of Sussex. 307, 314

15. R. Milner. *Communication und Concurrency.* Prentice Hall, 1989. 306

16. R. Milner, J. Parrow, and D. Walken *A calculus of mobile processes, (Parts I und II).* Information and Computation, *100:1-77, 1992.* 304, 306, 307

17. B. Pierce and D. Sangiorgi. *Typing und subtyping for mobile processes.* Journal of Mathematical Structures in Computer Science, *6(5):409-454, 1996.* 310, 319

18. J. Vitek and G. Castagna. Seal: A framework for secure mobile computations. In *Internet Programming Languages,* volume 1686 of Lecture Notes in Computer Science, Springer, 1999. 306

19. Y Yang, X. Guan, and J. You. *Typing evolving nmbients.* Information Processing Letters, *80(5):265-270, 2001.* 306, 316

20. N. Yoshida and M. Hennessy. Subtyping and locality in distributed higher order processes. In *Proc. CONCUR 1999,* volume 1664 of Lecture Notes in Computer Science, Springer, 1999. 311, 319

21. N. Yoshida and M. Hennessy. Assigning types to processes. In *Proc. LICS* 2000, IEEE Press, 2000. 319

22. P. Zimmer. Subtyping and typing algorithms for mobile ambients. In *Proc. FoSSaCS* 2000, volume 1784 of Lecture Notes in Computer Science, Springer, 2000. 311, 313, 319

Orchestrating Transactions in Join Calculus[*]

Roberto Bruni[1], Cosimo Laneve[2], and Ugo Montanari[1]

[1] Dipartimento di Informatica, Università di Pisa, Italia
{bruni,ugo}@di.unipi.it
http://www.di.unipi.it/~{bruni,ugo}
[2] Dipartimento di Scienze dell'Informazione, Università di Bologna, Italia
laneve@cs.unibo.it
http://www.cs.unibo.it/~laneve

Abstract. We discuss the principles of distributed transactions, then we define an operational model which meets the basic requirements and we give a prototyping implementation for it in join-calculus. Our model: (1) extends BizTalk with multiway transactions; (2) exploits an original algorithm, for distributed commit; (3) can deal with dynamically changing communication topology; (4) is almost language-independent. In fact, the model is based on a two-level classification of resources, which should be easily conveyed to distributed calculi and languages, providing them with a uniform transactional mechanism.

1 Introduction

Global computing requires data integration and process cooperation within and across sites and organizations. The design and execution of distributed applications for global computing thus heavily rely on *process orchestration services*, which are usually demanded to the coordination layer of the system. This is the case, for instance, for transaction managers in BizTalk and Javaspaces platforms, which handle distributed decisions in asynchronous environments (e.g. the web or WAN's).

In the orchestration of services, transactional activities must be modeled also when distributed components are designed and implemented separately (e.g. in e-commerce or on-line auction systems). To this purpose, the ordinary formulation of transaction in databases theory (see Table 1) is inadequate because:

1. distributed transactions may have several entry/exit points in parallel, rather than just one (*multiparty* or *multiway transactions*);
2. data integrity should be specialized for distributed, heterogeneous systems, where there is no explicit notion of data;
3. the communication topology of processes participating to a transaction may change dynamically. This requires a commit protocol among a number of participants which cannot be statically determined.

---

[*] Research supported by the MSR Cambridge Project *Network-Aware Programming and Interoperability*.

L. Brim et al. (Eds.): CONCUR 2002, LNCS 2421, pp. 321–337, 2002.
© Springer-Verlag Berlin Heidelberg 2002

Table 1. Data base transactions as defined in [13]

A *transaction* consists of a collection of actions that transforms a system from one consistent state to another and adheres to the so-called ACID properties:

Atomicity, A transaction's changes to the state are atomic: either all happen or none happen.

Consistency, A transaction is a correct transformation of the state. The actions taken as a group do not violate any of the integrity constraints associated with the state.

Isolation, Even though transactions execute concurrently, it appears to each transaction, T, that others executed either before T or after T, but not both.

Durability, Once a transaction completes successfully (commits), its changes to the state survive failures.

A standard example in business-to-business e-commerce is *dynamic pricing*, e.g. the reverse auction. In a reverse auction, a *buyer* issues a request for offers to the *market place* where several *sellers* may propose their bids. The number of sellers is not know *a priori*. Later on, the buyer chooses the optimal bid, emits a payment for the seller, and removes its request from the market place. The whole negotiation must look like an atomic activity. For instance, if the negotiation aborts, the offer must be neglected, the payment refused, and the initial situation must be restored.

Microsoft® BizTalk [17] is a system explicitly designed for process orchestration. This system provides a graphical environment for modeling processes as flowcharts, where several *shapes* can be composed and *boxed* into transactions. Each shape represents a basic action for sending/receiving data or redirecting the execution flow.

In BizTalk, transactions can be *short, long* or *timed*. Transactions consist of series of actions, with long and timed ones possibly grouping any combination of actions and transactions (up to two nesting levels). Short transactions retain automatic recovery, which implements database transactions as defined in Table 1. On-failure compensation in the other types of transactions is programmed by the users, and may be defined in a compositional way.

We note that BizTalk boxes correspond to a two-level classification of states, *observable* (i.e., outside the box) and *hidden* (i.e., inside the box). This partition also pervades another formalism, which has been recently defined to model transactional aspects in concurrent systems, the *zero-safe Petri nets* (ZS nets) [5,7]. BizTalk flowcharts may be easily encoded into ZS nets, while the converse encoding seems not possible. The reason is that BizTalk boxes provide a "static" specification of transactions boundaries, while the state partitioning gives a "dynamic" notion of them, which depends on the runtime behaviour (e.g. which processes communicated, which data were exchanged). This remark qualifies ZS nets as a possible formal model for orchestration services.

Building on the transactional mechanism of ZS nets we propose a fairly general notion of distributed transaction that can be easily adapted to BizTalk and other orchestration systems. This mechanism also supports multiway transactions, which retain several entry and exit points, and admit a number of participants which is statically unknown.

The feasibility of our model is demonstrated by implementing ZS nets in the join-calculus [10,11]. This formalism has been chosen for three reasons:

1. join calculus is a well-known calculus, with an assessed formal theory;
2. a distributed prototype implementation has been developed for the join calculus;
3. several comparisons between join calculus and Petri nets have been studied (see e.g. the type systems for join calculus in [8] that characterize a hierarchy of net models), making it easier to establish a formal correspondence between ZS nets and their encoding in join.

In the following, we shall work under the usual assumption that communications are reliable, i.e. that messages cannot get lost.

We discuss an implementation of ZS nets, which we call *distributed*, as opposed to the *centralized* approach that relies on a unique transaction coordinator (like in BizTalk's design). The distributed implementation is the core result of the paper. It exploits the whole expressive power of the join-calculus for the dynamic definition of local transaction controllers. Moreover, it exploits a *distributed* 2PC *protocol* (a variant of the *decentralized* 2PC protocol [1]) that, up-to our knowledge, is novel to this contribution.

In the decentralized 2PC, every process participating to a transaction is aware of the other processes involved in the same transaction. When a process is ready to commit, it sends a message to all the companion processes (first phase). At the same time it collects all the commit messages coming from the companion processes. When all the messages have been received, the process commits (second phase). Alternatively, if a process fails, it will send a failure message to every companion process, and roll back to its own initial state (in this paper we implement the ideal compensation mechanism of Table 1). Every process receiving a failure message also fails.

In the distributed 2PC protocol, the number of participants and their names are not statically fixed, and processes that are ready to commit know only the participants with whom have directly cooperated. For this reason, in the distributed 2PC protocol, the role of the coordinator is played by all participants. In particular, every participant builds, in linear time, its own transitive closure of the processes cooperating in the transaction. When the transitive closure is stable, the participant commits. Alternatively, the participant waits for a failure message, and restores the initial state when such message arrives.

Synopsis. In Sections 2 and 3, we give a brief account of the transactional mechanism of BizTalk, and discuss its modeling via ZS nets, where also multiway transactions can be designed. In Section 4, we present the distributed encoding of zs nets in join calculus. In Section 5 we discuss suitable extensions of the distributed encoding. Finally, some remarks and conclusions are drawn in Section 6.

Due to space limitation, we refer the interested reader to the forthcoming technical report [3] for the proofs of main results and for the comparison of the distributed implementation of zs nets against the centralized modeling with a unique transaction coordinator. Noticeably, while the centralized encoding can be carried out in a "flat" version of the join-calculus, where definitions are not nested (i.e. in high-level nets, according to [8]), the distributed encoding shows the expressiveness of the full language.

2 Coordinating Agents in Biztalk

Microsoft® *BizTalk Orchestration Visual Designer* provides a graphical environment for building business processes, which integrates three different views: the *flowchart* view, the *implementation* view, and the *data flow* view. We focus on flowcharts,[1] which are realized by connecting several basic shapes (see Figure 1(a)).

In Figure 1(b), we illustrate a simple BizTalk process sending the value v on channel a, then inputting a value on the variable x from channel b, and, later on, performing some calculation. A transaction is defined by boxing series of operations like in Figure 1(c), meaning that either all the operations succeed or the system is rolled-back to the initial state, e.g. the emission of the message v on channel a and the input of x from b depend on the successful termination of the *"compute"* operation.

Figure 2(a) illustrates a process which implements a *rendez-vous* between two transactions: a commit is performed provided both the transactions are ready to commit. The same diagram can also be used to model a remote procedure call ($send_a(v)$ plays the role of the invocation and $send_b(w)$ plays the role of the transmission of the result).

Transaction commits are demanded to the *Distributed Transaction Coordinator* (DTC) running on the server machine and coordinating a two-phase commit protocol (2PC). Roughly, the 2PC works as follows [13]:

1. the DTC sends a vote request to all participants;
2. upon vote request, each participant either votes **no** and aborts, or votes **yes**;
3. the DTC collects all votes. If all votes are **yes**, then the DTC sends **commit** to all participants. Otherwise, the DTC sends **abort** to all participants that voted **yes**;
4. each participant that voted **yes** waits for DTC response and decides accordingly.

---

[1] Our actual understanding of BizTalk's transactions is mostly based on documents available on the web through MSDN Library http://msdn.microsoft.com/library [15,17].

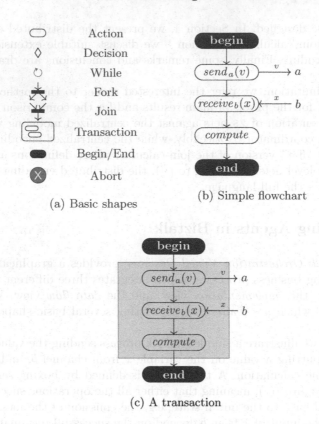

(a) Basic shapes

(b) Simple flowchart

(c) A transaction

Fig. 1. Flowcharts in BizTalk Orchestration Visual Designer

The correctness of the 2PC algorithm strongly relies on the knowledge by DTC of every participant to the transaction. To this aim, every transaction is paired with suitable components—the *COM+ components*—that record participants to the DTC. Actually, the process in Figure 2(a) shows up a further issue: it is required DTC become aware that the two transactions must commit together. This can be achieved by making communication *transactional*, which amounts to employ COM+ components (that, at run-time, report to DTC that the two transactions communicated). For long and timed transactions, users' compensation code can be given for rolling back in case of failure [14].

In the following we assume that long and timed transactions possess an *ideal compensation code* which implements the properties in Table 1. For instance, the process of Figure 2(a) either rendez-vous or nothing occurs. We also assume that transactions are not nested. In BizTalk, nested transactions allow to define a common programming pattern: a long (inter-companies) transaction grouping a sequence of short (intra-company) ones. The two assumptions above simplify the theory: we discuss the general case in Section 5.

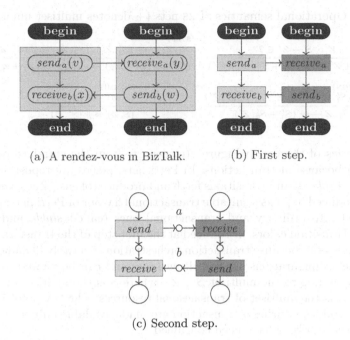

(a) A rendez-vous in BizTalk.   (b) First step.

(c) Second step.

Fig. 2. Alternative drawings of BizTalk transactions

2.1 BizTalk without Boxes

BizTalk flowcharts may be converted into a standard formalism for concurrent computations, the *Petri nets*; actually into a transactional flavour of them, the *zero-safe nets* [5]. We split this conversion into two steps:

First Step: Coloring Basic Shapes. In BizTalk, transactions are depicted by grouping basic shapes into (shadowed) boxes (Figures 1(c) and 2(a)). Since short transactions can be neither intersected nor nested, instead of using boxes, one may color basic shapes therein. Shapes included in different boxes have different colors; shapes outside boxes are white. Figure 2(b) illustrates this alternative drawing for Figure 2(a).

Second Step: Adding States. We insert circles in the pictures. Circles represent states, or *places* in Petri net terminology, and are drawn in the middle of every link. There are two kinds of circles: large ones (*stable places*) and small ones (*transactional places*), respectively for states *outside* transactions and states *within* some transaction. In case of a transition link, if the link connects two shapes of the same color (different from white) then the circle is small, otherwise it is large. In case of a communication, if the action is transactional then the circle is small, otherwise it is large. Begin and end shapes are regarded as stable places. This second step is shown in Figure 2(c) for the rendez-vous flowchart in Figure 2(a).

Table 2. Operational semantics of ZS nets (+ denotes multiset union)

(FIRING)

$$\frac{S + Z \vartriangleright S' + Z' \in T}{(S + S'', Z + Z'') \to_T (S' + S'', Z' + Z'')}$$

(STEP)

$$\frac{(S_1, Z_1) \to_T (S_1', Z_1') \quad (S_2, Z_2) \to_T (S_2', Z_2')}{(S_1 + S_2, Z_1 + Z_2) \to_T (S_1' + S_2', Z_1' + Z_2')}$$

(CONCATENATION)

$$\frac{(S_1, Z) \to_T (S_1', Z'') \quad (S_2, Z'') \to_T (S_2', Z')}{(S_1 + S_2, Z) \to_T (S_1' + S_2', Z')}$$

(COMMIT)

$$\frac{(S, \varnothing) \to_T (S', \varnothing)}{(S, \varnothing) \Rightarrow_T (S', \varnothing)}$$

The semantics of the net in Figure 2(c) departs from the standard one for Petri nets [16] because of transactions. In Petri nets, places are repositories of resources, called *tokens*, and transitions fetch and produce tokens.[2] Zero-safe nets have been introduced in [4] as a suitable transactional flavour of Petri nets: places are partitioned into ordinary and transactional ones (called *stable* and *zero*, respectively). Transition colors, introduced at the first step of the transformation are no longer relevant, because transaction orchestration is entirely demanded to zero places. Net configurations are called *markings* and can be viewed as pairs (S, Z)—corresponding to the multiset $S + Z$—where S is the multiset of stable resources and Z is the multiset of transactional resources. The key point is that stable tokens produced during a transaction are made available only at commit time, when all zero tokens have been consumed.

The operational semantics of ZS nets is defined by the two relations $\Rightarrow$ and $\to$ in Table 2, indexed by the set of transitions T. Transitions have the form $U \vartriangleright U'$, with U and U' multisets of stable and zero places. Rules FIRING and STEP are the ordinary ones for Petri nets, for the execution of one/many transition(s). However, sequences of steps differ from the ordinary transitive closure of $\to$: The rule CONCATENATION composes zero tokens in series but stable tokens in parallel, hence stable tokens produced by the first step cannot be consumed by the second step. Transactions are step sequences from stable markings to stable markings, when COMMIT can be applied. We present ZS nets as pairs (T, S) where S is the initial marking, and denote $(S, \varnothing) \Rightarrow_T (S', \varnothing)$ by $S \Rightarrow_T S'$.

The moves $S \Rightarrow_T S'$ define all the atomic activities of the net, and hence they can be performed in parallel and sequentially as the transitions of an ordinary net. It is worth noting that a step $S \Rightarrow_T S'$ can be itself the parallel composition of several transactions (by rule STEP). We refer the interested reader to [5] for the characterization of the set of minimal transactions—in the sense that they cannot be decomposed into smaller transactions—that depends on the "token philosophy" under consideration: either *collective* or *individual* according to the classification in [12].

---

[2] For simplicity, here we leave aside that tokens can carry values and transitions can have parameters, but our results in Section 4 can be smoothly lifted to the valued case.

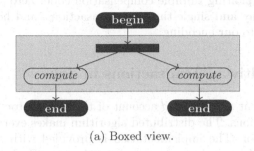

(a) Boxed view.

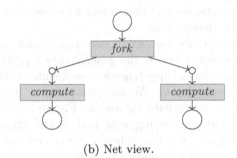

(b) Net view.

Fig. 3. A transaction with two exit points

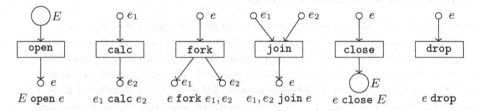

Fig. 4. Basic shapes of extended BizTalk

3   BizTalk with Multiway Transactions

BizTalk transactions possess exactly one entry and one exit point, meaning that *intra* thread coordination is mostly delegated to programmers (in contrast with *inter* thread coordination due to message exchanges, which is demanded to the DTC process). The analogy between BizTalk flowgraphs and ZS nets, detailed in the previous section, suggests that transactions can be generalized by allowing multiple entry and exit points—yielding *multiway transactions*. In Figure 3, we picture a flowgraph with two exit points, as it should appear in BizTalk and its counterpart in ZS nets.

Up-to our understanding, BizTalk limitation to single-threaded transaction shapes is motivated by implementation issues, rather than theoretical motivations. Indeed, rendez-vous are essentially multiway transactions and can be programmed in BizTalk exploiting suitable compensation code. Zero-safe nets deal uniformly with multiway and single-threaded transactions, and hence the distinction is transparent to our encoding.

4 Encoding Multiway Transactions in Join

In this section we present a *distributed* account of the 2PC protocol for Biztalk with multiway transactions. The distributed algorithm makes every participant acts as local coordinator. The implementation is provided with a distributed machine, the *distributed join calculus* [10,11]. Actually, since BizTalk flowgraphs may be converted into ZS nets, we find convenient to implement the latter ones of whom we have a neat understanding.

Without loss of generality, we restrict to nets made with the basic shapes in Figure 4 (which are as expressive as the general nets [6]), for E any stable place and e, e_1, e_2 any zero places (uppercase letters denote stable places, while lowercase letters denote zero places). We note that the ZS net in Figure 2(c) is not a basic ZS net. It is immediate to rewrite Figure 2(c) by adding four dummy *compute* shapes and considering *send* and *receive* shapes as *fork* and *join*, respectively. We remark that for ordinary Petri nets (i.e. without zero places) a straightforward encoding in join is possible.

4.1 Brief Intro to the Join Calculus

The join calculus [10] relies on a countable set of names ranged over by x, y, u, v, ...; tuples of names are written $\tilde{u}$. Table 3 collects the syntax and the semantics of the join calculus. The syntax includes processes P, definitions D, and join-patterns J. A process P can be the inert process 0, a message $x\langle\tilde{u}\rangle$, a parallel composition of processes, or a defining process def D in P. A definition D is a conjunction of reaction rules $J \triangleright P$ that associate join-patterns J to *guarded processes* P; the intended meaning is that, whenever messages match the pattern J, these messages can be replaced with a copy of the guarded process P where the content of the messages substitute the formal parameters. The only binders of the calculus are join-patterns, but the scope of names appearing in a join-pattern depends on their position: the scope of formal parameters—called *received names*—is the guarded process; the scope of *defined names*—i.e., names carrying messages—is the main process of the definition and, recursively, all guarded processes of the definition.

The semantics of the join calculus relies on the *reflexive chemical abstract machine* model [2]. In this model a solution is a multiset of active definitions and processes (separated by comma). Dynamically new definitions may become active. Moves are distinguished between *structural* $\equiv$, which heat or cool processes, and *reductions* $\rightarrow$, which are the basic computational steps (disjoint reductions can be executed in parallel). In Table 3, the rules only address the part of the solution which actually moves.

Table 3. Syntax and semantics of the join calculus

Syntax $P \stackrel{def}{=} 0 \mid x\langle \tilde{u} \rangle \mid P \mid P \mid \mathsf{def}\ D\ \mathsf{in}\ P$ $D \stackrel{def}{=} J \triangleright P \mid D \wedge D$ $J \stackrel{def}{=} x\langle \tilde{u} \rangle \mid J \mid J$

Structural moves $P \mid Q \equiv P, Q$ $\mathsf{def}\ D\ \mathsf{in}\ P \equiv D\sigma, P\sigma$ $D \wedge D' \equiv D, D'$
                                                        (σ renames defined names in D with fresh names)

Reduction $J \triangleright P, J\rho \rightarrow J \triangleright P, P\rho$ (ρ only renames received names in J)

The *distributed join calculus* is a distributed implementation of the join calculus, with notions of location, migration of processes, failure, and failure recovery [11]. In order to simplify the notation, the encoding in the sequel will be written in join calculus. Yet, the distributed versions shall be discussed informally.

4.2   Distributed 2PC

In the following encoding, we extend the join calculus with the data type *SET*, for finite sets and the standard operations of emptyset $\varnothing$, union $\cup$, and difference $\setminus$. Join patterns are extended with pattern matching on sets. We also use the operation **release** which takes a set of channels and sends an (empty) message on every channel in the set. We address channels which encode stable and zero tokens as stable and zero channels, respectively. Intuitively, a message $x\langle \tilde{u} \rangle$ models a token with value $\tilde{u}$ in the place x.

Definition 1 (Reflexive Encoding). *The join calculus process of a* ZS *net* (T, S) *is* $\mathsf{def}\ [\![T]\!]\ \mathsf{in}\ \{\![S]\!\}$, *where* $[\![T]\!] = \wedge_{t \in T}[\![t]\!]$ *with* $[\![t]\!]$ *defined in Figure 5, and* $\{\![S]\!\}$ *defined inductively as follows:* $\{\![\varnothing]\!\} = 0$ *and* $\{\![E + S]\!\} = E\langle\rangle \mid \{\![S]\!\}$.

A new thread is started either when (1) *a transition* open(E, e) *occurs*, or when (2) *a thread forks*. This is evidenced by controller definitions D in the join calculus agents $[\![E\ \mathsf{open}\ e]\!]$ and $[\![e\ \mathsf{fork}\ e_1, e_2]\!]$. Every thread has at most one active zero token at any time. A thread may terminate when its associated zero token has been consumed, i.e. when a `join`, or `close`, or `drop` is executed on that token. Zero channels carry two informations: (a) a channel name to notify the thread completion; (b) the *synchronization set* of the thread, namely a set of pointers to companion threads which belong to the same transaction. This synchronization set is built by recording thread pointers every time a fork or a join occurs (see the encodings of `fork` and `join`).

We comment the definition D in Figure 5. The channel *state* records the stable channels (if any) that must be released in case of failure. The *state* message is created when the thread starts and it is consumed when the thread terminates either with success or with failure. Successful termination occurs when the active zero token of the thread has been consumed—a message $put\langle \ell, F \rangle$ has been

$$\begin{aligned}
\llbracket E \text{ open } e \rrbracket &= E\langle\rangle \ \triangleright \ \text{def D in } e\langle put, \{lock\}\rangle \,|\, state\langle\{E\}\rangle \\
\llbracket e_1 \text{ calc } e_2 \rrbracket &= e_1\langle p, \ell\rangle \ \triangleright \ e_2\langle p, \ell\rangle \\
\llbracket e \text{ fork } e_1, e_2 \rrbracket &= e\langle p, \ell\rangle \ \triangleright \ \text{def D in } e_1\langle p, \ell\cup\{lock\}\rangle \,|\, e_2\langle put, \ell\cup\{lock\}\rangle \,|\, state\langle\varnothing\rangle \\
\llbracket e_1, e_2 \text{ join } e \rrbracket &= e_1\langle p_1, \ell_1\rangle \,|\, e_2\langle p_2, \ell_2\rangle \ \triangleright \ e\langle p_1, \ell_1\cup\ell_2\rangle \,|\, p_2\langle\ell_2\cup\ell_1, \varnothing\rangle \\
\llbracket e \text{ close } E \rrbracket &= e\langle p, \ell\rangle \ \triangleright \ p\langle\ell, \{E\}\rangle \\
\llbracket e \text{ drop} \rrbracket &= e\langle p, \ell\rangle \ \triangleright \ p\langle\ell, \varnothing\rangle
\end{aligned}$$

where D is the following definition:

$$\begin{aligned}
D \ &\overset{def}{=} & state\langle H\rangle \,|\, put\langle\ell, F\rangle \ &\triangleright \ commit\langle\ell\setminus\{lock\}, \ell, \{lock\}, F, H\rangle \\
&\wedge & state\langle H\rangle \ &\triangleright \ failed\langle\rangle \,|\, \mathsf{release}\langle H\rangle \\
&\wedge & commit\langle\{l\}\cup\ell, \ell', \ell'', F, H\rangle \ &\triangleright \ commit\langle\ell, \ell', \ell'', F, H\rangle \,|\, l\langle\ell', lock, fail\rangle \\
&\wedge \ commit\langle\ell, \ell', \ell'', F, H\rangle \,|\, lock\langle\ell''', l, f\rangle \ &\triangleright \ commit\langle\ell\cup(\ell'''\setminus\ell'), \ell'\cup\ell''', \ell''\cup\{l\}, F, H\rangle \\
&\wedge & commit\langle\varnothing, \ell, \ell, F, H\rangle \ &\triangleright \ \mathsf{release}\langle F\rangle \\
&\wedge & commit\langle\ell, \ell', \ell'', F, H\rangle \,|\, fail\langle\rangle \ &\triangleright \ failed\langle\rangle \,|\, \mathsf{release}\langle H\rangle \\
&\wedge & failed\langle\rangle \,|\, put\langle\ell, F\rangle \ &\triangleright \ failed\langle\rangle \\
&\wedge & failed\langle\rangle \,|\, lock\langle\ell, l, f\rangle \ &\triangleright \ failed\langle\rangle \,|\, f\langle\rangle \\
&\wedge & failed\langle\rangle \,|\, fail\langle\rangle \ &\triangleright \ failed\langle\rangle
\end{aligned}$$

Fig. 5. The encoding in the join calculus

emitted and

$$state\langle H\rangle \,|\, put\langle\ell, F\rangle \ \triangleright \ commit\langle\ell\setminus\{lock\}, \ell, \{lock\}, F, H\rangle$$

has been executed. In this case a *commit* message is produced. We assume that a thread cannot (nondeterministically) decide to fail anymore once *commit* has been emitted. This is a standard assumption: when the thread reaches this state, it logs the relevant infos. However, if another thread involved in the same transaction fails, the *commit* state must still be able to handle the failure.

A thread in *state*$\langle H\rangle$ may fail. This is modelled by a nondeterministic rule yielding the internal state *failed*$\langle\rangle$. (In real implementations, failures are e.g. triggered by time-outs of the communication with a specific other participant or of the whole transaction—see timed transactions in BizTalk.) In the state *failed*$\langle\rangle$, any thread in the same transaction is informed about the failure.

The commit protocol is a distributed variant of the 2PC, where the role of the coordinator is played by all participants. Up-to our knowledge, this algorithm is original to our contribution. It differs from the *decentralized* 2PC [1] because the number of participants and their names are not statically fixed. The protocol is detailed below.

The commit state is modeled by the *commit* message, carrying values $\langle\ell, \ell', \ell'', H, F\rangle$:

1. ℓ records the set of threads to which the signal of successful completion (i.e. the analogous of the **yes** vote) must still be sent;
2. ℓ' stores the synchronization set of the thread. The successful completion signal must be sent to every item of ℓ'. During the protocol, this set is augmented with the synchronization sets of the threads participating to the same transaction, until when it is *transitively closed*. Initially, ℓ' contains the pointers to the threads with whom there has been a direct interaction (a fork or a join), together with a pointer to itself;

3. ℓ'' records the participants who have already sent the success signal to the thread. Initially, ℓ'' contains the pointer to itself, thus avoiding self-addressed messages;

4. F and H store the stable channels to be released in case of successful and unsuccessful completion, respectively. In our case, they may be empty sets or singletons.

The *distributed* 2PC is based on the following steps performed by every thread:

1. **First Phase**. The thread sends a request message to every thread in its own synchronization set. This task is performed by the rule

$$commit\langle\{l\}\cup\ell,\ell',\ell'',F,H\rangle \;\triangleright\; commit\langle\ell,\ell',\ell'',F,H\rangle \mid l\langle\ell',lock,fail\rangle.$$

   The request message carries the synchronization set of the thread, together with the names for signaling the successful or unsuccessful completion.

2. **Second Phase**. The thread collects the messages sent by other threads and updates its own synchronization set. The name used to carry these information is *lock*, and the rule collecting the synchronization sets is:

$$commit\langle\ell,\ell',\ell'',F,H\rangle \mid lock\langle\ell''',l,f\rangle \;\triangleright\; commit\langle\ell\cup(\ell'''\setminus\ell'),\ell'\cup\ell''',\ell''\cup\{l\},F,H\rangle.$$

   A request message will be also sent to the new items in the synchronization set. Namely, the first and the second phases work in parallel.

3. When the synchronization set is transitively closed, namely when the union of synchronization sets of threads in ℓ' is equal to the set ℓ'' of successful termination messages, the commit protocol for the local thread terminates and the messages on channels in F may be emitted.

4. In case of a failure, the thread transits in the state *failed*, releases the stable channels in H, and replies to every *lock* message with a failure answer:

$$commit\langle\ell,\ell',\ell'',F,H\rangle \mid fail\langle\rangle \;\triangleright\; failed\langle\rangle \mid release\langle H\rangle$$
$$failed\langle\rangle \mid lock\langle\ell,l,f\rangle \;\triangleright\; failed\langle\rangle \mid f\langle\rangle$$

The proof of correctness of the distributed 2PC is split in two steps: (part 1) we show that if all coordinators are ready to commit, then all frozen resources will be released (assuming fairness); (part 2) we strengthen the result by dealing with failures of transactions.

In the following theorems let σ_i, $i\in\mathbb{N}$, be the renaming that indexes with i all the defined names in D. We write $A\langle\rangle$, when A is an empty set or a singleton $\{a\}$: In the former case it means 0, in the latter case it represents $a\langle\rangle$. Moreover, we let a *symmetric lock covering* be a finite family $\{\ell_i\}_{i\in I}$ such that $\ell_i\subseteq\{lock_j\mid j\in I\}$, with $lock_j\in\ell_i$ if and only if $lock_i\in\ell_j$ for all $i,j\in I$.

Theorem 1 (Correctness of the Distributed 2pc, Part 1). *Let* $P = \mid_{i\in I} commit_i\langle\ell_i,\ell_i\cup\{lock_i\},\{lock_i\},F_i,H_i\rangle$, *where* $\{\ell_i\}_{i\in I}$ *is a symmetric lock covering, and let* n *be the cardinality of* I. *The process* def $\bigwedge_{i\in I}\mathrm{D}\sigma_i$ *in* P *is* *strongly confluent, in the sense that it always converges after a finite number of steps bound by $O(n^2)$ to the configuration*

$$\text{def} \bigwedge_{i \in I} \mathsf{D}\sigma_i \text{ in } \left(\bigm|_{i \in I} F_i \langle \rangle \right).$$

Though the number of steps is $O(n^2)$, they are concurrently executed by n threads, thus the number of steps for each thread is linear in n. More precisely, in the worst case where all threads participate to the same transaction, each thread must (asynchronously) send and receive exactly n messages to commit.

The second theorem states that, when several coordinators fail, then all the participants to their transactions also fail. To determine the coordinators which participate to a transaction, we compute the transitive closure of the synchronization sets.

Theorem 2 (Correctness of the Distributed 2pc, Part 2). *Let $\{\ell_i\}_{i \in I}$ be a symmetric lock covering and let $P = |_{i \in I} P_i$, such that P_i may be one of the followings: (1) $P_i = commit_i \langle \ell_i, \ell_i \cup \{lock_i\}, \{lock_i\}, F_i, H_i \rangle$; or (2) $P_i = state_i \langle H_i \rangle \mid e_i \langle put_i, \ell_i \rangle$; or (3) $P_i = failed_i \langle \rangle \mid e_i \langle put_i, \ell_i \rangle \mid H_i \langle \rangle$. Let $L \subseteq I$ be the least set such that*

1. *if $P_i = state_i \langle H_i \rangle \mid e_i \langle put_i, \ell_i \rangle$ then $i \in L$;*
2. *if $P_i = failed_i \langle \rangle \mid e_i \langle put_i, \ell_i \rangle \mid H_i \langle \rangle$ then $i \in L$; and*
3. *L is transitively closed, namely if $i \in L$ and $lock_j \in \ell_i$, then also $j \in L$.*

The process def $\bigwedge_{i \in I} \mathsf{D}\sigma_i$ in P *is strongly confluent and converges to*

$$\text{def} \bigwedge_{i \in I} \mathsf{D}\sigma_i \text{ in } \left(\bigm|_{i \in I \setminus L} F_i \langle \rangle \right) \mid \left(\bigm|_{i \in L} H_i \langle \rangle \right) \mid G$$

where G is a parallel composition of messages on zero channels and failed messages with indexes in L (garbage).

The set G in Theorem 2 collects the active zero tokens of threads and failed messages of failed threads. These messages survive to the failure and may be consumed by future transactions, making fail any of them. In a real implementation, one may design an explicit garbage collection of these zero tokens.

Though definitions in D are generated for orchestrating threads, their task only last for the time strictly necessary to successfully conclude the transaction. A completeness result between the operational semantics of zs nets and our distributed encoding can thus be stated as below, where D plays the role of the dynamically generated controls.

Theorem 3 (Correctness). *If $S_1 \Rightarrow_T S_2$, then def $[\![T]\!]$ in $\{\![S_1]\!\} \rightarrow^*$ def $[\![T]\!] \wedge D$ in $\{\![S_2]\!\}$, where the names defined in D appear neither in $[\![T]\!]$ nor in $\{\![S_2]\!\}$.*

Theorem 3 handles the case where only successful computations are considered.

When failures occur, it is still possible to automatically normalize the reached state into a correct configuration. To this aim we define the normalization of a solution $\mathcal{S}$, noted as $norm(\mathcal{S})$, as the solution yielded by executing rules of coordinators D until termination, plus the release operations. (It is easy to check that these evaluations terminate.) The normalization process yields configurations which reflect stable configurations of ZS net. These are obtained by making all the active transactions failed, and rolling back the initial state (except for transactions that are already committing). In this normalized configuration, every remaining message on zero channels must be considered garbage since the corresponding thread is failed.

Theorem 4 (Completeness). *If* def $[\![T]\!]$ in $\{\![S_1]\!\}$ $\rightarrow^*$ P, *then* $norm(P) =$ def $[\![T]\!] \wedge D$ in $\{\![S_2]\!\} \mid Q$, *for some* S_2 *such that* $S_1 \Rightarrow^*_T S_2$ *and: (1)* $D = \wedge_{i \in I} D\sigma_i$; *(2)* Q *is a parallel composition of messages of the form* $failed_i\langle\rangle$ *and* $e\langle put_i, \ell_i \rangle$, *such that* $e\langle put_i, \ell_i \rangle \in Q$ *implies* $failed_i\langle\rangle \in Q$. *(Roughly, Q keeps track of all failed coordinators and controls.)*

It is worth noting that the encoding of Definition 1 characterizes threads according to the semantic interpretation of zs nets based on the individual token philosophy. Namely, threads are collected in a transaction provided they effectively interact together.

A running implementation of the reflexive encoding in Definition 1 has been developed by Hernan Melgratti, currently PhD student in Pisa. For more information and the full code we refer the interested reader to the URL http://www.di.unipi.it/~melgratt/D2PC/implementation.html.

4.3   Distributing Places and Coordinators

The join calculus processes encoding ZS nets in Definition 1 may be easily distributed by attaching (sub)definitions to locations. In particular, locations of coordinators D are mandatory: every coordinator is located in a different location. As regards places of the net, the distribution task is left to the ZS net programmer, which must suitably partition them in separate locations.

In Figure 6 we illustrate a ZS net modeling two transactions communicating on a transactional channel. Figure 7 illustrates a join process for the net in Figure 6 with a possible distribution of definitions. In particular, the sender and the receiver are in different locations, called locSend and locRec, respectively, and new threads are created as sub-locations.

5   Compensation and Nesting

There are two issues which have been expressly left aside: programmable compensations and nested transactions.

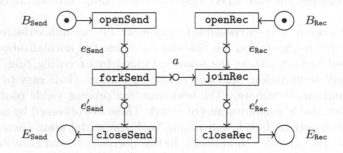

Fig. 6. Net modeling of a distributed transactions

$$
\begin{aligned}
\text{def } \texttt{locSend} : [\; &B_{\mathsf{Send}}\langle\rangle \; \triangleright \; \text{def } \mathtt{sub1} : [\mathsf{D}\,,\; state\langle\{B_{\mathsf{Send}}\}\rangle\,]\; \text{in } e_{\mathsf{Send}}\langle put, \{lock\}\rangle \\
&\wedge\; e_{\mathsf{Send}}\langle p, \ell\rangle \;\triangleright\; \text{def } \mathtt{sub2} : [\mathsf{D}\,,\; state\langle\varnothing\rangle\,] \\
&\qquad\qquad\qquad \text{in } e'_{\mathsf{Send}}\langle p, \ell\cup\{lock\}\rangle \mid a\langle put, \ell\cup\{lock\}\rangle \\
&\wedge\; e'_{\mathsf{Send}}\langle p, \ell\rangle \;\triangleright\; p\langle\ell, \{E_{\mathsf{Send}}\}\rangle\,, \\
&B_{\mathsf{Send}}\langle\rangle\,] \\
\wedge\; \texttt{locRec} : [\; &B_{\mathsf{Rec}}\langle\rangle \;\triangleright\; \text{def } \mathtt{sub3} : [\,\mathsf{D}\,,\; state\langle\{B_{\mathsf{Rec}}\}\rangle\,]\; \text{in } e_{\mathsf{Rec}}\langle put, \{lock\}\rangle \\
&\wedge\; e_{\mathsf{Rec}}\langle p_1, \ell_1\rangle \mid a\langle p_2, \ell_2\rangle \;\triangleright\; e'_{\mathsf{Rec}}\langle p_1, \ell_1\cup\ell_2\rangle \mid p_2\langle\ell_2\cup\ell_1, \varnothing\rangle \\
&\wedge\; e'_{\mathsf{Rec}}\langle p, \ell\rangle \;\triangleright\; p\langle\ell, \{E_{\mathsf{Rec}}\}\rangle\,, \\
&B_{\mathsf{Rec}}\langle\rangle\,] \\
\text{in } 0
\end{aligned}
$$

Fig. 7. Reflexive encoding of a distributed transactions

Regarding compensation, the fact is that zs-nets implement standard compensations of database transactions as defined in Table 1, assuming that tokens can be fetched or produced, but not "updated." If large databases must be managed or if shared memory is taken into account, then it is often the case that some trade-off can be negotiated between the atomicity assumption and efficiency, so that suitable compensation code is associated to programs to avoid keeping track of all memory modifications internal to the transaction (that should be rolled back in case of failure). In our distributed encoding, compensation can be easily accomodated replacing the default continuation H for failure (i.e. the stable tokens that initiated the transaction) by the address of the compensation code, which in general can be any join calculus process that the programmer associates with net transitions. Roughly, each thread can execute a suitable algorithm compensate$\langle H\rangle$ instead of release$\langle H\rangle$.

For what concern nesting, the issue has not been yet considered for zs-nets, but the intuition is that resources should be classified on different levels so that stable tokens are *tokens of level 0*, zero tokens are *tokens of level 1*, and so on. Then, at the generic level i the resources of levels $j < i$ are seen as stable for that level. Note that in the case of zs-nets, the maximum number of levels is statically assigned, which should suffice for modeling the two-level nesting of BizTalk. A much more interesting framework can be obtained by applying the zero-safe approach to the join calculus, where the nesting of definition and reflection can be used to dynamically generate new levels, a topic that we leave to future research.

6 Concluding Remarks

Transactional aspects should play a relevant role in global computing, though the ordinary concept of transaction must be stretched out to deal with issues of distributed computations, such as asynchrony, dynamically changing topology and mobility (a number of weakenings of the ACID properties for orchestrating distributed processes has been recently discussed in [9]). To this respect, both the design and implementation phases of process orchestration should be supported by well developed, easy-to-use tools. In particular, visual formalisms and prototyping platforms should be at disposal of system analysts, and well assessed programming paradigms be at disposal of developers.

The proposal in this paper aims to fill the above gaps. In fact, it extends in many directions the concept of transaction; it comes equipped with both a graphical presentation and a concurrent semantics; it can be implemented with a fully distributed commit, which is novel to the transaction community (to the best of our knowledge). Our proposal relies on the zero-safe approach, which promotes an abstract notion of transaction that can find application to many concurrent and distributed calculi, because it is based on the following three assumptions: (1) states are multisets (e.g. of resources or messages); (2) rules can concurrently rewrite parts of the state; and (3) transactions are defined by typing resources (as stable or zero).

The first two features are common to most calculi (e.g., π, spi, join, ambients); the third one is the key for having a basic, uniform, and formal notion of transaction. Roughly, to import transactions from the ZS approach, we just partition names into stable and zero. Then configurations are separated into those containing messages on stable names only, called *stable*, and the other ones, and the operational semantics can be given in the style of Definition 2. We plan to apply this technique to the join calculus, with the aim to exploiting reflection for modeling nested transactions. The foundations and pragmatics of this "transactional" join calculus will be the argument of future work.

The distributed 2PC looks suitable for orchestrating web transactions, because it is fully distributed and it does not require the election of a global coordinator. The second feature is relevant, because when the participants are e.g. threads running on servers of different companies it is often the case that not all the companies can agree on the choice of a unique coordinator.

To conclude, let us remark that the modeling of failures in our encoding refers to the impossibility of completing a transaction in the correct way, not to the failure of the distributed join interpreter. Dealing with failures in this broader sense is an ambitious goal that is out of the scope of the present paper and that we leave to future work.

Acknowledgements. We would like to thank Satish Thatte for his kind and patient clarification of several aspects related to the design of transactions in BizTalk. We also would like to thank the anonymous referees for their constructive comments and criticisms.

References

1. P. A. Bernstein, V. Hadzilacos, and N. Goodman. *Concurrency, Control and Recovery in Database Systems.* Addison-Wesley Longman, 1987. 323, 331
2. G. Berry and G. Boudol. The chemical abstract machine. *Theoret. Comput. Sci.,* 96(1):217–248, 1992. 329
3. R. Bruni, C. Laneve, and U. Montanari. Centralized and distributed orchestration of transactions in the join-calculus. Technical Report, University of Pisa. To appear. http://www.di.unipi.it/~bruni/publications/TRbis2002.ps.gz 324
4. R. Bruni and U. Montanari. Zero-safe nets, or transition synchronization made simple. *Proc. of EXPRESS'97*, vol. 7 of *Elect. Notes in Th. Comput. Sci.* Elsevier Science, 1997. 327
5. R. Bruni and U. Montanari. Zero-safe nets: Comparing the collective and individual token approaches. *Inform. and Comput.*, 156(1-2):46–89, 2000. 322, 326, 327
6. R. Bruni and U. Montanari. Transactions and zero-safe nets. *Advances in Petri Nets: Unifying Petri Nets*, vol. 2128 of *Lect. Notes in Comput. Sci.*, pp. 380–426. Springer, 2001. 329
7. R. Bruni and U. Montanari. Zero-safe net models for transactions in linda. *Proc. of ConCoord 2001*, vol. 54 of *Elect. Notes in Th. Comput. Sci.*, 2001. 322
8. M. Buscemi and V. Sassone. High-level Petri nets as type theories in the Join calculus. *Proc. of FoSSaCS 2001*, vol. 2030 of *Lect. Notes in Comput. Sci.*, pp. 104–120. Springer, 2001. 323, 324
9. A. Coratella, M. Felder, R. Hirsch, and E. Rodriguez. A framework for analyzing mobile transaction. *Journal of Database Management*, 12(13), 2001. 336
10. C. Fournet and G. Gonthier. The reflexive chemical abstract machine and the Join calculus. *Proc. of POPL'96*, pp. 372–385. ACM Press, 1996. 323, 329
11. C. Fournet, G. Gonthier, J.-J. Lévy, L. Maranget, and D. Rémy. A calculus of mobile agents. *Proc. of CONCUR'96*, vol. 1119 of *Lect. Notes in Comput. Sci.*, pp. 406–421. Springer, 1996. 323, 329, 330
12. R. J. van Glabbeek and G. D. Plotkin. Configuration structures. *Proc. of LICS'95*, pp. 199–209. IEEE Computer Society Press, 1995. 327
13. J. Gray and A. Reuter. *Transaction Processing: Concepts and Techniques.* Morgan Kaufmann, 1993. 322, 324
14. T. Hoare. *A Model for Long-Running Transactions in XLANG.* Preliminary draft, 2001. 325
15. B. Laskey and J. Parker. Microsoft biztalk server 2000: Building a reverse auction with biztalk orchestration, 2001. Microsoft Corporation. Available at [18]. 324
16. W. Reisig. *Petri Nets: An Introduction.* EATCS Monographs on Theoretical Computer Science. Springer, 1985. 327
17. U. Roxburgh. Biztalk orchestration: Transactions, exceptions, and debugging, 2001. Microsoft Corporation. Available at [18]. 322, 324
18. URL http://msdn.microsoft.com/library/en-us/dnbiz/html/bizorchestr.asp. 337

Simulation for Continuous-Time Markov Chains

Christel Baier[1], Joost-Pieter Katoen[2],
Holger Hermanns[2], and Boudewijn Haverkort[3]

[1] Institut für Informatik I, University of Bonn
Römerstraße 164, D-53117 Bonn, Germany
[2] Dept. of Computer Science, RWTH Aachen
Ahornstraße 55, D-52056 Aachen, Germany
[3] Faculty of Computer Science, University of Twente
P.O. Box 217, 7500 AE Enschede, The Netherlands

Abstract. This paper presents a simulation preorder for continuous-time Markov chains (CTMCs). The simulation preorder is a conservative extension of a weak variant of probabilistic simulation on fully probabilistic systems, i.e., discrete-time Markov chains. The main result of the paper is that the simulation preorder preserves safety and liveness properties expressed in continuous stochastic logic (CSL), a stochastic branching-time temporal logic interpreted over CTMCs.

1 Introduction

To compare the stepwise behaviour of states in transition systems, simulation ($\sqsubseteq$) and bisimulation relations ($\sim$) have been widely considered [31,25]. Bisimulation relations are equivalences such that two bisimilar states exhibit identical stepwise behaviour. On the contrary, simulation relations are preorders on the state space such that if $s \sqsubseteq s'$ ("s' simulates s") state s' can mimic all stepwise behaviour of s; the converse, i.e., $s' \sqsubseteq s$ is not guaranteed, so state s' may perform steps that cannot be matched by s. Thus, if $s \sqsubseteq s'$ then every successor of s has a corresponding, i.e., related successor of s', but the reverse does not necessarily hold. Simulation can be lifted to entire transition systems by comparing (according to $\sqsubseteq$) their initial states. Simulation relations are often used for verification purposes to show that one system correctly implements another, more abstract system. One of the interesting aspects of simulation relations is that they allow a verification by "local" reasoning.

In the setting of model checking, (bi)simulation relations can be used to combat the well-known state-space explosion problem [15]. Here, bisimulation relations possess the so-called *strong preservation* property, whereas simulation possesses *weak preservation*. Strong preservation means: if $s \sim s'$, then for all formulas Φ it follows $s \models \Phi$ iff $s' \models \Phi$. This property holds, for instance, for CTL (and CTL*) and strong bisimulation [12]. The use of simulation relies on the preservation of certain classes of formulas, not of all formulas (such as for $\sim$). For instance, if $s \sqsubseteq s'$ then for all safety formulas Φ it follows that $s' \models \Phi$

L. Brim et al. (Eds.): CONCUR 2002, LNCS 2421, pp. 338–354, 2002.
© Springer-Verlag Berlin Heidelberg 2002

implies $s \models \Phi$.[1] Note that the converse, $s' \not\models \Phi$, cannot be used to deduce that Φ does not hold in the simulated state s; hence, the name *weak* preservation. As simulation equivalence – defined as mutual simulation of states – is coarser than bisimulation equivalence it yields a "better abstraction", i.e., a smaller quotient. Simulation relations are the basis for abstraction techniques where the rough idea is to replace the large system to be verified by a small abstract model and to model check the abstract system.

This paper studies a simulation preorder for continuous-time Markov chains (CTMCs) [29,36] and investigates the preservation of properties expressed in continuous stochastic logic (CSL) [3,8]. CTMCs are an important class of stochastic processes that are widely used in practice to determine system performance and dependability characteristics. CSL is a continuous probabilistic variant of CTL and includes means to express both transient and steady-state performance measures. For instance, it allows one to stipulate that the probability of reaching a certain set of goal-states within a specified real-valued time bound, provided that all paths to these states obey certain properties, is at least/at most some probability value. Model-checking algorithms for CSL have been presented in [8,6], and prototypical software implementations are available: one based on sparse matrices [23] and a symbolic one based on multi-terminal BDDs [28]. Baier *et al.* [6] prove that lumping equivalence [13] – a continuous time variant of probabilistic bisimulation – preserves CSL; Desharnais and Panangaden [18] have recently shown the converse, namely that the equivalence induced by CSL implies lumping equivalence.

This paper proposes a novel simulation preorder ($\sqsubseteq_m$) for CTMCs. This notion extends probabilistic simulation ($\sqsubseteq_p$) on discrete-time Markov chains (DTMCs), as originally defined by Jonsson and Larsen [26]. The main result of the paper is that $\sqsubseteq_m$ weakly preserves CSL safety and liveness properties. This means that for $s \sqsubseteq_m s'$ we have that $s' \models \Phi_{safe}$ implies $s \models \Phi_{safe}$ for any CSL safety-formula Φ_{safe}, and that $s \models \Phi_{live}$ implies $s' \models \Phi_{live}$ for any CSL liveness-formula Φ_{live}. As a consequence, the validity of safety formulas and the refutation of liveness formulas carries over from the abstract state s' (wrt. $\sqsubseteq_m$) to the concrete state s. This result can be used to verify CSL-formulas for a CTMC by verifying the same formulas on a smaller or simpler CTMC which is an abstraction of it.

Organisation of the paper. Section 2 introduces CTMCs, presents the simulation preorder for CTMCs and some of its elementary properties. Section 3 recalls CSL and introduces its safe and live fragments. Section 4 discusses weak preservation of CSL-formulas. Section 5 defines simulation equivalence and compares this to other equivalence notions. Section 6 discusses related work. Section 7 concludes the paper. Proofs of the main results are provided in [9].

---

[1] Safety formulas are here to be understood as arbitrary formulas in $\forall$CTL*, the restriction of CTL* to universal path-quantifiers [14].

2   Simulation for CTMCs

Fully probabilistic systems. Let AP be a fixed, finite set of atomic propositions. A (labelled) fully probabilistic system (FPS) $\mathcal{D}$ is a tuple $(S, \mathbf{P}, L)$ where S is a countable set of *states*, $\mathbf{P} : S \times S \rightarrow [0, 1]$ is a *probability matrix* satisfying $\sum_{s' \in S} \mathbf{P}(s, s') \in [0, 1]$ for all $s \in S$, and $L : S \rightarrow 2^{AP}$ is a *labelling* function which assigns to each state $s \in S$ the set $L(s)$ of atomic propositions that are valid in s. If $\sum_{s' \in S} \mathbf{P}(s, s') = 1$ for all $s \in S$, then $\mathbf{P}(s, \cdot)$ (and $\mathcal{D}$) is called stochastic, otherwise it is called sub-stochastic. A (labelled) DTMC is an FPS with $\sum_{s' \in S} \mathbf{P}(s, s') \in \{0, 1\}$ for all $s \in S$.

Continuous-time Markov chains. A (labelled) CTMC $\mathcal{M}$ is a tuple $(S, \mathbf{R}, L)$ where S and L are as before, and $\mathbf{R} : S \times S \rightarrow \mathbb{R}_{\geqslant 0}$ is the *rate matrix*. (We adopt the same conventions as in [6,8], i.e., we do allow self-loops.) The exit rate $E(s) = \sum_{s' \in S} \mathbf{R}(s, s')$ denotes that the probability of taking a transition from s within t time units equals $1 - e^{-E(s) \cdot t}$. If $\mathbf{R}(s, s') > 0$ for more than one state s', a *race* between the outgoing transitions from s exists. That is, the probability $\mathbf{P}(s, s')$ of moving from s to s' in a single step equals the probability that the delay of going from s to s' "finishes before" the delays of any other outgoing transition from s; i.e., $\mathbf{P}(s, s') = \mathbf{R}(s, s')/E(s)$ if $E(s) > 0$ and 0 otherwise.

Definition 1. *For CTMC $\mathcal{M} = (S, \mathbf{R}, L)$, the embedded discrete-time Markov chain is given by $emb(\mathcal{M}) = (S, \mathbf{P}, L)$, where $\mathbf{P}(s, s') = \mathbf{R}(s, s')/E(s)$ if $E(s) > 0$, and $\mathbf{P}(s, s) = 1$ and $\mathbf{P}(s, s') = 0$ for $s \neq s'$ if $E(s) = 0$.*

Note that, by definition, the embedded DTMC $emb(\mathcal{M})$ of any CTMC $\mathcal{M}$ is stochastic, i.e., $\sum_{s'} P(s, s') = 1$ for any state s.

Definition 2. *For CTMC $\mathcal{M} = (S, \mathbf{R}, L)$ the uniformised CTMC is given by $unif(\mathcal{M}) = (S, \overline{\mathbf{R}}, L)$ where $\overline{\mathbf{R}}(s, s') = \mathbf{R}(s, s')$ for $s \neq s'$ and $\overline{\mathbf{R}}(s, s) = \mathbf{R}(s, s) + E - E(s)$ where constant $E \geqslant \max_{s \in S} E(s)$.*

E is called the *uniformisation rate* of $\mathcal{M}$, and is determined by the state with the shortest mean residence time, since $E \geqslant \max_{s \in S} E(s)$. All rates of self-loops in the CTMC $\mathcal{M}$ are "normalised" with respect to E, and hence the mean residence time is uniformly set to $1/E$ in $unif(\mathcal{M})$. In the literature [21,24], uniformisation is often defined by transforming CTMC $\mathcal{M}$ into the DTMC $emb(unif(\mathcal{M}))$. For technical convenience, we here define uniformisation as a transformation from CTMCs to CTMCs basically by adding self-loops to slower states (as e.g. in [33]).

Simulation for fully probabilistic systems. For labelled transition systems, state s' simulates s if for each successor t of s there is a successor t' of s' that simulates t. Simulation of two states is thus defined in terms of simulation of their successor states. In the probabilistic setting, the target of a transition is in fact a probability distribution, and thus, the simulation relation $\sqsubseteq$ needs to be lifted from states to distributions. This can be done using *weight functions* [26]. For countable set X, let $Dist(X)$ denote the collection of all, possibly sub-stochastic, distributions on X.

Definition 3. *Let $\mu \in Dist(X)$ and $\mu' \in Dist(Y)$ and $\sqsubseteq \ \subseteq X \times Y$. Then $\mu \preceq \mu'$ iff there exists a weight function $\Delta : X \times Y \to [0,1]$ for $\sqsubseteq$ such that:*

1. *$\Delta(x, y) > 0$ implies $x \sqsubseteq y$*
2. *$\mu(x) = K_1 \cdot \sum_{y \in Y} \Delta(x, y)$ for any $x \in X$*
3. *$\mu'(y) = K_2 \cdot \sum_{x \in X} \Delta(x, y)$ for any $y \in Y$,*

where $K_1 = \sum_{x \in X} \mu(x)$ and $K_2 = \sum_{y \in Y} \mu'(y)$.

Intuitively, a weight function Δ shows how the probability $\mu(x)$ can be distributed among the related states y such that $\mu'(y)$ equals the total amount of probability it gets distributed by Δ. (Note that $K_1 = K_2 = 1$ for stochastic μ and μ'.) Δ is a probability distribution on $X \times Y$ such that the probability to select (x, y) with $x \sqsubseteq y$ is one. In addition, the probability to select an element in $\sqsubseteq$ whose first component is x equals $\mu(x)$, and the probability to select an element in $\sqsubseteq$ whose second component is y equals $\mu'(y)$.

Example 1. Let $X = \{s, t\}$ and $Y = \{u, v, w\}$ with $\mu(s) = \frac{2}{9}$, $\mu(t) = \frac{2}{3}$ and $\mu'(u) = \frac{1}{3}$, $\mu'(v) = \frac{4}{9}$ and $\mu'(w) = \frac{1}{9}$; $K_1 = K_2 = \frac{8}{9}$. Note that μ and μ' are both sub-stochastic. Let $\sqsubseteq \ = (X \times Y) \setminus \{(s, w)\}$. We have $\mu \preceq \mu'$, as weight function Δ defined by $\Delta(s, u) = \Delta(s, v) = \Delta(t, w) = \frac{1}{8}$, $\Delta(t, v) = \frac{3}{8}$ and $\Delta(t, u) = \frac{1}{4}$ satisfies the constraints of Def. 3.

For fully probabilistic systems we consider a slight variant of probabilistic simulation by Jonsson and Larsen [26]:

Definition 4. *For FPS $(S, \mathbf{P}, L)$, let $\sqsubseteq_p$ be the coarsest binary relation on the state space S such that for all $s_1 \sqsubseteq_p s_2$:*

1. *$L(s_1) = L(s_2)$ and*
2. *$\mathbf{P}(s_1, \cdot) \preceq \mathbf{P}(s_2, \cdot)$, where $\preceq$ uses $\sqsubseteq_p$*

Relation $\sqsubseteq_p$ is symmetric if the transition probabilities are stochastic [26]. In this case, the simulation preorder agrees with probabilistic bisimulation [30]. Thus, for instance, $\sqsubseteq_p$ and probabilistic bisimulation $\sim_p$ coincide for an embedded DTMC of a CTMC.

Simulation for CTMCs. For CTMCs we modify $\sqsubseteq_p$ such that timing aspects are incorporated. Intuitively, we intend a simulation preorder to ensure that s_2 simulates s_1 iff (i) s_2 is "faster than" s_1 and (ii) the time-abstract behaviour of s_2 simulates that of s_1. An obvious attempt in this direction would be to refine Def. 4 by demanding that in addition to $\mathbf{P}(s_1, \cdot) \preceq \mathbf{P}(s_2, \cdot)$, we have $E(s_1) \leqslant E(s_2)$, i.e., s_2 should be on average at least as fast as s_1. However, such an approach turns out not to be very useful, as this would coincide with lumping equivalence [13] for uniformised CTMCs. Therefore, we present a more involved definition, which – in return – also enables a more radical state-space aggregation, since it incorporates a notion of *stuttering* [12,20].

Definition 5. *Let* $\mathcal{M} = (S, \mathbf{R}, L)$ *be a CTMC. Relation* $\sqsubseteq \ \subseteq \ S \times S$ *is a simulation iff for all states* $s_1, s_2 \in S$ *with* $s_1 \sqsubseteq s_2$ *we have that* $L(s_1) = L(s_2)$ *and there exist functions* $\Delta : S \times S \to [0, 1]$, $\delta_i : S \to [0, 1]$ *and sets* $U_i, V_i \subseteq S$ *(for* $i = 1, 2$*) with:*

$$U_i = \{\, u_i \in S \mid \mathbf{R}(s_i, u_i) > 0 \wedge \delta_i(u_i) > 0 \,\} \ and$$
$$V_i = \{\, v_i \in S \mid \mathbf{R}(s_i, v_i) > 0 \wedge \delta_i(v_i) < 1 \,\}$$

such that:

1. $v_1 \sqsubseteq s_2$ *for any* $v_1 \in V_1$ *and* $s_1 \sqsubseteq v_2$ *for any* $v_2 \in V_2$,
2. $\Delta(u_1, u_2) > 0$ *implies* $u_1 \in U_1$, $u_2 \in U_2$ *and* $u_1 \sqsubseteq u_2$,
3. $K_1 \cdot \displaystyle\sum_{u_2 \in U_2} \Delta(w, u_2) = \delta_1(w) \cdot \mathbf{P}(s_1, w)$ *and*

   $K_2 \cdot \displaystyle\sum_{u_1 \in U_1} \Delta(u_1, w) = \delta_2(w) \cdot \mathbf{P}(s_2, w)$, *for all* $w \in S$, *and*
4. $K_1 \cdot E(s_1) \leqslant K_2 \cdot E(s_2)$

where $K_i = \sum_{u_i \in U_i} \delta_i(u_i) \cdot \mathbf{P}(s_i, u_i)$ *for* $i = 1, 2$.

Definition 6. *The simulation relation* $\sqsubseteq_m$ *is defined by:* $s_1 \sqsubseteq_m s_2$ *iff there exists a simulation* $\sqsubseteq$ *such that* $s_1 \sqsubseteq s_2$.

The successor states of s_i are grouped into the subsets U_i and V_i. Although we do not require that U_i and V_i are disjoint, to understand the definition first consider $U_i \cap V_i = \varnothing$. (The fact that we allow a non-empty intersection has technical reasons that will be explained later). K_i denotes the total probability to move from s_i within one transition to a state in U_i. Vice versa, with probability $1 - K_i$, in state s_i a transition to some state in V_i is made (cf. Fig. 1). The first condition states that the grouping of successor states into V_i and U_i is such that any state in V_2 simulates s_1 and that s_2 simulates any state in V_1. Intuitively, we interpret the moves from s_i to a V_i-state as silent transitions (i.e., a τ-transition for action-labeled transition systems). The first condition thus guarantees that any such transition is a "stutter" step. The second and third condition require the existence of a weight function Δ that relates the conditional probabilities to move from s_1 to a U_1-state and the conditional probabilities for s_2 to move to a U_2-state. Thus, Δ is a weight function for the probability distributions

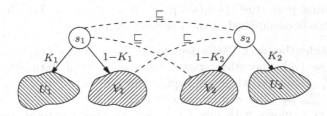

Fig. 1. Simulation scenario

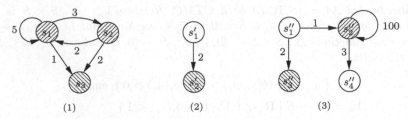

Fig. 2. Some examples of simulation refinement: $s_1 \sqsubseteq_m s_1'$ and $s_1' \sqsubseteq_m s_1''$

$\delta_i(\cdot) \cdot \mathbf{P}(s_i, \cdot)/K_i$. Intuitively, the transitions from s_i to a U_i-state are considered as observable moves and the second and third condition are the continuous versions of similar conditions for strong simulation ($\sqsubseteq_p$) in the discrete-time case. Finally, the fourth condition states that s_2 is "faster than" s_1 in the sense that the total rate to move from s_2 to a U_2-state is at least the total rate to move from s_1 to a U_1-state.

Example 2. Consider the three CTMCs depicted in Fig. 2 where states s_1, s_2, s_1', s_1'' and s_2'' are labelled with proposition a, and the other states by b. We have $s_1 \sqsubseteq_m s_1'$, since there exists a relation $\sqsubseteq \; = \{\, (s_1, s_1'), (s_3, s_2'), (s_2', s_3), (s_2, s_1') \,\}$ with $U_1 = \{\, s_3 \,\}, V_1 = \{\, s_1, s_2 \,\}, \delta_1(s_3) = 1$ and 0 otherwise, $U_2 = \{\, s_2' \,\}, V_2 = \varnothing$, $\delta_2(s_2') = 1$ and 0 otherwise, and $\Delta(s_3, s_2') = \Delta(s_2', s_3) = 1$ and 0 otherwise. It follows that $K_1 = \frac{1}{9}$ and $K_2 = 1$. (In the pictorial representation, the elements of U_i and V_i are indicated by the same patterns used in Fig. 1 for U_i and V_i). It is not difficult to check that indeed all constraints of Def. 5 are fulfilled, e.g., for the fourth constraint we obtain $\frac{1}{9} \cdot 9 \leqslant 1 \cdot 2$. Note that $s_1 \not\sqsubseteq_m s_2$ if $\mathbf{R}(s_2, s_3) > 2$ (rather than being equal to 2), since then $s_2 \sqsubseteq s_1'$ can no longer be established.

We further have $s_1' \sqsubseteq_m s_1''$ since there exists a relation $\sqsubseteq = \{\, (s_1', s_1''), (s_1', s_2''),$ $(s_2', s_3''), (s_3'', s_2'), (s_2', s_4''), (s_4'', s_2') \,\}$ with $U_1 = \{\, s_2' \,\}, V_1 = \varnothing, K_1 = 1$, and $\delta_1(s_2') = 1$ and 0 otherwise, $U_2 = \{\, s_3'' \,\}, V_2 = \{\, s_2'' \,\}, \delta_2(s_3'') = 1$ and 0 otherwise, $K_2 = \frac{2}{3}$ and $\Delta(s_3'', s_2') = \Delta(s_2', s_3'') = 1$. It is straightforward to check that indeed all constraints of Def. 5 are fulfilled.

In the examples so far, we have used the special case where $\delta_i(s) \in \{\, 0, 1 \,\}$ for any state s. In this case, δ_i is the characteristic function of U_i, and the sets U_i and V_i are disjoint. In general, though, things are more complicated and we need to construct U_i and V_i using *fragments* of states. That is, we deal with functions δ_i where $0 \leqslant \delta_i(s) \leqslant 1$. Intuitively, the $\delta_i(s)$-fragment of state s belongs to U_i, while the remaining part (the $(1 - \delta_i(s))$-part) of s belongs to V_i. The use of fragments of states is exemplified in the following example.

Example 3. Consider the two CTMCs depicted in Fig. 3. where $L(s_1) = L(s_3) = L(s_1') = L(s_3') = \{\, a \,\}$; the other states are labelled by b. Intuitively, s_1 is "slower than" s_1'. However, when we require the sets U_i, V_i in Def. 5 to be disjoint, then $s_1 \not\sqsubseteq_m s_1'$. This can be seen as follows. We have $s_1 \not\sqsubseteq_m s_3'$ (and hence, $V_2 = \varnothing$) as s_1 moves with rate 1 to a b-state while the total rate for s_3' to move to a b-state is smaller (i.e., $\frac{1}{2}$). Hence, the only chance to define the

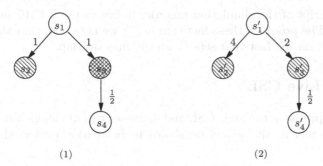

(1)   (2)

Fig. 3. An example of simulation using fragments of states

components in Def. 5 is $V_2 = \varnothing$ and $U_2 = \{s_2', s_3'\}$. Because s_3' and s_2 are not comparable with the simulation order (as they have different labels), we would have to define $U_1 = \{s_2, s_3\}$ and $V_1 = \varnothing$. But then, the weight-function condition is violated because s_1 moves with probability $\frac{1}{2}$ to a b-state while the probability for s_1' to reach a b-state within one step is $\frac{2}{3}$.

On the other hand, when we allow s_3 to be split: one half of s_3 belongs to U_1, one half to V_1, i.e., $\delta_1(s_3) = \frac{1}{2}$ and $U_1 = \{s_2, s_3\}$, $V_1 = \{s_3\}$ then we get that with $U_2 = \{s_2', s_3'\}$, $V_2 = \varnothing$ and $\sqsubseteq_m = \{(s_1, s_1'), (s_2, s_2'), (s_3, s_1'), (s_4, s_4'), (s_2, s_4')\}$ the conditional probabilities for the U_i-states are related via $\preceq$. Note that $K_1 = \frac{1}{2} + \frac{1}{4} = \frac{3}{4}$, $K_2 = 1$ and $\Delta(s_2, s_2') = \frac{2}{3}$, $\Delta(s_3, s_3') = \frac{1}{3}$.

Remark 1. It is interesting to observe what happens if $s_1 \sqsubseteq_m s_2$ and one of the states is absorbing. If s_2 is absorbing (i.e., $E(s_2) = 0$) then $K_1 \cdot E(s_1) = 0$. Hence, either s_1 has to be absorbing or $K_1 = 0$. In the latter case, we have $\delta_1(u_1) = 0$ for all $u_1 \in U_1$ (by condition 3. in Def. 5), i.e., all successor states of s_1 belong to V_1 and are simulated by s_2 (by condition 2. in Def. 5). Vice versa, for any state $u_2 \in U_2$:

$$0 < \delta_2(u_2) \cdot \mathbf{P}(s_2, u_2) = \sum_{u_1 \in U_1} \Delta(u_1, u_2).$$

Thus, $\Delta(u_1, u_2) > 0$ for some $u_1 \in U_1$. In particular, if $U_2 \neq \varnothing$ then $U_1 \neq \varnothing$, which implies that s_1 is non-absorbing. This shows that, if s_1 is absorbing then all successor states of s_2 belong to V_2 and simulate s_1 (by condition 2. of Def. 5).

The observation that an absorbing state s_1 is simulated by any state s_2 with the same labeling is natural for any type of simulation that abstracts from silent moves. The observation that any state s_2 which simulates an absorbing state s_1 can only perform stutter steps (non-observable transitions) can be viewed as the probabilistic counterpart to divergence for non-probabilistic systems. Note that in absorbing states of a CTMC just time advances.

Lemma 1. $\sqsubseteq_m$ *is a preorder.*

Lemma 2. *For CTMC $\mathcal{M} = (S, \mathbf{R}, L)$ and $s_1, s_2 \in S$ we have:*

$$s_1 \sqsubseteq_m^{\mathcal{M}} s_2 \text{ if and only if } s_1 \sqsubseteq_m^{\mathrm{unif}(\mathcal{M})} s_2.$$

Here, the superscript of the simulation preorder indicates the CTMC on which it is considered. The proofs of these facts are in [9]; we note here that the proof of Lemma 2 relies on the fact that sets U_i and V_i may overlap.

3 Safe and Live CSL

This section recapitulates the logic CSL and discusses two distinguished subsets of the logic that will in the sequel be shown to be weakly preserved by our simulation.

Paths in CTMCs. A path through a CTMC is an alternating sequence $\sigma = s_0\, t_0\, s_1\, t_1\, s_2 \ldots$ with $\mathbf{R}(s_i, s_{i+1}) > 0$ and $t_i \in \mathbb{R}_{>0}$ for all i.[2] The time stamps t_i denote the amount of time spent in state s_i. Let *Path* denote the set of paths through $\mathcal{M}$. $\sigma[i]$ denotes the $(i{+}1)$th state of σ, i.e. $\sigma[i] = s_{i+1}$. $\sigma@t$ denotes the state of σ occupied at time t, i.e. $\sigma@t = \sigma[i]$ with i the smallest index such that $t < \sum_{j=0}^{i} t_j$. Let Pr_s denote the unique probability measure on sets of paths that start in s (for a definition of the Borel space see [8]).

Continuous Stochastic Logic. CSL [8] is a branching-time temporal logic à la CTL where the state-formulas are interpreted over states of a CTMC and the path-formulas are interpreted over paths in a CTMC. CSL is a variant of the (equally named) logic by Aziz *et al.* [3] and incorporates (i) an operator to refer to the probability of the occurrence of particular paths, similar to PCTL [22], a (ii) real-time until-operator, like in TCTL [1], and (iii) a steady-state operator [8]. In this paper, we focus on a fragment of CSL (denoted CSL$^-$), distinguished in that we do not consider the next step and steady-state operator. (For simplicity, we also only consider time-intervals of the form $[0, t]$.) The omission of these operators will be justified later on. Besides the usual strong until-operator we incorporate a weak until-operator that will be used in the classification of safety and liveness properties. These properties are subjects of the weak preservation results we aim to establish.

Recall that AP is the set of atomic propositions. Let $a \in AP$, $p \in [0,1]$ and $\trianglelefteq\, \in \{\leqslant, \geqslant\}$ and $t \in \mathbb{R}_{\geqslant 0}$ (or ∞). The syntax of CSL$^-$ is:

$$\Phi ::= a \quad\Big|\quad \Phi \wedge \Phi \quad\Big|\quad \neg\Phi \quad\Big|\quad \mathcal{P}_{\trianglelefteq p}(\Phi\, \mathcal{U}^{\leqslant t}\, \Phi) \quad\Big|\quad \mathcal{P}_{\trianglelefteq p}(\Phi\, \mathcal{W}^{\leqslant t}\, \Phi).$$

$\mathcal{P}_{\trianglelefteq p}(\varphi)$ asserts that the probability measure of the paths satisfying φ meets the bound given by $\trianglelefteq p$. The operator $\mathcal{P}_{\trianglelefteq p}(.)$ replaces the usual (fair) CTL path quantifiers $\exists$ and $\forall$. The path-formula $\Phi\, \mathcal{U}^{\leqslant t}\, \Psi$ asserts that Ψ is satisfied at some time instant before t and that at all preceding time instants Φ holds (strong until). The weak until-operator $\mathcal{W}$ differs in that we do not require that Ψ eventually becomes true, i.e., $\Phi\, \mathcal{W}^{\leqslant t}\, \Psi$ means $\Phi\, \mathcal{U}^{\leqslant t}\, \Psi$ unless always Φ in the time-interval $[0, t]$ holds.

---

[2] For paths that end in an absorbing state s_k we assume a path to be represented as an infinite sequence $s_0\, t_0\, s_1 \ldots t_{k-1}\, s_k\, 1\, s_k\, 1\, s_k\, 1 \ldots$.

Semantics. The semantics of CSL for the boolean operators is identical to that for CTL and is omitted here. For the remaining state-formulas [8]:

$$s \models \mathcal{P}_{\trianglelefteq p}(\varphi) \text{ iff } Prob(s, \varphi) \trianglelefteq p$$

for path-formula φ. Here, $Prob(s, \varphi) = \mathrm{Pr}_s\{\sigma \in Path \mid \sigma \models \varphi\}$. The semantics of $\mathcal{U}^{\leqslant t}$ is defined by:

$$\sigma \models \Phi \mathcal{U}^{\leqslant t} \Psi \text{ iff } \exists x \leqslant t. (\sigma@x \models \Psi \wedge \forall y < x. \sigma@y \models \Phi) .$$

Note that the standard (i.e., untimed) until operator is obtained by taking t equal to ∞. The semantics of the weak until operator is defined by:

$$\sigma \models \Phi \mathcal{W}^{\leqslant t} \Psi \text{ iff } (\forall x \leqslant t. \sigma@x \models \Phi) \vee \sigma \models \Phi \mathcal{U}^{\leqslant t} \Psi.$$

The other boolean connectives are derived in the usual way, i.e., tt $= a \vee \neg a$, ff $= \neg$tt, $\Phi_1 \vee \Phi_2 = \neg(\neg\Phi_1 \wedge \neg\Phi_2)$, and $\Phi_1 \rightarrow \Phi_2 = \neg\Phi_1 \vee \Phi_2$. Temporal operators like $\Diamond$, $\Box$ and their real-time variants $\Diamond^{\leqslant t}$ or $\Box^{\leqslant t}$ can be derived, e.g.

$$\mathcal{P}_{\trianglelefteq p}(\Diamond^{\leqslant t} \Phi) = \mathcal{P}_{\trianglelefteq p}(\mathrm{tt} \, \mathcal{U}^{\leqslant t} \Phi) \text{ and } \mathcal{P}_{\trianglelefteq p}(\Box^{\leqslant t} \Phi) = \mathcal{P}_{\trianglelefteq p}(\Phi \mathcal{W}^{\leqslant t} \mathrm{ff}).$$

For instance, if *error* is an atomic proposition that characterizes all states where a system error has occurred then $\mathcal{P}_{<0.001}(\Diamond^{\leqslant 4} error)$ asserts that the probability for a system error within 4 time units is smaller than 0.001.

The until-operator and the weak until-operator are closely related. For any state s and CSL^--formula Φ and Ψ we have:

$$Prob(s, \Phi \mathcal{U}^{\leqslant t} \Psi) = 1 - Prob(s, (\neg\Psi) \mathcal{W}^{\leqslant t} \neg(\Phi \vee \Psi)) \qquad (1)$$

$$Prob(s, \Phi \mathcal{W}^{\leqslant t} \Psi) = 1 - Prob(s, (\neg\Psi) \mathcal{U}^{\leqslant t} \neg(\Phi \vee \Psi)) \qquad (2)$$

Hence, the following two formulas are equivalent:

$$\mathcal{P}_{\geqslant p}(\Phi \mathcal{W}^{\leqslant t} \Psi) \text{ and } \mathcal{P}_{\leqslant 1-p}((\neg\Psi) \mathcal{U}^{\leqslant t} \neg(\Phi \vee \Psi)).$$

A similar equivalence holds when the weak until- and the until-operator are exchanged. Note that a path satisfies $\neg((\neg\Phi) \mathcal{U}^{\leqslant t} (\neg\Psi))$ if Ψ always holds, a requirement that is released as soon as Φ becomes valid.

CSL safety and liveness properties. For the weak preservation results we distinguish between safety ("something bad never happens") and liveness ("something good will eventually happen") properties. In order to do so, negations may only be attached to atomic propositions. The syntax of CSL_{safe}, the set of safety formulas, is defined by:

$$\Phi ::= a \mid \neg a \mid \Phi \wedge \Phi \mid \Phi \vee \Phi \mid \mathcal{P}_{\geqslant p}(\Phi \mathcal{W}^{\leqslant t} \Phi) \mid \mathcal{P}_{\leqslant p}(\neg \Phi \mathcal{U}^{\leqslant t} \neg \Phi).$$

An example CSL safety formula is $\mathcal{P}_{\geqslant 0.99}(\Box^{\leqslant 100} \neg error)$ expressing that with probability at least 0.99 no error will occur in the next hundred time units. The syntax of CSL_{live}, the set of liveness formulas, is defined by:

$$\Phi ::= a \mid \neg a \mid \Phi \wedge \Phi \mid \Phi \vee \Phi \mid \mathcal{P}_{\geqslant p}(\Phi \mathcal{U}^{\leqslant t} \Phi) \mid \mathcal{P}_{\leqslant p}(\neg \Phi \mathcal{W}^{\leqslant t} \neg \Phi).$$

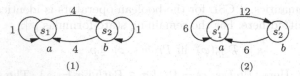

Fig. 4. Next and steady state behaviour is not preserved by $\sqsubseteq_m$

As a result of the aforementioned relationship between $\mathcal{U}$ and $\mathcal{W}$ (cf. equations (1) and (2)), there is a duality between safety and liveness properties for CSL, i.e., for any formula Φ_{safe} there is a liveness property equivalent to $\neg\Phi_{safe}$, and the same applies to liveness property Φ_{live}.

Next and steady state. Neither the next operator $\mathcal{P}_{\lhd p}(X\Phi)$, nor the steady-state operator $\mathcal{S}_{\lhd p}(\Phi)$ of [8] can become part of a CSL fragment that enables a weak preservation result for $\sqsubseteq_m$. This is shown by the following example.

Example 4. Consider the two CTMCs depicted in Fig. 4, where each state is decorated with the atomic propositions valid in the respective state. We have $s_1 \sqsubseteq_m s_1'$ and $s_2 \sqsubseteq_m s_2'$. The steady-state (or long-run) probability $\pi(s_i)$ of being in state s_i is spread evenly among s_1 and s_2, whereas it is spread unevenly among s_1' and s_2'; s_1' is less likely than s_2'. Concretely $\pi(s_1) = \pi(s_2) = \frac{1}{2}$ but $\pi(s_1') = \frac{1}{3}$ and $\pi(s_2') = \frac{2}{3}$. As a consequence, $s_1 \models \mathcal{S}_{\geqslant 0.5}(a)$, but $s_1' \not\models \mathcal{S}_{\geqslant 0.5}(a)$. On the other hand, $s_2 \models \mathcal{S}_{\leqslant 0.5}(b)$, while $s_2' \not\models \mathcal{S}_{\leqslant 0.5}(b)$. Furthermore, we have that $s_1 \models \mathcal{P}_{\leqslant 0.2}(Xa)$ and $s_2 \models \mathcal{P}_{\geqslant 0.2}(Xb)$, but $s_1' \not\models \mathcal{P}_{\leqslant 0.2}(Xa)$ and $s_2' \not\models \mathcal{P}_{\geqslant 0.2}(Xb)$.

The fact that the steady-state operator is not compatible with our simulation relation can be viewed as a specific instance of the well-known phenomenon that CTMCs cannot be ordered according to their steady-state performance [35,11].

4   Weak Preservation

This section is devoted to the main result of the paper: weak preservation of the two CSL fragments CSL$_{safe}$ and CSL$_{live}$ with respect to $\sqsubseteq_m$. To arrive there, requires to establish some crucial observations.

For a given CTMC $\mathcal{M}$ we first remark that the probability measures on CTMC $\mathcal{M}$ agree with those on the uniformised CTMC $unif(\mathcal{M})$. For arbitrary CSL path-formula φ we have:

Lemma 3. $\Pr_s^{\mathcal{M}}\{\sigma \in Path \mid \sigma \models \varphi\} = \Pr_s^{unif(\mathcal{M})}\{\sigma \in Path \mid \sigma \models \varphi\}.$

The above lemma implies that CSL satisfaction on $\mathcal{M}$ agrees with CSL satisfaction on $unif(\mathcal{M})$. We thus may safely assume that the exit rate of each state equals E.

Theorem 1. *For state s_1, s_2:*

1. *for CSL$_{safe}$-formula Φ_{safe}: $s_1 \sqsubseteq_m s_2 \implies (s_2 \models \Phi_{safe} \implies s_1 \models \Phi_{safe})$.*
2. *for CSL$_{live}$-formula Φ_{live}: $s_1 \sqsubseteq_m s_2 \implies (s_2 \not\models \Phi_{live} \implies s_1 \not\models \Phi_{live})$.*

Proof. It is first proven that sets $Sat(\Phi_{safe})$ are upward-closed, i.e., if $s_1 \sqsubseteq_m s_2$ and $s_1 \in Sat(\Phi_{safe})$ then $s_2 \in Sat(\Phi_{safe})$. This is not involved and omitted here. The proof is then by induction on the formula, where the interesting cases ($\mathcal{U}^{\leqslant t}$ and $\mathcal{W}^{\leqslant t}$) use Lemma 4 below. The statement for the CSL_{live}-formulas follows then by duality of the weak until- and until-operator. $\square$

The proof of the above theorem requires to establish the following fact (Lemma 4):

$$s_1 \sqsubseteq_m s_2 \text{ implies } Prob(s_1, \Phi_1 \mathcal{U}^{\leqslant t} \Phi_2) \leqslant Prob(s_2, \Phi_1 \mathcal{U}^{\leqslant t} \Phi_2), \qquad (3)$$

where sets $Sat(\Phi_i) = \{\, s \in S \mid s \models \Phi_i \,\}$ are upward-closed. The initial proof idea for this fact is to resort to the embedded uniformised CTMC of $\mathcal{M}$, using the result that:

$$Prob^{\mathcal{M}}(s_1, \Phi_1 \mathcal{U}^{\leqslant t} \Phi_2) = e^{-E \cdot t} \cdot \sum_{k=0}^{\infty} \frac{(E \cdot t)^k}{k!} \cdot Prob^{\mathcal{D}}(s_1, \Phi_1 \mathcal{U}^{\leqslant k} \Phi_2), \qquad (4)$$

where $\mathcal{D} = emb(unif(\mathcal{M}))$ and $\Phi_1 \mathcal{U}^{\leqslant k} \Phi_2$ means that Φ_2 can be reached within at most k steps via a Φ_1-path (for natural k) [22]. The advantage of this approach would be that the remaining proof obligation:

$$s_1 \sqsubseteq_m s_2 \text{ implies } Prob^{\mathcal{D}}(s_1, \Phi_1 \mathcal{U}^{\leqslant k} \Phi_2) \leqslant Prob^{\mathcal{D}}(s_2, \Phi_1 \mathcal{U}^{\leqslant k} \Phi_2), \text{ for any } k$$
$$(5)$$

could be verified by considering the discrete-time behaviour of the CTMC only. Whereas the proof of equation (4) is rather straightforward, the conjecture (5) turns out to be wrong. This is illustrated by the following (uniformised) CTMC $\mathcal{M}$:

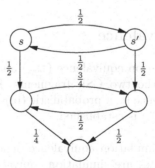

where only the absorbing state is labelled by proposition b. It is not difficult to check that state s' simulates state s. Indeed it follows that $Prob^{\mathcal{M}}(s, \Diamond^{\leqslant t} b) \leqslant Prob^{\mathcal{M}}(s', \Diamond^{\leqslant t} b)$ for any real time instant t. However, $Prob^{emb(\mathcal{M})}(s, \Diamond^{\leqslant k} b) = \frac{7}{16} \not\leqslant \frac{3}{8} = Prob^{emb(\mathcal{M})}(s', \Diamond^{\leqslant k} b)$ for $k = 3$. This contradicts (5). Thus, this initial proof attempt fails and we have to consider an alternative route. Alternative proof attempts along similar lines failed. We prove (3) therefore in a different way. The crux of the proof is to apply a number of transformations on the CTMC under consideration. The details of the proof are in [9]; the proof sketch is given below.

Lemma 4. *Let Φ_1 and Φ_2 be CSL-formulas such that the satisfaction sets $Sat(\Phi_i)$ are upward-closed, i.e., if $s_1 \sqsubseteq_m s_2$ and $s_1 \in Sat(\Phi_i)$ then $s_2 \in Sat(\Phi_i)$ for $i = 1, 2$. Then:*

$$s_1 \sqsubseteq_m s_2 \text{ implies } Prob(s_1, \Phi_1 \mathcal{U}^{\leqslant t} \Phi_2) \leqslant Prob(s_2, \Phi_1 \mathcal{U}^{\leqslant t} \Phi_2).$$

Proof. We only provide the proof sketch here; the full proof is given in [9]. Through a series of transformation steps we modify $\mathcal{M}$ to obtain a CTMC such that for any pair $s_1 \sqsubseteq_m s_2$:

- The probability to move from s_1 to a V_1-state equals the probability for the added self-loop $s_2 \to s_2$.
- The probability for the added self-loop $s_1 \to s_1$ equals the probability to move from s_2 to a V_2-state.
- The probabilities to move from s_1 and s_2 to a U_1- and U_2-state, respectively, are equal.
- s_2 is faster than s_1, i.e., the exit rate of s_2 exceeds the exit rate of s_1.

(The meaning of U_1, U_2, V_1 and V_2 is as in Def. 5.) The reasoning will then be as follows. The interesting case is $s_i \models \Phi_1 \wedge \neg\Phi_2$ for $i = 1, 2$. Hence, all states in V_1 and V_2 satisfy Φ_1 but not Φ_2. Thus, the only possibility for s_i to fulfill the path-formula $\Phi_1 \mathcal{U}^{\leqslant t} \Phi_2$ is to move to a U_i-state. Let $p(s, t, n)$ denote the probability for s to reach a Φ_2-state in at most t time units within at most n transitions via Φ_1-states. Then, $Prob(s_i, \Phi_1 \mathcal{U}^{\leqslant t} \Phi_2)$ equals $\lim_{n \to \infty} p(s_i, t, n)$. Via the introduction of (yet another) state s'_2 that has the same probabilistic behaviour as s_2 but the exit rate of s_1 we then establish $p(s'_2, t, n) \leqslant p(s_2, t, n)$. By induction on n it is subsequently shown that $p(s_1, t, n) \leqslant p(s'_2, t, n)$. $\qquad\square$

5 Simulation Equivalence

This section defines simulation equivalence ($\equiv_m$) and relates this notion to the equivalences induced by the two CSL fragments. Furthermore, the relationship with lumping equivalence [13], probabilistic (bi)simulation [30,26] and weak probabilistic bisimulation [7] is established.

Simulation equivalence. Simulation equivalence denotes the kernel of the simulation preorder. Two states are simulation equivalent if and only if they are mutually simulating each other:

Definition 7. $s_1 \equiv_m s_2$ *if and only if $s_1 \sqsubseteq_m s_2$ and $s_2 \sqsubseteq_m s_1$.*

Theorem 2. *Let $s_1 \equiv_m s_2$. Then:*

1. *for any CSL safety-formula Φ_{safe}: $s_1 \models \Phi_{safe}$ iff $s_2 \models \Phi_{safe}$*
2. *for any CSL liveness-formula Φ_{live}: $s_1 \models \Phi_{live}$ iff $s_2 \models \Phi_{live}$*

Lemma 5. CSL_{safe}*-equivalence and CSL_{live}-equivalence are simulations.*

Theorem 3. *For any states s_1, s_2:*

$s_1 \equiv_m s_2$ *iff* $(s_1, s_2$ *are* CSL_{safe}-*equivalent*) *iff* $(s_1, s_2$ *are* CSL_{live}-*equivalent*).

Thus, simulation is characterised by each of the two fragments of CSL we considered.

Lumping equivalence. Recall from [6] that two states s_1 and s_2 are lumping equivalent ($s_1 \sim_m s_2$) if there is some equivalence relation R on S with $(s_1, s_2) \in R$ satisfying that whenever $(s, s') \in R$ then $L(s) = L(s')$ and for all equivalence classes C in the quotient S/R,

$$\sum_{s'' \in C} \mathbf{R}(s, s'') = \sum_{s'' \in C} \mathbf{R}(s', s'').$$

Theorem 4. *For any state s_1, s_2:* $s_1 \sim_m s_2$ *implies* $s_1 \equiv_m s_2$.

The converse of the above theorem does not hold. For instance, two corresponding states in a CTMC $\mathcal{M}$ and $unif(\mathcal{M})$ simulate each other (if considered in the disjoint union of the state spaces), but are not lumping equivalent if the uniformisation rate E is chosen strictly larger than $max_{s \in S} E(s)$. Thus simulation equivalence strictly refines lumping equivalence.

Simulation on DTMCs. It is interesting to investigate the effect of our simulation relation if interpreted without the constraint on the total rates of states, i.e., on (embedded) DTMCs. For a given DTMC $(S, \mathbf{P}, L)$, let $\leqslant_p$ be the preorder obtained by omitting clause *4.* from Def. 5, and let $\equiv_p$ denote the induced simulation equivalence (cf. Def. 7). We have that strong probabilistic bisimulation ($\sim_p$) is finer than $\equiv_p$, and so is weak probabilistic bisimulation [7]: Let $\approx_p$ denote (state-labelled) weak probabilistic bisimulation. More specific, two states s_1 and s_2 are weakly probabilistic bisimilar ($s_1 \approx_p s_2$) if there is some equivalence relation R on S with $(s_1, s_2) \in R$ satisfying that whenever $(s, s') \in R$ then $L(s) = L(s')$ and for all equivalence classes C in the quotient S/R,

$$\mathbf{W}(s, C) = \mathbf{W}(s', C)$$

where $\mathbf{W}(s, C) = \sum_{s'' \in [s]_R} \mathbf{P}(s, s'') \mathbf{W}(s'', C)$ if $s \notin C$, and 1 otherwise ($[s]_R$ is the equivalence class of R containing s).[3]

Theorem 5. *For any state s_1, s_2 of a DTMC:* $s_1 \approx_p s_2$ *implies* $s_1 \equiv_p s_2$.

We claim that the converse direction of this theorem holds as well in the DTMC setting (but not for FPSs) though we have not formally shown this yet. Recall that $\sqsubseteq_p$ and $\sim_p$ agree on DTMCs, and we feel that a similar result may be expected for $\leqslant_p$ and $\approx_p$. Note that the probabilistic preorder is a side issue of our work since we are mainly interested in CTMC model checking.

---

[3] Here we define $\approx_p$ using the branching bisimulation style, see [7] for a proof that both styles coincide on DTMCs.

6   Related Work

Preservation and bisimulation. Aziz *et al.* [2] have shown that Larsen-Skou probabilistic bisimulation [30] on discrete-time Markov chains fully preserves any formula in the logic Probabilistic CTL (PCTL) [22]. This result has recently been generalised towards continuous-space Markov processes by Desharnais *et al.* [17]. Segala and Lynch [34] reported similar results for simple probabilistic automata, a model in which probabilistic choices and non-determinism co-exist. Baier *et al.* [6] have shown that lumping equivalence [13] preserves CSL; Desharnais and Panangaden [18] have recently shown the converse, namely that the equivalence induced by CSL implies lumping equivalence.

Simulation preorders. Based on the seminal works by Larsen and Skou [30] and Jonsson and Larsen [26] on probabilistic (bi)simulation several variants have been proposed, see e.g., [34,7,10,32,37]. Mostly related to this paper are the simulations of [16,34,19]. We discuss these works briefly.

D'Argenio *et al.* [16] investigated simulation on discrete-time Markov decision processes, and showed preservation of (untimed) probabilistic reachability properties. Opposed to their work, our approach stays in an entirely probabilistic setting – we do not abstract away probabilistic behaviour. This has the advantage that CSL model-checking algorithms can be applied to the abstract model as well as to the concrete model.

Segala and Lynch [34] presented weak and strong simulations for action-labelled probabilistic automata and showed that these notions are pre-congruences wrt. parallel composition. For divergence-free probabilistic automata they showed that strong simulation weakly preserves a "safe" fragment of PCTL [22]. In addition, a weak preservation result for weak simulation for a fragment of (a subset of) a variant of PCTL that abstracts from internal activities is shown.

Desharnais *et al.* [19] studied the approximation of continuous-space Markov processes by a series of finite (rational) Markov processes. They used a simulation preorder to capture the relationship between successive finite approximants and showed that this preorder weakly preserves a subset of PML, a probabilistic variant of Hennessy-Milner logic.

Testing preorders. Another important branch of preorders are the ones based on testing, a framework in which processes are compared by their (in)ability to pass a specified set of tests. For discrete-time probabilistic systems, a whole range of testing preorders have been proposed. A recent account can be found in [27] where also the relation between probabilistic may-testing and probabilistic simulation is established. Testing preorders for continuous-time probabilistic systems have received scant attention so far. A notable exception is the work by Bernardo and Cleaveland [11] who consider testing of action-labelled CTMCs. Similar to our simulation preorder, their tests allow one to discriminate models with respect to their transient evolution. To be more precise, two testing preorders are considered, one based on the probability of executing a successful computation whose average duration is not exceeding a time bound, and one based on the probability to reach success within a time bound. It is shown that these testing preorders coincide. CSL preservation results for testing are not known to us.

7   Concluding Remarks

This paper presented a simulation preorder ($\sqsubseteq_m$) for CTMCs and provided weak preservation results for safety- and liveness-fragments of CSL. We claim that the simulation preorder can be easily extended towards Markov reward models (by requiring that rewards of simulating states are related according to $\leqslant$) and that weak preservation results for fragments of the logic CSRL [5] can be obtained in a similar way as shown in this paper. As a next step, we plan to work on an algorithm for deciding $\sqsubseteq_m$ and to construct the quotient space w.r.t. simulation preorder or simulation equivalence, based on [7,10,4,32]. Moreover, we will investigate whether the concept of simulation can help to increase the efficiency of CSL model checking using an abstraction refinement methodology as in [16].

References

1. R. Alur, C. Courcoubetis and D. Dill. Model-checking in dense real-time. *Inf. and Comp.*, **104**(1): 2–34, 1993. 345
2. A. Aziz, V. Singhal, F. Balarin, R. Brayton and A. Sangiovanni-Vincentelli. It usually works: the temporal logic of stochastic systems. In P. Wolper (ed), *Computer-Aided Verification*, LNCS 939, pp. 155–165, 1995. 351
3. A. Aziz, K. Sanwal, V. Singhal and R. Brayton. Verifying continuous time Markov chains. In R. Alur and T. A. Henzinger (eds), *Computer-Aided Verification*, LNCS 1102, pp. 269–276, 1996. 339, 345
4. C. Baier, B. Engelen, and M. Majster-Cederbaum. Deciding bisimilarity and similarity for probabilistic processes. *J. of Comp. and System Sc.*, **60**(1):187–231, 2000. 352
5. C. Baier, B. R. Haverkort, H. Hermanns and J.-P. Katoen. On the logical characterisation of performability properties. In U. Montanari *et al.* (eds.), *Automata, Languages, and Programming*, LNCS 1853, pp. 780–792, 2000. 352
6. C. Baier, B. R. Haverkort, H. Hermanns and J.-P. Katoen. Model checking continuous-time Markov chains by transient analysis. In E. A. Emerson and A. P. Sistla (eds), *Computer-Aided Verification*, LNCS 1855, pp. 358–372, 2000. 339, 340, 350, 351
7. C. Baier, H. Hermanns. Weak bisimulation for fully probabilistic processes. In O. Grumberg (ed), *Computer-Aided Verification*, LNCS 1254, pp. 119-130. 1997. 349, 350, 351, 352
8. C. Baier, J.-P. Katoen and H. Hermanns. Approximate symbolic model checking of continuous-time Markov chains. In J. C. M. Baeten and S. Mauw (eds), *Concurrency Theory*, LNCS 1664, pp. 146–162, 1999. 339, 340, 345, 346, 347
9. C. Baier, J.-P. Katoen, H. Hermanns and B. Haverkort. Simulation for continuous-time Markov chains. Technical report, Univ. Twente, 2002. 339, 345, 348, 349
10. C. Baier and M. I. A. Stoelinga. Norm functions for probabilistic bisimulations with delays. In J. Tyurin (ed), *Found. of Software Science and Computation Structures*, LNCS 1784, pp. 1-16. 2000. 351, 352

11. M. Bernardo and R. Cleaveland. A theory of testing for Markovian processes. In C. Palamidessi (ed), *Concurrency Theory*, LNCS 1877, pp. 305–319, 2000. 347, 351

12. M. Brown, E. Clarke, O. Grumberg. Characterizing finite Kripke structures in propositional temporal logic. *Th. Comp. Sc.*, **59**: 115–131, 1988. 338, 341

13. P. Buchholz. Exact and ordinary lumpability in finite Markov chains. *J. of Appl. Prob.*, **31**: 59–75, 1994. 339, 341, 349, 351

14. E. Clarke, O. Grumberg and D. E. Long. Model checking and abstraction. *ACM Tr. on Progr. Lang. and Sys.*, **16**(5): 1512–1542, 1994. 339

15. E. Clarke, O. Grumberg and D. Peled. *Model Checking*. MIT Press, 1999. 338

16. P. R. D'Argenio, B. Jeannet, H. E. Jensen, and K. G. Larsen. Reachability analysis of probabilistic systems by successive refinements. In L. de Alfaro and S. Gilmore (eds), *Process Algebra and Probabilistic Methods*, LNCS 2165, pp. 39–56, 2001. 351, 352

17. J. Desharnais, A. Edalat and P. Panangaden. A logical characterisation of bisimulation for labelled Markov processes. In *IEEE Symp. on Logic in Computer Science*, pp. 478–487, 1998. 351

18. J. Desharnais and P. Panangaden. Continuous stochastic logic characterizes bisimulation of continuous-time Markov processes, 2001 (submitted for publication). (available at http://www-acaps.cs.mcgill.ca/~prakash/csl.ps). 339, 351

19. J. Desharnais, V. Gupta, R. Jagadeesan and P. Panangaden. Approximating labelled Markov processes. In *IEEE Symp. on Logic in Computer Science*, pp. 95–106, 2000. 351

20. R. J. van Glabbeek and W. P. Weijland. Branching time and abstraction in bisimulation semantics. *J. ACM*, **43**(3): 555–600, 1996. 341

21. D. Gross and D. R. Miller. The randomization technique as a modeling tool and solution procedure for transient Markov chains. *Oper. Res.* **32**(2): 343–361, 1984. 340

22. H. Hansson and B. Jonsson. A logic for reasoning about time and reliability. *Form. Asp. of Comp.* **6**: 512–535, 1994. 345, 348, 351

23. H. Hermanns, J.-P. Katoen, J. Meyer-Kayser and M. Siegle. A Markov chain model checker. In S. Graf and M. Schwartzbach (eds), *Tools and Algs. for the Construction and Analysis of Systems*, LNCS 1785, pp. 347–362, 2000. 339

24. A. Jensen. Markov chains as an aid in the study of Markov processes. *Skand. Aktuarietidskrift* **3**: 87–91, 1953. 340

25. B. Jonsson. Simulations between specifications of distributed systems. In J. C. M. Baeten and J. F. Groote (eds), *Concurrency Theory*, LNCS 527, pp. 346–360, 1991. 338

26. B. Jonsson and K. G. Larsen. Specification and refinement of probabilistic processes. In *IEEE Symp. on Logic in Computer Science*, pp. 266–277, 1991. 339, 340, 341, 349, 351

27. B. Jonsson, W. Yi and K. G. Larsen. Probabilistic extensions of process algebras. In J. Bergstra *et al.* (eds), *Handbook of Process Algebra*, Ch. 11, pp. 685–709, 2001. 351

28. J.-P. Katoen, M. Z. Kwiatkowska, G. Norman and D. Parker. Faster and symbolic CTMC model checking. In L. de Alfaro and S. Gilmore (eds), *Process Algebra and Probabilistic Methods*, LNCS 2165, pp. 23–38, 2001. 339

29. V. G. Kulkarni. *Modeling and Analysis of Stochastic Systems*. Chapman & Hall, 1995. 339

30. K. G. Larsen and A. Skou. Bisimulation through probabilistic testing. *Inf. and Comp.*, **94**(1): 1–28, 1992. 341, 349, 351

31. R. Milner. *Communication and Concurrency*. Prentice-Hall, 1989. 338
32. A. Philippou, I. Lee, and O. Sokolsky. Weak bisimulation for probabilistic systems. In C. Palamidessi (ed), *Concurrency Theory*, LNCS 1877, pp. 334–349, 2000. 351, 352
33. M. L. Puterman. *Markov Decision Processes: Discrete Stochastic Dynamic Programming*. John Wiley & Sons, 1994. 340
34. R. Segala and N. A. Lynch. Probabilistic simulations for probabilistic processes. *Nordic J. of Computing*, **2**(2): 250–273, 1995. 351
35. M. Silva. Private communication. 1993. 347
36. W. J. Stewart. *Introduction to the Numerical Solution of Markov Chains*. Princeton Univ. Press, 1994. 339
37. M. I. A. Stoelinga. *Verification of Probabilistic, Real-Time and Parametric Systems*. PhD Thesis, University of Nijmegen, 2002. 351

Weak Bisimulation is Sound and Complete for PCTL*

Josée Desharnais[1*], Vineet Gupta[2],
Radha Jagadeesan[3*], and Prakash Panangaden[4*]

[1] Département d'Informatique, Université Laval
Québec, Canada, G1K 7P4
[2] Stratify Inc.
501 Ellis Street, Mountain View CA 94043 USA
[3] Dept. of Computer Science, Loyola University-Lake Shore Campus
Chicago IL 60626, USA
[4] School of Computer Science, McGill University
Montreal, Quebec, Canada

Abstract. We investigate weak bisimulation of probabilistic systems in
the presence of nondeterminism, i.e. labelled concurrent Markov chains
(LCMC) with silent transitions. We build on the work of Philippou, Lee
and Sokolsky [17] for finite state LCMCs. Their definition of weak bisimulation destroys the additivity property of the probability distributions,
yielding instead *capacities*. The mathematics behind capacities naturally
captures the intuition that when we deal with nondeterminism we must
work with estimates on the possible probabilities.
Our analysis leads to three new developments:

- We identify an axiomatization of "image finiteness" for countable
  state systems and present a new definition of weak bisimulation for
  these LCMCs. We prove that our definition coincides with that of
  Philippou, Lee and Sokolsky for finite state systems.
- We show that bisimilar states have matching computations. The
  notion of matching involves *linear combinations* of transitions. This
  idea is closely related to the use of randomized schedulers.
- We study a minor variant of the probabilistic logic pCTL* — the
  variation arises from an extra path formula to address action labels.
  We show that bisimulation is sound and complete for this variant of
  pCTL*.

1 Introduction

The main object of this paper is to study systems that combine probability,
concurrency and nondeterminism. We focus in particular on weak bisimulation.
The importance of weak bisimulation comes from the need for abstraction. In
order to construct larger programs from smaller programs one works with the
composition mechanisms of the language. When doing so it is necessary to hide
internal actions and work with weak (rather than strong) bisimulation.

---

* Research supported by NSERC, NSF and MITACS.

L. Brim et al. (Eds.): CONCUR 2002, LNCS 2421, pp. 355–370, 2002.

In the purely probabilistic context, the study of strong bisimulation was initiated by Larsen and Skou [15], and an equivalence notion was developed, similar to the queuing theory notion of "lumpability" [14]. This theory has been extended to continuous state spaces and continuous distributions [4,8,9] and, in the discrete setting, to weak bisimulation [2].

The study of weak bisimulation for systems with probability and non-determinism is sensitive to the underlying model. The two principal models are the *alternating* model [13] - where there are two disjoint classes of states, probabilistic states and nondeterministic states - and the nonalternating model [20]. Weak bisimulation for finite-state systems in the alternating model with distinct nondeterministic and probabilistic states was defined by Philippou, Lee and Sokolsky [17] whereas weak bisimulation for the nonalternating model was studied by Segala and Lynch [20]. Our study is set in the context of the alternating model and follows [17].

We explore the subtle consequences of the benign looking definitions of [17]. The most significant change from ordinary probability theory is that the "probabilities" no longer satisfy additivity[1]. In the presence of nondeterminism, we are describing a *set* of probability distributions $\{Q_i\}$ for a given state s and a given weak transition label a. The "probabilities" ascribed by [17] arise by majorizing over this set, i.e. $P(s, a, E)$, the probability of reaching a set of states E from state s on weak transition labelled a, is given by $\max_i Q_i(E)$ for any subset of states E.

The second important change is that the notion of matching has changed radically. The essence of any bisimulation notion is that transitions of one process can be matched with transitions in the bisimilar process. In order to match computation paths on given weak labels we are forced to take linear combinations of computations. The "computations" (to be defined precisely later) now have a vector space structure. In example 2 we discuss this point in detail. Essentially randomized schedulers allow one to take just such linear combinations.

The three main points that we make can be summarized as follows.

- First, we generalize the definitions of [17] to a large class of infinite-state systems satisfying a compactness property. Informally, compactness is a topological formalization of finite branching. In this context, compactness enables us to capture a robust notion of "image finiteness" for weak transitions that hide internal actions. The compact systems that we consider include all finite state systems (including those with cycles).
- Second, we adapt the ideas on randomized schedulers from Segala's work on probabilistic IO automata [19]. On the one hand, randomized schedulers do not change the semantics (the sups that one computes are the same). On the other hand, these schedulers enable us to perform a fine-grained analysis of the structure of computations in bisimilar systems. This analysis permits us to establish that bisimilar states s, t satisfy a familiar property: "for every distribution of states induced by a resolution of non-deterministic

---

[1] Additivity: P is additive if for disjoint sets A, B, $P(A \cup B) = P(A) + P(B)$.

choices from s, there exists a resolution of non-deterministic choices from t that results in a matching distribution on states". We show simple examples that demonstrate that this matching property *requires* the presence of linear combinations.

— Third, we analyze the structure that arises by majorizing over a set of probability distributions. This structure is called a capacity — for our purposes, capacities are monotone functions from a Borel algebra to the reals that preserve sups (resp. infs) of increasing (resp. decreasing) sequences of sets. Capacities are not necessarily additive. Indeed, the capacities induced by the definitions of [17] only satisfy: $P(s, a, A) + P(s, a, B) \geq P(s, a, A \cup B)$ for disjoint sets of states A, B.

This loss of additivity has already been recognized in various situations in mathematics [5,7,16] and in economics [18][2], and a rich theory was already available for our use. This theory meshes very well with the idea that uncertainty in probability distributions should be captured by giving upper and lower bounds on probabilities and expectation values. We show that the key equations that are demanded by this theory are met by the capacities that arise in the context of weak bisimulation.

Soundness and Completeness of weak bisimulation for probabilistic logics. A fundamental application of these ideas and the original impetus for these investigations is the analysis of soundness and completeness of bisimulation for probabilistic logics. We study a minor variant of the probabilistic logic pCTL* [6] – the variation arises from an extra path formula to address action labels – and is inspired by the variants of probabilistic logics that deal with action labels [20,13] . We show that bisimulation is sound and complete for this variant of pCTL*. Our soundness and completeness proofs relies crucially on all three developments identified above.

Organization of this paper. The rest of this paper is organized as follows. First, in section 2, we review the basic definitions of the model (the "alternating model") and weak probabilistic bisimulation and associated results to make the paper self-contained. Section 3 identifies the class of countable systems to which our study applies. In section 4 we show that our definition is equivalent to that of Philippou, Lee and Sokolsky [17]. In section 5 we show that the capacities defined in the development of weak bisimulation satisfy the axioms required of capacities. Finally, in section 6, we use the machinery that has been developed to prove soundness and completeness results for the logic.

---

[2] Economic studies distinguish risk (the relative probabilities of the events are known) from uncertainty (there is no unique assignment of probabilities to events) - this is what computer scientists call nondeterminism. Risk is modelled using probability. The modelling of uncertainty is via a set of probability measures that are consistent with the known information. The structure obtained by majorizing this set of probability measures does not satisfy additivity and is a capacity.

2   Background and Definitions

We begin with a review of the underlying framework — our definitions are adapted from [17]. We work in the context of the "alternating model" for labelled concurrent Markov chains [13], labelled transition systems with non-determinism and probability.

Definition 1. *A labelled concurrent Markov chain (henceforth LCMC), is a tuple $\mathcal{K} = (K, \mathsf{Act}, \longrightarrow, k_0)$, where*
(1) $K = K_p \cup K_n$, a countable set, is partitioned into the probabilistic states, K_p, and the nondeterministic states K_n. k_0 is the start state.
(2) Act is a finite set of action symbols that contains a special action τ.
(3) The transition relation $\longrightarrow = \longrightarrow_p \cup \longrightarrow_n$ is partitioned into probabilistic and nondeterministic transitions. $\longrightarrow_n \subseteq K_n \times \mathsf{Act} \times K_p$ is image-finite, i.e. for each $s \in K_n$ and $a \in \mathsf{Act}$, the set $\{s' \in K_p \mid s \xrightarrow{a} s'\}$ is finite. $\longrightarrow_p \subseteq K_p \times (0,1] \times K_n$ satisfies that for each $s \in K_p$, $\sum_{(s,\pi,t) \in \longrightarrow_p} \pi = 1$.

A state is either probabilistic - in which case the transitions are probabilistic and unlabelled - or nondeterministic, in which case the transitions are finite-branching and labelled (possibly by a τ). The probabilistic branching can be countable at a state.

Every probabilistic state s induces a probability distribution Q on K_n given by $Q(t) = \sum_{(s,\pi,t) \in \longrightarrow_p} \pi$ for every $t \in K$. We sometimes write $s \to_p Q$ to emphasize this distribution. Indeed, one can take the view that the "real" states are the nondeterministic states and the probabilistic states are really just names for certain probability distributions.

The LCMC model does not need to be strictly alternating. One can work with a model that only restricts states to be either purely nondeterministic or purely probabilistic and does not enforce strict alternation.

We use some notation for sequences (of states or transitions). We use ε for the empty sequence and $\cdot$ for concatenation. Every sequence, say σ, of transitions has as an associated probability $\mathtt{prob}(\sigma)$, obtained by multiplying the probabilities occurring on the path. Thus, we attribute 1 to a nondeterministic transition in a path, and multiply together probabilities of all the probabilistic transitions. Similarly, every sequence σ of transitions has an associated weak sequence of labels $\mathtt{Weak}(\sigma) \in (\mathsf{Act} - \{\tau\})^*$, obtained by removing the labels of τ-transitions. Thus, probabilistic transitions and nondeterministic transitions with label τ do not contribute to the weak label. We use τ for the empty sequence as well as for the empty transition. Thus we will say that a path of τ transitions and probabilistic transitions has weak label τ.

We define *computations* of an LCMC as transition trees obtained by unfolding the LCMC from the root, resolving the nondeterministic choices (i.e. each nondeterministic state has at most one transition coming out of it) and taking all probabilistic choices at a probabilistic state. A computation can thus be viewed as a purely (sub)probabilistic labelled Markov chain. We refer to the set of all the probabilistic transitions from a probabilistic state as a *fan*.

Definition 2. *A computation of an LCMC is a (possibly infinite) subtree of the tree obtained by partially unfolding the LCMC. In a computation every nondeterministic state has at most one transition coming out of it and if a probabilistic transition is included then the entire fan of that probabilistic transition is included.*

We are interested in transitions with particular weak labels.

Definition 3. *Let $\mathcal{K}$ be a LCMC, $a \in \mathsf{Act}$. An a-computation from $s \in K$ is a computation such that every path from the root has weak label a or ε.*

It may seem peculiar to allow an a-computation to have paths labelled by ε. This is done to allow for a computation where the a transition has not happened yet (or may never happen). However, when we associate probability distributions with computations we will not count the paths labelled with ε, we insist that the paths that contribute to the distribution have weak label a.

Each computation induces a distribution on its leaf states in the standard way — the probability of a leaf node is the probability of the (unique) path going to it. We actually use a somewhat looser correspondence between computations and distributions. We allow many distributions to be induced by a given computation; the requirement of matching is weakened to an inequality. This will turn out to be very convenient when constructing certain sequences of weak transitions, for example in proving Lemma 1.

Definition 4. *Let $\mathcal{K}$ be a LCMC, $s \in K$, and let Q be a distribution on states. We write $s \overset{a}{\Rightarrow} Q$, if there is an a-computation such that for all $s_i \in K$, $Q(s_i) \leq \sum_\sigma \mathsf{prob}(\sigma)$ where the summation is taken over paths σ with weak label a that start in s and end in the leaf s_i.*

We extend this notation to linear combinations of distributions. $s \overset{a}{\Rightarrow} \sum_i \lambda_i \times Q_i$ is an a-transition from s to the distribution $\sum_i \lambda_i \times Q_i$. This is where the linear structure becomes explicit. Such a transition can be viewed as the "weighted superposition" of the transitions $s \overset{a}{\Rightarrow} Q_i$.

Definition 5. *Let $s_i \overset{a}{\Rightarrow} Q_i$ and let $\sum_i \lambda_i \leq 1$, where all $\lambda_i \geq 0$. Then we write: $\sum_i \lambda_i \times (s_i \overset{a}{\Rightarrow} Q_i)$ to denote the linear combination of the transitions $s_i \overset{a}{\Rightarrow} Q_i$. In the special case where all $s_i = s$, we write $s \overset{a}{\Rightarrow} \sum_i \lambda_i \times Q_i$ to represent an a-transition from s to the distribution $\sum_i \lambda_i \times Q_i$.*

We thus have linear (vector-space) structure on the space of computations and on the space of distributions. Note that when we write $s \overset{a}{\Rightarrow} Q$ we refer to the general case of transitions of the form $s \overset{a}{\Rightarrow} \sum_i \lambda_i \times Q_i$: when we want to refer to transitions that are not weighted combinations we use the term "basic". For $s \neq t$, the notation $\lambda \times (s \overset{a}{\Rightarrow} Q_1) + (1 - \lambda) \times (t \overset{a}{\Rightarrow} Q_2)$ is merely notational convenience. Note that $s \overset{a}{\Rightarrow} [\lambda \times Q_1 + (1-\lambda) \times Q_2]$ is reminiscent of the randomized schedulers [19].

Transitions from states to distributions as above are one way to the defintion of bisimulation. Another way is through transitions from states to sets of states,

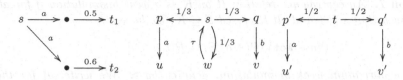

Fig. 1. (a)Additivity Fails   (b) Matching with linear combinations

which is how strong bisimulation is defined for labelled Markov processes in [4,9].
The "probability" from a state s to a subset of states via a path with weak label a
is defined by taking the supremum over all possible a-computations.

Definition 6. *Let $\mathcal{K}$ be a LCMC, $s \in K, E \subseteq K$. Then, the probability of going
from s to $E \subseteq K$ via a, denoted by $P(s, a, E)$, is defined as:*

$$P(s, a, E) = \sup\{\sum_{t \in E} Q(t) \mid s \overset{a}{\Rightarrow} Q\}.$$

The supremum in this definition is the source of the subtlety of weak bisimulation
— $P(s, a, .)$ does not satisfy additivity.

Example 1. Consider the transition system in figure 1(a). Then $P(s, a, \{t_1\}) =
0.5$, $P(s, a, \{t_2\}) = 0.6$, $P(s, a, \{t_1, t_2\}) = 0.6$. Thus additivity does not hold.
This example also illustrates in a trivial way why we must take the sup over all
computations in the definition of $P(s, a, E)$.

The next example shows the importance of allowing linear combinations when
matching computations with given weak labels.

Example 2. Consider the transition systems of figure 1(b). Intuitively we would
like to say that the states s and t are weakly bisimilar. We would also like to say
p, p' and q, q' are weakly bisimilar.

The probability of starting from s and reaching u on a weak a label is $1/2$
and the same is true for reaching u' from t. Note that we need to sum over all
possible paths that include the τ-loop if we want to get the answer $1/2$ starting
from s. Thus the a-computation from t that includes u' gives a probability of
$1/2$ to u' and can be matched by the infinite computation from s that loops
infinitely through w and gives probability $1/2$ to u. However, we have absolutely
no way of matching the distribution induced by the computation including only
one step from s. Indeed, this computation induces the distribution that gives
probability $1/3$ to each one of u, w and v. The only way to match it is to
take a linear combination, namely the distribution δ_t induced by the trivial
computation consisting only of state t, and the distribution P induced by the
one-step computation. The required combination is thus $1/3 \times \delta_t + 2/3 \times P$.

We are now ready to define weak bisimulation. Given an equivalence rela-
tion R, we say a set E is R-closed if $E = Cl_R(E) := \{s \mid \exists t \in E \text{ such that } tRs\}$.

Definition 7. *An equivalence relation R on K is a weak bisimulation if for all $s, t \in K$ such that $s\,R\,t$ and all R-closed $E \subseteq K$, we have:*

$$(\forall a \in \mathsf{Act})\,[P(s, a, E) = P(t, a, E)].$$

There is a maximum weak bisimulation, denoted by $\approx$. We write $[u]$ for the bisimulation class of the state u.

A LCMC $\mathcal{K}$ is *bisimulation collapsed* if for any state, the targets of all transitions are in distinct bisimulation classes.

The equational laws supported by this definition extend the usual ones for nondeterministic labelled transition systems or purely probabilistic transition systems. Indeed, the usual relations that witness the bisimulation are carried over essentially unchanged, for example, $\tau.\mathcal{K} \approx \mathcal{K}$, and unfolding a LCMC yields a weakly bisimilar system. See [3] for a full axiomatization of equational laws for finite processes (without loops, so the transition system is a tree).

We present a second definition of bisimulation which is similar to the one found in the non-probabilistic setting. It will be shown to be equivalent to the one above in Section 4 for *compact* LCMCs, defined in the next section.

Definition 8. *An equivalence relation R on K is a weak-$*$ bisimulation iff for all $s, t \in K$ such that $s\,R\,t$ we have:*

$$\forall s \overset{a}{\Rightarrow} Q\ \exists t \overset{a}{\Rightarrow} Q'\ (\forall R\text{-closed } E \subseteq K\ [Q(E) = Q'(E)])$$

We will denote it $\approx_*$.

3   The Compactness Condition

We consider countable-state LCMCs that satisfy a compactness condition. Intuitively speaking, the compactness condition can be viewed as the right generalization of "image-finiteness" for countable state LCMCs in the context of weak transitions that hide τ-labels.

We first consider some preliminary motivation for considering such a condition. In general, it is not the case – even for finitely branching systems – that there is a single computation that attains the supremum of definition 6.

Example 3. Let $\mathcal{K}$ be the LCMC described by the following diagram.

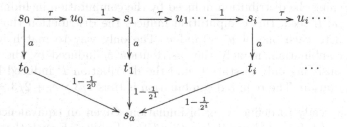

Clearly, $P(s_0, a, \{s_a\}) = 1$, but there is no single computation to witness this.

We diagnose the reason as the infinite (weak) branching at the state s_0. We now identify a large class of countable systems the class of systems that we will work with. Intuitively, this is a "compactness" condition that captures the essence of a "finite weak branching" requirement.

We begin with the definition of a metric d on distributions of states.

Definition 9. *The metric d on distributions of the states of a LCMC $\mathcal{K}$ is defined by $d(Q_1, Q_2) = sup_{A \subseteq K}|Q_1(A) - Q_2(A)|$.*

In this metric, any computation is the limit of finite depth computations.

Lemma 1. *Given any weak transition $s \overset{a}{\Rightarrow} P$, one can find a sequence of finite-depth computations with corresponding weak transitions $s \overset{a}{\Rightarrow} P_i$ with the P_i distributions converging to P in the metric d.*

Definition 10. *Let $\mathcal{K}$ be the LCMC and s be a state and a any label. We say s is a-compact if the set $\{Q \mid s \overset{a}{\Rightarrow} Q\}$ is compact[3] under metric d.*

A bisimulation collapsed LCMC $\mathcal{K}$ is compact if all states s are a-compact for all labels a (including τ).

A LCMC $\mathcal{K}'$ is compact if its bisimulation collapse is compact.

For labelled transition systems, the compactness condition is an image-finiteness condition. Here the probability of all paths is 1 and d is the discrete metric. So, an LTS is compact iff for all states s and all labels a, the set of states reachable on a weak transition labelled a is finite.

The definition is general enough to include all finite state systems. Weighted combinations of computations are crucial to this proof. The proof builds on the idea of Example 2. It shows that for any state s, there is a finite set of computations rooted at s such that any computation rooted at s can be built as a weighted combination of the elements of this set.

Theorem 1. *All finite state systems are compact.*

For compact countable-state systems, there is a single computation yielding the maximum probability, thus resolving the issue raised by Example 3.

Lemma 2. $P(s, a, E) = \sum_{s \in E} Q(s)$ *for some $s \overset{a}{\Rightarrow} Q$.*

4   Coincidence with the Definition of Philippou, Lee and Sokolsky

Our formulation of bisimulation (Definition 7) is different from the definition in [17]. However, the two definitions are equivalent.

We begin by presenting their definition below — we have recast it in terms of computations rather than schedulers. Recall that $[u]_R$ stands for the equivalence class of a state u for an equivalence relation R. Let C be an a-computation starting from s, we write $P^C(s, a, \cdot)$ for the distribution induced on the leaves of C.

---

[3] A subset A of a metric space is compact if every infinite subset $S \subseteq A$ has a limit point in A, i.e., $(\forall S \subseteq A)(\exists p \in A)(\forall \epsilon > 0)(\exists x \in S)\, d(p, x) < \epsilon$.

Definition 11. *An equivalence relation R on K is a PLS-weak bisimulation if for all $s, t \in K$ such that whenever sRt, then*

- *if $s \in K_n, a \in Act$ and $(s, a, s') \in \longrightarrow$, then there exists a computation C such that $P^C(t, a, [s']_R) = 1$.*
- *if $s \in K_p$ with $s \rightarrow_p Q$, then there exists a computation C such that*

$$\forall M \in K/R - [s]_R, P^C(t, \varepsilon, M) = \frac{Q(M)}{1 - Q([s]_R)}.$$

There is a maximum weak bisimulation, denoted by $\approx_{PLS}$.

The term $\frac{Q(M)}{1-Q([s]_R)}$ represents the conditional probability of reaching M from s in one step given that the system leaves the equivalence class of s in its first step.

For compact LCMCs (and hence all finite state LCMCs), $\approx$ and $\approx_{PLS}$ coincide. The proof of this theorem requires weighted combinations of computations, as illustrated by Example 2. The role of these weighted linear combinations is seen in the case $(2) \Rightarrow (3)$ in the following proof.

Theorem 2. *The following are equivalent for compact LCMCs.*

1. *$s \approx t$.*
2. *$s \approx_{PLS} t$.*
3. *$s \approx_* t$.*

Proof. We sketch the main ideas below.

- $(1) \Rightarrow (2)$: The key structural properties exploited in the proof are:
  - If t is a nondeterministic state, and s is a probabilistic state, such that t is weakly bisimilar to s, then there is a τ-transition from t to some t' such that t' is weakly bisimilar to s.
  - we can show that $\approx$-bisimilar probabilistic states have identical (upto $\approx$) probabilistic fans.
- $(2) \Rightarrow (3)$: We show this with $\approx_{PLS}$ as the equivalence relation in the Definition 8. Using Lemma 1, it suffices to prove the result for finite-depth computations Q. In this case, the proof proceeds by induction on depth.
  - Let C extend $s \stackrel{a}{\Rightarrow} Q$ by a nondeterministic transition $u \stackrel{b}{\rightarrow} u'$ at a leaf u. Let $Q(u) = p$. In this case, consider $t \stackrel{a}{\Rightarrow} Q'$, the extension of Q by matching transitions $v \stackrel{b}{\Rightarrow} Q_i$ from all the $v \approx_{PLS} u$ that are leaves.
  - The case when C extends $s \stackrel{a}{\Rightarrow} Q$ by adding a one-step probabilistic transition $u \rightarrow Q$ at a leaf u uses the ideas from example 2. There are two cases depending on whether $Q([u]) = 0$ or not. If $Q([u]) = 0$, $u \rightarrow Q$ can be matched by computations from all the $v \approx_{PLS} u$. If $Q([u]) = r > 0$, consider the transition from u to Q' where: $Q'[v] = \frac{Q[v]}{1-r}$, if $u \notin [v]$ and $Q'([u]) = 0$. For any $v \approx_{PLS} u$, this computation reaches its leaves with weak label τ and assign probabilities

in accordance with Q'. The required transition to Q from v is given by a linear combination (with coefficient $1 - r$) of this computation with the computation consisting only of v (with coefficient r).

Consider $t \stackrel{a}{\Rightarrow} Q'$, the extension of Q by matching transitions $v \stackrel{b}{\Rightarrow} Q_i$ from all the $v \approx_{PLS} u$ that are leaves.

In either case, the required transition from t is obtained by a linear combination $t \Rightarrow [\lambda \times Q' + (1 - \lambda) \times Q]$, where $\lambda = p/Q([u])$.

- (3) $\Rightarrow$ (1): This is immediate.

5 From Measures to Capacities

5.1 Background

In this section we first review the basic theory of capacities [5]. The original context that Choquet was interested in led him to impose several conditions that need not concern us here. We will present a simplified treatment and omit proofs of any results available in the literature.

We begin by recalling that the basic example 1(a) shows that we lose the additivity property crucial to the definition of a measure. We omit a few of the details in the following definitions[4].

Definition 12. *Let S be a set and let Σ be an algebra of subsets of S. A **capacity** on Σ is a non-negative real-valued set function $\nu : \Sigma \to \mathcal{R}$ such that*

- $\nu(\emptyset) = 0$
- *if $A \subseteq B$ in Σ then $\nu(A) \leq \nu(B)$,*
- *if $E_1 \subseteq E_2 \subseteq \ldots \subseteq E_n \subseteq \ldots$ with $\cup_i E_i = E$ then $\lim_{i \to \infty} \nu(E_i) = \nu(E)$,*
- *if $E_1 \supseteq E_2 \supseteq \ldots \supseteq E_n \supseteq \ldots$ with $\cap_i E_i = E$ then $\lim_{i \to \infty} \nu(E_i) = \nu(E)$.*

*If, in addition, it satisfies $\nu(A \cup B) \leq \nu(A) + \nu(B)$, it is said to be **subadditive**.*

For measures the two continuity properties are consequences of countable additivity. If we have a family of measures μ_i defined on Σ we can get subadditive capacities as follows[5].

$$\bar{\nu}(A) := \sup_i \mu_i(A)$$

We establish the key properties of the functions $\nu(E) = P(s, a, E)$ showing that they are capacities.

Lemma 3. *Let $s \in K$, $a \in \mathsf{Act}$. Then the function ν on the $\approx$-closed subsets of K defined as above is a subadditive capacity as per definition 12.*

Proof. We sketch the proof. Recall that for any C that is an a-computation from s, we write P^C for the induced distribution on the leaves. We have:

---

[4] Like the exact definition of the family of sets on which a capacity is defined.
[5] There are examples showing that not all capacities arise in this way.

- $E_1 \subseteq E_2 \Rightarrow P^C(s, a, E_1) \subseteq P^C(s, a, E_2)$.
- Let $\{E_i\}$ be an increasing sequence of $\approx$-closed sets of states. Then $P^C(s, a, \cup_i E_i) = \sup_i P^C(s, a, E_i)$.
- If $E_1 \cap E_2 = \emptyset$, $P^C(s, a, E_1 \cup E_2) = P^C(s, a, E_1) + P^C(s, a, E_2)$.

Thus, the first three properties and sub-additivity follow from basic properties of sup.

The proof of the fourth property crucially uses compactness. First note that ν is the sup of a family of measures, say Q_i. Measures are down-continuous - considered as functions from the σ-algebra - as an easy consequence of σ-additivity. Since the space is compact the convergence is uniform and the limit of a uniformly convergent family is continuous.

6   pCTL*

We now examine the relation between our processes and a minor variant of pCTL* [1,6], a standard modal logic used for expressing properties of probabilistic systems. We will largely elide formal definitions, instead focusing on explaining the key differences from the treatment of de Alfaro [6] for Markov decision processes (that lack τ and associate *unique* probability distributions with each label at a state).

The logic. There are two kinds of formulas — state formulas, denoted $\phi, \phi', \ldots$, and sequence formulas, denoted $\psi, \psi', \ldots$. These are generated by the following grammar:

$$\phi ::= \top \mid \neg\phi \mid \phi \wedge \phi' \mid E\psi \mid P_{\bowtie q}\psi$$
$$\psi ::= a \mid \phi \mid \neg\psi \mid \psi \wedge \psi' \mid \bigcirc\phi \mid \Diamond\phi \mid \psi\mathcal{U}\psi'$$

In the above, $\bowtie$ is drawn from $\{=, \leq, \geq, <, >\}$ q is a rational in $[0, 1]$, and $a \in \mathsf{Act}$.

We ignore *atomic formulas* which are first order logic formulas over some fixed sets of variables, functions and predicate symbols. One can assume that bisimilar states satisfy the same atomic formulas.

Silent transitions and behaviors We handle the presence of silent transitions by considering a "saturation" of the set of paths from a state, in the spirit of closure under "stuttering".

We define a *behavior* (adapting the definition of de Alfaro [6] to weak transition sequences) from a state s to be a sequence of states and labels $s = s_0, l_0, s_1, l_1, s_2, \ldots$ where $l_i \in \mathsf{Act}$ is the weak label for the transition from s_i to s_{i+1} and the probability of this transition is non-zero. Thus, we are permitting state repetition and skipping of intermediate states reached by τ transitions.

The non-probabilistic formulas For $a \in \mathsf{Act}$, the path formula a is true of behaviors $s_0, a, s_1, \ldots$ whose first weak label is a. Following standard definitions, the state formula $E\psi$ is true at a state s if there is a behavior $s = s_0, a, s_1, \ldots$ at s that satisfies the path formula ψ.

Policies and the probabilistic quantifier A basic policy [6], say η, is a partial function from state sequences to states — thus a policy resolves the nondeterminism completely. We also permit linear combinations of policies $\sum_i \lambda_i \eta_i$, where $\lambda_i > 0, \sum_i \lambda_i = 1$. Each policy η defines a computation $C(\eta, s)$ starting from each state s. We denote by $\mu_{\eta,s}$ the measure on the paths of $C(\eta, s)$ which is induced in a standard way[6].

The path formulas of pCTL* are interpreted on behaviours. We define an operation $C\updownarrow$ from paths to sets of behaviours by closing under repetition of states and under replacing subsequences of the form $s \xrightarrow{\tau} u \xrightarrow{\tau} t$ with $s \xrightarrow{\tau} t$. This is lifted to give a map from sets of paths to sets of behaviours. Now we define $\mu_{\eta,s}$ on behaviours (using the same name as on paths) by $\mu_{\eta,s}(B) = \mu_{\eta,s}(C\updownarrow^{-1}(B))$, where B is a set of behaviours.

Fix a policy η. A set of behaviors is measurable if the set of the corresponding paths in η is measurable. By a routine structural induction, we can show that the sets of behaviours that satisfy path formulas are measurable.

Following standard definitions, the state formula $P_{\bowtie q}\psi$ is true at a state s if for all policies η, the set B of behaviours that satisfy ψ satisfies $\mu_{\eta,s}(B) \bowtie q$.

Soundness of Bisimulation

The key to the proof, as might be expected, is to show that the paths and computations out of bisimilar states "match" sufficiently.

First, we consider behaviors. The following lemma is a standard use of the co-inductive definition of bisimulation.

Lemma 4. *Let $s \approx t$. Then, for any behavior $s = s_0, l_0, s_1, l_1, s_2, \ldots$ from s, there is a behavior, $t = t_0, l'_0, t_1, l'_1, t_2, \ldots$, from t such that:* $(\forall i)\ [s_i \approx t_i]$ *and* $(\forall i)\ [l_i = l'_i]$.

Based on this we define two behaviours to be equivalent if they satisfy the conclusions of Lemma 4.

Next, we move to policies and induced computations. For this, we follow the proof of Theorem 2 (in particular the implication (2) $\Rightarrow$ (3)). This proof has already shown that given a computation C from a state s, and given t bisimilar to s, there is a computation C' from t that assigns the same probabilities to the leaves of C. We will now generalize this to all paths — given a computation C_η induced by a policy η from a state s, we show that for any bisimilar state t, there is a policy η' that assigns at least the probabilities assigned by η to all the paths in C_η. We use the equivalence of our definitions with those of Philippou, Lee and Sokolsky [17]. The first case of their definition permits the simulation of nondeterministic edges. The second case of their definition permits the simulation of probabilistic branches.

Lemma 5. *Let s, t be bisimilar states. Let η be a policy and let $C(\eta, s)$ be the induced η-computation from s. Then, there is a policy η' such that every path in $C(\eta, s)$ is equivalent to a behaviour in $C(\eta', t)$ with the same probability.*

---

[6] We elide well-known measure-theoretic details in this paper.

Proof. It suffices to prove this for the case where η is a basic policy.

The proof is a routine induction. We write C_η for $C(\eta, s)$ and $C_{\eta'}$ for $C(\eta', t)$. C_η has countably many transitions. Consider any ordering o of these transitions such that a transition occurs after all the transitions leading upto it. We construct $C_{\eta'}$ by mimicking transitions in the order prescribed by o. Our induction hypothesis is that at the i'th stage: every path in the subtree induced by the first i transitions (as per o) is a behavior in $C_{\eta'}^i$ computation from t with the same probability.

Let the $i + 1$'st transition be a transition at u. Let p be the probability of the path from t to u in C_η. Let V be the set of leaves in $C_{\eta'}^i$ such that:

- $v \approx u$
- The path from s to u in C_η is a behavior corresponding to the path from t to v in $C_{\eta'}^i$

The measure of V in $C_{\eta'}^i$, say q, is at least p by the induction hypothesis.

There are two cases based on the kind of the $(i + 1)$st transition.

1. The $(i+1)$st transition is a nondeterministic transition $u \xrightarrow{b} u'$. This transition can be matched by computations from all elements of V: by definition these computations reach $[u']$ with probability 1 on weak label b.

2. The $(i + 1)$st transition is a probabilistic transition $u \to Q$. There are two cases depending on whether $Q([u]) = 0$ or not.

   If $Q([u]) = 0$, this transition can be matched by computations from all elements of V: by theorem 2 these computations reach the leaves with weak label τ and assign probabilities in accordance with Q.

   If $Q([u]) = r > 0$, consider the transition from u to Q' where: $Q'[v] = \frac{Q[v]}{1-r}$, if $u \notin [v]$ and $Q'([u]) = 0$. Pick any element $v \in V$. Since $v \approx u$, by theorem 2, this computation reaches the leaves with weak label τ and assign probabilities in accordance with Q'. The required transition to Q from v is given by a linear combination (with coefficient $1 - r$) of this computation with the computation consisting only of v (with coefficient r).

In either case, let $C_{\eta'}^{i'}$ be the extension of $C_{\eta'}^i$ by these matching transitions. $C_{\eta'}^{i+1}$ is got by a linear combination $t \Rightarrow [\lambda \times C_{\eta'}^{i'} + (1 - \lambda) \times C_{\eta'}^i]$, where $\lambda = p/q$.

Lemmas 4 and 5 yield the desired theorem by a standard induction on the structure of formulas.

Theorem 3. *If $s \approx t$, then for all pCTL* state formulas ϕ, $s \models \phi$ iff $t \models \phi$.*

Proof. We sketch the case of $P_{\geq q}\psi$. Let s satisfy $P_{\geq q}\psi$. Every policy induces a set of computations from s. For every computation from s, using lemma 5, there is a computation from t that attributes a larger measure to the set of behaviors from t that satisfy ψ. Hence, t satisfies $P_{\geq q}\psi$.

Completeness

We proceed now to completeness. Here the fact that we have a capacity plays a key role, as we use the downward continuity property of capacities.

We identify $\mathcal{L}$, a sub-fragment of the state formulas of the pCTL* variant above, that suffices for completeness. These are generated by the following grammar:

$$\phi ::= \top \mid \phi_1 \wedge \phi_2 \mid \phi_1 \vee \phi_2 \mid \neg\phi \mid \langle a \rangle_{\geq q} \phi$$

where $a \in \mathsf{Act}$ (including τ), q is a rational and $\langle a \rangle_{\geq q}\phi$ is shorthand for $\neg P_{<1-q}$ $[a \wedge \bigcirc\phi]$. Thus, a state s satisfies $\langle a \rangle_{\geq q}\phi$ iff there is a policy η such that the computation induced by η assigns probability greater than q to the states satisfying ϕ reachable on a weak a transition. More succinctly, s satisfies $\langle a \rangle_{\geq q}\phi$ if $P(s, a, \{t \mid t \text{ satisfies } \phi\}) \geq q$.

Theorem 4. *If two states satisfy the same formulas of $\mathcal{L}$, then they are bisimilar.*

Proof. Let R be the equivalence relation defined by the formulas of $\mathcal{L}$. Let s and t be two R-related states. We need to prove that for every R-closed set X, $P(s, \{a\}, X) = P(t, \{a\}, X)$, where $a \neq \tau$. By using formulas of the form $\langle a \rangle_{\geq q}\phi$, we obtain the required equality for sets of states X that are denotations of formulas, i.e. $X = \{s' \mid s' \text{ satisfies } \phi\}$, $\phi \in \mathcal{L}$.

Since the state space is countable every R-closed set is a countable union of equivalence classes. Every equivalence class is described by countably many formulas and - since we have negation - can be described as the intersection of countably many sets of the form $\{s|s \text{ satisfies } \phi\}$. Thus every R-closed set, say Y, is of the form

$$Y = \cup_{i=1}^{\infty} \cap_{j=1}^{\infty} X_{ij}$$

where the X_{ij} are the denotations of formulas.

We define

$$Y_i := \cap_{j=1}^{\infty}[\cup_{k=1}^{i} X_{kj}].$$

Note that Y_i forms an increasing family in the subset ordering. Furthermore $\cup_{i=1}^{\infty} Y_i = Y$ by distributivity. Now, for each i, the sets $Z_i^{(l)} := \cap_{j=1}^{l} \cup_{k=1}^{i} X_{kj}$ are a decreasing family as l increases and they are the denotations of formulas, since there is conjunction and disjunction in the logic. Thus the two capacities will agree on each $Z_i^{(l)}$ and by up continuity they will agree on Y_i and thus, by down continuity, they agree on Y.

The proof for $P(s, \varepsilon, X) = P(t, \varepsilon, X)$ is similar except for the use of the formulas $\langle \tau \rangle \phi$ and is omitted.

7   Conclusions

The main thrust of the present paper has been to elucidate the interaction between probability and nondeterminism. The definition of weak bisimulation that we have used generalizes the elegant treatment of Philippou, Lee and Sokolsky from finite state to countable systems. We have emphasized two features of their definition that were left implicit by them, namely the loss of additivity and the need for considering linear structure when matching weak transitions. The main new result of our analysis is that weak bisimulation is sound and complete for (a minor variant of) pCTL*.

It is worth taking a retrospective view of some of the mathematical ideas in the proofs. The basic loss that we have had to struggle with is the loss of σ-additivity. The heart of any completeness proof of this type is arguing that equality of the transition probabilities to sets of states defined by the logic forces equality of all the transition probabilities. Such an argument rests on theorems that guarantee equality of measures given equality on a suitable generating set for the σ-field. These uniqueness theorems heavily rely on σ-additivity. Thus we were led to consider what structure we do have given that we do not have a probability measure. The fact that we have capacities and in particular that capacities satisfy strong continuity properties (both upward and downward) turns out to be strong enough to rescue the uniqueness theorems that we need. What remains to argue is that we really have the property of a capacity. Here the compactness property turns out to be crucial.

In closely related work [11] we have shown that one can develop a metric for weak bisimulation analogous to our previous treatment of metrics for strong bisimulation [10]. In this work we heavily use linear programming and duality.

The present treatment is for discrete systems, we are considering two new directions: continuous state spaces and continuous time. We have preliminary results on continuous time, namely we have shown completeness for continuous stochastic logic [12].

References

1. A. Aziz, V. Singhal, F. Balarin, R. K. Brayton, and A. L. Sangiovanni-Vincentelli. It usually works:the temporal logic of stochastic systems. In *Proceedings of the Conference on Computer-Aided Verification*, number 939 in Lecture Notes In Computer Science. Springer-Verlag, 1995. 365
2. C. Baier and H. Hermanns. Weak bisimulation for fully probabilistic processes. In *Proceedings of the 1997 International Conference on Computer Aided Verification*, number 1254 in Lecture Notes In Computer Science. Springer-Verlag, 1997. 356
3. E. Bandini and R. Segala. Axiomatizations for probabilistic bisimulation. In *Proceedings of the 28th International Colloquium on Automata, Languages and Programming*, number 2076 in Lecture Notes In Computer Science, pages 370–381. Springer-Verlag, July 2001. 361
4. R. Blute, J. Desharnais, A. Edalat, and P. Panangaden. Bisimulation for labelled Markov processes. In *Proceedings of the Twelfth IEEE Symposium On Logic In Computer Science, Warsaw, Poland.*, 1997. 356, 360
5. G. Choquet. Theory of capacities. *Ann. Inst. Fourier (Grenoble)*, 5:131–295, 1953. 357, 364
6. L. de Alfaro. *Formal Verification of Probabilistic Systems*. PhD thesis, Stanford University, 1997. Technical Report STAN-CS-TR-98-1601. 357, 365, 366

7. C. Dellacherie. *Capacités et Processus Stochastiques.* Springer-Verlag, 1972. 357

8. J. Desharnais, A. Edalat, and P. Panangaden. A logical characterization of bisimulation for labeled Markov processes. In *proceedings of the 13th IEEE Symposium On Logic In Computer Science, Indianapolis*, pages 478–489. IEEE Press, June 1998. 356

9. J. Desharnais, A. Edalat, and P. Panangaden. Bisimulation for labeled Markov processes. *Information and Computation*, 2002. 356, 360

10. J. Desharnais, V. Gupta, R. Jagadeesan, and P. Panangaden. Metrics for labeled Markov processes. In Jos Baeten and Sjouke Mauw, editors, *Proceedings of CONCUR99*, number 1664 in Lecture Notes in Computer Science. Springer-Verlag, 1999. 369

11. J. Desharnais, V. Gupta, R. Jagadeesan, and P. Panangaden. The metric analogue of weak bisimulation for labelled Markov processes. In *Proceedings of the Seventeenth Annual IEEE Symposium On Logic In Computer Science*, July 2002. 369

12. J. Desharnais and P. Panangaden. Continuous stochastic logic characterizes bisimulation for continuous-time markov processes. Available from `http://www-acaps.cs.mcgill.ca/~prakash/pubs.html`, 2001. 369

13. Hans A. Hansson. *Time and Probability in Formal Design of Distributed Systems*, volume 1 of *Real-time Safety-critical Systems*. Elseiver, 1994. 356, 357, 358

14. J. G. Kemeny and J. L. Snell. *Finite Markov Chains*. Van Nostrand, 1960. 356

15. K. G. Larsen and A. Skou. Bisimulation through probablistic testing. *Information and Computation*, 94:1–28, 1991. 356

16. P. A. Meyer. *Probability and Potentials*. Blaisdell, 1966. 357

17. A. Philippou, I. Lee, and O. Sokolsky. Weal bisimulation for probabilistic processes. In C. Palamidessi, editor, *Proceedings of CONCUR 2000*, number 1877 in Lecture Notes In Computer Science, pages 334–349. Springer-Verlag, 2000. 355, 356, 357, 358, 362, 366

18. D. Schmeidler. Subjective probability without additivity. Technical report, Foerder Institute of Economic Research, 1984. 357

19. R. Segala. *Modeling and Verification of Randomized Distributed Real-Time Systems*. PhD thesis, MIT, Dept. of Electrical Engineering and Computer Science, 1995. Also appears as technical report MIT/LCS/TR-676. 356, 359

20. R. Segala and N. Lynch. Probabilistic simulations for probabilistic processes. In B. Jonsson and J. Parrow, editors, *Proceedings of CONCUR94*, number 836 in Lecture Notes In Computer Science, pages 481–496. Springer-Verlag, 1994. 356, 357

Decision Algorithms for Probabilistic Bisimulation*

Stefano Cattani[1] and Roberto Segala[2]

[1] School of Computer Science, The University of Birmingham
Birmingham B15 2TT, United Kingdom
[2] Dipartimento di Informatica, Università di Verona
Strada Le Grazie 15, Ca' Vignal 2 37134 Verona, Italy

Abstract. We propose decision algorithms for bisimulation relations defined on probabilistic automata, a model for concurrent nondeterministic systems with randomization. The algorithms decide both strong and weak bisimulation relations based on deterministic as well as randomized schedulers. These algorithms extend and complete other known algorithms for simpler relations and models. The algorithm we present for strong probabilistic bisimulation has polynomial time complexity, while the algorithm for weak probabilistic bisimulation is exponential; however we argue that the latter is feasible in practice.

1 Introduction

Randomization is attracting increasing attention in computer science, and consequently the study of modeling and verification techniques for randomized concurrent systems becomes fundamental. An evidence of this fact is the existence of a considerable literature about models for concurrent probabilistic systems and related techniques [1, 7, 9, 11, 16, 18, 24, 25]. This paper focuses on the model of probabilistic automata [21], an extension of labeled transition systems with probabilities, and on verification techniques based on probabilistic extensions of bisimulation relations [17] as defined in [22].

Probabilistic automata [21] extend labeled transition systems by generalizing the notion of a transition, which leads to a probability distribution over states rather than to a single state. Then, several notions and techniques for labeled transition systems can be extended directly to probabilistic automata. Among these, bisimulation relations [22, 8, 16] are the focus of this paper. Bisimulation was first defined in the context of CCS [17], and turned out to be a fundamental relation for its simplicity and the elegance of its axiomatization. It was first extended to a model with randomization in [16] and then extended to a model with nondeterminism and randomization in [8]. The model of [8] is also known as the alternating model of concurrent probabilistic systems as opposed to the non-alternating model given by probabilistic automata. The main restriction in the alternating model is that each state either enables several transitions that

---

* Supported in part by EPSRC grants GR/N22960 and GR/M13046

L. Brim et al. (Eds.): CONCUR 2002, LNCS 2421, pp. 371–386, 2002.
© Springer-Verlag Berlin Heidelberg 2002

lead to a single state (nondeterministic state), or a single unlabeled transition that leads to a probability distribution over states (probabilistic state). Probabilistic automata allow more general notions of bisimulation, which turn out to be different compared to the alternating model as soon as we use randomization to resolve nondeterminism. Such new bisimulation relations, both in their strong and weak versions, are studied in [22]. Bisimulation relations are also studied in the context of stochastic process algebras [12, 5, 10], where it is shown that bisimulation coincides with the notion of lumping for Markov chains [12].

A problem that is subject of considerable study is the search for decision algorithms for bisimulation [3, 20, 4]. The problem is solved already in the context of stochastic process algebras [3], in the context of the alternating model [20] and in the context of probabilistic automata with respect of strong bisimulation [2]. However, it is still open in the context of probabilistic automata, since the restrictions imposed to the alternating model seem to guarantee a lot of extra structure that simplifies decision procedures; in the non alternating model bisimulation gives rise to two different relations under deterministic and randomized schedulers respectively, while in the alternating model bisimulation gives rise to the same relation no matter whether randomization is used or not.

In this paper we give decision algorithms for strong bisimulation under randomized schedulers (strong probabilistic bisimulation) and for weak bisimulation under randomized schedulers (weak probabilistic bisimulation). The algorithms are instances of the well established partitioning technique [13, 19], where large equivalence classes are refined into smaller classes; thus, our presentation concentrates on how to define a splitter for each of the relations that we analyze. The splitter for strong probabilistic bisimulation considers two states s_1 and s_2 as equivalent if and only if for each transition that leaves s_1 there is a matching convex combination of transitions that leave from s_2 and vice versa, where the convex combination of transitions expresses the ability of the scheduler to use randomization. Operationally, if we take the extreme points of the convex hull generated by the transitions that are labeled by a specific action, then the extreme points of the convex hulls for s_1 and s_2 must coincide. The splitter for weak probabilistic bisimulation is based again on convex hulls; however, we have to consider arbitrary sequences of transitions that are labeled by internal actions. Since such transitions are potentially infinite, we identify a sufficiently powerful finite class of schedulers that can characterize the extremal points of the convex hulls to be examined.

The algorithms that we propose for the probabilistic relations are based on the problem of computing the extreme points of the convex hull generated by a set of n points in a d-dimensional space; the extreme points can be computed by solving $O(n)$ linear programming problems. Unfortunately, in the case of weak probabilistic bisimulation, the number of points generating the convex hull can be exponential in the number of states of the automaton. Despite the negative result concerning the complexity of our decision algorithms, we show that from a practical perspective our algorithms are feasible since the worst case scenarios are very unlikely to occur.

The rest of the paper is organized as follows. Section 2 contains some background on measure theory and convex hulls and describes our notational conventions; Section 3 introduces the model of probabilistic automata, and Section 4 describes the bisimulation relations of [22]; Section 5 describes the general structure of the decision algorithms, while Sections 6 and 7 describe the details of the algorithms for strong probabilistic bisimulation, and weak probabilistic bisimulation, respectively; finally, Section 8 contains some concluding remarks.

2   Preliminaries

Probability Spaces and Measures. A *σ-field* over a set X is a set $\mathcal{F} \subseteq 2^X$ that includes X and is closed under complement and countable union. Observe that 2^X is a σ-field over X. A *measurable space* is a pair $(X, \mathcal{F})$ where X is a set and $\mathcal{F}$ is a σ-field over X. The set X is also called the *sample space*. A measurable space $(X, \mathcal{F})$ is called *discrete* if $\mathcal{F} = 2^X$. Given a measurable space $(X, \mathcal{F})$, a *measure* over $(X, \mathcal{F})$ is a function $\mu : \mathcal{F} \to \mathbb{R}^{\geq 0}$ such that, for each countable collection $\{X_i\}_{i \in I}$ of pairwise disjoint elements of $\mathcal{F}$, $\mu[\cup_I X_i] = \sum_I \mu[X_i]$. A *probability measure* over a measurable space $(X, \mathcal{F})$ is a measure μ over $(X, \mathcal{F})$ such that $\mu[X] = 1$; a *sub-probability measure* over $(X, \mathcal{F})$ is a measure μ over $\mathcal{F}$ such that $\mu[X] \leq 1$. A measure over a discrete measurable space is called a *discrete measure*. Sometimes we refer to probability measures as *distributions*.

Given a set X, denote by $Disc(X)$ the set of discrete probability measures over the measurable space $(X, 2^X)$, and by $SubDisc(X)$ the set of discrete sub-probability measures over the measurable space $(X, 2^X)$. We call a discrete (sub-)probability measure a *Dirac* measure if either it assigns measure 1 to exactly one object or it assigns measure 0 to all objects. Given a discrete sub-probability measure μ of $SubDisc(X)$, denote by $\mu[\perp]$ the value $1 - \mu[X]$. In the sequel discrete sub-probability measures are used to describe progress. If the measure of the sample space is not 1, then it means that with some non-zero probability the system does not progress. We use the symbol $\perp$ to denote this fact.

In this paper we refer also to semi-Markov processes. A semi-Markov process is a pair (Q, μ) where Q is a set and $\mu : Q \times Q \to [0, 1]$ is a function, called a *transition function*, such that for each element $q \in Q$ the function is the probability of reaching an element from X when leaving from q.

Convex Sets and Convex Hulls. A subset S of $\mathbb{R}^d$ is *convex* if for each pair of points $s_1, s_2 \in S$, the segment joining s_1 and s_2, i.e., the set of points $T = \{ts_1 + (1 - t)s_2 \mid 0 \leq t \leq 1\}$, is entirely contained in S. Given a subset S of $\mathbb{R}^d$, the *convex hull* of S, denoted by $CHull(S)$, is the smallest convex set that contains S. A convex set S is said to be *finitely generated* if there is a finite set T, called a *generator*, such that $S = CHull(T)$. In such case there is also a unique minimum set T that generates S. We denote such minimum set T by $Gen(S)$. The elements of $Gen(S)$ are called the *extreme points* of S.

Given a set of points $S = \{s_1, \ldots, s_n\}$, we say that s is a *convex combination* of the points in S if there exists a set of non negative weights $t_1, \ldots, t_n$ such that

$\sum_{i=1}^{n} t_i = 1$ and $s = \sum_{i=1}^{n} t_i * s_i$. The definition is extended in the natural way to give the convex combination of an infinite countable set.

In the sequel, we rely on the fact that there are algorithms to determine the extreme points of the convex hull generated by a given set of n points. This is also known as the "redundancy removal for a point set S" in $\mathbb{R}^d$. This problem has a polynomial complexity as it can be reduced to solving $O(n)$ linear programming problems, for which many polynomial time algorithms are available [6].

3   Probabilistic Automata

Probabilistic Automata. A *probabilistic automaton* $\mathcal{A}$ is a tuple $(S, \bar{s}, \Sigma, \mathcal{D})$ where S is a set of states, $\bar{s} \in S$ is the *start state*, Σ is a set of *actions* and $\mathcal{D} \subseteq S \times \Sigma \times Disc(S)$ is the *transition relation*. The set of actions Σ is partitioned into two sets E and H of *external* and *hidden* actions, respectively. For the purpose of this paper, we will consider only automata with finite state sets.

For convenience, states are ranged over by r, q, s, actions are ranged over by a, b, c, internal actions are ranged over by τ, and discrete distributions are ranged over by μ. We also denote the generic elements of a probabilistic automaton $\mathcal{A}$ by $S, \bar{s}, \Sigma, E, H$ and $\mathcal{D}$, and we propagate primes and indices when necessary. Thus, the elements of a probabilistic automaton $\mathcal{A}'_i$ are $S'_i, \bar{s}'_i, \Sigma'_i, E'_i, H'_i$ and $\mathcal{D}'_i$.

An element of $\mathcal{D}$ is called a *transition*. A transition (s, a, μ) is said to leave from state s, to be labeled by a, and to lead to μ. We also say that s enables action a and that action a is enabled from s. Finally, we say that the transition (s, a, μ) is enabled from s. The transition (s, a, μ) is denoted alternatively by $s \xrightarrow{a} \mu$. Given a state q, denote by $\mathcal{D}(q)$ the set of transitions that leave from q, that is, $\mathcal{D}(q) = \{(s, a, \mu) \in \mathcal{D} \mid s = q\}$.

The reactive models of [7] are probabilistic automata where each state enables at most one transition for each action. In line with the process algebraic terminology, we call such probabilistic automata *deterministic*. Ordinary automata are probabilistic automata where each transition leads to a Dirac distribution; we call them *Dirac* automata. The alternating model [9] can be seen as probabilistic automata where each state either enables a unique transition labeled by an internal action or several transitions that lead to Dirac distributions.

Executions and Traces. A *potential execution* of a probabilistic automaton $\mathcal{A}$ is a finite or infinite sequence of alternating states and actions, $\alpha = s_0 a_1 s_1 a_2 s_2 \ldots$ starting from a state and, if the sequence is finite, ending with a state. Define the *length* of a potential execution α, denoted by $|\alpha|$, to be the number of occurrences of actions in α. If α is an infinite sequence, then $|\alpha| = \infty$. For a natural number $i \leq |\alpha|$, denote by $\alpha[i]$ the state s_i. In particular $\alpha[0]$ is the first state of α. For a finite execution α denote by $\alpha[\bot]$ the last state of α. We say that a potential execution α is a *prefix* of a potential execution α', denoted by $\alpha \leq \alpha'$ if the sequence α is a prefix of the sequence α'. An *execution* of a probabilistic automaton $\mathcal{A}$ is a potential execution of $\mathcal{A}$, $\alpha = s_0 a_1 s_2 a_2 s_2 \ldots$ such that for each $i < |\alpha|$ there exists a transition (s_{i-1}, a_i, μ_i) of $\mathcal{D}$ where $\mu_i[s_i] > 0$. An execution is said to be *initial* if $\alpha[0] = \bar{s}$. We denote by $execs(\mathcal{A})$ the set of executions of $\mathcal{A}$, and by $execs^*(\mathcal{A})$ the set of finite executions of $\mathcal{A}$.

The *trace* of a potential execution α, denoted by $trace(\alpha)$ is the sub-sequence of α composed by its external actions. A trace is used to observe the externally visible communication that takes place within a potential execution.

Combined Transitions. Nondeterminism in a probabilistic automaton arises from the fact that a state may enable several transitions. Resolving the nondeterminism in a state s means choosing one of the transitions that are enabled from s. However, being in a randomized environment, transitions may be chosen randomly. In this case we obtain an object which we call a combined transition.

Given a state s and a distribution $\sigma \in SubDisc(\mathcal{D}(s))$, define the *combined transition* according to σ to be the pair (s, μ_σ), where $\mu_\sigma \in SubDisc(\Sigma \times S)$ is defined for each pair (a, q) as

$$\mu_\sigma[(a,q)] = \sum_{(s,a,\mu)} \sigma[(s,a,\mu)]\,\mu[q]. \tag{1}$$

In practice a transition is chosen among the transitions enabled from s according to σ, and then the chosen transition is scheduled. The chosen transitions may be labeled by different actions, and thus the distribution that appears in a combined transition includes actions as well. Observe that, since σ is a sub-probability measure, we consider also the fact that with some non-zero probability no transition is scheduled from s. We denote a combined transition (s, μ) alternatively by $s \longrightarrow_C \mu$. Whenever there exists an action a such that $\mu[(a, S)] = 1$ we denote the corresponding combined transition alternatively by $s \xrightarrow{a}_C \mu'$ where $\mu' \in Disc(S)$ is defined for each state q as $\mu'[q] = \mu[(a,q)]$.

Schedulers. A *scheduler* for a probabilistic automaton $\mathcal{A}$ is a function $\sigma :$ $execs^*(\mathcal{A}) \to SubDisc(\mathcal{D})$ such that for each finite execution α, we have that $\sigma(\alpha) \in SubDisc(\mathcal{D}(\alpha[\bot]))$. In other words, a scheduler is the entity that resolves nondeterminism in a probabilistic automaton by choosing randomly either to stop or to perform one of the transitions that are enabled from the current state. The choices of a scheduler are based on the past history.

We say that a scheduler is *Dirac* if it assigns a Dirac distribution to each execution. We say that a scheduler is *simple* if for each pair of finite executions $\alpha_1, \alpha_2 \in execs(\mathcal{A})$ such that $\alpha_1[\bot] = \alpha_2[\bot]$ we have that $\sigma(\alpha_1) = \sigma(\alpha_2)$. Finally, we say that a scheduler is *determinate* is for each pair of finite executions $\alpha_1, \alpha_2 \in execs(\mathcal{A})$ such that $\alpha_1[\bot] = \alpha_2[\bot]$ and $trace(\alpha_1) = trace(\alpha_2)$ we have that $\sigma(\alpha_1) = \sigma(\alpha_2)$.

A Dirac scheduler is a scheduler that does not use randomization in its choices. We could call it a deterministic scheduler; however the name Dirac is more consistent with the rest of our terminology and avoids overloading of the term nondeterministic. Simple schedulers base their choices only on the current state without looking at the past history, while determinate scheduler may look at the externally visible part of the past history. Determinate scheduler were introduced in [20] for the purpose of defining a finite class of schedulers that would characterize probabilistic bisimulation in the alternate model. In this paper we use determinate schedulers for the same purpose as in [20].

Consider a scheduler σ and a finite execution α with last state q. The distribution $\sigma(\alpha)$ describes how to move from q. The resulting combined transition is the combined transition according to the distribution $\sigma(\alpha)$, which we denote by $(q, \mu_{\sigma(\alpha)})$.

Probabilistic Executions. The result of the action of a scheduler from a start state s can be represented as a semi-Markov process whose states are finite executions of $\mathcal{A}$ with start state s. These objects are called *probabilistic executions*.

Formally, the probabilistic execution of $\mathcal{A}$ identified by a scheduler σ and a state s is a semi-Markov process (Q, μ) where Q is the set of finite executions of $\mathcal{A}$ that start with s, and μ is 0 except for pairs of the form (q, qar), where it is defined as follows: $\mu[q, qar] = \mu_{\sigma(\alpha)}[(a, r)]$.

Given a probabilistic execution we can define a probability measure over executions as follows. The sample space is the set of executions that start with s; the σ-field is the σ-field generated by the set of *cones*, sets of the form $C_\alpha = \{\alpha' \in execs(\mathcal{A}) \mid \alpha \leq \alpha'\}$; the measure is the unique extension $\mu_{\sigma,s}$ of the measure defined over the cones by the following equation: $\mu_{\sigma,s}[C_{sa_1 s_1 \ldots a_n s_n}] = \prod_{i \in \{1, \ldots n\}} \mu_{\sigma(sa_1 s_1 \ldots a_{i-1} s_{i-1})}[(a_i, s_i)]$. This definition is justified by standard measure theoretical arguments [15]. In the sequel we denote a probabilistic execution alternatively by the probability measure over executions that it identifies.

Observe that any reachability property is measurable since it can be expressed as a countable union of cones. Furthermore, observe that the probability of a finite execution α is $\mu_{\sigma,s}[\alpha] = \mu_{\sigma,s}[C_\alpha]\mu_{\sigma(\alpha)}[\bot]$. The probability of α represents the probability of executing α and then stopping. The probability of the set of finite executions represents the probability of stopping eventually.

Weak Transitions. We are often interested in transitions that abstract from internal computation. Weak transitions as defined in [17] serve this purpose. In [23] weak transitions are generalized to probabilistic automata by stating that a weak transition is essentially a probabilistic execution that stops with probability 1 and whose traces at the stopping points consist of a unique action.

Formally, we say that there is a *weak transition* from state s to μ labeled by an action a, denoted by $s \overset{a}{\Longrightarrow} \mu$, if there is a probabilistic execution $\mu_{\sigma,s}$, with σ a Dirac scheduler, such that

1. $\mu_{\sigma,s}[execs^*(\mathcal{A})] = 1$, and
2. for each $\alpha \in execs^*(\mathcal{A})$, if $\mu_{\sigma,s}[\alpha] > 0$ then $trace(\alpha) = a$.
3. for each state q, $\mu_{\sigma,s}[\{\alpha \in execs^*(\mathcal{A}) \mid \alpha[\bot] = q\}] = \mu[q]$.

If we remove the Dirac condition on the scheduler σ, then we say that there is a *combined weak transition* from s to μ labeled by a, denoted by $s \overset{a}{\Longrightarrow}_C \mu$.

Condition 1 states that the probability of stopping is 1; Condition 2 states that at each stopping point only action a has occurred among the external actions; Condition 3 states that the distribution over states at the stopping points is μ.

4   Bisimulation

We can now define the bisimulation relations that we are interested to study following the approach of [23]. We distinguish between strong and weak bisimulations, and within each class we distinguish between bisimulations based on Dirac schedulers (strong bisimulation and weak bisimulation relations) and bisimulations based on general schedulers (strong probabilistic bisimulation and weak probabilistic bisimulation relations).

We first need to lift an equivalence relation on states to an equivalence relation on distributions over states. Following [16], two distributions are equivalent if they assign the same probabilities to the same equivalence classes. Formally, given an equivalence relation $\mathcal{R}$ on a set of states Q, we say that two probability distributions μ_1 and μ_2 of $Disc(Q)$ are equivalent according to $\mathcal{R}$, denoted by $\mu_1 \equiv_{\mathcal{R}} \mu_2$, iff for each equivalence class $\mathcal{C}$ of $\mathcal{R}$, $\mu_1[\mathcal{C}] = \mu_2[\mathcal{C}]$.

Strong Probabilistic Bisimulation. Let $\mathcal{A}_1, \mathcal{A}_2$ be two probabilistic automata. An equivalence relation $\mathcal{R}$ on $S_1 \cup S_2$ is a *strong probabilistic bisimulation* if, for each pair of states $q, r \in S_1 \cup S_2$ such that $q \mathcal{R} r$, if $q \xrightarrow{a} \mu$ for some distribution μ, then there exists a distribution μ' such that $\mu \equiv_{\mathcal{R}} \mu'$ and $r \xrightarrow{a}_C \mu'$.

The probabilistic automata $\mathcal{A}_1, \mathcal{A}_2$ are said to be strongly probabilistically bisimilar if there exists a strong probabilistic bisimulation $\mathcal{R}$ on $S_1 \cup S_2$ such that $\bar{s}_1 \mathcal{R} \bar{s}_2$. We denote a strong probabilistic bisimulation relation also by $\sim_c$.

The non probabilistic version of strong bisimulation [16, 8, 22] is obtained by disallowing combined transitions in the definition above. Strong probabilistic bisimulation was first defined in [22], but it also gives rise to meaningful relations for reactive systems and for the alternating model. However, in the two restrictive models strong bisimulation and strong probabilistic bisimulation coincide.

Weak Probabilistic Bisimulation. Let $\mathcal{A}_1, \mathcal{A}_2$ be two probabilistic automata. An equivalence relation $\mathcal{R}$ on $S_1 \cup S_2$ is a *weak probabilistic bisimulation* if, for each pair of states $q, r \in S_1 \cup S_2$ such that $q \mathcal{R} r$, if $q \xrightarrow{a} \mu$ for some distribution μ, then there exists a distribution μ' such that $\mu \equiv_{\mathcal{R}} \mu'$ and $r \xmapsto{a}_C \mu'$.

The probabilistic automata $\mathcal{A}_1, \mathcal{A}_2$ are said to be weakly probabilistically bisimilar if there exists a weak probabilistic bisimulation $\mathcal{R}$ on $S_1 \cup S_2$ such that $\bar{s}_1 \mathcal{R} \bar{s}_2$. We denote a weak probabilistic bisimulation relation also by $\approx_c$.

The non probabilistic version of weak bisimulation [22] is obtained by disallowing combined transitions in the definition above. Weak probabilistic bisimulation was first defined in [22]. Decision algorithms for weak probabilistic bisimulation in the alternating model are studied in [20]. Similarly to the strong case, there is a very close relationship between weak bisimulation and weak probabilistic bisimulation in the alternating model.

5   The Algorithms

In this section we define the general scheme of the algorithms that decide whether two probabilistic automata are bisimilar according to one of the definitions of

Section 4. The approach we use in all cases is the partitioning technique of [13, 19]: we start with a single equivalence class containing all the states and we refine it until we get the equivalence classes induced by the bisimulation relation under examination.

To refine a partition, we find an element (*splitter*) of the partition that violates the definition of bisimulation and then subdivide it further. Formally, given a probabilistic automaton $\mathcal{A} = (S, \bar{s}, \Sigma, \mathcal{D})$ and a partition $\mathcal{W}$ of S, we say that a triplet $(\mathcal{C}, a, \mathcal{W})$, $\mathcal{C} \in \mathcal{W}$ and $a \in \Sigma$, is a splitter if there are two states $s, t \in \mathcal{C}$ that prevent the partition from being a bisimulation.

Algorithm 1 describes the main structure of the decision procedure Decide-Bisim. It is based on two functions: function FindSplit returns a splitter $(\mathcal{C}, a, \mathcal{W})$ for the current partition $\mathcal{W}$ if one exists, and returns the empty set otherwise; function Refine, given a splitter $(\mathcal{C}, a, \mathcal{W})$, distinguishes the states in $\mathcal{C}$ that are incompatible, and divides $\mathcal{C}$ into subclasses, thus refining the current partition.

Algorithm 1. *Decide whether two probabilistic automata* $\mathcal{A}_1 = (S_1, \bar{s}_1, \Sigma_1, \mathcal{D}_1)$ *and* $\mathcal{A}_2 = (S_2, \bar{s}_2, \Sigma_2, \mathcal{D}_2)$ *are related according to some bisimulation* $\mathcal{R}$.

DecideBisim $(\mathcal{A}_1, \mathcal{A}_2) =$
    $\mathcal{W} = \{S_1 \cup S_2\};$
    $(\mathcal{C}, a, \mathcal{W}) = \text{FindSplit}(\mathcal{W});$
    while $\mathcal{C} \neq \emptyset$ do
        $\mathcal{W} = \text{Refine}(\mathcal{W}, \mathcal{C}, a);$
        $(\mathcal{C}, a, \mathcal{W}) = \text{FindSplit}(\mathcal{W});$
    if ($\bar{s}_1$ *and* $\bar{s}_2$ *are related*) then
        return $\mathcal{W};$
    else return false;

Algorithm 1 works as follows: it starts with one single equivalence class and then refines it through the while loop. It is easy to see that in each iteration, if a splitter is found, then the refinement produces a partition that is finer than the previous one. When no splitter is found, then DecideBisim simply checks whether the start states of $\mathcal{A}_1$ and $\mathcal{A}_2$ are equivalent according to the current partition.

Function FindSplit (see Algorithm 2) has a two phase structure which is independent of the relation we study. In the first phase, FindSplit computes information about the transitions enabled from each state s; then, in the second phase, it compares the information of each pair of states in the same equivalence class to check whether they should be separated.

Algorithm 2. *Finds a splitter in partition* $\mathcal{W}$.

FindSplit($\mathcal{W}$*)* $=$
    foreach $s \in S_a \cup S_b$, $a \in \Sigma$
        $I(s, a) = \text{ComputeInfo}(s, a, \mathcal{W})$
    foreach $\mathcal{C}_i \in \mathcal{W}$, $s, t \in \mathcal{C}_i$, $a \in \Sigma$
        if $I(s, a)/\mathcal{W} \neq I(t, a)/\mathcal{W}$
            return $(\mathcal{C}_i, a, \mathcal{W});$
    return $\emptyset;$

Finally, function Refine has a very simple structure: it refines each partition by comparing states pairwise and grouping those with the compatible information into new equivalence classes. We omit the pseudo code from this paper.

In the following sections we show how to compute the information $I(s, a)$ and how to compare such information for strong probabilistic bisimulation and weak probabilistic bisimulation. The technique can also be used for strong non probabilistic bisimulation as $I(s, a)$ is described by the finite set of transitions leaving state s and labeled by a (the resulting algorithm is proposed in [2]).

For strong (resp, weak) probabilistic bisimulation $I(s, a)$ describes the set of combined transitions (resp, weak combined transitions) that are enabled from s and labeled by a. In both cases, each transition can be described simply by the distribution over states that it leads to, which can be seen as well as a tuple in a n-dimensional space, where n is the number of states. Formally, if we express S as $\{s_1, s_2, \ldots, s_n\}$, thus numbering the states, a transition (s, a, μ) of $I(s, a)$ can be represented by the point $(p_1, p_2, \ldots, p_n)$ in $\mathbb{R}^n$ where $p_i = \mu(s_i)$ for each i in $\{1, \ldots, n\}$.

Define the *reachable space* for a point s with transitions labeled by a with respect to strong probabilistic bisimulation, denoted by $S_{\sim_c}(s, a)$, to be the set of points that are reachable from s with a combined transition $s \xrightarrow{a}_C \mu$. Similarly, define the reachable space with respect to weak probabilistic bisimulation, denoted $S_{\approx_c}(s, a)$ by considering combined weak combined transitions.

Theorem 1. *Let $\simeq$ be either strong probabilistic bisimulation or weak probabilistic bisimulation, $\mathcal{A}$ a probabilistic automaton, and s_1 and s_2 two states. Then, $s_1 \simeq s_2$ if and only if $\forall a \in \Sigma$ we have that $S_{\simeq}(s_1, a)/\simeq = S_{\simeq}(s_2, a)/\simeq$.*

Proof outline. The proof is straightforward in the case of strong probabilistic bisimulation, since we have to match strong transitions of one state with strong combined transitions of the other and vice versa. The result for weak probabilistic bisimulation is similar, after proving that the main condition in the definition of probabilistic weak bisimulation can be replaced by the following: for each pair of states q and r, such that $q \approx_c r$ if $q \xRightarrow{a}_c \mu$ for some distribution μ, then there exists a distribution μ' such that $\mu \equiv_{\approx_c} \mu'$ and $r \xRightarrow{a}_c \mu'$. □

It follows that the information $I(s, a)$ that we need in FindSplit coincides with the reachable spaces defined above. Such spaces are then quotiented with respect to the equivalence relation induced by the current partition $\mathcal{W}$. In the following sections we show that for strong probabilistic bisimulation and weak probabilistic bisimulation these spaces are convex sets and, despite being potentially infinite because of combined transitions, they are generated by a finite set of points.

Complexity. Assuming that the complexity to compute the information $I(s, a)$ is c and the complexity to compare such information is d, then the complexity of FindSplit is $O(n * c + n^2 * d)$, the complexity of Refine is $O(n^2 * d)$ and the overall complexity is $O(n * (n * c + n^2 * d))$, since the while loop can be repeated at most n times, corresponding to the worst case when all the states are in a different equivalence class. Note that our algorithm computes $I(s, a)$ at each iteration and an efficient implementation would avoid this.

6   Splitter for Strong Probabilistic Bisimulation

In the case of strong probabilistic bisimulation, $S_{\sim_c}(s, a)$ is a potentially infinite set, but it is easy to see that such set is the convex set generated by the (non combined) transitions leaving the state.

Proposition 1. *Given a probabilistic automaton $\mathcal{A}$, for each state s and each action a, the reachable space $S_{\sim_c}(s, a)$ is a convex space.*

Proof. We need to prove that, given two combined transitions $s \xrightarrow{a}_c \mu_1$ and $s \xrightarrow{a}_c \mu_2$, each of their convex combinations is still a legal combined transition. To prove this fact, observe that each transition $(s, a, (p * \mu_1 + (1 - p) * \mu_2))$, with $0 \leq p \leq 1$, can be seen as the combination of the two transitions $s \xrightarrow{a}_c \mu_1$ and $s \xrightarrow{a}_c \mu_2$ with weights p and $1 - p$, respectively. $\square$

Proposition 2. *Given a probabilistic automaton $\mathcal{A}$, each point reachable with a combined transition $s \xrightarrow{a}_c \mu$ is a convex combination of those points reachable with non combined transitions.*

Compute. From Propositions 1 and 2, the distributions that are reachable from s with non combined transitions labeled by a, are sufficient to characterize the set $S_{\sim_c}(s, a)$. Thus, we can apply any algorithms for the determination of the extreme points to obtain $Gen(S_{\sim_c}(s, a))$. This means that we have to apply linear programming algorithms to the points corresponding to each deterministic transition.

Compare. We have to verify that the generators computed are the same set.

Complexity. The algorithm proposed above is polynomial in the number of states n and the number of transitions m of the automaton. The computation of the generator of the convex set can be done by solving at most $O(m)$ linear programming problems, for which polynomial algorithms are available (e.g. [14]). The comparison of two sets of extreme points is again polynomial. In practice, we expect to have a limited number of transitions leaving each point, thus limiting the number of linear programming problems to solve for each point.

7   Splitter for Weak Probabilistic Bisimulation

Again we can prove that the set $S_{\approx_c}(s, a)$ is a convex set; however, since in a weak transition we can consider arbitrary sequences of transitions labeled by internal actions, we need to identify a finite set of points that includes the generator of $S_{\approx_c}(s, a)$. A weak combined transition can be seen as the result of the action of a scheduler. We show that the generator of $S_{\approx_c}(s, a)$ is included in the set of weak transitions generated by determinate and Dirac schedulers, which are finite. The idea of determinate schedulers originates from [20]. The proof proceeds in two steps: first we show that we can use determinate schedulers (Proposition 3); then we show that we can remove randomization from the schedulers (Proposition 4).

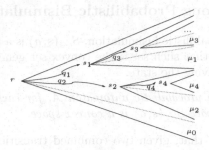

Fig. 1. Structure of the proof of Proposition 3

Proposition 3. *Given a probabilistic automaton $\mathcal{A}$, any point reachable with a weak transition under the control of a (generic) scheduler can be obtained as a convex combination of the points reachable with determinate schedulers.*

Proof. To simplify our proof we augment our probabilistic automaton by adding some state information that records the last external action that occurred. Thus we can limit our analysis to simple schedulers.

Consider a probabilistic execution induced by a scheduler σ starting from a state r. Let s be a state of the automaton and call $s_1, s_2, \ldots$ its occurrences in the probabilistic execution (see Figure 1). There can be at most countably many occurences of s. For each $i > 0$, let π_i be the probability not to reach any other occurrence of s from s_i, and let μ_i by the final distribution reached from s_i conditioned on not reaching s any more. If $\pi_i = 0$, then define μ_i arbitrarily. Let π_0 be the probability not to reach s from r if $s \neq r$, 0 otherwise, and let μ_0 by the final distribution reached from r conditioned on not reaching s. As before, μ_0 is arbitrary if $\pi_0 = 0$. For each $i > 0$, define σ_i as a scheduler that behaves like σ whenever s does not occur in the history and that treats the last occurrence of s as the occurrence s_i otherwise. Then σ_i is a scheduler that does not look at the past history whenever s is reached. Furthermore, the weak combined transition identified by σ_i leads to distribution $\rho_i = \pi_0\mu_0 + (1 - \pi_0)\mu_i$.

Observe that the distribution μ induced by σ satisfies the equation $\mu = \sum_{i\geq 0} p_i\mu_i$, where p_i is the probability to reach the occurrence s_i from r multiplied by π_i for $i > 0$, and $p_0 = \pi_0$; note that $\sum_{i>0} p_i = 1 - \pi_0$. By defining p_i' to be $p_i/(1 - \pi_0)$, it is immediate to show that $\mu = \sum_{i>0} p_i'\rho_i$, which means that the weak combined transition associated with σ can be expressed as a convex combination of the weak combined transitions associated with each of the σ_i's.

By repeating the above procedure on the other states for each of the schedulers σ_i, we end up with a collection of simple schedulers whose corresponding transitions can be combined to give the transition of σ. The process ends since the states of $\mathcal{A}$ are finite. $\qquad\square$

Proposition 4. *Given a probabilistic automaton $\mathcal{A}$, each point reachable with a weak transition under the control of a determinate scheduler can be obtained as a convex combination of the points reachable with Dirac determinate schedulers.*

Proof outline. Again we simplify the proof by augmenting our probabilistic automata so that we deal with simple schedulers. Then, we proceed state by state by replacing the combined transition returned by σ by one of the transitions that have non-zero probability. The resulting schedulers can be combined to lead to the distribution of σ. □

Compute. To compute $S_{\approx_c}(s, a)$ we first compute the set of points reachable by transitions generated by Dirac determinate schedulers and then solve the extreme point problem in the set of reachable points as we did in Section 6 for strong probabilistic bisimulation.

To compute the set of points reachable by transitions generated by Dirac determinate schedulers we first check all the possible ways to resolve non determinism by visiting the transition graph of $\mathcal{A}$ and resolving nondeterminism in each possible way at each state that is reached in the visit. Since we are restricted to Dirac determinate schedulers, each time we encounter a state before or after the occurrence of a external action the same decision must be taken.

Let σ be a Dirac simple scheduler for $\mathcal{A}$ (again we consider augmented automata for simplicity), and let the states of $\mathcal{A}$ be $s_0, s_1, \ldots, s_n$. For each i, let μ_i be the target distribution of the transition given by σ and x_i be the distribution reachable from s_i under the control of σ. The following linear system holds, where e_i is the vector with the ith component set to 1 and all others set to 0.

$$
\begin{cases}
x_0 = \mu_0[s_0] \cdot x_0 + \ldots + \mu_0[s_n] \cdot x_n + \mu_0[\bot] \cdot e_0 \\
\quad \vdots \\
x_n = \mu_n[s_0] \cdot x_0 + \ldots + \mu_n[s_n] \cdot x_n + \mu_n[\bot] \cdot e_n
\end{cases}
\tag{2}
$$

We are interested in the solution of the system above relative to state s. If such solution does not exist, then it means that scheduler σ does not describe a transition from s, and thus it should be discarded.

Compare. Once we have the set of extreme points, the problem is the same as with strong probabilistic bisimulation and we have to check whether the two generators are the same.

Complexity. Unfortunately, the algorithm described above is exponential: there can be exponentially many Dirac determinate schedulers to consider while resolving non determinism. In such a case, we have to run the extremal point algorithm on an exponential number of candidate points.

Example 1. The automaton of Figure 2 shows a scenario in which the exponential bound is reached. Assume that all $b_{i,j}$ states are in different equivalence classes (achievable by enabling different actions from the states), and that all the transitions shown are labeled by invisible actions. Let σ be a Dirac determinate scheduler; the distribution μ generated by σ is such that $\mu(b_{i,j_i}) = \frac{1}{2^i}$, $i = 1 \ldots k - 1$ and $\mu(b_{k,j_k}) = \frac{1}{2^{k-1}}$ for some combination of $j_i \in \{0, 1\}$ and probability 0 to all other states. We denote a scheduler σ with the set of indexes

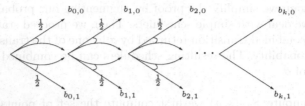

Fig. 2. An automaton with an exponential number of Dirac determinate schedulers

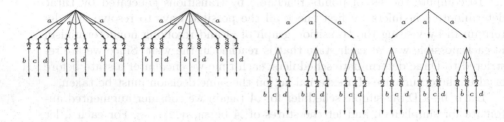

Fig. 3. Two non bisimilar probabilistic automata (left) and two non bisimilar alternating automata (right)

$\{j_i\}_{i \in 1..k}$ of the states reached with non zero probability under σ. It is clear that there are 2^k such schedulers. In order to show that all 2^k schedulers must be considered, it is necessary to show that no resulting point can be expressed as the convex combination of the others. Assume that the point reached with scheduler $\{j_i\}$ can be expressed as a convex combination of the other schedulers, then there must be another scheduler $\{l_i\}$ which has a positive weight in the convex combination. Since the two schedulers $\{j_i\}$ and $\{l_i\}$ are different, there must be an index k such that $j_k \neq l_k$, that is, they make a different choice at the k-th level. This leads to a contradiction, since $\{l_i\}$ would give a non zero probability to state b_{k,l_k} in the convex combination, while b_{k,l_k} has probability 0 under scheduler $\{j_k\}$.

The example above shows that, using the technique described in this section, all points reachable with Dirac determinate schedulers must be considered, resulting in an exponential complexity. We do not know whether this bound is inevitable or there are other techniques that avoid consideration of all these points, thus reaching a polynomial complexity.

However, despite the exponential complexity we have achieved, we argue that the algorithm is feasible in practice. Note that the worst case complexity bound is achieved when all states and transitions are reachable from a state via sequences of τ moves. We believe that such pathological cases are unlikely to occur since the sequences of τ moves in a typical probabilistic automaton are short.

In the description of the algorithms for both strong and weak probabilistic bisimulation, we have not considered efficiency: both algorithms can be made more efficient by not calculating the reachable states at each iteration and by reusing much of the previous computation. Making such improvement to the algorithms would not change their complexity classes; in particular, the algorithm for weak probabilistic bisimulation would still be exponential.

Comparison with the Alternating Model. A polynomial time algorithm for the alternating model was proposed in [20]. This algorithm uses the same partitioning technique we have used and it is based on the result that two states are weakly bisimilar if and only if the maximum probabilities of reaching each equivalence class are the same for each action. Informally, this works in the alternating model because for each probability distribution there is a state representing it, so checking maximum probabilities is enough to check exact probabilities. In our model a single state represents more than one probability distribution. Figure 3 shows how computing maximal probabilities fails to distinguish non bisimilar states for probabilistic automata, while it works in the alternating model. The start states of the two automata at the top of Figure 3 are not weakly bisimilar; however, the maximal probabilities of reaching each equivalence class (reachable with action b or c or d, respectively) are the same. The bottom part of Figure 3 shows the alternating automata obtained from those above by using the widely accepted decomposition of the transitions. In this case, the alternating automata first resolve the nondeterministic choice, then the probabilistic choice; this allows the algorithm to distinguish between non bisimilar states: the states reached after the a action have different maximal probabilities for each equivalence class.

8   Concluding Remarks

We have studied decision algorithms for bisimulation relations on probabilistic automata and we have obtained a polynomial time algorithm for strong probabilistic bisimulation and an exponential algorithm for weak probabilistic bisimulation. From a practical perspective we have argued that our exponential time algorithm should be feasible as the number of reachable equivalence classes from a state is small. It is still an open problem to find a decision algorithm for weak bisimulation, while the problem is solved already in the alternating model. However, given the results of [22], where it is shown that the probabilistic temporal logic PCTL is preserved by probabilistic bisimulation, we believe that the probabilistic version of our bisimulation relations is the most important.

References

[1] L. d. Alfaro. *Formal Verification of Probabilistic Systems*. PhD thesis, Stanford University, 1997. Available as Technical report STAN-CS-TR-98-1601. 371
[2] C. Baier, B. Engelen, and M. E. Majster-Cederbaum. Deciding bisimilarity and similarity for probabilistic processes. *Journal of Computer and System Sciences*, 60(1):187–231, 2000. 372, 379

[3] C. Baier and H. Hermanns. Weak bisimulation for fully probabilistic processes. Technical Report 99/12, University of Twente, 1999. 372

[4] C. Baier and M. Stoelinga. Norm functions for bisimulations with delays. In *Proceedings of FOSSACS*. Springer-Verlag, 2000. 372

[5] M. Bernardo, L. Donatiello, and R. Gorrieri. Modeling and analyzing concurrent systems with MPA. In *Proceedings of the Second Workshop on Process Algebras and Performance Modelling* (PAPM), Erlangen, Germany, pages 175–189, 1994. 372

[6] K. Fukuda. *Polyhedral computation FAQ.* http://www.ifor.math.ethz.ch/~fukuda/polyfaq/polyfaq.html, 2000. 374

[7] R. v. Glabbeek, S. Smolka, and B. Steffen. Reactive, generative, and stratified models of probabilistic processes. *Information and Computation*, 121(1), 1996. 371, 374

[8] H. Hansson. *Time and Probability in Formal Design of Distributed Systems*, volume 1 of *Real-Time Safety Critical Systems*. Elsevier, 1994. 371, 377

[9] H. Hansson and B. Jonsson. A calculus for communicating systems with time and probabilities. In *Proceedings of the 11th IEEE Symposium on Real-Time Systems*, Orlando, Fl., 1990. 371, 374

[10] H. Hermanns, U. Herzog, and J. Katoen. Process algebra for performance evaluation. To appear in *Theoretical Computer Science*. 372

[11] J. Hillston. PEPA: Performance enhanced process algebra. Technical Report CSR-24-93, Department of Computer Science, Univ. of Edimburgh (UK), 1993. 371

[12] J. Hillston. *A Compositional Approach to Performance Modeling*. PhD thesis, Department of Computer Science, Univ. of Edimburgh (UK), 1994. 372

[13] P. Kanellakis and S. Smolka. CCS expressions, finite state processes, and three problems of equivalence. *Information and Computation*, 86(1):43–68, 1990. 372, 378

[14] N. Karmakar. A new polynomial-time algorithm for linear programming. *Combinatorica 4*, pages 373–395, 1984. 380

[15] J. Kemeny, J. Snell, and A. Knapp. *Denumerable Markov Chains*. Graduate Texts in Mathematics. Springer-Verlag, second edition, 1976. 376

[16] K. Larsen and A. Skou. Bisimulation through probabilistic testing. In *Conference Record of the 16th ACM Symposium on Principles of Programming Languages*, Austin, Texas, pages 344–352, 1989. 371, 377

[17] R. Milner. *Communication and Concurrency*. Prentice-Hall International, Englewood Cliffs, 1989. 371, 376

[18] C. Morgan, A. McIver, and K. Seidel. Probabilistic predicate transformers. *ACM Trans. Prog. Lang. Syst.*, 18(3):325–353, May 1996. 371

[19] R. Paige and R. Tarjan. Three partition refinement algorithms. *SIAM J. Comput.*, 16(6):973–989, 1987. 372, 378

[20] A. Philippou, I. Lee, and O. Sokolsky. Weak bisimulation for probabilistic systems. In *Proceedings of CONCUR 2000*, pages 334–349. Springer-Verlag, 2000. 372, 375, 376, 377, 380, 384

[21] R. Segala. *Modeling and Verification of Randomized Distributed Real-Time Systems*. PhD thesis, MIT, Dept. of Electrical Engineering and Computer Science, 1995. Also appears as technical report MIT/LCS/TR-676. 371

[22] R. Segala and N. Lynch. Probabilistic simulations for probabilistic processes. In *Proceedings of CONCUR 94*, pages 481–496. Springer-Verlag, 1994. 371, 372, 373, 377, 384

[23] R. Segala and N. Lynch. Probabilistic simulations for probabilistic processes. *Nordic Journal of Computing*, 2(2):250–273, 1995. 376, 377

[24] K. Seidel. Probabilistic communicating processes. Technical Report PRG-102, Ph.D. Thesis, Programming Research Group, Oxford University, 1992. 371

[25] S. Wu, S. Smolka, and E. Stark. Composition and behaviors of probabilistic I/O automata. *Theoretical Comput. Sci.*, 176(1-2):1–38, 1999. 371

Axiomatizing an Algebra of Step Reactions for Synchronous Languages

Gerald Lüttgen[1] and Michael Mendler[2]

[1] Department of Computer Science, Sheffield University
211 Portobello Street, Sheffield S1 4DP, U.K.
g.luettgen@dcs.shef.ac.uk
[2] Fakultät für Wirtschaftsinformatik und Angewandte Informatik
Universität Bamberg, 96045 Bamberg, Germany
michael.mendler@wiai.uni-bamberg.de

Abstract. This paper introduces a novel algebra for reasoning about step reactions in synchronous languages, such as macro steps in Harel, Pnueli and Shalev's Statecharts and instantaneous reactions in Berry's Esterel. The algebra describes step reactions in terms of configurations which can both be read in a standard operational as well as in a model–theoretic fashion. The latter arises by viewing configurations as propositional formulas, interpreted intuitionistically over finite linear Kripke structures. Previous work by the authors showed the adequacy of this approach by establishing compositionality and full–abstraction results for Statecharts and Esterel. The present paper generalizes this work in an algebraic setting and, as its main result, provides a sound and complete equational axiomatization of step reactions. This yields, for the first time in the literature, a complete axiomatization of Statecharts macro steps, which can also be applied, modulo encoding, to Esterel reactions.

1 Introduction

Synchronous languages provide a popular framework for designing and programming *event–based reactive systems*. Prominent examples of such languages include Harel's *Statecharts* [2], which is a graphical language that extends finite–state machines by concepts of state hierarchy, concurrency, and event priority, and Berry's *Esterel* [1], which is a textual language having similar features to Statecharts. Today, both languages are supported by commercial tools that mainly focus on generating running code. The development of semantic–based verification tools, however, is still in its infancy, which is partly due to the lack of sufficiently simple compositional semantics.

The semantics of Statecharts, as conceived by Pnueli and Shalev [15], and of Esterel are based on the idea of *cycle–based reaction*, where first the input events, as defined by a system's environment, are sampled at the beginning of each cycle, then the system's reaction in form of the emission of further events is determined, and finally the generated events are output to the environment. Statecharts and Esterel differ in the details of what exactly constitutes a cycle,

L. Brim et al. (Eds.): CONCUR 2002, LNCS 2421, pp. 386–401, 2002.

which is also called a *macro step* in Statecharts and an *instantaneous reaction* in Esterel. Moreover, Esterel refers to events as signals. Both languages have in common that they obey the semantic principles of *synchrony* and *causality*. The synchrony requirement reflects the mechanism behind cycle–based reaction and is mathematically modeled via the *synchrony hypothesis*. This hypothesis ensures that reactions and propagations of events are instantaneous, which models an idealized system behavior and is practically justified by the observation that reactive systems usually perform much faster than their environments. Causality refers to the requirement that the reason for an event to be generated in a system reaction can be traced back to the input events provided by the environment. Esterel differs from Statecharts in that it further adopts the principles of *reactivity* and *determinism*. Reactivity implies that in each cycle, a system response, in the form of generated events, can be constructed for any input an environment may provide. Determinism requires for this response to be unique.

This brief discussion highlights the variety of possible choices when defining a semantics for step reactions, with different choices implying subtly different semantics. Recent research by the authors, aiming at a unifying semantic framework for synchronous languages, has concentrated on employing ideas from *intuitionistic logic* for describing step reactions [8,9,10]. Intuitionistic logic, in contrast to classical logic, is constructive and thus truly reflects the operational character of step reactions in the light of causality: it rejects the principle of the excluded middle, viz., that events are either always present or always absent throughout a reaction. This axiom cannot be maintained for a compositional semantics that allows the system environment to inject events *during* a step reaction. Indeed, our intuitionistic setting led to compositional and fully–abstract characterizations of Statecharts macro steps and Esterel reactions [9,10].

This paper introduces a simple yet expressive algebra for describing and reasoning about step reactions in terms of so–called *configurations* and presents an equational axiomatization for it. In particular, this gives for the first time in the literature a sound and complete axiomatization for Statecharts macro steps, which can also be applied, modulo encoding, to Esterel reactions. The step algebra's semantics is inspired by the authors' previous work and reads configurations as propositional formulas, interpreted intuitionistically over finite linear Kripke structures, to which we refer as *sequence structures* (cf. Sec. 2). Our axiomatization is then built on top of this algebra (cf. Sec. 3), and its proof of completeness combines techniques used in process algebras and logics (cf. Sec. 4). At its heart, the proof employs a process–algebraic notion of *normal form* that in turn is defined by model–theoretic means. Our axioms not only shed light on the semantics of step reactions, but also provide groundwork for an exact axiomatic comparison of popular synchronous languages.

2   Step Algebra

This section introduces our step algebra for reasoning about those step reactions that may be specified within *event–based synchronous language*. Usually, synchronous languages, such as *Statecharts* [2,15] or *Esterel* [1] (with its graphical front–end *SyncCharts*), enrich the notation of finite state machines by mechanisms for expressing hierarchy, concurrency, and priority. This makes it possible to refine a single state by a state machine, to run several state machines in parallel which may coordinate each other via broadcasting events, and to give some transitions precedence over others, respectively. The underlying semantics is based on a nested two–level execution model. The top–level synchronous computation cycle consists of a sequence of *macro steps*, each of which represents a single reaction of the system to some environment stimulus. If the notion of a reaction is understood, this synchronous level can be handled by conventional automata models and poses no semantic challenge. Hence, the interesting question is what exactly constitutes a reaction. Although the environment treats reactions as atomic, each individual reaction is indeed a computation in its own right, a sequence of *micro steps* in which concurrent components of the system under consideration are engaged. This introduces subtle issues regarding compositionality and full-abstraction, which are well documented in the literature (cf. Sec. 5). Moreover, many synchronous languages —and variants of Statecharts in particular— are distinguished by how exactly they define valid sets of concurrent transitions that can fire together in a single reaction. The work presented here features an algebra of individual reactions that arose from the systematic study of these problems and variations in the literature. We start off with an informal description of step reactions.

In event–based synchronous languages, each transition t is labeled by two sets of events, which are referred to as *trigger* and *action*, respectively. The trigger is a set of positive events P and negative events $\overline{N}$, taken from a countable universe of events Ev and their negated counterparts in $\overline{Ev} =_{df} \{\overline{e} : e \in Ev\}$, respectively. For convenience, we define $\overline{\overline{e}} =_{df} e$. Intuitively, t is enabled and forced to fire if the transition's environment signals all events in P but none in N. The effect of firing t is the generation of all events in the transition's action $A \subseteq Ev$. These events might in turn trigger transitions in different parallel components, thus enabling a *causal* chain reaction whose length is bounded by the number of parallel components within the program under consideration. A *step reaction* is then the set of all events that are already valid at the beginning of the step or generated during the step. When constructing steps in the suggested operational manner, it is possible to experience inconsistencies, namely when a firing transitions generates some event e, whose absence, i.e., its negation $\overline{e}$, was assumed when firing a previous transition in the step. Since an event cannot be both present and absent within the same step reaction, due to the principle of *global consistency*, the choice sequence leading to the inconsistency is rejected, and a different sequence must then be chosen. If no consistent sequence is possible, the step construction fails altogether. Alternatively, one could also say that the step construction remains unfinished; it waits for the environment to provide additional events to disable the transition(s) that produced the inconsistency.

The semantic subtlety of step reactions arises precisely from the capability of defining transitions whose enabledness disables other transitions, as well as from

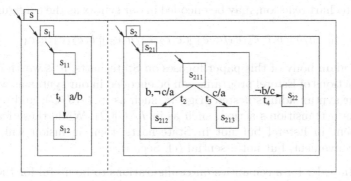

Fig. 1. Example Statechart

the interpretation of negated trigger events. In the light of this discussion, the key operators for combining transitions in synchronous languages are *parallel composition* and *event negation*. State hierarchy is merely a notational convenience rather than a semantically relevant operator. Observe that parallel composition and event negation also allow one to express *nondeterministic choice* [ ]. For example, a choice between two transitions $P_1, \overline{N_1}/A_1$ and $P_2, \overline{N_2}/A_2$ might be written as the parallel composition $P_1, \overline{N_1}, \overline{e_2}/A_1, e_1 \parallel P_2, \overline{N_2}, \overline{e_1}/A_2, e_2$, where e_1, e_2 are distinguished events not occurring in the triggers or actions of the two original transitions and where the comma notation stands for union, i.e., $X, Y =_{df} X \cup Y$ and $X, x =_{df} X \cup \{x\}$. Finally, we often write x for the singleton set $\{x\}$.

Syntax. For the purposes of this paper, it is convenient to work with a quite general syntax for reactions, which allows us to encode several dialects of synchronous languages, including Statecharts and Esterel. In fact, it may be seen as the smallest common superset of the kernel of both languages. The terms describing step reactions, to which we also refer as *configurations*, are defined inductively as follows:

$$C \quad ::= \quad 0 \mid A \mid I/C \mid C \parallel C$$

where $A \subseteq Ev$ and $I \subseteq Ev \cup \overline{Ev}$. Intuitively, 0 stands for the configuration with the empty behavior, $A \subseteq Ev$ denotes the signaling of all events in A, configuration I/C encodes that configuration C is triggered by the presence of the positive events in I and the absence of the negative events in I, and $C_1 \parallel C_2$ describes the parallel composition of configurations C_1 and C_2. Observe that the semantics of configuration 0 coincides with the semantics of $A = \emptyset$; nevertheless, it seems natural to include 0. For notational convenience, we let the transition slash / to have lower binding power than parallel composition $\parallel$ and interpret a nesting of transition slashes in a right–associative manner.

We illustrate our syntax by means of an example. Consider the Statechart depicted in Fig. 1 and assume that all components are in their initial states marked by small unlabeled arrows. Then the first Statechart step determining the initial Statechart reaction, may be encoded in our syntax as the configuration

$$C_{ex} \quad =_{df} \quad a/b \parallel b, \overline{c}, \overline{e_3}, \overline{e_4}/a, e_2 \parallel c, \overline{e_2}, \overline{e_4}/a, e_3 \parallel \overline{b}, \overline{e_2}, \overline{e_3}/c, e_4 \ .$$

Although the main body of this paper focuses on Statecharts, it is worth noting again that reactions of Esterel programs can be encoded in our syntax as well. In particular, our syntax admits nested triggers, such as in $I/(J/C)$, and parallel composition in a transition's action, such as in $I/(C\|D)$. While these features are only present in Esterel but not in Statecharts, their inclusion will prove notationally convenient, but not essential (cf. Sec. 5).

Semantics. In order for a semantics on configurations to be useful for the purposes of this paper, it must meet several requirements. First, it must be *compositional* to be axiomatizable, i.e., it must give rise to a semantic equivalence on configurations that is a congruence. Second, it should be compatible with the existing semantics of the synchronous languages of interest, in particular with Statecharts' and Esterel's semantics. Unfortunately, many semantics for synchronous languages, including the one of Statecharts as originally conceived by Harel, Pnueli and Shalev [2,15], are not compositional. Recent research by the authors has revealed an appealing model–theoretic framework for studying Statecharts' and Esterel's semantics, which is based on reading configurations as simple propositional formulas that are *intuitionistically* interpreted over finite linear Kripke structures [8,9,10]. This model–theoretic approach allows not only for a compositional semantics but also for establishing full–abstraction results. The present paper generalizes this work in an algebraic setting.

The key idea is to consider a single step reaction as a *stabilization* process, where the synchronous environment is only concerned with the final response, while the system under consideration takes care of the actual sequence of events that leads to the stationary state. The main feature that distinguishes a stabilization process from an arbitrary computation is that it is a *monotonically increasing approximation* of the final step reaction. This means that once an event from the final step reaction has become present or asserted by the firing of a transition generating it, the event will remain present until the stationary state is reached. Formally, we interpret configurations over finite, nonempty, strictly increasing sequences $M = (M_1, M_2, \ldots, M_n)$, where $n \in \mathbb{N}$ and $M_i \subseteq Ev$, to which we refer as *sequence structures*. 'Strictly increasing' means that $M_i \subsetneq M_{i+1}$, for all $1 \le i < n$. We say that M satisfies C, in signs $M \models C$, if the following holds for all $1 \le i \le n$:

$$
\begin{aligned}
&M_i \models 0 &&\textit{always} \\
&M_i \models A &&\textit{if } A \subseteq M_i \\
&M_i \models I/C &&\textit{if } (I \cap Ev \subseteq M_i \textit{ and } \overline{(I \cap \overline{Ev})} \cap M_n = \emptyset) \textit{ implies } M_i \models C \\
&M_i \models C_1 \| C_2 &&\textit{if } M_i \models C_1 \textit{ and } M_i \models C_2
\end{aligned}
$$

This definition is a shaved version of the standard semantics obtained when reading a configuration as a formula in propositional intuitionistic logic [16], i.e., when taking events to be atomic propositions and replacing $\overline{e}$ by the negation $\neg e$, concatenation of events in sets and '$\|$' by conjunction '$\wedge$', and the transition slash '$/$' by implication '$\supset$'. An empty trigger and the configuration 0 are identified with *true*. Then we have $M \models C$ if and only if C is valid in the intuitionistic Kripke structure M. Note that, for sequence structures $M = (M_1)$ of length one, the notions of sequence model and classical model coincide; hence, intuitionistic logic is a refinement of classical logic, and we simply write M_1 for (M_1). The utility of intuitionistic logic comes into play when ensuring global consistency within reaction sequences. This is because intuitionistic logic interprets negation globally for a sequence M, and not locally for single states M_i.

Our semantics suggests the following equivalence on configurations. Configurations C_1, C_2 are *step congruent*, in signs $C_1 \simeq C_2$, if $M \models C_1 \Leftrightarrow M \models C_2$ holds for all sequence structures M.

Proposition 1 (Congruence). *The equivalence $\simeq$ is indeed a congruence, i.e., $C_1 \simeq C_2$ implies $C_1\|D \simeq C_2\|D$ and $I/C_1 \simeq I/C_2$, for all configurations C_1, C_2, D and for all triggers $I \subseteq Ev \cup \overline{Ev}$.*

It was proved in [9] that step congruence $\simeq$ is *compositional* and *fully–abstract* with respect to Statecharts macro–step semantics, according to the operational semantics of Pnueli and Shalev [15]. More precisely, for any two Statecharts configurations C, D, we have $C \simeq D$ if and only if $C\|P$ and $D\|P$ have exactly the same step responses for all parallel environments P. The remainder of this paper presents an axiomatic characterization of our step congruence.

3   Axiomatization

Our axioms system is displayed in Table 1, where $A, B, N, P \subseteq Ev$, $I, I_1, I_2 \in Ev \cup \overline{Ev}$, and $e \in Ev$, and where C, C_1, C_2, C_3 are configurations. We write $\vdash C_1 = C_2$ to state that $C_1 = C_2$ can be derived from the axioms via standard equational reasoning. Axioms (A1)–(A6) and (B1)–(B4) are fairly natural and do not need much operational justification. When taking them together, it is easy to see that every configuration is equivalent to a flat parallel composition of transitions, without nested triggers and where ordering and duplication is immaterial. Note that Axioms (B3) and (B4) can actually be deduced from Axioms (A1)–(A6), (B1), and (B2) by induction on the structure of C. Because of their fundamental nature, however, we have included them as first–class axioms.

We concentrate on explaining the remaining, more interesting axioms. Axiom (C1) describes that, if the firing of a transition merely reproduces in its action some of the events required by its trigger, then we might just as well not fire the transition at all. Hence, it is equivalent to configuration 0. Axiom (C2) states that by adding in parallel to a configuration C a guarded version I/C of it, the behavior remains unchanged. This is intuitively clear since the extra I/C component, when and if it fires at all, only produces the behavior encoded by C, which is already present anyway. Logically speaking, guarding is a *weakening* operation. Axiom (C3) is perhaps the most important equation, as it emulates the firing of transitions. The left–hand side $A \| A, I/C$ represents a situation in

Table 1. Axioms for the step congruence

(A1)	$\emptyset = 0$	(A2)	$A \parallel B = A \cup B$
(A3)	$\emptyset/C = C$	(A4)	$I/0 = 0$
(A5)	$I_1, I_2/C = I_1/(I_2/C)$	(A6)	$I/(C_1 \parallel C_2) = I/C_1 \parallel I/C_2$
(B1)	$C_1 \parallel C_2 = C_2 \parallel C_1$	(B2)	$(C_1 \parallel C_2) \parallel C_3 = C_1 \parallel (C_2 \parallel C_3)$
(B3)	$C \parallel C = C$	(B4)	$C \parallel 0 = C$

(C1)	$P, I/P = 0$	
(C2)	$C = C \parallel I/C$	
(C3)	$A \parallel A, I/C = A \parallel I/C$	
(C4)	$P, \overline{N}/C = 0$	if $P \cap N \neq \emptyset$
(D1)	$P, \overline{N}/A = P, \overline{N}/A, B$	if $N \cap A \neq \emptyset$
(D2)	$P, \overline{N}/A = P, e, \overline{N}/A \parallel P, \overline{N}, \overline{e}/A$	if $N \cap A \neq \emptyset$
(D3)	$\overline{N}/C \parallel P, \overline{N}/A = \parallel \{\overline{N}, \overline{e}/C : e \in P\} \parallel P, \overline{N}/A$	if $N \cap A \neq \emptyset$ and $P \neq \emptyset$

which some events A have become present while at the same time there is a pending transition $A, I/C$ that is waiting, among other preconditions I, for the events in A. Hence, it is safe to cancel out all dependencies of C on A and to replace $A, I/C$ by I/C. Hence, Axiom (C3) is nothing but a version of the *cut* rule known from logic. Axiom (C4) deals with inconsistencies in triggers. If a configuration C is guarded by a trigger $P, \overline{N}$ in which some event is required to be both present and absent, i.e., $P \cap \overline{N} \neq \emptyset$, then this guarded configuration will never become active. In this case, $P, \overline{N}/C$ is obviously equivalent to 0.

The remaining Axioms (D1)–(D3) are concerned with conflicts between the trigger and action of a transition. They axiomatize the effect of transitions that produce a failure under certain trigger conditions. More precisely, these axioms involve a transition $P, \overline{N}/A$ with $N \cap A \neq \emptyset$, whose firing leads to a global inconsistency. Such a transition rejects the completion of all macro steps in which its trigger $P, \overline{N}$ is true. Thus, since $P, \overline{N}/A$ can never fire in a consistent way, the step construction cannot terminate in a situation in which trigger $P, \overline{N}$ holds true. In other words, whenever all P have become present the step construction must continue until at least one event in N is present, in order to inactivate the transition. If this does not happen the step construction fails. Axioms (D1)–(D3) formalize three different consequences of this. Axiom (D1) reflects the fact that, since $P, \overline{N}/A$ can never contribute to a completed step if $N \cap A \neq \emptyset$, we may add arbitrary other events B to its action, without changing its behavior. Logically, this axiom corresponds to the laws $e \wedge \neg e \equiv false$ and $false \supset B$, for any B. Axiom (D2) offers a second way of reading the inconsistency between triggers and actions. Since at completion time any event e is either present or absent, the same rejection that $P, \overline{N}/A$ produces can be achieved by $P, \overline{N}, e/A \parallel P, \overline{N}, \overline{e}/A$. This is because if e is present at completion time, then $P, \overline{N}, e/A$ raises the failure; if e is absent, then $P, \overline{N}, \overline{e}/A$ does the job. This corresponds to the law $\neg(\neg e \wedge \neg\neg e)$ in intuitionistic logic. To see this, simply instantiate P as *true* and A and N both as *false*. Then, Axiom (D2) turns into the equivalence $(true \wedge \neg false) \supset false \equiv ((true \wedge \neg false \wedge e) \supset false) \wedge (true \wedge \neg false \wedge \neg e) \supset false$, which simplifies to $\neg(\neg e \wedge \neg\neg e)$. Finally, consider Axiom (D3) that encodes the following intuition. Instead of saying that $P, \overline{N}/A$ generates a failure, if all events in P are present and all events in N are absent, we might say that, if all events in N are absent, then at least one of the events in P must be absent, provided the step under consideration is to be completed without failure. But then any parallel component of the form $\overline{N}/C$, which becomes active on the absence of all events in N, can be replaced by the parallel composition $\|\{\overline{N}, \overline{e}/C : e \in P\}$. The reason is that, if $\overline{N}/C$ fires at all in the presence of transition $P, \overline{N}/A$, then at least one of the weaker transitions $\overline{N}, \overline{e}/C$ will be able to fire at some point, depending on which of the events in P it is that will be absent to avoid failure. Again there is a logic equivalent for this, namely the law $\neg(p_1 \wedge p_2) \supset \neg p_1 \vee \neg p_2$ that holds for *linear* Kripke models. This can be seen by instantiating N and A as *false*, P as $p_1 \wedge p_2$, and C as $\neg p_1 \vee \neg p_2$. It is not difficult to show that then Axiom (D3) becomes equivalent to $((\neg p_1 \vee \neg p_2) \wedge \neg(p_1 \wedge p_2)) \equiv \neg(p_1 \wedge p_2)$, which in turn is logically equivalent to $\neg(p_1 \wedge p_2) \supset \neg p_1 \vee \neg p_2$. Last, but not least, it is important to note that configuration $P, \overline{N}/A$, for $N \cap A \neq \emptyset$, is not the same as configuration 0, since the former inevitably produces a failure if its trigger is true, while 0 does not respond at all, not even by failure.

Theorem 1 (Correctness). *Let* $\vdash C_1 = C_2$. *Then,* $C_1 \simeq C_2$.

The correctness of each of our axioms can be established directly along our notion of sequence models. However, since this is exactly the standard interpretation of propositional intuitionistic formulas over finite linear Kripke structures, one may simply employ the wealth of knowledge on intuitionistic logic for the proof [16].

4   Completeness

The proof of completeness of our step–congruence axiomatization employs a notion of *normal form*. As usual, the idea is to first show that every configuration can be rewritten into one in normal form using our axioms and then establish the desired completeness result for configurations in normal form. The purpose of the normal form is to lay out explicitly, in a canonical syntactic form, the behavior offered by a configuration relative to a fixed and finite set of relevant events. Typically, these are all the events that occur in the configurations we wish to normalize. For simplicity, let us take Ev to be this finite set; the complement A^c of any set $A \subseteq Ev$ is then also finite. A normal form relative to Ev is a parallel composition of simple transitions

$$(\|_{i \in I} P_i, \overline{N_i}/A_i) \ \| \ (\|_{j \in J} E_j, \overline{E_j^c}/Ev) \ .$$

The transitions are grouped into two categories, indexed by I and J, respectively. The former category encodes individual, partial or complete, step reactions, whereas the latter category records the conditions under which the step construction fails (to complete). A transition $P_i, \overline{N_i}/A_i$ of the first kind specifies that, if the events in P_i are known to be present and those in N_i are absent, then A_i is one possible reaction of the configuration to P_i. A transition $E_j, \overline{E_j^c}/Ev$ of the second kind enforces that the step construction cannot consistently complete with just the events in E_j present. In order to complete the reaction at least one event outside E_j must become available as well. In the light of this discussion, a normal form may be seen as a "response table", where, given a set of environment events, one may look up the associated partial or complete step reaction or learn about immanent failure. This response–table interpretation is reflected in a number of structural properties on normal–form configurations.

Definition 1. *A configuration C is in* normal form, *if it has the shape*

$$(\|_{i \in I} P_i, \overline{N_i}/A_i) \| (\|_{j \in J} E_j, \overline{E_j^c}/Ev),$$

where I, J are disjoint finite index sets, $E_j \subsetneq Ev$, for all $j \in J$; and if it satisfies:

1. *$P_i \subseteq A_i$ and $P_i \cap N_i = \emptyset$, for all $i \in I$;*
2. *$B \models C$ iff $\forall j \in J. B \neq E_j$;*
3. *$B \models C$ iff $\exists i \in I. B = N_i^c$;*
4. *$B \models C$ and $P \subseteq B$ implies $\exists i \in I. P_i = P$ and $B = N_i^c$;*
5. *$(P_i, N_i^c)^* = A_i$, for all $i \in I$ with $N_i \cap A_i = \emptyset$; and*
6. *$N_i \cap A_i = \emptyset$, for all $i \in I$.*

where $(P, N)^* =_{df} \bigcap \{E : (E, N) \models C, P \subseteq E \subseteq N\}$ and $B \subseteq Ev$ arbitrary.

Conds. (2)–(5) encode structural properties that refer to our model–theoretic semantics. It is through these that the normal form obtains its essential semantic relevance. The other conditions, Conds. (1) and (6), are simple local consistency requirements. Note that the side condition $N_i \cap A_i = \emptyset$ of Cond. (5) is redundant due to Cond. (6); however, its presence will simplify matters later. It seems important to stress that Conds. (2)–(5) could of course be rewritten in purely syntactic terms, simply by expanding the definition of $\models$ in the respective cases. This, however, would only obscure the purpose of these conditions, which is to permit an easy correspondence between syntax and semantics in the completeness proof. Note that there may be other notions of normal form; we do not claim that Def. 1 is necessarily the best choice for performing equivalence proofs.

Proposition 2. *For any configuration C there exists a configuration C' in normal form such that $\vdash C = C'$.*

Proof. Let C be an arbitrary configuration. Because of Axioms (A3)–(A6) we may assume without loss of generality that C is given as a flat parallel composition of simple transitions $P, \overline{N^c}/A$. We will rewrite C using our axioms in six steps, obtaining configurations C_i, for $1 \leq i \leq 6$, such that C_i satisfies normal–form Conds. (1) through (i). We say that C_i is in i–normal form, or i–nf for short. At each stage we define the J–*part* of C_i to be the collection of all transitions of the form $B, \overline{B^c}/Ev$, where $B \subsetneq Ev$. All other transitions make up the I–*part*. In this way each C_i naturally splits into the form $(\|_{i \in I} P_i, \overline{N_i}/A_i) \| (\|_{j \in J} E_j, \overline{E_j^c}/Ev)$ such that $E_j \subsetneq Ev$, for all $j \in J$.

We will employ the associativity and commutativity Axioms (B1) and (B2) for parallel composition without explicit mentioning, wherever convenient. Furthermore, observe that since all C_i have the same semantics, it does not matter whether we read validity $\models$ in Conds. (2)–(5) relative to C or C_i.

1. Assume Cond. (1) is violated by a transition $P, \overline{N}/A$ in C, i.e., $P \not\subseteq A$ or $P \cap N \neq \emptyset$. In the second case we can simply drop the transition because of Axioms (C4) and (B4). In the former case, we can transform $P, \overline{N}/A$ so that Cond. (1) is satisfied:

$$
\begin{aligned}
\vdash P, \overline{N}/A &= P, \overline{N}/A \parallel 0 & \text{(B4)} \\
&= P, \overline{N}/A \parallel P, \overline{N}/P & \text{(C1)} \\
&= P, \overline{N}/(A\|P) & \text{(A6)} \\
&= P, \overline{N}/A, P & \text{(A2)}
\end{aligned}
$$

Making these first adjustments yields C_1, with $\vdash C = C_1$, where C_1 is in 1–nf. All successive transformations to C_1 either introduce new transitions that satisfy Cond. (1) or, if not, we can repeat this step to clean out or transform the transitions such that Cond. (1) does hold.

2. Next we consider Cond. (2), starting off with direction ($\Longrightarrow$). Let $B \models C_1$, i.e., B is a classical model, and further $B = E_j$ for some $j \in J$. Then $B \subsetneq Ev$ and also $Ev \subseteq B$, since $B \models B, \overline{B^c}/Ev$. This is an obvious contradiction, whence this direction of Cond. (2) is automatically fulfilled in C_1.

   For the other direction ($\Longleftarrow$) we show that, for any $B \not\models C_1$, the equivalence $\vdash C_1 = C_1 \parallel B, \overline{B^c}/Ev$ is derivable. If we apply this for every such B we get our desired 2–nf C_2, subsuming the new transitions $B, \overline{B^c}/Ev$ in the J–part of the 2–nf. Note that always $Ev \models C$, which means $B \subsetneq Ev$ in such a case. The transformation $\vdash C_1 = C_1 \parallel B, \overline{B^c}/Ev$ is obtained in the following fashion. Since by assumption $B \not\models C_1$, there must be some transition $P, \overline{N}/A$ in C_1 such that $B \not\models P, \overline{N}/A$. Hence, $\vdash C_1 = C_1' \parallel P, \overline{N}/A$, where C_1' is C_1 without the transition $P, \overline{N}/A$. Now observe that $B \not\models P, \overline{N}/A$ implies $P \subseteq B$ and $N \cap B = \emptyset$, but $A \not\subseteq B$. We then reason as follows, abbreviating $P, \overline{N}/A \parallel B, \overline{B^c}/B$ by D.

$$
\begin{aligned}
\vdash P&, \overline{N}/A \\
&= P, \overline{N}/A \parallel B, \overline{B^c}/B & \text{(B4,C1)} \\
&= D \parallel B, P, \overline{B^c}, \overline{N}/A \parallel B, P, \overline{B^c}, \overline{N}/B & \text{(C2, A5, twice)} \\
&= D \parallel B, \overline{B^c}/A \parallel B, \overline{B^c}/B & (P \subseteq B,\ N \cap B = \emptyset,\ \text{i.e.,}\ N \subseteq B^c) \\
&= D \parallel B, \overline{B^c}/(A\|B) & \text{(A6)} \\
&= D \parallel B, \overline{B^c}/A, B & \text{(A2)} \\
&= D \parallel B, \overline{B^c}/Ev & (\text{D1},\ A \not\subseteq B,\ \text{i.e.,}\ A \cap B^c \neq \emptyset) \\
&= P, \overline{N}/A \parallel B, \overline{B^c}/B \parallel B, \overline{B^c}/Ev \\
&= P, \overline{N}/A \parallel B, \overline{B^c}/Ev & \text{(A6, A2)}
\end{aligned}
$$

   This shows $\vdash C_1 = C_1' \parallel P, \overline{N}/A = C_1' \parallel P, \overline{N}/A \parallel B, \overline{B^c}/Ev = C_1 \parallel B, \overline{B^c}/Ev$.

3. The direction ($\Longrightarrow$) of Cond. (3) can be trivially satisfied by inserting parallel transitions $B, \overline{B^c}/B$ for those $B \subsetneq Ev$ that satisfy $B \models C_2$, via Axioms (B4)

and (C1). This preserves Conds. (1) and (2). Note that we accommodate $B, \overline{B^c}/B$ in the I–part.

Suppose direction ($\Longleftarrow$) is violated by $B \not\models C_2$, for which there exists a transition $P_i, \overline{N_i}/A_i$ with $B = N_i^c$ in the I–part of C_2. We must have $N_i = B^c \neq \emptyset$, for otherwise $B = N_i^c = Ev$, contradicting $B \not\models C_2$. By Cond. (2), there exists a transition $B, \overline{B^c}/Ev$ in the J–part of C_2. Hence,

$$\vdash C_2 = C_2' \parallel P_i, \overline{B^c}/A_i \parallel B, \overline{B^c}/Ev \, .$$

We distinguish several cases. If $A_i = \emptyset$, then $P_i, \overline{B^c}/A_i$ is the same as $P_i, \overline{B^c}/\emptyset$ which can be eliminated from C_2 right away by Axioms (A1), (A4), and (B4). If $P_i \cap \overline{B^c} \neq \emptyset$, we can drop $P_i, \overline{B^c}/A_i$ by way of Axioms (B4) and (C4). Hence, assume that $A_i \neq \emptyset$ and $P_i \cap B^c = \emptyset$. Now, if $B = \emptyset$, then $B^c = Ev$ and $P_i = \emptyset$. Hence, we use Axioms (A2) and (A6) to derive $\vdash P_i, \overline{B^c}/A_i \parallel B, \overline{B^c}/Ev = \overline{Ev}/A_i \parallel \overline{Ev}/Ev = \overline{Ev}/Ev = B, \overline{B^c}/Ev$, which gets rid of the culprit $P_i, \overline{B^c}/A_i$. It remains to tackle the situation in which $B \neq \emptyset$. But then, since also $B^c \neq \emptyset$, we can use the equational rewriting

$$
\begin{aligned}
&\vdash P_i, \overline{B^c}/A_i \parallel B, \overline{B^c}/Ev \\
&= \overline{B^c}/(P_i/A_i) \parallel B, \overline{B^c}/Ev && \text{(A5)} \\
&= \parallel \{\overline{B^c}, \overline{e}/(P_i/A_i) : e \in B\} \parallel B, \overline{B^c}/Ev && \text{(D3)} \\
&= \parallel \{P_i, \overline{B^c}, \overline{e}/A_i : e \in B\} \parallel B, \overline{B^c}/Ev && \text{(A5)}
\end{aligned}
$$

to replace in C_2, effectively, the offending $P_i, \overline{B^c}/A_i$ by the parallel composition of transitions $P_i, \overline{B^c}, \overline{e}/A_i$, for $e \in B$, each of which has a negative trigger strictly larger than the one in $P_i, \overline{B^c}/A_i$ we started off with.

By iterating these transformations over all B's and i's such that $B \not\models C_2$ and $B = N_i^c$, Cond. (3) ($\Longleftarrow$) can be achieved. The normalization must terminate since the sets B to consider become smaller and smaller in the process. Note that the resulting configuration C_3 also satisfies Conds. (1) and (2), whence it is a 3–nf.

4. Cond. (4) may be achieved by inserting into C_3 the transitions $P, \overline{B^c}/P$, for all P, B such that $P \subseteq B \models C_3$. The insertions may be done via Axioms (B4) and (C1). Note that the resulting configuration C_4 still satisfies Conds. (1)–(3), since $P \subseteq B$ is equivalent to $P \cap B^c = \emptyset$, whence it is a 4–nf.

5. Consider an arbitrary transition $P_i, \overline{N_i}/A_i$, satisfying $N_i \cap A_i = \emptyset$, in the I–part of C_4. We will show how to enforce Cond. (5) for this transition. Under the assumptions, we know $P_i \subseteq A_i \subseteq N_i^c$ and $N_i^c \models C_4$ by Conds. (1) and (3). In order to show $(P_i, N_i^c)^* = A_i$, it is sufficient to establish the following two properties:

(a) $(A_i, N_i^c) \models C_4$; and

(b) $(X, N_i^c) \models C_4$ and $P_i \subseteq X \subseteq N_i^c$ implies $A_i \subseteq X$, for any $X \subseteq Ev$.

Assume that Property (5a) is not yet satisfied, i.e., $(A_i, N_i^c) \not\models C_4$. Then, there must be a transition $P, \overline{N}/A$ in C_4 such that $(A_i, N_i^c) \not\models P, \overline{N}/A$. This transition could be of the form $P_k, \overline{N_k}/A_k$, for some $k \in I$, or of the form $E_j, \overline{E_j^c}/Ev$, for some $j \in J$.

Because of $N_i^c \models C_4$, we have $N_i^c \models P, \overline{N}/A$. But then, $(A_i, N_i^c) \not\models P, \overline{N}/A$ means that $(A_i, N_i^c) \models P, \overline{N}$ and $(A_i, N_i^c) \not\models A$. Hence, in particular, $A_i \supseteq P$, $A_i \not\supseteq A$, and $N_i^c \cap N = \emptyset$, i.e., $N \subseteq N_i$.

We now show that $P_i, \overline{N_i}/A_i \parallel P, \overline{N}/A = P_i, \overline{N_i}/A_i, A \parallel P, \overline{N}/A$ by the following calculations, where $N_1 =_{df} N_i \setminus N$ and $A_1 =_{df} A_i \setminus P$:

$$
\begin{aligned}
& \vdash P_i, \overline{N_i}/A_i \parallel P, \overline{N}/A \\
&= P_i, \overline{N_1}, \overline{N}/A_1, P \parallel P, \overline{N}/A \\
&= P_i, \overline{N_1}, \overline{N}/A_1 \parallel P_i, \overline{N_1}, \overline{N}/P \parallel P, \overline{N}/A & (A2, A6) \\
&= P_i, \overline{N_1}, \overline{N}/A_1 \parallel \overline{N}/(P_i, \overline{N_1}/P \parallel P/A) & (A5, A6) \\
&= P_i, \overline{N_1}, \overline{N}/A_1 \parallel \overline{N}/(P_i, \overline{N_1}/P \parallel P_i, \overline{N_1}/(P/A) \parallel P/A) & (C2) \\
&= P_i, \overline{N_1}, \overline{N}/A_1 \parallel \overline{N}/(P_i, \overline{N_1}/(P \parallel P/A) \parallel P/A) & (A6) \\
&= P_i, \overline{N_1}, \overline{N}/A_1 \parallel \overline{N}/(P_i, \overline{N_1}/(P \parallel A) \parallel P/A) & (C3) \\
&= P_i, \overline{N_1}, \overline{N}/A_1, P, A \parallel P, \overline{N}/A & (A2, A5, A6) \\
&= P_i, \overline{N_i}/A_i, A \parallel P, \overline{N}/A
\end{aligned}
$$

This allows us to replace transition $P_i, \overline{N_i}/A_i$, for which $(A_i, N_i^c) \not\models C_4$ by the transition $P_i, \overline{N_i}/A_i, A$. If now $N_i \cap (A_i \cup A) = \emptyset$, i.e., $A_i \cup A \subseteq N_i^c$, then we find $(A_i \cup A, N_i^c) \models P, \overline{N}/A$ and $A_i \cup A \supsetneq A_i$ since $A_i \not\supseteq A$. Thus, using this technique, one can saturate the A_i until, for all transitions $P, \overline{N}/A$, there exists no $i \in I$ such that $N_i \cap A_i = \emptyset$ and $(A_i, N_i^c) \not\models P, \overline{N}/A$. This will ensure Property (5a), for all $i \in I$.

It remains to establish Property (5b). Let $(X, N_i^c) \models C_4$ for some $X \subseteq Ev$ such that $P_i \subseteq X \subseteq N_i^c$. Hence, $(X, N_i^c) \models P_i, \overline{N_i}/A_i$. Since $(X, N_i^c) \models P_i, \overline{N_i}$, we consequently know that $(X, N_i^c) \models A_i$, i.e., $A_i \subseteq X$ as desired. Let C_5 denote the 5–nf configuration resulting from this normalization step.

6. Let us assume that some transition $P, \overline{N}/A$ in C_5 violates Cond. (6). Then, using Axiom (D1) we rewrite $\vdash P, \overline{N}/A = P, \overline{N}/Ev$ first, and then by repeated applications of Axiom (D2) we obtain $\vdash P, \overline{N}/Ev = \parallel \{E, \overline{E^c}/Ev : P \subseteq E \subseteq N^c\}$. In this way, the offending original transition $P, \overline{N}/A$ in C_5 can be eliminated completely in terms of transitions indexed by J. This establishes Cond. (6) and does not destroy any of the conditions previously established. The result is a 6–nf C_6 with $\vdash C = C_6$.

Configuration C_6 is now the desired normal form of C.   □

Theorem 2 (Completeness). *Let $C_1 \simeq C_2$. Then, $\vdash C_1 = C_2$.*

Proof. Let, w.l.o.g., C_1, C_2 be in normal form such that $C_1 \simeq C_2$, i.e., $M \models C_1$ iff $M \models C_2$. Due to symmetry and Axioms (B1)–(B4), it suffices to show that every parallel component, i.e., transition, of C_1 also occurs in C_2.

Consider a transition of the form $P_i, \overline{N_i}/A_i$ occurring in C_1. Since C_1 is in normal form, we know by Cond. (3) that $N_i^c \models C_1$. Hence, by premise $C_1 \simeq C_2$, we have $N_i^c \models C_2$. We may now apply Cond. (4), since $P_i \subseteq N_i^c$ by Cond. (1), to obtain some $i' \in I$ such that $P_{i'}, \overline{N_{i'}}/A_{i'}$ is a transition in C_2 with $N_{i'} = N_i$ and $P_{i'} = P_i$. By Cond. (5), $A_{i'} = (P_{i'}, N_{i'}^c)^* = (P_i, N_i^c)^* = A_i$. Note that the definitions of $(P_{i'}, N_{i'}^c)^*$ in C_2 and $(P_i, N_i^c)^*$ in C_1 coincide, because of $C_1 \simeq C_2$.

Consider a transition of the form $E_j, \overline{E_j^c}/Ev$ in C_1. Since C_1 is in normal form, we know by Cond. (2) that $E_j \not\models C_1$. Hence, $E_j \not\models C_2$ by the premise $C_1 \simeq C_2$. Further, by Cond. (2) applied to normal form C_2, we conclude the existence of some $j' \in J$ such that $E_{j'}, E_{j'}^c/Ev$ is a transition in C_2 with $E_{j'} = E_j$.   □

5   Discussion and Related Work

There exists a wealth of related work on the semantics of synchronous languages, especially Statecharts. Our paper focused on the most popular original semantics of Harel's Statecharts, as defined by Pnueli and Shalev in their seminal paper [15]. Since this semantics combines the synchrony hypothesis and the causality principle, it cannot be compositional if step reactions are modeled by input–output–functions over event sets, according to a result by Huizing and Gerth [5]. Within the traditional style of labeled transition systems, researchers have then concentrated on providing compositionality for Pnueli and Shalev's semantics either by taking transition labels to be partial orders encoding causality [7,12] or by explicitly including micro–step transitions [11]. Our step algebra is related to the former kind of semantics, where causality is encoded via intuitionistically interpreted sequence structures. However, in contrast to the other mentioned work, our logical approach lends itself to establishing full–abstraction results [9] and the equational axiomatization of Statecharts presented here.

A different approach to axiomatizing Statecharts was suggested by de Roever et al. for an early and lateron rejected Statecharts semantics that does not obey global consistency [3]. In their setting, it is admissible for a firing transition to generate an event, whose absence was assumed earlier in the construction of the macro step under consideration. This leads to a very different semantics than the one of Pnueli and Shalev [15], for which Huizing, Gerth, and de Roever gave a denotational account in [6]. This denotational semantics provided the groundwork for an axiomatization by Hooman, Ramesh, and de Roever [4]. However, in contrast to our work that *equationally* axiomatized the step congruence underlying Pnueli and Shalev's semantics, Hooman et al. supplied a Hoare–style axiomatization for both liveness and safety properties of Statecharts, which was proved to be sound and complete with respect to the denotational semantics of Huizing et al. [6]. A similar approach was taken by Levi regarding a process–algebraic variant of Pnueli and Shalev's Statecharts and a real–time temporal logic [7]. It should be noted that the settings of de Rover et al. and of Levi deal with sequences of macro steps and not just single macro steps, as our step algebra does. However, extending the step algebra and its axiomatization to sequences of macro steps should not be difficult. In such a more general development the configuration algebra introduced here would play the role of a synchronization algebra [17], around which a macro–step process language would be built.

The results of this paper are not restricted to Statecharts but can also be applied to other languages, in particular to Berry's Esterel [1]. The authors have shown in [10], using the same model–theoretic framework of intuitionistic sequence structures as for Statecharts, how the instantaneous core of Esterel can be faithfully and compositionally encoded in terms of propositional formulas. This is done in such a way that the operational execution of the encoding produces the same responses as the execution of the original program under the semantics of Esterel [1]. It is not difficult to see that the propositional formulas corresponding to Esterel configurations build a subclass in our step algebra, when taking $Ev =_{\mathrm{df}} \{s{=}1, s{=}0 : s \text{ is a signal}\}$, where $s{=}1$ stands for signal s is present 'high' and $s{=}0$ for s is present 'low'. This subclass, however, requires the full syntax of our step algebra, which allows for nested transition triggers. For example, the instantaneous Esterel program **present** a **then present** b **else emit** c **end end** would be translated into the configuration $a{=}1/(b{=}0/c{=}1)$; see [10] for details. Because of the existence of this encoding of Esterel reactions into our step algebra, which preserves Esterel's semantics, the axiomatization presented here can directly be used to reason about Esterel reactions. For the sake of completeness, it needs to be mentioned that some initial work on axiomatizing Esterel has been carried out within an encoding of Esterel programs in a variant of the duration calculus [14]. However, this work aims at an axiomatic semantics for Esterel rather than an equational axiomatization of the underlying step congruence.

The step algebra presented in this paper focused on the most essential operators in synchronous languages. In the future we would like to enrich our algebra and its axiomatization to accommodate an operator for *event scoping*, or signal hiding, which is used in Esterel [1] and Argos [13]. Moreover, instead of encoding the external–choice operator $+$, as found in the hierarchy operator of Statecharts, via parallel composition and negated events, it is possible to include $+$ as a primitive operator in our step algebra. To do so, one only needs to add a silent, non–synchronizing event in the action of every transition; see [9].

Our syntax is a common superset of the kernel languages of Statecharts and Esterel. Specifically, the applications of Axioms (A5), (A6), and (C2) introduce nested triggers and parallel compositions in the action part of a transition, which do not exist in standard Statecharts configurations. However, it can be shown that any axiomatic proof can be performed properly within the Statecharts fragment, when using the following axioms instead of their original counterparts:

(A6') $\qquad I/A \parallel I/B = I/(A \cup B)$

(C2') $\qquad\qquad I/A = I/A \parallel I, J/A$

(C3') $\qquad I/A \parallel A, J/B = I/A \parallel A, J/B \parallel I, J/B$

(D3') $I, \overline{N}/B \parallel P, \overline{N}/A = \{I, \overline{N}, \overline{e}/B : e \in P\} \parallel P, \overline{N}/A$, if $N \cap A \neq \emptyset, P \neq \emptyset$

6   Conclusions and Future Work

This paper presented a uniform algebra, to which we referred as step algebra, for reasoning about step reactions in synchronous languages, such as those originating from Statecharts and Esterel. The algebra covers single reactions, and as such constitutes a first important step towards an axiomatization of Statecharts and related languages. Its semantics was inspired by previous work of the authors, which adapted ideas from intuitionistic logics for defining a compositional semantics for step reactions. Our main result is a sound and complete axiomatization of the resulting step congruence in our step algebra, whose completeness proof mixes techniques from process algebra and logic. This yields, for the first time in the literature, a complete axiomatization of Statecharts macro steps, in the sense of Pnueli and Shalev. Modulo a simple syntactic translation, this axiomatization can be adapted to instantaneous reactions in Esterel as well. We believe that our approach provides important groundwork for comparing popular synchronous languages by means of axioms, an approach that already proved successful in process algebra, and also for developing suitable compositional verification methods.

Regarding future work, we plan to integrate other operators employed in synchronous languages into our step algebra, in particular an operator for event scoping. Additionally, our algebra should be extended to step sequences, by adding prefixing operators and recursion.

Acknowledgments

We would like to thank the anonymous referees for their valuable comments and suggestions. The second author was supported by EPSRC grant GR/M99637 and the EC Types Working Group IST–EU–29001.

References

1. G. Berry. The constructive semantics of pure Esterel, 1999. Draft Version 3. Available at http://www-sop.inria.fr/meije/Personnel/Gerard.Berry.html.   386, 388, 398, 399
2. D. Harel. Statecharts: A visual formalism for complex systems. *SCP*, 8:231–274, 1987.   386, 388, 390
3. D. Harel, A. Pnueli, J. Pruzan-Schmidt, and R. Sherman. On the formal semantics of Statecharts. In *LICS '87*, pages 54–64. IEEE Computer Society Press, 1987.   398
4. J. J. M. Hooman, S. Ramesh, and W.-P. de Roever. A compositional axiomatization of Statecharts. *Theoretical Computer Science*, 101:289–335, 1992.   398
5. C. Huizing. *Semantics of Reactive Systems: Comparison and Full Abstraction.* PhD thesis, Eindhoven Univ. of Technology, 1991.   398
6. C. Huizing, R. Gerth, and W.-P. de Roever. Modeling Statecharts behavior in a fully abstract way. In *CAAP '88*, volume 299 of *LNCS*, pages 271–294, 1988.   398
7. F. Levi. *Verification of Temporal and Real-Time Properties of Statecharts.* PhD thesis, Univ. of Pisa-Genova-Udine, 1997.   398
8. G. Lüttgen and M. Mendler. Statecharts: From visual syntax to model-theoretic semantics. In *Integrating Diagrammatic and Formal Specification Techniques*, pages 615–621. Austrian Computer Society, 2001.   387, 389, 390
9. G. Lüttgen and M. Mendler. The intuitionism behind Statecharts steps. *ACM Trans. on Computational Logic*, 3(1):1–41, 2002.   387, 390, 391, 398, 399
10. G. Lüttgen and M. Mendler. Towards a model-theory for Esterel. In *Synchronous Languages, Applications, and Programming*, volume 65:5. ENTCS, 2002. To appear.   387, 390, 398, 399

11. G. Lüttgen, M. von der Beeck, and R. Cleaveland. Statecharts via process algebra. In *CONCUR '99*, volume 1664 of *LNCS*, pages 399–414, 1999. 398
12. A. Maggiolo-Schettini, A. Peron, and S. Tini. Equivalences of Statecharts. In *CONCUR '96*, volume 1119 of *LNCS*, pages 687–702, 1996. 398
13. F. Maraninchi. Operational and compositional semantics of synchronous automaton compositions. In *CONCUR '92*, volume 630 of *LNCS*, pages 550–564, 1992. 399
14. P. K. Pandya, Y. S. Ramakrishna, and R. K. Shyamasundar. A compositional semantics of Esterel in Duration Calculus. In *AMAST '95*, volume 936 of *LNCS*, 1995. 399
15. A. Pnueli and M. Shalev. What is in a step: On the semantics of Statecharts. In *TACS '91*, volume 526 of *LNCS*, pages 244–264, 1991. 386, 388, 390, 391, 398
16. D. van Dalen. Intuitionistic logic. In *Handbook of Philosophical Logic*, volume III, chapter 4, pages 225–339. Reidel, 1986. 390, 393
17. G. Winskel. A compositional proof system on a category of labelled transition systems. *Inform. and Comp.*, 87(1/2):2–57, 1990. 398

Regular Sets of Pomsets with Autoconcurrency

Jean Fanchon[1] and Rémi Morin[2]

[1] LAAS-CNRS
7, avenue du colonel Roche, F-31077 Toulouse, France
[2] LIF
39 rue F. Joliot-Curie, F-13453 Marseille cedex 13, France

Abstract. Partially ordered multisets (or pomsets) constitute one of the most basic models of concurrency. We introduce and compare several notions of regularity for pomset languages by means of contexts and residues of different kinds. We establish some interesting closure properties that allow us to relate this approach to SP-recognizability in the particular case of series-parallel pomsets. Finally we introduce the framework of compatible languages which generalizes several classical formalisms (including message sequence charts and firing pomsets of Petri nets). In this way, we identify regular sets of pomsets as recognizable subsets in the monoid of multiset sequences.

Partially ordered multisets or partial words constitute one of the most basic models of concurrency [14]. Process algebras like CCS and TCSP, and system models like Petri nets, have been given pomset semantics for many years, and several pomset algebras have been designed. Nevertheless the study of pomset languages from the point of view of recognizability or regularity still offers many interesting problems to investigate.

A key difficulty one encounters in the case of pomsets as opposed to words is the lack of a finite set of operators generating all of them [7]. As an alternative approach, different accepting finite devices for pomset languages have been defined such as, e.g., graph acceptors applied to pomsets [15] and asynchronous automata applied to restricted classes of pomsets without autoconcurrency [4]. In these works the recognizable languages have until now no characterization in an algebraic framework.

On the other hand, some restricted frameworks have been defined and investigated with an algebraic approach of recognizable sets of pomsets. In particular, the trace monoids [3], the concurrency monoids of stably concurrent automata [5] and more recently the monoid of basic message sequence charts [12] have been studied in details.

To our knowledge, until now little work has been done on languages of pomsets with autoconcurrency. The main exception is the algebra of series-parallel pomsets, for which Kleene-like results [11] and Büchi-like results [9] were established recently. In [6], a definition of recognizability by vertex substitution has been studied. It extends to the class of all pomsets the algebraic definition of [11] for SP-pomsets, and fulfills several closure properties.

L. Brim et al. (Eds.): CONCUR 2002, LNCS 2421, pp. 402–417, 2002.
© Springer-Verlag Berlin Heidelberg 2002

Investigating different interpretations of what a pomset language expresses, we introduce in this paper three candidate extensions to pomset languages of the definition of context known for word languages. The corresponding context equivalences $\asymp^{\mathcal{L}}$, $\asymp^{\mathcal{L}}_{\mathrm{w}}$, and $\asymp^{\mathcal{L}}_{\mathrm{s}}$ are shown to give rise to three distinct notions of regularity: More precisely we show

$$\asymp^{\mathcal{L}} \text{ is of finite index} \implies \asymp^{\mathcal{L}}_{\mathrm{w}} \text{ is of finite index} \implies \asymp^{\mathcal{L}}_{\mathrm{s}} \text{ is of finite index}$$

for a given pomset language $\mathcal{L}$ — but none of the converses holds in general. By means of several closure properties, we show also that these notions of regularity are weaker than the algebraic SP-recognizability [11] when we restrict to series-parallel pomsets.

In order to relate our three notions of regularity with the algebraic definition of recognizability in monoids, we introduce the class of *compatible languages*. The latter are characterized by their corresponding step sequences. They include Mazurkiewicz traces [3], local trace languages [10], subsets of message sequence charts [1, 13], pomset languages of stably concurrent automata [5], CCI sets of P-traces [2], and firing pomset languages of Place/Transition nets [8, 16] — but not series-parallel pomsets. Differently from the more general case of weak languages, we show that regularity of a compatible set of pomsets means exactly recognizability of the corresponding step extensions in the free monoid of multiset sequences. Thus, this wide framework of compatible pomset languages proves to have some interesting properties, although it generalizes many classical formalisms of concurrency theory. For this reason, we believe that these compatible languages deserve to be further investigated. In particular, realization of regular languages by labelled Petri nets and correspondence with MSO definability would lead to nice generalizations of results known in particular frameworks.

1 Basics

In this section, we present our main notations and definitions concerning pomsets. We recall the simple relationship between weak languages and basic languages of pomsets. We introduce the notion of *compatible languages* and show that this concept generalizes several classical frameworks of concurrency theory.

Preliminaries. In this paper, we consider a finite alphabet Σ. For any words $u, v \in \Sigma^*$, we write $u \leqslant v$ if u is a prefix of v, i.e. there is $z \in \Sigma^*$ such that $u.z = v$. The set of multisets over Σ is denoted by $\mathcal{M}(\Sigma)$ and $\mathcal{M}(\Sigma)^*$ denotes the set of finite sequences of multisets over Σ, also called *step sequences*.

A *pomset* over Σ is a triple $t = (E, \preccurlyeq, \xi)$ where $(E, \preccurlyeq)$ is a finite partial order and ξ is a mapping from E to Σ. A pomset is *without autoconcurrency* if $\xi(x) = \xi(y)$ implies $x \preccurlyeq y$ or $y \preccurlyeq x$ for all $x, y \in E$. A pomset can be seen as an abstraction of an execution of a concurrent system. In this view, the elements e of E are *events* and their label $\xi(e)$ describes the basic action of the system that is performed when the event e occurs. Furthermore, the order describes

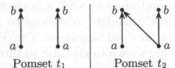

Fig. 1. Two pomsets with the same step extensions

the causal dependence between the events. In particular, a pomset is without autoconcurrency if two occurrences of an action cannot run simultaneously. We denote by $\mathbb{P}(\Sigma)$ the class of all pomsets over Σ. As usual, we shall identify isomorphic pomsets as a single object and consider only classes of pomsets closed under isomorphisms.

A *prefix* of a pomset $t = (E, \preccurlyeq, \xi)$ is the restriction $t' = (E', \preccurlyeq_{|E'}, \xi_{|E'})$ of t to some downward-closed subset E' of E. An *order extension* of a pomset $t = (E, \preccurlyeq, \xi)$ is a pomset $t' = (E, \preccurlyeq', \xi)$ such that $\preccurlyeq \subseteq \preccurlyeq'$. We denote by $\mathrm{OE}(t)$ the set of order extensions of t. A *linear extension* of t is an order extension that is linearly ordered. Now, words can naturally be considered as linear pomsets. Therefore, the set $\mathrm{LE}(t)$ of linear extensions of a pomset t over Σ may be identified to a subset of Σ^*: $\mathrm{LE}(t) = \mathrm{OE}(t) \cap \Sigma^*$.

More generally, any sequence of multisets $w \in \mathcal{M}(\Sigma)^*$ written $w = p_1 ... p_n$ can be identified with a pomset over the set of events $p_1 \uplus ... \uplus p_n$ such that each event of p_i is below each event of p_j for $1 \leqslant i < j \leqslant n$. For any pomset t, the set of *step extensions* $\mathrm{SE}(t)$ consists of the multiset sequences that are order extensions of t: $\mathrm{SE}(t) = \mathrm{OE}(t) \cap \mathcal{M}(\Sigma)^*$. As the next example shows, two distinct pomsets may share the same set of step extensions.

EXAMPLE 1.1. Consider the two pomsets t_1 and t_2 of Fig. 1. One easily checks that $\mathrm{SE}(t_1) = \mathrm{SE}(t_2)$.

Note that this phenomenon is typical of pomsets with autoconcurrency: For any two pomsets t_1 and t_2 *without* autoconcurrency, if $\mathrm{LE}(t_1) = \mathrm{LE}(t_2)$ then t_1 and t_2 are isomorphic. This holds also if $\mathrm{SE}(t_1) = \mathrm{SE}(t_2)$ since $\mathrm{LE}(t) = \mathrm{SE}(t) \cap \Sigma^*$.

Thus, pomsets with autoconcurrency are in general more expressive than their step extensions. We want here to study particular classes of pomsets (called *compatible sets*) that are faithfully described by the corresponding step extensions. As we shall observe below (Prop. 1.9), this includes the languages of firing pomsets of Place/Transition nets.

Weak and Basic Sets of Pomsets. The map OE from pomsets to sets of pomsets can be extended to languages of pomsets by putting $\mathrm{OE}(\mathcal{L}) = \bigcup_{t \in \mathcal{L}} \mathrm{OE}(t)$. Obviously, $\mathcal{L} \subseteq \mathrm{OE}(\mathcal{L}) = \mathrm{OE}(\mathrm{OE}(\mathcal{L}))$ for any language of pomsets $\mathcal{L}$. Now, a language is *weak* if it contains all its order extensions.

DEFINITION 1.2. *A language of pomsets $\mathcal{L}$ is* weak *if $\mathcal{L} = \mathrm{OE}(\mathcal{L})$.*

Typical examples of weak languages are the sets of firing pomsets of Petri nets. Consider for instance the example of a Producer-Consumer system illustrated by the Petri net of Fig. 2. In this net, p represents a production of one

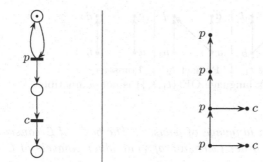

Fig. 2. Petri net $\mathcal{N}$ **Fig. 3.** Firing pomset t with autoconcurrency

item and c a consumption. Some concurrency may occur between p and c or even between distinct occurrences of c when the middle place contains several tokens. Usually, concurrent behaviors are described by partial orders. For instance here, a concurrent execution of the system is depicted in Fig. 3.

More generally, we let a *Petri net* be a quadruple $\mathcal{N} = (S, T, W, \mathrm{M}_{in})$ where

- S is a set of places and T is a set of transitions such that $S \cap T = \emptyset$;
- W is a map from $(S \times T) \cup (T \times S)$ to $\mathbb{N}$, called *weight function*;
- M_{in} is a map from S to $\mathbb{N}$, called *initial marking*.

We let $\mathrm{Mar}_{\mathcal{N}}$ denotes the set of all markings of $\mathcal{N}$ that is to say functions $\mathrm{M} : S \rightarrow \mathbb{N}$; a multiset p of transitions is *enabled* at $\mathrm{M} \in \mathrm{Mar}_{\mathcal{N}}$ if $\forall s \in S$, $\mathrm{M}(s) \geqslant \sum_{t \in T} p(t) \cdot W(s, t)$; in this case, we note $\mathrm{M}[p\rangle \mathrm{M}'$ where $\mathrm{M}'(s) = \mathrm{M}(s) + \sum_{t \in T} p(t) \cdot (W(t, s) - W(s, t))$ and say that the transitions of p may be *fired* concurrently and lead to the marking M'. A *multiset firing sequence* consists of a sequence of markings $\mathrm{M}_0, ..., \mathrm{M}_n$ and a sequence of multisets of transitions $p_1, ..., p_n$ such that $\mathrm{M}_0 = \mathrm{M}_{in}$ and $\forall k \in [1, n]$, $\mathrm{M}_{k-1}[p_k\rangle \mathrm{M}_k$. A *firing pomset* [8, 16] of $\mathcal{N}$ is a pomset $t = (E, \preccurlyeq, \xi)$ such that for all prefixes $t' = (E', \preccurlyeq', \xi')$ of t, and for all linear extensions $a_1...a_n \in \mathrm{LE}(t')$, the sequence $\{a_1\}...\{a_n\}.\xi(\min_{\preccurlyeq}(E \setminus E'))$ is a multiset firing sequence of $\mathcal{N}$. For instance, the pomset t of Fig. 3 is a firing pomset of the Producer-Consumer. Clearly, the language of firing pomsets of any Petri net is weak.

As far as the description of concurrency is concerned, some redundancy of information may appear in weak languages. In order to focus on restricted but representative parts of weak languages, we look at *basic* sets of pomsets.

DEFINITION 1.3. *A language of pomsets $\mathcal{L}$ is basic if $t_1 \in \mathrm{OE}(t_2)$ implies $t_1 = t_2$, for all $t_1, t_2 \in \mathcal{L}$.*

We can check easily that two basic sets that have the same order extensions are equal: $\mathrm{OE}(\mathcal{L}) = \mathrm{OE}(\mathcal{L}')$ implies $\mathcal{L} = \mathcal{L}'$ for all basic sets of pomsets $\mathcal{L}$ and $\mathcal{L}'$. Therefore the map OE from basic sets of pomsets to weak sets of pomsets is one-to-one. Actually, we shall see that this map is also onto.

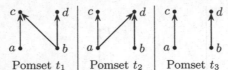

Pomset t_1 | Pomset t_2 | Pomset t_3

Fig. 4. The weak language $\mathrm{OE}(\{t_1, t_2\})$ is not compatible

DEFINITION 1.4. *Let $\mathcal{L}$ be a language of pomsets. The basis of $\mathcal{L}$ consists of all pomsets $t \in \mathcal{L}$ which are no order extension of some other pomsets of $\mathcal{L}$:*

$$\mathrm{Basis}(\mathcal{L}) = \{t \in \mathcal{L} \mid t' \in \mathcal{L} \wedge t \in \mathrm{OE}(t') \Rightarrow t = t'\}.$$

For any weak language $\mathcal{L}$, $\mathrm{OE}(\mathrm{Basis}(\mathcal{L})) = \mathcal{L}$ and $\mathrm{Basis}(\mathcal{L})$ is a basic set of pomsets. Thus, we obtain *a one-to-one correspondence between weak languages of pomsets and basic languages of pomsets.* However, as already observed in [10], this duality may not preserve some regularity properties such as MSO definability.

Compatible Sets of Pomsets. We focus now on the step extensions of a language $\mathcal{L}$: It consists of step sequences that are order extensions of $\mathcal{L}$. Formally, we put $\mathrm{SE}(\mathcal{L}) = \mathrm{OE}(\mathcal{L}) \cap \mathcal{M}(\varSigma)^\star$. Equivalently, we also have $\mathrm{SE}(\mathcal{L}) = \bigcup_{t \in \mathcal{L}} \mathrm{SE}(t)$. The *step compatible closure* $\overline{\mathcal{L}}$ of a language $\mathcal{L}$ is the set of all pomsets whose step extensions are step extensions of $\mathcal{L}$: $\overline{\mathcal{L}} = \{t \in \mathbb{P}(\varSigma) \mid \mathrm{SE}(t) \subseteq \mathrm{SE}(\mathcal{L})\}$. Obviously $\mathcal{L} \subseteq \overline{\mathcal{L}}$ and $\overline{\mathcal{L}} = \overline{\mathrm{OE}(\mathcal{L})}$ because $\mathrm{SE}(\mathcal{L}) = \mathrm{SE}(\mathrm{OE}(\mathcal{L}))$. Hence $\mathcal{L} \subseteq \mathrm{OE}(\mathcal{L}) \subseteq \overline{\mathcal{L}}$. We say that $\mathcal{L}$ is *compatible* if it is maximal among all languages that share the same step extensions.

DEFINITION 1.5. *A language of pomsets $\mathcal{L}$ is compatible if $\mathcal{L} = \overline{\mathcal{L}}$.*

We observe that any compatible set that includes t_1 or t_2 of Fig. 1 contains both of them because $\mathrm{SE}(t_1) = \mathrm{SE}(t_2)$ (Example 1.1). So neither $\{t_1\}$ nor $\{t_2\}$ is a compatible set of pomsets. Actually any compatible language is weak since $\mathcal{L} \subseteq \mathrm{OE}(\mathcal{L}) \subseteq \overline{\mathcal{L}}$. As the next example shows, the converse fails.

EXAMPLE 1.6. Consider the pomsets t_1, t_2 and t_3 of Fig. 4. Then the weak language $\mathcal{L} = \mathrm{OE}(\{t_1, t_2\})$ is not compatible since $t_3 \in \overline{\mathcal{L}} \setminus \mathcal{L}$.

It turns out that several classical formalisms of concurrency theory are included in the framework of compatible languages. For instance, the next result shows that languages of Mazurkiewicz traces [3], subsets of message sequence charts [1, 13], pomset languages of stably concurrent automata [5], and CCI sets of P-traces [2] are particular cases of basic languages of pomsets whose order extensions are *compatible* languages of pomsets (without autoconcurrency).

PROPOSITION 1.7. *Let $\mathcal{L}$ be a language of pomsets without autoconcurrency such that for all t_1, $t_2 \in \mathcal{L}$, if $\mathrm{LE}(t_1) \cap \mathrm{LE}(t_2) \neq \emptyset$ then $t_1 = t_2$. Then $\mathcal{L}$ is basic and $\mathrm{OE}(\mathcal{L})$ is compatible.*

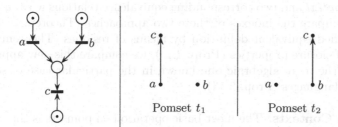

Fig. 5. A Petri net...   **Fig. 6.** ... and two of its firing pomsets

Proof. The language $\mathcal{L}$ is clearly basic. We take $t \in \overline{\mathrm{OE}(\mathcal{L})}$. Since $\overline{\mathcal{L}} = \overline{\mathrm{OE}(\mathcal{L})}$, we have $t \in \overline{\mathcal{L}}$. Note also that t is without autoconcurrency. Let $u_1 \in \mathrm{LE}(t)$. Since $t. \in \overline{\mathcal{L}}$, there is $t_1 \in \mathcal{L}$ such that $u_1 \in \mathrm{LE}(t_1)$. Assume now that u_2 is another linear extension of t that only differs from u_1 by the order of two adjacent actions, i.e. $u_1 = a_1.a_2...a_n$ and $u_2 = a_1...a_{k-1}.a_{k+1}.a_k.a_{k+2}...a_n$. Then the step sequence $w = \{a_1\}...\{a_{k-1}\}.\{a_k.a_{k+1}\}.\{a_{k+2}\}...\{a_n\}$ is also a step extension of t. Therefore there is $t_2 \in \mathcal{L}$ such that $w \in \mathrm{SE}(t_2)$. Since t_1 and t_2 share u_1 as a linear extension, we get $t_1 = t_2$ hence $u_2 \in \mathrm{LE}(t_1)$. Since all linear extensions of t can be obtained from u_1 by successive permutations of adjacent (independent) actions, we conclude that $\mathrm{LE}(t) \subseteq \mathrm{LE}(t_1)$. Since t and t_1 are without autoconcurrency, t is actually an order extension of t_1, hence $t \in \mathrm{OE}(\mathcal{L})$.   □

REMARK 1.8. In Prop. 1.7 above, the assumption that $\mathcal{L}$ is without autoconcurrency cannot be removed: The set of order extensions of the basic language which consists only of the pomset t_2 of Fig. 1 is not compatible since $\mathrm{SE}(t_1) = \mathrm{SE}(t_2)$ (Example 1.1).

As claimed above, the framework of compatible languages includes the partial word semantics of Place/Transition nets.

PROPOSITION 1.9. *The set of firing pomsets $\mathcal{L}$ of a Petri net $\mathcal{N}$ is compatible.*

Proof. Let $t = (E, \preccurlyeq, \xi)$ be a pomset of $\overline{\mathcal{L}}$. Let $t' = (E', \preccurlyeq_{|E'}, \xi_{|E'})$ be a prefix of t and $u' \in \mathrm{LE}(t')$ be a linear extension of t'. We put $M = \min_{\preccurlyeq}(E \setminus E')$ and $p = \xi(M)$. We consider a linear extension v' of the restriction of t to the events of $E \setminus (E' \cup M)$. Then $u'.p.v'$ is a step extension of t. Consequently, $u'.p.v' \in \mathrm{SE}(t_1)$ for some $t_1 \in \mathcal{L}$ and $u'.p$ is a step firing sequence of $\mathcal{N}$. Thus $t \in \mathcal{L}$ as well.   □

    To conclude this section, we consider the Petri net of Fig. 5. The basis Basis($\mathcal{L}$) of its firing pomsets contains the pomsets t_1 and t_2 of Fig. 6. Since $abc \in \mathrm{LE}(t_1) \cap \mathrm{LE}(t_2)$, not all compatible languages without autoconcurrency satisfy the condition of Prop. 1.7. Indeed, firing pomset languages of Petri nets are often much more involved than this restricted framework.

2   Regularity via Contexts and Residues

In this section, we investigate and relate several approaches that extend the usual notion of regularity from words to pomsets with autoconcurrency. We introduce two notions of *context* and two corresponding equivalence relations w.r.t. a given language. We compare the indexes of these two approaches (Theorem 2.4) and present a simplified equivalent definition by means of residues (Theorem 2.9). With the help of closure properties (Prop. 2.13), we compare this new approach of regularity to the more algebraic one known in the particular case of series-parallel pomset languages (Prop. 2.14).

Regularity via Contexts. The most basic operation on pomsets is the *strong concatenation*. Given two pomsets $t_1 = (E_1, \preccurlyeq_1, \xi_1)$ and $t_2 = (E_2, \preccurlyeq_2, \xi_2)$ over Σ, the product $t_1 \cdot t_2$ is the pomset that puts each event of t_2 after all events of t_1, i.e. $t_1 \cdot t_2 = (E_1 \uplus E_2, \preccurlyeq_1 \cup \preccurlyeq_2 \cup E_1 \times E_2, \xi_1 \cup \xi_2)$. This operation is the basis of the first notion of context which identifies a language and its order extensions. In other words, this approach adopts a weak interpretation of causality.

DEFINITION 2.1. *Let $\mathcal{L}$ be a language of pomsets and u be a pomset over Σ. The weak context of u w.r.t. $\mathcal{L}$ is $\mathcal{L} \backslash_{\mathrm{w}} u = \{(x, y) \in \mathbb{P}(\Sigma)^2 \mid x \cdot u \cdot y \in \mathrm{OE}(\mathcal{L})\}$. We say that u and v are* weak context equivalent *w.r.t. $\mathcal{L}$ if $\mathcal{L} \backslash_{\mathrm{w}} u = \mathcal{L} \backslash_{\mathrm{w}} v$. In that case we write $u \asymp_{\mathrm{w}}^{\mathcal{L}} v$ or simply $u \asymp_{\mathrm{w}} v$ if $\mathcal{L}$ is clear from the context.*

In the literature, many other products were designed in different frameworks, in particular for Mazurkiewicz traces, message sequence charts, or in the more general framework of stably concurrent automata. Following this trend, we introduce a weak product that somehow does not specify the causalities between the two components, giving rise to several possible pomsets. This operation is therefore better defined for languages than for single pomsets. Given two sets of pomsets $\mathcal{L}_1$ and $\mathcal{L}_2$, the *weak concatenation* $\mathcal{L}_1 \diamond \mathcal{L}_2$ consists of all pomsets $t = (E, \preccurlyeq, \xi)$ that can be split into a prefix belonging to $\mathcal{L}_1$ and a remaining part belonging to $\mathcal{L}_2$, i.e. such that $E = E_1 \uplus E_2$ where E_1 is downward-closed w.r.t. $\preccurlyeq$, $(E_1, \preccurlyeq_{|E_1}, \xi_{|E_1})$ belongs to $\mathcal{L}_1$ and $(E_2, \preccurlyeq_{|E_2}, \xi_{|E_2})$ belongs to $\mathcal{L}_2$. We can easily check that this weak concatenation is associative on sets of pomsets. We can now define our second kind of contexts.

DEFINITION 2.2. *Let $\mathcal{L}$ be a language of pomsets and u be a pomset over Σ. The context of u w.r.t. $\mathcal{L}$ is $\mathcal{L} \backslash u = \{(x, y) \in \mathbb{P}(\Sigma)^2 \mid (\{x\} \diamond \{u\} \diamond \{y\}) \cap \mathcal{L} \neq \emptyset\}$. Then u and v are* context equivalent *w.r.t. $\mathcal{L}$, and we write $u \asymp^{\mathcal{L}} v$, if $\mathcal{L} \backslash u = \mathcal{L} \backslash v$.*

We want now to compare these two equivalence relations. In the following lemma, we denote by $\mathrm{OE}(\mathcal{L} \backslash v)$ the set of pairs of pomsets (x, y) such that there are some pomsets x' and y' satisfying $x \in \mathrm{OE}(x')$, $y \in \mathrm{OE}(y')$, and $(x', y') \in \mathcal{L} \backslash v$.

LEMMA 2.3. *Let $\mathcal{L}$ be a language of pomsets and u be a pomset over Σ. Then*

$$\mathcal{L} \backslash_{\mathrm{w}} u = \bigcup_{v: u \in \mathrm{OE}(v)} \mathrm{OE}(\mathcal{L} \backslash v).$$

Proof. Consider first $(x, y) \in \mathcal{L} \backslash_{\mathrm{w}} u$. Then $x \cdot u \cdot y$ is an order extension of some pomset $t \in \mathcal{L}$. Therefore there are three pomsets x', u', and y' such that

$x \in \mathrm{OE}(x')$, $u \in \mathrm{OE}(u')$, $y \in \mathrm{OE}(y')$, and $t \in \{x'\} \diamond \{u'\} \diamond \{y'\}$. Thus $(x', y') \in \mathcal{L} \backslash u'$ and $(x, y) \in \mathrm{OE}(\mathcal{L} \backslash u')$. Conversely, assume now that $(x, y) \in \mathrm{OE}(\mathcal{L} \backslash v)$ for some pomset v which admits u as order extension. Then there are some pomsets x' and y' satisfying $x \in \mathrm{OE}(x')$, $y \in \mathrm{OE}(y')$, and $(x', y') \in \mathcal{L} \backslash v$. Thus $\{x'\} \diamond \{v\} \diamond \{y'\} \cap \mathcal{L}$ is not empty. Let t belong to this set. Clearly $x \cdot u \cdot y$ is an order extension of t, i.e. $(x, y) \in \mathcal{L} \backslash_{\mathrm{w}} u$. $\square$

As an immediate consequence, we observe that the equivalence relation $\asymp^{\mathcal{L}}$ is more restrictive than $\asymp^{\mathcal{L}}_{\mathrm{w}}$.

THEOREM 2.4. *Let $\mathcal{L}$ be a language of pomsets. If $\asymp^{\mathcal{L}}$ is of finite index then $\asymp^{\mathcal{L}}_{\mathrm{w}}$ is of finite index, too.*

Example 2.10 below will show that the converse fails: It may happen that $\asymp^{\mathcal{L}}_{\mathrm{w}}$ is of finite index while $\asymp^{\mathcal{L}}$ has infinitely many equivalence classes. A second basic relationship between these two kinds of contexts is obtained as follows.

LEMMA 2.5. *Let $\mathcal{L}$ be a language of pomsets and u be a pomset over Σ. Then $\mathcal{L} \backslash_{\mathrm{w}} u = \mathrm{OE}(\mathcal{L}) \backslash u$.*

Proof. Assume first that $(x, y) \in \mathcal{L} \backslash_{\mathrm{w}} u$. Then $t = x \cdot u \cdot y$ is a linear extension of some pomset of $\mathcal{L}$; it also belongs obviously to $\{x\} \diamond \{u\} \diamond \{y\}$ hence $(x, y) \in \mathrm{OE}(\mathcal{L}) \backslash u$. Conversely, if $(x, y) \in \mathrm{OE}(\mathcal{L}) \backslash u$ then there is some pomset v in $\{x\} \diamond \{u\} \diamond \{y\} \cap \mathrm{OE}(\mathcal{L})$; furthermore $x \cdot u \cdot y$ is an order extension of v: It belongs to $\mathrm{OE}(\mathcal{L})$ and consequently $(x, y) \in \mathcal{L} \backslash_{\mathrm{w}} u$. $\square$

This shows that for any weak language $\mathcal{L}$, $\asymp^{\mathcal{L}} = \asymp^{\mathcal{L}}_{\mathrm{w}}$. In particular, for word languages these two extensions are equivalent and correspond actually to the usual context equivalence for words. In the sequel, we choose the finer approach and focus on the weak concatenation.

DEFINITION 2.6. *A language of pomsets $\mathcal{L}$ is* regular *if $\asymp^{\mathcal{L}}$ is of finite index.*

Consider a weak language $\mathcal{L}$. By Lemma 2.5, $\asymp^{\mathrm{Basis}(\mathcal{L})}_{\mathrm{w}} = \asymp^{\mathcal{L}}$. Now if $\mathrm{Basis}(\mathcal{L})$ is regular then Theorem 2.4 asserts that $\asymp^{\mathrm{Basis}(\mathcal{L})}_{\mathrm{w}}$ is of finite index. In that way, we get the following result.

COROLLARY 2.7. *For all weak languages $\mathcal{L}$, if $\mathrm{Basis}(\mathcal{L})$ is regular then $\mathcal{L}$ is* regular.

Example 2.11 below will show that the converse fails: We exhibit a non-regular basic language $\mathcal{L}$ such that $\mathrm{OE}(\mathcal{L})$ is regular.

Regularity via Residues. Similarly to properties well-known for words or in monoids, we introduce now two notions of residue that will turn out to lead to an alternative definition for both $\asymp^{\mathcal{L}}$ and $\asymp^{\mathcal{L}}_{\mathrm{w}}$. This simpler approach will help us to present our counter-examples for the converses of Theorem 2.4 and Corollary 2.7 and to establish some closure properties of regularity (Prop. 2.13).

DEFINITION 2.8. *Let $\mathcal{L}$ be a class of pomsets and u be a pomset over Σ.*

1. *The* weak residue *of u w.r.t. $\mathcal{L}$ is $\mathcal{L}/_w\, u = \{y \in \mathbb{P}(\Sigma) \mid u \cdot y \in \mathrm{OE}(\mathcal{L})\}$. We say that u and v are* weak residue equivalent *w.r.t. $\mathcal{L}$ if $\mathcal{L}/_w\, u = \mathcal{L}/_w\, v$. In that case we write $u \asymp_w v$.*
2. *The* residue *of u w.r.t. $\mathcal{L}$ is $\mathcal{L}/u = \{y \in \mathbb{P}(\Sigma) \mid (\{u\} \diamond \{y\}) \cap \mathcal{L} \neq \emptyset\}$. We say that u and v are* residue equivalent *w.r.t. $\mathcal{L}$, and we write $u \asymp v$, if $\mathcal{L}/u = \mathcal{L}/v$.*

Note that if u is not a prefix of $\mathcal{L}$ then the residue $\mathcal{L}/u$ is empty. So all pomsets that are not prefixes of some pomset of $\mathcal{L}$ are residue equivalent. Clearly, if $\asymp$ (resp. $\asymp_w$) is of finite index then $\asymp$ (resp. $\asymp_w$) is of finite index, too. We show here that the converse holds.

THEOREM 2.9. *Let $\mathcal{L}$ be a language of pomsets.*

1. *$\asymp$ is of finite index if and only if $\asymp$ is of finite index.*
2. *$\asymp_w$ is of finite index if and only if $\asymp_w$ is of finite index.*

Proof. We assume that $\asymp$ is of finite index. For all $u \in \mathbb{P}(\Sigma)$, we define the equivalence relation $\equiv_u$ as follows: $v \equiv_u w$ if for all pomsets $z \in \mathbb{P}(\Sigma)$,

$$\{u\} \diamond \{v\} \diamond \{z\} \cap \mathcal{L} \neq \emptyset \iff \{u\} \diamond \{w\} \diamond \{z\} \cap \mathcal{L} \neq \emptyset.$$

We observe that

$$\{u\} \diamond \{v\} \diamond \{z\} \cap \mathcal{L} \neq \emptyset \Leftrightarrow \exists x \in \{u\} \diamond \{v\} : \{x\} \diamond \{z\} \cap \mathcal{L} \neq \emptyset \Leftrightarrow z \in \bigcup_{x \in \{u\} \diamond \{v\}} \mathcal{L}/x$$

Thus $v \equiv_u w$ iff $\bigcup_{x \in \{u\} \diamond \{v\}} \mathcal{L}/x = \bigcup_{x \in \{u\} \diamond \{w\}} \mathcal{L}/x$. Since there are only a finite number of different contexts $\mathcal{L}/x$, there is a finite number of possible unions of such sets, which shows that $\equiv_u$ has finite index for each $u \in \mathbb{P}(\Sigma)$. Furthermore there is only a finite number of possible different equivalences $\equiv_u$. Now $v \asymp w$ iff for all pomsets $u \in \mathbb{P}(\Sigma)$, $v \equiv_u w$. Therefore $\asymp$ is the intersection of a finite number of equivalences of finite index, and has thus a finite index. The proof for $\asymp_w$ is similar.   □

As shown in the sequel, this relationship provides us with simpler means for the study of regularity. It helps us in particular to exhibit some announced counter-examples (Theorem 2.4 and Cor. 2.7).

EXAMPLE 2.10. We consider the language $\mathcal{L} \subseteq \mathcal{M}(\Sigma)^\star$ which consists of all iterations of the step $\{a, b\}$ such as pomset t_5 of Fig. 7. These pomsets have no autoconcurrency: The events labelled a (resp. b) are linearly ordered. We let $\mathcal{L}'$ be the language consisting of all pomsets t' build from any pomset $t \in \mathcal{L}$ by adding a single causality relation from a 2^n-th a-event to the corresponding 2^n-th b-event. Such pomsets are illustrated by t'_3, t'_4 and t'_5 on Fig. 7. Then $\mathcal{L}$ has only 4 distinct residues: $\emptyset$, $\mathcal{L}/a$, $\mathcal{L}/b$, and $\mathcal{L}/\{a, b\}$. Therefore $\asymp^{\mathcal{L}}$ and $\asymp_w^{\mathcal{L}}$ are of finite index (Th. 2.9 and Th. 2.4). Since $\mathrm{OE}(\mathcal{L}) = \mathrm{OE}(\mathcal{L} \cup \mathcal{L}')$, $\asymp_w^{\mathcal{L}} = \asymp_w^{\mathcal{L} \cup \mathcal{L}'}$ is of finite index, too (Lemma 2.5). However we can easily see that $\mathcal{L} \cup \mathcal{L}'$ shows infinitely many residues, hence $\asymp^{\mathcal{L} \cup \mathcal{L}'}$ is of infinite index.

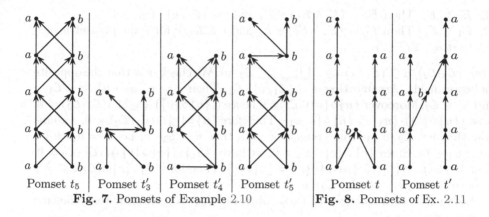

Pomset t_5 | Pomset t_3' | Pomset t_4' | Pomset t_5' | Pomset t | Pomset t'

Fig. 7. Pomsets of Example 2.10 | **Fig. 8.** Pomsets of Ex. 2.11

EXAMPLE 2.11. We consider the subset $\mathcal{L}_0$ of all pomsets t that consist of two rows of a-events and an additional b-event. The language $\mathcal{L} \subset \mathcal{L}_0$ restricts to the pomsets such that either the b-event covers the first a of each row, or covers the k-th a-event of one row and is covered by the $2k$-th a-event of the other row. Examples of such pomsets are depicted in Fig. 8. We claim that $\mathcal{L}$ is basic and not regular. However, we observe that $\precsim^{\mathrm{OE}(\mathcal{L})}$ has index 5: If t is not a prefix of some $t' \in \mathrm{OE}(\mathcal{L})$, then $\mathrm{OE}(\mathcal{L})/t = \emptyset$. Now $\mathrm{OE}(\mathcal{L})/\varepsilon = \mathrm{OE}(\mathcal{L})$, $\mathrm{OE}(\mathcal{L})/a = \mathrm{OE}(\mathcal{L}/a)$, and moreover for all pomsets t that are prefixes of $\mathcal{L}$ different from the empty pomset ε and the singleton pomset a, $\mathrm{OE}(\mathcal{L})/t$ depends only on whether b occurs in t. To be precise, let $\mathcal{L}_1$ be the language of all pomsets consisting of two rows of a. Then $\mathrm{OE}(\mathcal{L})/t$ equals $\mathrm{OE}(\mathcal{L}_1)$ if b occurs in t and $\mathrm{OE}(\mathcal{L}_0)$ otherwise.

We turn now our attention to some operations on pomsets languages that preserve regularity. First, the *parallel composition* of two pomsets $t_1 = (E_1, \preccurlyeq_1 , \xi_1)$ and $t_2 = (E_2, \preccurlyeq_2, \xi_2)$ executes t_1 and t_2 independently: $t_1 \| t_2 = (E_1 \uplus E_2, \preccurlyeq_1 \uplus \preccurlyeq_2, \xi_1 \uplus \xi_2)$. This composition is naturally extended to languages as follows: $\mathcal{L}_1 \| \mathcal{L}_2 = \{t_1 \| t_2 \mid t_1 \in \mathcal{L}_1 \wedge t_2 \in \mathcal{L}_2\}$. Similarly, the strong concatenation of $\mathcal{L}_1$ and $\mathcal{L}_2$ is $\mathcal{L}_1 \cdot \mathcal{L}_2 = \{t_1 \cdot t_2 \mid t_1 \in \mathcal{L}_1 \wedge t_2 \in \mathcal{L}_2\}$. Now the *strong iteration* of $\mathcal{L}$ is simply $\mathcal{L}^\star = \bigcup_{k \in \mathbb{N}} \mathcal{L}^k$ where $\mathcal{L}^0$ consists of the empty pomset and $\mathcal{L}^{k+1} = \mathcal{L} \cdot \mathcal{L}^k$.

LEMMA 2.12. *Let $\mathcal{L}$, $\mathcal{L}_1$ and $\mathcal{L}_2$ be some pomset languages. Then for all pomsets $u \in \mathbb{P}(\Sigma)$, we have:*

1. $(\mathcal{L}_1 \cup \mathcal{L}_2)/u = \mathcal{L}_1/u \cup \mathcal{L}_2/u$
2. $(\mathcal{L}_1 \| \mathcal{L}_2)/u = \bigcup_{u = u_1 \| u_2} (\mathcal{L}_1/u_1 \| \mathcal{L}_2/u_2)$
3. $(\mathcal{L}_1 \cdot \mathcal{L}_2)/u = (\mathcal{L}_1/u) \cdot \mathcal{L}_2 \cup (\bigcup_{v: u \in \mathcal{L}_1 \cdot v} \mathcal{L}_2/v)$
4. $(\mathcal{L}^\star)/u = \bigcup_{i \in \mathbb{N}} (\bigcup_{v: u \in \mathcal{L}^i \cdot v} (\mathcal{L}/v) \cdot \mathcal{L}^\star)$

Proof. We only sketch the third point. Consider a residue $r \in (\mathcal{L}_1 \cdot \mathcal{L}_2)/u$. For some pomset $w = (E, \preccurlyeq, \xi)$, we have $w \in (\mathcal{L}_1 \cdot \mathcal{L}_2) \cap (\{u\} \diamond \{r\})$. Therefore $w = u_1 \cdot u_2 = (E_1 \uplus E_2, \preccurlyeq, \xi)$ where $u_i = (E_i, \preccurlyeq_{|E_i}, \xi_{|E_i})$ belongs to $\mathcal{L}_i$. Similarly, $E = E_u \uplus E_r$ and E_u is a prefix of w. Recall that $x \preccurlyeq y$ for all $x \in E_1$ and all $y \in E_2$ because $w = u_1 \cdot u_2$. Consequently, only two cases may occur:

1. $E_u \subseteq E_1$. Then $E_r = (E_1 \setminus E_u) \uplus E_2$ and $r \in (\mathcal{L}_1/u) \cdot \mathcal{L}_2$.
2. $E_1 \subseteq E_u$. Then $E_2 = (E_u \setminus E_1) \uplus E_r$ and $r \in \mathcal{L}_2/v$ for some pomset v such that $u \in \mathcal{L}_1 \cdot \{v\}$.

Thus $(\mathcal{L}_1 \cdot \mathcal{L}_2)/u \subseteq (\mathcal{L}_1/u) \cdot \mathcal{L}_2 \cup (\bigcup_{v : u \in \mathcal{L}_1 \cdot v} \mathcal{L}_2/v)$. We check now that the opposite inclusion holds. Assume that $r \in (\mathcal{L}_1/u) \cdot \mathcal{L}_2$. Then $r = v \cdot u_2$ with $v \in \mathcal{L}_1/u$ and $u_2 \in \mathcal{L}_2$. Moreover $\{u\} \diamond \{v\} \cap \mathcal{L}_1 \neq \emptyset$ hence $((\{u\} \diamond \{v\}) \cdot \{u_2\}) \cap (\mathcal{L}_1 \cdot \mathcal{L}_2) \neq \emptyset$. Now $(\{u\} \diamond \{v\}) \cdot \{u_2\} \subseteq \{u\} \diamond \{v \cdot u_2\}$. Therefore $\{u\} \diamond \{r\} \cap (\mathcal{L}_1 \cdot \mathcal{L}_2) \neq \emptyset$. Assume now that $r \in \mathcal{L}_2/v$ for some pomset v such that $u \in \mathcal{L}_1 \cdot v$, i.e. $u = u_1 \cdot v$ for some $u_1 \in \mathcal{L}_1$. Since $\{v\} \diamond \{r\} \cap \mathcal{L}_2 \neq \emptyset$, we have $(\{u_1\} \cdot (\{v\} \diamond \{r\})) \cap \mathcal{L}_1 \cdot \mathcal{L}_2 \neq \emptyset$. Now $\{u_1\} \cdot (\{v\} \diamond \{r\}) \subseteq \{u_1 \cdot v\} \diamond \{r\} = \{u\} \diamond \{r\}$. Therefore $\{u\} \diamond \{r\} \cap (\mathcal{L}_1 \cdot \mathcal{L}_2) \neq \emptyset$ in both cases, i.e. $r \in (\mathcal{L}_1 \cdot \mathcal{L}_2)/u$. $\qquad\square$

Immediate consequences of these observations, we establish the following closure properties.

PROPOSITION 2.13. *The class of regular languages is closed under union, strong concatenation, strong iteration, and parallel composition.*

Consequently, the class of weak regular languages is also closed under union, strong concatenation, and strong iteration. However, the parallel composition of two non trivial weak languages is never weak. Moreover the class of regular languages is not closed under intersection nor complementation.

Comparison with SP-recognizability. The algebra of series-parallel pomsets on the alphabet Σ, denoted $SP(\Sigma)$, is the subset of $\mathbb{P}(\Sigma)$ generated by the singleton pomsets, identified with Σ, and the strong concatenation and parallel composition on pomsets. Note that the empty pomset does not belong to $SP(\Sigma)$. It is known [7] that $SP(\Sigma)$ is isomorphic to the quotient of the free term algebra $T(\Sigma, \bullet, \|)$ by the following set of equations :

1. Associativity: $t \bullet (t' \bullet t'') =_e (t \bullet t') \bullet t''$ and $t \| (t' \| t'') =_e (t \| t') \| t''$
2. Commutativity: $t \| t' =_e t' \| t$

We denote by $SP_k(\Sigma) \subseteq SP(\Sigma)$ the set of series-parallel pomsets (SP-pomsets for short) of width bounded by k, i.e. such that any antichain has at most k events. In the following, we denote in the same way a term of the initial algebra $T(\Sigma, \bullet, \|)$ and the unique associated pomset in $SP(\Sigma)$. We call SP-algebra any quotient of $SP(\Sigma)$, i.e. any finitely generated model of $T(\Sigma, \bullet, \|)/=_e$.

Let α be a symbol not in Σ. We define the set of unary SP-contexts $Ctxt(\alpha)$ as $Ctxt(\alpha) = \{C \in SP(\Sigma \cup \{\alpha\}) : |C|_\alpha = 1\}$, i.e. the set of SP-pomsets labelled on $\Sigma \cup \{\alpha\}$ (or SP-terms on $\Sigma \cup \{\alpha\}$) such that a single event (a single leaf of the term) is labelled by α. If $C \in Ctxt(\alpha)$ and $u \in SP(\Sigma)$, we denote by $C(u) \in SP(\Sigma)$ the pomset resulting from the substitution of α by u in C. Let $\mathcal{L} \subseteq SP(\Sigma)$ and $u \in SP(\Sigma)$, the *set of contexts* of u in $\mathcal{L}$ is $\mathcal{L}\backslash_\alpha u = \{C \in Ctxt(\alpha) : C(u) \in \mathcal{L}\}$. The *syntactic SP-congruence of* $\mathcal{L}$ is the equivalence on $SP(\Sigma)$ defined by $u \sim_\mathcal{L} v \Longleftrightarrow \mathcal{L}\backslash_\alpha u = \mathcal{L}\backslash_\alpha v$.

1. A subset $\mathcal{L} \subseteq SP(\Sigma)$ is *SP-recognizable* if there is a SP-homomorphism $\sigma : SP(\Sigma) \longrightarrow B$ on a finite SP-algebra B such that $\mathcal{L} = \sigma^{-1}(\sigma(\mathcal{L}))$.
2. Equivalently $\mathcal{L} \subseteq SP(\Sigma)$ is SP-recognizable if the *syntactic SP-congruence* of $\mathcal{L}$ is of finite index.

Note that *SP-recognizability* coincide for languages of linear pomsets $\mathcal{L} \subseteq \Sigma^*$ with the standard definition of recognizability/regularity for word languages.

Lodaya and Weil showed in [11] that *bounded width SP-pomset languages are SP-recognizable iff they are series-rational*, i.e. constructed from singletons by union, strong concatenation, strong iteration, and parallel composition. Proposition 2.13 asserts that regular languages are closed under these operations. Therefore series-rational languages are regular, and thus bounded width SP-recognizable languages are regular. We see now that this inclusion is strict.

PROPOSITION 2.14. *The class of bounded width SP-recognizable SP-pomset languages is strictly included in the class of regular languages of SP-pomsets.*

Proof. To show that the inclusion is strict, we consider a non-recognizable word language $\mathcal{L} \subseteq \Sigma^*$ and show that for all $k \geqslant 2$ the complement language $N = SP_k(\Sigma) \setminus \mathcal{L}$ is regular but not SP-recognizable.

First $N = SP_k(\Sigma) \setminus \mathcal{L}$ is regular. For all pomsets $u \in SP(\Sigma) \setminus SP_k(\Sigma)$, we have $N/u = \emptyset$ because $\forall v \in SP(\Sigma)$ $\{u\} \diamond \{v\} \subseteq SP(\Sigma) \setminus SP_k(\Sigma)$. For all pomsets $u \in SP_k(\Sigma)$, we have $N/u = SP_k(\Sigma)$ because for all $v \in SP_k(\Sigma)$ either $u\|v \in N$ or $u \cdot v \in N$.

For all $u \in SP(\Sigma) \setminus \Sigma^*$, there is no SP-context $C \in Ctxt(\alpha)$ such that $C(u) \in \mathcal{L}$. Thus $N\backslash_\alpha u = Ctxt(\alpha)$: All $u \in SP(\Sigma) \setminus \Sigma^*$ are SP-equivalent w.r.t. N. If $u \in \Sigma^*$ then for all $v \in \Sigma^*$ we have $(\alpha \cdot v)(u) \in N$ iff $v \notin \mathcal{L}/u$ i.e. $\alpha \cdot v \in N\backslash_\alpha u$ iff $v \notin \mathcal{L}/u$. Since $\mathcal{L}$ is not recognisable, there is an infinite number of sets $\Sigma^* \setminus \mathcal{L}/u$, and consequently an infinite number of sets $N\backslash_\alpha u$. Therefore N is not SP recognisable. $\square$

3   Recognizable Compatible Languages

In this section we compare the properties of a pomset language with those of its step extensions. We aim at relating the regularity of a language $\mathcal{L}$ to the usual property of recognizability of its step extensions $SE(\mathcal{L})$ within the monoid $\mathcal{M}(\Sigma)^*$. Recall that a subset $\mathcal{L}$ of a monoid $\mathbb{M}$ is called *recognizable* if there exists a finite monoid $\mathbb{M}'$ and a monoid morphism $\eta : \mathbb{M} \to \mathbb{M}'$ such that $\mathcal{L} = \eta^{-1} \circ \eta(\mathcal{L})$. Equivalently, $\mathcal{L}$ is recognizable if, and only if, the collection of all sets $\mathcal{L}/x = \{y \in \mathbb{M} \mid x \cdot y \in \mathcal{L}\}$ is finite. In particular the set of recognizable subsets of any monoid is closed under union, intersection and complement.

Since $SE(\mathcal{L})$ is preserved by order extensions, we shall consider weak languages only. We will easily observe that any weak regular language $\mathcal{L}$ describes a recognizable language $SE(\mathcal{L})$ of $\mathcal{M}(\Sigma)^*$. However two detailed examples will show that the converse fails. As main result, we prove that regularity corresponds to recognizability for compatible sets of pomsets (Def. 1.5 and Th. 3.5).

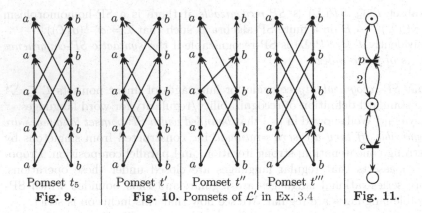

Pomset t_5 | Pomset t' | Pomset t'' | Pomset t'''
Fig. 9. | Fig. 10. Pomsets of $\mathcal{L}'$ in Ex. 3.4 | Fig. 11.

Towards an Algebraic Recognizability. Our first stage from regularity to recognizability of step extensions is the restriction of contexts to step sequences.

DEFINITION 3.1. *Let $\mathcal{L}$ be a class of pomsets and u be a pomset over Σ. The step context of u w.r.t. $\mathcal{L}$ is $\mathcal{L}\backslash_s u = \{(x, y) \in \mathcal{M}(\Sigma)^{\star 2} \mid x \cdot u \cdot y \in \mathrm{OE}(\mathcal{L})\}$. We say that u and v are step equivalent, and we write $u \asymp_s v$, if $\mathcal{L}\backslash_s u = \mathcal{L}\backslash_s v$.*

Clearly if $\asymp_w$ is of finite index then $\asymp_s$ is of finite index, too. As the next example will show, the converse fails even for weak languages. To see this, we use again an equivalent approach by means of residues: Similarly to the previous section, the *step residue* of u w.r.t. $\mathcal{L}$ is $\mathcal{L}/_s u = \{y \in \mathcal{M}(\Sigma)^\star \mid u \cdot y \in \mathrm{OE}(\mathcal{L})\}$ and two pomsets u and v are called *step residue equivalent*, written $u \overset{\cdot}{\asymp}_s v$, if $\mathcal{L}/_s u = \mathcal{L}/_s v$. Similarly to Theorem 2.9, we can prove that $\asymp_s$ is of finite index if and only if $\overset{\cdot}{\asymp}_s$ is of finite index.

EXAMPLE 3.2. We denote by t_n the pomset which consists of n linearly ordered a-events and n linearly ordered b-events such that the k-th event a is below the $(k + 2)$-th event b and symmetrically the k-th event b is below the $(k + 2)$-th event a, as shown on Fig. 9. For $n \geqslant 2$, we denote by t'_n the order extension of t_n with a single additional causality relation, from the $(n - 1)$-th event a to the n-th event b. Similarly we let t''_n be the order extension of t_n with a single additional causality relation, from the $(n - 1)$-th event b to the n-th event a. Now consider the language $\mathcal{L}$ which consists of all t_n for $n \neq 2^k$ together with all t'_{2^k} and all t''_{2^k}. We claim first that $\mathcal{L}$ is not regular because there are infinitely many distinct weak residues $\mathcal{L}/_w t_n$. However $\asymp_s^{\mathcal{L}}$ is of finite index. Note also that this gap appears for $\mathrm{OE}(\mathcal{L})$ as well, because $\asymp_w^{\mathcal{L}} = \asymp_w^{\mathrm{OE}(\mathcal{L})}$ and $\asymp_s^{\mathcal{L}} = \asymp_s^{\mathrm{OE}(\mathcal{L})}$.

We can also use these step residues to prove easily that any regular language is recognizable.

LEMMA 3.3. *If $\asymp_s$ is of finite index then $\mathrm{SE}(\mathcal{L})$ is recognizable in the monoid $\mathcal{M}(\Sigma)^\star$.*

Proof. We observe that $\mathrm{SE}(\mathcal{L})/u = \mathcal{L}_{/s}\,u \cap \mathcal{M}(\Sigma)^{\star}$ for all $u \in \mathcal{M}(\Sigma)^{\star}$. $\qquad\square$

As the next example shows, the converse fails even for weak languages.

EXAMPLE 3.4. We consider again the pomsets t_n of Example 3.2 and Figure 9. We let $\mathcal{L}'$ be the language consisting of all pomsets t' that are order extensions of some t_n with a single additional causality, either from a 2^k-th a-event to the corresponding $(2^k + 1)$-th b-event, or from a 2^k-th b-event to the corresponding $(2^k + 1)$-th a-event. Examples of such pomsets are depicted on Fig. 10. Consider the language $\mathcal{L}$ of all t_n. For all prefixes t of t_n, $-2 \leqslant |t|_a - |t|_b \leqslant 2$ and this number determines $\mathcal{L}/t$. Consequently $\mathcal{L}$ has 6 residues (including $\emptyset$) and $\asymp^{\mathcal{L}}$ and $\asymp^{\mathcal{L}}_s$ are of finite index (Th. 2.9 and Th. 2.4). Therefore $\mathrm{SE}(\mathcal{L})$ is recognizable in the monoid $\mathcal{M}(\Sigma)^{\star}$ (Lemma 3.3). We observe also that $\mathrm{SE}(\mathcal{L}) = \mathrm{SE}(\mathcal{L}')$. However we claim that $\asymp^{\mathcal{L}'}_s$ is of infinite index. Thus $\mathrm{SE}(\mathcal{L}')$ is recognizable in the monoid $\mathcal{M}(\Sigma)^{\star}$ but $\asymp^{\mathcal{L}'}_s$ is of infinite index. Furthermore $\mathcal{L}'' = \mathrm{OE}(\mathcal{L}')$ is a weak language such that $\asymp^{\mathcal{L}''}_s = \asymp^{\mathcal{L}'}_s$ is also of infinite index while $\mathrm{SE}(\mathcal{L}'') = \mathrm{SE}(\mathcal{L}')$ is a recognizable language of $\mathcal{M}(\Sigma)^{\star}$.

Characterization of Regular Compatible Languages. Let $\mathcal{L}$ be a weak language of pomsets. We have observed that the following implications hold:

$\mathcal{L}$ is regular $\Longrightarrow$ $\asymp^{\mathcal{L}}_s$ is of finite index $\Longrightarrow$ $\mathrm{SE}(\mathcal{L})$ is recognizable in $\mathcal{M}(\Sigma)^{\star}$

but none of the converses holds (Examples 3.2 and 3.4). We show now that this gap between regularity and recognizability vanishes for compatible languages.

THEOREM 3.5. *Let $\mathcal{L}$ be a compatible language of pomsets. The following are equivalent:*

(i) *$\mathcal{L}$ is regular.*
(ii) *$\asymp^{\mathcal{L}}_s$ is of finite index.*
(iii) *$\mathrm{SE}(\mathcal{L})$ is recognizable in the monoid $\mathcal{M}(\Sigma)^{\star}$.*

Proof. Since $\mathcal{L}$ is weak, $\asymp^{\mathcal{L}} = \asymp^{\mathcal{L}}_w$. By Lemma 3.3, we need just to show that (iii) implies (i). Since $\mathcal{L}$ is compatible, for all pomsets u and r,

$$u \cdot r \in \mathcal{L} \Longleftrightarrow \mathrm{SE}(u \cdot r) \subseteq \mathrm{SE}(\mathcal{L}) \Longleftrightarrow \mathrm{SE}(u) \cdot \mathrm{SE}(r) \subseteq \mathrm{SE}(\mathcal{L})$$

It follows that $\mathcal{L}/u = \overline{\mathcal{L}_u}$ where $\mathcal{L}_u = \bigcap_{v \in \mathrm{SE}(u)} \mathrm{SE}(\mathcal{L})/v$. Consequently, if $\mathrm{SE}(\mathcal{L})$ is recognizable then there are only finitely many residues $\mathcal{L}/u$. $\qquad\square$

This result shows that the duality between compatible languages and their corresponding step extensions identifies our notion of regularity with the algebraic recognizability in $\mathcal{M}(\Sigma)^{\star}$. As a consequence, we notice that our notion of regularity corresponds to the one considered for local trace languages [10].

Other Comparisons with Related Works. Recall first that $\mathrm{LE}(\mathcal{L})$ is regular as soon as $\mathcal{L}$ is regular because $\mathrm{LE}(\mathcal{L})/u = (\mathrm{SE}(\mathcal{L})/u) \cap \Sigma^{\star}$ for all words $u \in \Sigma^{\star}$. As the next example shows, the converse fails even for compatible sets of pomsets.

EXAMPLE 3.6. Consider the compatible set $\mathcal{L}$ of all firing pomsets of the Petri net depicted in Fig. 11. Since each place always contains at least one token, each transition is permanently enabled. Therefore $\mathrm{LE}(\mathcal{L}) = \{p, c\}^*$ is regular. Now, transition p produces a new token at each occurrence. Therefore the step $c^n = \{c, ..., c\}$ is enabled after a firing sequence s only if s contains at least $n - 1$ occurrences of p. Consequently $\mathrm{SE}(\mathcal{L})$ and $\mathcal{L}$ are not regular.

In practice however, it is often the case that regularity of $\mathrm{LE}(\mathcal{L})$ is equivalent to regularity of $\mathcal{L}$, as the next result shows.

PROPOSITION 3.7. *Let $\mathcal{L}$ be a language of pomsets. We assume that for all pomsets t_1 and t_2 such that t_1 is a prefix of some pomset of $\mathcal{L}$ and t_2 is a postfix of some pomset of $\mathcal{L}$, the following requirement is satisfied:*

$$(\forall u_1 \in \mathrm{LE}(t_1), \forall u_2 \in \mathrm{LE}(t_2), u_1.u_2 \in \mathrm{LE}(\mathcal{L})) \implies (\{t_1\} \diamond \{t_2\}) \cap \mathcal{L} \neq \emptyset$$

If $\mathrm{LE}(\mathcal{L})$ is recognizable in the free monoid Σ^* then $\mathcal{L}$ is regular.

This result applies to several frameworks of compatible languages: It shows in particular that for Mazurkiewicz traces and messages sequence charts, our notion of regularity corresponds precisely to the notion of regularity defined in these frameworks. As a consequence, for the particular case of message sequence charts, the notion regularity studied in this paper is stronger than the algebraic recognizability studied in [12].

Conclusion

In this paper we introduced a new general notion of regularity for pomset languages with autoconcurrency. We showed how this approach extends similar notions in classical frameworks of concurrency theory, such as Mazurkiewicz traces and message sequence charts. However a mismatch between regularity and algebraic recognizability appears in some particular cases such as series-parallel pomsets and message sequence charts. We showed that the particular class of compatible languages enjoys several nice properties and includes many formalisms from the literature. We believe that these languages are a good candidate for further generalizations, in particular for a connection between regularity and MSO-definability.

Acknowledgment

We thank Dietrich KUSKE for his useful observation that regular pomset languages are not closed under complementation.

References

[1] R. Alur and M. Yannakakis: *Model Checking of Message Sequence Charts*. CONCUR'99, LNCS **1664** (1999) 114–129   403, 406

[2] A. Arnold: *An extension of the notion of traces and asynchronous automata.* Theoretical Informatics and Applications **25** (1991) 355–393   403, 406

[3] V. Diekert and Y. Métivier: *Partial Commutations and Traces.* Handbook of Formal languages, vol. **3** (1997) 457–533   402, 403, 406

[4] M. Droste, P. Gastin, and D. Kuske: *Asynchronous cellular automata for pomsets.* Theoretical Computer Science Vol. **247** (2000) 1–38   402

[5] M. Droste and D. Kuske: *Logical definability of recognizable and aperiodic languages in concurrency monoids.* LNCS **1092** (1996) 233–251   402, 403, 406

[6] J. Fanchon: *A syntactic congruence for the recognizability of pomset languages.* RR 99008 (LAAS, Toulouse, 1999)   402

[7] J. L. Gischer: *The equational theory of pomsets.* Theoretical Comp. Science **61** (1988) 199–224   402, 412

[8] J. Grabowski: *On partial languages.* Fund. Informatica **IV(2)** (1981) 427–498   403, 405

[9] D. Kuske: *Infinite series-parallel posets: logic and languages.* LNCS **1853** (2000) 648–662   402

[10] D. Kuske and R. Morin: *Pomsets for Local Trace Languages — Recognizability, Logic & Petri Nets.* CONCUR 2000, LNCS **1877** (2000) 426–440   403, 406, 415

[11] K. Lodaya and P. Weil: *Series-parallel languages and the bounded-width property.* Theoretical Comp. Science **237** (2000) 347–380   402, 403, 413

[12] R. Morin: *Recognizable Sets of Message Sequence Charts.* STACS 2002, LNCS **2030** (2002) 332–342   402, 416

[13] M. Mukund, K. Narayan Kumar, and M. Sohoni: *Synthesizing distributed finite-state systems from MSCs.* CONCUR 2000, LNCS **1877** (2000) 521–535   403, 406

[14] V. Pratt: *Modelling concurrency with partial orders.* Int. J. of Parallel Programming **15** (1986) 33–71   402

[15] W. Thomas: *Automata Theory on Trees and Partial Orders.* TAPSOFT 97, LNCS **1214** (1998) 20–34   402

[16] W. Vogler: *Modular Construction and Partial Order Semantics of Petri Nets.* LNCS **625** (1992) 252–275   403, 405

The Fusion Machine
(Extended Abstract)

Philippa Gardner[1], Cosimo Laneve[2], and Lucian Wischik[2]

[1] Department of Computing, Imperial College, London
[2] Department of Computer Science, University of Bologna

Abstract. We present a new model for the distributed implementation of pi-like calculi, which permits strong correctness results that are simple to prove. We describe the *distributed channel machine* – a distributed version of a machine proposed by Cardelli. The distributed channel machine groups pi processes at their channels (or locations), in contrast with the more common approach of incorporating additional location information within pi processes. We go on to describe the *fusion machine*. It uses a form of concurrent constraints called *fusions* – equations on channel names – to distribute fragments of these processes between remote channels. This fragmentation avoids the movement of large continuations between locations, and leads to a more efficient implementation model.

1   Introduction

The pi calculus and its variants have made a significant impact in research on concurrency and distribution. However, we are aware of only two distributed implementations of the pi calculus: Facile [8] which uses a hand-shake discipline for communication, and an indirect encoding into the join calculus [5] which is then implemented on Jocaml [4]. Other related implementations [20, 6] add explicit location constructs to the pi calculus and use different mechanisms for distributed interaction.

There are two reasons for why pi calculus interaction has not been used for distributed interaction. First, synchronous rendezvous (as found in the pi calculus) seemed awkward to implement. Second, a model of distribution has generally been assumed, in which processes are grouped together at locations and use separate mechanisms for distributed versus local interaction. We propose a different distribution model, the *fusion machine*, which avoids the difficulty in synchronous rendezvous and leads to a simple connection between implementation and pi-like calculi.

In our distribution model, each channel exists at its own location (or is co-located with other channels). Each atomic process waiting to rendezvous over a channel is placed directly at that channel (location); thus, synchronous rendezvous is local. After rendezvous, a process' continuation is broken down into atomic processes. These are sent on to their appropriate channels, and are then ready to perform their own subsequent rendezvous. The task of breaking down

L. Brim et al. (Eds.): CONCUR 2002, LNCS 2421, pp. 418–433, 2002.

and sending is known as *heating* [2], and amounts to a directed implementation
of structural congruence. In some ways, our model can be regarded as a distributed version of the single-processor model first described by Cardelli [3] and
subsequently used in Pict [14, 17].

The fusion machine is distributed over channels, as outlined above. It also
uses explicit fusions [7], a form of concurrent constraints on channel names which
it implements with trees of forwarders between channels. These explicit fusions
enable atomic processes to be fragmented, so avoiding the movement of large
continuations between channels. The issue of fragmentation did not arise in the
single-processor channel machine used in Pict. In this machine, after a program is
involved in rendezvous, a *pointer* to its continuation is sent on to another channel
for subsequent rendezvous. In contrast, the (distributed) fusion machine would
require the entire continuation to be sent between channels. This explains why
fragmententation becomes relevant for a distributed implementation. We treat
fragmentation formally by showing that a calculus with limited continuations –
the *explicit solos calculus* – is as expressive as the full calculus with continuations.
This builds upon earlier results in [12, 10].

The differences between our model and that of Facile and Jocaml are as follows. Facile uses two classes of distributed entities: (co-)located processes which
execute, and channel-managers which mediate interaction. This forces it to use a
hand-shake discipline for rendezvous. Jocaml simplifies the model by combining
input processes with channel-managers. However, it uses a quite different form
of interaction, which does not relate that closely to pi calculus rendezvous. It
also forces a coarser granularity, in which every channel must be co-located with
at least one other. Like Jocaml, the fusion machine combines processes with
channel-managers. Unlike Jocaml, our machine has finer granularity and uses
the same form of interaction as the pi calculus.

To conclude the paper, we introduce a formal technique to argue about the
efficiency of our fusion machine in terms of the number of network messages
required to execute a program. As an example, we quantify the efficiency impact
of our encoding of continuations into the explicit solos calculus: it does no worse
than doubling the total message count.

The structure of the paper is as follows. Section 2 describes a distributed version
of the channel-machine, which is closely connected to the pi calculus. Section 3
presents the fusion machine, which is closer to the explicit fusion calculus and
solos calculus. Section 4 gives it a formal theory, and includes full abstraction
results. Section 5 adds a model of co-location to the machine, and uses this in a
proof of efficiency.

2   The Distributed Channel Machine

Cardelli described an abstract machine for synchronous rendezvous which runs
in a single thread of execution, in a shared address space. It contains *channel-
managers*, each of which contains pointers to programs; these programs are waiting to rendezvous on the channel. It also contains a *deployment bag* of pointers

to programs ready to be executed. The mode of operation of the machine is to move pointers between the channels and the deployment bag.

To make it distributed, we instead assume a collection of located channel-managers which run in parallel and which interact. Each channel-manager has its own thread of execution, its own address space and its own deployment bag. The mode of operation of a channel-manager is either to send some fragments across the network to other channel-managers, or to execute other fragments locally.

Assume a set of channel names ranged over by u, v, w, x, y, z. These might be Internet Protocol numbers and port numbers. At each location there is a channel-manager for exactly one channel name. We therefore identify locations, channels and names. Each channel-manager is made from two parts: atoms (A) which are waiting to rendezvous on the channel, and a deployment bag (D) of terms ready to be executed. We picture it as follows:

The *atoms* are a collection of output atoms out$x.P$ and a separate collection of input atoms in$(x).P$. In general they may be polyadic (communicating several names); but in this section we stick to monadic (single names) atoms for simplicity. The *deployment bag* is a multiset of terms – in this section, terms in the pi calculus.

As an example, the following machine is one representation of the program $\overline{u}x.P \mid u(y).Q \mid \overline{v}x.R \mid v(y).S$. Observe that each action $\overline{u}x.P$ is represented either as an atom at location u, or in any location's deployment bag.

There are two kinds of transition for each channel-manager. First, two matching atoms at the same location can *react*:

(react)

(If a replicated input or output atom were involved in the reaction, then a copy of it would be left behind.) Second, program fragments from the deployment bag might be deployed. This is also called *heating* in the process calculus literature.

(dep.par)

$$\begin{array}{c} u \\ \boxed{\begin{array}{c} A \\ \hline 0;D \end{array}} \end{array} \quad \overset{\cdot}{\longrightarrow} \quad \begin{array}{c} u \\ \boxed{\begin{array}{c} A \\ \hline D \end{array}} \end{array} \qquad\qquad\qquad\text{(dep.nil)}$$

$$\begin{array}{cc} u & v \\ \boxed{\begin{array}{c} A \\ \hline \overline{v}\,x.P;D \end{array}} & \boxed{\begin{array}{c} A' \\ \hline D' \end{array}} \end{array} \quad \overset{\cdot}{\longrightarrow} \quad \begin{array}{cc} u & v \\ \boxed{\begin{array}{c} A \\ \hline D \end{array}} & \boxed{\begin{array}{c} \text{out}x.P \\ A' \\ \hline D' \end{array}} \end{array} \qquad\text{(dep.out)}$$

$$\begin{array}{cc} u & v \\ \boxed{\begin{array}{c} A \\ \hline v(x).P;D \end{array}} & \boxed{\begin{array}{c} A' \\ \hline D' \end{array}} \end{array} \quad \overset{\cdot}{\longrightarrow} \quad \begin{array}{cc} u & v \\ \boxed{\begin{array}{c} A \\ \hline D \end{array}} & \boxed{\begin{array}{c} \text{in}(x).P \\ A' \\ \hline D' \end{array}} \end{array} \qquad\text{(dep.in)}$$

These heating transitions are all straightforward. They take a program fragment from the deployment bag, and either break it down further or send it to the correct place on the network. Cardelli's non-distributed machine uses similar rules with minor differences: it uses just a single deployment bag shared by all channel-managers; and because it uses a shared address space, it merely moves pointers rather than entire program fragments.

As for the restriction operator $(z)P$, it has three roles. First, it is a command which creates a new, globally unique channel – a *fresh* name. Second, through rules for alpha-renaming and scope extrusion, it indicates that an existing name should be understood to be globally unique, even though it might be syntactically written with a non-unique symbol. This second role is not relevant to an implementation. Third, it indicates that an existing channel is private, so that a separately-compiled program cannot refer to it by name. For example, it might mean that a machine is not listed in the Internet's Domain Name Service. We will write (z) to indicate a channel z that is not listed. The deployment of restrictions is as follows:

$$\begin{array}{c} u \\ \boxed{\begin{array}{c} A \\ \hline (z)P;D \end{array}} \end{array} \quad \overset{\cdot}{\longrightarrow} \quad \begin{array}{cc} u & (z') \\ \boxed{\begin{array}{c} A \\ \hline P\{z'/z\};D \end{array}} & \boxed{\begin{array}{c} - \\ \hline - \end{array}} \end{array} \quad z' \text{ fresh} \qquad\text{(dep.new)}$$

Theorem 1 (Full abstraction) *Two programs are (strongly barbed) congruent in the pi calculus if and only if they are (strongly barbed) congruent in the distributed channel machine.*

This straightforward theorem holds for both the single-processor channel machine and the distributed channel-machine, but as far as we know it has not been given before in the literature. (Cardelli's description of the channel machine anticipated the pi calculus by several years.) The proof is omitted, and will be provided in the full paper. Sewell has given a weaker result for the version of the machine used in Pict [15].

We remark that the full abstraction result for the join calculus is weaker than Theorem 1. This is because the join calculus encodes each pi channel with two join calculus channels that obey a particular protocol. Without a firewall, an encoded program would be vulnerable to any context which violates the protocol. Technically, the join calculus encoding is *non-uniform* as defined by Palamidessi [11]. As for the channel machine, we encode a pi calculus term P by deploying it in a dummy machine $x[P]$. Strictly speaking this is also a non-uniform encoding – but we could make it uniform by adding a structural rule $x[P], x[Q] \equiv x[P; Q]$. Such a rule would be usual in a calculus, but is not relevant in an implementation where different machines have different names by construction. Therefore we do not use it.

Efficiency of Continuations

This distributed version of the channel machine suffers from an efficiency problem. Consider for example the program $\overline{u}.\overline{v}.\overline{x}.\overline{y} \mid u.v.x.y.P$. In the machine, the continuation P would be transported first to u, then v, then x, then y. This is undesirable if the continuation P is large.

There have been two encodings of the pi calculus into a limited calculus without nested continuations. These might solve the efficiency problem. The first encoding, by Parrow [12], uses a sub-calculus of the pi calculus consisting of *trios* so that, for instance, $u(y).\overline{v}y$ becomes $t_1(\widetilde{x}).u(y).\overline{t}_2\widetilde{x}y \mid t_2(\widetilde{x}y).\overline{v}y.\overline{t}_3\widetilde{x}y$. Here, triggers t_1, t_2, t_3 guard each input and output command, and also transport the entire environment to every continuation. An encoded term could then be executed directly on the distributed channel machine.

The second encoding is based upon the *fusion calculus* of Parrow and Victor [13], a calculus in which the input command $u\widetilde{y}.P$ is not binding. The encoding [10] uses the sub-calculus with only *solos* $\overline{u}\widetilde{x}$ and $u\widetilde{x}$. It uses the reaction relation

$$(\widetilde{z})(\overline{u}\widetilde{x} \mid u\widetilde{y} \mid R) \;\rightarrow\; R\sigma$$

where every equivalence class generated by $\widetilde{x} = \widetilde{y}$ has exactly one element not in $\widetilde{z}$, and the substitution σ collapses each equivalence class to its one element.

A single-processor implementation of solos has been described [9]. However, it seems difficult to make a distributed implementation. This is because its reaction is not local: the channel-manager at u must look in the global environment to find sufficient names $(\widetilde{z})$ before it can allow reaction. Instead, we implement the solos calculus with the *explicit fusions* [7]. This allows local reaction as follows:

$$\overline{u}\widetilde{x} \mid u\widetilde{y} \mid R \;\rightarrow\; \widetilde{x}\text{=}\widetilde{y} \mid R.$$

The term $\widetilde{x}\text{=}\widetilde{y}$ is called an explicit fusion. It has delayed substitutive effect on the rest of the term R. In this respect it is similar to explicit *substitutions* [1]. As an example, in $\overline{u}x \mid vy \mid u\text{=}v$, the atom on u may be renamed to v. This yields $\overline{v}x \mid vy \mid u\text{=}v$. In contrast to Parrow's trios (which send the entire environment to every continuation), explicit fusions amount to a shared environment.

In fact, we prefer to use terms $\bar{u}\,\tilde{x}.\phi$ and $u\,\tilde{x}.\phi$ where ϕ is an explicit fusion continuation – instead of the arbitrary continuations of the channel machine, or the triple continuations of trios, or the empty continuations of the solos calculus. Technically, these fusion continuations allow for an encoding of arbitrary continuations that is uniform and a strong bisimulation congruence (Section 5).

3   Fusion Machine

In general, explicit fusions generate an equivalence relation on names such that any related names may react together. However, in our distributed setting, different names correspond to channel managers at different locations. If two (remote) atoms are related by the equivalence relation, we must send them to a common location in the network so they can react together. The decision as to where to send them must be taken locally. The problem is to find a data structure and an algorithm that allow such local decisions.

The data structure we use to represent each equivalence class is a directed tree. Then each channel can send its atoms to its parent, and related atoms are guaranteed to arrive eventually at a common ancestor. To store this tree, let each channel-manager contain a *fusion pointer* to its parent:

u	name of this channel-manager
F	fusion-pointer
A	atoms
D	deployment bag

The rule for sending an atom to a parent is called *migration*. (We write m to stand for either in or out).

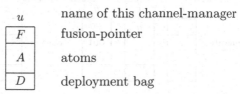

$$\begin{array}{c|c} u & v \\ \hline v & F' \\ \mathsf{m}x.\phi \; A & A' \\ D & D' \end{array} \quad \longrightarrow \quad \begin{array}{c|c} u & v \\ \hline v & F' \\ A & \mathsf{m}x.\phi \; A' \\ D & D' \end{array} \qquad \text{(migrate)}$$

To update the tree (i.e. to deploy a fusion term), we use a distributed version of Tarjan's *union find* algorithm [16]. This assumes a total order on names, perhaps arising from their Internet Protocol number and port number. The algorithm is implemented with just a single heating rule:

$$\begin{array}{c|c} u & x \\ \hline F & z \\ A & A' \\ x{=}y;\, D & D' \end{array} \quad \longrightarrow \quad \begin{array}{c|c} u & x \\ \hline F & y \\ A & A' \\ D & y{=}z;\, D' \end{array} \qquad \text{(dep.fu)}$$

where $x < y$ and, if x had no fusion pointer z originally, then we omit $y{=}z$ from the result. This rule amounts to u sending to x the message "fuse yourself to y".

To understand this rule, note that it preserves the invariant that the tree of names respects the total order on names, with greater names closer to the root. Therefore, each (dep.fu) transition takes a fusion progressively closer to the root, and the algorithm necessarily terminates. The effect is a distributed, concurrent algorithm for merging two trees.

Finally, we give the modified reaction rule which works with non-binding input and output.

$$
\begin{array}{c}
u \\
\boxed{\begin{array}{c} F \\ \mathsf{out}x.\phi \\ \mathsf{in}y.\psi;\ A \\ D \end{array}}
\end{array}
\quad \rightarrow \quad
\begin{array}{c}
u \\
\boxed{\begin{array}{c} F \\ A \\ x\text{=}y;\ \phi;\psi,D \end{array}}
\end{array}
\qquad \text{(react)}
$$

The following worked example illustrates $u\,x \mid \overline{u}\,y \mid \overline{x} \mid y \to^* x\text{=}y$.

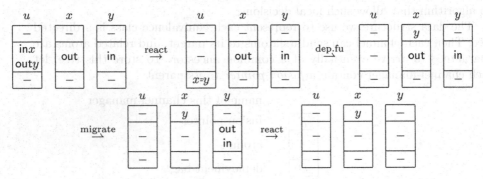

We ultimately imagine a hybrid machine which uses both continuations (as in the previous section) and fusions (as in this section). It will use continuations when the continuations are small enough to be efficient; at other times it will use fusions. The two areas are largely unrelated. Therefore, for simplicity, our formal treatment of the machine (next section) omits continuation (and replication). A formal account of the full hybrid machine may be found in [19]. Also, the efficiency results in Section 5 refer to the hybrid machine.

4   Fusion Machine Theory

We now develop a formalism for the fusion machine. We use this to prove that it is a fully abstract implementation of the *explicit solos calculus* (Table 1). For simplicity, we consider the calculus without replication.

We assume a countably infinite set $\mathcal{N}$ of names with a total order, ranged over by u,v,w,x,y,z. Let p range over $\{-\} \cup \mathcal{N}$, denoting pointers including the absent pointer $-$. We use the abbreviation $\widetilde{x}$ for tuples $x_1,\cdots,x_n$, and $\widetilde{x}\text{=}\widetilde{y}$ for $x_1\text{=}y_1 \mid \ldots \mid x_n\text{=}y_n$. Let ϕ, ψ range over explicit fusions $\widetilde{x}\text{=}\widetilde{y}$, and m over $\{\mathsf{out}, \mathsf{in}\}$.

Table 1. The explicit solos calculus

Terms P, **fusions** ϕ, **and contexts** E in the explicit solos calculus are given by

$$P \quad ::= \quad \mathbf{0} \quad | \quad \phi \quad | \quad \overline{u}\widetilde{x}.\phi \quad | \quad u\widetilde{x}.\phi \quad | \quad (x)P \quad | \quad P|P$$

$$\phi \quad ::= \quad \widetilde{x}\text{=}\widetilde{y}$$

$$E \quad ::= \quad \_ \quad | \quad (x)E \quad | \quad P|E \quad | \quad E|P$$

Structural congruence on terms $\equiv$ is the smallest congruence satisfying the following:

$$P|\mathbf{0} \equiv \mathbf{0} \quad P|Q \equiv Q|P \quad P|(Q|R) \equiv (P|Q)|R$$

$$x\text{=}x \equiv \mathbf{0} \quad x\text{=}y \equiv y\text{=}x \quad x\text{=}y \mid y\text{=}z \equiv x\text{=}z \mid y\text{=}z \quad (x)(x\text{=}y) \equiv \mathbf{0}$$

$$(x)(y)P \equiv (y)(x)P \quad (x)(P|Q) \equiv (x)P \mid Q \text{ if } x \notin \text{fn}(Q)$$

$$x\text{=}y \mid P \equiv x\text{=}y \mid P\{y/x\}$$

Reaction relation is the smallest relation $\to$ satisfying the following, and which is closed with respect to $\equiv$ and contexts: $\overline{u}\widetilde{x}.\phi \mid u\widetilde{y}.\psi \ \to\ \widetilde{x}\text{=}\widetilde{y} \mid \phi \mid \psi$.

Observation $P \downarrow u$ is the smallest relation satisfying

$$\overline{u}\widetilde{x}.\phi \downarrow u \qquad\qquad P \mid Q \downarrow u \quad \text{if } P \downarrow u$$

$$u\widetilde{x}.\phi \downarrow u \qquad\qquad (x)P \downarrow u \quad \text{if } P \downarrow u \text{ and } u \neq x$$

$$Q \downarrow u \quad \text{if } Q \equiv P \downarrow u$$

The *explicit fusion calculus* is obtained by allowing arbitrary continuations and replication: $!P \equiv P|!P$ with $P ::= \ldots \mid \overline{u}\widetilde{x}.P \mid u\widetilde{x}.P \mid !P$ and $E ::= \ldots \mid \overline{u}\widetilde{x}.E \mid u\widetilde{x}.E \mid !E$.

Bisimulation is as usual. A relation $\mathcal{S}$ is a strong barbed bisimulation if whenever $P \mathcal{S} Q$ then

- $P \downarrow u$ if and only if $Q \downarrow u$
- if $P \to P'$ then $Q \to Q'$ such that $P' \mathcal{S} Q'$
- if $Q \to Q'$ then $P \to P'$ such that $P' \mathcal{S} Q'$

Barbed congruence $P \sim Q$ holds whenever, for all contexts E, $E[P] \sim E[Q]$, where $\sim$ is the largest bisimulation.

Definition 2 (Fusion machine) *Fusion machines M, bodies B, and terms P are defined by the following grammar:*

$$M \quad ::= \quad \mathbf{0} \quad | \quad x[p\text{:}B] \quad | \quad (x)[p\text{:}B] \quad | \quad M,M \qquad\qquad \text{(machines)}$$

$$B \quad ::= \quad \text{out}\widetilde{x}.\phi \quad | \quad \text{in}\widetilde{x}.\phi \quad | \quad P \quad | \quad B;B \qquad\qquad \text{(bodies)}$$

$$P \quad ::= \quad \mathbf{0} \quad | \quad x\text{=}y \quad | \quad \overline{u}\widetilde{x}.\phi \quad | \quad u\widetilde{x}.\phi \quad | \quad (x)P \quad | \quad P|P \qquad \text{(terms)}$$

The *basic channel-manager* $x[p\text{:}B]$ denotes a channel-manager at channel x containing a fusion pointer to p and a *body* B. This body is an unordered collection of *atoms* $m\widetilde{x}.\phi$ and *terms* P; it combines the atoms and deployment bag of the previous section. The *local channel-manager* $(x)[p\!:\!B]$ denotes a channel-manager where the name x is not visible outside the machine. When not relevant, we omit parentheses $(\cdot)$ to address generically channel managers which may be local or global. We also omit the fusion-pointer $x[B]$ to stand for a machine with some unspecified fusion pointer. We write chan M to denote the set of names of all channel-managers in the machine, and lchan M for the names of only the local channel-managers. We write $x[\,]$ for $x[\mathbf{0}]$. In terms, the restriction operator $(x)P$ binds x in P; x is free in a term if it occurs unbound. We write fn P to denote the set of free names in P.

There are two well-formedness conditions on machines. First, recall from the previous section that there is exactly one channel-manager per channel. In the calculus, we say that a machine $x_1[B_1], \cdots, x_n[B_n]$ is *singly-defined* when $i \neq j$ implies $x_i \neq x_j$ (x_i or x_j may be local). Second, it does not make sense to write a program that refers to a machine which does not exist. We say that a machine is *complete* when it has no such 'dangling pointers'. Formally, define ptr M to be the smallest set containing all free names in all terms in the machine, all non-nil fusion pointers, and all names occurring in any atom $m\widetilde{x}.\phi$. Then a machine M is complete if ptr $M \subseteq$ chan M. A machine is *well-formed* when it is both singly-defined and complete. In the following, we consider only well-formed machines. In particular, when we write $x[P]$ it is shorthand for the (well-formed) machine $x[\text{-}\!:\!P], y_1[\,], \cdots y_n[\,]$ where $\{y_1, \cdots, y_n\} = \text{fn}(P)\backslash x$. Here, x stands for an arbitrary location where the user of the machine first deploys program P.

Definition 3 (Structural congruence) *The* structural congruence *for machines and atoms* $\equiv$ *is the least congruence and equivalence satisfying*

1. *Machines and bodies are chemical solutions [2] with* $\mathbf{0}$ *as unit*

   $M, \mathbf{0} \equiv M$ \qquad $M_1, M_2 \equiv M_2, M_1$ \qquad $M_1, (M_2, M_3) \equiv (M_1, M_2), M_3$

   $B; \mathbf{0} \equiv B$ \qquad $B_1; B_2 \equiv B_2; B_1$ \qquad $B_1; (B_2; B_3) \equiv (B_1; B_2); B_3$

2. *Fusion laws*

   $x\text{=}x \equiv \mathbf{0}$ \qquad $x\text{=}y \equiv y\text{=}x$

The fusion laws are a syntactic convenience, allowing us to write a fusion $x\text{=}y$ without explicitly stating that x and y are distinct names in a particular order. To the same end, we also let $x\text{=-}$ stand for $\mathbf{0}$. There is no need to incorporate the calculus congruence $P \equiv Q$ into the machine congruence: the congruence is already implemented by the machine heating transitions.

We remark that the machine has a minimal structural congruence, for ease of implementation: the rule $B_1; B_2 \equiv B_2; B_1$ models the fact that the implementation uses a non-ordered data structure, and so the rule takes no extra work to implement; and $M_1, M_2 \equiv M_2, M_1$ models the fact that machines on the Internet are not ordered. The usual rule $x[B_1], x[B_2] \equiv x[B_1; B_2]$, on the other hand, would not motivated by an implementation: therefore we do not use it.

It is easy to show that all rules in the structural congruence preserve well-formedness.

Definition 4 (Transitions) *The reduction transition* $\rightarrow$ *and the heating transition* $\rightharpoonup$ *are the smallest relations satisfying the rules below, and closed with respect to structural congruence. Each rule addresses generically both free and local channel-managers.*

$$u[\mathsf{out}\widetilde{x}.\phi;\,\mathsf{in}\widetilde{y}.\psi;\,B] \quad \rightarrow \quad u[\widetilde{x}{=}\widetilde{y};\,\phi;\,\psi;\,B] \qquad\qquad\qquad \text{(react)}$$

$$u[v:\mathsf{m}\widetilde{x}.\phi;\,B_1],\ v[B_2] \quad \rightharpoonup \quad u[v:B_1],\ v[\mathsf{m}\widetilde{x}.\phi;\,B_2] \qquad\qquad \text{(migrate)}$$

$$u[x{=}y;\,B_1],\ x[p:B_2] \quad \rightharpoonup \quad u[B_1],\ x[y:y{=}p;\,B_2], \quad \textit{if } x < y \qquad \text{(dep.fu)}$$

$$u[v\widetilde{x}.\phi;\,B_1],\ v[B_2] \quad \rightharpoonup \quad u[B_1],\ v[\mathsf{in}\widetilde{x}.\phi;\,B_2] \qquad\qquad\quad \text{(dep.in)}$$

$$u[\overline{v}\,\widetilde{x}.\phi;\,B_1],\ v[B_2] \quad \rightharpoonup \quad u[B_1],\ v[\mathsf{out}\widetilde{x}.\phi;\,B_2] \qquad\qquad\quad \text{(dep.out)}$$

$$u[(x)P \mid B] \quad \rightharpoonup \quad u[P\{x'/x\};\,B],\ (x')[{-}:\,], \quad x' \textit{ fresh} \qquad \text{(dep.new)}$$

$$u[P|Q;\,B] \quad \rightharpoonup \quad u[P;\,Q;\,B] \qquad\qquad\qquad\qquad\qquad\quad \text{(dep.par)}$$

$$u[0;\,B] \quad \rightharpoonup \quad u[B] \qquad\qquad\qquad\qquad\qquad\qquad\quad\ \text{(dep.nil)}$$

$$u[p:u{=}y;\,B] \quad \rightharpoonup \quad u[y:y{=}p;\,B], \quad \textit{if } u < y \qquad\qquad \text{(dep.fu}')$$

$$u[u\widetilde{x}.\phi;\,B] \quad \rightharpoonup \quad u[\mathsf{in}\widetilde{x}.\phi;\,B] \qquad\qquad\qquad\qquad \text{(dep.in}')$$

$$u[\overline{u}\,\widetilde{x}.\phi;\,B] \quad \rightharpoonup \quad u[\mathsf{out}\widetilde{x}.\phi;\,B] \qquad\qquad\qquad\quad \text{(dep.out}')$$

For every transition rule above, we close it under contexts:

$$\frac{M \rightarrow M', \quad \mathsf{chan}\,M' \cap \mathsf{chan}\,N = \emptyset}{M,N \rightarrow M',N} \qquad \frac{M \rightharpoonup M', \quad \mathsf{chan}\,M' \cap \mathsf{chan}\,N = \emptyset}{M,N \rightharpoonup M',N}$$

It is easy to show that all transition rules preserve well-formedness. In respect of this, note that *(dep.new)* generates a fresh name so as to preserve single-definition, and the context closure rule forces this name to be globally fresh.

Bisimulation

We now define barbed bisimulation on machines.

Definition 5 (Observation) *The* internal *observation* $M \downarrow u$ *is the smallest relation closed with respect to structural congruence and satisfying*

$$u[\mathsf{m}\widetilde{x}.\phi;\,B] \downarrow u$$
$$u[v:B],\,M \downarrow u \quad \textit{if } M \downarrow v$$
$$M_1,M_2 \downarrow u \quad \textit{if } M_1 \downarrow u \textit{ or } M_2 \downarrow u$$

The external *observation* $M \Downarrow u$ *holds if* $M \rightharpoonup^* M'$ *such that* $M' \downarrow u$ *and* $u \notin \mathsf{lchan}\,M'$.

This is standard apart from the middle rule. To understand it, consider the example $u[v:\,],\,v[\mathsf{out}x]$. This corresponds to the calculus term $u{=}v \mid \overline{v}\,x$, which has an observation on u because of the explicit fusion. So too we wish the machine to have an observation on u. As for the reverse case, of $u[v: \text{out}x], v[\,]$ being observable on v, this is observable after a single heating transition.

The symbol $\Downarrow$ is generally used for *weak* observation, which is blind to internal reactions. Note however that our external observation $\Downarrow$ is *strong* with respect to reactions, but weak with respect to heating. Similarly, we write $\Rightarrow$ for $\rightarrow^* \rightarrow \rightarrow^*$.

Definition 6 (Bisimulation) *A (strong) barbed bisimulation $\mathcal{S}$ between machines is a relation such that if $M \mathcal{S} N$ then*

1. *$M \Downarrow u$ if and only if $N \Downarrow u$*
2. *$M \Rightarrow M'$ implies there exists N' such that $N \Rightarrow N'$ and $M' \mathcal{S} N'$*
3. *$N \Rightarrow N'$ implies there exists M' such that $M \Rightarrow M'$ and $M' \mathcal{S} N'$*

Let $\overset{\cdot}{\sim}$, called barbed bisimilarity, *be the largest barbed bisimulation.*

Theorem 7 (Correctness)

1. *For programs P and Q in the explicit solos calculus, $P \overset{\cdot}{\sim} Q$ if and only if $x[P] \overset{\cdot}{\sim} x[Q]$.*
2. *There is a translation $(\cdot)^*$ from the pi calculus into the explicit solos calculus such that, for programs P and Q in the pi calculus without replication, $P \overset{\cdot}{\sim} Q$ if and only if $x[P^*] \overset{\cdot}{\sim} x[Q^*]$.*

Proof sketch. Consider the translation $\text{calc}\, M$ from machines to terms in the explicit solos calculus, defined by $\text{calc}\, M = (\text{lchan}\, M)[\![M]\!]$ where

$$
\begin{aligned}
[\![\mathbf{0}]\!] &= \mathbf{0} & [\![\mathbf{0}]\!]_u &= \mathbf{0} \\
[\![u[\text{-}: B]]\!] &= [\![B]\!]_u & [\![\text{out}\tilde{x}.\phi]\!]_u &= \overline{u}\,\tilde{x}.\phi \\
[\![u[v: B]]\!] &= u\text{-}v \mid [\![B]\!]_u & [\![\text{in}\tilde{x}.\phi]\!]_u &= u\,\tilde{x}.\phi \\
[\![M_1, M_2]\!] &= [\![M_1]\!] \mid [\![M_2]\!] & [\![P]\!]_u &= P \\
& & [\![B_1; B_2]\!]_u &= [\![B_1]\!]_u \mid [\![B_2]\!]_u
\end{aligned}
$$

It is straightforward to show that machine heating transitions imply structural congruence in the calculus, and that machine barbs and reactions imply barbs and reactions in the calculus.

The proof of the reverse direction is more difficult. Given $\text{calc}\, M \downarrow u$, then there is also a machine M' in which all the deployable terms in M have been deployed such that $\text{calc}\, M' \downarrow u$. We now consider the fusion pointers in M'. Let us write $u \rightsquigarrow v$ if there is a sequence of fusion pointers from u to v. Note that all transitions preserve the following properties of this relation: it is anti-reflexive, anti-symmetric and transitive, it respects the order on names ($x \rightsquigarrow y$ implies $x < y$) and it is confluent ($x \rightsquigarrow y$ and $x \rightsquigarrow z$ implies $y \rightsquigarrow z$ or $z \rightsquigarrow y$ or $y = z$). We are therefore justified in talking about a tree of fusion pointers. With this tree it is easy to prove that if $\text{calc}\, M' \downarrow u$, then also $M' \downarrow u$. It is a similar matter to show that the machine preserves calculus reactions.

Therefore, the translation calc preserves observation and reaction, and so $\text{calc}\, M \stackrel{\cdot}{\sim} \text{calc}\, N$ if and only if $M \stackrel{\cdot}{\sim} N$. The first part of the theorem is just a special case of this, since $\text{calc}\, x[P] \equiv P$.

As for the pi calculus result, we refer to Corollary 66 and Proposition 101 of [19]. Together these provide a translation from the pi calculus into the explicit solos calculus which preserves strong barbed bisimulation.   □

We now consider behavioural congruence. In this paper, our goal is that the fusion machine should provide an operational semantics for calculus programs: i.e. we wish to study how programs behave when placed in a machine. To this end, we define contexts E_m for the machine where holes are filled with terms.

Definition 8 (Contexts) *Machine contexts E_m are given by*

$$E_m \quad ::= \quad x[p\colon E_b] \quad | \quad (x)[p\colon E_b] \quad | \quad E_m, M \quad | \quad M, E_m$$
$$E_b \quad ::= \quad \_ \quad | \quad B; E_b \quad | \quad E_b; B$$

When we write $E_m[P]$, we implicitly assume it to be well-formed. The machine equivalence is defined as follows:

Definition 9 (Equivalence) *Two terms are judged equivalent by the machine, $P \sim_m Q$, if and only if for every context E_m, $E_m[P] \stackrel{\cdot}{\sim} E_m[Q]$.*

Theorem 10 (Full abstraction) *For terms P and Q in the explicit solos calculus, $P \sim Q$ if and only if $P \sim_m Q$.*

Proof sketch. In the forward direction, we extend the translation calc to contexts in the obvious way. Then, given a machine context E_m, we can construct a calculus context $E = \text{calc}\, E_m$ such that, for every P, $\text{calc}(E_m[P]) \equiv E[P]$.

The reverse direction is not so straightforward. Consider for example the context $E = \overline{u}\,x \mid (x)_-$. This has no direct equivalent in the machine: it is impossible in the machine for x to be a local channel-manager whose scope includes a hole, and also at the same time a free name. Instead, given a context E which can discriminate between P and Q, we will construct another context $E' = \overline{u}\,x' \mid (x)_-$ which also discriminates them, and which has no clash of names; therefore it can be represented in the machine.

Technically, we will define a translation $[\![\cdot]\!]_{\widetilde{y}}$ from calculus contexts E to triples $(\sigma, \widetilde{z}, R)$. This translation pushes out the bindings that surround the hole in E. In order to accomplish this structurally, we keep all the binders in $\widetilde{z}$ (suitably renamed to avoid clashes), and collect the necessary renamings of free names in σ. The intention is that for any terms P and Q, then $E[P] \stackrel{\cdot}{\sim} E[Q]$ if and only if $(\widetilde{z})(R|P) \stackrel{\cdot}{\sim} (\widetilde{z})(R|Q)$, where $[\![E]\!]_{\widetilde{y}} = (\sigma, \widetilde{z}, R)$ and $\widetilde{y}$ contains all the names occurring in E, P, and Q. The translation is defined as follows:

$$[\![\_]\!]_{\widetilde{y}} = (\emptyset, \emptyset, \mathbf{0})$$

$$[\![E|S]\!]_{\widetilde{y}} = (\sigma, \widetilde{z}, S\sigma|R) \qquad\qquad \text{where } [\![E]\!]_{\widetilde{y}} = (\sigma, \widetilde{z}, R)$$

$$[\![(x)E]\!]_{\widetilde{y}} = \begin{cases} (\sigma[x \mapsto x'], \widetilde{z}x, R) & \text{if } x \notin \widetilde{z} \\ (\sigma[x \mapsto x'], (\widetilde{z}, \sigma(x)), R) & \text{if } x \in \widetilde{z} \end{cases} \quad \begin{array}{l} \text{where } [\![E]\!]_{\widetilde{y}} = (\sigma, \widetilde{z}, R) \\ \text{and } x' \notin \{\widetilde{y}, \widetilde{z}, \text{ran}\,\sigma\} \end{array}$$

We can prove that the contexts E and $(\tilde{z})(R|_-)$ are equivalent up to renaming by σ. Since σ is by definition injective, the contexts have the same discriminating power. Hence, so does the machine context $E_m = (z_1)[\,], \ldots (z_n)[\,], x[R; _-]$. $\square$

Unsurprisingly, full abstraction does not also hold for the pi calculus: it is known that pi calculus congruence is not closed with respect to substitution, whereas explicit fusion contexts always allow substitution.

5   Co-location

We now refine the abstract machine with (co-)locations, to allow practical reasoning about efficiency. When two machines are running at the same physical location, and share an address space, we draw their diagrams as physically adjacent:

u	v
F	F'
A	A'
D	D'

Some optimisations are possible in this case. First, it is possible to migrate or deploy an arbitrarily large number of terms to an adjacent machine, in constant time and without requiring any inter-location messages. Second, we can use just a single thread to handle both channels. In the degenerate case, where all machine's channels are at the same location and handled by just a single thread, the machine is essentially the same as Cardelli's single-processor machine.

Co-location might be programmed with a *located restriction* command in the calculus, written $(x@y)P$, to indicate that the new channel x should be created physically adjacent to y. The deployment transition is

u	y		u	(x')	y	
F	F'		F	$-$	F'	
A	A'	$\rightarrow$	A	$-$	A'	(dep.new.at)
$(x@y)P; D$	D'		$P\{x'/x\}; D$	$-$	D'	

(To implement this efficiently, without sending any inter-location messages, we assume that u is able to generate the fresh channel name x' locally – even though that x' will reside outwith u. We could implement this by letting each channel name incorporate a Globally Unique Identifier.)

Note that bound input, as found in the distributed version of the channel machine, allows new names to be created at a location chosen at runtime. For instance, $\mathsf{in}(x).(y@x)P$ will create the name y at the location of whichever name substitutes x. By contrast, a fusion machine without bound input has no way to chose locations at runtime. Therefore, bound input should be retained.

Co-location Used in Encoding Continuations

As discussed in Section 3, we ultimately imagine a machine which uses both continuations and fusions, and which uses them to implement the full pi calculus and explicit fusion calculus with nested continuations. To avoid the cost of repeatedly transporting continuations, an optimising compiler can encode a term with nested continuations into one without. This section describes our encoding and discusses its efficiency.

Two different encodings have been given previously [12, 10]. The distinguishing features of ours are that it is a strong congruence rather than just preserving weak congruence, it is uniform, and it uses co-location for increased efficiency. As an example, we encode the term $\overline{u}.(\overline{v} \mid v)$ as

$$(v'@v, v''@v)(\overline{u}.(v\text{=}v'\text{=}v'') \mid \overline{v}' \mid v'').$$

Note that the commands $\overline{v}'$ and v'' will necessarily remain idle until after $\overline{u}$ has reacted. Then, since v' and v'' are co-located with v, it will take no inter-location messages to migrate them to v.

Technically, we will relate terms P to triples of the form $(\widetilde{x}, \phi, P')$. This triple should be understood as the term $(\widetilde{x})(\phi|P')$ in which P' contains no nested actions or unguarded explicit fusions, and the located restrictions $\widetilde{x}$ are alpha-renamable.

Definition 11 *The function* flat· *from terms in the explicit fusion calculus to terms in the explicit solos calculus is as follows. It makes use of an auxiliary translation* [·] *from terms in the explicit fusion calculus to triples* $(\widetilde{x}, \phi, P')$, *where* $\widetilde{x}$ *ranges over located restrictions and normal restrictions.*

$$[\![\mathbf{0}]\!] = (\emptyset, \emptyset, \mathbf{0})$$
$$[\![x\text{=}y]\!] = (\emptyset, x\text{=}y, \mathbf{0})$$

$[\![(z)P]\!] = (z\,\widetilde{x}, \phi, P')$ *where* $[\![P]\!]=(\widetilde{x}, \phi, P')$ *and* $z \notin \widetilde{x}$

$[\![\overline{u}\,\widetilde{z}.P]\!] = \big(u'@u, u\text{=}u', (\widetilde{x})(\overline{u}'\widetilde{z}.\phi \mid P')\big)$ *where* $[\![P]\!]=(\widetilde{x}, \phi, P')$, $\widetilde{x} \cap \widetilde{z}=\emptyset$, u' *fresh*

$[\![u\,\widetilde{z}.P]\!] = \big(u'@u, u\text{=}u', (\widetilde{x})(u'\widetilde{z}.\phi \mid P')\big)$ *where* $[\![P]\!]=(\widetilde{x}, \phi, P')$, $\widetilde{x} \cap \widetilde{z}=\emptyset$, u' *fresh*

$[\![P \mid Q]\!] = (\widetilde{x}\,\widetilde{y}, \phi|\psi, P'|Q')$ *where* $[\![P]\!]=(\widetilde{x}, \phi, P')$, $[\![Q]\!]=(\widetilde{y}, \psi, Q')$
                                                and $\widetilde{x} \cap (\{\widetilde{y}\} \cup \text{fn}(\psi|Q')) = \emptyset$
                                                and $\widetilde{y} \cap (\{\widetilde{x}\} \cup \text{fn}(\phi|P')) = \emptyset$

flat $P = (\widetilde{x})(\phi \mid P')$ *where* $[\![P]\!]=(\widetilde{x}, \phi, P')$

Theorem 12 *For any term P in the explicit fusion calculus, $P \sim$ flat P.*

This encoding is only defined on terms without replication. However, the encoding is a congruence even within replicated contexts. For instance, $!\overline{u}\,\widetilde{x}.P \sim$ $!\overline{u}\,\widetilde{x}.(\text{flat}\,P)$. Therefore, an optimising compiler can locally encode any part of a program, without needing to encode it all. The proof is substantial; it may be found in [19]. Other encodings of replication are also possible, in the style of [12] or [9].

Theorem 13 *If $x[P]$ takes n inter-location messages to evolve to M' in the fusion machine with continuations, then $x[\text{flat}\,P]$ needs to take no more than $2n$ inter-location messages in the machine without continuations to evolve to N', such that $M' \overset{\cdot}{\sim} N'$.*

Proof sketch. First, annotate the machine transitions from Definition 4 with 0 or 1 to indicate their cost. For instance, migration $u[v\!:\text{out}x], v[\,] \to^0 u[v\!:], v[\text{out}x]$ takes no messages if u and v are co-located, and one message $\to^1$ otherwise. Then, define a *costed simulation relation* where $P\,\mathcal{S}\,Q$ implies that transitions $P \to^i P'$ or $P \to^i P'$ can be matched by transitions in Q of cost no greater than $2i$. Construct $\mathcal{S} = \{(M, N)\}$ where for each term P contained in a channel-manager in M, then N contains flat P in any channel-manager. Then $\mathcal{S}$ is a costed simulation.   □

6   Conclusions

We have introduced the fusion machine, a distributed channel-based machine for implementing several pi-like calculi such as the synchronous and asynchronous pi calculi, the explicit fusion calculus and the explicit solos calculus. Our objective was to make an easily-implementable machine that corresponds closely to such pi-like calculi. This conjectured ease of implementation appears to be born out in a prototype implementation by Wischik [18] and in projects by students at the University of Bologna. With respect to the close correspondence with pi-like calculi, we have proved abstraction results which are stronger than those obtained for other implementations. On the contrary, the fusion calculus [13] and the solos calculus [10] are awkward to implement in the fusion machine, even though they are closely related to the explicit fusion calculus. This is because they only allow reaction after a global search for restricted names.

We are currently working on a full distributed implementation for the fusion machine, and on a fusion-based language incorporating transactions and failures. We also plan to use some structure richer than just co-location, perhaps to model firewalls or other ambient-like boundaries. We would also like to mention the Xspresso project at Microsoft Redmond – a project to develop a pi-like language with explicit fusions, and a corresponding distributed machine. The machine is similar to the fusion machine presented in this paper, although it implements fusions with an alternative to forwarder-trees – the hope is to make them more scalable, and robust in the presence of failure.

References

[1] M. Abadi, L. Cardelli, P.-L. Curien, and J.-J. Lévy. Explicit substitutions. *Journal of Functional Programming*, 1(4):375–416, 1991. 422

[2] G. Berry and G. Boudol. The chemical abstract machine. *Theoretical Computer Science*, 96:217–248, 1992. 419, 426

[3] L. Cardelli. An implementation model of rendezvous communication. In *Seminar on Concurrency*, LNCS 197:449–457, 1984. 419

[4] S. Conchon and F. L. Fessant. Jocaml: Mobile agents for objective-caml. In *ASA/MA'99*, pages 22–29. IEEE, Computer Society Press. 418

[5] C. Fournet and G. Gonthier. The reflexive chemical abstract machine and the join-calculus. In *POPL'96*, pages 372–385. ACM Press. 418

[6] C. Fournet, J.-J. Lévy, and A. Schmitt. An asynchronous, distributed implementation of mobile ambients. In *IFIP TCS 2000*, LNCS 1872:348–364. 418

[7] P. Gardner and L. Wischik. Explicit fusions. In *MFCS 2000*, LNCS 1893:373–382. 419, 422

[8] A. Giacalone, P. Mishra, and S. Prasad. FACILE: A symmetric integration of concurrent and functional programming. *International Journal of Parallel Programming*, 18(2):121–160, 1989. 418

[9] C. Laneve, J. Parrow, and B. Victor. Solo diagrams. In *TACS 2001*, LNCS, 2215:127–144. 422, 431

[10] C. Laneve and B. Victor. Solos in concert. In *ICALP'99*, LNCS 1644:513–523. 419, 422, 431, 432

[11] C. Palamidessi. Comparing the expressive power of the synchronous and the asynchronous pi-calculus. In *POPL'97*, pages 256–265. ACM Press. 422

[12] J. Parrow. Trios in concert. In *Proof, Language and Interaction: Essays in Honour of Robin Milner*, pages 621–637. MIT Press, 2000. 419, 422, 431

[13] J. Parrow and B. Victor. The fusion calculus: Expressiveness and symmetry in mobile processes. In *LICS'98*, pages 176–185. IEEE, Computer Society Press. 422, 432

[14] B. C. Pierce and D. N. Turner. Pict: A programming language based on the pi-calculus. In *Proof, Language and Interaction: Essays in Honour of Robin Milner*, pages 455–494. MIT Press, 2000. 419

[15] P. Sewell. On implementations and semantics of a concurrent programming language. In *CONCUR'97*, LNCS 1243:391–405. 421

[16] R. E. Tarjan. Efficiency of a good but not linear set union algorithm. *Journal of the ACM*, 22(2):215–225, 1975. 423

[17] D. N. Turner. *The Polymorphic Pi-Calculus: Theory and Implementation*. PhD thesis, University of Edinburgh, 1996. 419

[18] L. Wischik. Fusion machine prototype. http:// www.wischik.com/ lu/ research/ fusion-machine. 432

[19] L. Wischik. *Explicit Fusions: Theory and Implementation*. PhD thesis, Computer Laboratory, University of Cambridge, 2001. 424, 429, 431

[20] P. T. Wojciechowski. *Nomadic Pict: Language and Infrastructure Design for Mobile Computation*. PhD thesis, Computer Laboratory, University of Cambridge, 2000. 418

HOPLA—A Higher-Order Process Language

Mikkel Nygaard[1] and Glynn Winskel[2]

[1] BRICS*, University of Aarhus
[2] Computer Laboratory, University of Cambridge

Abstract. A small but powerful language for higher-order nondeterministic processes is introduced. Its roots in a linear domain theory for concurrency are sketched though for the most part it lends itself to a more operational account. The language can be viewed as an extension of the lambda calculus with a "prefixed sum", in which types express the form of computation path of which a process is capable. Its operational semantics, bisimulation, congruence properties and expressive power are explored; in particular, it is shown how it can directly encode process languages such as CCS, CCS with process passing, and mobile ambients with public names.

1 Introduction

We present an economic yet expressive language for higher-order nondeterministic processes that we discovered recently in developing a domain theory for concurrent processes. The language can be given a straightforward operational semantics, and it is this more operational account we concentrate on in the paper.

The language is typed. The type of a process describes the possible (shapes of) computation paths (or runs) the process can perform. Computation paths may consist simply of sequences of actions but they may also represent the input-output behaviour of a process. A typing judgement

$$x_1 : \mathbb{P}_1, \ldots, x_k : \mathbb{P}_k \vdash t : \mathbb{Q}$$

means that a process t yields computation paths in $\mathbb{Q}$ once processes with computation paths in $\mathbb{P}_1, \ldots, \mathbb{P}_k$ are assigned to the variables $x_1, \ldots, x_k$ respectively. The types $\mathbb{P}$ are built using a "prefixed sum," products, function spaces and recursive definition. It is notable that although we can express many kinds of concurrent processes in the language, the language itself does not have many features typical of process calculi built-in, beyond that of a nondeterministic sum and prefix operations.

In general, the language allows processes to be copied and discarded arbitrarily. In particular, the language will allow us to write terms which take a process as argument, copy it and then set those copies in parallel composition with each

---

* Basic Research in Computer Science (www.brics.dk), funded by the Danish National Research Foundation.

other. However some operations are by nature *linear* in certain arguments. Linearity, detected in the denotational semantics, translates into the property of preserving nondeterministic sums.

The operations associated with the prefix-sum type constructor are central to the expressiveness of the language. A prefix-sum type has the form $\Sigma_{\alpha \in A}\alpha.\mathbb{P}_\alpha$; it describes computation paths in which first an action $\beta \in A$ is performed before resuming as a computation path in $\mathbb{P}_\beta$. The association between an initial action β and ensuing type $\mathbb{P}_\beta$ is deliberate; performing an action should lead to a unique type. The prefix sum is associated with *prefix operations* taking a process t of type $\mathbb{P}_\beta$ to $\beta.t$ of type $\Sigma_{\alpha \in A}\alpha.\mathbb{P}_\alpha$, as well as a *prefix match* $[u > \beta.x \Rightarrow t]$, where u has prefix-sum type, x has type $\mathbb{P}_\beta$ and t generally involves the variable x. The term $[u > \beta.x \Rightarrow t]$ matches u against the pattern $\beta.x$ and passes the results of successful matches for x on to t. More precisely, prefix match is linear in the argument u so that the possibly multiple results of successful matches are nondeterministically summed together.

The language supports an operational semantics and bisimulation. It is expressive and, as examples, it is easy to translate CCS, a form of CCS with process passing, and mobile ambients with public names into the language. The translated languages inherit bisimulation. Linearity plays a role in deriving traditional expansion laws for the translations.

The reader may like to look ahead to the operational treatment of the language in Sects. 3–6 for a fuller description. These sections are essentially self-contained, with references to the account in Sect. 2 of the denotational semantics of the language, and how it arose from a process model of Girard's linear logic, only to highlight the correspondence to the operational semantics.

2   Denotational Semantics

2.1   Presheaf Models

Let $\mathbb{P}$ be a small category. The category of presheaves over $\mathbb{P}$, written $\widehat{\mathbb{P}}$, is the category $[\mathbb{P}^{op}, \mathbf{Set}]$ with objects the functors from $\mathbb{P}^{op}$ (the opposite category) to the category of sets and functions, and maps the natural transformations between them. In our applications, the category $\mathbb{P}$ is thought of as consisting of computation-path shapes where a map $e : p \rightarrow q$ expresses how the path p is extended to the path q. A presheaf $X \in \widehat{\mathbb{P}}$ specifies for a typical path p the set $X(p)$ of computation paths of shape p, and acts on $e : p \rightarrow q$ to give a function $X(e)$ saying how paths of shape q restrict to paths of shape p. In this way a presheaf can model the nondeterministic branching of a process. For more information of presheaf models, see [14,4].

A presheaf category has all colimits and so in particular all sums (coproducts); for any set I, the sum $\Sigma_{i \in I}X_i$ of presheaves X_i over $\mathbb{P}$ has a contribution $\Sigma_{i \in I}X_i(p)$, the disjoint union of sets, at $p \in \mathbb{P}$. The empty sum is the presheaf $\varnothing$ with empty contribution at each p. In process terms, a sum of presheaves represents a nondeterministic sum of processes.

2.2   A Linear Category of Presheaf Models

Because the presheaf category $\widehat{\mathbb{P}}$ is characterised abstractly as the free colimit completion of $\mathbb{P}$ we expect colimit-preserving functors to be useful. Define the category **Lin** to consist of small categories $\mathbb{P}, \mathbb{Q}, \ldots$ with maps $F : \mathbb{P} \to \mathbb{Q}$ the colimit-preserving functors $F : \widehat{\mathbb{P}} \to \widehat{\mathbb{Q}}$. **Lin** can be understood as a categorical model of classical linear logic, with the involution of linear logic, $\mathbb{P}^\perp$, given by $\mathbb{P}^{op}$. The tensor product of $\mathbb{P}$ and $\mathbb{Q}$ is given by the product of small categories, $\mathbb{P} \times \mathbb{Q}$, and the function space from $\mathbb{P}$ to $\mathbb{Q}$ by $\mathbb{P}^{op} \times \mathbb{Q}$. On objects $\mathbb{P}$ and $\mathbb{Q}$, products (written $\mathbb{P} \& \mathbb{Q}$) and coproducts are both given by $\mathbb{P} + \mathbb{Q}$, the sum of categories $\mathbb{P}$ and $\mathbb{Q}$; the empty category $\mathbb{O}$ is a zero object. While rich in structure, **Lin** does not support all operations associated with process languages; since all maps are linear (i.e.. colimit-preserving), when applied to the inactive process $\varnothing$, the result will be $\varnothing$. So, in particular, a prefix operation cannot be interpreted as a map of **Lin**.

There are (at least) two reasonable responses to this: One is to move to a model of affine-linear logic where maps are allowed to ignore their arguments in giving non-trivial output. One such model is the category **Aff**, where maps are connected-colimit preserving functors. In [18] we used the category **Aff** to interpret an expressive affine-linear process language. Unfortunately, its operational semantics is proving difficult, and has not yet been extended to higher order.

This leads us to consider a second answer. Following the discipline of linear logic, suitable nonlinear maps are obtained as linear maps whose domain is under an exponential. As for the exponential ! of linear logic, there are many possible choices—see [18]. One is to interpret $!\mathbb{P}$ as the finite-colimit completion of $\mathbb{P}$. With this understanding of $!\mathbb{P}$, it can be shown that $\widehat{\mathbb{P}}$ with the inclusion functor $!\mathbb{P} \to \widehat{\mathbb{P}}$ is the free filtered colimit completion of $!\mathbb{P}$—see [15]. It follows that maps $!\mathbb{P} \to \mathbb{Q}$ in **Lin** correspond, to within isomorphism, to continuous (i.e., filtered colimit preserving) functors $\widehat{\mathbb{P}} \to \widehat{\mathbb{Q}}$.

2.3   A Cartesian Closed Category of Presheaf Models

Define **Cts** to be the category consisting of small categories $\mathbb{P}, \mathbb{Q}, \ldots$ as objects and morphisms $F : \mathbb{P} \to \mathbb{Q}$ the continuous functors $F : \widehat{\mathbb{P}} \to \widehat{\mathbb{Q}}$; they compose as functors. Clearly **Lin** is a subcategory of **Cts**, one which shares the same objects. We have

$$\mathbf{Cts}(\mathbb{P}, \mathbb{Q}) \simeq \mathbf{Lin}(!\mathbb{P}, \mathbb{Q})$$

for all small categories $\mathbb{P}, \mathbb{Q}$. The category **Cts** is the coKleisli category of the comonad based on finite-colimit completions.[1] The unit of the corresponding adjunction is given by maps $copy : \mathbb{P} \to !\mathbb{P}$ of **Cts**, used to interpret prefixing below. We can easily characterize those maps in **Cts** which are in **Lin**:

Proposition 1. *Suppose* $F : \widehat{\mathbb{P}} \to \widehat{\mathbb{Q}}$ *is a functor which preserves filtered colimits. Then, F preserves all colimits iff F preserves finite coproducts.*

---

[1] We are glossing over 2-category subtleties as ! is really a pseudo functor.

In other words a continuous map is linear iff it preserves sums.

There is an isomorphism

$$!(\mathbb{P} \,\&\, \mathbb{Q}) \cong \,!\mathbb{P} \times \,!\mathbb{Q}$$

making **Cts** cartesian closed; this immediately allows us to interpret the simply-typed lambda calculus with pairing in **Cts**. Products $\mathbb{P} \,\&\, \mathbb{Q}$ in **Cts** are given as in **Lin** but now viewing the projections as continuous functors. The function space $\mathbb{P} \to \mathbb{Q}$ is given by $(!\mathbb{P})^{\mathrm{op}} \times \mathbb{Q}$.

The category **Cts** does not have coproducts. However, we can build a useful sum in **Cts** with the help of the coproduct of **Lin** and !. Let $(\mathbb{P}_\alpha)_{\alpha \in A}$ be a family of small categories. Their *prefixed sum*,

$$\Sigma_{\alpha \in A} \alpha.\mathbb{P}_\alpha \ ,$$

is based on the coproduct in **Lin** given by $\Sigma_{\alpha \in A} !\mathbb{P}_\alpha$ with corresponding injections $in_\beta : \,!\mathbb{P}_\beta \to \Sigma_{\alpha \in A} \alpha.\mathbb{P}_\alpha$, for $\beta \in A$. The *injections*

$$\beta.(-) : \mathbb{P}_\beta \to \Sigma_{\alpha \in A} \alpha.\mathbb{P}_\alpha$$

in **Cts**, for $\beta \in A$, are defined to be the compositions $\beta.(-) = in_\beta \circ copy$. As the notation suggests, $\beta.(-)$ is used to interpret prefixing with β.

The construction above satisfies a property analogous to the universal property of a coproduct. Suppose $F_\alpha : \mathbb{P}_\alpha \to \mathbb{Q}$ are maps in **Cts** for all $\alpha \in A$. Then, *within* **Lin**, we find a mediating map

$$F : \Sigma_{\alpha \in A} \alpha.\mathbb{P}_\alpha \to \mathbb{Q}$$

determined to within isomorphism such that

$$F \circ \alpha.(-) \cong F_\alpha$$

for all $\alpha \in A$. Since **Lin** is a subcategory of **Cts**, the mediating map F also belongs to **Cts**, but here it is not uniquely determined, not even up to isomorphism. Therefore, the prefixed sum is not a coproduct in **Cts**, but the linearity of the mediating map is just what we need for interpreting prefix match. Consider a prefix match term $[u > \beta.x \Rightarrow t]$ where t denotes a map $F_\beta : \mathbb{P}_\beta \to \mathbb{Q}$. We interpret it as the mediating map obtained for F_β together with constantly $\varnothing$ maps $F_\alpha : \mathbb{P}_\alpha \to \mathbb{Q}$ for $\alpha \in A$ different from β, applied to the denotation of u.

2.4   Rooted Presheaves and Operational Semantics

The category $!\mathbb{P}$ has an initial element $\bot$, given by the empty colimit, and a presheaf over $!\mathbb{P}$ is called *rooted* if it has a singleton contribution at $\bot$—see [14]. As an example, the denotation of $\beta.t$ with t closed is rooted. We can decompose any presheaf X over $!\mathbb{P}$ as a sum of rooted presheaves $\Sigma_{i \in X(\bot)} X_i$, each X_i a presheaf over $!\mathbb{P}$. This is the key to the correspondence between the denotational semantics and the operational semantics of Sect. 4. Judgements $t \xrightarrow{\beta} t'$, with t of prefix-sum type $\Sigma_{\alpha \in A} \alpha.\mathbb{P}_\alpha$ and $\beta \in A$, in the operational semantics will express that $copy[\![t']\!]$ is a rooted component of $[\![t]\!]$ restricted to $!\mathbb{P}_\beta$. In fact, derivations of transitions $t \xrightarrow{\beta} t'$ will be in 1-1 correspondence with such components.

3   A Higher-Order Process Language

The types of the language are given by the grammar

$$\mathbb{P}, \mathbb{Q} ::= \Sigma_{\alpha \in A} \alpha.\mathbb{P}_\alpha \mid \mathbb{P} \to \mathbb{Q} \mid \mathbb{P} \& \mathbb{Q} \mid P \mid \mu_j \boldsymbol{P}.\mathbb{P} .$$

P is drawn from a set of type variables used in defining recursive types; $\mu_j \boldsymbol{P}.\mathbb{P}$ abbreviates $\mu_j P_1, \ldots, P_k.(\mathbb{P}_1, \ldots, \mathbb{P}_k)$ and is interpreted as the j-component, for $1 \le j \le k$, of the "least" solution (given by a suitable ω-colimit in the category of small categories and functors) to the defining equations $P_1 = \mathbb{P}_1, \ldots, P_k = \mathbb{P}_k$, in which the expressions $\mathbb{P}_1, \ldots, \mathbb{P}_k$ may contain the P_j's. We shall write $\mu \boldsymbol{P}.\mathbb{P}$ as an abbreviation for the k-tuple with j-component $\mu_j \boldsymbol{P}.\mathbb{P}$.

The constructions of **Cts** form the basis of a syntax of terms:

$$t, u ::= x \mid rec\, x.t \mid \Sigma_{i \in I} t_i \mid \alpha.t \mid [u > \alpha.x \Rightarrow t] \mid \lambda x.t \mid t\, u \mid (t, u) \mid fst\, t \mid snd\, t$$

In a nondeterministic sum term, $\Sigma_{i \in I} t_i$, the indexing set I may be an arbitrary set; we write $t_1 + \cdots + t_k$ for a typical finite sum and $\varnothing$ when I is empty. The variable x in the match term $[u > \alpha.x \Rightarrow t]$ is a binding occurrence and so binds later occurrences of the variable in the body t. We shall take for granted an understanding of free and bound variables, and substitution on raw terms.

Let $\mathbb{P}_1, \ldots, \mathbb{P}_k, \mathbb{Q}$ be closed type expressions and assume that the variables $x_1, \ldots, x_k$ are distinct. A syntactic judgement $x_1 : \mathbb{P}_1, \ldots, x_k : \mathbb{P}_k \vdash t : \mathbb{Q}$ can be interpreted as a map $\mathbb{P}_1 \& \cdots \& \mathbb{P}_k \to \mathbb{Q}$ in **Cts**. We let Γ range over environment lists $x_1 : \mathbb{P}_1, \ldots, x_k : \mathbb{P}_k$, which we may treat as finite maps from variables to closed type expressions. The term formation rules are:

$$\frac{\Gamma(x) = \mathbb{P}}{\Gamma \vdash x : \mathbb{P}} \qquad \frac{\Gamma, x : \mathbb{P} \vdash t : \mathbb{P}}{\Gamma \vdash rec\, x.t : \mathbb{P}} \qquad \frac{\Gamma \vdash t_j : \mathbb{P} \quad \text{all } j \in I}{\Gamma \vdash \Sigma_{i \in I} t_i : \mathbb{P}}$$

$$\frac{\Gamma \vdash t : \mathbb{P}_\beta \quad \text{where } \beta \in A}{\Gamma \vdash \beta.t : \Sigma_{\alpha \in A} \alpha.\mathbb{P}_\alpha} \qquad \frac{\Gamma \vdash u : \Sigma_{\alpha \in A} \alpha.\mathbb{P}_\alpha \quad \Gamma, x : \mathbb{P}_\beta \vdash t : \mathbb{Q} \quad \text{where } \beta \in A}{\Gamma \vdash [u > \beta.x \Rightarrow t] : \mathbb{Q}}$$

$$\frac{\Gamma, x : \mathbb{P} \vdash t : \mathbb{Q}}{\Gamma \vdash \lambda x.t : \mathbb{P} \to \mathbb{Q}} \qquad \frac{\Gamma \vdash t : \mathbb{P} \to \mathbb{Q} \quad \Gamma \vdash u : \mathbb{P}}{\Gamma \vdash t\, u : \mathbb{Q}}$$

$$\frac{\Gamma \vdash t : \mathbb{P} \quad \Gamma \vdash u : \mathbb{Q}}{\Gamma \vdash (t, u) : \mathbb{P} \& \mathbb{Q}} \qquad \frac{\Gamma \vdash t : \mathbb{P} \& \mathbb{Q}}{\Gamma \vdash fst\, t : \mathbb{P}} \qquad \frac{\Gamma \vdash t : \mathbb{P} \& \mathbb{Q}}{\Gamma \vdash snd\, t : \mathbb{Q}}$$

$$\frac{\Gamma \vdash t : \mathbb{P}_j[\mu \boldsymbol{P}.\mathbb{P}/\boldsymbol{P}]}{\Gamma \vdash t : \mu_j \boldsymbol{P}.\mathbb{P}} \qquad \frac{\Gamma \vdash t : \mu_j \boldsymbol{P}.\mathbb{P}}{\Gamma \vdash t : \mathbb{P}_j[\mu \boldsymbol{P}.\mathbb{P}/\boldsymbol{P}]}$$

We have a syntactic substitution lemma:

Lemma 2. *Suppose* $\Gamma, x : \mathbb{P} \vdash t : \mathbb{Q}$ *and* $\Gamma \vdash u : \mathbb{P}$. *Then* $\Gamma \vdash t[u/x] : \mathbb{Q}$.

The semantic counterpart essentially says that the denotation of $t[u/x]$ is the functorial composition of the denotations of t and u.

4   Operational Semantics

With actions given by the grammar

$$a ::= \alpha \mid u \mapsto a \mid (a, -) \mid (-, a) \ ,$$

the operational rules below define a transition semantics for closed, well-formed terms:

$$\frac{t[rec\,x.t/x] \xrightarrow{a} t'}{rec\,x.t \xrightarrow{a} t'} \qquad \frac{t_j \xrightarrow{a} t'}{\Sigma_{i \in I} t_i \xrightarrow{a} t'} \, j \in I$$

$$\frac{}{\alpha.t \xrightarrow{\alpha} t} \qquad \frac{u \xrightarrow{\alpha} u' \quad t[u'/x] \xrightarrow{a} t'}{[u > \alpha.x \Rightarrow t] \xrightarrow{a} t'}$$

$$\frac{t[u/x] \xrightarrow{a} t'}{\lambda x.t \xrightarrow{u \mapsto a} t'} \qquad \frac{t \xrightarrow{u \mapsto a} t'}{t\,u \xrightarrow{a} t'}$$

$$\frac{t \xrightarrow{a} t'}{(t, u) \xrightarrow{(a, -)} t'} \qquad \frac{u \xrightarrow{a} u'}{(t, u) \xrightarrow{(-, a)} u'} \qquad \frac{t \xrightarrow{(a, -)} t'}{fst\,t \xrightarrow{a} t'} \qquad \frac{t \xrightarrow{(-, a)} t'}{snd\,t \xrightarrow{a} t'}$$

In the rule for lambda-abstraction, we must have $x : \mathbb{P} \vdash t : \mathbb{Q}$ and $\vdash u : \mathbb{P}$ for some $\mathbb{P}, \mathbb{Q}$.

To show that the rules are type-correct, we assign types to actions a using a judgement of the form $\mathbb{P} : a : \mathbb{P}'$. Intuitively, after performing the action a, what remains of a computation path in $\mathbb{P}$ is a computation path in $\mathbb{P}'$. For $\beta \in A$ we take $\Sigma_{\alpha \in A} \alpha.\mathbb{P}_\alpha : \beta : \mathbb{P}_\beta$ and inductively

$$\frac{\vdash u : \mathbb{P} \quad \mathbb{Q} : a : \mathbb{P}'}{\mathbb{P} \to \mathbb{Q} : u \mapsto a : \mathbb{P}'} \qquad \frac{\mathbb{P} : a : \mathbb{P}'}{\mathbb{P} \,\&\, \mathbb{Q} : (a, -) : \mathbb{P}'} \qquad \frac{\mathbb{P}_j[\mu \boldsymbol{P}.\mathbb{P}/\boldsymbol{P}] : a : \mathbb{P}'}{\mu_j \boldsymbol{P}.\mathbb{P} : a : \mathbb{P}'}$$

—with a symmetric rule for $(-, a)$. Notice that in $\mathbb{P} : a : \mathbb{P}'$, the type $\mathbb{P}'$ is unique given $\mathbb{P}$ and a.

Proposition 3. *Suppose* $\vdash t : \mathbb{P}$. *If* $t \xrightarrow{a} t'$ *then* $\mathbb{P} : a : \mathbb{P}'$ *and* $\vdash t' : \mathbb{P}'$.

We interpret $\mathbb{P} : a : \mathbb{P}'$ as a map $\mathbb{P} \to !\mathbb{P}'$ of **Lin** by letting the judgement for β above denote restriction to $!\mathbb{P}_\beta$, and inductively interpreting $u \mapsto a, (a, -), (-, a)$ as the denotation of a precomposed with the map given by application to $[\![u]\!]$, and first and second projections, respectively. The rules are then sound in the sense that if $t \xrightarrow{a} t'$ then (identifying a term with its denotation) $copy\,t'$ is a rooted component of $a(t)$. In fact, there is a 1-1 correspondence between derivations with conclusion $t \xrightarrow{a} t'$, for some t', and the rooted components of $a(t)$, so the rules are also complete.

As a side-remark, the operational rules incorporate evaluation in the following sense: Let values v be given by $v ::= \alpha.t \mid \lambda x.t \mid (t, u)$. Then we can define a nondeterministic evaluation-relation $\Downarrow$ such that

Proposition 4. *If* d *is a derivation of* $t \xrightarrow{a} t'$, *then there is a value* v *such that* $t \Downarrow v$ *and* $v \xrightarrow{a} t'$ *by a subderivation of* d.

5   Equivalences

After introducing some notation regarding relations, we explore four standard notions of equivalence for our language. A relation R between typing judgements is said to respect types if, whenever R relates

$$\Gamma_1 \vdash t_1 : \mathbb{P}_1 \quad \text{and} \quad \Gamma_2 \vdash t_2 : \mathbb{P}_2 \ ,$$

we have syntactic identities $\Gamma_1 \equiv \Gamma_2$ and $\mathbb{P}_1 \equiv \mathbb{P}_2$. Below, all our relations will respect types, so we'll often suppress the typing information, writing just $t_1 \ R \ t_2$.

Suppose Γ is an environment list

$$x_1 : \mathbb{P}_1, \ldots, x_k : \mathbb{P}_k \ .$$

A Γ-closure is a substitution $[\boldsymbol{u}/\boldsymbol{x}]$ such that for $1 \le j \le k$, $\vdash u_j : \mathbb{P}_j$. If R relates only closed terms, we write R° for its open extension, relating $\Gamma \vdash t_1 : \mathbb{P}$ and $\Gamma \vdash t_2 : \mathbb{P}$ if for all Γ-closures $[\boldsymbol{u}/\boldsymbol{x}]$ we have $t_1[\boldsymbol{u}/\boldsymbol{x}] \ R \ t_2[\boldsymbol{u}/\boldsymbol{x}]$.

We'll write R_c for the restriction of a type-respecting relation R to closed terms.

For a type-respecting relation R we write R also for the induced relation on actions, given as the least congruence on actions so that $u_1 \mapsto a \ R \ u_2 \mapsto a$ if $u_1 \ R \ u_2$.

5.1   Bisimulation

A type-respecting relation R on closed terms is a *bisimulation* [19,21] if the following holds. If $t_1 \ R \ t_2$, then

1. if $t_1 \xrightarrow{a} t_1'$, then $t_2 \xrightarrow{a} t_2'$ for some t_2' such that $t_1' \ R \ t_2'$;
2. if $t_2 \xrightarrow{a} t_2'$, then $t_1 \xrightarrow{a} t_1'$ for some t_1' such that $t_1' \ R \ t_2'$.

Bisimilarity, $\sim$, is the largest bisimulation.

Theorem 5. *Bisimilarity is a congruence.*

Proof. We use Howe's method [11] as adapted to a typed setting by Gordon [9]. In detail, we define the precongruence candidate $\hat{\sim}$ as follows:

$$\frac{}{x \hat{\sim} w} x \sim^\circ w \qquad \frac{t \hat{\sim} t' \quad rec\,x.t' \sim^\circ w}{rec\,x.t \hat{\sim} w} \qquad \frac{t_j \hat{\sim} t_j' \ \text{all} \ j \in I \quad \Sigma_{i \in I} t_i' \sim^\circ w}{\Sigma_{i \in I} t_i \hat{\sim} w}$$

$$\frac{t \hat{\sim} t' \quad \alpha.t' \sim^\circ w}{\alpha.t \hat{\sim} w} \qquad \frac{t \hat{\sim} t' \quad u \hat{\sim} u' \quad [u' > \alpha.x \Rightarrow t'] \sim^\circ w}{[u > \alpha.x \Rightarrow t] \hat{\sim} w}$$

$$\frac{t \hat{\sim} t' \quad \lambda x.t' \sim^\circ w}{\lambda x.t \hat{\sim} w} \qquad \frac{t \hat{\sim} t' \quad u \hat{\sim} u' \quad t' \, u' \sim^\circ w}{t \, u \hat{\sim} w}$$

$$\frac{t \hat{\sim} t' \quad u \hat{\sim} u' \quad (t', u') \sim^\circ w}{(t, u) \hat{\sim} w} \qquad \frac{t \hat{\sim} t' \quad fst\,t' \sim^\circ w}{fst\,t \hat{\sim} w} \qquad \frac{t \hat{\sim} t' \quad snd\,t' \sim^\circ w}{snd\,t \hat{\sim} w}$$

Following Howe we now have: (i) $\hat{\sim}$ is reflexive; (ii) $\hat{\sim}$ is operator respecting; (iii) $\sim^\circ \subseteq \hat{\sim}$; (iv) if $t \hat{\sim} t'$ and $t' \sim^\circ w$ then $t \hat{\sim} w$; (v) if $t \hat{\sim} t'$ and $u \hat{\sim} u'$ then $t[u/x] \hat{\sim} t'[u'/x]$ whenever the substitutions are well-formed; (vi) since $\sim$ is an equivalence relation, the transitive closure $\hat{\sim}^+$ of $\hat{\sim}$ is symmetric, and therefore, so is $\hat{\sim}_c^+$.

Now we just need to show that $\hat{\sim}_c$ is a simulation, because then $\hat{\sim}_c^+$ is a bisimulation by (vi), and so $\hat{\sim}_c^+ \subseteq \sim$. In particular, $\hat{\sim}_c \subseteq \sim$. By (i) and (v), it follows that $\hat{\sim} \subseteq \sim^\circ$, and so by (iii), $\hat{\sim} = \sim^\circ$. Hence, $\sim$ is a congruence because it is an equivalence relation and by (ii) it is operator respecting.

We prove that $\hat{\sim}_c$ is a simulation by induction on the derivations of the operational semantics and using (iv-v). In fact, we need an induction hypothesis slightly stronger than one might expect:

if $t_1 \hat{\sim}_c t_2$ and $t_1 \xrightarrow{a_1} t_1'$, then for all a_2 with $a_1 \hat{\sim}_c a_2$ we have $t_2 \xrightarrow{a_2} t_2'$ for some t_2' such that $t_1' \hat{\sim}_c t_2'$.

By (i), $a \hat{\sim}_c a$ for all actions a, from which it follows that $\hat{\sim}_c$ is a simulation. $\quad\square$

Proposition 6. *The following pairs of closed, well-formed terms are bisimilar:*

$$1. \qquad rec\, x.t \sim t[rec\, x.t/x]$$

$$2. \quad [\alpha.u > \alpha.x \Rightarrow t] \sim t[u/x]$$
$$3. \quad [\beta.u > \alpha.x \Rightarrow t] \sim \varnothing \quad if\ \alpha \neq \beta$$
$$4. \; [\Sigma_{i \in I} u_i > \alpha.x \Rightarrow t] \sim \Sigma_{i \in I}[u_i > \alpha.x \Rightarrow t]$$
$$5. \; [u > \alpha.x \Rightarrow \Sigma_{i \in I} t_i] \sim \Sigma_{i \in I}[u > \alpha.x \Rightarrow t_i]$$

$$6. \qquad (\lambda x.t)\, u \sim t[u/x]$$
$$7. \qquad \lambda x.(t\, x) \sim t$$
$$8. \qquad \lambda x.(\Sigma_{i \in I} t_i) \sim \Sigma_{i \in I}(\lambda x.t_i)$$
$$9. \qquad (\Sigma_{i \in I} t_i)\, u \sim \Sigma_{i \in I}(t_i\, u)$$

$$10. \qquad fst(t,u) \sim t$$
$$11. \qquad snd(t,u) \sim u$$
$$12. \qquad t \sim (fst\, t, snd\, t)$$
$$13. \quad (\Sigma_{i \in I} t_i, \Sigma_{i \in I} u_i) \sim \Sigma_{i \in I}(t_i, u_i)$$
$$14. \quad fst(\Sigma_{i \in I} t_i) \sim \Sigma_{i \in I}(fst\, t_i)$$
$$15. \quad snd(\Sigma_{i \in I} t_i) \sim \Sigma_{i \in I}(snd\, t_i)$$

In each case $t_1 \sim t_2$, we can prove that the identity relation extended by the pair (t_1, t_2) is a bisimulation, so the correspondence is very tight, as is to be expected since in the denotational semantics, we have $[\![t_1]\!] \cong [\![t_2]\!]$.

Proposition 7. *Let t_1, t_2 be closed terms of type $\mathbb{P} \to \mathbb{Q}$. The following are equivalent:*

1. $t_1 \sim t_2$;
2. $t_1\, u \sim t_2\, u$ for all closed terms u of type $\mathbb{P}$;
3. $t_1\, u_1 \sim t_2\, u_2$ for all closed terms $u_1 \sim u_2$ of type $\mathbb{P}$.

5.2   Applicative Bisimulation

A type-respecting relation R on closed terms is an *applicative bisimulation* [1] if the following holds:

1. If $\vdash t_1\ R\ t_2 : \Sigma_{\alpha \in A}\alpha.\mathbb{P}_\alpha$, we have
   (a) if $t_1 \xrightarrow{\beta} t_1'$, then $t_2 \xrightarrow{\beta} t_2'$ for some t_2' such that $\vdash t_1'\ R\ t_2' : \mathbb{P}_\beta$;
   (b) if $t_2 \xrightarrow{\beta} t_2'$, then $t_1 \xrightarrow{\beta} t_1'$ for some t_1' such that $\vdash t_1'\ R\ t_2' : \mathbb{P}_\beta$.
2. If $\vdash t_1\ R\ t_2 : \mathbb{P} \to \mathbb{Q}$ then for all $\vdash u : \mathbb{P}$ we have $\vdash t_1\ u\ R\ t_2\ u : \mathbb{Q}$.
3. If $\vdash t_1\ R\ t_2 : \mathbb{P}\ \&\ \mathbb{Q}$ then $\vdash fst\ t_1\ R\ fst\ t_2 : \mathbb{P}$ and $\vdash snd\ t_1\ R\ snd\ t_2 : \mathbb{Q}$.
4. If $\vdash t_1\ R\ t_2 : \mu_j\boldsymbol{P}.\mathbb{P}$ then $\vdash t_1\ R\ t_2 : \mathbb{P}_j[\mu\boldsymbol{P}.\mathbb{P}/\boldsymbol{P}]$.

Applicative bisimilarity, $\sim_A$, is the largest applicative bisimulation. We have

Proposition 8. *Bisimilarity and applicative bisimilarity coincide.*

Proof. Since $\sim$ is a congruence, it follows that $\sim$ is an applicative bisimulation, and so $\sim\,\subseteq\,\sim_A$. Conversely, we can show that $\sim_A$ is a bisimulation by structural induction on (typing derivations of) actions a, and so $\sim_A\,\subseteq\,\sim$.   □

5.3   Higher Order Bisimulation

A type-respecting relation R on closed terms is a *higher order bisimulation* [23] if the following holds: If $t_1\ R\ t_2$, then

1. if $t_1 \xrightarrow{a_1} t_1'$, then $t_2 \xrightarrow{a_2} t_2'$ for some a_2, t_2' such that $a_1\ R\ a_2$ and $t_1'\ R\ t_2'$;
2. if $t_2 \xrightarrow{a_2} t_2'$, then $t_1 \xrightarrow{a_1} t_1'$ for some a_1, t_1' such that $a_1\ R\ a_2$ and $t_1'\ R\ t_2'$.

Higher order bisimilarity, $\sim_H$, is the largest higher order bisimulation.

Proposition 9. *Bisimilarity and higher order bisimilarity coincide.*

Proof. Clearly, bisimilarity is a higher order bisimulation so that $\sim\,\subseteq\,\sim_H$. For the converse, we observe that the proof of Theorem 5 goes through if we replace $\sim$ by $\sim_H$, and so $\sim_H$ is a congruence. It then follows by structural induction on actions a that $\sim_H$ is a bisimulation, so that $\sim_H\,\subseteq\,\sim$.   □

5.4   Contextual Equivalence

Let the type $\mathbb{1}$ be given as $\bullet.\mathbb{O}$ where $\mathbb{O}$ is the empty prefixed sum. If $\vdash t : \mathbb{1}$ we'll write $t \xrightarrow{\bullet}$ if there exists a t' such that $t \xrightarrow{\bullet} t'$. Two terms $\Gamma \vdash t_1 : \mathbb{P}$ and $\Gamma \vdash t_2 : \mathbb{P}$ are said to be *contextually equivalent* [16,8] if $C(t_1) \xrightarrow{\bullet}$ iff $C(t_2) \xrightarrow{\bullet}$ for all contexts C such that $C(t_1), C(t_2)$ are closed and have type $\mathbb{1}$.

The following two terms can be shown contextually equivalent:

$$t_1 \equiv \alpha.\varnothing + \alpha.\beta.\varnothing \quad \text{and} \quad t_2 \equiv \alpha.\beta.\varnothing.$$

However, they are clearly not bisimilar, so contextual equivalence fails to take account of the nondeterministic branching of processes.

6   Examples

The higher-order language is quite expressive as the following examples show.

6.1   CCS

As in CCS [21], let N be a set of names and $\bar{N}$ the set of complemented names $\{\bar{n} \mid n \in N\}$. Let l range over labels $L = N \cup \bar{N}$, with complementation extended to L by taking $\bar{\bar{n}} = n$, and let τ be a distinct label. We can then specify a type $\mathbb{P}$ as

$$\mathbb{P} = \tau.\mathbb{P} + \Sigma_{n \in N} n.\mathbb{P} + \Sigma_{n \in N} \bar{n}.\mathbb{P} \ .$$

Below, we let α range over $L \cup \{\tau\}$. The terms of CCS can be expressed in the higher-order language as the following terms of type $\mathbb{P}$:

$$
\begin{array}{ll}
[\![x]\!] \equiv x & [\![rec\ x.P]\!] \equiv rec\ x.[\![P]\!] \\
[\![\alpha.P]\!] \equiv \alpha.[\![P]\!] & [\![\Sigma_{i \in I} P_i]\!] \equiv \Sigma_{i \in I}[\![P_i]\!] \\
[\![P|Q]\!] \equiv Par\ [\![P]\!]\ [\![Q]\!] & [\![P \setminus S]\!] \equiv Res_S\ [\![P]\!] \\
[\![P[f]]\!] \equiv Rel_f\ [\![P]\!] &
\end{array}
$$

Here, $Par : \mathbb{P} \to (\mathbb{P} \to \mathbb{P})$, $Res_S : \mathbb{P} \to \mathbb{P}$, and $Rel_f : \mathbb{P} \to \mathbb{P}$ are abbreviations for the following recursively defined processes:

$$
\begin{aligned}
Par \equiv\ & rec\ p.\lambda x.\lambda y.\Sigma_\alpha[x > \alpha.x' \Rightarrow \alpha.(p\ x'\ y)] + \\
& \Sigma_\alpha[y > \alpha.y' \Rightarrow \alpha.(p\ x\ y')] + \\
& \Sigma_l[x > l.x' \Rightarrow [y > \bar{l}.y' \Rightarrow \tau.(p\ x'\ y')]] \\
Res_S \equiv\ & rec\ r.\lambda x.\Sigma_{\alpha \notin (S \cup \bar{S})}[x > \alpha.x' \Rightarrow \alpha.(r\ x')] \\
Rel_f \equiv\ & rec\ r.\lambda x.\Sigma_\alpha[x > \alpha.x' \Rightarrow f(\alpha).(r\ x')]
\end{aligned}
$$

Proposition 10. *If $P \xrightarrow{\alpha} P'$ is derivable in CCS then $[\![P]\!] \xrightarrow{\alpha} [\![P']\!]$ in the higher-order language.*

Conversely, if $[\![P]\!] \xrightarrow{a} t'$ in the higher-order language, then $a \equiv \alpha$ and $t' \equiv [\![P']\!]$ for some α, P' such that $P \xrightarrow{\alpha} P'$ according to CCS.

It follows that the translations of two CCS terms are bisimilar in the general language iff they are strongly bisimilar in CCS.

We can recover the expansion law for general reasons. Write $P|Q$ for the application $Par\ P\ Q$, where P and Q are terms of type $\mathbb{P}$. Suppose

$$P \sim \Sigma_\alpha \Sigma_{i \in I(\alpha)} \alpha.P_i \quad \text{and} \quad Q \sim \Sigma_\alpha \Sigma_{j \in J(\alpha)} \alpha.Q_j.$$

Using Proposition 6 items 1 and 6, then items 2-4, we get

$$
\begin{aligned}
P|Q \sim\ & \Sigma_\alpha[P > \alpha.x' \Rightarrow \alpha.(x'|Q)] + \\
& \Sigma_\alpha[Q > \alpha.y' \Rightarrow \alpha.(P|y')] + \\
& \Sigma_l[P > l.x' \Rightarrow [Q > \bar{l}.y' \Rightarrow \tau.(x'|y')]] \\
\sim\ & \Sigma_\alpha \Sigma_{i \in I(\alpha)} \alpha.(P_i|Q) + \\
& \Sigma_\alpha \Sigma_{j \in J(\alpha)} \alpha.(P|Q_j) + \\
& \Sigma_l \Sigma_{i \in I(l), j \in J(\bar{l})} \tau.(P_i|Q_j) \ .
\end{aligned}
$$

6.2   Higher-Order CCS

In [10], Hennessy considers a language like CCS but where processes are passed at channels C; the language can be seen as an extension of Thomsen's CHOCS [23]. For a translation into our language, we follow Hennessy in defining types that satisfy the equations

$$\mathbb{P} = \tau.\mathbb{P} + \Sigma_{c \in C} c!.\mathbb{C} + \Sigma_{c \in C} c?.\mathbb{F} \qquad \mathbb{C} = \mathbb{P} \& \mathbb{P} \qquad \mathbb{F} = \mathbb{P} \to \mathbb{P} \ .$$

We are chiefly interested in the parallel composition of processes, $Par_{\mathbb{P},\mathbb{P}}$ of type $\mathbb{P} \& \mathbb{P} \to \mathbb{P}$. But parallel composition is really a family of mutually dependent operations also including components such as $Par_{\mathbb{F},\mathbb{C}}$ of type $\mathbb{F} \& \mathbb{C} \to \mathbb{P}$ to say how abstractions compose in parallel with concretions etc. All these components can be tupled together in a product and parallel composition defined as a simultaneous recursive definition whose component at $\mathbb{P} \& \mathbb{P} \to \mathbb{P}$ satisfies

$$\begin{aligned}
P|Q = \ &\Sigma_\alpha [P > \alpha.x \Rightarrow \alpha.(x|Q)] + \\
&\Sigma_\alpha [Q > \alpha.y \Rightarrow \alpha.(P|y)] + \\
&\Sigma_c [P > c?.f \Rightarrow [Q > c!.p \Rightarrow \tau.((f \ fst \ p)| \ snd \ p)]] + \\
&\Sigma_c [P > c!.p \Rightarrow [Q > c?.f \Rightarrow \tau.(snd \ p|(f \ fst \ p))]] \ ,
\end{aligned}$$

where, e.g., $P|Q$ abbreviates $Par_{\mathbb{P},\mathbb{P}} (P,Q)$. In the summations $c \in C$ and α ranges over $c!, c?, \tau$.

The bisimulation induced on higher-order CCS terms is perhaps the one to be expected; a corresponding bisimulation relation is defined like an applicative bisimulation but restricted to the types of processes $\mathbb{P}$, concretions $\mathbb{C}$, and abstractions $\mathbb{F}$.

6.3   Mobile Ambients with Public Names

We can translate the Ambient Calculus with public names [2] into the higher-order language, following similar lines to the process-passing language above. Assume a fixed set of ambient names $n, m, \ldots \in N$. Following [3], the syntax of ambients is extended beyond processes (P) to include concretions (C) and abstractions (F):

$$\begin{aligned}
P ::= \ &\varnothing \mid P|P \mid rep \ P \mid n[P] \mid in \ n.P \mid out \ n.P \mid open \ n!.P \mid \\
&\tau.P \mid mvin \ n!.C \mid mvout \ n!.C \mid open \ n?.P \mid mvin \ n?.F \mid x \\
C ::= \ &(P, P) \qquad F ::= \lambda x.P \ .
\end{aligned}$$

The notation for actions departs a little from that of [3]. Here some actions are marked with ! and others with ?—active (or inceptive) actions are marked by ! and passive (or receptive) actions by ?. We say actions α and β are *complementary* iff one has the form *open n*! or *mvin n*! while the other is *open n*? or *mvin n*? respectively. Complementary actions can synchronise together to form a τ-action. We adopt a slightly different notation for concretions $((P, R)$ instead of $\langle P \rangle R)$ and abstractions $(\lambda x.P$ instead of $(x)P)$ to make their translation into the higher-order language clear.

Types for ambients are given recursively by (n ranges over N):

$$\mathbb{P} = \tau.\mathbb{P} + \Sigma_n in\ n.\mathbb{P} + \Sigma_n out\ n.\mathbb{P} + \Sigma_n open\ n!.\mathbb{P} + \Sigma_n mvin\ n!.\mathbb{C} +$$
$$\Sigma_n mvout\ n!.\mathbb{C} + \Sigma_n open\ n?.\mathbb{P} + \Sigma_n mvin\ n?.\mathbb{F}$$
$$\mathbb{C} = \mathbb{P}\ \&\ \mathbb{P} \qquad \mathbb{F} = \mathbb{P} \to \mathbb{P}\ .$$

The eight components of the prefixed sum in the equation for $\mathbb{P}$ correspond to the eight forms of ambient actions τ, $in\ n$, $out\ n$, $open\ n!$, $mvin\ n!$, $mvout\ n!$, $open\ n?$ and $mvin\ n?$. We obtain the prefixing operations as injections into the appropriate component of the prefixed sum $\mathbb{P}$.

Parallel composition is really a family of operations, one of which is a binary operation between processes but where in addition there are parallel compositions of abstractions with concretions, and even abstractions with processes and concretions with processes. The family of operations

$$(-|-) : \mathbb{F}\ \&\ \mathbb{C} \to \mathbb{P},\ (-|-) : \mathbb{F}\ \&\ \mathbb{P} \to \mathbb{F},\ (-|-) : \mathbb{C}\ \&\ \mathbb{P} \to \mathbb{C},$$
$$(-|-) : \mathbb{C}\ \&\ \mathbb{F} \to \mathbb{P},\ (-|-) : \mathbb{P}\ \&\ \mathbb{F} \to \mathbb{F},\ (-|-) : \mathbb{P}\ \&\ \mathbb{C} \to \mathbb{C}$$

are defined in a simultaneous recursive definition:

Processes in parallel with processes:

$$P|Q = \Sigma_\alpha[P > \alpha.x \Rightarrow \alpha.(x|Q)] + \Sigma_\alpha[Q > \alpha.y \Rightarrow \alpha.(P|y)] +$$
$$\Sigma_n[P > open\ n!.x \Rightarrow [Q > open\ n?.y \Rightarrow \tau.(x|y)]] +$$
$$\Sigma_n[P > open\ n?.x \Rightarrow [Q > open\ n!.y \Rightarrow \tau.(x|y)]] +$$
$$\Sigma_n[P > mvin\ n?.f \Rightarrow [Q > mvin\ n!.p \Rightarrow \tau.((f\ fst\ p)|\ snd\ p)]] +$$
$$\Sigma_n[P > mvin\ n!.p \Rightarrow [Q > mvin\ n?.f \Rightarrow \tau.(snd\ p|(f\ fst\ p))]]\ .$$

Abstractions in parallel with concretions: $F|C = (F\ fst\ C)|\ snd\ C$.
Abstractions in parallel with processes: $F|P = \lambda x.((F\ x)|P)$.
Concretions in parallel with processes: $C|P = (fst\ C, (snd\ C|P))$.

The remaining cases are given symmetrically. Processes P, Q of type $\mathbb{P}$ will—up to bisimilarity—be sums of prefixed terms, and by Proposition 6, their parallel composition satisfies the obvious expansion law.

Ambient creation can be defined recursively in the higher-order language:

$$m[P] = [P > \tau.x \Rightarrow \tau.m[x]] +$$
$$\Sigma_n[P > in\ n.x \Rightarrow mvin\ n!.(m[x], \varnothing)] +$$
$$\Sigma_n[P > out\ n.x \Rightarrow mvout\ n!.(m[x], \varnothing)] +$$
$$[P > mvout\ m!.p \Rightarrow \tau.(fst\ p|m[snd\ p])] +$$
$$open\ m?.P + mvin\ m?.\lambda y.m[P|y]\ .$$

The denotations of ambients are determined by their capabilities: an ambient $m[P]$ can perform the internal (τ) actions of P, enter a parallel ambient ($mvin\ n!$) if called upon to do so by an in n-action of P, exit an ambient n ($mvout\ n!$) if P so requests through an out n-action, be exited if P so requests through an $mvout\ m!$-action, be opened ($open\ m?$), or be entered by an ambient ($mvin\ m?$);

initial actions of other forms are restricted away. Ambient creation is at least as complicated as parallel composition. This should not be surprising given that ambient creation corresponds intuitively to putting a process behind (so in parallel with) a wall or membrane which if unopened mediates in the communications the process can do, converting some actions to others and restricting some others away. The tree-containment structure of ambients is captured in the chain of *open m?*'s that they can perform.

By the properties of prefix match (Proposition 6, items 2-4), there is an expansion theorem for ambient creation. For a process P with $P \sim \Sigma_\alpha \Sigma_{i \in I(\alpha)} \alpha.P_i$, where α ranges over atomic actions of ambients,

$$m[P] \sim \Sigma_{i \in I(\tau)} \tau.m[P_i] +$$
$$\Sigma_n \Sigma_{i \in I(in\ n)} mvin\ n!.(m[P_i], \varnothing) +$$
$$\Sigma_n \Sigma_{i \in I(out\ n)} mvout\ n!.(m[P_i], \varnothing) +$$
$$\Sigma_{i \in I(mvout\ m!)} \tau.(fst\ P_i | m[snd\ P_i]) +$$
$$open\ m?.P + mvin\ m?.(\lambda y.m[P|y])\ .$$

7   Discussion

Matthew Hennessy's work on domain models of concurrency [10] is analogous to the domain theory we describe; our use of presheaf categories, functor categories of the form $[\mathbb{P}^{op}, \mathbf{Set}]$ for a category $\mathbb{P}$, is mirrored in Hennessy's work by domains of the form $[\mathbb{P}^{op}, \mathbf{2}]$ for a partial order $\mathbb{P}$ (here $\mathbf{2}$ is the partial order $0 < 1$). In this sense Hennessy's work anticipates the path-based domain theory used here.

Flemming Nielson's Typed Parallel Language (TPL) [17] is essentially a juxtaposition of value-passing CCS and simply-typed lambda calculus. Our language gains considerably in simplicity by integrating evaluation and transition semantics. The focus of TPL is a static type system in which processes are assigned a representation of their possible future communication possibilities, with no notion of causality. In contrast, our type system (which is also static) reflects that the capabilities of a process may change over time.

Andrew Gordon uses transition semantics and bisimulation to reason about the lambda calculus [9]. Our transitions correspond roughly to those of Gordon's "active" types, integrating evaluation and observation. "Passive" types include function space, for which Gordon uses transitions of the form $t \xrightarrow{@u} t\ u$ (where, in our notation, t has type $\mathbb{P} \to \mathbb{Q}$ and u has type $\mathbb{P}$). Such transitions have no counterpart in our semantics, because they would destroy the correspondence between derivations in the operational semantics and rooted components in the presheaf model.

Every presheaf category possesses a notion of bisimulation, derived from open maps [13,14]. Open maps are a generalization of functional bisimulations, or zig-zag morphisms, known from transition systems. Presheaves over $\mathbb{P}$ are open-map bisimilar iff there is a span of surjective open maps between them. The maps of **Lin** and **Aff** preserve open maps and so open-map bisimulation [7,4], giving congruence results for free when a process language is interpreted in these categories. Interestingly, although the operational bisimulation of Park/Milner is a congruence for the higher-order language, maps of **Cts** need not preserve open maps. This suggests that one should look at other notions of open map; in fact, as shown in [7], to every comonad T on **Lin** there is a corresponding notion of "T-open map", and thus a notion of "T-bisimulation". In the case of the exponential !, the corresponding !-bisimulation degenerates into isomorphism, but there are models where !-bisimulation and open-map bisimulation coincide, and one may hope to recover operational bisimulation as !-bisimulation for some choice of exponential (or expose it as a union of such bisimulations). In fact, it appears that the correspondence between the denotational and operational semantics can be proved abstractly, depending only on properties of the prefixed sum, so that it holds also for other choices of exponential.

The language has no distinguished invisible action τ, so there is the issue of how to support more abstract operational equivalences such as weak bisimulation, perhaps starting from [5].

Work is in progress on extending the idea of prefixed sum to include name-generation as in Milner's π-calculus. The π-calculus already has a presheaf semantics [6] but it has not been extended to higher order (see [22] for an operational extension). We hope to be able to link up with the work on the ν-calculus by Pitts and Stark [20] and Jeffrey and Rathke [12].

Acknowledgements

We thank the encyclopaedic Andy Pitts for helpful advice. Part of this paper was prepared during a pleasant visit of MN to DISI—the people there are thanked for their hospitality.

References

1. S. Abramsky. The lazy lambda calculus. In D. Turner (ed): *Research Topics in Functional Programming*. Addison-Wesley, 1990.   442
2. L. Cardelli and A. D. Gordon. Anytime, anywhere. Modal logics for mobile ambients. In *Proc. POPL'00*.   444
3. L. Cardelli and A. D. Gordon. A commitment relation for the ambient calculus. Note. October 6th, 2000.   444
4. G. L. Cattani. *Presheaf Models for Concurrency*. BRICS Dissertation Series DS-99-1, 1999.   435, 446
5. G. L. Cattani, M. Fiore, and G. Winskel. Weak bisimulation and open maps. In *Proc. LICS'99*.   447
6. G. L. Cattani, I. Stark, and G. Winskel. Presheaf models for the π-calculus. In *Proc. CTCS'97*, LNCS 1290.   447
7. G. L. Cattani and G. Winskel. Profunctors, open maps and bisimulation. Manuscript, 2000.   446, 447
8. A. D. Gordon and L. Cardelli. Equational properties of mobile ambients. In *Proc. FoSSaCS'99*.   442

9. A. D. Gordon. Bisimilarity as a theory of functional programming. In *Proc. MFPS'95*, ENTCS 1. 440, 446

10. M. Hennessy. A fully abstract denotational model for higher-order processes. *Information and Computation*, 112(1):55–95, 1994. 444, 446

11. D. J. Howe. Proving congruence of bisimulation in functional programming languages. *Information and Computation*, 124(2):103–112, 1996. 440

12. A. Jeffrey and J. Rathke. Towards a theory of bisimulation for local names. In *Proc. LICS'99*. 447

13. A. Joyal and I. Moerdijk. A completeness theorem for open maps. *Annals of Pure and Applied Logic*, 70:51–86, 1994. 446

14. A. Joyal, M. Nielsen, and G. Winskel. Bisimulation from open maps. *Information and Computation*, 127:164–185, 1996. 435, 437, 446

15. G. M. Kelly. *Basic concepts of enriched category theory*. London Math. Soc. Lecture Note Series 64, CUP, 1982. 436

16. J. H. Morris. *Lambda-Calculus Models of Programming Languages*. PhD thesis, MIT, December 1968. 442

17. F. Nielson. The typed λ-calculus with first-class processes. In *Proc. PARLE'89*, LNCS 366. 446

18. M. Nygaard and G. Winskel. Linearity in process languages. In *Proc. LICS'02*. 436

19. D. Park. Concurrency and automata on infinite sequences. In *Proc. 5th GI Conference*, LNCS 104, 1981. 440

20. A. M. Pitts and I. D. B. Stark. Observable properties of higher order functions that dynamically create local names, or: What's *new*? In *Proc. MFCS'93*, LNCS 711. 447

21. R. Milner. *Communication and Concurrency*. Prentice Hall, 1989. 440, 443

22. D. Sangiorgi. *Expressing Mobility in Process Algebras: First-Order and Higher-Order Paradigms*. PhD thesis, University of Edinburgh, 1992. 447

23. B. Thomsen. A calculus of higher order communicating systems. In *Proc. POPL'89*. 442, 444

A First Order Coalgebraic Model of π-Calculus Early Observational Equivalence[*]

Maria Grazia Buscemi[1] and Ugo Montanari[2]

[1] Dipartimento di Matematica e Informatica
Università di Catania, Italy
[2] Dipartimento di Informatica
Università di Pisa, Italy
buscemi@dmi.unict.it
ugo@di.unipi.it

Abstract. In this paper, we propose a compositional coalgebraic semantics of the π-calculus based on a novel approach for lifting calculi with structural axioms to coalgebraic models. We equip the transition system of the calculus with permutations, parallel composition and restriction operations, thus obtaining a bialgebra. No prefix operation is introduced, relying instead on a clause format defining the transitions of recursively defined processes. The unique morphism to the final bialgebra induces a bisimilarity relation which coincides with observational equivalence and which is a congruence with respect to the operations. The permutation algebra is enriched with a name extrusion operator δ à la De Brujin, that shifts any name to the successor and generates a new name in the first variable x_0. As a consequence, in the axioms and in the SOS rules there is no need to refer to the support, i.e., the set of significant names, and, thus, the model turns out to be first order.

1 Introduction

The π-calculus is the touchstone for several applications concerning higher order mobility, security and object orientation. The advantages of the π-calculus rely on its simplicity and its process algebra flavor. Its operational semantics is given in terms of a transition system and its abstract semantics is based on bisimilarity.

It is well known that labeled transition systems can be regarded as coalgebras for a functor in the category **Set**. A coalgebraic framework presents several advantages: morphisms between coalgebras (cohomomorphisms) enjoy the property of "reflecting behaviors" and thus they allow, for example, to characterize bisimulation equivalences as kernels of morphisms and bisimilarity as the bisimulation associated to the morphism to the final coalgebra.

However, in the above representation of transition systems, the states are seen as just forming a set, i.e., the algebraic structure modeling the construction of programs and the composition of states is disregarded.

---

[*] Research supported in part by FET Global project *PROFUNDIS* and by MIUR project *COMETA*.

L. Brim et al. (Eds.): CONCUR 2002, LNCS 2421, pp. 449–465, 2002.

The missing structure may be recovered by integrating coalgebras with algebras, as it is done by Turi and Plotkin [14]. They define *bialgebras* and prove that for them bisimilarity is a congruence. Roughly, bialgebras are structures that can be regarded both as algebras of coalgebras and as coalgebras of algebras. Morphisms between bialgebras are both algebra homomorphisms and coalgebra cohomomorphisms and, thus, the unique morphism to the final bialgebra, which exists under reasonable assumptions, induces a (coarsest) bisimulation congruence on any coalgebra.

A fully satisfactory coalgebraic theory for the π-calculus would take advantage of well understood verification techniques and of efficient algorithms for computing finite minimal realizations [13,12,4].

Here our goal is to provide a compositional coalgebraic semantics of the π-calculus. We will define a permutation algebra with parallel composition and restriction for the calculus and, then, we will prove that the labeled transition system of the π-calculus can be lifted to such an algebra, thus obtaining a bialgebra.

A similar task has been considered in [9,10]. There, a coalgebraic semantics of the π-calculus has been proposed, based on name permutations. The intuition is that the effects of permutations on the behavior of agents are the smallest information required to define an observational equivalence via ordinary bisimilarity, without restrictions due to name generation and passing. However, the proposed model is flat, i.e., it represents the calculus at an operational level, but it does not capture its algebraic structure. Rather, in the present paper we are mainly interested in a compositional interpretation of the π-calculus.

It is well known that, in the π-calculus, bisimilarity fails to be a congruence due to the input prefix. Thus, in order for this property to hold, our algebra structure will include operators of name permutation, parallel composition and restriction, but not prefix. First, we define *static* agents as π-agents whose outmost operation is either prefix, matching, recursion, or summation. We also define a bijective translation of π-agents into terms of our algebra. This function, in particular, maps static agents to constants in the algebra. Then we equip each constant with a set of reduction rules that mimic any possible transition the corresponding static agent can perform. Finally we prove that, for each π-agent, the number of static agents and associated reduction rules needed in all derivations of the agent is finite.

The compositional structure of our bialgebra also gives advantages in finite state verification methods [4]. Usually, such techniques glue components together and, then, apply model checking or other verification methods. However, in many cases, state explosion severely limits the applicability. Rather, a compositional approach gives a chance to minimize components before combining them, thus preventing state explosion, at some extent, and yielding a smaller state space.

The restriction operator of our permutation algebra has no name argument. Also extrusion and fresh input actions have no bound names. The reason is that the extruded, fresh or restricted name is assumed to be always the first one, i.e., x_0. To model name extrusion, we define a first order operator δ à la De

Brujin, that shifts any name to the successor, thus generating a new name in x_0. The advantage of this choice is that it does not need a notion of support, i.e., the set of names effectively present, which would yield a second order model. Similarly, Pitts's nominal logics [11] exploits a first order model, by relying on substitution algebras that do not need considering support names.

The coalgebraic semantics for the π-calculus proposed in [9,10] relies on the results about bialgebras in [2], where two sufficient conditions are spelled out for a labeled transition system to yield a coalgebra on the category $\mathbf{Alg}(\Gamma)$ of algebras satisfying a specification $\Gamma = (\Sigma, E)$. We follow a different strategy to prove that the transition system of the π-calculus can be lifted to yield a bialgebra. First, we consider a category $\mathbf{Alg}(\Sigma)$ of algebras where specification Σ does not contain axioms. Thus the powerset functor can be lifted to a functor on $\mathbf{Alg}(\Sigma)$ using the De Simone specification. Then, we construct a complete axiomatization (with auxiliary operators) of the π-calculus algebra and we prove that each axiom bisimulates. This is enough to ensure that the lifting can take place and thus, in particular, that bisimilarity is a congruence. The construction in [2] yields a category of bialgebras which satisfy the axioms, while in our case the algebraic specification is just a signature, without axioms. Thus our final coalgebra is larger. However, given a coalgebra which satisfies the axioms, its image in the final coalgebra is the same.

In [6], Fiore and Turi propose a semantic framework for name-passing process calculi. Their model is based on functor categories equipped with a differentiation functor δ modeling the introduction of an extra variable – the variable to be bound. Instead we work with permutation algebras enriched with the name extrusion operation δ. While we also rely on a functor category (when the algebraic specification is seen as a Lawvere theory), our setting is more uniform, since δ is at the same level of permutations and of any further operation (here parallel composition) added to the algebra. Another difference is that we deal with name permutations, rather than name substitutions, and, thus, we are able to define observational equivalence (rather than congruence) in a coalgebraic way. A difference with respect to [11] and [7] is that we assume a fixed ordering on names, while they do not need it.

The paper is organized as follows. Section 2 contains the background on permutations, π-calculus, and coalgebras. In Sect. 3 we define a category of coalgebras for mobile calculi and in Sect. 4 we introduce a permutation algebra for the π-calculus. In Sect. 5 we prove a general result to lift coalgebras in **Set** with structural axioms to coagebras on $\mathbf{Alg}(\Sigma)$ and in Sect. 6 we provide the coalgebraic semantics of the π-calculus, by applying such a result to the transition system of the calculus. Finally, Sect. 7 contains some concluding remarks.

2   Background

2.1   Names and Permutations

We need some basic definitions and properties on names and on name permutations. We denote with $\mathfrak{N} = \{x_0, x_1, x_2, \ldots\}$ the infinite, countable, totally ordered set of *names* and we use $x, y, z \ldots$ to denote names. A *name substitution* is a function $\sigma : \mathfrak{N} \to \mathfrak{N}$. We denote with $\sigma \circ \sigma'$ the composition of substitutions σ and σ'; that is, $\sigma \circ \sigma'(x) = \sigma(\sigma'(x))$. We use σ to range over substitution and we denote with $[y_1 \mapsto x_1, \cdots, y_n \mapsto x_n]$ the substitution that maps x_i into y_i for $i = 1, \ldots, n$ and which is the identity on the other names. We abbreviate by $[y \leftrightarrow x]$ the substitution $[y \mapsto x, x \mapsto y]$. The *identity substitution* is denoted by id. A *name permutation* is a bijective name substitution. We use ρ to denote a permutation. Given a permutation ρ, we define permutation ρ_{+1} as follows:

$$\frac{-}{\rho_{+1}(x_0) = x_0} \qquad \frac{\rho(x_n) = x_m}{\rho_{+1}(x_{n+1}) = x_{m+1}} \tag{1}$$

Essentially, permutation ρ_{+1} is obtained from ρ by shifting its correspondences to the right by one position.

2.2   The π-Calculus

Many versions of π-calculus have appeared in the literature. The π-calculus we present here is *early*, *monadic*, and has *synchronous* communications.

Let $\mathfrak{N}$ be the countable set of names introduced in the previous section. The π-calculus *agent terms*, ranged over by $p, q, \ldots$, are closed (wrt. variables X) terms defined by the syntax:

$$p ::= \mathbf{0} \mid \pi.p \mid p|p \mid p+p \mid (\boldsymbol{\nu}x)\,p \mid [x{=}y]p \mid \mathbf{rec}\,X.p \mid X$$

where recursion is guarded[1], and *prefixes*, ranged over by π, are defined as:

$$\pi ::= \tau \mid \bar{x}y \mid x(y).$$

The occurrences of y in $x(y).p$ and $(\boldsymbol{\nu}y)\,p$ are bound; *free names* and *bound names* of agent term p are defined as usual and we denote them with fn(p) and bn(p), respectively. Also, we denote with n(p) and n(π) the sets of (free and bound) names of agent term p and prefix π respectively.

If σ is a name substitution, we denote with $\sigma(p)$ the agent term p whose free names have been replaced according to substitution σ, in a capture-free way.

The *static* π-calculus agent terms, ranged over by s, are defined by the syntax:

$$s ::= \pi.p \mid p+p \mid [x{=}y]p \mid \mathbf{rec}\,X.p.$$

We define π-calculus *agents* (π-*agents* in brief) as agent terms up to a *structural congruence* $\equiv$; it is the smallest congruence that satisfies the following axioms:

(alpha)	$p \equiv q$ if p and q are alpha equivalent
(par)	$p|\mathbf{0} \equiv p \qquad p|q \equiv q|p \qquad p|(q|r) \equiv (p|q)|r$
(res)	$(\boldsymbol{\nu}x)\,(\boldsymbol{\nu}y)\,p \equiv (\boldsymbol{\nu}y)\,(\boldsymbol{\nu}x)\,p \qquad (\boldsymbol{\nu}x)\,p \equiv p \quad \text{if } x \notin \text{fn}(p)$
	$(\boldsymbol{\nu}x)\,(p|q) \equiv p|(\boldsymbol{\nu}x)\,q \quad \text{if } x \notin \text{fn}(p)$

---

[1]   Recursion is guarded in p iff in every subterm $\mathbf{rec}\,X.q$ of p, variable X appears within a context $\pi.\_$.

Note that $(\boldsymbol{\nu} x)\, \mathbf{0} \equiv \mathbf{0}$ is a particular case of the last axiom above. We do not consider axioms for summation $(+)$, matching $(=)$, and recursion $(\mathbf{rec}\,.)$, since, in this paper, we aim at introducing an algebra with only parallel composition and restriction. We remark that $p \equiv q$ implies $\sigma(p) \equiv \sigma(q)$ and $\mathrm{fn}(p) = \mathrm{fn}(q)$; so, it is possible to define substitutions and free names also for agents.

Below, we introduce an example of a static π-agent. Throughout the paper, we will adopt it as a running example.

Example 1. Let $p = \mathbf{rec}\, X.\, (\boldsymbol{\nu} y)\, \overline{y} x_2 \mathbf{0} \,|\, \overline{x_2} y.X$ be a static π-agent. Agent p generates new names and extrudes them on a channel x_2; in parallel, p sends name x_2 on each generated channel.

The *actions* an agent can perform are defined by the following syntax:

$$\alpha ::= \tau \;\mid\; xy \;\mid\; x(z) \;\mid\; \overline{x}y \;\mid\; \overline{x}(z)$$

and are called respectively *synchronization*, *free input*, *bound input*, *free output* and *bound output* actions; x and y are free names of α ($\mathrm{fn}(\alpha)$), whereas z is a bound name ($\mathrm{bn}(\alpha)$); moreover $\mathrm{n}(\alpha) = \mathrm{fn}(\alpha) \cup \mathrm{bn}(\alpha)$.

The standard operational semantics of the π-calculus is defined via labeled transitions $p \xrightarrow{\alpha} p'$, where p is the starting agent, p' is the target one and α is an action. We refer to [8] for further explanations of the transition relation.

The operational semantics we consider in this paper is reported in Table 1. It differs from the (standard) *early operational semantics* because it includes a bound input rule (π-INP$'$) and rule (π-CLOSE) replaces rule

$$(\pi\text{-}\mathrm{STD\text{-}CLOSE}) \quad \frac{p_1 \xrightarrow{\overline{x}(y)} q_1 \quad p_2 \xrightarrow{xy} q_2}{p_1 | p_2 \xrightarrow{\tau} (\boldsymbol{\nu} y)\,(q_1 | q_2)} \quad \text{if } y \notin \mathrm{fn}(p_2)$$

To understand why the two semantics are equivalent, let us consider the π-agents $p_1 = (\boldsymbol{\nu} y)\, \overline{x} y.\mathbf{0}$ and $p_2 = \overline{z} y.\mathbf{0} \,|\, x\,(z).\mathbf{0}$. A transition $p_1 | p_2 \xrightarrow{\tau} (\boldsymbol{\nu} y)\, \overline{z} y.\mathbf{0}$ should not be allowed because it would cause name y in the first component $\overline{z} y.\mathbf{0}$ of p_2 to be captured by restriction $(\boldsymbol{\nu} y)$. Indeed, on the one hand, if we start with $p_1 \xrightarrow{\overline{x}(y)} \mathbf{0}$ and $p_2 \xrightarrow{\overline{x} y} \overline{z} y.\mathbf{0}$, the above transition is prevented by the side condition of rule (π-STD-CLOSE); on the other hand, if by rule (π-INP) we get $p_2 \xrightarrow{x\,y} \overline{z} y.\mathbf{0}$, rule ($\pi$-CLOSE) cannot be applied since the input action is not bound, while if we employ rule (π-INP$'$) and we obtain $\overline{x}(y).\mathbf{0} \xrightarrow{\overline{x}(y)} \mathbf{0}$, then rule ($\pi$-PAR) cannot be applied to p_2, since y is both bound in $x\,(y)$ and free in $\overline{z}\,y.\mathbf{0}$.

2.3   Coalgebras

We recall that an algebra A over a signature Σ (Σ-algebra in brief) is defined by a carrier set $|A|$ and, for each operation $op \in \Sigma$ of arity n, by a function $op^A : |A|^n \to |A|$. A homomorphism (or simply a morphism) between two Σ-algebras A and B is a function $h : |A| \to |B|$ that commutes with all the operations in Σ, namely, for each operator $op \in \Sigma$ of arity n, we have

Table 1. Early operational semantics

$(\pi\text{-Tau})$ $\tau.p \xrightarrow{\tau} p$	$(\pi\text{-Out})$ $\bar{x}y.p \xrightarrow{\bar{x}y} p$
$(\pi\text{-Inp})$ $x(y).p \xrightarrow{xz} [z \mapsto y]p$	$(\pi\text{-Inp}')$ $x(y).p \xrightarrow{x(y)} p$
$(\pi\text{-Sum})$ $\dfrac{p_1 \xrightarrow{\alpha} q_1}{p_1 + p_2 \xrightarrow{\alpha} q_1}$ and symmetric	$(\pi\text{-Match})$ $\dfrac{p \xrightarrow{\alpha} q}{[x = x]p \xrightarrow{\alpha} q}$
$(\pi\text{-Rec})$ $\dfrac{p[\mathbf{rec}\,X.\,p/X] \xrightarrow{\alpha} q}{\mathbf{rec}\,X.\,p \xrightarrow{\alpha} q}$	$(\pi\text{-Par})$ $\dfrac{p \xrightarrow{\alpha} q}{p|r \xrightarrow{\alpha} q|r}$ if $\mathrm{bn}(\alpha) \cap \mathrm{fn}(r) = \emptyset$
$(\pi\text{-Res})$ $\dfrac{p \xrightarrow{\alpha} q}{(\nu y)\,p \xrightarrow{\alpha} (\nu y)\,q}$ if $y \notin \mathrm{n}(\alpha)$	$(\pi\text{-Open})$ $\dfrac{p \xrightarrow{\bar{x}y} q}{(\nu y)\,p \xrightarrow{\bar{x}(y)} q}$ if $x \neq y$
$(\pi\text{-Com})$ $\dfrac{p_1 \xrightarrow{\bar{x}y} q_1 \quad p_2 \xrightarrow{xy} q_2}{p_1|p_2 \xrightarrow{\tau} q_1|q_2}$	$(\pi\text{-Close})$ $\dfrac{p_1 \xrightarrow{\bar{x}(y)} q_1 \quad p_2 \xrightarrow{x(y)} q_2}{p_1|p_2 \xrightarrow{\tau} (\nu y)\,(q_1|q_2)}$

$op^B(h(a_1), \cdots, h(a_n)) = h(op^A(a_1, \ldots, a_n))$. We denote by $\mathbf{Alg}(\Sigma)$ the category of Σ-algebras and Σ-morphisms. The following definition introduces labeled transition systems whose states have an algebraic structure.

Definition 1 (transition systems). *Let Σ be a signature, and L be a set of labels. A transition system over Σ and L is a pair $lts = \langle A, \longrightarrow_{lts} \rangle$ where A is a nonempty Σ-algebra and $\longrightarrow_{lts} \subseteq |A| \times L \times |A|$ is a labeled transition relation. For $\langle p, l, q \rangle \in \longrightarrow_{lts}$ we write $p \xrightarrow{l}_{lts} q$.*

Let $lts = \langle A, \longrightarrow_{lts} \rangle$ and $lts' = \langle B, \longrightarrow_{lts'} \rangle$ be two transition systems. A morphism $h : lts \to lts'$ of transition systems over Σ and L (lts morphism, in brief) is a Σ-morphism $h : A \to B$ such that $p \xrightarrow{l}_{lts} q$ implies $f(p) \xrightarrow{l}_{lts'} f(q)$.

The notion of bisimulation on structured transition systems is the classical one.

Definition 2 (bisimulation). *Let Σ be a signature, L be a set of labels, and $lts = \langle A, \longrightarrow_{lts} \rangle$ be a transition system over Σ and L.*

A relation $\mathcal{R}$ over $|A|$ is a bisimulation if $p\,\mathcal{R}\,q$ implies:

- *for each $p \xrightarrow{l} p'$ there is some $q \xrightarrow{l} q'$ such that $p'\,\mathcal{R}\,q'$;*
- *for each $q \xrightarrow{l} q'$ there is some $p \xrightarrow{l} p'$ such that $p'\,\mathcal{R}\,q'$.*

Bisimilarity $\sim_{lts}$ *is the largest bisimulation.*

Given a signature Σ and a set of labels L, a collection of SOS rules can be regarded as a specification of those transition systems over Σ and L that have a transition relation closed under the given rules.

Definition 3 (SOS rules). *Given a signature Σ and a set of labels L, a sequent $p \xrightarrow{l} q$ (over L and Σ) is a triple where $l \in L$ is a label and p, q are Σ-terms with variables in a given set X.*

An SOS rule r over Σ and L takes the form:

$$\frac{p_1 \xrightarrow{l_1} q_1 \cdots p_n \xrightarrow{l_n} q_n}{p \xrightarrow{l} q}$$

where $p_i \xrightarrow{l_i} q_i$ as well as $p \xrightarrow{l} q$ are sequents.

We say that transition system lts = $\langle A, \longrightarrow_{lts}\rangle$ satisfies a rule r like above if each assignment to the variables in X that is a solution[2] to $p_i \xrightarrow{l_i} q_i$ for $i = 1, \ldots, n$ is also a solution to $p \xrightarrow{l} q$.

We represent with

$$\frac{\begin{array}{c}p_1 \xrightarrow{l_1} q_1 \cdots p_n \xrightarrow{l_n} q_n \\ \vdots\end{array}}{p \xrightarrow{l} q}$$

a proof, *with premises $p_i \xrightarrow{l_i} q_i$ for $i = 1, \ldots, n$ and conclusion $p \xrightarrow{l} q$, obtained by applying the rules in R.*

Definition 4 (transition specifications). *A transition specification is a tuple $\Delta = \langle \Sigma, L, R\rangle$ consisting of a signature Σ, a set of labels L, and a set of SOS rules R over Σ and L.*

A transition system over Δ is a transition system over Σ and L that satisfies rules R.

It is well known that ordinary labeled transition systems (i.e., transition systems whose states do not have an algebraic structure) can be represented as coalgebras for a suitable functor [13].

Definition 5 (coalgebras). *Let $F : \mathcal{C} \to \mathcal{C}$ be a functor on a category $\mathcal{C}$. A coalgebra for F, or F-coalgebra, is a pair $\langle A, f\rangle$ where A is an object and $f : A \to F(A)$ is an arrow of $\mathcal{C}$. A F-cohomomorphism (or simply F-morphism) $h : \langle A, f\rangle \to \langle B, g\rangle$ is an arrow $h : A \to B$ of $\mathcal{C}$ such that*

$$h; g = f; F(h). \tag{2}$$

We denote with **Coalg**(F) *the category of F-coalgebras and F-morphisms.*

Proposition 1. *For a fixed set of labels L, let $P_L : \text{Set} \to \text{Set}$ be the functor defined on objects as $P_L(X) = \mathcal{P}(L \times X + X)$, where $\mathcal{P}$ denotes the countable powerset functor, and on arrows as $P_L(h)(S) = \{\langle l, h(p)\rangle \mid \langle l, p\rangle \in S \cap L \times X\} \cup \{h(p) \mid p \in S \cap X\}$, for $h : X \to Y$ and $S \subseteq L \times X + X$. Then P_L-coalgebras are in a one-to-one correspondence with transition systems[3] on L, given by $f_{lts}(p) = \{\langle l, q\rangle \mid p \xrightarrow{l}_{lts} q\} \cup \{p\}$ and, conversely, by $p \xrightarrow{l}_{lts_f} q$ if and only if $\langle l, q\rangle \in f(p)$.*

---

[2] Given $h : X \to A$ and its extension $\hat{h} : T_\Sigma(X) \to A$, h is a solution to $p \xrightarrow{l} q$ for lts if and only if $\hat{h}(p) \xrightarrow{l}_{lts} \hat{h}(q)$.

[3] Notice that this correspondence is well defined also for transition systems with sets of states, rather than with algebras of states as required in Definition 1.

In [1] the generalized notion of lax cohomomorphism is given, in order to accommodate also the more general definition of lts morphisms in a (lax) coalgebraic framework. To make clear their intuition, let $f : A \to P_L(A)$ and $g : B \to P_L(B)$ be two P_L-coalgebras and let $h : A \to B$ be a P_L-morphism. If we split the morphism condition (2) for h in the conjunction of the two inclusions $f; P_L(h) \subseteq h; g$ and $h; g \subseteq f; P_L(h)$, then it is easily shown that the first inclusion expresses "preservation" of transitions, while the second one corresponds to "reflection". Thus, lts morphisms can be seen as arrows (i.e., functions in **Set**) that satisfy the first inclusion, while lts morphisms which also satisfy the reflection inclusion are P_L-morphisms. This observation will be useful in Sect. 5.

Definition 6 (De Simone format). *Given a signature Σ and a set of labels L, a rule r over Σ and L is in* **De Simone format** *if it has the form:*

$$\frac{\{x_i \xrightarrow{l_i} y_i \mid i \in I\}}{op(x_1, \ldots, x_n) \xrightarrow{l} p}$$

where $op \in \Sigma$, $I \subseteq \{1, \ldots, n\}$, p is linear and the variables y_i occurring in p are distinct from variables x_i, except for $y_i = x_i$ if $i \notin I$.

The following results are due to [14] and concern *bialgebras*, i.e., coalgebras in **Alg**(Σ). Bialgebras enjoy the property that the unique morphism to the final bialgebra, which exists under reasonable conditions, induces a bisimulation that is a congruence with respect to the operations, as noted in the introduction.

Proposition 2 (lifting of P_L). *Let $\Delta = \langle \Sigma, L, R \rangle$ be a transition specification with rules in De Simone format.*
*Define $P_\Delta : $ **Alg**$(\Sigma) \to$ **Alg**(Σ) as follows:*

- $|P_\Delta(A)| = P_L(|A|)$;
- *whenever* $\dfrac{\{x_i \xrightarrow{l_i} y_i \mid i \in I\}}{op(x_1, \ldots, x_n) \xrightarrow{l} p} \in R$ *then*

$$\frac{\langle l_i, p_i \rangle \in S_i, i \in I \quad q_j \in S_j, j \notin I}{\langle l, p[p_i/y_i, i \in I, \ q_j/y_j, j \notin I] \rangle \in op^{P_\Delta(A)}(S_1, \ldots, S_n)};$$

- *if $h : A \to B$ is a morphism in* **Alg**(Σ) *then* $P_\Delta(h) : P_\Delta(A) \to P_\Delta(B)$ *and $P_\Delta(h)(S) = \{\, \langle l, h(p) \rangle \mid \langle l, p \rangle \in S \cap (L \times |A|)\,\} \cup \{\, h(p) \mid p \in S \cap |A|\,\}$.*

Then P_Δ is a well-defined functor on **Alg**(Σ).

Corollary 1. *Let $\Delta = \langle \Sigma, L, R \rangle$ be a transition specification with rules R in De Simone format.*
Any morphism $h : f \to g$ in **Coalg**(P_Δ) *entails a bisimulation $\sim_h$ on lts$_f$, that coincides with the kernel of the morphism. Bisimulation $\sim_h$ is a congruence for the operations of the algebra.*
Moreover, the category **Coalg**(P_Δ) *has a final object. Finally, the kernel of the unique P_Δ-morphism from f to the final object of* **Coalg**(P_Δ) *is a relation on the states of f which coincides with bisimilarity on lts$_f$ and is a congruence.*

The theory described so far accounts for the lifting of the functor from **Set** to $\mathbf{Alg}(\Sigma)$; a further step is needed to lift a P_L-coalgebra to be a P_Δ-coalgebra. Indeed, the above step is obvious in the particular case of $f : A \to P_\Delta(A)$, with $A = T_\Sigma$ and f unique by initiality, namely when A has no structural axioms and no additional constants, and lts_f is the minimal transition system satisfying Δ.

As an example that in general the lifting may not succeed, let us consider the case of the chemical abstract machine $CHAM$. For our purposes, the signature Σ_c of a $CHAM$ is defined as:

$$\Sigma_c ::= \mathbf{0} \mid \_|\_ \mid a.\_ \mid \bar{a}.\_ \mid \texttt{redex}_a(\_,\_)$$

and E_c is the set of axioms for commutativity, associativity, id, $\mathbf{0}$ plus an axiom $\texttt{redex}_a(p,q) = a.p \mid \bar{a}.q$. The only reduction rule $\texttt{redex}_a(p,q) \longrightarrow p \mid q$ is in De Simone format. For P_{Δ_c} the usual poweralgebra functor on $\mathbf{Alg}(\Sigma_c)$, the transition system of $CHAM$ forms a P_L-coalgebra, but not a P_{Δ_c}-coalgebra [4]. And bisimilarity is not a congruence as, for example, $\mathbf{0} \sim a.p$ but $\bar{a}.p \not\sim a.p \mid \bar{a}.p$.

In Sect. 5, we will show how to lift a transition system with structural axioms from $\mathbf{Coalg}(P_L)$ to $\mathbf{Coalg}(P_\Delta)$, under appropriate conditions on the axioms.

3   A Category of Coalgebras for Mobile Calculi

In this section, we define a transition specification Δ_{pr} for mobile calculi with permutations (ρ), parallel composition ($|$), name restriction (ν) and extrusion (δ), and prove that the category $\mathbf{Coalg}(P_{\Delta_{pr}})$ of coalgebras over Δ_{pr} is well-defined. As mentioned in the Introduction, operators ν and δ do not have arguments, as the extruded or restricted name is assumed to be always the first one, i.e., x_0.

Definition 7. *Signature Σ_{pr} is defined as follows:*

$$\Sigma_{pr} ::= \mathbf{0} \mid \_|\_ \mid \nu.\_ \mid \delta.\_ \mid \rho\_$$

We adopt the convention that operators have decreasing binding power, in the following order: ρ, $|$, ν and δ. Thus, for example, $\nu.\delta.\rho p | q$ means $\nu.(\delta.((\rho p)|q))$.

Operators ρ are generic, finite name permutations, as described in Subsect. 2.1. Operator δ is meant to represent the substitution $[x_i \mapsto x_{i+1}]$, for $i = 0, 1, \dots$. Of course, this substitution is not finite, but, at least in the case of an ordinary agent p, it replaces a finite number of names, i.e., the free names of p.

We define the set L_{pr} of the labels:

$$L_{pr} = \{\tau,\ xy,\ x,\ \bar{x}\,y,\ \bar{x} \mid x, y \in \mathfrak{N}\}. \tag{3}$$

If $l \in L_{pr}$ then $\delta(l)$ and $\nu(l)$ are the labels obtained from l by respectively applying substitution δ and ν to its names, where $\nu(x_{i+1}) = x_i$ and $\delta(x_i) =$

---

[4] Indeed, axiom $\texttt{redex}_a(p,q) = a.p \mid \bar{a}.q$ does not satisfy the "bisimulation" condition required in Theorem 6.

x_{i+1}. Homomorphically, δ and ν are extended to π-agents, with δ and ν inactive on bound names. Note that in $\nu.\,p$, p is a value of a Σ_{pr}-algebra; in $\nu\,(p)$, p is a π-agent and $\nu\,(p)$ is defined only if $x_0 \notin \mathrm{fn}(p)$.

The correspondence between labels L_{pr} and the actions of the π-calculus is the obvious one for τ, $x\,y$, and $\overline{x}\,y$. In the case of bound output transitions, only the channel x on which the output occurs is observed in label $\overline{x}$, and similarly in the case of bound input transitions.

Definition 8 (transition specification Δ_{pr}). *The transition specification Δ_{pr} is the tuple $\langle \Sigma_{pr}, L_{pr}, R_{pr} \rangle$, where the signature Σ_{pr} is as in Definition 7, labels L_{pr} are defined in (3) and the rules R_{pr} are the SOS rules in Table 2.*

The most interesting rules are those in the second column, where α is an extrusion or the input of a fresh name. Intuitively, they follow the idea that substitutions on the source of a transition must be reflected on its destination by restoring the extruded or fresh name to x_0. Rule (DELTA') applies δ to q and then permutes x_0 and x_1, in order to have the extruded name back to x_0. Conversely, rule (RES') permutes x_0 and x_1 to make sure that the restriction operation applies to x_0 and not to the extruded name x_1. In rule (PAR') side condition $\mathrm{bn}(\alpha) \cap \mathrm{fn}(r) = \emptyset$, namely $x_0 \notin \mathrm{fn}(\delta.\,r)$, is *not necessary*. The intuitive reason is that x_0 does not appear in $\delta.\,r$, since δ shifts all the variables to the right.

Proposition 3. *Let $\Delta_{pr} = \langle \Sigma_{pr}, L_{pr}, R_{pr} \rangle$ be the transition specification in Definition 8. Rules R_{pr} are in De Simone format.*

Note that the rules of the π-calculus in Table 1 are not in De Simone format: the side condition on $\mathrm{fn}(r)$ prevents rule (π-PAR) from that.

Table 2. Structural operational semantics

(RHO) $\dfrac{p \overset{\alpha}{\Longrightarrow} q \quad \alpha \neq \overline{x}, x}{\rho p \overset{\rho(\alpha)}{\Longrightarrow} \rho q}$	(RHO') $\dfrac{p \overset{\alpha}{\Longrightarrow} q \quad \alpha = \overline{x}, x}{\rho p \overset{\rho(\alpha)}{\Longrightarrow} \rho_{+1} q}$
(PAR) $\dfrac{p \overset{\alpha}{\Longrightarrow} q \quad \alpha \neq \overline{x}, x}{p|r \overset{\alpha}{\Longrightarrow} q|r}$	(PAR') $\dfrac{p \overset{\alpha}{\Longrightarrow} q \quad \alpha = \overline{x}, x}{p|r \overset{\alpha}{\Longrightarrow} q|\delta.\,r}$
(DELTA) $\dfrac{p \overset{\alpha}{\Longrightarrow} q \quad \alpha \neq \overline{x}, x}{\delta.\,p \overset{\delta\,(\alpha)}{\Longrightarrow} \delta.\,q}$	(DELTA') $\dfrac{p \overset{\alpha}{\Longrightarrow} q \quad \alpha = \overline{x}, x}{\delta.\,p \overset{\delta\,(\alpha)}{\Longrightarrow} [x_0 \leftrightarrow x_1]\delta.\,q}$
(RES) $\dfrac{p \overset{\alpha}{\Longrightarrow} q \quad \alpha \neq \overline{x}, x}{\nu.\,p \overset{\nu\,(\alpha)}{\Longrightarrow} \nu.\,q}$ if $x_0 \notin \mathrm{n}(\alpha)$	(RES') $\dfrac{p \overset{\alpha}{\Longrightarrow} q \quad \alpha = \overline{x}, x}{\nu.\,p \overset{\nu\,(\alpha)}{\Longrightarrow} \nu.\,[x_0 \leftrightarrow x_1]q}$ if $x_0 \notin \mathrm{n}(\alpha)$
(OPEN) $\dfrac{p \overset{\overline{x}\,x_0}{\Longrightarrow} q \quad x \neq x_0}{\nu.\,p \overset{\nu\,(\overline{x})}{\Longrightarrow} q}$	(CLOSE) $\dfrac{p_1 \overset{\overline{x}}{\Longrightarrow} q_1 \quad p_2 \overset{x}{\Longrightarrow} q_2}{p_1|p_2 \overset{\tau}{\Longrightarrow} \nu.\,q_1|q_2}$
(COM) $\dfrac{p_1 \overset{\overline{x}\,y}{\Longrightarrow} q_1 \quad p_2 \overset{x\,y}{\Longrightarrow} q_2}{p_1|p_2 \overset{\tau}{\Longrightarrow} q_1|q_2}$	

Theorem 1. *Let $\Delta_{pr} = \langle \Sigma_{pr}, L_{pr}, R_{pr} \rangle$ be the transition specification in Definition 8. Then, functor $P_{L_{pr}}$ in **Set** can be lifted to functor $P_{\Delta_{pr}}$ in **Alg**(Σ_{pr}) and category **Coalg**$(P_{\Delta_{pr}})$ is well defined.*

4   A Σ_{pr}-Algebra for the π-Calculus

In this section we introduce a Σ_{pr}-algebra for the π-calculus, and we prove a finiteness result.

4.1   A Σ_{pr}-Algebra

We now define a Σ_{pr}-algebra and a bijective translation of π-agents to values of such an algebra.

Definition 9 (Σ_{pr}-algebra for the π-calculus). *Algebra B is defined as the initial algebra $B = T_{(\Sigma_{pr} \cup L, E_{pr} \cup E')}$ where:*

- *Σ_{pr} is as in Definition 7,*
- *constants L are*

$$L = \{ l_s \mid s \text{ is a static } \pi\text{-agent}\}$$

- *axioms E_{pr} are the axioms below:*

  (perm) $(\rho \circ \rho')p = \rho(\rho'(p))$ id $p = p$
  (par) $p|0 = p$ $p|q = q|p$ $p|(q|r) = (p|q)|r$
  (res) $\nu.\, 0 = 0$ $\nu.\, (\delta.\, p)|q = p|\nu.\, q$ $\nu.\, \nu.\, [x_0 \leftrightarrow x_1]p = \nu.\, \nu.\, p$
  (delta) $\delta.\, 0 = 0$ $\delta.\, p \mid q = (\delta.\, p) \mid \delta.\, q$ $\delta.\, \nu.\, p = \nu.\, [x_0 \leftrightarrow x_1]\delta.\, p$
  (rho) $\rho 0 = 0$ $\rho(p|q) = \rho p \mid \rho q$ $\rho \nu.\, p = \nu.\, \rho_{+1}p$ $\delta.\, \rho p = \rho_{+1}\delta.\, p$

- *axioms E' are*

$$\rho l_s = l_{\rho(s)} \qquad \delta.\, l_s = l_{\delta(s)}.$$

Axioms **(par)** and **(res)** correspond to the analogous axioms for the π-calculus. The other axioms rule how to invert the order of operators among each other, following the intuition that ν and δ decrease and increase variable indexes respectively. Axioms E_{pr} and E' can be applied from left to right to reduce every term p into a canonical form $p'(l_{s_1}, \ldots, l_{s_n})$, such that ρ and δ do not occur in context $p'(\_, \_, \ldots)$. Notice that other expected properties like $\nu.\, \delta.\, p = p$ and $[x_0 \leftrightarrow x_1]\delta.\, \delta.\, p = \delta.\, \delta.\, p$ can be derived from these axioms.

Definition 10 (translation $[\![\cdot]\!]$). *We define a translation on π-calculus agent terms $[\![\cdot]\!] : \Pi \to |B|$ as follows:*

$$[\![0]\!] = 0 \quad [\![p|q]\!] = [\![p]\!] | [\![q]\!] \quad [\![(\nu y)\, p]\!] = \nu.\, [\delta(y) \leftrightarrow x_0]\delta.\, [\![p]\!] \quad [\![s]\!] = l_s.$$

The translation of the restriction gives the flavor of the De Brujin notation: the idea is to split standard restriction in three steps. First, one shifts all names upwards to generate a fresh name x_0, then swaps $\delta(y)$ and x_0, and, finally, applies restriction on x_0, which now stands for what 'used to be' y.

Translation $[\![\cdot]\!]$ is also defined on actions as follows: $[\![\alpha]\!] = \alpha$, if $\alpha \neq \overline{x}(y), x(y)$; $[\![\overline{x}(y)]\!] = \overline{x}$; $[\![x(y)]\!] = x$.

Theorem 2. *If $p \equiv q$ then $[\![p]\!] = [\![q]\!]$.*

Theorem 3. *Function $[\![\cdot]\!]$ is bijective. I.e., let $\{\!|\cdot|\!\} : |B| \to \Pi$ be a translation defined as follows: $\{\!|0|\!\} = 0$; $\{\!|p|q|\!\} = \{\!|p|\!\}|\{\!|q|\!\}$; $\{\!|\nu.p|\!\} = (\nu x_i)\nu([\delta(x_i) \leftrightarrow x_0]\{\!|p|\!\})$, if $\delta(x_i) \notin \mathrm{fn}(\{\!|p|\!\})$; $\{\!|l_s|\!\} = s$; $\{\!|\rho p|\!\} = \rho(\{\!|p|\!\})$; $\{\!|\delta.p|\!\} = \delta(\{\!|p|\!\})$. Then, for every p in B, $[\![\{\!|p|\!\}]\!] = p$ and, for every π-agent q, $\{\!|[\![q]\!]|\!\} = q$.*

Definition 11 (transition system lts_g). *The transition system for algebra B is $lts_g = \langle B, \Longrightarrow_g \rangle$, where $\Longrightarrow_g$ is defined by the SOS rules in Table 2 plus the following axioms:*

$$(\textsc{Static})\ \frac{s \xrightarrow{\alpha} r\ \ \alpha \neq \overline{x}(y), x(y)}{l_s \overset{[\![\alpha]\!]}{\Longrightarrow}_g [r]} \qquad (\textsc{Static}')\ \frac{s \xrightarrow{\alpha} r\ \ \alpha = \overline{x}(y), x(y)}{l_s \overset{[\![\alpha]\!]}{\Longrightarrow}_g [\delta(y) \leftrightarrow x_0]\delta.[r]}$$

When no confusion arises, we will simply denote lts_g with lts and $\Longrightarrow_g$ with $\Longrightarrow$.

Theorem 4. *Transition system lts satisfies the specification Δ_{pr} in Def. 8.*

Example 2. Let us consider again π-agent $p = \mathbf{rec}\,X.\,(\nu y)\,\overline{y}x_2.0|\overline{x}_2y.X$. By rule $(\pi\text{-Rec})$ and $(\pi\text{-Open})$, p can reduce as $p \xrightarrow{\overline{x}_2(x_3)} \overline{x}_3x_2.0\,|\,p$. On the other hand, $[\![p]\!] = l_p$. By rule $(\textsc{Static}')$, l_p can reduce as $l_p \overset{\overline{x}_2}{\Longrightarrow} [\delta(x_3) \leftrightarrow x_0]\delta.[\![\overline{x}_3x_2.0\,|\,p]\!]$ and $[\delta(x_3) \leftrightarrow x_0]\delta.[\![\overline{x}_3x_2.0\,|\,p]\!] = [\![\overline{x}_0x_3.0]\!]\,|\,[x_4 \leftrightarrow x_0]\delta.l_p$.

At a second step, by rule $(\pi\text{-Rec})$ and $(\pi\text{-Open})$, p can reduce as $p \xrightarrow{\overline{x}_2(x_1)} \overline{x}_1x_2.0\,|\,p$, and by rule $(\pi\text{-Par})$ $\overline{x}_3x_2.0\,|\,p \xrightarrow{\overline{x}_2(x_1)} \overline{x}_3x_2.0\,|\,\overline{x}_1x_2.0\,|\,p$. On the other hand, $[\![\overline{x}_0x_3.0]\!]\,|\,[x_4 \leftrightarrow x_0]\delta.l_p \overset{\overline{x}_3}{\Longrightarrow} [\![\overline{x}_1x_4.0]\!]\,|\,[\![\overline{x}_0x_4.0]\!]\,|\,[\![\mathbf{rec}\,X.\,(\nu y)\,\overline{y}x_4.0|\overline{x}_4y.X]\!]$. Indeed, by rule $(\textsc{Static}')$, $l_p \overset{\overline{x}_2}{\Longrightarrow} [x_2 \leftrightarrow x_0]\delta.[\![\overline{x}_1x_2.0\,|\,p]\!]$ and $[x_2 \leftrightarrow x_0]\delta.[\![\overline{x}_1x_2.0\,|\,p]\!] = [\![\overline{x}_0x_3.0]\!]\,|\,[x_2 \leftrightarrow x_0]\delta.l_p$. Then, by $(\textsc{Delta}')$, $\delta.l_p \overset{\overline{x}_3}{\Longrightarrow} [x_0 \leftrightarrow x_1]\delta.[\![\overline{x}_0x_3.0]\!]\,|\,\delta.l_p = [\![\overline{x}_0x_4.0]\!]\,|\,\delta.\delta.l_p$. By rule $(\textsc{Rho}')$, $[x_4 \leftrightarrow x_0]\delta.l_p \overset{\overline{x}_3}{\Longrightarrow} [x_5 \leftrightarrow x_1][\![\overline{x}_0x_4.0]\!]\,|\,\delta.\delta.l_p = [\![\overline{x}_0x_4.0]\!]\,|\,\delta.\delta.l_p$. Finally, by rule $(\textsc{Par}')$, $[\![\overline{x}_0x_3.0]\!]\,|\,[x_4 \leftrightarrow x_0]\delta.l_p \overset{\overline{x}_3}{\Longrightarrow} [\![\overline{x}_1x_4.0]\!]\,|\,[\![\overline{x}_0x_4.0]\!]\,|\,\delta.\delta.l_p$, and $\delta.\delta.l_p = [\![\mathbf{rec}\,X.\,(\nu y)\,\overline{y}x_4.0|\overline{x}_4y.X]\!]$.

The two lemmata below will be useful to prove that the transition system of the π-calculus is equivalent to $lts = \langle B, \Longrightarrow \rangle$.

Lemma 1. *Let p and q be two π-agents. If $p \sim q$, then $\delta(p) \sim \delta(q)$ and $\rho(p) \sim \rho(q)$.*

Lemma 2.

1. *Let p and q be two π-agents. If $p \xrightarrow{\alpha} q$ and $\alpha \neq \overline{x}(y), x(y)$ then $[\![p]\!] \xrightarrow{[\alpha]} [\![q]\!]$;*
   if $p \xrightarrow{\alpha} q$ and $\alpha = \overline{x}(y), x(y)$ then $[\![p]\!] \xrightarrow{[\alpha]} [\delta(y) \leftrightarrow x_0]\delta. [\![q]\!]$.
2. *Let p and q be in B. If $p \stackrel{\alpha}{\Longrightarrow} q$ and $\alpha \neq \overline{x}, x$, then $\{[\![p]\!]\} \xrightarrow{\alpha} \{[\![q]\!]\}$; if $p \stackrel{\overline{x}}{\Longrightarrow}$
   q (resp. $p \stackrel{x}{\Longrightarrow} q$), then $\{[\![p]\!]\} \xrightarrow{\overline{x}(x_i)} \nu([\delta(x_i) \leftrightarrow x_0]\{[\![q]\!]\})$, (resp. $\{[\![p]\!]\} \xrightarrow{x(x_i)}$
   $\nu([\delta(x_i) \leftrightarrow x_0]\{[\![q]\!]\})$), for every x_i such that $\delta(x_i) \notin \mathrm{fn}(\{[\![q]\!]\})$.*

4.2 A Finiteness Result

We now prove that, for each π-agent p, the set of static agents and associated reduction rules needed in all derivations of p is finite up to name permutations. It is not larger than the set of the static subagents of p, closed with respect to name fusions.

Definition 12.

- *Let s be a static π-agent. We define $S(s)$ as follows: $S(q_1 + q_2) = S([\![q_1]\!]) \cup$
  $S([\![q_2]\!]) \cup \{q_1+q_2\}$; $S(\mathrm{rec}\,X.\,q) = [\mathrm{rec}\,X.\,q \mapsto X]S([\![q]\!]) \cup \{\mathrm{rec}\,X.\,q\}$; $S(X) =$
  $\emptyset$; $S([x = y]q) = S([\![q]\!]) \cup \{[x = y]q\}$.*
- *Let p be a term of B in the canonical form $p(l_{s_1}, \ldots, l_{s_n})$ such that ρ and δ
  do not occur in context $p(\_,\_,\ldots)$. We define $S(p)$ as follows: $S(\nu.\,p) = S(p)$;
  $S(p|q) = S(p) \cup S(q)$; $S(0) = \emptyset$; $S(l_s) = S(s)$.*

Notice that $S(s)$ is defined only for static agents, as, for the subagents q of s, it recalls $S([\![q]\!])$.

Lemma 3. *Let p and q be terms of B. If $p \stackrel{\alpha}{\Longrightarrow} q$ then for each $q' \in S(q)$ there is a $p' \in S(p)$ with $q' = \sigma p'$, for some name substitution σ (not necessarily a permutation).*

Theorem 5. *Let p be in B. The number of constants l_s (and respective axioms for $\Longrightarrow$) in all derivations of p is finite, up to name permutations.*

Proof. Set $S(p)$ is finite for every p, since it is defined by structural recursion. Thus, also its closure with respect to name fusion $\hat{S}(p) = \{\sigma q \mid q \in S(p), \sigma$ name substitution$\}$ is finite, when taken up to name permutations. But Lemma 3 guarantees that $p \stackrel{\alpha}{\Longrightarrow} q$ implies $\hat{S}(q) \subseteq \hat{S}(p)$.

The condition "up to name permutations" is not restrictive. Indeed, the idea is that, for each agent p, we can give a finite number of clauses $l_q \stackrel{\alpha}{\Longrightarrow} q'$ such that the transitions of static agents in all the derivations of p only use permutations of the form $l_{\rho q} \xrightarrow{\rho(\alpha)} \rho' q'$, with $\rho' = \rho$ or $\rho' = \rho_{+1}$ according to α.

Example 3. Let us consider again agent $p = \mathrm{rec}\,X.\,q$, with $q = (\nu y)\,\overline{y}x_2.0\,|$
$\overline{x}_2 y.X$. $S([\![p]\!]) = \{p\} \cup [\mathrm{rec}\,X.\,q \mapsto X]S([\![q]\!])$. Since $[\![q]\!] = \nu.\,l_{\overline{x}_0 x_3.0}\,|\,l_{\overline{x}_3 x_0.X}$, then
$S([\![q]\!]) = \{\overline{x}_0 x_3.0\} \cup \{\overline{x}_3 x_0.X\}$ and $S([\![p]\!]) = \{p\} \cup \{\overline{x}_0 x_3.0\} \cup \{\overline{x}_3 x_0.\mathrm{rec}\,X.\,q\}$.

5   Lifting Coalgebras on Set to Coalgebras on Alg(Σ)

Remark 1. Let A be a Σ-algebra and $h : X \to |A|$ be a function in **Set**. Then, h can be uniquely extended to $\hat{h} : T_\Sigma(X) \to A$ in **Alg**(Σ). For simplicity, in the sequel, we will also denote $\hat{h}$ by h.

Definition 13. *Let B be a Σ-algebra and $g : |B| \to P_L(|B|)$ be a coalgebra in* **Set** *satisfying $\Delta = \langle \Sigma, L, R \rangle$. Then, we define:*

  - *$A = T_\Sigma(|B|)$ and $h : A \to B$ as the unique extension in* **Alg**(Σ) *of $h(p) = p$, for $p \in B$;*
  - *$f : A \to P_\Delta(A)$ as the unique extension in* **Alg**(Σ) *of $f(p) = g(p)$, for $p \in B$.*

In the sequel, we want to find conditions under which P_L-coalgebra g can be lifted to a P_Δ-coalgebra and function h, as above defined, to a P_Δ-morphism. The observation in Subsect. 2.3 allows us to state, without any further condition, that h is a lax morphism between P_L-coalgebras f and g. The reflection inclusion, instead, will require appropriate hypotheses.

Property 1. Function h in Definition 13 is a lts morphism, namely, a lax P_L-coalgebra morphism. Furthermore, it is surjective.

We now assume to have an axiomatization E of B, with auxiliary operators Σ'.

Theorem 6. *Let $\Delta = \langle \Sigma, L, R \rangle$ be a transition specification with rules R in De Simone format, $B = T_{(\Sigma \cup \Sigma', E)}$, and let A, g, h, and f be as defined in Definition 13. If for all $t_l = t_r$ in E, with free variables $x_1, \ldots, x_n$ we have De Simone proofs as follows:*

$$\frac{x_i \overset{\alpha_i}{\Longrightarrow} y_i \quad i \in I}{t_l \overset{\alpha}{\Longrightarrow} t_l'} \quad implies \quad \frac{x_i \overset{\alpha_i}{\Longrightarrow} y_i \quad i \in I}{t_r \overset{\alpha}{\Longrightarrow} t_r'} \quad and \quad t_l' =^\dagger t_r' \quad (4)$$

and viceversa, where $t_l' =^\dagger t_r'$ means that $t_l' = t_r'$ is provable with axioms E, then the kernel of h is a bisimulation.

Proof. The hypotheses imply that if $h(t) = p$, then, there is a $(\Sigma \cup \Sigma', E)$ equational proof $t \equiv t_0 = t_1 = \ldots = t_m \equiv q$, with t_i ground terms, $t_i = t_{i+1}$ an instantiation of some axiom in E, and where $t \overset{\alpha}{\Longrightarrow}_f t'$ implies $p \overset{\alpha}{\Longrightarrow}_f q$, with $h(t') = q$ and viceversa. In fact, the latter bisimulation property holds for every pair t_i, t_{i+1} and it is easy to see that it is respected by transitive closure. By definition of f, $p \overset{\alpha}{\Longrightarrow}_f q$ if and only if $p \overset{\alpha}{\Longrightarrow}_g q$, and, thus, $t \overset{\alpha}{\Longrightarrow}_f t'$ implies $p \overset{\alpha}{\Longrightarrow}_g q$, with $h(t) = p$ and $h(t') = q$, and viceversa.

Corollary 2. *If Condition 4 holds and, therefore, h is a bisimulation, then the left diagram below commutes in* **Set**, *i.e., $h; g = f; P_L(h)$. Thus h not only is a lts morphism as by property 1, but also is a P_L-morphism.*

$$|A| \xrightarrow{\quad h \quad} |B| \qquad\qquad A \xrightarrow{\quad h \quad} B$$

$$f \downarrow \qquad\qquad \downarrow g \qquad\qquad f \downarrow \qquad\qquad \downarrow g$$

$$P_L(|A|) \xrightarrow[P_L(h)]{} P_L(|B|) \qquad P_\Delta(A) \xrightarrow[P_\Delta(h)]{} P_\Delta(B)$$

Theorem 7. *Let B, A, g, h, and f be defined as in Definition 13. If the left diagram above commutes in* **Set***, i.e., $h; g = f; P_L(h)$, then g can be lifted from* **Set** *to* **Alg**(Σ) *and the right diagram commutes in* **Alg**(Σ).

Corollary 3. *Let g be as defined in Definition 13 and let the right diagram above commute. Then in g bisimilarity is a congruence.*

6   A Bialgebra for the π-Calculus

In this section, we apply the results of Sect. 5 to the permutation algebra B and to the transition system $\langle B, \Longrightarrow_g \rangle$. We will prove that axioms E_{pr} satisfy the "bisimulation" condition in Theorem 6 and that $\langle B, \Longrightarrow_g \rangle$ is equivalent to the transition system of the π-calculus. parallel composition and restriction.

Theorem 8. *Let B be the algebra defined in Definition 9 with $E = E_{pr} \cup E'$ and $\Sigma' = L_{pr}$, $A = T_{\Sigma_{pr}}(|B|)$. Then, Condition 4 of Theorem 6 holds.*

Corollary 4. *Let B be the algebra defined in Definition 9. In $g : B \to P_{\Delta_{pr}}(B)$ bisimilarity is a congruence.*

Theorem 9. *Let p and q be π-agents. Then, $p \sim q$ if and only if $[\![p]\!] \sim_g [\![q]\!]$.*

Corollary 5. *Bisimilarity $\sim$ in the π-calculus is a congruence with respect to parallel composition and restriction.*

7   Conclusions

In this paper we have presented a general result about lifting calculi with structural axioms to coalgebraic models and we have applied such a result to the π-calculus. We have enriched the permutation algebra for the calculus defined in [9,10] with parallel composition, restriction and an extrusion operation δ. Since this algebra satisfies the condition required by our general theory (i.e., structural axioms bisimulate), the associated transition system can be lifted to obtain a bialgebra and, as a consequence, in the π-calculus, bisimilarity is a congruence with respect to parallel composition and restriction. To achieve this result, our algebra features no prefix operation: we rely, instead, on a clause format defining the transitions of recursively defined processes. Therefore, the bisimilarity induced by the unique morphism to the final bialgebra is the observational equivalence, rather than observational congruence, as in [6].

We expect that our coalgebraic model can be extended to treat weak bisimulation. Instead, we do not know how to adapt our model to deal with the late bisimilarity equivalence. In [5], late bisimilarity is seen in terms of early bisimulation. The idea is to split a bound input transition in two parts: in the first one, only the channel is observed; in the second one, there are infinitely many transitions, each labeled with a substitution for the input name. While the first transition is easy to model, the second kind of transitions requires a rule employing a substitution which is not a permutation.

We are rather confident that π-calculus observational congruences (both early and late) can be easily handled in our approach by considering algebras of name substitutions rather than name permutations. The same extension should accommodate also calculi with name fusions. More challenging would be to introduce general substitutions (on some first order signature), yielding models rather close to logic programming. By varying the underlying algebra, but otherwise employing similar constructions, we plan to show the flexibility of our uniform bialgebraic approach, where substitutions and extrusion are at the same level as the other operations of the algebra.

References

1. A. Corradini, M. Große-Rhode, R. Heckel. Structured transition systems as lax coalgebras. In *Proc. of CMCS'98*, ENTS 11. Elsevier Science, 1998. 456
2. A. Corradini, R. Heckel, and U. Montanari. Compositional SOS and beyond: A coalgebraic view of open systems. *Theoretical Computer Science* 280:163-192, 2002. 451
3. R. De Simone. Higher level synchronising devices in MEIJE-SCCS. *Theoretical Computer Science* 37(3):245–267, 1985.
4. G. Ferrari, U. Montanari, and M. Pistore. Minimizing Transition Systems for Name Passing Calculi: A Co-algebraic Formulation. In *Proc. of FoSSaCS'02*, LNCS 2303. Springer, 2002. 450
5. G. Ferrari, U. Montanari, and P. Quaglia. A pi-calculus with Explicit Substitutions. *Theoretical Computer Science* 168(1):53–103, 1996. 464
6. M. Fiore and D. Turi. Semantics of name and value passing. In *Proc. of LICS'01*, IEEE. Computer Society Press, 2001. 451, 463
7. M. Gabbay and A. Pitts. A new approach to abstract syntax involving binders. In *Proc. of LICS'99*, IEEE. Computer Society Press, 1999. 451
8. R. Milner, J. Parrow, and D. Walker. A calculus of mobile processes (parts I and II). *Information and Computation*, 100(1):1–77, 1992. 453
9. U. Montanari and M. Pistore. Pi-Calculus, Structured Coalgebras and Minimal HD-Automata. In *Proc. of MFCS'00*, LNCS 1983. Springer, 2000. 450, 451, 463
10. U. Montanari and M. Pistore. Structured Coalgebras and Minimal HD-Automata for the pi-Calculus. Technical Report 0006-02, IRST-ITC, 2000. Available at the URL: http://sra.itc.it/paper.epl?id=MP00. 450, 451, 463
11. A. M. Pitts. Nominal Logic: A First Order Theory of Names and Binding. In *Proc. of TACS'01*, LNCS 2215. Springer, 2001. 451
12. M. Pistore. *History Dependent Automata*. PhD. Thesis TD-5/99. Università di Pisa, Dipartimento di Informatica, 1999. Available at the URL: http://www.di.unipi.it/phd/tesi/tesi_1999/TD-5-99.ps.gz. 450

13. J. J. M. M. Rutten. Universal coalgebra: a theory of systems. *Theoretical Computer Science* 249(1):3–80, 2000. 450, 455
14. D. Turi and G. Plotkin. Towards a mathematical operational semantics. In *Proc. of LICS'97*, IEEE. Computer Society Press, 1997. 450, 456

Traces, Pomsets, Fairness and Full Abstraction for Communicating Processes

Stephen Brookes

Department of Computer Science, Carnegie Mellon University
5000 Forbes Avenue, Pittsburgh, PA 15213, USA

Abstract. We provide a denotational trace semantics for processes with synchronous communication and a form of weakly fair parallelism. The semantics is fully abstract: processes have the same trace sets if and only if their communication behaviors are identical in all contexts. The model can easily be adapted for asynchronously communicating processes, or for shared-memory parallel programs. We also provide a partial-order semantics, using pomsets adapted for synchronization and our form of fairness. The pomset semantics can also be adjusted to model alternative paradigms. The traces of a process can be recovered from the pomset semantics by taking all fair interleavings consistent with the partial order.

1 Introduction

Traces of various kinds are commonly used in semantic models of languages for parallel programming, with parallel execution usually interpreted as a form of fair interleaving. *Transition traces*, sequences of pairs of states, have been used for shared-memory parallel programs [27,5], for concurrent logic programs and concurrent constraint programs [4,34][1], and for networks of asynchronously communicating processes [8], assuming weakly fair execution. Transition traces also provide a semantics for a parallel Algol-like language [6,7]. *Communication traces*, sequences of input/output events, were the basis for an early model of CSP [19,20], later augmented with *refusal sets* to permit deadlock analysis in the *failures* model [11], and with *divergence traces* in the *failures-divergences* model [12][2]. *Pomset traces* provide a partial-order based framework based on "true concurrency" rather than interleaving [31,32].

Fairness assumptions [15], such as *weak process fairness*, the guarantee that each persistently enabled process is eventually scheduled, allow us to abstract away from unknown or unknowable implementation details. A fairness notion is "reasonable" if it provides a good abstraction of realistic schedulers, so that by

---

[1] The use of such sequences to model shared-memory programs dates back at least to Park [27]. The term *reactive sequence* is used in [4] for this kind of trace, which is also related to the *ask/tell* sequences of [34].

[2] Roscoe's book [33] gives a detailed account of these and related models of CSP. van Glabbeek's article [16] provides a wide-ranging and detailed survey of process algebras and notions of behavioral equivalence.

L. Brim et al. (Eds.): CONCUR 2002, LNCS 2421, pp. 466–482, 2002.

assuming this form of fairness one is able to deduce program properties which hold under any reasonable implementation. We are typically interested in *safety* and *liveness* properties [26]. A safety property has the general intuitive form that something "bad" never happens. A liveness property asserts that something "good" will eventually happen. Both kinds of property depend on the sequences of states through which a parallel system may pass during execution. Fairness plays a crucial role: it is often impossible to prove liveness properties without fairness assumptions.

CSP [19] is a language of synchronously communicating processes: a process attempting output must wait until another process attempts a matching input, and *vice versa*. The early denotational models of CSP [20,11,12,33], like many operational or denotational accounts of related languages such as CCS [22,23] and ACP [2,3], focussed mainly on finite behaviors and consequently did not take fairness into account. It is not easy to extend these models naturally to incorporate fairness. Moreover, there is a plethora of fairness notions, including strong and weak forms of process, channel, and communication fairness [15]. The extent to which these fairness notions provide tractable yet realistic abstractions for CSP-style processes is unclear, although weak process fairness has an intuitively appealing definition and can be ensured by a "reasonable" scheduler using a simple round-robin strategy. Costa and Stirling have shown how to provide an operational semantics for a CCS-like language assuming either weak or strong process fairness [13,14]. Older shows that one can treat some of these fairness notions denotationally by augmenting failure-style models still further, with detailed book-keeping information concerning processes, communications, and synchronizations which become persistently enabled but not scheduled [24,10,25]. Much of the difficulty is caused by the fact that synchronization requires cooperation between processes. Indeed, in Older's formulation even weak process fairness fails to be *equivalence robust* [1], in that there is a pair of computations, one fair and one unfair, which differ only in the interleaving order of independent actions [24]. In contrast, for processes communicating asynchronously one can model weak process fairness using transition traces, and weak process fairness can be given an equivalence-robust formulation [8,9].

The structural disparity between the simple trace semantics for asynchronous processes and the intricately book-keeping failure semantics for synchronous processes obscures the underlying similarities between the two paradigms. It seems to be widely believed that this disparity is inevitable, that traces are too simple a notion to support the combination of deadlock, fairness, and synchronized communication. This is certainly a valid criticism of the traditional trace-based accounts of CSP, which used prefix-closed sets of finite traces (augmented with refusal sets) and handled infinite traces implicitly based on their finite prefixes. Although these models give an accurate account of deadlock and safety properties, they do not adequately support liveness analysis since they do not admit fairness: the existence of a fair infinite trace for a process does not follow from the process's ability to perform each of its finite prefixes.

In this paper we show that, despite the above commentary, if we assume a reasonable weak (and robust) notion of fairness, it becomes possible to design a satisfactory trace semantics. Indeed, the *same* notion of trace can be used both for synchronously and asynchronously communicating processes. In each case we model a weak form of fairness consistent with a form of round-robin scheduling, so that we obtain a good abstraction of process behavior independent of implementation details[3]. The trace semantics is compositional, and supports safety and liveness analysis. Indeed our semantics is *fully abstract*, in the sense that two processes have the same trace set if and only if they exhibit identical communication behavior, including any potential for deadlock, in all program contexts. We do not augment traces with extraneous book-keeping information, or impose complex closure conditions. Instead we incorporate the crucial information about blocking directly in the internal structure of traces, in a manner reminiscent of Phillips-style refusal testing [30].

Our achievement is noteworthy, perhaps even surprising, given the history of separate development of semantic frameworks for the two communication paradigms. Traditional denotational models of asynchronous communication and synchronous communication have frustratingly little in common, as shown by the lack of family resemblance between failures and transition traces. In contrast, we treat both kinds of communication as straightforward variations on a trace-theoretic theme, so that we achieve a semantic unification of paradigms. Given prior results concerning the utility of trace semantics for shared-memory parallelism [5,6], and the availability of trace-based models for concurrent constraint programs [4], the unification goes further still.

We also provide a partial-order model for processes assuming synchronous communication and fair execution [31,32]. We define a semantics in which a process denotes a set of partially ordered multisets of actions (pomsets). Each pomset determines a set of traces, those obtainable by fair interleaving and synchronizations consistent with the partial order. The trace set of a process can be recovered in this way from its pomset semantics. The pomset semantics supports a style of reasoning which avoids dealing explicitly with interleaving, and this may help to tame the combinatorial explosion inherent in analyzing parallel systems. We can also adapt pomset semantics to model asynchronous communication, with a small number of simple changes to the semantic definitions.

We focus on a CSP-style language with blocking input and output, but our definitions and results can be adapted to handle alternative language design decisions, for example non-blocking guards, mixed boolean and input/output guards, and general recursive process definitions. We summarize the adjustments required to deal with asynchronous communication.

---

[3] By this we mean that a family of simple round-robin schedulers can be defined, such that each member of this family ensures weakly fair execution, and every weakly fair execution is allowed by some such scheduler. To handle synchronization we assume that if the process currently scheduled is waiting for communication the scheduler will use a round-robin strategy to see if another process is ready to perform a matching communication.

2 Syntax

Let P range over *processes*, G over *guarded processes*, given by the following
abstract grammar, in which e ranges over integer-valued expressions, b over
boolean expressions, h over the set **Chan** of channel names, x over the set **Ide**
of identifiers. We omit the syntax of expressions, which is conventional.

$$P ::= \mathbf{skip} \mid x{:=}e \mid P_1; P_2 \mid \mathbf{if}\ b\ \mathbf{then}\ P_1\ \mathbf{else}\ P_2 \mid \mathbf{while}\ b\ \mathbf{do}\ P \mid$$
$$\quad\ h?x \mid h!e \mid P_1 \| P_2 \mid P_1 \sqcap P_2 \mid G \mid \mathbf{local}\ h\ \mathbf{in}\ P$$
$$G ::= (h?x \to P) \mid G_1 \square G_2$$

As in CSP, $P_1 \sqcap P_2$ is "internal" choice, and $G_1 \square G_2$ is "external" choice[4].

The construct **local** h **in** P introduces a local channel named h with scope P.
One can also allow local variable declarations, as in **local** x **in** P, but we omit
the semantic details in what follows. We write $chans(P)$ for the set of channel
names occurring free in P. In particular, $chans(\mathbf{local}\ h\ \mathbf{in}\ P) = chans(P) - \{h\}$.

3 Actions

Let Z be the set of integers, with typical member v. An *action* has one of the
following forms:

- An *evaluation* of form $x{=}v$, where x is an identifier and v is an integer.
- An *assignment* of form $x{:=}v$, where x is an identifier and v is an integer.
- A *communication* $h?v$ or $h!v$, where h is a channel name and v is an integer.
- A *blocking action* of form δ_X, where X is a finite set of directions.

An input action $h?v$ or output action $h!v$ represents the *potential* for a process to
perform communication, and can only be completed when another process offers
a matching communication on the same channel ($h!v$ or $h?v$, respectively). We
write $match(\lambda_1, \lambda_2)$ when λ_1 and λ_2 are matching communication actions, and
we let $chan(h?v) = chan(h!v) = h$. Each communication action has a *direction*;
let $\mathbf{Dir} = \{h?, h! \mid h \in \mathbf{Chan}\}$ be the set of directions. A blocking action δ_X
represents an unrequited attempt to communicate along the directions in X.
When X is a singleton we write $\delta_{h?}$ or $\delta_{h!}$. When X is empty we write δ instead
of $\delta_{\{\}}$; the action δ is also used to represent a "silent" local action, such as a
synchronized handshake or reading or writing a local variable. We let $X \backslash h = X - \{h?, h!\}$. Let Σ be the set of actions, $\Lambda = \{h?v, h!v \mid h \in \mathbf{Chan}\ \&\ v \in Z\}$ be
the set of communications, and $\Delta = \{\delta_X \mid X \subseteq_{fin} \mathbf{Dir}\}$ be the set of blocking
actions.

---

[4] Our syntax distinguishes between guarded and general processes merely to enforce
the syntactic constraint that the "external choice" construct is only applicable to
input-guarded processes, as in Hoare's original CSP language. This allows certain
simplifications in the semantic development, but is not crucial.

4   Traces

A trace is a finite or infinite sequence of actions representing a potential behavior of a process. We model persistent waiting for communication and divergence (infinite local activity) as an infinite sequence of blocking actions. We assume that unless and until blocking or divergence occurs we only care about the non-silent actions taken by a process[5]. Accordingly, we assume when concatenating that $\delta\lambda = \lambda\delta = \lambda$ for all actions λ, and we suppress waiting actions which lead to successful communication, so that $\delta_{h?}^* h?v = h?v$ for example. A trace of the form $\alpha\delta_X{}^\omega$ describes an execution in which the process performs α then gets stuck waiting to communicate along the directions in X. For a trace β let $blocks(\beta)$ be the set of all directions which occur infinitely often in blocking steps of β. For example, $blocks(a!0(\delta_{b?}\delta_{c?})^\omega) = \{b?, c?\}$.

Let $\Sigma^\infty = \Sigma^* \cup \Sigma^\omega$ be the set of traces. We use ϵ for the empty sequence, and α, β, γ as meta-variables ranging over Σ^∞.

We write $\alpha\beta$ for the concatenation of β onto α, which is equal to α if α is infinite. For trace sets T_1 and T_2 we let $T_1 T_2 = \{\alpha_1\alpha_2 \mid \alpha_1 \in T_1 \ \& \ \alpha_2 \in T_2\}$. For a trace set T we define $T^0 = \{\delta\}$, $T^{k+1} = TT^k$ for $k \geq 0$, and $T^* = \bigcup_{n=0}^\infty T^n$. We also let T^ω be the set of all traces of form $\alpha_0\alpha_1\ldots\alpha_n\ldots$ where for each $n \geq 0$, $\alpha_n \in T$. Note that δ^ω is distinct from δ.

Given two traces α_1 and α_2, $\alpha_1\|\alpha_2$ is the set of all traces formed by merging them fairly, allowing (but not necessarily requiring) synchronization of matching communications. We let $\alpha\|\epsilon = \epsilon\|\alpha = \{\alpha\}$. When α_1 and α_2 are finite and non-empty, say $\alpha_i = \lambda_i\beta_i$, we use the standard inductive definition for $\alpha_1\|\alpha_2$:

$$(\lambda_1\beta_1)\|(\lambda_2\beta_2) = \quad \{\lambda_1\gamma \mid \gamma \in \beta_1\|(\lambda_2\beta_2)\} \ \cup \ \{\lambda_2\gamma \mid \gamma \in (\lambda_1\beta_1)\|\beta_2\}$$
$$\cup \ \{\delta\gamma \mid \gamma \in \beta_1\|\beta_2 \ \& \ match(\lambda_1, \lambda_2)\}$$

When α_1 and α_2 are infinite, we let $\alpha_1\|\alpha_2 = \{\}$ if some direction in $blocks(\alpha_1)$ matches a direction in $blocks(\alpha_2)$, since it is unfair to avoid synchronizing two processes which are blocked but trying to synchronize on a common channel. Otherwise, when α_1 and α_2 are infinite and $\neg match(blocks(\alpha_1), blocks(\alpha_2))$, we let $\alpha_1\|\alpha_2$ consist of all traces of form $\gamma_1\gamma_2\ldots$ where α_1 can be written as a concatenation of finite traces $\alpha_{1,1}\alpha_{1,2}\ldots$, α_2 can be written as a concatenation of finite traces $\alpha_{2,1}\alpha_{2,2}\ldots$, and for each $i \geq 1$ we have $\gamma_i \in \alpha_{1,i}\|\alpha_{2,i}$.

For example, $\delta_{h!}{}^\omega\|\delta_{h?}{}^\omega = \{\}$ and $(a!0\delta_{h!}{}^\omega)\|(b!1\delta_{h?}{}^\omega) = \{\}$. However, $\delta_{a!}{}^\omega \|\delta_{b?}{}^\omega$ is non-empty and can be written in the form $(\delta_{a!}{}^*\delta_{b?}\delta_{b?}{}^*\delta_{a!})^\omega$.

We write $chans(\alpha)$ for the set of channels occurring in input or output actions along α, and when $h \notin chans(\alpha)$ we let $\alpha\backslash h$ be the trace obtained from α by replacing every δ_X with $\delta_{X\backslash h}$. For instance, the trace $(a!0\,\delta_{h?}{}^\omega)\backslash h$ is $a!0\,\delta^\omega$.

5   Denotational Semantics

We now define a synchronous trace semantics for our programming language. We assume given the semantics of expressions: $\mathcal{T}(e) \subseteq \Sigma^* \times Z$ describes all

---

[5] Other notions of observable behavior, such as the assumption that we see all actions, including blocking steps, can be incorporated with appropriate modifications.

possible evaluation behaviors of e, and consists of all pairs (ρ, v) where ρ is a sequence of evaluation steps which yield value v for the expression. (We do not need to assume that expression evaluation is an atomic action.) For example, for an identifier y we have $T(y) = \{(y{=}v, v) \mid v \in Z\}$ and for a numeral $\underline{n}$ we have $T(\underline{n}) = \{(\delta, n)\}$. For a boolean expression b we assume given $T(b) \subseteq \Sigma^* \times \{\textbf{true}, \textbf{false}\}$, and we let $T(b)_{\textbf{true}} = \{\rho \mid (\rho, \textbf{true}) \in T(b)\}$ and, similarly, $T(b)_{\textbf{false}} = \{\rho \mid (\rho, \textbf{false}) \in T(b)\}$.

For a process P, the trace set $T(P) \subseteq \Sigma^\infty$ describes all possible executions, assuming fair interaction between the process and its environment.

Definition 1 (Synchronous Trace Semantics)
The synchronous trace semantics of processes is defined compositionally by:

$$T(\textbf{skip}) = \{\delta\}$$
$$T(x{:=}e) = \{\rho\, x{:=}v \mid (\rho, v) \in T(e)\}$$
$$T(P_1; P_2) = T(P_1)T(P_2) = \{\alpha_1\alpha_2 \mid \alpha_1 \in T(P_1) \,\&\, \alpha_2 \in T(P_2)\}$$
$$T(\textbf{if } b \textbf{ then } P_1 \textbf{ else } P_2) = T(b)_{\textbf{true}}\, T(P_1) \;\cup\; T(b)_{\textbf{false}}\, T(P_2)$$
$$T(\textbf{while } b \textbf{ do } P) = (T(b)_{\textbf{true}}\, T(P))^* T(b)_{\textbf{false}} \;\cup\; (T(b)_{\textbf{true}}\, T(P))^\omega$$
$$T(h?x) = \{h?v\, x{:=}v \mid v \in Z\} \cup \{\delta_{h?}{}^\omega\}$$
$$T(h!e) = \{\rho\, h!v,\; \rho\, \delta_{h!}{}^\omega \mid (\rho, v) \in T(e)\}$$
$$T(P_1\|P_2) = \bigcup\{\alpha_1\|\alpha_2 \mid \alpha_1 \in T(P_1) \,\&\, \alpha_2 \in T(P_2)\}$$
$$T(P_1 \sqcap P_2) = T(P_1) \cup T(P_2)$$
$$T(\textbf{local } h \textbf{ in } P) = \{\alpha\backslash h \mid \alpha \in T(P) \,\&\, h \notin chans(\alpha)\}$$
$$T(h?x \to P) = \{h?v\, x{:=}v\, \alpha \mid v \in Z \,\&\, \alpha \in T(P)\} \cup \{\delta_{h?}{}^\omega\}$$
$$T(G_1 \square G_2) = \{\alpha \in T(G_1) \cup T(G_2) \mid \alpha \notin \Delta^\omega\} \;\cup$$
$$\{\delta_{X \cup Y}{}^\omega \mid \delta_X{}^\omega \in T(G_1) \,\&\, \delta_Y{}^\omega \in T(G_2)\}$$

The traces of a guarded process G have two possible forms: either beginning with an input action $h?v \in \Lambda$, or an infinite sequence of blocking actions δ_X for the set $X = inits(G)$ given inductively in the obvious manner: $inits(h?x \to c) = \{h?\}$, $inits(G_1 \square G_2) = inits(G_1) \cup inits(G_2)$.

It is easy to prove that the above semantics satisfies standard algebraic laws, such as associativity of parallel composition and both forms of choice:

Theorem 1 *For all processes P_1, P_2, P_3 and all guarded processes G_1, G_2, G_3,*

$$T(P_1\|(P_2\|P_3)) = T((P_1\|P_2)\|P_3)$$
$$T(P_1 \sqcap (P_2 \sqcap P_3)) = T((P_1 \sqcap P_2) \sqcap P_3)$$
$$T(G_1 \square (G_2 \square G_3)) = T((G_1 \square G_2) \square G_3)$$

6 Operational Semantics

A state s is a mapping from program variables to values.[6] An action may or may not be enabled in a given state: the action $x{=}v$ is only enabled in a state for

---

[6] Since channels are only used for synchronized handshaking there is no need to treat channel contents as part of the state.

$$h?x, s \xrightarrow{h?v} x := v, s \qquad h?x, s \xrightarrow{\delta_{h?}} h?x, s$$

$$h!v, s \xrightarrow{h!v} \mathbf{skip}, s \qquad h!v, s \xrightarrow{\delta_{h!}} h!v, s$$

$$\frac{G_1, s \xrightarrow{\lambda} P_1, s' \quad \lambda \notin \Delta}{G_1 \square G_2, s \xrightarrow{\lambda} P_1, s'} \quad \frac{G_2, s \xrightarrow{\lambda} P_2, s' \quad \lambda \notin \Delta}{G_1 \square G_2, s \xrightarrow{\lambda} P_2, s'} \quad \frac{G_1, s \xrightarrow{\delta_X} G_1, s \quad G_2, s \xrightarrow{\delta_Y} G_2, s}{G_1 \square G_2, s \xrightarrow{\delta_{X \cup Y}} G_1 \square G_2, s}$$

$$\mathbf{while} \ b \ \mathbf{do} \ P, s \xrightarrow{\delta} \mathbf{if} \ b \ \mathbf{then} \ P; \mathbf{while} \ b \ \mathbf{do} \ P \ \mathbf{else} \ \mathbf{skip}, s$$

$$P_1 \sqcap P_2, s \xrightarrow{\delta} P_1, s \qquad P_1 \sqcap P_2, s \xrightarrow{\delta} P_2, s$$

$$\frac{P_1, s \xrightarrow{\lambda} P_1', s'}{P_1 \| P_2, s \xrightarrow{\lambda} P_1' \| P_2, s'} \qquad \frac{P_2, s \xrightarrow{\lambda} P_2', s'}{P_1 \| P_2, s \xrightarrow{\lambda} P_1 \| P_2', s'}$$

$$\frac{P_1, s \xrightarrow{\lambda_1} P_1', s \quad P_2, s \xrightarrow{\lambda_2} P_2', s \quad match(\lambda_1, \lambda_2)}{P_1 \| P_2, s \xrightarrow{\delta} P_1' \| P_2', s}$$

$$\frac{P, s \xrightarrow{\lambda} P', s' \quad chan(\lambda) \neq h}{\mathbf{local} \ h \ \mathbf{in} \ P, s \xrightarrow{\lambda} \mathbf{local} \ h \ \mathbf{in} \ P', s'} \qquad \frac{P, s \xrightarrow{\delta_X} P', s}{\mathbf{local} \ h \ \mathbf{in} \ P, s \xrightarrow{\delta_{X \setminus h}} \mathbf{local} \ h \ \mathbf{in} \ P', s'}$$

$$\frac{}{\mathbf{skip}, s \ \mathbf{term}} \qquad \frac{P_1, s \ \mathbf{term} \quad P_2, s \ \mathbf{term}}{P_1 \| P_2, s \ \mathbf{term}} \qquad \frac{P, s \ \mathbf{term}}{\mathbf{local} \ h \ \mathbf{in} \ P, s \ \mathbf{term}}$$

Fig. 1. Operational semantics for processes

which the value of x is v, and in fact a state is uniquely determined by the set of evaluation actions which it enables. We write $[s \mid x : v]$ for the state obtained from s by updating the value of x to v.

The operational semantics for expressions involves non-terminal transitions of form $e, s \xrightarrow{\mu} e', s$ and terminal transitions of form $e, s \xrightarrow{\mu} v$, where μ is an evaluation action and v is an integer. Similarly for boolean expressions. The operational semantics for processes involves transitions of form $P, s \xrightarrow{\lambda} P', s'$ and a termination predicate P, s **term**. Some transition rules are listed in Figure 1. (We omit several rules, including those dealing with sub-expression evaluation and the rules for sequential constructs, which are standard.) Note that an external choice $G_1 \square G_2$ is "resolved" only when a communication occurs.

A *transition sequence* of process P is a sequence of transitions of form

$$P, s_0 \xrightarrow{\lambda_0} P_1, s_0' \quad P_1, s_1 \xrightarrow{\lambda_1} P_2, s_1' \quad P_2, s_2 \xrightarrow{\lambda_2} P_3, s_2' \ \cdots$$

either infinite or ending in a terminal configuration. A *computation* is a transition sequence in which the state never changes between steps, so that $s_i' = s_{i+1}$. A transition sequence (or a computation) of P is *fair* if it contains a complete transition sequence for each syntactic sub-process of P, and no pair of sub-processes is permanently blocked yet attempting to synchronize. For example, the computation

$$a?x\|a!0, s \xrightarrow{\delta_a?} a?x\|a!0, s \xrightarrow{\delta_a!} a?x\|a!0, s \xrightarrow{\delta_a?} a?x\|a!0, s \xrightarrow{\delta_a!} \cdots$$

is not fair, because the two processes block on matching directions. However,

$$a?x\|a!0, s \xrightarrow{a?1} x:=1\|a!0, s \xrightarrow{x:=1} \text{skip}\|a!0, s' \xrightarrow{\delta_a!} \text{skip}\|a!0, s' \xrightarrow{\delta_a!} \cdots$$

where $s' = [s \mid x : 1]$, is fair because only one process is blocked; there is a fair computation of the process $a!1\|(a?x\|a!0)$ in which the first process performs $a!1$ and the second performs the above transition sequence. Similarly, the sequence

$$a!0\|b!1, s \xrightarrow{\delta_a!} a!0\|b!1, s \xrightarrow{\delta_b!} a!0\|b!1, s \xrightarrow{\delta_a!} a!0\|b!1, s \xrightarrow{\delta_b!} \cdots \text{ qualifies as fair,}$$

and corresponds to the trace $(\delta_a!\delta_b!)^\omega$ of process $a!0\|b!1$. We write $P \xrightarrow{\alpha}$ when P has a maximal fair transition sequence on which the actions form the trace α.

7 Semantic Properties

The denotational and operational characterizations of fair traces coincide:

Theorem 2 (Congruence of Operational and Denotational Semantics)
For every process P, $\mathcal{T}(P) = \{\alpha \mid P \xrightarrow{\alpha}\}$.

Suppose we can observe communication sequences, including persistent blocking and the values of non-local variables, but we cannot backtrack to try alternative runs. This notion of observable behavior suffices to allow safety and liveness analysis and is equivalent to observing traces. It is an obvious consequence of compositionality that our trace semantics is fully abstract for this notion of behavior:

Theorem 3 (Full Abstraction for Synchronous Trace Semantics)
Two processes P_1 and P_2 have the same trace sets iff they have the same observable behavior in all contexts.

This generalizes the analogous well known full abstraction results for failures semantics, which hold in a much more limited setting, without fairness [33]. The significance is not full abstraction *per se* but the construction of a *simple* trace-based semantics that incorporates a reasonable form of fairness and synchronized communication while supporting safety and liveness analysis.

To demonstrate that trace semantics distinguishes between processes with different deadlock capabilities, note that:

$$\delta_X{}^\omega \in \mathcal{T}((a?x \to P)\,\square\,(b?x \to Q)) \iff X = \{a?, b?\}$$

$$\delta_X{}^\omega \in \mathcal{T}((a?x \to P) \sqcap (b?x \to Q)) \iff X = \{a?\} \text{ or } X = \{b?\}.$$

If we run these processes in a context which is only capable of communicating on channel b, such as **local** a, b **in** $([-]\|b!0)$, the first process would behave like $x:=0$; **local** a, b **in** Q but the second would also have the possibility of behaving like **local** a, b **in** $((a?x \to P)\|b!0)$, which is deadlocked and has trace set $\{\delta^\omega\}$.

The following semantic equivalences, to be interpreted as equality of trace sets, illustrate how our model supports reasoning about process behavior.

Theorem 4 (Fair Synchronous Laws)
The following laws of equivalence hold in synchronous trace semantics:

1. local h in $(h?x; P)\|(h!v; Q)$ $=$ local h in $(x{:=}v; (P\|Q))$
2. local h in $(h?x; P)\|(Q_1; Q_2)$ $=$ Q_1; local h in $(h?x; P)\|Q_2$
   provided $h \notin \mathsf{chans}(Q_1)$
3. local h in $(h!v; P)\|(Q_1; Q_2)$ $=$ Q_1; local h in $(h!v; P)\|Q_2$
   provided $h \notin \mathsf{chans}(Q_1)$.

These properties reflect our assumption of fairness, and are particularly helpful in proving liveness properties. They are not valid in an unfair semantics: if execution is unfair there is no guarantee in the first law that the synchronization will eventually occur, and there is no guarantee in the second or third laws that the right-hand process will ever execute its initial (non-local) code.

8   Pomset Semantics

We now introduce a "truly concurrent" interpretation for our process language and show that it is a natural generalization of the trace semantics. We adapt Pratt-style "pomsets" to handle synchronization and our notion of fairness.

A *pomset* $(T, <)$ is a partially ordered countable multiset of actions: T is a multiset whose elements are drawn from the set Σ of actions, and $<$ is a partial order on T, representing a "precedence" relation on action occurrences in T. Actually we allow the precedence relation to be a pre-order: when T contains a pair of matching communication occurrences which precede each other this will force a synchronization. We also assume that every action dominates finitely many actions, so the precedence relation is well founded. We write $|T|$ for the cardinality of T, which is either finite or ω.

The *kernel* of an ordering relation $<$ is the subset consisting of the pairs (μ, μ') such that $\mu < \mu'$ and there is no μ'' such that $\mu < \mu'' < \mu'$. The full ordering relation can be recovered by taking the transitive closure of the kernel. We also elide non-final occurrences of δ, for example replacing $\mu < \delta < \mu'$ by $\mu < \mu'$. (This is analogous to our earlier convention for concatenating δ.)

Each pomset $(T, <)$ determines a set of traces, those traces containing all of the action occurrences from T in a linear order consistent with the precedence relation, *modulo* synchronization. We will refer to these as the traces *consistent* with the pomset. A single trace can be viewed as a pomset with a linear precedence order. A pomset consists of a number of connected components, or *threads*.

We define $T_1; T_2 = T_1$ if $|T_1| = \omega$, otherwise $T_1; T_2$ is the ordering on $T_1 \cup T_2$ obtained by putting T_2 after T_1. Likewise we define $T^0 = \{\delta\}$, $T^{k+1} = T; T^k$ for $k \geq 0$, and T^ω. $T_1\|T_2$ is the disjoint union of T_1 and T_2 ordered with the disjoint union of the orderings from T_1 and T_2. We say that a pomset is *fair* iff it does not contain a pair of concurrent threads which eventually block on a pair of matching directions. For example, the pomset $\{a!0\delta_{b!}{}^\omega, a?0\delta_{b?}{}^\omega\}$ is unfair. We write T *fair* to indicate that T is a fair pomset.

We define $T \preceq_h T'$ to mean that T' arises by choosing for each occurrence of $h?v$ (or $h!v$) in T a unique concurrent matching action occurrence $h!v$ (respectively, $h?v$) in T, and augmenting the ordering accordingly, with an arrow each way between the matched pairs. This can be formalized as a *synchronizing schedule* for channel h. For a given T and h there may be no such T', or there may be multiple such T', each corresponding to a sequence of synchronization choices. Given a pomset T' in which all visible actions on h are matched, we define $T'\backslash h$ to be the result of replacing all matching pairs by δ (i.e. enforcing synchronization), replacing every δ_X by $\delta_{X\backslash h}$, and eliding non-final δ actions.

We assume that the pomset semantics of expressions is given, so that for an expression e, $\mathcal{P}(e)$ is a set of pairs of the form (T, v), where $v \in Z$ and T is a pomset of evaluation actions. Intuitively, $(T, v) \in \mathcal{P}(e)$ means that if the evaluation trace of e is consistent with T then v is a possible final value. We also assume given the pomset semantics of boolean expressions, and we let $\mathcal{P}(b)_{\textbf{true}} = \{T \mid (T, \textbf{true}) \in \mathcal{P}(b)\}$ and similarly for $\mathcal{P}(b)_{\textbf{false}}$. A process P denotes a set (or "family") $\mathcal{P}(P)$ of pomsets.

Definition 2 (Synchronous Pomset Semantics)
The pomset semantics $\mathcal{P}(P)$ is given compositionally by:

$$\mathcal{P}(\textbf{skip}) = \{\{\delta\}\}$$
$$\mathcal{P}(x{:=}e) = \{T; \{x{:=}v\} \mid (T, v) \in \mathcal{P}(e)\}$$
$$\mathcal{P}(P_1; P_2) = \{T_1; T_2 \mid T_1 \in \mathcal{P}(P_1) \ \& \ T_2 \in \mathcal{P}(P_2)\}$$
$$\mathcal{P}(\textbf{if } b \textbf{ then } P_1 \textbf{ else } P_2) = \mathcal{P}(b)_{\textbf{true}}; \mathcal{P}(P_1) \cup \mathcal{P}(b)_{\textbf{false}}; \mathcal{P}(P_2)$$
$$\mathcal{P}(\textbf{while } b \textbf{ do } P) = (\mathcal{P}(b)_{\textbf{true}}; \mathcal{P}(P))^*; \mathcal{P}(b)_{\textbf{false}} \ \cup \ (\mathcal{P}(b)_{\textbf{true}}; \mathcal{P}(P))^\omega$$
$$\mathcal{P}(h?x) = \{\{h?v\} \mid v \in Z\} \cup \{\{\delta_{h?}{}^\omega\}\}$$
$$\mathcal{P}(h!e) = \{T; \{h!v\} \mid (T, v) \in \mathcal{P}(e)\} \cup \{\{\delta_{h!}{}^\omega\}\}$$
$$\mathcal{P}(P_1 \| P_2) = \{T_1 \| T_2 \mid T_1 \in \mathcal{P}(P_1) \ \& \ T_2 \in \mathcal{P}(T_2) \& (T_1 \| T_2) fair\}$$
$$\mathcal{P}(P_1 \sqcap P_2) = \mathcal{P}(P_1) \cup \mathcal{P}(P_2)$$
$$\mathcal{P}(\textbf{local } h \textbf{ in } P) = \{T'\backslash h \mid T \in \mathcal{P}(P) \ \& \ T \preceq_h T'\}$$
$$\mathcal{P}(h?x \rightarrow P) = \{\{h?v\}; T \mid v \in Z \ \& \ T \in \mathcal{P}(P)\} \ \cup \ \{\{\delta_h{}^\omega\}\}$$
$$\mathcal{P}(G_1 \square G_2) = \{T \in \mathcal{P}(G_1) \cup \mathcal{P}(G_2) \mid T \cap \Delta^\omega = \{\}\} \ \cup$$
$$\{\{\delta_{X\cup Y}{}^\omega\} \mid \{\delta_X{}^\omega\} \in \mathcal{P}(G_1) \ \& \ \{\delta_Y{}^\omega\} \in \mathcal{P}(G_2)\}$$

It can be proven by structural induction that every pomset $T \in \mathcal{P}(P)$ is fair.

An Example

Let $buff_1(in, mid)$ be **local** x **in while true do** $(in?x; mid!x)$, which behaves like a 1-place buffer. Let $buff_1(mid, out)$ be similarly defined. It is easy to prove using pomsets that with synchronized communication

$$buff_2(in, out) =_{\text{def}} \textbf{local } mid \textbf{ in } buff_1(in, mid) \| buff_1(mid, out)$$

behaves like a 2-place buffer. One can also use the semantics to analyze a variety of alternative buffer-like constructs, such as

$$\textbf{local } mid \textbf{ in } buff_2(in, mid) \| buff_2(mid, out)$$

and one can validate a number of general buffer laws as in [33].

9   Recovering Traces

The pomset semantics determines the trace semantics in a natural manner.

Definition 3 *The set of synchronous traces consistent with a pomset T, written $\mathcal{L}(T)$, consists of all traces which arise by fair interleaving the threads of T, possibly allowing synchronization.*

Equivalently, $\mathcal{L}(T)$ is the set of all linear orders on the multi-set T which extend the order of T, allowing for the possibility of synchronization.

Note that distinct pomset families may determine the same trace sets. For example the pomset families $\{\{a!0, b!1\}, \{a!0, \delta_{b!}{}^{\omega}\}, \{b!1, \delta_{a!}{}^{\omega}\}, \{\delta_{a!}{}^{\omega}, \delta_{b!}{}^{\omega}\}\}$ and $\{\{a!0\,b!1\}, \{b!1\,a!0\}, \{a!0, \delta_{b!}{}^{\omega}\}, \{b!1, \delta_{a!}{}^{\omega}\}, \{\delta_{a!}{}^{\omega}, \delta_{b!}{}^{\omega}\}\}$ both determine the trace set of $a!0\|b!1$.

Assuming that the pomset semantics of expressions is consistent with the trace semantics, i.e. that for all e, $\mathcal{T}(e) = \{(\rho, v) \mid \rho \in \mathcal{L}(T) \,\&\, (T, v) \in \mathcal{P}(e)\}$, with a similar assumption for boolean expressions, we can prove the analogous property for processes by structural induction:

Theorem 5 *For all processes P, $\mathcal{T}(P) = \bigcup\{\mathcal{L}(T) \mid T \in \mathcal{P}(P)\}$.*

Note the obvious but useful corollary:

Corollary 6 *For all P_1 and P_2, if $\mathcal{P}(P_1) = \mathcal{P}(P_2)$ then $\mathcal{T}(P_1) = \mathcal{T}(P_2)$.*

Many laws of process equivalence hold for pomset semantics, and can be proven without dealing with fully expanded trace sets. For example, the pomset semantics also satisfies standard algebraic laws, such as associativity of parallel composition and both forms of choice:

Theorem 7 *For all processes P_1, P_2, P_3 and all guarded processes G_1, G_2, G_3,*

$$\mathcal{P}(P_1\|(P_2\|P_3)) = \mathcal{P}((P_1\|P_2)\|P_3)$$
$$\mathcal{P}(P_1 \sqcap (P_2 \sqcap P_3)) = \mathcal{P}((P_1 \sqcap P_2) \sqcap P_3)$$
$$\mathcal{P}(G_1 \square (G_2 \square G_3)) = \mathcal{P}((G_1 \square G_2) \square G_3)$$

Using the above Corollary such laws transfer immediately to trace semantics, giving an alternative proof of the validity of these laws in the trace semantics. Pomset semantics thus provides a potentially more succinct model of process behavior and an alternative compositional approach to parallel program analysis.

Our pomset semantics and even our trace semantics make certain behavioral distinctions which might seem more consistent with the philosophy of "true concurrency" than with the trace-theoretic rationale for our models. In particular the so-called "interleaving law" [23,18,21] does not hold, and parallel composition cannot be "expanded away" and expressed equivalently as a guarded choice of interleavings. For example, $\mathcal{P}(a!0\|b!1)$ is given above, whereas $\mathcal{P}(a!0; b!1 \sqcap b!1; a!0)$ is the family

$$\{\{a!0\,b!1\}, \{b!1\,a!0\}, \{a!0\,\delta_{b!}{}^{\omega}\}, \{b!1\,\delta_{a!}{}^{\omega}\}, \{\delta_{a!}{}^{\omega}\}, \{\delta_{b!}{}^{\omega}\}\}$$

so that $a!0\|b!1$ is not pomset-equivalent to $(a!0; b!1) \sqcap (b!1; a!0)$. Indeed this distinction also holds in the trace semantics, since

$$T(a!0\|b!1) \cap \Delta^\omega = \delta_{a!}{}^\omega \| \delta_{b!}{}^\omega = (\delta_{a!}{}^* \delta_{b!} \delta_{b!}{}^* \delta_{a!})^\omega$$

$$T(a!0; b!1 \sqcap b!1; a!0) \cap \Delta^\omega = \{\delta_{a!}{}^\omega, \delta_{b!}{}^\omega\}.$$

This difference in trace sets can be explained intuitively, without appealing to considerations of true concurrency, since $a!0\|b!1$ can be observed (if placed in a suitable environment) waiting repeatedly for action on one of the two channels, whereas the other process makes a non-deterministic choice and thereafter fixates on one particular channel. Note that $a!0\|b!1$ also fails to be trace- or pomset-equivalent to $(a!0 \rightarrow b!1) \square (b!1 \rightarrow a!0)$, since

$$T((a!0 \rightarrow b!1) \square (b!1 \rightarrow a!0)) \cap \Delta^\omega = \{\delta_{\{a!,b!\}}{}^\omega\},$$

so neither form of non-deterministic choice can be used to expand away a parallel composition.

10   Asynchronous Communication

Now suppose that communication is asynchronous, as in non-deterministic Kahn-style networks, so that output actions are always enabled, and channels behave like unbounded queues; a process wishing to perform input from a channel must wait (only) if the queue is empty. We can easily adapt the trace semantics to model asynchronous communication. We only need to include blocking actions δ_X where X is a set of *input* directions[7]. We redefine $\alpha_1 \| \alpha_2$ to be the set of fair interleavings of α_1 with α_2, without allowing any synchronization. We say that α is *local for* h if the communications on h along α obey the queue discipline, and we redefine $\alpha \backslash h$ to replace all communications on h by δ and replace δ_X by $\delta_{X \backslash h}$.

Definition 4 *The set* $\mathcal{AT}(P)$ *of asynchronous traces of* P *is defined compositionally, exactly as for the synchronous traces but with modifications in the clauses for output, parallel composition, and local channels, which become:*

$$\mathcal{AT}(h!e) = \{\rho\, h!v \mid (\rho, v) \in T(e)\}$$
$$\mathcal{AT}(P_1 \| P_2) = \bigcup \{\alpha_1 \| \alpha_2 \mid \alpha_1 \in \mathcal{AT}(P_1) \ \& \ \alpha_2 \in \mathcal{AT}(P_2)\}$$
$$\mathcal{AT}(\text{local } h \text{ in } P) = \{\alpha \backslash h \mid \alpha \in \mathcal{AT}(P) \ \& \ \alpha \text{ local for } h\}$$

The asynchronous trace semantics also validates the associativity laws for parallel composition and both forms of choice.

The asynchronous operational semantics is obtained by making similar adjustments to the rules for output, parallel composition, and local channels, and

---

[7] It would obviously suffice to work with blocking actions decorated with the set of channel names h rather than the corresponding input directions h?, but we resist this temptation to emphasize the similarity with the synchronous case.

including channel contents as part of the state. The operational notion of fair transition sequence is as before, except that the transition relation no longer includes synchronizing steps. Again the denotationally characterized trace set coincides with the operationally characterized trace set, and we have full abstraction with respect to communication behavior.

Theorem 8 (Congruence of Denotational and Operational Semantics)
For every process P, $\mathcal{AT}(P)$ consists of the traces generated by the fair asynchronous transition sequences of P.

Theorem 9 (Full Abstraction for Asynchronous Trace Semantics)
Two processes P_1 and P_2 have the same asynchronous trace sets iff they have the same asynchronous communication behavior in all contexts.

We can define an asynchronous pomset semantics $\mathcal{AP}(P)$, again adjusting the clauses for output, parallel composition and local channels. We no longer need a side condition in the clause for $P_1 \| P_2$: every trace consistent with the disjoint union $T_1 \| T_2$ will represent a fair asynchronous behavior of the parallel process. We redefine $T \preceq_h T'$ to mean that T' arises by choosing, for each *input* occurrence $h?v$ in T an output occurrence $h!v$ in T which *justifies* it, all choices respecting the precedence order of T and the queue discipline of the channel, and augmenting the ordering so that each input is preceded by its justifying output. This can be viewed as imposing an *asynchronous schedule*. For a given T and h, there may be no such T', in which case T does not describe any traces which are local for h, or there may be multiple such T', each corresponding to a different sequence of scheduling choices. Given a pomset T' in which all inputs on h are justified in this manner, we define $T' \backslash h$ to replace each communication on h by δ, replace δ_X by $\delta_{X \backslash h}$, and elide non-final δ actions.

Definition 5 (Asynchronous Pomset Semantics)
The asynchronous pomset semantics is given compositionally as for the synchronous pomset semantics, with the following modifications:

$$\mathcal{AP}(h!e) = \{T; \{h!v\} \mid (T, v) \in \mathcal{P}(e)\}$$
$$\mathcal{AP}(P_1 \| P_2) = \{T_1 \| T_2 \mid T_1 \in \mathcal{AP}(P_1) \ \& \ T_2 \in \mathcal{AP}(P_2)\}$$
$$\mathcal{AP}(\textbf{local } h \textbf{ in } P) = \{T' \backslash h \mid T \in \mathcal{AP}(P) \ \& \ T \preceq_h T'\}$$

Definition 6 *The asynchronous trace set denoted by a pomset T, written $\mathcal{AL}(T)$, is the set of all traces which arise by fair interleaving the threads of T.*

Again the asynchronous traces of a process can be recovered naturally:

Theorem 10 *For all processes P, $\mathcal{AT}(P) = \bigcup \{\mathcal{AL}(T) \mid T \in \mathcal{AP}(P)\}$.*

Corollary 11 *For all P_1 and P_2, if $\mathcal{AP}(P_1) = \mathcal{AP}(P_2)$ then $\mathcal{AT}(P_1) = \mathcal{AT}(P_2)$.*

The process **local** mid **in** $buff_1(in, mid) \| buff_1(mid, out)$ behaves like a finite *unbounded* buffer if we assume asynchronous commuication, in contrast to the 2-place buffer which described its behavior under synchronous communication.

The following laws hold for *asynchronous* trace semantics, and are analogues of the first two laws given earlier for synchronous communication. The third law does not hold, because of the assumption that output is always enabled.

Theorem 12 (Fair Asynchronous Laws)
The following laws of equivalence hold in asynchronous trace semantics:

1. **local** h **in** $(h?x; P) \| (h!v; Q)$ = **local** h **in** $(x := v; P) \| Q$
2. **local** h **in** $(h?x; P) \| (Q_1; Q_2)$ = Q_1; **local** h **in** $(h?x; P) \| Q_2$
   provided $h \notin \mathsf{chans}(Q_1)$.

These laws also hold for asynchronous pomset semantics.

11   Related Work

Hoare's "trace model" of CSP [20] interpreted a process as a prefix-closed set of finite communication traces, recording only visible actions such as $h!v$ and $h?v$. Each such trace represents a *partial* behavior. Hoare's model did not treat infinite behaviors, and is mainly suitable for proving safety properties. The failures semantics of CSP [11] modelled a process as a set of failures (α, X) consisting of a finite sequence α of communications and a "refusal set" X. Our notion of trace subsumes failures: a process with failure (α, X) would have a trace $\alpha \delta_Y{}^\omega$, for some set Y disjoint from X. Our notion of trace is more general, allowing for instance traces of form $\alpha(\delta_A \delta_B)^\omega$ which cannot be represented in failure format. The extra generality is needed in order to cope properly with fair parallel composition. Our traces represent *entire* computations, so our trace sets are not prefix-closed. Again this is more than a philosophical difference: one cannot deduce the fair traces of a parallel process by looking at the prefixes of the traces of its constituent processes. The failures semantics and its later more refined extensions, all building on a prefix-closed trace set, were not designed with fairness in mind [33].

Our use of traces in which blocking actions play a crucial role is reminiscent of Phillips-style refusal testing, although Phillips did not incorporate fairness [30]. Refusal testing assumes that under certain circumstances one may detect that a process is *unable* to perform a communication; one may obviously view a process which is capable of performing δ_X as being (potentially) unable to perform $h?v$ for any $h? \in X$. It is not clear how to generalize Phillips's testing equivalence to deal properly with fairness.

Older's Ph.D. thesis [24] provides a framework capable of modelling several forms of fairness in the synchronous setting. She introduced generalized notions of fairness and blocking *modulo* a set of directions, and her models incorporated extensive book-keeping information concerning enabling, together with cleverly devised but complex closure conditions designed to achieve full abstraction [25,10]. As Older comments, it is questionable if these fairness notions are useful abstractions of realistic schedulers, since their implementation requires meticulous attention to so much enabling information. Moreover, these forms of fairness tend to lack equivalence robustness, being sensitive to subtle nuances in the formulation of the operational semantics [1].

In contrast we assume a robust yet simple form of weakly fair execution, suitably adapted to deal reasonably with synchronization to ensure that two processes waiting to perform matching communications will not be ignored forever. This property would be guaranteed for instance by any round-robin scheduler which runs each process for an randomly chosen number of steps, and also uses a round-robin strategy to look for matching communications if the chosen process blocks while attempting input or output. This form of fairness is a simple variant of weak process fairness and we believe this is a reasonable abstraction from the behavior of realistic implementations. Furthermore, in adopting this notion of fairness we avoid the need for separate book-keeping: the traces themselves can be designed to carry the relevant information in their δ actions. Older's notion of being blocked but fair *modulo* a set X of directions corresponds to a trace β such that $blocks(\beta) \subseteq X$. It would be interesting to see if the other forms of fairness discussed by Older can be treated within our framework.

Hennessy [17] gave an earlier treatment of a CCS-like language with weakly fair execution. Parrow [29] discusses various fairness notions for CCS-like processes. Costa and Stirling gave an operational semantics for a CCS-like language assuming either weak or strong process fairness [13,14].

Partial-order semantics of various kinds, such as Pratt-style pomsets [31,32], Winskel's event structures [35][8], and Petri nets [28] have been widely used, with parallel composition interpreted as so-called "true concurrency" rather than interleaving. Avoiding explicit interleaving can be advantageous, both in avoiding a combinatorial explosion and in side-stepping the need to define fairmerge operations. Indeed our motivation in developing a pomset formulation was to obtain an alternative and more tractable methodology for dealing with trace sets. The pomset union operation nicely handles weakly fair parallel composition in the absence of blocking. We show how to extend these ideas to incorporate blocking.

References

1. K. R. Apt, N. Francez, and S. Katz, *Appraising fairness in languages for distributed programming*, Distributed Computing, 2(4):226-241, 1988. 467, 480
2. J. A. Bergstra and J.-W. Klop, *Process Algebra for Synchronous Communication*, Information and Computation, 60(1/3):109–137, 1984. 467
3. J. A. Bergstra, J.-W. Klop, and J. Tucker, *Process algebra with asynchronous communication mechanisms*, Seminar on Concurrency, Springer LNCS 197, pp. 76–95, 1985. 467

---

[8] Event structures can be seen as pomsets equipped with a "conflict relation", although this characterization does not reflect their original, independent, development and subsequent usage.

4. F. de Boer, J. Kok, C. Palamidessi, and J. Rutten, *The failure of failures in a paradigm for asynchronous concurrency*, CONCUR'91, Springer LNCS 527, pp. 111-126, 1991. 466, 468

5. S. Brookes, *Full abstraction for a shared-variable parallel language*, Information and Computation, 127(2):145-163, June 1996. 466, 468

6. S. Brookes, *The Essence of Parallel Algol*, 11th LICS, pp. 164-173, July 1996. 466, 468

7. S. Brookes, *Idealized CSP: Combining Procedures with Communicating Processes*, Proc. MFPS XIII, ENTCS 6, Elsevier Science, 1997. 466

8. S. Brookes, *On the Kahn Principle and Fair Networks*, MFPS XIV, Queen Mary Westfield College, University of London, May 1998. 466, 467

9. S. Brookes, *Deconstructing CCS and CSP: Asynchronous Communication, Fairness and Full Abstraction*, MFPS XVI, 2000. 467

10. S. Brookes and S. Older, *Full abstraction for strongly fair communicating processes*, MFPS XI, ENTCS 1, Elsevier Science, 1995. 467, 480

11. S. Brookes, C. A. R. Hoare, and A. W. Roscoe, *A Theory of Communicating Sequential Processes*, JACM 31(3):560-599, July 1984. 466, 467, 479

12. S. Brookes, and A. W. Roscoe, *An improved failures model for CSP*, Seminar on concurrency, Springer-Verlag, LNCS 197, 1984. 466, 467

13. G. Costa and C. Stirling, *A fair calculus of communicating systems*, ACTA Informatica 21:417-441, 1984. 467, 480

14. G. Costa and C. Stirling, *Weak and strong fairness in CCS*, Technical Report CSR-16-85, University of Edinburgh, January 1985. 467, 480

15. N. Francez, **Fairness**, Springer-Verlag, 1986. 466, 467

16. R. van Glabbeek, *The Linear Time–Branching Time Spectrum*, **Handbook of Process Algebra**, Elsevier, 2001. 466

17. M. Hennessy, *An algebraic theory of fair asynchronous communicating processes*, Theoretical Computer Science, 49:121-143, 1987. 480

18. M. Hennessy and R. Milner, *Algebraic laws for nondeterminism and concurrency*, JACM 32(1):137–161, 1985. 476

19. C. A. R. Hoare, *Communicating Sequential Processes*, CACM 21(8):666–677, 1978. 466, 467

20. C. A. R. Hoare, *A Model for Communicating Sequential Processes*, Technical Monograph PRG-22, Oxford University, June 1981. 466, 467, 479

21. C. A. R. Hoare, **Communicating Sequential Processes**, Prentice-Hall, 1985. 476

22. R. Milner, *A Calculus of Communicating Systems*, Springer LNCS 92, 1980. 467

23. R. Milner, **Communication and Concurrency**, Prentice-Hall, London, 1989. 467, 476

24. S. Older, *A Denotational Framework for Fair Communicating Processes*, Ph.D. thesis, Carnegie Mellon University, December 1996. 467, 479

25. S. Older, *A Framework for Fair Communicating Processes*, Proc. MFPS XIII, ENTCS 6, Elsevier Science, 1997. 467, 480

26. S. Owicki and L. Lamport, *Proving liveness properties of concurrent programs*, ACM TOPLAS, 4(3): 455-495, July 1982. 467

27. D. Park, *On the semantics of fair parallelism*. **Abstract Software Specifications**, Springer-Verlag LNCS vol. 86, 504–526, 1979. 466

28. C. A. Petri, *Concepts of Net Theory*, Symposium on Mathematical Foundations of Computer Science, September 1973. 480

29. J. Parrow, *Fairness Properties in Process Algebras*, Ph. D. thesis, University of Uppsala, 1985. 480

30. I. Phillips, *Refusal testing*, Theoretical Computer Science, 50(2):241–284, 1987.
468, 479

31. V. Pratt, *On the Composition of Processes*, Proc. 9th ACM POPL Symp., 1982.
466, 468, 480

32. V. Pratt, *Modeling concurrency with partial orders*, International Journal on Parallel Processing, 15(1): 33–71, 1986.   466, 468, 480

33. A. W. Roscoe, **The Theory and Practice of Concurrency**, Prentice-Hall, 1998.
466, 467, 473, 475, 479

34. V. Saraswat, M. Rinard, and P. Panangaden, *Semantic foundations of concurrent constraint programming*, Proc. 18th ACM POPL Symposium, 1991.   466

35. G. Winskel, *Events in Computation*, Ph. D. thesis, Edinburgh University, 1980.
480

A Framework for the Analysis of Security Protocols*

Michele Boreale[1] and Maria Grazia Buscemi[2]

[1] Dipartimento di Sistemi e Informatica
Università di Firenze, Italy
[2] Dipartimento di Matematica e Informatica
Università di Catania, Italy
boreale@dsi.unifi.it buscemi@dmi.unict.it

Abstract. Properties of security protocols such as authentication and secrecy are often verified by explictly generating an operational model of the protocol and then seeking for insecure states. However, message exchange between the intruder and the honest participants induces a form of state explosion that makes the model infinite in principle. Building on previous work on symbolic semantics, we propose a general framework for automatic analysis of security protocols that make use of a variety of crypto-functions. We start from a base language akin to the spi-calculus, equipped with a set of *generic* cryptographic primitives. We propose a symbolic operational semantics that relies on unification and provides finite and effective protocol models. Next, we give a method to carry out trace analysis directly on the symbolic model. Under certain conditions on the given cryptographic primitives, our method is proven complete for the considered class of properties.

1 Introduction

Automatic methods for verifying properties of security protocols are very often based on explicit generation of the protocol model. The latter is then explored in order to check whether any insecure state is reachable. In particular, most methods based on finite state model-checking (see, e.g., [17,21,23,26]) follow a Dolev-Yao intruder model [12], which implies that a (hostile) environment has total control over the communication network. The assumption is that the environment can store, duplicate, hide or replace any message traveling on the network, and synthesize new messages by pairing, encryption and decryption of those already known.

To make standard finite-state model checking applicable to protocol analysis, two simplifying requirements are necessary: (a) there is a bound on the number of protocol runs, and (b) there is a bound on the number of possible messages the intruder can generate and send to honest participants at any moment. Discarding one of these two requirements leads to infinite models. Also, these bounds

---

* This work has been partially supported by EU within the FET - Global Computing initiative, projects MIKADO and PROFUNDIS and by MIUR project NAPOLI.

L. Brim et al. (Eds.): CONCUR 2002, LNCS 2421, pp. 483–498, 2002.

have to be chosen very carefully: due to the combinatorics of message generation, the size of the model tends to explode as multiple principals and data values are considered. It is known that discarding requirement (a) leads to undecidability of protocol analysis, unless severe restrictions are imposed on the analyzed protocols (see e.g.[5,11,13]). Rather, it is less clear to what extent requirement (b) can be relaxed, while preserving generality of protocol format, decidability and effectiveness.

For the case of shared-key encryption, approaches alternative to finite-state model checking have been pursued, based on notions of symbolic execution [4,7]. In this paper, we extend the symbolic semantics given in [7] to a general framework for the treatment of *generic* cryptographic primitives. We then spell out sufficient conditions on these primitives, under which verification can be performed symbolically and, hence, effectively. As an application, we consider an instance of this framework whose primitives correspond to the most common cryptographic funtions (shared and public key, digital signature and hashing).

As a base language, we consider a dialect of the spi-calculus [3]. Unlike the original spi-calculus and the languages in [4,7], where cryptographic functions are modelled as process operators, we adopt a uniform process syntax, much as that of [2], and consider a generic signature Σ of cryptographic functions. The latter may include constructors and destructors for various cryptographic operations, akin to [1]. The meaning of Σ-terms is provided by an evaluation relation $\downarrow$ that maps terms to values (or *messages*). On top of the evaluation relation, we introduce a deduction relation $\vdash$ that describes how the environment synthesize new messages from known ones. Protocol properties are formalised as correspondence assertions of the kind "every execution of action α must be preceded by some execution of action β", for given α and β.

The ("concrete") operational semantics of this language is, as expected, infinitary, because each input action gives rise to infinitely many transitions. To overcome this problem, we also define a symbolic operational semantics that is finitely branching and yields finite models of protocols with a fixed number of participants. Then, we give a method to carry out trace analysis directly on the symbolic traces.

Next, we provide some reasonable conditions on the given cryptosystem under which we can prove that the method is sound and complete with respect to the concrete semantics. In other words, every attack detected in the symbolic model corresponds to some attack in the concrete one, and vice-versa. Thus our symbolic method makes no approximation with respect to the infinitary, concrete model. For instance, type-dependent flaws (see e.g. [15]), which usually escape finite-state analysis, with our approach naturally emerge when present. The method is rather efficient in practice, because in the symbolic model there is no state-explosion induced by message exchange: every input action gives rise exactly to one symbolic transition. Experimentation with STA [27], a prototype tool based on this method, has given encouraging results [8].

A summary of our paper follows. The general framework is introduced in Section 2. Symbolic semantics, and its relationship to the concrete one, are the subject of Section 3. The verification method is introduced and discussed in Section 4 and applied to a specific protocol in Section 5. Throughout the paper, we shall consider public-key cryptography as a running example; other common crypto-primitives are discussed in Section 6. A few concluding remarks and directions for future work are in Section 7.

2   A General Framework

In this section, we present the main ingredients of our framework. We introduce the concept of *frame*, i.e., a structure consisting of a signature Σ, a set of (legal) messages and a function that evaluates terms to messages. Then, we generalize the notions of traces, configurations and security property, introduced in [7].

2.1   Frames

We consider two countable disjoint sets of *names* $m, n, \ldots \in \mathcal{N}$ and variables $x, y, \ldots \in \mathcal{V}$. The set $\mathcal{N}$ is in turn partitioned into a countable set of *local names* $a, b, \ldots \in \mathcal{LN}$ and a countable set of *environmental names* $\underline{a}, \underline{b}, \ldots \in \mathcal{EN}$: these two sets represent the basic data (keys, nonces,...) initially known to a process and to the environment, respectively. The set $\mathcal{N} \cup \mathcal{V}$ is ranged over by letters $u, v, \ldots$. Given a signature Σ of function symbols $f, g, \ldots$, each coming with its arity (constants have arity 0), we denote by $\mathcal{E}_\Sigma$ the algebra of terms (or *expressions*) on $\mathcal{N} \cup \mathcal{V} \cup \Sigma$, given by the grammar:

$$\zeta, \eta \quad ::= \quad u \mid f(\widetilde{\zeta})$$

where $\widetilde{\zeta}$ is a tuple of terms of the expected length. A *term context* $C[\cdot]$ is a term with a hole that can be filled with any expression ζ, thus yielding an expression $C[\zeta]$.

Definition 1 (frame). *A frame* $\mathcal{F}$ *is a triple* $(\Sigma, \mathcal{M}, \downarrow)$*, where:*

- *Σ is a signature;*
- *$\mathcal{M} \subseteq \mathcal{E}_\Sigma$ is a set of* messages *$M, N, \ldots$;*
- *$\downarrow \subseteq \mathcal{E}_\Sigma \times \mathcal{M}$ is an* evaluation relation.

In the sequel, we write $\zeta \downarrow M$ for $(\zeta, M) \in \downarrow$ and say that ζ *evaluates to* M. An evaluation relation evaluates expressions to messages. In typical frame instances the relation $\downarrow$ will be both a function and a congruence with respect to the operations in Σ, but we need not to assume these facts in the general framework.

Below, we define a deduction relation which expresses how the environment can generate new messages starting from an initial set of messages S. Unlike other approaches, our definition of deduction relation is not given by a set of deductive rules. Rather, we make use of the set $\mathcal{H}(S)$, which consists of all the expressions inductively built by applying functions of Σ to elements of S and of $\mathcal{EN}$. We denote by $\mathcal{P}_f(X)$ the set of finite subsets of X.

Definition 2 (deduction relation). *For $\mathcal{F} = (\Sigma, \mathcal{M}, \downarrow)$ a frame and $S \subseteq \mathcal{M}$, the set $\mathcal{H}_{\mathcal{F}}(S)$ is inductively defined by the following rules:*

$$\mathcal{H}^0_{\mathcal{F}}(S) \triangleq S \cup \mathcal{EN}$$
$$\mathcal{H}^{i+1}_{\mathcal{F}}(S) \triangleq \mathcal{H}^i_{\mathcal{F}}(S) \cup \{f(\tilde{\zeta}) : f \in \Sigma, \, \tilde{\zeta} \subseteq \mathcal{H}^i_{\mathcal{F}}(S)\}$$
$$\mathcal{H}_{\mathcal{F}}(S) \triangleq \bigcup_{i \geq 0} \mathcal{H}^i_{\mathcal{F}}(S)$$

The deduction relation $\vdash_{\mathcal{F}} \subseteq \mathcal{P}_f(\mathcal{M}) \times \mathcal{M}$ is defined by:

$$S \vdash_{\mathcal{F}} M \quad \triangleq \quad \exists \zeta \in \mathcal{H}_{\mathcal{F}}(S) : \zeta \downarrow M$$

A message M is deducible *from S if $S \vdash_{\mathcal{F}} M$.*

When no confusion arises, we simply write $\mathcal{H}(S)$ for $\mathcal{H}_{\mathcal{F}}(S)$ and $\vdash$ for $\vdash_{\mathcal{F}}$.

Throughout the paper, we study the case of public key encryption, which serves as a running example of application of our method.

Example: Public Key Encryption (1) Let us consider a system where primitives for pairing and public key encryption of messages can be arbitrarily nested, but non-atomic keys are forbidden. The frame $\mathcal{F}_{pk} = (\Sigma, \mathcal{M}, \downarrow)$ is defined in Table 1. The functions of Σ are: generation of public $((\cdot)^+)$ and private $((\cdot)^-)$ keys, encryption with a public key $(\{\!|\cdot|\!\}_{(\cdot)})$, decryption using a private key $(\mathsf{dec}^{\mathsf{pk}}_{(\cdot)}(\cdot))$, pairing $(\langle \cdot, \cdot \rangle)$ and selection $(\pi_i(\cdot))$. Public and private keys are represented by u^+ and u^-, respectively. Names and variables can be used to build compound messages via public-key encryption and pairing. In particular, $\{\!|M|\!\}_{m^+}$ represents the message obtained by encrypting M under m^+. The definition of evaluation relation makes use of an auxiliary relation $\rightsquigarrow$, that models the mechanisms of public key encryption under the perfect cryptography assumption. As an example of deducible message in $\mathcal{F}_{pk}$, if $S = \{\,\{\!|\langle a, b \rangle|\!\}_{k^+}, k^-\,\}$ then $S \vdash a$, since $\zeta = \pi_1(\mathsf{dec}^{\mathsf{pk}}_{k^-}(\{\!|\langle a, b \rangle|\!\}_{k^+})) \in \mathcal{H}(S)$ and $\zeta \downarrow a$. Note that, whatever S, the set of messages deducible from S is infinite.

2.2   Processes

Syntax As a base language, we consider a variant of the spi-calculus [3], parametrized by an arbitrary frame $\mathcal{F}$ (for readability, in the notation we omit explicit reference to $\mathcal{F}$). The syntax of *agent expressions*, in $\mathcal{A}$, is reported in Table 2. We consider a set $\mathcal{L}$ of *labels* which is ranged over by $\mathsf{a}, \mathsf{b}, \ldots$. The main difference from the spi-calculus is that, here, input and output labels $(\mathsf{a}, \mathsf{b}, \ldots)$ must not be regarded as channels – following the Dole-Yao model, we assume just one public network – but, rather, as 'tags' attached to process actions for ease of reference. Also, we have a single construct (let) for evaluating expressions that replaces the ad-hoc constructs found in the spi-calculus for encryption, decryption and other cryptographic operations. We do not consider restriction: it

Table 1. $\mathcal{F}_{pk}$, a frame for public key encryption

$$\Sigma \quad = \{(\cdot)^+, \quad (\cdot)^-, \quad \{\!\|\cdot\|\!\}_{(\cdot)}, \quad \langle \cdot, \cdot \rangle, \quad \pi_i(\cdot) \quad (i = 1, 2), \quad \mathsf{dec}^{\mathsf{pk}}_{(\cdot)}(\cdot)\}$$

Signature

$$M, N \qquad ::= u \mid u^+ \mid u^- \mid \{\!\|M\|\!\}_{u^+} \mid \langle M, N \rangle$$

Messages

$$\pi_i(\langle M_1, M_2 \rangle) \rightsquigarrow M_i \quad (i = 1, 2)$$

$$\mathsf{dec}^{\mathsf{pk}}_{u^-}(\{\!\|M\|\!\}_{u^+}) \rightsquigarrow M$$

$$\frac{\zeta \rightsquigarrow \zeta'}{C[\zeta] \rightsquigarrow C[\zeta']} \qquad \zeta \downarrow M \quad \triangleq \quad \zeta \rightsquigarrow^* M \qquad \text{Evaluation}$$

might be easily accommodated but it has little semantical significance, in the absence of replication/recursion.

Given the presence of binders for variables, notions of *free variables*, $\mathrm{v}(A) \subseteq \mathcal{V}$, and *alpha-equivalence* arise as expected. We shall identify alpha-equivalent agent expressions. For any M and u, $[^M\!/u]$ denotes the operation of substituting the free occurrences of u by M. An agent expression A is said to be *closed* or a *process* if $\mathrm{v}(A) = \emptyset$; the set of processes $\mathcal{P}$ is ranged over by $P, Q, \ldots$. Local names and environmental names occurring in A are denoted by $\mathrm{ln}(A)$ and $\mathrm{en}(A)$, respectively. A process P is *initial* if $\mathrm{en}(P) = \emptyset$.

Operational Semantics The semantics of the calculus is given in terms of a transition relation $\longrightarrow$, which we will sometimes refer to as 'concrete' (as opposed to the 'symbolic' one we shall introduce later on). We model the state of the system as a pair $\langle s, P \rangle$, where s records the current environment's knowledge (i.e., the sequence of messages the environment has "seen" on the network up

Table 2. Syntax for agents

$A, B ::=$		agents $\mathcal{A}$
	0	(null)
$\mid$	$a(x).\, A$	(input)
$\mid$	$\overline{a}\langle \zeta \rangle.\, A$	(output)
$\mid$	$\mathsf{let}\, y = \zeta\, \mathsf{in}\, A$	(evaluation)
$\mid$	$[\zeta = \eta]A$	(matching)
$\mid$	$A \parallel B$	(parallel composition)

The occurrences of variables x and y are bound.

to a given moment) and P is a process term. An *action* is a term of the form $a\langle M\rangle$ (*input* action) or $\bar{a}\langle M\rangle$ (*output* action), for a a label and M a message. The set of actions Act is ranged over by $\alpha, \beta, \ldots$, while the set Act^* of strings of actions is ranged over by $s, s', \ldots$. String concatenation is written '$\cdot$'. We denote by $act(s)$ and $msg(s)$ the set of actions and messages, respectively, appearing in s. A string s is *closed* if $v(s) = \emptyset$ and *initial* if $en(s) = \emptyset$. In what follows, we write '$s \vdash M$' for $msg(s) \vdash M$.

We, now, define *traces*, that is, sequences of actions that may result from the interaction between a process and its environment. In traces, each message received by a process (input message) can be synthesized from the knowledge the environment has previously acquired. In *configurations*, the latter is explicitly recorded.

Definition 3 (traces and configurations). *A* trace *is a closed string* $s \in Act^*$ *such that for each* s_1, s_2 *and* $a\langle M\rangle$, *if* $s = s_1 \cdot a\langle M\rangle \cdot s_2$ *then* $s_1 \vdash M$.

A configuration, *written as* $\langle s, P\rangle$, *is a pair consisting of a trace s and a process P. A configuration is* initial *if* $en(s, P) = \emptyset$. *Configurations are ranged over by* $\mathcal{C}, \mathcal{C}', \ldots$.

The concrete transition relation on configurations is defined by the rules in Table 3. Each action taken by the process is recorded in the configuration's first component. Rule (INP) makes the transition relation infinitely-branching, as M ranges over the infinite set $\{M : s \vdash M, M \text{ closed }\}$. In rule (OUT), ζ is evaluated before the action takes place. By rule (LET), the evaluation of ζ replaces any occurrence of y in P. No handshake communication is provided : all messages go through the environment (rule (PAR)).

2.3 Properties

We express security properties of a protocol in terms of the traces it generates. In particular, we focus on correspondence assertions of the kind 'for every generated

Table 3. Rules for the transition relation ($\longrightarrow$)

(INP)	$\langle s, \, a(x). \, P\rangle \longrightarrow \langle s \cdot a\langle M\rangle, \, P[M/x]\rangle$	$s \vdash M, \, M$ closed
(OUT)	$\langle s, \, \bar{a}\langle\zeta\rangle. \, P\rangle \longrightarrow \langle s \cdot \bar{a}\langle M\rangle, \, P\rangle$	$\zeta \downarrow M, \, M$ closed
(LET)	$\langle s, \, \text{let } y = \zeta \text{ in } P\rangle \longrightarrow \langle s, \, P[M/y]\rangle$	$\zeta \downarrow M, \, M$ closed
(MATCH)	$\langle s, \, [\zeta = \eta]P\rangle \longrightarrow \langle s, \, P\rangle$	$\zeta \downarrow M, \, \eta \downarrow N, \, M = N$
(PAR)	$\dfrac{\langle s, \, P\rangle \longrightarrow \langle s', \, P'\rangle}{\langle s, \, P \parallel Q\rangle \longrightarrow \langle s', \, P' \parallel Q\rangle}$	

plus symmetric version of (PAR).

trace, whenever action β occurs in the trace, then action α must have occurred at some previous point in the trace'. Given a configuration $\langle s, P \rangle$ and a trace s', we say that $\langle s, P \rangle$ *generates* s', written $\langle s, P \rangle \searrow s'$, if $\langle s, P \rangle \longrightarrow^* \langle s', P' \rangle$ for some P'. A substitution θ in a frame $\mathcal{F}$ is a finite partial map from $\mathcal{V}$ to the set of messages $\mathcal{M}$ of frame $\mathcal{F}$ such that $\theta(x) \neq x$, for each variable x. For any object t (i.e. variable, message, process, trace,...), we denote by $t\theta$ the result of simultaneously replacing each $x \in v(t) \cap \mathrm{dom}(\theta)$ by $\theta(x)$. We let ρ range over ground substitutions, i.e. substitutions that map variables to closed messages.

Definition 4 (satisfaction relation). *Let α and β be actions and s be a trace. We say that α occurs prior to β in s if whenever $s = s' \cdot \beta \cdot s''$ then $\alpha \in \mathrm{act}(s')$. For $v(\alpha) \subseteq v(\beta)$, we write $s \models \alpha \hookleftarrow \beta$, and say s satisfies $\alpha \hookleftarrow \beta$, if for each ground substitution ρ it holds that $\alpha\rho$ occurs prior to $\beta\rho$ in s. We say that a configuration $\mathcal{C}$ satisfies $\alpha \hookleftarrow \beta$, and write $\mathcal{C} \models \alpha \hookleftarrow \beta$, if all traces generated by $\mathcal{C}$ satisfy $\alpha \hookleftarrow \beta$.*

Assertions $\alpha \hookleftarrow \beta$ can express interesting secrecy and authentication properties. As an example, in the final step of many key-establishment protocols, a principal A sends a message of the form $\{N\}_k$ to a responder B, where $\{N\}_k$ is obtained by encrypting some authentication information N under a newly established shared-key k. Our scheme permits expressing that *every* message encrypted with k that is accepted by B during the execution of the protocol indeed originates from A, i.e. that B is really talking to A, and that k is authentic. If we denote by $\mathsf{final_A}$ and $\mathsf{final_B}$ the labels attached to A's and B's final action, respectively, then the above property might be formalized as an assertion $\overline{\mathsf{final_A}}\langle\{x\}_k\rangle \hookleftarrow \mathsf{final_B}\langle\{x\}_k\rangle$, for x a variable. An extended example is given in Section 5. In practice, all forms of authentication in Lowe's hierarchy [18] are captured by this scheme, except the most demanding one that requires one-to-one bijection between α's and β's. However, we expect our scheme can be easily adjusted to include this stronger form, by requiring that each β is preceded by *exactly* one occurrence of α.

Another property that can be set within our frame is *secrecy* in the style of [6]. In this case, it is convenient to fix a conventional 'absurd' action $\perp$ that is nowhere used in agent expressions. Thus, the formula $\perp \hookleftarrow \alpha$ means that action α should never take place. Now, the fact that a protocol, say P, does not leak a sensible datum, say d, can be expressed also by saying that the adversary will never be capable of synthesizing d. This can be formalized by extending the protocol to include a 'guardian' that at any time picks up one message from the network, $P \parallel \mathbf{g}(x).\mathbf{0}$, and then requiring that this guardian will never receive d, that is, $\langle \epsilon, P \parallel \mathbf{g}(x).\mathbf{0} \rangle \models \perp \hookleftarrow \mathbf{g}\langle d \rangle$.

3   Symbolic Semantics

The symbolic semantics we present in this section is based on the notion of symbolic frame. The latter is essentially a frame equipped with an additional symbolic evaluation relation, which is in agreement with its concrete counterpart.

Formally, let us denote by Subst the set of all substitutions in a given frame. A substitution θ is a *unifier* of t_1 and t_2 if $t_1\theta = t_2\theta$. We denote by $\mathrm{mgu}(t_1, t_2)$ a chosen *most general unifier* (mgu) of t_1 and t_2, that is, a unifier θ of t_1 and t_2 such that any other unifier is a composition of substitutions θ and θ', written $\theta\theta'$, for some θ'. Also, for t_1, t_1', t_2, t_2' terms, $\mathrm{mgu}(t_1 = t_1', t_2 = t_2')$ stands for $\mathrm{mgu}(t_2\theta, t_2'\theta)$, where $\theta = \mathrm{mgu}(t_1, t_1')$, if such mgu's exist.

Definition 5 (symbolic frame). *A symbolic frame is a pair $\mathcal{F}^s = (\mathcal{F}, \downarrow_s)$, where $\mathcal{F}$ is a frame, and $\downarrow_s \subseteq \mathcal{E}_\Sigma \times \mathsf{Subst} \times \mathcal{M}$ is a symbolic evaluation relation (we write $\zeta \downarrow_\theta M$ for $(\zeta, \theta, M) \in \downarrow_s$) such that, for any expression ζ and ground substitution ρ with $\mathrm{v}(\zeta) \subseteq \mathrm{dom}(\rho)$:*

(a) If $\zeta\rho \downarrow M$, then there exist N, θ, ρ_0 such that $\zeta \downarrow_\theta N$, $\rho = \theta\rho_0$ and $M = N\rho_0$, and

(b) If $\zeta \downarrow_\theta N$, $\rho = \theta\rho_0$, for some ρ_0, and $N\rho_0 \in \mathcal{M}$, then $\zeta\rho \downarrow N\rho_0$.

Example: Public Key Encryption (2) The symbolic frame $\mathcal{F}^s_{pk}$ is defined as the pair $(\mathcal{F}_{pk}, \downarrow_s)$, where $\downarrow_s$ is the reflexive and transitive closure of the relation $(\leadsto_s)$, as given in Table 4. $\mathcal{F}^s_{pk}$ is indeed a symbolic frame: Conditions (a) and (b) in Definition 5 are proven by straightforward induction on ζ.

We now come to symbolic counterparts of traces and configurations. Note that Condition (b) below states that only the environment can introduce variables into symbolic traces.

Definition 6 (symbolic traces and configurations). *A symbolic trace is a string $s \in Act^*$ such that: (a) $\mathrm{en}(s) = \emptyset$, and (b) for each s_1, s_2, α and x, if $s = s_1 \cdot \alpha \cdot s_2$ and $x \in \mathrm{v}(\alpha) - \mathrm{v}(s_1)$ then α is an input action. Symbolic traces are ranged over by $\sigma, \sigma', \ldots$. A symbolic configuration, written $\langle \sigma, A \rangle_s$, is a pair composed by a symbolic trace σ and an agent A, such that $\mathrm{en}(A) = \emptyset$ and $\mathrm{v}(A) \subseteq \mathrm{v}(\sigma)$.*

Table 4. Symbolic Evaluation Relation ($\downarrow_s$) for $\mathcal{F}^s_{pk}$

$$\mathrm{dec}^{\mathrm{pk}}_N(M) \overset{\theta}{\leadsto}_s x_1\theta \qquad\qquad \theta = \mathrm{mgu}(M = \{\![x_1]\!\}_{x_2^+}, N = x_2^-)$$

$$\pi_i(M) \overset{\theta}{\leadsto}_s x_i\theta \qquad (i = 1, 2) \qquad \theta = \mathrm{mgu}(M, \langle x_1, x_2 \rangle)$$

$$\{\![M]\!\}_x \overset{\theta}{\leadsto}_s \{\![M\theta]\!\}_{x^+} \qquad\qquad \theta = [x^+/x]$$

$$\frac{\zeta \overset{\theta}{\leadsto}_s \zeta'}{C[\zeta] \overset{\theta}{\leadsto}_s C\theta[\zeta']}$$

$$\zeta \downarrow_\theta M \overset{\triangle}{\Leftrightarrow} \zeta \overset{\theta_1}{\leadsto}_s \cdots \overset{\theta_n}{\leadsto}_s M \text{ and } \theta = \theta_1 \cdots \theta_n$$

Variables x_1 and x_2 are chosen fresh according to some arbitrary but fixed rule.

Note that, due to Condition (b) in the Definition 6, e.g. $\bar{\mathsf{a}}\langle x^+\rangle \cdot \mathsf{a}\langle\{\![h]\!\}_{x^+}\rangle$ is not a symbolic trace, while $\mathsf{a}\langle\{\![h]\!\}_{x^+}\rangle \cdot \bar{\mathsf{a}}\langle x^+\rangle$ is so. Once a symbolic frame $\mathcal{F}^s$ is fixed, configurations can be equipped with a symbolic transition relation, $\longrightarrow_s$, as defined by the rules in Table 5 (for the sake of readability we omit any explicit reference to $\mathcal{F}^s$). There, a function $\mathrm{new}_\mathcal{V}(\cdot)$ is assumed such that, for any given $V \subseteq_{\mathsf{fin}} \mathcal{V}$, $\mathrm{new}_\mathcal{V}(V)$ is a variable not in V. Note that, differently from the concrete semantics, input variables are *not* instantiated immediately (rule $(\textsc{Inp}_s)$). Rather, constraints on these variables are added as soon as they are needed, and recorded via mgu's. This may occur due to rules $(\textsc{Out}_s)$, $(\textsc{Let}_s)$ and $(\textsc{Match}_s)$. In the following example, after the first step, variable x gets instantiated to name b by a $(\textsc{Match}_s)$-reduction:

$$\langle \epsilon, \, \mathsf{a}(x).\,[x=b]P\rangle_s \;\; \longrightarrow_s \;\; \langle \mathsf{a}\langle x\rangle, \, [x=b]P\rangle_s \;\; \longrightarrow_s \;\; \langle \mathsf{a}\langle b\rangle, \, P[b/x]\rangle_s$$

Whenever $\langle \sigma, \, A\rangle_s \longrightarrow_s^* \langle \sigma', \, A'\rangle_s$ for some A', we say that $\langle \sigma, \, A\rangle_s$ *symbolically generates* σ', and write $\langle \sigma, \, A\rangle_s \searrow_s \sigma'$. The relation $\longrightarrow_s$ is finitely-branching if so is $\downarrow_s$ (this is the case, e.g., for the public key frame $\mathcal{F}^s_{pk}$). In this case, each configuration generates a finite number of symbolic traces. It is important to stress that many symbolic traces are in fact 'garbage' – jumbled sequences of actions that cannot be instantiated to any concrete trace. For instance, consider process $P \triangleq \mathsf{a}(y).\,\mathsf{let}\,x=\mathsf{dec}^{\mathsf{pk}}_{k-}(y)\,\mathsf{in}\,\bar{\mathsf{a}}\langle x\rangle.\,\mathbf{0}$. The initial configuration $\langle \epsilon, \, P\rangle_s$ symbolically generates the trace $\mathsf{a}\langle\{\![z]\!\}_{k+}\rangle \cdot \bar{\mathsf{a}}\langle z\rangle$, which is inconsistent, because the environment cannot provide k^+. The problem of detecting these inconsistent traces, that might give rise to 'false positives' when checking protocol properties, will be faced in the next section.

We define below the notion of consistency. Based on it, we state a theorem that lifts the concrete-symbolic correspondence given in Definition 5 to the transition relations. Its proof is an easy transition induction on $\longrightarrow_s$ and $\longrightarrow$.

Definition 7 (solutions of symbolic traces). *Given a symbolic trace σ and a ground substitution ρ, we say that ρ satisfies σ if $\sigma\rho$ is a trace. If this is this case, we also say that $\sigma\rho$ is a solution of σ, and that σ is consistent.*

Theorem 1 (concrete vs. symbolic semantics). *Let $\mathcal{F}^s$ be a symbolic frame, $\mathcal{C}$ an initial configuration and s a trace of $\mathcal{F}$. Then $\mathcal{C} \searrow s$ if and only if there is σ s.t. $\mathcal{C} \searrow_s \sigma$ and s is a solution of σ.*

4 A Verification Method

In this section, we first define *regular frames*, i.e., frames for which it is possible to determine a finite *basis* for the synthesis of messages. Next, we introduce a *refinement* procedure that checks consistency of symbolic traces. Finally, we present a verification method which is based on refinement and applies to regular frames.

Table 5. Rules for symbolic transition relation ($\longrightarrow_s$)

$$(\text{INP}_s) \qquad \langle \sigma, \, \mathsf{a}(x).A \rangle_s \; \longrightarrow_s \; \langle \sigma \cdot \mathsf{a}\langle x \rangle, \, A \rangle_s$$

$$(\text{OUT}_s) \qquad \langle \sigma, \, \overline{\mathsf{a}}\langle \zeta \rangle.A \rangle_s \; \longrightarrow_s \; \langle \sigma\theta \cdot \overline{\mathsf{a}}\langle M \rangle, \, A\theta \rangle_s \quad \zeta \downarrow_\theta M$$

$$(\text{LET}_s) \; \langle \sigma, \, \mathsf{let}\, y = \zeta \, \mathsf{in}\, A \rangle_s \; \longrightarrow_s \; \langle \sigma\theta, \, A\theta[M/y] \rangle_s \quad \zeta \downarrow_\theta M$$

$$(\text{MATCH}_s) \qquad \langle \sigma, \, [\zeta = \eta]A \rangle_s \; \longrightarrow_s \; \langle \sigma\theta, \, A\theta \rangle_s \qquad \zeta \downarrow_{\theta_1} M, \, \eta\,\theta_1 \downarrow_{\theta_2} N,$$
$$\theta_3 = \mathrm{mgu}(M\theta_2, N),$$
$$N\theta_3 \in \mathcal{M}, \, \theta = \theta_1\theta_2\theta_3$$

$$(\text{PAR}_s) \qquad \frac{\langle \sigma, \, A \rangle_s \; \longrightarrow_s \; \langle \sigma', \, A' \rangle_s}{\langle \sigma, \, A \parallel B \rangle_s \; \longrightarrow_s \; \langle \sigma', \, A' \parallel B' \rangle_s}$$

plus symmetric version of (PAR_s). In the above rules it is assumed that:
(i) $x = \mathrm{new}_\mathcal{V}(V)$ – where V is the set of free variables
 in the source configuration,
(ii) $y = \mathrm{new}_\mathcal{V}(V \cup \{x\})$ and $\mathrm{msg}(\sigma)\theta \subseteq \mathcal{M}$,
(iii) in rule (PAR_s), $B' = B\theta$ where $\sigma' = \sigma\theta \cdot \alpha$ or $\sigma' = \sigma\theta$.

Regular frames It is convenient to extend the syntax of messages with a new class of variables to be used as placeholders for generic messages known to the environment. Formally, we consider a new set $\widehat{\mathcal{V}}$ of *marked* variables, in bijection with $\mathcal{V}$ via a mapping $\hat{\cdot}$; thus, variables $x, y, z, \ldots$ have marked counterparts $\hat{x}, \hat{y}, \hat{z}, \ldots$. Marked messages (resp., traces) are messages (resp., traces) that may also contain marked variables. Also, for $S \subseteq \mathcal{M}$, the set $\mathcal{H}(S)$ in Definition 2 is extended to include marked variables, i.e., we re-define $\mathcal{H}_\mathcal{F}^0(S)$ as follows:

$$\mathcal{H}_\mathcal{F}^0(S) \triangleq S \cup \mathcal{EN} \cup \widehat{\mathcal{V}}.$$

The deduction relation ($S \vdash M$) remains formally unchanged. Note that in case S and M do not contain marked variables, this definition conservatively extends Definition 2. In practice, marked variables are treated as constants which are known to the environment. The satisfaction relation is extended to marked symbolic traces according to this intuition. For any $\hat{x}$ and any trace σ, we denote by $\sigma \backslash \hat{x}$ the longest prefix of σ not containing $\hat{x}$.

Definition 8. *Let σ be a marked symbolic trace and ρ be a ground substitution. We say that ρ satisfies σ if $\sigma\rho$ is a trace and, for each $\hat{x} \in \mathrm{v}(\sigma)$, it holds that $(\sigma \backslash \hat{x})\rho \vdash \rho(\hat{x})$. We also say that $\sigma\rho$ is a solution of σ, and that σ is consistent.*

The terminology introduced above agrees with Definition 7 when σ does not contain marked variables. We give now the definition of solved form, that lifts the concept of trace to the non-ground case (note that this definition is formally the same as Definition 3).

Definition 9 (solved forms). *Let σ be a marked symbolic trace. We say σ is in* solved form (sf) *if for every σ_1, $\mathsf{a}\langle M\rangle$ and σ_2 s.t. $\sigma = \sigma_1 \cdot \mathsf{a}\langle M\rangle \cdot \sigma_2$ it holds that $\sigma_1 \vdash M$.*

Regular frames enjoy a "finite-basis" property. Basically, this property states the existence of a finite set containing the building blocks of all messages that the attacker can synthesise out of a given σ. This requirement is stated by Condition 1, below. Condition 2 is a technical requirement about substitutions.

Definition 10 (regular frames). *A symbolic frame $\mathcal{F}^s$ is* regular *if there exists a function $\mathbf{b} : Act^* \longrightarrow \mathcal{P}_f(\mathcal{M})$ such that, for each solved form σ of $\mathcal{F}^s$ and for all ρ that satisfy σ:*

1. $\sigma\rho \vdash M$ if and only if $M \in \mathcal{H}(\mathbf{b}(\sigma\rho))$;
2. $\mathbf{b}(\sigma\rho) \subseteq \mathbf{b}(\sigma)\rho$.

For each σ, $\mathbf{b}(\sigma)$ is said a basis *of σ.*

Example: Public Key Encryption (3) Let us consider the frame $\mathcal{F}^s_{pk}$ defined in the previous sections. A basis function for this frame is defined by

$$\mathbf{b}_{pk}(\sigma) \stackrel{\triangle}{=} \{ M \mid \sigma \vdash M \text{ and either: } M = u, \text{ or } M = u^+, \text{ or } M = u^-,$$
$$\text{for } u \in \mathcal{LN} \cup \mathcal{V}, \text{ or } M = \{\!|N|\!\}_{u^+} \text{ for some } N \text{ and } u \text{ s.t. } \sigma \not\vdash \langle N, u^+\rangle\}$$

Condition 1 and Condition 2 of Definition 10 are proven by induction on M and σ, respectively. In practice, for a given σ, the set $\mathbf{b}_{pk}(\sigma)$ can be effectively computed by an iterative procedure, which repeatedly applies destructors ($\mathsf{dec}^{\mathsf{pk}}_{(\cdot)}(\cdot)$ and $\pi_i(\cdot)$) to messages in σ, until some fixed point is reached. This procedure always terminates. We omit the details.

Refinement In the refinement procedure, input messages in a symbolic trace are tentatively unified to messages that can be synthesized from the basis. By iterating this procedure, one can check whether a given symbolic trace can eventually be instantiated to a trace in the concrete model. In particular, given any symbolic trace σ, and a basis for it, we can compute the set of the most general instances of σ that are in solved form, denoted by $\mathbf{SF}(\sigma)$.

Definition 11 (refinement and $\mathbf{SF}(\sigma)$). *We let* refinement, *written $\succ$, be the least binary relation over marked symbolic traces of a regular frame given by the following rules. In (REF_1), σ' is the longest prefix of σ that is in solved form and $\sigma = \sigma' \cdot \mathsf{a}\langle M\rangle \cdot \sigma''$, for some σ'. Assume $N, N' \notin \mathcal{V} \cup \widehat{\mathcal{V}}$.*

$$(\mathrm{REF}_1) \; \frac{M = C[N] \quad N' \in \mathbf{b}(\sigma') \quad \theta = \mathrm{mgu}(N, N')}{\sigma \; \succ \; \sigma\theta\theta_0}$$

where $\theta \neq \epsilon$, $\theta_0 \stackrel{\triangle}{=} \{ x/\hat{x} \mid \hat{x} \in \mathrm{v}(\sigma) \text{ and } |(\sigma\theta)\backslash\hat{x}| < |\sigma\backslash\hat{x}| \}$;

$$(\mathrm{REF}_2) \; \frac{x \in \mathrm{v}(M)}{\sigma \; \succ \; \sigma[\hat{x}/x]}$$

For any symbolic trace σ, we let $\mathbf{SF}(\sigma) \triangleq \{\, \sigma' \mid \sigma\, (\succ)^* \,\sigma' \text{ and } \sigma' \text{ is in sf} \,\}$.

Rule (REF_1) implements the basic step of refinement: the subcomponent N of M gets instantiated, via θ, to an element of $\mathbf{b}(\sigma')$. E.g., consider $\sigma = \overline{c}\langle\{\!\{a\}\!\}_{k+}\rangle \cdot \overline{c}\langle\{\!\{b\}\!\}_{k+}\rangle \cdot c\langle\{\!\{x\}\!\}_{k+}\rangle$: its possible refinements are $\sigma \,\succ\, \sigma[a/x]$ and $\sigma \,\succ\, \sigma[b/x]$, and the refined traces are in sf. By rule (REF_2) a variable can be marked: this amounts to constraining its possible values to be messages known by the environment. (For technical reasons, marked variables sometimes need to be 'unmarked' back to plain variables, and this is achieved in (REF_1) via the renaming θ_0.)

The proposition below states that solutions of a symbolic trace σ can be completely characterized in terms of $\mathbf{SF}(\sigma)$.

Proposition 1. *Let $\mathcal{F}$ be a regular frame, σ be a symbolic trace and s a trace. Then s is a solution of σ if and only if s is a solution of some $\sigma' \in \mathbf{SF}(\sigma)$.*

Note that, since solved forms always have a solution (just map each variable to any name in $\mathcal{EN}$), the above proposition implies that σ is consistent if and only if $\mathbf{SF}(\sigma) \neq \emptyset$.

The verification method The method $\mathbf{M}(\mathcal{C}, \alpha \hookleftarrow \beta)$ described in Table 6 can be used to verify if $\mathcal{C} \models \alpha \hookleftarrow \beta$ or not. If the property is not satisfied, the method computes a trace violating the property, that is, an attack on $\mathcal{C}$. To understand how the method works, it is better to consider the simple case $\alpha = \bot$, i.e. verification of $\mathcal{C} \models \bot \hookleftarrow \beta$. This means verifying that, in the concrete semantics, no instance of action β is ever executed starting from $\mathcal{C}$. By the correspondence between symbolic and concrete semantics (Theorem 1), this amounts to checking that for each σ symbolically generated by $\mathcal{C}$, no solution of σ contains an instance of β. To verify this, the method proceeds as follows: for each such σ, and for each action γ in σ, it is checked whether there is a mgu θ for γ and β. If, for each σ, such a θ does not exist, or if it exists but $\sigma\theta$ is not consistent (i.e. $\mathbf{SF}(\sigma\theta) = \emptyset$, by the considerations following Proposition 1), then the property is true, otherwise it is not. The correctness of the method in the general case is stated in the following theorem. Its proof relies on Theorem 1 and on Proposition 1, plus routine calculations on unifiers.

Table 6. The verification method

$\mathbf{M}(\mathcal{C}, \alpha \hookleftarrow \beta)$
1. compute $\mathbf{Mod}_{\mathcal{C}} = \{\sigma \mid \mathcal{C} \searrow_s \sigma\}$;
2. **foreach** $\sigma \in \mathbf{Mod}_{\mathcal{C}}$ **do**
        foreach action γ in σ **do**
             if $\exists\, \theta = \mathrm{mgu}(\beta, \gamma)$ **and** $\exists\, \sigma' = (\sigma\theta\theta') \in \mathbf{SF}(\sigma\theta)$ s.t.
                 $\alpha\theta\theta'$ does not occur prior to $\beta\theta\theta'$ in σ'
             then return(No, σ');
3. **return**(Yes);

Theorem 2 (correctness and completeness). *Let $\mathcal{F}^s$ be a regular frame, $\mathcal{C}$ be an initial configuration of $\mathcal{F}^s$ and α and β be actions such that $\mathrm{v}(\alpha) \subseteq \mathrm{v}(\beta)$ and $\mathrm{v}(\beta) \cap \mathrm{v}(\mathcal{C}) = \emptyset$.*

- *If $\mathbf{M}(\mathcal{C}, \alpha \hookleftarrow \beta)$ returns* Yes *then $\mathcal{C} \models \alpha \hookleftarrow \beta$.*
- *If $\mathbf{M}(\mathcal{C}, \alpha \hookleftarrow \beta)$ returns* (No, σ) *then $\mathcal{C} \not\models \alpha \hookleftarrow \beta$. In particular, for any injective ground substitution $\rho : \mathrm{v}(\sigma) \longrightarrow \mathcal{EN}$, we have that $\mathcal{C} \searrow (\sigma\rho)$ and that $(\sigma\rho) \not\models \alpha \hookleftarrow \beta$.*

In practice, rather than generating the whole set of symbolic traces at once (step 1) and then checking the property, it is more convenient to work 'on-the-fly' and comparing every last symbolic action γ taken by the configuration against action β of the property $\alpha \hookleftarrow \beta$; the refinement procedure $\mathbf{SF}(\cdot)$ is invoked only when β and γ are unifiable.

5   An Example: The Needham-Schroeder Protocol

In this section, we analyze the Needham-Schroeder protocol within our framework. First, we give an informal description of the protocol (see, e.g., [17], for further details). Here, A is the initiator and B is the responder.

$$
\begin{array}{lll}
1. & A \longrightarrow B : \{NA, A\}_{kB^+} & (NA \text{ fresh nonce}) \\
2. & B \longrightarrow A : \{NA, NB\}_{kA^+} & (NB \text{ fresh nonce}) \\
3. & A \longrightarrow B : \{NB\}_{kB^+} &
\end{array}
$$

As reported in [17], there is a well-known attack on this protocol, in case A may also run the protocol with a dishonest participant I. The following is a formalization of the protocol according to our method. For readability, we adopt some abbreviations; for instance, we write 'a$(\{\![M, N]\!\}_{k^+})$. A' for 'a(x). let $y = \mathrm{dec}^{\mathrm{pk}}_{k^-}(x)$ in (let $z = \pi_1(y)$ in (let $w = \pi_2(y)$ in $([z = M][w = N]A)))$.

$$
A \stackrel{\triangle}{=} \overline{\mathrm{a1}}\langle\{\![NA, \mathrm{id_A}]\!\}_{kB^+}\rangle. \,\mathrm{a2}(\{\![NA, xNB]\!\}_{kA^+}). \,\overline{\mathrm{a3}}\langle\{\![xNB]\!\}_{kB^+}\rangle. \,\mathbf{0}
$$
$$
\| \quad \overline{\mathrm{a'1}}\langle\{\![N'A, \mathrm{id_A}]\!\}_{kI^+}\rangle. \,\mathrm{a'2}(\{\![N'A, xNI]\!\}_{kA^+}). \,\overline{\mathrm{a'3}}\langle\{\![xNI]\!\}_{kI^+}\rangle. \,\mathbf{0}
$$

$$
B \stackrel{\triangle}{=} \mathrm{b1}(\{\![yNA, \mathrm{id_A}]\!\}_{kB^+}). \,\overline{\mathrm{b2}}\langle\{\![yNA, NB]\!\}_{kA^+}\rangle. \,\mathrm{b3}(\{\![NB]\!\}_{kB^+}). \,\mathbf{0}
$$

$$
NS \stackrel{\triangle}{=} \langle\overline{\mathrm{disclose}}\langle kI, kA^+, kB^+, \mathrm{id_A}, \mathrm{id_B}, \mathrm{id_I}\rangle, \,(A \| B)\rangle
$$

$$
AuthAtoB \quad \stackrel{\triangle}{=} \quad \overline{\mathrm{a3}}\langle\{\![z]\!\}_{k^+}\rangle \hookleftarrow \mathrm{b3}\langle\{\![z]\!\}_{k^+}\rangle
$$

Our verification method finds a symbolic trace that refines to the following concrete trace, which violates the property *AuthAtoB*:

$$
\overline{\mathrm{disclose}}\langle kI, kA^+, kB^+, \mathrm{id_A}, \mathrm{id_B}, \mathrm{id_I}\rangle \cdot \overline{\mathrm{a'1}}\langle\{\![N'A, A]\!\}_{kI^+}\rangle \cdot \mathrm{b1}\langle\{\![N'A, A]\!\}_{kB^+}\rangle \cdot
$$
$$
\overline{\mathrm{b2}}\langle\{\![N'A, NB]\!\}_{kA^+}\rangle \cdot \mathrm{a'2}\langle\{\![N'A, NB]\!\}_{kA^+}\rangle \cdot \overline{\mathrm{a'3}}\langle\{\![NB]\!\}_{kI^+}\rangle \cdot \mathrm{b3}\langle\{\![NB]\!\}_{kB^+}\rangle.
$$

When fed with the above example, our prototype STA detects this attack in a fraction of second.

6   Other Cryptographic Primitives

We consider extending the symbolic frame $\mathcal{F}_{pk}^s$, that served as a running example in the previous sections, to deal with some of the most common cryptographic operations.

The set Σ is enriched by means of appropriate operators for shared-key encryption $\{\cdot\}_{(\cdot)}$ and decryption $\mathsf{dec}_{(\cdot)}^{\mathsf{sk}}(\cdot)$, digital signing $[\{\cdot\}]_{(\cdot)}$ and verifying $\mathsf{dec}_{(\cdot)}^{\mathsf{ds}}(\cdot)$ and hashing $H(\cdot)$. The syntax of messages is extended via the following additional clauses:

$$M, N ::= \quad \ldots \qquad \text{as in Table 2}$$
$$\mid \ \{M\}_u \ \mid \ [\{M\}]_{u^-} \ \mid \ H(M).$$

The symbolic and concrete evaluations are given in terms of an auxiliary relation $\rightsquigarrow$, defined as expected. In particular, hashing has no rules, digital signature rules are just the same as for public key, but the roles of u^+ and u^- are swapped. For shared key, the concrete and symbolic rules are given below:

$$\mathsf{dec}_u^{\mathsf{sk}}(\{M\}_u) \ \rightsquigarrow \ M \qquad \mathsf{dec}_v^{\mathsf{sk}}(\{M\}_u) \ \overset{\theta}{\rightsquigarrow}_s \ M\theta \quad \text{where } \theta = \mathrm{mgu}(u,v)\,.$$

A finite basis for this frame can be given by including into the basis given for public key also all messages of the form $\{M\}_u$ (resp. $[\{M\}]_{u^-}$, $H(M)$) s.t. $\sigma \not\vdash u$ (resp. $\sigma \not\vdash \langle M, u^- \rangle$, $\sigma \not\vdash M$).

7   Conclusions

We have proposed a framework for the analysis of security protocols and provided some sufficient conditions under which verification can be performed via a symbolic method. In contrast to finite-state model checking, our method can analyze the whole infinite state space generated by a limited number of participants. The method is efficient in practice, because the symbolic model is compact, and the refinement procedure at its heart is only invoked on demand and on single symbolic traces. However, claims on efficiency should generally be taken with some care, given that the protocol analysis problem is NP-hard even under very mild hypotheses (see e.g. [25]).

Early work on symbolic analysis is due to Huima. In [16], the execution of a protocol generates a set of equational constraints. Only an informal description is provided of the kind of equational rewriting needed to solve these constraints. More recent approaches based on symbolic analysis are exploited in [5,14]. The paper [5] extends the symbolic reachability analysis of [4] to hashing functions and public key cryptography and establishes some results on the complexity of the problem. Unlike our approach, symbolic execution and consistency check are not kept separate, and this may have a relevant impact on the size of the computed symbolic model. Another point worth noting is that, in [5], a brute-force method is needed to resolve variables in key position: such variables have to be instantiated to every possible name used by the participants; this fact may lead to state explosion, too. In [14], a procedure is provided to analyze the knowledge of the environment, based on a symbolic semantics akin to [7]. The approach applies to protocols with shared-key encryption and arbitrary messages as keys, but, like ours, it is proven complete only for atomic keys. Also, the method suffers from the same problem as [5] concerning brute-force instantiation.

Other recent developments of the symbolic approach are presented in [11] and [20]. Both of them do not rely on unification to build the symbolic model. The decision technique in [11] is based on a reduction to a set constraint problem which is in turn reduced to an automata-theoretic problem. Completeness is proven by assuming rather severe restrictions on protocol syntax. The technique in [20] focuses on reachability properties and is based on constraint solving. The symbolic reduction and the knowledge analysis are separated and the latter is performed by a procedure for solving a system of constraints.

In the future, we plan to focus on the verification of protocols that also exploit low-level cryptographic operations, such as modular exponentiation. As an example, we are confident that Diffie-Hellman key exchange can be smoothly set within our framework.

Acknowledgements

We thank the anonymous referees for helpful comments.

References

1. M. Abadi, B. Blanchet. Analyzing Security Protocols with Secrecy Types and Logic Programs. In *Conf. Rec. of POPL'02*, 2002. 484
2. M. Abadi, C. Fournet. Mobile Values, New Names, and Secure Communication. In *Conf. Rec. of POPL'01*, 2001. 484
3. M. Abadi, A. D. Gordon. A calculus for cryptographic protocols: The spi calculus. *Information and Computation*, 148(1):1-70, 1999. 484, 486
4. R. M. Amadio, S. Lugiez. On the reachability problem in cryptographic protocols. In *Proc. of Concur'00*, LNCS 1877, 2000. Full version: RR 3915, INRIA Sophia Antipolis. 484, 496
5. R. M. Amadio, S. Lugiez, V. Vanackère. On the symbolic reduction of processes with cryptographic functions. RR 4147, INRIA Sophia Antipolis, March 2001. 484, 496, 497
6. R. Amadio, S. Prasad. The game of the name in cryptographic tables. In *Proc. of Asian'00*, LNCS 1742, Springer-Verlag, 2000. RR 3733 INRIA Sophia Antipolis. 489
7. M. Boreale. Symbolic Trace Analysis of Cryptographic Protocols. In *Proc. of ICALP'01*, LNCS 2076, Springer-Verlag, 2001. 484, 485, 497
8. M. Boreale, M. Buscemi. Experimenting with STA, a Tool for Automatic Analysis of Security Protocols. In *Proc. of SAC'02*, ACM Press, 2002. 484

9. M. Boreale, R. De Nicola, R. Pugliese. Proof Techniques for Cryptographic Processes. In *Proc. of LICS'99*, IEEE Computer Society Press, 1999. Full version to appear in *SIAM Journal on Computing*.

10. E. M. Clarke, S. Jha, W. Marrero. Using State Space Exploration and a Natural Deduction Style Message Derivation Engine to Verify Security Protocols. In *Proc. of IFIP PROCOMET*, 1998.

11. H. Comon, V. Cortier, J. Mitchell. Tree automata with one memory, set constraints and ping-pong protocols. In *Proc. of ICALP'01*, LNCS 2076, Springer-Verlag, 2001. 484, 497

12. D. Dolev, A. Yao. On the security of public-key protocols. *IEEE Transactions on Information Theory*, 2(29):198-208, 1983. 483

13. N. Durgin, P. Lincoln, J. Mitchell, A. Scedrov. Undecidability of bounded security protocols. In *Proc. of Workshop on Formal Methods and Security Protocols*, 1999. 484

14. M. P. Fiore and M. Abadi. Computing Symbolic Models for Verifying Cryptographic Protocols. In *Proc. of 14th Computer Security Foundations Workshop*, IEEE Computer Society Press, 2001. 496, 497

15. J. Heather, G. Lowe, and S. Schneider. How to prevent type flaw attacks on security protocols. In *Proc. of 13th Computer Security Foundations Workshop*, IEEE Computer Society Press, 2000. 484

16. A. Huima. Efficient infinite-state analysis of security protocols. In *Proc. of Workshop on Formal Methods and Security Protocols*, Trento, 1999. 496

17. G. Lowe. Breaking and Fixing the Needham-Schroeder Public-Key Protocol Using FDR. In *Proc. of TACAS'96*, LNCS 1055, Springer-Verlag, 1996. 483, 495

18. G. Lowe. A Hierarchy of Authentication Specifications. In *Proc. of 10th IEEE Computer Security Foundations Workshop*, IEEE Computer Society Press, 1997. 489

19. W. Marrero, E. M. Clarke, S. Jha. Model checking for security protocols. Technical Report TR-CMU-CS-97-139, Carnegie Mellon University, 1997.

20. J. Millen, V. Shmatikov. Constraint solving for bounded-process cryptographic protocol analysis. In *Proc. of 8th ACM Conference on Computer and Communication Security*, ACM Press, 2001. 497

21. J. C. Mitchell, M. Mitchell, U Stern. Automated Analysis of Cryptographic Protocols Using Murφ. In *Proc. of Symp. Security and Privacy*, IEEE Computer Society Press, 1997. 483

22. L. C. Paulson. The inductive approach to verifying cryptographic protocols. *Journal of Computer Security*, 6:85–128, 1998.

23. A. W. Roscoe. Modelling and verifying key-exchange using CSP and FDR. In *Proc. of 8th Computer Security Foundations Workshop*, IEEE Computer Society Press, 1995. 483

24. A. W. Roscoe. Proving security protocols with model checkers by data independent techniques. In *Proc. of 11th Computer Security Foundations Workshop*, IEEE Computer Society Press, 1998.

25. M. Rusinowitch, M Turuani. Protocol Insecurity with Finite Number of Sessions in NP-Complete. In *Proc. of 14th Computer Security Foundations Workshop*, IEEE Computer Society Press, 2001. 496

26. S. Schneider. Verifying Authentication Protocols in CSP. *IEEE Transactions on Software Engineering*, 24(8):743-758, 1998. 483

27. STA: a tool for trace analysis of cryptographic protocols. ML object code and examples, 2001. Available at http://www.dsi.unifi.it/~boreale/tool.html. 484

On Name Generation and Set-Based Analysis
in the Dolev-Yao Model

Roberto M. Amadio[1] and Witold Charatonik[2,3]

[1] Laboratoire d'Informatique Fondamentale, Marseille
amadio@cmi.univ-mrs.fr
[2] Max-Planck-Institut für Informatik, Saarbrücken
[3] Uniwersytet Wrocławski, Wrocław
witold@mpi-sb.mpg.de

Abstract. We study the control reachability problem in the Dolev-Yao model of cryptographic protocols when principals are represented by tail recursive processes with generated names. We propose a conservative approximation of the problem by reduction to a non-standard *collapsed* operational semantics and we introduce checkable syntactic conditions entailing the equivalence of the standard and the collapsed semantics. Then we introduce a conservative and decidable *set-based* analysis of the collapsed operational semantics and we characterize a situation where the analysis is exact.

Keywords: cryptographic protocols, name generation, verification, set constraints.

1 Introduction

We study the control reachability problem for cryptographic protocols in the Dolev-Yao model [DY83] which is nowadays a widely used model abstracting the behaviour of cryptographic functions.

Most cryptographic protocols are programs of finite length without loops and then the control reachability problem can be solved in NPTIME [ALV01, RT01]. However, these finite programs usually can be executed any number of times in different sessions. In every session a participant may generate fresh *names* representing, *e.g.*, nonces or keys. A number of attacks are then possible relying on messages exchanged in previous or parallel sessions. Unfortunately, introducing recursive behaviours in cryptographic protocols leads quickly to an undecidable verification problem.

It has been observed by Durgin *et al.* [DLMS99] that name generation leads to undecidability of control reachability even when the height of the messages considered is *bounded*. When name generation is *not* allowed then the control reachability problem is still undecidable in general, and decidable in certain particular cases allowing a limited use of the pairing construct (also known as *ping-pong* protocols; see [DEK82]). To complete this picture, we show in [AC02] that

L. Brim et al. (Eds.): CONCUR 2002, LNCS 2421, pp. 499–514, 2002.
© Springer-Verlag Berlin Heidelberg 2002

the control reachability problem is undecidable *without pairs* and *with bounded height* messages when name generation is allowed.

It then appears that in order to obtain a decidable class of protocols we have to further restrict the use of name generation. The approach we explore in this paper is to bound the number of *parallel* sessions generating new names. This entails that there is a bound on the number of *fresh* names 'used' at any time by the principals.

Technically, we will concentrate on *tail-recursive* processes including an operation of *name generation*. In the standard operational semantics, whenever we execute a name generation instruction νc, we associate to c a fresh constant. Thus, during the execution the name c may get assigned constants from a countable set $C_0, C_1, C_2, \ldots$ In this paper, we introduce a non-standard *collapsed* operational semantics for name generation whose intuition is as follows: when a principal starts a new *session* a name generated in the session gets assigned a *new* constant while names generated in previous sessions are collapsed to an *old* constant. Thus a name generator νc operates over the finite set of constants $\{C^{old}, C^{new}\}$.

In our formal model, looping back models starting a new session. Then the collapsed semantics is a partial formalization of the idea that names generated in previous sessions can be confused. We note that the logical *length* of a session can be suitably adapted by unfolding the program. [1] As long as the behaviour of principals does *not* depend on name inequality, the collapsed semantics 'simulates' the standard one, *i.e.*, reachability of a control point in the standard semantics implies reachability of the same control point in the concrete one. Moreover, we introduce checkable syntactic conditions that guarantee the equivalence of the standard and the collapsed semantics (section 2).

Next, we provide a set-based analysis of the collapsed semantics. From an algorithmic point of view, the fact that the collapsed semantics operates over a *finite* signature is exploited to associate to a system of processes Eq a system of set constraints Φ_{Eq} such that the reachability of a control state in Eq implies the nonemptiness of a distinguished variable in the least solution of Φ_{Eq}. It turns out that the set constraints generated are a variant of those studied in [CP97, TDT00] so that the nonemptiness problem can be solved by a suitable adaptation of standard techniques (section 3). In particular, we give a general construction that handles the renaming operators introduced by the collapsed semantics and we point out a 'linear' subclass of definite set constraints that can be solved in PTIME.

In section 4, we characterize a situation –without name generation– where the set based analysis is exact and obtain a new decidable class of cryptographic protocols with a complexity ranging between simple and double exponential time. With name generation, the set-based analysis is conservative but not necessarily exact. In practice, it is difficult to find examples where the loss of precision is

---

[1] Clearly, if we adopted *iteration* rather than tail recursion, then it would be more difficult to design a sensible collapsed semantics; as shown by Stoller [Sto99] an attack may require exponentially many parallel sessions.

essential; an artificial example is given in section 4. A long version of this paper is available as a research report [AC02]: it includes all the proofs that have to be omitted here for lack of space and it also illustrates how our model can be used to formalize the standard property of *secrecy* as well as a more elusive property of *freshness*.

Related work We restrict our attention to authors who considered fully automatic methods to prove correctness of recursive cryptographic protocols in the Dolev-Yao model.

Monniaux [Mon99] introduces tree automata (which are related to set-constraints) to represent the knowledge of the adversary. In his study, he restricts his attention to protocols without recursion, but the approach has been generalized to handle recursion by the following authors. He already notices the lack of precision of the set based analysis pointed out in example 2.

At about the same time, Weidenbach [Wei99] applies the SPASS theorem prover to the analysis of a protocol by Neuman and Stubblebine. He reduces the verification problem to a proof search in monadic Horn clauses (again related to set-constraints). There is no general guarantee of termination for his method but some decidable subclasses are pointed out. Name generation is modelled by skolemisation –looking at the name generator as an existential– but no result is reported on the soundness or completeness of this modelling with respect to a standard operational semantics of name generation.

Later, Genet and Klay [GK00] and Goubault [Gou00] also rely on tree automata to produce a conservative approximation of cryptographic protocols. Genet and Klay consider a rather rough approximation where every action can be performed at any time and point out in their conclusion the need for a refined analysis of the control (a programme we carry on to some extent here). Goubault proposes to approximate a name generator by a superset of all values that it can generate in a run (which is quite different from the collapsed semantics studied here). In these two papers, no definite analysis is given of the complexity and the precision of the approximation schema.

Finally, Comon et al. [CCM01] introduce a special class of tree automata *with memory* that allows to decide in DEXPTIME secrecy properties for a class of cryptographic protocols strictly containing the ping-pong protocols. This work does not cover the notion of name generation and the class of protocols considered is *incomparable* with the one considered in theorem 4; their class goes beyond regular tree languages but, because of the so called *basicness condition*, only particular input filters are admitted.

2   Model

We begin by recalling the basic assumptions in the Dolev-Yao model (section 2.1). Then we introduce a particular family of tail recursive processes, their operational semantics, and the related control reachability problem (section 2.2). We propose a certain number of syntactic conditions and exhibit related fragments of the model where the control reachability problem is still undecidable (section 2.3). Finally, we define a collapsed semantics simulating the standard one and determine a checkable condition where the collapsed semantics is precise (section 2.4).

2.1 The Dolev-Yao Model

We recall that in the Dolev-Yao model communications are mediated by an adversary that can analyse the messages exchanged and synthesize new ones. To represent the set of messages we assume an infinite set of constants $\mathcal{N}$ and consider terms over the (infinite) signature $\Sigma = \mathcal{N} \cup \{E^2, \langle \_, \_ \rangle^2\}$. Thus we have two binary constructors: E for encryption and $\langle \_, \_ \rangle$ for pairing.

We use the following standard notation: $x, y, \ldots$ for (term) variables; V for the set of variables; $T_\Sigma(V)$ for the collection of finite terms over $\Sigma \cup V$; $t, t', \ldots$ for terms in $T_\Sigma(V)$; $\boldsymbol{t}$ for vectors of terms; $[t/x]$ for the substitution of t for x. We denote with $Var(t)$ the variables occurring in the term t.

The set of *messages* $\mathcal{M}$ is defined as the least set that contains $\mathcal{N}$ and such that: (1) if $t \in \mathcal{M}$ and $t' \in \mathcal{N}$ then $E(t, t') \in \mathcal{M}$ and (2), if $t, t' \in \mathcal{M}$ then $\langle t, t' \rangle \in \mathcal{M}$.

We abbreviate a message $E(\cdots E(t, D_n), \ldots, D_1)$ with $D_1 \cdots D_n t$ thus regarding nested encryptions as *words*. The functions S for *synthesis* and A for *analysis* are closure operators over the power set of messages $\mathcal{M}$ defined as follows:

- $S(T)$ is the least set that contains T and such that: (1) if $t_1, t_2 \in S(T)$ then $\langle t_1, t_2 \rangle \in S(T)$ and (2) if $t_1 \in S(T), t_2 \in T \cap \mathcal{N}$ then $E(t_1, t_2) \in S(T)$.
- $A(T)$ is the least set that contains T and such that: (1) if $\langle t_1, t_2 \rangle \in A(T)$ then $t_i \in A(T)$, $i = 1, 2$ and (2) if $E(t_1, t_2) \in A(T)$, $t_2 \in A(T) \cap \mathcal{N}$ then $t_1 \in A(T)$.

For the sake of simplicity, in this paper we restrict our attention to *symmetric* encryption where encryption and decryption keys coincide and moreover we make the rather standard assumption that keys are atomic names, *i.e.*, a pair or an encrypted message cannot be used as a key. However, our results are not strictly dependent on these hypotheses and we expect that they can been adapted to, *e.g.*, *public* keys and *complex* symmetric keys.

2.2 Tail-Recursive Processes

In a message, it is useful to distinguish between *data* and *key* positions.

Definition 1. *Let u, v be variables or constants and let $t \in T_\Sigma(V)$ be a term. We define two predicates $Occ_{Data}(u, t)$ and $Occ_{Key}(u, t)$ that are satisfied if u occurs in t in* Data *or* Key *position, respectively:*

> (1) $Occ_{Data}(u, u)$,
> (2) $Occ_{Data}(u, \langle t_1, t_2 \rangle)$ *if* $Occ_{Data}(u, t_i)$, $i = 1$ *or* $i = 2$,
> (3) $Occ_{Data}(u, E(t, v))$ *if* $Occ_{Data}(u, t)$.
> (4) $Occ_{Key}(u, \langle t_1, t_2 \rangle)$ *if* $Occ_{Key}(u, t_i)$, $i = 1$ *or* $i = 2$,
> (5) $Occ_{Key}(u, E(t, v))$ *if* $u = v$ *or* $Occ_{Key}(u, t)$.

Remark 1. Note that u may occur in t without occurring in either data or key position. This may happen only when no ground instance of t can produce a message, *i.e.*, when t contains a subterm $E(t_1, t_2)$ and t_2 is neither a constant nor a variable. Note also that we cannot syntactically outlaw such terms since they may be created from correct messages by communication, *e.g.*, $E(t_1, t_2)$ may be created from $E(t_1, x)$ by a communication that assigns the term t_2 to the variable x.

We fix a finite system Eq of k equations:

$$A_i = \nu c_i \, Q_i \text{ where } Q_i \equiv ?t_1^i.!s_1^i \dots ?t_{l_i}^i.!s_{l_i}^i.A_i' \text{ for } i = 1, \dots, k, \; l_i \geq 1 \qquad (1)$$

with distinct process identifiers A_i, $i = 1, \dots, k$ and where A_i' is either A_i or a special state err. The following definitions of configuration and reduction will refer to *this* system. The intuitive semantics is as follows: A_i generates a vector of fresh names c_i (this models the generation of fresh nonces or keys), it engages in an alternating sequence of input-output where it receives messages of the shape t_j^i and emits messages of the shape s_j^i, and finally either it loops back or it reaches an erroneous state. Example 1 shows how to translate a usual protocol description into such a system of equations. In general, we would introduce one equation for each participant and each role it plays in a protocol. If an arbitrary number of participants is allowed then a preliminary phase of abstraction is needed.

We will say that the terms t_j^i are *filters* and define the *filter variables* as

$$FVar(t_j^i) = Var(t_j^i) \backslash \bigcup_{h=1,\dots,j-1} Var(t_h^i) \, .$$

Similarly, the *key variables* are defined by $KVar(s_j^i) = \{z \in Var(s_j^i) \mid Occ_{Key}(z, s_j^i)\}$.

We suppose that there is always a ground instance of the terms t_j^i, s_j^i that can produce a message. If such a ground instance does not exist, then the thread will be blocked at the occurrence of the term, and an equivalent system is obtained by inserting at a corresponding position a filter which can be never satisfied.

The *filters* t_j^i must correspond to a combination of projections and decryptions. For this purpose, we require that filter variables occur in data position. Namely, if $x \in FVar(t_j^i)$ then x must occur in t_j^i in data position (cf. definition 1). This condition forbids, *e.g.*, to set $t_1^i = E(x, y)$, which in the operational semantics presented below would allow a principal to decrypt an encrypted message without knowing the key.

Finally, we require that the variables in an output are contained in the variables of the preceding input, *i.e.*, $Var(s_j^i) \subseteq FVar(t_j^i)$. We will see next that there is no loss of generality in this assumption.

We now turn to the formal operational semantics. For every vector of generated names νc_i, $i = 1, \dots, k$ in Eq, we reserve the vectors of distinct constants:

$$C_i^{old}, \, C_i^{new}, \, C_i^j, j = 0, 1, 2, \dots$$

We assume that no confusion arises with constants appearing in Eq or with constants related to another thread. We will see that the standard semantics of name generation relies only on the constants $C_i^j, j = 0, 1, 2, \ldots$ while the collapsed semantics presented in section 2.4 will rely on the constants C_i^{old}, C_i^{new}. We say that a thread P *relates to* the equation $A_i = \nu c_i \, Q_i$ if P is either A_i or an instance of $?t_j^i.!s_j^i \ldots ?t_{l_i}^i.!s_{l_i}^i.A_i', j \geq 1$.

Definition 2 (standard configuration). *A standard configuration is a pair* (R, T) *where:*

• $R \equiv (P_1, n_1) \mid \cdots \mid (P_k, n_k)$ *is the parallel composition of k pairs composed of a thread P_i relating to the ith equation and a counter n_i.*

• T *is a finite set of messages representing the knowledge of the adversary, and such that the constants $C_i^{old}, C_i^{new}, C_i^j$ for $i = 1, \ldots, k$ and $j > n_i$ do not occur in (R, T).*

We assume that parallel composition is associative and commutative and feel free to write R as $(P_i, n_i) \mid R'$, where R' might be empty.

Definition 3 (standard reduction). *We define a reduction relation on standard configurations as follows:*

$$
\begin{array}{llll}
\text{(unfold)} & ((A_i, n_i) \mid R, T) & \rightarrow \ ((\sigma_i^{n_i+1} Q_i, n_i + 1) \mid R, T), & (1) \\
\text{(i/o)} & ((?t.!s.P, n_i) \mid R, T) & \rightarrow \ ((\theta P, n_i) \mid R, T \cup \{\theta s\}), & (2) \\
\text{where:} & (1) \ \sigma_i^{n_i+1} = [C_i^{n_i+1}/c_i], & (2) \ \theta t \in S(A(T)) \text{ and } \theta s \in \mathcal{M} \ .
\end{array}
$$

The first rule (unfold) expands the recursive definition, instantiates the generated names c_i with fresh constants, and increments the related counter n_i. The second rule (i/o) inputs from the adversary a message θt matching a filter and outputs a message θs. Note that if θs is *not* a message then the reduction cannot take place. We can now state the control reachability problem.

Definition 4. *We fix $R_0 \equiv (A_1, 0) \mid \cdots \mid (A_k, 0)$ as initial control, $T_0 \neq \emptyset$ as initial knowledge of the adversary, and write $(R_0, T_0) \xrightarrow{*} \text{err}$ if $(R_0, T_0) \xrightarrow{*} ((\text{err}, n) \mid R', T')$ for some n, R', T'. The control reachability problem amounts to determine whether $(R_0, T) \xrightarrow{*} \text{err}$.*

2.3   Undecidable Fragments

It is convenient to introduce some *syntactic transformations* that do not affect the control reachability problem. Consider a thread $A = \nu c \, ?t_1.!s_1 \ldots ?t_n.!s_n.A_i'$ and suppose s_i is the first output that depends on filter variables of $t_1, \ldots, t_{i-1}$, say $x_1, \ldots, x_{i-1}$. If $d \equiv d_1, \ldots, d_j$ and $x \equiv x_1, \ldots, x_j$ then $\langle d \cdot x \rangle$ stands for $\langle d_1 x_1, \ldots, d_j x_j \rangle \equiv \langle E(x_1, d_1), \ldots, E(x_j, d_j) \rangle$. With this convention, we can rewrite the thread as

$$
\begin{aligned}
A = \ & \nu c \, \nu d_1, \ldots, d_{i-1} \, ?t_1.!\langle s_1, \langle d_1 \cdot x_1 \rangle \rangle \ldots. \\
& ?t_{i-1}.!\langle s_{i-1}, \langle d_{i-1} \cdot x_{i-1} \rangle \rangle. \\
& ?\langle t_i, \langle d_1 \cdot y_1 \rangle, \ldots, \langle d_{i-1} \cdot y_{i-1} \rangle \rangle!\, [y_1, \ldots, y_{i-1}/x_1, \ldots, x_{i-1}] s_i \ldots. \\
& ?t_n.!s_n.A_i'
\end{aligned}
$$

where d_j, y_j are fresh. In other terms, we store under the fresh keys d_j the parameters x_j and retrieve them again in the filter just preceding the output s_i. By iterating this transformation, we obtain an equivalent thread satisfying the condition $Var(s_j) \subseteq FVar(t_j)$.

Repeated outputs $?t.!s_1.!s_2$ can be encoded as $?t.!s_1.?x.!s_2$ with x fresh. Repeated inputs $?t_1.?t_2.!s$ can be encoded as $?t_1.!t_0.?t_2.!s$ where t_0 is a term in the initial knowledge. We will also write $?t_1.!s_1 \ldots ?t_n.!s_n.0$ to indicate that the thread stops at point 0. This can be encoded by inserting at the place of 0 a filter that can never be passed. Finally, we may generate names during a session as in $\ldots ?t.!s.\nu c\,?t'.!s'.\ldots$ which is equivalent to generate them at the very beginning.

Next we introduce four syntactic conditions on the system Eq. We anticipate that the syntactic transformations we have presented above can be performed while satisfying these conditions.

Definition 5 (variable dependency). *We say that the variables x and y are dependent in a term t if for some C there exists a subterm $E(t', C)$ of t with two distinct occurrences of x and y (x depends on itself if it occurs twice in t'). Otherwise, we say that x and y are independent in t.*

Definition 6 (syntactic conditions). *The system Eq satisfies the:*

(1) LINEARITY *condition if the filters t_j^i are linear, i.e., each variable in $FVar(t_j^i)$ occurs exactly once in t_j^i.*

(2) LOCALITY *condition if the filters t_j^i do not depend on previous filter variables, i.e., $Var(t_j^i) = FVar(t_j^i)$.*

(3) INDEPENDENCE *condition if for every i/o action $?t.!s$, assuming $\eta : KVar(s) \to \mathcal{N}$ is any assignment and $\langle s_1, \ldots, s_m \rangle \equiv \eta s$ the following holds for $l = 1, \ldots, m$: either (i) $\sharp Var(s_l) \leq 1$, or (ii) s_l is a linear term and the variables $Var(s_l)$ are independent in ηt.*

(4) DATA OR KEY *condition if every generated name occurs in the related thread either in data or key position (but not both, cf. definition 1), and moreover, if at least one generated name occurs in data position then every variable occurring in a filter can only occur in the related thread in data position.*[2]

Conditions (1–3) are partially motivated by the following undecidability result whose proof is based on a rather direct encoding of 2-counter machines. Conditions (1–3) will also play a role in the complexity and precision of the set-based analysis. Moreover, conditions (1–2) together with condition (4) will be used in section 2.4 to characterize the precision of the collapsed semantics.

---

[2] The restriction that filter variables occur only in data position is needed to avoid that a principal uses generated nonces as keys. The condition could be omitted if we included in the model a *typing* mechanism to distinguish nonces from keys.

Example 1. An example of cryptographic protocol satisfying all the four syntactic conditions in definition 6 is the Andrew Secure RPC Protocol from [CJ97]

$$
\begin{aligned}
&(1)\ A \to B : A, E(Na, Kab)\\
&(2)\ B \to A : E(\langle Na + 1, Nb\rangle, Kab)\\
&(3)\ A \to B : E(Nb + 1, Kab)\\
&(4)\ B \to A : E(\langle K'ab, N'b\rangle, Kab)
\end{aligned}
$$

We do not have addition in our syntax, but we take $x + 1$ as an abbreviation for $\langle x, 1\rangle$ where 1 is a constant symbol. Thus, we can model the protocol with the following two equations (note that the only variables here are x, y, z and w):

$$
\begin{array}{ll}
A_1 = \nu n_a & A_2 = \nu n_b, k'_{ab}, n'_b\\
(1)\quad !\langle A, E(n_a, K_{ab})\rangle. & (1)\quad ?\langle A, E(x, K_{ab})\rangle.\\
(2)\quad ?E(\langle n_a + 1, y\rangle, K_{ab}). & (2)\quad !E(\langle x + 1, n_b\rangle, K_{ab})).\\
(3)\quad !E(y + 1, K_{ab}). & (3)\quad ?E(n_b + 1, K_{ab}).\\
(4)\quad ?E(\langle z, w\rangle, K_{ab}).A_1 & (4)\quad !E(\langle k'_{ab}, n'_b\rangle, K_{ab}).A_2
\end{array}
$$

Other examples include a series of Woo and Lam Π protocols in [CJ97, section 6.3.10].

Theorem 1 (undecidability). *There are encodings of 2-counter machines showing that violation of one of the conditions* LINEARITY, LOCALITY, INDEPENDENCE *is sufficient for the undecidability of the control reachability problem.*

Remark 2. If we assume the DATA OR KEY condition then theorem 1 still holds. Moreover, if we violate the INDEPENDENCE condition then undecidability does not rely on name generation.

2.4　Collapsed Semantics

We introduce the notion of collapsed configuration and reduction mimicking definitions 2 and 3.

Definition 7 (collapsed configuration). *A* collapsed configuration *is a pair* (R, T) *where:*

- R *is the parallel composition of* k *threads* $P_1 \mid \cdots \mid P_k$ *with* P_i *relating to the* i^{th} *equation,*

- T *is a finite set of messages representing the knowledge of the adversary,*

and such that the constants C_i^j *for* $i = 1, \ldots, k$ *do not occur in* (R, T).

Definition 8 (collapsed reduction). *We define a reduction relation on collapsed configurations as follows:*

$$
\begin{aligned}
&\text{(unfold)}\ (A_i \mid R, T)\ \to\ (\sigma_i^{new} Q_i \mid \sigma_i^{old} R, \sigma_i^{old} T),\\
&\qquad\quad if\ \sigma_i^{new} = [C_i^{new}/c_i]\ and\ \sigma_i^{old} = [C_i^{old}/C_i^{new}]\\
&\text{(i/o)}\quad (?t.!s.P \mid R, T)\ \to\ (\theta P \mid R, T \cup \{\theta s\}),\quad if\ \theta t \in S(A(T))\ and\ \theta s \in \mathcal{M}\ .
\end{aligned}
$$

The notion of control reachability for collapsed configurations is an immediate adaptation of definition 4. Without name generation the collapsed semantics coincides with the standard semantics and therefore it follows from the remark 2 that the control reachability problem for the collapsed semantics is also undecidable in general.

We want to relate the control reachability problem for standard and collapsed configurations. Given any standard configuration (R, T) where $R \equiv (P_1, n_1) \mid \cdots \mid (P_k, n_k)$ we define a substitution τ_R as follows:

$$\tau_R(C_i^j) = \begin{cases} C_i^{new} & \text{if } j = n_i \\ C_i^{old} & \text{if } j < n_i . \end{cases}$$

We extend the definition of τ_R to standard configurations as follows:

$$\tau_R(R, T) = (\tau_R P_1 \mid \cdots \mid \tau_R P_k, \tau_R T) .$$

We can prove the following proposition by case analysis on the reduction rules.

Proposition 1 (simulation). *Let (R, T) be a standard configuration.*
(1) *If $(R, T) \to (R_1, T_1)$ then $\tau_R(R, T) \to \tau_{R_1}(R_1, T_1)$.*
(2) *If $((A_1, 0) \mid \cdots \mid (A_k, 0), T_0) \xrightarrow{*} \text{err}$ then $(A_1 \mid \cdots \mid A_k, T_0) \xrightarrow{*} \text{err}$.*

Next, we analyse the impact of the syntactic conditions on the precision of the collapsed semantics.

Proposition 2. *There are examples showing that the violation of one of the conditions* LINEARITY, LOCALITY, DATA OR KEY *is sufficient to compromise the precision of the collapsed semantics (even when condition* INDEPENDENCE *is satisfied).*

On the other hand, if the three conditions hold then the control reachability problem in the collapsed semantics is equivalent to the control reachability problem in the standard one.

Theorem 2 (precision of collapsed semantics). *Suppose the system Eq satisfies conditions* LINEARITY, LOCALITY, *and* DATA OR KEY. *Then $((A_1, 0) \mid \cdots \mid (A_k, 0), T_0) \xrightarrow{*} \text{err}$ iff $(A_1 \mid \cdots \mid A_k, T_0) \xrightarrow{*} \text{err}$.*

Another way to obtain the precision of the collapsed semantics, which was suggested to us by Y. Lakhnech, is to restrict our attention to tail-recursive processes that *publish* at the end of the session the names generated at its beginning. We say that the system Eq satisfies the condition PUBLISH if in the system (1) the Q_i's have the shape $?t_1^i.!s_1^i \ldots ?x.!c_i.A_i'$.

Proposition 3. *Suppose the system Eq satisfies conditions* LINEARITY, LOCALITY, *and* PUBLISH. *Then the collapsed semantics is precise in the sense of theorem 2.*

The condition PUBLISH allows to get rid of the restrictive condition DATA OR KEY. On the other hand, this condition puts the burden on the protocol which has to resist attacks coming from the publication of 'old' names.

3   Set Based Analysis

In this section we perform an analysis based on *set constraints* of the control reachability problem in the collapsed semantics. In section 3.1 we introduce a particular family of set constraints tailored to our needs, in section 3.2 we show how to generate them, and in section 3.3 we explain how to solve them.

3.1   A Family of Set Constraints

We will use a class of set constraints very close to *definite* set constraints with membership expressions [HJ90, CP97, TDT00], but there are few differences. First, we do not allow any expressions except variables on the right-hand side of inclusion, which is quite usual in set based program analysis [HJ94]; therefore, we are not interested in testing satisfiability but in computing the least solution (such constraints are always satisfiable—a trivial solution is a valuation assigning the set of all terms to each variable). Second, we use conditional inclusions of the form if $ne(S)$ then $S' \subseteq X$. This is not an essential extension since the emptiness test is an inherent part of every set constraint solving algorithm. Moreover, in a setting with more complicated expressions on the right-hand side of inclusion, such conditional inclusion is equivalent to $f(S, S') \subseteq f(S, X)$. Third, we use membership expressions as in [TDT00]. A not surprising, but probably new observation here is that if the formulas in the set comprehension part of these expressions are all linear then set constraints can be solved in polynomial time (see theorem 3(2)). Finally, we use a novel operation of renaming needed in the representation of the unfolding rule of the collapsed semantics (definition 8). To our knowledge, this operation was not present in any previous work on set constraints.

Syntax of Set Constraints We assume that a finite signature $\Sigma = \{f, \ldots\}$ of function symbols is given. Every function symbol has a fixed arity; symbols of arity 0 are also called constants and denoted with $c, \ldots$ We will use a set of *individual variables* $V = \{x, y, \ldots\}$ ranging over terms from T_Σ and a set of *set variables* $\Xi = \{X, Y, \ldots\}$ ranging over sets of terms 2^{T_Σ}.

Set expressions are given by the grammar:

$$S ::= X \mid f(S_1, \ldots, S_n) \mid \{x \mid t \in S\} \mid \sigma S,$$

where X ranges over Ξ and f over n-ary function symbols from Σ. The meta-variable t ranges over *linear* terms in $T_\Sigma(V)$ and may contain individual variables possibly different from x. The hypothesis that terms are linear can be removed at the price of an increase in the complexity of the solving algorithm (see [CP97, TDT00]).

The renaming operator σ is a substitution of the form $[c'/c]$ that replaces all occurrences of constant symbols from c with a respective symbol in c'. To ensure termination of the solving algorithm we assume that all renamings here are idempotent ($\sigma\sigma = \sigma$) and commutative ($\sigma\sigma' = \sigma'\sigma$) and come from a finite set *Sub*, so that a composition of renamings can be canonically represented by a subset of *Sub* taking conventionally the identity if the subset is empty. The assumption that the renamings operate on constant symbols is not essential—an extension to other function symbols is straightforward.

Set constraints are:

$$\Phi ::= S \subseteq X \mid \text{if } \bigwedge_i \text{ne}(S_i) \text{ then } S \subseteq X \mid \Phi_1 \wedge \Phi_2 \ .$$

As is usual, we identify a conjunction of constraints with the set of all conjuncts. We will require that for every inclusion $S \subseteq X$ in all subexpressions $\{x \mid t \in S'\}$ of S, the variable x occurs in the term t (this requirement is not essential, but it allows to avoid special rules in table 2 for handling the set of all terms). We will not require this in subexpressions of $\text{ne}(S)$.

Semantics of Set Constraints A *valuation* $\alpha : \Xi \to 2^{T_\Sigma}$ is a mapping assigning sets of ground terms to set variables. The semantics of set expressions relative to a valuation α is defined recursively as follows.

$$[\![X]\!]_\alpha = \alpha(X)$$
$$[\![f(S_1, \ldots, S_n)]\!]_\alpha = \{f(t_1, \ldots, t_n) \mid t_1 \in [\![S_1]\!]_\alpha, \ldots, t_n \in [\![S_n]\!]_\alpha\}$$
$$[\![\{x \mid t \in S\}]\!]_\alpha = \{t' \in T_\Sigma \mid \{y\} = Var(t)\backslash\{x\} \text{ and } \exists s \ [t'/x, s/y]t \in [\![S]\!]_\alpha\}$$
$$[\![\sigma S]\!]_\alpha = \{\sigma t \mid t \in [\![S]\!]_\alpha\} \ .$$

We note that if x does not occur in t and there is an instance of t in $[\![S]\!]_\alpha$ then $[\![\{x \mid t \in S\}]\!]_\alpha$ is the set of all terms T_Σ. Similarly, if x does not occur in t and there is no instance of t in $[\![S]\!]_\alpha$ then $[\![\{x \mid t \in S\}]\!]_\alpha$ is the empty set.

A valuation α is a *solution* of a constraint Φ if for all conjuncts $S \subseteq X$ in Φ we have $[\![S]\!]_\alpha \subseteq \alpha(X)$, and for all conjuncts if $\wedge_i \text{ne}(S_i)$ then $S' \subseteq X$ we have $[\![S']\!]_\alpha \subseteq \alpha(X)$ whenever $[\![S_i]\!]_\alpha \neq \emptyset$ for all i.

Obviously every constraint Φ is satisfiable—a trivial solution is a valuation assigning T_Σ to each variable (under this valuation each inclusion just expresses that a given set is a subset of the universe). In the following we want to find the least solution of a given constraint Φ. This *least solution* may be defined inductively by:

$$\alpha_0(X) = \emptyset,$$
$$\alpha_{i+1}(X) = \bigcup\{[\![S]\!]_{\alpha_i} \mid S \subseteq X \in \Phi \text{ or } (\text{if } \text{ne}(\wedge_j S'_j) \text{ then } S \subseteq X \in \Phi, [\![S'_j]\!]_{\alpha_i} \neq \emptyset)\},$$
$$\alpha(X) = \bigcup_{i \in \mathbb{N}} \alpha_i(X) \ .$$

3.2 Constraints Generation

Here we show how to generate set constraints from a system *Eq* satisfying the conditions LINEARITY, LOCALITY, and INDEPENDENCE. We prove that the generated constraints give a conservative approximation of the protocols. [3]

---

[3] The method can be generalized to protocols not satisfying the conditions above. To this end, it seems natural to rely on *non-linear* constraints in order to limit the loss of precision. In this case the constraints can be solved in DEXPTIME.

Under the syntactic conditions above a *control state* is a process R that can be decomposed in $P_1 \mid \cdots \mid P_k$ so that P_i is either A_i or err or $\sigma_i^{new}(?t_j^i.!s_j^i \ldots ?t_{l_i}^i.!s_{l_i}^i).$ A_i'. For a system of k threads each comprising n i/o alternations there are at most $(n+2)^k$ control states and for a reachable collapsed configuration (R,T), R is always a control state.

For every control state R we introduce a set variable T_R. Intuitively it will represent (an approximation of) the knowledge of the adversary at this control point, so for any reachable configuration (R,T) the variable T_R will contain the set $S(A(T))$. Moreover, we introduce a set variable T_{err} that will be empty if an erroneous configuration is not reachable.

Table 1 gives the rules to generate constraints. The rules are self-explanatory: (init) is for the initial configuration, (err) for determining T_{err}, (A_{1-3}) and (S_{1-2}) for analysis and synthesis, respectively. The rule (unfold) is for the unfolding step. Here we note that every renaming occurring in the (unfold) constraint is of the form $[C_i^{old}/C_i^{new}]$, so for two different renamings their domains are disjoint, and every domain is disjoint from any range. This gives idempotency and commutativity as required. Finally, the (i/o_{1-2}) rules cover the (i/o) reduction. In these rules, we get rid of the key variables in the output by considering all their possible instances (note that in the collapsed semantics the set $\mathcal{N}$ is finite). This is conceptually simple but may lead to inefficiency. In practice, one can introduce a limited form of intersection and write set expressions such as $\{x_i \mid t \in X\} \cap \mathcal{N}$.

Table 1. Constraints generated

(init)	$t \subseteq T_{R_0}$	(1)
(err)	$T_{err\mid R} \subseteq T_{err}$	(2)
(A_1)	$\{x \mid \langle x,y \rangle \in T_R\} \subseteq T_R$	(3)
(A_2)	$\{y \mid \langle x,y \rangle \in T_R\} \subseteq T_R$	(3)
(A_3)	if $ne(\{y \mid C \in T_R\})$ then $\{x \mid E(x,C) \in T_R\} \subseteq T_R$	(3)
(S_1)	$\langle T_R, T_R \rangle \subseteq T_R$	(3)
(S_2)	if $ne(\{y \mid C \in T_R\})$ then $E(T_R, C) \subseteq T_R$	(3)
(unfold)	$\sigma_i^{old} T_{A_i \mid R} \subseteq T_{\sigma_i^{new} Q_i \mid R}$	(4)
(i/o_1)	if $ne(\{y \mid \eta t \in T_R\})$ then $T_R \subseteq T_{R'}$	(5)
(i/o_2)	if $ne(\{y \mid \eta t \in T_R\})$ then $[S/x](\eta s) \subseteq T_{R'}$	(5)

(1) (R_0, T_0) initial configuration, $t \in T_0$.
(2) err $\mid R$ control state.
(3) For all R control state and $C \in \mathcal{N}$.
(4) $A_i \mid R$ control state.
(5) $R \equiv ?t.!s.R_1 \mid R_2$ control state, $R' \equiv R_1 \mid R_2$,
      $\{x_1, \ldots, x_n\} = Var(s) \backslash KVar(s)$,
      $\eta : KVar(s) \to \mathcal{N}$, $S_i \equiv \{x_i \mid \eta t \in T_R\}$.

The set constraints provide a conservative approximation of the collapsed semantics. The proof proceeds by induction on the length of the reduction $(R_0, T_0) \xrightarrow{*} (R, T)$. We will see in example 2 that due to the constraints generated by rule $(\mathsf{i}/\mathsf{o}_2)$ the analysis is not exact.

Proposition 4. *Let α be a solution of the constraints generated according to table 1. Then:*

(1) *If $(R_0, T_0) \xrightarrow{*} (R, T)$ then $S(A(T)) \subseteq \alpha(T_R)$.*

(2) *If $(R_0, T_0) \xrightarrow{*} \mathsf{err}$ then $\alpha(T_{\mathsf{err}}) \neq \emptyset$.*

3.3   Constraints Solving

We say that a constraint Φ is in a *shallow* form if in every expression of the form $f(S_1, \ldots, S_n)$, $\{x \mid t \in S\}$ or σS occurring in Φ the expressions $S, S_1, \ldots, S_n$ are set variables. Any set constraint can be transformed into an equivalent one in shallow form by replacing every occurrence of a nested subexpression S with a fresh set variable X_S and adding a conjunct $S \subseteq X_S$. For the rest of this section we assume that all constraints are in shallow form.

Given a constraint Φ in shallow form over a set of variables Ξ and a set of renamings Sub we construct a constraint Φ' over a set of variables $\Xi' = \{(Y, u) \mid Y \in \Xi, u \subseteq Sub\}$ and an *empty* set of renamings. Thus if in Φ we have n variables and k renaming we have $n \cdot 2^k$ variables in Φ'. If $X = (Y, u) \in \Xi'$ and $\sigma \in Sub$ then X^σ stands for $(Y, u \cup \{\sigma\})$. Then Φ' is obtained from Φ by first replacing all set variables Y by $(Y, \emptyset)$ and then all set expressions σX by X^σ. By this construction we get rid of the set expressions σS and we will see that the least solution of Φ' when restricted to the variables $(Y, \emptyset)$ gives the least solution of Φ.

We say that a constraint Φ is in a *solved* form if all its conjuncts are of the form $f(X_1, \ldots, X_n) \subseteq X$. A constraint in a solved form can be seen as a transition table of a tree automaton whose states are set variables. The least solution of such a constraint is then a valuation that assigns to a variable X the language recognized by this automaton with X as a final state.

Our constraints solving algorithm applies the rules in table 2 starting from Φ'. Each consequence is an inclusion between two terms from a set of bounded size; this is used to show the termination and to derive the upper bound. Then given the initial constraint Φ' we infer all consequences of Φ' under the rules and then simply remove all inclusions that are not in solved form.

Definition 9 (closed and solved form). *For a constraint Φ we denote by Φ^C the least set of constraints that contains Φ and is closed under all rules in table 2, and by Φ^S the restriction of Φ^C to the constraints in a solved form $f(X_1, \ldots, X_n) \subseteq X$.*

Theorem 3. *Let Φ be a linear constraint over Ξ, Sub and let Φ' be the associated constraint over $\Xi' = \Xi \times 2^{Sub}$.*

Table 2. Saturation rules for linear constraints

1. $\bigwedge_i \mathsf{ne}(X_i) \to \mathsf{ne}(f(X_1, \ldots, X_n))$
2. $\bigwedge_i \mathsf{ne}(\{x \mid t_i \in X_i\}), f(X_1, \ldots, X_n) \subseteq X \to \mathsf{ne}(\{x \mid f(t_1, \ldots, t_n) \in X\})$
   (provided $f(t_1, \ldots, t_n)$ occurs in Φ)
3. $\mathsf{ne}(S), S \subseteq X \to \mathsf{ne}(X)$
4. $\mathsf{ne}(X) \to \mathsf{ne}(\{x \mid y \in X\})$ (y can be x)
5. $S \subseteq X, X \subseteq Y \to S \subseteq Y$
6. $\{x \mid f(t_1, \ldots, t_i[x], \ldots, t_n) \in X\} \subseteq Y, f(X_1, \ldots, X_n) \subseteq X \to$
   if $\bigwedge_{j \neq i} \mathsf{ne}(\{x \mid t_j \in X_j\})$ then $\{x \mid t_i[x] \in X_i\} \subseteq Y$
7. $\{x \mid x \in X\} \subseteq Y \to X \subseteq Y$
8. $\bigwedge_i \mathsf{ne}(S_i)$, if $\bigwedge_i \mathsf{ne}(S_i)$ then $S \subseteq X \to S \subseteq X$
9. $f(X_1, \ldots, X_n) \subseteq X \to \sigma(f)(X_1^\sigma, \ldots, X_n^\sigma) \subseteq X^\sigma$

(1) *The least solution of Φ'^S restricted to the variables $(Y, \emptyset)$ of Ξ' is the least solution of Φ.*

(2) *The least solution of Φ can be computed in time $\mathsf{poly}(n \cdot 2^k)$ where n is the size of Φ and k is the number of renaming operations in Φ.*

4 Precision of the Set-Based Analysis

The use of the collapsed semantics and the related set-based analysis can be applied to all protocols from [CJ97]. However, most of them violate at least one of the conditions above (example 1 being an exception) and this leads to a loss of precision either in the collapsed semantics or in set-based analysis. It turns out that in general the set based analysis is *not* precise even under the four syntactic conditions given in definition 6.

Example 2. Consider the initial knowledge $T_0 = \{ABD, ACD\}$ and the system

$$A_1 = ?Ax.!x.?By.?Cz.\mathsf{err} .$$

The constraints generated do not express that after the first filter is passed either BD or CD are known but not both. Consequently, the following two filters are passed and the erroneous state is reached.

An approach to the characterization of the set-based analysis is to look at *iterated* threads *without* name generation. [4] A thread is iterated if a new copy of the thread is spawned as soon as the first input output action is performed. A system Eq of k iterated threads is then formalized by k equations:[5]

$$A_i = ?t_1^i.!s_1^i.(A_i \mid (?t_2^i.!s_2^i \ldots ?t_{l_i}^i.!s_{l_i}^i.U.)) \tag{2}$$

---

[4] *With* name generation a simple variant of the example 2 shows that precision is lost.
[5] This formalization is equivalent to the standard notion of replication in π-calculus.

where U can be either the terminated state 0 or the erroneous state err. Since we do not have generated names, the transformation given in section 2.3 does not apply and we just require that $Var(s_j^i)$ is a subset of $\bigcup_{l \leq j} FVar(t_l^i)$ rather than of $FVar(t_j^i)$.

It turns out that these programs can be *flattened* so that each thread includes just *one alternation of input and output* and it is thus expressed by a tail recursive definition $A =?t.!s.A$. Thus the following theorem 4 is also a result about the precision of the set based analysis for tail-recursive definitions without name generation and with one alternation of input and output.

Definition 10. *The system of iterated threads (2) satisfies, respectively, the* LINEARITY *and* INDEPENDENCE *conditions if for all equations* $i = 1, \ldots, k$ *the term* $\langle t_1^i, \ldots, t_{l_i}^i \rangle$ *is linear and the i/o action* $?\langle t_1^i, \ldots, t_{l_i}^i \rangle.!\langle s_1^i, \ldots, s_{l_i}^i \rangle$ *is independent in the sense of definition 6(3).*

Theorem 4. *Let* n *be the size of the system of iterated threads (2),* c *be the number of different keys, and* k *be the number of key variables. Suppose the system satisfies the* INDEPENDENCE *condition 10. Then the control reachability problem is* DEXPTIME-*hard and decidable in time* $\exp(n \cdot c^k)$. *Moreover, under the additional* LINEARITY *condition it is decidable in time* $\mathsf{poly}(n \cdot c^k)$.

We expect that the factor c^k can be reduced, but the exponential blowup in the non-linear case is unavoidable as we can reduce the satisfaction of unary definite set constraints (see [CPT00]) to control reachability for the class of iterated systems considered even when neither pairs nor key variables are used (see [AC02] for details).

The upper bound relies on the flattening transformation mentioned above. By this transformation every input-output action can be repeated in every reachable configuration. This property coupled with the INDEPENDENCE condition allows to match the constraint generated by the rule (i/o_2).

As a particular instance of this result, one can obtain yet another polynomial time decision procedure for ping-pong protocols which satisfy LINEARITY and do not contain variables in key position (see [DEK82] and [ALV01] for another decision procedure based on prefix-rewriting). Of course, the DEXPTIME lower bound implies that the class of decidable protocols considered in the theorem 4 above is strictly more expressive than the class of ping-pong protocols.

Acknowledgement

The first author is partly supported by ACI VERNAM and IST PROFUNDIS.

References

[ALV01]   R. Amadio, D. Lugiez, and V. Vanackere. On the symbolic reduction of processes with cryptographic functions. *Theoretical Computer Science* (to appear). Also RR 4147, INRIA. 499, 513

[AC02]   R. Amadio, W. Charatonik. On name generation and set-based analysis in the Dolev-Yao model. RR-INRIA 4379, January 2002. 499, 501, 513

[AM01]   R. Amadio, C. Meyssonnier. On the decidability of fragments of the asynchronous π-calculus. Journal of Nordic Computing (to appear). Also RR-INRIA 4241.

[CP97]   W. Charatonik and A. Podelski. Set constraints with intersection. In *Proc. 12th IEEE LICS*, 1997. 500, 508

[CPT00]   W. Charatonik, A. Podelski, and J.-M. Talbot. Paths vs. trees in set-based program analysis. In *Proc. 27th Annual ACM POPL*, 2000. 513

[CCM01]   H. Comon, V. Cortier, and J. Mitchell. Tree automata with one memory, set constraints, and ping-pong protocols. In *Proc. ICALP*, Springer Lecture Notes in Comp. Sci. 2076, 2001. 501

[CJ97]   J. Clark and J. Jacob. A survey of authentication protocol literature: Version 1.0. Available at http://www-users.cs.york.ac.uk/~jac/papers/drareview.ps.gz, 1997. 506, 512

[DEK82]   D. Dolev, S. Even, and R. Karp. On the security of ping-pong protocols. *Information and Control*, 55:57–68, 1982. 499, 513

[DLMS99]   N. Durgin, P. Lincoln, J. Mitchell, and A. Scedrov. Undecidability of bounded security protocols. In *Proc. Formal methods and security protocols, FLOC Workshop, Trento*, 1999. 499

[DY83]   D. Dolev and A. Yao. On the security of public key protocols. *IEEE Trans. on Information Theory*, 29(2):198–208, 1983. 499

[GK00]   T. Genet and F. Klay. Rewriting for cryptographic protocol verification. In *Proc. CADE*, Springer Lecture Notes in Comp. Sci. 1831, 2000. 501

[Gou00]   J. Goubault. A method for automatic cryptographic protocol verification. In *Proc. FMPPTA, Springer-Verlag*, 2000. 501

[HJ90]   N. Heintze and J. Jaffar. A decision procedure for a class of set constraints (extended abstract). In *Proc. 5th IEEE LICS*, 1990. 508

[HJ94]   N. Heintze and J. Jaffar. Set constraints and set-based analysis. In *Proc. Workshop on Principles and Practice of Constraint Programming*, Springer Lecture Notes in Comp. Sci. 874, 1994. 508

[Mon99]   D. Monniaux. Abstracting cryptographic protocols with tree automata. In *Proc. Static Analysis Symposium*, Springer Lect. Notes in Comp. Sci., 1999. 501

[RT01]   M. Rusinowitch and M. Turuani Protocol insecurity with finite number of sessions is NP-complete. RR INRIA 4134, March 2001. 499

[Sto99]   S. Stoller. A bound on attacks on authentication protocols. TR 526, Indiana University, CS Dept., july 1999. 500

[TDT00]   J.-M. Talbot, Ph. Devienne, and S. Tison. Generalized definite set constraints. *Constraints: An International Journal*, 5(1-2):161–202, January 2000. 500, 508

[Wei99]   C. Weidenbach. Towards an automatic analysis of security protocols in first-order logic. In *Proc. CADE 99*. Springer Lect. Notes in Comp. Sci. (LNAI) 1632, 1999. 501

On the Decidability of Cryptographic Protocols with Open-Ended Data Structures

Ralf Küsters

Institut für Informatik und Praktische Mathematik
Christian-Albrechts-Universität zu Kiel, Germany
kuesters@ti.informatik.uni-kiel.de

Abstract. Formal analysis of cryptographic protocols has mainly concentrated on protocols with closed-ended data structures, where closed-ended data structure means that the messages exchanged between principals have fixed and finite format. However, in many protocols the data structures used are open-ended, i.e., messages have an unbounded number of data fields. Formal analysis of protocols with open-ended data structures is one of the challenges pointed out by Meadows. This work studies decidability issues for such protocols. We propose a protocol model in which principals are described by transducers, i.e., finite automata with output, and show that in this model security is decidable and PSPACE-hard in presence of the standard Dolev-Yao intruder.

1 Introduction

Formal methods are very successful in analyzing the security of cryptographic protocols. Using these methods, many flaws have been found in published protocols. By now, a large variety of different methods and tools for cryptographic protocol analysis is available (see [16] for an overview). In particular, for different interesting classes of protocols and intruders, security has been shown to be decidable, usually based on the Dolev-Yao model [7] (see the paragraph on related work).

Previous work has mostly concentrated on protocols with *closed-ended data structures*, where messages exchanged between principals have fixed and finite format. In what follows, we will refer to these protocols as *closed-ended protocols*. In many protocols, however, the data structures are *open-ended* (see Section 2 for examples): the number of data fields that must be processed by a principal in one receive-send action is unbounded, where receive-send action means that a principal receives a message and reacts, after some internal computation, by sending a message. We will call protocols with open-ended data structures *open-ended*.

This paper addresses open-ended protocols, and thus, deals with one of the challenges pointed out by Meadows [16]. The goal is to devise a protocol model rich enough to capture a large class of open-ended protocols such that security is decidable; the long-term goal is to develop tools for automatic verification of open-ended protocols.

L. Brim et al. (Eds.): CONCUR 2002, LNCS 2421, pp. 515–530, 2002.

Open-ended protocols make it necessary to model principals who can perform in one receive-send action an unbounded number of *internal actions*; only then can they handle open-ended data structures. Therefore, the first problem is to find a good computational model for receive-send actions. It turns out that one cannot simply extend the existing models. More specifically, Rusinowitch and Turuani [20] describe receive-send actions by single rewrite rules and show security to be NP-complete. In this model, principals have unbounded memory. Furthermore, the terms in the rewrite rules may be non-linear, i.e., multiple occurrence of one variable is allowed, and thus, a principal can compare messages of arbitrary size for equality. To handle open-ended protocols, we generalize the model by Rusinowitch and Turuani in a canonical way and show that if receive-send actions are described by *sets* of rewrite rules, security is undecidable, even with i) finite memory and non-linear terms, or ii) unbounded memory and linear terms. Consequently, we need a computational model in which principals have finite memory and cannot compare messages of arbitrary size for equality.

For this reason, we propose to use transducers, i.e., finite automata with output, as the computational model for receive-send actions, since transducers satisfy the above restrictions — they have finite memory and cannot compare messages of arbitrary size for equality —, and still can deal with open-ended data structures. In Section 5.1 our so-called transducer-based model is discussed in detail. The main technical result of this paper is that in the transducer-based model, security is decidable and PSPACE-hard under the following assumptions: the number of sessions is bounded, i.e., a protocol is analyzed assuming a fixed number of interleaved protocol runs; nonces and complex keys are not allowed. We, however, put no restrictions on the Dolev-Yao intruder; in particular, the message size is unbounded. These are standard assumptions also made in most decidable models for closed-ended protocols [20,2,13].[1] Just as in these works, the security property we study in the present paper is secrecy.

The results indicate that from a computational point of view, the analysis of open-ended protocols is harder than for closed-ended protocols, for which security is "only" NP-complete [20]. The additional complexity comes from the fact that now we have, beside the Dolev-Yao intruder, another source of infinite behavior: the unbounded number of internal actions (i.e., paths in the transducers of unbounded length). This makes it necessary to devise new proof techniques to show decidability. Roughly speaking, using that transducers only have finite memory we will use a pumping argument showing that the length of paths in the transducers can be bounded in the size of the problem instance.

Related work. All decidability and undecidability results obtained so far only apply to closed-ended protocols. Decidability depends on the following parameters: bounded or unbounded number of sessions, bounded or unbounded message size, absence or presence of pairing, nonces, and/or complex keys.

Usually, if one allows for an unbounded number of sessions, security is undecidable [1,8,2,9], except when the message size is bounded and nonces are dis-

---

[1] In [20,13], however, complex keys are allowed.

allowed [8] (then security is EXPTIME-complete), or pairing is disallowed [6,2] (then security is in P). The situation is much better if one puts a bound on the number of sessions and disallows nonces. Then, even with pairing and unbounded message size, security is decidable [20,2,13] and NP-hard [20,2]; Rusinowitch and Turuani [20] show NP-completeness (with complex keys). Except for complex keys, we make exactly the same assumptions in our models.

To the best of our knowledge, the only contributions on formal analysis of open-ended protocols are the following: The recursive authentication protocol [5] has been analyzed by Paulson [18], using the Isabelle theorem prover, as well as by Bryans and Schneider [4], using the PVS theorem prover; the A-GDH.2 protocol [3] has been analyzed by Meadows [15] with the NRL Analyzer, and manually by Pereira and Quisquater [19], based on a model similar to the strand spaces model. As mentioned, decidability issues have not been studied so far.

Structure of the paper. In Section 2, we give examples of open-ended protocols. We then define a generic model for describing open-ended protocols (Section 3). In this model, receive-send actions can be arbitrary computations. In Section 4, we consider the instances of the generic model in which receive-send actions are specified by sets of rewrite rules, and show the mentioned undecidability result. The transducer-based model, the instance of the generic protocol model in which receive-send actions are given by transducers, is introduced in Section 5. This section also contains the mentioned discussion. In Section 6 the actual decidability and complexity results are stated. Finally, we conclude in Section 7.

Due to space limitations, in this paper we have largely omitted technical details, and rather focused on the introduction and the discussion of our transducer-based model. The detailed and often involved proofs of all our results can be found in the technical report [14]. It also shows how the recursive authentication protocol (see Section 2) can be described in our transducer-based model.

2   Examples of Open-Ended Protocols

An example of an open-ended protocol is the IKE Protocol [12], in which a principal needs to pick a *security association (SA)*, the collection of algorithms and other informations used for encryption and authentication, among an a priori unbounded list of SAs. Such a list is an open-ended data structure, since it has an unbounded number of data fields to be examined by a principal. An attack on IKE, found by Zhou [22] and independently Ferguson and Schneier [10], shows that when modeling open-ended protocols, the open-ended data structures must be taken into account, since otherwise some attacks might not be found. In other words, as also pointed out by Meadows [16], open-endedness is security relevant.

Other typical open-ended protocols are group protocols, for example, the recursive authentication protocol (RA protocol) [5] and the A-GDH.2 protocol [3], which is part of the CLIQUES project [21]. In the RA protocol, a key distribution server receives an a priori unbounded sequence of request messages (containing pairs of principals who want to share session keys) and must generate a corresponding sequence of certificates (containing the session keys). These sequences are open-ended data structures: In one receive-send action the server needs to process an unbounded number of data fields, namely the sequence of pairs of principals. Group protocols often allow for an unbounded number of receive-send actions in one protocol run. In our models, we will, however, always assume a fixed bound on the number of receive-send actions, since otherwise, just as in the case of an unbounded number of sessions, security in general leads to undecidability. Nevertheless, even with such a fixed bound it is still necessary to model open-ended data structures. In the RA protocol, a bound on the number of receive-send actions would imply that the sequence of requests generated by the principals is bounded. Nevertheless, the intruder can generate arbitrarily long request messages. Thus, the data structures are still open-ended, and the server should be modeled in such a way that, as in the actual protocol, he can process open-ended data structures.

In [14], we provide a formal description of the RA protocol in our transducer-based model.

3   A Generic Protocol Model

Our generic protocol model and the underlying assumptions basically coincide with the ones proposed by Rusinowitch et al. [20] and Amadio el al. [2] for closed-ended protocols. However, the important difference is that in the generic model, receive-send actions are, roughly speaking, binary relations over the message space, and thus can be interpreted as arbitrary computations. In the models of Rusinowitch el al. and Amadio et al. , receive-send actions are described by single rewrite rules or processes without loops, respectively.

Thus, the generic protocol model is a very general framework for open-ended protocols. In fact, it is much too general to study decidability issues. Therefore, in subsequent sections we will consider different instances of this model.

The main features of the generic protocol model can be summarizes as follows:

- a generic protocol is described by a finite set of principals;
- the internal state space of a principal may be infinite (which, for example, enables a principal to store arbitrarily long messages);
- every principal is described by a finite sequence of receive-send actions;
- receive-send actions are arbitrary computations.

We make the following assumptions:

- the intruder is the standard Dolev-Yao intruder; in particular, we do not put restrictions on the size of messages;
- principals and the intruder cannot generate nonces;
- keys are atomic;
- the number of sessions is bounded. More precisely, the sessions considered in the analysis are only those encoded in the protocol description itself.

These are standard assumptions also made in decidable models for closed-ended protocols. They coincide with the ones in [2], and except for complex keys, with those in [20,13].

Let us now give a formal definition of the generic protocol model.

3.1 Messages

The definition of messages is rather standard. Let $\mathcal{N}$ denote a finite set of *atomic messages*, containing keys, names of principals, etc. as well as the special atomic message secret. The *set of messages* (over $\mathcal{N}$) is the least set $\mathcal{M}$ that satisfies the following properties:

- $\mathcal{N} \subseteq \mathcal{M}$;
- if $m, m' \in \mathcal{M}$, then $mm' \in \mathcal{M}$;
- if $m \in \mathcal{M}$ and $a \in \mathcal{N}$, then $\mathsf{enc}_a(m) \in \mathcal{M}$;
- if $m \in \mathcal{M}$, then $\mathsf{hash}(m) \in \mathcal{M}$.

As usual, concatenation is an associative operation, i.e., $(mm')m'' = m(m'm'')$. Note that we only allow for atomic keys, i.e., in a message $\mathsf{enc}_a(\cdot)$, a is always an atomic message.

Let ε denote the *empty message* and $\mathcal{M}_\varepsilon := \mathcal{M} \cup \{\varepsilon\}$ the set of messages containing ε. Note that ε is not allowed inside encryptions or hashes, that is, $\mathsf{enc}_a() \notin \mathcal{M}_\varepsilon$ and $\mathsf{hash}() \notin \mathcal{M}_\varepsilon$.

Later, we will also consider terms, i.e., messages with variables. Let $V := \{v_0, \ldots, v_{n-1}\}$ be a set of variables. Then a *term* t (over V) is a message over the atomic messages $\mathcal{N} \cup V$, where variables are not allowed as keys, i.e., terms of the form $\mathsf{enc}_v(\cdot)$ for some variable v are forbidden. A *substitution* σ is a mapping from V into $\mathcal{M}_\varepsilon$. If t is a term, then $\sigma(t)$ denotes the message obtained from t by replacing every variable v in t by $\sigma(v)$.

The *depth* $\mathsf{depth}(t)$ *of a term* t is the maximum number of nested encryptions and hashes in t, i.e.,

- $\mathsf{depth}(\varepsilon) := 0$, $\mathsf{depth}(a) := 0$ for every $a \in \mathcal{N} \cup V$;
- $\mathsf{depth}(tt') := \max\{\mathsf{depth}(t), \mathsf{depth}(t')\}$;
- $\mathsf{depth}(\mathsf{enc}_a(t)) := \mathsf{depth}(t) + 1$; $\mathsf{depth}(\mathsf{hash}(t)) := \mathsf{depth}(t) + 1$.

3.2 The Intruder Model

We use the standard Dolev-Yao intruder model [7]. That is, an intruder has complete control over the network and can derive new messages from his current knowledge by composing, decomposing, encrypting, decrypting, and hashing messages. As usual in the Dolev-Yao model, we make the perfect cryptography assumption. We do not impose any restrictions on the size of messages.

The (possibly infinite) set of messages $\mathsf{d}(\mathcal{K})$ the intruder can derive from $\mathcal{K} \subseteq \mathcal{M}_\varepsilon$ is the smallest set satisfying the following conditions:

- $\mathcal{K} \subseteq \mathsf{d}(\mathcal{K})$;
- if $mm' \in \mathsf{d}(\mathcal{K})$, then $m \in \mathsf{d}(\mathcal{K})$ and $m' \in \mathsf{d}(\mathcal{K})$ (decomposition);
- if $\mathsf{enc}_a(m) \in \mathsf{d}(\mathcal{K})$ and $a \in \mathsf{d}(\mathcal{K})$, then $m \in \mathsf{d}(\mathcal{K})$ (decryption);
- if $m \in \mathsf{d}(\mathcal{K})$ and $m' \in \mathsf{d}(\mathcal{K})$, then $mm' \in \mathsf{d}(\mathcal{K})$ (composition);
- if $m \in \mathsf{d}(\mathcal{K})$, $m \neq \varepsilon$, and $a \in \mathcal{N} \cap \mathsf{d}(\mathcal{K})$, then $\mathsf{enc}_a(m) \in \mathsf{d}(\mathcal{K})$ (encryption);
- if $m \in \mathsf{d}(\mathcal{K})$ and $m \neq \varepsilon$, then $\mathsf{hash}(m) \in \mathsf{d}(\mathcal{K})$ (hashing).

3.3   Protocols

Protocols are described by sets of principals and every principal is defined by a sequence of receive-send actions, which, in a protocol run, are performed one after the other. Since we are interested in attacks, the definition of a protocol also contains the initial intruder knowledge. Formally, principals and protocols are defined as follows.

Definition 1. *A generic principal Π is a tuple (Q, I, n, α) where*

- *Q is the (possibly infinite) set of states of Π;*
- *I is the set of initial states of Π;*
- *n is the number of receive-send actions to be performed by Π;*
- *α is a mapping assigning to every $j \in \{0, \ldots, n-1\}$ a receive-send action $\alpha(j) \subseteq Q \times \mathcal{M}_\varepsilon \times \mathcal{M}_\varepsilon \times Q$.*

A generic protocol P is a tuple $(n, \{\Pi_i\}_{i<n}, \mathcal{K})$ where

- *n is the number of principals;*
- *$\{\Pi_i\}_{i<n}$ is a family of n generic principals, and*
- *$\mathcal{K} \subseteq \mathcal{M}_\varepsilon$ is the initial intruder knowledge.*

Note that receive-send actions are arbitrary relations. Intuitively, they take an input message (2. component) and nondeterministically, depending on the current state (1. component), return an output message (3. component) plus a new state (4. component). Later, when we consider instances of the generic protocol model, one receive-send action of a principal will consist of an unbounded number of internal actions. By allowing receive-send actions to be nondeterministic and principals to have a set of initial states, instead of a single initial state, one can model more flexible principals: for instance, those that nondeterministically choose one principal, who they want to talk to, or one SA from the list of SAs in the IKE Protocol.

We also remark that a protocol P is *not* parametrized by n. In particular, when we say that P is secure, we mean that P is secure given the n principals as defined in the protocol. We do not mean that P is secure for every number n of principals.

3.4 Attacks on Protocols

In an attack on a protocol, the receive-send actions of the principals are interleaved in some way and the intruder, who has complete control over the communication, tries to produce inputs for the principals such that from the corresponding outputs and his initial knowledge he can derive the secret message secret. Formally, an attack is defined as follows.

Definition 2. *Let $P = (n, \{\Pi_i\}_{i<n}, \mathcal{K})$ be a generic protocol with $\Pi_i = (Q_i, I_i, n_i, \alpha_i)$, for $i < n$. An attack on P is a tuple consisting of the following components:*

- *a total ordering $<$ on the set $\{(i,j) \mid i < n, j < n_i\}$ such that $(i,j) < (i,j')$ implies $j < j'$ (the execution order of the receive-send actions);*[2]
- *a mapping ψ assigning to every (i,j), $i < n$, $j < n_i$, a tuple*

$$\psi(i,j) = (q_i^j, m_i^j, m_i'^j, q_i^{j+1})$$

with

- *$q_i^j, q_i^{j+1} \in Q_i$ (the state of Π_i before/after performing $\alpha_i(j)$); and*
- *$m_i^j, m_i'^j \in \mathcal{M}_\varepsilon$ (the input message received and output message sent by $\alpha_i(j)$);*

such that

- *$q_i^0 \in I_i$ for every $i < n$;*
- *$m_i^j \in \mathsf{d}(\mathcal{K} \cup \{m_{i'}'^{j'} \mid (i',j') < (i,j)\})$ for every $i < n$, $j < n_i$;*
- *$(q_i^j, m_i^j, m_i'^j, q_i^{j+1}) \in \alpha_i(j)$ for every $i < n$, $j < n_i$.*

An attack is called successful *if secret $\in \mathsf{d}(\mathcal{K} \cup \{m_i'^j \mid i < n, j < n_i\})$.*

The decision problem we are interested in is the following:

ATTACK: Given a protocol P, decide whether there exists a successful attack on P.

A protocol guarantees *secrecy*, if there does not exist a successful attack. In this case, we say that the protocol is *secure*.

Whether ATTACK is decidable or not heavily depends on what kinds of receive-send actions a principal is allowed to perform. In the subsequent sections, we look at different instances of generic protocols, i.e., different computational models for receive-send actions, and study the problem ATTACK for the classes of protocols thus obtained.

---

[2] Although, we assume a linear ordering on the receive-send actions performed by a principal, we could as well allow partial orderings (as in [20]) without any impact on the decidability and complexity results.

4　Undecidability Results

We extend the model proposed by Rusinowitch and Turuani [20] in a straight-forward way such that open-ended protocols can be handled, and show that this extension leads to undecidability of security.

The model by Rusinowitch and Turuani can be considered as the instance of the generic protocol model in which receive-send actions are described by single rewrite rules of the form $t \to t'$, where t and t' are terms.[3] The internal state of a principal is given implicitly by the values assigned to the variables occurring in the rewrite rules – different rules may share variables. In particular, a principal has unbounded memory to store information for use in subsequent receive-send actions. Roughly speaking, a message m is transformed by a receive-send action of the form $t \to t'$ into the message $\sigma(t')$, where σ is a substitution satisfying $m = \sigma(t)$. In [20], it is shown that in this setting, ATTACK is NP-complete.

Of course, in this model open-ended data structures cannot be handled since the left hand-side of a rewrite rule t has a fixed and finite format, and thus, one can only process messages with a fixed number of data fields.

A natural extension of this model, which allows to deal with open-ended data structures, is to describe receive-send actions by sets of rewrite rules, which can nondeterministically be applied to the input message, where, as in the model of Rusinowitch and Turuani, rewriting means top-level rewriting: If the rule $t \to t'$ is applied to the input message m yielding $\sigma(t')$ as output, another rule (nondeterministically chosen from the set of rules) may be applied to $\sigma(t')$. To the resulting output yet another rule may be applied and so on, until no rule is or can be applied anymore. The applications of the rules are the internal actions of principals. The instance of the generic protocol model in which receive-send actions are described by sets of rewrite rules as described above is called *rule-based protocol model*. In [14], we give a formal definition of this model. In this model, we distinguish between input, output, and process rules, and also put further restrictions on the rewrite rules such that they can be applied only a finite (but a priori unbounded) number of times.

Theorem 1. *For rule-based protocols,* ATTACK *is undecidable.*

By reduction from Post's Correspondence Problem (PCP), this theorem is easy to show. It holds true, even for protocols consisting of only one principal, which may only perform one receive-send action. In other words, the undecidability comes from the internal actions alone.

However, the reduction does not work if only linear terms are allowed in rewrite rules. In linear terms, every variable occurs at most once, and therefore, one cannot compare submessages of arbitrary size for equality. Nevertheless, if principals can store one message and compare it with a submessage of the message being processed, we still have undecidability. Such protocols are called

---

[3] Since Rusinowitch and Turuani allow for complex keys, the terms are more general than the ones we use here. However, we will only consider terms as defined in Section 3.1.

linear-term one-memory protocols; see [14] for the formal definition and the proof of undecidability, which is again by a rather straightforward reduction from PCP.

Theorem 2. *For linear-term one-memory protocols,* ATTACK *is undecidable.*

5 The Transducer-Based Protocol Model

The previous section indicates that, informally speaking, when principals can process open-ended data structures and, in addition, can

1. compare submessages of arbitrary size (which is possible if terms are not linear), or
2. store one message and compare it with a submessage of the message being processed,

then security is undecidable. To obtain decidability, we need a device with only finite memory, and which does not allow to compare messages of arbitrary size. This motivates to use transducers to describe receive-send actions. In what follows, we define the corresponding instance of the generic protocol model. In Section 5.1, we will discuss capabilities and restrictions of our transducer-based model.

If Σ is a finite alphabet, Σ^* will denote the set of finite words over Σ, including the empty word ε.

Definition 3. *A transducer $\mathcal{A}$ is a tuple $(Q, \Sigma, \Omega, I, \Delta, F)$ where*

- *Q is the finite set of states of $\mathcal{A}$;*
- *Σ is the finite input alphabet;*
- *Ω is the finite output alphabet;*
- *$I \subseteq Q$ is the set of initial states of $\mathcal{A}$;*
- *$\Delta \subseteq Q \times \Sigma^* \times \Omega^* \times Q$ is the finite set of transitions of $\mathcal{A}$; and*
- *$F \subseteq Q$ is the set of final states of $\mathcal{A}$.*

A *path* π (of length n) in $\mathcal{A}$ from p to q is of the form $q_0(v_0, w_0)q_1(v_1, w_1)q_2 \ldots$ $(v_{n-1}, w_{n-1})q_n$ with $q_0 = p$, $q_n = q$, and $(q_i, v_i, w_i, q_{i+1}) \in \Delta$ for every $i < n$; π is called *strict* if $n > 0$, and v_0 and v_{n-1} are non-empty words. The word $v_0 \ldots v_{n-1}$ is the *input label* and $w_0 \ldots w_{n-1}$ is the *output label* of π. A path of length 0 has input and output label ε. We write $p(v, w)q \in \mathcal{A}$ ($p(v, w)q \in_s \mathcal{A}$) if there exists a (strict) path from p to q in $\mathcal{A}$ with input label v and output label w.

If $S, T \subseteq Q$, then $\mathcal{A}(S, T) := \{(p, v, w, q) \mid p \in S, q \in T, p(v, w)q \in \mathcal{A}\} \subseteq Q \times \Sigma^* \times \Omega^* \times Q$. The *output of $\mathcal{A}$ on input* $v \in \Sigma^*$ is defined by $\mathcal{A}(v) := \{w \mid$ there exists $p \in I$ and $q \in F$ with $(p, v, w, q) \in \mathcal{A}(I, F)\}$.

If $\Delta \subseteq Q \times (\Sigma \cup \{\varepsilon\}) \times (\Omega \cup \{\varepsilon\}) \times Q$, $\mathcal{A}$ is called *transducer with letter transitions* in contrast to transducers with word transitions. The following remark shows that it suffices to consider transducers with letter transitions.

Remark 1. Let $\mathcal{A} = (Q, \Sigma, \Omega, I, \Delta, F)$ be a transducer. Then there exists a transducer $\mathcal{A}' = (Q', \Sigma, \Omega, I, \Delta', F)$ with letter transitions such that $Q \subseteq Q'$, and $\mathcal{A}'(S,T) = \mathcal{A}(S,T)$ for every $S, T \subseteq Q$.

In order to specify the receive-send actions of a principal, we consider special transducers, so-called message transducers, which satisfy certain properties. Message transducers interpret messages as words over the finite alphabet $\Sigma_{\mathcal{N}}$, consisting of the atomic messages as well as the letters "$\mathtt{enc}_a$(", "$\mathtt{hash}$(", and ")", that is,

$$\Sigma_{\mathcal{N}} := \mathcal{N} \cup \{\mathtt{enc}_a(\mid a \in \mathcal{N}\} \cup \{\mathtt{hash}(,)\}.$$

Messages considered as words over $\Sigma_{\mathcal{N}}$ have always a balanced number of opening parentheses, i.e., "$\mathtt{enc}_a$(" and "$\mathtt{hash}$(", and closing parentheses, i.e., ")".

A message transducer reads a message (interpreted as a word) from left to right, thereby producing some output. If messages are considered as finite trees (where leaves are labeled with atomic messages and internal nodes are labeled with the encryption or hash symbol), a message transducer traverses such a tree from top to bottom and from left to right.

Definition 4. *A message transducer $\mathcal{A}$ (over $\mathcal{N}$) is a tuple $(Q, \Sigma_{\mathcal{N}}, I, \Delta, F)$ such that $(Q, \Sigma_{\mathcal{N}}, \Sigma_{\mathcal{N}}, I, \Delta, F)$ is a transducer with letter transitions, and*

1. *for every $x \in \mathcal{M}_\varepsilon$, $\mathcal{A}(x) \subseteq \mathcal{M}_\varepsilon$; and*
2. *for all $p, q \in Q$, $x \in \mathcal{M}$, and $y \in \Sigma_{\mathcal{N}}^*$, if $p(x,y)q \in_s \mathcal{A}$, then $y \in \mathcal{M}_\varepsilon$.*

The first property is a condition on the "external behavior" of a message transducer: Whenever a message transducer gets a message as input, then the corresponding outputs are also messages (rather than arbitrary words). Note that in an attack, the input to a message transducer is always a message. The second property imposes some restriction on the "internal behavior" of a message transducer. Both properties do not seem to be too restrictive. They should be satisfied for most protocols; at least they are for the transducers in the model of the recursive authentication protocol (as described in [14]).

An open issue is whether the properties on the internal and external behavior are decidable, i.e., given a transducer over $\Sigma_{\mathcal{N}}$ does it satisfy 1. and 2. of Definition 4. Nevertheless, in the model of the recursive authentication protocol it is easy to see that the transducers constructed satisfy the properties.

For $S, T \subseteq Q$, we define $M_{\mathcal{A}}(S,T) := \mathcal{A}(S,T) \cap (Q \times \mathcal{M}_\varepsilon \times \Sigma_{\mathcal{N}}^* \times Q)$. By the definition of message transducers, $M_{\mathcal{A}}(I, F) \subseteq (Q \times \mathcal{M}_\varepsilon \times \mathcal{M}_\varepsilon \times Q)$ if I is the set of initial states and F is the set of final states of $\mathcal{A}$. Thus, message transducers specify receive-send actions of principals (in the sense of Definition 1) in a natural way.

In order to define one principal (i.e., the whole sequence of receive-send actions a principal performs) by a single transducer, we consider so-called extended message transducers: $\mathcal{A} = (Q, \Sigma_{\mathcal{N}}, \Delta, (I_0, \ldots, I_n))$ is an *extended message-transducer* if $\mathcal{A}_{I_j, I_{j+1}} := (Q, \Sigma_{\mathcal{N}}, I_j, \Delta, I_{j+1})$ is a message transducer for all $j < n$. Given such an extended message transducer, it defines the principal (Q, I_0, n, α) with $\alpha(j) = M_{\mathcal{A}_{I_j, I_{j+1}}}(I_j, I_{j+1})$ for $j < n$. In this setting, an internal action of a principal corresponds to applying one transition in the extended message transducer.

Definition 5. *A* transducer-based protocol *P* *is a generic protocol where the principals are defined by extended message transducers.*

5.1 Discussion of the Transducer-Based Protocol Model

In this section, we aim at clarifying capabilities and limitations of the transducer-based protocol model. To this end, we compare this model with the models usually used for closed-ended protocols. To make the discussion more concrete, we concentrate on the model proposed by Rusinowitch and Turuani (see Section 4), which, among the decidable models used for closed-ended protocols, is very powerful. In what follows, we refer to their model as the *rewriting model*. As pointed out in Section 3, the main difference between the two models is the way receive-send actions are described. In the rewriting model receive-send actions are described by single rewrite rules and in the transducer-based model by message transducers.

Let us start to explain the capabilities of message transducers compared to rewrite rules.

Open-ended data structures. As mentioned in Section 4, with a single rewrite rule one cannot process an unbounded number of data fields. This is, however, possible with transducers.

For example, considering the IKE protocol (see Section 2), it is easy to specify a transducer which i) reads a list of SAs, each given as a sequence of atomic messages, ii) picks one SA, and iii) returns it. With a single rewrite rule, one could not parse the whole list of SAs.

The transducer-based model of the recursive authentication protocol (described in [14]) shows that transducers can also handle more involved open-ended data structures: The server in this protocol generates a sequence of certificates (containing session keys) from a *request message* of the form $\mathrm{hash}(m_0\mathrm{hash}(m_1 \cdots \mathrm{hash}(m_n) \cdots)$, where the m_i's are sequences of atomic messages and the nesting depth of the hashes is a priori unbounded (see [14] for the exact definition of the messages.)

Of course, a transducer cannot match opening and closing parenthesis, if they are nested arbitrarily deep, since messages are interpreted as words. However, often this is not necessary: In the IKE protocol, the list of SAs is a message without any nesting. In the recursive authentication protocol, the structure of request messages is very simple, and can be parsed by a transducer. Note that a transducer does not need to check whether the number of closing parenthesis in the request message matches the number of hashes because all words sent to a message transducer (by the intruder) are messages, and thus, well-formed.

Simulating rewrite rules. Transducers can simulate certain receive-send actions described by single rewrite rules. Consider for example the rule $\mathrm{enc}_k(x) \rightarrow$

hash(kx), where x is a variable and k an atomic message: First, the transducer would read "enc$_k$(" and output "hash(k", and then read, letter by letter, the rest of the input message, i.e., "x)" – more precisely, the message substituted for x – and simultaneously write it into the output.

Let us now turn to the limitations of the transducer-based model compared to the rewriting model. The main limitations are the following:

1. *Finite memory:* In the rewriting model, principals can store messages of arbitrary size to use them in subsequent receive-send actions. This is not possible with transducers, since they only have finite memory.
2. *Comparing messages:* In the rewriting model, principals can check whether submessages of the input message coincide. For example, if $t = $ hash(kx)x, with k an atomic message and x a variable, a principal can check whether plain text and hash match. Transducers cannot do this.
3. *Copying messages:* In the rewriting model, principals can copy messages of arbitrary size. For example, in the rule enc$_k$(x) $\rightarrow$ hash(kx)x, the message x is copied. Again, a transducer would need to store x in some way, which is not possible because of the finite memory. As illustrate above, a transducer could however simulate a rule such as enc$_k$(x) $\rightarrow$ hash(kx).
4. *Linear terms:* A transducer cannot simulate all rewrite rules with linear left and right hand-side. Consider for example the rule enc$_k$(xAy) $\rightarrow$ hash(yAx), where x and y are variables, and A is an atomic message. Since in the output, the order of x and y is switched, a transducer would have to store the messages substituted for x and y. However, this requires unbounded memory.

The undecidability results presented in Section 4 indicate that, if open-ended data structures are involved, the restrictions 1. and 2. seem to be unavoidable. The question is whether this is also the case for the remaining two restrictions. We will comment on this below.

First, let us point out some work-arounds. In 1., it often (at least under reasonable assumptions) suffices to store atomic messages such as principal names, keys, and nonces. Thus, one does not always need unbounded memory. One example is the recursive authentication protocol. In 4., it might be possible to modify the linear terms such that they can be parsed by a message transducer, and such that the security of the protocol is not affected. In the example, if one changes the order of x and y in the output, the rewrite rule can easily be simulated by a transducer. Finally, a work-around for the restrictions 2. to 4., is to put a bound on the size of messages that can be substituted for the variables. This approach is usually pursued in protocol analysis based on finite-state model checking (e.g., [17]), where transducers have the additional advantage of being able to process open-ended data structures. For messages of bounded size, all transformations performed by rewrite rules can also be carried out by message transducers. Moreover, in this setting message transducers can handle type flaws.

Of course, it is desirable to avoid such work-arounds if possible to make the analysis of a protocol more precise and reliable. One approach, which might lift some of the restrictions (e.g., 3. and 4.), is to consider tree transducers instead of word transducers to describe receive-send actions. It seems, however, necessary to devise new kinds of tree transducers or extend existing once, for example tree transducers with look-ahead, that are especially tailored to modeling receive-send actions. A second approach is to combine different computational models for receive-send actions. For instance, a hybrid model in which some receive-actions are described by rewrite rules and others by transducers might still be decidable.

6   The Main Result

The main technical result of this paper is the following:

Theorem 3. *For transducer-based protocols,* ATTACK *is decidable and PSPACE-hard.*

In what follows, we very briefly sketch the proof idea of the theorem. See [14] for the detailed proof.

The hardness result is easy to show. It is by reduction from the finite automata intersection problem, which has been shown to be PSPACE-complete by Kozen [11].

The decidability result is much more involved, because we have two sources of infinite behavior in the model. First, the intruder can perform an unbounded number of steps to derive a new message, and second, to perform one receive-send action, a principal can carry out an unbounded number of internal actions. Note that because transducers may have ε-transitions, i.e., not in every transition a letter is read from the input, the number of transitions taken in one receive-send action is not even bounded in the size of the input message or the problem instance.

While the former source of infinity was already present in the (decidable) models for closed-ended protocols [20,2,13], the latter is new. To show Theorem 3, one therefore not only needs to show that the number of actions performed by the intruder can be bounded, but also the number of internal actions of principals. In fact, it suffices to show the latter, since if we can bound the number of internal actions, a principal only reads messages of bounded length and therefore the intruder only needs to produce messages of size bounded by this length.

Roughly speaking, we can bound the number of internal actions of principals because principals (the extended message transducers describing them) have only finite memory and we can apply a pumping argument showing that long paths in a message transducer can be truncated. Of course, the pumping argument is much more involved than that for usual finite automata since we have to guarantee that i) the input label of the truncated path is still a message that can be produced by the intruder, and ii) the output label of the truncated path is such that it can be used by the intruder to perform a successful attack if this was possible with the output label of the original path. While property i) is relatively easy to achieve, property ii) is very involved. In what follows, we therefore concentrate on ii).

Proof idea of the pumping argument. First, we define a so-called *solvability preserving (quasi-)ordering* on messages, which allows to replace single messages in the intruder knowledge by new ones such that if in the original problem a successful attack exists, then also in the modified problem. This reduces the pumping argument to the following problem: Truncate paths in message transducers in such a way that the output of the original path is equivalent (w.r.t. the solvability preserving ordering) to the output of the truncated path. It remains to find criteria for truncating paths in this way. To this purpose, we introduce another quasi-ordering, the so-called *path truncation ordering*, which indicates at which positions a path can be truncated. To really obtain a bound on the length of paths, one then needs to show that the equivalence relation corresponding to the path truncation ordering has finite index – more accurately, an index that can be bounded in the size of the problem instance. With this, and the fact that message transducers have only finite memory, the length of paths can be restricted. Finally, to show the bound on the index, one needs to establish a bound on the depth of messages (i.e., the depth of nested encryptions and hashes) in successful attacks. Again, we make use of the fact that message transducers have only finite memory.

7   Conclusion

We have introduced a generic protocol model for analyzing the security of open-ended protocols, i.e., protocols with open-ended data structures, and investigated the decidability of different instances of this model. In one instance, receive-send actions are modeled by sets of rewrite rules. We have shown that in this instance, security is undecidable. These results indicated that to obtain decidability, principals should only have finite memory and should not be able to compare messages of arbitrary size. This motivated our transducer-based model, which complies to these restrictions, but still captures certain open-ended protocols. We have shown that in this model security is decidable and PSPACE-hard; it remains to establish a tight complexity bound. These results have been shown for the shared key setting and secrecy properties. We conjecture that they carry over rather easily to public key encryption and authentication.

As pointed out in Section 5.1, a promising future direction is to combine the transducer-based model with the models for closed-ended protocols and to devise tree transducers suitable for describing receive-send actions. We will also try to incorporate complex keys, since they are used in many protocols. We believe that the proof techniques devised in this paper will help to show decidability also in the more powerful models. Finally, encouraged by the work that has been done for closed-ended protocols, the long-term goal of the work started here is to develop tools for automatic verification of open-ended protocols, if possible by integrating the new algorithms into existing tools.

Acknowledgement

I thank Thomas Wilke for many helpful comments on this work, and Catherine Meadows for pointing me to the paper by Pereira and Quisquater.

References

1. R. M. Amadio and W. Charatonik. On name generation and set-based analysis in Dolev-Yao model. Technical Report RR-4379, INRIA, 2002. 516
2. R. M. Amadio, D. Lugiez, and V. Vanackère. On the symbolic reduction of processes with cryptographic functions. Technical Report RR-4147, INRIA, 2001. 516, 517, 518, 519, 527
3. G. Ateniese, M. Steiner, and G. Tsudik. Authenticated group key agreement and friends. In *Proceedings of the 5th ACM Conference on Computer and Communication Secruity (CCS'98)*, pages 17–26, San Francisco, CA, 1998. ACM Press. 517
4. J. Bryans and S. A. Schneider. CSP, PVS, and a Recursive Authentication Protocol. In *DIMACS Workshop on Formal Verification of Security Protocols*, 1997. 517
5. J. A. Bull and D. J. Otway. The authentication protocol. Technical Report DRA/CIS3/PROJ/CORBA/SC/1/CSM/436-04/03, Defence Research Agency, Malvern, UK, 1997. 517
6. D. Dolev, S. Even, and R. M. Karp. On the Security of Ping-Pong Protocols. *Information and Control*, 55:57–68, 1982. 517
7. D. Dolev and A. C. Yao. On the Security of Public-Key Protocols. *IEEE Transactions on Information Theory*, 29(2):198–208, 1983. 515, 519
8. N. A. Durgin, P. D. Lincoln, J. C. Mitchell, and A. Scedrov. Undecidability of bounded security protocols. In *Workshop on Formal Methods and Security Protocols (FMSP'99)*, 1999. 516, 517
9. S. Even and O. Goldreich. On the Security of Multi-Party Ping-Pong Protocols. In *IEEE Symposium on Foundations of Computer Science (FOCS'83)*, pages 34–39, 1983. 516
10. N. Ferguson and B. Schneier. A Cryptographic Evaluation of IPsec. Technical report, 2000. Available from http://www.counterpane.com/ipsec.pdf. 517
11. M. R. Garey and D. S. Johnson. *Computers and Intractability: A Guide to the Theory of NP-Completeness*. Freeman, San Francisco, 1979. 527
12. D. Harkins and D. Carrel. *The Internet Key Exchange (IKE)*, November 1998. RFC 2409. 517
13. A. Huima. Efficient infinite-state analysis of security protocols. In *Workshop on Formal Methods and Security Protocols (FMSP'99)*, 1999. 516, 517, 519, 527
14. R. Küsters. On the Decidability of Cryptographic Protocols with Open-ended Data Structures. Technical Report IFI-0204, CAU Kiel, Germany, 2002. Available from http://www.informatik.uni-kiel.de/reports/2002/0204.html. 517, 518, 522, 523, 524, 525, 527
15. C. Meadows. Extending formal cryptographic protocol analysis techniques for group protocols and low-level cryptographic primitives. In *Proceedings of the First Workshop on Issues in the Theory of Security (WITS'00)*, pages 87–92, 2000. 517
16. C. Meadows. Open issues in formal methods for cryptographic protocol analysis. In *Proc. of DISCEX 2000*, pages 237–250. IEEE Computer Society Press, 2000. 515, 517
17. J. Mitchell, M. Mitchell, and U. Stern. Automated Analysis of Cryptographic Protocols using Murphi. In *Proceedings of the 1997 IEEE Symposium on Security and Privacy*, pages 141–151. IEEE Computer Society Press, 1997. 526
18. L. C. Pauslon. Mechanized proofs for a recursive authetication protocol. In *10th IEEE Computer Security Foundations Workshop (CSFW-10)*, pages 84–95, 1997. 517

19. O. Pereira and J.-J. Quisquater. A Security Analysis of the Cliques Protocols Suites. In *Proceedings of the 14th IEEE Computer Security Foundations Workshop (CSFW-14)*, pages 73–81, 2001. 517

20. M. Rusinowitch and M. Turuani. Protocol Insecurity with Finite Number of Sessions is NP-complete. In *14th IEEE Computer Security Foundations Workshop (CSFW-14)*, pages 174– 190, 2001. 516, 517, 518, 519, 521, 522, 527

21. M. Steiner, G. Tsudik, and M. Waidner. CLIQUES: A new approach to key agreement. In *IEEE International Conference on Distributed Computing Systems*. IEEE Computer Society Press, pages 380–387, 1998. 517

22. J. Zhou. Fixing a security flaw in IKE protocols. *Electronic Letter*, 35(13):1072–1073, 1999. 517

Causality Semantics of Petri Nets with Weighted Inhibitor Arcs

H. C. M. Kleijn[1] and M. Koutny[2]

[1] LIACS, Leiden University
P.O.Box 9512, NL-2300 RA Leiden, The Netherlands
[2] Department of Computing Science, University of Newcastle upon Tyne
NE1 7RU, UK

Abstract. A causality semantics for weighted Place/Transition nets with weighted inhibitor arcs (PTI-nets) is proposed, by extending the standard approach based on the process semantics given through net unfolding and occurrence nets. It is demonstrated how processes corresponding to step sequences of PTI-nets can be constructed, and a non-algorithmic (axiomatic) characterisation is given of the processes that can be obtained in this way. Moreover, a framework is established allowing to separately consider behaviours, processes and causality, in order to facilitate the discussion of their mutual consistency for different Petri net classes.

Keywords: theory of concurrency, Petri nets, weighted inhibitor arcs, causality semantics, occurrence nets, step sequences.

1 Introduction

In a Place/Transition net (PT-net) the executability of a transition only depends on the presence of enough tokens in its input places. Adding inhibitor arcs means that one can also test whether some specific places are empty, which is particularly useful for communication protocols and performance analysis (see [5,8]). In general, this leads to universal computational power ([16]), and important decision problems, e.g., marking reachability, become undecidable ([12]).

In this paper, we consider causal relationships in concurrent runs of PTI-nets consisting of PT-nets with weighted inhibitor arcs which test whether a place does not contain more than a certain threshold number of tokens [1]. We continue the work of [13] on elementary net systems with inhibitor arcs — further developed in [14] — which employed *stratified order structures* (so-structures) to provide a causality semantics consistent with the operational semantics defined in terms of step sequences. Whereas for PT-nets an abstract causality semantics can be given in terms of partial orders alone, the presence of inhibitor arcs requires more involved information on the relationships between transition occurrences.

Consider the net NI_{expl} shown in figure 1(a). In addition to the weighted standard arcs (e.g., executing t adds 2 tokens to place p_3), there is an inhibitor

L. Brim et al. (Eds.): CONCUR 2002, LNCS 2421, pp. 531–546, 2002.

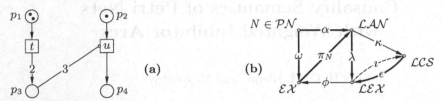

Fig. 1. (a) A PTI-net NI_{expl}, and (b) the semantical setup for a Petri net N in $\mathcal{PN}$

arc between place p_3 and transition u of weight 3. This means that u is enabled and can occur only if p_3 contains *at most* 3 tokens (and p_2 contains at least one); moreover, executing u has no effect on the tokens in p_3. Initially, both t and u are enabled and the seven non-empty execution sequences of NI_{expl} are: u, ut, utt, t, tu, tut and tt. In the *a priori* concurrency semantics for PTI-nets, as discussed in [7] and investigated in [13,14], t and u may also be executed simultaneously after executing t, since the inhibitor place p_3 of u holds less than 3 tokens *prior* to the occurrence of u. The resulting step sequence $t\{t,u\}$ cannot be adequately described by a causal partial order as any such order would also allow the execution sequence ttu which is not a valid behaviour of NI_{expl}.
Stratified order structures take care of these more involved relations between transition occurrences by providing next to a partial order a weak partial order. The former describes the standard causal relationships between the occurrences whereas the latter describes relationships as above: after the first occurrence of t, u *may precede* another occurrence of t but not vice versa, and hence the step $\{t,u\}$ after t may be sequentialised to ut, but not to tu.

For elementary net systems and PT-nets, an abstract partial order semantics follows immediately from their process semantics (see, e.g., [18,3,11]). Processes are constructed by unfolding the system according to a given run represented by a firing sequence σ. This leads to occurrence nets, which are (labelled) acyclic nets with non-branching place occurrences (conditions). By abstracting from the conditions of an occurrence net, one obtains a (labelled) partial order which describes the causal relationships between the events (transition occurrences) in σ: all labelled sequences which are linearisations of the partial order are also firing sequences of the net, and among them one can find σ.

To obtain a causality semantics for nets with zero-testing inhibitor arcs, also both [13] and [14] first develop a process semantics. Since in the *a priori* semantics not all concurrent runs of the system can be represented by a firing sequence, these processes are based on step sequences (e.g., for NI_{expl} with an inhibitor arc of weight 0 from p_4 to t, neither tut nor ttu are firing sequences though $t\{t,u\}$ is a valid step sequence).
Given a step sequence σ of an elementary net system with inhibitor arcs, [13] constructed an occurrence net with additional (activator) arcs, and testing whether a place is empty (inhibitor arc) is represented by testing whether its complement condition holds using an activator arc. The resulting activator occurrence net

is acyclic in a sense which includes all activator arcs ($\Diamond$–acyclic), and allows one to extract a (labelled) so-structure which describes the causality and weak causality between the events in σ: all step sequences which obey the constraints imposed by the so-structure are valid step sequences, and they also include σ.

To define a process semantics for unweighted PT-nets with unweighted inhibitor arcs, we first investigated in [14] the case that all inhibitor places are complemented. Then the approaches of [3] and [13] could be combined in a straightforward manner. To deal with the general case, additional conditions (z-conditions) were generated during the construction of a process for a given step sequence (the presence of a z-condition represents an empty inhibitor place). Since z-conditions may be branching (with respect to the ordinary arcs), this led to a new type of occurrence net with activator arcs.

As observed in [14], the process and causality semantics presented there could easily be generalised to PT-nets with weighted ordinary arcs. How to deal with weighted inhibitor arcs was less obvious. In this paper, we show that in case of complemented inhibitor places, the approach of [14] is readily adaptable. For general PTI-nets, however, we propose a novel process semantics using another kind of additional conditions connected to activator arcs. This is different from the use of the z-conditions in [14] and avoids references to the weights of inhibitor arcs. Moreover, it is no longer necessary to use occurrence nets with branching activator places. We describe how processes corresponding to step sequences of PTI-nets can be constructed, and a non-algorithmic (axiomatic) characterisation is given of the processes that can be obtained in this way.

Developing a causality semantics based on net unfoldings requires going through several behavioural notions and relations between them, no matter what kind of Petri nets one is interested in. That is, there is a general pattern of proceeding, which only differs in technical (though non-trivial) aspects between different net classes. In this paper, we decided to make such a pattern explicit, and developed a uniform framework for relating, in particular, behaviours, processes, and causality structures generated by nets. As a result, we will identify some interesting semantical characteristics (called the *aims*), and relatively few requirements (called the *properties*) which need to be established for a specific class of nets and/or behaviours to guarantee that the aims hold. This results in a clear separation of concerns when discussing different behavioural notions.

We will first introduce the semantical framework, and then show that the standard treatment of PT-nets adheres to it. After that we investigate PTI-nets with and without complemented inhibitor places. All proofs can be found in [15].

Basic notions and notations A multiset (over a set X) is a function $m : X \to \mathbb{N}$, and an *extended* multiset is a function $m : X \to \mathbb{N} \cup \{\infty\}$. The multiset $\mathbf{0}_X$ and the extended multiset $\mathbf{\Omega}_X$ are given by $\mathbf{0}_X(x) \overset{\mathrm{df}}{=} 0$ and $\mathbf{\Omega}_X(x) \overset{\mathrm{df}}{=} \infty$. A multiset m is finite if there are finitely many $x \in X$ such that $x \in m$ (i.e., $m(x) \geq 1$); the cardinality of such m is $|m| \overset{\mathrm{df}}{=} \sum_{x \in X} m(x)$. The sum $(+)$ and difference $(-)$ of multisets are defined as usual; moreover, for two extended multisets m and m', we have $m \leq m'$ if $m(x) \leq m'(x)$ for all $x \in X$. Any subset of X may be viewed as a multiset, and any multiset as an extended multiset.

A *labelling* is a function $\ell : X \rightarrow \mathbb{A}$, where $\mathbb{A}$ is a set of *labels*. For $Y \subseteq X$, $\ell(Y) \stackrel{\text{df}}{=} \{a \in \mathbb{A} \mid \exists y \in Y : a = \ell(y)\}$ and, if Y is finite, then $\ell\langle Y \rangle$ is the multiset over $\mathbb{A}$ given by $\ell\langle Y \rangle(a) \stackrel{\text{df}}{=} |\ell^{-1}(a) \cap Y|$, for every $a \in \mathbb{A}$.

A (weighted) *net* is $N \stackrel{\text{df}}{=} (P, T, W)$ such that P (*places*) and T (*transitions*) are disjoint finite sets, and $W : (T \times P) \cup (P \times T) \rightarrow \mathbb{N}$ is the *weight function*. We adopt the usual conventions for drawing nets, and assume that, for every $t \in T$, there are p, q such that $W(p, t) \neq 0 \neq W(t, q)$. The *pre-* and *post-multiset* of $t \in T$ are multisets of places, given by $\text{PRE}_N(t)(p) \stackrel{\text{df}}{=} W(p, t)$ and $\text{POST}_N(t)(p) \stackrel{\text{df}}{=} W(t, p)$. For a finite multiset of transitions U, $\text{PRE}_N(U) \stackrel{\text{df}}{=} \sum_{t \in U} U(t) \cdot \text{PRE}_N(t)$ and $\text{POST}_N(U) \stackrel{\text{df}}{=} \sum_{t \in U} U(t) \cdot \text{POST}_N(t)$. A *marking* of N is a multiset M of places, and a *step* is a finite non-empty multiset U of transitions. The latter is *enabled* at M if $M \geq \text{PRE}_N(U)$; then U can be *executed* leading to the marking $M' \stackrel{\text{df}}{=} M - \text{PRE}_N(U) + \text{POST}_N(U)$ and we write $M[U\rangle_N M'$. A *step sequence* from a marking M to M' is a possibly empty sequence $\sigma = U_1 \ldots U_n$ such that $M[U_1\rangle_N M_1 \cdots M_{n-1} [U_n\rangle_N M'$ for some markings $M_1, \ldots, M_{n-1}$; we write $M[\sigma\rangle_N M'$, while $M[\sigma\rangle_N$ means that $M[\sigma\rangle_N M'$ for some M'.

An *inhibitor net* is $NI \stackrel{\text{df}}{=} (P, T, W, I)$ such that $\text{UND}(NI) \stackrel{\text{df}}{=} (P, T, W)$ is a net, the *underlying* net of NI, and $I : (P \times T) \rightarrow \mathbb{N} \cup \{\infty\}$ is an extended multiset. If $I(p, t) = k \in \mathbb{N}$ then p is an *inhibitor place of* t and (p, t) is an *inhibitor arc* leading from p to t, drawn with a small circle as arrowhead and annotated with k if $k \geq 1$. The notations for transitions and places introduced above are defined for NI through $\text{UND}(NI)$. In addition, for every $t \in T$, $\text{INH}_{NI}(t)$ is the extended multiset of places given by $\text{INH}_{NI}(t)(p) \stackrel{\text{df}}{=} I(p, t)$ and, for a finite multiset U of transitions, $\text{INH}_{NI}(U)$ is the extended multiset of places given by $\text{INH}_{NI}(U)(p) \stackrel{\text{df}}{=} \min(\{\infty\} \cup \{\text{INH}_{NI}(t)(p) \mid t \in U\})$. Steps and markings of NI are those of $\text{UND}(NI)$. In NI, a step U is *enabled* at a marking M if it is enabled at M in $\text{UND}(NI)$ and $M \leq \text{INH}_{NI}(U)$. Thus, if a place p is an inhibitor place of some transition t occurring in U, then p should not contain more than $I(p, t)$ tokens. (In the *a posteriori* approach [6], the inequality for enabledness is strengthened and becomes $M + \text{POST}_{NI}(U) \leq \text{INH}_{NI}(U)$.) So, if $I(p, t) = 0$ then p must be empty. The step sequences of NI are defined as before, using the modified notion of enabledness.

An *activator net* is $NA \stackrel{\text{df}}{=} (P, T, W, Act)$ such that $\text{UND}(NA) \stackrel{\text{df}}{=} (P, T, W)$ is a net, the *underlying* net of NA, and $Act \subseteq P \times T$. $(p, t) \in Act$ is an *activator arc* from p to t, meaning that t can only be executed if p contains at least one token (the presence of a token is tested without being consumed by t). Activator arcs have small black dots as arrowheads. The notations for transitions and places introduced above are defined for NA through $\text{UND}(NA)$. In addition, for every $t \in T$, $\text{ACT}_{NA}(t)$ is the set of places p such that $(p, t) \in Act$ and, for a finite multiset U of transitions, $\text{ACT}_{NA}(U)$ is the union of sets $\text{ACT}_{NA}(t)$, for all $t \in U$. Steps and markings of NA are those of $\text{UND}(NA)$. A step $U : T \rightarrow \mathbb{N}$ is *enabled* at a marking M if it is enabled at M in $\text{UND}(NA)$ and, in addition, $M(p) \geq 1$ for all $p \in \text{ACT}_{NA}(U)$ (for alternative definitions see [6,20]). The step sequences of NA are defined as before, using the modified notion of enabledness.

For each kind of net, we can consider *labelled* versions as well as *marked* versions, which amounts to adding a final component (labelling or *initial* marking) to the tuple representing the net. All the notation relating to the structure and behaviour of the labelled (marked) net is inherited from the original net.

Finally, for functions $f : X \to \mathbb{P}(Y)$ and $g : Y \to \mathbb{P}(Z)$, we define the composition $g \circ f : X \to \mathbb{P}(Z)$ by $g \circ f(x) \stackrel{\mathrm{df}}{=} \bigcup_{y \in f(x)} g(y)$.

2 The Semantical Framework

The semantical framework within which we present our results is shown in figure 1(b). For a given Petri net model $\mathcal{PN}$, we use the following semantical domains:

- $\mathcal{EX}$ are executions, such as step sequences, employed by the operational (or behavioural) semantics of nets in $\mathcal{PN}$;
- $\mathcal{LAN}$ are labelled acyclic nets, such as occurrence nets, providing the structural description of abstract processes (histories) of nets in $\mathcal{PN}$;
- $\mathcal{LEX}$ are labelled executions, such as labelled step sequences, employed by the operational semantics of nets in $\mathcal{LAN}$;
- $\mathcal{LCS}$ are labelled causal structures, such as labelled partial orders, used to define an abstract causality semantics of nets in $\mathcal{PN}$.

The arrows in figure 1(b) indicate functions that will be instantiated later, and then used to relate the three views on semantics for the Petri net model $\mathcal{PN}$, captured respectively by $\mathcal{EX}$, $\mathcal{LAN}$ and $\mathcal{LCS}$. For each net model, it will be our aim to show that the different semantics agree in the sense that processes ($\mathcal{LAN}$) and causal structures ($\mathcal{LCS}$) describe relations between events consistent with the chosen operational semantics ($\mathcal{EX}$). This section explains how certain simple conditions (called *Properties*) guarantee such an agreement. As a result, we can later focus on the definitions of the semantical domains and functions appearing in figure 1(b), and after establishing their Properties, the desired results on the semantics will follow immediately.

Suppose that a Petri net model $\mathcal{PN}$ has been fixed, and that the N in figure 1(b) is an arbitrary net from $\mathcal{PN}$. We first consider the square-like part of the diagram (together with the diagonal), which essentially describes and relates two different ways in which a net in $\mathcal{PN}$ can be given a process semantics.

The function $\omega : \mathcal{PN} \to \mathbb{P}(\mathcal{EX})$ yields the non-empty set of executions of N, providing its *operational* semantics. The function $\alpha : \mathcal{PN} \to \mathbb{P}(\mathcal{LAN})$ associates with N a non-empty set of labelled acyclic nets (processes) from $\mathcal{LAN}$ satisfying certain *axioms*; a process is given an operational semantics through the function $\lambda : \mathcal{LAN} \to \mathbb{P}(\mathcal{LEX})$ which associates with it a non-empty set of *labelled* executions. A labelled execution can be interpreted as an ordinary execution (of the original net N) by *forgetting* some irrelevant information through the total function $\phi : \mathcal{LEX} \to \mathcal{EX}$. Finally, the partial function $\pi_N : \mathcal{EX} \to \mathbb{P}(\mathcal{LAN})$ defines, for each execution ξ of N, a non-empty set of labelled acyclic nets which can be viewed as operationally defined *processes* of ξ (note that π_N is only meaningful for the executions of N). Thus we require:

Property 1. ω, α, λ, ϕ, $\pi_N|_{\omega(N)}$ are total, and ω, α, λ, $\pi_N|_{\omega(N)}$ never return $\varnothing$.

Two aims can now be formulated which, when fulfilled, mean that the axiomatic and behavioural process definition as well as the operational semantics of nets in $\mathcal{PN}$ are in agreement: the axiomatic processes of N (defined through α) coincide with the operational processes of N (defined through $\pi_N \circ \omega$); and the operational semantics of N (defined through ω) coincides with the operational semantics of the processes of N (defined through $\phi \circ \lambda \circ \alpha$).

Aim 1. $\alpha = \pi_N \circ \omega$.

Aim 2. $\omega = \phi \circ \lambda \circ \alpha$.

These aims follow from a consistency property relating individual executions to individual processes: (i) any process defined from an execution ξ of N can also be defined axiomatically and then has ξ as one of its executions; and (ii) any labelled execution of a process LN of N can also be interpreted as an execution of N and then can be used to define LN operationally. Thus we require:

Property 2 (Consistency). For all $\xi \in \mathcal{EX}$ and $LN \in \mathcal{LAN}$,
$$\xi \in \omega(N) \wedge LN \in \pi_N(\xi) \text{ iff } LN \in \alpha(N) \wedge \xi \in \phi(\lambda(LN)) .$$

A corollary of Aims 1 and 2 is the consistency between the operational semantics of N and the operational semantics of its behaviourally defined processes.

Corollary 1. $\omega = \phi \circ \lambda \circ \pi_N \circ \omega$.

We now turn to the abstract causality semantics of processes which is represented by the triangle-like part on the right of the diagram in figure 1(b). By extracting from a labelled acyclic net the causal relationships between its labelled events one obtains an abstract representation of causality between events. This is formalised through a function $\kappa : \mathcal{LAN} \to \mathcal{LCS}$ which associates a labelled *causal* structure with each process in $\mathcal{LAN}$. To relate this abstract causality semantics to the operational semantics of processes, there is a total function $\epsilon : \mathcal{LCS} \to \mathbb{P}(\mathcal{LEX})$ and a partial function $\iota : \mathbb{P}(\mathcal{LEX}) \to \mathcal{LCS}$, which allow one to go back and forth between labelled causal structures and the labelled executions they are supposed to represent. We require:

Property 3. κ, ϵ, $\iota|_{\lambda(\mathcal{LAN})}$ are total, and ϵ never returns $\varnothing$.

The function ϵ associates with each labelled causal structure a set of labelled *executions* which should uniquely represent it. To formalise this, we have the partial function ι which, for any set of labelled executions with the same domain and labelling, yields — typically through some kind of *intersection* — the labelled causal structure, they are supposed to represent. We thus require:

Property 4 (Representation). $\iota \circ \epsilon = id_{\mathcal{LCS}}$.

Note that this implies that the domain of ι includes $\epsilon(\mathcal{LCS})$.
The causality in a process of N (defined through κ) should coincide with the causality structure implied by its operational semantics (through $\iota \circ \lambda$).

Aim 3. $\kappa = \imath \circ \lambda$.

To show the above we need to ensure that the observational semantics for the structures in $\mathcal{LCS}$ fits with the operational semantics chosen for $\mathcal{LAN}$.

Property 5 (Fitting). $\lambda = \epsilon \circ \kappa$.

Finally, we can relate the operational semantics of the net N and the set of labelled causal structures associated with it, in effect joining together the two parts of the diagram in figure 1(b) considered so far separately.

Corollary 2. $\omega = \phi \circ \epsilon \circ \kappa \circ \alpha$.

Aim 2 and corollaries 1 and 2 verify the consistency of the process and abstract causality semantics of the net N with its operational semantics given by the function ω (which captures the dynamics of the nets in $\mathcal{PN}$ and is in many cases given through a firing sequence or step sequence semantics).

To use the above setup in practice, all we need to do is to establish Properties 1–5, and then the semantical Aims 1-3 and their Corollaries 1-2 follow.

2.1   Executions and Causal Structures

This section instantiates for this paper $\mathcal{EX}$, $\mathcal{LEX}$, and $\mathcal{LCS}$ together with mappings ϕ, $\imath$, and ϵ; the associated Properties 1, 3, and 4 are established.

To model executions, we use step sequences ($\mathcal{STS}$), where a *step sequence* is a finite sequence of non-empty finite multisets. As labelled executions we use labelled step sequences ($\mathcal{LSTS}$). Each *labelled step sequence* is a pair $\varpi = (\sigma, \ell)$, where $\sigma = X_1 \ldots X_n \in \mathcal{STS}$ is a step sequence consisting of mutually disjoint sets, and ℓ is a labelling for $X_1 \cup \ldots \cup X_n$. With such a ϖ, we associate a step sequence $\phi(\varpi) \stackrel{\mathrm{df}}{=} \ell\langle X_1 \rangle \ldots \ell\langle X_n \rangle$. Thus ϕ is total and satisfies Property 1. Moreover, for $i \leq n$ and $x \in X_i$, $ind(\varpi, x) \stackrel{\mathrm{df}}{=} i$ where i is such that $x \in X_i$.

We use two kinds of labelled causal structures, labelled partial orders ($\mathcal{LPO}$) and labelled stratified order structures ($\mathcal{LSOS}$). A *labelled partially ordered set* (or *poset*) is a triple $lpo = (X, \prec, \ell)$, where X is a finite set, ℓ is a labelling for X, and $\prec \subseteq X \times X$ is a transitive and irreflexive relation. A poset can be thought of as an abstract history of a concurrent system, where $\prec$ is interpreted as *causality*. A *labelled stratified order structure* [10,13] (or *so-structure*) is a quadruple $lsos = (X, \prec, \sqsubset, \ell)$, where X is a finite set, ℓ is a labelling for X, and $\prec$ and $\sqsubset$ are two binary irreflexive relations over X such that $\prec$ is included in $\sqsubset$, $((x \sqsubset y \sqsubset z) \wedge (x \neq z) \Longrightarrow x \sqsubset z)$ and $((x \sqsubset y \prec z) \vee (x \prec y \sqsubset z) \Longrightarrow x \prec z)$. It is easily seen that $(X, \prec, \ell)$ is a poset and, furthermore, that $x \prec y$ implies $y \not\sqsubset x$. The first relation in an so-structure $lsos$, should be interpreted as an abstraction of the 'earlier than' relation (*causality*), and the second as an abstraction of the 'not later than' relation (see [13]).

The set $\epsilon_{\mathcal{LPO}}(lpo)$ of *labelled step sequences* of a poset $lpo = (X, \prec, \ell)$ comprises all $\varpi \in \mathcal{LSTS}$ with domain X and labelling ℓ such that $x \prec y$ implies

$ind(\varpi, x) < ind(\varpi, y)$, i.e., those labelled step sequences which respect the ordering $\prec$. Thus $\epsilon_{\mathcal{LPO}}$ is total and never returns $\varnothing$, and so satisfies Property 3.

The *poset intersection* of a non-empty set $LSTS$ of labelled step sequences with the same domain X and labelling ℓ is $\iota_{\mathcal{LPO}}(LSTS) \stackrel{\mathrm{df}}{=} (X, \prec, \ell)$, where $\prec$ is the binary relation on X such that $x \prec y$ whenever $ind(\varpi, x) < ind(\varpi, y)$ for all $\varpi \in LSTS$, i.e., $\iota_{\mathcal{LPO}}(LSTS)$ intersects all the orderings on the set X implied by the elements of $LSTS$. Thus $\iota_{\mathcal{LPO}}(LSTS)$ is a poset completely determined by the labelled step sequences in $LSTS$. Since the functions λ that we will consider yield non-empty sets of labelled step sequences with the same domain and labelling, it follows that $\iota_{\mathcal{LPO}}$ satisfies Property 3. Moreover, for a poset *lpo*, $\iota_{\mathcal{LPO}}(\epsilon_{\mathcal{LPO}}(lpo)) = lpo$ and so $\epsilon_{\mathcal{LPO}}$ and $\iota_{\mathcal{LPO}}$ together satisfy Property 4.

The set $\epsilon(lsos)$ of *labelled step sequences* of an so-structure $lsos = (X, \prec, \sqsubset, \ell)$ comprises all $\varpi \in \mathcal{LSTS}$ with domain X and labelling ℓ such that $x \prec y$ implies $ind(\varpi, x) < ind(\varpi, y)$, and $x \sqsubset y$ implies $ind(\varpi, x) \leq ind(\varpi, y)$, i.e., those labelled step sequences which respect both $\prec$ and $\sqsubset$. This ϵ is total, never returns the empty set and so satisfies Property 3.

The *so-structure intersection* of a non-empty set $LSTS$ of labelled step sequences with the same domain X and labelling ℓ is $\iota(LSTS) \stackrel{\mathrm{df}}{=} (X, \prec, \sqsubset, \ell)$, where $\prec$ and $\sqsubset$ are binary relations on X such that $x \prec y$ whenever $ind(\varpi, x) < ind(\varpi, y)$ for all $\varpi \in LSTS$, and $x \sqsubset y$ whenever $ind(\varpi, x) \leq ind(\varpi, y)$ for all $\varpi \in LSTS$. Then $\iota(LSTS)$ is an so-structure completely determined by its labelled step sequences ([13]). By the properties of the functions λ that we will consider, we have that ι satisfies Property 3; moreover, for an so-structure *lsos*, $\iota(\epsilon(lsos)) = lsos$ and so ϵ and ι together satisfy Property 4.

As labelled causal structures are often derived from locally defined information, we need suitable closure operations. For posets, all we need is the standard transitive closure. A structure $rs = (X, \prec, \ell)$ is *acyclic* if the transitive closure $\prec^+$ of $\prec$ is irreflexive. The *transitive closure* of rs is $rs^+ \stackrel{\mathrm{df}}{=} (X, \prec^+, \ell)$ which is a labelled partial order iff rs is acyclic. For so-structures, we need more complicated devices. The $\Diamond$-*closure* of a structure $rs = (X, \prec, \sqsubset, \ell)$ is $rs^\Diamond \stackrel{\mathrm{df}}{=} (X, \prec', \sqsubset', \ell)$, where $\prec' \stackrel{\mathrm{df}}{=} (\prec \cup \sqsubset)^* \circ \prec \circ (\prec \cup \sqsubset)^*$ and $\sqsubset' \stackrel{\mathrm{df}}{=} (\prec \cup \sqsubset)^* \backslash id_X$. Moreover, rs is $\Diamond$-*acyclic* if $\prec'$ is irreflexive. In operational terms, this means that in a system history described by rs, there are no event occurrences $e_1, e_2, \ldots, e_k$ such that each e_i has occurred *before or simultaneously with* e_{i+1}, while e_k has occurred *before* e_1. We have that $rs^\Diamond$ is an so-structure iff rs is $\Diamond$-*acyclic* ([13]).

2.2   Labelled Acyclic Nets

This section instantiates $\mathcal{LAN}$ together with mappings κ and λ; the associated Properties 1, 3, and 5 are established as well as Aim 3.

For PT-nets, labelled occurrence nets are used to represent execution histories (see, e.g., [3,4,11,18].) Such nets may be viewed as (partial) net unfoldings, where conflicts between transitions have already been resolved.

Definition 1 ($\mathcal{LAN}$ for PT-nets). *The class $\mathcal{LON}$ of labelled occurrence nets (or o-nets) comprises all labelled nets $ON = (B, E, R, \ell)$ such that:*

- $R \subseteq (B \times E) \cup (E \times B)$ and ℓ is a labelling for $B \cup E$.
- For every $b \in B$, $|\text{PRE}_N(b)| \leq 1$ and $|\text{POST}_N(b)| \leq 1$.
- The structure $rs_{ON} \overset{\text{df}}{=} (E, \prec_{loc}, \ell|_E)$ is acyclic, where $\prec_{loc} \overset{\text{df}}{=} R^2|_{E \times E}$.

As usual, we refer to the places of an occurrence net as *conditions*, and to its transitions as *events*. The relation $\prec_{loc}$ represents the *local* information about the causal relationships between events. Since rs_{ON} is acyclic, ON *generates* a poset $\kappa_{\mathcal{LPO}}(ON) \overset{\text{df}}{=} rs_{ON}^+ = (E, \prec_{loc}^+, \ell|_E)$ which provides a partial order description of the labelled event occurrences. Clearly, $\kappa_{\mathcal{LPO}}$ is total and so satisfies Property 3.

The default *initial* (*final*) marking of ON is MIN_{ON} (resp. MAX_{ON}) which consists of all conditions without incoming (resp. outgoing) arcs. The *labelled step sequences* of ON are defined by $\lambda(ON) \overset{\text{df}}{=} \{(\sigma, \ell|_E) \mid \text{MIN}_{ON}[\sigma\rangle_{ON}\text{MAX}_{ON}\}$. Thus $\lambda(ON) \subseteq \mathcal{LSTS}$ and $\lambda(ON) \neq \varnothing$ and so λ satisfies Property 1. Moreover, as promised, all labelled step sequences in $\lambda(ON)$ have the same domain and labelling. Furthermore, the operational semantics of an o-net ON fits with its partial order semantics, i.e., we have $\lambda(ON) = \epsilon_{\mathcal{LPO}}(\kappa_{\mathcal{LPO}}(ON))$ and so Property 5 is satisfied. We may conclude now that Aim 3 is satisfied and $\kappa_{\mathcal{LPO}}(ON) = \imath_{\mathcal{LPO}}(\lambda(ON))$.

Inhibitor arcs make the standard unfolding procedure more complicated, due to the fact that local information regarding the lack of tokens in a place cannot be explicitly represented in an o-net. Following [13] we add activator arcs which will be used to represent the presence of inhibitor arcs.

Definition 2 ($\mathcal{LAN}$ for inhibitor nets). *The class $\mathcal{LAON}$ of labelled activator occurrence nets (or ao-nets) comprises all labelled activator nets $AON = (B, E, R, Act, \ell)$ such that:*

- $R \subseteq (B \times E) \cup (E \times B)$, $Act \subseteq B \times E$ and ℓ is a labelling for $B \cup E$.
- For every $b \in B$, $|\text{PRE}_{AON}(b)| \leq 1$ and $|\text{POST}_{AON}(b)| \leq 1$.
- The structure $rs_{AON} \overset{\text{df}}{=} (E, \prec_{loc}, \sqsubset_{loc}, \ell|_E)$ is $\Diamond$-acyclic, where $\prec_{loc}$ and $\sqsubset_{loc}$ are relations respectively given by $R^2|_{E \times E} \cup (R \circ Act)$ and $Act^{-1} \circ R$.

Since rs_{AON} is $\Diamond$-acyclic, $R^2|_{E \times E}$ is acyclic in the usual sense, and so the labelled net underlying AON, $\text{UND}(AON) \overset{\text{df}}{=} (B, E, R, \ell)$, is an o-net. Similarly as for o-nets, the relations $\prec_{loc}$ and $\sqsubset_{loc}$ represent the *local* information about the causal relationships between the events contained in AON. Figure 2(a,b,c) shows how $\prec_{loc}$ and $\sqsubset_{loc}$ are constructed from ordinary arcs and activator arcs. The so-structure *generated* by AON is $\kappa(AON) = (E, \prec_{AON}, \sqsubset_{AON}, \ell|_E) \overset{\text{df}}{=} rs_{AON}^\Diamond$. Thus κ is total and satisfies Property 3.

The default *initial* (*final*) marking of AON is $\text{MIN}_{AON} \overset{\text{df}}{=} \text{MIN}_{\text{UND}(AON)}$ (resp. $\text{MAX}_{AON} \overset{\text{df}}{=} \text{MAX}_{\text{UND}(AON)}$) and the *labelled step sequences* of AON are given by

(a) $\boxed{e} \rightarrow \bigcirc \rightarrow \boxed{f}$ (b) $\boxed{e} \rightarrow \bigcirc \rightarrow\!\!\!\!- \boxed{f}$ (c) $\boxed{e} \rule{0pt}{0pt} \bigcirc \rightarrow \boxed{f}$

Fig. 2. (a,b) Two cases defining $e \prec_{loc} f$, and (c) one case defining $e \sqsubset_{loc} f$

$\lambda(AON) \stackrel{\mathrm{df}}{=} \{(\sigma, \ell|_E) \mid \mathrm{MIN}_{AON}[\sigma\rangle_{AON}\mathrm{MAX}_{AON}\}$. Thus $\lambda(AON) \subseteq \mathcal{LSTS}$ and $\lambda(AON) \neq \varnothing$ and so λ satisfies Property 1. Note that the labelled step sequences in $\lambda(AON)$ all have the same domain and labelling. It can be proved ([13]) that the operational semantics of an ao-net AON agrees with $\kappa(AON)$, as we have $\lambda(AON) = \epsilon(\kappa(AON))$ and so Property 5 is satisfied. We may conclude that Aim 3 is satisfied and $\kappa(AON) = \iota(\lambda(AON))$.

3   Process Semantics of PT-nets

This section shows how the case of PT-nets (see [3,11]) fits into our framework. The processes come from $\mathcal{LON}$. We instantiate ω, π_N, and α for PT-nets and establish Properties 1 and 2, from which Aims 1 and 2 then follow.

A *PT-net* is any marked net $N = (P, T, W, M_0)$. The set $\omega_{STS}(N) \stackrel{\mathrm{df}}{=} \{\sigma \mid M_0[\sigma\rangle_N\}$ is the set of *step sequences* of N. Thus ω_{STS} always returns a non-empty set and satisfies Property 1. The o-nets associated to N can be defined in two ways. First we consider the operational definition based on step sequences.

Definition 3 (π_N for PT-nets). *Let $\sigma = U_1 \ldots U_n$ be a step sequence of N. The set $\pi_N(\sigma)$ of processes generated by σ comprises all labelled nets N_n in sequences $N_0, \ldots, N_n$, where each $N_k = (B_k, E_k, R_k, \ell_k) \stackrel{\mathrm{df}}{=} (\biguplus_{i=0}^{k} B^i, \biguplus_{i=0}^{k} E^i, \biguplus_{i=0}^{k} R^i, \biguplus_{i=0}^{k} \ell^i)$ is constructed in the following way (here and later, the various net components do not contain any elements other than those specified explicitly).*

- *For each $0 \leq i \leq n$, $\ell^i : B^i \cup E^i \to P \cup T$ is a labelling defined below.*
- *$E^0 = \varnothing$ and for $1 \leq i \leq n$, E^i comprises a distinct event for each transition occurrence in U_i. The event corresponding to the j-th occurrence of t in U_i is t–labelled and denoted by $t^{i,j}$.*
- *B^0 comprises a distinct condition for each place occurrence in M_0. The condition corresponding to the j-th occurrence of s in M_0 is s–labelled and denoted by s^j.*
- *For $1 \leq i \leq n$ and for every $e \in E^i$, B^i comprises a distinct condition for each place occurrence in $\mathrm{POST}_N(\ell_i(e))$. The condition corresponding to the j-th occurrence of p in $\mathrm{POST}_N(\ell_i(e))$ is p–labelled and denoted by $p^{e,j}$.*
- *$R^0 = \varnothing$, and for $1 \leq i \leq n$ and every $e \in E^i$: we add an arc $(e, p^{e,j})$ to R^i for each $p^{e,j} \in B^i$; moreover, we choose a disjoint (i.e., $B_f \cap B_g = \varnothing$ whenever $f \neq g$) set of conditions $B_e \subseteq B_{i-1} \backslash \mathrm{dom}_{R_{i-1}}$ such that $\ell_i\langle B_e\rangle = \mathrm{PRE}_N(\ell_i(e))$ and add an arc (b, e) to R^i for each $b \in B_e$.*

For every step sequence σ of N, all processes generated by σ are o-nets. Moreover, $\pi_N|_{\omega_{STS}(N)}$ never returns the empty set and so Property 1 is satisfied. Next we give an axiomatic definition of processes based on the structure of the PT-net.

Definition 4 (α for PT-nets). *The set $\alpha(N)$ of processes of N comprises all o-nets $ON = (B, E, R, \ell)$ satisfying the following:*

- *ℓ is a labelling function for $B \cup E$ such that $\ell(B) \subseteq P$ and $\ell(E) \subseteq T$.*

- *For all $e \in E$, $\text{PRE}_N(\ell(e)) = \ell\langle\text{PRE}_{ON}(e)\rangle$ and $\text{POST}_N(\ell(e)) = \ell\langle\text{POST}_{ON}(e)\rangle$.*
- $M_0 = \ell\langle\text{MIN}_{ON}\rangle$.

Since every process generated by a step sequence σ of N satisfies definition 4 we have that $\pi_N(\sigma) \subseteq \alpha(N)$. Thus $\alpha(N)$ satisfies Property 1. Returning to definition 3, we observe that the successive addition of sets of events to construct the process actually defines an execution of the process. Consequently, any process generated by some step sequence σ of N will have a labelled step sequence from which σ can be extracted using the mapping ϕ which forgets the underlying identities of the events. Also the converse holds, because any labelled step sequence of a process satisfying definition 4 provides a way to construct a process satisfying definition 3. Thus Property 2 holds and the remaining aims for PT-nets are fulfilled: the operationally and axiomatically defined processes coincide (Aim 1) and the operational semantics of a PT-net corresponds with the operational semantics of its processes (Aim 2).

4   PT-nets with Inhibitor Arcs

In this section, we first consider PTI-nets in which all inhibitor places have complement places, extending and systematizing our previous results ([14]). We then deal with the general class of PTI-nets, for which we develop a novel approach. As in each case we use the semantic framework with $\mathcal{LAON}$ as the process domain, we only need to instantiate the mappings ω, π_N, and α, and establish the Properties 1 and 2, in order to guarantee that Aims 1 and 2 are both fulfilled.

A *PT-net with inhibitor arcs* (or *PTI-net*) is a marked inhibitor net $NI \overset{\text{df}}{=} (P, T, W, I, M_0)$. The set $\omega_{STS}(NI) \overset{\text{df}}{=} \{\sigma \mid M_0[\sigma\rangle_{NI}\}$ is the set of *step sequences* of NI, comprising all step sequences of NI starting from the initial marking M_0. Since the empty sequence is always a step sequence of NI, ω_{STS} is total and never returns the empty set; hence it satisfies Property 1. By $\text{UND}(NI) \overset{\text{df}}{=} (P, T, W, M_0)$ we denote the PT-net underlying NI.

A *PT-net with complemented inhibitor places* (or *PTCI-net*) is a PTI-net NCI in which every inhibitor place p has a designated *complement* place denoted by p^{cpl}, which means that $\text{PRE}_{NCI}(p) = \text{POST}_{NCI}(p^{cpl})$ and $\text{POST}_{NCI}(p) = \text{PRE}_{NCI}(p^{cpl})$. The joint token count on p and p^{cpl} is the same in every marking reachable from M_0 and equal to $\text{BND}_{NCI}(p) = \text{BND}_{NCI}(p^{cpl}) \overset{\text{df}}{=} M_0(p) + M_0(p^{cpl})$. Thus the inhibitor places of a PTCI-net NCI are bounded and, crucially, an inhibitor place p of a PTCI-net NCI contains no more than k tokens *iff* its complement p^{cpl} contains at least $\text{BND}_{NCI}(p) - k$ tokens.

In the processes of PT-nets, the *presence* of tokens is represented by conditions, but their *absence* cannot be tested. The idea of [13] was that an inhibitor arc which tests whether a place is empty, can be replaced by an activator arc which tests whether its complement place is not empty. To apply this idea in the non-safe case (as explored in [14]), the inhibitor places should be bounded and have complement places.

First we provide an operational definition which takes a step sequence of NCI and constructs a corresponding ao-net essentially as done for PT-nets but now adding on the way activator arcs to instances of complement places (with the number of activator arcs to be added determined by the bound of the inhibitor place and the weight of the adjacent inhibitor arc).

Definition 5 (π_N for PTCI-nets). *Let $\sigma = U_1 \ldots U_n \in \omega_{STS}(NCI)$. The set $\pi_{NCI}^{cpl}(\sigma)$ of complement activator processes (or ca-processes) generated by σ comprises all labelled activator nets N_n in sequences $N_0, \ldots, N_n$, where each $N_k = (B_k, E_k, R_k, Act_k, \ell_k) \overset{\text{df}}{=} (\biguplus_{i=0}^{k} B^i, \biguplus_{i=0}^{k} E^i, \biguplus_{i=0}^{k} R^i, \biguplus_{i=0}^{k} Act^i, \biguplus_{i=0}^{k} \ell^i)$ is constructed as in definition 3, except for the activator arcs Act^i, which are defined thus.*

> *$Act^0 = \varnothing$, and for $1 \leq k \leq n$ and every $e \in E^k$, if p is an inhibitor place of $\ell_k(e)$ then we choose a set A_e of exactly $\text{BND}_{NCI}(p) - \text{INH}_{NCI}(\ell_k(e))(p)$ conditions in $B_{k-1} \backslash dom_{R_{k-1}}$ labelled by p^{cpl}. After that we add an activator arc (b, e) to Act^i for each $b \in A_e$.*

Definition 5 is sound as the required sets A_e can always be found, though it may happen that $A_e \cap A_f \neq \varnothing$ for $e \neq f$ (hence conditions may have multiple adjacent activator arcs). One can check that, for every step sequence σ of NCI, $\pi_{NCI}^{cpl}(\sigma) \subseteq \mathcal{LAON}$. Moreover, $\pi_{NCI}^{cpl}|_{\omega_{STS}(NCI)}$ is total and never returns the empty set, and so Property 1 is satisfied.

Figure 3 shows a PTCI-net NCI and the construction of one of its ca-processes. Note that $\text{BND}_{NCI}(q) = \text{BND}_{NCI}(r) = 3$ and $r = q^{cpl}$. In this, and the next, diagram vertical dashed lines indicate the stages in which the net has been derived. We next give an axiomatic definition of ca-processes.

Definition 6 (α for PTCI-nets). *The set $\alpha^{cpl}(NCI)$ of complement activator processes (or ca-processes) of the PTCI-net NCI comprises all ao-nets $AON = (B, E, R, Act, \ell)$ such that $\text{UND}(AON)$ is a process of $\text{UND}(NCI)$ and, moreover, if $e \in E$ and p is an inhibitor place of $\ell(e)$ then*

$$|\ell^{-1}(p^{cpl}) \cap \text{ACT}_{AON}(e)| = \text{BND}_{NCI}(p) - \text{INH}_{NCI}(\ell(e))(p) .$$

Intuitively, the last condition means that if event e is enabled then there are enough tokens in p^{cpl} to ensure that p does not inhibit transition $\ell(e)$.

The ca-processes generated by step sequences of NCI satisfy $\pi_{NCI}^{cpl}(\sigma) \subseteq \alpha^{cpl}(NCI)$, for all $\sigma \in \omega_{STS}(NCI)$. Thus α^{cpl} satisfies Property 1. Moreover, each ca-process generated by a step sequence σ of NCI will have a labelled step sequence to which ϕ associates σ by forgetting about the identities of the events.

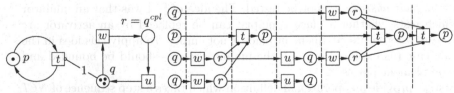

Fig. 3. A PTCI-net and a ca-process generated by $\{w, w\}t\{u, u\}\{w, w\}tt$

Conversely, every labelled step sequence of a ca-process from $\alpha^{cpl}(NCI)$ defines through ϕ a step sequence of NCI and can be used to construct the process according to definition 5. Thus the executions and ca-processes of NCI satisfy Property 2, and so the remaining aims are fulfilled, i.e., the operationally and axiomatically defined ca-processes coincide, and the operational semantics of a PTCI-net corresponds to that of its ca-processes.

Theorem 1 (Aims 1 and 2 for PTCI-nets). *For every PTCI-net NCI,*
$$\alpha^{cpl}(NCI) = \pi_{NCI}^{cpl}(\omega_{STS}(NCI)) \text{ and } \omega_{STS}(NCI) = \phi(\lambda(\alpha^{cpl}(NCI))).$$

We now turn to defining a process semantics for general PTI-nets. Since inhibitor places do not necessarily have complements, a new feature is needed to represent the test that an inhibitor place does not contain too many tokens. Our proposal is to add 'on demand' new artificial conditions with activator arcs to represent the testing by inhibitor arcs. Moreover, if a transition has an inhibitor place which is input or output to some other transition, then occurrences of these two transitions may have a causal relationship which should be faithfully reflected by the neighbourhood of the new condition. In the rest of this section, we consider a general PTI-net $NI = (P, T, W, M_0, I)$. Below, if two transitions, t and w, and a place p of NI are such that $\text{INH}_{NI}(t)(p) \neq \infty$ and $\text{PRE}_{NI}(w)(p) + \text{POST}_{NI}(w)(p) \neq 0$, then we denote $w \multimap t$. Similarly, if two events, e and f, and a condition b of an ao-net AON are such that $\text{ACT}_{AON}(e)(b) \neq 0 \neq \text{PRE}_{AON}(f)(b) + \text{POST}_{AON}(f)(b)$, then we denote $f \overset{b}{\multimap\!\bullet} e$, or simply $f \multimap\!\bullet e$.

The main idea behind the process construction presented next is to ensure that whenever $w \multimap t$, any two occurrences, f of w and e of t, are adjacent to a common condition so that $f \multimap\!\bullet e$, and thus are related in the corresponding causal structure. Note that this resembles the technique used in [19] to define a process semantics of PT-nets, where the construction always makes occurrences of transitions adjacent to a common place causally dependent.

First we define the operational process semantics and demonstrate how to construct an ao-net for a given step sequence of NI. Again, the construction follows the pattern established for PT-nets, but now new conditions — labelled by the special symbol λ — may have to be added on the way.

Definition 7 (π_N for PTI-nets). *Let $\sigma = U_1 \ldots U_n$ be a step sequence of NI. The set $\pi_{NI}(\sigma)$ of activator processes (or a-processes) generated by σ comprises all labelled activator nets N_n in sequences $N_0, \ldots, N_n$, where each $N_k = (B_k \uplus \widetilde{B}_k, E_k, R_k, Act_k, \ell_k) \overset{df}{=} (\biguplus_{i=0}^{k} B^i \uplus \biguplus_{i=0}^{k} \widetilde{B}^i, \biguplus_{i=0}^{k} E^i, \biguplus_{i=0}^{k} R^i, \biguplus_{i=0}^{k} Act^i, \biguplus_{i=0}^{k} \ell^i)$ is constructed as in definition 3, except that $\widetilde{B}^0 = Act^0 = \varnothing$ and, for $k \leq n$:*

- *All conditions in $\widetilde{B}^k$ are labelled by λ.*
- *If $e \in E^k$ and $f \in E^j$ (for $j < k$) are such that $\ell_k(f) \multimap \ell_k(e)$ then we create exactly one condition $b \in \widetilde{B}^k$ and add two arcs: $(f, b) \in R^k$ and $(b, e) \in Act^k$.*
- *If $f \in E^k$ and $e \in E^j$ (for $j \leq k$) are such that $\ell_k(f) \multimap \ell_k(e)$ then we create exactly one condition $b \in \widetilde{B}^k$ and add two arcs: $(b, f) \in R^k$ and $(b, e) \in Act^k$.*

The definition is illustrated in figure 4. For every $\sigma \in STS(NI)$, $\pi_{NI}(\sigma) \subseteq LAON$. Since $\pi_{NI}|_{\omega STS(NI)}$ is total and never returns $\varnothing$, Property 1 holds.

In the construction of definition 7, whenever an event f is introduced before an event e and $\ell(f) \multimap \ell(e)$, then this will *always* lead to $f \prec e$ in the generated so-structure. Similarly, whenever an event e is introduced not later than an event f and $\ell(f) \multimap \ell(e)$, then this will *always* lead to $e \sqsubset f$. Moreover, one can show that for a subclass of PTI-nets which includes those with unweighted inhibitor arcs (i.e., I always returns 0 or ∞) all these relationships are *necessary* to maintain the consistency with the operational semantics of NI. We next give an axiomatic definition of a-processes.

Definition 8 (α for PTI-nets). *The set $\alpha(NI)$ of* activator processes *(or a-processes) of NI comprises all ao-nets $AON = (B \uplus \widetilde{B}, E, R, Act, \ell)$ satisfying the following, for all $b \in \widetilde{B}$ and $e, f \in E$:*

1. *$\ell(B) \subseteq P$, $\ell(E) \subseteq T$, and the conditions in $\widetilde{B} = dom_{Act}$ are labelled by λ.*
2. *$M_0 = \ell\langle MIN_{AON} \cap B\rangle$.*
3. *$PRE_{NI}(\ell(e)) = \ell\langle PRE_{NI}(e) \cap B\rangle$ and $POST_{NI}(\ell(e)) = \ell\langle POST_{NI}(e) \cap B\rangle$.*
4. *There are unique events $g, h \in E$ such that $PRE_{AON}(b) + POST_{AON}(b) = \{g\}$, $b \in ACT_{AON}(h)$ and $\ell(g) \multimap \ell(h)$.*
5. *If $\ell(f) \multimap \ell(e)$ then there is exactly one $c \in \widetilde{B}$ such that $f \xrightarrow{c} e$.*
6. *If $PRE_{AON}(e) \cup ACT_{AON}(e) \subseteq S$ then $\ell\langle S \cap B\rangle \leq INH_{NI}(\ell(e))$, for every maximal set $S \subseteq B \uplus \widetilde{B}$ such that $(b,c) \notin R \circ \prec_{loc}^* \circ R$, for all $b, c \in S$.*

Intuitively, the last condition requires that all markings reachable from MIN_{AON} (and S is such marking) of AON properly reflect the inhibitor constraints present in NI: if an event is enabled at such a marking then there are not too many instances of its inhibitor places in the corresponding marking of NI.

It can be shown that $\pi_{NI}(\sigma) \subseteq \alpha(NI)$, for all $\sigma \in \omega STS(NI)$. Thus α satisfies Property 1. Any a-process generated by a step sequence σ of NI will have a labelled step sequence to which ϕ associates σ by forgetting about the identities of the events. Conversely, every labelled step sequence of an $AON \in \alpha(NI)$ defines through ϕ a step sequence σ of NI and can be used to construct AON

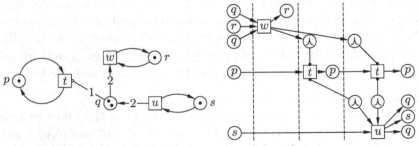

Fig. 4. A PTI-net and an a-process generated by the step sequence $\sigma = \{w\}\{t\}\{t, u\}$

as an element of $\pi_{NI}(\sigma)$. Thus Property 2 is satisfied. Hence also for PTI-nets the remaining aims are fulfilled.

Theorem 2 (Aims 1 and 2 for PTI-nets). *For every PTI-net NI, $\alpha(NI) = \pi_{NI}(\omega_{STS}(NI))$ and $\omega_{STS}(NI) = \phi(\lambda(\alpha(NI)))$.*

We conclude by remarking that for a subclass of PTCI-nets which includes those with unweighted inhibitor arcs (i.e., I always returns 0 or ∞), the two process semantics agree in the sense that they yield the same abstract causality semantics: for such nets *NCI* we have $\kappa(\alpha^{cpl}(NCI)) = \kappa(\alpha(NCI))$.

Future Work and Acknowledgements

We plan to develop a verification technique based on unfoldings of bounded PTI-nets (our preliminary investigations showed that the a-process semantics can be lifted to infinite step sequences so that the resulting ao-nets are finitely branching if the underlying PT-nets are bounded). Moreover, after developing an appropriate categorical model based on the present work we intend to compare it with the setup proposed in [2,6].

We would like to thank Eike Best and the anonymous referees for their helpful comments. This research was supported by travel grants from Nwo and the British Council, as well as the Epsrc grant GR/M94366 (Movie).

References

1. M. Ajmone Marsan, G. Balbo, G. Conte, S. Donatelli and G. Franceschinis: *Generalized Stochastic Petri Nets.* Wiley (1995). 531
2. P. Baldan, N. Busi A. Corridani and G. M. Pinna: Functorial Concurrent Semantics for Petri Nets with Read and Inhibitor Arcs. Proc. of *CONCUR 2000*, Springer-Verlag, LNCS 1877 (2000) 442–457. 545
3. E. Best and R. Devillers: Sequential and Concurrent Behaviour in Petri Net Theory. *Theoretical Computer Science* 55 (1988) 87–136. 532, 533, 538, 540
4. E. Best and C. Fernández: *Nonsequential Processes. A Petri Net View.* EATCS Monographs on Theoretical Computer Science, Springer-Verlag (1988). 538
5. J. Billington: Protocol Specification Using P-Graphs, a Technique Based on Coloured Petri Nets. In: Part II of [17] (1998) 331–385. 531
6. N. Busi and G. M. Pinna: Process Semantics for Place/Transition Nets with Inhibitor and Read Arcs. *Fundamenta Informaticae* 40 (1999) 165–197. 534, 545
7. G. Chiola, S. Donatelli, G. Franceschinis: Priorities, Inhibitor Arcs, and Concurrency in P/T Nets. Proc. of *ICATPN'1991*, Gjern (1991) 182–205. 532
8. S. Donatelli and G. Franceschinis: Modelling and Analysis of Distributed Software Using GSPNs. In: Part II of [17] (1998) 438–476. 531
9. R. Fräisse: *Theory of Relations.* North Holland (1986).
10. H. Gaifman and V. Pratt: Partial Order Models of Concurrency and the Computation of Function. Proc. of *LICS'87*, IEEE CS Press (1987) 72–85. 537
11. U. Goltz and W. Reisig: The Non-sequential Behaviour of Petri Nets. *Information and Control* 57 (1983) 125–147. 532, 538, 540

12. M. H. T. Hack: Decidability Questions for Petri Nets. PhD Thesis, M. I. T. (1976). 531

13. R. Janicki and M. Koutny: Semantics of Inhibitor Nets. *Information and Computation* 123 (1995) 1–16.   531, 532, 533, 537, 538, 539, 540, 541

14. H. C. M. Kleijn and M. Koutny: Process Semantics of P/T-Nets with Inhibitor Arcs. Proc. of *ICATPN'2000*, Springer-Verlag, LNCS 1825 (2000) 261–281.   531, 532, 533, 541

15. H. C. M. Kleijn and M. Koutny: Process Semantics of General Inhibitor Nets. Technical Report CS-TR-769, Dept. of Comp. Sci., University of Newcastle (2002). 533

16. J. L. Peterson: *Petri Net Theory and the Modeling of Systems.* Prentice Hall (1981). 531

17. W. Reisig and G. Rozenberg (Eds.): *Lectures on Petri Nets.* Springer-Verlag, LNCS 1491&1492 (1988).   545, 546

18. G. Rozenberg and J. Engelfriet: Elementary Net Systems. In: Part I of [17] (1998) 12–121.   532, 538

19. W. Vogler: Executions: a New Partial-order Semantics of Petri Nets. *Theoretical Computer Science* 91 (1991) 205–238.   543

20. W. Vogler: Partial Order Semantics and Read Arcs. Proc. of *MFCS'97*, Springer-Verlag, LNCS 1295 (1997) 508–517.   534

Refinement-Robust Fairness

Hagen Völzer*

Software Verification Research Centre
The University of Queensland, Australia

Abstract. We motivate and study the robustness of fairness notions under refinement of transitions and places in Petri nets. We show that the classical notions of weak and strong fairness are not robust and we propose a hierarchy of increasingly strong, refinement-robust fairness notions. That hierarchy is based on the conflict structure of transitions, which characterizes the interplay between choice and synchronization in a fairness notion. Our fairness notions are defined on non-sequential runs, but we show that the most important notions can be easily expressed on sequential runs as well. The hierarchy is further motivated by a brief discussion on the computational power of the fairness notions.

1   Introduction

In order to show a liveness property in a distributed system, i.e., a property of the form "something good will eventually happen", another liveness property has to be assumed first to rule out some runs of the system. The most basic liveness assumption is *sequential maximality*, that is that some transition must occur as long as some transition is enabled. However, this assumption is often too weak. Stronger liveness assumptions are usually called *fairness assumptions*. A fairness assumption constrains the nondeterminism in the system.

There is an impressively wide variety of fairness notions in the literature. Each fairness notion lies in a specific context of an application area, a specific language, and is often meant to represent a particular phenomenon. Phenomena expressed by fairness assumptions include progress of individual processes, general environment behaviour, behaviour of probabilistic choice, impartiality of arbiters and schedulers, and partial synchrony. Overviews over fairness can be found in [14,5,16]. More recent studies on fairness include [7,8,15].

Few interrelationships between fairness notions are known because of their different contexts and there is not much guidance on how to choose an appropriate fairness notion for a given model of a system. Apt, Francez, and Katz [1] propose three semantic criteria to aid in this choice. These criteria are *feasibility*, which is also called *machine closure*, then *equivalence robustness*, and *liveness*

---

* Postal address: Hagen Völzer, SVRC, The University of Queensland, Qld 4072, Australia; e-mail: voelzer@svrc.uq.edu.au, Phone: +61 7 3365 1647; Fax: +61 7 3365 1533. This research was funded in part by Australian Research Council Large Grant A49801500, A Unified Formalism for Concurrent Real-Time Software Development.

L. Brim et al. (Eds.): CONCUR 2002, LNCS 2421, pp. 547–562, 2002.

enhancement. Machine closure means that each finite run of the system can be extended to a fair run of the system, i.e., the system cannot get into a state in which it is impossible for the system to produce a fair run. Apt, Francez, and Katz consider two sequential runs to be *equivalent* if they both represent the same non-sequential run, i.e., if they only differ in the order of concurrent events. A fairness notion is *equivalence robust* if equivalent runs are either all fair or all unfair. *Liveness enhancement* means that there is at least one system where the fairness notion excludes more runs than sequential maximality.

Lamport [15] argues that from the three criteria only machine closure is relevant. However, Joung [7] has shown that equivalence robustness is important when one wants to implement a fairness notion for programs with multiparty interactions by a scheduler. Francez, Back, and Kurki-Suonio [6] argue that equivalence robustness is important in composing fairness assumptions.

As a further aid for choosing a fairness notion, we suggest *refinement-robustness* in this paper, that is a fair run always refines to a fair run and an unfair run always refines to an unfair run. This is important when we want to preserve liveness properties in refinement steps in design or implementation of a system. Refinement-robustness has extensively been studied for several equivalence notions for distributed systems, where, however, fairness assumptions have not been taken into account. A good starting point for this area is the work of van Glabbeek and Goltz [22]. We base our definitions on process semantics of Petri nets, which is robust under several refinement operations.

We study two types of refinement in this paper: the refinement of a transition into the sequential execution of two transitions (Fig. 1a) and, its dual, the refinement of a place into an output and an input place (Fig. 1b). We show that the traditional notions of weak and strong fairness are not robust. A refinement-robust version of weak fairness is *non-sequential maximality*, also called *progress*, that is an enabled transition eventually occurs unless a conflicting transition occurs. Progress has been identified as an adequate version of weak fairness for various partial-order semantics [19,13,18,23].

However, progress is not always sufficient. The limitation of progress is paradigmaticly characterized by the result that each starvation-free mutual exclusion algorithm needs a stronger assumption, which was proven by Kindler and Walter [11] and, independently, by Vogler [24]. We introduce the notion of *simple fairness*, a refinement-robust version of strong fairness, in this paper. Simple fairness is a generalization of *fair arcs* [10]. Simple fairness is also, in contrast to strong fairness, equivalence-robust. Furthermore, we show that progress and simple fairness are part of a hierarchy of increasingly strong, refinement-robust, fairness notions. That hierarchy corresponds to the conflict structure hierarchy in the sense that it collapses under the constraints of the conflict structure hierarchy.

Although we derive our notions from partial-order semantics, we show that the most important notions can be easily expressed on sequential runs.

Different fairness notions have different computational power in the sense that a stronger notion can be used to solve more synchronization- and coordina-

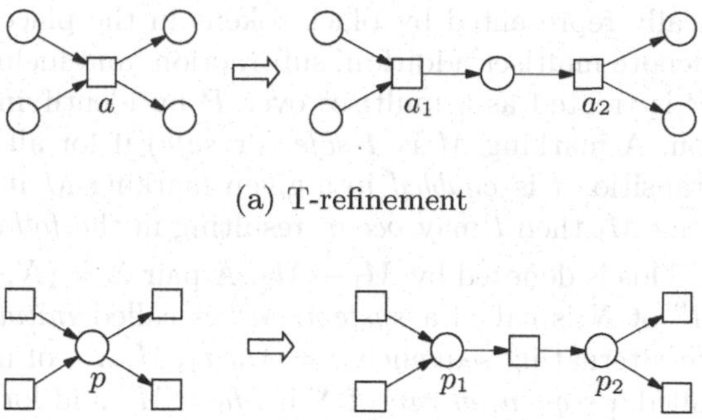

(a) T-refinement

(b) P-refinement

Fig. 1. Two refinement operations

tion problems. Weak fairness and strong fairness do not separate computational power very well because one can be simulated by the other (cf. [5]). We argue that our hierarchy better separates computational power.

We proceed as follows. After recalling some preliminaries, we motivate T- and P-refinement in Section 3. We then introduce the new hierarchy and study its properties including its relationship with classical fairness notions. An informal discussion on different aspects of fairness and on the computational power of fairness notions follows. Finally, we give characterizations on sequential runs for some of the proposed notions.

2   Preliminaries

This section collects some preliminaries which include Petri nets, their concurrent runs and their conflict structure hierarchy.

Petri nets. A *Petri net* (or *net* for short) $N = (P, T, F)$ consists of two disjoint non-empty, countable sets P and T and a binary relation $F \subseteq (P \times T) \cup (T \times P)$. Elements of P, T, and F are called *places*, *transitions*, and *arcs* of the net respectively. An $x \in P \cup T$ is also called an *element* of N. We graphically represent a place by a circle, a transition by a square, and an arc by an arrow between the corresponding elements. For each element x, we define the *preset* of x by ${}^\bullet x = \{y \mid (y, x) \in F\}$ and the *postset* of x by $x^\bullet = \{y \mid (x, y) \in F\}$. For a set X of elements, we set ${}^\bullet X = \bigcup_{x \in X} {}^\bullet x$ and $X^\bullet = \bigcup_{x \in X} x^\bullet$. The set of *minimal elements* is defined by ${}^\circ N = \{x \mid {}^\bullet x = \varnothing\}$. For each element x of N, we define the set of *predecessors* of x by $\downarrow x = \{y \mid y F^+ x\}$, where F^+ denotes the transitive closure of F. We restrict our attention to nets in which, for each transition t, the preset ${}^\bullet t$ and the postset $t^\bullet$ are non-empty and finite.

Systems and sequential runs. A *marking* M of a net is a finite multiset over P. A marking is graphically represented by black tokens in the places of the net. By $+, -$, and $\leq$ we denote multiset addition, subtraction, and inclusion, respectively. A subset of P is treated as a multiset over P by identifying it with its characteristic function. A marking M is *1-safe* (or *safe*) if for all places p, we have $M(p) \leq 1$. A transition t is *enabled* in a given marking M if ${}^\bullet t \leq M$. If t is enabled in a marking M_1 then t may *occur*, resulting in the *follower marking* $M_2 = (M_1 - {}^\bullet t) + t^\bullet$. This is denoted by $M_1 \xrightarrow{t} M_2$. A pair $\Sigma = (N, M^0)$ of a net N and a marking M^0 of N is called a *system*; M^0 is called *initial marking* of Σ. A finite or infinite alternating sequence $\sigma = M_0, t_1, M_1, \dots$ of markings and transitions of Σ is called a *sequential run* of Σ if $M_0 = M^0$ and for all positions $i \geq 0$ of σ, we have $M_i \xrightarrow{t_{i+1}} M_{i+1}$. A system is *safe* if, for all sequential runs σ and all positions i of σ, the marking M_i is safe.

Assumption. We restrict our attention to safe systems since safe systems rule out auto-concurrency, that is a transition being concurrent to itself, and auto-conflict, that is a transition being in conflict with itself. These phenomena raise new issues when dealing with fairness, which are beyond the scope of this paper.

Concurrent runs. Let N be a net. N is *acyclic* if for each element x of N, we have $x \notin \downarrow x$. N is *predecessor-finite* if for each element x of N, the set $\downarrow x$ is finite. Let $K = (B, E, <)$ be an acyclic, predecessor-finite net. A place $b \in B$ is called *condition* and a transition $e \in E$ is called *event*. K is a *causal net* if ${}^\circ K$ is finite and for each condition b of K we have $|{}^\bullet b| \leq 1$ and $|b^\bullet| \leq 1$. Since K is acyclic, the transitive closure of $<$, denoted $<$, is a partial order, which we call *causal order*. We write $x_1 \leq x_2$ for $x_1 < x_2 \vee x_1 = x_2$. Two different elements are *concurrent*, denoted $x_1 \mathbin{\text{co}} x_2$, if neither $x_1 < x_2$ nor $x_2 < x_1$. A finite set of pairwise concurrent conditions is called a *co-set* in this paper. A maximal co-set is called a *cut*. Let C be a cut and D a co-set. D is *reachable from* C if for all $b \in C$ and for all $b' \in D$, we have $b \leq b' \vee b \mathbin{\text{co}} b'$. If, for two cuts C and C', we have $C' = (C \setminus {}^\bullet e) \cup e^\bullet$ for some event e then we write $C \xrightarrow{e} C'$.

Let $\Sigma = (N, M^0)$ be a system with $N = (P, T, F)$ and let $K = (B, E, <)$ be a causal net. Let $l : B \cup E \to P \cup T$ be a mapping such that $l(B) \subseteq P$ and $l(E) \subseteq T$. The pair $\rho = (K, l)$ is a *non-sequential* (or *concurrent*) *run* of Σ if $l({}^\circ K) = M^0$ and for each event e of K, we have $l({}^\bullet e) = {}^\bullet l(e)$ and $l(e^\bullet) = l(e)^\bullet$. $\mathfrak{R}(\Sigma)$ denotes the set of all non-sequential runs of Σ.

Let $\rho = (K, l)$ be a concurrent run of a system Σ. An alternating sequence $\tau = C_0, e_1, C_1, \dots$ of cuts and events of ρ is a *sequentialization* of ρ if $C_0 = {}^\circ K$, for all positions $i \geq 0$ of τ, we have $C_i \xrightarrow{e_{i+1}} C_{i+1}$, and for each event e of ρ, there is a position i of τ such that $e = e_i$. A co-set D of ρ is *visible* in τ if there exists a position i of σ such that $D \subseteq C_i$. The sequential run $l(\tau) = l(C_0), l(e_1), l(C_1), \dots$ of Σ is also called *interleaving* of ρ. By $IL(\rho)$, we denote the set of all interleavings of ρ. In a safe net, $\{IL(\rho) \mid \rho \text{ is a concurrent run}\}$ is a partition on the set of all sequential runs of Σ.

Conflict structure of transitions. Conflict structure constraints are here defined not as usual with respect to whole nets, but rather with respect to single transitions and slightly renamed. Let N be a net. Two different transitions t_1 and t_2 are *in conflict* if ${}^\bullet t_1 \cap {}^\bullet t_2 \neq \varnothing$. A transition t of N is

a) *conflict free* if for all $p \in {}^\bullet t$, we have $|p^\bullet| = 1$,
b) *loop-conflict free* if for all $p \in {}^\bullet t$, we have ${}^\bullet p \cap p^\bullet \subseteq \{t\}$,
c) *free* if for all $p, q \in {}^\bullet t$, we have $p^\bullet = q^\bullet$, and
d) *simple* if for all $p, q \in {}^\bullet t$, we have $p^\bullet \subseteq q^\bullet \vee q^\bullet \subseteq p^\bullet$.

We have: t is conflict free $\Rightarrow t$ is loop conflict free, and we have: t is conflict free $\Rightarrow t$ is free $\Rightarrow t$ is simple.

3   T- and P-refinement

In this section, we motivate T- and P-refinement, but first we discuss some properties of weak and strong fairness.

3.1   Weak and Strong Fairness

First we recall the definition of weak and strong fairness. Let Σ be a system, σ a sequential run and t a transition of Σ. We say t is *recurrent* in σ if there are infinitely many positions i of σ such that $t = t_i$. The run σ is not *weakly fair* with respect to t if t is not recurrent in σ and there is a position i such that for all positions $j \geq i$, we have M_j enables t (we also say: ${}^\bullet t$ is *eventually always marked*). We say that σ is not *strongly fair* with respect to t if t is not recurrent and for each position i of σ there is a position $j \geq i$ such that M_j enables t (we also say: ${}^\bullet t$ is *always eventually marked*). Weak fairness is sometimes also called *justice* and strong fairness is also called *compassion* in the literature. It is straight-forward to verify that weak and strong fairness are machine-closed and liveness enhancing.

Proposition 1. *a) Weak fairness is equivalence-robust (in safe systems) and b) strong fairness is not equivalence-robust.*

Proof. a) Let ρ be a run of a system Σ, σ a fair and σ' an unfair interleaving of ρ wrt t. Consider a suffix of ρ where t does not occur and that corresponds to a suffix of σ' where t is always enabled. There is a pair of cuts C, C' in that suffix such that $C \xrightarrow{e} C'$ and C enables t but C' does not. (Such a pair exists because there are cuts where t is not enabled due to the existence of a fair interleaving and there are cuts that enable t due to the existence of an unfair interleaving.) The event e consumes at least one token from ${}^\bullet t$ that is not reproduced by e. However, e eventually also occurs in σ', where it, due to safeness, also disables t. This contradicts the unfairness of σ'. For part b), consider the net in Fig. 2c. Consider the unique infinite run ρ; the interleaving $(a_1 a_2 c_1 c_2)^\infty$ of ρ is strongly fair and the interleaving $(a_1 c_1 a_2 c_2)^\infty$ is not strongly fair wrt b.

Non-equivalence-robustness of strong fairness is a known phenomenon [1,13]. Equivalence robustness of weak fairness strongly depends on the model. In particular, Prop. 1a does not hold for unsafe systems. The issue of equivalence robustness dissolves if we define fairness on concurrent runs rather than on sequential runs. This has motivated some research on fairness for non-sequential models [19,12,13,17]. A fairness notion A on sequential runs can be lifted to non-sequential runs in a natural way: a non-sequential run ρ is not fair according to A if all interleavings of ρ are not fair according to A. This is called *(maximal) equivalence completion* [6,8]. Let weak and strong fairness be defined on non-sequential runs by equivalence completion.

3.2 Refinement Robustness

The rest of the paper is not concerned with the three criteria of Apt, Francez, and Katz. All fairness notions in the sequel satisfy these. Instead, we propose to study the behaviour of fairness notions under syntactic transformations such as refinement. Consider now Σ_1 in Fig. 2a. Σ_1 terminates under weak fairness for b. If we refine Σ_1 now in a design or implementation step by replacing transition a by the sequential execution of two transitions a_1 and a_2, we get the system Σ_2 in Fig. 2b. Σ_2 does not terminate under weak fairness for b. Hence, our refinement step was not property preserving.

The reason for this is a known problem of weak fairness. The formalization of eventually always enabled does not coincide with our intuition of continuous enabledness. If a is assumed to have a duration then b is not continuously enabled in the infinite run of Σ_1. As a way out, Francez [5] proposes to use overlapping semantics (split semantics). Another solution is to use non-sequential maximality instead of weak fairness [19,18,12], which will be discussed in Sect. 4. Strong fairness behaves similarly. Σ_2 in Fig. 2b terminates under strong fairness for b but Σ_3 in Fig. 2c does not.

Consider now Σ_4 in Fig. 3a. Σ_4 terminates under strong fairness for c, because, in an infinite run of Σ_4, B and C are, although independent of each other, always eventually available together *at the same time*, i.e., in a global state. This is not preserved by P-refinement. If we refine the places B and C as

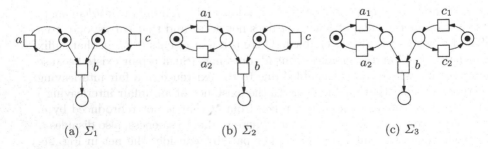

(a) Σ_1 (b) Σ_2 (c) Σ_3

Fig. 2. Non-robustness of weak and strong fairness

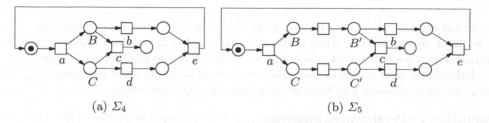

(a) Σ_4 (b) Σ_5

Fig. 3. Non-robustness of strong fairness under P-refinement

in Fig. 1b then we get the system Σ_5 (Fig. 3b), which does not terminate under strong fairness for c.

As a semantics that is not preserved under T-refinement is only suitable in models where transitions are assumed to be unrefinable and instantaneous, so is a semantics that is not preserved under P-refinement only suitable for models that assume that conditions are atomic and unrefinable. Examples for refinable conditions with durations are: if place p in Fig. 1b represents a channel then p_1 could represent the condition that a message has been sent and p_2 that a message has arrived; if p represents that a container is full then p_1 could represent that the container is half full and p_2 that the container is full.

We now make refinement-robustness precise. For the purpose of this paper, a *fairness assumption* is a mapping f that assigns to each system Σ a set $f(\Sigma) \subseteq \mathfrak{R}(\Sigma)$ of runs of Σ such that $f(\Sigma)$ is machine-closed wrt Σ. For example, the intersection of weak fairness wrt a and strong fairness wrt b is a fairness assumption for every system. A refinement φ is considered to be mapping that maps a net to a net, a system to a system and also a concurrent run to a concurrent run (by T-refining a transition t in a concurrent run ρ we mean that each occurrence of t in ρ is refined; P-refinement is analogous).

Definition 1 (Refinement robustness). *A fairness assumption f is robust under a refinement φ if we have $f(\varphi(\Sigma)) = \varphi(f(\Sigma))$ for all systems Σ.*

Note that the vacuous fairness assumption $f(\Sigma) = \mathfrak{R}(\Sigma)$ is robust under T- and P-refinement[1]. We now conclude this section.

Theorem 1. *Weak and strong fairness are not robust under T- and P-refinement.*

Note that the examples in Fig. 2 serve as counterexamples for T- as well as for P-refinement.

---

[1] Note that, due to the desired robustness under P-refinement, other T-refinement-robust partial-order models such as ST-traces may not be suitable here.

4   Refinement-Robust Fairness

To find a refinement-robust version of strong fairness on a non-sequential run ρ, we have to characterize when a transition is enabled in ρ, which reduces to characterize when concurrent conditions are available at the same time[2]. We use the following notion of *coexistence*. Two concurrent conditions are *coexistent* if both are never consumed or both are consumed by the same event.

Definition 2 (Persistence, insistence). *Let Σ be a system and $\rho = (K, l)$ a concurrent run of Σ. A co-set D of ρ is* persistent *if $D^\bullet = \varnothing$ and* coexistent *if $e \in D^\bullet \Rightarrow D \subseteq {}^\bullet e$. Let Q be a set of places of Σ. A co-set D of ρ is called a* Q-set *if $l(D) = Q$. We say Q is*

a) persistent *in ρ if there is a persistent Q-set in ρ,*
b) insistent *in ρ if for each cut C of ρ, there is a reachable Q-set,*
c) strictly insistent *in ρ if, for each cut C of ρ, there is a reachable coexistent Q-set,*
d) strongly insistent *in ρ if there are sets $Q_1, Q_2 \subseteq Q$ with $Q_1 \cup Q_2 = Q$ such that Q_1 is persistent in ρ and Q_2 is strictly insistent in ρ.*

Proposition 2. *We have: Q is persistent in $\rho \Rightarrow Q$ is strictly insistent in ρ $\Rightarrow Q$ is strongly insistent in $\rho \Rightarrow Q$ is insistent in ρ.*

Proof. A persistent co-set is also coexistent by definition. A persistent co-set is reachable from every cut. All claims except the last follow now directly. For the last claim, let Q be strongly insistent in ρ. Then, there is a persistent Q_1-set D_1 and, for each cut C of ρ, a reachable coexistent Q_2-set D_C. Then, $D_1 \cup D_C$ is a Q-set that is reachable from C.

Proposition 3. *Let Q be a set of places and ρ a concurrent run of a system Σ. Let σ be an interleaving of ρ.*

a) *If Q is persistent in ρ then Q is eventually always marked in σ.*
b) *If Q is strongly insistent in ρ then Q is always eventually marked in σ.*

Proof. a) A persistent co-set D of ρ is visible in σ as soon as all events in ${}^\bullet D$ have occurred. b) A coexistent co-set D that is not persistent is visible immediately before the consuming event $e \in D^\bullet$ occurs.

We are now prepared to define various fairness notions.

Definition 3 (Progress, free fairness, simple fairness, hyperfairness). *Let Σ be a system, t a transition, and ρ a concurrent run of Σ. We say ρ is*

a) *not* progressive *wrt t if ${}^\bullet t$ is persistent in ρ,*
b) *not* freely-fair *wrt t if t is not recurrent and ${}^\bullet t$ is strictly insistent in ρ,*

---

[2] Such a notion is the notion of *strong concurrency* proposed by Reisig [21]. However, Reisig's notion is not robust under P-refinement.

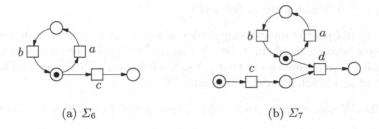

(a) Σ_6 (b) Σ_7

Fig. 4. Two systems

c) not simply-fair *wrt t if t is not recurrent and* $^\bullet t$ *is strongly insistent in* ρ, *and*
d) not hyperfair *wrt t if t is not recurrent and* $^\bullet t$ *is insistent in* ρ.

Note that, due to safeness, persistence of $^\bullet t$ implies that t is not recurrent.

Proposition 4. *We have:* ρ *is hyperfair wrt* $t \Rightarrow \rho$ *is simply-fair wrt* $t \Rightarrow \rho$ *is freely-fair wrt* $t \Rightarrow \rho$ *is progressive wrt* t.

Proof. The claims are immediate consequences of Proposition 2.

The systems in Fig. 2 and Fig. 3 terminate only under hyperfairness. Σ_6 in Fig. 4a terminates under free fairness but not under progress wrt c. Σ_7 in Fig. 4b terminates under simple fairness but not under free fairness wrt d. For free fairness all interleavings (observers) have to agree always eventually on an enabling of t (i.e. the enabling is visible in each interleaving) while, for simple fairness, all interleavings only have to agree that t has been enabled always eventually.

Progress is known as non-sequential maximality. Free and simple fairness are new according to our knowledge, where simple fairness is a generalization of fair arcs [10]. Hyperfairness wrt t excludes so-called *conspiracies* wrt t [3,2]. A conspiracy wrt a transition t occurs when all resources of t are always, independently of each other, eventually available, but never together at the same time[3]. To exclude conspiracies, Attie, Francez, and Grumberg [2] propose another notion of hyperfairness and Best [3] proposes the notion of ∞-*fairness* for the same purpose. Both notions are different from ours. Lamport's hyperfairness [15], designed as a generalization of Attie, Francez, and Grumberg's notion, is identical with Best's ∞-fairness. We treat hyperfairness and conspiracies in detail elsewhere [25]. Our notion of hyperfairness has been defined as 0-transition fairness by Merceron [17] as a theoretical way to define fairness on non-sequential runs. It coincides with Reisig's notion of *quasifairness* [20] as we will show in Prop. 5 below. Kwiatkowska's notion of strong event fairness [12] is similar.

---

[3] Originally, the situation has been described by Dijkstra in his five philosophers example. There, a philosopher may experience a conspiracy by his two neighbours when these eat alternatingly in such a way that the philosopher never has his two forks at the same time.

Proposition 5. *A run ρ is not hyperfair wrt t if and only if there is an interleaving σ of ρ that is not strongly fair wrt t.*

Proof. ($\Rightarrow$) To obtain the interleaving, order independent events in such a way that the $\bullet t$-sets become visible in σ. ($\Leftarrow$) For each cut C of ρ, there is a position i of σ such that M_i represents a cut that is reachable from C. Hence, we can find, for each cut of ρ, a reachable cut that enables t.

Theorem 2. *All notions from Def. 3 are robust under T- and P-refinement.*

Proof. Persistence and coexistence of co-sets are robust under refinement. The claim follows in a straight-forward way.

Theorem 2 implies that linear-time process semantics with fairness from Def. 3 is preserved under T- and P-refinement.

Corollary 1. *If a system is equipped with a fairness assumption[4] f that is a countable conjunction of assumptions from Def. 3 and if we define $\Sigma_1 \equiv \Sigma_2$ if $f(\Sigma_1) = f(\Sigma_2)$ then $\equiv$ is preserved under T- and P-refinement, i.e., we have $\Sigma_1 \equiv \Sigma_2 \Rightarrow \varphi(\Sigma_1) \equiv \varphi(\Sigma_2)$. Moreover, we have $\Sigma_1 \equiv \Sigma_2 \Leftrightarrow \varphi(\Sigma_1) \equiv \varphi(\Sigma_2)$.*

5   The Hierarchy and Its Relationships

We study the relationship of the fairness notions from Def. 3 with the classical notions of weak and strong fairness in this section. Since hyperfairness and Best's ∞-fairness have a similar motivation, we include ∞-fairness in our comparison. A sequential run σ is not ∞-*fair* wrt a transition t if t is not recurrent in σ and from each marking M_i of σ, it is possible to enable t, i.e., $\sigma_i = M^0, \ldots, M_i$ can be extended to a finite run σ' of Σ such that the final marking of σ' enables t.

A fairness notion f is *stronger* (*strictly stronger*) than a fairness notion g if for all systems Σ, we have $f(\Sigma) \subseteq g(\Sigma)$ ($f(\Sigma) \subset g(\Sigma)$). We will prove all relationships depicted in Fig. 5a, where an arrow represents increasing strength; dotted relationships are derived. All relationships are strict and there are no more relationships than those depicted. Note that the left column of relationships is implied by Proposition 4.

Theorem 3. *Let Σ be a system, t a transition and ρ a run of Σ.*

a) ρ is not progressive wrt $t \Rightarrow \rho$ is not weakly fair wrt t;
b) ρ is not simply-fair wrt $t \Rightarrow \rho$ is not strongly fair wrt t;
c) ρ is not strongly fair wrt $t \Rightarrow \rho$ is not hyperfair wrt t;
d) ρ is not hyperfair wrt $t \Rightarrow \rho$ is not ∞-fair wrt to t.

Proof. a) follows from Prop. 3a), b) follows from Prop. 3b), c) follows from Prop. 5, and d) is obvious.

---

[4] We also equip the replacements in Fig. 1 with a fairness assumption such that a_1 inherits the assumption from a and we assume progress for a_2 and for the transition between p_1 and p_2.

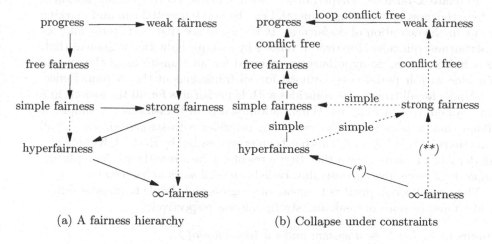

(a) A fairness hierarchy   (b) Collapse under constraints

Fig. 5. Relationships between various fairness notions

As an example for the completeness of Fig. 5a, consider Σ_1 in Fig. 2a, which shows that simple fairness is not stronger than weak fairness. Σ_1 terminates under weak fairness for b but not under simple fairness for b.

We show now that the hierarchy corresponds to the conflict structure hierarchy in the sense that it collapses under the constraints of the conflict structure hierarchy. Fig. 5b illustrates our results, where dotted lines denote derived relationships. The relationships labelled by (*) and (**) will be explained below.

Theorem 4.

a) If t is simple then ρ is hyperfair wrt t if and only if ρ is simply-fair wrt t.
b) If t is free then ρ is simply-fair wrt t if and only if ρ is freely-fair wrt t.
c) If t is conflict-free then ρ is freely-fair wrt t if and only if ρ is progressive wrt t.
d) If t is loop-conflict free then ρ is weakly fair wrt t if and only if ρ is progressive wrt t.

Proof. a) ($\Rightarrow$) follows from Prop. 4. For ($\Leftarrow$), let ρ be not hyperfair wrt t. Then, t is not recurrent in ρ. Furthermore, $^\bullet t$ is insistent in ρ. Let C be a cut of ρ and D_C be a $^\bullet t$-set that is reachable from C. Let $D_1 \subseteq D_C$ be the persistent part and $D_2 = D_C \setminus D_1$. If D_2 is not coexistent then there exist two different events $e_1, e_2 \in D_2^\bullet$, which contradicts t being simple. Parts b) and c) are similar. Part d) ($\Rightarrow$) follows from Thm. 3a. For ($\Leftarrow$), let ρ be not weakly fair wrt t and assume that $^\bullet t$ is not persistent in ρ. We consider a suffix of σ where t is always enabled and t never occurs. Since $^\bullet t$ is not persistent, a token $p \in {}^\bullet t$ is eventually consumed by a conflict transition t' of t. This token is immediately reproduced since we assumed that t is always enabled. Hence $t' \in {}^\bullet p \cap p^\bullet$.

To relate ∞-fairness to hyperfairness, we first define a corresponding notion of ∞-hyperfairness by replacing sequential run by non-sequential run and marking by cut in the definition of ∞-fairness. It is easy to see that ∞-fairness and ∞-hyperfairness coincide. Moreover, it follows by a simple induction argument that, for a finite system, ∞-hyperfairness assumed for all transitions of the system coincides with hyperfairness assumed for all transitions of the system. Hence, ∞-fairness for all transitions coincides with hyperfairness for all transitions in a finite system ((*) in Fig. 5b). When, additionally, all transitions are simple, it follows that ∞-fairness for all transitions coincides with strong fairness for all transitions ((**) in Fig. 5b). This has been proven earlier by Best [3]. Kindler and van der Aalst [9] have shown that Best's result can be strengthened by replacing *simple* by a more liberal constraint, called *extended asymmetric choice*.

The next theorem justifies to speak of progress and simple fairness as refinement-robust versions of weak and strong fairness respectively.

Theorem 5. *Let Σ be a system and t a transition of Σ.*

a) *If Σ' is derived from Σ by P-refining all places in $^\bullet t$ then:*
   1. *strong fairness wrt t and simple fairness wrt t coincide in Σ',*
   2. *weak fairness wrt t and progress wrt t coincide in Σ'.*
b) *If Σ' is derived from Σ by T-refining all conflict transitions of t then weak fairness wrt t and progress wrt t coincide in Σ'.*

Proof. a) 1. Let ρ be not strongly fair wrt t and, to obtain a contradiction, assume that ρ is simply-fair. Let σ be an interleaving of ρ. Let $Q_p \subseteq {}^\bullet t$ a maximal subset of preconditions of t that is persistent in ρ and D_p the corresponding set of conditions. We consider a suffix of ρ where t does not occur and there is no coexistent $({}^\bullet t \setminus Q_p)$-set in that suffix. Let D be a ${}^\bullet t$-set in that suffix. Since $D' = D \setminus D_p$ is not coexistent there a two different events $e_1, e_2 \in D'^\bullet$. Assume that e_1 occurs before e_2 in σ. Let $b \in {}^\bullet e_2 \cap D'$ and let e_b be the event that produces b. Then, e_b and e_1 are concurrent. Therefore we find an interleaving σ' where e_1 occurs before e_b, which implies that D is not visible in σ'. Moreover σ' can be constructed such that all subsequent ${}^\bullet t$-sets become invisible in σ'. Therefore, t is not always eventually enabled in σ' and hence σ' is strongly fair wrt t, which contradicts our assumption that ρ is not strongly fair wrt t. The parts a) 2. and b) follow from Thm. 4d and the fact that t is loop-conflict free in Σ'.

6   Remarks

6.1   Aspects of Fairness

In concurrent programs, two types of fairness assumptions are often distinguished: *fairness wrt concurrency* and *fairness wrt choice*. Progress is pure fairness wrt concurrency: it stipulates that the occurrence of an enabled transition is not delayed by concurrent events. Choices are not influenced by progress. The

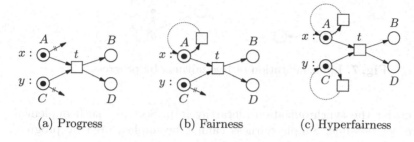

| (a) Progress | (b) Fairness | (c) Hyperfairness |

Fig. 6. Three synchronization assumptions

difference between free fairness and progress is pure fairness wrt choice: a run that is progressive but not freely-fair neglects a particular outcome of a recurrent choice. Simple fairness and hyperfairness additionally deal with situations where the above two aspects overlap. Such situations are usually called *confusion*. Simple fairness and hyperfairness are better explained by interpreting them together with progress as a hierarchy of *synchronization assumptions*.

We describe the assumptions here for two-party synchronization. Fig. 6a shows an object x in state A and an object y in state C. Both objects can synchronize in transition t, that is they change their state simultaneously through the occurrence of t. If object x is in state A we also say x is *ready* for t. Progress means that both objects eventually synchronize in t if both wait for each other when ready for t, i.e., neither object engages in another transition departing from A and C, respectively (Fig. 6a). Fairness means that both objects eventually synchronize in t if one object waits for the other and the other object is always eventually ready, i.e., it also waits or it always returns to the state where it is ready for t (Fig. 6b). Hyperfairness means that both objects synchronize in t when both objects are always, independently of each other, eventually ready (Fig. 6c).

6.2 Computational Power

Fairness notions have different computational power. By assuming a stronger fairness notion, it is possible to solve more synchronization- and coordination problems (such as mutex) than by assuming a weaker notion. Consider Fig. 7. It shows a local transformation such that for each environment, free fairness for a and b is implemented by progress in the sense that each run of the refined system that is progressive wrt a and b corresponds to a run of the abstract system that is freely-fair wrt a and b. A similar transformation can be found for implementing strong fairness by weak fairness if both are formulated wrt transition labels (actions) not just wrt transitions[5] (cf. [5]).

---

[5] This transformation is local to the *conflict cluster* of t, that is the set of transitions that are transitively in conflict with t.

Fig. 7. Implementation of free fairness by progress

However, for the synchronization hierarchy from Sect. 6.1 such implementations are not possible. Simple fairness cannot be implemented by progress, which follows from the result that mutex is solvable by simple fairness but not by progress (cf. [11,24,25]). Hyperfairness cannot be implemented by simple fairness, which follows from the result that a generalized mutex problem is solvable by hyperfairness but not by simple fairness (cf. [25]).

6.3   Definitions for Sequential Runs

In this section, we show that free and simple fairness can be easily expressed on sequential runs. For progress, this is well-established (by Kwiatkowska [13] and by Peled and Pnueli [18] for Mazurkiewicz traces and by Vogler [23] for partial words and interval semi words.)

Definition 4. *Let Σ be a system, σ a sequential run and t a transition of Σ. A set Q of places of Σ is persistent in σ if there is a position i of σ such that $Q \subseteq M_i$ and $\forall j > i : {}^\bullet t_j \cap Q = \varnothing$ and strongly insistent in σ if it is persistent or there are infinitely many positions j of σ such that $Q \subseteq {}^\bullet t_j$.*

With Def. 4, the definition of progress, free fairness, and simple fairness on sequential runs is analogous to Def. 3. It is straight-forward to verify that the equivalence completions of the resulting interleaving notions coincide with the corresponding non-sequential notions from Def. 3. Note that the resulting interleaving notions are equivalence-robust. Hyperfairness could also be expressed on interleavings, which is, however, much more complicated.

7   Conclusion

It is easy to see that Theorem 2 can be generalized to more general refinement of transitions and places by suitable nets, for example when a transition t is refined by a causal net that has the same input/output behaviour as t (cf. [4]). In further work, we will study the behaviour of fairness under composition and the generalization of the proposed notions to unsafe and high-level nets.

Acknowledgement

We would like to thank the anonymous referees for their helpful comments and suggestions.

References

1. K. R. Apt, N. Francez, and S. Katz. Appraising fairness in languages for distributed programming. *Distr. Comput.*, 2:226–241, 1988. 547, 552
2. P. C. Attie, N. Francez, and O. Grumberg. Fairness and hyperfairness in multi-party interactions. *Distr. Comput.*, 6:245–254, 1993. 555
3. E. Best. Fairness and conspiracies. *IPL*, 18:215–220, 1984. Erratum ibidem 19:162. 555, 558
4. W. Brauer, R. Gold, and W. Vogler. A survey of behaviour and equivalence preserving refinements of Petri nets. *LNCS* 483. Springer, 1990. 560
5. N. Francez. *Fairness*. Springer, 1986. 547, 549, 552, 559
6. N. Francez, R.-J. J. Back, and R. Kurki-Suonio. On equivalence-completions of fairness assumptions. *Formal Aspects of Computing*, 4:582–591, 1992. 548, 552
7. Y.-J. Joung. On fairness notions in distributed systems, part I: A characterization of implementability. *Information and Computation*, 166:1–34, 2001. 547, 548
8. Y.-J. Joung. On fairness notions in distributed systems, part II: Equivalence-completions and their hierarchies. *Information and Computation*, 166:35–60, 2001. 547, 552
9. E. Kindler and W. van der Aalst. Liveness, fairness and recurrence in Petri nets. *IPL*, 70(6):269–274, June 1999. 558
10. E. Kindler and R. Walter. Message passing mutex. In J. Desel, ed., *Structures in Concurrency Theory*, Workshops in Computing, pp. 205–219, Springer, 1995. 548, 555
11. E. Kindler and R. Walter. Mutex needs fairness. *IPL*, 62:31–39, 1997. 548, 560
12. M. Z. Kwiatkowska. Event fairness and non-interleaving concurrency. *Formal Aspects of Computing*, 1:213–228, 1989. 552, 555
13. M. Z. Kwiatkowska. *Fairness for Non-Interleaving Concurrency*. Technical report no. 22, University of Leicester, Department of Computing Studies, May 1989. 548, 552, 560
14. M. Z. Kwiatkowska. Survey of fairness notions. *Information and Software Technology*, 31(7):371–386, 1989. 547
15. L. Lamport. Fairness and hyperfairness. *Distr. Comput.*, 13(4):239–245, 2000. 547, 548, 555
16. D. Lehmann, A. Pnueli, and J. Stavi. Impartiality, justice, and fairness: The ethics of concurrent termination. In *Proc. 8th ICALP, LNCS* 115, pp. 264–277, 1981. 547
17. A. Merceron. Fair processes. In *Adv. in Petri Nets, LNCS* 266. Springer, 1987. 552, 555
18. D. Peled and A. Pnueli. Proving partial order properties. *TCS*, 126:143–182, 1994. 548, 552, 560
19. W. Reisig. Partial order semantics versus interleaving semantics for CSP-like languages and its impact on fairness. In *Proc. 11th ICALP, LNCS* 172, pp. 403–413. Springer, July 1984. 548, 552
20. W. Reisig. Das Verhalten Verteilter Systeme. GMD-Bericht 170, GMD, 1987. R. Oldenbourg Verlag. 555
21. W. Reisig. A strong part of concurrency. In *Adv. in Petri Nets, LNCS* 266, pp. 238–272. Springer, 1987. 554
22. R. van Glabbeek and U. Goltz. Refinement of actions and equivalence notions for concurrent systems. *Acta Informatica*, 37:229–327, 2001. 548
23. W. Vogler. Fairness and partial order semantics. *IPL*, 55:33–39, 1995. 548, 560

24. W. Vogler. Efficiency of asynchronous systems and read arcs in Petri nets. In *Proceedings ICALP'97, LNCS* 1256, pp. 538–548. Springer, 1997. 548, 560

25. H. Völzer. *Fairneß, Randomisierung und Konspiration in Verteilten Algorithmen.* PhD thesis, Humboldt-Universität zu Berlin, Institut für Informatik, Dec. 2000. in German, http://dochost.rz.hu-berlin.de/dissertationen/ voelzer-hagen-2000-12-08. 555, 560

Decidability of Strong Bisimilarity for Timed BPP

Sławomir Lasota[1,2] *

[1] LSV, CNRS UMR 8643 & ENS Cachan, France
[2] Institute of Informatics, Warsaw University, Poland
sl@mimuw.edu.pl

Abstract. We investigate a timed extension of the class of Basic Parallel Processes (BPP), in which actions are durational and urgent and parallel components have independent local clocks. The main result is decidability of strong bisimilarity, known also as performance equivalence, in this class. This extends the earlier decidability result for plain BPP [8] as well as decidability for timed BPP with strictly positive durations of actions [3]. Both ill-timed and well-timed semantics are treated. Our decision procedure is based on decidability of the validity problem for Presburger arithmetic.

1 Introduction

One important problem in verification of concurrent systems is to check whether two given systems P and Q are equivalent under a given notion of equivalence. For process algebras generating infinite-state systems the equivalence checking problem is not decidable in general, hence restricted classes of processes have been defined and investigated. We study here Basic Parallel Processes (BPP) [7], an extension of recursively defined finite-state systems by an operator of parallel composition. Strong bisimilarity [19] is a well accepted behavioural equivalence which often remains decidable for infinite-state systems. An elegant proof of decidability of bisimilarity for BPP was given in [8], while all other equivalences in van Glabbeek's spectrum are undecidable in BPP [15,17].

In order to deal with timing aspects of systems, process algebras were extended with an appropriate notion of time (see eg. [20], [1], [14], [10], [9], [2]). A substantial effort have also been directed toward defining a robust notion of equivalence taking performance into consideration, e.g., equivalence that relates only those processes that exhibit the same behavior at the same speed. The bisimilarity investigated in [14,10,9] applies to discrete-time process algebras where parallel components have their own local clocks and actions are *durational* and *urgent*. Urgent actions take place as soon as possible and can only

---

* This work has been supported by the fellowship of the Foundation for Polish Science, during the author's post-doc stay at Laboratoire Specification et Verification, ENS Cachan. Partially supported by the KBN grant 7 T11C 002 21 and by the Research Training Network *Games*.

L. Brim et al. (Eds.): CONCUR 2002, LNCS 2421, pp. 562–578, 2002.

be delayed in order to wait for a communication with another process. The semantics allows for runs which are *ill-timed*, i.e. the observed time of an action need not to increase along a run, but *well-caused*, i.e., causally-related local clock values do increase along a run.

Equivalence checking of finite-state timed processes attracted some attention [6,11]. For instance, in [6] bisimilarity was proved decidable for finite timed transition systems. In contrast to this, there are not many results on verification of infinite-state timed systems. We can mention here [22], where the tableau-based technique of [8] was adapted to timed-arc BPP nets. One relevant result [3] is the decidability and surprisingly polynomial-time complexity of strong bisimilarity for timed BPP when durations of actions are strictly positive. Due to this latter restriction, process algebra does not subsume plain BPP. Only when the restriction is omitted, the process algebra obtained is a timed extension of BPP, since BPP embeds naturally into it as the case when all durations equal zero and no time delay is used in process definitions.

As the main result of this paper, we prove decidability of bisimilarity for the timed extension of BPP, called TBPP in the sequel. In fact, our formulation of the process algebra is simpler and more general than in [14,10,3], as durations are implicitly assigned to each rewrite rule rather than to each action. In particular, duration of an action can be chosen in a nondeterministic way.

Outline: After basic definitions in Section 2, we prove in Section 3 a series of decomposition results. They allow us to overcome in Section 4 the main difficulty: while the set of plain BPP processes, up to a structural congruence, forms a finitely-generated commutative semigroup, this is not the case in TBPP, since parallel components of a process can be arbitrarily spread out over time. Then Section 5 contains the decision procedure. We exploit decidability of the validity problem for Presburger arithmetic [21] in the way suggested by Jančar in [18] for untimed systems. In Section 6 we extend our decidability result to TBPP with communication and to TBPP under *well-timed* semantics. The last section contains a few remarks.

2   Definitions

Let *Const* be a finite set of *process constants*, ranged over by X, Y, etc. The set of TBPP process expressions (processes) over *Const*, ranged over by P, Q, P_1, etc. is given by

$$P ::= \mathbf{0} \mid X \mid P\|P \mid 1{\triangleright}P$$

where $\mathbf{0}$ denotes the *empty* process, $\_\|\_$ stands for a parallel composition and $1{\triangleright}P$ denotes a process which behaves like P but delayed by one time unit. Processes not involving the delay operator $1{\triangleright}\_$ are called *untimed* processes or BPP processes [7]. For $t \in \mathbb{N}$, a natural number, we write $t{\triangleright}P$ as a shorthand for $\underbrace{1{\triangleright}(1{\triangleright}(\ldots(1{\triangleright}P)\ldots))}_{t \text{ times}}$.

We do not distinguish between processes related by a *structural congruence*, i.e.,
the smallest congruence induced by:

- associativity and commutativity of parallel composition,
- nilpotency and time cancellation for **0**: $\mathbf{0}\|P = P$, $1\triangleright\mathbf{0} = \mathbf{0}$,
- clock distribution law [10]: $1\triangleright(P_1\|P_2) = 1\triangleright P_1\|1\triangleright P_2$.

From now on, equality of processes in understood up to the structural congruence. This allows us to consider only processes in the following *timed normal form*:

$$t_1\triangleright\alpha_1\|t_2\triangleright\alpha_2\| \ \ldots \ \|t_n\triangleright\alpha_n \tag{1}$$

where $n \geq 0$, $0 \leq t_1 < t_2 < \ldots < t_n$ and $\alpha_1 \ldots \alpha_n$ are non-empty untimed processes, i.e., not involving the delay operator and **0**. When $n = 0$, (1) denotes the empty process **0**. We assume here and later that delay operator binds stronger than parallel composition.

Due to associativity, commutativity and nilpotency laws, each untimed process can be seen as a finite multiset of process constants, or equivalently as an element of the free commutative semigroup over *Const*. This observation was a key point in the decision procedure for strong bisimilarity of BPP [8]. Unfortunately, in TBPP we lose this finite-generation property: TBPP processes can be rather seen as elements of the free commutative semigroup over $\mathbb{N} \times Const$.

A TBPP process definition consists of a finite set *Const* of process constants, a finite set *Act* of *actions* and a finite set of process rewrite rules of the form $X \xrightarrow{a} P$, where P is a process over *Const* in timed normal form and $a \in Act$. We assume at least one rewrite rule for each $X \in Const$. Each process definition Δ induces a labeled transition system, whose states are processes, and whose transitions are labeled by pairs (t, a), with t a natural number and $a \in Act$. The transitions are derived from the following SOS rules (recall that $\_\|\_$ is commutative):

$$\frac{(X \xrightarrow{a} P) \in \Delta}{X \xrightarrow{0,a} P} \qquad \frac{P \xrightarrow{t,a} P'}{P\|Q \xrightarrow{t,a} P'\|Q} \qquad \frac{P \xrightarrow{t,a} P'}{1\triangleright P \xrightarrow{t+1,a} 1\triangleright P'} \tag{2}$$

A transition $P \xrightarrow{t,a} Q$ is to mean "P does a at time t and becomes Q". The transition system obtained is finitely-branching despite that it has infinite labeling set. According to the right-most rule, delay operator is preserved during the transition and thus is used to record the value of a clock associated to a process. Following [10],[14] and [3], we allow for *ill-timed runs*, i.e., we *do not* exclude $P \xrightarrow{t_1,a_1} P' \xrightarrow{t_2,a_2} P''$ when $t_1 > t_2$. This is due to the middle rule, which allows for a transition in one component independently from values of clocks in other components. It was argued convincingly in [1] that ill-timed semantics brings no semantical problems since the ill-timed runs are well-caused and on the other hand greatly simplifies the technical treatment. While we agree with the first point, in Section 6 we demonstrate that deciding strong bisimilarity is even easier for well-timed semantics.

If we restrict ourselves to BPP processes only, and if all right-hand sides of rewrite rules in Δ are BPP processes, each transition derived from rules (2) is performed at time $t = 0$. Hence the time becomes irrelevant and we essentially obtain a BPP process definition.

The rules (2) require some further comment. In [3] the transition system for TBPP was defined for an arbitrary *duration function* $f : Act \to \mathbb{N} \setminus \{0\}$, assigning a positive duration to each action. Consequently, instead of the first rule in (2) a rule

$$\frac{(X \xrightarrow{a} P) \in \Delta}{X \xrightarrow{0,a} f(a) \triangleright P}$$

was used, following [10,14]. A rewrite rule $X \xrightarrow{a} P$ of [3] can be obviously expressed in our framework by the rule $X \xrightarrow{a} t \triangleright P$, where $t = f(a)$. On the other hand, our rules are more general in at least two respects: first, zero-durations are allowed; second, a duration is assigned to each rewrite rule separately rather then to each action (a rule $X \xrightarrow{a} t_1 \triangleright \alpha_1 \| \ldots \| t_n \triangleright \alpha_n$ is implicitly assigned duration $t_1 \geq 0$, in fact).

Given a process definition Δ, two processes P_1 and P_2 are *(strongly) bisimilar* w.r.t. Δ, denoted $P_1 \sim_\Delta P_2$ (or $P_1 \sim P_2$ when Δ is understood in the context), if they are related by some bisimulation R, that is a binary relation over processes such that whenever $(P, Q) \in R$, for each $a \in Act$ and $t \geq 0$,

– if $P \xrightarrow{t,a} P'$ then $Q \xrightarrow{t,a} Q'$ for some Q' such that $(P', Q') \in R$
– if $Q \xrightarrow{t,a} Q'$ then $P \xrightarrow{t,a} P'$ for some P' such that $(P', Q') \in R$.

In [3] and [10], such relations were called *performance relations* and *R-bisimulations*, respectively, and the induced equivalence was called *performance equivalence*. The equivalence was also called *timed bisimilarity*, eg. in [6]. We prefer to call it *bisimilarity* to avoid introducing unnecessary names and to emphasize that we generalize bisimilarity on BPP. In the following sections we show the decidability of the following problem:

Problem: STRONG BISIMILARITY FOR TBPP
Instance: A TBPP process definition Δ and two process
   constants X, Y
Question: $X \sim_\Delta Y$?

We do not lose generality by only restricting to constants, since checking $P \sim Q$, for arbitrary P, Q is equivalent to checking $X_P \sim X_Q$, where X_P and X_Q are new fresh constants and their only rewrite rules are: $X_P \xrightarrow{a} P$ and $X_Q \xrightarrow{a} Q$. The rest of this section is devoted to an example illustrating the main difficulty of the problem.

Example 1. Assume that two processes $X \| 3 \triangleright (Y \| Z)$ and $(Y \| Y) \| 3 \triangleright (Z \| Z \| Z)$ are bisimilar. Decomposition results in Lemmas 1 and 2 in Section 3 imply that $3 \triangleright (Y \| Z)$ and $3 \triangleright (Z \| Z \| Z)$ are then bisimilar too. So we can substitute one for another and consider $X\|3\triangleright(Y\|Z)$ and $(Y\|Y)\|3\triangleright(Y\|Z)$, which are *almost identical* according to terminology from the next section, i.e., differ only at time 0. At first sight, this short deduction suggests that we are not very far from the bisimilarity checking problem for BPP, as we only need to consider BPP processes X and $Y\|Y$ in a context $\_\|3\triangleright(Y\|Z)$, roughly. But this is not really true. Assume that Z has a rewrite rule $Z \xrightarrow{a} Y\|Z$. According to Lemma 5 in the next section, a transition in the context part can always be matched by identical transition in the context part, e.g., $X\|3\triangleright(Y\|Z) \xrightarrow{3,a} X\|3\triangleright(Y\|Y\|Z)$ is matched by $(Y\|Y)\|3\triangleright(Y\|Z) \xrightarrow{3,a} (Y\|Y)\|3\triangleright(Y\|Y\|Z)$. But nevertheless we must take into account an infinite number of contexts: $\_\|3\triangleright(Y^i\|Z)$, for $i > 0$. Moreover, if Y has for instance a rule $Y \xrightarrow{b} Y\|1\triangleright Y$, contexts that are arbitrarily spread out through the time domain $\mathbb{N}$ must be considered. $\qquad\square$

In particular, all proof methods for decidability of bisimilarity for BPP work no more for TBPP, since they are based on the fact that the set of BPP processes is a finitely-generated commutative semigroup. This difficulty is overcome in Lemma 7 in Section 4, where we prove that one can restrict to a sufficiently large initial fragment of the time domain and ignore transitions which lead out of this fragment.

3   Decomposition and Almost-Identical Pairs

From now on we assume that Δ is an arbitrary fixed process definition and that all processes are in timed normal form (1). For such $P = t_1\triangleright\alpha_1\|t_2\triangleright\alpha_2\|\ldots\|t_n\triangleright\alpha_n$, which is *non-empty*, i.e., $n > 0$, we put:

- $head(P) := t_1\triangleright\alpha_1$,
- $tail(P) := t_2\triangleright\alpha_2\|\ \ldots\ \|t_n\triangleright\alpha_n$,
- $minclock(P) := t_1$,
- $now(P) := \alpha_1\|(t_2 - t_1)\triangleright\alpha_2\|\ \ldots\ \|(t_n - t_1)\triangleright\alpha_n$.

Note that $head(P)$, $tail(P)$ and $now(P)$ are in timed normal form again, $head(now(P))$ is untimed, $P = head(P)\|tail(P)$ and $P = minclock(P)\triangleright now(P)$.

Bisimilarity is not only compositional (i.e. a congruence) w.r.t. parallel composition and the delay operator but it is also partially decompositional:

Lemma 1 (Decomposition w.r.t. $1\triangleright\_$). *For non-empty P and Q, $P \sim Q$ implies*

1. *$minclock(P) = minclock(Q)$ and*
2. *$now(P) \sim now(Q)$.*

Proof. 1. $minclock(P) = minclock(Q)$ as the earliest action of P must be matched in Q and vice versa. 2. The relation $\{(t\triangleright now(P), t\triangleright now(Q)) : t \geq 0,\ P \sim Q\}$ is a bisimulation. $\qquad\square$

Lemma 2 (Partial decomposition w.r.t. _‖_). *For non-empty P and Q, $P \sim Q$ implies tail$(P) \sim$ tail(Q).*

Proof. The relation $\{(\text{tail}(P), \text{tail}(Q)) : P \sim Q, P \text{ and } Q \text{ are non-empty}\}$ is a bisimulation, since any action in tail(P) at time $t > \text{minclock}(P) = \text{minclock}(Q)$ must be matched in tail(Q). □

Example 2. Strong bisimilarity is not fully decompositional w.r.t. _‖_, $P \sim Q$ does not imply head$(P) \sim$ head(Q). As a counterexample, consider a process definition:

$$A \xrightarrow{a} 1 \triangleright B \qquad A' \xrightarrow{a} 1 \triangleright C \qquad B \xrightarrow{b} B \qquad C \xrightarrow{c} C$$

We have $A\|1\triangleright(B\|C) \sim A'\|1\triangleright(B\|C)$ but $A \nsim A'$. □

By Lemmas 1 and 2, if two processes are bisimilar, say $t_1\triangleright\alpha_1\| \ \ldots \ \|t_n\triangleright\alpha_n$ and $u_1\triangleright\beta_1\| \ \ldots \ \|u_n\triangleright\beta_m$, then necessarily they involve the same time stages, that is to say $n = m$ and $t_i = u_i$, for $i \leq n$.

> **Assumption.** In Sections 3, 4 and 5, whenever we consider a pair (P,Q) of processes, we silently assume that $P = t_1\triangleright\alpha_1\| \ \ldots \ \|t_n\triangleright\alpha_n$ and $Q = t_1\triangleright\beta_1\| \ \ldots \ \|t_n\triangleright\beta_n$, for some $n \geq 0$, $0 \leq t_1 < t_2 < \ldots < t_n$ and non-empty untimed processes $\alpha_1, \ldots, \alpha_n, \beta_1, \ldots, \beta_n$. We omit routine verification that all pairs mentioned throughout the following sections are of this form.

Lemma 2 suggests to study pairs of processes in a particularly simple form:

Definition 1. (Almost-identical pairs) *Processes P and Q are called* almost-identical *if minclock$(P) = $ minclock$(Q) = 0$ and tail$(P) = $ tail(Q).*

We will apply Lemma 2 to decompose a pair of processes into a number of almost-identical pairs. As a consequence, we will be able to ignore all pairs which are not almost-identical (Lemma 3 below). Before the formal definition of decomposition, we give an example to explain the idea.

Example 3. Consider a pair:

$$P = \quad 2 \triangleright (X\|Y) \quad \| \quad 7 \triangleright (X\|X\|Y) \quad \| \quad 10 \triangleright (Z\|Z) \quad \| \quad 16 \triangleright Y$$
$$Q = \quad 2 \triangleright (X\|X\|Z) \quad \| \quad 7 \triangleright (X\|Z) \quad \| \quad 10 \triangleright (X\|X) \quad \| \quad 16 \triangleright Y$$

(P,Q) can be decomposed into four pairs (P_i, Q_i), $i \leq 4$. The rule is as follows: head(P_i) and head(Q_i) is the i-th component of P and Q, respectively, while tail$(P_i) = $ tail(Q_i) contains the components of P from all later time stages.

$$
\begin{aligned}
P_1 &= & (X\|Y) &\quad\| & 5 \triangleright (X\|X\|Y) &\quad\| & 8 \triangleright (Z\|Z) &\quad\| & 14 \triangleright Y \\
Q_1 &= & (X\|X\|Z) &\quad\| & 5 \triangleright (X\|X\|Y) &\quad\| & 8 \triangleright (Z\|Z) &\quad\| & 14 \triangleright Y \\
P_2 &= & & & (X\|X\|Y) &\quad\| & 3 \triangleright (Z\|Z) &\quad\| & 9 \triangleright Y \\
Q_2 &= & & & (X\|Z) &\quad\| & 3 \triangleright (Z\|Z) &\quad\| & 9 \triangleright Y \\
P_3 &= & & & & & (Z\|Z) &\quad\| & 6 \triangleright Y \\
Q_3 &= & & & & & (X\|X) &\quad\| & 6 \triangleright Y \\
P_4 &= & & & & & & & Y \\
Q_4 &= & & & & & & & Y.
\end{aligned}
$$

It can be shown using Lemmas 1 and 2 that $P \sim Q \iff \forall i \le 4.P_i \sim Q_i$. The last pair is identical and hence can be ignored, therefore to show $P \sim Q$ it is sufficient to consider only the first three: $P \sim Q \iff \forall i \le 3.P_i \sim Q_i$. The formal definition follows. $\qquad\square$

Definition 2. (Decomposition set) *A decomposition set* $\mathbb{DS}(P,Q)$ *of a pair* (P,Q) *is defined recursively by (for brevity, $\bar{P}$ stands for $now(P)$ and $\bar{Q}$ stands for $now(Q)$)*

$$
\mathbb{DS}(P,Q) := \begin{cases} \{(\bar{P}, head(\bar{Q})\|tail(\bar{P}))\} \cup \mathbb{DS}(tail(\bar{P}), tail(\bar{Q})) & \text{if } P \ne Q \\ \emptyset & \text{if } P = Q. \end{cases}
$$

Note that all pairs in $\mathbb{DS}(P,Q)$ are almost-identical by definition.

Lemma 3. $P \sim Q$ *iff* $\mathbb{DS}(P,Q) \subseteq \sim$.

Proof. By induction on the size of P, Q. As for $P = Q$ we are immediately done, assume that P, Q are non-identical, hence non-empty and that the lemma holds for a pair $(tail(now(P)), tail(now(Q)))$, i.e.,

$$
tail(now(P)) \sim tail(now(Q)) \iff \mathbb{DS}(tail(now(P)), tail(now(Q))) \subseteq \sim .
\tag{3}
$$

IF-IMPLICATION: If $\mathbb{DS}(P,Q) \subseteq \sim$, then also $\mathbb{DS}(tail(now(P)), tail(now(Q))) \subseteq \sim$, as a subset of $\mathbb{DS}(P,Q)$. Hence, by induction assumption (3),

$$
tail(now(P)) \sim tail(now(Q)).
\tag{4}
$$

Moreover, from $\mathbb{DS}(P,Q) \subseteq \sim$ we derive

$$
now(P) \sim head(now(Q))\|tail(now(P)),
\tag{5}
$$

since this pair is in $\mathbb{DS}(P,Q)$. By (4) and (5) and the congruence property of $\sim$ we conclude $now(P) \sim now(Q)$ hence $P \sim Q$.
ONLY-IF-IMPLICATION: Assume $P \sim Q$. By Lemma 1 and 2, (4) holds again. By (3), $\mathbb{DS}(tail(now(P)), tail(now(Q))) \subseteq \sim$. Now, we only need to show (5), which follows by (4) and by $\sim$ being a congruence:
$now(P) \sim now(Q) = head(now(Q))\|tail(now(Q)) \sim head(now(Q))\|tail(now(P))$. $\quad\square$

In Definitions 3, 5 and 6 below we introduce a series of computationally more and more tractable notions of bisimulation.

Definition 3. (Decompositional bisimulation) *A binary relation R over processes is a* decompositional bisimulation *if whenever $(P, Q) \in R$, for each $a \in Act$ and $t \geq 0$,*

- *if $P \xrightarrow{t,a} P'$ then $Q \xrightarrow{t,a} Q'$ for some Q' such that $\mathbb{DS}(P', Q') \subseteq R$*
- *if $Q \xrightarrow{t,a} Q'$ then $P \xrightarrow{t,a} P'$ for some P' such that $\mathbb{DS}(P', Q') \subseteq R$.*

Lemma 4. *$P \sim Q$ iff P and Q are related by a decompositional bisimulation.*

Before the proof, we need a definition of a *bisimulation-base*. It is an adaptation of the well-know notion due to Caucal [4,5,7].

Definition 4. *For a binary relation R, let $\overset{R}{\equiv}$ denote the smallest congruence w.r.t. parallel composition and delay operator containing R. We call R a* bisimulation-base *if whenever $(P, Q) \in R$, for each $a \in Act$ and $t \geq 0$,*

- *if $P \xrightarrow{t,a} P'$ then $Q \xrightarrow{t,a} Q'$ for some Q' such that $(P', Q') \in \overset{R}{\equiv}$*
- *if $Q \xrightarrow{t,a} Q'$ then $P \xrightarrow{t,a} P'$ for some P' such that $(P', Q') \in \overset{R}{\equiv}$.*

Proof of Lemma 4. By Lemma 3, $\sim$ is a decompositional bisimulation. Hence we only need to show the IF-direction. This is shown in two steps:

1. each decompositional bisimulation is a bisimulation-base,
2. if R is a bisimulation-base, then $\overset{R}{\equiv}$ is a bisimulation.

Point 1. is immediate, since each pair (P', Q') belongs to the congruence generated by its decomposition set, $(P', Q') \in \overset{\mathbb{DS}(P',Q')}{\equiv}$. The proof of 2. amounts to showing that the two clauses in the definition of bisimulation hold for $\overset{R}{\equiv}$. This can be done by a straightforward induction on the depth of inference of $P \overset{R}{\equiv} Q$. □

Bisimilarity is closed under identical transitions performed in identical parts of almost-identical processes:

Lemma 5. *Whenever P and Q are almost-identical, $P \sim Q$ and $tail(P) \xrightarrow{t,a} P'$ then $head(P) \| P' \sim head(Q) \| P'$.*

Proof. Note that, by assumption, t is necessarily strictly positive. Thus the answer of Q to the transition $P \xrightarrow{t,a} head(P) \| P'$ is performed in $tail(Q)$, since the time t must be matched exactly. Hence for some Q', $tail(Q) \xrightarrow{t,a} Q'$ and $head(P) \| P' \sim head(Q) \| Q'$. By Lemma 2 and the congruence property of $\sim$, $head(Q) \| Q' \sim head(Q) \| P'$, which completes the proof. □

To make our notation more succinct, we introduce a closure operator on binary relations over processes as follows: let $R^{\rightarrow}$ be the smallest relation containing R

such that whenever an almost-identical pair (P, Q) is in $R^{\rightarrow}$ and $\mathrm{tail}(P) \xrightarrow{t,a} P'$ then $(\mathrm{head}(P)\|P', \mathrm{head}(Q)\|P') \in R^{\rightarrow}$. Lemma 5 can be then shortly rephrased by $\sim^{\rightarrow} \subseteq \sim$.

Due to Lemma 3, it is sufficient to consider almost-identical pairs. Lemma 5 allows us to refine the notion of decompositional bisimulation for almost-identical pairs in Definition 5 below and to strengthen Lemma 4 in Lemma 6 below.

Definition 5. *A binary relation R over processes is an* almost-identical decompositional bisimulation *if it only contains almost-identical pairs and*

1. *whenever $(P, Q) \in R$, for each $a \in Act$,*
   - *if $P \xrightarrow{0,a} P'$ then $Q \xrightarrow{0,a} Q'$ for some Q' such that $\mathbb{DS}(P', Q') \subseteq R$*
   - *if $Q \xrightarrow{0,a} Q'$ then $P \xrightarrow{0,a} P'$ for some P' such that $\mathbb{DS}(P', Q') \subseteq R$*
2. *$R^{\rightarrow} \subseteq R$.*

Roughly, the Defender's invention in the Bisimulation Game is restricted only to moves at time 0, since all transitions performed at time $t > 0$ are matched identically.

Lemma 6. *Let P and Q be almost-identical. $P \sim Q$ iff P and Q are related by an almost-identical decompositional bisimulation.*

Proof. By Lemma 5, $\sim$ restricted to only almost-identical pairs is an almost-identical decompositional bisimulation. On the other hand, each almost-identical decompositional bisimulation is obviously a decompositional bisimulation. $\square$

4   Bounded Bisimulations

Having elaborated an appropriate notion of bisimulation, we are ready to face the main difficulty of the problem. It turns out that we can restrict ourselves to only a finite initial fragment of the time domain $\mathbb{N}$, without losing the completeness of almost-identical decompositional bisimulations w.r.t. $\sim$ as stated in Lemma 6. The restriction is imposed by a "horizon" $2 \cdot H$, where H is defined as

$$H := \max\{\mathrm{maxclock}(P) : X \xrightarrow{a} P \in \Delta\}$$

and $\mathrm{maxclock}(P)$ of a non-empty process P in timed normal form (1) is to denote t_n and $\mathrm{maxclock}(\mathbf{0}) = 0$. Intuitively, H is the maximal *scope* of a single transition: in effect of a transition performed at time t, say, only process components at time between t and $t + H$ can be modified.

Definition 6. *A binary relation R over processes is a* bounded almost-identical decompositional bisimulation *(bounded bisimulation in short) if it only contains almost-identical pairs (P, Q) with $\mathrm{maxclock}(P) \leq 2 \cdot H$ and $\mathrm{maxclock}(Q) \leq 2 \cdot H$, and whenever $(P, Q) \in R$, for each $a \in Act$,*

1. – if $P \xrightarrow{0,a} P'$ then $Q \xrightarrow{0,a} Q'$ for some Q' such that $\mathbb{DS}(P',Q') \subseteq R$
    – if $Q \xrightarrow{0,a} Q'$ then $P \xrightarrow{0,a} P'$ for some P' such that $\mathbb{DS}(P',Q') \subseteq R$
2. for $0 < t \le H$, if $tail(P) \xrightarrow{t,a} P'$ then $(head(P)\|P', head(Q)\|P') \in R$.

Having restricted in Lemma 6 non-identical responses of the Defender to transitions at $t{=}0$, we restrict ourselves further and take into consideration only transitions at time $t{\le}H$. Intuitively, H is chosen sufficiently large to guarantee that the additional restriction has no impact on the relevant part of the Bisimulation Game played at time 0. If one reminds that the scope of transitions performed at time 0 does not go beyond $0 \ldots H$, then all transitions (and the identically-matching responses) that are performed at time $t > 0$ belonging to that scope are clearly taken into consideration. This guarantees that each bounded bisimulation can be extended to an almost-identical decompositional bisimulation, by closing under identically-matched transitions performed at time $t{>}H$.

Lemma 7. *Let P and Q be almost-identical with $maxclock(P) \le 2{\cdot}H$. Then $P \sim Q$ iff P and Q are related by a bounded bisimulation.*

Proof. ONLY-IF-IMPLICATION: $\sim$ restricted to only those almost-identical pairs (P,Q) with $maxclock(P) \le 2{\cdot}H$ is a bounded bisimulation.
IF-IMPLICATION: Relying on Lemma 6, we will show that if R is a bounded bisimulation then $R^{\to}$ is an almost-identical decompositional bisimulation. Point 2. in Definition 5 is immediate, i.e., $(R^{\to})^{\to} \subseteq R^{\to}$. For the proof of Point 1. we will need the following notation. For $P = t_1{\triangleright}\alpha_1\| \ldots \|t_n{\triangleright}\alpha_n$ and $t \ge 0$, let

$$head_t(P) = t_1{\triangleright}\alpha_1\| \ldots \|t_i{\triangleright}\alpha_i,$$
$$tail_t(P) = t_{i+1}{\triangleright}\alpha_{i+1}\| \ldots \|t_n{\triangleright}\alpha_n,$$

where i is chosen so that $t_j <= t$ for all $1 \le j \le i$ and $t_j > t$ for all $i{+}1 \le j \le n$. In particular $head(P) = head_0(P)$ and $tail(P) = tail_0(P)$, when $minclock(P) = 0$.

We need to show Point 1. in Definition 5 only for pairs in $R^{\to} \setminus R$. Let (P,Q) be any pair in $R^{\to} \setminus R$. So there exists a pair $(P_0, Q_0) \in R$ such that P is obtained from P_0 and Q is obtained from Q_0 by a finite sequence of transitions performed in $tail(P_0) = tail(Q_0)$. W.l.o.g. we can assume that the transitions performed at time less or equal to H precede in the sequence those performed at time strictly greater than H. Thus we can further assume that all transitions in the sequence are performed at time greater than H, since all earlier transitions performed at time less or equal H do not lead out of R. To be more precise, there is $(P_0, Q_0) \in R$ such that

$$head_H(P_0) = head_H(P), \qquad\qquad head_H(Q_0) = head_H(Q), \qquad (6)$$

and there exists $m > 0$, $t_1, \ldots, t_m > H$ and $a_1, \ldots, a_m \in Act$ such that

$$tail_H(P_0) \xrightarrow{t_1,a_1} \ldots \xrightarrow{t_m,a_m} tail_H(P). \qquad (7)$$

Recall that both (P_0, Q_0) and (P, Q) are almost-identical pairs, hence

$$Q_0 = \text{head}_H(Q_0)\|\text{tail}_H(P_0) \qquad \text{and} \qquad Q = \text{head}_H(Q)\|\text{tail}_H(P).$$

Now we will show only the first clause in Point 1. – the second clause follows by the identical reasoning. Here is the simple idea underlying the pedantic analysis to follow: all transitions performed at time 0 by P or Q have its scope inside $\text{head}_H(P)$ or $\text{head}_H(Q)$, respectively, hence by (6) the matching of a transition of P_0 by Q_0 can be re-used for P and Q. Assume that P has a transition labelled by $(0, a)$. This means that $\text{head}_H(P) \xrightarrow{0,a} P'$ for some P' with $\text{maxclock}(P') \leq H$ and $P \xrightarrow{0,a} P'\|\text{tail}_H(P)$. Hence $\text{head}_H(P)\|\text{tail}_H(P_0) = P_0 \xrightarrow{0,a} P'\|\text{tail}_H(P_0)$.

$$\underbrace{\text{head}_H(P)\|\text{tail}_H(P_0)}_{P_0} \xrightarrow{t_1,a_1} \cdots \xrightarrow{t_m,a_m} \underbrace{\text{head}_H(P)\|\text{tail}_H(P)}_{P}$$
$$\Big\downarrow 0,a \qquad\qquad\qquad\qquad\qquad\qquad \Big\downarrow 0,a$$
$$P'\|\text{tail}_H(P_0) \xrightarrow{t_1,a_1} \cdots \xrightarrow{t_m,a_m} P'\|\text{tail}_H(P)$$

$(P_0, Q_0) \in R$ and R is a bounded bisimulation, hence there exists a Q' such that $\text{maxclock}(Q') \leq H$, $\text{head}_H(Q_0) \xrightarrow{0,a} Q'$ and

$$\mathbb{DS}(P'\|\text{tail}_H(P_0), Q'\|\text{tail}_H(P_0)) \subseteq R. \tag{8}$$

This means that $Q \xrightarrow{0,a} Q'\|\text{tail}_H(P)$ and we have the following picture again:

$$Q'\|\text{tail}_H(P_0) \xrightarrow{t_1,a_1} \cdots \xrightarrow{t_m,a_m} Q'\|\text{tail}_H(P)$$
$$\Big\uparrow 0,a \qquad\qquad\qquad\qquad\qquad\qquad \Big\uparrow 0,a$$
$$\underbrace{\text{head}_H(Q)\|\text{tail}_H(P_0)}_{Q_0} \xrightarrow{t_1,a_1} \cdots \xrightarrow{t_m,a_m} \underbrace{\text{head}_H(Q)\|\text{tail}_H(P)}_{Q}$$

We only need to show that

$$\mathbb{DS}(P'\|\text{tail}_H(P), Q'\|\text{tail}_H(P)) \subseteq R^{\rightarrow}.$$

Consider any pair $(\bar{P}, \bar{Q}) \in \mathbb{DS}(P'\|\text{tail}_H(P), Q'\|\text{tail}_H(P))$. By (8) it is sufficient to show that there exists a pair $(\bar{P}_0, \bar{Q}_0) \in \mathbb{DS}(P'\|\text{tail}_H(P_0), Q'\|\text{tail}_H(P_0))$ such that

$$\text{tail}(\bar{P}_0) = \text{tail}(\bar{Q}_0) \xrightarrow{\bar{t}_1,\bar{a}_1} \cdots \xrightarrow{\bar{t}_m,\bar{a}_m} \text{tail}(\bar{P}) = \text{tail}(\bar{Q}), \tag{9}$$

for some sequences $\bar{t}_1, \ldots, \bar{t}_m > 0$, $\bar{a}_1, \ldots, \bar{a}_m \in Act$. Let $(\text{tail}_H(P))^{-u}$ denote process $\text{tail}_H(P)$ in which all time prefixes are decreased by u; analogously $(\text{tail}_H(P_0))^{-u}$. It is crucial now to observe that by the very definition of $\mathbb{DS}(\_,\_)$ we have

$$\bar{P} = \bar{P}'\|(\text{tail}_H(P))^{-u} \quad \text{and} \quad \bar{Q} = \bar{Q}'\|(\text{tail}_H(P))^{-u},$$

for some u such that $0 \leq u \leq H$ and some $(\bar{P}', \bar{Q}') \in \mathbb{DS}(P', Q')$, Moreover, if we put:

$$\bar{P}_0 := \bar{P}' \| (\text{tail}_H(P_0))^{-u} \quad \text{and} \quad \bar{Q}_0 := \bar{Q}' \| (\text{tail}_H(P_0))^{-u},$$

then we have $(\bar{P}_0, \bar{Q}_0) \in \mathbb{DS}(P' \| \text{tail}_H(P_0), Q' \| \text{tail}_H(P_0))$, by the very definition of $\mathbb{DS}(\_,\_)$ again. Now if we put $\bar{t}_i := t_i - u$ and $\bar{a}_i := a_i$, by (7) it is routine to check that (9) holds. $\square$

5   Decision Procedure

Our algorithm is composed of two semi-decision procedures, analogously as in the case of BPP. The TBPP processes are *finitely branching*, hence bisimulation inequivalence $\not\sim$ is semi-decidable. The semi-decision procedure is essentially the same as for BPP [4] and is based on the fact that $\sim$ is the intersection of a countable chain of decidable approximations. Furthermore, our development in Section 4 enables us to prove also semi-decidability of $\sim$ essentially in the same way as it was done for BPP. The semi-decision procedure for $\sim$ proposed below is motivated by the idea of Jančar [18] to use Presburger arithmetic.

For BPP, the crucial observation was that BPP processes can be seen as elements of the free commutative semigroup over *Const* with the semigroup operation $\_\|\_$, isomorphic to $\mathbb{N}^{Const}$ with vector addition $\_+\_$. The TBPP processes can be rather seen as elements of $\mathbb{N}^{\mathbb{N} \times Const}$. But due to Lemma 7, we can essentially restrict ourselves to only processes P with $\text{maxclock}(P) \leq 2 \cdot H$, i.e., to $\mathbb{N}^{\{0,\ldots,2 \cdot H\} \times Const}$. This allows us to apply Theorem 1 below.

Definition 7. *A linear subset of $\mathbb{N}^n$, $n > 0$, is a set of the form*

$$v + span\{w_1, \ldots, w_k\} = \{v + n_1 w_i + \ldots + n_k w_k : n_1, \ldots, n_k \in \mathbb{N}\}.$$

I.e., each linear set is determined by a base $v \in \mathbb{N}^n$ and periods $\{w_1, \ldots, w_k\} \subset \mathbb{N}^n$. A semi-linear set is a finite union of linear sets.

Every binary relation over $\mathbb{N}^n$, i.e., a subset of $\mathbb{N}^n \times \mathbb{N}^n$, can be seen naturally as a subset of $\mathbb{N}^{2 \cdot n}$. In the sequel we silently identify $\mathbb{N}^n \times \mathbb{N}^n$ and $\mathbb{N}^{2 \cdot n}$.

Theorem 1 ([12,16,18]). *Each congruence in $(\mathbb{N}^n, \_+\_)$, $n > 0$, is semi-linear.*

By Theorem 1, $\sim$ restricted to the almost-identical pairs (P, Q) with $\text{maxclock}(P) \leq 2 \cdot H$ is semi-linear, as it is obviously a congruence w.r.t. $\_\|\_$. Hence we refine Lemma 7 as follows:

Corollary 1. *Let P and Q be almost-identical with $\text{maxclock}(P) \leq 2 \cdot H$. Then $P \sim Q$ iff P and Q are related by a semi-linear bounded bisimulation.*

Lemma 8. *For a semi-linear binary relation R over $\mathbb{N}^{\{0,\ldots,2 \cdot H\} \times Const}$, given by a finite set of base-periods pairs, it is decidable whether R is a bounded bisimulation.*

Proof. Given R, we can effectively construct a closed formula in Presburger arithmetic ϕ_R such that ϕ_R is valid iff R is a bounded bisimulation. The validity problem for Presburger arithmetic is decidable (see for instance [21]), hence this gives a decision procedure required.

Let $Const = \{X_1, \dots, X_N\}$. The formula ϕ_R involves several tuples of variables of the form $\{x_{t,i}\}_{0 \le t \le 2 \cdot H, 1 \le i \le N}$, denoted in short $\bar{x}$. A valuation of each such tuple corresponds to a TBPP process.

The structure of ϕ_R follows directly the two points in Definition 6 (we omit the second clause in the first point of Definition 6, which is symmetric to the first clause):

$$\forall \bar{x}, \bar{y}. \ (\bar{x}, \bar{y}) \in R \Longrightarrow \quad (\bar{x}, \bar{y}) \text{ is an almost-identical pair } \wedge$$

$$\left(\bigwedge_{r_x \in \Delta} \forall \bar{x}'. \ \bar{x} \xrightarrow{0, r_x} \bar{x}' \implies \exists \bar{y}'. \ \bigvee_{r_y \in \Delta \text{ labelled as } r_x} (\bar{y} \xrightarrow{0, r_y} \bar{y}' \wedge \mathbb{DS}(\bar{x}', \bar{y}') \subseteq R) \right) \wedge$$

$$\left(\bigwedge_{r \in \Delta} \bigwedge_{1 \le t \le H} \forall \bar{x}'. \ \bar{x} \xrightarrow{t, r} \bar{x}' \implies \exists \bar{y}'. \ (\bar{y} \xrightarrow{t, r} \bar{y}' \wedge (\bar{x}', \bar{y}') \in R)) \right)$$

We argue that all ingredients of ϕ_R are expressible in Presburger arithmetic. First, it is well-known that semi-linear sets are expressible in Presburger arithmetic [13]. Hence there exists a formula to denote "$(\bar{x}, \bar{y}) \in R$", with free variables $\bar{x}, \bar{y}$. Further, "$(\bar{x}, \bar{y})$ is an almost-identical pair" is easily expressible by a conjunction of $2 \cdot H \times N$ equations. "$\mathbb{DS}(\bar{x}', \bar{y}') \subseteq R$" is expressible by a conjunction of $2 \cdot H + 1$ formulas of the form "$\bar{x} \ne \bar{y} \Rightarrow (\bar{x}, \bar{y}) \in R$". Finally, let

$$r = (X_i \xrightarrow{a} 0 \triangleright P_0 \| \dots \| H \triangleright P_H) \in \Delta,$$

for some $1 \le i \le N$, where $P_u = X_1^{p_{u,1}} \| \dots \| X_N^{p_{u,N}}$, $p_{u,j} \ge 0$ for $0 \le u \le H$ and $1 \le j \le N$. Now "$\bar{x} \xrightarrow{t, r} \bar{x}'$", $0 \le t \le H$, is a shorthand for

$$x_{t,i} > 0 \ \wedge \ x_{t,i} + p_{0,i} = x'_{t,i} + 1 \ \wedge$$

$$\bigwedge_{1 \le j \le N, \ 0 \le u \le H, \ (u,j) \ne (0,i)} x'_{t+u,j} = x_{t+u,j} + p_{u,j}.$$

$\square$

Corollary 1 and Lemma 8 form the core of the semi-decidability proof. The semi-decision procedure for $\sim$ consists of enumerating base-periods representations of all the semi-linear binary relations over $\mathbb{N}^{\{0,\dots,2 \cdot H\} \times Const}$ and checking whether any of them is a bounded bisimulation. Hence we have proved:

Theorem 2. *Strong bisimilarity is decidable for TBPP.*

6   Extensions

The proposed method of bisimilarity checking is quite robust and can be easily extended and adapted to other frameworks. Below we briefly sketch the proof of decidability of $\sim$ when communication is allowed and when well-timed semantics is considered instead of ill-timed one.

Communication. Assume that *Act* contains a distinguished silent action τ. Moreover, assume that for each $a \neq \tau$, there exists a complementary action $\bar{a} \in Act$ such that $\bar{\bar{a}} = a$. Two different synchronization rules have been proposed for timed processes, for $a \neq \tau$:

$$\frac{P \xrightarrow{t_1,a} P' \quad Q \xrightarrow{t_2,\bar{a}} Q' \quad t = \max\{t_1,t_2\}}{P\|Q \xrightarrow{t,\tau} P'\|Q'} \quad (10) \qquad \frac{P \xrightarrow{t,a} P' \quad Q \xrightarrow{t,\bar{a}} Q'}{P\|Q \xrightarrow{t,\tau} P'\|Q'} \quad (11)$$

According to the rule (10), proposed in [14], the busy waiting is allowed, when one of components is able to execute an action before the other. The second rule (11), studied in [1], prevents from any waiting and two processes can synchronize only if they are ready to perform complementary actions at the same time (see [10] for a detailed discussion).

We consider the second rule first. It is routine to verify that all the facts proved in Sections 3 and 4 are still valid; in particular, $\sim$ is still a congruence. Moreover, Lemma 8 from Section 5 still holds, since the Presburger formula constructed in the proof can be easily adapted for τ-moves arising from communication. Hence the decision procedure is exactly the same as in Section 5 and we conclude:

Theorem 3. *Strong bisimilarity is decidable for TBPP with rule (11).*

When the rule (10) is chosen, even Lemma 2 from Section 3 does not hold and it is not clear how to adapt our proof for this case.

Well-timed semantics. In well-timed semantics a transition $P \xrightarrow{t,a} P'$ is allowed exclusively at time $t = \text{minclock}(P)$. We lose now all the decomposition properties from Section 3 except from Lemma 1. Hence we can consider only pairs (P,Q) with

$$\text{minclock}(P) = 0 = \text{minclock}(Q).$$

We put additionally $\text{minclock}(\mathbf{0}) = 0$, so that the empty process is not ruled out. Two such P, Q are bisimilar iff they are related by some *0-bisimulation*, that is a binary relation R over processes such that whenever $(P,Q) \in R$, for each $a \in Act$,

- if $P \xrightarrow{0,a} P'$ then $Q \xrightarrow{0,a} Q'$ for some Q' such that $(\text{now}(P'), \text{now}(Q')) \in R$
- if $Q \xrightarrow{0,a} Q'$ then $P \xrightarrow{0,a} P'$ for some P' such that $(\text{now}(P'), \text{now}(Q')) \in R$.

Moreover, due to the bound H on maxclock(_) of all right-hand sides of rewrite rules, there always exists a 0-bisimulation containing only pairs (P,Q) with $\text{maxclock}(P) \leq H$ and $\text{maxclock}(Q) \leq H$, called a *bounded 0-bisimulation* below (note that $\text{maxclock}(P)$ needs not be equal to $\text{maxclock}(Q)$, even when P and Q are bisimilar). Strong bisimilarity is a congruence again, hence by Theorem 1 we derive:

Lemma 9. *Assume $\text{maxclock}(P) = 0 = \text{maxclock}(Q)$. $P \sim Q$ iff P and Q are related by a semi-linear bounded 0-bisimulation.*

Lemma 10. *For a semi-linear binary relation R over $\mathbb{N}^{\{0,\ldots,H\} \times Const}$, given by a finite set of base-periods pairs, it is decidable whether R is a bounded 0-bisimulation.*

Proof. Similarly as in Lemma 8, given R, we can effectively construct a formula in Presburger arithmetic ϕ_R such that ϕ_R is valid iff R is a bounded 0-bisimulation. $\square$

Similarly as in Section 5, Lemmas 9 and 10 form a core of the semi-decision procedure: it consists of enumerating (base-periods representations of) all the semi-linear binary relations over $\mathbb{N}^{\{0,\ldots,H\} \times Const}$ and checking whether any of them is a bounded 0-bisimulation. Hence we have proved:

Theorem 4. *Strong bisimilarity is decidable for TBPP with rule (11), under well-timed semantics.*

7   Final Remarks

The main result of our paper is decidability of strong bisimilarity, also known as performance equivalence, for timed BPP. The decision procedure is based on decidability of validity problem for Presburger arithmetic. Nevertheless we believe that after the crucial development of Sections 3 and 4, also other proof methods known for plain BPP could be used here. For instance, the decision procedure could be also based on searching for a finite bisimulation base [4] or for a successful tableau [8,7]. In the latter case, we suppose that the method proposed in [22], being a generalization of the tableau method of [8], could be further generalized to capture our setting.

Exact complexity of the problem rests still unknown, similarly as in the case of BPP. Since our problem subsumes bisimilarity checking for BPP, the recent PSPACE lower bound of Srba [23] applies as well.

Following many papers in the area, we considered only processes in *normal form*, i.e., without action prefix and summation. While each BPP process can be effectively transformed into normal form [7], this is not the case for timed BPP. However, one more advantage of our new formulation is that the minor extension of the process algebra satisfies the *expansion law* [19], in contrast to the process algebra as considered in [14,10,9,3]. Therefore we hope that only a slight effort is needed to extend our result to the language with action prefix and summation.

Acknowledgements

The author is very grateful to Philippe Schnoebelen for many fruitful discussions and to anonymous reviewers for constructive suggestions helpful in improving the presentation.

References

1. L. Aceto and D. Murphy. Timing and causality in process algebra. *Acta Informatica*, 33(4):317–350, 1996. 562, 564, 575
2. J. C. M. Baeten and C. A. Middelburg. Process algebra with timing: real time and discrete time. In *J. Bergstra, A. Ponse, S. Smolka, eds., Handbook of Process Algebra, chapter 10*, pages 627–684, 2001. 562
3. B. Bérard, A. Labroue, and P. Schnoebelen. Verifying performance equivalence for timed Basic Parallel Processes. In *Proc. 3rd Int. Conf. Foundations of Software Science and Computation Structures (FOSSACS'2000), LNCS 1784*, pages 35–47, 2000. 562, 563, 564, 565, 576
4. O. Burkart, D. Caucal, F Moller, and B. Steffen. Verification of infinite structures. In *J. Bergstra, A. Ponse, S. Smolka, eds., Handbook of Process Algebra, chapter 9*, pages 545–623, 2001. 569, 573, 576
5. D. Caucal. Graphes canoniques des graphes algebraiques. *Informatique Theoretique et Applications (RAIRO)*, 24(4):339–352, 1990. 569
6. K. Čerāns. Decidability of bisimulation equivalence for parallel timer processes. In *Proc. CAV'92, LNCS 663*, 1992. 563, 565
7. S. Christensen. *Decidability and Decomposition in process algebras*. PhD thesis, Dept. of Computer Science, University of Edinbourg, UK, 1993. PhD Thesis CST-105-93. 562, 563, 569, 576
8. S. Christensen, Y. Hirshfeld, and F. Moller. Bisimulation equivalence is decidable for Basic Parallel Processes. In *Proc. 4th Int. Conf. Concurrency Theory (CONCUR'93), LNCS 713*, pages 143–157, 1993. 562, 563, 564, 576
9. F. Corradini. On performance congruences for process algebras. *Information and Computation*, 145(2):191–230, 1998. 562, 576
10. F. Corradini, R. Gorrieri, and M. Roccetti. Performance preorder and competitive equivalence. *Acta Informatica*, 34(11):805–835, 1997. 562, 563, 564, 565, 575, 576
11. F. Corradini and M. Pistore. Specification and verification of lazy timed systems. In *Proc. 21th Int. Symp. math. Found. Comp. Sci. (MFCS'96), LNCS 1113*, pages 279–290, 1996. 563
12. S. Eilenberg and M. P. Schuetzenberger. Rational sets in commutative monoids. *J. of Algebra*, 13:173–191, 1969. 573
13. S. Ginsburg and E. Spanier. Semigroups, Presburger formulas, and languages. *Pacific J. of Mathematics*, 16(2):285–296, 1966. 574
14. R. Gorrieri, M. Roccetti, and E. Stancampiano. A theory of processes with durational actions. *Theoretical Computer Science*, 140(1):73–94, 1995. 562, 563, 564, 565, 575, 576
15. Y. Hirshfeld. Petri nets and the equivalence problem. In *Proc. Computer Science Logic (CSL'93), LNCS 832*, pages 165–174, 1993. 562
16. Y. Hirshfeld. Congruences in commutative semigroups. LFCS report ECS-LFCS-94-291, Laboratory for Foundations of Computer Science, University of Edinbourg, 1994. 573
17. H. Hüttel. Undecidable equivalences for basic parallel processes. In *Proc. TACS'94, LNCS 789*, pages 454–464, 1994. 562
18. P. Jančar. Decidability questions for bisimilarity of Petri nets and some related problems. In *Proc. 11th International Symposium on Theoretical Aspects of Computer Science (STACS'94), Caen, France, LNCS 775*, pages 581–592, 1994. 563, 573
19. R. Milner. *Communication and Concurrency*. Prentice Hall, 1989. 562, 576

20. F. Moller and C. Tofts. Relating processes with respect to speed. In *Proc. 2nd Int Conf. Concurrency Theory (CONCUR'91), LNCS 527*, pages 424–438, 1991. 562

21. D. C. Oppen. A $2^{2^{2^{pn}}}$ upper bound on the complexity of Presburger arithmetic. *J. of Comp. and System Sciences*, 16:323–332, 1978. 563, 574

22. J. Srba. Note on the tableau technique for commutative transition systems. In *Proc. 5th Foundations of Software Science and Computation Structures (FOSSACS'02), LNCS 2303*, pages 387–401, 2002. 563, 576

23. J. Srba. Strong bisimilarity and regularity of Basic Parallel Processes is PSPACE-hard. In *Proc. 19th International Symposium on Theoretical Aspects of Computer Science (STACS'02), LNCS 2285*, 2002. 576

Undecidability of Weak Bisimilarity for Pushdown Processes

Jiří Srba *

Basic Research in Computer Science (**BRICS**),
Centre of the Danish National Research Foundation
Department of Computer Science, University of Aarhus
Ny Munkegade bld. 540, 8000 Aarhus C, Denmark
{srba}@brics.dk

Abstract. We prove undecidability of the problem whether a given pair of pushdown processes is weakly bisimilar. We also show that this undecidability result extends to a subclass of pushdown processes satisfying the normedness condition.

1 Introduction

An important question in the area of verification of infinite-state systems is that of *equivalence checking* [1]. A prominent role is played by the bisimulation equivalence [17] as it possesses many pleasant properties. *Strong bisimilarity* is decidable both for Basic Process Algebra (BPA) [3] and Basic Parallel Processes (BPP) [2], two basic models of purely sequential, respectively parallel, computations. There are even polynomial time algorithms for *normed* subclasses of BPA and BPP [7, 8] (a process is normed iff from every reachable state there is a computation leading to the empty process). This strongly contrasts with the fact that all other equivalences (including language equivalence) in van Glabbeek's spectrum (see [25, 26]) are undecidable for BPA [5] and BPP [9].

The answers to the strong bisimilarity problems for processes generated by *pushdown automata* (PDA) are even more involved than those for BPA and BPP. A pushdown automaton can be seen as a BPA process extended with a finite control unit. From the language point of view, there is no difference between PDA and BPA, since both formalisms describe the class of context-free languages. On the other hand the situation is different when considering strong bisimilarity as the equivalence relation. The PDA class is strictly more expressive than BPA w.r.t. strong (and weak) bisimilarity, and hence the decidability problems are more difficult to handle. Nevertheless, Stirling proved decidability of strong bisimilarity for normed PDA [22] and the same question for the whole class of PDA was positively answered by Senizergues [19].

Let us draw our attention to the notion of *weak bisimilarity*. Weak bisimilarity is a more general equivalence than strong bisimilarity, in the sense that it allows

---

* The author is supported in part by the GACR, grant No. 201/00/0400.

L. Brim et al. (Eds.): CONCUR 2002, LNCS 2421, pp. 579–594, 2002.

to abstract from internal behaviour of processes by introducing a *silent action* τ, which is not observable [15]. Decidability of weak bisimilarity for BPA and BPP are well known open problems. The problems are open even for normed BPA and BPP. Some partial positive results were achieved e.g. in [6, 23]. It is also known that weak bisimilarity is decidable for *deterministic* PDA (follows from [18] as mentioned e.g. in [14]).

Our contribution is the undecidability of weak bisimilarity for PDA (and even for its normed subclass). To the best of our knowledge, this is the first undecidability result for weak bisimilarity on a class of infinite-state systems where strong bisimilarity remains decidable. Similar result is only known for bisimilarity between Petri nets and finite-state systems where strong bisimilarity is decidable [12] whereas weak bisimilarity is undecidable [11].

A full proof of our result is provided in Section 3. The technique is based on an effective encoding of the halting problem for 2-counter Minsky machine into the bisimilarity checking problem for a pair of pushdown processes. We use a game-theoretic characterization of weak bisimilarity to make the proof more understandable. In this setting two processes are weakly bisimilar if and only if a player called 'defender' has a winning strategy in the bisimulation game against a player called 'attacker'. The intuition of our encoding is that a configuration of a Minsky machine, consisting of an instruction label and the values of counters, is represented by a pair of pushdown processes. The label is remembered in the control state and the values of counters are stored in the stack. The problem is, of course, that we have only sequential access to the stack but we need to enable (at least a limited) parallel access to both counters. The key idea is a technique how to manage these stack contents in such a way that the players faithfully simulate the computation of the Minsky machine. The goal is to establish that the attacker has a winning strategy in the bisimulation game iff the machine halts, or equivalently that the defender has a winning strategy iff the machine diverges.

2   Basic Definitions

A *labelled transition system* is a triple $(S, \mathcal{A}ct, \longrightarrow)$ where S is a set of *states* (or *processes*), $\mathcal{A}ct$ is a set of *labels* (or *actions*), $\longrightarrow \subseteq S \times \mathcal{A}ct \times S$ is a *transition relation*, written $\alpha \stackrel{a}{\longrightarrow} \beta$, for $(\alpha, a, \beta) \in \longrightarrow$.

As usual we extend the transition relation to the elements of $\mathcal{A}ct^*$, i.e., $\alpha \stackrel{\epsilon}{\longrightarrow} \alpha$ for every $\alpha \in S$ and $\alpha \stackrel{aw}{\longrightarrow} \beta$ if $\alpha \stackrel{a}{\longrightarrow} \alpha'$ and $\alpha' \stackrel{w}{\longrightarrow} \beta$ for every $\alpha, \beta \in S$, $a \in \mathcal{A}ct$ and $w \in \mathcal{A}ct^*$. We also write $\alpha \longrightarrow^* \beta$ whenever $\alpha \stackrel{w}{\longrightarrow} \beta$ for some $w \in \mathcal{A}ct^*$, $\alpha \stackrel{a}{\not\longrightarrow}$ whenever there is no β such that $\alpha \stackrel{a}{\longrightarrow} \beta$, and $\alpha \not\longrightarrow$ whenever $\alpha \stackrel{a}{\not\longrightarrow}$ for all $a \in \mathcal{A}ct$.

A *process* is a pair (α, T) where $T = (S, \mathcal{A}ct, \longrightarrow)$ is a labelled transition system and $\alpha \in S$. We say that $\beta \in S$ is *reachable in* (α, T) iff $\alpha \longrightarrow^* \beta$. We call (α, T) a *finite-state process* iff the set of its reachable states is finite.

Assume that the set of actions $\mathcal{A}ct$ contains a distinguished *silent action* τ. The notation $\alpha \stackrel{\tau^*}{\longrightarrow} \beta$ means that there is an integer $n \geq 0$ such that $\alpha \stackrel{\tau^n}{\longrightarrow} \beta$, where τ^n is a word consisting of n occurrences of τ. The *weak transition relation* $\Longrightarrow$ is defined as follows:

$$\overset{a}{\Longrightarrow} \overset{\mathrm{def}}{=} \begin{cases} \overset{\tau^*}{\longrightarrow} \circ \overset{a}{\longrightarrow} \circ \overset{\tau^*}{\longrightarrow} & \text{if } a \in \mathcal{A}ct \smallsetminus \{\tau\} \\ \overset{\tau^*}{\longrightarrow} & \text{if } a = \tau. \end{cases}$$

Let $T = (S, \mathcal{A}ct, \longrightarrow)$ be a labelled transition system. A binary relation $R \subseteq S \times S$ is a *weak bisimulation* iff whenever $(\alpha, \beta) \in R$ then for each $a \in \mathcal{A}ct$:

- if $\alpha \overset{a}{\longrightarrow} \alpha'$ then $\beta \overset{a}{\Longrightarrow} \beta'$ for some β' such that $(\alpha', \beta') \in R$
- if $\beta \overset{a}{\longrightarrow} \beta'$ then $\alpha \overset{a}{\Longrightarrow} \alpha'$ for some α' such that $(\alpha', \beta') \in R$.

Processes (α_1, T) and (α_2, T) are *weakly bisimilar*, and we write $(\alpha_1, T) \approx (\alpha_2, T)$ (or simply $\alpha_1 \approx \alpha_2$ if T is clear from the context), iff there is a weak bisimulation R such that $(\alpha_1, \alpha_2) \in R$. Given a pair of processes (α_1, T_1) and (α_2, T_2) such that T_1 and T_2 are different labelled transition systems, we write $(\alpha_1, T_1) \approx (\alpha_2, T_2)$ iff $(\alpha_1, T) \approx (\alpha_2, T)$ where T is the disjoint union of T_1 and T_2.

Remark 1. If we assume that τ does not appear in the set of actions $\mathcal{A}ct$ then the relations $\Longrightarrow$ and $\longrightarrow$ coincide. We call the corresponding notion of bisimilarity *strong bisimilarity* and denote it by $\sim$.

Weak bisimilarity has an elegant characterisation in terms of *bisimulation games*.

Definition 1 (Bisimulation game).
A bisimulation game *on a pair of processes* (α_1, T) *and* (α_2, T) *where* $T = (S, \mathcal{A}ct, \longrightarrow)$ *is a two-player game between an 'attacker' and a 'defender'. The game is played in rounds on pairs of states from* $S \times S$. *In each round the players change the current states* β_1 *and* β_2 *(initially* α_1 *and* α_2*) according to the following rule.*

1. *The attacker chooses an* $i \in \{1, 2\}$, $a \in \mathcal{A}ct$ *and* $\beta_i' \in S$ *such that* $\beta_i \overset{a}{\longrightarrow} \beta_i'$.
2. *The defender responds by choosing a* $\beta_{3-i}' \in S$ *such that* $\beta_{3-i} \overset{a}{\Longrightarrow} \beta_{3-i}'$.
3. *The states* β_1' *and* β_2' *become the current states.*

A play *is a maximal sequence of pairs of states formed by the players according to the rule described above, and starting from the initial states* α_1 *and* α_2. *The defender is the winner in every infinite play. A finite play is lost by the player who is stuck. Note that the attacker gets stuck in current states* β_1 *and* β_2 *if and only if both* $\beta_1 \not\longrightarrow$ *and* $\beta_2 \not\longrightarrow$.

We remind the reader of the fact that if the attacker chooses a move under the action τ in one of the processes, the defender can (as one possibility) simply answer by doing "nothing", i.e., by staying in the same state of the other process. The following proposition is a standard one (see e.g. [21, 24]).

Proposition 1. *Processes (α_1, T) and (α_2, T) are weakly bisimilar iff the defender has a winning strategy (and nonbisimilar iff the attacker has a winning strategy).*

Let $Q = \{p, q, \ldots\}$, $\Gamma = \{X, Y, \ldots\}$ and $\mathcal{A}ct = \{a, b, \ldots\}$ be finite sets of *control states*, *stack symbols* and *actions*, respectively, such that $Q \cap \Gamma = \emptyset$ and $\tau \in \mathcal{A}ct$ is the distinguished *silent action*. A *pushdown automaton* (PDA) is a finite set

$$\Delta \subseteq Q \times \Gamma \times \mathcal{A}ct \times Q \times \Gamma^*$$

of *rewrite rules*, written $pX \xrightarrow{a} q\alpha$ for $(p, X, a, q, \alpha) \in \Delta$. A pushdown automaton Δ generates a labelled transition system $T(\Delta) = (Q \times \Gamma^*, \mathcal{A}ct, \longrightarrow)$ where $Q \times \Gamma^*$ is the set of states[1], $\mathcal{A}ct$ is the set of actions, and the transition relation $\longrightarrow$ is defined by

$$pX\beta \xrightarrow{a} q\alpha\beta \quad \text{iff} \quad (pX \xrightarrow{a} q\alpha) \in \Delta$$

for all $\beta \in \Gamma^*$.

A *pushdown process* (or simply a *process*) is a pair $(p\alpha, T(\Delta))$ where $T(\Delta)$ is the transition system generated by a pushdown automaton Δ and $p\alpha$ is a state of $T(\Delta)$. We often abbreviate the notation $(p\alpha, T(\Delta))$ to $(p\alpha, \Delta)$ or even to $p\alpha$ if Δ is clear from the context.

A process $(p\alpha, \Delta)$ is *normed* iff for every reachable state $q\beta$ there is a finite computation which empties the stack, i.e., there is a state $r\epsilon \in Q \times \Gamma^*$ such that $q\beta \longrightarrow^* r\epsilon$. We say that $(p\alpha, \Delta)$ is *weakly (or strongly) regular* iff there is some finite-state process (γ, T) such that $(p\alpha, \Delta) \approx (\gamma, T)$ (or $(p\alpha, \Delta) \sim (\gamma, T)$).

Notation 1. Let i be a natural number and $A \in \Gamma$. We use the notation A^i for a sequence of i occurrences of A, i.e., $A^0 \overset{\text{def}}{=} \epsilon$ and $A^{i+1} \overset{\text{def}}{=} A^i A$. For example pX^2Y^3 is an abbreviation for $pXXYYY$.

Example 1. Let $Q \overset{\text{def}}{=} \{p, p_1, p', p_1', p_2', p_3'\}$, $\Gamma \overset{\text{def}}{=} \{X, Y\}$ and $\mathcal{A}ct \overset{\text{def}}{=} \{a, b, c, \tau\}$ and let Δ be the following pushdown automaton.

$$pX \xrightarrow{a} p_1 X \qquad pX \xrightarrow{\tau} p'X \qquad p_1 X \xrightarrow{c} p_1 X$$

$$p'X \xrightarrow{a} p_1'X \qquad p_1'X \xrightarrow{c} p_1'X$$
$$p'X \xrightarrow{\tau} p_2'X \qquad p_2'X \xrightarrow{c} p_3'$$
$$p_2'X \xrightarrow{\tau} p_2'YX \qquad p_2'Y \xrightarrow{\tau} p_2'YY \qquad p_2'Y \xrightarrow{b} p_2'$$

A fraction of the transition system $T(\Delta)$ is depicted in Figure 1. Let us consider processes (pX, Δ) and $(p'X, \Delta)$. We show that $(pX, \Delta) \approx (p'X, \Delta)$ by describing a winning strategy for the defender in the bisimulation game starting from pX and $p'X$. The attacker has the following four possibilities in the first round: $pX \xrightarrow{a} p_1 X$, or $pX \xrightarrow{\tau} p'X$, or $p'X \xrightarrow{a} p_1'X$, or $p'X \xrightarrow{\tau} p_2'X$. In order to

---

[1] We write $p\alpha$ instead of $(p, \alpha) \in Q \times \Gamma^*$. A state $p\epsilon \in Q \times \Gamma^*$, where ϵ is the symbol for *empty stack*, is usually written only as p.

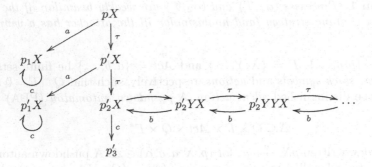

Fig. 1. Transition system generated by Δ

avoid the situation where the defender can reach a pair of syntactically equal states, the attacker is forced to choose the first move, namely $pX \xrightarrow{a} p_1X$.

The defender answers by playing $p'X \Longrightarrow p'_1X$. Now the game continues from p_1X and p'_1X, however, these two states are obviously weakly bisimilar and hence the defender has a winning strategy. This implies that $(pX, \Delta) \approx (p'X, \Delta)$.

In this example we also recall some of our previous definitions. The process (pX, Δ) can terminate (empty its stack) since $pX \longrightarrow^* p'_3$ but it is not normed — it can reach e.g. the state p_1X from which there is no terminating computation. On the other hand the process (p'_2Y^iX, Δ) is normed for any $i \geq 0$.

Also note that (pX, Δ) is not weakly regular because it has infinitely many reachable and weakly nonbisimilar states. Consider the states p'_2Y^iX and p'_2Y^jX for $i \neq j$. Obviously, $pX \longrightarrow^* p'_2Y^iX$ and $pX \longrightarrow^* p'_2Y^jX$. We leave it to the reader to find a winning strategy for the attacker from the pair p'_2Y^iX and p'_2Y^jX and thus show that $(p'_2Y^iX, \Delta) \not\approx (p'_2Y^jX, \Delta)$.

3   Undecidability of Weak Bisimilarity

We shall prove that weak bisimilarity of pushdown processes is undecidable.

Problem:	Weak bisimilarity of pushdown processes
Instance:	A pushdown automaton Δ and a pair of processes $(p_1\alpha_1, \Delta)$ and $(p_2\alpha_2, \Delta)$.
Question:	$(p_1\alpha_1, \Delta) \approx (p_2\alpha_2, \Delta)$?

The proof is by reduction from the halting problem of Minsky machine [16] with two counters.

Definition 2 (Minsky machine with two counters).
A Minsky machine R with two counters c_1 and c_2 is a finite sequence

$$R = (L_1 : I_1, \quad L_2 : I_2, \quad \ldots, \quad L_{n-1} : I_{n-1}, \quad L_n : \texttt{halt})$$

where $n \geq 1$, $L_1, \ldots, L_n$ are pairwise different labels, and $I_1, \ldots, I_{n-1}$ are instructions of the following two types:

- *increment:* $c_r := c_r + 1;$ goto L_j
- *test and decrement:* if $c_r = 0$ then goto L_j else $c_r := c_r - 1;$ goto L_k

where $1 \le r \le 2$ *and* $1 \le j, k \le n$.

A *configuration* of a Minsky machine R is a triple (L_i, v_1, v_2) where L_i is the instruction label $(1 \le i \le n)$, and $v_1, v_2 \in \mathbb{N}$ are nonnegative integers representing the values of counters c_1 and c_2, respectively. Let $Conf$ be the set of all configurations of R. The transition relation $\hookrightarrow \subseteq Conf \times Conf$ between configurations is defined in the obvious and natural way. We remind the reader of the fact that the computation of the machine R is deterministic, i.e., if $c \hookrightarrow d$ and $c \hookrightarrow e$ then $d = e$ for all $c, d, e \in Conf$.

It is a well known fact that the problem whether a Minsky machine R *halts* with the initial counter values set to zero (in other words the problem whether $(L_1, 0, 0) \hookrightarrow^* (L_n, v_1, v_2)$ for some $v_1, v_2 \in \mathbb{N}$) is undecidable [16]. If R does not halt we say that it *diverges*.

Our aim is to show that there is an effective construction such that given a Minsky machine R it defines a pushdown automaton Δ and a pair of processes $p_1\alpha_1$ and $p_2\alpha_2$ with the property that R halts if and only if $(p_1\alpha_1, \Delta) \not\approx (p_2\alpha_2, \Delta)$. This proves that weak bisimilarity of pushdown processes is an undecidable problem.

Let us fix a Minsky machine

$$R = (L_1 : I_1, \quad L_2 : I_2, \quad \dots, \quad L_{n-1} : I_{n-1}, \quad L_n : \text{halt}).$$

We construct Δ in stages. First, we define the sets of control states, stack symbols and actions. Let $\mathcal{I}nc \overset{\text{def}}{=} \{i \mid 1 \le i < n$ and I_i is of the type 'increment'$\}$ and $\mathcal{D}ec \overset{\text{def}}{=} \{i \mid 1 \le i < n$ and I_i is of the type 'test and decrement'$\}$.

$$Q \overset{\text{def}}{=} \{\text{equal}, \text{equal}_1, \text{equal}_2, \text{empty}_1, \text{empty}_2, \text{empty}'_1, \text{empty}'_2\} \cup$$
$$\bigcup_{i \in \mathcal{I}nc} \{p_i, p'_i\} \cup \bigcup_{i \in \mathcal{D}ec} \{p_i, p'_i, u_i, u'_i, q_i, q'_i, t_i, t'_i\} \cup \{p_n, p'_n\}$$

$$\Gamma \overset{\text{def}}{=} \{C_1, C_2, S\}$$

$$\mathcal{A}ct \overset{\text{def}}{=} \{a, b, c, d, e, c_1, c_2, c'_1, c'_2, \text{halt}, \tau\}$$

The intuition is that a configuration $(L_i, v_1, v_2) \in Conf$ is represented by a pair of processes $p_i\gamma S$ and $p'_i\gamma'S$ where $\gamma, \gamma' \in \{C_1, C_2\}^*$ such that the number of occurrences of C_1 and C_2 in γ (and also in γ') is equal to v_1 and v_2, respectively. Using this representation, our task is now to design rewrite rules to simulate step by step the computation of R. Let us define formally a mapping $value : \{C_1, C_2\}^* \mapsto \mathbb{N} \times \mathbb{N}$ by the following inductive definition (the operation of addition is component-wise).

$$value(\epsilon) \overset{\text{def}}{=} (0, 0)$$
$$value(C_1\gamma) \overset{\text{def}}{=} value(\gamma) + (1, 0) \qquad \text{for all } \gamma \in \{C_1, C_2\}^*$$
$$value(C_2\gamma) \overset{\text{def}}{=} value(\gamma) + (0, 1) \qquad \text{for all } \gamma \in \{C_1, C_2\}^*$$

As a part of the bisimulation game we will find useful the following rewrite rules which enable to check whether two given stacks contain the same number of occurrences of C_1 and C_2. In the rules below X ranges over the set $\{C_1, C_2, S\}$.

$$\text{equal } X \xrightarrow{a} \text{equal}_1 X \qquad \text{equal } X \xrightarrow{b} \text{equal}_2 X$$

$$\text{equal}_1 C_1 \xrightarrow{c_1} \text{equal}_1 \qquad \text{equal}_1 C_2 \xrightarrow{\tau} \text{equal}_1$$
$$\text{equal}_2 C_2 \xrightarrow{c_2} \text{equal}_2 \qquad \text{equal}_2 C_1 \xrightarrow{\tau} \text{equal}_2$$

Proposition 2. *Let* $\gamma, \gamma' \in \{C_1, C_2\}^*$. *Then*

$$\text{equal } \gamma S \approx \text{equal } \gamma' S \quad \text{iff} \quad \text{value}(\gamma) = \text{value}(\gamma').$$

We continue by defining further rewrite rules to check whether the number of occurences of C_1 (or C_2) is zero.

$$\text{empty}_1 C_1 \xrightarrow{c_1} \text{empty}_1 \qquad \text{empty}_1 C_2 \xrightarrow{c_2} \text{empty}_1$$
$$\text{empty}_1' C_1 \xrightarrow{c_1'} \text{empty}_1' \qquad \text{empty}_1' C_2 \xrightarrow{c_2} \text{empty}_1'$$

$$\text{empty}_2 C_1 \xrightarrow{c_1} \text{empty}_2 \qquad \text{empty}_2 C_2 \xrightarrow{c_2} \text{empty}_2$$
$$\text{empty}_2' C_1 \xrightarrow{c_1} \text{empty}_2' \qquad \text{empty}_2' C_2 \xrightarrow{c_2'} \text{empty}_2'$$

Proposition 3. *Let* $\gamma, \gamma' \in \{C_1, C_2\}^*$ *be such that* $\text{value}(\gamma) = \text{value}(\gamma') = (v_1, v_2)$ *for some* $v_1, v_2 \in \mathbb{N}$. *Let* $r \in \{1, 2\}$. *Then*

$$\text{empty}_r \, \gamma S \approx \text{empty}_r' \, \gamma' S \quad \text{iff} \quad v_r = 0.$$

Let us now define the rewrite rules that are connected with the increment instructions of R. Assume again that X ranges over the set $\{C_1, C_2, S\}$. For all $i \in \mathcal{I}nc$ such that I_i is of the type

$$L_i: \ c_r := c_r + 1; \ \texttt{goto} \ L_j$$

where $1 \leq j \leq n$ and $1 \leq r \leq 2$, we add the following two rules.

$$p_i X \xrightarrow{a} p_j C_r X \qquad p_i' X \xrightarrow{a} p_j' C_r X$$

Lemma 1. *Let* $(L_i, v_1, v_2) \in \mathcal{C}onf$ *be such that* I_i *is the 'increment' instruction and* $(L_i, v_1, v_2) \hookrightarrow (L_j, v_1', v_2')$. *Let* $\gamma, \gamma' \in \{C_1, C_2\}^*$ *be such that* $\text{value}(\gamma) = \text{value}(\gamma') = (v_1, v_2)$. *There is a unique continuation of the bisimulation game from the pair* $p_i \gamma S$ *and* $p_i' \gamma' S$ *such that after one round the players reach the pair* $p_j \overline{\gamma} S$ *and* $p_j' \overline{\gamma'} S$ *satisfying* $\text{value}(\overline{\gamma}) = \text{value}(\overline{\gamma'}) = (v_1', v_2')$.

Proof. Obvious — see Figure 2.   □

Fig. 2. Instruction L_i: $c_r := c_r + 1$; goto L_j

We proceed by giving the rules for the 'test and decrement' instructions. For all $i \in \mathcal{Dec}$ such that I_i is of the type

$$L_i: \text{ if } c_r = 0 \text{ then goto } L_j \text{ else } c_r := c_r - 1; \text{ goto } L_k$$

where $1 \le j, k \le n$ and $1 \le r \le 2$, we define the rewrite rules in three parts. The intuitive meaning is that if $v_r \ne 0$ and the stacks γS and $\gamma' S$ contain on their tops the symbol C_r, we can do immediately the branching according to the rules defined later in the third part. However, if it is not the case, the first two parts of the rewrite rules enable the defender to rearrange the stack contents (while preserving the number of occurrences of C_1 and C_2) in such a way that C_r will appear as the first symbol on the stacks. Recall that X ranges over the set $\{C_1, C_2, S\}$.

$$p_i X \xrightarrow{a} q_i X \qquad\qquad p_i X \xrightarrow{a} u_i' X$$

$$
\begin{array}{lll}
p_i' X \xrightarrow{a} u_i' X & u_i' X \xrightarrow{\tau} q_i' X & u_i' X \xrightarrow{e} u_i' X \\
u_i' C_1 \xrightarrow{\tau} u_i' & u_i' C_2 \xrightarrow{\tau} u_i' & \\
u_i' X \xrightarrow{\tau} u_i' C_1 X & u_i' X \xrightarrow{\tau} u_i' C_2 X &
\end{array}
$$

$$q_i X \xrightarrow{c} \text{equal } X \qquad q_i' X \xrightarrow{c} \text{equal } X$$

Assume a bisimulation game played from $p_i \gamma S$ and $p_i' \gamma' S$. The purpose of the previously defined rules is to enable the defender to rearrange the sequence of C_1 and C_2 in γ'. Details are discussed in the proof of Lemma 2, here we give only a short description. If the attacker plays $p_i \gamma S \xrightarrow{a} q_i \gamma S$, the defender must answer by $p_i' \gamma' S \xRightarrow{a} q_i' \overline{\gamma'} S$ for some $\overline{\gamma'} \in \{C_1, C_2\}^*$. Now the attacker can check the invariant that $value(\gamma) = value(\overline{\gamma'})$ by using the rules $q_i X \xrightarrow{c} \text{equal } X$ and $q_i' X \xrightarrow{c} \text{equal } X$.

$$q_i' X \xrightarrow{a} t_i' X \qquad\qquad q_i' X \xrightarrow{a} u_i X$$

$$
\begin{array}{lll}
q_i X \xrightarrow{a} u_i X & u_i X \xrightarrow{\tau} t_i X & u_i X \xrightarrow{e} u_i X \\
u_i C_1 \xrightarrow{\tau} u_i & u_i C_2 \xrightarrow{\tau} u_i & \\
u_i X \xrightarrow{\tau} u_i C_1 X & u_i X \xrightarrow{\tau} u_i C_2 X &
\end{array}
$$

$$t_i X \xrightarrow{c} \text{equal } X \qquad t_i' X \xrightarrow{c} \text{equal } X$$

These rules are completely symmetric to the previous ones. In the bisimulation game starting from $q_i \gamma S$ and $q_i' \overline{\gamma}' S$, if the attacker plays $q_i' \overline{\gamma}' S \xrightarrow{a} t_i' \overline{\gamma}' S$, the defender must choose some $\overline{\gamma} \in \{C_1, C_2\}^*$ and play $q_i \gamma S \xRightarrow{a} t_i \overline{\gamma} S$. The attacker can again check whether $value(\overline{\gamma}) = value(\overline{\gamma}')$. The current states become $t_i \overline{\gamma} S$ and $t_i' \overline{\gamma}' S$ satisfying $value(\gamma) = value(\gamma') = value(\overline{\gamma}) = value(\overline{\gamma}')$.

The third part of the rewrite rules defined below is here to perform a branching according to whether C_r occurs in γ and γ' or not. The correctness is discussed later.

$$t_i C_r \xrightarrow{a} p_k \qquad\qquad t_i' C_r \xrightarrow{a} p_k'$$

$$t_i C_{3-r} \xrightarrow{b} p_j C_{3-r} \qquad\qquad t_i' C_{3-r} \xrightarrow{b} p_j' C_{3-r}$$
$$t_i S \xrightarrow{b} p_j S \qquad\qquad t_i' S \xrightarrow{b} p_j' S$$

$$t_i C_{3-r} \xrightarrow{d} empty_r\, C_{3-r} \qquad\qquad t_i' C_{3-r} \xrightarrow{d} empty_r'\, C_{3-r}$$

Finally, we add one extra rule to distinguish whether the last instruction halt was reached. Recall that X ranges over the set $\{C_1, C_2, S\}$.

$$p_n X \xrightarrow{\text{halt}} p_n X$$

Lemma 2. *Let* $(L_i, v_1, v_2) \in \mathcal{C}onf$ *be such that* I_i *is the 'test and decrement' instruction*

$$L_i: \text{ if } c_r = 0 \text{ then goto } L_j \text{ else } c_r := c_r - 1; \text{ goto } L_k$$

and let $\gamma, \gamma' \in \{C_1, C_2\}^*$ *be such that* $value(\gamma) = value(\gamma') = (v_1, v_2)$. *Assume a bisimulation game played from the pair*

$$p_i \gamma S \text{ and } p_i' \gamma' S.$$

a) *The attacker has a strategy such that he either wins, or after three rounds the players reach the states*
  1. $p_k \overline{\gamma} S$ *and* $p_k' \overline{\gamma}' S$ — *if* $v_r \neq 0$ *and* $(L_i, v_1, v_2) \hookrightarrow (L_k, v_1', v_2')$ — *where* $value(\overline{\gamma}) = value(\overline{\gamma}') = (v_1', v_2')$, *or*
  2. $p_j \overline{\gamma} S$ *and* $p_j' \overline{\gamma}' S$ — *if* $v_r = 0$ *and* $(L_i, v_1, v_2) \hookrightarrow (L_j, v_1, v_2)$ — *where* $value(\overline{\gamma}) = value(\overline{\gamma}') = (v_1, v_2)$.

b) *The defender has a strategy such that he either wins, or after three rounds the players reach the states*
  1. $p_k \overline{\gamma} S$ *and* $p_k' \overline{\gamma}' S$ — *if* $v_r \neq 0$ *and* $(L_i, v_1, v_2) \hookrightarrow (L_k, v_1', v_2')$ — *where* $value(\overline{\gamma}) = value(\overline{\gamma}') = (v_1', v_2')$, *or*
  2. $p_j \overline{\gamma} S$ *and* $p_j' \overline{\gamma}' S$ — *if* $v_r = 0$ *and* $(L_i, v_1, v_2) \hookrightarrow (L_j, v_1, v_2)$ — *where* $value(\overline{\gamma}) = value(\overline{\gamma}') = (v_1, v_2)$.

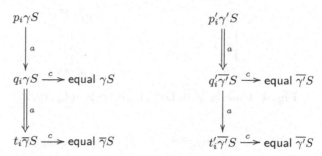

Fig. 3. Instruction 'test and decrement' — first two rounds

Proof. We begin with part a). First two rounds of the bisimulation game are depicted in Figure 3. The game starts from $p_i\gamma S$ and $p'_i\gamma' S$ such that $value(\gamma) = value(\gamma') = (v_1, v_2)$. We show that after two attacker's moves the players either reach a pair $t_i\overline{\gamma}S$ and $t'_i\overline{\gamma'}S$ such that $\overline{\gamma}, \overline{\gamma'} \in \{C_1, C_2\}^*$ and $value(\overline{\gamma}) = value(\overline{\gamma'}) = (v_1, v_2)$, or the attacker has an immediate winning strategy. The attacker starts by playing $p_i\gamma S \xrightarrow{a} q_i\gamma S$. The defender must respond by playing $p'_i\gamma' S \overset{a}{\Longrightarrow} q'_i\overline{\gamma'}S$ for some $\overline{\gamma'} \in \{C_1, C_2\}^*$ because of the following remark.

Remark 2. The defender's $\overset{a}{\Longrightarrow}$-answer must start with the transition $p'_i\gamma' S \xrightarrow{a} u'_i\gamma' S$, followed by a finite number of τ-labelled transitions using the rules that enable to remove an arbitrary part of the stack $\gamma' S$ and add an arbitrary sequence from the symbols C_1 and C_2. Thus the defender can reach the state $u'_i\overline{\gamma'}S$ for any sequence $\overline{\gamma'} \in \{C_1, C_2\}^*$. Also note that he must finish the sequence of τ-moves by $u'_i\overline{\gamma'}S \xrightarrow{\tau} q'_i\overline{\gamma'}S$. If not, then the attacker has an immediate winning move in the next round by playing $u'_i\overline{\gamma'}S \xrightarrow{e} u'_i\overline{\gamma'}S$ to which the defender has no answer because there is no $\overset{e}{\Longrightarrow}$-move from $q_i\gamma S$.

The bisimulation game continues from the states $q_i\gamma S$ and $q'_i\overline{\gamma'}S$. Whenever $value(\gamma) \neq value(\overline{\gamma'})$ then the attacker plays $q_i\gamma S \xrightarrow{c}$ equal γS to which the defender has only one possible answer $q'_i\overline{\gamma'}S \xrightarrow{c}$ equal $\overline{\gamma'}S$. Now the attacker has a winning strategy because of Proposition 2.

Let us so assume that $value(\gamma) = value(\overline{\gamma'})$. In the second round the attacker switches the states and performs the move $q'_i\overline{\gamma'}S \xrightarrow{a} t'_i\overline{\gamma'}S$. The game is now completely symmetric to the situation in the first round. The defender must answer with $q_i\gamma S \overset{a}{\Longrightarrow} t_i\overline{\gamma}S$ for some $\overline{\gamma} \in \{C_1, C_2\}^*$ such that $value(\overline{\gamma}) = value(\overline{\gamma'}) = (v_1, v_2)$.

In the third round played from $t_i\overline{\gamma}S$ and $t'_i\overline{\gamma'}S$ the attacker's strategy splits into two parts, according to whether $v_r \neq 0$ or $v_r = 0$.

1. Let $v_r \neq 0$ and hence $(L_i, v_1, v_2) \hookrightarrow (L_k, v'_1, v'_2)$. See Figure 4.
   - If $\overline{\gamma} = C_r\overline{\overline{\gamma}}$ for some $\overline{\overline{\gamma}}$ then the attacker plays $t_i\overline{\gamma}S \xrightarrow{a} p_k\overline{\overline{\gamma}}S$ and the defender must answer by $t'_i\overline{\gamma'}S \xrightarrow{a} p'_k\overline{\overline{\gamma'}}S$ where $\overline{\gamma'} = C_r\overline{\overline{\gamma'}}$. (If $\overline{\gamma'} = C_{3-r}\overline{\overline{\gamma'}}$ then the attacker wins immediately since $t'_i\overline{\gamma'}S$ cannot perform

Fig. 4. Case $v_r \neq 0$, i.e., $(L_i, v_1, v_2) \hookrightarrow (L_k, v_1', v_2')$

$$t_i \overline{\gamma} S \xrightarrow{\ d\ } \text{empty}_r\ \overline{\gamma} S \qquad\qquad t_i' \overline{\gamma'} S \xrightarrow{\ d\ } \text{empty}_r'\ \overline{\gamma'} S$$

$$\downarrow b \qquad\qquad\qquad\qquad\qquad\qquad \downarrow b$$

$$p_j \overline{\gamma} S \qquad\qquad\qquad\qquad\qquad p_j' \overline{\gamma'} S$$

Fig. 5. Case $v_r = 0$, i.e., $(L_i, v_1, v_2) \hookrightarrow (L_j, v_1, v_2)$

any $\overset{a}{\Longrightarrow}$-move.) Now the players reached the pair $p_k \overline{\gamma} S$ and $p_k' \overline{\overline{\gamma'}} S$ as required. Obviously $value(\overline{\gamma}) = value(\overline{\gamma'}) = (v_1', v_2')$.

- If $\overline{\gamma} = C_{3-r} \overline{\overline{\gamma}}$ for some $\overline{\overline{\gamma}}$ then the attacker plays $t_i \overline{\gamma} S \xrightarrow{\ d\ } \text{empty}_r\ \overline{\gamma} S$ to which the defender has only one possible answer (if any), namely $t_i' \overline{\gamma'} S \xrightarrow{\ d\ } \text{empty}_r'\ \overline{\gamma'} S$. Since $value(\overline{\gamma}) = value(\overline{\gamma'}) = (v_1, v_2)$ and $v_r \neq 0$, the attacker has a winning strategy because of Proposition 3.
- The case $\overline{\gamma} = \epsilon$ is impossible since we assume that $v_r \neq 0$.

2. Let $v_r = 0$ and hence $(L_i, v_1, v_2) \hookrightarrow (L_j, v_1, v_2)$. See Figure 5. The assumption $v_r = 0$ implies that $\overline{\gamma}, \overline{\gamma'} \in \{C_{3-r}\}^*$. Hence the attacker can play $t_i \overline{\gamma} S \xrightarrow{\ b\ } p_j \overline{\gamma} S$ and the defender has only one answer $t_i' \overline{\gamma'} S \xrightarrow{\ b\ } p_j' \overline{\gamma'} S$. The players reached the pair $p_j \overline{\gamma} S$ and $p_j' \overline{\gamma'} S$ as required. Recall that $value(\overline{\gamma}) = value(\overline{\gamma'}) = (v_1, v_2)$.

Let us now prove part b). First two rounds can be seen again in Figure 3. The initial states are $p_i \gamma S$ and $p_i' \gamma' S$ such that $value(\gamma) = value(\gamma') = (v_1, v_2)$. We claim that the defender has a strategy such that he either wins, or after two rounds the players reach the states $t_i C_r^{v_r} C_{3-r}^{v_3-r} S$ and $t_i' C_r^{v_r} C_{3-r}^{v_3-r} S$ (for definitions of $C_r^{v_r}$ and $C_{3-r}^{v_3-r}$ see Notation 1). In the first round the attacker has three possible moves: (i) $p_i \gamma S \xrightarrow{\ a\ } q_i \gamma S$, (ii) $p_i \gamma S \xrightarrow{\ a\ } u_i' \gamma S$ or (iii) $p_i' \gamma' S \xrightarrow{\ a\ } u_i' \gamma' S$. The moves (ii) and (iii) are good for the defender since he can immediately win by playing (ii) $p_i' \gamma' S \overset{a}{\Longrightarrow} u_i' \gamma S$ or (iii) $p_i \gamma S \overset{a}{\Longrightarrow} u_i' \gamma' S$. Obviously, two syntactically equal states are also weakly bisimilar. Hence we can assume that the attacker's first move is $p_i \gamma S \xrightarrow{\ a\ } q_i \gamma S$. The defender answers by $p_i' \gamma' S \overset{a}{\Longrightarrow} q_i' C_r^{v_r} C_{3-r}^{v_3-r} S$. Recall that $value(\gamma) = (v_1, v_2)$ and thus the attacker loses by taking (i) $q_i \gamma S \xrightarrow{\ c\ }$ equal γS or (ii) $q_i' C_r^{v_r} C_{3-r}^{v_3-r} S \xrightarrow{\ c\ }$ equal $C_r^{v_r} C_{3-r}^{v_3-r} S$ as his next move since the defender can respond by playing (i) $q_i' C_r^{v_r} C_{3-r}^{v_3-r} S \xrightarrow{\ c\ }$ equal $C_r^{v_r} C_{3-r}^{v_3-r} S$ or (ii) $q_i \gamma S \xrightarrow{\ c\ }$

equal γS. The pair of states equal γS and equal $C_r^{v_r} C_{3-r}^{v_3-r} S$ is weakly bisimilar because of Proposition 2 and the defender has a winning strategy.

From the pair $q_i \gamma S$ and $q_i' C_r^{v_r} C_{3-r}^{v_3-r} S$ we have a symmetric situation to the previous one. So after the second round either the defender can win, or he can force the attacker to reach the states $t_i C_r^{v_r} C_{3-r}^{v_3-r} S$ and $t_i' C_r^{v_r} C_{3-r}^{v_3-r} S$. Now the game splits into two parts according to whether $v_r \neq 0$ or $v_r = 0$.

1. Let $v_r \neq 0$ and hence $(L_i, v_1, v_2) \hookrightarrow (L_k, v_1', v_2')$. See Figure 4. Then there is a unique continuation of the game reaching the states $p_k C_r^{v_r - 1} C_{3-r}^{v_3-r} S$ and $p_k' C_r^{v_r - 1} C_{3-r}^{v_3-r} S$. Obviously $value(C_r^{v_r - 1} C_{3-r}^{v_3-r}) = (v_1', v_2')$.

2. Let $v_r = 0$ and hence $(L_i, v_1, v_2) \hookrightarrow (L_j, v_1, v_2)$. See Figure 5. Consider the game starting from $t_i C_{3-r}^{v_3-r} S$ and $t_i' C_{3-r}^{v_3-r} S$ (note that $C_r^{v_r} = C_r^0$ is the empty string here). There is either a continuation of the game such that the players reach the states $p_j C_{3-r}^{v_3-r} S$ and $p_j' C_{3-r}^{v_3-r} S$, and $value(C_{3-r}^{v_3-r}) = (v_1, v_2)$ — or the attacker performs the $\xrightarrow{d}$-move but then the defender wins because of Proposition 3.

$\square$

We arrived at the point where we are ready to prove our main theorem.

Theorem 1. *Weak bisimilarity of pushdown processes is undecidable.*

Proof. Let R be a Minsky machine and let Δ be the pushdown automaton constructed above. We prove that R halts if and only if $p_1 S \not\approx p_1' S$.

Assume that R halts, i.e., $(L_1, 0, 0) \hookrightarrow^* (L_n, v_1, v_2)$ for some $v_1, v_2 \in \mathbb{N}$. Then the attacker has a winning strategy starting from $p_1 S$ and $p_1' S$. Using repeatedly Lemma 1 and part a) of Lemma 2 we can easily see that the attacker either wins, or the players reach the states $p_n \gamma S$ and $p_n' \gamma' S$ for some $\gamma, \gamma' \in \{C_1, C_2\}^*$ such that $value(\gamma) = value(\gamma') = (v_1, v_2)$. From the pair $p_n \gamma S$ and $p_n' \gamma' S$ the attacker immediately wins by playing $p_n \gamma S \xrightarrow{halt} p_n \gamma S$ to which the defender has no answer from $p_n' \gamma' S$. Hence $p_1 S \not\approx p_1' S$.

On the other hand if R diverges, i.e., there is an infinite computation starting from $(L_1, 0, 0)$, the defender has a winning strategy. Using repeatedly Lemma 1 and part b) of Lemma 2 he can force the attacker to simulate the computation of R in the bisimulation game. Because the computation of R is infinite, so is the bisimulation game starting from $p_1 S$ and $p_1' S$. Since any infinite bisimulation game is won by the defender (Definition 1), we get that $p_1 S \approx p_1' S$. $\square$

Let us now study the rewrite rules defined above to see whether we can prove the even stronger undecidability result for the normed subclass of pushdown processes. As it can be observed, the pushdown processes $p_1 S$ and $p_1' S$ are almost normed. There are only a few exceptions: computations of the pushdown automaton from $p_1 S$ and $p_1' S$ can get stuck with nonempty stacks by reaching e.g. the states $p_n' \gamma' S$, $equal_1 S$, $equal_2 S$, $empty_1 S$, or there is an infinite loop where only the increment instructions appear.

It would be easy to fix these problems by adding some extra rules but we didn't want to confuse the reader by mentioning these rules during the development of the undecidability proof. In fact, we can derive undecidability of weak bisimilarity for normed pushdown processes from the following lemma.

Lemma 3. *Let Δ be a pushdown automaton, and $(p_1\alpha_1, \Delta)$ and $(p_2\alpha_2, \Delta)$ a pair of processes. We can construct in polynomial time a pushdown automaton Δ' and a pair of normed processes $(p_1\alpha_1', \Delta')$ and $(p_2\alpha_2', \Delta')$ such that*

$$(p_1\alpha_1, \Delta) \approx (p_2\alpha_2, \Delta) \quad \text{if and only if} \quad (p_1\alpha_1', \Delta') \approx (p_2\alpha_2', \Delta').$$

Proof. Let Δ be a pushdown automaton with the set of control state Q, stack symbols Γ and actions $\mathcal{A}ct$. We define Δ' with the corresponding sets $Q' \stackrel{\text{def}}{=} Q \cup \{p_d\}$, $\Gamma' \stackrel{\text{def}}{=} \Gamma \cup \{D\}$ and $\mathcal{A}ct' \stackrel{\text{def}}{=} \mathcal{A}ct \cup \{f\}$ such that p_d, D and f are new symbols. In particular, D is the symbol for a new bottom of the stack. Let $\Delta' \stackrel{\text{def}}{=} \Delta \cup \{pX \stackrel{f}{\longrightarrow} p_d \mid p \in Q \text{ and } X \in \Gamma'\} \cup \{p_dX \stackrel{\tau}{\longrightarrow} p_d \mid X \in \Gamma'\}$. We define $\alpha_1' \stackrel{\text{def}}{=} \alpha_1 D$ and $\alpha_2' \stackrel{\text{def}}{=} \alpha_2 D$. Obviously, $(p_1\alpha_1', \Delta')$ and $(p_2\alpha_2', \Delta')$ are normed processes. The validity of $(p_1\alpha_1, \Delta) \approx (p_2\alpha_2, \Delta)$ iff $(p_1\alpha_1', \Delta') \approx (p_2\alpha_2', \Delta')$ is easy to see from the fact that $(p_d\gamma, \Delta') \approx (p_d\gamma', \Delta')$ for any $\gamma, \gamma' \in \Gamma'^*$. $\square$

Corollary 1. *Weak bisimilarity of normed pushdown processes is undecidable.*

Remark 3. Observe that the construction in Lemma 3 gives immediately a polynomial time reduction from weak bisimilarity between pushdown processes and finite-state processes to the normed instances of the problems. It is also easy to see that it preserves the property of being weakly regular, i.e., $(p_1\alpha_1, \Delta)$ is weakly regular iff $(p_1\alpha_1', \Delta')$ is weakly regular.

4   Conclusion

We proved that weak bisimilarity of pushdown processes is undecidable. This result confirms that decidability issues for weak bisimilarity are more complex than those for strong bisimilarity, even though not many examples of infinite-state systems which give similar conclusions have been found so far. In particular, the decidability questions of weak bisimilarity for BPA and BPP are still open. Another interesting problem is decidability of strong/weak regularity for PDA.

Remark 4. It is obvious that the presented reduction from 2-counter machines to weak bisimilarity of pushdown processes can be extended to work for an arbitrary number of counters and hence we think that the problem lies beyond arithmetical hierarhy: the technique of Jančar [10] for showing high undecidability of weak bisimilarity for Petri nets can be adapted also to our case.

In the following table we provide a summary of the state of the art for bisimilarity problems of pushdown processes. The notation $\sim$ FS ($\approx$ FS) stands for strong (weak) bisimilarity checking between pushdown processes and finite-state processes.

	PDA	normed PDA
strong bisimilarity	decidable [19] EXPTIME-hard [13]	decidable [22] EXPTIME-hard [13]
weak bisimilarity	undecidable	undecidable
∼ FS	∈ PSPACE [13] PSPACE-hard [14]	∈ PSPACE [13] PSPACE-hard [14], Remark 5
≈ FS	∈ PSPACE [13] PSPACE-hard [14]	∈ PSPACE [13] PSPACE-hard [14], Remark 3
strong regularity	? PSPACE-hard [14]	∈ P [4], Remark 6 NL-hard [20]
weak regularity	? PSPACE-hard [14]	? PSPACE-hard [14], Remark 3

Remark 5. The reduction from [14] (Theorem 8) uses unnormed processes but can be modified to work also for the normed case. An important observation is that the stack size of the PDA from Theorem 8 is bounded by the number of variables in the instance of QSAT from which the reduction is done.

Remark 6. Strong regularity of normed PDA is equivalent to the boundedness problem. Boundedness (even for unnormed PDA) is decidable in polynomial time using the fact that the set of all reachable configurations of a pushdown process is a regular language L and a finite automaton recognizing L can be constructed in polynomial time [4].

Acknowledgement

I would like to thank my advisor Mogens Nielsen for his comments and suggestions. I also thank Marco Carbone for useful remarks, Petr Jančar for drawing my attention to high undecidability issues mentioned in Remark 4, and Richard Mayr for several discussions concerning Remark 5. Finally, my thanks go to the anonymous referees for their detailed reviews.

References

[1] O. Burkart, D. Caucal, F. Moller, and B. Steffen. Verification on infinite structures. In J. Bergstra, A. Ponse, and S. Smolka, editors, *Handbook of Process Algebra*, chapter 9, pages 545–623. Elsevier Science, 2001. 579

[2] S. Christensen, Y. Hirshfeld, and F. Moller. Bisimulation is decidable for basic parallel processes. In *Proc. of CONCUR'93*, volume 715 of *LNCS*, pages 143–157. Springer-Verlag, 1993. 579

[3] S. Christensen, H. Hüttel, and C. Stirling. Bisimulation equivalence is decidable for all context-free processes. *Information and Computation*, 121:143–148, 1995. 579

[4] J. Esparza, D. Hansel, P. Rossmanith, and S. Schwoon. Efficient algorithms for model checking pushdown systems. In *Proc. of CAV'00*, volume 1855 of *LNCS*, pages 232–247. Springer-Verlag, 2000. 592

[5] J. F. Groote and H. Hüttel. Undecidable equivalences for basic process algebra. *Information and Computation*, 115(2):353–371, 1994. 579

[6] Y. Hirshfeld. Bisimulation trees and the decidability of weak bisimulations. In *Proc. of INFINITY'96*, volume 5 of *ENTCS*. Springer-Verlag, 1996. 580

[7] Y. Hirshfeld, M. Jerrum, and F. Moller. A polynomial algorithm for deciding bisimilarity of normed context-free processes. *Theoretical Computer Science*, 158(1–2):143–159, 1996. 579

[8] Y. Hirshfeld, M. Jerrum, and F. Moller. A polynomial-time algorithm for deciding bisimulation equivalence of normed basic parallel processes. *Mathematical Structures in Computer Science*, 6(3):251–259, 1996. 579

[9] H. Hüttel. Undecidable equivalences for basic parallel processes. In *Proc. of TACS'94*, volume 789 of *LNCS*, pages 454–464. Springer-Verlag, 1994. 579

[10] P. Jančar. High undecidability of weak bisimilarity for Petri nets. In *Proc. of CAAP'95*, volume 915 of *LNCS*, pages 349–363. Springer-Verlag, 1995. 591

[11] P. Jančar and J. Esparza. Deciding finiteness of Petri nets up to bisimulation. In *Proc. of ICALP'96*, volume 1099 of *LNCS*, pages 478–489. Springer-Verlag, 1996. 580

[12] P. Jančar and F. Moller. Checking regular properties of Petri nets. In *Proc. of CONCUR'95*, volume 962 of *LNCS*, pages 348–362. Springer-Verlag, 1995. 580

[13] A. Kučera and R. Mayr. On the complexity of semantic equivalences for pushdown automata and BPA. In *Proc. of MFCS'02*, LNCS. Springer-Verlag, 2002. To appear. 592

[14] R. Mayr. On the complexity of bisimulation problems for pushdown automata. In *Proc. of IFIP TCS'00*, volume 1872 of *LNCS*. Springer-Verlag, 2000. 580, 592

[15] R. Milner. *Communication and Concurrency*. Prentice-Hall, 1989. 580

[16] M. L. Minsky. *Computation: Finite and Infinite Machines*. Prentice-Hall, 1967. 583, 584

[17] D. M. R. Park. Concurrency and automata on infinite sequences. In *Proc. of 5th GI Conference*, volume 104 of *LNCS*, pages 167–183. Springer-Verlag, 1981. 579

[18] G. Sénizergues. The equivalence problem for deterministic pushdown automata is decidable. In *Proc. of ICALP'97*, volume 1256 of *LNCS*, pages 671–681. Springer-Verlag, 1997. 580

[19] G. Sénizergues. Decidability of bisimulation equivalence for equational graphs of finite out-degree. In *Proc. of FOCS'98*, pages 120–129. IEEE Computer Society, 1998. 579, 592

[20] J. Srba. Strong bisimilarity and regularity of basic process algebra is PSPACE-hard. In *Proc. of ICALP'02*, LNCS. Springer-Verlag, 2002. To appear. 592

[21] C. Stirling. Local model checking games. In *Proc. of CONCUR'95*, volume 962 of *LNCS*, pages 1–11. Springer-Verlag, 1995. 581

[22] C. Stirling. Decidability of bisimulation equivalence for normed pushdown processes. *Theoretical Computer Science*, 195(2):113–131, 1998. 579, 592

[23] C. Stirling. Decidability of weak bisimilarity for a subset of basic parallel processes. In *Proc. of FOSSACS'01*, volume 2030 of *LNCS*, pages 379–393. Springer-Verlag, 2001. 580

[24] W. Thomas. On the Ehrenfeucht-Fraïssé game in theoretical computer science (extended abstract). In *Proc. of TAPSOFT'93*, volume 668 of *LNCS*, pages 559–568. Springer-Verlag, 1993. 581

594   Jiří Srba

[25] R. J. van Glabbeek. *Comparative Concurrency Semantics and Refinement of Actions*. PhD thesis, CWI/Vrije Universiteit, 1990. 579
[26] R. J. van Glabbeek. The linear time—branching time spectrum. In *Proc. of CONCUR'90*, volume 458 of *LNCS*, pages 278–297. Springer-Verlag, 1990. 579

Why Is Simulation Harder than Bisimulation?

Antonín Kučera [*,1] and Richard Mayr[2]

[1] Faculty of Informatics, Masaryk University
Botanická 68a, 60200 Brno, Czech Republic
tony@fi.muni.cz
[2] Department of Computer Science, Albert-Ludwigs-University Freiburg
Georges-Koehler-Allee 51, D-79110 Freiburg, Germany
mayrri@informatik.uni-freiburg.de

Abstract. Why is deciding simulation preorder (and simulation equivalence) computationally harder than deciding bisimulation equivalence on almost all known classes of processes? We try to answer this question by describing two general methods that can be used to construct direct one-to-one polynomial-time reductions from bisimulation equivalence to simulation preorder (and simulation equivalence). These methods can be applied to many classes of finitely generated transition systems, provided that they satisfy certain abstractly formulated conditions. Roughly speaking, our first method works for all classes of systems that can test for 'non-enabledness' of actions, while our second method works for all classes of systems that are closed under synchronization.

1   Introduction

In the last decade, a lot of research effort has been devoted to the study of decidability/complexity issues for checking various semantic equivalences between certain (classes of) processes. Formally, a *process* is (associated with) a state in a *transition system*.

Definition 1. *A transition system is a triple* $\mathcal{T} = (T, Act, \rightarrow)$ *where* T *is a set of* states, *Act is a finite set of* actions, *and* $\rightarrow \subseteq T \times Act \times T$ *is a transition relation.*

We write $t \xrightarrow{a} \bar{t}$ instead of $(t, a, \bar{t}) \in \rightarrow$ and we extend this notation to elements of Act^* in the natural way. A state $\bar{t}$ is *reachable* from a state t, written $t \rightarrow^* \bar{t}$, if $t \xrightarrow{w} \bar{t}$ for some $w \in Act^*$. A state $\bar{t}$ is an *a-successor* of a state t if $t \xrightarrow{a} \bar{t}$. The set of all *a*-successors of t is denoted by $succ(t, a)$. Assuming some implicit linear ordering on $succ(t, a)$, we denote by $t(a, j)$ the jth *a*-successor of t for each $1 \leq j \leq |succ(t, a)|$. The *branching degree* of $\mathcal{T}$, denoted $d(\mathcal{T})$, is the least number n such that $n \geq |\bigcup_{a \in Act} succ(t, a)|$ for every $t \in T$. If there is no such n then $d(\mathcal{T}) = \infty$.

The notion of 'behavioral sameness' of two processes can be formally captured in many different ways (see, e.g., [vG99] for an overview). Among those

---

* Supported by the Grant Agency of the Czech Republic, grant No. 201/00/0400.

L. Brim et al. (Eds.): CONCUR 2002, LNCS 2421, pp. 594–609, 2002.
© Springer-Verlag Berlin Heidelberg 2002

behavioral equivalences, *simulation* and *bisimulation* equivalence enjoy special attention.

Definition 2. *Let $\mathcal{S} = (S, Act, \rightarrow)$ and $\mathcal{T} = (T, Act, \rightarrow)$ be transition systems. A relation $\mathcal{R} \subseteq S \times T$ is a* simulation *iff whenever $(s, t) \in \mathcal{R}$, then*

- *for each $s \xrightarrow{a} \bar{s}$ there is some $t \xrightarrow{a} \bar{t}$ such that $(\bar{s}, \bar{t}) \in \mathcal{R}$.*

A process s is simulated *by t, written $s \sqsubseteq t$, iff there is a simulation $\mathcal{R}$ such that $(s, t) \in \mathcal{R}$. Processes s, t are* simulation equivalent, *written $s \simeq t$, iff they can simulate each other.*

A bisimulation is a simulation whose inverse is also a simulation; a more explicit definition follows.

Definition 3. *Let $\mathcal{S} = (S, Act, \rightarrow)$ and $\mathcal{T} = (T, Act, \rightarrow)$ be transition systems. A relation $\mathcal{R} \subseteq S \times T$ is a* bisimulation *iff whenever $(s, t) \in \mathcal{R}$, then*

- *for each $s \xrightarrow{a} \bar{s}$ there is some $t \xrightarrow{a} \bar{t}$ such that $(\bar{s}, \bar{t}) \in \mathcal{R}$;*
- *for each $t \xrightarrow{a} \bar{t}$ there is some $s \xrightarrow{a} \bar{s}$ such that $(\bar{s}, \bar{t}) \in \mathcal{R}$.*

Processes s and t are bisimulation equivalent (bisimilar), *written $s \sim t$, iff they are related by some bisimulation.*

Simulations (and bisimulations) can also be viewed as *games* [Sti98, Tho93] between two players, the attacker and the defender. In a simulation game the attacker wants to show that $s \not\sqsubseteq t$, while the defender attempts to frustrate this. Imagine that there are two tokens put on states s and t. Now the two players, attacker and defender, start to play a *simulation game* which consists of a (possibly infinite) number of *rounds* where each round is performed as follows: The attacker takes the token which was put on s originally and moves it along a transition labeled by (some) a; the task of the defender is to move the other token along a transition with the same label. If one player cannot move then the other player wins. The defender wins every infinite game. It can be easily shown that $s \sqsubseteq t$ iff the defender has a winning strategy. The only difference between a simulation game and a *bisimulation game* is that the attacker can *choose* his token at the beginning of every round (the defender has to respond by moving the other token). Again we get that $s \sim t$ iff the defender has a winning strategy.

Let **A**, **B** be classes of processes. The problem whether a given process s of **A** is simulated by a given process t of **B** is denoted by **A** $\sqsubseteq$ **B**. Similarly, the problem if s and t are simulation equivalent (or bisimilar) is denoted by **A** $\simeq$ **B**, (or **A** $\sim$ **B**, respectively).

One reason why simulation preorder/equivalence and bisimilarity found their way to many practical applications is their special computational tractability—both equivalences are decidable in polynomial time for finite-state processes (in fact, they are **P**-complete [BGS92, SJ01]) and remain decidable even for certain classes of infinite-state processes [Mol96]. By contrast, all trace-based equivalences are **PSPACE**-complete for finite-state systems and become undecidable for infinite-state systems. Further evidence is provided by recent results on equivalence-checking between infinite and finite-state systems—see [KM02b] for an overview. Although the formal definitions of simulation and bisimulation are quite similar, one cannot immediately transfer techniques and algorithms developed for one of the two equivalences to the other one. Nevertheless, there *is* some kind of connection between them—for example, in [KM02b] it has been shown that simulation equivalence can be 'reduced' to bisimulation equivalence in the following sense: given a transition system T, one can define a transition system T' with the same set of states as T such that for all states s, t we have that s, t are simulation equivalent in T iff s, t are bisimilar in T'. Although this 'reduction' works for arbitrary finitely-branching transition systems, it is not effective in general (the only known class of infinite-state processes where the method is effective is the class of one-counter nets [JKM00]; for finite-state processes, the method is even efficient, i.e., polynomial-time). Actually, our present knowledge indicates that there cannot be any general efficient reduction from simulation equivalence to bisimilarity, because all of the existing results confirm a general rule saying that

"simulation is computationally harder than bisimilarity."

Indeed, bisimilarity tends to be 'more decidable' and 'more tractable' than simulation; to the best of our knowledge, there is (so far) no counterexample violating this 'rule of thumb' (maybe except for some artificial constructions). But why is that? One possible answer is that bisimilarity is so much finer than simulation equivalence that it has 'more structure' and becomes easier to decide. However, this is a rather vague statement. In this paper we try to provide a more convincing explanation/justification for the aforementioned rule. We show that there are possibilities how to 'transfer' winning strategies for both players from a bisimulation game to a simulation game. More precisely, given two states s and t in transition systems S and T, we show how to construct states s' and t' in transition systems S' and T' in such a way that $s \sim t$ iff $s' \sqsubseteq t'$ (or $s' \simeq t'$). We propose two methods how to achieve that. The point is that both methods are applicable to certain (quite large) classes of models of concurrent systems where they result in *effective* and *polynomial-time* reductions. In fact, we formulate abstract conditions on process classes **A** and **B** under which the problem **A** $\sim$ **B** is polynomially reducible to the problem **A** $\sqsubseteq$ **B** (or **A** $\simeq$ **B**). Roughly speaking, the first method (introduced in Section 2) applies to models with a finite branching degree where one can in some sense identify what actions are not enabled. Examples include (subclasses of) pushdown systems, queue systems, etc. The second method (Section 3) is applicable to models closed under (synchronized) parallel composition. Examples are, e.g., Petri nets with various extensions/restrictions. The applicability and limitations of each method are discussed in greater detail in the respective sections.

Although the two methods do not cover all of the existing models of concurrent processes (see Section 4), they reveal a kind of general relationship between winning strategies in bisimulation and simulation games. Moreover, it is now clear that simulation is harder than bisimulation not by coincidence but due to some fundamental reason—one can polynomially reduce bisimilarity to simulation preorder/equivalence by general reductions whose underlying principle is independent of concrete process models. Hence, the paper presents a new piece of generic knowledge rather than a collection of technical results.

2   Reducing Bisimilarity to Simulation – Method 1

For the rest of this section, we fix a finite set of actions $Act = \{a_1, \ldots, a_k\}$ and two transition systems $\mathcal{S} = (S, Act, \rightarrow)$, $\mathcal{T} = (T, Act, \rightarrow)$ with a finite branching degree. Moreover, we put $d = \max\{d(\mathcal{S}), d(\mathcal{T})\}$. Our aim is to define two other transition systems $\mathcal{S}'$ and $\mathcal{T}'$ which extend the systems $\mathcal{S}$ and $\mathcal{T}$ by some new states and transitions in such a way that for all $s \in S, t \in T$ we have that $s \sim t$ iff $s' \sqsubseteq t'$, where s' and t' are the 'twins' of s and t in $\mathcal{S}'$ and $\mathcal{T}'$, respectively. Since, in the considered simulation game, the attacker plays within $\mathcal{S}'$ and the defender plays within $\mathcal{T}'$, we call $\mathcal{S}'$ an *A-extension* of $\mathcal{S}$, and $\mathcal{T}'$ a *D-extension* of $\mathcal{T}$. The idea behind the construction of $\mathcal{S}'$ and $\mathcal{T}'$ can be intuitively described as follows: one round of a bisimulation game between s and t is emulated by at most two rounds of a simulation game between s' and t'. The rules of the bisimulation game allow the attacker to make his move either from s or from t. If he chooses s and plays $s \overset{a_i}{\rightarrow} s(a_i, j)$, we can easily emulate his attack by $s' \overset{a_i}{\rightarrow} s(a_i, j)'$ (remember that $s(a_i, j)$ is the jth a_i-successor of s). The defender's response $t \overset{a_i}{\rightarrow} t(a_i, \ell)$ is emulated by $t' \overset{a_i}{\rightarrow} t(a_i, \ell)'$ (t' has the 'same' a_i-successors as t). If the attacker chooses t and plays $t \overset{a_i}{\rightarrow} t(a_i, j)$, the emulation is more complicated and takes two rounds. First, to each successor $t(a_i, j)$ of t we associate a unique action λ_i^j.

Now, we add to s' a family of transitions $s' \overset{\lambda_i^j}{\rightarrow} s'$ for all $1 \le i \le k$ and $1 \le j \le d$. To emulate the move $t \overset{a_i}{\rightarrow} t(a_i, j)$ in our simulation game, the attacker performs the λ_i^j-loop on s'. In our bisimulation game, the attack $t \overset{a_i}{\rightarrow} t(a_i, j)$ would be matched by (some) move $s \overset{a_i}{\rightarrow} s(a_i, \ell)$. First, we name the successors of s by a family of δ_i^j actions. Now, the response $s \overset{a_i}{\rightarrow} s(a_i, \ell)$ is emulated by $t' \overset{\lambda_i^j}{\rightarrow} r[a_i, j, \ell]$, where $r[a_i, j, \ell]$ is a newly added state. It finishes the first round, i.e., the first emulation phase. In the second round, t' is in a way *forced* to go to $t(a_i, j)'$ and the only response available to $r[a_i, j, \ell]$ is to enter $s(a_i, \ell)'$, which finishes the emulation. The mentioned 'forcing' is achieved by allowing $r[a_i, j, \ell]$ to go to a 'universal' state (i.e., to a state which can simulate everything) under all but one action δ_i^ℓ. It means that if any other action (different from δ_i^ℓ) is used by t' in the second round, the attacker loses the simulation game. Hence, his only chance is to play a δ_i^ℓ-transition; our construction ensures that the only such transition is $t' \overset{\delta_i^\ell}{\rightarrow} t(a_i, \ell)'$. Our construction also guarantees that any 'bad' move of one of the two players in the simulation game (which is not consistent with the above given scenario) is immediately 'punished' by allowing the other player to win. Formal definitions and proofs follow.

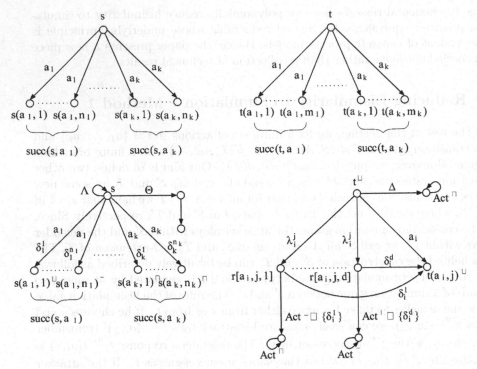

Fig. 1. States s of $\mathcal{S}$ and t of $\mathcal{T}$, and the corresponding states s' of $\mathcal{S}'$ and t' of $\mathcal{T}'$ (some of the out-going transitions of t' are omitted)

Let $\Lambda = \{\lambda_i^j \mid 1 \le i \le k, 1 \le j \le d\}$ and $\Delta = \{\delta_i^j \mid 1 \le i \le k, 1 \le j \le d\}$ be finite sets of actions such that Λ, Δ, and Act are pairwise disjoint. We define $Act' = Act \cup \Lambda \cup \Delta \cup \{\gamma\}$ where γ is a fresh action.

Definition 4. *An A-extension of $\mathcal{S}$ (see Fig.1) is a transition system $\mathcal{S}' = (S', Act', \rightarrow)$ together with an injective mapping $f : S \to S'$ satisfying the following conditions (where $f(s)$ is abbreviated to s'):*

- *If $s \xrightarrow{a} \bar{s}$ is a transition of $\mathcal{S}$, then $s' \xrightarrow{a} \bar{s}'$ is a transition of $\mathcal{S}'$.*
- *$s' \xrightarrow{\lambda} s'$ is a transition of $\mathcal{S}'$ for every $s \in S$ and $\lambda \in \Lambda$.*
- *For all $s \in S$, $1 \le i \le k$, and $1 \le j \le d$ we have the following:*
  - *if $j \le |succ(s, a_i)|$ then $s' \xrightarrow{\delta_i^j} s(a_i, j)'$ is a transition of $\mathcal{S}'$ (remember that $s(a_i, j)$ is the jth a_i-successor of s in $\mathcal{S}$);*
  - *if $j > |succ(s, a_i)|$ then there is a transition $s' \xrightarrow{\delta_i^j} q_j$ to some state $q_j \in S'$ which can perform the action γ. This family of δ_i^j-transitions is indicated by a Θ-labeled arrow in Fig. 1. Also observe that we do not impose any additional restrictions on q_j (i.e., q_j can also emit other actions).*
- *For each $s \in S$ the state s' has only the transitions admitted above.*

A simple observation about A-extensions is

Lemma 5. *If S is deterministic, then S has a deterministic A-extension.*

A state u is *universal* if $u \xrightarrow{a} u$ for every $a \in Act'$ (u can also have other out-going transitions). Observe that a universal state can simulate *any* process which emits actions of Act'. In the next definition, we write $t \xrightarrow{a} U$ to indicate that $t \xrightarrow{a} u$ for some universal state u.

Definition 6. *A D-extension of T (see Fig. 1) is a transition system $T' = (T', Act', \rightarrow)$ together with an injective mapping $g : T \rightarrow T'$ satisfying the following conditions (where $g(t)$ is abbreviated to t'):*

- *If $t \xrightarrow{a} \bar{t}$ is a transition of T, then $t' \xrightarrow{a} \bar{t}'$ is a transition of T'.*
- *$t' \xrightarrow{\delta} U$ for every $t \in T$ and $\delta \in \Delta$.*
- *For all $t \in T$, $1 \le i \le k$, and $1 \le j \le d$ we have the following:*

  - *If $j \le |succ(t, a_i)|$ then $t' \xrightarrow{\lambda_i^j} r[a_i, j, \ell]$ is a transition of S' for each $1 \le \ell \le d$. Here $r[a_i, j, \ell]$ is a state of T' which has*

    * *exactly one δ_i^ℓ-transition $r[a_i, j, \ell] \xrightarrow{\delta_i^\ell} t(a_i, j)'$ (remember that $t(a_i, j)$ is the jth a_i-successor of t in T);*
    * *a transition $r[a_i, j, \ell] \xrightarrow{a} U$ for each $a \in Act' - \{\delta_i^\ell\}$.*

  - *If $j > |succ(t, a_i)|$ then there is a transition $t' \xrightarrow{\lambda_i^j} U$.*
- *For each $t \in T$ the state t' has only the transitions admitted above.*

Theorem 7. *Let $s \in S$ and $t \in T$. Let S' be an A-extension of S and T' a D-extension of T. We have that $s \sim t$ iff $s' \sqsubseteq t'$.*

Proof. We start with the '$\Longrightarrow$' direction. Let us suppose that $s \sim t$. We show that the defender has a winning strategy in a simulation game initiated in (s', t'). Let $\mathcal{R} = \{(s', t') \mid s \in S, t \in T, s \sim t\}$. We prove that $\mathcal{R}$ can be extended to a simulation relation (which means that indeed $s' \sqsubseteq t'$). Let $(s', t') \in \mathcal{R}$. We show that the defender can play in such a way that after at most two rounds he achieves either a configuration from $\mathcal{R}$, or a configuration where he 'obviously' wins. So, let $s' \xrightarrow{a} p$ be an attacker's move. We consider three possibilities:

- If $a \in Act$, then $p = \bar{s}'$ for some $\bar{s} \in S$. Since $s \sim t$, there is $t \xrightarrow{a} \bar{t}$ such that $\bar{s} \sim \bar{t}$. Hence, the defender can respond by $t' \xrightarrow{a} \bar{t}'$ and thus enter a configuration from $\mathcal{R}$.
- If $a \in \Delta$, then there is a transition $t' \xrightarrow{a} U$ (cf. Definition 6). Hence, the defender can use this transition and from that point on he can simulate 'everything'.
- If $a = \lambda_i^j$, then $p = s'$ and there are two possibilities:
  - The state t has fewer than j a_i-successors. Then there is a transition $t' \xrightarrow{\lambda_i^j} U$ and the defender wins.

- Otherwise, let us consider the attack $t \xrightarrow{a_i} t(a_i, j)$ in the *bisimulation* game between s and t. Since $s \sim t$, there is a move $s \xrightarrow{a_i} s(a_i, \ell)$ such that $s(a_i, \ell) \sim t(a_i, j)$. In our simulation game, the defender uses the $t' \xrightarrow{\lambda_i^j} r[a_i, j, \ell]$ transition as a response. The current game situation (after playing one round) is $(s', r[a_i, j, \ell])$. Now, if the attacker plays $s' \xrightarrow{\delta_i^\ell} s(a_i, \ell)'$, the defender can respond by $r[a_i, j, \ell] \xrightarrow{\delta_i^\ell} t(a_i, j)'$ and enter a configuration from $\mathcal{R}$. If the attacker uses any other attack, the defender can go to a universal state and thus he wins.

Now we show the '$\Longleftarrow$' direction, i.e., we assume $s' \sqsubseteq t'$ and prove $s \sim t$. To do that, we demonstrate that $\mathcal{R} = \{(s, t) \mid s \in S, t \in T, s' \sqsubseteq t'\}$ is a bisimulation. So, let $(s, t) \in \mathcal{R}$. An attack which comes from the first component is easy to handle—if $s \xrightarrow{a} \bar{s}$, then also $s' \xrightarrow{a} \bar{s}'$ and since $s' \sqsubseteq t'$, there is $t' \xrightarrow{a} \bar{t}'$ such that $\bar{s}' \sqsubseteq \bar{t}'$. Hence, $t \xrightarrow{a} \bar{t}$ where $(\bar{s}, \bar{t}) \in \mathcal{R}$. Now let us consider an attack $t \xrightarrow{a_i} t(a_i, j)$. To find an appropriate response for the defender, let us examine the *simulation* game between s' and t'. Here, the attacker can play $s' \xrightarrow{\lambda_i^j} s'$. The defender must respond by some $t' \xrightarrow{\lambda_i^j} r[a_i, j, \ell]$ (there is surely no transition $t' \xrightarrow{\lambda_i^j} U$). If the ℓ was greater than the number of a_i-successors of s, the defender's response would be definitely wrong because then the attacker could win in two rounds by performing the transitions $s' \xrightarrow{\delta_i^\ell} q_\ell \xrightarrow{\gamma} q$. So, we see that the ℓ must be less than or equal to the number of a_i-successors of s. The attacker can further play $s' \xrightarrow{\delta_i^\ell} s(a_i, \ell)'$, and the defender can respond only by $r[a_i, j, \ell] \xrightarrow{\delta_i^\ell} t(a_i, j)'$. Thus, we obtain that $s(a_i, \ell)' \sqsubseteq t(a_i, j)'$. It means that, in our bisimulation game, the defender can use the transition $s \xrightarrow{a_i} s(a_i, \ell)$ and enter a configuration from $\mathcal{R}$.

$\square$

2.1 Applications

Theorem 7 allows to construct direct one-to-one polynomial-time reductions from the problem $\mathbf{A} \sim \mathbf{B}$ to the problem $\mathbf{A} \sqsubseteq \mathbf{B}$ (and $\mathbf{A} \simeq \mathbf{B}$) for many process classes $\mathbf{A}$ and $\mathbf{B}$. All we need to show is that the syntax of $\mathbf{A}$ and $\mathbf{B}$ admits an efficient construction of A- and D-extensions, respectively. It can be done, e.g., for (various subclasses of) pushdown automata, BPA systems, one-counter automata, queue automata (where the queue can be tested for emptiness), channel systems, 1-safe Petri nets, and others (the list is surely not exhaustive; interested reader can probably add some of his own favorite models). To illustrate this, we discuss the model of pushdown automata in greater detail. The limitations of our first method are mentioned at the end of this section.

A *pushdown automaton (PDA)* is a tuple $\mathcal{M} = (Q, \Gamma, Act, \eta)$ where Q is a finite set of *control states*, Γ is a finite *stack alphabet*, Act is a finite *input alphabet*, and $\eta : (Q \times \Gamma) \to \mathcal{P}(Act \times (Q \times \Gamma^*))$ is a *transition function* with finite image (here $\mathcal{P}(M)$ denotes the powerset of M). In the rest of this paper we adopt a more intuitive notation, writing $pA \xrightarrow{a} q\beta \in \eta$ instead of $(a, (q, \beta)) \in \eta(p, A)$. To $\mathcal{M}$ we associate the transition system $\mathcal{T}_{\mathcal{M}}$ where $Q \times \Gamma^*$ is the set of states (we write $p\alpha$ instead of (p, α)), Act is the set of actions, and the transition relation is defined by $pA\alpha \xrightarrow{a} q\beta\alpha$ iff $pA \xrightarrow{a} q\beta \in \eta$. The set of all states of $\mathcal{T}_{\mathcal{M}}$ is also denoted by $States(\mathcal{T}_{\mathcal{M}})$.

A PDA $\mathcal{M} = (Q, \Gamma, Act, \eta)$ is

- *deterministic* if for all $p \in Q$, $A \in \Gamma$, and $a \in Act$ there is at most one $q\beta \in Q \times \Gamma^*$ such that $pA \xrightarrow{a} q\beta$;
- *normed* if for every $p\alpha \in Q \times \Gamma^*$ there is $q \in Q$ such that $p\alpha \rightarrow^* q\varepsilon$;
- *stateless* if $|Q| = 1$;
- *one-counter automaton* if $\Gamma = \{I, Z\}$ and each element of η is either of the form $pZ \xrightarrow{a} qI^j Z$ where $j \in \mathbb{N}_0$ (such transitions are called *zero-transitions*), or of the form $pI \xrightarrow{a} qI^j$ where $j \in \mathbb{N}_0$ (these transitions are *non-zero-transitions*). Hence, the Z can be viewed as a bottom marker (which cannot be removed), and the number of pushed I's represents the counter value.

The classes of all pushdown processes, stateless pushdown processes, one-counter processes, and finite-state processes are denoted by **PDA**, **BPA**, **OC**, and **FS**, respectively. The normed subclasses of **PDA** and **BPA** are denoted by **nPDA** and **nBPA** (one could also consider normed **OC** processes, but these are not so important). If **A** is any of the so-far defined classes, then **det-A** denotes the subclass of all deterministic processes of **A**. For example, **det-nBPA** is the class of all deterministic normed **BPA** processes. Let

- $\mathcal{D} = \{\textbf{PDA}, \textbf{BPA}, \textbf{OC}, \textbf{nPDA}, \textbf{nBPA}, \textbf{FS}\}$,
- $\mathcal{A} = \mathcal{D} \cup \{\textbf{det-A} \mid \textbf{A} \in \mathcal{D}\}$.

Lemma 8. *Let $\textbf{A} \in \mathcal{A}$ and let $\mathcal{M} \in \textbf{A}$ be an automaton of $\textbf{A}$. Then there is $\mathcal{M}' \in \textbf{A}$ and a mapping $f : States(\mathcal{T}_{\mathcal{M}}) \rightarrow States(\mathcal{T}_{\mathcal{M}'})$ constructible in polynomial time (in the size of $\mathcal{M}$) such that $\mathcal{T}_{\mathcal{M}'}$ together with f is an $\textbf{A}$-extension of $\mathcal{M}$.*

Proof. We construct $\mathcal{M}'$ by extending $\mathcal{M}$. First, if $\mathcal{M}$ is not a one-counter automaton, it can possibly empty its stack and therefore we add a new 'bottom' symbol Z to the stack alphabet. The mapping f then maps every configuration $p\alpha$ to $p\alpha Z$ (in the case of one-counter automata, f is just identity). The λ_i^j-loops are added by extending the transition function with all rules of the form $pX \xrightarrow{\lambda_i^j} pX$. Since the outgoing transitions of a given state $pX\alpha$ are completely determined by p and X, we can also easily add the δ_i^j-transitions; the family of Θ-transitions (see Fig. 1) is implemented by changing the top stack symbol to a fresh symbol Y, without changing the control state (this works both for PDA and BPA; in the case of one-counter automata we instead change the control to a newly-added control state without modifying the stack). Then, the action γ is emitted and Y is removed from the stack. Note that this construction preserves normedness and determinism. Obviously, the reduction works in polynomial time (and even in logarithmic space). $\qquad\square$

The next lemma can be proved in a similar way. Note that the construction does not preserve determinism (see Fig. 1).

Lemma 9. *Let $D \in \mathcal{D}$ and let $\mathcal{M} \in D$ be an automaton of D. Then there is $\mathcal{M}' \in D$ and a mapping $f : States(\mathcal{T}_{\mathcal{M}}) \to States(\mathcal{T}_{\mathcal{M}'})$ constructible in polynomial time (in the size of $\mathcal{M}$) such that $\mathcal{T}_{\mathcal{M}'}$ together with f is an D-extension of $\mathcal{M}$.*

Now, we can formulate two interesting corollaries of Theorem 7.

Corollary 10. *Let $A \in \mathcal{A}$ and $D \in \mathcal{D}$. The problem $A \sim D$ is polynomially reducible to the problem $A \sqsubseteq D$.*

Corollary 11. *Let $A, B \in \mathcal{D}$ such that $B \subseteq A$. Then the problem $A \sim B$ is polynomially reducible to the problem $A \simeq B$.*

Proof. There is a general one-to-one reduction from the problem $\mathbf{A} \sqsubseteq \mathbf{B}$ to the problem $\mathbf{A} \simeq \mathbf{B}$, which is applicable also in our case—given two processes s and t, we construct other processes s' and t' with transitions $s' \xrightarrow{a} s$, $s' \xrightarrow{a} t$, and $t' \xrightarrow{a} t$. We see that $s \sqsubseteq t$ iff $s' \simeq t'$. $\qquad\square$

Our first method is applicable to a wide variety of models, but it has its limitations. For example, in the case of A-extensions there can be difficulties with the family of Θ-transitions. In order to implement them, the model must be able to (somehow) 'detect' the missing transitions. It is not always possible; for example, general Petri nets cannot test a place for emptiness and hence the Θ-transitions cannot be implemented. Nevertheless, the method is applicable to some subclasses/extensions of Petri nets. For example, 1-safe Petri nets *can* in a way test their places for emptiness—to construct an A-extension of a given 1-safe net $\mathcal{N}$, we just equip each place p with its 'twin' $\bar{p}$ and restructure the transitions so that they have the same effect on the 'old' places and preserve the following invariant: $\bar{p}$ is marked iff p is unmarked. It is quite easy; then, we can easily implement the family of Θ-transitions (by testing appropriate 'twins' for being marked). Another example are Petri nets with inhibitor arcs, where our first method applies without any problems.

Hence, we can extended the $\mathcal{A}$ and $\mathcal{D}$ classes by many other models and the obtained corollaries are still valid. In this way one can 'generate' a long list of results, of which some were already known while others are new. Some of these results are 'exotic' (for example, **det-nPDA** $\sim$ **1-PN** is polynomially reducible (and hence not harder than) **det-nPDA** $\sqsubseteq$ **1-PN** where **1-PN** is the class of 1-safe Petri nets; both problems are decidable but their complexity has not yet been analyzed in detail). However, some of the obtained consequences actually improve our knowledge about previously studied problems. For example, **PDA** $\sim$ **FS** is known to be **PSPACE**-hard [May00] while the best known lower bound for **PDA** $\sqsubseteq$ **FS** was **coNP** [KM02b]. Our method allows to improve this lower bound to **PSPACE**[1].

---

[1] Very recently [KM02a], the authors proved that **PDA** $\sqsubseteq$ **FS** is actually **EXPTIME**-complete and **PDA** $\sim$ **FS** is **PSPACE**-complete.

3 Reducing Bisimilarity to Simulation – Method 2

As in the previous section, we first fix a finite set of actions $Act = \{a_1, \ldots, a_k\}$ and two transition systems $\mathcal{S} = (S, Act, \rightarrow)$, $\mathcal{T} = (T, Act, \rightarrow)$ with a finite branching degree. We also define $d = \max\{d(\mathcal{S}), d(\mathcal{T})\}$.

Definition 12. *By a parallel composition of transition systems* $\mathcal{T}_1 = (T_1, Act, \rightarrow)$ *and* $\mathcal{T}_2 = (T_2, Act, \rightarrow)$ *we mean a transition system* $\mathcal{T}_1 \| \mathcal{T}_2 = (T_1 \times T_2, Act, \rightarrow)$ *where* $(t_1, t_2) \xrightarrow{a} (\bar{t}_1, \bar{t}_2)$ *iff either* $t_1 \xrightarrow{a} \bar{t}_1$ *and* $\bar{t}_2 = t_2$, *or* $t_2 \xrightarrow{a} \bar{t}_2$ *and* $\bar{t}_1 = t_1$.

Intuitively, our second method works for all classes of systems that are closed under parallel composition and synchronization (see Definition 17). The idea is as follows: For $\mathcal{S}$ and $\mathcal{T}$ one constructs new systems A-$comp(\mathcal{S}, \mathcal{T})$ and D-$comp(\mathcal{S}, \mathcal{T})$ by composing (and synchronizing) $\mathcal{S}$ and $\mathcal{T}$. Hence, the sets of states of A-$comp(\mathcal{S}, \mathcal{T})$ and D-$comp(\mathcal{S}, \mathcal{T})$ subsume $S \times T$ (to prevent confusion, states of A-$comp(\mathcal{S}, \mathcal{T})$ are marked by a horizontal bar; hence, $\overline{(s, t)}$ is a state of A-$comp(\mathcal{S}, \mathcal{T})$ while (s, t) is a state of D-$comp(\mathcal{S}, \mathcal{T})$). The goal is to obtain the property that, for all $s \in S, t \in T$ we have that $s \sim t$ iff $\overline{(s, t)} \sqsubseteq (s, t)$. Note that each player has his own copy of $\mathcal{S}$ and $\mathcal{T}$.

The simulation game proceeds as follows: The attacker (playing in A-$comp(\mathcal{S}, \mathcal{T})$) chooses either $\mathcal{S}$ or $\mathcal{T}$ and makes a move there. Let us assume that the attacker chooses $\mathcal{S}$ (the other case is symmetric). Then the defender (playing in D-$comp(\mathcal{S}, \mathcal{T})$) must make exactly the same move in his copy of $\mathcal{S}$ as the attacker, but also some move in his copy of $\mathcal{T}$. The defender can choose which move in $\mathcal{T}$ he makes, provided it has the same action as the attacker's move. Furthermore, the defender 'threatens' to go to a universal state (that can simulate everything) unless the attacker does a specific action in the next round. In the next round the attacker must make exactly the same move in his (the attacker's) copy of $\mathcal{T}$ as the defender did in his (the defender's) copy of $\mathcal{T}$ in the previous round. The defender responds to this by ending his threat to become universal. Otherwise the defender can make his side universal and wins the simulation game.

This construction ensures that the two copies of $\mathcal{S}$ and $\mathcal{T}$ on both sides are kept consistent. One round of the bisimulation game between $\mathcal{S}$ and $\mathcal{T}$ is thus emulated by two rounds of the simulation game between A-$comp(\mathcal{S}, \mathcal{T})$ and D-$comp(\mathcal{S}, \mathcal{T})$.

Of course, it is possible that for a given state s there are several different outgoing arcs labeled with the same action a_i. However, we need to construct new systems where outgoing transitions are labeled uniquely. Our notation is similar to the one used in the previous section: Let $\Lambda = \{\lambda_i^j \mid 1 \leq i \leq k, 1 \leq j \leq d\}$ and $\Delta = \{\delta_i^j \mid 1 \leq i \leq k, 1 \leq j \leq d\}$ be finite sets of actions such that Λ, Δ, and Act are pairwise disjoint. We define $Act' = \Lambda \cup \Delta$.

For any state s in S, the action δ_i^j is used to label the j-th outgoing arc that was previously labeled by action a_i. Note that the action δ_i^j can occur many times in the transition system. It is only unique among the labels of the outgoing arcs of any single state. Similarly, the actions λ_i^j are used to label the outgoing arcs of states t in T.

Figure 2 illustrates the construction. The first row shows parts of the original systems S and T. The second row shows A-$comp(S,T)$. The labels of the transitions have been changed as described above, and the modified systems have been put in parallel without any synchronization. The last row shows (a fragment of) D-$comp(S,T)$. Here the systems S and T have been composed and synchronized in such a way as to ensure the properties of the simulation game as described above.

Definition 13. *We define transition systems* $S' = (S, Act', \rightarrow)$ *and* $T' = (T, Act', \rightarrow)$ *where*

- *for every transition* $s \xrightarrow{a_i} s(a_i, j)$ *in* S *there is a transition* $s \xrightarrow{\delta_i^j} s(a_i, j)$ *in* S';
- *for every transition* $t \xrightarrow{a_i} t(a_i, \ell)$ *in* T *there is a transition* $t \xrightarrow{\lambda_i^\ell} t(a_i, \ell)$ *in* T';
- *there are no other transitions in* S' *and* T'.

The A-*composition* A-$comp(S,T)$ *of* S *and* T *(see Fig.2) is the parallel composition* $S' \| T'$. *Configurations in* A-$comp(S,T)$ *are denoted by* $\overline{(s,t)}$.

Remark 14. Observe that A-$comp(S,T)$ is always deterministic, even if S and T are nondeterministic.

A state u is *universal* if $u \xrightarrow{a} u$ for every $a \in Act'$ (u can also have other outgoing transitions). Observe that a universal state can simulate *any* process which emits actions of Act'. In the next definition, we write $t \xrightarrow{a} U$ to indicate that $t \xrightarrow{a} u$ for some universal state u.

Definition 15. *The* D-*composition* D-$comp(S,T)$ *of* S *and* T *(see Fig. 2) is the transition system* $D = (D, Act', \rightarrow)$, *where* D *is the set*

$$\{(s,t) \mid s \in S, t \in T\} \cup \{(s,t)' \mid s \in S, t \in T\} \cup \{(s,t)'' \mid s \in S, t \in T\}$$

and the transition relation of D *is defined as follows. Let* $1 \le i \le k$, $1 \le j \le n_i$ *and* $1 \le \ell \le m_i$.

- *If there are transitions* $s \xrightarrow{a_i} s(a_i, j)$ *in* S *and* $t \xrightarrow{a_i} t(a_i, \ell)$ *in* T *then there are transitions* $(s,t) \xrightarrow{\delta_i^j} (s(a_i, j), t(a_i, \ell))'$ *and* $(s,t) \xrightarrow{\lambda_i^\ell} (s(a_i, j), t(a_i, \ell))''$ *in* D.
- $(s(a_i, j), t(a_i, \ell))' \xrightarrow{\lambda_i^\ell} (s(a_i, j), t(a_i, \ell))$
- $(s(a_i, j), t(a_i, \ell))' \xrightarrow{b} U$, *for each* $b \in Act' - \{\lambda_i^\ell\}$.
- $(s(a_i, j), t(a_i, \ell))'' \xrightarrow{\delta_i^j} (s(a_i, j), t(a_i, \ell))$
- $(s(a_i, j), t(a_i, \ell))'' \xrightarrow{c} U$, *for each* $c \in Act' - \{\delta_i^j\}$.

Theorem 16. *Let* $s \in S$, $t \in T$, *and let* $\overline{(s,t)}$ *and* (s,t) *be the corresponding states in* A-$comp(S,T)$ *and* D-$comp(S,T)$, *respectively. We have that* $s \sim t$ *iff* $\overline{(s,t)} \sqsubseteq (s,t)$.

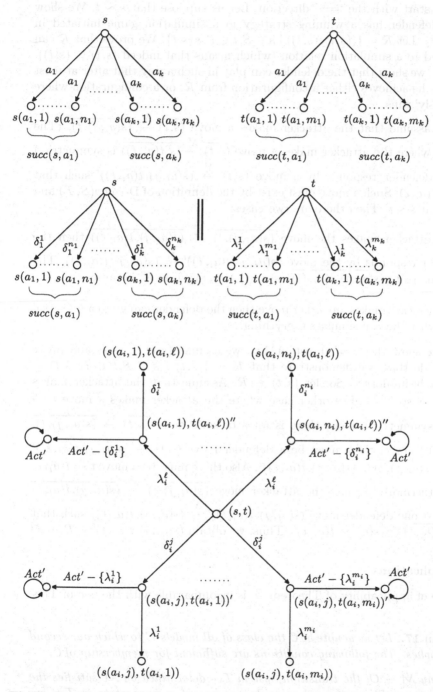

Fig. 2. States s and t of $\mathcal{S}$ and $\mathcal{T}$, then the A-composition of $\mathcal{S}$ and $\mathcal{T}$, and finally the D-composition of $\mathcal{S}$ and $\mathcal{T}$

Proof. We start with the '$\Longrightarrow$' direction. Let us suppose that $s \sim t$. We show that the defender has a winning strategy in a simulation game initiated in $(\overline{(s,t)}, (s,t))$. Let $\mathcal{R} = \{(\overline{(s,t)}, (s,t)) \mid s \in S, t \in T, s \sim t\}$. We prove that $\mathcal{R}$ can be extended to a simulation relation (which means that indeed $\overline{(s,t)} \sqsubseteq (s,t)$). To do that, we show that the defender can play in such a way that after at most two rounds he achieves either a configuration from $\mathcal{R}$, or a configuration where he 'obviously' wins.

Let us assume that the attacker makes a move $\overline{(s,t)} \xrightarrow{\delta_i^j} \overline{(s(a_i,j),t)}$. (The other case where the attacker makes a move $\overline{(s,t)} \xrightarrow{\lambda_i^\ell} \overline{(s,t(a_i,\ell))}$ is symmetric.) Then the defender responds by a move $(s,t) \xrightarrow{\delta_i^j} (s(a_i,j),t(a_i,\ell))'$ such that $s(a_i,j) \sim t(a_i,\ell)$. Such a move must exist by the definition of D-*comp*$(\mathcal{S},\mathcal{T})$ and the fact that $s \sim t$. Then there are two cases:

- If the attacker makes the move $\overline{(s(a_i,j),t)} \xrightarrow{\lambda_i^\ell} \overline{(s(a_i,j),t(a_i,\ell))}$ then the defender responds by the move $(s(a_i,j),t(a_i,\ell))' \xrightarrow{\lambda_i^\ell} (s(a_i,j),t(a_i,\ell))$. The resulting pair $(\overline{(s(a_i,j),t(a_i,\ell))}, (s(a_i,j),t(a_i,\ell)))$ is in $\mathcal{R}$, because $s(a_i,j) \sim t(a_i,\ell)$.
- If the attacker makes any other move then the defender can go to a universal state where he can simulate everything.

Now we show the '$\Longleftarrow$' direction, i.e., we assume $\overline{(s,t)} \sqsubseteq (s,t)$ and prove $s \sim t$. To do that, we demonstrate that $\mathcal{R} = \{(s,t) \mid s \in S, t \in T, \overline{(s,t)} \sqsubseteq (s,t)\}$ is a bisimulation. So, let $(s,t) \in \mathcal{R}$. Assume that the attacker makes a move $s \xrightarrow{a_i} s(a_i,j)$. (The other case where the attacker makes a move $t \xrightarrow{a_i} t(a_i,\ell)$ is symmetric.) Thus, there is an attacker's move $\overline{(s,t)} \xrightarrow{\delta_i^j} \overline{(s(a_i,j),t)}$. Since $\overline{(s,t)} \sqsubseteq (s,t)$ there must be a defender move $(s,t) \xrightarrow{\delta_i^j} (s(a_i,j),t(a_i,\ell))'$ such that $\overline{(s(a_i,j),t)} \sqsubseteq (s(a_i,j),t(a_i,\ell))'$. Also there must be a move $t \xrightarrow{a_i} t(a_i,\ell)$ in $\mathcal{T}$. Furthermore, against the attacker move $\overline{(s(a_i,j),t)} \xrightarrow{\lambda_i^\ell} \overline{(s(a_i,j),t(a_i,\ell))}$ there is just one defender move $(s(a_i,j),t(a_i,\ell))' \xrightarrow{\lambda_i^\ell} (s(a_i,j),t(a_i,\ell))$ such that $\overline{(s(a_i,j),t(a_i,\ell))} \sqsubseteq (s(a_i,j),t(a_i,\ell))$. Thus, we obtain $(s(a_i,j),t(a_i,\ell)) \in \mathcal{R}$. $\square$

3.1   Applications

The range of applicability of Theorem 16 is incomparable with the one of Theorem 7.

Definition 17. *Let us denote by $\mathcal{C}$ the class of all models C to which our second method applies. The following conditions are sufficient for membership of $\mathcal{C}$.*

1. *For any $\mathcal{M} \in \mathcal{C}$, the transition system $\mathcal{T}_\mathcal{M}$ determined by $\mathcal{M}$ satisfies the following condition: the out-going transitions of a given state in $\mathcal{T}_\mathcal{M}$ are determined by a finite number of labeled 'transition rules' which are a part of $\mathcal{M}$. The transition rules must be injective in the sense that each rule*

generates at most one out-going transition in every state of T_M. The label of this outgoing transition is the same as the label of the associated transition rule.

2. C *is efficiently closed under parallel composition (i.e., for all $M_1, M_2 \in C$ there is $M_3 \in C$ computable in polynomial time such that $T_{M_3} = T_{M_1} \| T_{M_2}$).*

3. C *is efficiently closed under synchronization in the following sense: for any two given transition rules it is possible to (efficiently) define a new transition rule that has the effect of both.*

4. C *subsumes the class of finite automata.*

For example, the above conditions are satisfied by 1-safe Petri nets, general Petri nets, reset Petri nets, transfer Petri nets [Pet81], VASS (vector addition systems with states) [BM99], FIFO-channel systems [AJ93], etc. However, there are also some classes that not in C. For example, Basic Parallel Processes [Chr93] are not in C, because they are not closed under synchronization (condition 3). Pushdown automata are not in C, because they are not closed under parallel composition (condition 2). PA-processes [BK85] are not in C, because they are not closed under synchronization and because their transition rules are not injective (they do not satisfy conditions 1 and 3).

Lemma 18. *Let C be a process model satisfying the above conditions and let $M_1, M_2 \in C$. Then there is $M' \in C$ constructible in polynomial time such that $T_{M'}$ is (isomorphic to) A-comp(T_{M_1}, T_{M_2}).*

Proof. Follows immediately from condition 1 (which enables efficient renaming of actions) and condition 2 (efficient parallel composition).   □

Lemma 19. *Let C be a process model satisfying the above conditions and let $M_1, M_2 \in C$. Then there is $M' \in C$ constructible in polynomial time such that $T_{M'}$ is (isomorphic to) D-comp(T_{M_1}, T_{M_2}).*

Proof. M' is obtained by constructing the synchronization of M_1 and M_2 according to Definition 15 (this is possible by conditions 1 and 3). It is also necessary to include the states of the form $(s, t)'$ and $(s, t)''$ into the new system. This is possible because C subsumes the class of finite automata (condition 4) and is thus also closed under synchronization with them (condition 3).   □

Corollary 20. *Let C be a process model satisfying the above conditions, and let **det-**C be the subclass of all $M \in C$ which generate a deterministic transition system. Then the problem $C \sim C$ is polynomially reducible to **det-**$C \sqsubseteq C$ (and also to $C \simeq C$).*

Proof. Immediately from Theorem 16, Remark 14, Lemma 18, and Lemma 19. The reduction to $C \simeq C$ is achieved in the same way as in Corollary 11.   □

4   Conclusion

We have described two general methods to construct direct one-to-one reductions from bisimulation equivalence to simulation preorder (or simulation equivalence) on labeled transition systems. On many classes of finitely generated transition systems these reductions are even effectively computable in polynomial time. Generally speaking, the first method is effective for all classes of systems that can test for non-enabledness of actions, like finite-state systems, pushdown automata, context-free processes (BPA), one-counter machines, FIFO-channel systems with explicit test for queue-emptiness, 1-safe Petri nets, Petri nets with inhibitor arcs, and various subclasses of all these. The second method is effective for all classes of systems that are closed under parallel composition and synchronization like 1-safe Petri nets, general Petri nets, reset Petri nets, transfer Petri nets, VASS (vector addition systems with states) [BM99] and FIFO-channel systems [AJ93].

Thus, for all these classes of systems, deciding simulation preorder/equivalence must be computationally at least as hard as deciding bisimulation equivalence. This provides a formal justification of the general rules of thumb mentioned in Section 1. It is interesting to compare these results to the results in [KM02b], where an abstract, (but not generally effective) one-to-one reduction from simulation equivalence to bisimulation equivalence on general labeled transition systems was presented (i.e., a reduction in the other direction). Therefore, these results further clarify the relationship between simulation equivalence and bisimulation equivalence.

For some classes of systems both methods are effective, e.g., for finite-state systems, FIFO-channel systems with explicit test for emptiness, or for 1-safe Petri nets. However, for general Petri nets only the second method works (the first one fails since Petri nets cannot test for non-enabledness of actions). For pushdown automata it is vice-versa. They can test for non-enabledness of actions, but are not closed under parallel composition.

Finally, there remain a few classes of systems for which none of our methods is effective, like Basic Parallel Processes (BPP) and PA-processes. Also for these classes, simulation preorder/equivalence is computationally harder than bisimulation equivalence [KM02b], but no effective *direct* reduction from bisimulation equivalence to simulation preorder is known for them yet (although effective indirect reductions exist).

References

[AJ93]   P. A. Abdulla and B. Jonsson. Verifying programs with unreliable channels. In *Proceedings of LICS'93*, pages 160–170. IEEE Computer Society Press, 1993. 607, 608

[BGS92]   J. Balcázar, J. Gabarró, and M. Sántha. Deciding bisimilarity is P-complete. *Formal Aspects of Computing*, 4(6A):638–648, 1992. 595

[BK85]   J. A. Bergstra and J. W. Klop. Algebra of communicating processes with abstraction. *Theoretical Computer Science*, 37:77–121, 1985. 607

[BM99]   A. Bouajjani and R. Mayr. Model-checking lossy vector addition systems. In *Proceedings of STACS'99*, volume 1563 of *LNCS*, pages 323–333. Springer, 1999. 607, 608

[Chr93]   S. Christensen. *Decidability and Decomposition in Process Algebras*. PhD thesis, The University of Edinburgh, 1993. 607

[JKM00]   P. Jančar, A. Kučera, and F. Moller. Simulation and bisimulation over one-counter processes. In *Proceedings of STACS 2000*, volume 1770 of *LNCS*, pages 334–345. Springer, 2000. 596

[KM02a]   A. Kučera and R. Mayr. On the complexity of semantic equivalences for pushdown automata and BPA. In *Proceedings of MFCS2002*, LNCS. Springer, 2002. To appear. 602

[KM02b]   A. Kučera and R. Mayr. Simulation preorder over simple process algebras. *Information and Computation*, 173(2):184–198, 2002. 596, 602, 608

[May00]   R. Mayr. On the complexity of bisimulation problems for pushdown automata. In *Proceedings of IFIP TCS'2000*, volume 1872 of *LNCS*, pages 474–488. Springer, 2000. 602

[Mol96]   F. Moller. Infinite results. In *Proceedings of CONCUR'96*, volume 1119 of *LNCS*, pages 195–216. Springer, 1996. 595

[Pet81]   J. L. Peterson. *Petri Net Theory and the Modelling of Systems*. Prentice-Hall, 1981. 607

[SJ01]   Z. Sawa and P. Jančar. P-hardness of equivalence testing on finite-state processes. In *Proceedings of SOFSEM'2001*, volume 2234 of *LNCS*, pages 326–335. Springer, 2001. 595

[Sti98]   C. Stirling. The joys of bisimulation. In *Proceedings of MFCS'98*, volume 1450 of *LNCS*, pages 142–151. Springer, 1998. 595

[Tho93]   W. Thomas. On the Ehrenfeucht-Fraïssé game in theoretical computer science. In *Proceedings of TAPSOFT'93*, volume 668 of *LNCS*, pages 559–568. Springer, 1993. 595

[vG99]   R. van Glabbeek. The linear time—branching time spectrum. *Handbook of Process Algebra*, pages 3–99, 1999. 594

Author Index

Lecture Notes in Computer Science

For information about Vols. 1–2341
please contact your bookseller or Springer-Verlag